Advanced Language & Literature

STRONG ROOTS FOR AP®, COLLEGE, AND BEYOND

Advanced Language & Literature

STRONG ROOTS FOR AP®, COLLEGE, AND BEYOND

SECOND EDITION

Renée H. Shea
Bowie State University, Maryland

John Golden
Cleveland High School, Portland, Oregon

Carlos A. Escobar
Felix Varela Senior High School, Miami, Florida

Lance Balla
Henry M. Jackson High School, Mill Creek, Washington

bedford, freeman & worth
high school publishers
Boston | New York

Senior Vice President, Humanities, Social Sciences, and High School: Chuck Linsmeier
Executive Program Director, High School: Ann Heath
Executive Program Manager, HS Humanities: Nathan Odell
Development Editor: Mara Weible
Director of Media Editorial: Adam Whitehurst
Senior Media Editor: Kimberly Morté
Executive Marketing Manager, High School: Lisa Erdely
Senior Director, Content Management Enhancement: Tracey Kuehn
Senior Managing Editor: Michael Granger
Senior Manager of Publishing Services: Andrea Cava
Senior Workflow Project Manager: Lisa McDowell
Production Supervisor: Robin Besofsky
Director of Design, Content Management: Diana Blume
Interior Design: Jerilyn DiCarlo
Cover Design: William Boardman
Icon Credits: (chapter numbers) KRAGHOVBET/Shutterstock; (lightbulb, conversation bubbles, magnifying glass, pencil) PureSolution/Shutterstock
Director, Rights and Permissions: Hilary Newman
Text Permissions Researcher: Elaine Kosta, Lumina Datamatics, Inc.
Photo Researchers: Krystyna Borgen and Donna Ranieri, Lumina Datamatics, Inc.
Director of Digital Production: Keri deManigold
Lead Media Project Manager: Jodi Isman
Project Management: Aravinda Doss, Lumina Datamatics, Inc.
Editorial Services: Lumina Datamatics, Inc.
Composition: Lumina Datamatics, Inc.
Cover Image: Crystal Autumn by Erin Hanson
Printing and Binding: LSC Communications

Library of Congress Control Number: 2020947170
ISBN 978-1-319-24428-6 (Student Edition)
ISBN 978-1-319-25004-1 (Instructor's Annotated Edition)

Printed in the United States of America.
1 2 3 4 5 6 26 25 24 23 22 21

Acknowledgments
Text acknowledgments and copyrights appear at the back of the book on pages 1183–86, which constitute an extension of the copyright page. Art acknowledgments and copyrights appear on the same page as the art selections they cover.

For information, write: BFW Publishers, One New York Plaza, Suite 4500, New York, NY 10004
hsmarketing@bfwpub.com

TO

Arthur and Dolores Cunningham

Richard Golden

Diane, Lucas, and Sienna Escobar

Joan Balla

About the Authors

Renée H. Shea was professor of English and modern languages and director of freshman composition at Bowie State University in Maryland. A College Board® faculty consultant for more than thirty years in AP® Language, Literature, and Pre-AP® English, she has been a reader and question leader for both AP® English exams. Renée served as a member of the Development Committee for AP® Language and Composition and the English Academic Advisory Committee for the College Board, as well as the SAT® Critical Reading Test Development Committee. She is co-author of the Bedford, Freeman and Worth textbooks *The Language of Composition, Literature & Composition*, *Foundations of Language & Literature*, and *American Literature & Rhetoric*, as well as two volumes in the NCTE High School Literature series (on Amy Tan and Zora Neale Hurston).

John Golden teaches at Cleveland High School in Portland, Oregon. He was an advisor to the College Board 6–12 English Language Arts Development Committee. An English teacher for over twenty years, John has developed curriculum and led workshops for the College Board's Pacesetter® and SpringBoard® English programs. He is the author of the Bedford, Freeman and Worth textbook *Foundations of Language & Literature* and the producer of *Teaching Ideas: A Video Resource for AP® English* (Bedford/St. Martin's, 2008), as well as *Reading in the Dark: Using Film as a Tool in the English Classroom* (NCTE, 2001), *Reading in the Reel World: Teaching Documentaries and Other Nonfiction Texts* (NCTE, 2006), and *The NCTE Centennial Film: Reading the Past, Writing the Future* (2010).

© 2021 Macmillan, Photo by Steven Lemon

Carlos A. Escobar teaches 10th grade English and AP® English Literature and Composition at Felix Varela Senior High School in Miami, Florida, where he is also the AP Program Director. In addition, Carlos has been a College Board Advisor for AP English Literature and a member of the AP® English Literature Test Development Committee. He has mentored new AP English teachers and presented at various local and national AP® workshops and conferences. As part of the College Board's Instructional Design Team, Carlos contributed to the development, review, and publication of the 2019 *AP English Literature and Composition Course and Exam Description*. To prepare students for the 2020 AP examination, he designed and delivered daily, live YouTube lessons streamed globally by the College Board. Carlos has co-authored three Teacher's Editions for Bedford, Freeman and Worth including *Literature & Composition* 2e, *Advanced Language & Literature* 1e, and *Foundations of Language & Literature* 1e. He is also a co-author on the third edition of *Literature & Composition*.

Courtesy of Lance Balla

Lance Balla is a former curriculum developer and current principal at Henry M. Jackson High School in Washington. He was an AP® teacher for almost twenty years, and a College Board faculty consultant for over ten years. He has also been a reader and table leader for the AP® Literature and Composition exam. Lance is a member of the College Board English Academic Advisory Committee, has been a co-author on of the College Board's SpringBoard program, and was a member of the SAT® Critical Reading Test Development Committee. His awards and recognitions include the White House Distinguished Teacher Award, the Teacher Recognition Award from the U.S. Department of Education, the Washington State Award for Professional Excellence, and the Woodring College of Education Award for Outstanding Teaching.

Meet the Advisory Board

Courtesy of Natalie Castillo

Natalie Castillo
Miami-Dade County Public Schools, Florida

Courtesy of Miles Hillis

David Hillis
Clackamas High School, Oregon

Sandra M. Thomas/Courtesy of Christian Cicoria

Christian Cicoria
American School of Paris, France

Courtesy of Brett Noble

Brett Noble
KIPP ENC College Prep Public Schools, North Carolina

©2021 Macmillan, Photo by Steven Lemon

Katherine E. Cordes
Skyview High School, Montana

Courtesy of Bryan Sandala

Bryan Sandala
School District of Palm Beach County, Florida

Courtesy of Samir Dayal/Joy LeDuc Photography

Samir Dayal
Bentley University, Massachusetts

Courtesy of Doranna Tindle

Doranna Tindle
Friendship Charter Schools, Washington, D.C.

Karl Weinrich/Courtesy of Natalie Fallert

Natalie Fallert
Rockwood School District, Missouri

GUIDED TOUR OF

Advanced Language & Literature, Second Edition

Welcome to the second edition of *Advanced Language & Literature*, a textbook designed specifically to prepare students for AP® English, college, and beyond. We, the authors of this book, are deeply committed to the idea that equity of access requires equity of preparation. And that means helping ALL students gain the skills, background knowledge, and earned confidence to be able to walk into either an AP® or a college English course in the future knowing that they belong there, and that they can be successful.

This Guided Tour of the book will introduce you to its structure and features.

Here's How It Works

Advanced Language & Literature is divided into two main parts:

Opening Chapters

1. Making Meaning
2. Understanding Literature
3. Understanding Argument and Rhetoric
4. Understanding Inquiry and Evidence-Based Argument

Building Key Skills

These skill-building instructional chapters lay the groundwork for the skills students will develop and master throughout the course. These chapters use very brief accessible texts to ***introduce, model, and practice fundamental academic skills.***

Thematic Chapters: *The chapters intentionally alternate between literature and nonfiction to help provide a fully balanced language arts curriculum.*

Chapter — Thematic Focus	Genre Focus	Skill Focus
5 Changing the World	*Nonfiction*	*Personal Experience in Argument*
6 Self-Discovery	*Literature*	*Character and Theme in Prose*
7 The Individual in School	*Nonfiction*	*Rhetorical Situation*
8 Cultures, Conflicts, and Connections	*Literature*	*Speaker and Meaning in Poetry*
9 Our Robotic Future	*Nonfiction*	*Evidence in Argument*
10 Utopia/Dystopia	*Literature*	*Style and Meaning in Prose*
11 Do the Right Thing	*Nonfiction*	*Style and Tone in Argument*
12 Power	*Literature*	*Figurative Language and Meaning in Poetry*

What Makes *Advanced Language & Literature* Different?

Texts that Students Will Actually Want to Read

The readings in this book are **fresh, engaging, and vital**. From works by Trevor Noah to N. K. Jemisin, from Mindy Kaling to Sandra Cisneros, from Cory Doctorow to Kurt Vonnegut, the texts in these chapters were selected with sophomore readers in mind. Additionally, we have included a wide range of authors who reflect the diversity of today's world and address topics relevant to today's students, such as institutional racism, climate change, gun violence, immigration, utopia/dystopia, power, and others.

Trevor Noah

Jeff Schear/Getty Images

N. K. Jemisin

Laura Hanifin ©2015/ Courtesy of N. K. Jemisin

Mindy Kaling

James Veysey/Shutterstock

Richard Blanco

Johnny Louis/Getty Images

Stephen Hawking

Eleanor Bentall/Getty Images

Spiraling Skill Development Throughout the Book

Skill development is at the heart of any great English course that is dedicated to preparing students for success in AP® and college, and there are no quick solutions. Building skills is a year-long process. That's why *Advanced Language & Literature* includes a variety of resources to help identify needs, introduce key skills, deepen skill development, and build mastery through practice throughout the book:

Step 1. Skill-Building Opening Chapters. These brief chapters lay a strong foundation by introducing fundamental skills with brief, high-interest texts, and reinforcing those skills with incremental practice.

Step 2. Skill Workshops. Each thematic chapter begins with a short, engaging workshop on a key skill in the chapter, called the Skill Focus. This workshop advances student understanding a step beyond what they learned in the opening chapters, drilling down into more specific techniques, concepts, and academic moves. Each Skill Workshop ends with a Culminating Activity that can act as a formative assessment to determine students' current abilities with that key skill.

Step 3. Skill Focus Questions. Each text in a thematic chapter asks one or more questions about the specific skill students developed in the Skill Workshop.

skill workshop

Understanding Personal Experience in Argument

As we discussed in Chapter 3, many different types of evidence can help you prove a point or make your case. You certainly can and should use facts, statistics, data, and quotations from experts. However, the role that your own personal experience with an issue can play in developing and supporting your argument is often overlooked. If, for instance, you are writing about why school should start later in the day, your own experi-

writing workshop

Using Personal Experience in an Argument

You may have read some of the speeches earlier in this chapter and seen the impact an effective argument can have on the world. For example, Martin Luther King Jr. made the case for nonviolent economic boycotts to improve conditions for workers in Memphis; Malala Yousafzai presented her argument for universal education in the face of religious extremism before an international audience; and Nelson Mandala presented a case for a time when a movement might be required to turn to violence to achieve its aims. Real arguments matter in the real world. The ability to communicate your ideas about a topic — especially one that affects you personally — is an essential skill both in the classroom and in your life outside of it.

While a balanced argument — appealing to ethos, logos, and pathos — is usually the most effective, pathos can be the most powerful appeal in your arsenal when used wisely. Talking about your personal experience is a good way to unlock it.

Step 4. Writing Workshops. At the end of each thematic chapter, a Writing Workshop leads students through the process of writing a full essay demonstrating the specific skill they have been practicing throughout the chapter.

Powerful Tools for Differentiating Instruction

With a classroom of students of multiple skill levels, it is important to have access to a wide range of resources that allow for differentiation by *task, text,* and *process*.

Text-Based Questions | **Differentiate by Task**

The questions in *Advanced Language & Literature* offer a range of options to determine how well students can demonstrate an understanding, make an interpretation, and analyze a text for its stylistic choices. These questions can be answered with short responses or through full essays, as determined by curriculum needs and students' skill level. Each text includes the following question types:

- **Understanding and Interpreting** questions lay the foundation for analysis. These questions guide students to an understanding of the content and move them toward an interpretation.
- **Analyzing Language, Style, and Structure** questions ask students to look at craft — how the writer's choices create meaning at the level of word, sentence, and beyond. Each set of these questions includes at least one **Vocabulary-in-Context** question, perfect for supporting language acquisition and looking closely at diction.
- **Topics for Composing** prompts include extended essay and project ideas, ranging from reflecting on personal connections to building researched arguments and more — all delivered in a variety of modes, from written to verbal, visual to project-based.

▼ Leveled Text Sets | **Differentiate by Text**

Each thematic chapter has three text sections of increasing complexity that allow you to tailor curricular choices to students' needs and interests — while keeping all students exploring the same theme and developing the same skills. With at least twelve texts per chapter, you and your students will have a wide range of texts from which to choose.

Section 1	**Foundational**	These entry-level texts are brief, high-interest, and relatively straightforward in terms of content, context, and structure.
Section 2	**Grade-Level**	These texts represent a level of complexity that a 10th grade student should reasonably be able to read and analyze with a bit of teacher support and additional context.
Section 3	**Challenging**	The most challenging texts in each chapter, these texts have rich language, sophisticated ideas, or unfamiliar contexts. These texts approach the level of challenge seen in actual AP® English classes.

Support for ELL Students | **Differentiate by Process**

Teachers know that English Language Learners are capable of high-level academic work, but they need the right supports. That's why — in addition to the supports already built into the book, such as **Key Context** notes, **Vocabulary in Context** questions, and **Foundational Texts** — we are offering ELL **Essential Guide handouts** for every page of the book. These handouts offer a suite of ELL supports, such as a summary that previews the text, additional context or information to help build background knowledge, detailed help with vocabulary, and more. A **Glossary/Glosario** in the back of the book provides helpful definitions and examples of academic vocabulary in both English and Spanish.

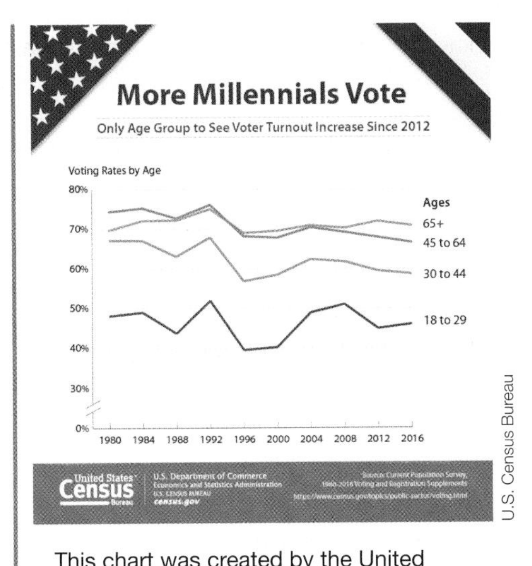

U.S. Census Bureau

This chart was created by the United States Census Bureau.

What conclusions can you draw from this chart about voting rates by age, especially trends in recent years? How would this chart help or hinder Bystricky's argument? Conduct brief research to identify the latest data on youth voting.

Visual Texts | Images with a Purpose

Today's students live in a visual world, and it's never been more important to equip them with the analysis and critical thinking skills to navigate it. That's why every image in *Advanced Language & Literature* is included for a specific pedagogical purpose, comes with a contextualizing caption and analytical question, and provides opportunities for differentiation.

ELL Support | Essential Tools to Build Understanding

Teachers know that English Language Learners are capable of high-level academic work, they just need the right supports. That's why — in addition to the supports already built into the book like **Key Context** notes, **Vocabulary in Context** questions, and Foundational Texts — we are offering **Essential Guide handout** for every reading that offers a suite of ELL supports, such as a summary of the text to support comprehension, additional context to help build background knowledge, specific help with word- and sentence-level challenges in the text, and more.

Extending Beyond the Text | Authentic Engagement and Ready-Made Enrichment

These boxed features accompanying readings throughout the book are enrichment ideas placed right at point-of-use. They challenge students to encounter other perspectives, put texts in conversation, grapple with counterarguments, and draw connections to real-world issues.

In "I Have Been to the Mountaintop," King says, "Men, for years now, have been talking about war and peace. But now, no longer can they just talk about it. It is no longer a choice between violence and nonviolence in this world; it's nonviolence or nonexistence. That is where we are today." A contemporary of King's, Malcolm X, sometimes took a different view of the need for violence in an unjust society. Read the following excerpt from *The Autobiography of Malcolm X: As Told to Alex Haley*.

STF/AFP/Getty Images

***from* The Autobiography of Malcolm X: As Told to Alex Haley**

Malcolm X and Alex Haley

They called me "the angriest Negro in America." I wouldn't deny that charge. I speak exactly as I feel. "I *believe* in anger. The Bible says there is a *time* for anger." They called me "a teacher, a proposer of violence." I would say point blank, "That is a lie. I'm not for meaningless violence;

▶ Essential Questions | **Real Life in the Classroom**

Anticipating the question that many students ask — "Why are we reading this?" — every thematic chapter begins with an opportunity for students to engage with essential questions, which ask about real-life connections. Then, at the end of each thematic chapter, we've included what we call "Continuing the Conversation." This feature includes engaging writing/speaking prompts that provide opportunities for students to respond to the ideas in the chapter and to make connections to themselves, other texts, and the world at large. Whether you want to have students write an argument, reflect on the theme, start a movement, get creative, or do some serious research, these prompts ensure that the real world is never far from the classroom.

Throughout this chapter, you have been reading texts and thinking about how people create change in the world. At the beginning of the chapter and after each of the readings, you had opportunities to consider ideas related to the following essential questions:

ESSENTIAL QUESTIONS

- What conditions are required to make change happen?
- How does one gain the appropriate amount and type of power to create change?
- How does effective, persuasive communication help to bring about change?
- When — if ever — is violence an appropriate means for creating change?

The sections that follow will give you an opportunity to revisit and respond to some of those questions as you think further about creating change by connecting these ideas to yourself, to texts you've read, and to the world outside of the classroom.

▶ Speaking and Listening | **Instruction and Practice for Effective Communication**

It's clear today that we can all use more effective communication and civil discourse. Whether you're interested in building a classroom community or preparing students to engage in academic dialogue, *Advanced Language & Literature* includes instruction and practice opportunities through **Speaking & Listening Focus** boxes in every opening chapter. In addition, several activities in the opening chapters end with a **Talk It Through** section to give students a chance to engage with each other verbally, exchange ideas, and deepen understanding. Finally, at least one prompt for speaking and listening can be found in the **Topics for Composing** after each piece in every thematic chapter.

SPEAKING & LISTENING FOCUS

Listening Actively

Part of the process of learning about others who may be different from you includes having a conversation with them. One of the most important elements of having a successful conversation is the ability to listen actively. Here are some processes you can follow to try to engage fully as you listen to someone:

1. **Prepare to listen.** Put away anything that could be distracting (phone, watch, food, and so on); make eye contact with the speaker.

2. **Be quietly attentive.** Do not interrupt, and keep an open mind. Maybe take notes in a manner that will not disturb the speaker. As you listen, nod, smile, or laugh when appropriate. You can vocalize with sounds like "hmm," "okay," and so on, but do not interrupt until the speaker is finished talking.

3. **Ask follow-up questions.** Once the speaker has finished, you want to be able to demonstrate you have listened closely and give the speaker an opportunity to

Innovative Approaches to Writing Instruction

Advanced Language & Literature recognizes that sophomores come into English class with a wide variety of writing skills. In addition to the core instruction found in the **Opening Skill-Building Chapters** and a wide variety of essential and creative **Topics for Composing** that follow each reading, the book includes the following approaches to support student writers:

Step-by-Step Writing Workshops | Guided Instruction and Practice

Each thematic chapter includes a Writing Workshop that leads students through the process of writing a full essay that they will need to demonstrate in both AP® English and college. Students practice essential writing skills such as brainstorming, writing thesis statements, using evidence, organizing an essay, and developing an effective introduction and conclusion.

▼ Revision and Grammar Workshops | Targeted Help That's There When You Need It

Not all students commit the same kinds of errors with grammar and conventions, or need to revise their writing in the same way. So, at the end of the book, we include eight Revision Workshops and fifteen Grammar Workshops with scaffolded activities that guide students from understanding to application in their own writing. These activities are far more effective than the old, skill-and-drill approach, and they help teachers to meet their students' individual writing needs.

Revision Workshops
Effective Topic Sentences and Unified Paragraphs
Effective Thesis and Essay Structure
Balanced Evidence and Commentary
Appropriate Evidence and Support
Effective Transitions
Effective Syntax
Effective Diction
Effective Introductions and Conclusions

Grammar Workshops (sample topics)
Active and Passive Voice
Adjectives and Adverbs
Capitalization
Comma Splices and Run-On Sentences
Commonly Confused Words
Fragments
Misplaced and Dangling Modifiers
Parallelism and More!

Helpful References | Guides and Glossaries to Help All Students

Also in the back of the book is a handy reference guide to Vocabulary and Word Roots to help students strengthen vocabulary, a glossary and glosario of academic and literary terms to support the understanding of all students, and a Guide to MLA Documentation Style to help students document their sources properly.

A Complete Package to Support Teachers and Students

Teacher's Edition | Written by Teachers for Teachers

As a classroom teacher, you not only need to make adjustments in the texts and the tasks your students encounter, but also in the *ways* that they encounter them. The

Teacher's Edition gives you lots of suggestions — all written by veteran classroom teachers — to make adjustments in the following categories:

1. **Building Context:** Recommendations for short research on background information students may need to understand the context of a text.
2. **Check for Understanding:** Short, focused questions to be asked at key places in a text that might cause confusion for students.
3. **Close Reading:** Places in a text that merit close reading for word choice, syntax, and other stylistic elements.
4. **Differentiation:** Suggestions for scaffolding, speaking and listening opportunities, collaborative learning, inquiry, varying modes of expression, and connections to self, other texts, and the world.

In this exceptionally valuable resource, the authors and a team of master teachers provide helpful marginal annotations throughout to support your teaching of students at all levels, including called-out passages for close reading, useful teaching ideas, important spots to check for understanding, and help building context.

This Teacher's Edition is designed to help teachers in the three key components of an effective classroom: planning, teaching, and assessing.

Digital Options | **More than Just an E-book**

Advanced Language & Literature is available in our fully interactive digital platform. In this platform, students can read, highlight, and take notes on any device, on-line or off-line. You have the ability to assign every question from the book as well as supplemental quizzes and activities, and students' results automatically sync to your gradebook. You can also access the Teacher's Resource Materials, test bank, adaptive quizzing, and more.

Teacher's Resource Materials | **Everything You Need to Build a Great Course**

The Teacher's Resource Materials include a whole host of valuable tools, from suggested responses to questions, ELL Essential Guides to each instructional section and reading in the book, classroom strategies and how-tos, vocabulary-in-context worksheets, key passages for annotation, answers to accompany the exercises in the grammar workshops, and more. All items in the Teacher's Resource Materials can be accessed via the book's e-book platform, or through links embedded throughout the Teacher's Edition e-book.

Assessment | **Your Home for Quizzing**

Our test bank includes hundreds of quizzes and more than 1500 questions that take students from understanding to close rhetorical, literary, and stylistic analysis. Our authors and editors analyzed hundreds of items from national assessments and AP® exams to target key skills. The test bank lets teachers quickly create paper, and online tests in minutes. The platform is fully customizable, allowing teachers to enter their own questions, edit existing questions, set time limits, incorporate multimedia, and scramble answers and change the order of questions to prevent plagiarism. Detailed results reports feed into a grade book.

LearningCurve | Game-like Adaptive Quizzing

Embedded in the book's digital platform is the LearningCurve adaptive quizzing engine. LearningCurve is adaptive game-like quizzing that helps students focus on the material they need the most help with. When they get a question wrong, feedback tells them why and links them to content review — and then they get a chance to try again. LearningCurve has hundreds of topics to support student learning, such as: Active and Passive Voice, Appropriate Voice, Argument: Arguable Claims, Argument: Reasoning and Logical Fallacies, Basic Sentence Patterns, Building Vocabulary, and many many more.

Contents

3 Understanding Rhetoric and Argument 77

Understanding Inquiry and Evidence-Based Arguments 123

7 The Individual in School (nonfiction) 371

9 Our Robotic Future (nonfiction) 559

10 Utopia and Dystopia (literature) 669

12 Power (literature) 919

Revision Workshops 1064

Grammar Workshops 1101

Acknowledgments

To our gifted and committed colleagues:
We are fortunate to have had the assistance of some amazing teachers at key times in the creation of this second edition of *Advanced Language & Literature*. Some of you reviewed the last edition, or previewed materials, whereas others participated in focus groups, but all of you shared with us your enthusiasm, expertise, and experience. This book changed substantially thanks to your insights, and we are profoundly grateful.

Our thanks to the reviewers of this edition, including Marc Andres, Margaret Annen, Sara Behrens, Debra Berry, Kathleen Bielas, Wendy Bivins, Deborah Bookout, Julie Bowles, Matthew Brennan, Sharon Brown, Zachary Brown, Lisa Bullington, Tammy Carpenter, Asani Charles, Lauren Djigo, Valarie Dufrene, Amanda Edwards, Jen Furphey, Jenna Gardner, Shelly Haddock, Cindy Hancock, Carolyn Harman, Lindsey Hayes, Thomas Holman, Mindy Hunter, Karen Judge, Dora King, Brenda Larabee, Gary Lemco, Jennifer Letus, John Manear, Dina Marks, Nicole Mendenhall, Catherine Moore, Patrick Morse, Jamie Mozzone, Richard Murphy, Natalie Nielsen, Heidi Norcross, Ifeoma Okolo, Frazier O'Leary, Michael Park, Jill Pecora, John Peruggia, Rosemarie Poluchowicz, Bertha Redner, Mary Roidt Ringhand, Amy Rousseau, Tom Rutt, Stephanie Salazar, Josh Seematter, Kerry Shepherd, Stephanie Smith, Darla Smyth, Emily Snedeker, Angie Stephenson, Joanna Stubenrauch, Lori Svatora, Kristin Thompson, Marina Vladova, Amy Willeford, Suanne Adams Willman, and Sheena Zadai.

Thank you to those of you who consulted on the first edition as well. Without you, there wouldn't be a second edition. Our thanks to Eva Arce, Lisa Baker, Vinetta Bell, April Ramsey Boyce, Claudette Brassil, Pam Cannon, Rebecca Chowske, Christian Cicoria, Patricia Conquest, Penny Crofford, Elizabeth Davis, Lisa Drance, Alex Gordin, Diana Halluska, Karen Hansen, Tamara Harrington, Stephen Heller, Joyce Herr, Amy Holthause, Ann Jackson, Carol Jago, Kristina Janeway, Elaine Jones, Yvonne Kaatz, Lynn Knowles, Joanne Krajeck, Jamie Mandel, Teri Marshall, Andie Martin, Debra McIntire, Lynn Meier, Chelsie Messenger, Jean Mullooly, Katherine Myers, Theresa Neman, Christine Palmer, Jo Palmore, Cheryl Petersohn, Rebecca Rogers, Ellen Ryan, Tracy Scholz, Pat Sherbert, Suzanne Skipper, Shannon Smith, Paul Stevenson, Violet Turner, Sarah Brown Wessling, and Robyn Westrem.

To the whole team at Bedford, Freeman, and Worth: Thank you for caring so deeply about teachers and their students. How lucky are we to have Nathan Odell steering this project; he is creative, thoughtful, and able to see things most people cannot. Mara Weible, who entered the project at a pivotal moment, faced a steep learning curve, and never faltered; she brought a collaborative spirit and willingness to learn, listen, and challenge. Everyone should have a chance to write for a publisher like Ann Heath, who supported this project in every imaginable way. But a book like this takes a village, so thanks also to Corrina Santos, and Carla Duval, Charles Linsmeier, Hilary Newman,

Elaine Kosta, Donna Ranieri, Lou Bruno, Andrea Cava, Jogender Taneja, Aravinda Doss, and many more who made this book happen. For sales and marketing, we thank the brilliant Lisa Erdely, Nicole Sheppard, Sara Whittern, Tiffani Tang, and the amazing team of sales reps who are always so generous in sharing the knowledge they gain from working directly with teachers.

To any we have neglected to thank by name, rest assured that it is merely an error of the head and not of the heart. Thank you.

Advanced Language & Literature

STRONG ROOTS FOR AP®, COLLEGE, AND BEYOND

db Waterman

Making Meaning

English is typically the only subject that is required for all four years of high school. Have you wondered why this is the case? Here is an actual hallway conversation from the beginning of the school year between two sophomores who (probably unintentionally) were wrestling with this question:

> **STUDENT A:** What English class are you in?
>
> **STUDENT B:** English 2.
>
> **STUDENT A:** What's that?
>
> **STUDENT B:** Don't know. Same as English 1, but one harder?

You might conclude that the two students really don't know much about why they've been studying English. However, their conversation may also reflect your own feelings about English class: you do most of the same things each year (read books, write essays, give speeches), but the process gets a little harder and you probably read different books.

So, what is English *for,* then?

And why is English so important that, if you have grown up in the United States, you have likely studied it every year for the past ten years? One easy answer is that you must learn to read, write, and speak effectively so that you can function as a literate citizen in society. Thoughtful reading and effective communication will help you secure a job that suits your needs and interests, understand politics and cast informed votes, and protect your future with sound financial decisions.

It's about all of those practical things, sure, but it's about loftier goals as well. It's about encountering ideas, developing empathy, thinking about identity, reflecting on values, understanding differences, and communicating with others. In other words, by studying English, you are becoming a thinking, feeling, fully functioning member of society. And because of the topics covered, the texts you read, and the activities you engage in, English class is a place where you can get to know more about yourself and others.

Knowing Yourself

If you jumped on a plane to Greece, you would be able to see the ruins of the Oracle of Delphi, which dates from around 1400 BC. People came from all over the ancient world to ask a priestess of the Greek god Apollo to predict their futures.

Historians suspect that the Oracle's prophesies were likely only hallucinations caused by methane gas and carbon dioxide released from fissures in the earth on which the temple was built. However, there is one truthful aspect of the Oracle that still resonates with us today. Carved into the stone near the entrance of the site is a saying that translates as "Know Yourself." This phrase has endured because it's a simple idea. And yet, getting to know yourself can be a challenging process.

The artist Frida Kahlo created a number of self-portraits in an effort to address the Oracle's charge to "know yourself," including this one called *Self-Portrait on the Borderline between Mexico and the United States.* **Looking carefully at this painting, what would you say Kahlo might identify as the main factors contributing to her sense of self?**

Who *are* you? Simple, right? You have a name, an age, a gender identity, a race, or an ethnicity. You also might play a sport, an instrument, or a particular video game. That's also part of who you are, along with a religion you may practice, the city or town you live in, the size and type of family you come from, and so on. But the saying at Delphi wasn't "Describe Yourself," but "*Know* Yourself." It urges you to understand how those elements of yourself — age, interests, family — affect what you think, feel, believe, and do. That's the difficult part; to really *know* yourself means to consider how all of those factors work together to define you and to distinguish you from others.

Look at this poem called "Knoxville, Tennessee" by Nikki Giovanni, in which the speaker of the poem describes various people, places, objects, and experiences that contribute to the speaker's sense of self:

Knoxville, Tennessee

Nikki Giovanni

I always like summer
best
you can eat fresh corn
from daddy's garden
and okra
and greens
and cabbage
and lots of
barbecue
and buttermilk
and homemade ice-cream
at the church picnic
and listen to
gospel music
outside
at the church
homecoming
and go to the mountains with
your grandmother
and go barefooted
and be warm
all the time
not only when you go to bed
and sleep ■

Town Hens, 1995 (acrylic ink, gouache)/Graa Jensen, Lisa/LISA GRAA JENSEN/Private Collection/Bridgeman Images

Imagine that the figure in this painting *Town Hens* by Lisa Graa Jensen were to write a poem similar to "Knoxville, Tennessee." **What main details would she likely include?**

Notice all of the family connections (*daddy* and *grandmother*), the food (*okra, greens, ice-cream, etc.*), the settings (*garden, church picnic, mountains, bed*), as well as the sights, sounds, and tastes of childhood (*gospel music, barefoot, warm all the time*). This speaker is someone who is truly trying to understand him- or herself by recognizing that a sense of self is at least partly the product of past influences.

Knowing Yourself

Write a short response in which you try to address the motto at Delphi to "Know Yourself." Choose one or two of the following prompts to guide you, or respond to one of your own:

- How have you been encouraged, supported, challenged, or discouraged by your family, friends, teachers, and others in your life?
- In what ways might your age, race, gender identity, sexual orientation, ethnicity, social class, or other factors influence how you see yourself?
- What are some of your favorite things (foods, music, movies, TV shows, videos, or clothes, for example), and how do they influence you or reveal something about you to others?
- If you regularly participate in clubs, sports, or other organized activities, how do they help shape and define you?
- What elements from your past and present environments seem important to your sense of self? How do they help shape your identity?

Knowing Others

Once you have considered just how complicated a directive "Know Yourself" really is, you can apply that understanding to other people. Unlike the ancient Greeks, you don't need to turn to the Oracle of Delphi to see beyond what you can directly observe. In the twenty-first century, a simple Google search can put you in touch with the words, images, and sounds of people of various ages, interests, classes, genders, and backgrounds. The experiences and interests of some of these people may overlap with your own. But it's more likely that they are different from you — from a different place, with different interests, background knowledge, and points of reference. Even the words they use to describe their experiences may be unfamiliar to you.

For example, take a look at this excerpt from a popular sports blog discussing a particular basketball play:

> In this standard high pick-and-roll, you have Bargnani setting up at the top of the key by the 3-point line, setting a ball screen for Jose Calderon. Calderon does a good job of setting up the screen, coming off Bargnani, and using it effectively. In terms of setting ball screens, versatility means the ability to do different things when the point guard comes off your screen. As a shooting 7-footer, Bargnani can either pop out or roll to the rim, and while he favors popping out, doing so close to 79 percent of the time, his size makes him

a threat when rolling to the rim as well. So in this case, when JaVale McGee leaves him to hedge on this ball screen, Bargnani dives into the paint.

Now, unless you play or watch basketball regularly, there are a number of words and phrases that you probably recognize, but not in the way they are used here: *guard, paint, screen, hedge, key, pop, roll, dives,* and so on. Someone with limited basketball knowledge might reasonably ask why a basketball player would suddenly dive into paint in the middle of a game or "favor popping out." Obviously, this is just one example of a group with specialized interests that may or may not overlap with your own. Others might include people who write or play music, those who code, people who knit, row, game, and so on. Sadly, our distinctive groups can also divide us, sometimes complicating communication among groups separated by race, gender, social class, sexual orientation, ethnicity, politics, or other factors, including interests and background knowledge.

How do we begin to bridge these gaps in understanding? Appreciating what a difficult undertaking it is to "Know Yourself" can actually help us to "Know Others." We can begin by asking questions we have about others' experiences and considering what lies outside our own sphere of experiences — what we don't know. Throughout this year in English class, you will read texts written by people who might have backgrounds, views, and experiences that differ greatly from your own. These texts will give you opportunities to practice identifying what you don't know and what you want to know. You will also learn how to ask questions that will help you understand the texts, their authors, and the characters and situations they portray. The questions and conversations you will have about these texts are a necessary part of beginning to understand the world around you.

Knowing Others

Write a brief response about your own gaps in knowledge, expertise, background, and interests. Consider using one or two of the following prompts to guide you:

1. Think about someone whose age, race, gender identity, socioeconomic status, or other circumstances are different from your own. Describe those differences and why they interest you. What elements of your own experience make it difficult for you to understand how this person might see him- or herself and the world? What questions could you ask this person to help bridge the gaps between the two of you?
2. Identify groups that you are not currently a part of at your school or in your community that have their own unique, specialized vocabulary (like the basketball example earlier). What elements of your own experience make it difficult for you to understand these groups? What questions could you ask people in these groups to help you bridge the gaps between your experiences and theirs?
3. How has the town or city where you live, or the school you attend, limited your experiences? If you live in a large city, for instance, how might your experiences be different from those of someone who lives in a small town? What questions could you ask people from a different location to help you bridge the gaps between your experiences and theirs?

SPEAKING & LISTENING FOCUS

Listening Actively

Part of the process of learning about others who may be different from you includes having a conversation with them. One of the most important elements of having a successful conversation is the ability to listen actively. Here are some processes you can follow to try to engage fully as you listen to someone:

1. Prepare to listen. Put away anything that could be distracting (phone, watch, food, and so on); make eye contact with the speaker.

2. Be quietly attentive. Do not interrupt, and keep an open mind. Maybe take notes in a manner that will not disturb the speaker. As you listen, nod, smile, or laugh when appropriate. You can vocalize with sounds like "hmm," "okay," and so on, but do not interrupt until the speaker is finished talking.

3. Ask follow-up questions. Once the speaker has finished, you want to be able to demonstrate you have listened closely and give the speaker an opportunity to expand or clarify ideas. The most effective way to do this is to ask questions, such as the following:

- So, what I heard you say was ___________. Is that correct? What did I miss?
- Can you say more about ___________?
- What do you think is most important to know about ___________?
- Why do you feel it is important to ___________?

Notice that these questions help demonstrate that you listened actively and provide the speaker with an opportunity to dig even deeper.

Practice

1. Review the responses you wrote earlier for the activities called "Knowing Yourself" (p. 6) and "Knowing Others" (p. 8), and prepare to share with a partner.
2. If possible, pair up with a classmate whom you don't know well already, and who might have at least some differences from you in background, knowledge, or interests.
3. Take turns with sharing responses and listening. Try to discuss your ideas and questions without reading what you've written. Your partner should listen actively, as described in Steps 1 and 2.
4. When you finish, your partner should say, "What I heard you say was ___________," and try to recount the most important details of what you said. Your partner should give you an opportunity to clarify or add by asking, "What did I miss?"
5. After you add or clarify, your partner should ask you one or two follow-up questions like those listed in Step 3 above to prompt you to dig a little deeper into one or more of the topics. Try to elaborate with more details, description, or explanation.
6. Switch roles so that both you and your partner have spoken and listened. The goal is to demonstrate active listening and to ensure that you and your partner each have the chance to share fully.

Reflection

Reflect on your conversation with your partner. What were some of the similarities and differences between what you and your partner chose to write about and discuss? Did you or your partner have to explain any terms or concepts? If so, what were they? What did you learn from each other by listening actively? What was it like speaking to a partner who was listening actively? What was it like being responsible for accurately recalling what your partner was saying?

Making Connections, Asking Questions, and Annotating Texts

In English class, one of your primary tasks is to read and create texts — poems, stories, editorials, speeches, and many others. And inevitably, as you encounter these texts, who you are will impact how you understand them and what you create. You bring different aspects of who you are — your age, race, gender identity, ethnicity, sexual orientation, religious beliefs, family background, and so on — to everything you encounter. If you were writing an editorial on, say, the topic of criminal justice reform, your piece would likely reflect any experiences you or those close to you have had with racial profiling, crime, or law enforcement. If you were reading a poem about a winter day, whether you love or hate snow is going to change how you respond to the poem. We cannot separate our experiences from what and how we read and write. Nor should we — our experiences make us who we are.

But connecting who you are to what you're reading or writing is where you start the process of understanding — not where you end it. When you read texts written by people whose backgrounds and experiences differ from your own, there are always opportunities to expand your knowledge by listening, engaging, researching, and above all, asking questions. Two essential habits to develop as you encounter a text are to make connections (*What seems familiar?*) and to ask questions (*What is unknown or unfamiliar?*). In the chart that follows, you will see some prompts that can guide you as you work with the texts you read:

Making Connections	Asking Questions
• What about this text reminds you of an experience in your past? • What do you know about the topic or ideas because of your life, experience, or beliefs? • How does this text make you feel? • How is this text similar to or different from another text you know? • How does this text reflect something about a community you belong to?	• What in this text is unfamiliar? • What does this text seem to say about the world? • What confuses or interests you about the text? • What questions do you have about the author's language choices? Are there words or phrases you aren't familiar with?

Whenever you read a text, try to slow down to make connections and ask questions. It's also important to write down your thoughts about the text, so that you can continue to explore them. This process of marking up a text as you read it is called

annotation. Annotation is a conversation between you and the text, and it's done by marking up that text. Looking back at these annotations after you finish reading will help you understand the text better.

A Model Annotation: Making Connections, Asking Questions

As an example of what this process might look like, here is a model annotated excerpt from a *New York Times* editorial by culture critic Lindy West about the need for more diverse representations in movies and TV shows. This article was annotated by a female high school student.

from We Got Rid of Some Bad Men. Now Let's Get Rid of Some Bad Movies

Lindy West

Bad men like Harvey Weinstein, Kevin Spacey, and LOTS of others (Connection)

What does this word mean? (Question)

Hollywood is both a perfect and bizarre vanguard in the war for cultural change.

I like the way she shows two sides of Hollywood — how it brings us joy but also does damage. (Connection)

Perfect because its reach is so vast, its influence so potent; bizarre because television and movies are how a great many toxic ideas embedded themselves inside of us in the first place.

When I was growing up, I didn't chafe at the shallow, exploitative representations of my gender that I saw on screen; I took notes. I added item after item to my mental lists of how to be a woman and the things I should yearn for and tolerate from men.

This is how little girls are taught to take in media. I always had princess movies and dolls around when I was a kid that were telling me something about being a woman. And not good ☹ (Connection)

From makeover shows, I learned that I was ugly. From romantic comedies, I learned that stalking means he loves you and persistence means he earned you — and also that I was ugly.

We learn this from everywhere, regardless of genre. It's easier for me — I'm a cis white girl and have seen myself in media forever, but some girls don't even get that. (Connection)

From Disney movies, I learned that if I made my waist small enough (maybe with the help of a witch), a man or large hog-bear might marry me, and that's where my story would end.

Is this an allusion to "Beauty and the Beast?" (Question)

"The Smurfs" taught me that boys can have distinct personalities, like being smart or grumpy, and girls can have only one (that personality is "high heels"). From "The Breakfast Club," I learned that rage and degradation are the selling points of an alluring bad boy, not the red flags of an abuser. From pretty much all media, I learned that complicated women are "crazy" and complicated men are geniuses.

Or hormonal. Or worse... (Connection)

That's essentially a random sample, and pulled from media I actually *like*. You could make a parallel list about race, sexuality, ability, poverty — every vector of identity that has historically been funneled through, for instance, the 82.4 percent of film directors who are white men (according to a 2015 report by the Directors Guild of America).

Logic for people who don't believe her yet. If personal anecdotes aren't fact enough... (Connection)

Do you know how noise-canceling headphones work? (I don't really, but I'm going to embarrass myself for the sake of the metaphor.) They have a built-in microphone that measures the ambient noise around you, then generates an exact inversion of that sound wave and adds it to the mix in your headphones. When a frequency meets its opposite — when the peaks of one match up with the valleys of another — the result is called phase cancellation. The two waves cancel each other out. Silence.

Was I supposed to be paying attention in Science class? (Question)

What we could really use from Hollywood is about 100 years of phase cancellation. We need new work that actively challenges and counterbalances old assumptions, that offers radical models for how to conceive of ourselves and how to treat each other.

I like her view of a new Hollywood — how can consumers of media help make that a reality? (Question)

You should notice that these annotations reflect the reader's own experiences, revealing the questions and ideas she has about the piece. Your annotations of the very same text might look quite different based on your age, experience, gender identity, race, and so on. Regardless of the perspectives you bring to the text, however, the process of making connections and asking questions remains the same.

Annotating a Text

Read the following poem by Aimee Nezhukumatathil, and annotate the text by making connections and asking questions.

On Listening to Your Teacher Take Attendance

Aimee Nezhukumatathil

Breathe deep even if it means you wrinkle
your nose from the fake-lemon antiseptic

of the mopped floors and wiped-down
doorknobs. The freshly soaped necks

and armpits. Your teacher means well,
even if he butchers your name like

he has a bloody sausage casing stuck
between his teeth, handprints

on his white, sloppy apron. And when
everyone turns around to check out

your face, no need to flush red and warm.
Just picture all the eyes as if your classroom

is one big scallop with its dozens of icy blues
and you will remember that winter your family

took you to the China Sea and you sank
your face in it to gaze at baby clams and sea stars

the size of your outstretched hand. And when
all those necks start to crane, try not to forget

someone once lathered their bodies, once patted them
dry with a fluffy towel after a bath, set out their clothes

for the first day of school. Think of their pencil cases
from third grade, full of sharp pencils, a pink pearl eraser.

Think of their handheld pencil sharpener and its tiny blade. ■

Talking It Through

After you have read and annotated the poem, share your annotations with a partner and compare notes. How are your connections and questions similar to or different from your partner's? Discuss your annotations with each other, using the following prompts to guide your conversation:

- Do you or someone you know have a name that some teachers have difficulty pronouncing correctly? How does having the name mispronounced affect you (or the person you know)?
- Where in the poem does the speaker express feelings similar to some that you have had in school? Even if the circumstances differ, which moments in the poem trigger memories of your own experiences?
- Does the teacher or do the classmates in this poem remind you of people you've encountered? In what ways?
- Are you confused or curious about any ideas or images in the poem?
- What words, phrases, topics, or descriptions were unclear to you?

Discuss with each other how the process of annotating, specifically asking questions and making connections, may have helped you to begin making meaning from the poem.

Look at this piece called *The Exam Room* by Cyril Edward Power. **What connections and questions come to mind? How is the environment in this painting similar to or different from the classroom described by Nezhukumatathil?**

Reading for Understanding, Interpretation, and Style

In the previous activity, you annotated the text by making connections and asking questions, but that is only one step in your work with texts in an English class. Ultimately, the goal is to try to draw conclusions about the meaning of a text. In general, there are three ways that you read a text to get at its meaning, often in this order:

1. Reading for understanding
2. Reading for interpretation
3. Reading for style

Reading for Understanding

Before you can do any deeper reading and analysis, you have to be able to state what the text is literally saying. The goal of reading for understanding is to be able to **summarize** the text, to identify the main idea and the key supporting details that reinforce that idea.

A paragraph or short excerpt often has a single main idea with two or more supporting details, though longer works can have multiple related main ideas. Sometimes the main idea is directly stated by the author, but more often it is left unstated. For instance, think back on the excerpt from the *New York Times* editorial about representation in the media by Lindy West (p. 11). An effective summary based on a main idea and some supporting details might read as follows:

> Lindy West contends that Hollywood portrays a limited range of images representing beauty and femininity. She includes several supporting details, such as examples from *The Smurfs* and *The Breakfast Club* and a statistic about the percentage of white male directors.

This is an accurate summary of the excerpt that demonstrates an overall understanding of the text.

Reading for Interpretation

When reading for interpretation, you are concerned primarily with explaining what the text means — its significance. Significance refers to the ideas that give us insight into ourselves, the world around us, or the author's message. When interpreting, you need to have a reasonable explanation for why you think your conclusion is accurate. When we discuss meaning in nonfiction texts (editorials, speeches, essays, documentaries, etc.), we usually speak of the author's **purpose** — what the author is hoping to communicate to readers. But in literature (poetry, short stories, drama, fiction films, etc.), we express our interpretation as the **theme** of the text, a point the author is trying to make about life, the world, people, or other topics. Earlier, you made connections and asked questions about Aimee Nezhukumatathil's poem "On Listening to Your Teacher Take Attendance" (p. 13). After doing so, you could attempt to interpret the poem's meaning — the theme — by asking yourself, "What does the author want me to think about school, teachers, and ethnicity based on this situation?" You might conclude that she is suggesting that when people treat you differently because of your race, ethnicity, or other factors, you can draw strength from those differences. Now, this is not *THE* theme of the poem, but it is one possible theme. It is a reasonable conclusion about the message of the poem based on the available evidence in the text. There are many other likely interpretations as well.

Reading for Style

A final way of determining the meaning of a text is to read for style, to understand why the text was created in the way it was. Style is the particular way writers, visual artists, and songwriters, for example, express themselves through the words they choose, the images they invoke, the rhythms they select. When reading a print text for style, you conduct a close reading, focusing on the individual words, sentences, and structure of the text to understand how the writer creates a specific intended effect on the reader. The main question you should consider when reading for style is this: why did the writer make this specific choice? While oftentimes, the style of a piece might be created for its own sake — achieving an interesting sound, rhythm, or image — style can also help reinforce the meaning or theme of the work as a whole. In the poem "On Listening to Your Teacher Take Attendance," Nezhukumatathil makes specific choices to communicate her idea that when people treat you differently because of your race, ethnicity, or other factors, you can draw strength from those differences to fight back. Notice that she chooses to have the speaker describe the teacher as a butcher with "sausage casing stuck between his teeth, handprints on his white, sloppy apron" to show just how damaging his mispronunciation was, but the speaker refuses to be embarrassed and instead finds strength in her differences, especially in these lines:

> and you will remember that winter your family
>
> took you to the China Sea and you sank
> your face in it to gaze at baby clams and sea stars
>
> the size of your outstretched hand.

In this excerpt from her graphic memoir, *Passing for Human*, Liana Finck describes an aspect of her identity as an artist.

What is an interpretation that you could make about why she draws? How does her style—the choices she makes with words and images—help her to communicate this idea?

By looking closely at Nezhukumatathil's style — her choices of words, images, and subjects — we understand more about the message of the poem: Power imbalances based on race and culture can have lasting effects on an individual.

All three of these ways of reading — for understanding, interpretation, and style — work together to help us determine the meaning of a text. And in general, the order these were presented in will be the order in which you will apply them to most texts. You can't really make an interpretation until you have an understanding of a text. Similarly, reading for style requires an examination of specific word choices that usually is better reserved for when you have drawn some possible interpretations.

KEY QUESTIONS

- When you are reading for understanding, ask yourself, "What is this text literally saying?"
- When you are reading for interpretation, ask yourself, "What is the author trying to communicate to the reader?"
- When you are reading for style, ask yourself, "Why did the author create the text this way?"

A Model Analysis: Making Meaning

Let's take this process of making meaning from a text step by step by working with this photograph: *Life Goes On, Checa, Ecuador, 2011* by Phil Douglis. Whether it's analyzing a poem, teasing apart an argument, or thinking about a photograph, the basic

Phil Douglis, *Life Goes On, Checa, Ecuador, 2011.*

thought process remains the same: make connections, ask questions, and try to determine the meaning of the work by reading for understanding, interpretation, and style. Let's try this with the photograph on page 17.

1. **Make Connections and Ask Questions:** You probably recognized the pig and the cross. Depending on where you live and your own experiences, you may also have seen images like the falling-down chain-link fence before, or have heard the phrase that makes up the title of the photograph: *Life Goes On*. Perhaps, though, you have questions about the location of this photograph. What is Ecuador like? Is that a cemetery on the other side of the fence? Is the pig a pet or livestock? What is the cross doing there?
2. In drawing a conclusion about the meaning of a text, you should go through the three steps described in the previous section:
   - **Understanding**: What is literally happening in this photograph? Well, we see a pig near a road on one side of a fence that is falling down with a cross on the other side.
   - **Interpretation**: What is the photographer trying to communicate to the audience? Interpreting this photograph, you might conclude something similar to what the photographer, Phil Douglis, says about his work: "The image symbolizes the fact that life continues to be lived, even in the constant presence of death itself." Again, this is only one possible interpretation; even the creator of the work doesn't have the final word on what it means.
   - **Style**: What choices did the photographer make to communicate his ideas about life in the presence of death? The most significant choice he made was to frame his photograph so that the pig and the cross are close to one another, and neatly separated by the leaning fence post. It is also a color photograph; had the photo been black-and-white instead, it might have had a more stark, depressing feel.

Making Meaning

Earlier in this chapter, you read part of an editorial by Lindy West about gender stereotypes in Hollywood. Below are the concluding paragraphs of that editorial. As you read and reread them, use annotations to make connections and ask questions. Your annotations should show that you are reading for understanding, interpretation, and style.

from We Got Rid of Some Bad Men. Now Let's Get Rid of Some Bad Movies

Lindy West

One of the most breathtaking things about #MeToo — just behind the iron-jawed fury of its deponents — is how swiftly and decisively it pulled conversations about sexual predation from the conceptual to the concrete. After decades of debates and doubts and dissertations and settlements and nondisclosure agreements and whisper networks and stasis and silence, all of a sudden, in one great gust, powerful men are toppling. Talk has become action. The seemingly untouchable have lost jobs, reputations, and legacies overnight. Choices have consequences, even if you are Harvey Weinstein. This is new.

But in the rush of catharsis, it's important not to lose track of some of those old conceptual conversations, because we never came close to finishing them. We are not done talking about *why* so many men feel entitled to space, power, and other people's bodies. We are not done talking about our culture's hostility toward women's sexual pleasure. We are not done talking about how to get justice for "imperfect" victims, and how to let go of perpetrators we love. We are not done talking about how to decide which abusers deserve a path to redemption, and what that path might look like. We are not done talking about the legal system. We are not done talking about sex. We are not done talking about race.

Unseating a couple (or a score, or even a generation) of powerful abusers is a start, but it's not an end, unless we also radically change the power structure that selects their replacements and the shared values that remain even when the movement wanes. Art didn't invent oppressive gender roles, racial stereotyping, or rape culture, but it reflects, polishes, and sells them back to us every moment of our waking lives. We make art, and it simultaneously makes us. Shouldn't it follow, then, that we can change ourselves by changing the art we make? ■

Talking It Through

Once you have finished annotating the text, share your connections and questions with a partner and discuss possible interpretations of this section. What is West trying to communicate to her readers? What stylistic choices does West make in this piece to help the reader understand her purpose? While you can certainly look back at the first part of this editorial on page 11 for additional information, try to focus your interpretations on this section. Also, refer to the Key Questions on page 17 to help you with this step and return to your annotations as needed.

Considering Context

As you encounter a text, you're almost always going to have some questions. You might be confused by unfamiliar vocabulary or complex sentence structures, for example. Questions about **context**, however, might keep you from being able to draw a conclusion about possible meanings. Contextual challenges often occur when you do not know enough about the author, time period, or subject matter to understand what you are reading. These, in turn, can lead to misunderstanding or confusion. If you didn't know, for example, that the Christian cross is commonly used in cemeteries, you might have trouble analyzing the photo *Life Goes On*

(p. 17). Or, maybe you didn't know what #MeToo refers to in the editorial by Lindy West. It would be far more difficult to make an accurate interpretation without that context. Part of your work in an English class will be knowing when you do not have all the background information you need and taking the steps to gain this information by conducting brief research, talking with classmates, and finding ways to answer your questions.

For another example of how considering context can affect understanding, look at the photograph at the bottom of this page by Thomas Hoepker. It was taken on September 11, 2001, the day of a major terrorist attack on the World Trade Center in New York City, which can be seen smoldering in the background of the photo. Five years after the attack, *New York Times* commentator Frank Rich saw the photo and drew this conclusion:

> This is a country that likes to move on, and fast. The young people in Mr. Hoepker's photo aren't necessarily callous. They're just American. In the five years since the attacks, the ability of Americans to dust themselves off and keep going explains both what's gone right and what's gone wrong on our path to the divided and dispirited state the nation finds itself in today.

Rich's conclusion was not accurate, however, because he lacked context for the photograph. In response to the *New York Times* piece, one of the people in the

Thomas Hoepker/Magnum Photos

Thomas Hoepker, photograph taken overlooking Manhattan on September 11, 2001.

photograph wrote an email to the online magazine *Slate*, saying "A snapshot can make mourners attending a funeral look like they're having a party." He went on to say that, like most people who watched the Towers fall, he and his companions were in a "profound state of shock and disbelief," and that Thomas Hoepker did not ask permission to take the photograph or interview them to determine their state of mind. "Had Hoepker walked fifty feet over to introduce himself he would have discovered a bunch of New Yorkers in the middle of an animated discussion about what had just happened." Instead, Thomas Hoepker took the photograph and Frank Rich drew his conclusion without fully understanding the context of the situation. Look back at the photograph now that you know more about the context. Do you see the scene differently now? Would the writer Frank Rich and the photographer Thomas Hoepker have reached a different conclusion if they had known more about their subjects?

As you encounter texts that leave you with more questions than connections, finding out about their context can provide you with the framework necessary to make a valid interpretation and help you avoid drawing faulty conclusions. Thinking back on the poem in a previous activity, "On Listening to Your Teacher Take Attendance," learning information about the China Sea, scallops, and even Nezhukumatathil's own background might give you valuable context for forming a reasonable conclusion. Context will play an important role in your work with the literature and nonfiction found in this book. Much of what you will read here is either written by or about people from different countries with different cultures and customs.

KEY QUESTIONS

The following questions will likely come up as you deal with contextual challenges:

- Who are the author, speaker, or characters of the text? What do we know about them?
- What is the setting or occasion for the text? What is the time period? Where does it take place? Did a significant historical or cultural event inspire the creation of this text?
- Who is the intended audience for this text? Do people familiar with this topic use specific terminology or references?
- What do you already know about the topic? What background information do you need? Do you need to conduct brief research on the topic to give you more context?
- What is the purpose of the text? Why was the text created? To inform? To persuade? To sell something? To entertain?

activity Considering Context

1. Look at the painting reproduced here without reading the context of the artist and the situation depicted. Jot down some connections and some questions. Then, write a description of what you think is happening in this painting. Your description should be detailed enough to make sense to someone who has not seen the painting.

Guernica, 1937, oil on canvas by Pablo Picasso (1881–1973); Museo Nacional Centro de Arte Reina Sofia, Madrid, Spain/Bridgeman Images; © 2020 Estate of Pablo Picasso/Artists Rights Society (ARS), New York

2. After you finish your description, read the background information that follows and try to answer some of the questions about context listed on page 21. If you need to, conduct some additional research on the painting.

   BACKGROUND: Pablo Picasso painted *Guernica* in 1937 in response to the bombing of Guernica, Spain by German and Italian forces during the Spanish Civil War. The bombing resulted in nearly one thousand civilian deaths. The painting is almost 12 feet high and 25 feet wide.

Talking It Through

With this context in mind, meet with a partner to revisit each other's original description of the painting. Have you been able to answer some of your own questions about the painting? Discuss how learning about the context affected your understanding of the painting.

culminating activity

The following texts are typical of the sort you will encounter this year — one is a nonfiction essay and the other is a short piece of fiction. Each text also includes a bit of context about the author and the text itself.

For each piece, complete the following steps:

1. Annotate the text or write a response in which you make connections and ask questions.
2. Determine a possible meaning of the piece based on the evidence by reading for understanding, interpretation, and style. (For a refresher on these terms, see pp. 14–17.) Write a brief response to share your conclusions.

from A Quilt of a Country

Anna Quindlen

Anna Quindlen (b. 1953) is an American novelist and newspaper columnist. Her novels include *One True Thing* and *Black and Blue*, and her nonfiction books include *A Short Guide to a Happy Life* and *How Reading Changed My Life*. Quindlen won the Pulitzer Prize in 1992 for her column in the *New York Times*, and she wrote a regular column for *Newsweek* from 2000 to 2009.

KEY CONTEXT This article appeared in *Newsweek* on September 26, 2001, about two weeks after the September 11 terrorist attacks. Militants associated with the Islamic extremist group Al Qaeda hijacked airplanes and carried out suicide attacks against targets in the United States, including the World Trade Center in New York City, and the Pentagon in Washington, DC. Almost three thousand people were killed during the attacks, which led to major U.S. initiatives to combat terrorism, as well as a lot of self-reflection on the part of Americans about what makes their country unique.

America is an improbable idea. A mongrel nation built of ever-changing disparate parts, it is held together by a notion, the notion that all men are created equal, though everyone knows that most men consider themselves better than someone. "Of all the nations in the world, the United States was built in nobody's image," the historian Daniel Boorstin wrote. That's because it was built of bits and pieces that seem discordant, like the crazy quilts that have been one of its great folk-art forms, velvet and calico and checks and brocades. Out of many, one. That is the ideal.

The reality is often quite different, a great national striving consisting frequently of failure. Many of the oft-told stories of the most pluralistic nation on earth are stories not of tolerance, but of bigotry. Slavery and sweatshops, the burning of crosses and the ostracism of the other. Children learn in social-studies class and in the news of the lynching of blacks, the denial of rights to women, the murders of gay men. It is difficult to know how to convince them that this amounts to "crown thy good with brotherhood," that amid all the failures is something spectacularly successful. Perhaps they understand it at this moment, when enormous tragedy, as it so often does, demands a time of reflection on enormous blessings. . . .

What is the point of this splintered whole? What is the point of a nation in which Arab cabbies chauffeur Jewish passengers through the streets of New York — and in which Jewish cabbies chauffeur Arab passengers, too, and yet speak in theory of hatred, one for the other? What is the point of a nation in which one part seems to be always on the verge of fisticuffs with another, blacks and whites, gays and straights, left and right, Pole and Chinese and Puerto Rican and Slovenian? Other countries with such divisions have in fact divided into new nations with new names, but not this one, impossibly interwoven even in its hostilities. . . .

Once these disparate parts were held together by a common enemy, by the fault lines of world wars and the electrified fence of communism. . . . Today the citizens of the United States have come together once more because of armed conflict and enemy attack. Terrorism has led to devastation — and unity. . . .

When photographs of the faces of all those 5
who died in the World Trade Center destruction are assembled in one place, it will be possible to trace in the skin color, the shape of the eyes and the noses, the texture of the hair, a map of the world. These are the representatives of a mongrel nation that somehow, at times like this, has one spirit. Like many improbable ideas, when it actually works, it's a wonder. ■

Everything, Then Silence

Justin Herrmann

Justin Herrmann is the author of the short fiction collection *Highway One, Antarctica*. His stories have appeared in journals including *River Styx*, *SmokeLong Quarterly*, and *Crab Orchard Review*. He lives with his family in Alaska.

KEY CONTEXT The narrator of the story appears to be an MMA (mixed-martial arts) fighter. Unlike traditional boxing, MMA is a full-contact sport that allows striking and grappling, both standing and on the ground. A&W is a fast-food restaurant and brand of root beer.

Sipping floats at an A&W in Marion, Indiana with a son I hadn't seen in a decade, my top incisors were stuck in another man's foot, I presumed being extracted at the local ER. It was my third knockout loss in a row.

Son poked around in his float with a fat red straw like he might uncover answers deep in his glass to questions I pretended not to hear.

Feeling was coming back in parts of my face. I realized I hadn't touched my float, and wouldn't be able to. I could feel, however, each curve of a pill bottle pressed thankfully against my thigh. Son asked about my nickname, Sausage.

Nicknames. His mother shouted plenty in the single-wide he was conceived in — though none were as original as Sausage, where neighbors covered their windows with foil, where neighbors felt safe enough within their thin walls to weep loudly.

Sausage was anointed by a commentator 5
the only time a fight of mine was televised. Said I string together garbage techniques nobody else uses: triple jabs, crescent kicks, standing elbows. It was meant, briefly, as a compliment. First round,

everything I threw landed. Everything, including me, was covered with someone else's blood. It ended as my first time getting knocked out.

"Everything," I said, "makes us who we are, whether we want it or not."

If my son was pleased with that answer, he showed it by taking substantial sips from his float, then said, "What's it feel like? Going out cold?"

I laughed hard at that, which caused everything to hurt, including my hands, which best I recall didn't land a punch.

The only employee darkened the open sign. A rag, sanitizer, and ancient hands waiting. I started saying that pretty well answered his question, but by then he was slurping loud just like his mother used to, so I said, "Feels same as raising you."

*

I dropped son off in a subdivision near a reservoir, one that submerged an entire town. Houses, graves, roads, all buried. I reckon there's not a single truth remembered from the world below.

I drove all night towards Tampa, though I knew my next fight wouldn't be medically cleared. One eye had swollen in a way that traffic coming at me looked like a laser light show, like one I saw at SeaWorld when I was small, Alabama playing in the background. ■

db Waterman

Understanding Literature

Humans tell stories. And it is through these stories that we communicate, entertain, and make sense of our world. Think about times that you get together with your family or friends. Much of your conversation likely consists of telling stories about something that happened to you, something you saw on the internet, or something that is going on in another person's life. As professor and writer Jonathan Gottschall observes in a TED Talk, "This is what we are doing all the time, every day, in our lives: We are trying to impose the order of story structure on the chaos of existence."

Storytelling seems to have originated with humanity itself, even before the written word. The cave drawings in the Chauvet Cave in France, which were created over forty thousand years ago, portray the animals with which the artists interacted while hunting and herding. Aside from depicting typical herbivores, such as horses and bison, the paintings shed light on the variety of predatory animals that coexisted with humans during the Ice Age, including panthers and lions. They are simple narratives, lacking all the plot twists and drama we've come to appreciate, but they're stories nonetheless.

When we listen to other people's stories, we see ourselves in them; stories help us empathize and identify with others. Or, as Atticus Finch in *To Kill a Mockingbird* puts it, "You never really understand a person . . . until you climb into his skin and walk around in it." These stories come in many forms, or genres, including those we refer to as *literature*—imaginative texts such as novels, films, plays, and poetry. Literature is both an exploration of ourselves and of everything beyond ourselves. In fact, researchers at Ohio State University have "found that after reading literary fiction . . . people performed better on tests measuring empathy, social perception, and emotional intelligence—skills that come in especially handy when you are trying to read someone's body language or gauge what they might be thinking." So, if telling stories makes us human, reading stories puts us in touch with our humanity.

Patrick Aventurier/Getty Images

The drawings in the Chauvet Cave in France depict various animals along a single section of the cave wall. **What story do you think this particular section is depicting? Do any interactions between the animals seem familiar to you?**

activity

Reflecting on Your Relationship with Storytelling

Describe your experiences with stories. What kinds of stories are important to you? Where do you typically read, watch, or hear stories? What makes the experience of engaging with stories so enjoyable?

Talking It Through

Meet with a partner or group and share some of your thoughts and ideas. What's similar about your responses? What's different?

Thinking Abstractly about Literature

The stories we tell as part of the human experience can be complex. Those who tell stories often use structure and language creatively to convey meaning. That's why, in English class, we do more than tell stories — we tend to analyze them as well. Analyzing means looking carefully at the parts of something in order to better understand the whole. You might analyze the gears and springs in a clock to understand how it works, for instance.

Now, you might be thinking that analysis is where English classes become confusing and overwhelming. You might even find yourself agreeing with Melinda, the narrator of the young adult novel *Speak* by Laurie Halse Anderson. In the following excerpt from the novel, Melinda describes how her teacher, whom she calls "Hairwoman," teaches *The Scarlet Letter* by Nathaniel Hawthorne:

> It's Nathaniel Hawthorne Month in English. Poor Nathaniel. Does he know what they've done to him? We are reading *The Scarlet Letter* one sentence at a time, tearing it up and chewing on its bones.
>
> It's all about SYMBOLISM, says Hairwoman. Every word chosen by Nathaniel, every comma, every paragraph break — these were all done on purpose. To get a decent grade in her class, we have to figure out what he was really trying to say. Why couldn't he just say what he meant? Would they pin scarlet letters on his chest? B for blunt, S for straightforward?

Melinda brings up two key complaints that are often raised by students studying literature:

1. The study of literature is mostly about hunting for hidden symbols and meanings in order to get a good grade.
2. Authors don't really mean to do whatever English teachers say they do. They can't possibly think about all of this as they write their stories. It's all made up.

Melinda's concerns convey that she doesn't understand that literature is composed of abstractions. Authors work through implication, metaphor, symbolism, and imagery to convey both literal and figurative meanings, concrete and abstract ideas. You'll need to be willing to think abstractly to engage with literature. When Romeo sees Juliet on the balcony, he says, "But, soft! What light through yonder window breaks? It is the east, and Juliet is the sun." Obviously, Romeo isn't saying that Juliet is literally the sun, but rather that her beauty is like that of the sun, or maybe that seeing her is like the start of a brand-new day for him. Abstract language often leaves room for multiple plausible interpretations. In this chapter, we're going to help you develop your abstract thinking skills, which are essential not only to interpreting literature, but also to understanding the complexities of our world.

How do we deal with abstraction? We actively engage with the text to make meaning from it. In fact, reading the text is only the beginning of the larger process of analysis: interpreting what we read. In the example from *Speak*, Melinda seems to be reading just for understanding, but this chapter will focus on the other two ways we read to reach the deeper meanings of a text: reading for interpretation and reading for style. Both of those types of reading require analysis. As novelist and artist Douglas Coupland describes it, "Storytelling is ultimately a creative act of pattern recognition. Through characters, plot, and setting, a writer creates places where previously invisible truths become visible. Or the storyteller posits a series of dots that the reader can connect."

This is a promotional poster for *Edward Scissorhands* (1990). **How does this poster visually illustrate the conflict Edward faces? What are other films you know that ask their audiences to think abstractly about the characters, subjects, settings, or situations?**

As for Melinda's second point — questioning whether authors intentionally mean to do what English teachers say they do — she is probably half right. Language and storytelling are rich, complex things that even an author can't fully control. Sometimes the meaning we find in a piece of literature is just a happy accident, a pattern that readers found and the author neither noticed nor intended. When Joseph Heller, author of *Catch-22*, was asked whether readers sometimes found meaning in his work he had not intended, he said, "This happens often, and in every case there is good reason for the inference; in many cases, I have been able to learn something about my own book, for readers have seen much in the book that is there, although I was not aware of it being there." This is part of what makes reading so much fun: readers are empowered to make discoveries as they develop reasonable interpretations of texts. Where Melinda is half wrong, however, is that there absolutely *are* times when authors intend to develop an idea abstractly through implication, metaphor, or symbolism. In doing so, they present the idea in

Thinking Abstractly

activity

Look at this painting by Salvador Dalí, *The Persistence of Memory* (1931). As Burton does with the scissors in *Edward Scissorhands*, Dalí treats the clocks metaphorically. After analyzing the details of how Dalí presents the clocks, try to make an interpretation about what he might be suggesting about time. What does the title tell you about Dalí's intended meaning in this piece? What is an alternative title for the painting that might reflect your conclusion?

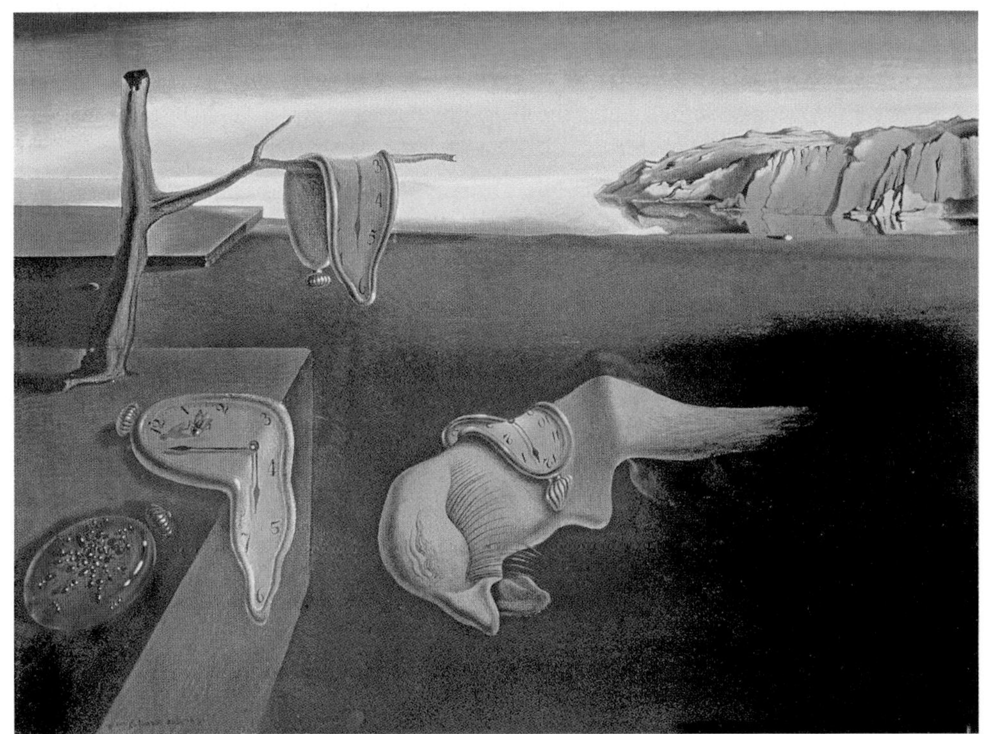

Persistence of memory (Soft Watches). Painting by Salvador Dali (1904–1989), 1931. Oil on canvas. New York, Museum of Modern Art (MOMA)/Dali, Salvador (1904–89) ©Luisa Ricciarini/Bridgeman Images; © 2020 Salvador Dalí, Fundació Gala-Salvador Dalí, Artists Rights Society (ARS), New York

a more interesting, powerful, or nuanced way than they would if they were "blunt" or "straightforward." American writer Ralph Ellison agrees that "man is a symbol-making and -using animal. . . . The great writers all used symbol as a means of controlling the form of their fiction."

Consider Tim Burton's film *Edward Scissorhands* (1990). The film is about a mechanical man, played by Johnny Depp, whose creator died before he could finish building him, leaving him with scissors instead of hands. Circumstances cause Edward to leave his safe, solitary home and integrate into society. It's clear that the scissors are a metaphor. Burton could have given Edward normal hands, or even, say, salad tongs for hands. So, to address Melinda's point, yes, Burton chose scissors on purpose because they work metaphorically. Scissors can be both useful tools and dangerous weapons, which exactly mirrors the conflicting reactions Edward encounters as he tries to protect those he loves, often from himself.

Eventually Melinda from *Speak* begins thinking abstractly and realizes something else, too—writing that is completely literal wouldn't be all that interesting to read:

> I can't whine too much. Some of it is fun. It's like a code, breaking into his head and finding the key to his secrets. Like the whole guilt thing. Of course you know the minister feels guilty and Hester feels guilty, but Nathaniel wants us to know this is a big deal. If he kept repeating, "She felt guilty, she felt guilty, she felt guilty," it would be a boring book and no one would buy it.

Theme in Literature

In Chapter 1, you explored the three ways that we read a text to help us determine its meaning: understanding, interpretation, and style. When we read a piece of literature for **understanding**, we should be able to produce an accurate **summary** of it, including the most significant subjects it explores. When we read a piece of literature for **interpretation**, however, we should be able to make a statement of **theme** — what the author might be suggesting about the main subjects of the text. For William Shakespeare's *Romeo and Juliet*, we might identify the following:

Summary: The children of two feuding households fall in love, which results in disastrous consequences.

Main Subjects: love, family feuds, friendship

Possible Theme: Through *Romeo and Juliet*, William Shakespeare suggests that love is a powerful force that, once unleashed, cannot be controlled.

Note that we have said "possible" theme above, because a complex piece of literature like *Romeo and Juliet* usually has multiple themes. The goal in this chapter is to make sure that you practice going beyond reading for understanding — an essential first step — to being able to read a literary text for its theme.

Let's further explore the concept of theme using Aesop's fable "The Tortoise and the Hare," in which the arrogant hare, thinking there's no way that the slow tortoise can beat him in a race, takes a nap in the middle of the competition. In the end, the moral is stated: "Slow but steady wins the race." This example fits our definition of theme, since it identifies the idea of the text and reveals something about the real world.

Read this version of "The Tortoise and the Hare" and identify the theme. **How is the theme of this version different from that of the original?**

Sometimes the theme is clearly and explicitly stated in a text, as in the 2002 movie version of *Spider-Man*, when Uncle Ben tells Peter Parker, "With great power comes great responsibility." More often, however, the theme of a work is implied: It is slowly established as the story progresses.

At this point, you might be thinking that the theme is just something you can make up, and that you can interpret literature any way you like because your interpretation is just based on your opinion. While the answers in an English class are not always as concrete as they might be in a math class, there can, in fact, be right and wrong answers. Just because readers may differ in their interpretations of a piece of literature does not mean that *any* interpretation is valid. An interpretation needs to be backed up by evidence, just like in any other class. As we said earlier, the act of interpreting literature is about seeing how the details add up to a big idea; therefore, the most important part of analyzing literature is that you build your interpretation through analysis. To say that young love has no value in the world and should be dismissed as childish nonsense would be an incorrect interpretation of *Romeo and Juliet*. Upon examining the text, we would find too much evidence showing that this is simply not what the text is saying.

Identifying Theme

Choose one text from the following list of fairy tales, fables, and films that you may have heard, read, or seen, or choose one of your own. Briefly summarize the plot and write two to three subjects that are important in the text. Then, identify the theme using one of the identified subjects, and provide evidence from the text that supports your thematic statement. Remember, the theme may be explicitly stated, but it is more likely to be implied throughout the work.

1. *The Three Little Pigs*
2. *Little Red Riding Hood*
3. *Beauty and the Beast*
4. *The Wizard of Oz*
5. The *Harry Potter* series
6. A superhero film

Interpreting Theme

When you're asked to analyze literature, especially a long text like a novel or a play, it can be overwhelming if you don't know what to look for. It's certainly tempting and a whole lot easier to just search, "What is the theme of ___________?" But any information you gather in that way is secondhand, which means that you can be accused of cheating and the results may not be accurate. Moreover, you miss the opportunity to engage with a text on your own terms, making connections and asking questions that can lead to an original interpretation of the work. Writer Francine Prose describes her own experience reading for theme in high school English:

> When I was a high school junior, our English teacher assigned a term paper on . . . blindness in Oedipus Rex and King Lear. We were supposed to go through the two tragedies and circle every reference to eyes, light, darkness, and vision, then draw some conclusion on which we would base our final essay. . . .
>
> Tracing those patterns and making those connections was fun. Like cracking a code that the playwright had embedded in the text, a riddle that existed just for me to decipher. I felt as if I were engaged in some intimate communication with the writer, as if the ghosts of Sophocles and Shakespeare had been waiting patiently all those centuries for a bookish sixteen-year-old to come along and find them.
>
> I believed that I was learning to read in a whole new way.

What Prose does here is read for interpretation like we explored in Chapter 1: She reads closely, asks questions, and makes connections between the two characters. While Prose does not reveal exactly what interpretation she arrived at, she implies that she drew an interesting conclusion about the works in the term paper she was assigned.

While reading a text carefully and thinking abstractly, you should mark it with your ideas or annotations. But what exactly should you be looking for? First of all, let's recall that in Chapter 1 we discussed that each reading of a text allows us to make new discoveries. Don't be discouraged if you don't see everything at once. We certainly don't. As you make connections and ask questions through your annotations, keep these four topics in mind:

- **Curiosities.** Things you find puzzling, intriguing, or ambiguous. This is where you try to think abstractly, as described on pages 28–32.
- **Repetitions.** Repeated images, words, phrases, settings, structures, rhymes, and so on.
- **Opposites.** Contrasts like light/dark, good/evil, or characters or settings that seem to be in opposition.
- **Links.** Connections and **allusions**, including references in the text to art, history, literature, or religion that the writer expects the reader to know.

Look carefully at *The Third of May 1808*, a painting by Francisco Goya that depicts the Spanish resistance to the army of Napoleon, who had conquered Spain. The subject of the painting is war, but what is Goya suggesting about war in this painting? We can apply the four ideas above to answer this question and determine a possible theme.

Erich Lessing/Art Resource, NY

Francisco Goya, *The Third of May 1808*.

Curiosities

You might find it curious that, despite what looks to be his imminent death, the man in the center has thrown his arms wide in defiance — or is it submission? You might find it curious that the people in the background seem to blend into the landscape.

Repetitions

You might notice that each soldier on the right has a hood on, and that you can't see these soldiers' faces.

Opposites

You probably notice the opposites in the painting right away; the man about to be executed is in bright light, while his executioners are in dark. In addition, you can see opposites in the straight, formal line of soldiers contrasting with the chaotic alignment of the civilians.

Links

As the central character in this painting is wearing white and holding his arms out, Goya might be suggesting a Christ-like pose and indicating the righteousness of his sacrifice.

From these observations and patterns, you could probably draw a reasonable conclusion regarding Goya's thoughts on war. Through the details in *The Third of May 1808,* Goya suggests that war is inhumane and that it takes the heroism and sacrifice of average citizens to liberate a country.

Interpreting Theme

As you read the poem "Famous" by Naomi Shihab Nye, make connections and ask questions about the curiosities, opposites, repetitions, and links that come to mind. Propose a reasonable interpretation of what Nye might be suggesting about being famous. Be sure to include specific references to the poem to support your interpretation.

Famous

Naomi Shihab Nye

The river is famous to the fish.
The loud voice is famous to silence,
which knew it would inherit the earth
before anybody said so.
The cat sleeping on the fence is famous to the birds
watching him from the birdhouse.
The tear is famous, briefly, to the cheek.
The idea you carry close to your bosom
is famous to your bosom.

The boot is famous to the earth,
more famous than the dress shoe,
which is famous only to floors.
The bent photograph is famous to the one who carries it
and not at all famous to the one who is pictured.
I want to be famous to shuffling men
who smile while crossing streets,
sticky children in grocery lines,
famous as the one who smiled back.
I want to be famous in the way a pulley is famous,
or a buttonhole, not because it did anything spectacular,
but because it never forgot what it could do. ■

Elements of Fiction

You are probably familiar with the standard elements of storytelling — point of view, characterization, plot and conflict, setting, and symbol — but have you ever really wondered why English teachers insist that these are important? The reason is that each of these elements is a tool that authors use to craft their stories, and thus convey their ideas — the themes of their work. In this next section, you will have an opportunity to review these elements and consider how writers use them to help develop a work's theme.

Point of View

One of the very first and most significant choices a writer makes is the perspective from which the story will be told. The options for point of view in a novel or short story include the following:

First Person The narrator uses pronouns such as "I," "me," "we," and "us" and is often, but not always, the main character in the story.

> **Example:** "My name is Christopher John Francis Boone. I know all the countries of the world and their capital cities and every prime number up to 7,057."
>
> –Mark Haddon, *The Curious Incident of the Dog in the Night-time*

Third Person The narrator uses "he," "she," "they," and "them" and is not usually a character within the story. There are a few different types of third-person narration:

- An *omniscient* narrator is one who knows what every character is thinking and can move easily through time.

> **Example:** "They accepted the pleasures of morning, the bright sun, the whelming sea and sweet air, as a time when play was good and life so full that hope was not necessary and therefore forgotten."
>
> –William Golding, *Lord of the Flies*

- A *limited omniscient narrator* is one who knows the thoughts of only one character.

  Example: "When he had been younger, Harry had dreamed and dreamed of some unknown relation coming to take him away, but it had never happened; the Dursley's were his only family."

  –J. K. Rowling, *Harry Potter and the Sorcerer's Stone*

- An *objective narrator* is one who reports the actions and dialogue of the characters and describes the setting but does not move into the thoughts of any of the characters.

  Example: "The woman brought two glasses of beer and two felt pads. She put the felt pads and the beer glasses on the table and looked at the man and the girl. The girl was looking off at the line of hills. They were white in the sun and the country was brown and dry."

  –Ernest Hemingway, "Hills Like White Elephants"

Second Person While it is used very rarely, some authors choose a second person narration, which uses the pronoun "you" to address the reader directly. Essentially, it treats the reader like a character within the story.

Example: "You are amongst them, of course. Your curiosity got the better of you, as curiosity is wont to do. You stand in the fading light, the scarf around your neck pulled up against the chilly evening breeze, waiting to see for yourself exactly what kind of circus only opens once the sun sets."

–Erin Morgenstern, *The Night Circus*

KEY QUESTIONS

When connecting point of view to theme, consider the following:

- What does the perspective reveal and what does it hide from readers about the story?
- Why did the storyteller choose this specific point of view to tell the story?

Characterization

Because the characters are often the focus of the action in a text, one of the most significant ways to determine a central idea, or theme, is to closely examine them. For example, by focusing on Harry Potter's decision to sacrifice himself to save others from Lord Voldemort at the very end of the series, J. K. Rowling illustrates the idea that the evil of the world will only be conquered by remembering the importance of community, family, and friendship.

As you probably know, the two main characters in a piece of literature are the **protagonist** (main character) and the **antagonist** (who opposes the main character). It is important to remember that the protagonist is not necessarily good, and the antagonist is not necessarily bad. Some of Edgar Allan Poe's short stories, for instance, feature protagonists who are murderers and antagonists who are potential victims.

The way an author brings a character to life is called **characterization**, and there are two basic techniques:

Direct characterization is when the author explicitly comments on or describes a character (for example, by having the narrator state that a character is tall, short, mean, or friendly).

Indirect characterization is when the author develops the character through things the character does and says, or what others say to or about the character. The reader is expected to infer certain aspects of the character through this type of characterization. For example, if the narrator states, "The young woman got up and offered her seat on the bus to the old woman," the reader might conclude, without being explicitly told, that the young woman is kind and polite.

The essential components that authors tend to include for characterization are the following:

- physical descriptions
- actions, gestures, movements
- dialogue
- what other characters say or think about a character
- how other characters behave toward him or her
- character motivations
- character internal thoughts

KEY QUESTIONS

When thinking about how character relates to theme, focus on these questions:

- What do characters' actions, inactions, traits, and motivations reveal about them?
- How does character development throughout the work connect to the author's central ideas?

Plot and Conflict

The **plot** of a story refers not only to the events that take place in the text, but also to the arrangement of these events. You may have studied the classic plot structure of exposition, rising action, climax, falling action, and resolution. However, flashbacks, flashforwards, and subplots can add greater complexity to the way writers structure their stories.

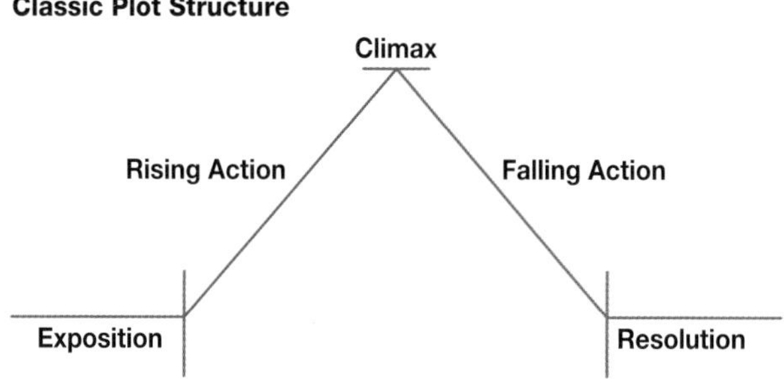

The story of Homer's *The Odyssey*, for example, is that of a general in the Greek army who wins a war against Troy and spends the next ten years trying to get home to Ithaca. He experiences many adventures along the way, including a battle with the Cyclops. The plot of *The Odyssey*, however, is far more complex. It begins when a council of the Greek gods determines the fate of Odysseus, who is already many years into his journey home. From there, the reader meets Odysseus's nearly grown son and we see what life is like in Ithaca without Odysseus. Only then do we get the stories, told in flashback, of Odysseus's adventures. The story is not told chronologically or linearly. In other words, paying attention to these aspects of the plot enhances our appreciation of the story as a whole. When analyzing literature, remember that authors can present a story in any manner they wish, so you should always ask yourself why the events of the story unfold the way that they do.

The key to every plot is **conflict**, which is generally summarized as a struggle between a protagonist and an antagonist. However, it doesn't have to be limited to clashes between two characters. The main types of conflicts are listed below with examples from literature and movies:

- **One Character vs. Another Character.** Harry Potter against Voldemort; Dorothy against the Wicked Witch
- **Character vs. Society.** Katniss going up against the Capitol; Atticus Finch battling the racism of the American South in the 1930s
- **Character vs. Nature.** Odysseus against the winds of the Mediterranean; Frodo against the snowstorm on the mountainside
- **Character vs. Self.** Luke Skywalker against his own immaturity and impulsiveness; Odysseus against his own arrogance

KEY QUESTIONS

When thinking about how plot relates to theme, consider the following questions:

- Why is the story told in the chosen order?
- What are the significant conflicts and how are they resolved — or not?

Setting

Setting provides context in a piece of literature. It establishes the location, time period, and cultural background. It also creates a specific atmosphere that provokes an emotional response in the audience. Think about a horror or mystery film you have seen. Many scenes probably took place at night, with lots of shadows, maybe in creepy abandoned houses. Obviously, these settings create feelings of suspense and unease. Like all of these literary elements, however, setting is also used as a tool by authors to illustrate meaning in their work. For instance, Harper Lee set *To Kill a Mockingbird* in the American South during the Jim Crow era because that setting is appropriate for commenting on race in American society.

KEY QUESTIONS

When thinking about how the setting of a piece of literature relates to its theme, ask yourself the following questions:

- What details of time and place create a specific feeling?
- How does the setting contribute to an understanding of the work as a whole?

Symbolism

Earlier in this chapter, you examined a poster from the movie *Edward Scissorhands.* The scissors act as a **symbol**, which may be an object, a person, a situation, or events or actions that have both literal and metaphorical meaning in a work of literature. In *Edward Scissorhands*, the character literally has scissors for hands. However, the scissors metaphorically represent his difficulty in connecting with other people. Our stories are filled with symbols: Cinderella's glass slipper; the poison in *Romeo and Juliet*; the dawning of a new day at the end of a horror film. They all have meanings beyond their literal use in the work. In Edgar Allan Poe's poem "The Raven," for example, the black bird is literally sitting in the room with the narrator, but it is also a metaphor for the narrator's feelings of loss and depression. In the movie *Citizen Kane*, an abandoned sled symbolizes the main character's lost childhood. You can often recognize symbols in a piece of literature by noting their repeated use and links to ideas outside of the text.

KEY QUESTIONS

When thinking about how symbolism in a piece of literature connects to the theme, ask yourself the following questions:

- What larger significance do the objects, situations, or events have?
- How do they help to illustrate a deeper meaning of the work?

Applying Elements of Fiction

Look carefully at the images that follow. Choose one image and write brief responses to the following questions, applying your knowledge of the elements of fiction described above:

1. **Characterization:** Who are the people in the picture? What do you imagine their names, ages, professions, interests, and physical and emotional qualities might be? What are they doing here?
2. **Setting:** Describe the location of this story for someone who has not seen the image. Can you identify the time of day, season, time period, or other physical details of the surroundings?
3. **Conflict:** What has happened, or what will happen? What is the main conflict?
4. **Point of View:** Write a sentence or two from the point of view of one of the figures in the image. Then, rewrite those same sentences from the third or second person point of view.
5. **Symbolism:** What in the image might hold some kind of larger significance? What might it represent?

Now, pull together what you've written to create a very brief short story that demonstrates your knowledge of the main elements of fiction. Be sure to choose a point of view and remain consistent throughout your short story.

Wednesday April 3 2002: Angola's parliament has approved an amnesty for the rebel UNITA movement which has agreed to end 27 years of hostility, 2002 (oil on panel)/McLaughlin, Ben/Private Collection/Bridgeman Images

Untitled, 2009 (oil on card)/McLaughlin, Ben (Contemporary Artist)/Private Collection/Bridgeman Images

00.40 A night with Beyonce, 2012 (oil on card laid on panel)/McLaughlin, Ben (Contemporary Artist)/Private Collection/Bridgeman Images

A Model Analysis: Connecting Elements of Fiction to Theme

Now that we've discussed the elements of fiction, let's see how they function in a story. Read the short story "Sticks" by George Saunders and then observe how we use our analysis of the elements of fiction to draw a conclusion about the possible themes of the work.

Sticks

George Saunders

Every year Thanksgiving night we flocked out behind Dad as he dragged the Santa suit to the road and draped it over a kind of crucifix he'd built out of metal pole in the yard. Super Bowl week the pole was dressed in a jersey and Rod's helmet and Rod had to clear it with Dad if he wanted to take the helmet off. On the Fourth of July the pole was Uncle Sam, on Veteran's Day a soldier, on Halloween a ghost. The pole was Dad's only concession to glee. We were allowed a single Crayola from the box at a time. One Christmas Eve he shrieked at Kimmie for wasting an apple slice. He hovered over us as we poured ketchup saying: good enough good enough good enough. Birthday parties consisted of cupcakes, no ice cream. The first time I brought a date over she said: what's with your dad and that pole? and I sat there blinking.

We left home, married, had children of our own, found the seeds of meanness blooming also within us. Dad began dressing the pole with more complexity and less discernible logic. He draped some kind of fur over it on Groundhog Day and lugged out a floodlight to ensure a shadow. When an earthquake struck Chile he lay the pole on its side and spray painted a rift in the earth. Mom died and he dressed the pole as Death and hung from the crossbar photos of Mom as a baby. We'd stop by and find odd talismans from his youth arranged around the base: army medals, theater tickets, old sweatshirts, tubes of Mom's makeup. One autumn he painted the pole bright yellow. He covered it with cotton swabs that winter for warmth and provided offspring by hammering in six crossed sticks around the yard. He ran lengths of string between the pole and the sticks, and taped to the string letters of apology, admissions of error, pleas for understanding, all written in a frantic hand on index cards. He painted a sign saying LOVE and hung it from the pole and another that said FORGIVE? and then he died in the hall with the radio on and we sold the house to a young couple who yanked out the pole and the sticks and left them by the road on garbage day. ■

Point of View

Saunders chooses a first-person narrator for this story, which prevents the reader from knowing exactly what is going on in the other characters' thoughts. We normally look for the first-person pronoun "I" in this type of narration. But the story opens with the word "we." Notice how the narrator speaks for himself (or herself, depending on your interpretation) and the siblings in this sentence, but the voice telling the story belongs to a single person. The reader perceives the world only through what one of the man's grown children chooses to tell.

Characters

We mainly understand the father's character through his interactions with the pole because his exchanges with his children are limited. His relationship with his family is clearly damaged by his inability to talk about his thoughts and emotions. This makes him seem odd and he is thrust into further isolation. The narrator's words and actions reveal that their father's isolation shapes their own development, particularly when the narrator admits that all of the siblings "found the seeds of meanness blooming also within."

Plot/Conflict

In fewer than 400 words, Saunders presents us with the progression of a man and his family through time. The children "[flock] out behind dad" when they are young, eventually marry and move out, and ultimately sell their childhood home when their father dies. There appears to be a conflict between the father's meanness — both in terms of temperament and his thrifty nature — and the rest of the family. A more subtle conflict, however, exists within the characters themselves as they struggle to confront their own emotions.

Setting

The bulk of the recollection centers on the yard of the narrator childhood home. The timeframe of the story, however, spans from when the siblings are children living with their parents to when they are adults and contending with their parents' deaths. Interestingly, time is marked by the presence of holidays: Thanksgiving, Christmas, the Fourth of July, Veteran's Day, Halloween, and Groundhog Day.

Symbolism

Several aspects of the story function as symbolism. The pole is the dominant symbol, specifically because it is described as a "crucifix." In a Christian context, this is associated with death, torment, forgiveness, and resurrection. The "six crossed sticks" are referred to as the "offspring" of the pole, which may thereby represent the narrator and the family. We can also consider the symbolism attached to some of the holidays that are mentioned. For example, instead of commenting on the importance of family and being grateful for what we have, Saunders simply mentions Thanksgiving.

Possible Themes

Saunders touches upon many subjects in this short story: communication, family, forgiveness, love. One possible theme is the inevitability of children turning out like their parents. While we repeatedly see the father substituting his interactions with the pole for actual communication with his family, the narrator does not seem much different. Note how the narrator shares the news of their parents' deaths, moving away from home, and selling their childhood home with the same matter-of-fact tone that they used when stating that "the pole was Uncle Sam" on the Fourth of July. In fact, the link with their father is undeniable when they freely admit that the father's meanness was "blooming also within" both the narrator and the siblings.

Connecting Elements of Fiction to Theme

Carefully read the following excerpt from *The Scarlet Letter*, the novel by Nathaniel Hawthorne that Melinda, the narrator from *Speak*, complained about, and annotate the text by making connections and asking questions, as you did in Chapter 1. In addition, look for curiosities, repetitions, opposites, and links (p. 35). As you read the excerpt a second time, think about how Hawthorne uses point of view, characterization, plot and conflict, setting, and symbol. Finally, draw a conclusion about what Hawthorne might be suggesting about guilt and punishment in this excerpt.

from The Scarlet Letter

Nathaniel Hawthorne

This novel, published in 1850, focuses on life in Massachusetts during the Puritan era of the 1640s. Puritans were a group of religious dissidents from England who left their parent country to establish a religious utopia in the New World. They led strict and pious lives and banned nonreligious entertainment, games, and even the celebration of holidays.

The main character in this story is a young woman, Hester Prynne, whose husband is presumed to be lost at sea. She is convicted of adultery after giving birth to a child, Pearl. In addition to being imprisoned for what the Puritans considered to be a crime, Hester was ordered to embroider a scarlet *A*, and to wear it on the outside of her clothes.

In this excerpt, Hester has just been released from prison. The townspeople, all strict Puritans, see Hester, Pearl, and the scarlet *A* for the first time since her conviction. She is ordered to stand on a scaffold for three hours so that everyone can see her.

When the young woman — the mother of this child — stood fully revealed before the crowd, it seemed to be her first impulse to clasp the infant closely to her bosom; not so much by an impulse of motherly affection, as that she might thereby conceal a certain token, which was wrought or fastened into her dress. In a moment, however, wisely judging that one token of her shame would but poorly serve to hide another, she took the baby on her arm, and with a burning blush, and yet a haughty smile, and a glance that would not be abashed, looked around at her townspeople and neighbours. On the breast of her gown, in fine red cloth, surrounded with an elaborate embroidery and fantastic flourishes of gold thread, appeared the letter A. It was so artistically done, and with so much fertility and gorgeous luxuriance of fancy, that it had all the effect of a last and fitting decoration to the apparel which she wore, and which was of a splendour in accordance with the taste of the age, but greatly beyond what was allowed by the sumptuary regulations of the colony.

The young woman was tall, with a figure of perfect elegance, on a large scale. She had dark and abundant hair, so glossy that it threw off the sunshine with a gleam, and a face which, besides being beautiful from regularity of feature and richness of complexion, had the impressiveness belonging to a marked brow and deep black eyes. She was lady-like, too, after the manner of the feminine gentility of those days; characterized by a certain state and dignity, rather than by the delicate, evanescent, and indescribable grace which is now recognized as its indication. And never had Hester Prynne appeared more lady-like, in the antique interpretation of the term, than as she issued from the prison. Those who had before known her, and had expected to behold her dimmed and obscured by a disastrous cloud, were astonished, and even startled, to perceive how her beauty shone out, and made a halo of the misfortune and ignominy in which she was enveloped. It may be true, that, to a sensitive observer, there was something exquisitely painful in it. Her attire, which, indeed, she had wrought for the occasion, in prison, and had modelled much after her own fancy, seemed to express the attitude of her spirit, the desperate recklessness of her mood, by its wild and picturesque peculiarity. But the point which drew all eyes, and, as it were, transfigured the wearer — so that both men and women, who had been familiarly acquainted with Hester Prynne, were now impressed as if they beheld her for the first time — was that SCARLET LETTER, so fantastically embroidered and illuminated upon her bosom. It had the effect of a spell, taking her out of the ordinary relations with humanity, and inclosing her in a sphere by herself. ■

The Scarlet Letter, 1861 (oil on canvas)/Merle, Hugues (1823–81)/Walters Art Museum, Baltimore, USA/Bridgeman Images

The young lady stood fuuly revealed/Thomson, Hugh (1860–1920)/IVAN LAWRENCE ESQ./Private Collection/Bridgeman Images

Look at these two images showing Hester Prynne.

What are the similarities and differences in how each artist portrays Hester? Which of these visual interpretations seems more in line with Hawthorne's description of her in the text?

SPEAKING & LISTENING FOCUS

Discussing Interpretations of Literature

Determining meaning in a piece of literature is a complex process because literature is often abstract, with multiple plausible interpretations. One of the best ways to deepen your ability to analyze literature is to participate in discussions with others; each person can bring a different perspective to a work because of his or her own life experiences, gender identity, culture, race, and other factors. Therefore, it's essential to make every effort to hear all voices when you are discussing literature with a group. Be sure to take the following steps:

1. Respond personally. Taking turns, members of the group should share their personal responses to the piece of literature. This is not yet the place for analysis; group members should share what they liked or didn't like about the piece, what it reminded them of, or what personal connections they can make with the characters, setting, conflict, and so on.

2. Consider evidence. To move from personal response to analysis, have each group member share an interpretation of a character, the theme, or tone of the work. After each person shares, the rest of the group should try to support that person's interpretation by pointing to specific evidence from the text. Repeat this process for each member of the group. After everyone has had the opportunity to share an interpretation, decide as a group which of the interpretations you discussed has the most evidence to support it.

3. Analyze style. Finally, move on to discussing the style of the piece (see Chapter 1, p. 15). Group members should spend a few minutes working independently to identify a sentence or two that illustrates the stylistic choices of the piece. It might be an interesting sound, rhythm, or image. Then, spend some time sharing and discussing the sentences each group member identified. Think back to the second step and the interpretation your group thought would have the most evidence to support it. Which of the stylistic elements you've identified as a group seems most closely connected to that interpretation?

Practice

In small groups, discuss the excerpt from *The Scarlet Letter* using the steps outlined above. Although you've already completed an activity with this excerpt from the novel, you will see that engaging in these speaking and listening steps will enhance your understanding and appreciation of the excerpt from the novel.

Reflection

How did discussing the piece in a group add to or change your original interpretation of the work? What did you learn by discussing the piece with others?

Elements of Drama

Drama is a form of storytelling in which actors who are on stage perform before a live audience. It shares most of its elements with fiction, such as plot, characterization, setting, and symbols. It's less likely that drama will have a specific point of view, though it's not unheard of to have a narrator. The use of a narrator occasionally makes the point of view third person. Let's take a look at how the elements of storytelling function in drama.

Plot

While plot in drama also adheres to an arc that ranges from exposition to resolution, the main structure is often divided into **acts** and **scenes**. When analyzing a drama's plot structure, pay attention to the acts and scenes marked by the playwright and how characters change as you proceed through these sections.

Although many plays are told chronologically, playwrights have found other inventive ways of structuring their plays. For example, in *Death of a Salesman*, Arthur Miller uses the characters' placement on stage to convey whether the events belong to the past or present.

Character

Dialogue, or characters' conversations with each other, is pivotal to characterization in drama. Aside from engaging in dialogue with another actor, sometimes a single actor delivers an extended speech, which we call a **monologue**. When a monologue is not spoken to another character, but is a verbal expression of a character's thoughts, we call it a **soliloquy**. Because soliloquies allow the audience to enter the character's mind, they are critical to the analysis of characterization.

How actors move on stage, called **blocking**, and how they interact with others also reveal aspects of the characters they are playing. As you read, visualize these actors on stage. Your interpretation of how the scene should be blocked can influence your understanding of the characters. When reading a play, pay close attention to **stage directions** — the instructions of how actors should speak or interact with others — because these details might provide insight into the characters' thoughts, motivations, and emotions.

Setting

Cues regarding a play's setting can be conveyed through dialogue, stage directions, and props. Since we aren't reading lengthy descriptions of the scenery, the way we would in novels and short stories, we have to pay close attention to every detail. The audience knows, for instance, that Henrik Ibsen's *A Doll's House* takes place in December because we see a Christmas tree on stage. In Tennessee Williams's *A Streetcar Named Desire*, the streetcars, music, and climate place us in New Orleans. It's important to recognize, however, that setting is not simply the backdrop of a play;

Robbie Jack/Corbis Entertainment/Getty Images

Look at this still from a 2009 London production of *A Doll's House*, by Henrik Ibsen.
Even if you don't know much about the plot of the play, what conclusions might you draw about it from the set, the props in the background, and the ways that the characters are dressed and positioned?

it is a critical element that influences characters' feelings and subsequent actions. In Williams's play, for instance, as the oppressive heat in New Orleans assaults the characters, their interactions become more volatile and destructive.

Symbolism

Symbols in drama are sometimes props, actions, or statements by characters. Since we do not have detailed paragraphs that highlight the presence and importance of a symbol, we need to read the stage directions very carefully to identify the props that will be on stage. In fact, while symbolism in prose may be presented in a subtle manner, it may be even more difficult to identify it in drama if you don't pay attention to all the props that are on the stage. Sometimes, actors will interact with these objects. For example, Mama's relationship with her precious plant in *A Raisin in the Sun* represents her nurturing character and hope for the future. Other times, the symbol will be mentioned only briefly — and perhaps not even appear on the stage. Examples of this type of symbolism are Desire and Cemeteries, the two streetcars mentioned in Williams's play. Their names are clear indicators that our desires could lead to our deaths.

activity

Literary Elements and Theme in Drama

Carefully read the following excerpt from *A Raisin in the Sun*, by Lorraine Hansberry. First, annotate or respond to the text by making connections and asking questions, as you did in Chapter 1. In addition, look for curiosities, repetitions, opposites, and links (p. 35). Then, write a brief response describing how Hansberry uses characterization, plot and conflict, setting, and symbol. Use your observations to identify a possible theme that emerges from this excerpt.

from A Raisin in the Sun

Lorraine Hansberry

The play takes place in Chicago in the 1950s. The Younger family has been having financial difficulties, but recently Mama has received an insurance settlement after the death of her husband. Her son, Walter, wants to use the money for a risky business investment.

WALTER . . . Do you know what this money means to me? Do you know what this money can do for us? (*puts it back*) Mama — Mama — I want so many things . . .

MAMA Yes, son —

WALTER I want so many things that they are driving me kind of crazy . . . Mama — look at me.

MAMA I'm looking at you. You a good-looking boy. You got a job, a nice wife, a fine boy and —

WALTER A job. (*looks at her*) Mama, a job? I open and close car doors all day long. I drive a man around in his limousine and I say, "Yes, sir; no, sir; very good, sir; shall I take the Drive, sir?" Mama, that ain't no kind of job . . . that ain't nothing at all. (*very quietly*) Mama, I don't know if I can make you understand.

MAMA Understand what, baby?

WALTER (*quietly*) Sometimes it's like I can see the future stretched out in front of me — just plain as day. The future, Mama. Hanging over there at the edge of my days. Just waiting for me — a big, looming blank space — full of nothing. Just waiting for me. But it don't have to be. (*Pause. Kneeling beside her chair.*) Mama — sometimes when I'm downtown and I pass them cool, quiet-looking restaurants where them white boys are sitting back and talking 'bout things . . . sitting there turning deals worth millions of dollars . . . sometimes I see guys don't look much older than me —

MAMA Son — how come you talk so much 'bout money?

WALTER (*with immense passion*) Because it is life, Mama!

MAMA (*quietly*) Oh — (*very quietly*) So now it's life. Money is life. Once upon a time freedom used to be life — now it's money. I guess the world really do change . . .

WALTER No — it was always money, Mama. We just didn't know about it. ■

Talking It Through

With a partner, discuss how drama is similar to and different from fiction. How would this excerpt from *A Raisin in the Sun* be different if it were written as a piece of fiction, or if the story "Sticks" (p. 44) were written as a piece of drama?

Elements of Poetry

Unlike fiction and drama, poetry doesn't necessarily tell a story—though it might. Poetry is a type of literature that artfully expresses an idea, conveys an experience, or describes an object. It can have characters, point of view, conflict (though plot is rare), setting, and certainly symbols. A number of important elements, however, are unique to studying poetry. Let's start by talking a bit about how we read poetry, and what we look for.

Making Meaning – Looking for Shifts

Working with poetry involves connecting the dots between language, sound, and structure in order to understand not just what the poem means, but how the poet created that meaning. That's a lot to take in, so let's first go back to some of the ideas that you might remember from Chapter 1. When you read a poem closely, you still read it in three ways:

1. Reading for understanding
2. Reading for interpretation
3. Reading for style

When you first encounter a poem, begin with a literal reading: try to understand what the words are saying. One of the most common mistakes students make is skipping this step entirely, moving right to interpretation, and ending up off the mark. Once you understand the poem literally, look at the ideas in the poem and come to an interpretation of its meaning and significance. Finally, read it for style, to appreciate and understand how the author uses language to create that meaning, and to create interesting sounds. The addition of sound here is a bit of a departure if you're used to reading fiction. Poetry is often intended to be read aloud, performed even, so sometimes creating an interesting sound is an end in itself.

When you're reading poetry in these ways, look for patterns and *where patterns shift*. Almost every poem has one or more **shifts**, and they are the key to understanding and interpreting poetry. Sometimes words mark moments where these changes occur – these might be transition words or conjunctions, like "but" or "yet." These shifts in subject, tone, rhythm, rhyme, or any other element almost always reveal a point in the poem in which the meaning is emphasized. As a result, they give you insight into how to interpret it.

Look, for instance, at the poem "The Red Hat" by Rachel Hadas.

The Red Hat

Rachel Hadas

It started before Christmas. Now our son
officially walks to school alone.
Semi-alone, it's accurate to say:
I or his father track him on the way.
He walks up on the east side of West End,
we walk on the west side. Glances can extend
(and do) across the street; not eye contact.
Already ties are feelings and not fact.
Straus Park is where these parallel paths part;
he goes alone from there. The watcher's heart
stretches, elastic in its love and fear,
toward him as we see him disappear,
striding briskly. Where two weeks ago,
holding a hand, he'd dawdle, dreamy, slow,
he now is hustled forward by the pull
of something far more powerful than school.

The mornings we turn back to are no more
than forty minutes longer than before,
but they feel vastly different—flimsy, strange,
wavering in the eddies of this change,
empty, unanchored, perilously light
since the red hat vanished from our sight. ■

Rachel Hadas's poem centers on a parent's account of her son growing up, as evidenced by his desire to start walking to school by himself. While there is a change in the dynamics of the family, where exactly does the poem itself shift?

Since the poem consists of two stanzas, or distinct groupings of lines, let's see if there is a shift between these. To do so, two questions should be considered: 1) What is going on in each stanza? and 2) What is the tone, or attitude toward the subject, in each stanza? The answers to these questions make us realize something certainly changes at this point in the poem.

Notice that in line 17 the speaker is no longer recounting the experience of walking the child to school, as she does in the first 16 lines. Now the poem shifts from sharing the perspective of that walk to focusing on the speaker's analysis of the change her family has undergone. The shift signals that this is an important point the poet wants to make: The transition from being needed by their children to watching their children grow up can be a difficult and traumatic experience for parents; in fact, it can leave them feeling "empty, unanchored," as it does the speaker.

FPG/Getty Images

This image from the 1930s shows a child walking to school.

What feelings does this photograph evoke, and how are those feelings similar to or different from those that Rachel Hadas might be trying to convey in her poem?

As we look at the elements of poetry, it's important to understand that poets make choices about each one of them as they create their work. As is the case in this poem, poets often use shifts to signal important moments to their readers.

Speaker

One of the most important elements in poetry is the **speaker**. When discussing poetry, the main voice of the poem is called the *speaker* rather than the *narrator*, since there isn't necessarily storytelling or narration happening in a poem. While poems are often on personal topics, we can't assume that the speaker is the author. It might be, or the author might be taking on a **persona**, meaning playing a character. Just as in fiction, where understanding the main character is key to understanding the story's themes, understanding the speaker in poetry is key to understanding the theme of a poem. A very common task in poetry analysis is to show how the language of the poem reveals who the speaker is. Speaker and meaning work hand in hand.

For instance, if you want to characterize the speaker of "The Red Hat," you might say that it is a parent learning to cope with the idea of a child growing up and venturing out alone. And in that statement, by examining the speaker, you have expressed a possible theme of the poem.

Speaker and Shifts

Read A. E. Housman's "When I Was One-and-Twenty" and identify the phrases that reveal who the speaker is. In a brief response, describe the speaker based on what you learn from these phrases. Then, describe the shift the speaker experiences in the poem. Remember to look for transition words or conjunctions, like "but" or "yet." In your response, identify any words that help you recognize shifts in the poem.

When I Was One-and-Twenty

A. E. Housman

When I was one-and-twenty
I heard a wise man say,
"Give crowns and pounds and guineas
But not your heart away;
Give pearls away and rubies
But keep your fancy free."
But I was one-and-twenty,
No use to talk to me.

When I was one-and-twenty
I heard him say again,
"The heart out of the bosom
Was never given in vain;
'Tis paid with sighs a plenty
And sold for endless rue."
And I am two-and-twenty,
And oh, 'tis true, 'tis true. ■

Structure

Structure in poetry includes all of the things that give the poem its shape. This includes things like lines, stanzas, rhyme, meter, and form.

As we discuss structure, we'll use this poem as a model: William Shakespeare's Sonnet 116. For now, just give the poem a first reading, thinking about what elements of structure stand out the most.

Sonnet 116

William Shakespeare

Let me not to the marriage of true minds *A*
Admit impediments. Love is not love *B*
Which alters when it alteration finds, *A*
Or bends with the remover to remove. *B*
O no! it is an ever-fixed mark *C*
That looks on tempests and is never shaken; *D*
It is the star to every wand'ring bark, *C*
Whose worth's unknown, although his height be taken. *D*
Love's not Time's fool, though rosy lips and cheeks *E*
Within his bending sickle's compass come; *F*
Love alters not with his brief hours and weeks, *E*
But bears it out even to the edge of doom. *F*
If this be error and upon me prov'd, *G*
I never writ, nor no man ever lov'd. ■ *G*

Lines and Stanzas

The fundamental building block of poetry is the line, rather than the sentence. A **line** is a word or group of words arranged in a single row of a poem. A line or group of lines may form a complete sentence, but that is not always the case. The poet decides how to arrange the line(s) to reinforce meaning, produce a visual effect, or create specific sounds.

Poets can combine lines into groups called **stanzas**. A stanza in a poem is like a paragraph in prose, both visually and in terms of its content. The lines that make up a stanza usually share an idea or a tone. We refer to stanza types based on the number of lines they contain. The most common are **couplets**, which have two lines, and **quatrains**, which have four. In Sonnet 116, Shakespeare uses three quatrains and a couplet. Though not separated by spaces, the stanzas are defined by the rhyme scheme and reinforced by the sentence structure.

When observing the way that lines and stanzas are structured in a poem, we should pay attention to how the poet uses punctuation, since the purpose of punctuation is to guide how we read in terms of both sound and meaning. Poets play with this idea, using punctuation or skipping it as they see fit, to reinforce their meaning. When a line of poetry continues to another line to complete its meaning, we call that **enjambment**. Because the enjambed line is missing end punctuation (period, question mark, exclamation mark), it is easy to spot. In prose, would you ever move from one sentence to the next without end punctuation? Not without confusing your readers. Poetry allows for this kind of movement, and it is the reader's responsibility to consider its significance. **Caesura** is the opposite of enjambment. It refers to stops or pauses created by punctuation that occur within a line of poetry. On occasion, caesura solely serves its grammatical purpose. At other times, the pause signals a significant moment or creates a sound in the poem.

Let's look at part of William Shakespeare's Sonnet 116, which you read in full on page 56. Notice that Shakespeare uses both enjambment and caesura within the first four lines:

Let me not to the marriage of true minds   *Enjambed line*
Caesura   Admit impediments. Love is not love
Which alters when it alteration finds,
Or bends with the remover to remove.

The use of these tools helps Shakespeare stick to his designated structure (the sonnet), which requires a certain number of lines, syllables per line, and rhymes. Or perhaps the line break between lines 1 and 2 is acting out the "impediment" that Shakespeare refers to. Your job as a reader of poetry is to think about how and why the poet uses stanzas, enjambment, and caesura, and to look for shifts in the use of those elements. Maybe the poet uses them to preserve a structure, or perhaps to affect the sound of the poem, or even to shift its meaning.

Rhyme

People often associate poetry with rhyming. What happens, however, if a poem does not rhyme at all? Is it still a poem? And if it does rhyme, where do we expect the rhymes to appear? Most of us are familiar with rhymes that occur at the end of a line. We call this **end rhyme**. Look back at Shakespeare's Sonnet 116 and notice the end rhyme.

We call exact rhymes **true rhymes**, but sometimes words are meant to be bound by rhyme even if the sound they share is not identical. Take a look at the rhymes in Shakespeare's Sonnet 116. While "minds" and "finds" are true rhymes, "love" and "remove" are not — but they come close. We call these close rhymes **slant** or **near rhymes**.

Sometimes end rhymes form a pattern, which we can discern by identifying the poem's **rhyme scheme**. To identify the rhyme scheme, label the first end rhyme with the letter A and assign that letter to all the lines in the poem that end with the same sound. The next new sound is labeled B, and so on. The lines from Shakespeare's Sonnet 116 have been marked to show the rhyme scheme. Identifying a poem's rhyme scheme is a relatively quick way to see shifts in a poem's structure, which sometimes indicate shifts in meaning and sound.

Meter

Meter is the rhythm of the poem. It consists of two parts: 1) the pattern of stressed and unstressed syllables and 2) the number of times that pattern is repeated in a line of poetry. In a prior English class, you may have heard of **iambic pentameter**. This term indicates that a line of poetry consists of five (*penta* means five) iambs. An iamb is a combination of an unstressed syllable followed by a stressed one. Iambic pentameter is among the most common forms, because it closely follows natural speech patterns in English, and particularly because it was used heavily by William Shakespeare. In Sonnet 116 he writes:

With | **in** | his | **ben** | ding | **si** | ckle's | **com** | pass | **come**

Note that the line is made up of ten syllables that consist of five iambs, or sets of unstressed and stressed syllables.

Scansion, the process of analyzing poetic lines to determine meter, can become complicated. However, you can start by counting the number of beats — or syllables — found in each line. Our main objective is to identify patterns or shifts in the poem's structure and to try to make connections between these patterns or shifts and the poem's meaning.

Form

Certain combinations of structure, rhyme, and meter create poetic forms that poets can choose to follow. While poets can write without parameters, poetic forms are a way of constraining the poet and thus presenting an additional creative challenge. Throughout high school, you may encounter many different poetic forms, such as the ballad, elegy, haiku, lyric, ode, and villanelle.

For now, we'd like to focus on one of the most popular — the sonnet. Sonnets are fourteen-line, one-stanza, iambic pentameter poems. **Italian** (**Petrarchan**) **Sonnets** were popularized by the Italian poet Francesco Petrarch in the fourteenth century. Those following his structure use ABBAABBA as the rhyme scheme for the first eight lines, or the octet. The last six lines, or the sestet, however, might use either CD or CDE patterns. In the sixteenth century, the sonnet form was reimagined by William Shakespeare to better suit the lack of common word-endings in English. This new type of sonnet became known, naturally, as the **English** (**Shakespearean**) **Sonnet**. By using ABABCDCDEFEFGG as the rhyme scheme, Shakespeare allowed for more variety in end rhymes.

If we examine Sonnet 116 in its entirety, we can see how it abides by the conventions of Shakespearean Sonnets: fourteen lines, three quatrains and one couplet, iambic pentameter, ABABCDCDEFEFGG rhyme scheme.

Recognizing a conventional form, such as the sonnet, can give you two chief advantages as you read a poem. First, the structure can guide your reading by grouping the text by recognizable features. In the Shakespearean sonnet we just read, for example, note that the rhyme scheme changes every four lines. Additionally, each four-line cluster, or quatrain, comes to an end-stop, as marked by a period. This format makes the sonnet more approachable because you can read each quatrain as a distinct chunk instead of reading all fourteen lines straight through. Once you make sense of the first quatrain, you can proceed to the next, and so on. When you recognize poetic forms, you can also notice meaningful deviations from those forms, which might highlight key ideas in a text. For example, if a poet chooses to disrupt the expected rhyme scheme at a moment when the speaker professes love to his beloved, a careful reader should consider why the poet is drawing attention to that point in the poem with an unexpected change in form.

Annotating for Structure

First, annotate A. E. Stallings's poem "The School of Dreams" by making connections and asking questions, as you did in Chapter 1. In addition, look for curiosities, repetitions, opposites, and links (p. 35). Then, annotate the poem by making observations about its structure, rhyme, and meter. Remember that all poems won't necessarily employ each of the topics we discussed. To make sure that your observations are as complete as possible, share your annotations with a partner.

The School of Dreams

A. E. Stallings

It is an afternoon
With chalk dust in the light.
The dusk is coming soon
And the answer is not right.

The answer is not right
And the bell is going to ring,
And red ink, like a blight,
Has tainted everything:

The leaves upon the trees,
The leaves that fall and rest,
The light, that by degrees,
Is failing in the west,

Everything will burn
With a shade of shame,
Because it is your turn,
Because you hear your name,

And cannot solve for *y*.
Minutes go to waste,
The slate blank as a sky,
Imperfectly erased.

The bell is going to chime.
There's nothing you can do
But to flip a dime
Between false and true.

The problem still remains,
It isn't what you think.
Failure's in your veins,
Red as any ink. ■

Sound

A critical element in poetry is sound. Sound effects are created by grouping the vowel and consonant sounds of words in interesting ways. They might create a rhythm, or they might create a rhyme. **Alliteration**, or the repetition of beginning sounds in neighboring words, can be used to draw special attention to a portion of a poem. Sometimes, poets repeat vowel sounds or consonant sounds to emphasize the importance of a series of words. Repeating vowel sounds is called **assonance** and repeating consonant sounds is called **consonance**. These repetitions may enhance the harmonious sound of a poem, which we call **euphony**, or introduce harsh, discordant sounds, which we call **cacophony**. But not all sounds are created through repetition. For instance, **onomatopoeia** is a type of sound created by a word that sounds like the sound it represents — like "bam" or "crack." And sometimes poets choose turns of phrase simply because they sound appealing. Poets use all of these tools to incorporate particular sounds into their poetry. Those sounds might reinforce the meaning of the poem, or the sound might be an end unto itself. Look back, for instance, at how Rachel Hadas uses sounds to bring to life the experience of a parent watching her son grow up in her poem "The Red Hat" (p. 53). Notice how the alliteration in lines 5 and 6, for instance, emphasizes the physical separation between where her son walks and where she and her husband stand: "He walks up on the east side of West End, / we walk on the west side." Alliteration further marks the distance between parent and child when, in line 9, the speaker notes that "parallel paths part" at this point in their journey. Since she is clearly having a difficult time accepting this change, it is natural that the speaker's reflections will include some cacophonous sounds, namely those created by the words "strange," "change," "unanchored," and "vanished." When analyzing how individual words contribute to the meaning of a poem, be sure to consider their sounds as part of their effect.

activity

Annotating for Sound

Read "You Go to My Head," a poem from *Becoming Billie Holiday*, Carole Boston Weatherford's collection of poems chronicling the life of legendary jazz singer Billie Holiday. Annotate the poem, noting how the speaker uses language to create sounds. Make an interpretation about how those sounds reinforce the poem's meaning.

You Go to My Head

Carole Boston Weatherford

I sang my songs so much
that they became
the soundtrack for my dreams,
the melody of my moods,
a room I lived in,
and a balm for my wounds.

I sang my songs enough
to know them backward
and forward, enough
to wonder if they could lift me
from hometown haunts
to center stage.
I'd sung my songs enough
to think I could take on
Baltimore's best talent
at the Harlem Theatre
Amateur Hour
and maybe even win.

If you sing a song enough,
it can go to your head that way.

Talking It Through

After completing your annotations, share your observations with a partner. What sounds did you find particularly interesting? How does sound contribute to shifts in meaning?

A Model Analysis: Connecting Elements of Poetry to Theme

So far in our work with poetry, we've been focusing on the individual poetic elements. Now it's time to connect each of those elements to see how a poet uses them to characterize the speaker and communicate a theme. In "The Passionate Shepherd to His Love" by Christopher Marlowe, the speaker makes promises to his beloved in an effort to win her love. Read the poem carefully. Then, read the sample observations about how poetic elements help to characterize the speaker and convey its theme.

The Passionate Shepherd to His Love

Christopher Marlowe

Come live with me and be my love,
And we will all the pleasures prove
That valleys, groves, hills, and fields,
Woods, or steepy mountain yields.

And we will sit upon the rocks,
Seeing the shepherds feed their flocks,
By shallow rivers to whose falls
Melodious birds sing madrigals.

And I will make thee beds of roses
And a thousand fragrant posies,
A cap of flowers, and a kirtle
Embroidered all with leaves of myrtle;

A gown made of the finest wool
Which from our pretty lambs we pull;
Fair lined slippers for the cold,
With buckles of the purest gold;

A belt of straw and ivy buds,
With coral clasps and amber studs:
And if these pleasures may thee move,
Come live with me, and be my love.

The shepherds' swains shall dance and sing
For thy delight each May morning:
If these delights thy mind may move,
Then live with me and be my love. ■

Structure

The poem consists of six four-line stanzas, or quatrains. Within each stanza, the first two lines rhyme with each other and the last two lines rhyme with each other. Each stanza is therefore made up of two rhymed couplets. It's clear that Marlowe has deliberately established a pattern throughout the poem, and he chooses not to deviate from that pattern.

Rhyme

Marlowe maintains the structure of rhymed couplets throughout the poem. The rhyme scheme is therefore AABBCCDD, and so on. Notice Marlowe's use of near rhyme with the words "love," "move," and "prove." Due to the limited number of words that rhyme directly with "love," the use of near rhyme with this particular word is quite common in poetry, especially considering how often love is the subject. Marlowe rhymes the word "love" three times in the poem. This is clearly meant to place the idea of love at the center of the poem.

Meter

Typically, every other syllable in this poem is stressed. The first two lines, for example, are stressed as such:

> Come **live** with **me** and **be** my **love**,
> And **we** will **all** the **plea**sures **prove**

Since each line has four sets of iambs, or pairs of unstressed and stressed syllables, then the poem's meter is iambic tetrameter.

Form

While Marlowe's poem has a set rhyme scheme and meter, it does not abide by a particular conventional form.

Sound

Sound is mainly produced by the regular rhyme scheme and persistent meter. This combination adds a sing-song effect to the poem. To add to the musical quality of the poem, Marlowe includes many moments that are marked by alliteration, such as the pairing of "pleasures prove," "we will," and "coral clasps."

Shifts

The first two stanzas portray a passive life wherein the speaker and his beloved take in the landscape that surrounds them. Stanzas 3 through 5, however, portray a frenzy of activity on the part of the speaker, as he gathers and creates a series of love tokens meant to entice his love. Ultimately, the poem shifts again in the final stanza, as the speaker presents an idyllic life in which his beloved will be entertained by the "shepherds' swains."

Theme

The musical element of the poem, along with the lover's pleas and promises, place love at the center of the poem. Specifically, the speaker suggests that young, passionate love is characterized by idealized promises, as opposed to practical observations. This shepherd feels like he has all of nature at his disposal as he tries to woo his beloved. Additionally, the repetitions — or patterns — we observed in rhyme and meter might suggest the lover's persistence in his pursuit.

The Agreeable Lesson, 1748 (oil on canvas) (detail of 123277)/Boucher, Francois (1703–70) National Gallery of Victoria, Melbourne, Australia/ Bridgeman Images

Consider the two figures and the setting in Francois Boucher's 1748 painting *The Agreeable Lesson*.

To what extent does the painting reflect the tone and ideas Marlowe presents in his poem?

Connecting Elements of Poetry to Theme by Writing a Poem

In this activity, you will explore poetic elements and theme through your own writing. Although writing your own poem may seem challenging right now, the process will empower you to work with structure, rhyme, form, meter, sound, and shifts to convey theme.

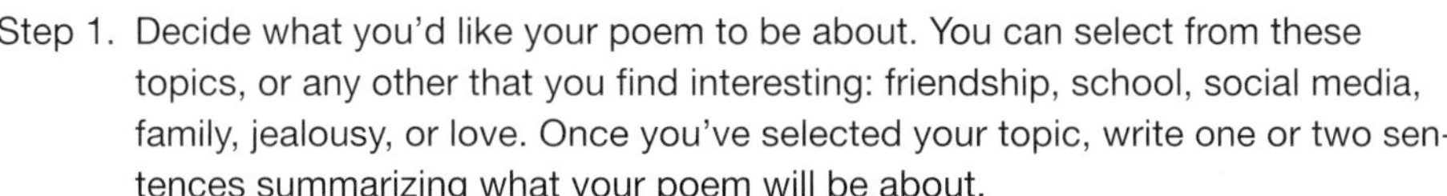

Step 1. Decide what you'd like your poem to be about. You can select from these topics, or any other that you find interesting: friendship, school, social media, family, jealousy, or love. Once you've selected your topic, write one or two sentences summarizing what your poem will be about.

Step 2. Based on your summary, what themes would you like to explore in your poem? For instance, if your poem is about friendship, what message(s) would you like to convey about friendship?

Step 3. Next, decide on your poem's structure. Do you want to work within a form? How many lines and stanzas do you envision for your poem? To fully practice working with the elements of poetry, your poem should consist of at least five lines. Should your poem rhyme? Should the lines be of the same length? How would your poem shift? Once you have made these determinations, explain why your decisions match your poem's meaning.

You have essentially created a blueprint for a poem by thinking about what it should be about, what ideas it should present, and what it should look and sound like. Poets do not sit down to write and haphazardly end up with the final version of their poems. Instead, they think about how each element can help their message reach their readers.

Step 4. Now it's time to use the information you completed in Steps 1-3 to create your own poem. As you write, you might find that you need to deviate from your plan just a bit.

Talking It Through

After completing your poem, share it with a partner, and discuss how writing the poem deepened your understanding of the elements of poetry.

Language and Style

In this chapter, you have been thinking about and practicing the various ways to read literary texts. Now it's time to begin asking how the building blocks themselves are constructed. Think back to setting, for instance. When we say that a setting creates a "dreary" atmosphere, how exactly does the author convey that dreariness? Or, think back to characterization. How exactly does the reader get the impression that the main character is arrogant? The answer is **style**. Style is a term that refers to all the language choices authors make in their writing.

Notice in this short passage from *A Tale of Two Cities* how Charles Dickens uses language to create his setting and evoke a very specific feeling. (We have underlined some words for emphasis.)

> There was a <u>steaming</u> mist in all the hollows, and it had <u>roamed</u> in its <u>forlornness</u> up the hill, like an <u>evil</u> spirit, seeking rest and finding none. A <u>clammy</u> and intensely <u>cold</u> mist, it made its slow way through the air in <u>ripples</u> that visibly followed and <u>overspread</u> one another, as the waves of an <u>unwholesome</u> sea might do. It was dense enough to shut out everything from the light of the coach-lamps but these its own workings, and a few yards of road; and the <u>reek</u> of the <u>labouring</u> horses steamed into it, as if they had made it all.

The stylistic choices of "reek," "clammy," "unwholesome," and "evil" create a setting so dismal and depressing that it almost seems hopeless.

While style is important in fiction and drama, it is also crucial to poetry. In poetry, style is often employed for its own sake, to create something that sounds beautiful, or

This painting by Edwin Septimus Scott was created for an illustrated version of *A Tale of Two Cities.* **Look closely at the painting and identify words and phrases from the text that might have inspired Scott to create it the way he did.**

Illustration for A Tale of Two Cities (colour litho)/Scott, Septimus Edwin (1879–1965)/LOOK AND LEARN (M IMAGES)/Private Collection/Bridgeman Images

to convey a surprising idea or powerful image. Look, for instance, at this section from a poem called "America" by Claude McKay, and notice how the language choices — the style — bring the ideas to life and fill them with power:

> Although she feeds me bread of bitterness,
> And sinks into my throat her tiger's tooth,
> Stealing my breath of life, I will confess
> I love this cultured hell that tests my youth.
> Her vigor flows like tides into my blood,
> Giving me strength erect against her hate,
> Her bigness sweeps my being like a flood.

Reading purposefully to assess how an author's style affects the meaning of a work of literature is what we call close reading, or close analysis. Close reading is about carefully examining the author's craft and seeing how each choice contributes to the style of the piece.

So far, we've discussed style as a broad term to describe an author's language choices. Next, we'll look at four specific components that contribute to an author's style:

- Diction
- Syntax
- Figurative Language
- Imagery

Each of these components builds on and supports the others. These essential language choices allow writers to create the settings, characters, conflicts, and other literary elements described earlier in this chapter.

Diction

Like artists who paint in watercolor, pastel, or oil, writers select the types of words they need to fulfill their purposes. **Diction** refers to word choice in a speech or text.

Denotation and Connotation. To fully understand the idea of diction, we have to recognize the differences between two essential terms:

- **Denotation** is the literal meaning of a word, free from any associated meanings.
- **Connotation** is the cultural or emotional associations attached to a word.

An easy way to understand the difference between the two is to think about the word *home*. The denotation is simply "the place where one resides," but think about the connotative meanings of the word: comfort, safety, warmth. You can see this even more clearly when you contrast *home* with another word the writer might have chosen — *house*, which has a more impersonal connotation.

Formal and Informal. In addition to creating a variety of associations for the reader, diction choices can also create a certain level of formality through the use of very proper words or technical jargon, or a casual feeling through the intentional use of slang.

Syntax

Authors also make stylistic choices regarding **syntax**, or sentence structure. To some extent, grammar dictates how writers construct their sentences. However, there are certain choices they can make to achieve an intended purpose, such as reversing the expected word order. Note how the inversion in this example changes the emphasis of the sentence: "My job, I cannot quit," as opposed to the more typical "I cannot quit my job." By placing the words "my job" first, the former emphasizes the job, while the latter begins with "I cannot quit" to direct our attention to the quitting itself.

The following are some components to consider when analyzing syntax:

Length of Sentences

Syntax often gives a text a particular rhythm. Short sentences, for example, can create a choppy rhythm or a sense of urgency, whereas longer sentences can feel smooth and flowing. If you are familiar with musical dynamics, you might think of short sentences as being *staccato*, while long sentences are *legato*. Often, writers will use changes in sentence length or sentence types to create rhythmic effects. The most common is to follow a series of long sentences with a short one to create impact, but the sequence can work the other way as well.

Types of Sentences

There are a number of sentence types a writer can use. The most common is the **declarative sentence**, but writers can also use sentence **fragments**, **interrogative sentences**, and **exclamatory sentences**.

To show a relationship between two ideas in the same sentence, writers use types of sentences called complex sentences and compound sentences. **Complex sentences** make one idea subordinate to another idea. **Compound sentences** combine two ideas and put them on equal footing.

COMPLEX	As the sun went down, night fell on the city.
COMPOUND	The sun went down, and night fell on the city.

Two other types of sentences often used for effect are cumulative and periodic sentences. **Cumulative sentences** put the main idea first, then add details. **Periodic sentences** start with details and build to the main idea.

CUMULATIVE SENTENCE	The dirty snow fell, blackened by soot, tar, and the grime of the city.
PERIODIC SENTENCE	Blackened by soot, tar, and the grime of the city, the dirty snow fell.

Punctuation

How (or whether) a writer uses punctuation is also a matter of syntax. William Faulkner, for instance, regularly includes run-on sentences to reflect the rambling thoughts of his characters. Punctuation is especially important in poetry because of its concise nature and the liberties that poets can take as they convey their ideas.

If you are just starting to consider syntax, be on the lookout for times when *form follows function,* which is when the syntax itself emphasizes a point the author is making. For example, read the following passage from a classic detective novel, *The Maltese Falcon*, by Dashiell Hammett, and notice how detective Sam Spade's short, simple, declarative sentences reveal his no-nonsense approach to his job:

> When a man's partner is killed he's supposed to do something about it. It doesn't make any difference what you thought of him. He was your partner and you're supposed to do something about it. Then it happens we were in the detective business. Well, when one of your organization gets killed it's bad business to let the killer get away with it. It's bad all around — bad for that one organization, bad for every detective everywhere.

Figurative Language

Authors use **figurative language** when they choose words or phrases that are not meant to be taken literally, just as you do when you say something like "I'm so hungry that I could eat a horse." You are not literally going to eat a horse, but you are using figurative language (hyperbole, in this case) to communicate just how hungry you are. Some of the most common elements of figurative language are the following:

- **Metaphor.** a direct comparison between unlike things
- **Simile.** a comparison between unlike things using "like" or "as"
- **Hyperbole.** a deliberate exaggeration or overstatement (often for the sake of humor)
- **Personification.** giving human qualities to inanimate objects
- **Allusion.** a reference to something well-known from literature, art, history, mythology, or religion

Imagery

Another element of style that writers have at their disposal is **imagery**, words and phrases that appeal to the readers' senses by evoking sights, sounds, smells, tastes, and touch. Keep in mind that imagery can be both literal and figurative.

LITERAL IMAGERY	The wind shook the trees.
FIGURATIVE IMAGERY	The trees danced with the wind.

Writers communicate the worlds they create through imagery; they want their readers to feel as if they are experiencing their worlds, not just reading about them.

Annotating for Elements of Style

Read the final stanza of the poem "Renascence" by Edna St. Vincent Millay, a poem inspired by the view from a mountaintop in Maine. First, annotate by first making connections and asking questions, as you did in Chapter 1. Then, annotate by looking for how Millay uses elements of style (diction, syntax, figurative language, and imagery) to describe this setting and the speaker's perception of it.

from Renascence

Edna St. Vincent Millay

The world stands out on either side
No wider than the heart is wide;
Above the world is stretched the sky,—
No higher than the soul is high.
The heart can push the sea and land
Farther away on either hand;
The soul can split the sky in two,
And let the face of God shine through.
But East and West will pinch the heart
That can not keep them pushed apart;
And he whose soul is flat—the sky
Will cave in on him by and by. ■

Talking It Through

Work in groups or pairs to identify and discuss the elements of style that lead you to an understanding of the speaker's perception of the setting.

Analyzing Style and Tone

All the elements of style work together to produce meaning and to convey the author's, narrator's, or speaker's attitude toward the subject of the text. By carefully considering how authors present ideas, readers can determine what feelings the work expresses about the subject. This is what we call **tone**. In your study of literature, you will often be asked to analyze the tone of a text. To do this, you will focus on the author's stylistic choices.

You've probably heard the term *tone* before in the expression "tone of voice." With your tone of voice, you can make what you say sound angry, happy, sarcastic, and so on. You use your tone of voice to indicate your attitude toward what you are saying. In writing, tone works similarly.

There are many possible ways to describe the tone in a piece of literature. Here are just a few:

Positive Tone	Negative Tone
sentimental, light, fanciful, sympathetic, benevolent, vibrant, joyful, complimentary	angry, sharp, cold, condescending, detached, sarcastic

A Model Analysis: Connecting Style to Tone

Read this opening paragraph from *The Catcher in the Rye* by J. D. Salinger. The sample analysis following the excerpt demonstrates how examining stylistic choices can reveal the tone of a work.

from The Catcher in the Rye

J. D. Salinger

If you really want to hear about it, the first thing you'll probably want to know is where I was born, and what my lousy childhood was like, and how my parents were occupied and all before they had me, and all that David Copperfield kind of crap, but I don't feel like going into it, if you want to know the truth. In the first place, that stuff bores me, and in the second place, my parents would have about two hemorrhages apiece if I told anything pretty personal about them. They're quite touchy about anything like that, especially my father. They're nice and all. I'm not saying that—but they're also touchy as hell. Besides, I'm not going to tell you my whole goddam autobiography or anything. I'll just tell you about this madman stuff that happened to me around last Christmas just before I got pretty run-down and had to come out here and take it easy. ■

Let's consider the elements of style in this paragraph that establish narrator Holden Caulfield's sarcastic and condescending tone.

Diction

His choice of the words "lousy," "crap," and "goddam" show that Holden doesn't care if he offends someone with his slang or profanity.

Syntax

The first sentence is one long rush, like a sudden outpouring of thoughts. The narrator then switches to some shorter sentences when he makes it clear that he is not going to reveal much, especially about his parents.

Figurative Language

Holden uses hyperbole when he says that his parents would have "two hemorrhages apiece." This reveals his sarcastic tone and his willingness to exaggerate to make a point.

Tone

Caulfield's tone in this novel is famously casual, off-handed, dismissive. But a literary work rarely has only a single tone. Even Holden's softens later in the novel. A piece may begin with one tone and switch to another to illustrate a particular point. A doctor in a story, for instance, might start off with a very clinical and detached tone, but then move to a more sympathetic tone to reflect her compassion and growing engagement in the lives of her patients.

activity

Analyzing Style and Tone

Read this poem by Paul Laurence Dunbar and annotate it by making connections and asking questions, as you did in Chapter 1. In addition, look for curiosities, repetitions, opposites, and links (p. 35). Then, analyze how the diction, syntax, figurative language, and imagery help to create the speaker's tone.

Sympathy

Paul Laurence Dunbar

I know what the caged bird feels, alas!
  When the sun is bright on the upland slopes;
When the wind stirs soft through the springing grass,
And the river flows like a stream of glass;
  When the first bird sings and the first bud opes,
And the faint perfume from its chalice steals—
I know what the caged bird feels!

I know why the caged bird beats his wing
  Till its blood is red on the cruel bars;
For he must fly back to his perch and cling
When he fain would be on the bough a-swing;
  And a pain still throbs in the old, old scars
And they pulse again with a keener sting—
I know why he beats his wing!

I know why the caged bird sings, ah me,
    When his wing is bruised and his bosom sore,—
When he beats his bars and he would be free;
It is not a carol of joy or glee,
    But a prayer that he sends from his heart's deep core,
But a plea, that upward to Heaven he flings—
I know why the caged bird sings! ■

Analyzing Style and Theme

Earlier in the chapter we discussed that all the elements employed by writers make up their particular style. Considering the choices writers make helps us recognize the themes that their texts convey. In other words, the diction, syntax, figurative language, and imagery all work towards a common purpose: transmitting the ideas and concerns of the writer. As careful readers, then, we must closely observe these elements to analyze a text and be able to discuss its themes.

A Model Analysis: Connecting Style to Theme

While sometimes the goal of analyzing style is to pick up on the speaker's tone and figure out how that tone is created, at other times we want to look at how these stylistic moves help create the meaning of the work as a whole: the theme.

Read the poem "Magic Lesson" by Debora Kuan, and then look at some methods for analyzing each stylistic element. These observations will then be used to draw a conclusion about a possible theme of the work.

Magic Lesson

Debora Kuan

This is my face,
a spinning plate.
I'm unraveling
as a mother does

a knot from a bow
to astonish you.

In time, you'll master
the fact that every woman
has been sawed in half
at least a dozen times
before sunset.

Some of us walk through
that wall.
Some of us burrow beneath it.

The rest spend their lives as
bespoke assistants.
Younger siblings.
Bottom drawers
unsticking.
And then a lifetime ignites.

For you, I'll wish for something else.

I want you to be
a student of impossible binds,
a magician of
a bloom from a fist,
a dove from a dove from a dove. ■

Diction

There is a contrast between the negative words that refer to the present, such as "unraveling," "sawed," and "bottom drawers," and the positive words that refer to the future, such as "magician," "bloom," and "dove."

Syntax

The poet strings a single sentence across many lines, connecting many ideas together, and giving a sense of chaos — or "unraveling." In contrast, the sixth stanza is a brief sentence on a single line. It breaks the pattern of longer, more rambling sentences and signals the primary shift in the poem, from the life that the speaker has led to the life she wishes women will have in the future.

Figurative Language

The comparison of the speaker's face to "a spinning plate" conveys her state of mind. Then, as the speaker proceeds through her day, she is "sawed in half" multiple times before sunset. Life's demands chip away at this speaker. Eventually, out of this turbulence, "a lifetime ignites." This metaphor linking life to a bomb leads the speaker to utter her desire: "For you, I'll wish for something else."

Imagery

The imagery presented in lines 1–20 is markedly different from that found in the final stanza (ll. 22–26). Line 22 is where this shift occurs. In context, the negative images of "bespoke assistants," "younger siblings," and "bottom drawers" give way to the more positive presentations of "student," "magician," "bloom," and "dove."

Possible Themes

As the poem progresses, contrasts in word choice and imagery convey hope for a future in which women's social roles will be more positive, active, and fulfilling than they have been in the past. Guided by the simile in line 4, you may also perceive a theme centered on the subject of parenthood. Kuan could be arguing that parents always long for a better world for their children than the one in which they themselves have lived.

activity

Analyzing Style and Theme

Read this excerpt from the opening of the novel *Things Fall Apart* by Chinua Achebe and annotate it by making connections and asking questions, as you did in Chapter 1. In addition, look for curiosities, repetitions, opposites, and links (p. 35). Then, make observations about its diction, syntax, figurative language, and imagery.

from Things Fall Apart

Chinua Achebe

Chinua Achebe's *Things Fall Apart* (1958) tells the story of the Igbo people of Nigeria in the late 1800s. The novel opens just prior to the start of British colonial rule in this African nation and centers on the lives of Okonkwo, his three wives, and their children. Okonkwo, unlike his father, is one of the most respected leaders of the village of Umuofia.

Okonkwo was well known throughout the nine villages and even beyond. His fame rested on solid personal achievements. As a young man of eighteen he had brought honor to his village by throwing Amalinze the Cat. Amalinze was the great wrestler who for seven years was unbeaten, from Umuofia to Mbaino. He was called the Cat because his back would never touch the earth. It was this man that Okonkwo threw in a fight which the old men agreed was one of the fiercest since the founder of their town engaged a spirit of the wild for seven days and seven nights.

The drums beat and the flutes sang and the spectators held their breath. Amalinze was a wily craftsman, but Okonkwo was as slippery as a fish in water. Every nerve and every muscle stood out on their arms, on their backs and their thighs, and one almost heard them stretching to breaking point. In the end Okonkwo threw the Cat.

That was many years ago, twenty years or more, and during this time Okonkwo's fame had grown like a bush-fire in the harmattan. He was tall and huge, and his bushy eyebrows and wide nose gave him a very severe look. He breathed heavily, and it was said that, when he slept, his wives and children in their houses could hear him breathe. When he walked, his heels hardly touched the ground and he seemed to walk on springs, as if he was going to pounce on somebody. And he did pounce on people quite often. He had a slight stammer and whenever he was angry and could not get his words out quickly enough, he would use his fists. He had no patience with unsuccessful men. He had had no patience with his father. ■

Talking It Through

Share your findings with a partner so that you can each have a better understanding of the stylistic elements of the text. Then, draw conclusions about the possible themes that emerged as you analyzed the excerpt.

culminating activity

1. The following poem is by the eighteenth-century English poet William Blake. Read and annotate the poem by making connections and asking questions, as you did in Chapter 1. In addition, look for curiosities, repetitions, opposites, and links (p. 35). Then, write a response in which you identify a possible theme for the poem. Discuss how devices such as diction, syntax, figurative language, and imagery develop this theme.

The Tyger

William Blake

Tyger Tyger, burning bright,
In the forests of the night;
What immortal hand or eye,
Could frame thy fearful symmetry?
In what distant deeps or skies
Burnt the fire of thine eyes?
On what wings dare he aspire?
What the hand, dare seize the fire?
And what shoulder, & what art,
Could twist the sinews of thy heart?
And when thy heart began to beat,
What dread hand? & what dread feet?
What the hammer? what the chain,
In what furnace was thy brain?
What the anvil? what dread grasp,
Dare its deadly terrors clasp!
When the stars threw down their spears
And water'd heaven with their tears:
Did he smile his work to see?
Did he who made the Lamb make thee?
Tyger Tyger burning bright,
In the forests of the night:
What immortal hand or eye,
Dare frame thy fearful symmetry? ■

2. The following passage is from the short story "The Tell-Tale Heart," by Edgar Allan Poe. Read the passage carefully and annotate by making connections and asking questions, as you did in Chapter 1. In addition, look for curiosities, repetitions, opposites, and links (p. 35). Then, in a written response, analyze how the author reveals the character of the unnamed narrator. In your analysis, consider how diction, syntax, figurative language, and imagery contribute to the characterization.

from The Tell-Tale Heart

Edgar Allan Poe

In this scene, the narrator has just murdered an old man, who lived in a room in the narrator's house, for no stated reason other than he felt disturbed by the old man's vulture-like eye. Just as he finishes burying the old man beneath the floorboards, the police knock on the narrator's door.

As the bell sounded the hour, there came a knocking at the street door. I went down to open it with a light heart, — for what had I now to fear? There entered three men, who introduced themselves, with perfect suavity, as officers of the police. A shriek had been heard by a neighbor during the night; suspicion of foul play had been aroused; information had been lodged at the police office, and they (the officers) had been deputed to search the premises.

I smiled, — for what had I to fear? I bade the gentlemen welcome. The shriek, I said, was my own in a dream. The old man, I mentioned, was absent in the country. I took my visitors all over the house. I bade them search — search well. I led them, at length, to his chamber. I showed them his treasures, secure, undisturbed. In the enthusiasm of my confidence, I brought chairs into the room, and desired them here to rest from their fatigues, while I myself, in the wild audacity of my perfect triumph, placed my own seat upon the very spot beneath which reposed the corpse of the victim.

The officers were satisfied. My manner had convinced them. I was singularly at ease. They sat, and while I answered cheerily, they chatted of familiar things. But, ere long, I felt myself getting pale and wished them gone. My head ached, and I fancied a ringing in my ears: but still they sat and still chatted. The ringing became more distinct: — it continued and became more distinct: I talked more freely to get rid of the feeling: but it continued and gained definiteness — until, at length, I found that the noise was not within my ears.

No doubt I now grew very pale; — but I talked more fluently, and with a heightened voice. Yet the sound increased — and what could I do? It was a low, dull, quick sound — much such a sound as a watch makes when enveloped in cotton. I gasped for breath — and yet the officers heard it not. I talked more quickly — more vehemently; but the noise steadily increased. I arose and argued about trifles, in a high key and with violent gesticulations, but the noise steadily increased. Why would they not be gone? I paced the floor to and fro with heavy strides, as if excited to fury by the observation of the men — but the noise steadily increased. Oh God! what could I do? I foamed — I raved — I swore! I swung the chair upon which I had been sitting, and grated it upon the boards, but the noise arose over all and continually increased. It grew louder — louder — louder! And still the men chatted pleasantly, and smiled. Was it possible they heard not? Almighty God! — no, no! They heard! — they suspected! — they knew! — they were making a mockery of my horror! — this I thought, and this I think. But any thing was better than this agony! Any thing was more tolerable than this derision! I could bear those hypocritical smiles no longer! I felt that I must scream or die! — and now — again! — hark! louder! louder! louder! louder! —

"Villains!" I shrieked, "dissemble no more! I admit the deed! — tear up the planks! — here, here! — it is the beating of his hideous heart!" ■

ZUMA Press, Inc./Alamy

Understanding Rhetoric and Argument

It may seem odd that this book includes a chapter about something that most people try to avoid, an argument. Arguing with friends often leads to hurt feelings, and arguing with teachers or parents may lead to punishments. But there is another, more positive meaning of the term **argument:** using language, reason, and evidence to influence the thoughts and behaviors of others. And that kind of argument will be the focus of this chapter.

You have heard and even likely used the word *argument* in this sense. For example, if a friend comes up with a list of reasons why you should take a robotics course, you might respond with something like, "Yeah, you've made a good argument. I think I might take robotics next year." You and your friend did not have a disagreement that involved anything unpleasant; your friend was simply trying use concrete points to convince you to do something — in this case, learn a particular skill that might be useful in the future.

Let's flip the scenario. If you wanted to convince your friend to take robotics with you, what argument would you make? Would you beg and plead because you didn't know anyone else in the class? Would you point out the benefits of the course for a college application? Would you entice your friend with the idea of a trip to the World Robotics Competition? The approach you chose would depend on your audience — what you know about your friend's personality and interests. These choices, *how* you approach an argument, are what we call **rhetoric**.

Simply put, rhetoric refers to the strategies we use to make an argument achieve its purpose: to persuade our target audience. Rhetoric, which had its beginnings in ancient Greece, also gives us a vocabulary for analyzing the effectiveness of arguments, whether written, spoken, or visual. It reminds us, too, that argument is not a matter of winning, losing, or wearing an opponent down: It's a matter of strategy and persuasion.

Changing Minds, Changing the World

Argument and rhetoric are not just for politicians. They are how ideas get shared, how minds get changed, how movements begin. Argument and rhetoric can change the world. The philosopher Plato said that "rhetoric is the art of ruling the minds of men."

In the early seventeenth century, Galileo Galilei presented evidence supporting Nicolaus Copernicus's theory that the Earth revolved around the sun, despite the claim of most scientists and religious leaders at the time that the Earth was the center of the universe. Though Galileo was arrested and imprisoned for his position, eventually his ideas prevailed because of the compelling evidence he and others presented.

In 1852, Harriet Beecher Stowe published the novel *Uncle Tom's Cabin*, which became one of the best-selling books of the nineteenth century. The book's depictions of the cruel realities of slavery in the United States before the Civil War greatly expanded support for abolition. Upon meeting Stowe, President Abraham Lincoln reportedly said, "So this is the little lady who started this great war."

Heritage Images/Getty Images

This 19th century painting by Joseph-Nicolas Robert-Fleury shows Galileo defending himself before the Vatican Tribunal of the Inquisition.

How does this painting visually represent the challenges that Galileo faced?

In 2009, Malala Yousafzai began blogging about the Taliban, which had taken control of her town in Pakistan and banned girls from attending school. Despite threats of violence, she continued posting to her blog to express her point of view. On October 9, 2012, a Taliban fighter boarded her school bus, asked for her by name, and shot her three times. Yousafzai recovered and has since continued to advocate for education for girls, leading Pakistan to pass its very first Right to Education bill. She was honored with the Nobel Peace Prize in 2014.

In 2018, teenage Swedish environmental activist Greta Thunberg began organizing school walkouts to call attention to the effects of climate change on younger generations. Her climate strikes became a worldwide movement. Thunberg addressed the United Nations in 2019, sounding a defiant alarm in support of radical changes to how we treat the environment.

While historic figures often change the world all by themselves, more often we change the world by joining a movement and lending our voices to many others in order to bring about change. In the aftermath of the deaths of Breonna Taylor, George Floyd, and many others killed by police officers, millions of protesters have taken to the streets proclaiming that "Black Lives Matter." This movement and message resulted in

Pat Bagley/Cagle Cartoons, Inc.

This political cartoon by artist Pat Bagley is from 2012, soon after Yousafzai was shot by the Taliban. **How does Bagley make his argument about the power of Malala's message?**

significant changes in the ways that many thought about race and privilege, and led to many cities and states addressing issues of police brutality and other results of systemic racism.

As you can see, making strong arguments allows us to influence the world around us — across boundaries such as age, gender identity, or ethnicity. The change we create may be globally, locally, or personally significant.

Just as important as developing our own arguments is being able to critically examine the arguments intended to influence us. Companies try to sell us their products; politicians try to secure our votes; researchers present evidence to convince us of their findings and conclusions; people on social media challenge our points of view. We have to be careful consumers, voters, readers, viewers, and listeners, so that we can make informed choices in all areas of our lives and not be manipulated by faulty arguments.

In analyzing rhetoric, carefully observe what writers or speakers say and how they say it. Look for patterns in their language, evidence, or reasoning, and draw conclusions about whether their use of rhetoric is effective, manipulative, flawed, masterful, or somewhere in between.

Considering an Argument

Read the following excerpt from an argument about college admission policies that give preference to legacy applicants, those whose parents attended the school. On your first read, annotate or respond to the text by making connections and asking questions (p. 10). On your second read, identify anything the authors do to persuade readers.

from End Legacy College Admissions

The Editorial Board of the *New York Times*

For nearly a century, many American college and university admissions officers have given preferential treatment to the children of alumni.

The policies originated in the 1920s, coinciding with an influx of Jewish and Catholic applicants to the country's top schools. They continue today, placing a thumb on the scale in favor of students who already enjoy the benefits of being raised by families with elite educations. Of the country's top 100 schools (as determined by the editors at *U.S. News & World Report*), roughly three-quarters have legacy preferences in admissions. These anachronistic policies have been called "affirmative action for the rich" and "affirmative action for whites."

Preferential treatment for legacy admissions is anti-meritocratic, inhibits social mobility, and helps perpetuate a de facto class system. In short, it is an engine of inequity. Little wonder that it is unpopular with most Americans, yet supported by the affluent who both oversee the college admissions process and are its primary beneficiaries.

Legacy admissions are no ordinary leg up. In 2011, a Harvard researcher who studied thirty of the nation's most selective schools found that all legacy applicants had a 23 percent higher probability of admission, while "primary legacy" students (those with a parent who attended the school as an undergraduate, rather than, say, a grandparent or aunt) had a 45 percent higher probability compared with their peers, all other things being equal.

A federal trial last year over the admission practices at Harvard University focused on 5
how the school's affirmative action policies may have affected Asian-American applicants. That case is still being considered by a judge. But in the course of the trial some eye-popping numbers came to light. Between 2010 and 2015, the admission rate for legacy applicants at Harvard was higher than 33 percent. It was 6 percent for non-legacies. More than 20 percent of the white applicants admitted to the school during that period were legacy students.

Backers of legacy preference point out that at Harvard and other schools across the country, the student body — and with it the pool of alumni — has gotten more diverse over time. That means that the composition of the legacy population is also diversifying. At Harvard, evidence from the trial showed, some 80 percent of legacy admissions for the class of 2014 were white, while only 60 percent of legacies in the class of 2019 were white. Would ending legacy preference equate to pulling up the ladder ahead of a more diverse group of students who could leverage their legacy status?

Not in the least. Consideration of race in admissions can be defended not only as a remedy for past injustices but also as an imperative for schools seeking to represent the population at large. But continuing to give applicants an advantage simply because of where their parents went to school is, as one critic called it, "a form of property transfer from one generation to another." ■

Talking It Through

With a partner, share your impressions of the excerpt from the editorial. How is the piece trying to change minds and change the world? Do you or your partner agree with the editorial? Why or why not?

Arguable Claims

Central to every argument is a **claim**, the position taken by the person making the argument. The claim is a statement of what the author is hoping to prove, to persuade the audience to believe. For the examples we just discussed, the claims could be summarized as follows:

Galileo: The Earth revolves around the sun.

Stowe: Slavery is inhumane and should be eliminated.

Yousafzai: Education should be available to everyone, regardless of gender identity.

Thunberg: The climate crisis is real, and humanity needs to reduce its carbon footprint.

Black Lives Matter: Excessive police violence is caused by systemic racism.

A. F. Branco ©2019/Creators Syndicate, Inc.

Dave Whamond/Cagle Cartoons, Inc.

What claim is each of these editorial cartoons making about Greta Thunberg and her climate justice movement? How do they communicate these claims to their audience?

If you think carefully about these claims, you'll notice something a bit odd: At this point in time, the claims put forth by Galileo and Stowe seem indisputable. It is a verifiable scientific truth that the Earth revolves around the sun. Slavery is absolutely inhumane and was long ago outlawed in the United States. It's a testament to the power of these arguments that these issues are no longer subject to debate.

However, what made all of these arguments effective was that at one point each of these claims *was* controversial and the subject of debate. In the case of Yousafzai's claim that education should be available to everyone regardless of gender identity, the matter might seem indisputable to you, but in her homeland it is still a matter of ongoing debate. And proponents of the Black Lives Matter movement continue to face significant challenges in fully implementing their antiracist policies in police departments around the country.

So, the first step in crafting a strong argument is to develop an arguable claim. After all, what's the point of trying to persuade someone of something that's already a proven fact? Finding an arguable claim is also about more than just personal preference. "I like popcorn better than potato chips" is not arguable. However, "popcorn is a more nutritious snack than potato chips" is a statement that requires support and that can serve as the basis of an argument. You would consider what "nutritious" means in terms of calories, fat, fiber, vitamins, or various other measures. After defining what you mean by "nutritious," you would compare the relevant values of those two snack foods — perhaps across brands — to support your position. It's an arguable claim, in part because you would need to convince readers that your understanding of "nutritious" is valid and your examination of the two foods is fair.

In the article on page 80 about the college admissions process, the claim could be stated as "legacy admissions are harmful to American society." Even if you might agree with this claim, it is definitely arguable. Ideas about what is "harmful" to society vary greatly. And there are thousands of students who apply each year as "legacies" who would probably not want to see this policy changed.

KEY QUESTIONS

When writing or analyzing a claim, be sure to ask yourself the following questions:

- To what extent is the claim arguable?
- Why is the claim worth making?
- Is the claim directly stated or is it implied?

Finding the Claim

Read the following excerpts from two arguments about climate change. Identify the central claim of each and restate it in your own words. Then, meet with a partner to discuss which of the claims you agree or disagree with and why.

from The Uninhabitable Earth

David Wallace-Wells

It is worse, much worse, than you think. The slowness of climate change is a fairy tale, perhaps as pernicious as the one that says it isn't happening at all, and comes to us bundled with several others in an anthology of comforting delusions: that global warming is an Arctic saga, unfolding remotely; that it is strictly a matter of sea level and coastlines, not an enveloping crisis sparing no place and leaving no life undeformed; that it is a crisis of the "natural" world, not the human one; that those two are distinct, and that we live today somehow outside or beyond or at the very least defended against nature, not inescapably within and literally overwhelmed by it; that wealth can be a shield against the ravages of warming; that the burning of fossil fuels is the price of continued economic growth; that growth, and the technology it produces, will allow us to engineer our way out of environmental disaster; that there is any analogue to the scale or scope of this threat, in the long span of human history, that might give us confidence in staring it down.

from Don't Even Think About It

George Marshall

Because weather events can never be ascribed with certainty to climate change, we are therefore prone to interpret them in light of our prior assumptions and prejudices. If we regard climate change as a myth, we regard variable and extreme weather as proof that weather can be naturally variable and extreme. If we are disposed to accept that climate change is a real and growing threat, we are liable to regard extreme weather as evidence of growing destabilization.

These selective processes are called *biases* by cognitive psychologists because they draw on preformed assumptions and intuitions to influence decisions . . .

Research finds that these cognitive biases are guiding our interpretation of extreme weather events and climate science as a whole. When asked about recent weather in their own area, people who are already disposed to believe in climate change will tend to say it's been warmer. People who are unconvinced about climate change will say it's been colder. Farmers in Illinois, invited to report their recent experiences of the weather, emphasized or played down extreme events depending on whether or not they accepted climate change.

The Rhetorical Situation of an Argument

Imagine that you are making the argument to your parents or guardians that you ought to have a later curfew. Your claim might be something like: *Because I am mature and responsible, I should be able to stay out until midnight*. Now, let's consider how the *context* can affect the argument. What if you were nine years old when you made this argument? Would it be received differently than if you made it when you were fifteen or sixteen or even eighteen? What if you had just made the honor roll at school? What about the **audience** of your argument — the individuals or groups you are trying to persuade? Would your parents react differently if they had recently read a newspaper story about a child being abducted? If you knew that one of your parents was having a difficult time at work, would you try to ease into your argument slowly and carefully?

The point here is that all arguments exist within a context, which directly influences not only *what* is presented but also *how* it is presented. We call this the **rhetorical situation**. The easiest way to examine the choices we make when building or analyzing an argument is to consider three key elements, represented in the following diagram, which is often referred to as the **rhetorical triangle**.

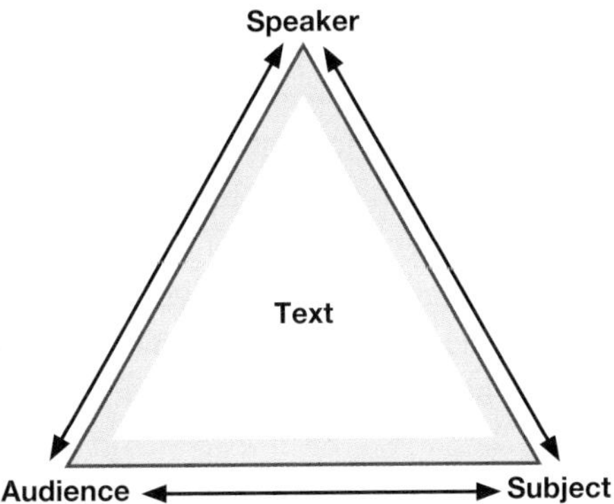

When we develop or analyze arguments, we're looking at the interaction among these three key elements — **speaker (writer)**, **subject**, and **audience** — and how those three elements determine the form and content of the argument (the text).

Think about changing just one of them. If, for instance, you're asked to persuade a group of fourth graders about the importance of reading both widely and often, how would you approach them? Would you present research studies and all sorts of statistical data? Not likely. You might if you were asked to make a formal presentation to a group of adults, but what would get the fourth graders' attention? A personal story? Maybe a video clip of celebrities or famous athletes talking about what reading means to them?

Considering the rhetorical triangle is an essential place to start when you are thinking about an argument. However, when you begin analyzing or writing an argument, you might want to consider the acronym **SOAPSTone**: Subject, Occasion, Audience, Purpose, Speaker (the writer of a text or creator of an artwork, for example), and Tone (the attitude the speaker takes toward the subject). SOAPSTone is a useful starting point for organizing your ideas, whether you're analyzing someone else's argument or planning one of your own.

Subject

What is the speaker's general topic or content? Harriet Beecher Stowe's subject was slavery in the United States. Remember that the subject can be stated in a few words or a phrase, while the claim is the speaker's position on the subject. Part of your analysis of subject is determining if the writer has chosen a narrow or broad subject, and whether that subject is sufficiently developed.

Occasion

What circumstances give rise to the argument? Is there a controversy already in play? Is the speaker responding to an accusation or an existing or urgent situation? When Greta Thunberg began her climate strikes, for example, there was growing evidence of the effects of greenhouse gases on climate change. These findings and others led Thunberg to sound the alarm and argue for action to preserve the environment.

Audience

While there are often multiple audiences for any argument, speakers usually have a primary audience in mind for their claim and will tailor the argument depending on the expectations, prejudices, anticipated objections, and interests of that audience. As Galileo was proposing his theories about our solar system, for example, his greatest opponent was the Roman Catholic Church, so he tried to be careful not to offend religious leaders when making his argument.

Purpose

What is the speaker's intention? What does the speaker want the audience to do? In many cases, texts are designed to inspire action: vote, buy, stop, start, do something. But sometimes the goal is simply to have the audience consider a different perspective or a new angle on an idea. In some cases, there is more than one purpose, an immediate and specific one and then a broader, ongoing one. For example, the leaders of the Black Lives Matter movement want to call attention to the systemic racism that exists in society, and they propose significant changes to the use-of-force policies of police officers.

Speaker

Who is putting forward the claim? Speakers usually represent themselves, but sometimes they speak for or are heavily influenced by a corporation, a political party, or some other group of individuals. What do you know about the person or people behind the ideas? Might their age, gender identity, race, or socioeconomic status, for example, influence what they have to say? What about their interests, biases, or political leanings? We know, for instance, that Harriet Beecher Stowe was a committed abolitionist, and we also know that she was a devout Christian. Both aspects of her background greatly influenced how she presented her argument in *Uncle Tom's Cabin*.

Tone

What is the speaker's attitude toward the subject and the audience? Tone can be described as *adoring, bitter, casual, accusatory, angry, frustrated, critical, cynical, sarcastic, despairing, factual, formal, grim, hopeless, optimistic, outraged, respectful*, and so on. In her speech before the United Nations, Greta Thunberg said, "This is all wrong. I shouldn't be up here. I should be back in school on the other side of the ocean. Yet you all come to us young people for hope. How dare you! You have stolen my dreams and my childhood with your empty words." Her tone is one of exasperation and barely hidden disgust at the inaction of the adults she addressed in her speech.

KEY QUESTION

When thinking about the rhetorical situation, ask yourself the following question:

- How do the subject, occasion, audience, purpose, speaker, and tone influence the way the argument is expressed?

Analyzing the Rhetorical Context

Read the speech that follows and annotate it by making connections and asking questions (p. 10). Then, read it a second time and annotate the text for examples of any SOAPSTone elements that apply.

Challenger Speech

Ronald Reagan

The following speech was delivered the evening of January 28, 1986, after the space shuttle *Challenger* exploded during liftoff earlier that day. All seven crew members, including Christa McAuliffe, a high school teacher, perished. President Reagan was scheduled to deliver the State of the Union address to Congress that evening, but given the tragedy, he gave this speech from the Oval Office instead.

Ladies and gentlemen, I'd planned to speak to you tonight to report on the state of the Union, but the events of earlier today have led me to change those plans. Today is a day for mourning and remembering. Nancy and I are pained to the core by the tragedy of the shuttle *Challenger*. We know we share this pain with all of the people of our country. This is truly a national loss.

Nineteen years ago, almost to the day, we lost three astronauts in a terrible accident on the ground. But, we've never lost an astronaut in flight; we've never had a tragedy like this. And perhaps we've forgotten the courage it took for the crew of the shuttle; but they, the *Challenger* Seven, were aware of the dangers, but overcame them and did their jobs brilliantly. We mourn seven heroes: Michael Smith, Dick Scobee, Judith Resnik, Ronald McNair, Ellison Onizuka, Gregory Jarvis, and Christa McAuliffe. We mourn their loss as a nation together.

For the families of the seven, we cannot bear, as you do, the full impact of this tragedy. But we feel the loss, and we're thinking about you so very much. Your loved ones were daring and brave, and they had that special grace, that special spirit that says, "Give me a challenge and I'll meet it with joy." They had a hunger to explore the universe and discover its truths. They wished to serve, and they did. They served all of us. We've grown used to wonders in this century. It's hard to dazzle us. But for twenty-five years the United States space program has been doing just that. We've grown used to the idea of space, and perhaps we forget that we've only just begun. We're still pioneers. They, the members of the *Challenger* crew, were pioneers.

And I want to say something to the schoolchildren of America who were watching the live coverage of the shuttle's takeoff. I know it is hard to understand, but sometimes painful things like this happen. It's all part of the process of exploration and discovery. It's all part of taking a chance and expanding man's horizons. The future doesn't belong to the fainthearted; it belongs to the brave. The *Challenger* crew was pulling us into the future, and we'll continue to follow them.

I've always had great faith in and respect for our space program, and what happened 5
today does nothing to diminish it. We don't hide our space program. We don't keep secrets and cover things up. We do it all up front and in public. That's the way freedom is, and we wouldn't change it for a minute. We'll continue our quest in space. There will be more shuttle flights and more shuttle crews and, yes, more volunteers, more civilians, more teachers in space. Nothing ends here; our hopes and our journeys continue. I want to add that I wish I could talk to every man and woman who works for NASA or who worked on this mission and tell them: "Your dedication and professionalism have moved and impressed us for decades. And we know of your anguish. We share it."

There's a coincidence today. On this day 390 years ago, the great explorer Sir Francis Drake died aboard ship off the coast of Panama. In his lifetime the great frontiers were the oceans, and a historian later said, "He lived by the sea, died on it, and was buried in it." Well, today we can say of the *Challenger* crew: Their dedication was, like Drake's, complete.

The crew of the space shuttle *Challenger* honored us by the manner in which they lived their lives. We will never forget them, nor the last time we saw them, this morning, as they prepared for the journey and waved goodbye and "slipped the surly bonds of earth" to "touch the face of God." ■

Talking It Through

Discuss this speech with a partner. Who was President Reagan's audience? What was his purpose? How do you think his audience and purpose affected his tone, including the words and examples he chose to use?

Using Evidence

You have probably witnessed or participated in an exchange like this at some point in your life:

Child: I don't want to. Why do I have to?

Parent: Because I said so.

Child: But that's not fair!

The parent may have "won" this argument, but it's clear that the child is far from convinced. That's understandable because the parent offers no evidence to support his or her position. Successful arguments — those that influence the intended audience — require evidence to support the claim. Evidence is the heart of an argument: without effective evidence, you're basically just asserting your opinion again and again. Learning how to use and analyze evidence effectively, therefore, is very important. If you recall the rhetorical triangle, one of the key components of writing and analyzing an argument is understanding the intended audience of the argument, and thinking about what might be convincing to members of that audience. Effective writers know how to appeal to their audiences by including types of evidence that their readers will find appealing. Keep in mind, too, that you can cite evidence either to support your argument directly or to show your understanding of another viewpoint.

When considering what evidence to gather in support of your argument, keep in mind that any evidence you use should be relevant and reliable. When you support your argument with information that's common knowledge or comes from your own experience, you generally don't need to provide detailed information about the source. For any support you gather from outside sources, however, include information about where the ideas come from (we'll discuss this in more detail in the next chapter). Providing information about your sources makes your argument stronger and gives credit to the original author or authors. The discussion that follows describes various types of sources and how they can support a claim. Keep in mind that most successful arguments use a combination of types of evidence. Relying too heavily on one type or another may result in an argument that seems unbalanced or doesn't hold up to scrutiny.

Personal Experience and Anecdotes

A story about personal experience can be used as effective evidence if it is relevant to the claim. Or, a writer might provide an anecdote about the experience of others as a way to support a claim. This sort of evidence can help writers build a connection with readers and possibly stir up readers' emotions. If you were writing an argument about why people should have better access to health care, for example, your inclusion of a story about a family member's experiences in the hospital could be powerful evidence. Personal experience alone, however, is unlikely to be as convincing as an argument that includes other types of evidence as well.

Facts and Data/Statistics

Quantitative data, which takes the form of numbers, counts, percentages, and other information that can be measured, may sound dull, but a well-chosen statistic or data set can be very compelling either in paragraph form or as a chart or table. Because this kind of information is often rooted in scientific research, many writers and readers find it convincing. If you were writing about ways to improve your school's graduation rate, for example, including the current percentages of graduates from schools in your area would probably make a lot of sense. But studies can have flawed methods and data is subject to interpretation, so you have to be careful about where your statistics come from. Data can be manipulated or framed in a way that serves a particular agenda, or it can be outdated.

Scholarly Research and Expert Opinion

Using evidence from those who have specialized knowledge strengthens your argument in two ways. First, you boost your credibility by showing that your argument is not based solely on personal opinion. Second, you back up your thinking by pointing to those who have made it their career to study a topic in great depth and can therefore provide reliable information. So, if you're writing an argument in favor of requiring vaccinations for entrance to college, for example, then evidence from physicians who have researched the topic or someone who works at the U.S. Centers for Disease Control and Prevention could be very effective. In the same way, if you're writing about national security, providing the viewpoint of someone who serves or has served as Secretary of State would add authority to your argument.

KEY QUESTIONS

When thinking about the types of evidence found in an argument, ask yourself the following key questions:

- How does the writer balance the types of evidence in the argument?
- Is there sufficient evidence to support the claim?
- Is the evidence relevant to the claim?

Analyzing Evidence

Read the following text and identify the different types of evidence the writer uses. Explain how the evidence helps the writer to support his claim.

I'm a multimillionaire — and I think the tax system doesn't serve most Americans

Stephen Prince

I am a multimillionaire in Tennessee, one of the more deeply conservative states in America. In my circle of friends here, I'm often met with scorn for wanting to tax myself and all of my fellow wealthy friends. I'm called a "class traitor" by some, and altruistic by others, but neither is quite true.

The way I see it, the reason for any law is to temper the worst vices of individual human nature, so our society can work for everybody. Not just for the rich or the poor or even just for the middle class — but for everyone.

For instance, I like to drive fast, but we have speed limits because speeding is dangerous. Thus, I obey speed limit laws even though I have convinced myself that I'm an excellent high-speed driver.

The same principle stands for the economy and the laws that govern it. Increasingly, a small percentage of people have most of the money in our country because our laws have made it easier for us to keep it. In 1973, the top 1% of income earners received 9% of the nation's combined income. Today we receive more than 23%.

These imbalances are not sustainable and, more importantly, they just aren't right. 5
The top 1% now owns almost half the wealth of this country and received 83% of the benefits from the Tax Cuts and Jobs Act. I netted between $2-3m that I neither asked for nor needed from the Tax Cuts and Jobs Act.

My gains were offset by across-the-board budget cuts that slashed public services working families depend on to make ends meet. Add that to the ongoing issue of stagnating wages and thousands of job losses at the very same companies that benefit most from that tax bill, and you can start to draw a line between the rampant deregulation of our economy and the current flashing red warning signs of a recession.

Take wages, for example. Millions of workers still make under $15 an hour, because the Tennessee senator Lamar Alexander, who represents me in Congress, refuses to bring the minimum wage bill to the floor. He is adhering to a mantra I hear too often down here: American people just don't need it. But in a 70% consumer-driven economy, my business needs it just as much as the workers do.

Tax cuts for the rich at the expense of the working class is not a sustainable system for our economy. From my vantage, as a CEO in manufacturing, it's clear that my peers do not, by and large, take their tax savings and reinvest them in higher wages and job creation — all the things that might help stave off a recession. Instead, they tend to keep it all to themselves, because our tax laws allow them to.

It's akin to an open highway with no speed limits. And it's not a question of if an economic crash occurs — it's when.

When an economic downturn does happen, rich and poor alike would be better 10
served by an administration that has invested in the majority of Americans.

Fixing the problem doesn't mean I need to write checks to the treasury, as many of my friends down here often suggest. That would only be a drop in the ocean, for an inequality problem that exists in the trillions of dollars. Individual actions aren't enough to counter an entire system that supports and incentivizes the worst of human greed.

Rather, fixing the problem means that our elected officials need to implement a tax system that puts my money, and the money of all multimillionaires and billionaires, to its best use: running our military, building our roads and bridges, educating our youth, providing healthcare. This kind of tax policy acknowledges that government has to be paid for, and those of us who have derived the most from this country must pay more simply because we can.

If we stay on our current trajectory, we will be the first generation to leave much, much less of a country than we were given by our parents. To avoid it, it's time to put up more guardrails against the greed of the 1%. ■

Choosing Evidence

Discuss the types of evidence that you might use to write one of the following arguments. Explain why the evidence you suggest would effectively appeal to your audience and fit your purpose.

1. A social media post asking friends to make a financial contribution to a specific local group or organization (such as a homeless shelter or your local humane society)
2. A personal statement (or essay) for a part-time job application. Argue that you're the one to hire
3. A proposal to your school board or principal, in which you argue to replace individually written essays and exams with more collaborative projects in a specific course or in the curriculum in general

Detecting Bias

Bias refers to a speaker or writer having an identifiable preference for — or a prejudice against — one particular side of an issue. True objectivity is impossible, especially when someone is advocating one view over another. Nevertheless, it is important to understand the influences that a speaker or writer might bring to a subject. For example, religious or political affiliation might play a part in the position a writer takes on a particular issue. That's unavoidable, but it's essential that we understand *how* it influences the writer's viewpoint.

Similarly, place and time affect a writer's perspective. For example, if the mayor of a major city argues that a Fortune 500 company should build its headquarters in her city, we would expect her viewpoint to be biased toward the best interests of her city and her legacy. Her view can't be entirely dismissed, but it does reflect some self-interest.

The key is to understand what the potential sources of bias might be in a particular argument — for example, the politics, religion, age, position/job, geographical region, or socioeconomic status of the writer — and to scrutinize if and how that bias affects the argument.

KEY QUESTIONS

As you examine an argument for bias, keep the following questions in mind:

- What facts or perspectives has the writer left out?
- Is the writer affiliated with a company, political party, cultural movement, or other group that might suggest a hidden agenda?
- Does the author at least acknowledge, rather than dismiss or flat-out ignore, other perspectives on the issue?
- Does the author's choice of words seem reasonable, or is it deliberately intended to stir up fear or anger?

activity

Analyzing Bias

Read the following excerpt of an editorial written in 2019 by Facebook founder Mark Zuckerberg, who is trying to explain the business principles of his company at a time when many people were criticizing Facebook for profiting from users' private data. Zuckerberg has a lot of obvious biases. After you read the excerpt, try to explain how these biases affect what he includes in his argument — and what he leaves out. You may need to conduct quick research on some of the criticisms of Facebook's practices to know what he excludes from this piece.

from The Facts About Facebook

Mark Zuckerberg

Facebook turns 15 next month. When I started Facebook, I wasn't trying to build a global company. I realized you could find almost anything on the internet — music, books, information — except the thing that matters most: people. So I built a service people could use to connect and learn about each other. Over the years, billions have found this useful, and we've built more services that people around the world love and use every day.

Recently I've heard many questions about our business model, so I want to explain the principles of how we operate.

I believe everyone should have a voice and be able to connect. If we're committed to serving everyone, then we need a service that is affordable to everyone. The best way to do that is to offer services for free, which ads enable us to do.

People consistently tell us that if they're going to see ads, they want them to be relevant. That means we need to understand their interests. So based on what pages people like, what they click on, and other signals, we create categories—for example, people who like pages about gardening and live in Spain—and then charge advertisers to show ads to that category. Although advertising to specific groups existed well before the internet, online advertising allows much more precise targeting and therefore more-relevant ads.

The internet also allows far greater transparency and control over what ads you see 5
than TV, radio or print. On Facebook, you have control over what information we use to show you ads, and you can block any advertiser from reaching you. You can find out why you're seeing an ad and change your preferences to get ads you're interested in. And you can use our transparency tools to see every different ad an advertiser is showing to anyone else.

Still, some are concerned about the complexity of this model. In an ordinary transaction, you pay a company for a product or service they provide. Here you get our services for free—and we work separately with advertisers to show you relevant ads. This model can feel opaque, and we're all distrustful of systems we don't understand. . . .

There's the important question of whether the advertising model encourages companies like ours to use and store more information than we otherwise would.

There's no question that we collect some information for ads—but that information is generally important for security and operating our services as well. For example, companies often put code in their apps and websites so when a person checks out an item, they later send a reminder to complete the purchase. But this type of signal can also be important for detecting fraud or fake accounts. . . .

Ultimately, I believe the most important principles around data are transparency, choice, and control. We need to be clear about the ways we're using information, and people need to have clear choices about how their information is used. We believe regulation that codifies these principles across the internet would be good for everyone.

It's important to get this right, because there are clear benefits to this business model. 10
Billions of people get a free service to stay connected to those they care about and to express themselves. And small businesses—which create most of the jobs and economic growth around the world—get access to tools that help them thrive. . . . That's the world we're building for every day, and our business model makes it possible. ■

Talking It Through

Working with a partner, one of you pretend to be Zuckerberg and the other a reporter interviewing him. The reporter should ask questions of Zuckerberg about what evidence he included in or excluded from the editorial. Afterward, discuss whether Zuckerberg's biases get in the way of what he was trying to communicate.

Rhetorical Appeals

So far in our discussion of analyzing arguments, we have identified claims, recognized the importance of the rhetorical situation, and examined various types of evidence. Now it's time to focus on the **appeals** writers use to make arguments as persuasive as possible. The Greek philosopher Aristotle broke down persuasion into three basic ways of appealing to an audience:

- **Logos.** reason and logic
- **Pathos.** emotion
- **Ethos.** credibility

While we will discuss each of these individually, keep in mind that most writers use a variety of appeals to make their cases, rarely relying on a single appeal throughout an entire argument.

Logos

The appeal to reason can be very powerful in our data-driven society. Arguments based on logos rely primarily on clear reasoning, statistical data, research, and historical fact, and they generally use an objective tone. An argument about the need for increased security in schools, for instance, might appeal to logos by examining data about the relationship between increased security and decreased violence in school settings. Notice how the author of the editorial on the following page uses statistics and historical patterns to make the case for increased immigration.

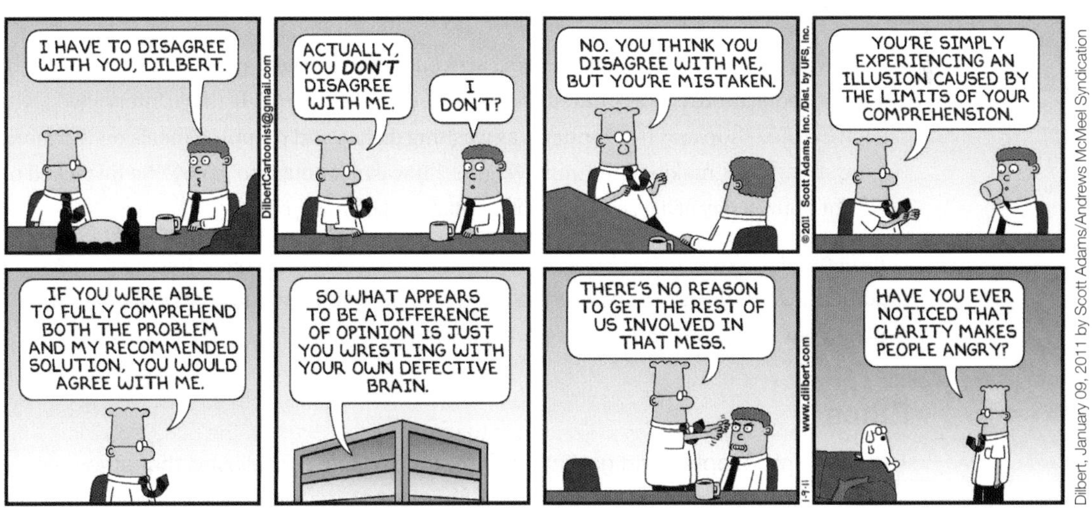

How does this Dilbert cartoon poke fun at the appeal to logos?

> Between 1950 and 2000, 47.2 million additional women and 31.4 million additional men entered the labor force. If jobs had been scarce, we should have seen the unemployment rate increase. . . . It didn't. . . . The unemployment rate for men, which was 4.8 percent in 1950, was down to 3.9 percent in 2000. . . . The same thing has happened with immigrants. [Despite increased immigration, 2018 saw] the lowest unemployment rate in 17 years.

Pathos

While a strong argument requires appeals to logos to be convincing, too much logos can also feel a little empty and robotic. As a result, pathos needs to play a role in connecting with your audience. The appeal to emotion can be evoked by descriptive and vivid language, or even an image. Let's return to the speech given by former president Ronald Reagan after the space shuttle *Challenger* disaster (p. 87). Notice the appeals to pathos in this paragraph:

> But we feel the loss, and we're thinking about you so very much. Your loved ones were daring and brave, and they had that special grace, that special spirit that says, "Give me a challenge and I'll meet it with joy." They had a hunger to explore the universe and discover its truths. They wished to serve, and they did. They served all of us.

The very language is filled with emotion that underscores the tragedy of the loss: those who died "were daring and brave," with a "special grace . . . special spirit." They "had a hunger to explore" and "wished to serve." Every word strikes a note of admiration and affirmation that honors the sacrifice this crew made. Similarly, look at the following section of an article about the founders of the clothing store Forever 21 coming to the United States from South Korea. Think about how it communicates the challenges immigrants face:

> Do Won Chang and his wife, Jin Sook, arrived . . . in 1981 with not much more than a high school education. . . . He immediately scoured newspaper job listings, interviewed with a local coffee shop and by Monday was washing dishes and prepping meals on the morning shift. "I was making minimum wage. . . . It wasn't enough to get by." So he tacked on eight hours a day at a gas station and . . . started [cleaning offices].

But be careful. While it can be a powerful strategy, pathos alone results in a weak argument. Once the emotional response wears off and logic kicks in, your audience will assess your argument with a more critical eye.

Ethos

The Greek philosopher and godfather of rhetoric, Aristotle, believed that ethos, an appeal to the credibility and authority of the speaker, was the most important of the three appeals. If the writer is not seen as trustworthy or knowledgeable on the subject, and free from obvious bias, then all the logic and emotion in the world is unlikely to sway an audience. There are two primary ways to appeal to ethos:

- demonstrate authority
- demonstrate shared values

Some speakers have a certain amount of ethos because of who they are, such as a respected neuroscientist who presents an argument on the effects of caffeine on the brain. But what if that scientist wanted to talk to the school board about increasing security at her son's school? Does being a well-respected neuroscientist help? A bit, sure, but it's not really relevant to the issue at hand. At that point, the scientist would have to establish her ethos as a parent who shares the values and concerns of other parents in the room. Read this excerpt from an opinion piece on immigration by a research fellow at Stanford University's Hoover Institution, and notice how the writer establishes ethos as someone who is not only a scholar on immigration, but has directly experienced it:

> [Being an undocumented immigrant] means going about my day in fear of being found out. It means rarely trusting people, even those closest to me, with who I really am. It means keeping my family photos in a shoebox rather than displaying them on shelves in my home, so friends don't ask about them . . . And it has meant relying on a sort of 21st-century underground railroad of supporters, people who . . . took risks for me.

KEY QUESTIONS

When thinking about the appeal to logos, ask yourself the following question:

- How does the writer use evidence and logic to appeal to the audience's reason?

When thinking about pathos, ask yourself the following questions:

- How does the writer appeal to the audience's emotions?
- Are these appeals effective, or do they go overboard to become overly sentimental, dramatic, or manipulative?

When thinking about ethos, ask yourself the following questions:

- What values or concerns does the speaker share with the audience?
- How does the speaker establish his or her good character?

activity Analyzing Appeals

Look over the following advertisements. For each one, identify the central claim, the likely intended audience, and the appeal which is most strongly at work.

Talking It Through

In pairs or small groups, rate the advertisements by which were the most and the least persuasive based on how successful you think they were at incorporating their appeals. Discuss how susceptible you are to various appeals. Does one type tend to work more effectively to persuade you? Why or why not?

activity Using Appeals

Read through the following scenarios and choose one to imagine yourself facing. Write a short piece in which you try to employ all three major appeals—ethos, pathos, and logos. Afterward, write a reflection about why you think some appeals were more effective than others for the scenario you chose.

1. You are the spokesperson for a student group hoping to convince your school's administration that your school day should start one hour later.
2. You are speaking to your town's governing council about an issue in which you have an interest, such as building a new park, ending a curfew, or supporting more school funding.
3. You are trying to persuade a group of teenagers who are angry about the verdict in a controversial court case to make their protest in an orderly, peaceful manner.
4. You are the President of the United States and you are trying to convince Congress and the public to support (or oppose) funding for a colony on Mars within ten years.

Counterarguments

Addressing **counterarguments** — that is, opposing viewpoints — is an important element of effective argument because it demonstrates that you are reasonable and you have given your position careful thought. For instance, if you were arguing against adding armed security guards at your school, you might reference a counterargument that security guards are beneficial to the learning environment because they make students feel safe, but then refute that argument by pointing to research showing that security guards more regularly target students of color, making security conditional upon race and ethnicity. In this way, you indicate that you have recognized and considered a position counter to your own as part of the process of developing your viewpoint. The result is that you not only appeal to logos by sounding reasonable but also establish your ethos as a fair-minded person who has taken the time to consider multiple perspectives.

When you work with counterargument, an effective strategy is **concession** and **refutation**. You start out by making a concession, agreeing with some aspect of the opposition to show that you respect the views of others, even those you disagree with. Then — and here's the trick — you refute the argument by pointing out how the opposition either doesn't account for important issues or is outweighed by other considerations.

For instance, in an article examining the controversial issue of requiring all police officers to wear body cameras, *New York Times* writer David Brooks opens by acknowledging the reasons one might argue in favor of body cams:

> First, [in] too many cases . . ., police officers have abused their authority and then covered it up. Second, . . . cops would be less likely to abuse their authority if they were being tracked. Third, human memory is . . . unreliable. . . . We might be able to reduce . . . wrongful convictions and acquittals if [police wear body cameras].

By starting with the reasons why some people support body cams — the counterargument to his position — Brooks avoids sounding confrontational. In fact, he sounds downright agreeable. This encourages his readers, even those who might disagree, to be receptive to what he has to say. But once he has raised the counterarguments, he refutes the opposition by asking his readers to consider something that those in favor of body cams have not said:

> Cop-cams strike a blow for truth, but they strike a blow against relationships. Society will be more open and transparent, but less humane and trusting.

So, yes, body cams can be beneficial, he says, but overall, they will make us less trusting of each other.

Edgar Argo/Cartoon Stock

What point is this cartoon making about the importance of acknowledging counterarguments? What is the intended humor of the cartoon?

Counterarguments

Earlier in this chapter we included an excerpt from an editorial about ending legacy admissions to colleges (p. 80). What follows is another excerpt from the editorial. As you read, identify the counterarguments the writer uses. Then, discuss with a partner or small group the ways that the writer refutes the counterarguments and whether or not this approach is effective to the overall argument.

from End Legacy College Admissions

The Editorial Board of the *New York Times*

Schools make various arguments about the value of legacy preference. Most often, they argue that it helps with donations, which in turn helps fund financial aid programs for needy students and the construction of facilities that help the entire organization.

Research, however, has cast serious doubt on this line of reasoning. A group of researchers studied data from the top 100 schools in the country (again ranked by U.S. News) from 1998 to 2008 and found that "there is no statistically significant evidence of a causal relationship between legacy preference policies and total alumni giving among top universities."

Another argument that college presidents make is that multigenerational enrollment helps improve the institutional ethos, tightening the bonds of community for those lucky enough to be admitted. That may be so, but it comes at a high cost in unfairness. College admission is a zero-sum proposition — for every legacy admitted, another promising applicant is denied the career and economic opportunity that a top degree can provide.

Little wonder that American universities are a global outlier when it comes to legacy preference. Oxford and Cambridge Universities, for instance, gave up the practice decades ago. In the United States, schools like Texas A&M University and the University of Georgia dropped legacy admissions and continue to thrive, while schools like the Massachusetts Institute of Technology historically haven't used them. In a 2012 blog post, Chris Peterson, an assistant director in the M.I.T. admissions office, put the issue in stark terms. "I personally would not work for a college which had legacy admission because I am not interested in simply reproducing a multigenerational lineage of educated elite. And if anyone in our office ever advocated for a mediocre applicant on the basis of their 'excellent pedigree' they would be kicked out of the committee room. So to be clear: if you got into M.I.T., it's because you got into M.I.T. Simple as that." ■

SPEAKING & LISTENING FOCUS

Differences of Opinion

When you are dealing with important and complex issues, there are bound to be differences of opinion. And there should be. We are not robots with preprogrammed ideas and thoughts; we learn and grow from discussion and debate. But this does not mean yelling and screaming at each other like we might see on cable news or hear on sports radio. A good discussion about an issue on which people disagree requires active listening and a genuine respect for each other's perspectives. The following steps can help you when you find yourself in a discussion with someone whose views on a topic differ from your own:

1. Identify disagreement. Respectfully identify where your discussion partner's ideas differ from your own. Consider using the following sentence starters to help you:

- While I agree with you about ___________, I do not agree with you about ___________.
- Although you make an interesting point about ___________, I wonder if ___________.
- Then again, I think that ___________.
- Another way to look at it could be ___________.
- I think it is also important to consider that ___________.
- I see your point, but what do you think about ___________?

2. Identify agreement. On which points do you and your partner agree? Consider using the following statements or asking the following questions to see where you and your partner have common ground on your topic:

- Though we disagree about ___________, it seems we agree that ___________.
- What are other perspectives about this that we have not considered yet?
- On the whole, I think we can agree that ___________.

3. Create a plan. Identify next steps that the two of you agree need to be taken on your issue. Consider using the following sentence stems to help you:

- We need to gather more information about ___________ in order to ___________.
- This issue will be "solved" when ___________.
- Fifty years from now, people discussing this issue will likely say ___________.
- Actions that we each can take on this issue are ___________.

Practice

Working with a partner, choose a topic that you are both interested in and that has multiple sides to it. Possible topics could include the following: *Are professional athletes paid too much? Should homework be eliminated? Should all vehicles be required to be electric? Should the use of cell phones by students be restricted in school? Should the voting age be lowered to 16? Should zoos be eliminated?* Flipping a coin, determine which partner will take which side. If necessary, conduct some brief research to determine the best evidence to support your assigned position. When you are both ready, hold a discussion using the steps identified above.

Reflection

What was it like to discuss your issue using these steps? In what ways did you each demonstrate active listening? What new perspectives did you gain on the issue?

Logical Fallacies

When you're examining an argument, including your own, you want to be on the lookout for gaps in logic, called **logical fallacies**. In some cases, a speaker or writer may deliberately try to manipulate an audience through a logical fallacy. In other instances, however, a logical fallacy may be the result of unclear thinking. There are many types of fallacies, but here are five very common ones:

Ad Hominem

Latin for "to the person," this fallacy takes place when a speaker attacks the character of his or her opponents rather than countering the opponents' ideas. This is a way to shift attention from the issue to the person. For instance, in an argument in favor of the construction of a new school building, someone might point out that a person holding an opposing view was recently fined for reckless driving. That fact may not be admirable, but it's not relevant to the person's credibility regarding new school construction.

Bandwagon Appeal

Go with the crowd! That's essentially the fallacy that occurs when someone argues that something is true or right because a number of people believe it. So, for instance, someone might argue that because millions have used the latest herbal diet supplement, it must be both safe and effective. Advertisers often use bandwagon appeals in an attempt to persuade consumers that large sales are proof of excellence or — perhaps with even faultier logic — that because a celebrity endorses a product, you should use it.

Either-Or Fallacy

This fallacy (also known as "false dilemma") occurs when a speaker reduces a complex issue to two artificial options. "You're either with us or you're with the terrorists" exemplifies the either-or fallacy. Such thinking cuts off the possibility of middle ground or compromise. In addition, this fallacy can artificially limit choices, as is the case in the following argument: "You want to cut diesel emissions, but diesels produce fewer greenhouse gases. So, do you care about climate change, or not?" Of course, it's possible to care about both air pollution and climate change.

Hasty Generalization

This fallacy occurs when an inference or a conclusion is drawn on the basis of insufficient evidence. For instance, if you make an argument that a company is guilty of ageism because your grandfather applied for a job and was not hired, you risk making a hasty generalization. If, indeed, there is a pattern of failing to hire people over a certain age, then you might have a case — but not hiring one person is not a pattern. Note that stereotypes are often formed as a result of hasty generalizations, such as, women are bad drivers; men won't ask for directions; Midwesterners are overly friendly.

Slippery Slope

This fallacy relies on fear. Also known as the "floodgates fallacy," the slippery slope occurs when someone argues that if you allow X to occur, Y will surely follow. If you argue, for example, that convicted felons should be allowed to vote after they have served their sentences, someone might respond that soon criminals will be running the country. In other words, by doing one thing, you're on a slippery slope to a far worse and (usually exaggerated) situation.

Identifying Logical Fallacies

Read the following article about whether students should have access to cellphones during school. As you read, identity any possible logical fallacies, and then meet with a partner to discuss how the fallacies might affect the writer's argument.

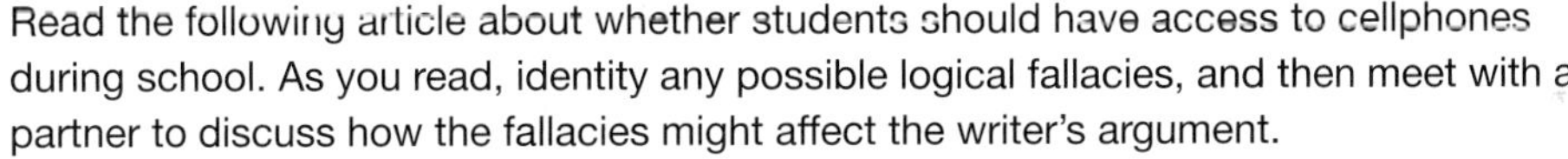

Cellphones at School: Should Your Kid Have One?

Edward Baig

Lawmakers in France recently passed a ban on the use of smartphones in schools, impacting students in their early to midteens. In U.S. school districts where digital device policies are all over the map, parents and teachers are divided on how to curb or permit phone use in the classroom.

Some schools have students stash their phones in their lockers — as they do for middle schoolers in my Northern New Jersey town. Others have kids place them in a canvas "pocket chart" — essentially a hanging shoe organizer — in the classroom.

What most everyone agrees on is that screen-time addiction is a problem for young and old, an issue that companies such as Apple, Google and Facebook are finally tackling with recently announced software updates. You hear all too often how kids who are fixated

Edward C. Baig, "Cellphones at school: Should your kid have one?" USA Today, August 14, 2018.

on smartphone screens are only modeling the behavior of their parents. (It's also not unheard of that a teacher also may use a phone in the classroom, to check on his or her own family at home.)

According to nonprofit family media watchdog Common Sense Media, 24 percent of kids from 8 to 12 years old have their own smartphone and 67 percent of their teenage counterparts do, with tweens using an average of about six hours' worth of entertainment media daily.

Compounding the confusion is the age at which families give their kids a 5
phone — often, but not always, when the youngster is about to enter middle school. But what effect does a kid who has a phone that's visible at school have on a classmate who doesn't have his or her own handset?

Some schools implement "one-to-one" programs to provide computers, tablets, or other mobile devices to each student. Other cash-strapped districts may have to share tech gear in the classroom. And some educators may even encourage students to bring their own devices for class use.

It's safe to assume that most schools aren't about to dictate to a parent that a kid can or cannot use a device on the way to or from school, though some do actually ask families to sign commitments to temper tech use. . . .

"When we're asking these 12 to 13 year olds to carry the phone and not be on them, we 100 percent know that's not happening," says Delaney Ruston, a physician and director of the documentary "Screenagers: Growing Up in the Digital Age." "You can go into any classroom or ask any middle schooler, and they will tell you consistently how they and/or their friends are sneaking being on the phones during class times."

The consequences? According to the "Away For The Day" initiative Ruston developed with the team behind "Screenagers" to try to institute policies requiring phones to be put away, 56 percent of middle schools allow students to carry phones on them all day, yet 82 percent of parents don't want their kids using phones there.

The Away For The Day website cites various academic studies that point to 10
potential negative outcomes of classroom phone use. In one such study, 75 percent of teachers reported that the attention spans of students have decreased. In another study, students regularly interrupted by text messages had test scores that were 10.6 percent lower.

Ruston believes that putting the phones away can improve a child's emotional well-being in school and help with their focus in and out of the classroom.

And while she recognizes that a teacher might ask a kid to pull out a phone during a given lesson, "to do X, Y, Z . . . the reality is that many of these kids now on their personal device have gotten so many notifications that they're actually not going to do whatever the teacher is saying they should be doing, but instead sending and receiving messages or going onto their video games."

"You're already going to have those struggles with (school supplied) educational devices," Ruston adds, "but it gets exponentially more challenging when it's a personal device."

Even if a device on a student's desk is turned off, the worry is that it still becomes a distraction.

Ruston also dismisses the safety argument. She pointed to an NPR report in which 15
security experts have said that letting a kid have a phone in the classroom during a lockdown makes them less safe, not more. When students should be quiet, for example, a ringing or vibrating phone might alert an assailant where kids are hiding. Parents trying to reach youngsters in an emergency might jam communications and interfere with first responders. And the kids might miss instructions from the authorities.

But Ruston concedes that "that's not to say there's not an emotional upside for a parent." ■

Interpreting an Argument

As you may remember from Chapter 1, there are many different purposes for reading. However, when you are reading for interpretation of an argument, you will be concerned primarily with explaining what the text means — its significance. Significance refers to the ideas that give us insight into ourselves, the world around us, or the author's message. When interpreting, you need to focus on having a reasonable explanation for why you think your conclusion is an accurate one. When we discuss meaning in argumentative texts, we generally speak of the author's purpose: What are the reasons why the author may have written the text and what does he/she hope to communicate to his/her readers? To draw a reasonable interpretation of an argument, you will need to examine it for the elements we have been discussing so far: claim, elements of the rhetorical situation, evidence, rhetorical appeals, and counterarguments.

Look at the first part of an argument that proposes that high school students should be required to apply to their high schools, as if it were college; it has been annotated for the elements of an argument you have been examining throughout this chapter.

from High Schools Shouldn't Guarantee Admission

Leslie Nguyen-Okwu

My mother stole my education for me, before I ever strapped on my first bubblegum-pink backpack and entered the brooding halls of kindergarten. In our gritty neighborhood, the schools were close to failing, the textbooks fell apart and the walls crumbled. But if you drove a short 15 minutes west, you'd find

Appeals to pathos.

schools that stood tall and gleaming, beacons of education. Their doors opened only to the most privileged students in the city — which shut resoundingly in my face. Back then, school-enrollment fraud was, and still is, illegal. But my mother cheated the system and rustled up a fake address to sneak me into an award-winning magnet school — you know, one of those "shinier" schools.

The aftertaste of a failed high school education can linger throughout a person's life, simply because they reside in a crappy ZIP code like I did. Today, some 900,000 students remain trapped in low-performing high schools where resources are scant, the curriculum is as bland as bran, and the students — disproportionately Black and Latino — are rarely encouraged to reach their full potential. Many studies illuminate just how low-quality schools can undercut grades in college too and limit opportunities to explore new interests that ultimately lead to full-blown career choices.

Different types of evidence — facts and data, as well as personal experience.

As racial, ethnic and socioeconomic divides continue to be stubborn features of our education landscape, here's one way to level the playing field: All students must apply to high school, admission not guaranteed.

Here is her central claim.

Yes, school choice already exists in some form or another: Rich parents can "opt out" of public schools, whether by sending their kids to private school or moving houses; others can apply to public or private charter schools in their cities, hoping for the best.

She acknowledges a part of the counterargument: We already have what she is proposing, so what's the point?

But a nationwide mandatory high school application process for all would fall neatly in step with the ideals of American meritocracy. Call it school choice on steroids. Not everyone will go to an all-star school like Stuyvesant in New York City, but at least high-achieving students will no longer be kept down by the system or miss out on all the rich academic and social experience of high school that they

She concedes and refutes here by saying, "Yes, but this goes much further."

deserve — so long as they submit a polished essay, stellar test scores and some excellent extracurriculars.

Teenagers should have options when it comes to their schooling, much like we all have choices at the grocery store or in the various doctors we can select from in our neighborhood. That means 14-year-old Devon should have a fighting chance for a spot at a public charter school that focuses on the arts and Rosa can finally apply for a nontraditional high school like the Public Museum School in Michigan.

Is this a fallacy? Schools are not really like supermarkets.

Principal Chris Hanks says his school boasts lessons on topics like microbiotics and outer space inside an 80-year-old museum and typically accepts only students who score above a certain percentile in math or reading across the district. Just because a kid doesn't live in a certain neighborhood shouldn't mean they're bound to a school that's not right for them.

Specific evidence from an expert in the field of education.

After examining the key elements, we can try to determine a reasonable interpretation of the argument by asking ourselves about the rhetorical appeals and strategies the author employs to achieve her purpose in this article. Is the argument persuasive? Why or why not? For this piece, we could say that Leslie Nguyen-Okwu is making the claim that every student should have to apply to high school to ensure that everyone who has the ability to succeed has the right to attend. She makes her case by appealing to our emotions when she describes the poor conditions of some schools and contrasting them with the benefits of the better schools. Overall, her argument in this section is successful because she uses various types of evidence, including data, statistics, and expert opinion.

Interpreting an Argument

Read the second part of Leslie Nguyen-Okwu's argument that follows. Read it once and annotate by making connections and asking questions, as we discussed in Chapter 1 (p. 10). Then, read it a second time, annotating for elements such as claim, rhetorical situation, evidence, rhetorical appeals, and counterarguments. Finally, write a brief response that describes how the author uses the elements of an argument to make her case. How persuasive is this section of the argument?

from High Schools Shouldn't Guarantee Admission

Leslie Nguyen-Okwu

Moreover, students would be encouraged — nay, forced — to think about their futures and to deeply deliberate the kind of careers they would like to lead for the rest of their lives, as early as the eighth grade. Just look at Germany's three-pronged education tracks to find preteens who already have a profound clarity on what they want to do in life and how they'll achieve it, long before they learn how to drive.

Of course, Germany's uber-elite *gymnasiums* have drawn criticism too. Rather than acting as a great equalizer, its schools for so-called gifted and talented students have become more like breeding grounds of privilege. A mandatory application process for high school would likewise favor more affluent families who have the spare cash to drop on application prep and personal tutors to ensure their spoiled progeny will get into the best high school, again reinforcing inequality. And some experts, like Michael Dannenberg, the director of Strategic Initiatives for Policy at Education Reform Now, say our efforts are better served by improving the lot of schools we already have, rather than forcing students to compete for a limited number of spots at top-tier high schools. "We've got a quality problem on the supply side," he says. "School choice without accountability is reckless. It undermines the school choice movement if it's done without attention to outcomes and education accountability standards."

So, choice isn't the only solution at play here — a point made even more poignant when you consider the fact that attending a public, private or charter high school makes little difference in terms of student achievement, according to both the National Center for Education Evaluation and Regional Assistance (NCEE) and the Center on Education Policy at George Washington University. But then again, if applications work so well for colleges, then why not spread the benefits at the high school level too and aim to close our achievement gap before it's too late?

I would know. All those years ago, my mother's well-meaning scam was discovered a few months after my first day of kindergarten. My last day at the glittery school came in the winter — not even halfway through the academic year. All I can remember is the drooping farewell cake from my teacher and the tears streaming down my face. ■

Interpreting Visual Arguments

As you have seen throughout this chapter, writers and speakers use a variety of tools to persuade their audiences of their claims: evidence, appeals, refutation of counterarguments, and so on. But you have also likely noticed many visuals in this chapter — advertisements, editorial cartoons, and others — that present and try to prove a claim. While visual arguments can use many of the tools that written or spoken arguments can, some additional, specialized vocabulary will help you interpret visual arguments.

Visual Element	Questions to Ask
Color and Lighting	What colors, if any, are used, and how do they contrast with other colors in the visual text? How is lighting used? What is emphasized through color choices?
Framing and Focus	Every artist, photographer, or filmmaker must decide what to show, and what to leave out—what goes inside the frame, and what goes outside of it. Does the viewer see the scene close up, or from a great distance? What is in focus, or out of focus? Does the viewer see the subject from above, below, or behind? What elements are centered, or off to one side? What does not appear in the frame?
Layout and Design	How has the visual information been categorized, organized, and presented? In a pie chart? Bar graph? Is information listed chronologically or by quantity? Is there blank space? If so, how is it used? How would you describe any lines in the design: thick, thin, squiggly?
Fonts and Symbols	What fonts or styles are used for the words? Does the font communicate a particular tone? What is labeled or captioned? How are speech balloons, if any, used?

Let's apply these terms to the advertisement on page 112 sponsored by the American Academy of Pediatrics, which is making the claim that children should be immunized.

Color and Lighting

The lighting and colors are soft and welcoming, just like what we would want in a doctor's office or a baby's nursery. They are muted and let us focus on how cute the baby is.

Framing and Focus

We see a close-up of the baby, healthy and happy and looking directly at the viewer, clearly intending to say to us, "Keep me this way."

Layout and Design

While the baby is the focus, prominently featured in the center of the ad, notice how the main text about immunizations appears above and below the baby, forcing the viewer to read the warnings about immunizations with the baby in mind.

Fonts and Symbols

The main message — consider the dangers of not immunizing — is in bold and in the larger-sized? font, while the details of the possible effects appear much smaller. And featured prominently in large font in the lower right-hand corner is the icon and name of the ad's sponsor, The American Academy of Pediatrics, a source of authority and expertise.

Images as Rhetoric

Visual arguments can be so powerful because they often communicate their messages viscerally and emotionally, sometimes without the need for words. Now that we've learned about some visual elements, let's circle back and think about how to apply the rhetorical concepts that we've been using for written texts to visual texts. Like written texts, images have an author (the speaker), an audience, a subject, an occasion, a purpose, and even a tone. They can appeal to emotions and logic. Whenever you analyze an image and think about its visual elements, you should also try to connect them back to these fundamental rhetorical concepts.

For instance, photojournalist Jacob Riis documented the bleak living conditions in New York City in the late 1800s in a book called *How the Other Half Lives: Studies among the Tenements of New York*. Riis, the creator of the image on the next page, wanted to document conditions in the tenements for an audience of upscale readers

Jacob A. Riis

of the daily newspapers in New York City. Because these readers had probably never seen the portions of the city Riis captures, he uses an objective tone to push his claim. The person in this photograph doesn't look miserable; he has dignity. This builds Riis's credibility and ethos. He's not just going for shock, or solely pathos; he's documenting the situation accurately for his audience, who Riis likely hoped would be outraged by the conditions. Notice how the framing of the photograph is wide and captures the man's surroundings. Riis's purpose here is not to make a portrait, but rather to document squalid living conditions. The framing helps him achieve his purpose. The lighting also creates a starkness and desperateness to the man's situation, appealing to pathos. His photographs led to significant reforms in housing laws; in other words, his argument, communicated visually, worked.

Interpreting Visual Arguments

Look over the advertisement on the next page created by Crisis Relief Singapore, a relief agency that supports volunteer efforts in disaster areas around the world. Identify the claim the ad is making, and then analyze how the visual elements assist the creators in persuading their audience.

Language and Style in an Argument

So far in this chapter, you have been focusing on the content of an argument — claim, evidence, appeals, and so on. You may recall from Chapter 1, however, that another way of determining the meaning of a text is to **read for style** (p. 15), to examine why the text was created in the way it was. When reading an argument for style, you are conducting a close reading, focusing on the individual words, sentences, structure of the text in order to understand how the writer created the text to make it as persuasive as possible.

The language of an argument is more than just icing on the argumentative cake. A writer's stylistic choices can make an argument both memorable and persuasive. Not everyone has the stylistic genius of Abraham Lincoln or Martin Luther King Jr., but you can study their brilliant arguments, along with others, to learn to make effective stylistic choices in your own writing.

KEY QUESTIONS

Consider the following questions when reading for style:

- Why did the writer make this specific choice?
- What effect does that choice have?

Connotative Language

As you may recall from Chapter 2, **connotation** refers to the ideas and emotions associated with a word's literal meaning. Connotative language adds impact to an argument by stirring emotions or by painting a visual picture. Leslie Nguyen-Okwu uses connotative language to set the stage for the argument you read earlier (p. 107) about recommended changes in the admission process of high schools:

> My mother stole my education for me, before I ever strapped on my first bubble-gum-pink backpack and entered the brooding halls of kindergarten. In our gritty neighborhood, the schools were close to failing, the textbooks fell apart and the walls crumbled. But if you drove a short 15 minutes west, you'd find schools that stood tall and gleaming, beacons of education. Their doors opened only to the most privileged students in the city — which shut resoundingly in my face.

The language draws readers in. We're right there with her, feeling the rejection and separation she describes. Her language choices — "stole," "brooding," "crumbled," "gleaming" — add emotional intensity as we begin reading the argument. Such skillful use of language is intended to make us more receptive to an argument about the dangers of certain admissions policies, but her stylistic choices in this opening get our attention first.

Figurative Language

You might be used to thinking about metaphors and similes as literary tools, but, like other kinds of **figurative language**, they can serve as a rhetorical strategy to give an idea more impact. Figurative language often appeals to our emotions and helps us to look at things from a different perspective. In his speech following the terrorist attacks on September 11, 2001, President George W. Bush — known for his practical and straightforward language — used one brief but effective figure of speech. He warned the enemies of the United States: "Terrorist attacks can shake the foundations of our biggest buildings, but they cannot touch the foundation of America. These acts shatter steel, but they cannot dent the steel of American resolve." The figurative language choices reinforce the idea of American strength. But the use of figurative language in argument isn't reserved only for speeches. In the editorial you read earlier about why high schools shouldn't guarantee admission to specific students, Leslie Nguyen-Okwu writes, "Rather than acting as a great equalizer, its schools for so-called gifted and talented students have become more like breeding grounds of privilege." Now, these elite schools are not literally breeding grounds, but the use of the simile conveys the inevitability of sustained inequalities.

Allusion

Another type of figurative language in fiction and poetry is an allusion. An **allusion** is a cultural reference — a myth, a famous painting, a famous historical figure or event that the writer assumes the reader will recognize. In argument, that can still hold true, but speakers and writers need to choose allusions not only for their broad cultural relevance, but also for their appeal to a specific audience. Thus, a historical allusion might resonate with one community, while a sports allusion might be effective for another audience, and a pop culture reference might work where a historical allusion would otherwise fall flat. An editorial arguing for stricter gun control might refer to Columbine, Sandy Hook, or Parkland, all sites of school shootings that an audience would likely (and sadly) recognize. In his speech after the space shuttle *Challenger* was destroyed, President Reagan uses an allusion to Sir Francis Drake. Because he couldn't be certain that his audience would know about a British explorer who died hundreds of years earlier, he also subtly defines his allusion: "On this day 390 years ago, the great explorer Sir Francis Drake died aboard ship off the coast of Panama. In his lifetime the great frontiers were the oceans, and a historian later said, 'He lived by the sea, died on it, and was buried in it.'" His use of the allusion to Drake puts the actions of the crew of the *Challenger* in the larger historical context of explorers throughout time.

Parallel Structure

Parallelism means using similar grammatical structures to emphasize related ideas. Parallel structure may involve a single word, a phrase, a clause, a full sentence, or even a series of paragraphs. In President Reagan's speech about the *Challenger*, he said of the astronauts, "They had a hunger to explore the universe and discover its truths. They wished to serve, and they did. They served all of us," keeping all of the focus and emphasis on them. In his speech to mark the fiftieth anniversary of the civil rights march in Selma, Alabama, President Barack Obama uses parallel structure to stress the unity of a diverse nation. Toward the end of his speech, he says, "Look at our history." He then goes through various people that he claims mark our nation's history:

> We are Lewis and Clark and Sacajawea, pioneers who braved the unfamiliar, followed by a stampede of farmers and miners, and entrepreneurs and hucksters. . . .
>
> We're the immigrants who stowed away on ships to reach these shores, the huddled masses yearning to breathe free — Holocaust survivors, Soviet defectors, the Lost Boys of Sudan. . . .
>
> We're the slaves who built the White House. . . . We're the ranch hands and cowboys. . . .
>
> We're the inventors of gospel and jazz and blues, bluegrass and country, and hip-hop and rock and roll, and our very own sound with all the sweet sorrow and reckless joy of freedom.

After this catalog of all the different people and voices who make up this country, Obama concludes, "That's what America is." The similar structure at the beginning of each sentence, along with the different endings, allows for differences while stressing the similarities that Obama claims are the hallmark of the United States.

Rhetorical Questions

A rhetorical question is one that asks the audience to reflect on an issue but does not elicit a direct response. For example, someone arguing against stricter gun control laws might ask, “What is a law-abiding citizen supposed to do when only the criminals have guns?” Greta Thunberg, speaking to the United Nations about climate change, asks her audience, “How dare you pretend that this can be solved with just ‘business as usual’ and some technical solutions?” She does not intend for her audience to answer but instead uses the rhetorical question to shame her audience for its inaction. Rhetorical questions allow you to frame the issue, engage your readers, and offer a transition from one idea or issue to the next.

Analyzing Language and Style

Following are the opening paragraphs from Elie Wiesel’s acceptance speech when he was awarded the Nobel Peace Prize in 1986. How do Wiesel’s stylistic choices help him to support his claim that it’s essential to speak out against injustice, rather than remain silent?

from Nobel Prize Speech

Elie Wiesel

It is with a profound sense of humility that I accept the honor you have chosen to bestow upon me. I know: your choice transcends me. This both frightens and pleases me.

It frightens me because I wonder: do I have the right to represent the multitudes who have perished? Do I have the right to accept this great honor on their behalf? . . . I do not. That would be presumptuous. No one may speak for the dead; no one may interpret their mutilated dreams and visions.

It pleases me because I may say that this honor belongs to all the survivors and their children, and through us, to the Jewish people with whose destiny I have always identified.

I remember: it happened yesterday or eternities ago. A young Jewish boy discovered the kingdom of night. I remember his bewilderment, I remember his anguish. It all happened so fast. The ghetto. The deportation. The sealed cattle car. The fiery altar upon which the history of our people and the future of mankind were meant to be sacrificed.

I remember: he asked his father: “Can this be true?” This is the twentieth century, not 5
the Middle Ages. Who would allow such crimes to be committed? How could the world remain silent?

And now the boy is turning to me: “Tell me,” he asks. “What have you done with my future? What have you done with your life?”

And I tell him that I have tried. That I have tried to keep memory alive, that I have tried to fight those who would forget. Because if we forget, we are guilty, we are accomplices.

And then I explained to him how naive we were, that the world did know and remain silent. And that is why I swore never to be silent whenever and wherever human beings endure suffering and humiliation. ■

A Model Analysis: Connecting Content and Style

Let's see how content and style work together by examining this advertisement from the shoe and apparel company Nike featuring NFL quarterback Colin Kaepernick.

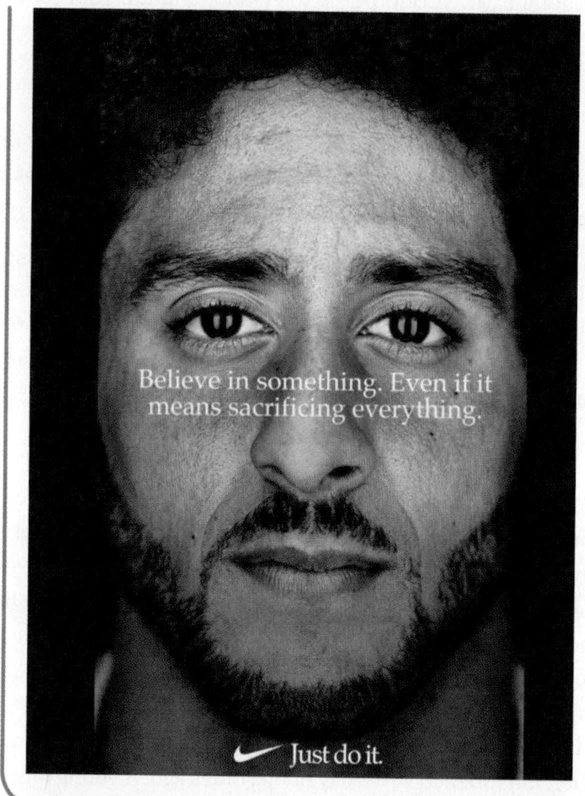

Rhetorical Situation

We should always begin our analysis of an argument by considering the speaker (writer), subject, and audience. In this case, the speaker is Nike, a shoe and apparel company that regularly use sports figures to endorse its products. The subject requires some context: In 2016, Colin Kaepernick, a quarterback for the San Francisco 49ers football team, decided to kneel — instead of standing — during the playing of the national anthem at the beginning of games in order to silently protest police brutality. Kaepernick was criticized for his action by some team owners and politicians, and the following year, no NFL team would hire him. Because Nike's culture and media reach is so wide, the audience for this ad might be difficult to narrow down. However, by choosing a subject that transcends sports, it's clear that Nike is trying to appeal to consumers beyond those who watch football. This ad was part of a large campaign that included print ads, billboards, and videos.

Appeal to Ethos

Clearly, Kaepernick has the authority to be selling sporting goods since he is a sports star himself. However, the main use of ethos is found in how the text of the ad addresses the audience as "we." It does not say that Kaepernick believes in "something" (though he does) and has sacrificed "everything" (which he did), but it suggests that "we" should. What is implicit is that Nike shares those values as well, and is a company "we" should support.

Appeal to Pathos

How does Nike appeal to our emotions? First, the company uses Kaepernick's story, which most of the audience is familiar with. Second, the ad features his dramatically lit face looking directly at the camera, with a look of determination and clarity.

Appeal to Logos

The logic and evidence here are implied, rather than directly stated. Kaepernick took a stand for justice. Nike is taking a stand for Kaepernick. By supporting Nike, you too can support justice. There is a subtle logic here that Nike is asking its audience to follow.

Language and Style

The stylistic elements of the ad come through both in the language and syntactical choices at work throughout, as well as the visual choices. Words such as "believe" and "sacrificing" carry positive associations. In addition, the short, declarative sentences are intended to speak directly and clearly to the audience, which matches the declaration of Nike's slogan, "Just Do It." Also, the words "something" and "everything" not only rhyme, but they show connection and growth from one to the other. The directness of the language is mirrored by the starkness of the visuals, in particular, the choice of black and white, which generally creates a realistic and serious tone. Additionally, while the audience likely knows who Kaepernick is, the ad does not show him in his football uniform, emphasizing how his actions aren't that far from action we could take in the real world.

Interpretation

While overall, the makers of this ad want the audience to buy Nike products, their real goal is probably to create positive associations between the selfless, social justice actions that Kaepernick took and the company itself. Nike is just like Kaepernick in that it believes in something more than just selling shoes and is willing to sacrifice some short-term sales from those who do not agree with Kaepernick politically. The ad is suggesting that we, Kaepernick, and Nike are all together in this fight for a better world, so we should all "Just do it."

culminating activity

Following is a newspaper article by Lenore Skenazy that was originally published in 2008 in the *New York Sun* and was subsequently reprinted in newspapers throughout the United States. A syndicated columnist and National Public Radio commentator, Skenazy received so much feedback on her article, both positive and negative, that she expanded her ideas into a book titled *Free-Range Kids: Giving Our Children the Freedom We Had without Going Nuts with Worry* (2010).

After reading and annotating the piece, write a response to one of the following prompts:

1. Analyze the rhetorical appeals and strategies Skenazy employs to achieve her purpose in this article. Overall, is her argument persuasive? Why or why not?
2. Do you believe a nine-year-old in your community should be allowed to travel (on a subway, bus, bicycle) without adult supervision? Why or why not? Write a brief editorial for your local newspaper explaining your position. As you write, be sure to consider the rhetorical situation and rhetorical strategies you have learned throughout this chapter.

Why I Let My 9-Year-Old Ride the Subway Alone

Lenore Skenazy

I left my 9-year-old at Bloomingdale's (the original one) a couple weeks ago. Last seen, he was in first floor handbags as I sashayed out the door.

Bye-bye! Have fun!

And he did. He came home on the subway and bus by himself.

Was I worried? Yes, a tinge. But it didn't strike me as that daring, either. Isn't New York as safe now as it was in 1963? It's not like we're living in downtown Baghdad.

5 Anyway, for weeks my boy had been begging for me to please leave him somewhere, anywhere, and let him try to figure out how to get home on his own. So on that sunny Sunday I gave him a subway map, a MetroCard, a $20 bill, and several quarters, just in case he had to make a call.

No, I did not give him a cell phone. Didn't want to lose it. And no, I didn't trail him, like a mommy private eye. I trusted him to figure out that he should take the Lexington Avenue subway down, and the 34th Street crosstown bus home. If he couldn't do that, I trusted him to ask a stranger. And then I even trusted that stranger not to think, "Gee, I was about to catch my train home, but now I think I'll abduct this adorable child instead."

Long story short: My son got home, ecstatic with independence.

Long story longer, and analyzed, to boot: Half the people I've told this episode to now want to turn me in for child abuse. As if keeping kids under lock and key and helmet and cell phone and nanny and surveillance is the right way to rear kids. It's not. It's debilitating — for us and for them.

And yet —

"How would you have felt if he didn't come home?" a New Jersey mom of four, Vicki Garfinkle, asked.

Guess what, Ms. Garfinkle: I'd have been devastated. But would that just prove that no mom should ever let her child ride the subway alone?

No. It would just be one more awful but extremely rare example of random violence, the kind that hyper parents cite as proof that every day in every way our children are more and more vulnerable.

"Carlie Brucia — I don't know if you're familiar with that case or not, but she was in Florida and she did a cut-through about a mile from her house . . . and midday, at 11 in the morning, she was abducted by a guy who violated her several times, killed her, and left her behind a church."

That's the story that the head of safetynet4kids.com, Katharine Francis, immediately told me when I asked her what she thought of my son getting around on his own. She runs a company that makes wallet-sized copies of a child's photo and fingerprints, just in case.

Well of course I know the story of Carlie Brucia. That's the problem. We all know that story — and the one about the Mormon girl in Utah and the one about the little girl in Spain — and because we do, we all run those tapes in our heads when we think of leaving our kids on their own. We even run a tape of how we'd look on Larry King.

"I do not want to be the one on TV explaining my daughter's disappearance," a father, Garth Chouteau, said when we were talking about the subway issue.

These days, when a kid dies, the world — i.e., cable TV — blames the parents. It's simple as that. And yet, Trevor Butterworth, a spokesman for the research center STATS.org, said, "The statistics show that this is an incredibly rare event, and you can't protect people from very rare events. It would be like trying to create a shield against being struck by lightning."

Justice Department data actually show the number of children abducted by strangers has been going down over the years. So why not let your kids get home from school by themselves?

"Parents are in the grip of anxiety and when you're anxious, you're totally warped," the author of *A Nation of Wimps*, Hara Estroff Marano, said. We become so bent out of shape over something as simple as letting your children out of sight on the playground that it starts seeming on par with letting them play on the railroad tracks at night. In the rain. In dark non-reflective coats.

The problem with this everything-is-dangerous outlook is that over-protectiveness is a danger in and of itself. A child who thinks he can't do anything on his own eventually can't.

Meantime, my son wants his next trip to be from Queens. In my day, I doubt that would have struck anyone as particularly brave. Now it seems like hitchhiking through Yemen.

Here's your MetroCard, kid. Go. ■

Imageplotter Travel/Alamy

Understanding Inquiry and Evidence-Based Arguments

One of the myths about writing is that it's all about loneliness and isolation: the writer toils alone, usually after midnight, rarely talking to anyone — or at least not talking about what she's writing. While it's true that when we actually sit down to write, we need some time to ourselves to focus and draft our ideas, the thinking process that prepares us to write is often collaborative. We start with an idea that we bounce off of someone; we read what somebody else has to say about an issue; we engage in online comments; or maybe we just talk face-to-face with one or two people. We have a *conversation*.

In this chapter, we focus on how to enter an academic conversation by writing an evidence-based argument, one that includes sources of information, data, and viewpoints. We think of an evidence-based argument as a conversation because, like any face-to-face conversation, it involves listening, speaking, consulting outside sources to learn more about a subject, and discussing those sources. Instead of reacting right away, writers listen to what others are writing or saying. You may have heard someone comment: "He says whatever pops into his head." It's not meant as a compliment! It's a reminder that our first opinions are not always our wisest opinions.

Another key part of writing an evidence-based argument is reflection. As you encounter new information, take a step back and think about how it changes your thinking on the issue. How do we find value in a range of viewpoints, even those that we initially might want to dismiss? You might think about reflection as having a conversation with yourself.

It is also important to take stock of the rhetorical context that you learned about in Chapter 3 as you explore an issue. Are you reading a series of comments posted on social media; reading an article in a well-regarded print publication (such as the *Atlantic* magazine or the *New York Times*); researching professional journals in a specific discipline, such as biology or history; watching a TED Talk given by an expert on a particular subject; or listening to a political speech? Once you have a sense of the context of a conversation and you've considered what's being said, you're ready to join in with an informed opinion.

activity

Entering the Conversation

The following is a brief excerpt from *Reality Is Broken: Why Games Make Us Better and How They Can Change the World*, a book by Jane McGonigal. Read through the excerpt, and think about how she uses an outside source to support her position.

from Reality Is Broken

Jane McGonigal

Jane McGonigal is a game designer and author who studies how gaming can solve serious problems in real life. In this section from her book, McGonigal discusses how *World of Warcraft* (*WoW*) keeps its players motivated. She draws on the research of psychologist Sonja Lyubomirsky to make her point.

When you're on a *WoW* quest, there's never any doubt about what you're supposed to do or where or how. It's not a game that emphasizes puzzle solving or trial-and-error investigation. You simply have to get the job done, and then you will collect your reward.

Why do we crave this kind of guaranteed productivity? In *The How of Happiness,* Sonja Lyubomirsky writes that the fastest way to improve someone's everyday quality of life is to "bestow on the person a specific goal, something to do and to look forward to." When a clear goal is attached to a specific task, she explains, it gives us an energizing push, a sense of purpose. That's why receiving more quests every time we complete one in *World of Warcraft* is more of a reward than the experience points and the gold we've earned. Each quest is another clear goal with actionable steps. ■

Talking It Through

With a partner, discuss how Jane McGonigal uses the research of psychologist Sonja Lyubomirsky to support her position on video games. Describe what the inclusion of Lyubomirsky's research adds to McGonigal's writing.

The Process of Inquiry

In general, joining a conversation with an informed opinion involves conducting some research. The novelist Zora Neale Hurston, also trained as an anthropologist, described research as a "formalized curiosity. It is poking and prying with a purpose." In other words, Hurston asserts that the process of inquiry, which is what research is all about, starts with being curious about something, not just randomly but with a purpose. If we return to the McGonigal example, we might imagine that her curiosity led her to inquire into what motivates people to stick with a task — and enjoy it. Seeking more information led her to conduct some research about why people set goals and either do or do not achieve their purposes. This research then led her to Lyubomirsky's work, which she included in her own thinking about the topic of video games. Essentially, McGonigal engaged in what is called the inquiry process.

The inquiry process has five basic "academic moves" that we will model in this chapter. You do not necessarily have to complete these steps in a strict order. Instead, move freely among them throughout your inquiry process, as you learn more about your topic and think about additional questions. True inquiry is not straightforward: not everything you find through your research will immediately be useful. However, most of what you find will at least lead you to another line of inquiry that might be. Here is a summary of the five basic moves of inquiry that we will practice throughout this chapter:

- **Identify and Focus:** At this stage, you think about your topic, ask questions about it, and form an initial opinion, which you can revisit throughout the inquiry process.
- **Investigate and Analyze:** This move occurs when you locate and critically examine information to develop a more informed opinion about the topic.
- **Draw Connections:** The more you read and learn about your topic, the more important it will be to see how the information you gather relates to other information you have found. This move occurs when you draw connections among the ideas and opinions that other people have about your topic.

What point does this cartoon make about the challenges of developing informed opinions about a topic?

- **Integrate and Present:** One of the goals of inquiry is to share your findings and your informed opinion with others. In this move, you bring all the pieces of your inquiry together and present your argument and your evidence. The process of integrating information and ideas — both your own and those you find in other sources — is called *synthesis*.
- **Reflect and Revisit:** Throughout your inquiry process, you have the opportunity to revisit your original opinion for the purpose of revising, adding to, and questioning it. This move occurs when you weigh new evidence and rethink your opinion or position as you learn more about it, always challenging yourself to keep an open mind about new ideas and perspectives.

To help you imagine what an inquiry process might look like from start to finish, we will walk through a sample inquiry, including an analysis of sources and integration of ideas into an evidence-based argument. An inquiry process involves immersing yourself in your subject or a question by reading a variety of sources, exploring viewpoints, and analyzing data. Not every source you find or link you follow will pay off as something you can use in your argument. However, the more you read and research, the better informed you'll be. To practice these steps, we will explore an issue that you are likely to have at least some experience with or knowledge about — the role of sports in high school.

Identify and Focus

The initial phase of forming an opinion and reflecting on that opinion will look a lot like how you learned to approach a text in Chapter 1: Make connections and ask questions. Start by laying out what you think and what you know. Then, figure out what you want to learn more about. Remember that forming an initial opinion is only a first step. You should not feel you need to defend this opinion at all costs. This is not a competition. The goal is to make your opinion more nuanced by recognizing the complexity of the situation. Complex issues are not black and white; your thinking shouldn't be either.

Forming an Initial Opinion

1. **Think about the Issue:** The primary mission of high school is to educate students, and yet a lot of funding, time, effort, and social importance tend to be placed on sports. What are the benefits and drawbacks of sports in high school?
2. **Make Connections:** Jot down some notes about your personal experiences with sports in high school. Do you or friends play sports? Why do you choose to play or not play? How pervasive are sports in your school? How much of your thinking is based on how you *feel* about the issue rather than what you *think* or *know* about it?

3. **Ask Questions:** What are you curious about regarding this issue? What information do you think you need to understand this issue? List at least four questions that you would like to find answers to. For example, *How much money does my school spend to support sports?*
4. **Form an Initial Opinion:** At this point, what do you think is the most appropriate role of sports in high school? Should sports be supported, expanded, eliminated, or changed? Why? When responding, you can focus on your own school or on high schools in general.

Talking It Through

With a partner, share your initial opinion on the benefits and drawbacks of sports in high school. How did your connections differ from your partner's? How did those differences influence your opinions? What questions are both of you curious or concerned about? On what points do you and your partner agree?

Investigate and Analyze

Now that you have formed an initial opinion on the issue of high school sports, it's time to find out more and identify possible answers to your questions. Information is everywhere, so the challenge of research is to identify *good* information rather than merely to locate information on the topic. In the sections that follow, we've identified some texts for you to work with. However, it's still up to you to analyze them by applying the critical reading you practiced in Chapter 3 to determine if the sources are reliable and to figure out how they relate to your opinion.

Approaching a Source

The best advice to any researcher, whether it's a fifth grader just starting out or an experienced scholar, is to keep an open mind and a skeptical eye at the same time. That might sound contradictory, but it's not really. You don't want to dismiss a source right away, particularly if you are tempted to do so because it expresses a viewpoint that differs from your own. Ask yourself what makes the position compelling to the person who wrote or spoke it. Whether you comment on the source with annotations or by writing a response of some sort is up to you; just make sure that you're fully engaged with the source.

Approaching a Source

The following excerpt is from an essay by Mark Edmundson, an English professor at the University of Virginia, about his experience playing high school football. The essay was published in the *Chronicle of Higher Education*. As you read, practice being both open minded and skeptical. Then, answer the questions that follow the source.

Do Sports Build Character? Or Damage It?

Mark Edmundson

I liked the transforming aspect of the game: I came to the field one thing — a diffident guy with a slack body — and worked like a dog and so became something else — a guy with some physical prowess and more faith in himself. Mostly, I liked the whole process because it was so damned hard. I didn't think I could make it, and no one I knew did either. My parents were ready to console me if I came home bruised and dead weary and said that I was quitting. In time, one of the coaches confessed to me that he was sure I'd be gone in a few days . . . But football was something I could do, though I was never going to be anything like a star. It was hard, it took some strength of will, and — clumsily, passionately — I could do it. . . .

No one really noticed my improvements, least of all the coaches. But I did, and I took great pleasure in them. Football became a prototype for every endeavor in later life that required lonely painstaking work and that was genuinely demanding. Through the game, I learned to care more about how I myself judged this or that performance of mine and less about how the world did. ■

Questions

1. What's your open-minded response? What observations can you make about what makes this subject important to the writer?
2. What's your skeptical response? Does anything seem unclear or somehow confusing? What questions might you raise about the piece?
3. How has this source influenced your initial position regarding the value of sports in high school? Does it validate it? Challenge it? To what extent does it add an idea you hadn't thought of?

Examining Sources

Approaching a source with an open mind and a skeptical eye is an informal way to begin your research. It can help you identify which sources might be useful to your argument. Before using a source in your writing, make a more formal examination, assessing its relevance, currency, authority, accuracy, and bias. You should apply these criteria to everything you read, not just in school but all the time. Learning to internalize a process like this into your life is called building a habit of mind. These steps in particular are key to thinking critically about the information you encounter every day.

Relevance: If your source is not clearly related to your topic, then it's not likely to advance your argument. Keep in mind, however, that sometimes a source does not seem directly related but it might have a more philosophical connection. If you're writing about an environmental issue such as fracking, for instance, the nineteenth century American naturalist Henry David Thoreau might not seem to have a direct connection to the issue. However, his attitude toward the relationship between the human and natural worlds might provide a relevant source for your more contemporary discussion. Similarly, the preceding excerpt by Mark Edmundson seems relevant to the topic of high school sports because it discusses the value of the hard work he put into football.

Currency: The issue here is whether your source is current enough to be useful to your argument. If your argument is about the financial burden of a college education for your generation, for example, you'll need up-to-date sources regarding tuition costs and student loans. If a source you're considering discusses college costs from twenty years ago, you'll need to find something more current. However, if you want to draw comparisons that show, for example, the skyrocketing costs of college over the last two decades, the older statistics would be useful. Edmundson recounts his football playing experience that took place in the 1970s. If you were considering using Edmundson as a source, you'd have to consider whether his experiences from fifty years ago are still applicable to today's high school sports.

Authority: The age of social media has changed our notion of authority in some ways. More people than ever before have the ability to broadly share information and ideas — and opinions. It has also opened the floodgates for unqualified people to pose as experts — and even to claim to know more than experts. When you are researching sources, pay attention to credentials — relevant education and experience — that qualify a person to speak on an issue. If you're writing about conflict in the Middle East, for example, a journalist writing on the subject for a respected news outlet is a more reliable

RGJ-Richard Jolley/Cartoon Stock

What does this editorial cartoon suggest about the ways that we can receive news these days? When you want to be informed about your community, your country, and the world, where do you turn for news? Do you consider your preferred source(s) to be reliable and balanced? How do you know?

source than any of the anonymous commenters reacting to the journalist's article online. Is Edmundson an "authority" on high school sports? He was a football player and he is also identified as an English professor, so he has some experience on both sides of the issue that qualifies him to talk about the balance between sports and academics.

Accuracy: In this era of so called "fake news" and manipulated information, accuracy has taken on a whole new meaning and can be difficult to gauge. If you're not an expert, how would you know if the source you've found is accurate? Analyze it carefully, approach it critically, ask questions about the author, look for fully documented citations, and be on the lookout for excessive misspellings and typos that might demonstrate that it was published without being checked for errors or vetted for accuracy. If you have any doubts about a source's accuracy, especially one you locate online, consider double checking the information with at least one other source. You can never be too careful. How do we know if what Edmundson writes is accurate? It's mostly a memoir, so we can't really double check his own recollections. However, it was published in the *Chronicle of Higher Education*, a respected journal with a very detailed and well-maintained website. As a result, we might be willing to conclude that its editors did a thorough job checking Edmundson's accuracy.

Bias: As we mentioned in Chapter 3, a significant concern for all sources is bias — that is, how a source's take on an issue might be skewed by the author's viewpoint, context, or affiliations. When trying to identify bias, consider the author's tone. Is it professional? Does the author attempt to be objective? If the answer to either of those questions is "no," proceed with extreme caution. Also keep any outside influences in mind. If you're reading a research study, try to determine who paid for it. If a university has sponsored the research, that's a good sign. If a corporation has backed the study, you might consider what vested interest the corporation could have in the topic. Or perhaps the source of the study is an organization with political affiliations? Is Edmundson biased? It's clear that his football experiences were good ones, but do his fond memories influence his judgment and perspective about the value of high school sports? The answer is probably "yes," but just about every source you encounter will have some level of bias; your work is to determine the extent to which a personal preference makes the source unbalanced or if the source is deliberately manipulative.

KEY QUESTIONS

As you examine a source, consider the following key questions:

- Is this source relevant to my topic?
- Does this source provide current information?
- Is this source authoritative?
- Is this source accurate?
- Is this source biased?

Examining a Source

Read through the following text and examine it with the elements described earlier: relevance, currency, authority, accuracy, and bias. Be sure to look carefully at the context of the piece before reading, and feel free to conduct additional brief research to help you to examine this source.

from Address of President Roosevelt in the Chapel of the University of Minnesota, April 4, 1903

Theodore Roosevelt

In 1903, football as an organized sport was still relatively new and played only at the college level, but it had been coming under attack for its brutality and the on-field deaths of players. President Roosevelt was a fan of the game. Two years after this speech, he arranged for the presidents of several colleges to adopt new safety rules, which has led to Roosevelt being called the man who "saved football."

There is a twofold side to the work done in any institution of this kind. In the first place the institution is to turn out scholars and men proficient in the different technical branches for which it trains them. It should be the aim of every university which seeks to develop the liberal side of education to turn out men and women who will add to the sum of productive achievement in scholarship; who will not merely be content to work in the fields that have already been harrowed a thousand times by other workers, but who will strike out for themselves and try to do new work that counts; so in each technical school if the institution is worthy of standing in the front rank, it will turn out those who in that particular specialty stand at the head. But in addition to this merely technical work, the turning out of the scholar, the professional man, the man or woman trained on some special line, each university worthy the name must endeavor to turn out men and women in the fullest sense of the word, good citizens, men and women who will add by what they do to the sum of noble work in the whole community.

It is a good thing that so much attention should be given to physical development. I believe in rough games and in rough, manly sports. I do not feel any particular sympathy for the person who gets battered about a good deal so long as it is not fatal, and if he feels any sympathy for himself I do not like him. I believe thoroughly in the sound and vigorous body. I believe still more in the vigorous mind. And I believe most of all in what counts for more than body, for more than mind, and that is character. That is the sum of the forces that make the man or the woman worth knowing, worth revering, worth holding to. Play hard while you play, but do not mistake it for work. If a young fellow is twenty it is a good thing that he should be a crack half-back; but when he is forty I am sorry, if he has never been anything else except once at twenty a good half-back. Keep the sense of proportion. Play hard; it will do you good in your work. But work hard and remember that this is the main thing.

Finally, in closing, I think it is a safe thing to take a motto that I heard from the lips of an old football player once: "Don't flinch, don't foul, and hit the line hard." ■

Talking It Through

Meet with a partner to share your examination of the source and try to come to consensus on the following question: Would you use this source in an argument about the benefits and drawbacks of high school sports? Why or why not?

Draw Connections

So far, you have formed an initial opinion about the role of sports in high school and have begun investigating the issue and critically examining sources. In this section, you will read and draw connections among six sources to explore the benefits and drawbacks of sports in high school and to make sure that your opinion is an informed one. Following each source is an activity to help you practice working with sources, and to determine which sources might be useful as solid evidence to support a position. These activities include comparing sources, evaluating a source for credibility, connecting a source to your own view, and addressing a counterargument (see Chapter 3, pp. 100–101) — all analytical moves. As you read, use the following chart to keep track of what distinct point each piece makes, how it relates to your initial opinion, and how these sources connect to each other:

Author/ title	Position on high school sports	Quotation(s) that best illustrate the author's ideas about sports	Your reaction and/or connection to other authors

SOURCES

1. **Amanda Ripley** ■ School Should Be About Learning, Not Sports
2. **Programme for International Student Assessment (PISA)** ■ How U.S. Students Compare with Their International Peers
3. **Mark Edmundson** ■ *from* Do Sports Build Character? Or Damage It?
4. **Frederick M. Hess and Amy Cummings** ■ *from* The Misguided Sliming of High School Sports
5. **Erin Shortell** ■ *from* Sports vs. Education: A False Choice
6. **Edward Koren** ■ Two Scoreboards

1 School Should Be About Learning, Not Sports

Amanda Ripley

Following is an article that Amanda Ripley wrote for the feature "Room for Debate" in the *New York Times* (2015). Ripley is an author and senior fellow at the New American Foundation, a nonpartisan research organization based in Washington, D.C.

In the world's smartest countries, school is about learning. Full stop. There is no confusion about the academic hurdles kids must clear to have full and interesting adult lives. Kids play sports, of course, but outside of school, through recreation centers, club teams or pick-up games on dirt fields with no adults in sight.

When these same kids come to the U.S. to live or study abroad, they are surprised by the Olympic villages they encounter in our high schools. Here, school is about learning, but it's also about training to compete in games that the majority of kids will never get paid to play. It's about pep rallies, booster clubs, trophy cases and cheerleaders decorating football players' lockers after they fill them with brownies.

Those messages shape kids' priorities. When I surveyed former exchange students about their impressions of America, 9 out of 10 said that teenagers here cared more about sports than their peers back home. "Doing well at sports was in the U.S. just as important as having good grades," observed one German student.

This mash-up makes school more fun, without a doubt. "The biggest difference was definitely the school spirit," one student from Finland noted. "It was amazing to see how school wasn't just about the grades. In my home country, school is just for learning."

5 The problem is the dishonesty. By mixing sports and academics, we tempt kids into believing that it's O.K. if they don't like math or writing — that there is another path to glory. Less obvious is that this path ends abruptly, whereupon they get to spend 50 years in an economy that lavishly rewards those with higher-order skills and ruthlessly punishes those without.

Kids notice when they have a sub in math class because the football coach (I mean teacher) has an away game. It is not lost on them that their local newspapers devote an entire section to high school sports and say nothing about the trials and travails of the AP English class. This hypocrisy eats away at the focus and integrity of our schools.

Imagine if medical schools dedicated hours of every day (and a chunk of their budgets and staff) to the culinary arts — to perfecting tiered wedding cakes and artisan breads. We could argue that this approach keeps med students from dropping out, but we would sound insane.

Competitive sports is not about exercise. If it were, we'd have the fittest kids in the world. It's about a fantasy with a short shelf life. If we want to build school spirit and teach kids about grit, hold a pep rally for the debate team. Those kids are training to rule the real world. ■

Understanding the Source

Analyze the overall argument Ripley makes by completing these sentence templates. These templates take you step-by-step through the process of thoroughly understanding the source.

1. **Summarize.** In "School Should Be About Learning, Not Sports," Amanda Ripley makes the central claim that __________.
2. **Identify Evidence.** One way she supports her position is __________. Another point she raises as evidence for her argument is __________.
3. **Identify Counterarguments.** One counterargument she addresses is that __________.

2 How U.S. Students Compare with Their International Peers

Programme for International Student Assessment (PISA)

The following bar graph compares rankings of high school students from the United States to their international counterparts in science, math, and reading. The Programme for International Student Assessment (PISA) is a worldwide study by the Organization for Economic Cooperation and Development in member and non-member nations intended to evaluate educational systems by measuring 15-year-old school pupils' academic performance.

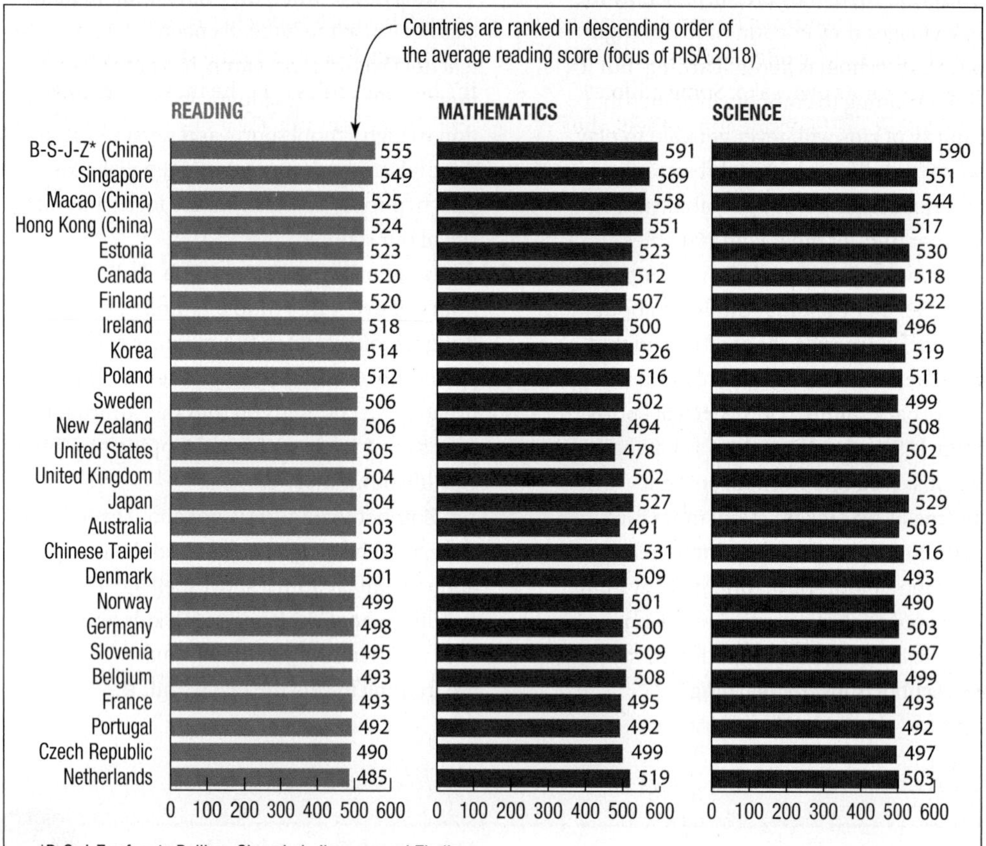

Countries are ranked in descending order of the average reading score (focus of PISA 2018)

	READING	MATHEMATICS	SCIENCE
B-S-J-Z* (China)	555	591	590
Singapore	549	569	551
Macao (China)	525	558	544
Hong Kong (China)	524	551	517
Estonia	523	523	530
Canada	520	512	518
Finland	520	507	522
Ireland	518	500	496
Korea	514	526	519
Poland	512	516	511
Sweden	506	502	499
New Zealand	506	494	508
United States	505	478	502
United Kingdom	504	502	505
Japan	504	527	529
Australia	503	491	503
Chinese Taipei	503	531	516
Denmark	501	509	493
Norway	499	501	490
Germany	498	500	503
Slovenia	495	509	507
Belgium	493	508	499
France	493	495	493
Portugal	492	492	492
Czech Republic	490	499	497
Netherlands	485	519	503

Axis (each panel): 0 100 200 300 400 500 600

*B-S-J-Z refers to Beijing, Shanghai, Jiangsu, and Zhejiang

Interpreting Quantitative Data by Asking Questions

After studying the graph, work in pairs or small groups to arrive at a series of questions that you believe would help you interpret it. For instance, you might ask, *What are teacher qualifications or salaries in the top-ranking countries?* Generate a few questions about information that you would like to know before drawing firm conclusions about what appears to be the lagging educational achievement of the United States. After generating your questions, what conclusions can you draw from this chart? Why might Ripley use this chart in her argument, or choose not to use it?

3 *from* Do Sports Build Character? Or Damage It?

Mark Edmundson

The following excerpt is from a later part of the essay by Mark Edmundson that you read earlier (p. 128). You may recall that Edmundson is an English professor at the University of Virginia. The essay about his experience playing high school football was published in the *Chronicle of Higher Education*.

Athletes, as everyone who went to an American high school will tell you, can be courtly, dignified individuals. But they're often bullies; they often seek violence for its own sake. Some athletes take crude pleasure in dominating others; they like to humiliate their foes, off the field as well as on it.

All too often, the players who go all out on the field but can't readily turn it off elsewhere are the best players. They're the most headlong, the most fearless, the most dedicated. And when they encounter a modulated, more controlled antagonist in a game, often they, the more brutal players, win.

Lawrence Taylor was one of the best players ever to appear in the National Football League. With his speed and ferocity, and his ability to run down the opposing quarterback, he made football into a different, more violent game. But he was often as much in a fury off the field as on. By his own account, Taylor led the life of a beast — drunk, brawling, high on coke, speeding in his car: He was a peril to anyone who came near him.

His coach, Bill Parcells, allowed him to cultivate this off-field character, knowing that it contributed to his prowess when he played. If the best players are the ones who are the least controlled, the ones in whom passion for preeminence trumps reason, then it is not entirely clear that one can say what American coaches and boosters love to say, that sports builds character. If having a good character means having a coherent, flexible internal structure, where the best part rules over the most dangerous, then sports may not always be conducive to true virtue.

5 My own experience in high school confirms this view. Playing football made me more confident; it gave me powers of resolve that I'd draw on later in life, and I'm grateful for those things. But it also made me more brutal. I came to crave the physical stimulation of the game — I came to like hitting and even being hit. When the season ended, I found myself recreating the feeling of football in a string of fistfights and all-in brawls.

I didn't become a thug — far from it. But I did let the part of me that sought power and standing — over others — go way too far. Having been down that road, the chances of my taking it again are greater, I suspect, than they are for others. Once the path has been cut, it stays open. I once shocked a colleague, and myself, by admitting that if someone ran a light and smashed up my car (which I loved more than I should), the chances of my popping him in the jaw were probably much greater than the chances of the average professional guy doing so. Once the punch in the mouth is part of your repertoire — once you've done it a few times as an adult — it never really goes away. ■

Comparing Sources

Use the sentence templates below to analyze how Edmundson's position supports or challenges Ripley's ideas.

1. **Understand.** Mark Edmundson, a professor at the University of Virginia, cites his own experience to argue that ___________.
2. **Connection.** His experience relates to Ripley's argument in that ___________.
3. **Interpret.** I think that Edmundson's ideas support/undermine Ripley's argument in that___________.

4 *from* The Misguided Sliming of High School Sports

Frederick M. Hess and Amy Cummings

Frederick M. Hess is the director of education policy studies at the American Enterprise Institute, where Amy Cummings is a research associate. This article was published in 2019 in the *National Review*, self-described as a leading conservative magazine and website that covers news, politics, current events, and culture with detailed analysis and commentary.

In recent years, high school sports have had a tough go of it. Football's concussion problem has spawned headlines such as CBS's "Young Athletes Abandon Football as Concussions Rock High School Teams." But it's not just football. The indefensible actions of some pro athletes, especially with regards to domestic violence and sexual misconduct, have colored views of sporting culture more generally. Meanwhile, for many progressives, sports are seen as celebrating problematic notions of competition, toxic masculinity, and gender segregation.

The manifold benefits of school sports can too readily get lost, especially the crucial role that athletics can play in supporting academic success and building character.

Despite assertions that sports detract from academics, there's evidence that they can just as readily complement the scholastic mission of schools. A widely cited 2003 study by Oxford University's Herbert Marsh and the University of Sydney's Sabina Kleitman in the *Journal of Sport & Exercise Psychology* reported, using nationally representative longitudinal data, that participating in high school sports had a positive effect on academics in high school and college. Students who played high school sports got better grades, selected more challenging courses, had higher educational and occupational aspirations, were more likely to enroll in college, and had higher levels of educational attainment. What's more, these results held up across socioeconomic status, gender, race, and ability.

A decade ago, in the *Economics of Education Review*, Mathematica's Stephen Lipscomb used a fixed-effects strategy to test whether participating in high school sports affected academic performance. He found that sports participation associated with a 2 percent increase in math and science test scores and a 5 percent increase in bachelor's-degree attainment expectations. Other scholarship has reported that participating in high school sports significantly reduces a student's likelihood of dropping out of high school and, for young women, that it is associated with higher odds of college completion.

5 None of this is remotely new. Three decades ago, Alyce Holland and Thomas Andre published an influential review of the research on high school extracurricular participation in the *American Educational Research Journal,* reporting that participation in sports was associated with higher self-esteem and feelings of control over one's life. In a finding that won't surprise many who've participated in sports, they found that athletics participation was also correlated with improved race relations and heightened young adult involvement in political and social activities. Educators and reformers who are seeking ways to promote values such as self-control, responsibility, and good citizenship should keep in mind that schools already house programs with a track record of doing just that. . . .

The point is not to make outsize claims about the restorative powers of school sports. These studies all have methodological limitations, and we should not treat the results as gospel. Meanwhile, there *are* real physical risks in some sports, some of the benefits are due to self-selection, some poorly run sports programs do breed destructive behavior, and there are times and places when school sports can clash with education's academic mission.

None of these cautions, however, should excuse the pooh-poohing of high school sports by zealots, the dismissal of sports by reformers, and the distortions by media outlets seeking salacious tales of sports' ill effects. School reformers are now reconsidering their all-consuming fascination with reading and math scores and expressing new interest in social and emotional learning, citizenship, and character. That makes this a propitious time to remember all that sports can offer. After all, the skills that sports aspire to teach — perseverance, self-discipline, leadership, and being good at teamwork — are the very ones that help produce successful graduates and responsible citizens. ■

Acknowledging the Counterargument

activity

Use the Hess and Cummings text to consider counterarguments, which you read about in Chapter 3 (pp. 100–101). These sentence templates can help you point out specific ways in which Hess and Cummings address counterarguments to strengthen their own position.

1. **Understand:** In their discussion of high school sports, Hess and Cummings acknowledge viewpoints different from their own. For example, ___________.
2. **Concession:** They concede that ___________.
3. **Refutation:** However, they argue that ___________.

5 *from* Sports v. Education: A False Choice

Erin Shortell

This essay appeared on the website of the *Harvard Political Review* in a section called "Equality: So What?" in 2013. Erin Shortell was a student staff writer for the website.

While sports participation has risen, American educational rankings in comparison to other countries across the world have troublingly continued to plummet. In the 2012 Summer Olympics, the U.S. walked away with more gold medals than any other country. Yet Americans accept not first but 31st in global math education, 23rd in global science education, and 14th in reading when compared to these global competitors.

It is more fun to sit back and relax with a cold beer on Super Bowl Sunday if one is not worried about the fact that only 77% of American students graduate from high school and that six other countries have higher graduation rates. It is easier to cheer for a favorite basketball team than to acknowledge that 24 countries currently outpace the U.S. rate of educational improvement. As long as this attitude persists, America's academic standings relative to other nations show little promise of rebounding. American children are increasingly falling behind as their international competitors in today's globalized world pull ahead.

Contrary to cultural undercurrents, sports participation and academic success are not mutually exclusive. The education attainable through sports can be incredibly valuable in other arenas of life. As Neal McCluskey, associate director of the Cato Institute's Center for Educational Freedom, told the HPR: "There is some good evidence to suggest that we culturally focus maybe too much on sports, [rather] than on academics. But, that said, we don't actually know that the values you learn [in sports] don't ultimately help with being successful in life." In an interview with the HPR, New York middle school teacher and softball and bowling coach Marni Torgersen listed the skills learned on sports teams that, in her experience, translate into success in the classroom: leadership, resilience, self-discipline, patience, persistence, time management, and self-esteem.

Sports participation is an incredible opportunity, as long as it is balanced with concern for academics. If Americans viewed sports not as an alternative but as a complement to education, then the two enterprises might excel simultaneously. Former Harvard Graduate School of Education professor Eleanor Duckworth believes that athletic participation can improve academic performance: "People can be very fascinated by academics and intrigued by athletics and good at both. They enhance each other."

5 It is not always easy to strike that balance. Giovanni Galvano went on to play soccer in Italy following his graduation last June from a New York high school. Discussing the challenges of balancing school and soccer, the 18-year-old Galvano says, "When work gets heavy with soccer it's easy to have work in class become insufficient and vice versa, but that could be avoided. It then becomes a time management challenge." Although Galvano was extremely passionate about soccer and knew that he would pursue athletics after high school, he challenged himself academically by taking college-level courses. ■

Examining Sources

Analyze this source according to the criteria introduced earlier in this chapter (p. 128) by considering its relevance, currency, authority, accuracy, and bias.

Talking It Through

Share your analysis with a partner and discuss why you would or would not use Shortell as a source in your own argument.

6 Two Scoreboards

Edward Koren

Edward Koren, writer and illustrator of children's books, has published over 1000 cartoons in various venues. "Two Scoreboards," which was published in the *New Yorker* magazine in 2002, comments on the relationship between academics and sports in American high schools.

Edward Koren/The New Yorker Collection/The Cartoon Bank

Analyzing and Interpreting a Political Cartoon

Discuss the cartoon on the previous page as an argument. (See Chapter 3, pp. 110–114, for help with analyzing visual arguments.) Start by analyzing the rhetorical moves that Koren makes. Use that analysis as a basis of your interpretation of the cartoon as either a criticism of high school sports or as support for them. Use the following questions to guide your analysis and interpretation:

- What is the basic visual image that defines this cartoon? In what ways might it function metaphorically instead of literally?
- Does the cartoon suggest that there are only two sides to the debate surrounding the relationship between sports and academics? If the image hints at more nuanced views, how does it do so?
- The basketball court is familiar terrain for sports, but not academic testing. What does this setting suggest about Koren's attitude toward testing?
- What purpose does the American flag serve? . . . in his argument?
- Of the texts you have examined in this section, which author(s) might agree with Koren's argument? Why?

Considering Sources in Conversation

Once you have examined each source, assessing its relevance, currency, authority, accuracy, and bias, you can decide which sources would contribute meaningfully to your position and how they might relate to each other. Thinking about how sources connect or clash can deepen your understanding of the issue you are writing about and help you present a stronger position.

Remember to keep an open mind throughout the inquiry process. As you consider sources together and how they relate to your own ideas, you may find that you want to adjust your original position on the issue.

Reflecting on What You've Learned

Return to your initial opinion, which you drafted in response to the activity on page 126, on the subject of the drawbacks and benefits of high school sports. Freewrite for a few minutes on the issues that engaging with these sources have raised for you — issues that were not part of your original response. What new considerations have confirmed or challenged your position, or led you to modify it? Revise your claim to reflect your deeper understanding of the topic of high school sports. You will repeat this kind of "reflection and revision" move throughout your inquiry process.

SPEAKING & LISTENING FOCUS

Considering Sources in Conversation

One of the most important steps of writing an argument based on evidence is the process of understanding how the ideas in your sources connect with each other. A way of practicing this process is to take on the role of one of the authors you have read in this chapter while talking to a partner who has adopted the role of another author. Following are the steps you should take when using role play to understand how to put sources in conversation with one another:

1. Pick an Author. Assume the role of one of the authors by drawing the name out of a hat or being assigned one of them by your teacher. Don't worry if it's someone you disagree with; that might actually make the role play more interesting for you.

2. Find Examples. Look carefully once again at the text (article or image) created by the author whose role you're playing. To present his or her ideas, you'll want to draw specific examples from the text.

3. Role Play. Find a classmate playing the part of a different author. Engage the person in a discussion. To make sure you're having a meaningful conversation, ask each other questions like the following:

- What's your position on the topic?
- Why do you believe that?
- What's your best evidence for your position?
- Have you considered ___________?
- What are your qualifications for writing on this topic? Do you have any biases toward the topic?
- After a few minutes, move to another "author" and repeat the process.

Practice

Throughout this chapter, you have been reading texts and thinking about the following questions:

- To what extent are participation in high school sports and the pursuit of academic excellence incompatible activities?
- Should high schools severely cut back their sports programs? Why or why not?

Try out the role-playing steps described above with the authors of the texts you have read so far. Be sure to speak as "I" rather than saying, for instance, "Ripley would say" or "Hess believes."

Reflection

How did speaking as the author of one of the sources deepen your understanding of that source? How did the role playing, especially listening to others, deepen your understanding of the issues?

Researching Additional Sources

At this point, you've read a lot of different texts on the question of whether high school sports are a distraction from academics, a benefit to it, or something in between. There are likely areas that interest you that the sources haven't addressed yet. Or these sources may have raised topics that you feel warrant further investigation. These questions should lead you to do your own research. This move demonstrates how the inquiry process is recursive, in that it takes you back to investigating and analyzing.

As you look for additional sources, keep in mind that useful information and ideas are not limited to written texts. Consider a powerful photograph or a political cartoon, for example, as well as multimedia sources such as a TED Talk or a documentary film. You might also consider interviewing an expert — not necessarily someone who has published extensive scholarly studies but someone with first-hand experience, such as a coach or a student athlete (from high school or college). These are all potential sources that can contribute a meaningful viewpoint.

Locating and Examining Your Own Source

By whatever means you and your teacher think most appropriate, locate an additional source that might address your further questions and areas of interest regarding the relationship between sports and academics in high school. Then, examine your new potential source with the same critical eye you've applied to the texts provided in this chapter. The chart below can help you think about how this new source might contribute to your position. If, after examining your source, you feel that it is not appropriate for your argument, locate another that might work better and repeat these steps.

Source Information: (author, title, publication)	**Notes**
Relevance:	
Currency:	
Authority:	
Accuracy:	
Bias:	
Contribution to My Position/ Connection to Other Sources:	

Talking It Through

Share your analysis of your source with a partner (who will share a different source with you). Remember to listen actively (see p. 8 from Chapter 1) to each other. During your partner's presentation to you, keep in mind that your purpose is not to judge but to comment and discuss the value the new source might have for your partner's argument. If your source — or your partner's — seems like it will be useful, consider adding it to the chart you began on page 132.

Integrate and Present

Throughout this chapter, you have explored some of the inquiry moves with the main goal of learning more about your topic of high school sports. By now, you have an opinion that is more informed than the one you started with. It's time to put that new knowledge to work by connecting what you've been learning to a point you want to make about the topic. The ultimate goal of inquiry is not to just keep researching and examining sources. Rather, it is to use the sources to answer your questions from the beginning of the process and to present your findings to an audience in the form of a source-based argument on the topic. As you read in Chapter 3, the claim of an argument is the position that you want your audience to adopt, and the strongest claims are supported with evidence. The next step, therefore, is to connect your sources to the point you want to make about high school sports and to establish your ethos by demonstrating to your audience that you have carefully considered a wide range of perspectives.

activity

Connecting Claim and Evidence

Review the graphic organizer you developed as you read the sources in this chapter (p. 132). Think about how each source relates to the revised claim that you developed in response to the activity on page 140 and how you could use each source, whether to provide support or a counterargument you can refute. Identify at least three sources, perhaps including the one you located through your research, that you think most closely relate to the point you are trying to make about high school sports. You might not use all of the sources in your argument, but this exercise will help you decide which ones are more and less useful for developing it.

Source	Main point	How I might use the source in my argument

Now that you have your sources connected to your claim, the next step is to ensure that your own ideas remain central. You don't want outside sources to replace your argument; you want them to inform it. You might want to look again at the example of Jane McGonigal in her analysis of video games (p. 124). Notice how she cites ideas and directly quotes psychology researcher Sonja Lyubormirsky. McGonigal uses her source not to replace her own voice but to strengthen her argument with an authority. The next section will show you how to use commentary to keep the emphasis on your own writing and ideas.

Using Commentary

One important way to keep the focus on your own ideas is to make sure that you include commentary with every piece of evidence to connect it with your claim in some way. The following structure can help you:

- Make your point.
- Provide evidence (possibly a quotation).
- Provide commentary on how the evidence supports your point.

It's important to keep in mind that summary, though sometimes useful for giving your readers an overview of another writer's argument, is not a substitute for analysis. When you summarize, you restate the major ideas from a text in your own words without injecting any of your own ideas. For example, the following use of Hess and Cummings as evidence is ineffective because it only summarizes what they have to say, without letting readers know what role the source plays in the writer's argument:

> Researchers Hess and Cummings argue that high school sports have gotten unfair criticism because of the current obsession with standardized test scores, particularly in reading and math. They do not dispute the importance of academic achievement but rather point out that sports develop character traits that are valuable to students far beyond the high school classroom.

It's much more effective to specifically *connect* a source's argument to your own claim. For instance, the following revision of the previous paragraph includes commentary about the source to make it more effective:

> Although it is true that very few high school athletes make sports a career, just participating fosters habits that are valuable in college, career, and life in general. *[Point]* Hess and Cummings argue that the current "all-consuming fascination with reading and math scores" has caused many in education to undervalue skills and habits that serve us well no matter *[Evidence]*

what we do after high school: "perseverance, self-discipline, leadership, and being good at teamwork" are ones Hess and Cummings cite as examples. By pitting sports against academics, we make the mistake of an either-or choice when, in fact, sports and academics together can reinforce one another. After all, maybe additional perseverance and self-discipline will contribute to higher test scores.

Commentary

It's important to remember that this is not the *only* way to go about integrating sources, but it's an effective way to make sure that you include commentary as well as direct reference to your sources. In the examples that follow, we'll show you some variations on this structure.

Supporting Your Ideas

Develop a paragraph using a source you read in this chapter or a source you researched independently to support your position on the relationship between high school academics and sports. You can use the point, evidence, commentary structure if you like.

Using Visuals as Evidence

So far, we've been using quotations from print texts as evidence. But what if you want to reference a cartoon, or a documentary, or a billboard? How do you integrate the message from a visual into your writing? If you insert a visual into your text, the same rules about commentary apply. You must discuss the visual and make it clear to the reader how the visual connects to your argument. What is your interpretation of the visual? How does it convey meaning? How does that meaning relate to your own ideas and those of your other sources? (See pp. 110–114 in Chapter 3 for help with interpreting visuals.) If you discuss a visual that does not actually appear in the body of your writing, be sure to include a careful description, so that even readers who cannot see the image will be able to grasp how it supports your argument. The following example uses the political cartoon from p. 139 as evidence.

Context

Who can deny that sports are more fun than the usual academic classroom? Team spirit is contagious; competition is exciting. We're proud of our home team, and we support them whether we're cheering them on, fundraising with car washes, or wearing team colors on game days. In his cartoon,

Edward Koren lets the illustration with no caption or commentary speak for itself: the bleachers are filled with fans focused on the athletes on the game side of the court while the competing team of academics has an empty court. Maybe if academic activities could be conducted with more engagement, maybe even the team spirit of collaboration, students would become as engaged as they are with sports. That could go a long way towards evening the score.

Evidence — Commentary — Point

This paragraph demonstrates how well a visual image can serve as a source even though there are no actual quotations. There are clear and concrete references to the source, in this case a cartoon, and commentary linking it to the writer's point.

Integrating Counterarguments

Addressing a counterargument (pp. 100–101) is one way to strengthen your writing by avoiding a binary argument: either it's all this or all that. Counterarguments are very useful in the introduction, as you set up the issue. However, you can also use them throughout to add nuance to your argument and demonstrate to your audience that you have thoroughly considered the issue. Notice that the general pattern for introducing the counterargument is a bit different from the structure we have already discussed, mostly because we need both to concede and refute the counterargument. Here's one typical way of structuring a counterargument:

What some don't seem to understand is that the discipline needed to be successful on the field often provides the grit necessary to keep working in school, where success also takes a lot of work. Ripley is right to value the "higher order skills" that bring entrance to college and good jobs, but when she says that "school is about learning. Full stop," she ignores the other lessons that sports provide. Being a member of a team, losing with grace as well as winning with humility, and developing discipline as a habit of mind and body are all learned skills that have academic benefits.

Point — Evidence + concession — Evidence + refutation — Commentary

In this example, the writer positively acknowledges part of Ripley's argument (concession), and then takes issue with another of her points (refutation). Note also that the final sentence is a fairly lengthy commentary on what Ripley ignores in her limited definition of "learning." Another virtue of this paragraph that's worth noting is that it both opens and closes with the writer's own words — that is, a topic sentence related to the writer's thesis and a final commentary. That move emphasizes that the writer's own voice is in control with sources used for support and examples.

activity

Integrating a Counterargument

Return to the paragraph you developed in the activity on page 145 and add a few sentences in which you raise and refute a counterargument. The counterargument can be one you identified in one of the texts you read in this chapter or in a source you located on your own. The following sentence stems can help you integrate and refute the counterargument.

Raising the counterargument:

- "On the other hand, ___________ suggests that ___________"
- "In contrast, ___________ disagrees, suggesting instead that ___________."
- "Another factor to consider is what ___________ raises, recommending that ___________"

Refuting the counterargument:

- "And yet, ___________"
- "What ___________ fails to recognize is ___________."
- "While that is certainly true, it's also true that ___________."

Citing Sources and Using Quotations

Whenever you write with sources, be sure to give credit for any ideas that are not your own. When a textbook chapter (like this one) or a timed exam provides you with a group of sources, you will likely be expected to cite authors within your own sentence or in parentheses following a quotation. In online publications, writers often use hyperlinks to the sources cited. When you are writing a full-fledged research paper, however, you should include full citations within the text and a list of Works Cited at the end, so that your readers can locate your sources in their original form. Your teacher will indicate whether you should follow the documentation format of the Modern Language Association (MLA, which is in an Appendix at the back of this book), the *Chicago Manual of Style*, or the American Psychological Association (APA).

Once you've identified quotations you want to use in your argument, make sure you integrate them as effectively as possible into your own writing. There are quite a few options for how to go about weaving quotations into your writing. In this section, we'll look at a handful of the most common ones.

Integrating Sentence Quotations

If you want to use an entire sentence from one of your sources, there are two ways to do that. In both cases, you want to build context before you quote and provide commentary following it.

PHRASE + SIGNAL WORD + COMMA

Based on her comparison of American schools with their international counterparts, investigative journalist Amanda Ripley asserts, "Here, school is about learning, but it's also about training to compete in games that the majority of kids will never get paid to play."

Note that this example is only the context and quotation; in a full paragraph, some commentary in the writer's own words would follow — maybe a comment about the improbability that most students will become professional athletes.

When you use this format, you are incorporating a quoted sentence into your own sentence. Therefore, all you need is a comma to introduce the source material because the result is a single sentence. Notice, too, that the period is enclosed inside the quotation mark.

We call the verb that introduces the quotation a "signal word." Instead of repeating "says" again and again, try to use verbs that provide more information about the writer's tone or purpose. Here are a few examples to draw from:

argues	believes	observes
reports	suggests	concedes
claims	advocates	recommends
supports	contends	asserts

While the sentence construction just discussed is the most common way to integrate a quotation into your own writing, another way is to write your own introductory sentence, follow it with a colon, then quote a complete sentence from your source. Let's use the same example from Ripley to see the difference.

SENTENCE + COLON

Investigative journalist Amanda Ripley points out that international students are often surprised by American high schools' intense focus on sports: "Here, school is about learning, but it's also about training to compete in games that the majority of kids will never get paid to play."

This is a perfectly acceptable — and grammatically correct — way of using a quotation, but you probably noticed that it doesn't flow as well as the previous method. Without a transition between the writer's voice and the quotation, it feels a bit like two blocks of text. The best advice is to use this method sparingly.

Integrating Word or Phrase Quotations

Although using a complete sentence of quoted material might be necessary to capture an especially interesting idea or eloquent wording, selecting only a few words or a phrase from your source has several advantages. On a practical level, this approach makes your overall writing more succinct, which tends to be easier to follow and is appreciated by readers who want you to get right to the point. Perhaps even more important, by integrating your own words with those of your source, your voice remains primary as the source informs and supports your argument. Your sentences flow more smoothly.

> **INTEGRATED PHRASE**
>
> Ripley contends that when American high schools emphasize sports over academics, they are failing to prepare students for a work world "that lavishly rewards those with higher-order skills and ruthlessly punishes those without."

This example also illustrates that integrating quotations into your own sentence shows that you've understood the source well enough to pick and choose relevant parts and incorporate those into your own line of reasoning.

Putting Sources into Conversation with One Another

When you are writing an evidence-based essay, it's tempting to select one source per paragraph or idea. That works most of the time, but you can also use different perspectives to your own advantage by putting sources into conversation with one another. For instance, Ripley, a critic of high school sports, would likely disagree with researchers Hess and Cummings, who think that sports are worthwhile. Let's look at how their different views might work in your own argument.

> At a time when most school budgets are lean at best, academics cannot be undercut by sports without serious consequences to the future of our students. Dr. Frederick M. Hess, the director of education policy studies at the American Enterprise Institute, found that students who played sports had "higher levels of educational attainment." While it is true that participating in sports can help develop those skills, working hard and behaving honestly are values also developed in the classroom. To undermine the whole purpose of school—learning—by glorifying sports does a disservice to students and their communities. Ripley hits the mark when she suggests that it might be a good idea to "hold a pep rally for the debate team."

The student writer's voice is in control throughout the paragraph from the opening topic sentence. The writer uses the differing views of two sources to illustrate a conflict, quote sufficiently to give authority to that conflict, and weave their own commentary throughout.

Integrating Sources into Your Own Writing

Continue developing your own argument on the relationship between high school and sports by returning to the response you have been writing. Revise the response so that it integrates one quotation as a full sentence and another with a word or phrase. Choose both quotations from the same source, or try using two different sources.

Reflecting on the Inquiry Process

Hopefully you have seen throughout this chapter that inquiry rarely follows a linear path: The process is recursive, moving forward, then circling back, then moving forward again. Throughout your inquiry process, you're not marching through a series of steps from beginning to end, checking them off as you go. Rather, you are continually revisiting steps in a series of loops or spirals that show your thinking at work. A source you read might push you to add a new question to your inquiry, or a discussion you have with a classmate might cause you to reconsider your opinion entirely. Whenever you are truly engaged in a topic, doing real inquiry, you will move easily among those steps.

Reflecting on the Inquiry Process

Now that you've practiced putting sources into a conversation and integrating them into your own writing, look back at your original opinion on the benefits and drawbacks of high school sports, as well as the notes you took on the sources and the responses you've been writing. With a partner or small group, discuss the following: What most influenced the development of your final position? Was it a specific reading? An activity? A conversation with a classmate? Your own research? And, finally, what questions do you still have? How has your own recursive inquiry process shaped your views on the issue?

culminating activity

Climate Change and Meat

As climate change becomes an increasingly urgent concern, there has been considerable debate about the environmental impact of the production and consumption of meat. Some question whether that effect is too minor to be of consequence, while others argue that changes in farming practices can help curb greenhouse gas emissions. Some believe that individual efforts to decrease or even eliminate meat in their diet is the best way to limit humanity's carbon footprint.

Read the following sources carefully, including the introductory information for each one. Write an evidence-based response that refers to at least three of the sources and develops your position on whether reducing meat consumption is essential to curbing climate change.

1. **Jonathan Safran Foer** ■ *from* Why We Must Cut Out Meat and Dairy before Dinner in Order to Save the Planet
2. **Lynne Curry** ■ *from* The "Eat Less Meat" Movement Is Growing. Does It Distort Science?
3. **Tom Toles** ■ The Meat Cooked Faster Than I Expected (Cartoon)
4. **Frank M. Mitloehner** ■ *from* Yes, Eating Meat Affects the Environment, But Cows Are Not Killing the Climate
5. **Karl Tate** ■ The Role of Animal Farts in Global Warming (Infographic)

1 *from* Why We Must Cut Out Meat and Dairy before Dinner in Order to Save the Planet

Jonathan Safran Foer

The following selection was taken from a 2019 article that appeared in the *Guardian*, a British newspaper, by novelist and journalist Jonathan Safran Foer.

We cannot save the planet unless we significantly reduce our consumption of animal products. This is not my opinion, or anyone's opinion. It is the inconvenient science. Animal agriculture produces more greenhouse gas emissions than the entire transportation sector (all planes, cars, and trains), and is the primary source of methane and nitrous oxide emissions (which are 86 and 310 times more powerful than CO_2, respectively). Our meat habit is the leading cause of deforestation, which releases carbon when trees are burned (forests contain more carbon than do all exploitable fossil-fuel reserves), and also diminishes the planet's ability to absorb carbon. According to a recent report from the Intergovernmental Panel on Climate Change, even if we were to do everything else that is necessary to save the planet, it will be impossible to meet the goals of the Paris Climate Accord if we do not dramatically reduce our consumption of animal products.

Why is this subject avoided? Conversations about meat, dairy, and eggs make people defensive. They make people annoyed. It's far easier to vilify the fossil fuel industry and its lobbyists — which are without a doubt deserving of our vilification — than to examine our own eating habits. No one who isn't a vegan is eager to go there, and the eagerness of vegans can be a further turnoff. But we have no hope of tackling climate change if we can't speak honestly about what is causing it, as well as our potential to change in response.

It is hard to talk about our need to eat fewer animal products both because the topic is so fraught and because of the sacrifice involved. Most people like the taste of meat, dairy, and eggs. Most people have eaten animal products at almost every meal since they were children, and it's hard to change lifelong habits, even when they aren't freighted with pleasure and identity. Those are meaningful challenges, not only worth acknowledging but necessary to acknowledge. Changing the way we eat is simple compared with converting the world's power grid, or overcoming the influence of powerful lobbyists to pass carbon-tax legislation, or ratifying a significant international treaty on greenhouse gas emissions — but it isn't simple. . . .

Climate change is a crisis that will always be simultaneously addressed together and faced alone. The four highest impact things an individual can do to tackle the planetary crisis are: have fewer children; live car-free; avoid air travel; and eat a plant-based diet. Most people are not in the process of deciding whether to have a baby. Few drivers can simply decide to stop using their cars. A sizable portion of air travel is unavoidable. But everyone will eat a meal relatively soon and can immediately participate in the reversal of climate change. Furthermore, of those four high-impact actions, only plant-based eating immediately addresses methane and nitrous oxide, the most urgently important greenhouse gases.

5 Different studies suggest different dietary changes in response to climate change, but the ballpark is pretty clear. The most comprehensive assessment of the livestock industry's environmental impact was published in *Nature* in October 2018. After analysing food-production systems from every country around the world, the authors concluded that while undernourished people living in poverty across the globe could actually eat a little more meat and dairy, the average world citizen needs to shift to a plant-based diet in order to prevent catastrophic, irreversible environmental damage. The average US and UK citizen must consume 90% less beef and 60% less dairy.

No animal products for breakfast or lunch would come close to achieving that. It might not amount to precisely the reductions that are asked for, but it's about right, and easy to remember.

Emphasizing individual responsibility doesn't need to distract from corporate and federal responsibility. We absolutely need structural change — we need a global shift away from fossil fuels and towards renewable energy. We need to enforce something akin to a carbon tax, mandate environmental-impact labels for products, replace plastic with sustainable solutions, and build walkable cities. We need to end subsidies to the factory farming industry, and hold it accountable for the environmental destruction it incurs. We need to ethically address the west's relationship to the global south. We might even need a political revolution. These changes will require shifts that individuals alone cannot realize. But putting aside the fact that collective revolutions are made up of individuals, led by individuals, and reinforced by thousands of individual revolutions, we would have no chance of achieving our goal of limiting environmental destruction if individuals don't make the very individual decision to live differently.

Climate change is the greatest crisis humankind has ever faced, and it is one that will always be simultaneously addressed together and faced alone. We cannot keep eating the kinds of meals we have known and also keep the planet we have known. We must either let some eating habits go or let the planet go. It is that straightforward, and that fraught. ■

2 *from* The "Eat Less Meat" Movement Is Growing. Does It Distort Science?

Lynne Curry

The following selection is from a 2019 article from *The Counter*, an online publication by a non-profit called The New Food Economy. According to its website, it provides independent reporting "to investigate the forces shaping how and what we eat." Lynne Curry is a food journalist and author of a cookbook on using grassfed beef.

Emissions related to agriculture are a primary cause of the current climate crisis — and, as major consumers of beef, Americans carry a large share of the blame. Although the American diet has shifted away from beef toward chicken, we still eat four times as much beef per capita, on average, as the rest of the world.

The solution seems apparent: We should eat less meat. Order the beefless burger and you can save the planet, eliminate cruelty to animals, and improve your health.

But a rising chorus of farming advocates says that notion gets it wrong, or at best only partly right. . . .

Ariel Greenwood, who ranches in Montana and New Mexico, rejects the eat-less-meat message as short-sighted and misleading. "There are many, many ways to raise meat, and dismissing all meat as being destructive is asinine because it ignores the significant variation in production methods and ecosystems in which meat can be produced," says Greenwood, who is also co-owner of Grass Nomads LLC, a company that helps clients sustainably manage their grasslands. . . .

5 In June, six months after his company launched a reformulated version of its non-meat Impossible Burger, Impossible Foods CEO Pat Brown declared his mission to end animal agriculture by 2035. "The use of animals to produce food for human consumption has long been taken for granted as an indispensable part of the global food system," Brown wrote. "Now, finally, this disastrously resource-intensive and inefficient system is being recognized by environmentalists and, increasingly, by the public for what it is: a destructive and unnecessary technology."

Predictably, his call to action ignited a backlash. . . .

Georgia rancher Will Harris responded to Brown's statement with evidence from a recent lifecycle analysis of grass-fed beef raised at his White Oak Pastures, a celebrated model of sustainable agriculture. The carbon footprint of his pasture-raised beef measured significantly less than conventional beef, chicken, and even the Beyond Burger, a plant-based burger from Beyond Meat. The study, which indicated that Harris' farm offset more carbon emissions than it produced, has inspired a new conversation about what it refers to as the "full carbon story for regenerative agriculture systems."

". . . And since analog burgers cost twice as much as an organic grass-fed burger — about $12 per pound for Beyond Burger, versus under $6 a pound for organic grass-fed ground beef at Walmart — [says dietician and nutritionist Diana] Rodgers . . ., "I don't see how that is changing anything for the better."

Ryan Katz-Rosense and Sarah J. Martin, co-authors of the forthcoming book *Green Meat? Sustaining Eaters, Animals, and the Planet,* have identified three pathways for the future of protein — "re-modernization," "replacement," and "restoration."

10 "The evidence suggests our planet is traveling in all three directions at once," the authors write.

The meat industry, controlled by four transnational corporations — Cargill, JBS, Tyson Foods, and Smithfield Foods — leads the "re-modernization" camp through increased efficiencies in factory farming to produce cheap and abundant protein. "Replacement" innovators are disrupting the meat industry with protein substitutes, from plant-based proteins to lab-grown meats. Both of these dominant pathways, proposing industrialization, commodity crops, and concentration as the way forward, have attracted billions of dollars in investments.

The "restoration" pathway is a radical departure from modern food production. It promotes ecological and social health through a focus on soil health, a farming system called regenerative agriculture. . . .

The "eat less meat" effort focuses on decreasing the demand for animal protein, based on the assumption that all meat is the same. "When it comes to resource use and environmental impacts," the World Resource Institute's website states, "the type of food eaten matters as much, if not more than how that food is produced."

But the organic community, which has insisted for years that production practices matter, is finding its voice. That chorus is chanting: "It's not the cow, it's the how." . . .

As a nation, we take pride in personal sacrifice for a larger cause — except that this time, skeptics say, it will not suffice. The problem's too big for individual self-denial to work on its own.

[Andrew] Gunther [director of a sustainable livestock farming organization] says, "It's not as simple as stop eating meat and being a vegetarian. . . . It's a system, not a product. It's education, not a solution." ■

3 The Meat Cooked Faster Than I Expected

Tom Toles

Following is a political cartoon by the award-winning artist Tom Toles, whose work is syndicated in numerous publications.

Tom Toles/May 8, 2014/Andrews McMeel Syndication

4 *from* Yes, Eating Meat Affects the Environment, But Cows Are Not Killing the Climate

Frank M. Mitloehner

This excerpt is from a 2018 article published on the website theconversation.com by Frank M. Mitloehner, professor of animal science and air quality extension specialist, University of California, Davis.

My research focuses on ways in which animal agriculture affects air quality and climate change. In my view, there are many reasons for either choosing animal protein or opting for a vegetarian selection. However, foregoing meat and meat products is not the environmental panacea many would have us believe. And if taken to an extreme, it also could have harmful nutritional consequences.

A healthy portion of meat's bad rap centers on the assertion that livestock is the largest source of greenhouse gases worldwide. For example, a 2009 analysis published by the Washington, D.C.-based Worldwatch Institute asserted that 51 percent of global greenhouse gas (GHG) emissions come from rearing and processing livestock.

According to the U.S. Environmental Protection Agency, the largest sources of U.S. GHG emissions in 2016 were electricity production (28 percent of total emissions), transportation (28 percent), and industry (22 percent). All of agriculture accounted for a total of 9 percent. All of animal agriculture contributes less than half of this amount, representing 3.9 percent of total U.S. greenhouse gas emissions. That's very different from claiming livestock represents as much or more than transportation.

Why the misconception? In 2006 the United Nations Food and Agriculture Organization published a study titled "Livestock's Long Shadow," which received widespread international attention. It stated that livestock produced a staggering 18 percent of the world's greenhouse gas emissions. The agency drew a startling conclusion: Livestock was doing more to harm the climate than all modes of transportation combined. . . .

5 In its most recent assessment report, the FAO estimated that livestock produces 14.5 percent of global greenhouse gas emissions from human activities. There is no comparable full life-cycle assessment for transportation. However, as Steinfeld has pointed out, direct emissions from transportation versus livestock can be compared and amount to 14 versus 5 percent, respectively.

Many people continue to think avoiding meat as infrequently as once a week will make a significant difference to the climate. But according to one recent study, even if Americans eliminated all animal protein from their diets, they would reduce U.S. greenhouse gas emissions by only 2.6 percent. According to our research at the University of California, Davis, if the practice of Meatless Monday were to be adopted by all Americans, we'd see a reduction of only 0.5 percent.

Moreover, technological, genetic, and management changes that have taken place in U.S. agriculture over the past 70 years have made livestock production more efficient and less greenhouse gas-intensive. According to the FAO's statistical database, total direct greenhouse gas emissions from U.S. livestock have declined 11.3 percent since 1961, while production of livestock meat has more than doubled. . . .

Removing animals from U.S. agriculture would lower national greenhouse gas emissions to a small degree, but it would also make it harder to meet nutritional requirements. Many critics of animal agriculture are quick to point out that if farmers raised only plants, they could produce more pounds of food and more calories per person. But humans also need many essential micro- and macronutrients for good health. . . .

The world population is currently projected to reach 9.8 billion people by 2050. Feeding this many people will raise immense challenges. Meat is more nutrient-dense per serving than vegetarian options, and ruminant animals largely thrive on feed that is not suitable for humans. Raising livestock also offers much-needed income for small-scale farmers in developing nations. Worldwide, livestock provides a livelihood for 1 billion people.

Climate change demands urgent attention, 10
and the livestock industry has a large overall environmental footprint that affects air, water, and land. These, combined with a rapidly rising world population, give us plenty of compelling reasons to continue to work for greater efficiencies in animal agriculture. I believe the place to start is with science-based facts. ■

5 The Role of Animal Farts in Global Warming

Karl Tate

The following infographic appeared on the site LiveScience.com in 2015. It was created by Karl Tate, an infographic artist working for LiveScience and other sites.

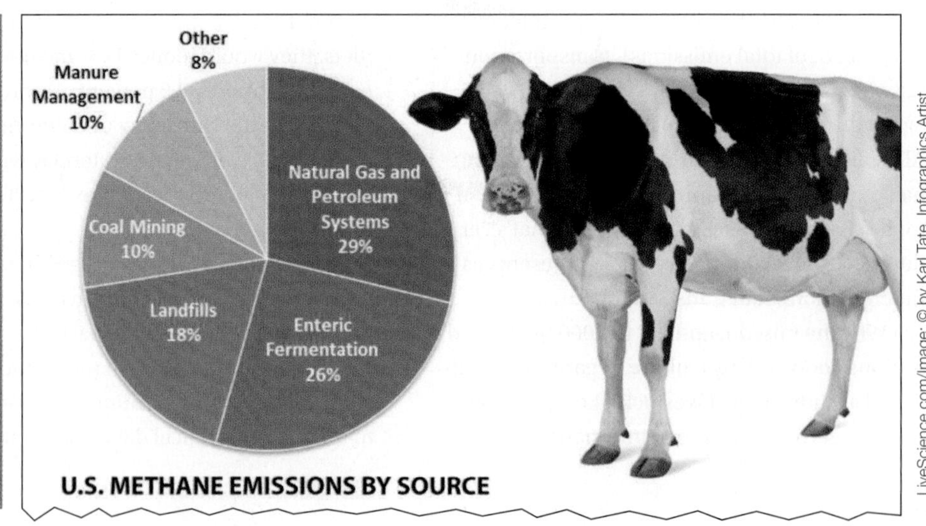

LiveScience.com/Image: © by Karl Tate, Infographics Artist

HOW COWS CONTRIBUTE TO GLOBAL WARMING

Ruminants are herbivores that regurgitate their food to re-chew it. Microorganisms in the animal's gut break down carbohydrates into simpler molecules.

Ruminants including cattle and deer produce large amounts of methane, a greenhouse gas with an impact on the atmosphere 23 times greater than that of carbon dioxide. The production of methane by this process is called enteric fermentation, and it accounts for more than a quarter of methane emissions in the United States (chart, above).

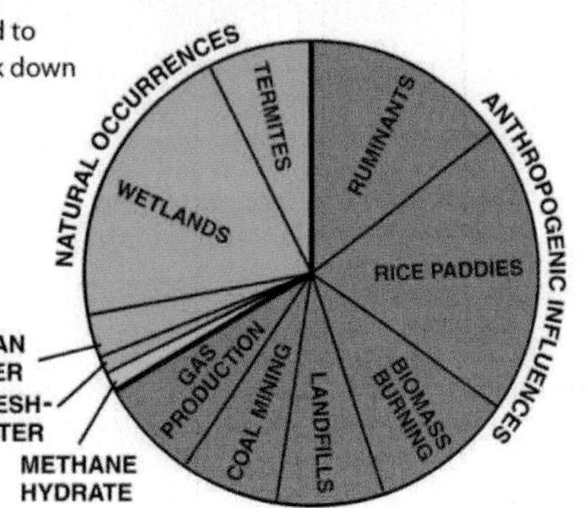

RIGHT: Naturally occurring and human-caused (anthropogenic) sources of methane.

METHANE EMITTED PER ANIMAL PER YEAR

265 lbs. (120 kilograms)

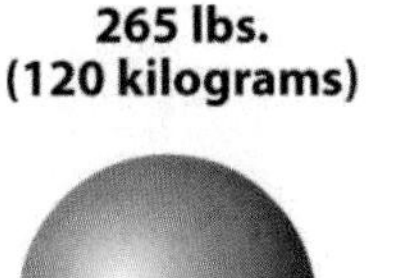

Cattle

17.6 lbs. (8 kg)

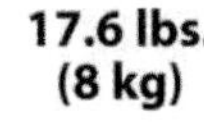

Sheep

3.3 lbs. (1.5 kg)

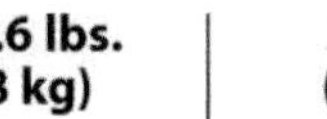

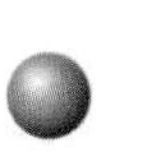

Pigs

0.26 lbs. (0.12 kg)

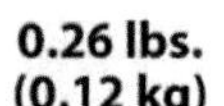

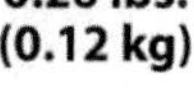

Humans

SOURCES: NASA GODDARD INSTITUTE FOR SPACE SCIENCE; ENVIRONMENTAL PROTECTION AGENCY; U.S. DEPT. OF ENERGY TECHNOLOGY LABORATORY; SHUTTERSTOCK

CHILDREN
FIRST

Changing the World

Essential Questions:

- **What conditions are required to make change happen?**
- **How does one gain the appropriate amount and type of power to create change?**
- **How does effective, persuasive communication help to bring about change?**
- **When — if ever — is violence an appropriate means for creating change?**

With so much injustice in the world, as well as racism, sexism, and other forms of discrimination, at some point in your life, you've probably said to someone, "If I could change the world, I'd ___________." Maybe you'd focus on a big topic such as climate change. Perhaps you'd look at a local issue like a school policy that prevents younger students from taking certain classes. The point is that our world is far from perfect, and there are a number of issues that need to be addressed. In this chapter, while you will read speeches, editorials, and other pieces that address topics such as gun control, sexual harassment, labor rights, and others, the focus is not on the issues themselves. Rather, it is on HOW the changes the speakers and writers propose can come about. Because most people, especially those who are in power, are resistant to change, those who hope to change the world need to give careful thought to what will persuade others and move them to participate. What roles do dialogue and communication play? Should violence ever be used in an effort to bring about justice? How can people avoid becoming cynical and disillusioned?

activity Changing the World

With a partner or in a small group, brainstorm a list of times when significant change occurred, such as the civil rights movement in the 1950s and 1960s, or the Black Lives Matter movement in the first part of the 21st century. Conduct brief research as needed to add to your list. Then, choose one of these events or movements to discuss with your partner or group. Consider who promoted the change, who was trying to prevent it, and what finally caused the change to come about. If necessary, conduct additional research to add to your background knowledge.

Texts in Conversation

Throughout this chapter, you will read about a number of people who have tried — or are still trying — to bring about meaningful change across a wide range of topics. As you read, keep track of some of their different approaches to creating change, make connections among them, and respond to them with your own reactions. At the end of the chapter, you'll have an opportunity to write your own pieces about change, using the texts you read as evidence and inspiration. If it would help you, use a graphic organizer like the following:

Author/ title	How does the author advocate for change?	Quotation(s) that illustrate the author's ideas about change	Your reaction and/or connections to other texts

skill workshop

Understanding Personal Experience in Argument

As we discussed in Chapter 3, many different types of evidence can help you prove a point or make your case. You certainly can and should use facts, statistics, data, and quotations from experts. However, the role that your own personal experience with an issue can play in developing and supporting your argument is often overlooked. If, for instance, you are writing about why school should start later in the day, your own experience getting up for your first period class would likely provide relevant and highly effective support. This workshop will focus on examining how personal experience can be used to develop and support an argument, and also on recognizing its limitations. In addition to analyzing the use of personal experience in the argument put forward in a speech by Malala Yousafzai, you will write your own brief argument that includes an effective use of personal experience as evidence to support a claim.

Speech to the United Nations Youth Assembly

Malala Yousafzai

FRANCK ROBICHON/POOL/EPA-EFE/Shutterstock

Nobel Peace Prize winner Malala Yousafzai (b. 1997) is a Pakistani woman who, at the age of eleven, began writing a blog about the hardships of her life under Taliban rule. The blog specifically addressed the Taliban's ban on education for girls. Though she protected her identity with a pseudonym, her writing soon became widely read and led to appearances on television, where Yousafzai spoke out for education rights for girls around the world. On October 9, 2012, the Taliban made an attempt to assassinate Yousafzai while she was riding a bus home from school. She was shot in the head but survived the attack. Yousafzai has since become a symbol for social justice, human rights, and resistance to Taliban rule.

KEY CONTEXT On July 12, 2013, young people were given control of the United Nations for the first time in the sixty-eight-year history of the organization. More than one hundred organizations came together, along with hundreds of young education advocates from around the world. The advocates included Malala Yousafzai, who made her first public speech since recovering from the Taliban's assassination attempt. Below is the speech she gave on that day.

FOCUS FOR READING As you read this speech for the first time, annotate the text by making connections and asking questions (see p. 10). Then, go back and annotate it again looking specifically for moments in which Yousafzai's argument relies on descriptions of her own personal experiences, also called anecdotes. Comment on how those descriptions support her argument.

Dear brothers and sisters, do remember one thing. Malala Day is not my day. Today is the day of every woman, every boy and every girl who have raised their voice for their rights. There are hundreds of human rights activists and social workers who are not only speaking for human rights, but who are struggling to achieve their goals of education, peace and equality. Thousands of people have been killed by the terrorists and millions have been injured. I am just one of them.

So here I stand . . . one girl among many.

I speak — not for myself, but for all girls and boys.

I raise up my voice — not so that I can shout, but so that those without a voice can be heard.

Those who have fought for their rights:

Their right to live in peace.

Their right to be treated with dignity.

Their right to equality of opportunity.

Their right to be educated.

Dear Friends, on the 9th of October 2012, the Taliban shot me on the left side of my forehead. They shot my friends too. They thought that the bullets would silence us. But they failed. And then, out of that silence came thousands of voices. The terrorists thought that they would change our aims and stop our ambitions but nothing changed in my life except this: Weakness, fear and hopelessness died. Strength, power and courage [were] born. I am the same Malala. My ambitions are the same. My hopes are the same. My dreams are the same.

Dear sisters and brothers, I am not against anyone. Neither am I here to speak in terms of personal revenge against the Taliban or any other terrorist group. I am here to speak up for the right of education of every child. I want education for the sons and the daughters of all the extremists especially the Taliban.

I do not even hate the Talib who shot me. Even if there is a gun in my hand and he stands in front of me, I would not shoot him. This is the compassion that I have learnt from Muhammad — the prophet of mercy, Jesus Christ and Lord Buddha. This is the legacy of change that I have inherited from Martin Luther King, Nelson Mandela and Muhammad Ali Jinnah. This is the philosophy of non-violence that I have learnt from Gandhi Jee, Bacha Khan and Mother Teresa. And this is the forgiveness that I have learnt from my mother and father. This is what my soul is telling me: be peaceful and love everyone.

Dear sisters and brothers, we realize the importance of light when we see darkness. We realize the importance of our voice when we are silenced. In the same way, when we were in Swat, the north of Pakistan, we realized the importance of pens and books when we saw the guns.

The wise saying, "The pen is mightier than sword" was true. The extremists are afraid of books and pens. The power of education frightens them. They are afraid of women. The power of the voice of women frightens them. And that is why they killed 14 innocent medical students in the recent attack in Quetta. And that is why they killed many female teachers and polio workers in Khyber Pukhtoon Khwa and FATA. That is why they are blasting schools every day. Because they were and they are afraid of change, afraid of the equality that we will bring into our society.

I remember that there was a boy in our school who was asked by a journalist, "Why are the Taliban against education?" He answered very simply. By pointing to his book, he said, "A Talib doesn't know what is written inside this book." They think that God is a tiny, little conservative being who would send girls to . . . hell just because of going to school. The terrorists are misusing the name of Islam and Pashtun society for their own personal benefits. Pakistan is [a] peace-loving democratic country. Pashtuns want education for their daughters and sons. And Islam is a religion of peace, humanity and brotherhood. Islam says that it is not only each child's right to get education, rather it is their duty and responsibility.

Honorable Secretary General, peace is necessary for education. In many parts of the world especially Pakistan and Afghanistan, terrorism, wars and conflicts stop children [from going] to their schools. We are really tired of these wars. Women and children are suffering in many parts of the world in many ways. In India, innocent and poor children are victims of child labor. Many schools have been destroyed in Nigeria. People in Afghanistan have been affected by the hurdles of extremism for decades. Young girls have to do domestic child labor and are forced to get married at early age. Poverty, ignorance, injustice, racism and the deprivation of basic rights are the main problems faced by both men and women.

Dear fellows, today I am focusing on women's rights and girls' education because they are suffering the most. There was a time when women social activists asked men to stand up for their rights. But, this time, we will do it by ourselves. I am not telling men to step away from speaking for women's rights; rather I am focusing on women to be independent [and] to fight for themselves.

Dear sisters and brothers, now it's time to speak up.

So today, we call upon the world leaders to change their strategic policies in favor of peace and prosperity.

We call upon the world leaders that all the peace deals must protect women and children's rights. A deal that goes against the dignity of women and their rights is unacceptable.

We call upon all governments to ensure free compulsory education for every child all over the world.

We call upon all governments to fight against terrorism and violence, to protect children from brutality and harm.

We call upon the developed nations to support the expansion of educational opportunities for girls in the developing world.

We call upon all communities to be tolerant — to reject prejudice based on cast[e], creed, sect, religion or gender. To ensure freedom and equality for women so that they can flourish. We cannot all succeed when half of us are held back.

We call upon our sisters around the world to be brave — to embrace the strength within themselves and realize their full potential.

Dear brothers and sisters, we want schools and education for every child's bright future. We will continue our journey to our destination of peace and education for everyone. No one can stop us. We will speak for our rights and we will bring change through our voice. We must believe in the power and the strength of our words. Our words can change the world.

Because we are all together, united for the cause of education. And if we want to achieve our goal, then let us empower ourselves with the weapon of knowledge and let us shield ourselves with unity and togetherness.

Dear brothers and sisters, we must not forget that millions of people are suffering from poverty, injustice and ignorance. We must not forget that millions of children are out of schools. We must not forget that our sisters and brothers are waiting for a bright peaceful future.

So let us wage a global struggle against illiteracy, poverty and terrorism and let us pick up our books and pens. They are our most powerful weapons.

One child, one teacher, one pen and one book can change the world.

Education is the only solution. Education First. ■

Making a Claim

One of the most important components of any argument is its claim, the central point the writer or speaker is trying to prove to the audience. While Yousafzai addresses many topics, her claim is likely found in this statement from the very end of her speech: "Education is the only solution. Education First." She clearly believes that education is the most important element to creating lasting change; her claim is arguable because some might suggest that addressing poverty is the only solution, or eliminating gender discrimination. Yousafzai has a lot of relevant personal experience, so it is easy and appropriate for her to use herself and her story as evidence. In the discussion that follows, we will examine more closely how she does this. Throughout this workshop, you will consider topics and claims that you have personal experience with as well, so that you can see how this type of evidence can work in an argument.

Writing a Claim

1. Consider the following prompts to help you begin identifying a topic for your own argument. Respond to as many prompts as needed to help you to identify a topic:
   - Describe a time when you suffered an injustice of some kind. The experience might be tied to your race, gender, ethnicity, or another part of your identity. If no experience comes to mind from your own life, consider writing about the experience of someone close to you.

- Identify something that should be changed at your school. For example, should specific courses be added or removed? Should the school day begin later in the morning? Does your school need new athletic fields?
- What do you wish your family or friends would do differently? Go on more trips? Give more allowance? Let you stay out later? Try a new activity?
- Describe a change you would like to see in your community. Improvements to a local park? More recycling centers? Additional bike lanes?

2. Once you have identified a possible topic, write a draft of a claim about the topic. In other words, what change are you proposing and hoping to convince your audience to support or act on?

Using Personal Experience as Evidence

As you noticed when you read and annotated Yousafzai's speech, much of it is about telling her story. However, her speech is not just a narrative. Her goal is not simply to tell the story of her attack, but rather to prove her claim that education is the only solution to "poverty, injustice, and ignorance." She uses her own personal experiences to support that claim. Reread the following section of the speech:

> Dear Friends, on the 9th of October 2012, the Taliban shot me on the left side of my forehead. They shot my friends too. They thought that the bullets would silence us. But they failed. And then, out of that silence came thousands of voices. The terrorists thought that they would change our aims and stop our ambitions but nothing changed in my life except this: Weakness, fear and hopelessness died. Strength, power and courage [were] born. I am the same Malala. My ambitions are the same. My hopes are the same. My dreams are the same.

Notice how Yousafzai uses her experience to stir our emotions — by recounting the shooting and then by inviting us to share her defiance in her own ambitions and strength. Using personal experience is an extremely effective way to appeal to pathos (p. 96). Notice, however, how she refers to other people and their voices in between the personal elements. In fact, she even switches the pronoun usage from "me" to "our," showing how her personal experiences are related to those of other people.

This is the ultimate aim of using personal experience within an argument: You want to show how your own experiences are not unique to you. They can stand in for other people's perspectives as well. Personal experience also adds to Yousafzai's ethos as an expert with first-hand information on this topic; she is a voice that needs to be listened to specifically because of her experiences.

While you likely have not endured as dramatic a personal experience as Yousafzai, you still have many experiences you can draw on, such as the following:

1. Descriptions of a specific event or incident that happened directly to you.
2. Descriptions of an event that you witnessed or heard about happening to someone else that you know and trust.

3. Ideas that you have gained from your general experiences based on your race, gender, age, ethnicity, participation in school, work, particular groups, and so on.
4. Feelings that you have about a topic, rooted in a specific incident or experience.

skill workshop

activity

Writing Using Personal Experience as Evidence

1. Return to the topic that you chose in response to the activity on pages 163–164. Write down as many experiences as possible that you've had in connection with this topic. At this point do not worry about relevance or effectiveness; just try to get a lot of ideas down on paper. The list above of what might qualify as personal experiences can help you generate ideas.
2. Now focus on the claim you developed in response to the activity on pages 163–164. Choose one or two of your best examples and explain to a partner why you think they might be effective in helping you to prove your claim. Provide and receive feedback on how effective and relevant these experiences might be for your topic.

Balancing Personal Experience with Other Evidence

Of course, relying too much on personal experience is risky. If, for example, you argue for a later start to your school day and support your argument with a detailed, emotional account of how hard it is for you to get out of bed and how much coffee you have to drink just to get yourself to class even five minutes late, any members of your audience who are "morning people" won't relate at all to what you are saying. They might not find that evidence convincing because their experiences are completely different.

Your voice and your experiences matter a great deal. But when your personal experience is connected to and supported with additional types of evidence, your argument becomes even stronger and more difficult for critics to dismiss. So, in your argument about the later school start time, perhaps you should sandwich your experiences between university research that explains how sleep patterns differ for adolescents and adults and data from your school showing that attendance is the worst for first period. Additional evidence does not suggest that your own experience is not valid. Your personal experience will humanize your argument, giving your audience a chance to connect emotionally, but the other types of evidence will act as a balance to your experiences, helping to convince your audience that your argument is valid because it is grounded in more than just your opinion.

Reread the following excerpt from Yousafzai's speech. Notice that the paragraph begins and ends with her personal experiences, but in between are references to other people and ideas:

> I do not even hate the Talib who shot me. Even if there is a gun in my hand and he stands in front of me, I would not shoot him. <u>This is the compassion that I have learnt from Muhammad — the prophet of mercy, Jesus Christ and Lord Buddha. This is the legacy of</u>

> change that I have inherited from Martin Luther King, Nelson Mandela and Muhammad Ali Jinnah. This is the philosophy of non-violence that I have learnt from Gandhi Jee, Bacha Khan and Mother Teresa. And this is the forgiveness that I have learnt from my mother and father. This is what my soul is telling me: be peaceful and love everyone.

Yousafzai offers a wide range of support for her position that goes beyond her own personal experiences; because her evidence includes references to Christian, Muslim, and Buddhist religions, and political leaders from across the world, it broadens her appeal outside of her native Pakistan.

activity

Using Balanced Evidence

1. Return to the topic you have been thinking about for your own argument. Conduct brief research to locate an additional piece of evidence or two that might support your claim. Possible types of evidence include data or statistics, research, and information from an expert on the subject (see Chapter 3).
2. Meet with the same partner you worked with to complete the activity on page 165. Provide and receive feedback on how effective and relevant this additional evidence might be for your topic.

culminating activity

Write a brief argument that includes a claim, a relevant personal experience for support, and one other type of evidence. This argument should not be a full essay; it is a response that demonstrates that you can use personal experience and additional relevant evidence effectively in an argument.

When 16-Year-Olds Vote, We All Benefit

Bill Bystricky

Bill Bystricky is a writer living in Maryland. He has written about youth rights for *Yes!*, *Wiretap*, and *The Pro-Youth Pages*, among other publications. He is the founder of Growing Democracy, a group that assists youth seeking to lower the voting age.

Courtesy of Bill Bystricky

The March for Our Lives in Washington, D.C., on March 24, when high school students rallied against gun violence, demonstrated that teenage citizens have voices that deserve to be heard and needs that deserve to be addressed by our leaders. In order for teenagers to have a fighting chance at winning, however, they need votes.

Several nations, including Austria, Argentina, and Brazil, already have 16-year-olds voting, and the United States is slowly moving in that direction, with one city at a time implementing a voting age of 16.

While progress is slow, the benefits are clear. Teenagers, not yet distracted by the stresses of college or full-time work, have the time and have supportive adults around to help them navigate the complexities of voter registration. By starting their voting lives at a time when it's easy, youth begin a habit of voting instead of a habit of staying home.

It should be no surprise, then, that the voter-suppression crowd hates the #Vote16 movement.

5 I helped organize campaigns that lowered the voting age to 16 in three Maryland cities, and in every case, the same arguments were used against us.

Kids will just vote the same way their parents do, claim parents who overestimate their influence. But ScotCen Social Research's 2013 study[1] of 16-year-old voters in Scotland found they were no more influenced by their parents than older voters were.

Teenagers would just vote for celebrities, claim others. But exit polls show it was voters over 40 who elected a reality TV star as president[2] and an action movie star as governor of California[3]. In both elections, the youngest voters voted for more qualified candidates.

Kids' brains aren't fully developed yet, claim people who get their science news from Facebook. But actual scientists know better.

---

[1] Eichorn, Jan. "Will 16 and 17 Year Olds Make a Difference in the Referendum?" ScotCen Social Research, November 2013. http://www.scotcen.org.uk/media/205540/131129_will-16-and-17-years-olds-make-a-difference.pdf

[2] Roper Center. "How Groups Voted in 2016." https://ropercenter.cornell.edu/how-groups-voted-2016

[3] Edison Media Research and Mitofsky International. "California Recall Election Exit Poll." *The Washington Post,* October 7, 2003. https://www.washingtonpost.com/wp-srv/politics/replacementballotexitpoll.html

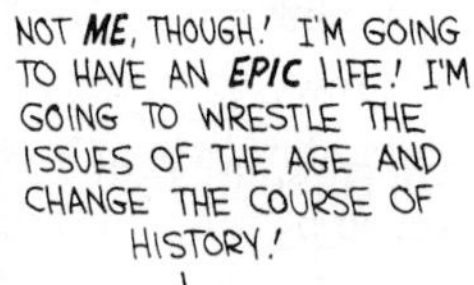

Cartoonist Bill Watterson often addresses philosophical questions in his *Calvin and Hobbes* comic strip. **What point is Watterson making here about creating change? How might Bystricky react to this point, based on this article?**

As Laurence Steinberg, a professor of psychology at Temple University, wrote, "the skills necessary to make informed decisions are firmly in place by 16. By that age, adolescents can gather and process information, weigh pros and cons, reason logically with facts, and take time before making a decision. Teenagers may sometimes make bad choices, but statistically speaking, they do not make them any more often than adults do."

Of all the arguments made against #Vote16, the most infuriating may be this: *They don't want to vote. Kids are apathetic.*

For me, this one is personal. I taught social 10 studies. And in every classroom, I encountered the same barrier. "What difference does it make if we understand how government works? We can't even vote!" students would tell me.

Many students saw no point in developing an informed opinion when no decision-maker was asking for theirs. They saw no point in learning from history when they were barred from even a small say in America's path forward.

Excluded from America's democracy, too many teenagers respond with sour grapes, telling themselves bitterly that *democracy* is just a word. They develop the habits that look from a distance like apathy, habits that can linger for years. And then adults use that disconnection as the reason to keep youth excluded.

It's amazing, though, how easily this cycle can be broken. When teenagers hear about the mere possibility of being included in elections — even just local elections — the bitterness melts, and hopeful youth emerge from the shadows in droves.

In 2013, a city council member in Takoma Park, Maryland, proposed his city lowering its voting age to 16. No other U.S. city had done this, and other council members dismissed the idea. Then local high school students heard about the proposal. On the night the matter was up for discussion, numerous students sacrificed late hours on a school night to ask their city council for a small voice in local elections. Councilmember Tim Male noted that 5 percent of the city's entire population aged 16–17 showed up to the meeting. "If we had 5 percent turnout of this entire community at a city council meeting, we'd have 600–800 people. There are 200 chairs in this room. That would never happen."

Impressed by these youth, the city council 15 passed the proposal, and youth brought their enthusiasm into the voting booth. In the first local election after the change, the turnout rate

Voting Rates by Age

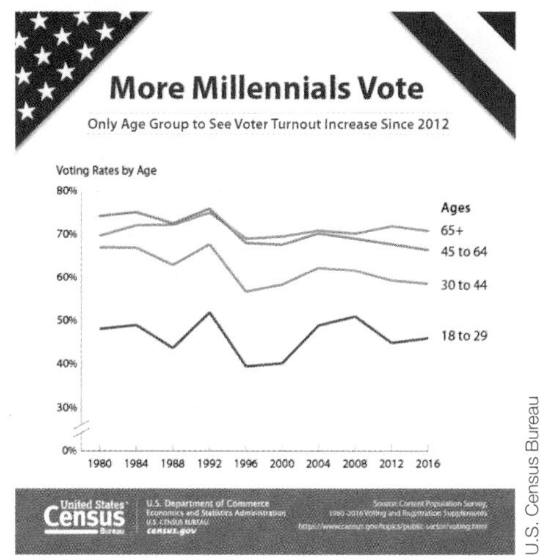

U.S. Census Bureau

This chart was created by the United States Census Bureau.

What conclusions can you draw from this chart about voting rates by age, especially trends in recent years? How would this chart help or hinder Bystricky's argument? Conduct brief research to identify the latest data on youth voting.

for voters younger than 18 was four times that of older voters[4].

But that's Takoma Park, an affluent suburb of Washington where many parents are among America's policy leaders. Their kids grow up informed and engaged. Surely, critics said, that couldn't happen in a more typical city.

The next campaign arose in working-class Hyattsville. This time, teenagers turned out in such numbers that the council chambers had standing room only[5]. The architects had never planned for a Hyattsville city council meeting to draw such attendance, but on this freezing cold night, teenagers had walked, carpooled, or taken public transit to plead for the right to take part in the same local elections most adults blow off.

Among them was Juwan Blocker, who got a ride from an English teacher. And after he saw that his voice really mattered when his city lowered its voting age to include him, Blocker's engagement grew, and he continued taking part as he became an adult.

"I got involved in running for the school board twice and got elected as a student member," he says. "And now I'm here at the age of 20 running for a full term on the board of education. So it definitely impacted me and others."

20 That shouldn't be too surprising. A study published in the *Journal of Youth Studies*[6] found that "political interest of 16- and 17-year-olds was higher after lowering the voting age."

Two years after Takoma Park lowered its voting age, Male emailed me and told me how young people's involvement has become everyday.

"[It's now] normal for older people to stand in line with younger people to vote," he said. "Normal for 16- to 17-year-olds to be at campaign events and asking questions of candidates. Normal to see 16- to 17-year-olds at council meetings. And best of all, as an elected representative, it has become normal for me to get requests from 16- to 17-year-olds — for information or representation or services that the city provides."

Blocker found his increased engagement even rubbed off on his parents. Before, he says, his parents were only occasional voters, but now they vote in every election. That too is

---

[4] Wogan, J. B. "Takoma Park Sees High Turnout Among Teens After Election Reform." *Governing*, November 7, 2013. https://www.governing.com/news/headlines/gov-maryland-city-sees-high-turnout-among-teens-after-election-reform.html

[5] Schneider, Elena. "Students in Maryland Test Civic Participation and Win Right to Vote." *The New York Times*, January 9, 2015. https://www.nytimes.com/2015/01/10/us/politics/students-in-maryland-test-civic-participation-and-win-right-to-vote.html

[6] Zeglovits, Eva & Martina Zandonella. "Political interest of adolescents before and after lowering the voting age: the case of Austria." *Journal of Youth Studies*, 16:8, 1084-1104, May 24, 2013. DOI: 10.1080/13676261.2013.793785

unsurprising. Research from Denmark[7] has shown that parents who live with voting children are more likely to vote than parents without voting-age children in their household. A lower voting age rejuvenates democracy across generations. ■

[7] Dahlgaard, Jens Olav. "The surprising consequence of lowering the voting age." *The Washington Post*, March 1, 2018. https://www.washingtonpost.com/news/monkey-cage/wp/2018/02/28/the-surprising-consequence-of-lowering-the-voting-age/?noredirect=on

Understanding and Interpreting

1. Starting with the March for Our Lives protests, Bystricky says that for the teenagers to be able to win — meaning to succeed in bringing about change — they need votes. What connection does he make between winning and voting?
2. Paragraph 3 include some reasons to support lowering the voting age to 16. Which of those reasons seem to be the strongest at this point in the argument?
3. Explain what Bystricky means when he writes in paragraph 12, "They develop the habits that look from a distance like apathy, habits that can linger for years. And then adults use that disconnection as the reason to keep youth excluded."
4. Bystricky offers two specific examples of local governments in Maryland that considered lowering their voting age: Takoma Park and Hyattsville. What is similar and different about these examples, and why did Bystricky likely choose to include both of them?
5. Who do you think is the intended audience for this argument? How do you know, based on what Bystricky includes?

Analyzing Language, Style, and Structure

1. **Vocabulary in Context.** In paragraph 17, Bystricky refers to the "architects." What does this word mean in the context of his argument? How is his use of this word similar to or different from other uses you have encountered?
2. **Skill Focus.** Reread paragraphs 9 through 12. How does Bystricky use his own personal experiences as a social studies teacher to refute a counterclaim and support his position? How was his argument strengthened or weakened by the inclusion of his own experiences?
3. Paragraphs 6, 7, and 8 all follow the same structure: Bystricky raises a counterargument and tries to refute it. How successful is he at addressing those who disagree with his proposal?
4. Look back carefully at some of Bystricky's word choices, including "voter-suppression crowd" (par. 4), "more qualified candidates" (par. 7), and "actual scientists" (par. 8). What do his language choices reveal about his potential biases?
5. Re-examine Bystricky's piece looking at the appeals (ethos, logos, pathos) he uses. Which appeals are most strongly at work in his argument? Why might these have been effective or ineffective in persuading his audience?
6. Why might Bystricky have chosen to end his piece with the observation by Juwan Blocker and the research from Denmark?

Topics for Composing

1. **Analysis.** We know that Bystricky's central claim is that 16-year-olds should be allowed to vote. Examine Bystricky's argument by evaluating how effectively he uses evidence, appeals, reasoning, and language choices to persuade his audience to agree with his claim.
2. **Argument.** Is Bystricky right? Should 16-year-olds be allowed to vote? Use evidence from his piece, or conduct additional research for evidence to support your position.
3. **Connection.** Bystricky says the following about his own students: "They saw no point in learning from history when they were barred from even a small say in America's path forward." How engaged are you and your friends in politics? Are there local or national issues that you wish that you could vote on? Would being able to vote have affected your attitude toward the issues?
4. **Speaking and Listening.** Interview students, teachers, and staff members, and ask them why 16-year-olds should or should not be allowed to vote. Try to gather responses from as many people as possible at your school, and take careful notes on the reasons they offer. Once you have enough responses, look for patterns in your findings. For example, have adults tended to respond in one way and students in another? Present your findings to your class using a graph, word cloud, or other visual representation.
5. **Research.** Are there currently any proposals in your state, city, or town to lower the voting age? If so, what objections do opponents raise? If there are no such proposals in your area, identify representatives in your local or city government who might be interested in hearing about this proposal. Then, write a letter or an email to that person sharing your perspective on the issue.
6. **Creative Writing.** Bystricky shares accounts of students approaching their city councils to propose the right to vote. Write an imaginary dialogue between a young person and a councilperson who opposes the idea of allowing anyone under the age of 18 to vote. Try to communicate elements of each person's character and motivations through your choice of dialogue.

The Road to Change

David Hogg

Emma McIntyre/Getty Images

David Hogg (b. 2000) was a student at Marjory Stoneman Douglas High School in Parkland, Florida, the site of a school shooting on February 14, 2018, that left 17 people dead and many others wounded. In the aftermath of the shooting, Hogg and several of his classmates became outspoken advocates for stricter gun-control legislation, helping to form the organization March for Our Lives to raise awareness of gun violence. The following piece was originally published in a collection in 2018 called *We Say #Never Again*, written by Parkland student journalists.

It is hard to believe that all of this has happened in the same calendar year. From our lives as normal high school students, to activists born of tragedy, to caricatures of the gun lobby and many of their supporters, 2018 has changed our lives forever and set us on a path to effect sane gun laws for America once and for all.

The shooting at our school also sent me and my friends on a journey into the heart of our country, and on this journey we have discovered that Americans are more divided than ever before. These divisions are exploited and encouraged by those at the top, the people we once called "leaders," who are supposed to make our democracy function, smooth over our differences, and lead us toward solutions to our problems. Instead, our "leaders" too often have us at each other's throats and encourage us to think the very worst of each other, which only hardens positions and hearts, reinforces biases, and closes minds and ears. This is no way for adults to behave, and no way to solve problems, much less run a country.

This is the world that we are trying to change. These polarized politics existed before February 14, 2018, and it is obviously not just about gun violence and not just about the Second Amendment. There are deep cultural chasms in the country — regional, religious, economic, political — and all of us find it too easy to go to our corners with our tribes when a serious and divisive issue comes up. The mistrust in this country is just intolerable. This politics of dehumanization dehumanizes us all and makes it easier to be perpetual, intractable enemies, forever unable to even talk to each other. But the dirty little secret is that this just plays into the hands of the powerful lobbies, because that way the status quo prevails, kids remain at risk in their schools and communities, and nothing ever changes for the better. It is only by looking each other in the eye and speaking from the heart that we will have a chance to understand each other, respectfully explain ourselves to each other, *rehumanize* each other, and defeat the deeply troubling vision that we have discovered of an America forever reduced to warring camps. I believe in my heart that very few people want to live like that.

As I begin to write this — from Bismarck, North Dakota — the March For Our Lives group is preparing for a rally in our Road to Change tour. This evening, we are projected to have a good group at the rally — here to talk about sensible solutions to our undeniable problem of gun violence, register to vote, maybe volunteer, but that crowd is also expected to be dwarfed by protesters. And one task that we could not have counted on having to do when we first got started in this effort is having to clear up so much slander that has been spread about us — in my case, especially, the nonsense that I was not at Marjory Stoneman Douglas High School that day, that I was not even a student there, that I am a professional "crisis actor," that I am ABC news anchor David Muir, that I am a shape-shifting lizard, etc., etc., etc.

These are the times in which we live. 5

When my friends and I survived the murder of seventeen of our schoolmates, we felt compelled to enter into an arena that was alien to us — politics — with the goal of being engaged citizens and appealing for commonsense laws to change the circumstances that made our friends' murders possible. I am not sure what we thought the response of the world would be, but to see a fictional villainous version of yourself emerge from internet trolls and ideologues and Alex Jones, well, that certainly is something I never imagined. And because there have been so many outrageous and untrue things written and said about us, the protesters we meet often expect the absolute worst at first. They are angry and worked up, calling us "gun grabbers" and things like that. It takes a long time to undo that misconception, to show a human face, to persuade people who have been conditioned to hate us and our views that we aren't the bogeymen that they have been told we are.

All of this takes patience and kindness, qualities that sometimes honestly are in short supply. But it is the only thing to do, because, to quote that wise saying, you've got to be the change you wish to see in the world. And screaming and yelling and calling people stupid is not only rude, but it will also accomplish precisely nothing. When you are going to new towns and asking to be heard, the most important thing you can do is listen to the people who live there. Hear their stories, learn their perspectives, find connections, because they are there. Before we are Democrats or Republicans, red

JIM WATSON/AFP/Getty Images

This photograph was taken during the March for Our Lives Rally in Washington, DC, in 2018. In the center of the picture is Emma Gonzalez, who became politically active after the tragedy at her school, along with David Hogg and other Parkland students.

What message does this photo seem to communicate, and how might Hogg respond to the photo based on what you have read?

or blue, we are all human. We all have experienced loss and pain and joy. We all have families and friends and hometowns. As John Kennedy once said when talking about resolving the differences of a different time, "We all inhabit this small planet. We all breathe the same air. We all cherish our children's future. And we are all mortal."

Please do not misunderstand me — our goals to make America safer do involve political solutions, and politics asks you to make choices. One candidate over another, one value judgment over another, one solution over another. Democracy is by nature about choices, and choices can be divisive. We will fight for our goals, we will not relent, and we will not give up. But we in March For Our Lives have learned through this baptism by fire in 2018 that the world is not improved by vilifying each other. In addition to being childish and wrong, vilification is also inefficient, in that it is a terrible way to achieve your desired result, and so we'll leave the vilification to other people as we set about in good faith to convert our pain and loss into action that changes our world for the better.

We will continue to talk to any audience in any town anywhere to convey the simple, strong message that commonsense legislation does not mean taking your guns away — it means saving lives. And we will continue to work during the coming election and all the elections to follow to support moral candidates who will value lives over lobbyist dollars and common sense over ideology. And we will continue to describe things as they are, and to tell the truth — about who is and who is not a captive of the gun lobby, which seeks to keep us afraid and keep us divided. We will continue to use the technologies available to us to address the whole world, even as we cherish meeting and talking to new individuals in town after town, whether we agree or disagree.

What is this editorial cartoon suggesting about David Hogg and about CNN? In what ways does this cartoon reflect what Hogg says in his article about how he has been portrayed?

10 The anger we felt after February 14 may have been our initial adrenaline in this marathon, but love and compassion will be what keep us going. We won't reach everybody — some people will have no interest in hearing our perspective, and that's okay. But we will reach a lot more people than have been reached in the past, when all sides have been stuck in their well-dug trenches, hurling rocks and mortars at each other.

And in this spirit, sure enough, around Independence Day, our Road to Change tour found itself in Dallas, Texas, a proud place of independent-minded people who like to openly carry their weapons in public places, but who also live in a state where a majority — 51 percent — favor more commonsense gun laws. And even more Texans than that favor universal background checks. *In Texas.* As we were doing everywhere, we were in Dallas to talk and to listen. As several of us stepped outside the venue where our rally was taking place to meet the protesters who had assembled there, an armed man asked me why I wanted to take his gun away. I told him that I didn't, and that members of my family owned guns. A larger group gathered around, both people with guns and people without, and ninety minutes later, after a sometimes contentious, sometimes very emotional conversation, that man thanked us for helping him understand why we are doing what we are doing. It was as if he had never experienced an honest exchange of ideas before. It was as if he had never been accorded that level of respect for his thoughts. We thanked the man in return.

In the days after that encounter, a few stories appeared in the press. One headline read: "Parkland students and gun owners got into a heated debate that ended in tears and hugs." Of all the headlines in this terribly sad and wondrous year, that headline just might be my favorite.

Onward. ■

Understanding and Interpreting

1. How does Hogg build his ethos in the first two paragraphs of his piece? Why might he have felt the need to do so?
2. In paragraph 3, Hogg describes the divisions between "tribes" in the United States. What does he say causes these divisions? What is his proposed solution?
3. What does Hogg mean in paragraph 6 when he says that he has to "show a human face"? Why does he think this is so important for creating change?
4. Why might Hogg have used the quote by John Kennedy in paragraph 7?
5. Reread paragraph 8 and explain what Hogg identifies as the challenges that he and his group face in a democracy like that of the United States.
6. In paragraphs 11 and 12, Hogg describes the encounter with the group of people in Dallas. What message is the reader expected to draw from that example?

Analyzing Language, Style, and Structure

1. **Vocabulary in Context.** In paragraph 3, Hogg writes, "There are deep culture chasms in the country." What does the word "chasm" mean in this context? What is a "chasm" in the natural world? How does that meaning relate to Hogg's use of the word?
2. **Skill Focus.** Reread paragraphs 4 through 6. Think about how Hogg inserts himself and his experiences into the argument. In what ways do these moments strengthen or weaken his argument?
3. Why does Hogg use quotation marks around the word "leaders" in paragraph 2?
4. What does Hogg accomplish by writing "etc., etc., etc." at the end of paragraph 4?
5. Look back at some of the word choices Hogg has made to describe his group's gun control proposals, such as "sensible solutions," "our undeniable problem," and "laws." How do these phrases reflect his position, and how might someone who disagrees with his position react to these word choices?
6. Throughout his piece, Hogg has used "we" to refer to himself and his fellow students. In paragraph 7, however, he uses "we" a little differently. Describe this shift and its likely effect on readers.
7. At the end of paragraph 10, Hogg compares the fight he and his group are in to warfare. What does he hope to accomplish with this analogy? Is it effective or not?
8. Why did Hogg repeat "In Texas" and put it in italics in paragraph 11?
9. What is the effect of the single word paragraph that ends this essay?

Topics for Composing

1. **Analysis.** Explain why listening and generating dialogue are crucial when trying to create lasting change, according to Hogg.
2. **Argument.** Consider Hogg's statement that "Americans are more divided than ever before. These divisions are exploited and encouraged by those at the top." Do you agree or disagree? Support your position with examples from your own experiences or from what you have read or seen in the news.
3. **Argument.** The Second Amendment to the U.S. Constitution says, "A well-regulated Militia, being necessary to the security of a free State, the right of the people to keep and bear Arms, shall not be infringed." Using the Second Amendment as at least one piece of

evidence to support your position, write an argument for or against tighter gun control legislation.

4. **Connection.** In paragraph 5, Hogg says, "These are the times in which we live." How are your experiences with "the times" similar to or different from what Hogg describes?
5. **Speaking and Listening.** Hold a conversation with a partner or a small group about a contentious issue that you all feel strongly about. As you discuss the issue, be sure to listen actively to each other. When you are done, discuss what it was like to talk through an issue that you are all passionate about, especially if you disagreed with one another. What have you learned from Hogg that might help you and those who disagree with you move beyond disagreement, toward understanding and change?
6. **Research.** Hogg states that some people, including politicians, are "captive to the gun lobby." Conduct research to find out what the "gun lobby" is. What are their goals and what methods do they use to achieve them? Based on your research, is Hogg's animosity toward the gun lobby reasonable or extreme?

I'm Not Ready for the Redemption of Men

Amber Tamblyn

David Livingston/Getty Images

Amber Tamblyn (b. 1983) is an American actress, director, poet, and activist. She appeared in the soap opera *General Hospital* as a child, appeared in the film series *The Sisterhood of the Traveling Pants*, starred in the TV show *Joan of Arcadia*, and had recurring roles on shows such as *House*, *Two and a Half Men*, and *Inside Amy Schumer*. Tamblyn was one of the founding members of the Time's Up Organization, working against sexual harassment in the workplace. In addition, she wrote an explosive editorial called "I'm Done with Not Being Believed," in which she recounted the numerous incidents of sexual harassment she faced as a Hollywood actress. This piece, a follow-up to that editorial, was published in the *New York Times* on November 27, 2017.

KEY CONTEXT Several incidents of sexual harassment and sexual abuse triggered the #MeToo movement, within which Tamblyn plays a significant role. While the phrase "Me Too" connected to sexual assault is traced back to activist Tarana Burke, the term and the hashtag grew to prominence with the allegations of abuse against movie producer Harvey Weinstein by many famous actresses, including Alyssa Milano, in 2017. This piece also refers to other men, including the comedian Louis C. K., who admitted to several incidents of sexual misconduct in 2017. The comedian had a film pulled from distribution and his tour canceled in the aftermath, though he soon after began appearing onstage again.

Recently, I was sitting on my couch between two influential, Emmy-winning writers, one a man and one a woman. We were talking about consequences. The comedian Louis C. K.'s entire life seemed to have been canceled overnight. His movie wasn't being released, and his representatives dropped him after five women accused him of sexual harassment, behavior he then admitted. In just the past week, more famous and admired men have lost their jobs for such behaviors. Enter Charlie Rose and Matt Lauer right behind him and then Garrison Keillor.

The man on the couch next to me was disconcerted, making an argument that while Louis C. K.'s actions certainly merited serious consequences, what he did and what Harvey Weinstein did are two very different things. We shouldn't lump them all together, he insisted. The woman was firm with her response: "Yes, we can and we will. Choosing consequences doesn't belong to you anymore."

The man balked with frustration. "What do you want?" he asked her. "What's the ultimate thing you would want to happen to him, for what he did? That he never works in this business again?" The woman said, simply: "Yes. That's the price you pay." The man was quiet for a moment, thinking, until he found the question he'd been looking for the entire conversation. "Tell me something: Do you believe in redemption?"

It's a valid question. But it's also a question that makes me deeply suspicious of its timing. Why do we need to talk about the redemption of men when we are right in the middle of the salvation of women? Not even the middle, but the very beginning? Why are we obligated to care about salvaging male careers when we have just begun to tell the stories that have plagued us for lifetimes? It seems some men like a revolution only when it's their kind of war.

Throughout history, women haven't been in 5
a position to come forward with their stories and be taken seriously as a rule. That's the reason we sometimes wait 20 years to report something — harassment, assault — if we say anything at all. We haven't been silent because we forgot or made our stories up. We've been silent because we've been silenced. But women now feel comfortable telling such stories. And maybe even more important, we are seeing consequences for those actions. This is more than a watershed moment — it's a flash-flood point.

extending beyond the text

Read this excerpt written in response to news reports that New York Attorney General Eric Schneiderman had sexually abused at least four women. Note the language and word choices that Howe uses to describe this incident, as well as the #MeToo movement in general.

from After #MeToo, What's Next?

Neil Howe

#MeToo has claimed its latest victim: New York Attorney General Eric Schneiderman, one of the movement's most prominent advocates, has resigned amid accusations of sexual abuse. This comes on the heels of Bill Cosby's conviction on three counts of sexual assault. The nationwide reckoning on sexual harassment began late last year in the wake of accusations against Hollywood mogul Harvey Weinstein. Since then, a torrent of new allegations has surfaced, toppling the careers of dozens of powerful men as millions of victims have come forward. Those behind this #MeToo movement have launched a global conversation, one that Time magazine's editor-in-chief called "one of the highest velocity shifts in our culture since the 1960s."

Based on your examination of what Howe says and the words he uses to say it, how would you describe his attitude toward #MeToo?

Not everyone in my industry is in support of how quickly things are moving. There's a lot of collateral-damage dread, a cloud of unease that has covered the industry lately with talk of potentially harmful side effects of such decisive actions. What if an innocent man is falsely accused? What if the repercussion doesn't fit the crime? What ever happened to innocent until proved guilty?

That's why the male writer wanted to talk about redemption. The idea appeals to the men I've been talking with, I believe, because they want a sense of normalcy restored. They want measured discussion of consequences, not swift punishment. They want us to leave poor Al Franken and his harmless grabbing alone. I've heard several male friends talk about text chains they are on with other men only; they describe it as a safe space to talk about how they feel in this moment. They feel afraid, disoriented and discounted. And I understand their need for such comfort and security. I am a woman. I know nothing other than needing such comfort and security, for my entire life.

We're in the midst of a reckoning. It's what toxic masculinity's own medicine tastes like. And people should allow the consequences to unfold, regardless of how it affects those they consider to be friends. The only way to enforce seismic, cultural change in the way men relate to women is to draw a line deep in the sand and say: This is what we will no longer tolerate. You're either with our bodies or against our bodies. The punishment for harassment is you disappear. The punishment for rape is you disappear. . . . The punishment for coercion is you disappear.

Angelica Frausto in series "I'm Tired of Performing Trauma," The Nib, InkWell Management

What is artist Angelica Frausto suggesting about #MeToo in this short graphic story? How does she communicate this point visually? How do you think Tamblyn would respond to this visual?

This new rule upsets many people, men and women. But what they don't seem to understand is, no one is saying a disappearance from the public eye has to be forever. (Well, Harvey Weinstein is forever.) I'm not talking about banishment. I'm talking about ceding the floor. The power of celebrity and cultural approval must disappear for the time being so that all women see and believe that consequences do exist.

10 In that discussion about redemption on my couch, the woman said to the man: "Look, do I believe Louis C. K. is going to come back in a year or so with a lot of reflection about what he did? Yes, I do. When he goes back out on that standup tour someday, I'll roll my eyes and say, 'All right, get on with it, then.' But for now, his old power is over. He's going to have to find a new power if he ever wants to come back."

A new power. Can there be one for men, free of humiliation, shame and violent assault against women? Women who are their wives, daughters, mothers and friends sitting next to them on couches? And what would it take to achieve it? That's the question for men and their text chains right now, not the question of how soon they can ask about redemption. Redemption must be preceded by atonement. It is earned, not offered. If you want amends, you have to make them. You have to acknowledge the line in the sand. Once you do this, the next step is simple: Pick a side. Choose us. ■

Understanding and Interpreting

1. Tamblyn starts her piece by describing a conversation between a man and a woman, both Hollywood writers, who are discussing the comedian Louis C. K. Summarize their two points of view. Where do they agree and disagree with each other? What is the effect of talking about a man and a woman (rather than two men or two women) expressing these viewpoints?
2. What does Tamblyn mean when she asks, "Why do we need to talk about the redemption of men when we are right in the middle of the salvation of women?" (par. 4).
3. Tamblyn claims that perpetrators should face swift consequences for their actions. In paragraph 6, she addresses a key counterargument to her claim. How does she characterize and address this counterargument from others in the entertainment industry?
4. What is Tamblyn's response to those who claim that some men are feeling "afraid, disoriented, and discounted" (par. 7)?
5. Tamblyn states that she is trying to "enforce seismic, cultural change" (par. 8). What does she say must happen to create and maintain this change?
6. Explain what Tamblyn means by "ceding the floor" (par. 9).
7. The woman on the couch says that Louis C. K. will need a new power if he wants to come back into the public space. According to Tamblyn in the last paragraph, what will this new power require?
8. Overall, do you think that Tamblyn is optimistic or pessimistic about the chances that Hollywood will change? What leads you to this conclusion?

Analyzing Language, Style, and Structure

1. **Vocabulary in Context.** In paragraph 4, Tamblyn asks why we should care about salvaging male careers. What does the word "salvaging" mean in this context? What are other things that can be salvaged? What connotation does the word carry in this context?
2. **Skill Focus.** Even though Tamblyn does not include any stories about her own relevant experiences in this piece, she does have a presence as a woman working in Hollywood during

the time of #MeToo. How does this presence come across in this piece? How does it help her communicate her point?

3. Tamblyn oftentimes casts this conflict in terms of warfare. Explain her use of the following analogy here: "It seems like men like a revolution only when it's their kind of war" (par. 4)?
4. Look back through her piece, and note when Tamblyn uses the pronouns "we" (especially in par. 5), "our" (par. 8), or "us" (par. 11). What effect does she create with these pronouns? Does their use make her argument stronger or more limited? Why?
5. Paragraph 5 starts off with "Throughout history," and includes a summary and explanation of what preceded the #MeToo movement. What purpose does this paragraph play in her argument? Why might she have placed it where she did?
6. Reread paragraph 8. What does Tamblyn achieve through the repetition and parallelism at the end of the paragraph?
7. In paragraph 9, Tamblyn uses the "yes, but" method of addressing those who might think differently. Describe how Tamblyn uses this approach and explain how effective it might be for making her argument.

Topics for Composing

1. **Analysis.** The word "redemption" appears in the title and is repeated throughout. Explain how Tamblyn defines redemption and under what conditions perpetrators can ever attain it. How does the idea of "redemption" relate to lasting change, according to Tamblyn?
2. **Argument.** What is the most appropriate punishment for personalities, politicians, athletes, and other famous people who are in positions of power and have been credibly accused of sexually inappropriate behavior that is not necessarily illegal?
3. **Connection.** Tamblyn refers to "toxic masculinity" in her piece. Writer Harris O'Malley defines this phrase as "a narrow and repressive description of manhood, designating manhood as defined by violence, sex, status, and aggression. It's the cultural ideal of manliness, where strength is everything while emotions are a weakness." Explain whether you agree or disagree with this definition, based on your own understanding of the term and personal experiences of gender norms.
4. **Connection.** Several of the men accused during #MeToo, including John Hockenberry, Jian Ghomeshi, and others, have written responses online defending their actions and trying to clear their names. Choose one, read it carefully, and write an explanation about how Tamblyn would respond. Would it meet her definition of "atonement"?
5. **Speaking and Listening.** Talk with someone of a different gender or with someone who does not identify as either gender about your reaction to the issues raised in this piece. Listen carefully to the other person's response and then discuss the ways that people's gender identities may or may not affect attitudes toward #MeToo.
6. **Research.** Find out what has happened to some of the "famous and admired men who have lost their jobs" in the wake of #MeToo. How long did they stay out of the public eye? Did their careers suffer?
7. **Multimodal.** Create a poster appropriate for your school in which you present information and resources that support people who have experienced sexual abuse or misconduct. Be sure to consider a combination of text and images that would not only be engaging for the viewer, but also appropriate for hanging in a public space.
8. **Exposition.** Define "cancel" or "call-out" culture, using this article and other sources. Who are some people who have been "canceled," and how has this kind of protest affected them and society?

How to Get People to Change Their Minds

Denise Cummins

Denise D. Cummins

Denise D. Cummins, PhD, is a research psychologist, a fellow of the Association for Psychological Science, and the author of over 40 scholarly works, including *Good Thinking: Seven Powerful Ideas That Influence the Way We Think.* She has held faculty and research positions at Yale University, the University of California, and the University of Illinois. In addition, Cummins has been an invited scientist at the Max Planck Institute for Human Development in Berlin. The following piece appeared in *Psychology Today* on February 25, 2016.

As the saying goes, "All the world is mad except for me and thee, and I'm not too sure of thee."

This is the reaction many of us have when people express opinions that differ markedly from our own. And then, of course, we try to change their minds.

If we were all entirely rational, then our beliefs would be grounded in logic and evidence, and changing our beliefs would simply be a matter of presenting a logical argument backed up by objective evidence. In fact, this is how we educate students to "think critically." It is also how our politicians and lawmakers debate issues.

Yet this is rarely effective.

5 Consider [the] study by Lord, Ross and Leppner (1979), which used a very realistic procedure to examine whether logic and evidence lead people to change their minds: People supporting and opposing capital punishment were asked to read two studies, one that confirmed and one that disconfirmed their existing beliefs about the death penalty. The studies were fictional, but were described as actual published research. They were then asked of each study, "Has this study changed the way you feel toward capital punishment?", and "Has this study changed your beliefs about the deterrent efficacy of the death penalty?" Then they were given summaries of several prominent criticisms of the study, and the authors' rebuttals to the criticisms.

The results? The two groups became more certain of their original position, and, as a result, the groups became more polarized in their beliefs!

Why? Because people are likely to examine relevant evidence in a biased manner, accepting evidence that is consistent with their views

"Research suggests that using facts and logic to try to change someone's mind just makes them believe their original position even more. So I'm thinking we just forget this unit and enjoy some extra recess."

©Mark Anderson, www.Andertoons.com

As you know, persuasive writing is a common assignment in an English class.

To what extent might Cummins agree with the student in this image?

without further scrutiny while subjecting evidence that contradicts their views to intense scrutiny.

Researchers at Cornell University recently took a different approach[1] to the question of how to get people to change their minds: They analyzed social media.

ChangeMyView is an active . . . community of over 200,000 members on Reddit that allows users to present their opinions and to invite others to contest them. If the ensuing discussion causes them to change their minds, they acknowledge that they've changed their minds and explain what in particular it was that they found persuasive. Some of the opinions posted included: "People don't define who they are, their genetics and environment do," "Zoos are immoral," and "I think that the vast majority of Bernie supporters are selfish and ill-informed." That last one received over a thousand comments in one day.

10 The researchers analyzed a number of factors, including the number of people who responded, the order in which their responses occurred in the discussion, and how the responses were worded.

Some of the results jibed with common sense:

- Persuasive arguments tended to use calm words rather than emotional words (such as *terrorist*) or "dominant" words that imply control (such as *completion*).
- They tended to be longer, including greater numbers of sentences and paragraphs. In other words, one-liners and rants rarely persuade people.
- It was also heartening to find that posts containing citation links to external sites were more persuasive. So evidence does seem to play a role in changing minds.
- Original posters who use the word "I" rather than "we" when describing their opinion tend to be more open to persuasion, as are those who avoid using dominant, emotional, or "superlative" words (such as "worst" and "dumbest").

Other results were more surprising:

- Words that are emotionally neutral or slightly "downbeat" are more persuasive than upbeat, happy words.

[1] Tan, Chenhao, et al. "Winning Arguments: Interaction Dynamics and Persuasion Strategies in Good-faith Online Discussions." Cornell University, February 2, 2016. https://arxiv.org/pdf/1602.01103v1.pdf

- Using words that are different from the ones used by the original poster is more effective than using the same words. The researchers interpreted this to mean that different words signal a different point of view.
- "Hedging" language (such as "it could be the case") is usually labeled "weak" because it signals uncertainty. Yet arguments containing such language were, surprisingly, more persuasive than those without. The researchers suggest that is because "they may make an argument easier to accept by softening its tone." In other words, people are not open to persuasion when they feel they are being bulldozed, conquered, proved wrong, or dominated by their opponent.
- Arguments presented early in the thread are more likely to persuade than those presented later, and that was true regardless of the expertise of the responder. In fact, the first two challengers were three times more likely to succeed at persuading than the tenth challenger. In back-and-forth dialogues between the original poster and a responder, the results were crystal clear: If you haven't persuaded the person by the fourth round, you never will.
- Initial analyses indicated that the greater the number of challengers, the higher the likelihood of success in changing the original poster's mind. But subsequent analyses indicated single-challenger threads consistently outperformed multiple-challenger threads in terms of conversion rate. According to the authors, *"This observation suggests that the sheer number of challengers is not necessarily associated with higher chances of conversion."*

Perhaps the most interesting outcome (and least surprising from an educator's viewpoint) is that using specific examples is a powerful persuasion technique. One picture is worth a thousand words, and one example is worth an hour of lecture.

This artwork by illustrator Gérard DuBois appeared in an article called "Why Facts Don't Change Our Minds" in *The New Yorker*. **What point is the artist making about our ability to digest new information? Consider the images in the piece as well as the figure's posture and expression. Why would Cummins likely agree or disagree with what the image seems to convey?**

I was disappointed to find, however, that the researchers did not investigate one type of specific example that is perhaps the most persuasive of all, and that is analogy and metaphor. As I said in a previous post:

> When Federal Reserve Chief Ben Bernanke appeared on the TV news show 60 Minutes to persuade us to bail out the banking system, he didn't bother with charts, figures, or lengthy argument. Instead, he used something far more powerful: Analogy and metaphor.
>
> Imagine, he explained, that you have an irresponsible neighbor who smokes in bed, and sets fire to his house. Should you call the fire department, or should you simply walk

away and let him face the consequences of his actions? What if your house — indeed all the houses in the entire neighborhood — are also made of wood? We all agree, he argued, that under those circumstances, we should focus on putting out the fire first. Then we can turn to the issues of assigning blame or punishment, re-writing the fire code, and putting fail-safes in place.

15 This was a powerful analogy. It communicated the clear and present danger to the economy and the urgency of implementing his proposed solution . . . Lawyers use analogies frequently to draw parallels between an undecided case and a case that has already been decided (a precedent) . . . Some legal scholars, such as Lloyd Weinreb, go so far as to argue that without analogy, a court's decision is incomplete. It is that important in explaining and justifying legal judgments.

[A]rguments based on analogies and metaphors are so powerful that you need to know how to evaluate them so that you are not misled. ■

Understanding and Interpreting

1. According to Cummins in paragraph 3, what does it mean to "think critically"? What does Cummins suggest about this skill?
2. Summarize what Cummins concludes about the findings of the study by Lord, Ross, and Leppner.
3. Explain why, according to the study by researchers at Cornell University, certain language choices are more effective than others at persuading people to change their minds.
4. Why might the number of challengers to an argument affect its ability to persuade readers?
5. In paragraph 14, Cummins describes what she feels is a component of effective arguments: the use of analogy and metaphor. Explain how this component works in an argument and why, according to Cummins, it can be so effective.

Analyzing Language, Style, and Structure

1. **Vocabulary in Context.** In paragraph 6, Cummins uses the word "polarized," which is a scientific term applied to a nonscientific context. What does the word mean here, and how is that meaning similar to or different from its scientific use? What other scientific terms can you think of that are also used in nonscientific contexts?
2. **Skill Focus.** According to Cummins, what did the researchers conclude about the effect of personal experience in argument?
3. Cummins begins her piece with a common saying. Why might she have done so? What does it accomplish?
4. Evaluate Cummins's piece for its use of rhetorical appeals (ethos, logos, pathos). Where is her argument strongest in its use of appeals, and where could her argument have been strengthened by additional appeals?

Topics for Composing

1. **Analysis.** In paragraphs 3 and 4, Cummins says changing beliefs by "presenting a logical argument backed up by objective evidence . . . is rarely effective." Evaluate Cummins's

argument. To what extent does her argument use objective evidence, personal experience, and other tools of persuasion. Point to specific examples from her text in your response.

2. **Argument.** See Cummins's bullet lists summarizing the research results on pages 182–183. In these lists, Cummins notes which rhetorical moves or strategies make arguments more and less persuasive, according to the research. Select one of these points to focus on and write an argument that either supports or refutes the researchers' conclusions. You can refer to your own experiences and/or conduct additional research to support your point of view.
3. **Connection.** Has a conversation or something you've watched or read ever succeeded in changing your mind on an issue you care deeply about? If so, why was the message and its delivery so effective? If not, why did the message fail to persuade you? In your discussion, be sure to consider elements Cummins describes.
4. **Speaking and Listening.** Try out Cummins's suggestions by holding a debate about an issue in which one person or group uses only objective evidence, while another uses a variety of types of evidence. Afterward, evaluate each side's approach. Was one approach more effective than the other? Explain your response.
5. **Research.** Go to Reddit or a similar site where ideas on various topics are discussed. Find an idea that interests you and examine the arguments, using the results that Cummins identifies on pages 182–183. What did you notice about the language (calm, downbeat, upbeat, emotionally neutral, hedging, etc.), the types of evidence, and the number of challengers? To what extent do your observations back up or refute Cummins's own discussion?
6. **Multimodal.** Create two posters about an issue that you feel strongly about. Use the same visuals and clear claim in both. But, in one of the posters, use the types of language and evidence that Cummins identifies as least effective. In the other, use what she identifies as most effective, including the use of analogy and metaphor. Show your posters to as many people as possible. Determine whether your conclusions match those of Cummins.
7. **Creative Writing.** Write a short scene from a play in which one character tries to persuade another character of an idea. Describe the set, costumes, props, lighting, and other aspects of the stage. Be sure that the dialogue you use reflects the characters and uses some of the approaches that Cummins recommends.

What if We're All Coming Back?

Michelle Alexander

Ben Garvin/The New York Times/Redux Pictures

A civil rights lawyer and advocate, and a *New York Times* columnist, Michelle Alexander (b. 1967) is the author of *The New Jim Crow: Mass Incarceration in the Age of Colorblindness*. As director of the Racial Justice Project at the ACLU of Northern California, she led a national campaign against racial profiling by law enforcement. Alexander was a law clerk for Justice Harry Blackmun at the U.S. Supreme Court. A visiting professor at the Union Theological Seminary in the City of New York, she explores the moral and spiritual aspects of mass incarceration. The following piece was published in the *New York Times* on October 29, 2018.

I can't say that I believe in reincarnation, but I understand why some people do. In fact, I had a bizarre experience as a teenager that made me wonder if I had known someone in a past life.

I was walking to school one day, lost in thought. I turned the corner onto a wide, tree-lined street and noticed a man on the other side heading my direction. For an instant, we held each other's gaze and a startling wave of excitement and recognition washed over me. We spontaneously ran toward each other, as if to embrace a long-lost friend, relative or lover. But just as we were close enough to see the other's face, we were both jolted by the awareness that we didn't actually know each other.

We stood in the middle of the street, bewildered. I mumbled, "I'm so sorry — I thought I knew you." Equally embarrassed, he replied: "Oh, my God, this is so strange. What's happening right now?" We backed away awkwardly — me, a teenage black girl; he, a middle-aged white man. I never saw him again.

The incident shook me deeply. This was not a case of mistaken identity. Something profound and mysterious happened and we both knew it. Still, I'm not among the 33 percent of Americans (including 29 percent of Christians) who believe in reincarnation. Lately, though, I've been thinking that if more of us did believe we were coming back, it could change everything.

At first, I thought about reincarnation in the 5
narrowest possible terms, wondering what future life I'd earn if karma proved real. It's a worrisome thing to contemplate. It's easier to speculate about what kind of future lives other people deserve. Maybe Bull Connor — that white supremacist Alabama politician who ordered that black schoolchildren protesting segregation be attacked with police dogs and fire hoses — has already been born again as a black child in a

What point is this cartoon making, and how does it compare to what Alexander is suggesting?

neighborhood lacking jobs and decent schools but filled with police officers who shoot first and ask questions later. Maybe he's now subjected to the very forms of bigotry, terror and structural racism that he once gleefully inflicted on others.

This kind of thought experiment is obviously dangerous, since it can tempt us to imagine that people have somehow earned miserable fates and deserve to suffer. But considering future lives can also be productive, challenging us to imagine that what we do or say in this life matters and might eventually catch up with us. Would we fail to respond with care and compassion to the immigrant at the border today if we thought we might find ourselves homeless, fleeing war and poverty, in the next life? Imagining ourselves in those shoes makes it harder to say: "Well, they're not here legally. Let's build a wall to keep those people out." After all, one day "those people" might be you.

Once I entered college, I found myself less interested in karma and more interested in politics. It occurred to me that if we're born again at random, we can't soothe ourselves with fantasies that we'll come back as one of the precious few on the planet who live comfortably. We must face the fact that our destiny is inextricably linked to the fate of others. What kind of political, social and economic system would I want — and what would I fight for — if I knew I was coming back somewhere in the world but didn't know where and didn't know who I'd be?

In law school, I discovered that I wasn't the first to ponder this type of question. In his landmark 1971 book, "A Theory of Justice," the political philosopher John Rawls urged his audience to imagine a wild scene: A group of people gathered to design their own future society behind "a veil of ignorance." No one knows his or her place in society, class position or social status, "nor does he know his fortune in the distribution of natural assets and abilities, his intelligence and strength and the like." As Rawls put it, "If a man knew that he was wealthy, he might find it rational to advance the principle that various taxes for welfare measures be counted unjust; if he knew he was poor, he would most likely propose the contrary principle." If denied basic information about one's circumstances, Rawls predicted that important social goods, such as rights and liberties, power and opportunities, income and wealth, and conditions for self-respect would be "distributed equally unless an unequal distribution of any or all of these values is to everyone's advantage."

Back then, I was struck by how closely Rawls's views mirrored my own. I now believe, however, that the veil of ignorance is quite distorted in an important respect. Rawls's veil encourages us to imagine a scenario in which we're equally likely to be rich or poor or born with natural talents or limitations. But the truth is, if we're reborn in 50 years, there's only a small chance that any of us would be rich or benefit from white privilege.

Almost half the world — more than three 10
billion people — live on less than $2.50 per day. At least 80 percent of humanity lives on less than $10 per day. Less than 7 percent of the world's population has a college degree. The vast majority of the earth's population is nonwhite, and roughly half are women. Unless radical change sweeps the globe, the chances are high that any of us would come back as a nonwhite woman living on less than $2.50 per day. And given what we now know about climate change, the chances are very good that we would find ourselves suffering as a result of natural disasters — hurricanes, tsunamis, droughts and floods — and enduring water and food shortages and refugee crises.

This month, the world's leading climate scientists released a report warning of catastrophic consequences as soon as 2040[1] if global warming increases at its current rate. Democratic politicians expressed alarm, yet many continue to accept campaign contributions from the fossil fuel industry that is responsible for such a large percentage of the world's greenhouse gas emissions[2].

It's nearly impossible to imagine that our elected officials would be so indifferent if they knew climate scientists were foretelling a future that they would have to live without any of the privileges they now enjoy.

Rawls was right: True morality becomes possible only when we step outside the box of our perceived self-interest and care for others as much as we care for ourselves. But rather than imagining a scenario in which we're entirely ignorant of what the future holds, perhaps we ought to imagine that we, personally, will be born again into the world that we are creating today through our collective and individual choices.

Who among us would fail to question capitalism or to demand a political system free from corporate cash if we knew that we'd likely live our next life as a person of color, earning

[1] Davenport, Coral. "Major Climate Report Describes a Strong Risk of Crisis as Early as 2040." *The New York Times*, October 7, 2018. https://www.nytimes.com/2018/10/07/climate/ipcc-climate-report-2040.html?module=inline

[2] Griffin, Paul. "CDP Carbon Majors Report 2017." CDP, July 2017. https://b8f65cb373b1b7b15feb-c70d8ead6ced550b4d987d7c03fcdd1d.ssl.cf3.rackcdn.com/cms/reports/documents/000/002/327/original/Carbon-Majors-Report-2017.pdf?1499691240

extending beyond the text

The British philosopher John Stuart Mill (1806–1873) supported the philosophy of "utilitarianism," which sought to create the greatest amount of good for the greatest number. Read the following excerpt from his book *Utilitarianism* (1861):

from Utilitarianism

John Stuart Mill

> This firm foundation is that of the social feelings of mankind; the desire to be in unity with our fellow creatures, which is already a powerful principle in human nature, and happily one of those which tend to become stronger, even without express inculcation, from the influences of advancing civilisation. The social state is at once so natural, so necessary, and so habitual to man, that, except in some unusual circumstances or by an effort of voluntary abstraction, he never conceives himself otherwise than as a member of a body; and this association is riveted more and more, as mankind are further removed from the state of savage independence. . . .
>
> They are also familiar with the fact of co-operating with others, and proposing to themselves a collective, not an individual interest as the aim (at least for the time being) of their actions. So long as they are co-operating, their ends are identified with those of others; there is at least a temporary feeling that the interests of others are their own interests. Not only does all strengthening of social ties, and all healthy growth of society, give to each individual a stronger personal interest in practically consulting the welfare of others; it also leads him to identify his *feelings* more and more with their good, or at least with an even greater degree of practical consideration for it. He comes, as though instinctively, to be conscious of himself as a being who *of course* pays regard to others. The good of others becomes to him a thing naturally and necessarily to be attended to, like any of the physical conditions of our existence.

How is Mill's approach similar to or different from Alexander's?

less than $2.50 a day, in some part of the world ravaged by climate change while private corporations earn billions building prisons, detention centers and border walls for profit?

Not I. And I'm willing to bet, neither would 15
you. We don't have to believe in reincarnation to fight for a world that we'd actually want to be born into. ■

Understanding and Interpreting

1. Reread paragraph 5 and explain how karma works, according to Alexander. In paragraph 6, why does Alexander conclude that thinking about reincarnation in these narrow terms could also be dangerous?
2. In describing her expanded thinking in college, what does Alexander suggest about the differences between karma and being born again at random?
3. Summarize the essential lessons that Alexander learned from reading the work of political philosopher John Rawls. In paragraphs 8 through 10, how does Alexander build on or repurpose Rawls's ideas?
4. Explain how Alexander uses the following idea from Rawls (found in paragraph 13) to support her own theories about combating climate change: "True morality becomes possible only when we step outside the box of our perceived self-interest and care for others as much as we care for ourselves." (par. 13)
5. Overall, based on what you have read, is Alexander hopeful or pessimistic about the future?

Analyzing Language, Style, and Structure

1. **Vocabulary in Context.** The word "alarm" is a common one that you encounter regularly, but look at its use in the following sentence in paragraph 11: "Democratic politicians expressed alarm, yet many continue . . ." What is its meaning in this context? What is something that you might express alarm about?
2. **Skill Focus.** Alexander starts her piece with a short narrative about an interaction with a stranger on the street. What was she likely trying to accomplish by including that personal experience? To what extent do you think it was an effective way to introduce her topic?
3. For the most part, Alexander adopts a neutral tone to describe the development of her moral philosophy, but look closely at paragraphs 10 through 12. How do her language choices create an emotional reaction in her readers? Explain why she may have made these language choices.
4. Paragraph 14 is one long rhetorical question. How is it intended to connect with her readers and lead them to the concluding paragraph?
5. Alexander has structured her piece in an unusual way in that her main point — using the idea of reincarnation to advocate for global environmental and economic action — doesn't come until more than halfway through the essay. Why might she have chosen to structure it this way? If she had placed her main point near the beginning, how might the effect have been different?

Topics for Composing

1. **Analysis.** Overall, why does Alexander believe that thinking about reincarnation is an effective tool for creating change in the world?
2. **Argument.** To what extent do you believe that thinking about reincarnation is an effective tool for combating issues like climate change? What are other factors that her proposal does not

account for, Use your own ideas and experiences, as well as additional research to support your position.

3. **Connection.** How might it affect your thinking if you were likely to live your "next life as a person . . . earning less than $2.50 a day"? What changes might you make in your world today?
4. **Speaking and Listening.** Locate a speech online of someone who is discussing the issue of global climate change. Listen to the speech carefully and write an explanation of why you do or do not think the speech was an effective one. Focus on both the content and the delivery of the speech.
5. **Research.** What world religions include belief in reincarnation or karma? Choose one to learn about, and compare its approach to reincarnation or karma to Alexander's ideas on the subject.
6. **Exposition.** Alexander identifies climate change and economic and racial inequalities as main issues that can be discussed effectively in terms of reincarnation. What are other issues that she does not identify that could also be explored with this line of thinking? Explain how this thought experiment could help provide perspective on these issues.

from Speech at UCLA

Dolores Huerta

Cathy Murphy/Getty Images

Dolores Huerta (b. 1930) is a labor organizer and civil rights activist. Along with Cesar Chavez in the 1960s, Huerta formed the United Farm Workers union, the first in the world to successfully gain bargaining and other rights for agricultural workers. One of her many accomplishments was the highly successful Delano Grape Strike, which was a widespread boycott of the fruit to push for better working conditions for those who picked it. Huerta is also credited with popularizing the phrase used by many protesters "Si, se puede," which roughly translates as "Yes, it can be done." She has won numerous awards for her activism, including the Presidential Medal of Freedom, during the ceremony for which President Obama quoted her as saying, 'Don't wait to be invited. Step in there." Huerta delivered the following speech to students at UCLA on February 22, 1978.

KEY CONTEXT Huerta references a hunger strike that Cesar Chavez, her friend and co-founder of the United Farm Workers union, went on for 24 days in 1968 to support the grape boycott. Presidential candidate Robert Kennedy visited him to show his support.

I saw the Martin Luther King movie the other day, how many of you saw that? The film that they have on the Martin Luther King struggle, did any of you see that? They had it on NBC the other day. In seeing that they were showing all of the things that had changed in the South like integration, people having the right to vote, and the tremendous changes that were made in a twelve-year period. And I remember we were organizing the union at the same time that these civil rights, the big organization was going on in the South, and we were almost organizing simultaneously when King was organizing. And I thought to myself, of all of the things that have changed for the farm workers in the last twelve years. . . .

Farm workers had no unemployment insurance. It wasn't until Governor Jerry Brown got in and there was an Assemblyman here from

Justin Chin/Bloomberg/Getty Images

Sonu Mehta/Hindustan Times/Getty Images

Erik McGregor/Pacific Press/Getty Images

These are images of various protests from around the world.

What similarities and differences do you notice among these images? Based on what you have read, how might Huerta respond to these images?

Los Angeles, Jack Benton, who really helped push that bill. [Governor] Reagan vetoed the bill four times. We first got it out of the Assembly back in 1961. I remember one of the farm workers said at that hearing, "They are going to get a person to the moon before we get unemployment insurance for farm workers," and they did. A man landed on the moon before farm workers got unemployment insurance. Isn't that incredible? But we finally got unemployment insurance that we finally have now. And Cesar said, "We won't get unemployment insurance until we organize the union."

There was a time when farm workers couldn't get any kind of welfare. Again, if they were out of work, they couldn't get it. Back in 1963, we did a big campaign and we got farm workers covered under welfare so if farm workers were out of work they could at least get welfare. Of course they had no kind of job security. When Robert Kennedy ran for the presidency back in 1968, farm workers who had a Robert Kennedy bumper sticker on their cars were immediately fired from their jobs. And they couldn't take any kind of activity, like registering to vote, or do any political action because they were fired. So, when you see where we are at now, we have come a long way in the changes that have been made. . . .

When we think of how the changes were made, the way that you make change, social change is so simple, but people don't believe it. You know I've been in the movement now since I was twenty-five years old maybe some of you are younger than I was then and I look back and I see all of the things we've done, and even to myself it's hard for me to believe how we made the changes that we made and how we made them. The changes that were made were made by people that were like the poorest of all, people that didn't know how to read or write, people who had no resources, and when we think of the changes that we were able to make for farm workers, it's really kind of a mindblower. Because the kind of action that has been taken, the kind of political action has always been very simple things. About this time ten years ago, Cesar Chavez started his first fast. He did this because we had been on strike at that time for about five years — no, for three years — and we still didn't have any contract and the contributions stopped coming in, everybody was living on Campbell's Tomato Soup and Pork and Beans because that's what we got in donations. Tons of Campbell's Soup and tons of Pork and Beans, and a lot of the farm workers were getting kind of desperate. So Cesar started his first fast for nonviolence in 1968. He did a twenty-five day fast and he didn't eat for twenty-five days, and this was to commit farm workers in all of our movement to the philosophy of nonviolence. And of course a lot of people thought he was crazy. Some people said that Cesar was trying to play God and some people who were very anti-religious were furious over the fact that Cesar would do something so crazy. They thought that doing the daily work of the union was more important than fasting. This was some of our staff people. And a lot of people left the union because they didn't agree with Cesar fasting, they tried to pressure Cesar to stop fasting.

Myself, I was in New York working on the boycott and I kept getting calls from Delano where people were saying "Cesar's crazy, he's trying to have this fast but you should call him up and tell him to start eating." I said, "Well look, this is his decision." I didn't do what they asked me to do, and we let Cesar continue his fast, and, of course, it was a very glorious thing that he did. The day that Cesar ended his fast, Robert Kennedy was there with him, and there was something like nine thousand farm workers. But that was a very simple thing that Cesar did, he just fasted. We sort of picked up on that idea of Cesar's fast, and then we thought, why couldn't the whole country do a little fast? Let's ask everybody not to eat grapes. That's a kind of a simple thing, right? It doesn't take a lot, just don't eat grapes. And so we asked the whole country and the whole world not to eat grapes, and they didn't. And as a result of that, people not eating grapes, we had our first big national grape boycott and we got our first contract. That was a really simple thing, but it had a tremendous impact. Because we were going to the heart of the growers, and that is their pocketbook. And we have to remember that when you are dealing with corporations and you are dealing with businesses you can't, like when you go to school you are taught to be rational, to be objective, to believe what you read and to weigh things, and do all of these things. You have to be very careful when you are in school and learn all of these things because it can be an entrapment. Luckily, farm workers many times — because they don't have school they go by their guts — they know what's right and they know what's wrong and they aren't afraid to take action.

That's a very important thing when you are in school, that you never lose that, don't ever forget to go by what you think is right and wrong down deep inside of your gut because all the time that you are in school you are going to be taught how to

extending beyond the text

Professor Brayden King of Kellogg's Management & Organizations department has researched what conditions are necessary for a successful protest. Read this except from a blog post he wrote.

from How Protests Matter

Brayden King

[A] study of mine (coauthored with Sarah Soule) shows that protests generate information that people use to evaluate their targets. We show that protests against corporations lead to a .4 to 1% decline in the stock price of that company during a two-day window around the protest. The result demonstrates that when activists protest, investors listen. The protests are generating some type of information, which likely varies across protests, that makes investors worry about the value of the asset. In some cases, the protest may cause investors to be concerned about the soundness of a particular corporate policy or practice but in other cases they may interpret the protest as a signal that consumers will be unhappy with the company. The point is that the protest generates information and shifts public attention to a problem that prior to the protest was ignored. If it wasn't being ignored prior to the protest, then the price would never have fluctuated because the information would already be reflected in the stock price.

Explain how Huerta might react to Professor King's conclusions.

conform. And I am saying this from experience because I was in college, and I was a schoolteacher, and I quit teaching schools to come back and help Cesar build a union. So I know where I come from, and I had to unlearn about being rational, objective, and being logical, right? Because when you are dealing with a big social fight and trying to make changes, the people that you are dealing with are not going to be rational and they are not going to do things on the basis of justice — they respond to only one thing and that is economic power. So somehow, you have to hit them in that pocketbook where they have their heart and their nerves and then they feel the pain. Otherwise, they can give you a thousand arguments on why something can't be done. . . .

A lot of the work that was done was done by picketing. What is picketing? That is just marching, [it's] just walking up and down in front of a store asking people not to buy grapes or not to buy lettuce, or not to — whatever it is we happen to be boycotting. Now that doesn't seem like that could be powerful, but it is! It's just amazing how powerful it is. Just walking up and down in front of a store. I always relate picketing to praying in a way; when people pray together they say that it has a lot of effect, except you are not praying just by yourself, you are praying with your feet and your hands and your whole body. Because it is like a petition you are out in front of the store and you are asking, trying to reach that man's conscience, or the people's conscience, trying to give them a message and you do this by displaying your whole body and that is the thing that counts the most. It's your own body, your own person; this is what counts more than anything else.

Probably some of you think to yourselves that I'm not a Martin Luther King, I'm not a Cesar Chavez, I'm just plain old me, and what can plain old me do? Well, this is where you really have to think about it and about what plain old you can do. Plain old you can do a lot of things, you can make real great changes for this country, just plain old you — if you make a commitment. Just like farm workers have done, all of the changes that have been brought and farm workers have done is because farm workers have made a commitment and they lent their whole bodies to go out there and do something. It was, again, like during the Civil Rights struggle when people went in and sat in and got beaten up and what have you — it was their bodies that made that difference. So don't ever think that plain old you can't make the difference; it's like dropping a little stone in a pool; it's just one little stone, a little pebble, but it makes all kinds of waves that reach way out. That's what your action does, what you do goes way way out. Sometimes this may be hard if we haven't been in political action before or social action, and you think, "How can I do this?" or think, "I don't know how," because you've never had the opportunity to learn or been lucky enough to be on a picket line or a sit-in or some type of demonstration to make change. And we have to do these things, it doesn't happen by osmosis, you know, or long distance, you've got to be present and it's got to happen to you. . . .

Build up those muscles because you are going to need them, you are going to need them. This country needs a lot of changes and we have to make them. We can't say, "I am going to wait for somebody else to do them," say, "I am going to do it. In whatever way I can, I am going to do it." In Spanish, in our union, we have a saying called — whenever we start these impossible tasks like they told Cesar — "You can't organize a union, Cesar," and "You can't start a national boycott." The unions told us we couldn't do a national boycott; now they are doing it. We always say, *"Sí se puede."* Who knows what that means, *"Sí se puede?"* It can be done, right? *Sí se puede* means it can be done. ■

Understanding and Interpreting

1. Reread paragraphs 2 and 3, in which Huerta traces some of the history of the farm workers union. What is the key information that she communicates here? What purpose does it serve in her larger argument?
2. Huerta claims at several points in her speech that creating change really comes down to doing simple things. She offers three examples of simple things: fasting, boycotting, and picketing. Explain how, to Huerta, these are simple things and how they lead to change.
3. Throughout her speech, Huerta talks about hitting the corporations in the pocketbook. What does this mean, and how can it lead to change?
4. Huerta says that she had to unlearn "about being rational, objective, and being logical" (par. 6). According to Huerta, did she need to do this, and why is this a significant statement to make considering her audience?
5. In the last paragraph, Huerta tells her audience to "build up those muscles." What are the muscles she's describing? What does she want her audience to do with them?

Analyzing Language, Style, and Structure

1. **Vocabulary in Context.** In paragraph 8, Huerta says, "it doesn't happen by osmosis." "Osmosis" is a scientific term, but Huerta is applying it in a nonscientific context here. What does it mean in this context? How is this meaning influenced by its scientific meaning?

2. **Skill Focus.** Huerta recounts her personal experiences throughout her speech. Choose one place where you think her inclusion of her own experiences was particularly effective. Explain why you think it helped her to prove a point she is trying to make.
3. Huerta chooses to open her speech by discussing Martin Luther King, Jr. Considering her audience and her purpose, why was this likely an effective choice?
4. In paragraph 7, Huerta makes an analogy between picketing and praying. Explain this comparison, and determine whether it is effective in this context.
5. Near the end of her speech, Huerta begins to directly address her audience: "Probably some of you think to yourselves . . ." and "plain old you." Why does Huerta choose to directly address her audience at this point and to use these particular phrases?
6. In paragraph 8, Huerta uses a simile to describe the actions that people take as being "like dropping a little stone in a pool." Explain the meaning and effect of this simile in this context. How does it relate to Huerta's purpose?
7. What you have read here is only an excerpt of her speech at UCLA. While this portion ends with the phrase "*Sí se puede*," her full speech continued afterward. At the conclusion of her speech, the audience shouted "*Sí se puede!*" What is the impact of this phrase? Why is it so essential to her purpose?
8. This speech was delivered in front of a group of college students. While Huerta clearly had points she wanted to make, it also feels a little extemporaneous — not planned — in its delivery. Identify language choices, sentence structures, or other choices that reflect this extemporaneous feeling. Explain how this approach helped or hindered the presentation of her argument.

Topics for Composing

1. **Analysis.** Overall, what message is Huerta hoping to communicate to the college students about change? What evidence does she use to illustrate and support her points?
2. **Argument.** Is it true that "in school you are going to be taught how to conform," as Huerta suggests? Provide evidence from your own experiences in school — and additional research, if needed — to support your position.
3. **Connection.** What issue is so important to you that you would "lend your whole body" to it, as Huerta urges? How have you already (or how might you) become involved? How would your actions compare to those suggested by Huerta in her speech?
4. **Speaking and Listening.** Deliver a speech to your class or a small group about an issue that matters to you and that could be addressed, at least in part, with a boycott designed to hit someone "in the pocketbook." Be specific about the nature of the boycott you propose and how it would lead to some significant change.
5. **Research.** Huerta discusses a number of ways to protest and create change. She spends significant time on the role that a boycott can play. What makes a successful boycott? Research successful and unsuccessful boycotts in the past and identify the key factors that the successful boycotts have in common. What changes occurred as a result of the boycotts?

central text

Bully and the Pulpit

DeRay Mckesson

DeRay Mckesson (b. 1985) is an American social activist who became a strong supporter of the Black Lives Matter movement through protests against police brutality in Ferguson, Missouri, and Baltimore, Maryland. He is the host of the podcast *Pod Save the People*, and the author of *On the Other Side of Freedom: The Case for Hope* (2018), from which the following excerpt is taken.

Paras Griffin/Getty Images

KEY CONTEXT In this piece, Mckesson refers to a literal bully who traumatized him as a child, as well as the metaphorical bully of white supremacy. Mckesson describes white supremacy's bullying influence throughout American history, during slavery and the legal oppression of the Jim Crow Era (late 1800s through mid-1900s), as well as its modern manifestations, including racial profiling and police brutality. Keep both the literal and the metaphorical representations in mind as you read Mckesson's discussions of bullying.

The less you think about your oppression, the more your tolerance for it grows. —Assata Shakur

When I was nine years old, my babysitter put water on a grease fire and our house burned to the ground. My father, sister, and I moved to Grandma's house then, to a different part of town—leaving our small but separate bedrooms to now share a bed in her living room—about fifteen minutes away. And my sister and I started going to a new school. The thing that I remember most vividly from that year is the walk home from school.
I remember the sweaty palms, the dry mouth, the bravado, the focus, the running.
I remember Uncle Barry sometimes meeting us at the top of the hill.

And I remember the fear.

There was a bully on our block on the walk home, always present even when I couldn't see him. And every day, the ten minutes between the school parking lot and my grandmother's yard were full of anxiety. I've thought a lot about that year since then, especially after teaching sixth grade and seeing the way children are taught about power—about who has it and who doesn't; how to wield it and how to share it; and how one gains or loses it. And most important, what it is.

I've thought a lot more about the role of the bully too—about how he moves, adapts, and survives over time; about his source of legitimacy; about the impact of his power. Of late, I've thought about the bully in the context of our present world versus the world that we aim to create for the future, and considering him has transformed the way I think about both.

5 THE CURRENCY OF the bully is fear. It is what he trades in and what he feeds on—fear and confusion. He is violent in the obvious ways that we see and feel, in the physical assaults, but also in the quieter ways, the belittling and the taunts, the mental assaults. His goals are straightforward: to harm you and then convince you that no damage was done or that you deserved it. He aims to strip you of your power,

The Wolf and the Lamb, c.1819-20 (oil on panel)/ Mulready, William (1786-1863)/ROYAL COLLECTION/ Royal Collection Trust © Her Majesty Queen Elizabeth II, 2020/Bridgeman Images

This painting is titled *The Wolf and the Lamb.*

Why is that an appropriate title based on the scene depicted? How is this scene similar to what Mckesson describes about his experiences?

to normalize the interaction so that you are simultaneously traumatized and left questioning if what you experienced actually happened, if what you felt was real.

Every day after school I anticipated him, even though he did not always show up in the ways I expected. But I was prepared, mentally and physically. I realize now that his power lay partly in his omnipresence — ever present in my mind even when he wasn't there in the flesh. And long after the bruises from the bully had healed, I was left living in a world where I expected violence, where the anticipation of trauma served as a survival mechanism. It was a world that looked subtly different from the one that I used to inhabit, a world without agency.

The bully aims to become the center of your everything. For me, the block was no longer the block where my grandmother lived, but the block with the bully. His trauma trapped me in the present where time, space, and my sense of self all folded in on themselves.

There were many days when I just wanted to get home. I didn't want to fight, I didn't want to run, I didn't want to find another way. I wanted to see my grandmother, my grandfather, my father. I wanted things to be normal. I now realize that the bully wants his tyranny to become the norm. And when he succeeds, he creates a burden that incessantly grinds on your spirit. It threatens your joy; it steals your innocence. The threat and the fear and the burden transform you. In the most literal sense, it changes the way that everyone in its orbit interacts with one another.

In the face of the bully, there are seemingly only two options: to challenge him or to accept him. I never understood the notion of "fight or flight" in this context, because "flight" would only be a temporary reprieve and not an actual stance. I couldn't avoid the street forever, and I shouldn't have had to. "Fight" feels like an equally false option — overcoming the bully should not rest on adopting his tactics. When we accept these options, we run, we fight, we push back, because it seems like these are the only things we can do. In a world of incessant battles and their accompanying exhaustion, survival can become the overriding

extending beyond the text

Read the following poem by Danez Smith.

alternate names for black boys

Danez Smith

1. smoke above the burning bush
2. archnemesis of summer night
3. first son of soil
4. coal awaiting spark & wind
5. guilty until proven dead
6. oil heavy starlight
7. monster until proven ghost
8. gone
9. phoenix who forgets to un-ash
10. going, going, gone
11. gods of shovels & black veils
12. what once passed for kindling
13. fireworks at dawn
14. brilliant, shadow hued coral
15. (I thought to leave this blank but who am I to name us nothing?)
16. prayer who learned to bite & sprint
17. a mother's joy & clutched breath

Explain what Smith suggests about the way that some people view African American males. Which of these names might Mckesson agree with, based on what you have read in this piece? How is the tone of this poem similar to or different from Mckesson's tone?

theme in how we think about living, and fear something that we unconsciously accept.

And sometimes, even as we challenge the bully, we come to accept him as just a part of our world.

Bullies don't just happen, they are enabled. There were bystanders who lived on my grandmother's block who chose to do nothing every single day. I think those people simply thought of bullying as another feature of childhood, a condition of growing up—just "kids being kids" or "boys being boys." They didn't suppose that simple child's play could have any lasting negative consequences, and thus did not consider themselves responsible for ending it. So they chose a third option that, in some ways, was the most dangerous: they chose to ignore him, to pretend that he and his tyranny were not what they were. And then there was the bully's family. They loved and cared for him but never corrected his behavior. Indeed, they never held a mirror up to show him what he was becoming.

When the world around you seems to accept bullying as normal, it's hard to imagine a world without it. And if the burden is inevitable, why fight against it?

I am no longer on the walk home, but I still know the bully.

We would recognize him today as much as Bull Connor[1] and Jim Crow[2], the poll tax, police violence, the Black Codes, and redlining were recognized in their own time. The bully is the ideology of white supremacy. It is the notion that the lives of white people are inherently worth more than those of anyone else.

[1] Bull Connor was a white politician in Birmingham, Alabama, during the civil rights movement. Connor urged the police under his authority to use extreme measures to respond to protesters, including using fire hoses and attack dogs. — Eds.

[2] The term Jim Crow refers to the time period of the late 1800s to mid-1900s in America, particularly in the South, when local and state laws enforced racial segregation, keeping African Americans from having the same access as whites to voting, education, and the justice system. — Eds.

In many ways, we live in one of the bully's 15
golden ages, a time when the mere mention of white supremacy is an anachronism. Absent the hoods and burning crosses, we presume the bully dead. But he's still operating in the shadows; he's just working through insidious means. The fact that many people refuse to acknowledge him means that we cannot dismantle what he has wrought. And in our blindness we've created a host of studies to explain away his legacy. In the meantime, he is at work. When we see 21 percent of kids of color in poverty, that is white supremacy at work. When we see a president refusing to allow immigrants from majority people-of-color countries into this country, that is white supremacy at work. Defunding public education, gerrymandering, and scaling back the Voting Rights Act are all manifestations of this ideology.

Bailey Graham

This is a painting called *The Odd Girl* by Bailey Graham, who made the following statement about herself: "Though I was bullied and alone, it didn't hit me very often, but when it did, it hurt. I found solitude in my creativity, and slowly I became what I created."

What do you see in this image that reflects what Graham says of her being bullied, and what connections might Mckesson make to this image?

While we are able to share the pain that we experience, to organize, and to act in ways and with speed not heretofore possible, many of the tools that we now have at our disposal have simultaneously been turned against us. The platform that facilitated community building in Ferguson and beyond is now the preferred venue for our president to lie and mislead the public. We now know that our election was manipulated through the abuse of social media information on Facebook and the like. So though the tactics of the bully are tried and true, there is an unprecedented sophistication to the bullies of our time.

I know the world better since that year that I lived at my grandmother's house. I know that there's no avoiding the bully — not when you move off that street, or exit that grade, or graduate from that school. In truth, the bully only becomes more vicious, more insidious, more institutionalized as time passes.

Paradoxically, many white people have been the collateral damage of policies enacted to uphold white supremacy. And thus we are all of us at risk. It's the trick of the bully that some of us may not realize the risk. Indeed, there are those who don't realize that the bully is coming for them too; they have not yet learned the fear. But white supremacy is about the fleecing of power to gain more power. So while the bully may not be after you today, he will surely target your car or hop over your fence in due time — because the bully is aiming to amass power, regardless of its victims.

In the face of this ever-present threat, silence is tempting. Indeed, responding can be tiring and it may even seem futile in the midst of the onslaught. You just want the pain to end. Or to acknowledge the risk and walk confidently down the street despite it. While understandable, silence too easily becomes acceptance. But neither offers us a path to address the bully. The bully will take your lunch money, then tell you to go buy lunch; steal your car, then give you a driver's license. The bully likes to perform innocence when confronted, suggesting that we can all just move on, but we know this is one of his tricks.

extending beyond the text

The following is an interview from the Lambda Literary site with Mckesson. Read his responses to the question about the idea of reparations, which is the idea that people whose ancestors were enslaved would receive some kind of compensation.

from DeRay Mckesson on Changing the Institution of Policing

Nahshon Dion Anderson

> **[P]lease share your thoughts on reparations. Who should benefit? Will there ever be a time to "move on"?**
> I think that reparations are a true expression of acknowledgement and repair. We need to acknowledge how we got here and what happened, and then we need to repair it. That seems so basic to me. I'm shocked that that word is really charged to people, but the notion — the work behind the word — is just seen as common sense. There was harm done, so we should talk about it, and we should fix the harm. What does it mean when there are generations of people who worked for no pay? That has long-lasting consequence. We should probably do something about that, right? It just seems like common sense to me.

Explain how his answer to this question connects with his central idea in "The Bully and the Pulpit."

To acknowledge the existence of the bully and his accompanying risks is not the same as accepting him as a permanent feature of our world. I know that if we accept trauma and fear, it wins.

Bullies don't just go away. Their legacies don't just disappear. The bully must be confronted intentionally, his impact named and addressed. Even so, it seems there's no clear consensus on how to deal with the bully on our blocks. Do we confront him? Match violence with violence? Do we ignore him, or try to kill him with kindness? I don't think there's a silver bullet to handling the bully, no one-size-fits-all strategy. But the right strategy has to be rooted in a context bigger than the immediate one, has to be rooted in more than aiming to end the presence of the bully himself. We must focus on the type of world we want to live in and devise a plan for getting *there,* as opposed to devising a strategy centered on opposition.

Still, there may yet be a general blueprint for beating the bully. He is effective on the street because he knows the street. He knows which neighbors turn a blind eye. He knows what sections of the street have the lowest traffic and are farthest from the objecting gaze of concerned neighbors. The bully picks his spots. So we need to identify and name the things that enable him, in order to address them head-on and remove them from the playing field. Then we need to expose the bully and all the ways he is able to perpetrate his actions, stripping him of the agency that he seeks to strip from us.

We need to remind the peers of the bully that they benefit from bullying even if they are not themselves the transgressors. Indeed, they benefit from it, but they are tarnished by it.

Charles Moore/Getty Images

This is Bull Connor, the Commissioner of Public Safety in Birmingham, Alabama, during the civil rights movement.

Mckesson says that we can recognize in Bull Connor the bully of white supremacy. How does this photo depict Bull Connor as a bully and as a symbol of the oppressive force of white supremacy?

To chip away at the humanity of select groups is to chip away at humanity itself.

As long as the trauma, the pain he causes, is present, the work of exposing the bully will be present. We identify what props him up and we remove it: If he is propped up by the death of a people, then empowering and rescuing become part of that exposure. If he is propped up by artificial division or the propagation of false information, then partnering together and focusing on truth are part of that exposure. If he is propped up by his effort to pull us apart, to widen the gap between winners and losers, then standing in solidarity with the disenfranchised and oppressed becomes part of that exposure. If he is propped up by a shift in the focus of the work, then reminding ourselves of our main objectives becomes part of that exposure.

25 When we think about engaging and defeating the bully, we must remember that it isn't just about getting home, it's about thriving, and that our goal is not to switch places with the bully, but to end bullying.

This is by no means an easy task. The presence of the bully is difficult to overcome and the residue is difficult to shake. I stress the importance of imagining our ideal world because we naturally gravitate toward methods for achieving our desired outcomes. Indeed, we focus on tactics — how do we beat the bully? — but we don't always remember to prepare for the day when the bully is no more. We will need a vision for that time too. If we don't have a vision for our desired future, how can we plan to achieve it? If you cannot imagine it, you cannot fight for it. When we confront the bully, we are confronting our fear and reclaiming our imagination. There are those who cannot imagine a block without a bully. We must all imagine the block without a bully, otherwise we cannot get there.

When I am most in fear of succumbing to the bully, of allowing him to redefine my space, my world, I am reminded that the street existed before the bully did. We were free before we were enslaved. We are born to love before we know pain.

When I was nine, I didn't know how to challenge the bully. I thought I was alone. The task of conquering my fear, of exposing him, loomed so large in my mind's eye that I was overcome by it. If I hadn't gone to Ferguson and stood toe to toe with other protesters on the streets calling for justice, naming our bully, and saying enough is enough, I'm not sure I'd have the courage to confront him today.

In each generation there is a moment when young and old, inspired or disillusioned, come together around a shared hope, imagine the world as it can be, and have the opportunity to bring that world into existence. Our moment is now. ■

Understanding and Interpreting

1. Reread paragraphs 1 through 3. Which details of Mckesson's experiences with the bully stand out most to you? Why do you think they stand out? How do they affect your understanding of Mckesson's personal story as evidence?
2. While the majority of the first half of the essay focuses on Mckesson's experiences with his literal bully, in paragraph 4, he writes, "Of late, I've thought about the bully in the context of our present world versus the world that we aim to create for the future, and considering him has transformed the way I think about both." Describe the shift Mckesson makes here and explain why it is important to his argument.
3. Explain what Mckesson means when he says that a bully "wants his tyranny to become the norm" (par. 8).

4. In paragraphs 9 through 11, Mckesson explains the different ways that we can respond to bullies. What are the pros and cons of these methods as Mckesson describes them?
5. In paragraph 15, Mckesson offers evidence that white supremacy is not an anachronism, a thing of the past. How does this evidence support his theory that white supremacy is still alive today?
6. Mckesson raises a counterargument to confronting the bully in paragraph 19. What is this counterargument and how does he attempt to refute it? Is he successful?
7. Remember that oftentimes when Mckesson is talking about a bully, he's also talking about white supremacy. With that in mind, explain what Mckesson might be suggesting about white supremacy and white privilege in paragraphs 22 to 24.
8. Why, according to Mckesson in paragraph 24, is it essential that the bully (and white supremacy) be exposed?
9. Despite all of the challenges that Mckesson describes in this piece, he is mostly optimistic about the future. Reread the final paragraph and explain what he includes to communicate his optimism.

Analyzing Language, Style, and Structure

1. **Vocabulary in Context.** In paragraph 5, Mckesson says that "the currency of the bully is fear." What does the word "currency" mean in this context?
2. **Vocabulary in Context.** In paragraph 6, Mckesson describes "a world without agency." What does the word "agency" mean in this context? How is Mckesson's use of the word similar to or different from other uses you have encountered? What are some things that you either do or do not have agency over?
3. **Skill Focus.** Mckesson includes multiple examples from his own personal experience with a bully throughout his essay. To what extent are these examples useful or not useful in his argument about fighting against white supremacy?
4. Mckesson does not explicitly raise the issues of race and white supremacy until paragraph 14. Why might Mckesson have waited so long to bring up his main purpose for writing?
5. Reread the following portion of a sentence from paragraph 17: "the bully only becomes more vicious, more insidious, more institutionalized as time passes." The words "more vicious" seem like a typical way to describe a bully, but what does Mckesson mean by "institutionalized"? What might he be trying to accomplish with this word choice?
6. Reread paragraphs 18 and 19 in which Mckesson uses analogies to describe the bully ("target your car or hop over your fence," "take your lunch money," and others). Knowing that he is also talking about the bully as white supremacy, explain the meaning and effect of these analogies.
7. In the middle of paragraph 21, Mckesson employs a number of rhetorical questions. What is the likely intention behind this choice, and how effective was it?
8. Mckesson's title is a pun on a phrase that you may or may not know. President Theodore Roosevelt referred to his office as a "bully pulpit," a platform from which to push his agenda. Explain the meaning and effect of Mckesson's title based on this background information and what you read in this piece.
9. Structurally, Mckesson returns to his bullying story at the end of his piece. What is different for Mckesson and different for the reader by the end?

Topics for Composing

1. **Analysis.** Explain Mckesson's extended metaphor comparing white supremacy to a bully. What are the most significant similarities? Why did he choose this metaphor for his argument?
2. **Argument.** To what extent is Mckesson correct in characterizing the social media information that appears on Facebook and other sites as "abuse"? In what ways do your experience and additional research support or contradict this characterization?
3. **Connection.** Mckesson writes, "I stress the importance of imagining our ideal world because we naturally gravitate toward methods for achieving our desired outcomes." What do you imagine your ideal world to be? What are the bullying forces in your own life? How might you confront them in a manner that's similar to the way that Mckesson is working to confront the bully of white supremacy?
4. **Speaking and Listening.** According to the National Center for Education Statistics and Bureau of Justice, about 20 percent of students ages 12 to 18 have experienced bullying. Ask friends, family members, teachers, and others about their experiences with bullying, as victims, perpetrators, or bystanders. Listen carefully to their stories, taking notes if appropriate, and share your findings with your class or a small group. In what ways were their experiences and conclusions about bullying similar to or different from those described by Mckesson?
5. **Research.** Mckesson refers to the historical period of Jim Crow as an example of white supremacy. Research more about this time period and explain what has changed in America — and what has not — since that time.
6. **Research.** The Black Lives Matter movement, of which Mckesson is a part, gained national recognition in response to the killings of Michael Brown in Ferguson, Missouri, and Eric Garner in New York City by police officers in 2014, and expanded their reach in the aftermath of the killing of George Floyd in Minneapolis in 2020. Research the movement: its activities, aims, accomplishments, opposition, and influence since then.
7. **Creative Writing.** Write a short story from the point of view of a bully. Include details of setting, characterization, and conflict that illustrate some of the ideas of power and fear that Mckesson presents in his piece.

from An Ideal for Which I Am Prepared to Die

Nelson Mandela

Chris Jackson/Getty Images

Nobel Peace Prize recipient Nelson Mandela (1918–2013) was a South African political activist who eventually became the president of South Africa from 1994 to 1999. His actions as a political activist fighting for equality resulted in his spending twenty-seven years in prison.

KEY CONTEXT Long before he became the president of South Africa and a Nobel Prize winner, Nelson Mandela fought against a system known as apartheid, the racial segregation of people within South Africa. As a result, Mandela faced constant persecution from the ruling political party in South Africa at the time, the National Party. Mandela was arrested four times, in 1952, 1956, 1962, and then again in 1963, when he was tried along with ten other defendants in what is called the Rivonia Trial. Due to a justice system that was beholden to the ruling National Party, Mandela was convicted and sentenced to life in prison. Following intense international pressure, he was released in 1993.

The text that follows is an excerpt from Mandela's courtroom speech at the opening of the defense case in the Rivonia Trial. Although he was eventually convicted of the charges, the speech became a rallying point for opposition leaders. It is considered to be one of the most compelling and important speeches made by Mandela in his illustrious career.

I am the first accused. I hold a bachelor's degree in arts and practised as an attorney in Johannesburg for a number of years in partnership with Oliver Tambo. I am a convicted prisoner serving five years for leaving the country without a permit and for inciting people to go on strike at the end of May 1961. . . .

I must deal immediately and at some length with the question of violence. Some of the things so far told to the court are true and some are untrue. I do not, however, deny that I planned sabotage. I did not plan it in a spirit of recklessness, nor because I have any love of violence. I planned it as a result of a calm and sober assessment of the political situation that had arisen after many years of tyranny, exploitation, and oppression of my people by the whites.

I admit immediately that I was one of the persons who helped to form Umkhonto we Sizwe[1], and that I played a prominent role in its affairs until I was arrested in August 1962. . . .

[1] The military wing of the African National Congress, translated as "Spear of the Nation." —Eds.

I, and the others who started the organisation, did so for two reasons. Firstly, we believed that as a result of Government policy, violence by the African people had become inevitable, and that unless responsible leadership was given to canalise and control the feelings of our people, there would be outbreaks of terrorism which would produce an intensity of bitterness and hostility between the various races of this country which is not produced even by war. Secondly, we felt that without violence there would be no way open to the African people to succeed in their struggle against the principle of white supremacy. All lawful modes of expressing opposition to this principle had been closed by legislation, and we were placed in a position in which we had either to accept a permanent state of inferiority, or to defy the government. We chose to defy the law. We first broke the law in a way which avoided any recourse to violence; when this form was legislated against, and then the government resorted to a show of force to crush opposition to its policies, only then did we decide to answer violence with violence.

But the violence which we chose to adopt was not terrorism. We who formed Umkhonto were all members of the African National Congress, and had behind us the ANC tradition of non-violence and negotiation as a means of solving political disputes. We believe that South Africa belongs to all the people who live in it, and not to one group, be it black or white. We did not want an interracial war, and tried to avoid it to the last minute. . . .

In the words of my leader, Chief Lutuli, who became President of the ANC in 1952, and who was later awarded the Nobel Peace Prize:

> Who will deny that thirty years of my life have been spent knocking in vain, patiently, moderately, and modestly at a closed and barred door? What have been the fruits of moderation? The past thirty years have seen

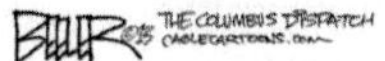

NELSON MANDELA
1918–2013

Nate Beeler/Cagle Cartoons

Consider this political cartoon created in response to Mandela's passing in 2013.

In what ways does this cartoon capture the essence of Mandela's rebellion against apartheid? Based on your understanding of this excerpt from his speech, why do you believe that this image is or is not an appropriate representation of him?

> the greatest number of laws restricting our rights and progress, until today we have reached a stage where we have almost no rights at all.

. . . What were we, the leaders of our people, to do? Were we to give in to the show of force and the implied threat against future action, or were we to fight it and, if so, how?

We had no doubt that we had to continue the fight. Anything else would have been abject surrender. Our problem was not whether to fight, but was how to continue the fight. We of the ANC had always stood for a non-racial democracy, and we shrank from any action which might drive the races further apart than they already were. But the hard facts were that fifty years of non-violence had brought the African people nothing but more and more repressive legislation, and fewer and fewer rights. It may not be easy for this court to understand, but it is a fact that for a long time the people had been talking of violence — of the day when they would fight the white man and win back their country — and we, the leaders of the ANC, had nevertheless always prevailed upon them to avoid violence and to pursue peaceful methods. When some of us discussed this in May and June of 1961, it could not be denied that our policy to achieve a non-racial state by non-violence had achieved nothing, and that our followers were beginning to lose confidence in this policy and were developing disturbing ideas of terrorism. . . .

At the beginning of June 1961, after a long and anxious assessment of the South African situation, I, and some colleagues, came to the conclusion that as violence in this country was inevitable, it would be unrealistic and wrong for African leaders to continue preaching peace and non-violence at a time when the government met our peaceful demands with force.

10 This conclusion was not easily arrived at. It was only when all else had failed, when all channels of peaceful protest had been barred to us, that the decision was made to embark on violent forms of political struggle, and to form Umkhonto we Sizwe. We did so not because we desired such a course, but solely because the government had left us with no other choice. In the Manifesto of Umkhonto published on 16 December 1961, which is exhibit AD, we said:

> The time comes in the life of any nation when there remain only two choices — submit or fight. That time has now come to South Africa. We shall not submit and we have no choice but to hit back by all means in our power in defence of our people, our future, and our freedom. . . .

Four forms of violence were possible. There is sabotage, there is guerrilla warfare, there is terrorism, and there is open revolution. We chose to adopt the first method and to exhaust it before taking any other decision.

In the light of our political background the choice was a logical one. Sabotage did not involve loss of life, and it offered the best hope for future race relations. Bitterness would be kept to a minimum and, if the policy bore fruit, democratic government could become a reality. This is what we felt at the time, and this is what we said in our manifesto (exhibit AD):

> We of Umkhonto we Sizwe have always sought to achieve liberation without bloodshed and civil clash. We hope, even at this late hour, that our first actions will awaken everyone to a realisation of the disastrous situation to which the nationalist policy is leading. We hope that we will bring the government and its supporters to their senses before it is too late, so that both the government and its policies can be changed before matters reach the desperate state of civil war.

The initial plan was based on a careful analysis of the political and economic situation

Welcome in Our Peace World, 1993 (wood,paint, wire, synthetic fibre) Segogela, JohannesMashego (b.1936) / South African; Brooklyn Museumof Art, New York, USA. Gift of Jerome L. and EllenStern/Bridgeman Images

This is a photograph of an art display made of wood, paint, wire, and synthetic fiber created by Johannes Mashego Segogela called *Welcome in Our Peace World*. According to the Brooklyn Museum, the artwork "addresses the South African transition from the armed liberation struggle against whites-only apartheid rule into the new democratic era, [and] suggests the need for South Africans to cast their weapons into the furnace."

What aspects of this image remind you of the struggle that Mandela describes in his speech?

of our country. We believed that South Africa depended to a large extent on foreign capital and foreign trade. We felt that planned destruction of power plants, and interference with rail and telephone communications, would tend to scare away capital from the country, make it more difficult for goods from the industrial areas to reach the seaports on schedule, and would in the long run be a heavy drain on the economic life of the country, thus compelling the voters of the country to reconsider their position.

Attacks on the economic life-lines of the country were to be linked with sabotage on government buildings and other symbols of apartheid. These attacks would serve as a source of inspiration to our people. In addition, they would provide an outlet for those people who were urging the adoption of violent methods and would enable us to give concrete proof to our followers that we had adopted a stronger line and were fighting back against government violence.

In addition, if mass action were successfully organised, and mass reprisals taken, we felt that sympathy for our cause would be roused in other countries, and that greater pressure would be brought to bear on the South African government.

This then was the plan. Umkhonto was to perform sabotage, and strict instructions were given to its members right from the start, that on no account were they to injure or kill people in planning or carrying out operations. . . .

Umkhonto had its first operation on 16 December 1961, when Government buildings in Johannesburg, Port Elizabeth and Durban were attacked. The selection of targets is proof of the policy to which I have referred. Had we intended to attack life we would have selected targets where people congregated and not empty buildings and power stations. . . .

Above all, we want equal political rights, because without them our disabilities will be permanent. I know this sounds revolutionary to the whites in this country, because the majority of voters will be Africans. This makes the white man fear democracy.

But this fear cannot be allowed to stand in the way of the only solution which will guarantee racial harmony and freedom for all. It is not true that the enfranchisement of all will result in racial domination. Political division, based on colour, is entirely artificial and, when it disappears, so will the domination of one colour group by another. . . .

This then is what the ANC is fighting. Their struggle is a truly national one. It is a struggle of the African people, inspired by their own suffering and their own experience. It is a struggle for the right to live.

During my lifetime I have dedicated myself to this struggle of the African people. I have fought against white domination, and I have fought against black domination. I have cherished the ideal of a democratic and free society in which all persons live together in harmony and with equal opportunities. It is an ideal which I hope to live for and to achieve. But if needs be, it is an ideal for which I am prepared to die. ■

David Rogers/Getty Images

This is a photograph of the captain of the Springboks, the South African team that won the Rugby World Cup, and Mandela, just after being elected president and wearing a Springboks jersey and hat. During the apartheid era, the Springboks were seen as a symbol of white supremacy.

What does this photograph represent for the future of South Africa and what in his speech demonstrates that Mandela would be capable of this kind of gesture?

Understanding and Interpreting

1. Look back at the Key Context section before this piece and think about the charges that Mandela stands trial for. What does the nature of those charges tell you about the political context of this speech?
2. What distinction does Mandela make between “violence” and “terrorism” (pars. 5-7), and how does this distinction serve his argument?
3. Explain the concept of a “non-racial democracy” (par. 8). Why is it of central concern to Mandela and the ANC?
4. According to Mandela, why is sabotage the better form of political violence? Do you think he makes his case convincingly for this choice of violence?
5. Why, according to Mandela, does the white man fear democracy in South Africa?

Analyzing Language, Style, and Structure

1. **Vocabulary in Context.** In paragraph 16, Mandela says that the attacks will "provide an outlet" for some people. What does the word "outlet" mean in this context? How is Mandela's use of the word similar to or different from other uses you have encountered?
2. **Vocabulary in Context.** In paragraph 10, Mandela says that "channels of peaceful protest" were closed to him. What does the word "channels" mean in this context?
3. **Skill Focus.** Mandela gave this speech in the courtroom as part of his defense. With that context in mind, why was it essential that he include personal experiences in his argument about the necessity to commit political violence?
4. How does opening with an acknowledgement about his use of violence to create change help Mandela establish his overall purpose?
5. What reasons does Mandela provide for the formation of the resistance group Umkhonto? How effectively do these reasons justify the organization's actions for creating change?
6. What purpose does quoting Chief Lutuli serve in Mandela's argument (par. 6)? In your response, consider both the quotation itself and the speaker.
7. In what ways does Mandela use the prospect of civil war in South Africa to explain the choice to adopt a more violent approach?
8. Explain how Mandela's statement that "[p]olitical division, based on colour, is entirely artificial and, when it disappears, so will the domination of one colour group by another" (par. 21) is linked to his argument about change as a whole.

Topics for Composing

1. **Analysis.** How does Mandela justify abandoning nonviolent protest? How does he make the case for sabotage as his preferred alternative? How does this reasoning support his overall argument in this speech?
2. **Argument.** Mandela put his life on the line, and ultimately sacrificed his freedom in pursuit of his cause. Consider a current political, social, or economic issue of great importance to you. Write an argument in which you explain the issue, why you believe it's important, why you believe others should agree with your position, and what you would be willing to do in order to support your position. It can be an issue related to your school, your local community, the entire nation, or even the global community.
3. **Connection.** Locate online and read Martin Luther King's "Letter from a Birmingham Jail" and consider the similarities between that speech and Mandela's. Specifically, consider the ways in which both King and Mandela use the circumstances of their imprisonment to advance their causes.
4. **Speaking and Listening.** Prepare for and hold a discussion with classmates in which you address one or more of the following questions: Was Nelson Mandela justified in the use of violence to overthrow apartheid? What does it mean that he was awarded the Nobel Peace Prize in spite of his call for violent opposition? Can violence ever be justified?
5. **Research.** When Mandela was released from prison, many South Africans thought he would be angry and would seek revenge because the government had mistreated him. Instead, he helped to create the Truth and Reconciliation Commission (TRC), which tried to heal the damage done by the years of apartheid. Research the TRC's work and write an examination of its lasting impact in South Africa and around the world.

6. **Research.** Mandela was called a rebel and was ultimately imprisoned for his political views as he strove for justice. In spite of his long imprisonment, he inspired lasting change in his country and around the world. Research other leaders who have also been imprisoned for their activism and were nonetheless able to motivate powerful and lasting change. Select one whom you find particularly compelling. Then share the ways in which the leader you selected influenced or changed the world.
7. **Multimodal.** Mandela gave numerous speeches during his career as a political activist. Research other speeches he made, and then select one that you find inspiring. Create a visual presentation using words from the speech you select and images (from various sources) that capture the tone of the speech.

I Have Been to the Mountaintop

Martin Luther King Jr.

Marvin Koner/Corbis/Getty Images

Dr. Martin Luther King Jr. (1929–1968) was a Baptist minister and civil rights leader whose contributions improved race relations in America in the twentieth century. Through his political activism, King played a vital role in ending the legal segregation that was widespread in the South at the time. King's leadership was instrumental in the creation of the Civil Rights Act of 1964 and the Voting Rights Act of 1965, two significant legislative acts of the twentieth century that expanded equality for African American citizens. King also helped to organize the 1963 March on Washington, where he delivered his legendary "I Have a Dream" speech. For his work in civil rights, King was awarded the Nobel Peace Prize in 1964.

KEY CONTEXT In March of 1968, Martin Luther King Jr. traveled to Memphis, Tennessee, to lend his support and inspiration to the black sanitation and public works employees who were on strike for better wages and fair treatment. Violence between police and protestors had broken out at the rally on March 28. This speech, "I Have Been to the Mountaintop," was delivered to an audience of supporters on April 3, 1968, in response to that violence of a few days before. Tragically, this speech was King's last, as he was assassinated the following day by James Earl Ray, who confessed to the murder and died in prison in 1998.

Thank you very kindly, my friends. As I listened to Ralph Abernathy and his eloquent and generous introduction and then thought about myself, I wondered who he was talking about. It's always good to have your closest friend and associate to say something good about you. And Ralph Abernathy is the best friend that I have in the world. I'm delighted to see each of you here tonight in spite of a storm warning. You reveal that you are determined to go on anyhow.

Something is happening in Memphis; something is happening in our world. And you know, if I were standing at the beginning of time, with the possibility of taking a kind of general and panoramic view of the whole of human history up to now, and the Almighty said to me, "Martin Luther King, which age would you like to live in?" I would take my mental flight by Egypt and I would watch God's children in their magnificent trek from the dark dungeons of Egypt through, or rather across the Red Sea, through the wilderness on toward the promised land. And in spite of its magnificence, I wouldn't stop there.

I would move on by Greece and take my mind to Mount Olympus. And I would see Plato, Aristotle, Socrates, Euripides and Aristophanes assembled around the Parthenon. And I would watch them around the Parthenon as they discussed the great and eternal issues of reality. But I wouldn't stop there.

I would go on, even to the great heyday of the Roman Empire. And I would see developments around there, through various emperors and leaders. But I wouldn't stop there.

I would even come up to the day of the 5
Renaissance, and get a quick picture of all that the Renaissance did for the cultural and aesthetic life of man. But I wouldn't stop there.

I would even go by the way that the man for whom I am named had his habitat. And I would watch Martin Luther as he tacked his ninety-five theses on the door at the church of Wittenberg. But I wouldn't stop there.

I would come on up even to 1863, and watch a vacillating President by the name of Abraham Lincoln finally come to the conclusion that he had to sign the Emancipation Proclamation. But I wouldn't stop there.

I would even come up to the early thirties, and see a man grappling with the problems of the bankruptcy of his nation. And come with an eloquent cry that we have nothing to fear but "fear itself." But I wouldn't stop there.

Joe Heller/Cagle Cartoons, Inc.

This political cartoon by Joe Heller of the *Green Bay Press-Gazette* depicts the *Stone of Hope* statue at the Martin Luther King Jr. Memorial in Washington, D.C., along with one of King's quotations. **Choose a quotation from this speech that would be a suitable replacement for the one in this cartoon. Explain why you chose the quotation you did, and how it works with the image in the cartoon to capture King's legacy.**

Strangely enough, I would turn to the Almighty and say, "If you allow me to live just a few years in the second half of the twentieth century, I will be happy."

Now that's a strange statement to make, because the world is all messed up. The nation is sick. Trouble is in the land; confusion all around. That's a strange statement. But I know, somehow, that only when it is dark enough can you see the stars. And I see God working in this period of the twentieth century in a way that men, in some strange way, are responding.

Something is happening in our world. The masses of people are rising up. And wherever they are assembled today, whether they are in Johannesburg, South Africa; Nairobi, Kenya; Accra, Ghana; New York City; Atlanta, Georgia; Jackson, Mississippi; or Memphis, Tennessee — the cry is always the same: "We want to be free."

And another reason that I'm happy to live in this period is that we have been forced to a point where we are going to have to grapple with the problems that men have been trying to grapple with through history, but the demands didn't force them to do it. Survival demands that we grapple with them. Men, for years now, have been talking about war and peace. But now, no longer can they just talk about it. It is no longer a choice between violence and nonviolence in this world; it's nonviolence or nonexistence. That is where we are today.

And also in the human rights revolution, if something isn't done, and done in a hurry, to bring the colored peoples of the world out of their long years of poverty, their long years of hurt and neglect, the whole world is doomed. Now, I'm just happy that God has allowed me to live in this period to see what is unfolding. And I'm happy that He's allowed me to be in Memphis.

I can remember — I can remember when Negroes were just going around as Ralph has said, so often, scratching where they didn't itch, and laughing when they were not tickled. But that day is all over. We mean business now, and we are determined to gain our rightful place in God's world.

And that's all this whole thing is about. We aren't engaged in any negative protest and in any negative arguments with anybody. We are saying that we are determined to be men. We are determined to be people. We are saying — We are saying that we are God's children. And that we are God's children, we don't have to live like we are forced to live.

Now, what does all of this mean in this great period of history? It means that we've got to stay together. We've got to stay together and maintain unity. You know, whenever Pharaoh wanted to prolong the period of slavery in Egypt, he had a favorite, favorite formula for doing it. What was that? He kept the slaves fighting among themselves. But whenever the slaves get together, something happens in Pharaoh's court, and he cannot hold the slaves in slavery. When the slaves get together, that's the beginning of getting out of slavery. Now let us maintain unity.

Secondly, let us keep the issues where they are. The issue is injustice. The issue is the refusal of Memphis to be fair and honest in its dealings with its public servants, who happen to be sanitation workers. Now, we've got to keep attention on that. That's always the problem with a little violence. You know what happened the other day, and the press dealt only with the window-breaking. I read the articles. They very seldom got around to mentioning the fact that one thousand three hundred sanitation workers are on strike, and that Memphis is not being fair to them, and that Mayor Loeb is in dire need of a doctor. They didn't get around to that.

Now we're going to march again, and we've got to march again, in order to put the issue where it is supposed to be — and force everybody to see that there are thirteen hundred of God's children here suffering, sometimes going hungry, going through dark and dreary nights wondering how this thing is going to come out. That's the issue. And we've got to say to the nation: We know how it's coming out. For when people get caught up with that which is right and they are willing to sacrifice for it, there is no stopping point short of victory.

We aren't going to let any mace stop us. We are masters in our nonviolent movement in disarming police forces; they don't know what to do. I've seen them so often. I remember in Birmingham, Alabama, when we were in that majestic struggle there, we would move out of the 16th Street Baptist Church day after day; by the hundreds we would move out. And Bull Connor would tell them to send the dogs forth, and they did come; but we just went before the dogs singing, "Ain't gonna let nobody turn me around."

20 Bull Connor next would say, "Turn the fire hoses on." And as I said to you the other night, Bull Connor didn't know history. He knew a kind of physics that somehow didn't relate to the transphysics that we knew about. And that was

extending beyond the text

In "I Have Been to the Mountaintop," King says, "Men, for years now, have been talking about war and peace. But now, no longer can they just talk about it. It is no longer a choice between violence and nonviolence in this world; it's nonviolence or nonexistence. That is where we are today." A contemporary of King's, Malcolm X, sometimes took a different view of the need for violence in an unjust society. Read the following excerpt from *The Autobiography of Malcolm X: As Told to Alex Haley*.

STF/AFP/Getty Images

from The Autobiography of Malcolm X: As Told to Alex Haley

Malcolm X and Alex Haley

They called me "the angriest Negro in America." I wouldn't deny that charge. I speak exactly as I feel. "I *believe* in anger. The Bible says there is a *time* for anger." They called me "a teacher, a proposer of violence." I would say point blank, "That is a lie. I'm not for meaningless violence; I'm for justice. I feel that if white people were attacked by Negroes — if the forces of law prove unable, or inadequate, or reluctant to protect those whites from those Negroes — then those white people should protect and defend themselves from those Negroes, using arms if necessary. And I feel that when the law fails to protect Negroes from whites' attack, then those Negroes should use arms, if necessary to defend themselves."

"Malcolm X Advocates Armed Negroes!"

What was wrong with that? I'll tell you what was wrong. I was a black man talking about physical defense against the white man. The white man can lynch and burn and bomb and beat Negroes — that's all right: "Have patience" . . . "The customs are entrenched" . . . "Things are getting better."

Well, I believe it's a crime for anyone who is being brutalized to continue to accept that brutality without doing something to defend himself.

Based on what you've read in the speech by King and this excerpt from Malcolm X, on what points might they agree and disagree?

the fact that there was a certain kind of fire that no water could put out. And we went before the fire hoses; we had known water. If we were Baptist or some other denominations, we had been immersed. If we were Methodist, and some others, we had been sprinkled, but we knew water. That couldn't stop us.

And we just went on before the dogs and we would look at them; and we'd go on before the water hoses and we would look at it, and we'd just go on singing "Over my head I see freedom in the air." And then we would be thrown in the paddy wagons, and sometimes we were stacked in there like sardines in a can. And they would throw us in, and old Bull would say, "Take 'em off," and they did; and we would just go in the paddy wagon singing, "We Shall Overcome." And every now and then we'd get in jail, and we'd see the jailers looking through the windows being moved by our prayers, and being moved by our words and our songs. And there was a power there which Bull Connor couldn't adjust to; and so we ended up transforming Bull into a steer, and we won our struggle in Birmingham. Now we've got to go on in Memphis just like that. I call upon you to be with us when we go out Monday.

Now about injunctions: We have an injunction and we're going into court tomorrow morning to fight this illegal, unconstitutional injunction. All we say to America is, "Be true to what you said on paper." If I lived in China or even Russia, or any totalitarian country, maybe I could understand some of these illegal injunctions. Maybe I could understand the denial of certain basic First Amendment privileges, because they hadn't committed themselves to that over there. But somewhere I read of the freedom of assembly. Somewhere I read of the freedom of speech. Somewhere I read of the freedom of press. Somewhere I read that the greatness of America is the right to protest for right. And so just as I say, we aren't going to let dogs or water hoses turn us around, we aren't going to let any injunction turn us around. We are going on.

We need all of you. And you know what's beautiful to me is to see all of these ministers of the Gospel. It's a marvelous picture. Who is it that is supposed to articulate the longings and aspirations of the people more than the preacher? Somehow the preacher must have a kind of fire shut up in his bones. And whenever injustice is around he tell it. Somehow the preacher must be an Amos, and saith, "When God speaks who can but prophesy?" Again with Amos, "Let justice roll down like waters and righteousness like a mighty stream." Somehow the preacher must say with Jesus, "The Spirit of the Lord is upon me, because he hath anointed me, and he's anointed me to deal with the problems of the poor."

And I want to commend the preachers, under the leadership of these noble men: James Lawson, one who has been in this struggle for many years; he's been to jail for struggling; he's been kicked out of Vanderbilt University for this struggle, but he's still going on, fighting for the rights of his people. Reverend Ralph Jackson, Billy Kiles; I could just go right on down the list, but time will not permit. But I want to thank all of them. And I want you to thank them, because so often, preachers aren't concerned about anything but themselves. And I'm always happy to see a relevant ministry.

It's all right to talk about "long white robes 25
over yonder," in all of its symbolism. But ultimately people want some suits and dresses and shoes to wear down here! It's all right to talk about "streets flowing with milk and honey," but God has commanded us to be concerned about the slums down here, and his children who can't eat three square meals a day. It's all right to talk about the new Jerusalem, but one day, God's preacher must talk about the new New York, the new Atlanta, the new Philadelphia, the new Los Angeles, the new Memphis, Tennessee. This is what we have to do.

Now the other thing we'll have to do is this: Always anchor our external direct action with the power of economic withdrawal. Now, we are poor people. Individually, we are poor when you compare us with white society in America. We are poor. Never stop and forget that collectively — that means all of us together — collectively we are richer than all the nations in the world, with the exception of nine. Did you ever think about that? After you leave the United States, Soviet Russia, Great Britain, West Germany, France, and I could name the others, the American Negro collectively is richer than most nations of the world. We have an annual income of more than thirty billion dollars a year, which is more than all of the exports of the United States, and more than the national budget of Canada. Did you know that? That's power right there, if we know how to pool it.

We don't have to argue with anybody. We don't have to curse and go around acting bad with our words. We don't need any bricks and bottles. We don't need any Molotov cocktails. We just need to go around to these stores, and to these massive industries in our country, and say, "God sent us by here, to say to you that you're not treating his children right. And we've come by here to ask you to make the first item on your agenda fair treatment, where God's children are concerned. Now, if you are not prepared to do that, we do have an agenda that we must follow. And our agenda calls for withdrawing economic support from you."

And so, as a result of this, we are asking you tonight, to go out and tell your neighbors not to buy Coca-Cola in Memphis. Go by and tell them not to buy Sealtest milk. Tell them not to buy — what is the other bread? — Wonder Bread. And what is the other bread company, Jesse? Tell them not to buy Hart's bread. As Jesse Jackson has said, up to now, only the garbage men have been feeling pain; now we must kind of re-distribute the pain. We are choosing these companies because they haven't been fair in their hiring policies; and we are choosing them because they can begin the process of saying they are going to support the needs and the

Martin Luther King's ideas concerning civil rights and equality were not for only his generation. **Explain how this political cartoon attempts to express King's full influence as his ideas continue to shape modern American culture based on what you have read in this speech.**

rights of these men who are on strike. And then they can move on downtown and tell Mayor Loeb to do what is right.

But not only that, we've got to strengthen black institutions. I call upon you to take your money out of the banks downtown and deposit your money in Tri-State Bank. We want a "bank-in" movement in Memphis. Go by the savings and loan association. I'm not asking you something that we don't do ourselves at SCLC. Judge Hooks and others will tell you that we have an account here in the savings and loan association from the Southern Christian Leadership Conference. We are telling you to follow what we are doing. Put your money there. You have six or seven black insurance companies here in the city of Memphis. Take out your insurance there. We want to have an "insurance-in."

Now these are some practical things that we can do. We begin the process of building a greater economic base. And at the same time, we are putting pressure where it really hurts. I ask you to follow through here.

Now, let me say as I move to my conclusion that we've got to give ourselves to this struggle until the end. Nothing would be more tragic than to stop at this point in Memphis. We've got to see it through. And when we have our march, you need to be there. If it means leaving work, if it means leaving school — be there. Be concerned about your brother. You may not be on strike. But either we go up together, or we go down together.

Let us develop a kind of dangerous unselfishness. One day a man came to Jesus, and he wanted to raise some questions about some vital matters of life. At points he wanted to trick Jesus, and show him that he knew a little more than Jesus knew and throw him off base. . . .

Now that question could have easily ended up in a philosophical and theological debate. But Jesus immediately pulled that question from mid-air, and placed it on a dangerous curve between Jerusalem and Jericho. And he talked

extending beyond the text

Because of King's famous "I Have a Dream" speech, we tend to think of him as always optimistic and noble. However, the reality is that he often had doubts about the future of the civil rights movement. He shared some of these thoughts publicly. Read this portion from a speech called "The Other America" that he delivered in 1967 at Stanford University.

from The Other America

Martin Luther King Jr.

Now the other thing that we've gotta come to see now that many of us didn't see too well during the last ten years — that is that racism is still alive in American society, and much more wide-spread than we realized. And we must see racism for what it is. It is a myth of the superior and the inferior race. It is the false and tragic notion that one particular group, one particular race is responsible for all of the progress, all of the insights in the total flow of history. And the theory that another group or another race is totally depraved, innately impure, and innately inferior.

Contrast his tone in this excerpt with the tone of "I've Been to the Mountaintop," as well as his "I Have a Dream" speech, which you can find online.

about a certain man, who fell among thieves. You remember that a Levite and a priest passed by on the other side. They didn't stop to help him. And finally a man of another race came by. He got down from his beast, decided not to be compassionate by proxy. But he got down with him, administered first aid, and helped the man in need. Jesus ended up saying, this was the good man, this was the great man, because he had the capacity to project the "I" into the "thou," and to be concerned about his brother.

Now you know, we use our imagination a great deal to try to determine why the priest and the Levite didn't stop. At times we say they were busy going to a church meeting, an ecclesiastical gathering, and they had to get on down to Jerusalem so they wouldn't be late for their meeting. At other times we would speculate that there was a religious law that "One who was engaged in religious ceremonials was not to touch a human body twenty-four hours before the ceremony." And every now and then we begin to wonder whether maybe they were not going down to Jerusalem — or down to Jericho, rather to organize a "Jericho Road Improvement Association." That's a possibility. Maybe they felt that it was better to deal with the problem from the causal root, rather than to get bogged down with an individual effect.

But I'm going to tell you what my imagination tells me. It's possible that those men were afraid. You see, the Jericho road is a dangerous road. I remember when Mrs. King and I were first in Jerusalem. We rented a car and drove from Jerusalem down to Jericho. And as soon as we got on that road, I said to my wife, "I can see why Jesus used this as the setting for his parable." It's a winding, meandering road. It's really conducive for ambushing. You start out in Jerusalem, which is about 1200 miles — or rather 1200 feet above sea level. And by the time you get down to Jericho, fifteen or twenty minutes later, you're about 2200 feet below sea level. That's a dangerous road. In the days of Jesus it came to be known as the "Bloody Pass." And you know, it's possible that the priest and the Levite looked over that man on the ground and wondered if the robbers were still around. Or it's possible that they felt that the man on the ground was merely faking. And he was acting like he had been robbed and hurt, in order to seize them over there, lure them there for quick and easy seizure. And so the first question that the priest asked — the first question that the Levite asked was, "If I stop to help this man, what will happen to me?" But then the Good Samaritan came by. And he reversed the question: "If I do not stop to help this man, what will happen to him?"

That's the question before you tonight. Not, "If I stop to help the sanitation workers, what will happen to my job?" Not, "If I stop to help the sanitation workers what will happen to all of the hours that I usually spend in my office every day and every week as a pastor?" The question is not, "If I stop to help this man in need, what will happen to me?" The question is, "If I do not stop to help the sanitation workers, what will happen to them?" That's the question.

Let us rise up tonight with a greater readiness. Let us stand with a greater determination. And let us move on in these powerful days, these days of challenge to make
35 America what it ought to be. We have an opportunity to make America a better nation. And I want to thank God, once more, for allowing me to be here with you.

You know, several years ago, I was in New York City autographing the first book that I had written. And while sitting there autographing books, a demented black woman came up. The only question I heard from her was, "Are you Martin Luther King?" And I was looking down writing, and I said, "Yes." And the next minute I felt something beating on my chest. Before I knew it I had been stabbed by this demented woman. I was rushed to Harlem Hospital. It was a dark Saturday afternoon. And that blade had gone through, and the X-rays

Bettmann/Getty Images

This is a photograph of a conflict between the police and the striking sanitation workers in Memphis that King was in town to support.
Look closely at this image. Based on what you read in this speech, explain what King might have found so distressing about the situation.

revealed that the tip of the blade was on the edge of my aorta, the main artery. And once that's punctured, you're drowned in your own blood— that's the end of you.

It came out in the *New York Times* the next morning, that if I had merely sneezed, I would have died. Well, about four days later, they allowed me, after the operation, after my chest had been opened, and the blade had been taken out, to move around in the wheel chair in the hospital. They allowed me to read some of the mail that came in, and from all over the states and the world, kind letters came in. I read a few, but one of them I will never forget. I had received one from the President and the Vice-President. I've forgotten what those telegrams said. I'd received a visit and a letter from the Governor of New York, but I've forgotten what that letter said. But there was another letter that came from a little girl, a young girl who was a student at the White Plains High School. And I looked at that letter, and I'll never forget it. It said simply,

> *Dear Dr. King,*
> *I am a ninth-grade student at the White Plains High School.*
> And she said,
> *While it should not matter, I would like to mention that I'm a white girl. I read in the paper of your misfortune, and of your suffering. And I read that if you had sneezed, you would have died. And I'm simply writing you to say that I'm so happy that you didn't sneeze.*

And I want to say tonight—I want to say tonight that I too am happy that I didn't sneeze. Because if I had sneezed, I wouldn't have been around here in 1960, when students all over the South started sitting-in at lunch counters. And I knew that as they were sitting-in, they were really standing up for the best in the American dream, and taking the whole nation back to those great wells of democracy which were dug deep by the Founding Fathers in the Declaration of Independence and the Constitution.

If I had sneezed, I wouldn't have been around here in 1961, when we decided to take a ride for freedom and ended segregation in interstate travel.

If I had sneezed, I wouldn't have been around here in 1962, when Negroes in Albany, Georgia, decided to straighten their backs up. And whenever men and women straighten their backs up, they are going somewhere, because a man can't ride your back unless it is bent.

If I had sneezed — If I had sneezed I wouldn't have been here in 1963, when the black people of Birmingham, Alabama, aroused the conscience of this nation, and brought into being the Civil Rights Bill.

If I had sneezed, I wouldn't have had a chance later that year, in August, to try to tell America about a dream that I had had.

If I had sneezed, I wouldn't have been down in Selma, Alabama, to see the great Movement there.

If I had sneezed, I wouldn't have been in Memphis to see a community rally around those brothers and sisters who are suffering.

I'm so happy that I didn't sneeze.

And they were telling me —. Now, it doesn't matter, now. It really doesn't matter what happens now. I left Atlanta this morning, and as we got started on the plane, there were six of us. The pilot said over the public address system, "We are sorry for the delay, but we have Dr. Martin Luther King on the plane. And to be sure that all of the bags were checked, and to be sure that nothing would be wrong with the plane, we had to check out everything carefully. And we've had the plane protected and guarded all night."

And then I got into Memphis. And some began to say the threats, or talk about the threats that were out. What would happen to me from some of our sick white brothers?

Well, I don't know what will happen now. We've got some difficult days ahead. But it really doesn't matter with me now, because I've been to the mountaintop.

And I don't mind.

Like anybody, I would like to live a long life. Longevity has its place. But I'm not concerned about that now. I just want to do God's will. And He's allowed me to go up to the mountain. And I've looked over. And I've seen the Promised Land. I may not get there with you. But I want you to know tonight, that we, as a people, will get to the promised land!

And so I'm happy tonight.

I'm not worried about anything.

I'm not fearing any man!

Mine eyes have seen the glory of the coming of the Lord!! ■

Understanding and Interpreting

1. King claims that if he were given the choice to live in any time period, he would choose the second half of the twentieth century, even though the world is "all messed up" (par. 10). Explain King's reasoning.
2. Explain what King means by "It is no longer a choice between violence and nonviolence in this world; it's nonviolence or nonexistence. That is where we are today." (par. 12). What are some examples of nonviolent solutions that King offers in his speech? How do those solutions support his overall argument for the best methods for creating change?
3. In Birmingham, Alabama, civil rights protestors were abused by the authorities. Specifically, Bull Connor, the Commissioner of Public Safety for the city, ordered that protestors be sprayed

with high-powered fire hoses. Explain why King suggests that the protesters would be able to overcome Connor's abuse.

4. In paragraph 26, King turns his attention to the economic power of the community. What is the advantage of focusing on the kinds of goods people purchase? How will this lead to the changes that King is promoting?
5. King tells the audience that "either we go up together, or we go down together" (par. 31). How is this message of change through unity reinforced in other parts of King's speech? Why is this message so important to the overall themes in the speech?
6. When King references the Promised Land (par. 52), he is talking about the land where, according to the Old Testament, the Jewish people would finally be able to live in peace and freedom after years of captivity in Egypt. What is the promised land that King is assuring the members of his audience they all will one day find?
7. This speech would be King's last, as he was shot to death by an assassin on April 4, 1968, just one day after he delivered this speech. Characterize King's attitude toward the threats he faced and explain why he thought it was important to share those feelings with the crowd.

Analyzing Language, Style, and Structure

1. **Vocabulary in Context.** What is the meaning of the word "determined" in paragraphs 14 and 15? How is this usage similar to or different from other, more common usages of the word?
2. **Skill Focus.** King uses personal experience at various times throughout his speech. Why, for instance, does he refer to a trip that he and his wife took to Jericho? How does King's recounting of this trip reinforce one of his main ideas about change?
3. **Skill Focus.** The speech includes a letter King received from a young white girl after he had been stabbed and almost killed at a book signing in New York City. What is the effect of the inclusion of the story of his stabbing and of the girl's reaction to it? How does this personal experience help to illustrate a point King is trying to make?
4. When King uses an allusion to Abraham Lincoln (par. 7), he describes the former president as "vacillating" and indicates that Lincoln "had to sign the Emancipation Proclamation." What do these specific language choices indicate about how King views Lincoln's role in freeing the slaves?
5. In paragraph 8, King refers to the early 1930s and a man struggling with the "bankruptcy of his nation." King is literally describing the Great Depression and the economic hardships of the time, but what effect does the word "bankruptcy" have when applied to a whole country or a people as King applies it here?
6. King argues that the Egyptian pharaohs maintained their power by keeping the "slaves fighting among themselves" (par. 16). How does this analogy connect to the situation in the United States in the 1960s, and to the situation in Memphis specifically?
7. Explain why King brings up China and Russia (par. 22), as well as other totalitarian countries during a speech that focuses on events in Memphis, Tennessee.
8. An ordained Baptist minister himself, King references other religious leaders, as well as the Bible, frequently. How does King characterize the roles of faith and religion in the struggle for change?
9. Explain what King means when he talks about a "dangerous unselfishness." How does his example about Jesus in paragraphs 32 and 33 reinforce King's meaning?

Topics for Composing

1. **Analysis.** Overall, what is the tone that King takes toward the likelihood of successful change in the future? What specific language choices, allusions, or examples help him convey this tone?
2. **Argument.** King preached nonviolent protest as the best way to achieve the goals of the civil rights movement. Current events illustrate that complete equality for all has not yet been achieved. Write an argument in which you support or challenge the position that Martin Luther King's approach to social and political change has been effective. Use specific examples from current events in support of your argument.
3. **Connection.** While King's "I Have Been to the Mountaintop" speech may be unfamiliar to many people, his "I Have a Dream" speech is widely known and includes one of his most famous lines: "I have a dream that my four little children will one day live in a nation where they will not be judged by the color of their skin but by the content of their character." In what ways do the ideas offered in "I Have Been to the Mountaintop" reflect this basic principle from his "I Have a Dream" speech?
4. **Speaking and Listening.** One of the hallmarks of Martin Luther King Jr.'s speeches is their inspirational quality. They are memorable not only for their eloquence but for spurring people to action. Watch clips of King deliver this or another speech. In addition to his words and phrases, what is it about his voice, gestures, and delivery that makes it effective and memorable? Try delivering one or more of the lines from the speech for yourself. How is it different to speak the line out loud rather than read it?
5. **Research.** Not all civil rights leaders agreed with Dr. King's nonviolent approach to gaining equality. Research other strategies used during the civil rights era and discuss whether they were effective or counterproductive in bringing about change.
6. **Creative Writing.** Like most of King's speeches, "I Have Been to the Mountaintop" includes beautiful, searing, and emotional word choices. Go back through the speech and highlight 15-20 words or phrases you find striking. Write those words out and organize them into a "found poem," in which you rearrange King's words into your own structures for your own purpose. You can add a few words of your own, if needed, but the majority of your "found poem" will come from King's speech. What did you learn about King's language as you were creating your poem?

Thoughts on Peace in an Air Raid

Virginia Woolf

Born Adeline Virginia Stephen, Virginia Woolf (1882–1941) is considered one of the most important twentieth century authors. Born into an affluent household in London, Woolf and her sisters were schooled at home. Encouraged by her father, she began writing professionally in 1900. She is perhaps best known for her essay "A Room of One's Own," (1929) an important early feminist text, arguing for both a literal and figurative space for women writers.

Culture Club/Hulton Archive/Getty Images

KEY CONTEXT This essay was published in 1940, during what is often referred to as the Battle of Britain, a year-long air battle between English and German forces in World War II over London and other major cities in England.

The Germans were over this house last night and the night before that. Here they are again. It is a queer experience, lying in the dark and listening to the zoom of a hornet, which may at any moment sting you to death. It is a sound that interrupts cool and consecutive thinking about peace. Yet it is a sound — far more than prayers and anthems — that should compel one to think about peace. Unless we can think peace into existence we — not this one body in this one bed but millions of bodies yet to be born — will lie in the same darkness and hear the same death rattle overhead. Let us think what we can do to create the only efficient air-raid shelter while the guns on the hill go pop pop pop and the searchlights finger the clouds and now and then, sometimes close at hand, sometimes far away, a bomb drops.

Up there in the sky young Englishmen and young German men are fighting each other. The defenders are men, the attackers men. Arms are not given to Englishwomen either to fight the enemy or to defend herself. She must lie weaponless tonight. Yet if she believes that the fight going on up in the sky is a fight by the English to protect freedom, by the Germans to destroy freedom, she must fight, so far as she can, on the side of the English. How far can she fight for freedom without firearms? By making arms, or clothes or food. But there is another way of fighting for freedom without arms: we can fight with the mind. We can make ideas that will help the young Englishman who is fighting up in the sky to defeat the enemy.

But to make ideas effective, we must be able to fire them off. We must put them into action. And the hornet in the sky rouses another hornet in the mind. There was one zooming in *The Times* this morning — a woman's voice saying, "Women have not a word to say in politics." There is no woman in the Cabinet; nor in any responsible post. All the idea-makers who are in a position to make ideas effective are men. That is a thought that damps thinking, and encourages irresponsibility. Why not bury the head in the pillow, plug the ears, and cease this futile activity of idea-making? Because there are other tables besides officer tables and conference tables. Are we not leaving the young Englishman without a weapon that might be of value to him if we give up private thinking, tea-table thinking, because it seems useless? Are we not stressing our disability because our ability exposes us perhaps to abuse, perhaps to contempt? "I will not cease from mental fight," Blake wrote. Mental fight means thinking against the current, not with it.

That current flows fast and furious. It issues in a spate of words from the loudspeakers and the politicians. Every day they tell us that we are a free people, fighting to defend freedom. That is the

"Women of Britain Come into the Factories", propaganda poster, c.1940 (litho) English School, (20th century) / English. The Stapleton Collection/Bridgeman Images

This is a British propaganda poster from World War II targeted to women.

How did the creators of this image attempt to convince women to begin working in the factories? How effective do you think it was? Based on what you've read, to what extent would Woolf agree or disagree with its message?

current that has whirled the young airman up into the sky and keeps him circling there among the clouds. Down here, with a roof to cover us and a gas-mask handy, it is our business to puncture gas-bags and discover seeds of truth. It is not true that we are free. We are both prisoners tonight — he boxed up in his machine with a gun handy; we lying in the dark with a gas-mask handy. If we were free we should be out in the open, dancing, at the play, or sitting at the window talking together. What is it that prevents us? "Hitler!" the loudspeakers cry with one voice. Who is Hitler? What is he? Aggressiveness, tyranny, the insane love of power made manifest, they reply. Destroy that, and you will be free.

5 The drone of the planes is now like the sawing of a branch overhead. Round and round it goes, sawing and sawing at a branch directly above the house. Another sound begins sawing its way in the brain. "Women of ability" — it was Lady Astor[1] speaking in *The Times* this morning — "are held down because of a subconscious Hitlerism in the hearts of men." Certainly we are held down. We are equally prisoners tonight — the Englishmen in their planes, the Englishwomen in their beds. But if he stops to think he may be killed; and we too. So let us think for him. Let us try to drag up into consciousness the subconscious Hitlerism that holds us down. It is the desire for aggression; the desire to dominate and enslave. Even in the darkness we can see that made visible. We can see shop windows blazing; and women gazing; painted women; dressed-up women; women with crimson lips and crimson fingernails. They are slaves who are trying to enslave. If we could free ourselves from slavery we should free men from tyranny. Hitlers are bred by slaves.

A bomb drops. All the windows rattle. The anti-aircraft guns are getting active. Up there on the hill under a net tagged with strips of green and brown stuff to imitate the hues of autumn leaves guns are concealed. Now they all fire at once. On the nine o'clock radio we shall be told "Forty-four enemy planes were shot down during the night, ten of them by anti-aircraft fire." And one of the terms of peace, the loudspeakers say, is to be disarmament. There are to be no more guns, no army, no navy, no air force in the future. No more young men will be trained to fight with arms. That rouses another mind-hornet in the chambers of the brain — another quotation. "To fight against a real enemy, to earn undying honour and glory by shooting total strangers, and to come home with my breast covered with medals and decorations, that was the summit of my hope. . . . It was for this that my whole life so far had been dedicated, my education, training, everything. . . ."

Those were the words of a young Englishman who fought in the last war. In the face of them, do the current thinkers honestly believe that by writing "Disarmament" on a sheet of paper at a conference table they will have done all that is needful? Othello's occupation will be gone; but he will remain Othello[2]. The young airman up in the sky is driven not only by the voices of loudspeakers; he is driven by voices in himself — ancient instincts, instincts fostered and cherished by education and tradition. Is he to be blamed for those instincts? Could we switch off the maternal instinct at the command of a table full of politicians? Suppose that imperative among the peace terms was: "Child-bearing is to be restricted to a very small class of specially selected women," would we submit? Should we not say, "The maternal instinct is a woman's glory. It was for this that my whole life has been dedicated, my education, training, everything. . . ." But if it were necessary, for the sake of humanity, for the peace of the world, that child-bearing should be restricted, the maternal instinct subdued; women would attempt it. Men would help them. They

[1] Nancy Witcher Astor (1879–1964), Viscountess Astor, first woman to serve in the British House of Commons. — Eds.

[2] Venetian general, title character in *Othello* by William Shakespeare. — Eds.

extending beyond the text

The following poem, "*Dulce et Decorum Est*" was written by Wilfred Owen, who fought — and died — in World War I.

Dulce et Decorum Est

Wilfred Owen

Bent double, like old beggars under sacks,
Knock-kneed, coughing like hags, we cursed through sludge,
Till on the haunting flares we turned our backs,
And towards our distant rest began to trudge.
Men marched asleep. Many had lost their boots,
But limped on, blood-shod. All went lame; all blind;
Drunk with fatigue; deaf even to the hoots
Of gas shells dropping softly behind.

Gas! GAS! Quick, boys! — An ecstasy of fumbling
Fitting the clumsy helmets just in time,
But someone still was yelling out and stumbling
And flound'ring like a man in fire or lime. —
Dim through the misty panes and thick green light,
As under a green sea, I saw him drowning.

In all my dreams before my helpless sight,
He plunges at me, guttering, choking, drowning.

If in some smothering dreams, you too could pace
Behind the wagon that we flung him in,
And watch the white eyes writhing in his face,
His hanging face, like a devil's sick of sin;
If you could hear, at every jolt, the blood
Come gargling from the froth-corrupted lungs,
Obscene as cancer, bitter as the cud
Of vile, incurable sores on innocent tongues, —
My friend, you would not tell with such high zest
To children ardent for some desperate glory,
The old Lie: *Dulce et decorum est*
Pro patria mori.[1]

[1]Latin for "It is sweet and fitting to die for one's country." — Eds.

Explain how Woolf might respond to what the speaker of the poem calls "the old Lie."

would honour them for their refusal to bear children. They would give them other openings for their creative power. That too must make part of our fight for freedom. We must help the young Englishmen to root out from themselves the love of medals and decorations. We must create more honourable activities for those who try to conquer in themselves their fighting instinct, their subconscious Hitlerism. We must compensate the man for the loss of his gun.

The sound of sawing overhead has increased. All the searchlights are erect. They point at a spot exactly above this roof. At any moment a bomb may fall on this very room. One, two, three, four, five, six. . . . the seconds pass. The bomb did not fall. But during those seconds of suspense all thinking stopped. All feeling, save one dull dread, ceased. A nail fixed the whole being to one hard board. The emotion of fear and of hate is therefore sterile, unfertile. Directly that fear passes, the mind reaches out and instinctively revives itself by trying to create. Since the room is dark it can create only from memory. It reaches out to the memory of other Augusts — in Bayreuth, listening to Wagner; in Rome, walking over the Campagna; in London. Friends' voices come back. Scraps of poetry return. Each of those thoughts, even in memory, was far more positive, reviving, healing, and creative than the dull dread made of fear and hate. Therefore if we are to compensate the young man for the loss of his glory and of his gun, we must give him access to the creative feelings. We must make happiness. We must free him from the machine. We must bring him out of his prison into the open air. But what is the use of freeing the young Englishman if the young German and the young Italian remain slaves?

The searchlights, wavering across the flat, have picked up the plane now. From this window one can see a little silver insect turning and twisting in the light. The guns go pop pop pop. Then they cease. Probably the raider was brought

Wartime pilots and the Battle of Britain Artist:Wood, Gerry (b.1938) / English. Terror From the Skies.Wartime pilots and the Battle of Britain. Original coverartwork from Look and Learn no. 652 (13 July 1974).©Look and Learn/Bridgeman Images

This image called "Terror From the Skies. Wartime pilots and the Battle of Britain" was the cover artwork from *Look and Learn*, a children's magazine. **How is this portrayal of the airmen similar to or different from how Woolf portrays them?**

down behind the hill. One of the pilots landed safe in a field near here the other day. He said to his captors, speaking fairly good English, “How glad I am that the fight is over!” Then an Englishman gave him a cigarette, and an Englishwoman made him a cup of tea. That would seem to show that if you can free the man from the machine, the seed does not fall upon altogether stony ground. The seed may be fertile.

10 At last all the guns have stopped firing. All the searchlights have been extinguished. The natural darkness of a summer’s night returns. The innocent sounds of the country are heard again. An apple thuds to the ground. An owl hoots, winging its way from tree to tree. And some half-forgotten words of an old English writer come to mind: “The huntsmen are up in America. . . .”[3] Let us send these fragmentary notes to the huntsmen who are up in America, to the men and women whose sleep has not yet been broken by machine-gun fire, and in the belief that they will rethink them generously and charitably, perhaps shape them into something serviceable. And now, in the shadowed half of the world, to sleep. ■

[3] “The huntsmen are up in America, and they are already past their first sleep in Persia.” — Sir Thomas Browne (1605–1682), from “The Garden of Cyrus.” — Eds.

Understanding and Interpreting

1. According to Woolf, why might the sound of the planes in the raid compel “one to think about peace” more than prayers and anthems?
2. By the second paragraph, it becomes clear that this is as much a piece about gender as it is about war. What is Woolf suggesting about the differences between men and women, and their roles in war?
3. Explain what Woolf believes “damps thinking and encourages irresponsibility” (par. 3)?
4. Explain what Woolf means when she quotes William Blake: “Mental fight means thinking against the current, not with it” (par. 3).
5. What does Woolf mean by the term “subconscious Hilterism”? Does she believe that it will be defeated when Hitler and Germany are defeated? How do you know? What does she mean when she says, “Hitlers are bred by slaves” (par. 5)?
6. Woolf writes that “We must compensate the man for the loss of his gun” (par. 7). What does she mean? How does this statement relate to the rest of the text?
7. Explain the significance of the sentence: “But what is the use of freeing the young Englishman if the young German and the young Italian remain slaves?” (par. 8). Keep in mind that England was at war with Germany and Italy at this time.
8. Woolf envisions what might happen to the enemy pilot who was shot down (par. 9). What is Woolf suggesting about war and peace through this imaginary scene?
9. Reread the final line of the essay. What is Woolf’s hope for those in America to do?

Analyzing Language, Style, and Structure

1. **Vocabulary in Context.** The title of the essay is “Thoughts on Peace in an Air Raid,” and Woolf uses the word “think” regularly throughout the piece. Locate two or three different uses of the word and explain its meaning within the different contexts.
2. **Skill Focus.** Woolf avoids specific references to herself throughout this essay. For example, she does not use the words “I” or “me.” However, she does make herself known at times.

Identify places where the reader gets a sense of Woolf's personal experiences. Explain how they help to support the points she is making about war and peace.

3. Several times Woolf uses a hornet as an analogy to war (pars. 1 and 3). Explain the analogy and why she might have used it.
4. Woolf personifies the "current" in paragraph 4. What does the current represent and what is accomplished through her use of personification?
5. In paragraph 3 Woolf writes, "But to make ideas effective, we must be able to fire them off." Explain the analogy to weapons. Then explain how this analogy relates to her larger ideas about the role and power of women.
6. Woolf regularly draws comparisons between "up there" (airmen) and "down here" (women). What are the differences? How are men and women "equally prisoners" in war (par. 4)?
7. Reread the beginning of paragraph 5, in which Woolf uses figurative language to describe the drone of the planes. What does she compare the sound to, and what is the effect of this particular simile?
8. What is the effect of including the words from the young Englishman who fought in the previous world war who described his desire to earn "undying honor and glory" (par. 6)?
9. How does Woolf use the section on reducing childbearing to help make her argument about subconscious Hitlerism (par. 7)? Is she, in fact, suggesting that childbearing is restricted to a class of "specially selected women"?
10. Reread paragraph 8 in which Woolf describes the moment when a bomb may fall directly on her room. Note the contrast between the moment when all thoughts stop and when the thoughts begin again. What language choices does she use to illustrate that contrast?
11. Review the structure of Woolf's essay, tracing the start of the raid, the middle, and the ending. What is the effect of framing her essay within the context of a single night's air raid?

Topics for Composing

1. **Analysis.** Overall, what is the main point that Woolf makes about how to create peace in the world? What role do women play in the process she imagines?
2. **Argument.** Woolf says, "All the idea makers who are in a position to make ideas effective are men" in 1940. Take a position and write an argument on whether this statement is true or not true today. You can refer to your own experience or conduct research to support your response.
3. **Connection.** Identify a characterization of gender in the essay that you either strongly agree or disagree with. Explain how your personal experiences relate to your conclusion.
4. **Speaking and Listening.** Working with a partner, choose a paragraph from this essay that struck you because of the language, ideas, or other elements. Read it aloud to each other twice, taking turns so each person gets to read once and listen once. What particular words stood out to you when you read it aloud? How was your understanding of the essay different after reading it aloud, rather than reading it silently to yourself?
5. **Research.** In 1940, when Woolf was writing this essay, women were not allowed to serve in combat positions. Conduct research to find out what roles women played in World War II. Compare and contrast your findings with the roles that women can play in the armed services today. How much has changed? How much has remained the same?
6. **Multimodal.** Use some combination of drawing, painting, construction, or found images to recreate the air raid and the civilians below as depicted in this essay. Be sure that your piece captures not only the elements of war, but also the ideas of gender and possibilities for peace that Woolf presents.

The Censors (fiction)

Luisa Valenzuela
Translation by Frank Thomas Smith

JAVIER LIRA/Notimex/Newscom

Luisa Valenzuela (b. 1938) is an Argentine novelist, who began her career as a journalist in Buenos Aires and published her first story at the age of seventeen. She is one of Argentina's most significant writers, best known for her experimental style, classified as "magical realism." Valenzuela wrote her most popular work in response to the military dictatorship that ruled Argentina from 1976 to 1983. She remains one of the most widely translated female South American writers. The following story was originally published in 1976.

FOCUS FOR READING Throughout this chapter, you have been reading speeches, editorials, and essays about various ways to bring about change in the world. Unlike those other texts, the following is a work of fiction, even though it is based on real-life events that Valenzuela witnessed in Argentina. As you read this short story, consider how the author uses characters, setting, conflicts, and theme to explore the idea of changing the world.

Poor Juan! He was caught off guard that day and he couldn't realize that what he thought was a stroke of luck was really an accursed trick of fate. Those things happen when you're not careful, and as sure as you're hearing me one gets careless very, very often. Juancito let happiness — an otherwise disturbing sentiment — overwhelm him when, from a confidential source, he received Mariana's new address, now in Paris, and he knew that she hadn't forgotten him. Without thinking twice, he sat down at his desk and wrote a letter. *The* letter. The same one that now prevents him from concentrating on his work during the day and doesn't let him sleep when night comes (what did he put in that letter, what had stuck to that sheet of paper that he sent to Mariana?)

Juan knew there wouldn't be any problem with the text, that the text is irreproachable, innocuous. But the rest? He knows that they probe the letters, sniff them, feel them, read between the lines and their insignificant punctuation, even the accidental stains. He knows that the letters pass from hand to hand through the vast censorship bureaus and that few finally pass the tests and are able to continue their journey. Usually it's a question of months, years if complications arise, a long time in which the freedom and perhaps even the life of the sender and receiver are in suspense. And that's what has our Juan so deeply depressed: the idea that something could happen to Mariana, in Paris, through his fault. Mariana, of all people, who must feel so safe, so at ease there where she always dreamed of living. But he knows that the Secret Commandos of Censorship operate the world over and are granted a large discount on airline fares; therefore there's nothing to prevent them from going even to the darkest Paris *quartier*, kidnap Mariana and go home convinced of the nobility of their earthly mission.

So you have to outsmart them, you have to do what everyone does: try to sabotage the mechanism, throw sand in the gears, that is, go to the source of the problem in order to obstruct it.

That was the plan when Juan, like so many others, applied to be a censor. Not because of conviction like a few others or because he needed work like still others, no. He applied simply in order to try to intercept his own letter, not at all an original idea, but a comforting one. He was hired immediately, because more censors are needed every day and there's no time to be squeamish about references.

The Directorate of Censorship was aware of the secret motive behind the desire of more than one to work in the bureau, but they were in no condition to be too strict and anyway — What for? They knew how difficult it would be for those poor innocents to find the letter they were looking for, and even if they did, what importance does a letter or two that slips [through] the barrier cracks [have] compared to the others that the new censor would shoot down. That's how our Juan was able to join the Censorship Bureau of the Ministry of Communications.

The building, seen from outside, had a festive air because of the smoked glass that reflected the sky, an air that was in total contrast to the austere atmosphere of its interior. And little by little Juan became accustomed to the climate of concentration which his new work required, and the knowledge that he was doing everything possible for his letter — that is for Mariana — assuaged his anxieties. He wasn't even worried when, the first month, he was assigned to Section K where the envelopes are

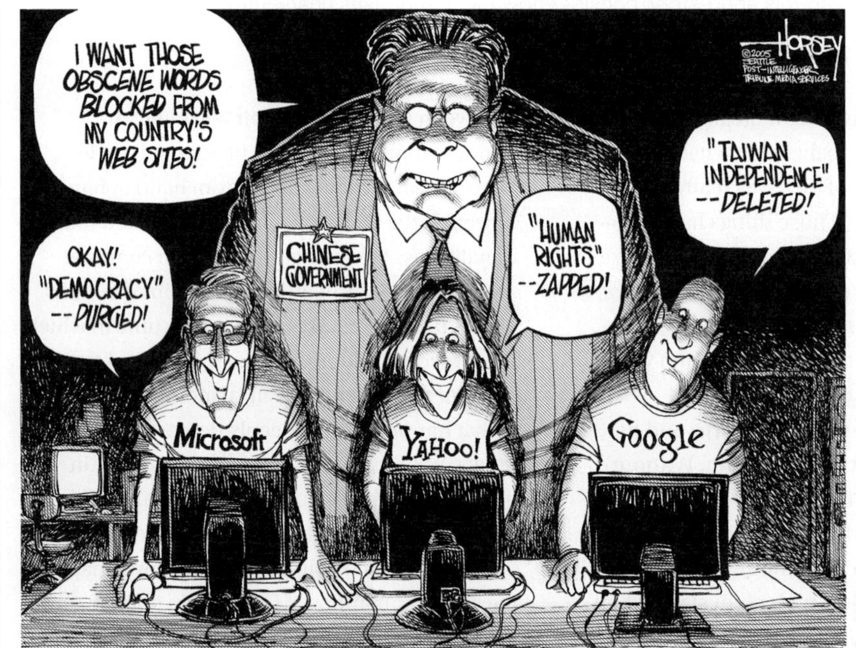

This editorial cartoon makes a statement about the relationship between an authoritarian government and large technology companies.

How would you describe that relationship, based on the image? How is this censorship similar to or different from the censorship described in the story?

extending beyond the text

Juan lives in a world where the government controls every aspect of communication. Read the following news release about a group of high school journalists who fought back against the censorship in their school.

from "Courage in Student Journalism Award" Goes To Burlington, Vermont High School Editors Who Successfully Fought Censorship

Student Press Law Center

Students from Burlington, Vermont who broke a story about alleged inappropriate behavior by a faculty member and triumphed over both censorship and prior review are being honored with the "Courage in Student Journalism Award."

"We fought back on a policy that restricted the rights of student journalism, keeping in mind that the outcome of our battle would set a precedent for the future journalists of Burlington," Julia Shannon-Grillo and Jenna Peterson, Co-Editors-in-Chief of The *BHS Register,* said in a brief statement this week.

"As a result, we were able to help write a new policy that allows us to be a reliable news source for the community and protects the freedom of the student press."

The *BHS Register* at Burlington High School broke the news of an investigation by the Vermont Agency of Education into six counts of alleged unprofessional conduct by the school's director of guidance.

To confirm details, the young journalists filed a public records request with the state agency. The day after the story was published online in September 2018, the school's then-interim principal ordered it to be taken down.

The *BHS Register* staff contacted the Student Press Law Center for legal guidance on how to respond to the administrator's action in light of a new state law that protects the basic First Amendment rights of student journalists. . . .

The students decided to keep links to their story up on social media that redirected readers to a page that said: "This article has been censored by Burlington High School administration."

Outrage over the censorship spread. Many teachers, parents and community residents publicly supported the right for the story to be published and multiple local and national news organizations covered the incident.

Along with assistance from the Student Press Law Center, The *BHS Register* also received steadfast support from the Vermont Press Association and the New England First Amendment Coalition. The latter two groups released a statement condemning the censorship.

Explain what these students did to "change the world," and consider what similar protections your own school's journalists might or might not have.

opened with painstaking care to see if they contain some explosive.

It's true that on the third day a letter blew a fellow-worker's hand off and disfigured his face, but the bureau chief claimed it had been mere negligence on the victim's part and Juan and the other employees could continue working as before, although with much less assurance. At quitting time another fellow worker tried to organize a strike to demand more pay for hazardous work, but Juan didn't participate and after thinking it over a while he denounced him to the authorities in order to be promoted.

Once doesn't form a habit, Juan thought as he left the chief's office, and when they transferred him to Section J where they unfold the letters with infinite care to see if they contain poisonous powder, he felt that he had ascended a step and could therefore return to his healthy habit of not getting involved in external affairs.

From J, thanks to his merits, he rose rapidly until reaching E, where the work became more interesting, for there begins the reading and analysis of the letters. In that Section he could even cherish hopes of coming across his own missive written to Mariana which, judging by the time elapsed, should have reached this level after a very long procession through the other departments.

10 Little by little there were days when his work so absorbed him that the noble mission that brought him to the Bureau became momentarily blurred. Days of crossing out long paragraphs with red ink, of tossing many letters into the Condemned Basket. Days of horror at the subtle and scheming ways people found to transmit subversive messages. Days of intuition so sharp that behind a simple "the weather is unsettled" or "prices are sky high," he detected the vacillating hand of someone whose secret intention was to overthrow the Government.

So much zeal brought him rapid promotion. We don't know if it made him very happy. In Section B the amount of letters which reached him daily was minimal — very few cleared the previous hurdles — but as compensation he had to read them often, put them under the magnifying glass, look for microdots with the electronic microscope and so tune his sense of smell that upon returning home at night he was exhausted. He barely managed to heat up some soup, eat some fruit and fall asleep with the satisfaction of having complied with his duty. Only his Sainted Mother worried about him, and tried without success to guide him back onto the right path. She'd say, although it wasn't necessarily true: Lola called, says she's with the girls in the café, that they miss you, are expecting you. But Juan didn't want to have anything to do with nonessentials: any distractions could cause him to lose the astuteness of his senses and he needed them alert, sharp, attentive, tuned, in order to be the perfect censor and detect deceit. His was a true patriotic labor. Self-denying and sublime.

His Basket of Condemned Letters soon became the best nourished but also the most subtle in the whole Censorship Bureau. He was at the point of feeling proud of himself, he was at the point of knowing that he had finally found his true path, when his own letter to Mariana reached his hands. Naturally he condemned it without remorse. And just as naturally he couldn't prevent them from executing him at dawn, one more victim of his devotion to work. ■

Understanding and Interpreting

1. What plan does Juan devise at the beginning of the story? What motivates him to conceive of this plan?
2. An essential way to understand a theme of this story is to trace the development of Juan's character. Describe what he is like and how he has changed at these key points:
   - Before he takes the censor job (pars.1–3)
   - In his first months on the job
   - When he arrives in Section B (last two paragraphs)
3. On his third day of work, Juan reported the man who was organizing a strike to his superiors. What does this action reveal about Juan? How is it a crucial turning point in the story?

4. While we can make assumptions about what the government is trying to censor, the only examples we see in this story are in paragraph 10, when Juan reads the phrases "the weather is unsettled" and "prices are sky high." Based on these examples, what do you think the government is trying to accomplish through its censorship?
5. Reread the last two sentences in paragraph 11. Explain the meaning of the phrase "self-denying" in the context of Juan's story. What is Valenzuela suggesting when she says that this describes a "patriotic labor."

Analyzing Language, Style, and Structure

1. **Vocabulary in Context.** Describing government workers, Valenzuela says they are "convinced of the nobility of their earthly mission." What does the word "nobility" mean in this context? How is this usage different from other uses you know of?
2. Throughout the piece, Valenzuela uses the word "they" to refer to the government. What is the effect of this word choice?
3. Verbal irony, sometimes called "sarcasm," is when words are used to express something contrary to truth or when someone says the opposite of what they really feel or mean. Explain how the following are examples of verbal irony and what effect they have on the reader:
   - "go home convinced of the nobility of their earthly mission" (par. 2)
   - "The building, seen from outside, had a festive air because of the smoked glass that reflected the sky." (par. 6)
   - "he had finally found his true path" (last paragraph)
4. In paragraph 11, Valenzuela writes, "So much zeal brought him rapid promotion. We don't know if it made him very happy." This is the first use of the pronoun *we* to refer to the narrator of this story. What does this pronoun choice suggest? Why might she have used *we* as opposed to *I*?
5. In the last paragraph, Valenzuela uses and repeats the word "naturally" to describe Juan's and the government's actions. How does this word choice help to communicate a point that Valenzuela is making about government and individuals?

Topics for Composing

1. **Analysis.** Juan set out to change the world that his government had made: "try to sabotage the mechanism, throw sand in the gears, that is, go to the source of the problem in order to obstruct it" (par. 2). Explain why Juan fails in his attempt to change the world. Consider what it is about the system or about his own personality that prevents him from succeeding.
2. **Argument.** While this story is fictional, it is based on real actions that governments have taken to censor the information their citizens can share with one another. Is government monitoring and censorship of its citizens ever appropriate? Take a position on this question and write an argument explaining and defending your position. Be sure to consider the balance between security and privacy.
3. **Connection.** You may have read other texts in this chapter written by people who, like the fictional Juan, set out to change the world. Imagine that one of those authors has the opportunity to explain to Juan where he went wrong. Adopting the persona of that author, what feedback would you give Juan about his plan and decisions he made along the way? What advice would you offer to save him from himself and the system in which he finds himself trapped? Address Juan in a letter, an email, a speech, or any mode that you think would best communicate your feedback to him.

4. **Speaking and Listening.** Hold a class or small group discussion about how free you are from censorship in your daily life. Are there environments in which you feel you can't say or write what's on your mind for fear of repercussions? How does your own experience of censorship affect you and those around you?
5. **Research.** Conduct research on the U.S. Patriot Act — originally passed in response to the 9/11 terrorist attacks in 2001 — to determine what the U.S. government can and cannot do to read and possibly censor private communication between citizens. Are there any connections between the Patriot Act and what occurs in this short story?
6. **Research.** Research the history of a country's government censorship, particularly in an authoritarian regime, such as the Soviet Union or East Germany during the Cold War, or Argentina in the 1970s. How extensive were these government operations? How successful were they in keeping information from citizens?
7. **Creative Writing.** Try out being a censor like Juan by creating what is called "erasure poetry," a form of found poetry writers generate by crossing out or obscuring part of an existing text, creating a wholly new work from what remains. Working with a newspaper article, a letter, or any other text that interests you, mark out what Juan might find objectional in his job. What is different about this new text that you've created with your erasures?

writing workshop

Using Personal Experience in an Argument

You may have read some of the speeches earlier in this chapter and seen the impact an effective argument can have on the world. For example, Martin Luther King Jr. made the case for nonviolent economic boycotts to improve conditions for workers in Memphis; Malala Yousafzai presented her argument for universal education in the face of religious extremism before an international audience; and Nelson Mandala presented a case for a time when a movement might be required to turn to violence to achieve its aims. Real arguments matter in the real world. The ability to communicate your ideas about a topic — especially one that affects you personally — is an essential skill both in the classroom and in your life outside of it.

While a balanced argument — appealing to ethos, logos, and pathos — is usually the most effective, pathos can be the most powerful appeal in your arsenal when used wisely. Talking about your personal experience is a good way to unlock it. Fundamentally, humans are attracted to stories. We remember them, and we respond emotionally to them.

In this workshop, you will use the following prompt to apply your own experiences to an argument:

> *Select a topic that is important and meaningful to you about which you can take a position that is debatable. Write an argumentative essay in which you use evidence that includes, but is not limited to, your own personal experiences.*

Throughout this workshop, we will refer to the moves that DeRay Mckesson makes in "Bully and the Pulpit" (p. 196) as a model for your own essay, highlighting how he connects his childhood experience of being bullied to the larger issues of social justice he took up as an adult.

Step 1: Gathering Ideas

This step allows you to slow down a bit and consider the topic you might want to write about and the personal connections you might have to it — *before* you write.

Finding a Topic

One of the first challenges we face with argumentative writing assignments is finding something to write about. DeRay Mckesson wasn't assigned to write a persuasive essay; he had important ideas about race and power that he wanted to communicate to others. These ideas are deeply rooted in his personal experiences as an African American male in the United States. As you explore topics, be sure to choose one that you are genuinely interested in and with which you have some kind of personal experience. This will make your writing authentic and meaningful not only in the classroom but also in the real world.

It is also important to think about *questions* you have, rather than *topics* you might write about. Although you might be tempted to jump right to the point you want to make, it is better to take some time and ask as many questions as you can about the topic first. For instance, if you are interested in sports and you regularly play and watch sports, you might ask questions such as these:

- Why are professional sports players paid so much?
- What are the ethical considerations of watching football, considering the risk of brain injury for the players?
- What are acceptable uses of performance-enhancing drugs in sports?
- What are the differences between the support that female athletes receive and the support that male athletes receive?

Try to pose questions that will take you beyond "yes" or "no" answers, and remember that no issue is black and white. Your job will be to investigate the nuances of the issue. Focusing on questions such as these will allow you to begin narrowing down your broad topic (sports, for example) into more specific ones (such as safety, or salaries), while at the same time keeping your options open to argumentative possibilities within your topic. Because you will also be including personal experience in your argument, you'll want to make sure that the topic is somehow relevant to you personally.

Finding a Topic

1. Look over the list of topics below and write two or three questions that you have about each one. Avoid questions that can be answered with "yes" or "no," such as "Should cell phones be banned in schools?" Try writing questions that reasonable people might have different opinions about. Eventually, you will select one question that you will use throughout the rest of this workshop. Again, be sure that you have some personal experiences with the questions — or their answers.
   - Education
   - Sports
   - The environment
   - Entertainment
   - Local or national politics
   - Technology
   - Topics of your own
2. In small groups, take a few minutes to share and discuss each person's questions.

Gathering Information

Once you've decided on a particular question that you have a genuine interest in, you can begin gathering information and developing an informed opinion on the subject. While you will certainly want to consult a wide variety of sources, including research studies, statistics, and articles by experts, the goal here is to start with what you know. Draw on your own experiences, as well as those of others around you, to begin informing your view on the subject. Look at the following excerpt from DeRay Mckesson's "Bully and the Pulpit" and notice how he incorporates into his argument an anecdote about his being bullied:

> When I am most in fear of succumbing to the bully, of allowing him to redefine my space, my world, I am reminded that the street existed before the bully did. We were free before we were enslaved. We are born to love before we know pain.
>
> When I was nine, I didn't know how to challenge the bully. I thought I was alone. The task of conquering my fear, of exposing him, loomed so large in my mind's eye that I was overcome by it. If I hadn't gone to Ferguson and stood toe to toe with other protesters on the streets calling for justice, naming our bully, and saying enough is enough, I'm not sure I'd have the courage to confront him today.

When you have a genuine interest in the argument you plan to write, there is likely some kind of personal experience that you (or people you know) have had with your topic.

If, for instance, your question is "Why do some school districts receive more funding than others?" you can think about the facilities and class sizes at your own school, and you can ask your family members or friends about the schools they have attended.

Gathering Information

Choose one of the questions that you wrote for the activity on page 236. Write three to five examples from either your own experiences or those of people you know that could give you information about your question. While these personal experiences might eventually be used as evidence, at this point, you are still at the information-gathering stage. Feel free to ask friends, classmates, and relatives, or to conduct surveys to learn more about experiences others have had with the question you've selected. If you cannot identify personal examples that might illustrate elements of your question, consider choosing a different topic that is more directly related to your experience and interests.

Investigating the Issue

Personal experience is a good place to start an argument. It gets you invested in the issue. Nevertheless, personal experience is not enough to give you the complete picture. You need to encounter multiple perspectives on the issue, look into the details of the situation, and investigate every angle possible. You need to go from having an opinion to having an *informed* opinion.

Begin by seeking answers to your questions. Who might have expertise on the issue you've chosen to write about? Scientists? Psychologists? Politicians?

It's likely that your investigation will uncover just as many new questions as it does answers. Learn to embrace that complexity. Understanding that every issue is complicated and that issues almost never have a clear answer will prevent you from writing an argument that is closed-minded, unreasonable, and not persuasive to anyone who doesn't already agree with you.

Investigating the Issue

Return to the question you developed in response to the activity on page 236, and begin conducting research to identify the following:

1. Who are three to five experts in the fields to which your question relates? These will be people who are referenced in many articles or in the bibliographies of multiple Wikipedia pages.
2. About what aspects of your topic might reasonable people disagree?
3. List two or three interesting facts or research results related to your question.

If you cannot find a wide range of information or differing views about your question that align in some significant way with your own personal experience on the issue, consider choosing a different topic. It is far better to switch topics at this point than to continue forward with one that might not work well.

Step 2: Planning the Essay

This step of the workshop is designed to move you closer to the actual writing of the essay. The following discussion will help you make sure that you have a clear point to address, enough evidence to support it, and an organizational structure that will help you prove your point.

Making a Claim

So far in this workshop, you have not been asked to write about your own position on the question you have been exploring. This is intentional. Too often, writers go into a topic already knowing their position, which can blind them to the complexity of the issue. But now, after conducting research and thinking about your own personal experiences with the topic, it's time to consider how you would present your position. You cannot have a successful argument if you do not have a **claim**, which is what you are hoping to prove, or convince your audience to believe. All strong arguments have a claim that the reader can identify and debate.

In his piece "The Bully and the Pulpit," Mckesson uses the metaphor of the bully on his block to illustrate how to confront the destructive power of white supremacy:

> The presence of the bully is difficult to overcome and the residue is difficult to shake. I stress the importance of imagining our ideal world because we naturally gravitate toward methods for achieving our desired outcomes. Indeed, we focus on tactics — how do we beat the bully? — but we don't always remember to prepare for the day when the bully is no more. We will need a vision for that time too. If we don't have a vision for our desired future, how can we plan to achieve it? If you cannot imagine it, you cannot fight for it. When we confront the bully, we are confronting our fear and reclaiming our imagination. There are those who cannot imagine a block without a bully. We must all imagine the block without a bully, otherwise we cannot get there.

You can see in the underlined sentence that Mckesson claims we need to be able to imagine a different future, one without the bully — white supremacy — if we are going to move past our fears.

It's important to remember that an argument's claim must be debatable. Without a debate, there is nothing to prove. So, when making a claim, be sure that it is something with which some people might reasonably disagree. You should also avoid simply stating a preference ("chocolate is better than vanilla"). There is no way to prove a claim like that using hard evidence. In addition, you should avoid a claim that just states a fact that is easily proved or disproved ("smoking causes cancer"). If it's a fact proven by numerous studies, it's not debatable. Mckesson's claim might seem undeniable because it has the force of history and justice behind it, but a reasonable person might argue that there are different, more direct ways to address the impacts of white supremacy.

Your claim should answer the question you have been exploring and either state your main reasons for believing what you do, or include a call for an action that ought to be taken (or both). Be sure that your claim takes a stance on an issue that is important to you. Avoid including the phrases "I think," "I believe," or "in my opinion." The purpose of an argument is to say what you think or believe, so these phrases are redundant.

Making a Claim

Consider the question you have been using throughout this workshop, and write a claim or thesis that stakes out your own position on the question. Share it with a partner, and be sure that it meets all of the expectations of a strong claim.

Developing Personal Experience as Evidence

In Step 1, when you gathered information about your question, you did so for the purpose of identifying personal connections to the topic and learning as much as possible about it before coming to an informed position in the form of your claim. Now it is time to begin making your case — by turning the information you gained into evidence that you can use to support your claim. A good argument includes a wide range and variety of evidence; this workshop focuses specifically on how you can use personal experience as evidence in your argument. Throughout "The Bully and the Pulpit," DeRay Mckesson talks about his experiences with the bully on his block when he was a child. For example, look back at the beginning of his essay:

> When I was nine years old, my babysitter put water on a grease fire and our house burned to the ground. My father, sister, and I moved to Grandma's house then, to a different part of town — leaving our small but separate bedrooms to now share a bed in her living room — about fifteen minutes away. And my sister and I started going to a new school. The thing that I remember most vividly from that year is the walk home from school. I remember the sweaty palms, the dry mouth, the bravado, the focus, the running. I remember Uncle Barry sometimes meeting us at the top of the hill.
>
> And I remember the fear.

> There was a bully on our block on the walk home, always present even when I couldn't see him. And every day, the ten minutes between the school parking lot and my grandmother's yard were full of anxiety.

Notice all of the details of the house, the physical and emotional descriptions of his fear. At points like this, Mckesson's essay probably feels more like a narrative than an argumentative piece because of all of the details he includes. But it is the inclusion of these personal experiences that gives this piece its power. When Mckesson switches soon after to make the comparison between this bully and white supremacy, the reader is ready to follow him because we have made an emotional connection with him.

Sadly, many of Mckesson's readers have probably directly suffered bullying or know someone who has, so his appeal to pathos here is extraordinarily effective. But the inclusion of his personal experience does more than just appeal emotionally; it also helps to establish his ethos, his position of authority on this topic because he has directly experienced the bullying that he uses to help the reader recognize the similarities to the power of white supremacy.

Personal experience, as you may remember from the Skill Workshop (pp. 160–166), can take a number of different forms:

1. Descriptions of a specific event or incident that happened directly to you.
2. Descriptions of an event that you witnessed or heard about happening to someone else that you know and trust.
3. Ideas that you have gained from your general experiences based on your race, gender, age, ethnicity, participation in particular groups, and so on.
4. Feelings that you have about a topic, rooted in a specific incident or experience.

Developing Personal Experience as Evidence

After considering how Mckesson successfully incorporates his story into his argument, try to do the same by settling on a specific experience or two that might be relevant to the claim that you wrote earlier in this workshop.

1. Choose one or two of those experiences and share them with a partner. Your partner will listen closely as you describe your experiences and will help you to clarify and deepen your own understanding by asking questions such as the following:
   - What specific details do you remember of the setting or other people?
   - What emotions were you feeling at the time?
   - What did you learn from this experience?
   - How does this experience relate to the claim you are trying to prove?
2. After discussing your experiences with a partner, write out one or two of those experiences with as much detail and description as you can. Be sure that the story you are writing is relevant to the claim you are hoping to prove.

Locating Additional Support

As you have seen throughout this workshop and in Mckesson's essay, personal experience can be a powerful and compelling source of evidence. However, an argument generally requires additional support to be persuasive. Sometimes readers will too easily dismiss an argument that relies solely on personal experience, saying something to the effect of, "Sure that might be true for you, but what about for other people?" Mckesson recognizes that some of his readers might not find his personal stories fully persuasive, so he adds evidence to make a stronger case:

> In many ways, we live in one of the bully's golden ages, a time when the mere mention of white supremacy is an anachronism. Absent the hoods and burning crosses, we presume the bully dead. But he's still operating in the shadows; he's just working through insidious means. The fact that many people refuse to acknowledge him means that we cannot dismantle what he has wrought. And in our blindness, we've created a host of studies to explain away his legacy. In the meantime, he is at work. When we see 21 percent of kids of color in poverty, that is white supremacy at work. When we see a president refusing to allow immigrants from majority people-of-color countries into this country, that is white supremacy at work. Defunding public education, gerrymandering, and scaling back the Voting Rights Act are all manifestations of this ideology.

Notice that he provides several concrete examples that demonstrate white supremacy's lasting power, including education funding, poverty, and voting rights. The inclusion of these examples helps Mckesson make his point about the need to imagine a world without white supremacy. While the centerpiece of the argument that you are writing is the personal experience you have had with this issue, like Mckesson, you will need to bolster your claim with additional types of evidence. In addition to personal experience, the main types of evidence (p. 90) that appear in an argument are facts, scholarly research, expert opinion, data, and statistics.

Locating Additional Support

Locate additional relevant and convincing evidence (conduct further research, if necessary). Be sure to find various types of evidence (facts, scholarly research, expert opinion, and data and statistics) that can appeal to both logos and pathos (p. 95). Then, identify the two or three most relevant and credible pieces of evidence (p. 138) to support your claim.

Organizing the Essay

At some point in your education, you may have heard that an essay is supposed to have five paragraphs: an introduction, three body paragraphs, and a conclusion. This argumentative essay you are writing might, in fact, have five paragraphs. Or, it might have four, fourteen, or any other number in between or beyond. The number of paragraphs you need will depend on the complexity of your argument, and the amount of personal experience you include. This is not to say that there are no guidelines at all for how you make your argument. The body of your essay is the place where you prove the claim that you wrote earlier. How you go about organizing the body of your essay is up to you, but here are a few possibilities, probably in order of increasing complexity, challenge, and sophistication:

- **Organize by reason**: With this approach, you would go through each of your main reasons for supporting your position, usually starting with your strongest reason and addressing the main counterargument last. Each reason would be a separate paragraph.
- **Organize by counterargument**: With this approach, your entire essay is organized by the arguments **against** your thesis. In each separate paragraph, you raise an objection to your claim and refute it.
- **Organize by problem and solution**: With this approach, you would describe the problem that your topic raises by documenting your own personal experiences with the issue and maybe supplementing it with additional sources. Then, you would offer a solution to the problem, which is your main claim. You might have one or more paragraphs about the problem and then an equal number about the proposed solution.

Organizing Your Essay

Sketch out an outline that the body of your essay could take. Where will you likely include your personal experiences? Where will you probably address the counterarguments, the ideas of those who might think differently about your claim? Discuss with a partner about why you chose this particular approach and what the benefits and challenges of this structure might be.

Step 3. Drafting the Essay

At this point in the workshop, you have all of the pieces in place to begin drafting your essay. This step will walk you through some of the factors to consider when you are writing your body paragraphs, as well as ideas to help you with starting and ending your essay.

Writing Body Paragraphs

In Chapter 4, we introduced a common structure for paragraphs, which we described with three key terms: Point, Evidence, Commentary (p. 144). Essentially, each of your body paragraphs will have a topic sentence that identifies a component of your claim (sometimes at the very beginning of the paragraph, sometimes embedded within it), evidence that supports the topic sentence, and your own commentary about how that evidence supports that part of your claim. You will include as much or as little evidence as you need to make your point, though it is always important to follow every piece of evidence with commentary. In this way, you will be sure to "connect the dots" for your reader and keep the emphasis on your own voice and ideas.

Again, this structure is not intended as a formula. Rather, it is suggested as a guide for you to use when it suits you and your argument. You can see how elements of this structure are in place in the following section from Mckesson's essay:

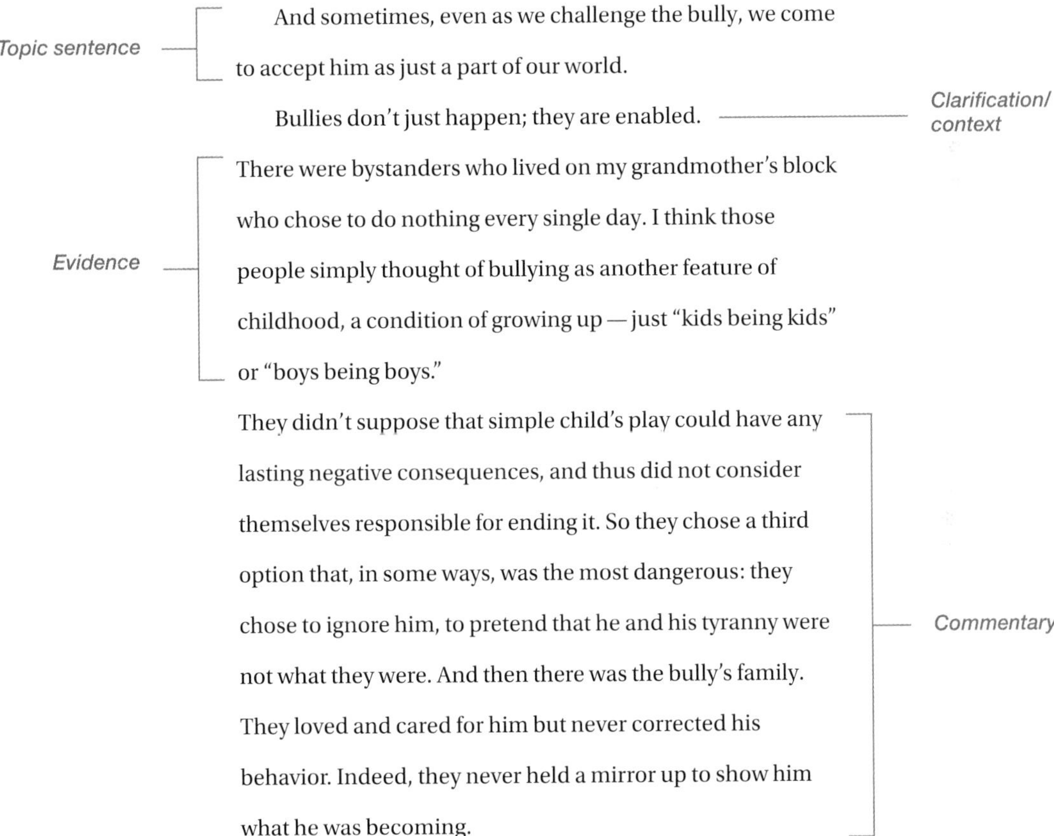

Mckesson often goes back and forth between commentary and evidence. Again, the structure suggested above is not a rigid formula. The point here is that evidence should never stand on its own. It should be accompanied by commentary from you, the writer. In an argumentative essay, telling your audience what the evidence proves, and why it is relevant to your overall argument, makes it more likely that your audience will understand and appreciate what you have to say.

Addressing Counterarguments

An essential part of making your argument is to address counterarguments (p. 100), those ideas that challenge your claim. These ideas are not necessarily against your entire position, but they might represent a different course of action, or might go beyond what you are willing to propose.

Some writers prefer to address the counterargument at the beginning of their piece, immediately conceding and refuting their opponents' points. Other writers may wait until later in their argument, after they have made their strongest points. Mckesson addresses a key counterargument toward the end of his essay when he points out that not everyone believes in the same approach to confronting the bully of white supremacy. Notice how he raises several other possibilities, and then works to explain why his approach might be the best:

> In the face of the bully, there are seemingly only two options: to challenge him or to accept him. I never understood the notion of "fight or flight" in this context, because "flight" would only be a temporary reprieve and not an actual stance. I couldn't avoid the street forever, and I shouldn't have had to. "Fight" feels like an equally false option — overcoming the bully should not rest on adopting his tactics. When we accept these options, we run, we fight, we push back, because it seems like these are the only things we can do. In a world of incessant battles and their accompanying exhaustion, survival can become the overriding theme in how we think about living, and fear something that we unconsciously accept.

The basic approach to addressing counterarguments is to acknowledge and concede any valid points your opponents might make, and then to refute the main thrust of their arguments. Unaddressed counterarguments linger in the minds of thoughtful readers who say, "Yeah, but what about ___________?" Your job as a successful writer of arguments includes anticipating all reasonable objections to your claim and presenting evidence that your point of view is the most reasonable.

It may be tempting to use a phrase such as "Some people say ___________," but this only prompts readers to question, "Who?" Instead, try to fully understand and describe the opposition's position, and respectfully identify any noteworthy experts who hold that view.

Writing Your Body Paragraphs

After reviewing the claim you wrote on page 239 and the organizational structure you identified on page 242, draft the body paragraphs for your argument. In addition to ensuring that you have balanced personal experience with some outside sources, be sure that at least one of your paragraphs introduces and refutes a key counterargument. Use the Point-Evidence-Commentary structure described above as a guide, but you should not be restricted by it as a formula. Remember that the number of paragraphs you need will depend on your purpose and the complexity of your topic. Share your body paragraphs with a partner or in a small group to help you make sure that your points are clear, that your evidence is balanced with commentary, and that you fully and ethically present and refute the counterargument.

Writing the Introduction

One of the most difficult parts of writing anything is figuring out how to start. Think of your opening as having three parts:

1. The hook
2. Context
3. Your claim or thesis

The Hook

Regardless of who the members of your audience are, they have demands on their time and a lot of options for what to read. You have to make them want to read *your* piece. So, begin your argument by "hooking" your readers with some kind of attention grabber. This might be a shocking fact, a startling statistic, or (since this has been the focus of this workshop) perhaps a profound personal story that is related to but different from the personal experience you offer as evidence in the body of your essay. If you think back to the rhetorical appeals discussed in Chapter 3, you can see that a successful hook often relies on an appeal to pathos — emotion. Pathos is the spice of an argument. It makes it interesting and gives it flavor, but it should be used sparingly. The hook is a great place to use it. As you saw above, Mckesson's hook is his devastating story about being bullied as a child, which powerfully draws his readers into the rest of his argument.

The Context

Another thing to think about when starting your argument is how much background you need to provide to your audience. If your audience does not understand the context of your argument, you have little chance of persuading them of your claim. The amount of context you need to include will vary based on the complexity of the issue or the specificity of the evidence you will likely use. For example, while Mckesson starts his essay with the story of his being bullied, his argument isn't really about childhood bullies. As a result, he has to provide his readers with a bit of context so they can see that he's using the story of the bully as a metaphor of a larger societal issue:

> I've thought a lot more about the role of the bully too — about how he moves, adapts, and survives over time; about his source of legitimacy; about the impact of his power. Of late, I've thought about the bully in the context of our present world versus the world that we aim to create for the future, and considering him has transformed the way I think about both.

Writing Your Introduction

Write a draft of your introductory paragraph by putting together the following components:

- Your hook (ethos, logos, or pathos)
- Appropriate and necessary context — the background information your audience will need to understand what follows
- Your claim, which you developed earlier, and which you may have revised after conducting additional research

Writing the Conclusion

Just as pathos can provide an effective hook for introducing your essay, more often than not, it is also a powerful approach to concluding it. Writers often want to get their readers to feel something before they ask them to take some kind of action. Look at the conclusion of Mckesson's essay, which is filled with appeals to emotion:

> When I was nine, I didn't know how to challenge the bully. I thought I was alone. The task of conquering my fear, of exposing him, loomed so large in my mind's eye that I was overcome by it. If I hadn't gone to Ferguson and stood toe to toe with other protesters on the streets calling for justice, naming our bully, and saying enough is enough, I'm not sure I'd have the courage to confront him today.
>
> In each generation there is a moment when young and old, inspired or disillusioned, come together around a shared hope, imagine the world as it can be, and have the opportunity to bring that world into existence. Our moment is now.

Notice, too, that Mckesson's conclusion includes a call to action — "Our moment is now." In addition to pathos, a good conclusion to an argument usually addresses a "So what?" statement that tells readers what you want them to think about, or do, and why it matters. What reforms should take place? What studies should be conducted? What viewpoint should be reevaluated? What programs should be funded? This is a final opportunity for you to connect directly with your readers. Mckesson's choice is to focus on bringing everyone "together around a shared hope."

Writing Your Conclusion

Write a conclusion to your argumentative essay that includes a final appeal to emotion and a call to action. Your conclusion might even be another place to return to a personal experience that you described earlier in your essay.

Step 4. Finalizing the Essay

Now that you have a complete draft of your argumentative essay, you can move on to the final phase in the writing process: revising and editing. These two acts are sometimes thought of as being the same, but they're not. Revision is when you look back at large-scale structural elements of your essay, such as how well you are supporting your claim, what kinds of evidence are you using, how effective your word choices are, and to what extent you have led your reader easily through your essay. Editing, on the other hand, focuses on fine tuning the language, grammar, punctuation, spelling, and other conventions. Editing is usually the very last thing you do before you finalize your piece, looking carefully for any errors that you tend to make. The following are suggestions for you to consider as you finalize your essay:

Revising

Oftentimes, revision can be more effective when you discuss these questions with a partner.

- Look back at your **claim**. Since you wrote this early on in the workshop, does it still relate to the argument you wrote? See Revision Workshop 1: Effective Thesis and Essay Structure (p. 1064) if you need more assistance.
- Look back at the **personal experience** you used as evidence. Is it detailed and evocative, like Mckesson's story of being bullied? Is it relevant to your claim? Are there places in which more personal experiences would make sense? Review the Skill Workshop at the beginning of this chapter (p. 160) if you need additional ideas.
- Look back at your **other evidence**. Does this evidence balance out and effectively bolster the personal experience? See Revision Workshop 4: Appropriate Evidence and Support (p. 1076) for help with this aspect of your argument.
- Have you attempted to address the main **counterarguments** for your position? Have you refuted them successfully? Are you fair and ethical in how you refute their arguments? Review Chapter 3 (p. 100) if you have trouble identifying and refuting counterarguments.

- Look back at your **body paragraphs**. Have you balanced the evidence with your own **commentary** about how that evidence supports your claim? See Revision Workshop 3: Balanced Evidence and Commentary (p. 1073) if you need more help with this part of your essay.
- Evaluate your **organizational structure**. Is it clear enough for the reader to follow? Are there other approaches to the organization that might be more effective? See Revision Workshop 5: Effective Transitions (p. 1082) or Revision Workshop 2: Effective Topic Sentences and Unified Paragraphs (p. 1068) if you think that your reader may have trouble following your essay.
- Does your **introduction** hook the reader and provide context to understand the claim? Does your **conclusion** include an appeal to pathos and a call to action? If not, consider looking at Revision Workshop 8: Effective Introductions and Conclusions (p. 1097).
- Are your **language choices** appropriate for your purpose and audience and as effective as they could be? See Revision Workshop 6: Effective Syntax (p. 1087) or Revision Workshop 7: Effective Diction (p. 1093) to further develop your style and voice.

Editing

Remember, editing is the very last thing you'll do before finalizing your essay. You and your teacher know better than anyone the types of spelling, grammar, and convention errors you are focusing on in your writing development. Refer to one or more of the Grammar Workshops (starting on p. 1101) in the back of the book if you encounter an issue and aren't sure how to address it.

Continuing the Conversation

Throughout this chapter, you have been reading texts and thinking about how people create change in the world. At the beginning of the chapter and after each of the readings, you had opportunities to consider ideas related to the following essential questions:

ESSENTIAL QUESTIONS

- What conditions are required to make change happen?
- How does one gain the appropriate amount and type of power to create change?
- How does effective, persuasive communication help to bring about change?
- When — if ever — is violence an appropriate means for creating change?

The sections that follow will give you an opportunity to revisit and respond to some of those questions as you think further about creating change by connecting these ideas to yourself, to texts you've read, and to the world outside of the classroom.

Connections to Self

Think back on the texts you have read, responses you have written, discussions you have participated in, and ideas you have considered during your work with this chapter. Use these questions to help explore how the issues in this chapter connect to your life and experience.

1. Describe a change that you would like to see at your school or in your town. What power do you have, personally, to bring about that change?
2. Explain how your personal, academic, social, and other skills might help you bring about a desired change.
3. How do you tend to respond when you talk with someone whose position on a topic is different from your own? How do you try to convince that person of your position?

Connections to Texts

Use these questions to make connections among the texts in this chapter, and consider what insights the texts provide into the issue of Changing the World. As you respond, be sure to make specific references to **two or more texts** you read in this chapter.

1. In her piece "What if We're All Coming Back" (p. 185), Michelle Alexander proposes that one way to help people consider the effects of climate change is to encourage them to imagine that they will be reincarnated after death. Use her same thought experiment with the topic of another chapter text. Explain how the idea of

reincarnation might or might not help create the proposed change. To what extent do you think Alexander's method is an effective approach to creating change?

2. Some of the authors in this chapter focus on how power (or the lack of power) affects how change can be created. In what ways do they view power similarly or differently? How do their views compare to your own sense of how power and change are related? You might want to consider the following texts in your response: "When 16-Year-Olds Vote, We All Benefit" (p. 167), Dolores Huerta's speech at UCLA (p. 190), and "Bully and the Pulpit" (p. 196).
3. Create a dialogue between two of the authors in this chapter. What topics related to creating change would they discuss? How would they respond to each other?
4. Which of the authors in this chapter would you like to have dinner with? Why? What questions would you ask about that author's choices and advocacy for change? Or, which author would you definitely not want to have dinner with? Why? If you were stuck next to that author at dinner, what questions would you ask?
5. Which of the texts in this chapter had the most significant effect on the way you think about change? Why?

Connections to World

Think back on the texts you have read, responses you have written, discussions you have participated in, and ideas you have considered during your work with this chapter. Use the following questions to help explore how the issues in this chapter play out in the world at large.

1. Identify political, cultural, or social leaders who are currently trying to create meaningful change. How effective are their approaches to creating change? What suggestions would you offer them?
2. What prevents meaningful change in the world from happening easily? Why are some people, institutions, and organizations reluctant to change?
3. What is the most important change that we need in the world? What are the best approaches to try to achieve that change?
4. Examine how two or more authors in this chapter approach the idea of using violence to create change in the world. You might want to consider the following texts in your response: "An Ideal for which I am Prepared to Die" (p. 205), "Thoughts on Peace in an Air Raid" (p. 222), "I Have Been to the Mountaintop" (p. 211), and "Bully and the Pulpit" (p. 196).

Evidence-Based Argument

Write an argument in response to one of the following prompts in which you support your claim with examples from **at least three of the texts** in this chapter.

Prompt 1: Write about a time that you created some kind of change. It could be something that took place at school, in your home, in your community, or elsewhere. Note that it does not need to be a major change. What were the steps that you took to create this change? Which of the authors from this chapter would likely support and or oppose your approach to creating that change?

Prompt 2: Is violence ever an appropriate approach to bringing about change? Why or why not? Refer to at least three texts you read.

Prompt 3: To what extent are humans capable of long-lasting and meaningful change? Refer to at least three texts you read.

Stevens, Nelson (b. 1938) © Copyright Towards Identity, 1970. Oil on canvas, 120.6 x 120.6 cm (47 1/2 x 47 1/2 in.). Image courtesy the artist and Galerie Myrtis. Gift of Dr. James and Jetta Jones, 1999.940. The Art Institute of Chicago/Art Resource, NY

Self-Discovery

Essential Questions:

- **What roles do individuals play within their close social circles and within society as a whole?**
- **How does identity shift over time?**
- **What kinds of events and influences can cause identity to shift?**
- **How does setting affect social interactions?**
- **How do factors such as race, culture, gender identity, socioeconomic status, immigration status, and sexual orientation influence what we know and learn about ourselves?**

Self-discovery is the continual process by which we learn to understand parts of ourselves and our identities. We know that identities change — you are probably not exactly the same person that you were in elementary school, and you might not even be exactly the same person that you were last month. Why do our identities change? What factors lead to those changes? And what allows and encourages you to discover these changes in yourself and your identity? David Bowie, a pop singer who began his career in the late 1960s, changed his identity with almost every album he released. He even wrote a song in 1971 called "Changes," in which he sang about all the versions of himself he had created. In some ways, are we all like Bowie, constantly reinventing ourselves?

A significant factor in our awareness and discovery of ourselves is the society we live in. We might think of society as the group with which we share a country, city, town, or region. But we also have a society made up of our peers, which is probably different from our home life. So, when we discover something about ourselves or think about who we are, we have to consider how we fit into large and small circles, broad and specific contexts. And, of course, our identity is greatly influenced by factors that surround us — our culture.

Self-Discovery

In small groups, talk about how you thought of yourself in elementary school and in middle school, and how you think of yourself now. How have you changed? What aspects of your personality are more prominent now? Which ones no longer apply? What factors do you think have contributed most to who you are today?

Texts in Conversation

All of the poems and stories you'll encounter in this chapter include characters and speakers who explore personal identity and achieve some kind of self-discovery. Some come to realize that they are different from those who surround them or chafe under their family's expectations. As you read, think about how these characters define their own identities and those of the people around them. Trace these individuals, their discoveries, and the factors that contribute to their sense of self. A graphic organizer like this one can help you keep track of the individuals you'll encounter and their journeys.

Author / Title	Main character, speaker, or narrator	Evidence from the text related to moment of self-discovery	Description of the specific change in self-perception	Connections to yourself and other texts

skill workshop

Understanding Character and Theme in Prose

As you may recall from Chapter 2, analyzing a story's characters helps us understand the main ideas, or themes, presented by a writer. Our task as readers is to pay attention to every detail associated with those characters. That means looking at what the author *tells* us about each character, which we call **direct characterization**, and what the author *shows* us about the character through actions, dialogue, and interactions with other characters, which we call **indirect characterization**.

While the protagonist is usually the focus of an analysis of character and theme, minor characters and the antagonist can also help us understand ideas the author aims to convey. In fact, all characters contribute to the idea of the story in some way. This workshop will focus on how we gather, organize, and interpret textual details regarding a character to draw conclusions about the theme of a text.

Abuela Invents the Zero

Judith Ortiz Cofer

Poet, novelist, and essayist Judith Ortiz Cofer was born in Puerto Rico in 1952 and grew up in New Jersey. The following story is from her 1995 collection *An Island Like You: Stories from the Barrio.*

FOCUS FOR READING As you read this story for the first time, annotate the text by making connections and asking questions (see p. 10). Then, go back and annotate it again, looking specifically for moments in which the characters are developed.

"You made me feel like a zero, like a nothing," she says in Spanish, *un cero, nada*. She is trembling, an angry little old woman lost in a heavy winter coat that belongs to my mother. And I end up being sent to my room, like I was a child, to think about my grandmother's idea of math.

It all began with Abuela coming up from the Island for a visit — her first time in the United States. My mother and father paid her way here so that she wouldn't die without seeing snow, though if you asked me, and nobody has, the dirty slush in this city is not worth the price of a ticket. But I guess she deserves some kind of award for having had ten kids and survived to tell about it. My mother is the youngest of the bunch. Right up to the time when we're supposed to pick up the old lady at the airport, my mother is telling me stories about how hard times were for *la familia* on *la isla*, and how *la abuela* worked night and day to support them after their father died of a heart attack. I'd die of a heart attack too if I had a troop like that to support. Anyway, I had seen her only three or four times in my entire life, whenever we would go for somebody's funeral. I was born here and I have lived in this building all my life. But when Mami says, "Connie, please be nice to Abuela. She doesn't have too many years left. Do you promise me, Constancia?" — when she uses my full name, I know she means business. So I say, "Sure." Why wouldn't I be nice? I'm not a monster, after all.

So we go to Kennedy to get *la abuela*, and she is the last to come out of the airplane, on the arm of the cabin attendant, all wrapped up in a black shawl. He hands her over to my parents like she was a package sent airmail. It is January, two feet of snow on the ground, and she's wearing a shawl over a thin black dress. That's just the start.

Once home, she refuses to let my mother buy her a coat because it's a waste of money for the two weeks she'll be in *el Polo Norte*, as she calls New Jersey, the North Pole. So since she's only four feet eleven inches tall, she walks around in my mother's big black coat looking ridiculous. I try to walk far behind them in public so that no one will think we're together. I plan to stay very busy the whole time she's with us so that I won't be asked to take her anywhere, but my plan is ruined when my mother comes down with the flu and Abuela absolutely *has* to attend Sunday mass or her soul will be eternally damned. She's more Catholic than the Pope. My father decides that he should stay home with my mother and that I should escort *la abuela* to church. He tells me this on Saturday night as I'm getting ready to go out to the mall with my friends.

"No way," I say.

I go for the car keys on the kitchen table: he usually leaves them there for me on Friday and Saturday nights. He beats me to them.

"No way," he says, pocketing them and grinning at me.

Needless to say, we come to a compromise very quickly. I do have a responsibility to Sandra and Anita, who don't drive yet. There is a Harley-Davidson fashion show at Brookline Square that we *cannot* miss.

"The mass in Spanish is at ten sharp tomorrow morning, *entiendes*?" My father is dangling the car keys in front of my nose and pulling them back when I try to reach for them. He's really enjoying himself.

"I understand. Ten o'clock. I'm out of here." I pry his fingers off the key ring. He knows that I'm late, so he makes it just a little difficult. Then he laughs. I run out of our apartment before he changes his mind. I have no idea what I'm getting myself into.

Sunday morning I have to walk two blocks on dirty snow to retrieve the car. I warm it up for Abuela as instructed by my parents, and drive it to the front of our building. My father walks her by the hand in baby steps on the slippery snow. The sight of her little head with a bun on top of it sticking out of that huge coat makes me want to run back into my room and get under the covers.

I just hope that nobody I know sees us together. I'm dreaming, of course. The mass is packed with people from our block. It's a holy day of obligation and everyone I ever met is there.

I have to help her climb the steps, and she stops to take a deep breath after each one, then I lead her down the aisle so that everybody can see me with my bizarre grandmother. If I were a good Catholic, I'm sure I'd get some purgatory time taken off for my sacrifice. She is walking as slow as Captain Cousteau exploring the bottom of the sea, looking around, taking her sweet time. Finally she chooses a pew, but she wants to sit in the other end. It's like she had a spot picked out for some unknown reason, and although it's the most inconvenient seat in the house, that's where she has to sit. So we squeeze by all the people already sitting there, saying, "Excuse me, please, *con permiso,* pardon me," getting annoyed looks the whole way. By the time we settle in, I'm drenched in sweat. I keep my head down like I'm praying so as not to see or be seen. She is praying loud, in Spanish, and singing hymns at the top of her creaky voice.

I ignore her when she gets up with a hundred other people to go take communion. I'm actually praying hard now — that this will all be over soon. But the next time I look up, I see a black coat dragging around and around the church, stopping here and there so a little gray head can peek out like a periscope on a submarine. There are giggles in the church, and even the priest has frozen in the middle of a blessing, his hands above his head like he is about to lead the congregation in a set of jumping jacks.

I realize to my horror that my grandmother is lost. She can't find her way back to the pew. I am so embarrassed that even though the woman next to me is shooting daggers at me with her eyes, I just can't move to go get her. I put my hands over my face like I'm praying, but it's really to hide my burning cheeks. I would like for her to disappear. I just know that on Monday my friends, and my enemies, in the barrio will have a lot of senile-grandmother jokes to tell in front of me. I am frozen to my seat. So the same woman who wants me dead on the spot does it for me. She makes a big deal out of getting up and hurrying to get Abuela.

The rest of the mass is a blur. All I know is that my grandmother kneels the whole time with her hands over *her* face. She doesn't speak to me on the way home, and she doesn't let me help her walk, even though she almost falls a couple of times.

When we get to the apartment, my parents are at the kitchen table, where my mother is trying to eat some soup. They can see right away that something is wrong. Then Abuela points her finger at me like a judge passing a sentence on a criminal. She says in Spanish, "You made me feel like a zero, like a nothing." Then she goes to her room.

I try to explain what happened. "I don't understand why she's so upset. She just got lost and wandered around for a while," I tell them. But it sounds lame, even to my own ears. My mother gives me a look that makes me cringe and goes in to Abuela's room to get her version of the story. She comes out with tears in her eyes.

"Your grandmother says to tell you that of all the hurtful things you can do to a person, the worst is to make them feel as if they are worth nothing."

20 I can feel myself shrinking right there in front of her. But I can't bring myself to tell my mother that I think I understand how I made Abuela feel. I might be sent into the old lady's room to apologize, and it's not easy to admit you've been a jerk — at least, not right away with everybody watching. So I just sit there not saying anything.

My mother looks at me for a long time, like she feels sorry for me. Then she says, "You should know, Constancia, that if it wasn't for the old woman whose existence you don't seem to value, you and I would not be here."

That's when *I'm* sent to *my* room to consider a number I hadn't thought much about — until today. ■

Gathering Textual Evidence

When analyzing a character, the first step is simply to begin gathering evidence. Try to avoid forming an interpretation early on because that might limit your view of the character. Keep an open mind at this phase. As we work, we'll focus on the development of two characters: Abuela and Connie, the narrator.

Considering main characters from the following angles can help you develop a complete picture:

- Descriptions of the character
- The character's actions
- Dialogue involving the character
- The character's internal thoughts
- Other characters' observations about the character

To see how viewing a character through these angles might work, consider these sample annotations focused on the characterization of Abuela in the first two paragraphs of the story:

"You made me feel like a zero, like a nothing," she says in Spanish, *un cero, nada*. She is trembling, an angry little old woman lost in a heavy winter coat that belongs to my mother. And I end up being sent to my room, like I was a child, to think about my grandmother's idea of math.

The text opens with Abuela's words.

Narrator views Abuela as angry, small, and old.

It all began with Abuela coming up from the Island for a visit — her first time in the United States. My mother and father paid her way here so that she wouldn't die without seeing snow, though if you asked me, and nobody has, the dirty slush in this city is not worth the price of a ticket. But I guess she deserves some kind of award for having had ten kids and survived to tell about it. My mother is the youngest of the bunch. Right up to the time when we're supposed to pick up the old lady at the airport, my mother is telling me stories about how hard times were for *la familia* on *la isla*, and how *la abuela* worked night and day to support them after their father died of a heart attack. I'd die of a heart attack too if I had a troop like that to support. Anyway, I had seen her only three or four times in my entire life, whenever we would go for somebody's funeral. I was born here and I have lived in this building all my life. But when Mami says, "Connie, please be nice to Abuela. She doesn't have too many years left. Do you promise me, Constancia?" — when she uses my full name, I know she means business. So I say, "Sure." Why wouldn't I be nice? I'm not a monster, after all.

Is Abuela close to dying?

Abuela had 10 kids! She's tough.

The narrator insists on describing Abuela as old.

Connie's mother recognizes all of Abuela's hard work.

Abuela's age and her imminent death have been repeated.

activity Gathering Evidence

Now that you've looked at sample annotations focused on the characterization of Abuela, look back on your previous annotations of this text, or create a new set of annotations that focus on the character of Connie. Make sure that your annotations for Connie identify multiple ways that Cofer characterizes her, including the following aspects of direct and indirect characterization:

- Descriptions of the character
- The character's actions
- Dialogue involving the character
- The character's internal thoughts
- Other characters' observations about the character

Organizing and Analyzing Textual Evidence

Now that you've made annotations related to the characterization of Connie, let's return to our discussion of Abuela, so that we can show you how the next steps — organizing and analyzing evidence from the text — might work. Let's review the annotations related to the direct and indirect characterizations of Abuela and organize our findings.

A table like the one that follows will help you see how the different types of details might or might not align. For instance, it might help you identify a conflict between a character's internal thoughts and her actions. Or you might notice that a character changes over time. For example, words used to describe the character might shift from "timid" to "bold," signaling a significant change in personality. You might not find details addressing each row in the table, and that's okay. The goal is to read and reread the text and capture the important details and moments that define the character's identity and show development. To show you what this might look like, we've organized and begun analyzing textual evidence related to Abuela's character development in this sample table.

Character Development: Abuela

Aspects of characterization	**Textual evidence**	**What the evidence says about the character**
Descriptions of the character	"little old woman" "creaky voice"	Abuela is old and maybe sounds weak.
The character's actions	"had ten kids" "worked night and day to support them" "baby steps" "praying loud" "points her finger at me like a judge passing a sentence on a criminal"	Abuela worked really hard for her family, especially because of how many kids she had. Religion is very important to her. Although she seems old and fragile, she is stern.
Dialogue involving the character	"You made me feel like a zero."	Abuela is hurt and has no problems voicing that feeling.
The character's internal thoughts	"tears in her eyes" "It's a waste of money" to buy her a coat since she's only visiting for "two weeks."	The "tears" suggest that Abuela feels humiliated. She never expected her granddaughter to be ashamed of her. She is also practical and very conscious of money.
Other characters' observations about the character	"doesn't have too many years left" "more Catholic than the Pope" "bizarre grandmother"	What others say about her supports our earlier observations about her advanced age and religion.

Organizing and Analyzing Textual Evidence

Now that you've read through the table with sample notes about Abuela's character development, re-create the table and fill it with your own notes and observations about Connie. Once you've filled out your table, share your findings with a partner. Discuss the details you wrote and add anything you might have missed.

Analyzing Characterization

We now have a lot of information, evidence, and ideas to work with, and we can start pulling it all together. Using Abuela as an example again, let's think back on the organized textual evidence and observations about her in the sample table on page 259. To write a paragraph describing and analyzing Abuela's character, we need to make claims about the nature of her character and support our ideas with the textual evidence we've gathered. Our analysis will consist of four steps: Draw conclusions about the character, connect those conclusions to evidence, compose an interpretive statement, and draft a paragraph that analyzes the character.

Step 1: Draw Conclusions about the Character

Based on the notes we have gathered on Abuela — particularly those observations we made in the final column of our chart on page 259 — we can try to come up with a list of traits that seem significant for her character. Let's begin with the following traits:

- **a.** Religious
- **b.** Maternal
- **c.** Hardworking
- **d.** Practical
- **e.** Frail
- **f.** Strong

Step 2: Connect These Conclusions to Evidence Gathered

We need to make sure that we can attach each of the traits listed in Step 1 to specific textual evidence from our chart on page 259. At this stage, we are selecting quotations that best support the observations we've made about Abuela. We can organize our ideas into the following table:

Traits	Textual evidence
Religious	"more Catholic than the Pope"
Maternal	Abuela had "ten kids." She's tough.
Hardworking	"worked night and day to support them"
Practical	Feels that "it's a waste of money" to buy her a coat since she's only visiting for "two weeks"
Frail	a "little old woman" yet strong in other ways
Strong	"points her finger at me like a judge passing a sentence on a criminal"

Step 3: Make an Interpretative Statement about the Character

Let's look at our evidence and observations to develop a statement summarizing Abuela's identity. Who is she, really? Since family and religion seem to be most important to her, we can say the following:

> Abuela is a deeply religious woman who has worked hard for her family and is strong despite her frail appearance.

Step 4: Draft a Paragraph Analyzing the Character

Now we can combine our interpretive statement about Abuela with the evidence and observations we have gathered in our chart to compose a paragraph analyzing her. Remember that a common pattern for writing an evidence-based paragraph is Point-Evidence-Commentary (p. 144). A piece of evidence never stands on its own; always tell your audience why it's significant. Here's an example:

> Abuela, in Judith Ortiz Cofer's "Abuela Invents the Zero," is a deeply religious woman who has worked hard for her family and is strong despite her frail appearance. She demonstrates religious devotion by "praying loud . . . and singing hymns." In fact, her granddaughter says that "she's more Catholic than the Pope." It is also clear that she is equally devoted to her family. Not only did Abuela have "ten kids," but she "worked night and day to support them." Now that she is elderly and frail, she certainly deserves for her granddaughter to "be nice to [her]." Despite her weakened condition, Abuela is still a strong woman who isn't afraid to assert herself. She realizes that her granddaughter is ashamed of being seen with her. Quite directly, Abuela "points her finger" at her granddaughter and tells her, "You made me feel like a zero, like a nothing." Abuela's frail outward appearance belies the strength of her character.

Analyzing Characterization

Think back on the four-step process we've shown you with Abuela's character and how those steps led to our sample character analysis (pp. 260–261). With the work you've already done with Connie's character in mind, it's time for you to work toward your own character analysis.

1. Revisit the notes, textual evidence, and observations you gathered in your chart on page 260. Identify three to five traits that seem important to Connie's character development.
2. Connect these traits to the evidence you've gathered.

Traits	Textual evidence

3. Use the information in the table you just completed to write an interpretive statement regarding Connie's character. Who is she, really? How would you describe the nature of her character?
4. After developing a sentence or two that defines Connie's character, write a paragraph connecting that analysis to the evidence you've gathered. The paragraph from Step 4 on page 261 should serve as a model for your own.

Connecting Characterization to Theme

It's critical that we learn to draw conclusions about characters through the process that we just followed: identifying direct and indirect characterization, organizing and analyzing textual evidence, making a claim regarding the character's significance, and supporting our claim with the evidence. Character analysis, however, is not the end goal for careful readers. Examination and interpretation of characters can help us identify subjects that are central to the text — subjects such as friendship, religion, or bravery. After all, it's important to remember that authors often create characters to help them convey ideas about life, which we refer to as *theme*. Cofer, for example, does not create Connie and Abuela simply because she likes these characters. Why, then, are they in the story? What ideas do they represent? What ideas can we explore when we think about them? When we pay close attention to how characters think, act, see themselves, and are seen by others, and even how they change, we begin to understand the themes of the work as a whole.

For example, by focusing on how Abuela is described, what she does, and what's important to her, we can generate a list of subjects that arise in the text. With the character analysis of Abuela (p. 261) in mind, we might identify the following subjects as being central to the story:

1. Sacrifice
2. Respect
3. Family
4. Religion
5. Homeland

We can then take one of these subjects — such as respect — and create a theme statement. To do this, we ask ourselves, *What is the author's idea or message about respect in "Abuela Invents the Zero"?* Since our purpose is to see the relationship between characterization and theme, we must also consider the following: How does Abuela's character help Cofer communicate her idea on the theme of respect?

A brief response about the theme of respect in the short story, and the role that Abuela plays in conveying that theme, might look like this:

> Abuela's interactions with her family reveal that respect is important to her. In fact, Abuela is respectful of all people, whether they are younger or older than she is. Judith Ortiz Cofer, through "Abuela Invents the Zero," suggests that respect is critical to the health of a relationship. Being disrespectful, like Connie is towards her grandmother at church, is an affront to the love, commitment, and appreciation that should be the basis of all relationships. For Cofer, respect cements the bonds between family members so that love and appreciation can then flourish.

culminating activity

Reread your character analysis of Connie to identify three to five subjects that are significant to the story. Although your list might overlap with the sample list we provided in relation to Abuela's character at the top of this page (sacrifice, respect, family, religion, homeland), focusing on Connie should reveal others. Then, imagine what Cofer's message might be regarding one of those subjects, and think about how Connie's character helps us understand that theme. Write a paragraph, modeled after the one above on the theme of respect, in which you identify a theme in "Abuela Invents the Zero" based on your analysis of Connie. All of the work you've done to prepare for and write this analysis will help you approach and understand the characters and themes of the other texts in this chapter.

from Friends with Boys

Faith Erin Hicks

Nathan Boone

Faith Erin Hicks is an artist, a writer, and an animator who lives in Nova Scotia, Canada. She is most well-known for her long-running web comic called *Demonology 101*, which tells the story of a teenage demon named Raven as she struggles to live a normal life in the human world.

KEY CONTEXT This excerpt from Hicks's graphic novel *Friends with Boys* focuses on Maggie's first days in a public school after being homeschooled her entire life. These are the main characters in *Friends with Boys*:

Maggie

Her brother, Daniel

Her other brother, Zander

SANDFORD
HIGHSCHOOL
TUES WED THURS FRI
HISTORY HISTORY HISTORY
ART ART
FREE FREE
BIOLOGY BIOLOGY

HI-FIVE
THMP THMP
THMP
EEEEE
HAHAHAHA

I... I DON'T WANT TO BE HERE.
HI.
SO. HOW'S THE FIRST DAY GOING?

THERE ARE TOO MANY PEOPLE IN THIS BUILDING, DANIEL.
YEAH, IT'S DIFFERENT FROM A SCHOOL OF FOUR–
IT'S COMPLETELY DIFFERENT! I CAN'T DO THIS!
I CAN'T GO TO SCHOOL WITH ALL THESE PEOPLE! DID YOU SEE HOW MANY OF THEM THERE ARE??
IT'S LIKE THOSE COMMUTER TRAINS IN JAPAN!
THEY KEEP PACKING THE PEOPLE IN, AND SOME GUY AT THE BACK GETS CRUSHED TO DEATH. I COULD DIE!
THERE'S NO WAY I CAN DO THIS. I CAN'T!
YOU CAN.
I CAN'T!
OKAY, WELL THEN, YOU HAVE TO.

MAYBE DAD WOULD LET ME DO HIGH SCHOOL AT HOME–
SO YOU'RE GONG TO STAY HOME YOUR WHOLE LIFE?
WHAT ABOUT GOING AWAY TO COLLEGE? OR TRAVELING? YOU'RE NEVER GOING TO DO ANY OF THAT BECAUSE IT'S AWAY FROM HOME?
NOOO. C'MON, THAT'S NOT FAIR. I JUST... IT'S ***SCARY***.
IT'LL GET LESS SCARY.
I PROMISE.
BUT CAN'T THINGS GO BACK TO THE WAY THEY WERE? I ***LIKED*** BEING AT HOME.
I KNOW.

YOU LIKED BEING HOMESCHOOLED TOO, DIDN'T YOU?
NO, I LIKE IT HERE BETTER
REALLY? I DIDN'T KNOW THAT.
YEP. NOW LET'S FIND YOUR CLASS.
BUT WHAT ABOUT MY RITE OF PASSAGE?
THINK OF ME AS YOUR SPIRIT GUIDE.
HI DANIEL!
HEY.
SEE YOU TONIGHT?
ABSOLUTELY.
WHO WAS THAT?
FELLOW DRAMATIC ARTS ENTHUSIAST. DRAMA CLUB MEETS TONIGHT.

DANIEL! HAVE A GOOD SUMMER?
IT WAS KICKASS. AND I HAVE THE BRUISES TO PROVE IT.

SEE YOU TONIGHT?
YOU BET.

ARE YOU POPULAR?
NAH, I JUST KNOW A LOT OF PEOPLE.

HERE'S YOUR CLASSROOM.

SEE, NOT SCARY AT ALL.

CHESS CLUB!
TRYOUTS!
LUNCH

HELLO!

I'M LUCY, AND THIS IS MY BROTHER ALISTAIR. ARE YOU NEW IN TOWN?
NO, JUST NEW IN HIGH SCHOOL.
HOW'S IT GOING SO FAR?
UM... OKAY, I GUESS.
CITIZENS, LEND ME YOUR EARS!

?
IN TWO WEEKS, CITIZENS, YOUR BELOVED CHAMPIONSHIP-WINNING VOLLEYBALL TEAM WILL BE PLAYING ITS FIRST GAME OF THE SEASON!
SCHOOL PATRIOTS, I CALL ON YOU TO COME OUT AND CHEER US ON!
WOMEN OF SANFORD HIGH, I ESPECIALLY REQUEST YOUR PRESENCE AT THE GAME.
MATT, COULD YOU BE ANY CHEESIER?
FOR YOU ETHEREAL BEAUTIES, I CERTAINLY COULD BE.
HA HA HA HA HA HAHA HA HA

ICED TEA

AWKWARD SILENCE
WHATEVER
REMEMBER, TWO WEEKS, CITIZENS! BE A PART OF HISTORY!

SO ARE YOU FRIENDS WITH DANIEL? I SAW YOU WITH HIM BEFORE CLASS–
HE'S MY BROTHER.
OH... ARE WE LEAVING?
YEP.
SORRY, GOTTA GO!
NICE MEETING YOU!
PLAY PRACTICE

FIRST DAY.
HI, ZANDER.
OH HEY. HOW'D THE FIRST DAY GO?
ONLY FREAKED OUT ONCE.
YOU DID BETTER THAN ME.

MAKEOUT STAIRWELL
AVOID!!
FIRST PERIOD
THIRD PERIOD
THEATRE
LOCKER BAY
PEOPLE SLEEP HERE
COURT YARD
LIBRARY
GRADE 9 BATHROOMS
NICE PLACE TO EAT LUNCH
ENTER HERE
DAYS THAT FOLLOW—

HEY, GOOD FOR YOU. YOU FOUND THE GRADE NINE BATHROOMS.
NOW ALL YOU NEED IS TO FIND YOUR PEOPLE.

MORE DAYS FOLLOW—
DANIEL LIVES HERE (AND LLOYD)
THEATRE
LOCKER BAY
PEOPLE SLEEP HERE
SOCCER FIELDS THAT WAY
THE FOOD IS TERRIBLE!
COURT YARD
CAFETERIA
B3
B4
B5
D2 D3 D4 D5 D6 D7
E1 E2 E3
E1 E2 E3
E4 E5 E6
D1
I don't have any classes here
SPORTS?
SOCCER AND TRACK (smelly boys)
NICE PLACE TO EAT LUNCH
GRADE 9 BATHROOMS (seriously this is the only place we're allowed to pee.!!)
QUIET AFTER LUNCH (ZANDER IS SOMETIMES HERE)
ENGLISH (my favorite
A3
A4
A5
J3 J4
HOME

extending beyond the text

Education reporter Emily Files explores a new approach to the often-dreaded school lunchroom in “Wisconsin School Breaks Up Lunchtime Cliques with Assigned Seating.” Consider how her reporting relates to the environment presented by Faith Erin Hicks in *Friends with Boys*.

from “Wisconsin School Breaks Up Lunchtime Cliques with Assigned Seating”

Emily Files

There’s a scene in the movie *Mean Girls* where new student Cady Heron gets a lesson from her friend, Janice Ian, about the social hierarchy of the high school cafeteria.

Where you sit in the cafeteria is crucial,” Janice says. She then maps out the cliques, including preps, jocks and, of course, the “plastics.”

The scene is an exaggeration of a common experience: the stress of finding your place in a school cafeteria. But Wisconsin resident Smitha Chintamaneni can’t relate.

“I’ve never had that experience,” she said. “I’ve never been at the cool kids’ table or the nerd table. We never had that at my school.”

5 Chintamaneni is an alum of the University School of Milwaukee, a private K-12 school in the suburb of River Hills. One of the most unusual things about the University School is its long-standing tradition of assigned lunch seating.

For new students, the seating rules can be a welcome relief. Sophomore Kylie Burger went to public elementary and middle schools before coming to the University School her freshman year of high school.

“At first I was really hyped,” said Kylie, 15. “I moved a lot with middle school, and usually I would sit alone. So I was excited to not sit alone at a table all year.” . . .

At the University School, Kylie said the assigned seating doesn’t fix everything. Like any high school, there are still cliques.

“The lunch system is more kind of a relief from [the cliques,]” Burger said. “It doesn’t reduce it in any way, from my experience. But it definitely, like, gives you a break.”

10 Burger said there are times she would rather sit with her friends. But she thinks it’s a good thing that at this school, no one sits alone. ■

How do you think Maggie would react to this assigned seating plan? Do you think it would improve her outlook on school in general? Think about your own school’s cafeteria. How do you think that mandated seating would impact both lunchtime and the school’s overall culture?

Understanding and Interpreting

1. What seems to be Maggie's biggest fear about attending high school outside her home environment? Is this a reasonable fear, or is she being overly cautious? Explain.
2. Maggie talks about her first day of school as a "rite of passage" (p. 272), an event which is normally considered to be a transition between significant stages in one's life. Looking carefully at all of the panels after she is first on her own, describe at least three rites of passage that Maggie faces on her first day. Does she overcome these challenges or not? Explain.
3. What prompts Lucy to approach Maggie? Why do they seem to get along?
4. How would you characterize the relationship that Maggie has with her brothers? What textual and visual evidence can you use to support your response?
5. Look back at the two maps that Maggie draws to help her navigate both the building and the social environment of the school (pp. 282 and 284). First, what do the places that she chooses to identify reveal about her as a character and her attempts to understand school? Second, what does she add to the second map? What does this addition show about her development at school?

Analyzing Language, Style, and Structure

1. **Vocabulary in Context.** What does the word "ethereal" mean in the context of Matt's reference to the girls in the lunchroom (p. 277)?
2. **Skill Focus.** The first four pages of this piece have no dialogue at all. What does this reveal about Maggie's character and Hicks's ideas about school life?
3. How does Hicks establish Maggie as an outcast on her first day of school? In your response, consider how Maggie's body language and facial expressions — as well as those of the people around her — help you arrive at your answer.
4. How does the author distinguish flashbacks from the present? What do the flashbacks reveal about Maggie?
5. When Matt first enters the cafeteria he says, "Lend me your ears." This quotation comes from Mark Antony's moving speech regarding the death of Caesar in William Shakespeare's *Julius Caesar*. What is Hicks suggesting about Matt with this allusion?
6. Look closely at the panels that show the two boys in the cafeteria (pp. 278–280). The author does not provide much context for their characterization: we don't really know who the boys are or why they are fighting. In other words, we are just like Maggie, who is watching from the side. What strategies does Hicks use — lines, shading, framing, angles, text, or other tools of the comic book artist — to portray these characters and their interactions?
7. Hicks creates black and white rather than color images to tell Maggie's story. How does this decision relate to the message of the text? As part of your response, refer to how the use of black and white in a specific panel, or graphic frame, contributes to your impression.

Topics for Composing

1. **Analysis.** Overall, what does Maggie's difficulty with adjusting to public school suggest about how she views herself? Citing specific details from the text, discuss what Maggie discovers about herself as she tries to understand her new environment and find her place in it.

2. **Argument.** Identify two or three character traits that a person would need to make new friends and adjust to a new school environment. How do these characteristics make it easier to accomplish these goals? As part of your argument, consider how not having the traits you selected could make it harder for someone to adjust and make friends.
3. **Connection.** Select a panel in which you can closely identify with what a character is experiencing. Discuss the visual cues Faith Erin Hicks uses to bring that character's experience to life. Then, compare and contrast your experience to what the character is going through. If you were to draw a panel of a similar experience from your life, what visual cues might you use to share your story?
4. **Speaking and Listening.** Imagine the moment when Maggie enters her house after the first day of school and her mother asks her how her day went. Prepare a two-minute response from Maggie's perspective that you will deliver in front of the class. Make sure that your response is informed by details from the text.
5. **Research.** How do different educational settings impact the way students perceive themselves? Locate research studies that examine different settings, such as public, private, boarding, and home schools, and their impact on how students think and feel about themselves. Summarize at least two research articles and determine how the writers' conclusions compare.
6. **Creative Writing.** Throughout the excerpt, a number of panels have no words. In these panels, Faith Erin Hicks uses the facial expressions and body language of the characters to convey how school impacts the way students perceive themselves. Select one panel in which there are no words and write text that would be appropriate for the scene. The text can be the thoughts of a single character or dialogue between characters. Explain what your text reveals about the scene.
7. **Multimodal.** Look back at the two maps that Maggie draws to help her navigate her new school. Think about how different areas of your own school make you feel. Where do you feel most at ease, and where do you feel like you don't belong? Create your own map for a section of your school; include text and images relevant to your experiences. Your artistic choices should help viewers of your map understand your feelings toward the spaces you include.

When I Grow Up I Want to Be a List of Further Possibilities

Chen Chen

Jess X. Snow

Poet Chen Chen (b. 1989) holds an MFA from Syracuse University and a PhD from Texas Tech University. He is currently the Jacob Ziskind Visiting Poet-in-Residence at Brandeis University. Chen's poems have appeared in *Poetry*, *Poem-a-Day*, *The Best American Poetry*, and *The Best American Nonrequired Reading*. His book *When I Grow Up I Want to Be a List of Further Possibilities* won multiple awards and was longlisted for the National Book Award.

To be a good
ex/current friend for R. To be one last

inspired way to get back at R. To be relationship
advice for L. To be advice

for my mother. To be a more comfortable
hospital bed for my mother. To be

no more hospital beds. To be, in my spare time,
America for my uncle, who wants to be China

for me. To be a country of trafficless roads
& a sports car for my aunt, who likes to go

fast. To be a cyclone
of laughter when my parents say

their new coworker is *like that,* they can tell
because he wears pink socks, see, you don't, so you can't,

can't be one of them. To be the one
my parents raised me to be —

a season from the planet
of planet-sized storms.

To be a backpack of PB&J & every
thing I know, for my brothers, who are becoming

their own storms. To be, for me, nobody,
homebody, body in bed watching TV. To go 2D

& be a painting, an amateur's hilltop & stars,
simple decoration for the new apartment

with you. To be close, J.,
to everything that is close to you —

blue blanket, red cup, green shoes
with pink laces.

To be the blue & the red.
The green, the hot pink. ■

Tree of My Life, 1919, (oil on canvas)/Stella, Joseph (1877–1946)/CHRISTIES IMAGES/ Private Collection/Bridgeman Images

Joseph Stella's 1919 painting *Tree of My Life* features a central tree trunk surrounded by a vibrant array of flora and fauna.

What does this depiction suggest about how Stella views life? How might the speaker in Chen's poem relate to this painting?

Understanding and Interpreting

1. Readers often forget to pay attention to a poem's title. Read the title of this poem and consider why Chen might have thought it was appropriate. What is the relationship between this poem's title and its first line?
2. Throughout the poem, the speaker refers to people by their initials only (for example, R. and J.). What might this reveal about the relationships between the speaker and people in his life? How would the poem affect you differently if the speaker had used full names?
3. Poets often use metaphors to enhance what they want a poem to communicate. For example, the speaker in Chen's poem says that he wants "to be a more comfortable / hospital bed" (ll. 5–6). What does he mean? How does his use of this metaphor enhance your understanding of the speaker's desire?
4. Lines 13 to 15 refer to the speaker's sexual orientation and how he thinks it is perceived by his parents. Based on what the speaker presents as his parents' words — as noted in italics in lines 13 to 15 — how does he believe his parents view him?
5. The poem ends with the speaker's desire to be a series of colors — adjectives for the objects in lines 27 to 28. Why does the speaker include this as a possibility of what he would like to be?

Analyzing Language, Style, and Structure

1. **Vocabulary in Context.** In lines 11 and 12, the speaker mentions a "cyclone / of laughter." What does the word "cyclone" mean in this context? What effect does the phrase "cyclone / of laughter" have at this moment in the poem?
2. **Skill Focus.** While the speaker of the poem is not a child, the title begins with the phrase "when I grow up." How is the speaker characterized throughout the poem? What does this characterization suggest about the broader theme of growing up?
3. The word "storms" is repeated in lines 18 and 21. Aside from its denotation, how do the connotations of this word enrich your understanding of these lines?
4. The repetition of words at the beginning of phrases, called anaphora, is a major feature of the poem's structure. Discuss how the repetition of "to be" affects your reading of the poem. Explain how it relates to the title.
5. Why do you think the speaker mentions so many individuals in the poem? Note the inclusion of R., L., mother, uncle, aunt, parents, brothers, and J.
6. Overall, what tone is created by the poem's list of "further possibilities" for the speaker? How does the speaker seem to feel about his current identity?

Topics for Composing

1. **Analysis.** The speaker in Chen's poem provides a list of many aspirations. Based on details from the text, how would you describe the speaker? What does he ultimately want to be when he "grow[s] up"? Use direct evidence from the poem to support your interpretation.
2. **Argument.** To what extent is it possible to please everyone within your social circle? Is such an impulse naïve or a natural part of forming close relationships? Consider evidence from the poem and your own experiences to support the position you choose to argue.
3. **Connection.** Review the list of possibilities that Chen creates in this poem. Identify and explain which "to be" statement most relates to your own relationship with friends and family.
4. **Speaking and Listening.** Work with a partner to discuss your interpretation of the poem. Then, reread the poem to each other aloud at least two times. How does the experience of listening to the poem multiple times affect your interpretation of and reaction to it?
5. **Creative Writing.** Think about how you could improve your relationship with those around you. Identify three possibilities you want for your own future. Include them as additional stanzas to this poem.
6. **Multimodal.** Create a digital collage that compiles the possibilities that the speaker wishes for himself. In addition to including words and pictures, embed hyperlinked features that take us to videos that further relate to the speaker's desires.

Good with Boys

Kristen Iskandrian

Hannah Slamen

Kristen Iskandrian grew up in Philadelphia and currently lives in Alabama. Her parents were Iraqi immigrants who spoke six languages, including Arabic and English. Iskandrian's stories have appeared in numerous publications, including *Ploughshares* and *McSweeney's*. Her debut novel, *Motherest*, was published in 2017. "Good with Boys" was first published in *Zyzzyva* and then in *The Best American Short Stories 2018*.

I WAS GOING to sleep in a museum — with any luck, next to Esau Abraham, a boy so gorgeously Jewish he held the entire Old Testament in his name, in the perfect contours of his face. I had this theory about boys, that if they just got close enough to me, and sort of focused in, they would forget about the obvious deterrents, the glasses, the frizzy hair, the underdeveloped body. I was zany, I really went for it. . . . Everyone talks about personality like it's a bad thing but the fact is, without one, you've got nowhere to go but ugly.

It's the beautiful people, isn't it, who most often wind up dead or alone.

We took a bus, not a yellow school bus but one of those real ones, with plush red seats and TVs, although we weren't allowed to turn the TVs on. Esau Abraham's mom, Mrs. Abraham, was on the bus, one of the parent chaperones. This was a problem but not necessarily a deal-breaker. She loved her son. She wanted what was best for him. We could be allies.

Someone opened up a giant bag of Cheetos. We were going to have dinner in the museum cafeteria but a bus ride demanded snacks. The bag got passed around, and soon the smell of powdered cheese was upon us all like a pollen. I knew even as a kid that kids were disgusting, the constant hand to mouth, the reckless tactility. Most of us did not wash our hands after we used the restroom — a fact I'd empirically uncovered by spending a lot of time in the bathroom. I hid in stalls to avoid certain things, which was my right, which was all of our right.

The bus driver was a middle-aged woman who clipped her turns close. The second time we bounced off a curb, Mrs. Abraham jostled up to the front and rapped on the Plexiglas. "Hey," she said. "This is a bus full of kids you're driving. Can you please be more careful?"

"Lady, I been driving kids a long time. They love it rough."

She wasn't wrong. We did like it rough. The higher we bounced, the better.

The year before we'd gone to the planetarium. Esau Abraham wasn't at our school then. I had big plans for Sam Bell — got behind him in line so that I could sit next to him — but as we entered the darkened room, Allison nudged ahead of me. "Sam," she'd said. "Sam, you dropped this," and handed him a VISITOR button. His VISITOR button was fastened to his shirt, so we all knew it was a big fat lie. But I gained a lot of admiration for her just then.

We hit a pothole and I flew a couple inches into the air. "Take it easy!" yelled Mrs. Abraham.

"Not much I can do about the roads!" the bus driver called back gleefully.

There was a rumor that the local news team would be at the museum when we got there, since this was the first time an elementary school class — or any class — had been invited to spend the night. As an event, it was just hitting all the right chords for me: a sleepover, not at my house, at the museum of natural history, with boys.

I just loved boys so much, it was a sickness, it was a secret. I had to pretend I didn't love them as much as I actually did. I didn't want to be boy crazy. Once boy craziness became your signifier you couldn't be taken seriously. Your art would be ignored. I worked so hard on mine, I fully expected to have a gallery showing of my gouaches and charcoal sketches within the year. Esau Abraham was a really good drawer and I looked forward to our future collaborations, the font of mutual encouragement we would fill together.

When we pulled up to the museum and the bus came to an especially jarring stop, I slung my overnight bag over my shoulder, tucked my sleeping bag under my arm, and squeezed into the aisle behind Mrs. Abraham. I leaned in and breathed in to see if I could learn anything additional about Esau. She smelled like Vicks Vapo-Rub and faintly, confusingly, bacon. In the dusk, we gathered on the wide sidewalk in front of the museum. Sure enough, a news man was

Photograph by Deniz Durmus. © The Natural History Museum of Los Angeles County

This is a photograph of a *Tyrannosaurus Rex* at the Natural History Museum of Los Angeles County. Sleepovers in natural history museums have become popular events.

What is it about a natural history museum that makes it a unique place to spend the night? What might that tell you about why the author of "Good with Boys" chose such a setting for this story?

talking to Ms. Green, our teacher. What a moment for her, for all of us. She was smiling and talking with her hands, her rosy face exuberant. I could tell she felt famous, and honestly, I think we all did.

Once inside, we were led to the Discovery Room, where we were told to find a place for our bags and sleeping bags. I was startled; I did not expect this to happen so soon. The Discovery Room had a hodgepodge of hands-on exhibits, some insects and fish, a family of stuffed wolves behind glass, and an enormous sculpture of the human brain that you could walk inside. Each of the four lobes was a different color and came with a mini audio tour.

Obviously, the Discovery Room would 15
also be where I "discovered" more about Esau Abraham, if you catch my drift.

Esau followed his mother to a small enclave created by an aquarium flanked by two bookshelves.

"Here, Esau, this is a good spot for us," she said, taking his navy blue sleeping bag from him and laying it on the floor. "We can look at the fish while we fall asleep!" She unrolled hers — red with a tartan print on the inside — right next to his.

My unsinkable heart sank. I had to be strategic. I put my things down on the other side of the bookshelf closest to Esau. I quickly tested the space and realized that if I stretched all the way out, my head would be more or less in line with his, about four feet apart. Three feet and eleven and three-quarters inches too many.

What could I do but wait, which was of course the one thing I was terrible at. My great aunt told me once, when you dislike doing something, you have to do it more, do it over and over, any chance you got, until you not necessarily liked it — liking wasn't the goal — but just felt neutral toward it. Neutrality, she said, was the whole purpose. Real Buddhist talk for a woman — my namesake — with a severe QVC addiction. But I thought of her now, and tried to make this situation apply. How to wait more? How to wait over and over? Impossible. Thanks for nothing, Aunt Jill.

Most of the other girls in the class had spread their stuff out in a long rectangle on the other side of the room, closer to the brain. Coyness was never a virtue I cared very much about. Once it was lights out, once Ms. Green and the other chaperones were asleep, those girls would have twice as much work to do, with twice as much risk. Me, I was staying right here, close to my target. Mrs. Abraham was squeezing hand sanitizer onto Esau's open palms. I had to be careful not to watch him too much when he was with his mother. It was a turn-off. I took off my glasses and cleaned them on the bottom of my shirt. The only thing worse than a girl with glasses, I reasoned, was a girl with dirty glasses.

I was good with boys because I knew what they wanted. I could enter the simple machines of their minds and see how their gears turned. Most of them needed a lot of oil. To be told, a lot, how correct their opinions were, because most of them believed that opinions were like facts — provable and true. *Thinking* something, for a boy, meant not-thinking all other things. When two even vaguely conflicting ideas rubbed together, they either quickly chose one and discarded the other, or abandoned them both for a new and better topic, often something they felt absolutely certain about, like a cool video game, or whose bra was visible beneath her shirt, or what was I even doing there anyway. Over time, I could make them talk to me, just by simply existing. I occupied a genderless place where I neither quickened the blood like the obvious girls, nor inspired the bravado often necessary around other boys. Around me, they got to take five. Being a safe harbor may seem dull and sexless (so to speak — nobody's having sex) but it's actually a place of power. . . .

Mrs. Abraham went off to use the bathroom.

"Hi, Esau," I said casually, coming from around the bookshelf.

"Hi," he said. "Aren't you supposed to be over there, with the other girls? It's just boys over here."

"Oh really? I didn't even notice. It looks pretty crowded over there. I might just stay put."

Esau rubbed his hands on his jeans. "I wish we could sleep in the brain."

"Are we not allowed to?" This was a possibility I hadn't considered.

"I don't think so. There's not really a lot of room in there."

Mrs. Abraham came back from the bathroom. "Who's this?" she asked brightly, glancing from Esau to me.

"Hi Mrs. Abraham," I stuck out my hand. "I'm Jill."

"Well hi, sweetie. Did you find a spot for your stuff? Looks like the girls are going to be on the other side of the room tonight. Probably a good idea, right?" Her eyes were roving over my shoulder to where I'd painstakingly placed my things. I noticed from this close distance that the majority of her eyebrows were drawn on. I was a mothers' favorite and a grandmothers' favorite and I had to decide whether I would risk my reputation and stay put, or oblige her and move. But before I could say or do anything, Ms. Green was summoning all of us to the doors. It was time to eat dinner, she said — pizzas had arrived — after which we had forty-five minutes to spend as we wished, in approved areas of the museum.

I got my two slices of pizza and fruit punch juice box and sat with a table of girls. My best friend Sarah was dabbing her pizza with a napkin.

"Why did you put your stuff on the boys' side?" she asked. I punctured the foil circle with my straw. "I didn't actually realize there were 'sides,'" I said. "Seems like the whole point of being here is to, you know, mix it up."

Sarah chewed carefully. She was a very careful chewer. She told me once that you were supposed to chew every bite thirty-five times before swallowing it. "Well, I don't think we're allowed to sleep on the same side. They were supposed to put us in separate rooms but the other rooms have to be kept really cold or something, that's what I heard."

A girl named Caroline tossed her long, pretty hair. "They'll probably come to our side after everyone's asleep, and try to be gross. I heard Nick say he was going to steal our underwear."

"Nick's an idiot," I said. "Who even brought underwear? It's not like we're staying here for a week."

Caroline shrugged. "I brought extra, just in case. My mom always says to pack extra underwear, because you never know."

"Yeah, like, you could pee your pants or something!" Lauren shouted out, and everyone laughed.

I didn't laugh. I tried not to roll my eyes. Caroline definitely wanted her underwear to be stolen. I could see right through her. I didn't like this kind of game-playing. I didn't like silliness, the silliness so often ascribed to our sex. I was constantly trying to get out from under it, kill it as savagely as possible, like a slug you pour salt on even after it's dead.

If you wanted a boy's attention, you had to get it. You had to take it.

After dinner, I kept my eye on Esau. His mother was talking to Ms. Green and the two other parent chaperones. With a few other boys he headed toward Ornithology, which was fortunate, since it was adjacent to the Mineralogy wing, where I wanted to spend my time. I had some money to spend in the gift shop tomorrow and I was definitely going to get a few new polished rocks and minerals for my collection. Some agate, maybe. I did not want to lose sight of the educational purpose of this trip. I knew, deep in my bedrock layer, that Esau Abraham would come and Esau Abraham would go. I knew I had to keep a firm hold on my interests outside of boys. I stood looking at an exhibit containing necklaces of jade, peridot, and pink topaz, right next to the clusters of Mississippi pearls so creamy they seemed edible, and I felt stirred, filled with longing.

My desire for boys and my desire for certain other things — often inexplicable, sometimes beautiful, frequently plain, occasionally attainable, like a tiny plastic fifty-cent notebook charm complete with even tinier pencil, for my charm bracelet; sometimes not, like these exquisite jewels that came from places in the earth that no longer even exist — were knotted together as intricately as a DNA double helix. I wanted and wanted and wanted. I believed, like my Great Aunt Jill, that objects had the power to protect me from harm — the harm of loneliness and my own impermanence — and I believed that boys had the same power.

My little voice told me, take what you want. Take what you can. Heal in the long shadows of the taking. My little voice and Aunt Jill's little voice, maybe, were the same.

I realized I was standing with my hands and forehead pressed to the glass. I heard a few

extending beyond the text

In a *New York Times* article titled "The Value of Childhood Crushes," Bonnie Rough, an essayist and a journalist who has written books on parenting and sexuality, considers how young love is perceived in different parts of the world. As part of her investigation, she compares the language used to describe young love in the Netherlands with the way it is described — or dismissed — in the United States. Read what she says about this topic and think about how it relates to Jill.

> . . . I found that Dutch speakers use the term verliefd zijn — "being in love" — with equal credence for children, teenagers and adults.
>
> For Americans, being "in love" is usually reserved for older teenagers and adults. We use trivializing terms like "puppy love" or "boy crazy" for younger adolescents.

What do you think the role of young love is in the process of forming an identity? What role does it play for Jill in this story? To what extent do your experiences align with Rough's observations of society's perception of childhood crushes?

people enter the room and then Esau's voice, "Adam — wait up!"

"Where are you guys going?" I asked, straightening up.

"Adam wants to go to the dinosaur room, right?" Esau asked. Adam was a shy boy, shyer than Esau, and obsessed with Abraham Lincoln.

"I'm not sure we're allowed upstairs. I think we're supposed to stay just on this floor, " I said, unsure of why I was taking the rule-abiding position, especially since I was planning on breaking a few unspoken rules later that night.

Esau looked at Adam. "I could ask my mom," he said.

"Let's just go," I said. Being alone with Esau plus Adam was better than being alone without Esau. And it was fun to take the lead, exciting. "We can pretend we didn't know."

The three of us walked quickly to the lighted exit sign. I opened the heavy door to the stairwell and held it for Adam and Esau. I saw Mrs. Abraham craning her neck behind a few kids wandering between Botany and Mineralogy, looking, surely, for her son.

We hurried up a flight of stairs, laughing, which was the sound of our nervous bodies trying to expel their nervousness.

The Vertebrate Paleontology wing was cold and very dimly lit. We fell silent immediately upon entering, tiny insects beneath the impossibly tall ceilings. The air smelled like stone — no, like bone. For a minute we stood there without moving, just inside the entrance. I felt a tingle in my body like a sustained high note, like I myself was an echo chamber for our collective giddiness. This would be a double trespass, I thought to myself. Once for being a forbidden area, twice for being an ancient era. We were moving through time in two directions, forward and backward. I wanted to be in charge of this moment, of being in this ideal place alone with two boys, like some better version of *From the Mixed-up Files of Mrs. Basil E. Frankweiler*, one of my all-time favorite books. Surely it wasn't too much to ask, to believe, that here under the spell of these skeletons and this flattering lighting they would both fall in love with me, and that although I would choose Esau, we would all remain friends and vow to undertake future adventures together. What good was a relationship, after all, with nobody around to witness it?

Adam broke off, breaking my trance, and hastened toward the crown jewel of the entire wing: the seventy-two-foot long *Haplocanthosaurus delfsi*. His footsteps were loud and sloppy.

Esau started to follow.

"Wait, Esau," I said, putting a hand on his arm. "Wanna see the T. rex's cousin?"

I actually didn't know anything about dinosaurs, but I had seen a sign earlier: the Late Cretaceous *Nanotyrranus lancensis*, for which the museum had recently acquired a skull.

Esau glanced over at Adam. "Sure — I just want to check out whatever-that-is real quick."

"Oh — yeah. Definitely. Me, too." I followed him, suddenly feeling less in charge. Esau stood close to Adam, his striking cheekbones slightly pink.

Adam reached with his index finger toward one of the dinosaur's tail bones. He reached and reached, but was still at least a foot off. He hoisted himself up to kneel on the platform and tried again, giggling, reaching. When he started to lose his balance, Esau caught his arm, pulling him down. The two of them in a heap on the floor, their laughter eddying through the room like ink in water. I stood above them, surprised by my anger, which felt like a betrayal to all of us, the same kind of massive bummer that happens when an adult walks into a youth situation.

"Ha ha," I joined in weakly, wanting them to get up off the floor.

Finally, they did. I tried not to look at how Esau was looking at Adam, tried not to register it as anything but boyish camaraderie. I felt a pang of something — sadness, but also panic, and desperation, like I'd been given the chance to re-enter a good dream and had messed it up somehow. I would do anything to get back in, is how I felt. I studied Adam, trying to memorize him so that I could be more like him, look more like him.

He started to say something, but was cut off by the jarring click of an intercom, a loud voice coming from the walls: All students please report to the Discovery Room. Once again, all students please report to the Discovery Room.

"Crap," I said.

Esau's face clouded over, exactly the way clouds cloud over the sky. "Let's go," he said.

We followed him quickly, wordlessly. When we got back down to the main floor, Mrs. Abraham was waiting outside the Discovery Room.

"Where were you?" she said. She grabbed Esau in a hug and cast a disapproving look toward Adam and me. "I was really starting to worry!"

"We just," Esau mumbled, "we wanted to see the dinosaurs real quick. Sorry, Mom."

Maybe I could win him back with righteousness, maybe I could get his mom on my side. "Yeah, I'm really sorry too, Mrs. Abraham. It was actually my idea."

"I see," she said. Her face did something I couldn't decipher.

"Well, you're here now. Go get in line with the girls, Jill. It's time for all of us to get ready for bed. Tomorrow morning they're going to release the monarch butterflies, bright and early."

Reluctantly, I moved my stuff across the room. I followed the other girls into the bathroom, where we changed into our pajamas and brushed our teeth.

"Where'd you go?" Sarah asked, when we were side by side at the sink. She was wearing a soft pink pajama set with satin trim.

How is a sleepover perceived differently by mother and daughter in this cartoon? How does their interaction reflect how Iskandrian depicts the sleepover in the story?

"Just, upstairs. To the dinosaurs." I spit. I was wearing a giant Snoopy nightshirt.

"Esau's mom was freaking out. It was kind of funny," she said, dabbing her mouth on a paper towel. "And, P.S., could you be any more obvious?"

We got in our sleeping bags. Ms. Green gave us one final lecture on good conduct, standing there in the center of the room wearing some kind of a sweatsuit. I lay and looked at the ceiling, listening to the whispers and giggles all around me, and felt anxious. Across the way, the boys were mostly quiet. Someone let out an enormous belch, and there were staggered titters around the room. In less time than you would imagine, there was absolute silence, the climax of this much-anticipated day folding noiselessly into itself.

I was awake and grew more and more alert. I thought about Esau, I prickled with Esau. I needed his undivided attention. What was this broken mirror inside of me, that showed me I was ugly, showed me I was wrong, but persisted in its reflection that I was better than other people? Could low self-esteem loop all the way around and become narcissism?

I heard breathing, a body intermittently shifting, rolling over. I felt like I was part of the museum, part of an exhibit, the control group of an experiment — proximity to sleep as a kind of stimulant, maybe, since my head buzzed as if from caffeine. Surrounded by bodies, bones, all the inert matter proffered by our tiny planet, I felt neon.

I don't know what time it was when I knelt cautiously on my sleeping bag, and then stood, and then tiptoed soundlessly to where Esau was lying. It seemed as though the darkness itself was carrying me. I squatted against the bookshelf and could just barely see him, his face wholly at rest, his lips slightly parted. If I could just get him away from his mother, if I could somehow communicate through the thick silence —

"Get back to bed, missy." Mrs. Abraham's voice was a sharp whisper.

I fled. I tried not to cry. I didn't cry. I slept, a hideous sleep of humiliating dreams.

The next morning, we stood shivering in the damp grass of the museum courtyard, squinting at the early sun streaming into our faces. One of the other parent chaperones had lightly slapped my arm to wake me — apparently she and Sarah and several others had tried over the course of twenty minutes, but I wouldn't budge, and now I was holding up the rest of the class — so I'd thrown on my clothes and rolled up my sleeping bag and raced to meet the line. My mouth felt mossy and the chilly, bright air made me feel extra exposed.

Predictably, Esau stood close to Adam. I watched them openly; I didn't care about butterflies. Esau looked as though he had slept at a spa, his pretty skin glowing, his eyes fresh. Adam was oblivious, infuriatingly unremarkable—if this were a play he'd be chorus, back row—but what did my opinions matter? I wasn't in charge of anything. I leaned a little against Sarah, whose tallness usually got on my nerves, and watched three men from the museum set down covered cages on the long table we were standing around. I leaned on Sarah a bit more, bracing myself for a long boring lecture about butterflies and their dumb habits. But the three men merely counted to three and unlatched the doors, and all of us were made to forget for a second, as wings filled the air, what was hurting. ■

Understanding and Interpreting

1. Note that Jill refers to Esau Abraham by his full name throughout the beginning of the story. At what point does she begin to call him Esau? What does this shift suggest about these two characters and their relationship?
2. Paragraph 8 relates Jill's "big plans for Sam Bell" during an earlier field trip to the planetarium. Based on this recollection and the current trip to the museum, what role do field trips play among children in general and for Jill, specifically?
3. Reread Aunt Jill's advice regarding what to do "when you dislike doing something" (par. 19). Summarize Aunt Jill's argument and explain its connection to Jill's current situation. What does Jill's attitude toward her aunt's advice reveal about her?
4. What does Jill mean when she says that boys "needed a lot of oil" (par. 21)? Provide an example from the text where Jill acts accordingly.
5. Summarize Jill's observations about the things she desires and how they are "knotted together" (par. 42) with her feelings towards boys.
6. What does Jill recognize about Esau's relationship with Adam — and where she fits in within that relationship — that leads her to study Adam (par. 60)?
7. Reread the descriptions of Sarah's and Jill's pajamas (pars. 71 and 72). What do these descriptions reveal about how Jill perceives herself in relation to the other girls?
8. Explain the significance of the "broken mirror" (par. 75) that exists within Jill. How does the existence of this "mirror" shape the events of the story?
9. Overall, what is the hurt to which Jill alludes in the final paragraph? Identify examples from the story where the hurt is evident.

Analyzing Language, Style, and Structure

1. **Vocabulary in Context.** What does the word "font" mean in the context of paragraph 12: "the font of mutual encouragement"? What meaning do you usually associate with the word "font"?

2. **Skill Focus.** From the outset, Iskandrian's characterization of Jill is complex. Focusing on the first four paragraphs of the story, identify details that convey contradictions in Jill's character.
3. Think about both the denotation and connotations of the word "allies" (par. 3). What does Jill's idea about being allied with Mrs. Abraham suggest about how she views the field trip?
4. What is the function of the simile in paragraph 4 in which "powdered cheese" is compared to "pollen"? In your response, consider the natural processes associated with pollen.
5. The short story ends with an image of butterflies being released from their cages. Identify the significance of this image and explain how it relates to Jill.
6. An aphorism is a concise statement that conveys a general truth, as understood by the speaker dispensing the advice. Socrates, for example, is believed to have said, "The unexamined life is not worth living." Identify a statement of truth that Jill presents in the story and determine the extent to which events in the story support that belief.

Topics for Composing

1. **Analysis.** Consider Jill's behavior towards the other girls, the boy she likes, and the grown-ups in the story. How would you characterize Jill? How does this characterization reflect a central idea, or theme, in the story?
2. **Argument.** Jill confesses, "I just loved boys so much, it was a sickness . . ." (par. 12). Does acknowledging and demonstrating this type of attraction damage a person's chances of being taken seriously, regardless of his or her abilities? Use current events, personal observations, and material from the story to support your response.
3. **Connection.** Think about what field trips represent for you and your friends. How does the way you view yourself influence your behavior on a field trip? Even though Jill is not yet in high school, are there elements of her experience that you can relate to, despite the age difference?
4. **Speaking and Listening.** Suppose that Jill were to confide in Sarah what was "hurting" her (par. 81). Write a short script that imagines Jill's explanation and Sarah's response to this admission. Share your script with a classmate, group, or your class. Discuss the extent to which you captured each character's identity.
5. **Research.** Look up the Biblical stories of Esau, Abraham, and Adam. Determine why Iskandrian might have selected these names for her story. What might the names reveal about these characters' identities?

section two

On Turning Ten

Billy Collins

GARY DOAK/Alamy

Billy Collins (b. 1941) was Poet Laureate of the United States from 2001–2003 and New York State Poet from 2004–2006. He has authored twelve poetry collections and edited various poetry publications. Collins recently retired as a Distinguished Professor of English at Lehman College of the City University of New York. "On Turning Ten" appeared in *The Art of Drowning*, published in 1995.

The whole idea of it makes me feel
like I'm coming down with something,
something worse than any stomach ache
or the headaches I get from reading in bad light—
a kind of measles of the spirit,
a mumps of the psyche,
a disfiguring chicken pox of the soul.

You tell me it is too early to be looking back,
but that is because you have forgotten
the perfect simplicity of being one
and the beautiful complexity introduced by two.
But I can lie on my bed and remember every digit.
At four I was an Arabian wizard.
I could make myself invisible
by drinking a glass of milk a certain way.
At seven I was a soldier, at nine a prince.

But now I am mostly at the window
watching the late afternoon light.
Back then it never fell so solemnly
against the side of my tree house,
and my bicycle never leaned against the garage

as it does today,
all the dark blue speed drained out of it.

This is the beginning of sadness, I say to myself,
as I walk through the universe in my sneakers.
It is time to say good-bye to my imaginary friends,
time to turn the first big number.

It seems only yesterday I used to believe
there was nothing under my skin but light.
If you cut me I could shine.
But now when I fall upon the sidewalks of life,
I skin my knees. I bleed. ■

Darrin Bell/Cartoonist Group

While Billy Collins's poem provides us with the thoughts of a boy turning 10, this cartoon presents us with a father thinking about his son reaching the same milestone.

How do the father's body language and dialogue convey his emotions? How does this father's perspective compare to that of the poem's speaker?

Understanding and Interpreting

1. What does the word "it" refer to in line 1? Why do you think the speaker uses a pronoun instead of clearly naming his subject?
2. In the first stanza, turning ten is compared to several maladies, from a "stomach ache" (l. 3) to a "disfiguring chicken pox of the soul" (l. 7). How does thinking about these illnesses help you understand the speaker's feelings about turning ten? Provide evidence from the poem to support your claim.
3. In the second stanza, the speaker addresses someone directly. Whom might he be addressing? How does the speaker's view of himself differ from his view of the person he is addressing in the poem?

4. The speaker describes the age of one as "perfect simplicity" (l. 10) and the age of two as "beautiful complexity" (l. 11). What situations, experiences, and identity shifts do these descriptions conjure up in your mind?
5. What does the description of the bicycle in lines 21 to 23 suggest about the speaker's perception of his surroundings?
6. According to the speaker, in what ways is 10 "the first big number?"

Analyzing Language, Style, and Structure

1. **Vocabulary in Context.** What does the word "solemnly" mean in the context of line 19 of this poem? What does this description of the "late afternoon light" suggest about the transition that the speaker is experiencing?
2. **Skill Focus.** Billy Collins's poem focuses on growing up. How would you describe the speaker's attitude toward changes in his identity? Refer to specific descriptions and word choices to support your claim. What does the speaker's attitude reveal about the poem's overall approach to the theme of growing up?
3. At the end of the second stanza, the speaker compares himself to "an Arabian wizard," "a soldier," and "a prince." What qualities do you associate with each of these figures? What do these metaphors reveal about the speaker's view of himself at each of the corresponding ages?
4. The word "But" in line 17 marks a shift in the poem. Identify the change that occurs and discuss how it affects the meaning of the poem as a whole.
5. Identify the repetition of the word "light," and consider its many uses in the poem. How does Collins use "light" to explore the theme of growing up?
6. Discuss the effect of ending the poem with such a short sentence: "I bleed." How would the impact of those words be different if they were incorporated into the previous sentence instead of standing on their own?

Topics for Composing

1. **Analysis.** Note the speaker's descriptions of life prior to turning ten and his perception of how things will change. Characterize the speaker's attitudes toward youth and aging. Then, explain what these attitudes reveal about the speaker's changing identity.
2. **Argument.** The speaker of this poem is clearly troubled by the idea of turning ten. Based on your own experiences and research, should parents take these types of concerns seriously when they stem from young children? How should parents respond? Make sure to support your position with specific examples.
3. **Connection.** Think back to when you were ten years old. To what extent were your thoughts similar to those of the speaker? How does your experience with growing up influence your perception of the speaker and his concerns?
4. **Speaking and Listening.** Select a stanza from the poem and determine the mood of the speaker within that stanza. Perform a reading of the stanza that conveys the mood you have identified. Think about the pace of your reading and the words you should emphasize to create the desired effect.
5. **Creative Writing.** Select an age that marked a major transition in your life. Write a poem at least two stanzas long that describes that time in your life and how it changed the way you see yourself.

Suburbia!

Amy Silverberg

Amy Silverberg (b. 1988) is a writer, stand-up comic, and doctoral fellow in fiction at the University of Southern California. Her short stories have been published in various magazines and literary journals, and she writes for television as well. "Suburbia!" first appeared in the *Southern Review* and then was selected for the collection *Best American Short Stories 2018*.

John Michael Bond

"LET'S MAKE A BET," my father said, on my fifteenth birthday. I remember very clearly being fifteen; or rather, I remember what fifteen feels like to a fifteen-year-old. The age is a diving board, a box half-opened.

We were sitting in stiff wooden chairs on the porch, watching the evening settle over the neighborhood, all of that harmless diffuse light softening the world.

"I bet you'll leave here at eighteen and you'll never come back," he said. "Not once."

We lived two hours outside of Los Angeles, in a suburb attached to a string of other suburbs, where the days rarely distinguished themselves unless you did it for them.

"You don't even think I'll come back and visit?" I said.

"No," he said. "I don't." My father was a reasonable man. He did not generalize. He was not prone to big, grandiose statements, and he rarely gambled. I felt hurt and excited by the suggestion.

"What about Mom?" I asked.

"What about her?"

I shrugged. It seemed she had little to do with his prediction.

"And James?" I asked.

"Not sure about James," he said. "I can't bet on that one."

James was — and still is — my younger brother. I felt little responsibility to him. At ten, he was brilliant and anxious and very much my parents' problem. My mother adored him, though she thought she had fooled me into thinking we were equal. Make no mistake: we were equally loved but not equally preferred. If parents don't have favorites, they do have allies.

Inside, my mother was cooking dinner while James followed her around the kitchen, handing her bits of paper he'd folded into unusual shapes. Even then, he had a knack for geometry.

"Where will I go?" I asked my father. My grades were aggressively mediocre. I'd planned — vaguely, at fifteen — to transfer somewhere after a few years at the local junior college.

"It doesn't matter where," he said, waving away a fly circling his nose.

Next door, the quiet neighbor kid, Carl, walked his miniature pinscher, also called Carl, back and forth across his lawn. The weather was balmy.

"What happens if I do come back?" I asked.

"You'll lose," he said. "You'll automatically forfeit the bet."

I hated to lose, and my father knew it.

"Will I see you again?" I asked. I felt nostalgic in a way that felt new, at fifteen, as though the day had already turned shadowy and distant, a predetermined memory. I felt nostalgic for my father and his partly bald head and his toothpaste breath, even as he sat next to me, running his palms over his hairy knees.

"Of course," he said. "Your mother and I will visit."

My mother appeared on the porch with my brother, his finger slung into the back pocket of her jeans. "Dinnertime," she said, and I kissed my father's cheek as though I were standing on a train platform. I spent all of dinner feeling that way too, staring at him from across the table, mouthing goodbye.

My eighteenth birthday arrived the summer after I'd graduated from high school. To celebrate, I saw the musical *Wicked* at a theater in Los Angeles with four of my friends. The seats were deep and velvety feeling. My parents drove us, and my father gave us each a glass of champagne in the parking lot before we entered the theater. We used small plastic cups he must have bought especially for the occasion. I pictured him browsing the plastics aisle, looking at all the cups, deciding.

A week after my birthday, my father woke me up, quieter than usual. He seemed solemn. I still had my graduation cap tacked up on the wall, its yellow tassel hanging jauntily. My mother had taken the dress I'd worn that day to the dry cleaner, and it still lay pooled on the floor in its plastic.

"Are you ready to go?" he asked.

"Where are you taking me?" I wanted to know.

"To the train station," he said. "It's time for you to go."

My father had always liked the idea of traveling. Even just walking through an airport gave him a thrill — it made him buoyant, seeing all those people hurrying through the world on their way to somewhere else. He had a deep interest in history, and the architecture of places he'd never seen in person. It was the great tragedy of his life that he became a real estate agent. As for my mother, it was the great tragedy of her life that her husband was unhappy and didn't take any pains to hide it. I can see that now, even if I didn't see it then.

"Where's Mom?" I asked. "And where's James?"

"The grocery store," my father said. James loved the grocery store — the order of things, all neat in their rows. "Don't cry," Dad said then, smoothing my pillowcase, still warm with sleep. He had a pained look on his face. "Don't cry," he said again. I hadn't noticed it had started. My whole body felt emotional in those days, like I was an egg balanced on a spoon.

"You'll be good," he said. "You'll do good."

"But what about junior college?" I asked. "What about plans?" I'd already received a stack of glossy school pamphlets in the mail. True, I didn't know what to do with them yet, but I had them just the same.

"No time," my father said, and the urgency in his voice made me hurry.

We stood on the platform at the train station — just as I'd pictured at fifteen, like I were a character in a history book, *Manifesting My Own Destiny*! He held my face in both palms and squeezed, a gentle vise. The sky was bright blue and wide open, as though it had been shelled from a duller sky.

"Whoa!.... I thought you read the book? It says that we need to *gently ease* them out of the nest."

Eric Hodecker/CartoonStock

This cartoon depicts a conflict between two different parenting styles within a family. **Characterize the parenting techniques of the two grown birds. How do they compare to how Maria's parents approach parenting?**

"You'll miss me," I said. I said it like a question.

"Of course," he said.

"Will I do OK?"

"Of course," he said. "Of course, of course, of course." The series of "of courses" worried me, as though he were trying to convince us both of something.

"Doth protest too much," I said.

"Ha!" My father pointed at a pigeon pecking its head in an odd little dance.

We hugged for a long time. My dad was tall, and he rested his chin against the top of my head. "Don't forget to shake my hand," he whispered into my hair. "We have an agreement, after all." He made a choking noise — a sob? — and ruffled my too-long bang. He stuffed a sweaty wad of money into my palm. I put it in my purse. He handed me another.

"That's it," he said. "I wish I had more."

"Where will I go?"

"I don't know," he said. "Wherever you want, I guess! You can buy a ticket when you get on the train. You used to talk about New York all the time." That's true, I did — but in an abstract, watercolor way. I knew nothing about living on my own, especially in a city that "stayed up all night." I was usually in bed by eleven, quick to fall asleep, books always splitting open onto my chest after I'd only read a few paragraphs. In fact, I'd only just started doing my own laundry last week, and I had to keep calling upstairs to my mother, about the separation of darks and lights, and when to put in the detergent. When?!

I could hardly manage to think about my mother, who was very pretty, I realized all of the sudden, and maybe always had been. (My mother had red hair, and I once heard a man at the post office tell her that from far away she looked like she was on fire. He had an odd look on his face, a half smile, as if he'd won something.)

"Shouldn't I wait to say bye?" I asked. "Won't Mom be mad?"

"It's for the best," my father said. "She'll only try to convince you to stay."

"But what about my friends," I said. "I haven't said bye to anyone!" I started thinking of odd people — our neighbor Carl and his miniature pinscher, my debate coach Mrs. Swanson who told me I touched my face too much when I talked, the boy with the unusually deep voice who worked the counter at CVS. "And James?"

"You'll see them again," he said.

"OK," I said, turning away from him. I hoped my back looked brave. From the train, I watched him through the window until I couldn't see him anymore, and the hand he'd been waving became like the minute hand of a clock — tiny — and then nothing at all.

After all that, I only went to LA. I didn't have enough money to get to New York, and anyway, that would have taken a long time on the train. On the ride, I met my first adult friend. He was sloshing down the aisles like he was drunk. He wasn't drunk though, just prone to motion sickness. His name was Charlie.

Charlie came with questions, I could tell. They animated his face before he spoke. He had just graduated from college, he told me. He had had three beers in the dining car, he volunteered, but was not drunk, just prone to motion sickness.

"Are you on your way back to school?" was his first question.

"No," I said, "I'm just leaving home. I might not even go to college."

He leaned forward. I wasn't scared, just curious. He had a harmless face — too round for murder. My mom was a big believer in physiognomy, and it had stuck with me. Your long limbs, she would say, means you'll always be efficient. I'll always be awkward, I'd say, but she assured me I was misreading my own body.

"Are you a runaway?" he asked.

"No," I said, "not exactly." I didn't want him to get the wrong idea about my family, that it was bad somehow, damaged. But then I wondered what sort of value that might have, the wrong idea about me — that I'd withstood something traumatic, that I was wise or strong. I decided the fewer words I said, the better. I'd be a person who spoke very little, but when I spoke, it would be especially important.

"I just left," I said, "I got up one day and left. Didn't even say bye to my mom."

"That's terrible," he said. "I'm sorry."

A silence fell over the two of us, one that made my pulse bang in all the wrong places — my wrist, my throat — and I asked him to tell me more about college. He'd studied political science, he said, "a stupid major, because it only made me cynical." That's what I wanted to be, too, I decided right then: cynical. It seemed fitting for the new personality I was cultivating.

"So," he said, leaning closer. "What were your parents like?"

I understood where this question was leading. "Terrible," I said. I felt the pinprick of tears somewhere behind my eyes. "Scary-awful."

Just then the slot of air between us lessened. He was leaning even closer. He had very nice teeth, prep-school teeth. I, too leaned closer. "I'm so sorry," he said.

"Don't worry. I'm on my own now."

"Geez, I should never complain about my parents," he said. "They really are nice to me. I mean my dad asks stupid questions all the time, and never listens to what I tell him, but geez, nothing like you went through."

I nodded. Maybe I would be an actress. Why not?

Charlie said I could stay at his place until I found something more permanent. He lived off of Pico in a brown stucco apartment with palm trees cemented in the sidewalk. Someone had scrawled the words *Here fur good* on one of the garage doors. Charlie had two roommates who were rarely there, and when they were there, they were always on their way out. I only ever saw them in motion — dashes of solid-colored T-shirts, streaks of floppy, surfer-boy hair. They seemed used to having a visitor.

"Hey, Boss," they'd say, like it had always been my nickname.

"Maria," I'd correct them.

"Right," they'd say. "Cool." Or, in a singsong voice, "Maria, Maria, how do you solve a problem like Maria," before closing the front door.

I was always worried about becoming a problem.

Suburban Home Contrasted with Skyscrapers, c.1945 (screenprint)/ Unknown Artist, (20th century)/GRAPHICA ARTIS/Private Collection/ Bridgeman Images

This screenprint titled *Suburban Home Contrasted with Skyscrapers* juxtaposes various features of the two settings. **What does this image convey about the city, as opposed to the suburban home that is depicted? How does your assessment of the city in this image compare with your understanding of Maria's life in the suburbs?**

I'd spoken to my father a few times. "You're doing great," he assured me. My mother got on the phone, tearful sounding sometimes, but mostly relegated to curt sentences with her voice all choked up, like the sadness was lodged in her throat. I thought their voices sounded different, higher pitched somehow, or smaller.

I wondered if my mother knew about the bet, but I couldn't tell her; I couldn't sell out my father. Regardless, she never told me to come home, just asked if I was happy. "Are you?" "Yes," I'd say, "I'm pretty sure I am."

After a few months, James started writing me emails. He was thirteen now, and had become suddenly articulate. When we were living together I hadn't realized it, or else, he had kept it from me. Maybe he was just better on paper. I started to rethink his and my mother's relationship — maybe they were true confidants, as young as he was, and as mom-like as she was.

75 The boys I lived with all loved horror films, and I would write James long movie reviews about whatever we'd just watched. He seemed to like it. I was getting to know the boys better — though they still usually called me Boss — and I would write to James about them, too.

"How are Mom and Dad," I'd write. "How's school?"

"I'm writing poetry," James wrote, "and I no longer care much for math."

"And Mom and Dad? What about them?"

"I'm thinking of going to boarding school," he said. "In fact, I'm sure I'll go." Sometimes he'd only respond with poetry: "I have perceived that to be with those I like is enough . . . I do not ask any more delight, I swim in it as in a sea," and so on.

80 "What is that?" I wrote back. "Some kind of prayer? That's not an answer! How are Mom and Dad?!?"

"Walt Whitman," he wrote, "and you really should read more."

The seasons changed. I moved into a small studio apartment by myself, and I did laundry remarkably often at a Laundromat down the street. Charlie said he was sad to see me go. I'd gotten a job as a waitress and I took classes at Santa Monica College in accounting and studio art. Eventually, I even managed to buy myself a used Jetta. "Wow," my father said when I told him about it over the phone, "that all sounds amazing." He kept telling me I was bohemian, that I was following my own path. He said it in a weird, far-off voice like he must have been sitting on the porch again, looking into the distance, at the purplish foothills.

Often, customers at the restaurant asked if I was an actress. All the waitresses in LA were actresses, and I had straight teeth and too-long legs, so sometimes I said yes. That was very meta, I thought — acting if only by telling people I was an actress. *Meta* was a new word I'd learned in community college, in the accounting class, of all things. Still, sometimes, at night, I'd rub my eyes and the tips of my fingers would be wet. I'd been crying and hadn't known it. I was quick to cry, but I wasn't sure if it was connected to any particular emotion. Like my mother said, sometimes I misread my own body. That hadn't changed.

After a while, I got a promotion at the restaurant, and suddenly I was a manager, telling the other actress-waitresses which territory of tables to serve. Sometimes, in the kitchen, they'd talk about their auditions — how often they were told to say, "Hi, welcome to Applebee's!" over and over — but more cheerful this time; no, more intense. "A waitress playing a waitress," I'd say. "Very meta!"

85 I started seeing Charlie every weekend. There was something about him I liked, a familiarity. We'd run errands — the grocery store, the comic book shop — so that the time we spent together passed easily. Being with him felt similar to being alone, only better, heightened. That's the best way I can describe it — we glided right alongside each other.

I started asking my father when he would come visit. "I'm no longer adjusting to my new life!" I said. "I'm adjusted. I'm an adult.

extending beyond the text

In this excerpt from an interview with Kathleen Boland, the editorial assistant of the *Southern Review*, Amy Silverberg discusses the setting of her story.

Kathleen Boland: "Suburbia!" revolves around the distance between Maria's suburban hometown and the city of Los Angeles. Though these locations are geographically close, they're emotionally distant, a truth made all too clear in the bet made by Maria's father.

Amy Silverberg: I grew up an hour away from Los Angeles, and even though I lived so close, I rarely came to the city unless my parents had a reason to take me. I was under eighteen; I didn't have my own car. I think a city — even if it's geographically close — always feels like night and day in comparison. Really, living in a city has always seemed emblematic of adulthood to me, of being able to make one's own choices, create one's own life. I suppose I set the story in L.A. because I live here, and it has, for me, a strange and particular identity which I associate with people moving here to "start their lives" and "make their dreams come true." Those are clichés, of course, but it's true that so many waitresses *are* actresses, and comedians, and writers — I'm always sitting in the back of a café listening to people tell each other about the auditions they bombed or nailed. I'm a stand-up comic, and everyone I know is working a day job, trying to juggle their shifts around so they can make it to a show, that kind of thing. It's a unique kind of striving. And even while I'm in the hustle (though my day job is teaching and not in the service industry), I find it endlessly interesting and stressful and worth writing about.

How does reading this interview enhance your understanding and appreciation of "Suburbia!"?

I'm living an adult life, as an adult person." He started piling up excuses and handing them over one by one. Even over the phone, I knew they were stacked up, like plates — I can't explain it. I felt angry and gypped. "You're not holding up your end of the bargain," I said. "You told me we'd see each other!"

"It's complicated," my dad said, "but I love you and miss you. We all do. It's not what you think." After a while, I started wondering why I shouldn't just go home. What did I even stand to lose?

"You can't," my father would say when I asked about it, and something about the weight of his words held me in place.

Still, I became resentful. I started noticing all of the things I'd inherited from my father that I didn't like. My mother, too! She was not exempt. I listed these things in my emails to James: passive-aggressiveness, knobby knees, indecision, weak ankles that made ice-skating difficult, an allergy to shrimp . . . the list went on. "Dad chose to be a real estate agent," I wrote in one email, "what sort of job is that?!"

"You're saying that out of anger," my brother wrote. Then, he'd include another poem. He'd moved on to a life I couldn't begin to imagine, in which he made his own lattes and collected vintage typewriters. "Mom's into poetry now," he wrote. Of course she is, I thought. "But you still want to go to boarding school?" I asked. "I'm already packing," he wrote.

Charlie loved movies, and there was a line he liked to quote whenever I complained about not understanding my family: "The awful thing about life is this: everybody has their reasons."

"I'm paraphrasing," he'd say. Meanwhile, I'd built my own kind of life for myself. Whatever it was, I knew it was distinctly mine. One week I ate every meal at the Russian deli across from my apartment. The next week, I called in sick to work and went out for a lobster dinner. The week after that, I spent the day in Venice Beach, watching the musclemen and skateboarders greet each other on the boardwalk. Still, my freedom made me restless. I saw Charlie almost every day now, usually after long shifts at the restaurant that made my clothes smell smoky like barbecue. He said my freedom made me brave. I never told him the truth about my parents, that they weren't awful, only strange. Actually, they had always been kind.

"I'm tied down," Charlie said, "by my parents' expectations. You just get to do whatever you want." Charlie worked at a law firm. He was rarely able to do what he wanted. "With you," he said, "I feel the rope around me slacken." By now, I knew he was subtly trying to sleep with me, and maybe always had been. We'd watch movies on the couch, and we'd start on opposite ends, and when the movie finished, he'd be right up against me, like we were two blocks getting ready to build.

"You're so brave," he said one night, after we'd eaten SpaghettiOs from a can. We were sitting at my small Formica kitchen table, and he kept dipping his head toward me, like he was trying to close the gap between our mouths. It's not that I didn't want to. The shape of his lips told me it would be good, and though I hadn't kissed that many people, I'd kissed enough to know shape mattered. It was the lie that kept me from pressing my lips to his.

"I haven't been honest about my parents," I said.

"Oh?" he said. "You can tell me anything. Anything they did to you—"

"I'm not as brave or as cynical as you think." Then I told him the whole story of the bet with my father.

"Well, you should go home and see them," he said.

"But then I'd lose."

"Who cares?" he shouted, and smacked the table. And maybe he was right. But I did care. I hated to lose. What's more, I hated to disappoint my father.

"I'll go with you," he said.

We took the train. "Remember when we met?" he asked. And of course I did. This time, he talked about his job at the law firm as we rode out of LA, buildings flipping by like cards in a deck. He hated his job.

"Then quit it," I said. It was a simple answer, and I said it simply. He looked like he wanted to kiss me, and this time I let him, or I kissed him, and he let me. It was one of those kisses that felt equal—where you're giving as much as you take. Also, I was right about how the shape of his mouth would feel, and happy that I'd read my body correctly. There was pleasure in knowing what you wanted and acting accordingly. It was a different kind of freedom.

We kissed for most of the train ride, so that by the time we arrived at my stop, I felt dizzy and short of breath, as though I'd run the whole way. Once we reached the platform, we took an Uber to my house, debating the entire time whether or not I should have told my parents I was coming—prepared my dad at least. I had decided not to; I wanted to catch them off guard. Charlie thought I should have told them. He thought it would have been more considerate. "Consideration?" I scoffed. "I've already outgrown it."

When we drove up the familiar street toward my cul-de-sac, I didn't realize I was nervous until I felt my insides twist up. Still, the neighborhood looked like you might expect it to—neat, prim, safe.

"Why are you nervous?" Charlie asked. "To see them?"

"No," I said. "Nervous to lose the bet." More so, I couldn't remember the last time I'd so blatantly gone against my father's wishes, if I ever had before.

"Is this it?" the driver asked, looking at his GPS again, and then at the empty lot. The curb was still painted with the numbers of my address, but the land was filled with grass and dandelions and other unnameable weeds.

"This can't be right," I said.

I saw a glimmer of something in the empty lot. Where were my parents? My brother? From afar, the something shone in the sun like a tin can. When I came upon it, though, I saw that it was an exact replica of the house I grew up in, just tiny, a little smaller than a toaster. I got down on my knees, then lowered my body to the ground as though I were preparing to do push-ups. "Hello!" I shouted through the windows. I flicked open the front door with my fingernail. "Hello?" The tiny curtains blew with my breath. The mailbox I remembered from my childhood was still there — sponge-painted red, a task I had completed when I was in elementary school — only teeny now.

I thought I heard something coming from inside the tiny house: a tiny, high-pitched voice. I saw my tiny father in the tiny foyer, shaking his head at me.

"I told you not to come," he said. "You didn't listen!"

Charlie was behind me. "What is it?" he asked. "What's that little box?"

"My house," I said. The way he stood, the shadow he produced made it difficult to see anything else. "Back up," I said.

"I didn't want you to see us like this," my father said. My mother appeared alongside him.

"It's OK," I told him, "don't worry." Still lying flat, I talked to my parents through the tiny doorway, and told them a few details about my life, mostly about junior college and waitressing and Charlie. My mother was trying not to cry. I could see her red hair, like the tip of a match now.

"How are you?" I asked. I wanted to reach out and stroke the top of her head with the pad of my finger.

"OK," she said. Her voice was soft, a faint whistle, and I had to lean close to hear it. "Dad and I are seeing a couples' therapist," she told me, and I wondered if the therapist was also miniature. My dad turned away, embarrassed.

"That's great," I said. "And James likes boarding school?"

"Loves it," my dad said, brightening again. "You should see him now. We hardly recognize him."

I looked around for Charlie, wanting him to get down on his knees at my parents' tiny door and introduce himself. But no, he was waiting in the car, giving us our privacy. From where I crouched, he also looked smaller. I thought this was a funny thing, the way the past and the future could both shrink down to a manageable size, like a pill to be swallowed, or the head of a match. ■

Observe Albert's surroundings and determine why he "hated growing up in a small town." **How do both this picture and "Suburbia!" use physical dimensions as a metaphor?**

Understanding and Interpreting

1. Maria describes her hometown as being a "suburb attached to a string of other suburbs" (par. 4). Based on this characterization, how would you describe her attitude towards it? Specifically, imagine how Maria might have felt about being part of this community before the bet with her father. How might her attitude then have been different from her attitude at the time of the telling of the story?
2. Summarize the bet Maria's father proposes. Why do you think he initiates this bet with his daughter? What might he know about Maria that she has not discovered about herself yet?
3. Why does Maria feel a sense of nostalgia and longing during dinner, even if her eventual departure isn't for another three years? What do these feelings reveal about how Maria sees herself and her place within her family?
4. Why does Maria call her father's career path "the great tragedy of his life" (par. 29)? What does "the great tragedy" of her mother's life reveal about her mother? What do these details about her parents suggest about how Maria perceives them?
5. To what extent is Maria truthful about her family history when she speaks to Charlie? Why does Maria choose to lie about some aspects of her life?
6. Notice the shift that begins with paragraph 82. In addition to the changes in season, what other changes are occurring for Maria? Her father? What remains the same?
7. From what he knows about Maria, what makes Charlie describe her as brave? To what degree is this assessment accurate?
8. Describe Maria's and Charlie's reactions to her parents and their home at the end of the story. What do these reactions suggest about their perceptions of themselves and others?

Analyzing Language, Style, and Structure

1. **Vocabulary in Context.** Maria explains that the idea of travelling always made her father "buoyant" (par. 28). What does the word usually refer to? What does it mean in this context? What does Maria convey about her father with her use of the word "buoyant"?
2. **Skill Focus**. When thinking about being fifteen, Maria describes it as a "diving board" and a "box half-opened" (par. 1). In what ways does being fifteen serve as an invitation for self-discovery for Maria? What does she discover about herself after her fifteenth birthday?
3. Instead of providing a gradual exposition as is commonly observed at the beginning of stories, *Suburbia!* opens in *medias res*, or in the middle of the action. Immediately, the father introduces the key feature in the story — the bet. How does this affect your reading of the story?
4. Note that Maria describes James and her mother as allies. What does this observation reveal about Maria's sense of self and the way she sees herself within the context of her family?
5. Silverberg manipulates the passage of time throughout the story. Aside from allowing the short story's plot to span many years, how are these time jumps significant to understanding Maria's path toward self-discovery?
6. Revisit the story's title. How does it relate to the story? How would the effect of the title change if it were missing the exclamation mark?
7. The story is realistic until the final moments when Maria encounters the shrunken house. What does this surprising detail suggest about what Maria has discovered about herself and her family since she left for Los Angeles?

8. The word "box" appears in paragraph 1 ("a box half-opened") and again in paragraph 112 ('What's that little box?'). This image thereby creates a structural frame for the story. Explain how the box is significant to this story's meaning.

Topics for Composing

1. **Analysis.** Maria's identity is first shaped by her life at home. Then, it is altered by her life in Los Angeles. How would you characterize Maria? How does this description convey a possible thematic concern in the story?
2. **Argument.** To what extent are our personalities shaped by our surroundings or innately part of who we are? Use both your own experiences and details from the text to support your position.
3. **Connection.** Think about how you feel about your hometown and evaluate how it makes you feel about yourself. Is your personality better suited for a smaller town, a larger city, or somewhere else? Explain.
4. **Speaking and Listening.** While you can infer the father's motives for placing the bet, he never directly expresses his rationale to Maria. Adopting the perspective of her father, record a video of yourself delineating to Maria the reasons for the bet. Make sure that your remarks are supported by the events that take place throughout the story.
5. **Research.** In this story, Silverberg makes various allusions, or references, to outside texts. Choose one from the list below and research its historical and cultural significance. Then, discuss how it relates to the story and specific characters.
   a. *Wicked*
   b. Manifest Destiny
   c. "Doth protest too much"
   d. Walt Whitman
6. **Creative Writing.** The emails between Maria and James are pivotal to our understanding of these characters and their relationship. Imagine yourself as Maria and write an email to James prior to your return home. Consider what this email would reveal about how she views herself, particularly in relation to home.

The Seven Ages of Man

William Shakespeare

William Shakespeare (1564–1616) is considered one of the greatest playwrights in history. His plays *Hamlet*, *King Lear*, *Macbeth*, *Othello*, *Julius Caesar*, *Romeo and Juliet*, and many others are among the most widely read and performed plays in the English language. While many of Shakespeare's best-known works are classified as tragedies, he also wrote a number of very popular comedies and histories, including *A Midsummer Night's Dream*, *As You Like It*, *The Taming of the Shrew*, *Antony and Cleopatra*, and *Richard III*.

GL Archive/Alamy

KEY CONTEXT The excerpt that follows is from the comedy *As You Like It* (1603), which is about a group of exiled noblemen and women who find love amid mistaken identities in a forest in rural France. The speech below, one of Shakespeare's most famous, is delivered as a monologue by the often-gloomy Jaques, one of the exiled lords. In it, Jaques describes what he sees as the life cycle of mankind, from childhood to old age, with five "ages" in between.

All the world's a stage,
And all the men and women merely players.
They have their exits and their entrances,
And one man in his time plays many parts,
His acts being seven ages. At first the infant,
Mewling and puking in the nurse's arms.
Then the whining schoolboy, with his satchel
And shining morning face, creeping like snail
Unwillingly to school. And then the lover,
Sighing like furnace, with a woeful ballad
Made to his mistress' eyebrow. Then a soldier,
Full of strange oaths, and bearded like the pard,[1]
Jealous in honor, sudden, and quick in quarrel,
Seeking the bubble reputation
Even in the cannon's mouth. And then the justice,
In fair round belly with good capon[2] lined,
With eyes severe and beard of formal cut,
Full of wise saws and modern instances;
And so he plays his part. The sixth age shifts
Into the lean and slippered pantaloon,[3]
With spectacles on nose and pouch on side,
His youthful hose, well saved, a world too wide
For his shrunk shank;[4] and his big manly voice,
Turning again toward childish treble, pipes
And whistles in his sound. Last scene of all,
That ends this strange eventful history,
Is second childishness and mere oblivion,
Sans teeth, sans eyes, sans taste, sans everything. ■

[1]pard: leopard. — Eds.
[2]capon: rooster intended for eating. — Eds.
[3]pantaloon: A stock character in the Italian commedia dell'arte, the pantaloon is an absurd, doddering old man. — Eds.
[4]shank: calf. — Eds.

FSL Interior: Seven Ages of Man Stained Glass Window 1985; Julie Ainsworth. Used by permission of the Folger Shakespeare Library.

In a reading room at the Folger Shakespeare Library in Washington, D.C., there is a large stained glass window created by artist Nicola d'Ascenzo that represents each of the seven ages of man.

Examine each section of the stained glass window shown here and explain which words or phrases from Jaques's speech you think likely contributed to d'Ascenzo's interpretation.

Understanding and Interpreting

1. Explain the opening metaphor: "All the world's a stage, / And all the men and women merely players." How is life similar to being an actor on stage?
2. The speaker attributes "strange oaths" (l. 12) and the pursuit of "the bubble reputation" (l. 14) to soldiers. What do these phrases reveal about the speaker's attitude toward soldiers and their priorities?
3. The sixth stage — the pantaloon — marks a drastic change in a person because there are physical and mental changes present. Characterize the speaker's reaction to this stage based on the details provided. Does the speaker seem more or less critical of this stage than of other stages?
4. How is the final stage similar to and different from the other stages? Explain what is significant about any similarities or differences you notice.
5. Paraphrase the seven ages in seven sentences. Be sure to identify how the speaker characterizes humanity at each age.

Analyzing Language, Style, and Structure

1. **Vocabulary in Context.** Jaques uses the word "saws" in line 18. What does this word usually mean? What does "saws" mean in the context of Jaques's description of the fifth stage of life?

2. **Skill Focus.** Consider the ideas about life and its many cycles conveyed by Jaques's speech. What does Jaques discover about life and himself in the process of describing these stages?
3. What is the effect of the word "merely" in the second line? How would the tone be different if that word were not included?
4. Jaques uses a number of similes to describe the stages men and women go through in life. Paraphrase each of the following similes and explain how each contributes to the overall tone:
   a. "creeping like snail" (l. 8)
   b. "Sighing like furnace" (l. 10)
   c. "bearded like the pard" (l. 12)
5. In addition to using similes, Jaques also uses imagery to describe many of the stages of life. Paraphrase each of the following lines and explain how each contributes to how humans are characterized at each stage:
   a. "Mewling and puking in the nurse's arms" (l. 6)
   b. "In fair round belly with good capon lined" (l. 16)
   c. "big manly voice, / Turning again toward childish treble, pipes / And whistles in his sound" (ll. 23–25)
6. There are several places where Jaques mocks human behavior. Identify one of these lines, explain what he is mocking, and provide the specific words that convey the mockery.
7. Each of the stages does not receive the same number of lines: some are longer and some are shorter. Look back through the speech to identify the "ages" with the fewest and most lines. What significance can you place on these choices?
8. What is the effect of the repetition of the word "sans" in the last line? What does this repetition suggest about the speaker's outlook on the final stage of life?

Topics for Composing

1. **Analysis.** Towards the end of the poem, Jaques refers to life as a "strange eventful history" (l. 26). How do this phrase and the seven ages Jaques describes convey his attitude toward life and the roles people play within it?
2. **Argument.** Shakespeare wrote these descriptions of the stages of life over 400 years ago. Does any part of Jaques's description of the "schoolboy" still hold true? Think about what it's like to be a student in the twenty-first century. What are the defining characteristics of school-age children or adolescents today? Defend your position with personal experience, research, and the text.
3. **Connection.** Select a character from another text in the chapter, or one that you have encountered on your own, that you think is emblematic of one of the stages described by Jaques. Identify the character and explain how he or she embodies the stage as envisioned by Shakespeare.
4. **Speaking and Listening.** *As You Like It* was first performed in 1603. How would this excerpt from the play be similar or different if it were written today? Consider differences in available professions, life expectancy, technology, medicine, transportation, and so on. Then, work with a group to write, either in poetry or prose, "The Seven Ages of a Twenty-First-Century Person" to reflect today's stages of life. Within your group, finalize the text and select the props, costumes, and movements needed to perform it. Each group will stage their performance in front of the whole class.

central text

Rules of the Game

Amy Tan

Amy Tan (b. 1952) grew up in California. She has a Master of Arts in linguistics, and has written several best-selling novels, including *The Valley of Amazement* (2013). In her work, Tan draws on her Chinese heritage to depict the clash of traditional Chinese culture with modern-day American customs. This short story, "Rules of the Game," became the basis for her critically acclaimed and popular novel *The Joy Luck Club* (1989).

Tim Mosenfelder/Getty Images

I was six when my mother taught me the art of invisible strength. It was a strategy for winning arguments, respect from others, and eventually, though neither of us knew it at the time, chess games.

"Bite back your tongue," scolded my mother when I cried loudly, yanking her hand toward the store that sold bags of salted plums. At home, she said, "Wise guy, he not go against wind. In Chinese we say, Come from South, blow with wind — poom! — North will follow. Strongest wind cannot be seen."

The next week I bit back my tongue as we entered the store with the forbidden candies. When my mother finished her shopping, she quietly plucked a small bag of plums from the rack and put it on the counter with the rest of the items.

My mother imparted her daily truths so she could help my older brothers and me rise above our circumstances. We lived in San Francisco's Chinatown. Like most of the other Chinese children who played in the back alleys of restaurants and curio shops, I didn't think we were poor. My bowl was always full, three five-course meals every day, beginning with a soup of mysterious things I didn't want to know the names of.

We lived on Waverly Place, in a warm, clean, two-bedroom flat that sat above a small Chinese bakery specializing in steamed pastries and dim sum. In the early morning, when the alley was still quiet, I could smell fragrant red beans as they were cooked down to a pasty sweetness. By daybreak, our flat was heavy with the odor of fried sesame balls and sweet curried chicken crescents. From my bed, I would listen as my father got ready for work, then locked the door behind him, one-two-three clicks.

At the end of our two-block alley was a small sandlot playground with swings and slides well-shined down the middle with use. The play area was bordered by wood-slat benches where old-country people sat cracking roasted watermelon seeds with their golden teeth and scattering the husks to an impatient gathering of gurgling pigeons. The best playground, however, was the dark alley itself. It was crammed with daily mysteries and adventures. My brothers and I would peer into the medicinal herb shop, watching old Li dole out onto a stiff sheet of white paper the right amount of insect shells, saffron-colored seeds, and pungent leaves for his ailing customers. It was said that he once cured a woman dying of an ancestral curse that had eluded the best of American doctors. Next to the pharmacy was a printer who specialized in gold-embossed wedding invitations and festive red banners.

Farther down the street was Ping Yuen Fish Market. The front window displayed a tank crowded with doomed fish and turtles struggling to gain footing on the slimy green-tiled sides. A hand-written sign informed tourists, "Within this store, is all for food, not for pet." Inside, the butchers with their bloodstained white smocks deftly gutted the fish while customers cried out their orders and shouted, "Give me your freshest," to which the butchers always protested, "All are freshest." On less crowded market days, we would inspect the crates of live frogs and crabs which we were warned not to poke, boxes of dried cuttlefish, and row upon row of iced prawns, squid, and slippery fish. The sanddabs made me shiver each time; their eyes lay on one flattened side and reminded me of my mother's story of a careless girl who ran into a crowded street and was crushed by a cab. "Was smash flat," reported my mother.

At the corner of the alley was Hong Sing's, a four-table cafe with a recessed stairwell in front that led to a door marked "Tradesmen." My brothers and I believed the bad people emerged from this door at night. Tourists never went to Hong Sing's, since the menu was printed only in Chinese. A Caucasian man with a big camera once posed me and my playmates in front of the restaurant. He had us move to the side of the picture window so the photo would capture the roasted duck with its head dangling from a juice-covered rope. After he took the picture, I told him he should go into Hong Sing's and eat dinner. When he smiled and asked me what they served, I shouted, "Guts and duck's feet and octopus gizzards!" Then I ran off with my friends, shrieking with laughter as we scampered across the alley and hid in the entryway grotto of the China Gem Company, my heart pounding with hope that he would chase us.

My mother named me after the street that we lived on: Waverly Place Jong, my official name for important American documents. But my family called me Meimei, "Little Sister." I was the youngest, the only daughter. Each morning before school, my mother would twist and yank on my thick black hair until she had formed two tightly wound pigtails. One day, as she struggled

Gavin Hellier/Alamy

This picture, taken in San Francisco's Chinatown, shows a blend of Chinese and American cultures.

Where do you see elements of each? In what ways is Waverly's environment similar to the one pictured here?

to weave a hard-toothed comb through my disobedient hair, I had a sly thought.

10 I asked her, "Ma, what is Chinese torture?" My mother shook her head. A bobby pin was wedged between her lips. She wetted her palm and smoothed the hair above my ear, then pushed the pin in so that it nicked sharply against my scalp.

"Who say this word?" she asked without a trace of knowing how wicked I was being. I shrugged my shoulders and said, "Some boy in my class said Chinese people do Chinese torture."

"Chinese people do many things," she said simply. "Chinese people do business, do medicine, do painting. Not lazy like American people. We do torture. Best torture."

My older brother Vincent was the one who actually got the chess set. We had gone to the annual Christmas party held at the First Chinese Baptist Church at the end of the alley. The missionary ladies had put together a Santa bag of gifts donated by members of another church. None of the gifts had names on them. There were separate sacks for boys and girls of different ages. One of the Chinese parishioners had donned a Santa Claus costume and a stiff paper beard with cotton balls glued to it. I think the only children who thought he was the real thing were too young to know that Santa Claus was not Chinese. When my turn came up, the Santa man asked me how old I was. I thought it was a trick question; I was seven according to the American formula and eight by the Chinese calendar. I said I was born on March 17, 1951. That seemed to satisfy him. He then solemnly asked if I had been a very, very good girl this year and did I believe in Jesus Christ and obey my parents. I knew the only answer to that. I nodded back with equal solemnity.

Having watched the older children opening their gifts, I already knew that the big gifts were not necessarily the nicest ones. One girl my age got a large coloring book of biblical characters, while a less greedy girl who selected a smaller box received a glass vial of lavender toilet water. The sound of the box was also important. A ten-year-old boy had chosen a box that jangled when he shook it. It was a tin globe of the world with a slit for inserting money. He must have thought it was full of dimes and nickels, because when he saw that it had just ten pennies, his face fell with such undisguised disappointment that his mother slapped the side of his head and led him out of the church hall, apologizing to the crowd for her son who had such bad manners he couldn't appreciate such a fine gift.

As I peered into the sack, I quickly fingered 15
the remaining presents, testing their weight, imagining what they contained. I chose a heavy, compact one that was wrapped in shiny silver foil and a red satin ribbon. It was a twelve-pack of Life Savers and I spent the rest of the party arranging and rearranging the candy tubes in the order of my favorites. My brother Winston chose wisely as well. His present turned out to be a box of intricate plastic parts; the instructions on the box proclaimed that when they were properly assembled he would have an authentic miniature replica of a World War II submarine.

Vincent got the chess set, which would have been a very decent present to get at a church Christmas party, except it was obviously used and, as we discovered later, it was missing a black pawn and a white knight. My mother graciously thanked the unknown benefactor, saying, "Too good. Cost too much." At which point, an old lady with fine white, wispy hair nodded toward our family and said with a whistling whisper, "Merry, merry Christmas."

When we got home, my mother told Vincent to throw the chess set away. "She not want it. We not want it," she said, tossing her head stiffly to the side with a tight, proud smile. My brothers had deaf ears. They were already lining up the chess pieces and reading from the dog-eared instruction book. I watched Vincent and Winston play during Christmas week. The chessboard seemed to hold elaborate secrets waiting to be untangled. The chessmen were more powerful than old Li's magic herbs that cured ancestral curses. And my brothers wore such serious faces that I was sure something was at stake that was greater than avoiding the tradesmen's door to Hong Sing's.

"Let me! Let me!" I begged between games when one brother or the other would sit back with a deep sigh of relief and victory, the other annoyed, unable to let go of the outcome. Vincent at first refused to let me play, but when I offered my Life Savers as replacements for the buttons that filled in for the missing pieces, he relented. He chose the flavors: wild cherry for the black pawn and peppermint for the white knight. Winner could eat both.

As our mother sprinkled flour and rolled out small doughy circles for the steamed dumplings that would be our dinner that night, Vincent explained the rules, pointing to each piece. "You have sixteen pieces and so do I. One king and queen, two bishops, two knights, two castles, and eight pawns. The pawns can only move forward one step, except on the first move. Then they can move two. But they can only take men by moving crossways like this, except in the beginning, when you can move ahead and take another pawn."

"Why?" I asked as I moved my pawn. "Why can't they move more steps?" "Because they're pawns," he said.

"But why do they go crossways to take other men? Why aren't there any women and children?"

"Why is the sky blue? Why must you always ask stupid questions?" asked Vincent. "This is a game. These are the rules. I didn't make them up. See. Here in the book." He jabbed a page with a pawn in his hand. "Pawn. P-A-W-N. Pawn. Read it yourself."

My mother patted the flour off her hands. "Let me see book," she said quietly. She scanned the pages quickly, not reading the foreign English symbols, seeming to search deliberately for nothing in particular.

"This American rules," she concluded at last. "Every time people come out from foreign country, must know rules. You not know, judge say, Too bad, go back. They not telling you why so you can use their way go forward. They say, Don't know why, you find out yourself. But they knowing all the time. Better you take it, find out why yourself." She tossed her head back with a satisfied smile.

I found out about all the whys later. I read the rules and looked up all the big words in a dictionary. I borrowed books from the Chinatown library. I studied each chess piece, trying to absorb the power each contained.

I learned about opening moves and why it's important to control the center early on; the shortest distance between two points is straight down the middle. I learned about the middle game and why tactics between two adversaries are like clashing ideas; the one who plays better has the clearest plans for both attacking and getting out of traps. I learned why it is essential in the endgame to have foresight, a mathematical understanding of all possible moves, and patience; all weaknesses and advantages become evident to a strong adversary and are obscured to a tiring opponent. I discovered that for the whole game one must gather invisible strengths and see the endgame before the game begins.

I also found out why I should never reveal "why" to others. A little knowledge withheld is a great advantage one should store for future use. That is the power of chess. It is a game of secrets in which one must show and never tell.

I loved the secrets I found within the sixty-four black and white squares. I carefully drew a handmade chessboard and pinned it to the wall next to my bed, where I would stare for hours at imaginary battles. Soon I no longer lost any games or Life Savers, but I lost my adversaries. Winston and Vincent decided they

People Playing With A Giant Chess Set on A Square, Amsterdam, Netherlands (photo)/UNIVERSAL IMAGES GROUP/Bridgeman Images

In Peter Langer's photograph *People Playing with a Giant Chess Set on a Square, Amsterdam*, chess is portrayed as an outdoor social pastime.

How would you describe the attitude of the players and that of the spectators? How does this portrayal of the game and its players compare to what chess represents for Waverly?

were more interested in roaming the streets after school in their Hopalong Cassidy cowboy hats.

On a cold spring afternoon, while walking home from school, I detoured through the playground at the end of our alley. I saw a group of old men, two seated across a folding table playing a game of chess, others smoking pipes, eating peanuts, and watching. I ran home and grabbed Vincent's chess set, which was bound in a cardboard box with rubber bands. I also carefully selected two prized rolls of Life Savers. I came back to the park and approached a man who was observing the game.

"Want to play?" I asked him. His face widened with surprise and he grinned as he looked at the box under my arm.

"Little sister, been a long time since I play with dolls," he said, smiling benevolently. I quickly put the box down next to him on the bench and displayed my retort.

Lau Po, as he allowed me to call him, turned out to be a much better player than my brothers. I lost many games and many Life Savers. But over the weeks, with each diminishing roll of candies, I added new secrets. Lau Po gave me the names. The Double Attack from the East and West Shores. Throwing Stones on the Drowning Man. The Sudden Meeting of the Clan. The Surprise from the Sleeping Guard. The Humble Servant Who Kills the King. Sand in the Eyes of Advancing Forces. A Double Killing Without Blood.

There were also the fine points of chess etiquette. Keep captured men in neat rows, as well-tended prisoners. Never announce "Check" with vanity, lest someone with an unseen sword slit your throat. Never hurl pieces into the sandbox after you have lost a game, because then you must find them again, by yourself, after apologizing to all around you. By the end of the summer, Lau Po had taught me all he knew, and I had become a better chess player.

A small weekend crowd of Chinese people and tourists would gather as I played and defeated my opponents one by one. My mother would join the crowds during these outdoor exhibition games. She sat proudly on the bench, telling my admirers with proper Chinese humility, "Is luck."

A man who watched me play in the park suggested that my mother allow me to play in local chess tournaments. My mother smiled graciously, an answer that meant nothing. I desperately wanted to go, but I bit back my tongue. I knew she would not let me play among strangers. So as we walked home I said in a small voice that I didn't want to play in the local tournament. They would have American rules. If I lost, I would bring shame on my family.

"Is shame you fall down nobody push you," said my mother.

During my first tournament, my mother sat with me in the front row as I waited for my turn. I frequently bounced my legs to unstick them from the cold metal seat of the folding chair. When my name was called, I leapt up. My mother unwrapped something in her lap. It was her chang, a small tablet of red jade which held the sun's fire. "Is luck," she whispered, and tucked it into my dress pocket. I turned to my opponent, a fifteen-year-old boy from Oakland. He looked at me, wrinkling his nose.

As I began to play, the boy disappeared, the color ran out of the room, and I saw only my white pieces and his black ones waiting on the other side. A light wind began blowing past my ears. It whispered secrets only I could hear.

"Blow from the South," it murmured. "The wind leaves no trail." I saw a clear path, the traps to avoid. The crowd rustled. "Shhh! Shhh!" said the corners of the room. The wind blew stronger. "Throw sand from the East to distract him." The knight came forward ready for the sacrifice. The wind hissed, louder and louder. "Blow, blow, blow. He cannot see. He is blind now. Make him lean away from the wind so he is easier to knock down."

"Check," I said, as the wind roared with laughter. The wind died down to little puffs, my own breath.

My mother placed my first trophy next to a new plastic chess set that the neighborhood Tao society had given to me. As she wiped each piece with a soft cloth, she said, "Next time win more, lose less."

"Ma, it's not how many pieces you lose," I said. "Sometimes you need to lose pieces to get ahead."

"Better to lose less, see if you really need."

At the next tournament, I won again, but it was my mother who wore the triumphant grin.

"Lost eight piece this time. Last time was eleven. What I tell you? Better off lose less!" I was annoyed, but I couldn't say anything.

I attended more tournaments, each one farther away from home. I won all games, in all divisions. The Chinese bakery downstairs from our flat displayed my growing collection of trophies in its window, amidst the dust-covered cakes that were never picked up. The day after I won an important regional tournament, the window encased a fresh sheet cake with whipped-cream frosting and red script saying "Congratulations, Waverly Jong, Chinatown Chess Champion." Soon after that, a flower shop, headstone engraver, and funeral parlor offered to sponsor me in national tournaments. That's when my mother decided I no longer had to do the dishes. Winston and Vincent had to do my chores.

"Why does she get to play and we do all the work," complained Vincent. "Is new American rules," said my mother. "Meimei play, squeeze all her brains out for win chess. You play, worth squeeze towel."

By my ninth birthday, I was a national chess champion. I was still some 429 points away from grand-master status, but I was touted as the Great American Hope, a child prodigy and a girl to boot. They ran a photo of me in *Life* magazine next to a quote in which Bobby Fischer said, "There will never be a woman grand master." "Your move, Bobby," said the caption.

The day they took the magazine picture I wore neatly plaited braids clipped with plastic barrettes trimmed with rhinestones. I was playing in a large high school auditorium that echoed with phlegmy coughs and the squeaky rubber knobs of chair legs sliding across freshly

extending beyond the text

Read the following article from *Good Housekeeping*. In it, the author, Marisa Lascala, discusses the "tiger mom" parenting style.

from **What Is Tiger Mom Parenting?**

Marisa Lascala

The term "Tiger Mom" burst onto the scene in 2011 when Amy Chua, a Yale law professor and mother of two daughters, published a book about her parenting style called *The Battle Hymn of the Tiger Mother.* In it, she ascribes tiger parenting to Chinese parents (though she admits she uses the terms "Chinese" and "Western" loosely — and, really, anybody can adopt this style).

"Western parents try to respect their children's individuality, encouraging them to pursue their true passions, supporting their choices, and providing positive reinforcement and a nurturing environment," she writes in her book, which was excerpted by the *Wall Street Journal*. "By contrast, the Chinese believe that the best way to protect their children is by preparing them for the future, letting them see what they're capable of, and arming them with skills, work habits, and inner confidence that no one can ever take away."

While some find Chua's methods extreme — she once told her four-year-old daughter to re-do a handmade birthday card because it didn't meet her standards — others say there's a lot of warmth as well, and that the high expectations produce results.

How does Chua's book title, *The Battle Hymn of the Tiger Mother,* seem appropriate to the parenting style she describes? Would Waverly consider her mom a "Tiger Mom"? Which parenting style seems most prevalent in your household and in your classmates' households?

waxed wooden floors. Seated across from me was an American man, about the same age as Lau Po, maybe fifty. I remember that his sweaty brow seemed to weep at my every move. He wore a dark, malodorous suit. One of his pockets was stuffed with a great white kerchief on which he wiped his palm before sweeping his hand over the chosen chess piece with great flourish.

In my crisp pink-and-white dress with scratchy lace at the neck, one of two my mother had sewn for these special occasions, I would clasp my hands under my chin, the delicate points of my elbows poised lightly on the table in the manner my mother had shown me for posing for the press. I would swing my patent leather shoes back and forth like an impatient child riding on a school bus. Then I would pause, suck in my lips, twirl my chosen piece in midair as if undecided, and then firmly plant it in its new threatening place, with a triumphant smile thrown back at my opponent for good measure.

I no longer played in the alley of Waverly Place. I never visited the playground where the pigeons and old men gathered. I went to school, then directly home to learn new chess secrets, cleverly concealed advantages, more escape routes.

But I found it difficult to concentrate at home. My mother had a habit of standing over me while I plotted out my games. I think she thought of herself as my protective ally. Her lips would be sealed tight, and after each move I made, a soft "Hmmmmph" would escape from her nose.

"Ma, I can't practice when you stand there like that," I said one day. She retreated to the kitchen and made loud noises with the pots and pans. When the crashing stopped, I could see out of the corner of my eye that she was standing in the doorway. "Hmmmmph!" Only this one came out of her tight throat.

My parents made many concessions to allow me to practice. One time I complained that the bedroom I shared was so noisy that I couldn't think. Thereafter, my brothers slept in a bed in the living room facing the street. I said I couldn't finish my rice; my head didn't work right when my stomach was too full. I left the table with half-finished bowls and nobody complained.

55 But there was one duty I couldn't avoid. I had to accompany my mother on Saturday market days when I had no tournament to play. My mother would proudly walk with me, visiting many shops, buying very little. "This my daughter Wave-ly Jong," she said to whoever looked her way.

One day after we left a shop I said under my breath, "I wish you wouldn't do that, telling everybody I'm your daughter." My mother stopped walking.

Crowds of people with heavy bags pushed past us on the sidewalk, bumping into first one shoulder, than another.

"Aii-ya. So shame be with mother?" She grasped my hand even tighter as she glared at me.

I looked down. "It's not that, it's just so obvious. It's just so embarrassing." "Embarrass you be my daughter?" Her voice was cracking with anger. "That's not what I meant. That's not what I said."

60 "What you say?"

I knew it was a mistake to say anything more, but I heard my voice speaking, "Why do you have to use me to show off? If you want to show off, then why don't you learn to play chess?"

My mother's eyes turned into dangerous black slits. She had no words for me, just sharp silence.

I felt the wind rushing around my hot ears. I jerked my hand out of my mother's tight grasp and spun around, knocking into an old woman. Her bag of groceries spilled to the ground.

"Aii-ya! Stupid girl!" my mother and the woman cried. Oranges and tin cans careened down the sidewalk. As my mother stooped to help the old woman pick up the escaping food, I took off.

65 I raced down the street, dashing between people, not looking back as my mother screamed shrilly, "Meimei! Meimei!" I fled down an alley, past dark, curtained shops and merchants washing the grime off their windows. I sped into the sunlight, into a large street crowded with tourists examining trinkets and souvenirs. I ducked into another dark alley, down another street, up another alley. I ran until it hurt and I realized I had nowhere to go, that I was not running from anything. The alleys contained no escape routes.

My breath came out like angry smoke. It was cold. I sat down on an upturned plastic pail next to a stack of empty boxes, cupping my chin with my hands, thinking hard. I imagined my mother, first walking briskly down one street or another looking for me, then giving up and returning home to await my arrival. After two hours, I stood up on creaking legs and slowly walked home. The alley was quiet and I could see the yellow lights shining from our flat like two tiger's eyes in the night. I climbed the sixteen steps to the door, advancing quietly up each so as not to make any warning sounds. I turned the knob; the door was locked. I heard a chair moving, quick steps, the locks turning — click! click! click! — and then the door opened.

"About time you got home," said Vincent. "Boy, are you in trouble."

He slid back to the dinner table. On a platter were the remains of a large fish, its fleshy head still connected to bones swimming upstream in vain escape. Standing there waiting for my punishment, I heard my mother speak in a dry voice.

"We not concerning this girl. This girl not have concerning for us." Nobody looked at me. Bone chopsticks clinked against the inside of bowls being emptied into hungry mouths.

70 I walked into my room, closed the door, and lay down on my bed. The room was dark, the ceiling filled with shadows from the dinnertime lights of neighboring flats.

In my head, I saw a chessboard with sixty-four black and white squares. Opposite me was my opponent, two angry black slits. She wore a triumphant smile. "Strongest wind cannot be seen," she said.

Her black men advanced across the plane, slowly marching to each successive level as a single unit. My white pieces screamed as they scurried and fell off the board one by one. As her men drew closer to my edge, I felt myself growing light. I rose up into the air and flew out the window. Higher and higher, above the alley, over the tops of tiled roofs, where I was gathered up by the wind and pushed up toward the night sky until everything below me disappeared and I was alone.

I closed my eyes and pondered my next move. ■

Understanding and Interpreting

1. Line 1 establishes that Waverly's mother teaches her the "art of invisible strength." In paragraph 2, the mother states, "Strongest wind cannot be seen." How are these two ideas related and how do they shape Waverly's character?
2. Waverly's mother tells her, "Bite back your tongue" (par. 2). What does she mean by this? How do you think this instruction influences Waverly's personality?
3. Paragraphs 3 through 8 of the story are devoted to a detailed description of Waverly's neighborhood, which is located in San Francisco's Chinatown. What are some of the challenges that Waverly must face growing up in a Chinese community, while at the same time striving to find her place in the surrounding Western culture?
4. Waverly asks her mother to explain what Chinese torture is after a classmate tells her that "Chinese people do Chinese torture" (par. 11). Her mother responds by explaining that Chinese people do many things well, including torture. What message is Waverly's mother trying to convey about Chinese culture and her own standards and expectations?
5. The exchanging of gifts often involves a complex set of social or cultural rules. When Waverly and her brothers go to the annual Christmas party held at the First Chinese Baptist Church, she describes the subtle rules that the children must follow while the gifts are being distributed (pars. 13–15). In what ways do these rules align with Western expectations? In what ways are they specifically related to Waverly's culture?
6. When Waverly begins winning many chess matches and her reputation begins to grow, her mother sits "proudly" and watches her. Yet claims it is only luck that allows Waverly to win. Is this a dismissive statement or is there another reason that Waverly's mother responds in this manner? Does this example of "proper Chinese humility" (par. 34) diminish Waverly's confidence in herself? Explain.
7. As Waverly becomes a national chess champion and is touted as the Great American Hope (par. 48), her family dynamic begins to change. How does her newfound success change her relationship with her brothers and her mother?
8. A sense of doomed captivity is created by the description of the animals found in the Ping Yuen Fish Market (par. 7). At the end of the story, however, a feeling of liberation prevails as Waverly feels "pushed up toward the night sky" (par. 72). What enables Waverly to shift her focus from captivity to liberation within the confines of the story?

9. At the end of the story, Waverly imagines her mother as an opponent in a chess match. The story concludes with Waverly's final thought: "I closed my eyes and pondered my next move." Explain the meaning of this statement in the context of the story as a whole.

Analyzing Language, Style, and Structure

1. **Vocabulary in Context.** At the beginning of the story, Waverly shares that her mother taught her "the art of invisible strength" at the age of six. What does the word "art" mean in context in the first paragraph? How is this usage different from other ways you have seen the word used?
2. **Skill Focus.** Select three statements uttered by Waverly's mother that reveal the nature of her character. Based on your three statements, describe Waverly's mother, paying particular attention to the concepts that are important to her. Then, consider how Tan presents these ideas. Does she criticize, agree with, or dismiss them?
3. In paragraphs 5–8, Waverly provides detailed descriptions of the bakery, the playground, the medicinal herb shop, the fish market, and a neighborhood café. Citing specific examples from the text, explain how she conveys the specific qualities of her neighborhood. Discuss what her descriptions reveal about Waverly's attitude toward the American and Chinese cultures that are part of her identity.
4. Whenever Waverly recounts conversations with her mother, she re-creates the dialogue accurately, without correcting her mother's grammatical errors. What is the effect of presenting these conversations in this way, rather than changing her mother's responses to standard English?
5. Tan begins her story by having Waverly describe her neighborhood. She then moves into a detailed explanation of Waverly's first exposure to chess and her initial learning process. Suddenly, Waverly explains that she has become a national chess competitor (par. 48). What is the effect of Tan's spending considerable narrative time describing the backstory and very little time describing how Waverly moved up the ranks to become a competitor on the national level?
6. The story is framed by a quotation from Waverly's mother, "Strongest wind cannot be seen" (pars. 2 and 71). In what ways does this quotation serve as an appropriate opening, as well as a conclusion, to Waverly's narrative?

Topics for Composing

1. **Analysis.** Waverly is shaped by both Chinese and American influences. What do these cultures allow her to learn about herself? How do they contribute to how she identifies herself? How does this characterization assist Tan in making a point about the tensions that can exist between family members of different generations?
2. **Argument.** Consider what success means to you. Think about the character traits normally present in successful people. Identify the trait that plays the greatest role in helping people reach success and explain why it is so crucial. As part of your response, provide evidence from your own observations and your interpretation of the interactions between Waverly and her mother.
3. **Connection.** Rules play a major role in this story; most of the important rules, however, seem to be unwritten. Think about your experience in school. What are some of the unwritten rules that govern how you approach the classes you attend each day? How do you learn these rules? What influence do these rules have on your identity?

4. **Speaking and Listening.** At one point in the story, the late chess grand master Bobby Fischer is quoted as saying, "There will never be a woman grand master." Does Waverly appear to agree with this assertion? Does her mother? Consider the following questions during a class discussion: Is Fischer's attitude still a common one regarding women in sports? If so, where do you see evidence of that attitude? If you think it is no longer common, what evidence do you see of an equal playing field for women and men in sports?
5. **Research.** The Chinatown neighborhood is a prominent presence in this story. How common are these communities in the United States? How many people do they serve? Conduct research to determine which Chinatown enclaves are the largest in the United States.
6. **Multimodal.** Use a combination of found images, drawing, painting, text, and other elements to create a profile poster that captures Waverly's identity. One half of the poster should reflect her personality when she is with her family. The other half should convey who she is while competing in chess tournaments.

In Defense of Small Towns

Oliver de la Paz

Photo courtesy of Papandrea Photography

Oliver de la Paz was born in the Philippines in 1972 and was raised in Ontario, Oregon. He earned an MFA from Arizona State University with a special concentration in poetry. He has authored five poetry collections, including *Requiem for the Orchard* (2010) in which "In Defense of Small Towns" was published.

When I look at it, it's simple, really. I hated life there. September,
once filled with animal deaths and toughened hay. And the smells

of fall were boiled-down beets and potatoes
or the farmhands' breeches smeared with oil and diesel

as they rode into town, dusty and pissed. The radio station
split time between metal and Tejano, and the only action

happened on Friday nights where the high school football team
gave everyone a chance at forgiveness. The town left no room

for novelty or change. The sheriff knew everyone's son and despite that,
we'd cruise up and down the avenues, switching between

brake and gearshift. We'd fight and spit chew into Big Gulp cups
and have our hearts broken nightly. In that town I learned

to fire a shotgun at nine and wring a chicken's neck
with one hand by twirling the bird and whipping it straight like a towel.

But I loved the place once. Everything was blonde and cracked
and the irrigation ditches stretched to the end of the earth. You could

ride on a bicycle and see clearly the outline of every leaf
or catch on the streets each word of a neighbor's argument.

Nothing could happen there and if I willed it, the place would have me
slipping over its rocks into the river with the sugar plant's steam

or signing papers at a storefront army desk, buttoned up
with medallions and a crew cut, eyeing the next recruits.

If I've learned anything, it's that I could be anywhere,
staring at a hunk of asphalt or listening to the clap of billiard balls

against each other in a bar and hear my name. Indifference now?
Some. I shook loose, but that isn't the whole story. The fact is

I'm still in love. And when I wake up, I watch my son yawn,
and my mind turns his upswept hair into cornstalks

at the edge of a field. Stillness is an acre, and his body
idles, deep like heavy machinery. I want to take him back there,

to the small town of my youth and hold the book of wildflowers
open for him, and look. I want him to know the colors of horses,

to run with a cattail in his hand and watch as its seeds
fly weightless as though nothing mattered, as though

the little things we tell ourselves about our pasts stay there,
rising slightly and just out of reach. ■

Streetlights (w/c on paper)/Hutchings, LaVere (1918-1999)/Private Collection/Bridgeman Images

American watercolorist LaVere Hutching's *Streetlights* captures the essence of a small town.

What do the details in this painting suggest about life in a small town? How does this portrayal align with the speaker's attitude in Oliver de la Paz's poem?

Understanding and Interpreting

1. Note how the speaker spent his free time as an adolescent. How do these activities influence his perception of himself and his environment?
2. In line 1, the speaker says that he "hated life there." In what ways and to what degree do lines 1 to 14 support this assertion?

3. Explain how high school football games in a small town might give "everyone a chance at forgiveness" (line 8). Did the speaker recognize this aspect of the games while he lived in the small town, or is this discovery made upon reflection years later?
4. What does the speaker mean when he says, "nothing could happen there" in line 19?
5. Why did the speaker leave his small hometown? How does the speaker view himself, now that he has left? Does he seem to have distanced himself from the small town altogether?
6. In the first line of the poem, the speaker states that he "hated life there." However, he also "loved the place once" according to line 15. Later on, lines 25 to 26 introduce the notion of "indifference." How would you ultimately characterize the speaker's feelings towards his hometown?

Analyzing Language, Style, and Structure

1. **Vocabulary in Context.** Refer to the phrase "his body / idles" (ll. 29–30). Explain what the word "idles" means in this context. To what does the word "idle" normally apply? What does this word usually mean? What is the effect of using the word "idles" in these lines of the poem?
2. **Skill Focus.** When thinking about his son, the speaker realizes how the small town of his youth shaped his own identity. How would the speaker like that small town to shape his son?
3. In the first line, the speaker says, "I hate life there." Reread lines 1 through 8 and notice the imagery Paz uses to describe the town. Choose 2–3 images and explain how they help Paz to communicate the speaker's tone toward the town. Then, reread lines 30 to 36. What images does Paz use here at the end of the poem? How do they contrast with the earlier imagery? How does this shift in imagery help Paz communicate an idea about changing perceptions as we age?
4. Notice the short syntax of the sentence beginning with the word "but" in line 15. How does this sentence signal a shift in the poem? How is the remainder of the poem different from the first 14 lines?
5. Late in the poem, the speaker watches his son as he wakes up: "I watch my son yawn, / and my mind turns his upswept hair into cornstalks / at the edge of a field. Stillness is an acre, and his body / idles, deep like heavy machinery" (ll. 27–30). Examine Paz's use of figurative language here and explain what it reveals about the speaker's changing feelings toward his hometown.
6. The poem is composed of 16 unrhymed couplets. How does this format contribute to how we perceive the speaker? If the poem followed a stricter structure in terms of rhyme and meter, how might that change our perception of the speaker and his subject?

Topics for Composing

1. **Analysis.** Consider the title of the poem. Why does the speaker feel he needs to defend small towns? What negative opinions or stereotypes are associated with them? Ultimately, what is the speaker's defense for the value of small towns?
2. **Argument.** The speaker creates a clear distinction between small towns and larger cities. Think about how these two settings provide distinct life experiences. Considering all the points made in the poem and your own understanding of life in big cities and small towns, which is actually better and why?
3. **Connection.** Think about how your hometown has shaped your identity. To what extent are you a product of the place where you were raised? How do your feelings for this setting compare to the speaker's emotions towards his small town?
4. **Speaking and Listening.** Work in small groups to come up with a "defense" of your town or city. Follow De La Paz's structure by beginning with a critique, and ending by pointing out what there is to love about the place. Deliver your presentation to the class as though it were a sales pitch to entice new residents to move there.

5. **Research.** Conduct research on a large city and a small town of your choosing. For each, try to find information on popular attractions and pastimes for the inhabitants. Based on your research, do the disparities between these two settings, as described by the speaker, continue to exist? To what extent does life seem different in each place?
6. **Creative Writing.** To describe the landscape of the town, the speaker writes, "Everything was blonde and cracked" (l. 15). Think about details from your town or a town you have visited and write a metaphor to describe the way it looks. Then, provide a rationale for why the metaphor perfectly captures or highlights particular characteristics of the town.

Glory

Lesley Nneka Arimah

Glen Stubbe/ZUMA Press Inc/Alamy

Lesley Nneka Arimah (b. 1983) was born in the United Kingdom, grew up in Nigeria, and currently resides in Las Vegas. "Glory" appeared in her debut collection *What It Means When A Man Falls From The Sky* (2017). For her stories, Arimah has received a Commonwealth Short Story Prize and an O. Henry Award. Most recently, she won the 2019 Caine Prize for African Writing.

KEY CONTEXT The Igbo are an ethnic group in Nigeria for whom the concept of *chi*, or spiritual identity, is significant. They believe a person's chi has more to do with success than a person's morality does. A person with a bad chi can be a good person but have terrible luck. Notice what Glory's grandfather says about her chi and how his remark informs the rest of her life.

When Glory's parents christened her Glorybetogod Ngozi Akunyili, they did not foresee Facebook's "real name" policy, nor the weeks she would spend populating forms and submitting copies of her bills and driver's license and the certificate that documented her birth on September 9, 1986, a rainy Tuesday, at 6:45 A.M., after six hours of labor and six years of barrenness. Pinning on her every hope they had yet to realize, her parents imagined the type of life that well-situated Igbos imagined for their children. She would be a smart girl with the best schooling. She would attend church regularly and never stray from the Word (amen!). She would learn to cook like her grandmother, her father added, to which her mother countered, "Why not like her mother?" and Glorybetogod's father hemmed and hawed till his wife said maybe he should go and eat at his mother's house. But back to Glorybetogod, whom everyone called Glory except her grandfather, who called her "that girl" the first time he saw her.

"That girl has something rotten in her, her chi is not well."

Husband pulled wife out of the room to prevent a brawl ("I don't care how old that drunk is, I will fix his mouth today") and begged his father to accept his firstborn grandchild. He didn't see, as the grandfather did, the caul of misfortune covering Glory's face, which would affect every decision she made, causing her to err on the side of wrong, time and time again. When Glory was five, she decided after much consideration to stick her finger into the maw of a sleeping dog. At seven, shortly after her family relocated to the United States, Glory thought it a good idea to walk home when her mother was five minutes late picking her up from school, a decision that saw her lost

extending beyond the text

Read the following information regarding the importance of names in Igbo culture. These results are from a research study sponsored by Covenant University in Nigeria.

Personal Name in Igbo Culture

Hilary I. Okagbue et al.

Igbo is one of the major tribes in Nigeria and the language is spoken by over 25 million people and characterized by dialects. The Igbo people are originally from the eastern part of Nigeria but can be found in virtually every country of the world. Similar to any other ethnic groups in Africa, naming in Igbo is [a] premeditated venture that is designed to speak to the future of the newly born child. Igbo people are not careless in naming because of their belief that names are tied to destinies and as such have religious, philosophical, psychological, historical, social and linguistic interpretations. . . .

Igbo personal names are gender sensitive because of the patriarchal nature of Igbo people. The males are often named based on issues such as gods or deities, physical and spiritual objects, intellectual prowess and dexterity in trade or agriculture, natural or mysterious phenomena, sportsmanship and craftsmanship, animals and so on. On the other hand, female names are often associated with good lineage, fruitfulness, beauty and [intelligence], moral responsibility, favor, good luck and tidings, joy, happiness, wealth, purity and so on.

How does this information on the importance of names in Igbo culture inform your understanding of Glory and her family? What importance do the meanings of names have in your culture?

and sobbing in a Piggly Wiggly parking lot before night fell. She did a lot of things out of spite, the source of which she couldn't identify — as if she'd been born resenting the world.

That's how, much to her parents' embarrassment, their Glory was nearing thirty, chronically single, and working at a call center in downtown Minneapolis. She fielded calls from disgruntled homeowners on the brink of foreclosure, reading from a script that was intricate and logical and written by people who had never before spoken on the phone to a human being. In all their calculations about her future, Glory's parents had never imagined that on April 16, 2013, at 5:17 P.M., Glory would receive another email refusing to restore her Facebook page. Nor could they have conceived that Glory would be the sort of person for whom this misfortune would set rolling an avalanche of misery, which led her to contemplate taking her life.

She called her mother, hoping to be talked out of it, but got her voicemail and then a text saying, "What is it now?" (Glory knew better than to respond.) A call to her father would yield a cooler response, and so she spent her evening on the edge of her bed, neck itching like crazy, contemplating how a bottle of Moscato and thirty gel-filled sleeping pills would go together. The note she wrote read:

> I was born under an unlucky star and my destiny has caught up with me. I'm sorry Mummy and Daddy that I didn't complete law school and become the person you'd hoped. But it was also your fault for putting so much pressure on me. Goodbye.

All of this was true, and not. She was unlucky, yes, but it was less Fate and more her terrible decision-making and laziness that saw her flunk out of college, along with her propensity for arguing with professors and storming out, never to return. She eventually graduated with a shameful G.P.A. Then came law school, to which she gained entrance through a favor of a friend of a friend of her father's, thinking that her argumentative tendencies could be put to good use. But she managed to screw that up too, choosing naps instead of class, happy hours instead of studying. She was unable to do right, no matter how small the choice. These foolish little decisions incremented into probation, then a polite request to leave, followed by an impolite request to leave after she staged a protest in the dean's office.

It was also true that her parents put pressure on her. Yet theirs was the sort of hopeful pressure that would have encouraged a better person.

Glory fell asleep after a glass and a half of wine and woke to find the pills a melted, bitter mass in her fist. In the morning light, her melodramatic note mortified her, and she tore it up and flushed it down the toilet. At work, avoiding the glare of her supervisor and the finger he pointed at the clock, she switched on her headphones to receive the first call: Mrs. Dumfries. Her husband had died and she had no clue where any paperwork was. Could Glory help her keep her house? Glory read from her script, avoiding the "no" she was never allowed to utter. Then there was Glen, who was actually Greg, who was also Peter, who called every day at least four or five times and tried to trick the customer-service reps into promises they couldn't keep. Little did he know that even if Glory promised him his childhood home, complete with all the antiques that had gone missing after the foreclosure, she would only be fired and he would be stuck in the same two-bedroom apartment with his kids. All day the calls came in, and Glory had to say no without saying "no," and the linguistic acrobatics required to evade this simple answer wore away her nerves.

At lunch, she ate one of the burritos that came three for a dollar at the discount grocery store and a nice-looking sandwich that belonged to one of her co-workers, and checked her email again. Even though her Facebook account hadn't yet been restored, she walked by the lobby of the advertising agency that dominated the top two floors of the building.

Before she reached the glass doors, she 10
paused by the wall to the right, on which the agency had mounted the logos of the companies it represented. She took a photo of herself in front of the logo of the jewelry mega-chain. When her Facebook page was restored, she would post the picture, with the caption: "Worked on my favorite account today. The best part is the free samples!"

Then her cousin in Port Harcourt would like her post, and another friend would confess her envy, and others still would say how (OMG!) she was *sooo* lucky. And for a moment, she would live the sort of life her parents imagined for her those many, many years ago.

After her lunch break, she sank back into her seat and was about to switch her headset on when he walked in. Glory knew he was Nigerian right away by his gait. And when he spoke, a friendly greeting as he shook her supervisor's hand, her guess was confirmed. He wore a suit, slightly ill fitting, but his shoulders made up for it. He joined a group of trainees across the room.

He had an air of competence that she found irritating, reading from the script as though he had memorized it and managing to make it sound compassionate and genuine. At one point, he noticed her staring, and every time she looked at him after that, he was looking at her, too.

She culled bits and pieces of him over the rest of the day, eavesdropped on impressed supervisors who sang his praises. He was getting an M.B.A. at the U. He had grown up in Nigeria but visited his uncle in Atlanta every summer. After his M.B.A., he was going to attend law school. His parents were both doctors.

Glory knew what he was doing, because she did it as well: sharing too many details of her life with these strangers, signaling why she didn't belong here earning $13.50 an hour. She was something better than a "customer-service representative" — everyone should know that this title was only temporary. Except in his case, it was all true.

He smiled at her when she was leaving, a smile so sure of reciprocation that Glory wanted to flip him off. But the home training that lingered caused her to avert her eyes instead and hurry to catch the bus.

Jaron Su

Jaron Su's *Social Media Syndrome* depicts a figure whose face is obscured by tentacles, using a cell phone.

What does this painting suggest about the role of social media in people's lives? What is Glory's relationship to social media in this story? To what extent do you think it reflects the ideas in this painting?

Her phone dinged. "Why did you call me, do you need money again?" A text from her mother. *No*, she wanted to respond, *I'm doing fine*, but she didn't. After a week, her mother might send $500 and say this was the last time and she'd better not tell her father. Glory would use the money to complete her rent or buy new shoes, or squirrel it away to be nibbled bit by bit — candy here, take-out there — till it disappeared.

Then, when her mother couldn't restrain herself anymore, Glory would receive a stern, long-winded lecture via email, about how she wouldn't have to worry about such things if she were married, and why didn't she let her father introduce her to some of the young men at his work? And Glory would delete it, and cry, and retrace all the missteps that had led her to this particular place. She knew her birth story, and what her grandfather had said, but it never made a difference when the time came to make the right choice. She was always drawn to the wrong one, like a dog curious to taste its own vomit.

The next day, Glory arrived at work to see the man sitting in the empty spot next to hers.

"Good morning."

"Hi."

"My name is Thomas. They told me you are also from Nigeria? You don't sound it."

"I've been here since I was six. I hope you don't think I should have kept my accent that long."

He flinched at her rudeness, but pressed on.

"I don't know many Nigerians here. Maybe you can introduce me?"

Glory considered the handful of women she knew who would *love* to be introduced to this guy, still green and fresh. But they saw little of her real life, thought Glory an ad exec with a fabulous living, and any introductions would jeopardize that.

"Sorry, I don't really know anyone, either. You should try talking to someone with real friends."

He laughed, thinking she was joking, and his misunderstanding loosened her tongue. It was nice to talk to someone new who had no expectations of her.

"So, why are you slumming it here with the rest of us? Shouldn't you be interning somewhere fabulous?"

"This is my internship. I actually work in corporate, but thought I should get a better understanding of what happens in the trenches."

"Wait, you're here voluntarily? Are you crazy?"

He laughed again.

"No, it's just . . . You wouldn't understand."

"I'm not stupid," Glory said, thinking he thought that of her. . . .

She ignored his "Whoa, where did that come from?" and switched on her headset, turning her dial to the busiest queue. The calls came in one after the other, leaving Thomas little chance to apologize if he wanted to.

An hour later, he pressed a note into Glory's palm. *I'm sorry*, it read. *Can I treat you to lunch?*

Her pride said no, but her stomach, last filled with the sandwich she had stolen yesterday afternoon, begged a yes.

She snatched up his pen. *I guess*.

"Mom, I'm seeing someone." Glory typed and deleted that sentence over and over, never sending it. Her mother would call for sure, and then she'd dissect every description of Thomas till he was flayed to her satisfaction. Her father would ask to hear the "young man's intentions" and the cloying quality of their attention would ruin it.

Thomas would delight them. He went to church every Sunday — though he'd learned to stop inviting her — and he had the bright sort of future that was every parent's dream. He prayed over his meals, before he went to bed, when he woke up. He prayed for her.

Glory despised him. She hated the sheen of accomplishment he wore, so dulled on her. She hated his frugal management of money. She hated that when she pressed him for sex, he demurred, saying that they should wait till they were more serious.

Glory couldn't get enough of him. She loved that he watched Cartoon Network with the glee of a teenager; loved that he could move through a crowd of strangers and emerge on the other side with friends. He didn't seem to mind her coarseness, how her bad luck had deepened her bitterness so that she wished even the best of people ill. He didn't seem to mind how joy had become a finite meal she begrudged seeing anyone but herself consume.

She wanted to ask him what he saw in her, but was afraid the answer would be qualities she knew to be an illusion.

They talked of Nigeria often, or at least he did, telling her about growing up in Onitsha and how he wanted to move back someday. He said "we" and "us" like it was understood that she would go back with him, and she began to savor a future she had never imagined for herself.

She'd been to Nigeria many times, but it was the one thing she kept from him, enjoying, then loathing, then enjoying how excited he was to explain the country to her. He didn't know that what little money she scraped together was spent on a plane ticket to Nigeria every thirteen months, or that over the past few years, she had arrived the day after her grandmother's death, then the day after her great-aunt's death, and then her uncle's, so that her grandfather asked her to let him know when she booked her ticket, so that he could prepare to die. Thomas still didn't know she was unlucky.

She kept it secret to dissuade any probing, not yet aware that people like Thomas were never suspicious, as trusting of the world's goodness as children born to wealth. When she visited her grandfather, with whom she had negotiated a relative peace, they sat together in his room watching TV, Glory getting up only to fetch food or drink for them. Nobody knew why she made the trips as often as she did, or why she eschewed the bustle of Lagos for his sleepy village. She couldn't explain that her grandfather knew her, saw her for what she was — a black hole that compressed and eliminated fortune and joy and happiness — and still opened his home to her, gave her a room and a bed, the mattress so old the underside bore stains from when her mother's water broke.

Near the end of her last stay, their conversation had migrated to her fate.

"There is only disaster in your future if you do not please the gods."

The older she got, the more she felt the truth of it: the deep inhalation her life had been so far, to prepare her for the explosive exhalation that would eventually flatten her.

50 "Papa, you know I don't have it in me to win anyone's favor, let alone the gods."

They were both dressed in shorts and singlets, the voltage of the generator being too low to carry anything that cooled. Glory sat on the floor, moving every half hour to relish the chill of the tiles. Her grandfather lounged on the bed.

When he began one of his fables, she closed her eyes.

"A porcupine and a tortoise came to a crossroads, where a spirit appeared before them. 'Carry me to the heart of the river and let me drink,' the spirit said. Neither wanted to be saddled with the spirit, but they could not deny it with no good reason.

"'I am slow,' said the tortoise, 'it will take us many years to reach it.'

55 "'I am prickly,' said the porcupine, 'the journey will be too painful.'

"The spirit raged.

"'If you don't get me to the heart of the river by nightfall and give me a cup to drink, I will extinguish every creature of your kind.'

"The tortoise and the porcupine conferred. 'What if you carry me,' said the tortoise, 'while I carry the spirit? We will surely make it by nightfall.'

"'I have a better idea,' said the porcupine. 'These are no ordinary quills on my back. They are magic quills capable of granting any wish. The only condition is that you must close your eyes and open them only after your wish is granted.'

60 "The tortoise and the spirit each plucked a quill, eager for desires out of reach. They closed their eyes. That's when the porcupine snatched the quill from the tortoise and jammed it into the flesh of his throat. He filled the spirit's hands with blood, which it drank, thinking the gurgling it heard to be that of the river. But spirits know the taste of blood, and this one lashed out at the porcupine, only to find that it could move no faster than a tortoise. The porcupine continued on his way."

Her grandfather's long pause signaled the end.

"Are you hearing me?"

"Yes, but what does it mean?"

"If you can't please the gods, trick them."

65 The time with her grandfather had eased the pressure building in her, but then she came back stateside to another stream of catastrophes. Keys left on the plane. An accident in which her foot slipped on the pedal made smooth by the car-insurance check she had forgotten to mail. A job lost for lack of transportation, which is how she ended up disappointing former homeowners in the petri dish of a large call center.

Thomas, on the other hand, was a lucky man. He always seemed to find money lying around in the street, although never so large an amount as to induce alarm or guilt. He got what he wanted, always, and attributed it to ingenuity and perseverance, unaware of the halo of fortune resting on his head. When she had him write the request to restore her Facebook page, it was back up in a day. He would have been appalled to know that she sometimes followed him when they parted ways after work, watching with fascination as he drew amity from everyone who came close.

Some of that luck rubbed off on her, and she found herself receiving invitations to long-standing events she hadn't even known existed. Igbo Women's Fellowship of the Midwest. Daughters of Biafra, Minnesota Chapter. Party, Party, a monthly event rotated among different homes. Sometimes, as she watched Thomas charm a crowd with little effort, she wondered how it was that one person could be so blessed and another not. They had been born in the same state to parents of similar means and faith. Even taking into account the rewards of his maleness, it seemed to Glory that they should have been in the same place. She began to think of his luck as something that had been taken from her, and viewed this relationship as a way to even her odds. . . .

But the more he said "us" and "we," the less quickly she deleted that "Mom, I'm seeing someone" text. One day, instead of sending it, she posted a picture of her and Thomas on her Facebook wall, setting off a sequence that involved her Port Harcourt cousin calling another cousin who called another and so on and so forth, until the news got to her mother, who called her right away. It took thirty-seven minutes.

Glory waited till just before the call went to voicemail to pick up.

"Hello?"

"Who is he? Praise God! What is his name?"

"Thomas Okongwu."

Her mother started praising God again. Glory couldn't help but laugh. It had been years since any news she delivered over the phone had given her mother cause for joy, and she felt a blush of gratitude. She told her mother about Thomas and his ambitions, getting more animated as her mother got more excited. She ignored the occasional hint of disbelief on the other end of the line, as if her mother couldn't quite believe her daughter had gotten something right.

After that, it was like *everything* she did was right. Her job, long pilloried, was now a good thing. No career, her father said, meant that she could fully concentrate on her children when they came along. That she was terrible at managing money became a nonissue. You see, she had picked the perfect man to make up for her weaknesses. Kind where she was not, frugal where she was not. Successful.

Glory stared at her father's email. . . . She moved it to a folder she had long ago titled EVIDENCE, meant to make the case if she chose to never speak to her father again.

When Thomas asked if she'd like to meet his mother, who was free to travel as his father was not, Glory knew the right answer and gave it. But she panicked at having to impress this woman. Her parents had been easy. Thomas was impressive. She was not.

"Why do you want me to meet her?" The question was a bit coy, but Glory wanted some reassurance to hold on to.

Thomas shrugged.

"She asked to meet you."

"So, you didn't ask her if she wanted to meet me?"

After a patient rolling of eyes, Thomas gripped her shoulders and shook her with gentle exasperation.

"You're always doing this. Of course I want you to meet her and of course she wants to meet you. You're all she ever talks about now, look."

Thomas dialed his cell phone, and after a pause, he said, "Hey, Mum, she's right here. I'll let you talk, but don't go scaring her off."

Glory heard the woman laugh on the line and say something that made her son laugh too. Then the warm phone was pressed to her ear, and a voice just shy of being too deep for a woman greeted her.

Glory tried to say all the right things about herself and her family, which meant not saying much about herself. She wanted this woman to like her, and, even beyond that, to admire her, something she wasn't sure she could accomplish without lies. She had already pretended to quit her advertising job on her Facebook wall — a "sad day indeed," an old college friend had said, worded so that Glory suspected he knew the truth. (She unfriended him right away.) But Thomas's mother could not be so easily dismissed. Glory trotted out her parents' accomplishments — engineer mother,

Olumide Egunlae

Observe the faces in the painting *Portrait* by Nigerian-born artist Olumide Egunlae. The distortions are suggestive of masks, which are an important part of Nigerian art and culture.

What ideas do you think Egunlae is conveying through the faces in his painting? What masks does Glory wear throughout Arimah's story?

medical-supply-business-owner father — to shore up her pedigree. Then she mentioned more recent social interests of hers, like the Igbo women's group, leaving out Thomas's hand in that. All the while, her inner voice wondered what the hell she was doing. *Tricking the gods*, she replied.

The day Thomas's mother flew in, Glory cooked for hours at his apartment, soliciting recipes from her own mother, who took much joy in walking her through every step over the phone. By the time he left for the airport, his apartment was as fragrant as a buka, with as large a variety of dishes awaiting eager bellies.

His mother was tall and Glory felt like a child next to her. His mother was also warm, and she folded Glory into a perfumed, bosomy hug.

"Welcome, Ma," Glory said, then wanted to kick herself for sounding so deferential.

"My dear, no need to be so formal, I feel like I've known you for years, the way my son goes on and on. It's me who should be welcoming you into the family."

His mother complimented each dish, tasting a bit of one after the other and nodding before filling her plate. It was a test, and Glory passed and felt gratified.

Thomas squeezed her leg under the table, a reassuring pressure that said, *See? Nothing to worry about.* But what did a person like him know about worry? When his mother questioned her about her work, it was clear she assumed Glory worked in corporate with Thomas, and neither of them dissuaded her. Yet it rankled Glory, who couldn't decide whether Thomas had stretched the truth into a more presentable fit or had simply overlooked the possibility that his mother would make such an assumption.

It didn't seem to matter to Thomas's mother, who expressed her delight that Glory would soon leave and come to stay with her in Nigeria, something Glory and Thomas had never discussed. He squeezed her leg again, the pressure less reassuring: *Please don't argue with my mother.*

Glory felt it then, that peculiar itch at the back of her neck that flared up when she came to a crossroads. She ignored the sensation and returned Thomas's squeeze, and he relaxed, changing the subject to his mother's schedule for the next day, which he and Glory would have off.

Thomas excused himself, leaving the two women to talk alone. He promised to be back in an hour and left to run an errand. Every minute that passed without Thomas by her side, Glory felt as though a veil was slipping off her, revealing more and more of her true nature. She didn't say or do anything different, but she felt his

"Rosie No. 1", by Tim Okamura, 2016, oil on canvas, 40×60

Tim Okamura's 2016 painting *Rosie no. 1* is based on Norman Rockwell's 1943 *Rosie the Riveter*.

Consider the pose, colors, and overall composition of this painting to determine how the figure is characterized. Which part of "Glory" most closely depicts Glory in a manner that matches the painting?

mother close off a bit, leaning back as though to consider what manner of girl she was.

After thirty minutes, his mother's pleasantness cooled to politeness and Glory excused herself to the bathroom before it chilled further. *You have to come back now*, she texted Thomas. *Now!*

And he did, interrupting a lie his mother could have uncovered with very little research. Perfect timing as always. Always perfect.

Not long after, the ease between the two women returned, but the more they talked, the more his mother touched on the expectation that Glory would drop everything and go back to Nigeria and live there with her hypothetical children, in her mother-in-law's house. If the idea had been hers, Glory might not have minded it — but this was being discussed as a given, not a choice. Thomas was most comfortable in Nigeria and would move back when he was done with schooling to join his wife, who would already be settled. And Thomas was a man who got what he wanted. All the "we" and "us" now felt less like a collaboration and more like a general compelling his troops. It surprised Glory to realize that she was not the only one scheming.

After they took his mother to her hotel, Thomas and Glory idled in the parking lot, each waiting for the other to break the silence. Then, offering neither apology nor explanation, Thomas placed a box in Glory's lap. She opened it, the hinge levering to reveal a ring that, just a year ago, she would never have imagined receiving anytime soon, or ever. The itch returned to her neck.

A part of Glory had always thought to win her parents' good graces by her own merit. She believed that one day, she would eventually stumble into accomplishments that she could hold up as her own, that the seeming chaos of her life would coalesce into an intricate puzzle whose shape one could see only when it was complete. That this ring was to be her salvation — she couldn't bear it. And yet, salvation it was. Acceptance into many proper folds. Lies she would never again have to tell. She could lose herself in the whirlwind of Thomas, golden child turned golden man.

But then Glory thought of the first time she had turned her luck with something truly reckless, the thing with the dog. She had felt itchy all over and there was her uncle's dog, napping. A thought wormed into her head, that the itch would go away if she touched the dog's tongue, and it was suddenly the right and only thing to do. She rubbed the scar on her thumb, thinking of all the times she had picked stupid over sensible, knowing, just knowing, she'd gotten it right. She could not afford to get it wrong this time.

She looked at the ring, and resentment and elation warred till one overcame the other and Glory made another decision. ■

Understanding and Interpreting

1. How is Facebook's "real name" policy an obstacle for Glory? In what ways does Glory's full name shape her identity? How does the shortened version of her name impact her sense of self?
2. Based on paragraph 1, what traits and behaviors are important to Glory's family? How do these details relate to the way Glory views herself throughout the story?
3. Summarize the evidence provided to support Glory's grandfather's observation about her chi. Do you see this as evidence that the grandfather's assessment of her chi is correct?
4. In reference to Glory's parents, the narrator states that "theirs was the sort of hopeful pressure that would have encouraged a better person" (par. 7). Do you agree with this assessment? How would you characterize her parents' encouragement?
5. Why is Glory so intent on restoring access to her Facebook account? Consider the picture in front of the "logo of the jewelry mega-chain" that she would like to post (par. 10).
6. Paragraph 17 offers a description of how Glory might spend $500, if her mother were to send her money. What do these imagined expenditures suggest about her character?
7. Describe Thomas's "sheen of accomplishment" (par. 41). Why does Glory despise this quality?
8. In paragraph 46, Glory visits her grandfather. Why is she drawn to him, despite his impression of her from the moment of her birth?
9. Fables are traditional ways that Igbo convey lessons. Summarize the fable Glory's grandfather tells her and explain how its meaning relates to the story as a whole: "If you can't please the gods, trick them."
10. At the end of the story, which impulse do you think wins, elation or resentment? How do you think Glory decides to respond to Thomas's proposal? Support your answer with evidence from the text.

Analyzing Language, Style, and Structure

1. **Vocabulary in Context.** The word "chronically" (par. 4) is often used to describe an illness. What does it mean in the phrase "chronically single"? What does this usage reveal about Glory and her parents?
2. **Skill Focus.** By introducing the idea of chi early in the story, Arimah encourages readers to question how much of a person's future is predetermined. If we think of fate as forces Glory does not control, how would you characterize the role of fate in Glory's life? To what extent is she in control of how her life turns out?
3. Glory's identity is deeply influenced by both Igbo culture and American culture. In the early part of this story, how does Arimah use word choice to establish the importance (and tension) of these two cultures to Glory's character?
4. How is Glory's job at the call center ironic? Consider why people call her and what she is tasked to do for them.

5. Thomas is said to have a "halo of fortune" (par. 66). What does that description tell us about Thomas's character? What is Glory's attitude towards Thomas's good luck? What does that attitude reveal about her?
6. Notice the details describing Glory and Thomas when his mother visits (beginning par. 86). To what extent do they seem well suited to each other?

Topics for Composing

1. **Analysis.** Glory is disingenuous — or she outright lies — at different points in the story. Identify these moments in the story and determine how lying might relate to a theme in "Glory." What might Arimah be suggesting about why people lie, to whom they lie, and what they lie about? Use textual evidence to support your assertions.
2. **Argument.** Think about the rewards and challenges associated with belonging to two distinct cultures. Overall, is this complex identity beneficial to someone living in America? Aside from your own observations, use details from the text to support your argument.
3. **Connection.** Think of how you use social media platforms. To what extent can you relate to Glory's interactions with Facebook? Does your social media identity align with your real-world identity?
4. **Speaking and Listening.** The limited omniscient point of view (par. 38) allows us to enter Glory's mind and perceive the world through her eyes. At one point, she wants to ask Thomas "what he saw in her" (par. 43). Imagine that Glory asks Thomas that question. Write a response from Thomas's perspective. Be prepared to read your answer to the class as well as to comment on your classmates' responses.
5. **Research.** Name some ways that Nigerian immigrants retain their cultural practices while living in the United States. Are there festivals, food shops, or clothing stores that help foster Nigerian culture? Aside from these sources, how else do they sustain their connection to Nigeria?
6. **Creative Writing.** Think about a lesson that Glory should learn about identity or self-discovery. Then write a fable that conveys that lesson. You can reread the grandfather's fable or look up other Igbo fables for ideas.

Eveline

James Joyce

Irish author James Joyce (1882–1941) is considered one of the most influential writers of the twentieth century. His masterpiece, *Ulysses*, takes the myth of the *Odyssey* and updates it to contemporary Ireland. The following story is taken from his collection *Dubliners*, which he finished writing in 1904 at the age of twenty-two, but was not able to publish until 1914.

Lebrecht Authors/Bridgeman Images

KEY CONTEXT In the collection *Dubliners*, Joyce depicts everyday life in Dublin at the start of the twentieth century. Throughout the stories, Joyce relies on epiphany, a sudden moment of realization or illumination, to capture a life-altering moment in his characters' lives.

She sat at the window watching the evening invade the avenue. Her head was leaned against the window curtains and in her nostrils was the odour of dusty cretonne[1]. She was tired.

Few people passed. The man out of the last house passed on his way home; she heard his footsteps clacking along the concrete pavement and afterwards crunching on the cinder path before the new red houses. One time there used to be a field there in which they used to play every evening with other people's children. Then a man from Belfast bought the field and built houses in it — not like their little brown houses but bright brick houses with shining roofs. The children of the avenue used to play together in that field — the Devines, the Waters, the Dunns, little Keogh the cripple, she and her brothers and sisters. Ernest, however, never played: he was too grown up. Her father used often to hunt them in out of the field with his blackthorn stick; but usually little Keogh used to keep nix[2] and call out when he saw her father coming. Still they seemed to have been rather happy then. Her father was not so bad then; and besides, her mother was alive. That was a long time ago; she and her brothers and sisters were all grown up; her mother was dead. Tizzie Dunn was dead, too, and the Waters had gone back to England. Everything changes. Now she was going to go away like the others, to leave her home.

Home! She looked round the room, reviewing all its familiar objects which she had dusted once a week for so many years, wondering where on earth all the dust came from. Perhaps she would never see again those familiar objects from which she had never dreamed of being divided. And yet during all those years she had never found out the name of the priest whose yellowing photograph hung on the wall above the broken harmonium[3] beside the coloured print of the promises made to Blessed Margaret Mary Alacoque. He had been a school friend of her father. Whenever he showed the photograph to a visitor her father used to pass it with a casual word:

"He is in Melbourne now."

She had consented to go away, to leave her home. Was that wise? She tried to weigh each side of the question. In her home anyway she had shelter and food; she had those whom she had known all her life about her. Of course she had to work hard, both in the house and at business. What would they say of her in the Stores when they found out that she had run away with a fellow? Say she was a fool, perhaps; and her place would be filled up by advertisement. Miss Gavan would be glad. She had always had an edge on her, especially whenever there were people listening.

"Miss Hill, don't you see these ladies are waiting?"

"Look lively, Miss Hill, please."

She would not cry many tears at leaving the Stores.

But in her new home, in a distant unknown country, it would not be like that. Then she would be married — she, Eveline. People would treat her with respect then. She would not be treated as her mother had been. Even now, though she was over nineteen, she sometimes felt herself in danger of her father's violence. She knew it was that that had given her the palpitations. When they were growing up he had never gone for her like he used to go for Harry and Ernest, because she was a girl but latterly he had begun to threaten her and say what he would do to her only for her dead mother's sake. And no she had nobody to protect her. Ernest was dead and Harry, who was in the church decorating business, was nearly always down somewhere in the country. Besides, the invariable squabble for money on Saturday nights had begun to weary her unspeakably. She always gave her entire wages — seven shillings — and

[1]Heavy cotton fabric used for upholstery. — Eds.
[2]Keep watch. — Eds.
[3]A small organ powered by a foot-operated bellows. — Eds.

Bettmann/Getty Images

This photo shows Dublin at about the time "Eveline" was set.

How would you describe the mood in this image? What details lead you to that description? How does the mood in this image of Dublin compare to the mood that Joyce creates in "Eveline"?

Harry always sent up what he could but the trouble was to get any money from her father. He said she used to squander the money, that she had no head, that he wasn't going to give her his hard-earned money to throw about the streets, and much more, for he was usually fairly bad on Saturday night. In the end he would give her the money and ask her had she any intention of buying Sunday's dinner. Then she had to rush out as quickly as she could and do her marketing, holding her black leather purse tightly in her hand as she elbowed her way through the crowds and returning home late under her load of provisions. She had hard work to keep the house together and to see that the two young children who had been left to her charge went to school regularly and got their meals regularly. It was hard work — a hard life — but now that she was about to leave it she did not find it a wholly undesirable life.

She was about to explore another life with Frank. Frank was very kind, manly, open-hearted. She was to go away with him by the night-boat to be his wife and to live with him in Buenos Ayres where he had a home waiting for her. How well she remembered the first time she had seen him; he was lodging in a house on the main road where she used to visit. It seemed a few weeks ago. He was standing at the gate, his peaked cap pushed back on his head and his hair tumbled forward over a face of bronze. Then they had come to know each other. He used to meet her outside the Stores every evening and see her home. He took her to see *The Bohemian Girl* and she felt elated as she sat in an unaccustomed part of the theatre with him. He was awfully fond of music and sang a little. People knew that they were courting and, when he sang about the lass that loves a sailor, she always felt pleasantly confused. He used to call her Poppens out of fun. First of all it had been an excitement for her to have a fellow and then she had begun to like him. He had tales of distant countries. He had started as a deck boy at a pound a month on a ship of the Allan Line going out to Canada. He told her the names of the ships he had been on and the names of the different services. He had sailed through the Straits of Magellan and he told her stories of the terrible Patagonians. He had fallen on his feet in Buenos Ayres, he said, and had come over to the old country just for a holiday. Of course, her father had found out the affair and had forbidden her to have anything to say to him.

"I know these sailor chaps," he said.

One day he had quarrelled with Frank and after that she had to meet her lover secretly.

The evening deepened in the avenue. The white of two letters in her lap grew indistinct. One was to Harry; the other was to her father. Ernest had been her favourite but she liked Harry too. Her father was becoming old lately, she noticed; he would miss her. Sometimes he could be very nice. Not long before, when she had been laid up for a day, he had read her out a ghost story and made toast for her at the fire. Another day, when their mother was alive, they had all gone for a picnic to the Hill of Howth. She remembered her father putting on her mother's bonnet to make the children laugh.

Her time was running out but she continued to sit by the window, leaning her head against the window curtain, inhaling the odour of dusty cretonne. Down far in the avenue she could hear a street organ playing. She knew the air. Strange that it should come that very night to remind her of the promise to her mother, her promise to keep the home together as long as she could. She remembered the last night of her mother's illness; she was again in the close dark room at the other side of the hall and outside she heard a melancholy air of Italy. The organ-player had been ordered to go away and given sixpence. She remembered her father strutting back into the sickroom saying:

"Damned Italians! coming over here!"

As she mused the pitiful vision of her mother's life laid its spell on the very quick of her being — that life of commonplace sacrifices closing in final craziness. She trembled as she heard again her mother's voice saying constantly with foolish insistence:

"Derevaun Seraun! Derevaun Seraun![4]"

Bridgeman Images

Toulouse-Lautrec's *Woman at the Window* gives us the impression of a woman deep in thought. **Based on the details in the painting, how would you characterize this woman? What do her appearance and surroundings reveal about her life? In what ways does she seem similar to and different from Eveline?**

She stood up in a sudden impulse of terror. Escape! She must escape! Frank would save her. He would give her life, perhaps love, too. But she wanted to live. Why should she be unhappy? She had a right to happiness. Frank would take her in his arms, fold her in his arms. He would save her.

She stood among the swaying crowd in the station at the North Wall. He held her hand and she knew that he was speaking to her, saying something about the passage over and over again. The station was full of soldiers with brown baggages. Through the wide doors of the sheds she caught a glimpse of the black mass of the boat, lying in beside the quay[5] wall, with

[4]Gaelic for "The end of pleasure is pain." — Eds.

[5]Concrete walkway along or extending out over a body of water used as a loading area for ships. Similar to a pier, or jetty. — Eds.

illumined portholes. She answered nothing. She felt her cheek pale and cold and, out of a maze of distress, she prayed to God to direct her, to show her what was her duty. The boat blew a long mournful whistle into the mist. If she went, tomorrow she would be on the sea with Frank, steaming towards Buenos Ayres. Their passage had been booked. Could she still draw back after all he had done for her? Her distress awoke a nausea in her body and she kept moving her lips in silent fervent prayer.

20 A bell clanged upon her heart. She felt him seize her hand:

"Come!"

All the seas of the world tumbled about her heart. He was drawing her into them: he would drown her. She gripped with both hands at the iron railing.

"Come!"

No! No! No! It was impossible. Her hands clutched the iron in frenzy. Amid the seas she sent a cry of anguish.

25 "Eveline! Evvy!"

He rushed beyond the barrier and called to her to follow. He was shouted at to go on but he still called to her. She set her white face to him, passive, like a helpless animal. Her eyes gave him no sign of love or farewell or recognition. ■

Understanding and Interpreting

1. What is the purpose of the recollection in the second paragraph? How does that memory contribute to Eveline's perception of herself and her situation?
2. How would you describe the complex relationship Eveline has with her father? In what ways does it change over time? How do these changes relate to the way Eveline views herself?
3. Eveline thinks of Frank in fairly general terms: he is "very kind, manly, open-hearted" (par. 10). What more specific information does James Joyce give us? What is it about Frank that appeals to Eveline? What does her interest in him reveal about her?
4. Joyce characterizes the existence of Eveline's mother as "that life of commonplace sacrifices closing in final craziness" (par. 16). In what ways is Eveline influenced by her mother's life? How does her perception of her mother's experience affect the way Eveline thinks of marriage?
5. "Eveline" focuses on the central character's decision-making process. What are the conflicting forces pulling Eveline in different directions? Identify and discuss at least three.
6. Why do you suppose that Eveline's eyes gave "no sign of love or farewell or recognition" (par. 26)? What does Joyce aim to convey by this final description?

Analyzing Language, Style, and Structure

1. **Vocabulary in Context.** Joyce uses the word "marketing" (par. 9) in a way that is probably unfamiliar to you. To understand this usage, consider the root of the word, along with what Eveline is doing. Explain the relationship between this usage of "marketing" and the "provisions" that Eveline carries.
2. **Skill Focus.** How does Eveline define her identity at home? How does she feel this identity will be altered if she moves to Buenos Aires with Frank? What does this realization reveal about the relationship between setting and identity in the story?
3. What is the feeling Joyce conveys in the opening paragraph? What specific words and images contribute to that feeling?

4. Much of "Eveline" centers on Eveline's home life, both before and after her mother's death. Joyce ends paragraph 2 with the sentence, "Now she was going to go away like the others, to leave her home." He opens the next paragraph with the one word exclamation, "Home!" What does this repetition suggest about the meaning(s) of home to Eveline?
5. Joyce explores the difficulty characters experience in making important life decisions. What are Eveline's thoughts regarding whether or not she should leave? Why does she consider staying? Why is leaving so attractive? Pay attention to concrete descriptive details, connotative language, and imagery.

Topics for Composing

1. **Analysis.** Think about how Eveline's house is a source of both comfort and pain. How does Eveline's relationship to her home shape her identity?
2. **Argument.** Eveline contemplates how her life might change if she were to move to Argentina. Argue whether or not moving from one place to another is an effective way to re-create your identity and shape your self-perception. Consider details from the text as well as your own experiences to support your argument.
3. **Connection.** Eveline stands at a crossroads in this text. Identify a time when you had to make a pivotal decision in your life. Explain how your decision shaped your identity, and how Eveline's decision shaped hers.
4. **Speaking and Listening.** Critics of "Eveline" disagree on their interpretations of the ending. Many conclude that Eveline's inability to leave with Frank is essentially accepting a life sentence as a housekeeper, even a servant, to her family. Others argue that in choosing to stay with her father, she defies Frank and thus shows at least the promise of becoming an independent woman. Which interpretation do you find most plausible? Working with a group, develop a defense of one of these perspectives and prepare to discuss it with the whole class.
5. **Creative Writing.** Joyce writes that, as "the evening deepened in the avenue" (par. 13), Eveline sits with two letters in her lap, one to her father, the other to her brother Harry. What do you imagine she has written in those letters? Write one of them based on the details you've gathered from the text.

Chameleon (nonfiction)

Trevor Noah

Jeff Schear/Getty Images

Trevor Noah was born in South Africa in 1984 to a white European father and a black South African mother. Noah is a successful comedian, writer, and television host. Since 2015, he's hosted Comedy Central's *The Daily Show*, a satirical late-night program. "Chameleon" is an excerpt from his debut book *Born a Crime* (2016), which earned him two NAACP Image Awards.

KEY CONTEXT Apartheid refers to a political and social system in South Africa that lasted from 1948 to 1994. Under apartheid, the white minority systematically marginalized and suppressed the black majority of the country through the legalization of discriminatory practices. During this period, the only officially recognized languages were English and Afrikaans, neither of which are indigenous.

FOCUS FOR READING Throughout this chapter you have been reading poems and short stories about the process of self-discovery. Unlike those other texts, the following is a work of nonfiction—a memoir. As you read the following excerpt from *Born a Crime*, consider how Noah uses elements such as characters, setting, and conflicts to explore the idea of self-discovery.

One afternoon I was playing with my cousins. I was a doctor and they were my patients. I was operating on my cousin Bulelwa's ear with a set of matches when I accidentally perforated her eardrum. All hell broke loose. My grandmother came running in from the kitchen. "*Kwenzeka ntoni*?!" "What's happening?!" There was blood coming out of my cousin's head. We were all crying. My grandmother patched up Bulelwa's ear and made sure to stop the bleeding. But we kept crying. Because clearly we'd done something we were not supposed to do, and we knew we were going to be punished. My grandmother finished up with Bulelwa's ear and whipped out a belt and she beat the s*** out of Bulelwa. Then she beat the s*** out of Mlungisi, too. She didn't touch me.

Later that night my mother came home from work. She found my cousin with a bandage over her ear and my gran crying at the kitchen table.

"What's going on?" my mom said.

"Oh, Nombuyiselo," she said. "Trevor is so naughty. He's the naughtiest child I've ever come across in my life."

"Then you should hit him."

"I can't hit him."

"Why not?"

"Because I don't know how to hit a white child," she said. "A black child, I understand. A black child, you hit them and they stay black. Trevor, when you hit him he turns blue and green and yellow and red. I've never seen those colors before. I'm scared I'm going to break him. I don't want to kill a white person. I'm so afraid. I'm not going to touch him." And she never did.

My grandmother treated me like I was white. My grandfather did, too, only he was even more extreme. He called me "Mastah." In the car, he insisted on driving me as if he were my chauffeur. "Mastah must always sit in the backseat." I never challenged him on it. What was I going to say? "I believe your perception of race is flawed, Grandfather." No. I was five. I sat in the back.

There were so many perks to being "white" in a black family, I can't even front. I was having a great time. My own family basically did what the American justice system does: I was given more lenient treatment than the black kids. Misbehavior that my cousins would have been punished for, I was given a warning and let off. And I was way naughtier than either of my cousins. It wasn't even close. If something got broken or if someone was stealing granny's cookies, it was me. I was trouble. 10

My mom was the only force I truly feared. She believed if you spare the rod, you spoil the child. But everyone else said, "No, he's different," and they gave me a pass. Growing up the way I did, I learned how easy it is for white people to get comfortable with a system that awards them all the perks. I knew my cousins were getting beaten for things that I'd done, but I wasn't interested in changing my grandmother's perspective, because that would mean I'd get beaten, too. Why would I do that? So that I'd *feel* better? Being beaten didn't make me feel better. I had a choice. I could champion racial justice in our home, or I could enjoy granny's cookies. I went with the cookies.

• • •

At that point I didn't think of the special treatment as having to do with color. I thought of it as having to do with Trevor. It wasn't, "Trevor doesn't get beaten because Trevor is white." It was, "Trevor doesn't get beaten because Trevor is Trevor." Trevor can't go outside. Trevor can't walk without supervision. It's because I'm me; that's why this is happening. I had no other points of reference. There were no other mixed kids around so that I could say, "Oh, this happens to us."

Nearly one million people lived in Soweto. Ninety-nine point nine percent of them were black — and then there was me. I was famous in my neighborhood just because of the color of my skin. I was so unique people would give directions using me as a landmark. "The house on Makhalima Street. At the corner you'll see a light-skinned boy. Take a right there."

Whenever the kids in the street saw me they'd yell, "*Indoda yomlungu*!" "The white man!" Some of them would run away. Others would call out to their parents to come look. Others would run up and try to touch me to see if I was real. It was pandemonium. What I didn't understand at the time was that the other kids genuinely had no clue what a white person was. Black kids in the township didn't leave the township. Few people had televisions. They'd seen the white police roll through, but they'd never dealt with a white person face-to-face, ever.

I'd go to funerals and I'd walk in and the bereaved would look up and see me and they'd stop crying. They'd start whispering. Then they'd wave and say, "Oh!" like they were more shocked by me walking in than by the death of their loved ones. I think people felt like the dead person was more important because a white person had come to the funeral. 15

After a funeral, the mourners all go to the house of the surviving family to eat. A hundred people might show up, and you've got to feed them. Usually you get a cow and slaughter it and your neighbors come over and help you cook. Neighbors and acquaintances eat outside in the yard and in the street, and the family eats indoors. Every funeral I ever went to, I ate indoors. It didn't matter if we knew the deceased or not. The family would see me and invite me in. "*Awunakuvumela umntana womlungu ame ngaphandle. Yiza naye apha ngaphakathi*," they'd say. "You can't let the white child stand outside. Bring him in here."

As a kid I understood that people were different colors, but in my head white and black and brown were like types of chocolate. Dad was the white chocolate, mom was the dark chocolate, and I was the milk chocolate. But we were all just chocolate. I didn't know any of it had anything to do with "race." I didn't know what race was. My mother never referred to my dad as white or to me as mixed. So when the other kids in Soweto called me "white," even though I was light brown, I just thought they had their colors mixed up, like they hadn't learned them properly. "Ah, yes, my friend. You've confused aqua with turquoise. I can see how you made that mistake. You're not the first."

I soon learned that the quickest way to bridge the race gap was through language. Soweto was a melting pot: families from different tribes and homelands. Most kids in the township spoke only their home language, but I learned several languages because I grew up in a house where there was no option but to learn them. My mom made sure English was the first language I spoke. If you're black in South Africa, speaking English is the one thing that can give you a leg up. English is the language of money. English comprehension is equated with intelligence. If you're looking for a job, English is the difference between getting the job or staying unemployed. If you're standing in the dock, English is the difference between getting off with a fine or going to prison.

After English, Xhosa was what we spoke around the house. When my mother was angry she'd fall back on her home language. As a naughty child, I was well versed in Xhosa threats. They were the first phrases I picked up, mostly for my own safety — phrases like "*Ndiza kubetha entloko.*" "I'll knock you upside the head." Or "*Sidenge ndini somntwana.*" "You idiot of a child." It's a very passionate language. Outside of that, my mother picked up different languages here and there. She learned Zulu because it's similar to Xhosa. She spoke German because of my father. She spoke Afrikaans because it is useful to know the language of your oppressor. Sotho she learned in the streets.

Bloomberg/Getty Images

Doris Salcedo's modern art installation, titled *Shibboleth*, is a crack in the floor. A shibboleth is a distinctive aspect of language used to identify someone — like how an accent might tell you where a person is from geographically.

Consider what this fissure suggests about the borders that divide people, whether they be due to immigration or race. How are language and race figurative cracks for Noah? How does he bridge these divides between people?

Living with my mom, I saw how she used 20
language to cross boundaries, handle situations, navigate the world. We were in a shop once, and the shopkeeper, right in front of us, turned to his security guard and said, in Afrikaans, "*Volg daai swartes, netnou steel hulle iets.*" "Follow those blacks in case they steal something."

My mother turned around and said, in beautiful, fluent Afrikaans, "*Hoekom volg jy nie daai swartes sodat jy hulle kan help kry waarna hulle soek nie?*" "Why don't you follow these blacks so you can help them find what they're looking for?"

"*Ag, jammer*!" he said, apologizing in Afrikaans. Then — and this was the funny thing — he didn't apologize for being racist; he merely apologized for aiming his racism at us. "Oh, I'm so sorry," he said. "I thought you were like the other blacks. You know how they love to steal."

I learned to use language like my mother did. I would simulcast — give you the program in your own tongue. I'd get suspicious looks from people just walking down the street. "Where are you from?" they'd ask. I'd reply in whatever language they'd addressed me in, using the same accent that they used. There would be a brief moment of confusion, and then the suspicious look would disappear. "Oh, okay. I thought you were a stranger. We're good then."

It became a tool that served me my whole life. One day as a young man I was walking down the street, and a group of Zulu guys was walking behind me, closing in on me, and I could hear them talking to one another about how they were going to mug me. "*Asibambe le autie yomlungu. Phuma ngapha mina ngizoqhamuka ngemuva kwakhe.*" "Let's get this white guy. You go to his left, and I'll come up behind him." I didn't know what to do. I couldn't run, so I just spun around real quick and said, "*Kodwa bafwethu yingani singavele sibambe umuntu inkunzi? Asenzeni. Mina ngikulindele.*" "Yo, guys, why don't we just mug someone together? I'm ready. Let's do it."

They looked shocked for a moment, and then they started laughing. "Oh, sorry, dude. We thought you were something else. We weren't trying to take anything from you. We were trying to steal from white people. Have a good day, man." They were ready to do me violent harm, until they felt we were part of the same tribe, and then we were cool. That, and so many other smaller incidents in my life, made me realize that language, even more than color, defines who you are to people.

I became a chameleon. My color didn't change, but I could change your perception of my color. If you spoke to me in Zulu, I replied to you in Zulu. If you spoke to me in Tswana, I replied to you in Tswana. Maybe I didn't look like you, but if I spoke like you, I was you.

• • •

As apartheid was coming to an end, South Africa's elite private schools started accepting children of all colors. My mother's company offered bursaries, scholarships, for underprivileged families, and she managed to get me into Maryvale College, an expensive private Catholic school. Classes taught by nuns. Mass on Fridays. The whole bit. I started preschool there when I was three, primary school when I was five.

In my class we had all kinds of kids. Black kids, white kids, Indian kids, colored kids. Most of the white kids were pretty well off. Every child of color pretty much wasn't. But because of scholarships we all sat at the same table. We wore the same maroon blazers, the same gray slacks and skirts. We had the same books. We had the same teachers. There was no racial separation. Every clique was racially mixed.

Kids still got teased and bullied, but it was over usual kid stuff: being fat or being skinny, being tall or being short, being smart or being dumb. I don't remember anybody being teased about their race. I didn't learn to put limits on what I was supposed to like or not like. I had a wide berth to explore myself. I had crushes on white girls. I had crushes on black girls. Nobody asked me what I was. I was Trevor.

It was a wonderful experience to have, but the downside was that it sheltered me from reality. Maryvale was an oasis that kept me from the truth, a comfortable place where I could avoid making a tough decision. But the real world doesn't go away. Racism exists. People are getting hurt, and just because it's not happening to you doesn't mean it's not happening. And at some point, you have to choose. Black or white. Pick a side. You can try to hide from it. You can say, "Oh, I don't pick sides," but at some point life will force you to pick a side.

At the end of grade six I left Maryvale to go to H. A. Jack Primary, a government school. I had to take an aptitude test before I started, and, based on the results of the test, the school counselor told me, "You're going to be in the smart classes, the A classes." I showed up for the first day of school and went to my classroom. Of the thirty or so kids in my class, almost all of them were white. There was one Indian kid, maybe one or two black kids, and me.

Then recess came. We went out on the playground, and black kids were *everywhere*. It was an ocean of black, like someone had opened a tap and all the black had come pouring out. I was like, *Where were they all hiding?* The white kids I'd met that morning, they went in one direction, the black kids went in another direction, and I was left standing in the middle, totally confused. Were we going to meet up later on? I did not understand what was happening.

I was eleven years old, and it was like I was seeing my country for the first time. In the townships you don't see segregation, because everyone is black. In the white world, any time my mother took me to a white church, we were the only black people there, and my mom didn't separate herself from anyone. She didn't care. She'd go right up and sit with the white people. And at Maryvale, the kids were mixed up and hanging out together. Before that day, I had never seen people being together and yet not together, occupying the same space yet choosing not to associate with each other in any way. In an instant I could see, I could feel, how the boundaries were drawn. Groups moved in color patterns across the yard, up the stairs, down the hall. It was insane. I looked over at the white kids I'd met that morning. Ten minutes earlier I'd thought I was at a school where they were a majority. Now I realized how few of them there actually were compared to everyone else.

Ejor/Getty Images

This photograph was taken in South Africa during the period of apartheid.

What do you notice about the relationship between the words and the people in the photo? How does the photograph align with Noah's depiction of his experience growing up in South Africa?

I stood there awkwardly by myself in this no-man's-land in the middle of the playground. Luckily, I was rescued by the Indian kid from my class, a guy named Theesan Pillay. Theesan was one of the few Indian kids in school, so he'd noticed me, another obvious outsider, right away. He ran over to introduce himself. "Hello, fellow anomaly! You're in my class. Who are you? What's your story?" We started talking and hit it off. He took me under his wing, the Artful Dodger to my bewildered Oliver.

Through our conversation it came up that I spoke several African languages, and Theesan thought a colored kid speaking black languages was the most amazing trick. He brought me over to a group of black kids. "Say something," he told them, "and he'll show you he understands you." One kid said something in Zulu, and I replied to him in Zulu. Everyone cheered. Another kid said something in Xhosa, and I replied to him in Xhosa. Everyone cheered. For the rest of recess Theesan took me around to different black kids on the playground. "Show them your trick. Do your language thing."

The black kids were fascinated. In South Africa back then, it wasn't common to find a white person or a colored person who spoke African languages; during apartheid white people were always taught that those languages were beneath them. So the fact that I did speak African languages immediately endeared me to the black kids.

"How come you speak our languages?" they asked.

"Because I'm black," I said, "like you."

"You're not black."

"Yes, I am."

"No, you're not. Have you not seen yourself?"

They were confused at first. Because of my color, they thought I was a colored person, but speaking the same languages meant that I belonged to their tribe. It just took them a moment to figure it out. It took me a moment, too.

At some point I turned to one of them and said, "Hey, how come I don't see you guys in any of my classes?" It turned out they were in the B classes, which also happened to be the black classes. That same afternoon, I went back to the A classes, and by the end of the day I realized that they weren't for me. Suddenly, I knew who my people were, and I wanted to be with them. I went to see the school counselor.

"I'd like to switch over," I told her. "I'd like to go to the B classes."

She was confused. "Oh, no," she said. "I don't think you want to do that."

"Why not?"

"Because those kids are . . . you know."

"No, I don't know. What do you mean?"

"Look," she said, "you're a smart kid. You don't want to be in that class."

"But aren't the classes the same? English is English. Math is math."

"Yeah, but that class is . . . those kids are gonna hold you back. You want to be in the smart class."

"But surely there must be some smart kids in the B class."

"No, there aren't."

"But all my friends are there."

"You don't want to be friends with those kids."

"Yes, I do."

We went back and forth. Finally she gave me a stern warning.

"You do realize the effect this will have on your future? You do understand what you're giving up? This will impact the opportunities you'll have open to you for the rest of your life."

"I'll take that chance."

I moved to the B classes with the black kids. I decided I'd rather be held back with people I liked than move ahead with people I didn't know.

Being at H. A. Jack made me realize I was black. Before that recess I'd never had to choose, but when I was forced to choose, I chose black. The world saw me as colored, but I didn't spend my life looking at myself. I spent my life looking at other people. I saw myself as the people around me, and the people around me were black. My cousins are black, my mom is black, my gran is black. I grew up black. Because I had a white father, because I'd been in white Sunday school, I got along with the white kids, but I didn't belong with the white kids. I wasn't a part of their tribe. But the black kids embraced me. "Come along," they said. "You're rolling with us."

extending beyond the text

Jason Larkin's photography book *Waiting* is a collection of photographs of South Africans waiting for public transportation. In an interview with Alex King in the magazine *Huck*, Larkin explores the significance of this waiting as a byproduct of the era of apartheid.

Jason Larkin

Alex King: What drew your attention to people waiting around Johannesburg?
Jason Larkin: While living in South Africa and working on my previous project, waiting had a much more pronounced and tangible reality to it, an awareness that came through strongly in the daily news reports of life across the country, as well as day-to-day conversations. But for me, it was a physical appearance of people waiting in public and out in the streets that really grabbed my attention.

Of course, like anywhere else, much of the waiting I realised was for people to simply get to and from work. However as I talked with those waiting I soon realised how long this waiting could take, and the implications of this. The geographical zoning that democratic South Africa has inherited, as well as an apartheid era transport system, means workers can wait hours to start a long ride home, making the daily commute an evident legacy of an unjust system that still persists today.

Alex King: What did you learn from the *Waiting* project?
Jason Larkin: Waiting is obviously not a reality exclusive to South Africans. But waiting for so long for transport home, or for jobs so far away from where they live is a legacy of the apartheid zoning that the new South Africa has inherited. If you spend four hours of your day waiting and travelling home you have much less time to spend with families, less time to do what you'd like to, start a new business, be competitive, etc.

How does the "waiting" that Larkin describes compare to the type of oppression that Noah experienced in apartheid South Africa? In what way is American society also "waiting"? In your response, define the "waiting" and discuss how it is grounded in the history of America.

With the black kids, I wasn't constantly trying to be. With the black kids, I just was.

• • •

Before apartheid, any black South African who received a formal education was likely taught by European missionaries, foreign enthusiasts eager to Christianize and Westernize the natives. In the mission schools, black people learned English, European literature, medicine, the law. It's no coincidence that nearly every major black leader of the anti-apartheid movement, from Nelson Mandela to Steve Biko, was educated by the missionaries — a knowledgeable man is a free man, or at least a man who longs for freedom.

The only way to make apartheid work, therefore, was to cripple the black mind. Under apartheid, the government built what became known as Bantu schools. Bantu schools taught no science, no history, no civics. They taught metrics and agriculture: how to count potatoes, how to pave roads, chop wood, till the soil. "It does not serve the Bantu to learn history and science because he is primitive," the government said. "This will only mislead him, showing him pastures in which he is not allowed to graze." To their credit, they were simply being honest. Why educate a slave? Why teach someone Latin when his only purpose is to dig holes in the ground?

Mission schools were told to conform to the new curriculum or shut down. Most of them shut down, and black children were forced into crowded classrooms in dilapidated schools, often with teachers who were barely literate themselves. Our parents and grandparents were taught with little singsong lessons, the way you'd teach a preschooler shapes and colors. My grandfather used to sing the songs and laugh about how silly they were. *Two times two is four. Three times two is six. La la la la la.* We're talking about fully grown teenagers being taught this way, for generations.

What happened with education in South 65
Africa, with the mission schools and the Bantu schools, offers a neat comparison of the two groups of whites who oppressed us, the British and the Afrikaners. The difference between British racism and Afrikaner racism was that at least the British gave the natives something to aspire to. If they could learn to speak correct English and dress in proper clothes, if they could Anglicize and civilize themselves, one day they might be welcome in society. The Afrikaners never gave us that option. British racism said, "If the monkey can walk like a man and talk like a man, then perhaps he is a man." Afrikaner racism said, "Why give a book to a monkey?" ■

Understanding and Interpreting

1. How would you describe the dynamics of Trevor Noah's family? Where does he see himself fitting in? How is the opening description of children playing emblematic of his family dynamics?
2. Explain how Noah's grandparents think about his whiteness. How does their perception of his skin color affect how they treat him?
3. Noah writes, "There were so many perks to being 'white'." Why does he place the word "white" in quotation marks (par. 10)?
4. Noah compares his treatment as a child to the "American justice system." In what ways are they similar?
5. Noah states that his mother "used language to cross boundaries." How does he use language in the same way throughout the text?
6. Noah asserts, "I became a chameleon" (par. 26). Identify specific moments in the text that support or illustrate his use of this metaphor.

7. Review Noah's experience at H. A. Jack Primary, and identify the stated purpose of A and B classes. Then, determine the unspoken functions of this division and how it impacts how Noah views himself.
8. How does Noah compare the prospect for growth under British colonial rule and under the enforcement of apartheid?

Analyzing Language, Style, and Structure

1. **Vocabulary in Context.** Reread the following phrase: "There were so many perks to being 'white' in a black family, I can't even front" (par. 10). What does "front" mean in that context? How is this similar to or different from other uses that you know of the word?
2. **Skill Focus.** In this excerpt, Noah is in a constant state of self-discovery. Identify at least two aspects of himself that he discovers through his interactions with different people. Explain how he responds to these realizations and how these relate to Noah's ideas about identity and fitting in.
3. Noah includes a biblical allusion when he writes, "If you spare the rod, you spoil the child" (par. 11). How does this allusion contribute to the characterization of his family's treatment of him?
4. What is Noah's tone when he relates the story of when kids would see him in the street and "run away" or "run up and try to touch" him (par. 14)?
5. Why does Noah include phrases in African languages such as Tswana, Xhosa, and Zulu? How do these languages contribute to how Noah views himself and how he is perceived by others?
6. What does Noah's repetition of the word "tribe" contribute to his purpose for the text?
7. Note that after the section recalling his own experiences at school, Noah includes a brief historical discussion on education during the period of apartheid. What is the purpose of weaving this historical section into his memoir?

Topics for Composing

1. **Analysis.** Reread the text and pay particular attention to what Noah writes about race, skin color, and setting. How does he suggest that these elements work together to shape a person's complex sense of self? How do they contribute to his own understanding of himself?
2. **Argument.** Consider obstacles or challenges that seem to be unique to multiracial or multilingual people in the United States. Select a few to focus on. Based on your own observations of race and culture and Noah's approach to diffusing conflict, what approach do you think would be most effective for overcoming such obstacles?
3. **Connection.** When have you ever been a chameleon, as Noah describes it? What did you learn from your experience? What connections do you see between your experience and Noah's?
4. **Speaking and Listening.** Find recordings online of the various languages referenced in the excerpt. Do you perceive the differences between them? How do they compare to English or other languages you might speak?
5. **Research.** How much variety in language, race, and ethnicity exists in South Africa? From at least two sources, gather demographic information about South Africa to determine the diversity that exists in that country.
6. **Multimodal.** Research the main historical events that helped to establish and then eradicate apartheid. Then, create a digital timeline of these events. Each marker on your timeline should be hyperlinked to a video or picture that you'll use to convey the history of apartheid.

Writing an Analysis of Character and Theme

In this Writing Workshop, you'll develop and write an analysis of a literary text, focusing on how the characters reveal a theme of the work. This will develop your analytical and interpretive skills, which are critical not just in English class, but in all sorts of real-world scenarios. This kind of work strengthens our abilities to read carefully, make thoughtful observations and connections, develop evidence-based interpretations, and communicate our ideas in a clear, well-organized, and thoroughly supported way.

You began thinking about characterization in Chapter 2, especially direct and indirect characterization. Then, in this chapter's Skill Workshop, you learned how to use the details in a text to draw conclusions about a character and a text's theme. You will now use those skills to write a complete essay in response to the following prompt:

> *Choose a text from this chapter, or from another source, that has an interesting character. Write an essay that explains how the writer's description of the character you have chosen helps to develop a theme in the text. In your essay, analyze how the author uses direct and indirect characterization to develop the character. In addition, show how the author uses this character and selection of detail to convey a theme.*

To help you with the process of writing this essay, we will model each of the specific steps by focusing on the Central Text in this chapter: "Rules of the Game" by Amy Tan (p. 316).

Step 1: Gathering Ideas

Before you dive right into responding to the prompt, in this step we will slow down a bit and model the ways that you will annotate a text of your choosing and begin to find a focus for your essay.

Reading Closely

You've read the story you chose once on your own. Now it's time to reread and annotate it with the prompt in mind. As discussed in Chapter 2, you need to focus on what the narrator tells you about the character directly. In addition, think about what you can infer based on the character's dialogue, thoughts, and interactions with other characters. Considering the prompt, your annotations should focus on the following:

1. Details that directly characterize the character
2. Details that indirectly characterize the character
3. Details that help convey the story's themes

Our annotations for the first page of "Rules of the Game" focusing on the character of Waverly might look like this:

She recognizes what her mother taught her from a very early age.

I was six when my mother taught me the art of invisible strength. It was a strategy for winning arguments, respect from others, and eventually, though neither of us knew it at the time, chess games.

Childish tantrum

"Bite back your tongue," scolded my mother when I cried loudly, yanking her hand toward the store that sold bags of salted plums. At home, she said, "Wise guy, he not go against wind. In Chinese we say, Come from South, blow with wind — poom! — North will follow. Strongest wind cannot be seen."

Learns from past mistakes

The next week I bit back my tongue as we entered the store with the forbidden candies. When my mother finished her shopping, she quietly plucked a small bag of plums from the rack and put it on the counter with the rest of the items.

She acknowledges that her mother wanted something better for her children.

My mother imparted her daily truths so she could help my older brothers and me rise above our circumstances. We lived in San Francisco's Chinatown. Like most of the other Chinese children who played in the back alleys of restaurants and curio shops, I didn't think we were poor. My bowl was always full, three five-course meals every day, beginning with a soup of mysterious things I didn't want to know the names of.

She doesn't perceive herself as being poor. At least she remembers her childhood being comfortable enough.

We lived on Waverly Place, in a warm, clean, two-bedroom flat that sat above a small Chinese bakery specializing in steamed pastries and dim sum. In the early morning, when the alley was still quiet, I could smell fragrant red beans as they were cooked

Chinese culture is a big part of her life and the memories seem pleasant.

down to a pasty sweetness. By daybreak, our flat was heavy with the odor of fried sesame balls and sweet curried chicken crescents. From my bed, I would listen as my father got ready for work, then locked the door behind him, one-two-three clicks.

Annotating the Text

As the prompt on page 355 indicated, you need to select a text that has a character you find interesting. With these model annotations in mind, turn to the text you have chosen to work with and annotate it by identifying the direct and indirect characterization that informs your understanding of the character. In other words, your annotations should focus on descriptions of the character as well as dialogue and other elements that help you draw conclusions about the character.

Gathering and Organizing Textual Evidence

As we saw in this chapter's Skill Workshop, transferring our annotations onto a table can help us organize our findings and build our analysis of the character. In working toward an essay, we would likely gather details from the entire text of "Rules of the Game." But for the purposes of providing a model, we will focus on the brief section that we annotated on pages 356–357:

Character: Waverly Place Jong

Descriptions of the character	Waverly is describing herself as a six-year-old.
The character's actions	"I cried loudly, yanking her hand. . . ."
Dialogue involving the character	The mother tells Waverly that she needs to "bite back" her tongue.
The character's internal thoughts	"I didn't think we were poor."
Other characters' observations about the character	The mother wants Waverly to "rise above" their circumstances.

Gathering and Organizing Textual Evidence

Create a table like the one on page 357. Then look back over your annotations of the complete work you have chosen and fill your table with material you've identified. Since every good characterization essay needs textual evidence, pair with a classmate who selected the same story you've chosen and compare notes. Make sure to comment on the notes each of you took and make appropriate additions and deletions to your table.

Interpreting the Evidence

To build an interpretation of Waverly's character, we would follow the process described in the Skill Workshop (pp. 254–263). We must first draw conclusions about the character. Then, we need to connect these conclusions to the evidence gathered. At this point, we can make an interpretative statement about the character. At the end of this process, we can write a paragraph analyzing the character.

If we implement this process using Waverly, we find that the evidence we just gathered allows us to conclude that she is a girl struggling to figure out who she is amidst strong external influences: her mother, her culture, and even her economic status. As we continue to interpret her character based on the details we've collected, our understanding of Waverly deepens.

Interpreting Your Evidence

Look at the notes you've gathered on your character. Using the process described above, write a few statements interpreting the character you've chosen. Make sure you include descriptions of your character, conclusions you've drawn based on your observations, and the textual evidence that supports your assertions.

Identifying Theme

Amy Tan creates a short story that centers on a young girl who displays a capacity for being both childish and mature, depending on the situation. But, beyond its plot, what is the story actually about? When trying to identify what themes an author might be exploring through a character's development, it can help to pose questions such as the following: *What is important to the character? What people and things does she care about? How connected does the character feel to the people and places around her? What problems does the character face at home and within her broader environment? What does she learn about herself?* Asking questions such as these about Waverly reveals that the story is not only about her relationship with her mother, but also about her need to exist in both the Chinese and American cultures around her. In addition, it is about her reaction to growing up. In short, the more we think about Waverly in this story, the more we realize that "Rules of the Game" is about the difficulties of carving out an identity amid cultural and family tensions.

Identifying Theme

Review the interpretive statements you wrote about the character from the story you've selected. Then, think about what the short story is actually about. By this, we don't mean plot; instead, we're referring to the thematic concerns the author develops throughout the story. Remember to ask questions about your character like the ones we asked about Waverly in the previous section to help you identify the thematic concerns the author develops throughout the story you selected.

Write three to four sentences summarizing your observations about the work's major thematic concerns. Then, pair with your partner again and share each other's observations. You should help one another determine if you've indeed identified a theme or are simply summarizing the story's plot.

Step 2: Planning The Essay

So far in this workshop, you have selected your text for analysis, done a close reading with careful annotations focused on a character, and identified a theme for the text. Before you actually begin writing your response, this step will walk you through developing your thesis, identifying relevant support, and considering an appropriate organizational structure.

Developing a Working Thesis

As we've noted in other chapters and workshops, a thesis statement is the part of your introduction where you explicitly state the claim you are making. In the case of this example and workshop, it is a specific claim developed in response to a prompt — the claim that will be explained and defended with reasoning and textual evidence throughout the body of the essay.

Let's consider a few possible thesis statements for our sample essay:

WEAK THESIS

By analyzing Waverly in Amy Tan's "Rules of the Game," we can understand the author's thematic purpose.

This thesis merely echoes the prompt; it provides no answers or direction.

WEAK THESIS

Amy Tan's "Rules of the Game" is about a girl named Waverly who argues with her mother and who becomes a chess champion.

Does this thesis answer any part of the prompt? It seems to offer a reductive summary of the story — and nothing else.

WEAK THESIS

In "Rules of the Game," Amy Tan discusses the difficulties of growing up, particularly due to parental and cultural conflicts.

While this statement addresses theme, it makes no specific claim about Waverly. Remember that the prompt asks us to consider how the story's character sheds light on its theme.

WORKING THESIS

Through the character of Waverly Place Jong, who reconciles her mother's expectations with her own desires while transforming herself into a poised chess champion, Amy Tan discusses the difficulties of carving out an identity amid cultural and family tensions in "Rules of the Game."

This thesis statement tells us something about who Waverly is and how her character serves to convey the story's theme. It provides a reasonable starting point. A thesis statement can be a work in progress, as long as it presents a claim that clearly and completely addresses the question you're trying to answer. You can always refine your thesis statement as you develop your essay.

Developing Your Working Thesis

Return to your selected story and write a thesis statement that addresses all parts of the prompt listed on page 355. Share your thesis with a classmate and answer the following questions for each other's thesis statements:

1. Does the thesis avoid merely restating the prompt?
2. Does the thesis avoid merely summarizing the story?
3. Does the thesis reveal an interpretation of the character?
4. Does the thesis make a claim about the story's theme?

Gathering Support

Before selecting the textual support that you'll include in your essay, make sure you understand the demands of your thesis. For example, based on our working thesis, what exactly do we need to prove? Let's look back at our thesis:

WORKING THESIS

Through the character of Waverly Place Jong, who reconciles her mother's expectations with her own desires while transforming herself into a poised chess champion, Amy Tan discusses the difficulties of carving out an identity amid cultural and family tensions in "Rules of the Game."

There are several points in this thesis that need to be proven:

Point 1: Waverly's mother has expectations for her that do not align with Waverly's own desires.

Point 2: Waverly tries to meet her mother's expectations while simultaneously seeking her own happiness.

Point 3: Waverly carves out an identity amidst clashing cultural demands.

Point 4: Waverly must contend with tensions within her own family as she seeks to carve out her identity.

The evidence you gather for your essay must be strategic: each quotation must be directly related to your thesis or to one of the points that you've identified. You can assess the quality of your evidence by placing it in a chart such as the one that follows:

Quotation	How the quotation supports my point
" 'Bite back your tongue,' scolded my mother when I cried loudly. . . ."	Throughout the text, Waverly's mother instructs her on what her behavior ought to be, such as when she tells her to "bite back" her tongue.

Gathering Support

Return to your working thesis and identify the points that need be addressed. Then, turn to the story you have chosen and gather evidence to support that thesis. Remember that whether you use note cards, take notes in a document, or fill in a chart is up to you. This activity is a good opportunity to try out a system and see how it works. If you are unable to identify at least four or five quotations from the text that support your thesis, you might want to consider revising your thesis.

Organizing the Essay

As we discussed earlier, effective essay writing requires careful planning and a systematic approach. Now that you have developed a thesis statement, defined the points that need to be proven in the essay, and gathered appropriate textual evidence, you need to consider the order in which you'll present this information.

For an essay on how characterization reveals theme, you might consider these two organizational structures:

- **Element by element:** First analyze character; then discuss theme. With this approach, you will first interpret the character without truly delving into the story's theme. Once you have fully analyzed the character, your essay will transition to a discussion of theme. To complete this approach successfully, make sure that you build a logical connection between the two parts of your essay so that they don't seem disjointed. Make it clear that the author presents the character in a particular way in order to convey theme, or a central idea in a text.

- **Blending elements:** In this approach, you will introduce an aspect of the character, then connect it to theme, continuously connecting characterization and theme throughout your essay. This method is more complex because you will be developing your arguments on both topics at the same time. To ensure that you don't simply repeat your interpretation of theme throughout the essay, focus on how your understanding of theme deepens as your interpretation of the character becomes more complex.

Organizing Your Essay

Review the two organizational structures discussed and consider which one might work best for your essay. Sketch an outline for the body of your essay based on the structure you selected. As you complete this activity, you might decide that a different structure is best suited for your essay. If so, sketch a new outline for your essay.

Step 3: Drafting the Essay

Now that you have a working thesis, lots of relevant evidence, and an idea about how you want to organize your essay, it's time to begin drafting it. Let's start by focusing on the elements of a body paragraph. Then, we'll focus on how you might start and conclude your essay.

Drafting Body Paragraphs

For the sample essay in this workshop, we have decided to blend elements. First, we will discuss various aspects of Waverly's character. Then, we will connect them to a theme of "Rules of the Game."

Regardless of how you organize your essay, each of the body paragraphs must include the following:

1. A topic sentence — a statement around which the paragraph will be developed and which asserts a minor claim connected to the thesis statement
2. Textual evidence — direct and indirect quotations taken from the text
3. Commentary — your own interpretation of the textual evidence and the ideas you've presented in the paragraph

Here is a sample body paragraph:

Topic sentence

Waverly Place Jong at times exhibits a slightly mischievous nature which is both normal for a young child and a precursor to subsequent, pre-adolescent behaviors. At the age of

Textual evidence

six, for instance, she "crie[s] loudly" as she pulls her mother towards the salty plums she wants. A few years later, she tells her mother that she wishes she would not tell "everybody" that they're related. These instances depict the natural tendency young people have to distance themselves from their parents as they assert their independence and individuality. Tan never questions Waverly's love for her mother, but she certainly presents the common experience of the younger generation being embarrassed by the older one. The friction seen here is heightened as Waverly becomes more irritated by her mother's shadow constantly looming over her.

Textual evidence

Commentary

Notice that this paragraph describes Waverly and discusses the big ideas (identity, generational conflict, parenting) that are central to the story. Note that the last sentence of the paragraph smoothly guides readers into the next body paragraph. To determine how many body paragraphs we should write, we can look through the points we identified as critical to our thesis (p. 360) and organize them according to the structure we selected on page 361. Each body paragraph we write should follow the same structure we used in the model above: Include a topic sentence that addresses an aspect of our thesis. Then, provide evidence and commentary that supports the point we are making.

Drafting Your Body Paragraphs

Write a body paragraph based on the thesis statement you created. Make sure that you include the following:

1. A topic sentence
2. Textual evidence
3. Commentary

As you work on developing the topic sentence for this body paragraph, you might come up with multiple sentences that could serve as topic sentences in this essay. Make sure you keep those, since they might be useful when you write the rest of the body paragraphs. Before completing those paragraphs, however, show a draft of your initial paragraph to a classmate to get feedback on how well you have used your evidence and commentary to support your topic sentence and how well these components align with your thesis. Once you receive feedback, draft the remaining body paragraphs needed to fully support your thesis. Remember to organize them according to the structure you identified earlier in this workshop (p. 361). Be sure that each body paragraph includes a topic sentence related to your working thesis, evidence, and commentary.

Writing the Introduction

We know that an essay begins with an introduction and that the thesis statement should be included within it. But what else should we write in the introduction?

Although there may be variations to this approach, an introduction should generally have three parts:

a. The hook
b. The context
c. The thesis (claim)

The Hook

The hook is how you grab your reader's attention. How you set up your thesis depends on the task at hand and the requirements of your assignment. However, some options include an interesting anecdote, a startling statistic, an observation, or a question. Whatever approach you choose, make sure the hook is related to the theme that you will ultimately discuss. Keep in mind that this section is called "the hook" because it should make readers want to keep reading.

The Context

Provide context to build a bridge between your hook and your thesis. While you may have started with a question about family, you might now refine your scope by saying something more specific about the subject of your essay. Perhaps it's about sibling rivalries, growing up in a large family, or dealing with parental conflicts.

The Thesis

Since you've already worked on your thesis, incorporating it into a paragraph will give you an additional opportunity to edit and revise it. Generally, the thesis appears at the end of the introduction.

Here is a possible introduction for the sample essay we've been developing:

Human beings are shaped by both their immediate home environments and their greater cultural surroundings. Tensions among personal desires, parental demands, and societal expectations contribute to each person's character and sense of identity. Through the character of Waverly Place Jong, who reconciles her mother's expectations with her own desires while transforming herself into a poised chess champion, Amy Tan discusses the difficulties of carving out an identity amid cultural and family tensions in "Rules of the Game."

Hook

Context

Thesis

activity

Writing Your Introduction

It's time to draft an introduction that includes your working thesis. Remember to grab your readers' attention with a hook and to connect that hook clearly to your thesis by providing context. Once you have drafted your introduction, use labels to show where your hook, context, and thesis appear.

Writing the Conclusion

Based on the purpose of your essay, a conclusion might summarize your argument, present a call to action, or present a deeper understanding of the topic. The essay we've been developing on character and theme might conclude with a deeper understanding of why Amy Tan crafts Waverly's character as she does or by sharing some final insights into the story's central theme. The conclusion might look like this:

> While Waverly's development through the short story might seem like her own personal story, Amy Tan is actually using her character to discuss a natural progression common to all children as they age. Waverly's early interactions with her mother lay the foundation for subsequent clashes. At the heart of these rifts is a universal desire for children to assert their independence from their parents while simultaneously seeking to be accepted by their peers. Exploring the various ways that Waverly is depicted marks the transition from early childhood to the beginning of pre-adolescence, a time when all children begin to distance themselves from their parents in an effort to assert themselves as individuals.

Writing Your Conclusion

Draft your own conclusion to the essay you've been developing. Make sure that you do not simply repeat what you've already stated; instead, provide a broader understanding that is now — after you've thoroughly analyzed the story — clear to you and those who read your essay.

Step 4: Finalizing the Essay

Now that you have a complete draft of your essay, you can move on to the final steps in the writing process: revising and editing. These two acts are sometimes thought of as being the same, but they're not. Revision is when you look back at large-scale structural elements of your essay, such as how well you are supporting your claim, what kinds of evidence you might be missing, how effective your word choices are, and to what extent you have led your reader easily through your essay. Editing, on the other hand, focuses on fine-tuning the language, grammar, punctuation, spelling, and other conventions. Editing is usually the very last thing you do before you finalize your piece, looking carefully for any errors you may have made. The following are suggestions for you to consider as you finalize your essay.

Revising

Revising gives you a good opportunity to think again about your essay's purpose and audience. In most cases, your audience will be your teacher or an external evaluator in the case of a standardized test. In both situations, that means using a somewhat formal tone, but your writing can still be engaging for you and your audience.
Reread your essay for the following:

- Look back at your **thesis**. Since you wrote this early on in the workshop, does it still relate to the analysis you ended up writing? If you need more assistance with this, be sure to look at Revision Workshop 1: Effective Thesis and Essay Structure (p. 1064).
- Look back at your **focus**. Is it still at the center of your argument, or are you finding yourself just cataloging stylistic choices without tying them back to the focus? If you need more assistance with this, be sure to look at Revision Workshop 2: Effective Topic Sentences and Unified Paragraphs (p. 1068).
- Look back at some of your **body paragraphs**. Have you balanced the evidence with your own **commentary** about how that evidence supports your thesis? If you need more assistance with this, be sure to look at Revision Workshop 4: Appropriate Evidence and Support (p. 1076).

- Does your essay draw a clear connection between the **characterization** and the possible **theme** of the story? Be sure to look back at the Skill Workshop (p. 254) at the beginning of this chapter if you need more practice with this.
- Does your **introduction** grab the reader's attention and effectively preview your topic? Does your **conclusion** wrap up in a way that highlights your focus? Review Revision Workshop 8: Effective Introductions and Conclusions (p. 1097) if you need additional support with these parts of your essay.

Editing

Remember, editing is the very last thing you'll do before finalizing your essay. You and your teacher know better than anyone the types of spelling, grammar, and convention errors you need to focus on in your writing development. Be sure to refer to one or more of the Grammar Workshops (starting on p. 1101) in the back of the book if you encounter an issue and aren't sure how to overcome it.

Continuing the Conversation

Throughout this chapter, you have been reading texts and thinking about self-discovery and identity. At the beginning of the chapter and after each of the readings, you had opportunities to consider ideas related to the following essential questions:

- What roles do individuals play within their close social circle and within society as a whole?
- How does identity shift over time?
- What kinds of events and influences can cause identity to shift?
- How does setting affect social interactions?
- How do factors such as race, culture, gender identity, socioeconomic status, immigration status, and sexual orientation influence what we know and learn about ourselves?

The sections that follow will give you an opportunity to revisit and respond to some of those questions as you think further about self-discovery and identity by connecting these ideas to yourself, to texts you read, and to the world outside of the classroom.

Connections to Self

Think back on the texts you have read, responses you have written, discussions you have participated in, and ideas you have considered during your work with this chapter. Use the following questions to help explore how the issues in this chapter connect to your life and experience:

1. How do characteristics such as race, gender identity, and cultural background contribute to the way you view yourself? What other factors play a role in your identity?
2. How has growing older impacted how you perceive your place within your community and your relationship with the adults who surround you?
3. Consider a moment of self-discovery in your life. How did internal and external factors contribute to that discovery? How was your experience similar to that of a character's in this chapter?
4. Which of the texts in this chapter had the most significant effect on the way you think about self-discovery and identity? How has your understanding of these topics changed because of that text?

Connections to Texts

Use the following questions to make connections among the texts in this chapter. Consider what insights the texts provide into the concept of self-discovery. As you respond, be sure to make specific references to one or more texts you read in this chapter.

1. Some of the characters in this chapter must contend with growing up. To what extent is growing up seen as positive or negative development by these characters? In your analysis, refer to texts such as *When I Grow Up I Want To Be a List of Further Possibilities*, *Good with Boys*, *Suburbia!,* and *On Turning Ten*.
2. Reflecting on past events can spur self-discoveries. Select at least two characters or speakers from this chapter and discuss how reflection shapes their identities. In your analysis, you might consider texts such as *Rules of the Game*, *Suburbia!*, and *Good with Boys*.
3. Some of the writers in this chapter focus on how love shapes their characters' identities. The processes of loving, being loved, and seeking love allow characters to understand themselves in new ways. What do the characters in texts such as *Good with Boys*, *Glory*, and *Eveline* learn about themselves as they pursue love?
4. Setting can influence people's self-perceptions, particularly if they feel connected to or isolated from their surroundings. Think about how setting functions in texts such as *Friends with Boys*, *Suburbia!*, *Glory*, and *In Defense of Small Towns*. How do at least two characters from your chosen texts discover something about themselves as they interact with their settings?

Connections to World

Think back on the texts you have read, responses you have written, discussions you have participated in, and ideas you have considered during your work with this chapter. Use these questions to help explore how the issues in this chapter play out in the world at large.

1. What laws or cultural practices allow people to forge their own identities? Which ones prevent people from forging their own identities?
2. To what extent are people's identities a reflection of the world around them?
3. What effect do factors such as gender identity, race, and cultural background have on the roles individuals assume in the world?
4. How does contact with another culture, through travel, studying a different language, or learning about other cultures spur self-discovery? What role do these journeys have on a person's identity?

Hill Street Studios/DigitalVision/Getty Images

nonfiction

The Individual in School

Essential Questions:

- **What is the purpose of education?**
- **To what extent is school necessary for becoming educated?**
- **What effect do the pressures to conform to an institution like school have on a person's individuality?**
- **What roles do race, gender identity, and ethnicity play in a school setting?**
- **How might schools in the future look similar to and different from today's schools?**

At this point in your life, you have spent nearly ten years in school, which translates into roughly ten thousand hours. On most days, you spend more time doing school-related work than you spend engaged in any activity other than sleeping. The award-winning author Kurt Vonnegut wrote that high school "is closer to the core of the American experience than anything else I can think of." Clearly, school is one of the most significant influences on your life. The question is, what kind of influence does it have on you?

There are some who believe that, in addition to teaching students the skills and knowledge they need to be successful later in life, school is supposed to produce model citizens by indoctrinating students in the behaviors, attitudes, and beliefs of the dominant social and political culture. Consider the following statement about the purpose of school from Henry Ward Beecher, a popular clergyman of the mid-nineteenth century who sought to abolish slavery:

> The common schools are the stomachs of the country in which all people that come to us are assimilated within a generation. When a lion eats an ox, the lion does not become an ox but the ox becomes a lion.

In other words, a main purpose of school is to assimilate those who are different so that everyone becomes the same "lion." Contrast Beecher's view with this passage from *Democracy and Education*, written by education reformer John Dewey in 1916:

> How one person's abilities compare in quantity with those of another is none of the teacher's business. It is irrelevant to his work. What is required is that every individual shall have opportunities to employ his own powers in activities that have meaning. Mind, individual method, originality . . . signify the quality of purposive or directed action.

It is clear from this passage that Dewey does not think that school should be about assimilation, but rather about individuals having the opportunity to develop their own skills and knowledge as determined by their unique needs and interests.

The Individual in School

1. Read the quotations from Henry Ward Beecher and John Dewey again and make two lists:
   a. a list of times when you have been directly or indirectly asked to **conform** to aspects of the institution of school
   b. a list of times when you have been in a position to develop some aspect of your own **individuality** while in school
2. With a partner or small group, share your lists and discuss which of the two preceding quotations most accurately reflects your experiences in school.
3. Write your own statement about the purpose of school and the individual's role within a school.

Texts in Conversation

Throughout this chapter, you will have opportunities to think about the role of an individual's identity within the larger community of school. You will read nonfiction pieces about the pressures of popularity in high school, the positive and negative effects that teachers have, and the arguments for and against public schooling. At the end of the chapter, you will have an opportunity to add your own expert voice to the conversation, having logged so many hours as a part of the school community yourself. A graphic organizer like this one can help you keep track of the important parts of each text and how it relates to other texts you encounter.

Author and title	Author's attitude toward school's effect on the individual	Quotation(s) that illustrate the author's ideas about school	Your reaction and/or connections to other texts

Skill Workshop

Understanding Rhetorical Situation

Every day, you are bombarded with messages: a text from a friend inviting you to a party, a pop-up advertisement trying to get you to click, a politician asking for your support, or a parent giving you a lecture about your future. Every one of these texts — long or short, visual or print, spoken or written — has been composed in a particular way for a particular purpose. In Chapter 3, we introduced the term rhetorical situation (p. 87) and discussed how to understand texts by analyzing the elements of SOAPStone — subject, occasion, audience, purpose, speaker, and tone.

In this Skill Workshop, we'll consider rhetorical situation by examining a text whose subject is close to your own experience: the importance and drawbacks of getting good grades. Focusing on "What Straight-A Students Get Wrong" by Adam Grant, we'll look closely at how the relationship among subject, speaker, and audience influences and often determines the overall approach a writer takes, the evidence presented, even the language used. Then, you'll have a chance to practice this essential skill with a rhetorical analysis of another text.

What Straight-A Students Get Wrong

Adam Grant

Adam Grant is an organizational psychologist at the University of Pennsylvania's prestigious Wharton School of Business. He is a contributing opinion writer to the *New York Times,* where this piece was published. He is also the author of *Originals: How Nonconformists Move the World* and host of the podcast *WorkLife*.

Lange Studio/Courtesy Penguin Random House _LC

FOCUS FOR READING As you give this piece a first read, annotate the text by making connections and asking questions (p. 10). Then, read it again, looking specifically for how the author presents himself to his audience, why he presents himself that way, and what the effect is.

A decade ago, at the end of my first semester teaching at Wharton, a student stopped by for office hours. He sat down and burst into tears. My mind started cycling through a list of events that could make a college junior cry: His girlfriend had dumped him; he had been accused of plagiarism. "I just got my first A-minus," he said, his voice shaking.

Year after year, I watch in dismay as students obsess over getting straight A's. Some sacrifice their health; a few have even tried to sue their school after falling short. All have joined the cult of perfectionism out of a conviction that top marks are a ticket to elite graduate schools and lucrative job offers.

I was one of them. I started college with the goal of graduating with a 4.0. It would be a reflection of my brainpower and willpower, revealing that I had the right stuff to succeed. But I was wrong.

The evidence is clear: Academic excellence is not a strong predictor of career excellence. Across industries, research shows that the correlation between grades and job performance is modest in the first year after college and trivial within a handful of years. For example, at Google, once employees are two or three years out of college, their grades have no bearing on their performance. (Of course, it must be said that if you got D's, you probably didn't end up at Google.)

5 Academic grades rarely assess qualities like creativity, leadership and teamwork skills, or social, emotional and political intelligence. Yes, straight-A students master cramming information and regurgitating it on exams. But career success is rarely about finding the right solution to a problem — it's more about finding the right problem to solve.

In a classic 1962 study, a team of psychologists tracked down America's most creative architects and compared them with their technically skilled but less original peers. One of the factors that distinguished the creative architects was a record of spiky grades. "In college our creative architects earned about a B average," Donald MacKinnon wrote. "In work and courses which caught their interest they could turn in an A performance, but in courses that failed to strike their imagination, they were quite willing to do no work at all." They paid attention to their curiosity and prioritized activities that they found intrinsically motivating — which ultimately served them well in their careers.

Getting straight A's requires conformity. Having an influential career demands originality. In a study of students who graduated at the top of their class, the education researcher Karen Arnold found that although they usually had successful careers, they rarely reached the upper echelons. "Valedictorians aren't likely to be the future's visionaries," Dr. Arnold explained. "They typically settle into the system instead of shaking it up."

This might explain why Steve Jobs finished high school with a 2.65 G.P.A., J. K. Rowling graduated from the University of Exeter with roughly a C average, and the Rev. Dr. Martin Luther King Jr. got only one A in his four years at Morehouse.

If your goal is to graduate without a blemish on your transcript, you end up taking easier classes and staying within your comfort zone. If you're willing to tolerate the occasional B, you can learn to program in Python while struggling to decipher "Finnegans Wake." You gain experience coping with failures and setbacks, which builds resilience.

10 Straight-A students also miss out socially. More time studying in the library means less time to start lifelong friendships, join new clubs or volunteer. I know from experience. I didn't meet my 4.0 goal; I graduated with a 3.78. (This is the first time I've shared my G.P.A. since applying to graduate school 16 years ago. Really, no one cares.) Looking back, I don't wish my grades had been higher. If I could do it over again, I'd study less. The hours I wasted memorizing the inner workings of the eye would have been better spent trying out improv comedy and having more midnight conversations about the meaning of life.

So universities: Make it easier for students to take some intellectual risks. Graduate schools can be clear that they don't care about the difference between a 3.7 and a 3.9. Colleges could just report letter grades without pluses and minuses, so that any G.P.A. above a 3.7 appears on transcripts as an A. It might also help to stop the madness of grade inflation, which creates an academic arms race that encourages too many students to strive for meaningless perfection. And why not let students wait until the end of the semester to declare a class pass-fail, instead of forcing them to decide in the first month?

Employers: Make it clear you value skills over straight A's. Some recruiters are already on board: In a 2003 study of over 500 job postings, nearly 15 percent of recruiters actively selected against students with high G.P.A.s (perhaps questioning their priorities and life skills), while more than 40 percent put no weight on grades in initial screening.

Straight-A students: Recognize that underachieving in school can prepare you to overachieve in life. So maybe it's time to apply your grit to a new goal — getting at least one B before you graduate. ■

Identifying Purpose

Every text — an advertisement, a meme, a poem, or an opinion piece like this one you just read — is created for a purpose. The writer, artist, poet, or songwriter is trying to communicate something to an audience. An essential starting point of rhetorical analysis of a text is identifying why the writer created the text. Dr. Martin Luther King Jr.'s purpose in his "I Have a Dream" speech, for example, was to convince his audience to support a civil rights movement working toward an America where people "will not be judged by the color of their skin, but by the content of their character." Based on the title "What Straight-A Students Get Wrong," you might conclude that Grant is criticizing straight-A students. Upon further reading, however, you could determine that his purpose is to convince his audience that students who focus on activities promoting leadership, socialization, and cooperation will be more successful.

Identifying Audience

One of the key elements of analyzing the rhetorical situation is knowing who the intended audience is. Think about how your communication changes depending on your audience. For example, you likely make different decisions about whether to include abbreviations, emojis, or memes in your messaging, depending on whether your audience is a friend, a parent, or a teacher. Professional writers are always conscious of their audiences. They tailor their content to meet the needs and backgrounds of the people they intend to reach. A quick Google search gave us the following information about Grant's readers of the *New York Times*:

- The largest group of readers is between 35 and 44 years old; about a third are under 30.
- Most are politically liberal (over 80% Democrats and Independents).
- More than 50% are college graduates; another 24% have some college education.
- Nearly 40% have annual income levels of $75,000 or more.

So, Grant's audience is generally an academically successful population, and many of them are old enough to have children of their own. They might, therefore, be reluctant to consider that school — which has benefited them — could be damaging their children.

Grant almost certainly had these factors in mind as he crafted his opinion piece. As he wrote, he needed to think about how to convince this particular audience to reconsider some of their previously held views.

Analyzing Audience

Reread the paragraphs below. Knowing what you do about Grant's audience, where do you see signs of his efforts to reach those specific readers? In these paragraphs, what details or word choices, for example, seem aimed at the group of people described on page 375?

> A decade ago, at the end of my first semester teaching at Wharton, a student stopped by for office hours. He sat down and burst into tears. My mind started cycling through a list of events that could make a college junior cry: His girlfriend had dumped him; he had been accused of plagiarism. "I just got my first A-minus," he said, his voice shaking.
>
> Year after year, I watch in dismay as students obsess over getting straight A's. Some sacrifice their health; a few have even tried to sue their school after falling short. All have joined the cult of perfectionism out of a conviction that top marks are a ticket to elite graduate schools and lucrative job offers.
>
> I was one of them. I started college with the goal of graduating with a 4.0. It would be a reflection of my brainpower and willpower, revealing that I had the right stuff to succeed. But I was wrong.

Selecting Evidence for an Intended Audience

Another essential part of a rhetorical analysis is to consider the type of evidence a speaker selects to appeal to the intended audience. From Chapter 3, you might recall that the main types of evidence are the following:

1. Personal experience and anecdotes
2. Facts and data or statistics
3. Scholarly research and expert opinion

When Grant describes how he behaved as a student, he uses personal experience — a strategy you discussed in Chapter 5 — to show his audience that he is one of them. Yet he knows that these educated, engaged readers will also expect hard evidence. In fact, he announces that he will give them just that: "The evidence is clear." Then, he cites research, followed by his commentary. He cites "a classic 1962 study," which on the face of it might seem outdated. Characterizing the study as "classic" indicates that it still has relevance. He quotes one of the authors, Donald MacKinnon, but the rest of the paragraph is his own commentary on the issue at hand: an obsession with straight-A grades.

Grant introduces a source with commentary.

In a classic 1962 study, a team of psychologists tracked down America's most creative architects and compared them with their technically skilled but less original peers. One of the factors that distinguished the creative architects was a record of spiky grades. "In college our creative architects earned about a B average," Donald MacKinnon wrote. "In work and courses which caught their interest they could turn in an A performance, but in courses that failed to strike their imagination, they were quite willing to do no work at all." They paid attention to their curiosity and prioritized activities that they found intrinsically motivating—which ultimately served them well in their careers.

Grant uses a quotation as evidence.

Grant's closing commentary

Grant is keenly sensitive to his audience. Based on what he knows about his *New York Times* readership, he can assume that many of his readers are successful and creative like the architects in the study. So instead of hammering away at how unimportant high grades are, he makes his argument by emphasizing what is even more important — focusing on things that are "intrinsically motivating" in school contributes to career success.

Analyzing the Appeal of Evidence to Audience

Throughout his argument, Grant is careful not to denigrate high grades, which his audience probably values. Reread the following two paragraphs and explain how Grant furthers his own argument through the evidence he selects without alienating his audience.

> Getting straight A's requires conformity. Having an influential career demands originality. In a study of students who graduated at the top of their class, the education researcher Karen Arnold found that although they usually had successful careers, they rarely reached the upper echelons. "Valedictorians aren't likely to be the future's visionaries," Dr. Arnold explained. "They typically settle into the system instead of shaking it up."
>
> This might explain why Steve Jobs finished high school with a 2.65 G.P.A., J. K. Rowling graduated from the University of Exeter with roughly a C average, and the Rev. Dr. Martin Luther King Jr. got only one A in his four years at Morehouse.

Considering the Occasion

Now that we have a sense of the way that audience affects the argument, let's step back a moment and consider the occasion of Grant's piece. Sometimes the occasion is obvious: a national or international event, like the speech you read in Chapter 3 about the explosion of the space shuttle *Challenger*. But Grant's opinion piece doesn't have such a dramatic occasion. In instances like this, occasion can have a broader meaning of the context of the time and place of the argument.

When you consider 2018 and the general climate surrounding education, the occasion certainly plays a part. More students were applying to the most competitive colleges, often at the urging of their parents, and studies were revealing higher anxiety and depression rates among high school and college students. So, although Grant does not write his column in response to a specific incident, nor does he cite this context directly, he is writing within an environment of concern about the increasing pressure in educational settings. The scenario that he describes in his opening paragraph with the college student crying may seem extreme. Perhaps it is, but, sadly, it is not unusual. It signals the lack of perspective that a focus exclusively on grades to measure worth and success can lead to. Given that context, his audience, people aware of current events, would understand the urgency of his message.

activity Analyzing Occasion

Reread the following two paragraphs and explain how the occasion we've described in this workshop may have affected what Grant chose to include.

> If your goal is to graduate without a blemish on your transcript, you end up taking easier classes and staying within your comfort zone. If you're willing to tolerate the occasional B, you can learn to program in Python while struggling to decipher "Finnegan's Wake." You gain experience coping with failures and setbacks, which builds resilience.
>
> Straight-A students also miss out socially. More time studying in the library means less time to start lifelong friendships, join new clubs or volunteer. I know from experience. I didn't meet my 4.0 goal; I graduated with a 3.78. (This is the first time I've shared my G.P.A. since applying to graduate school 16 years ago. Really, no one cares.) Looking back, I don't wish my grades had been higher. If I could do it over again, I'd study less. The hours I wasted memorizing the inner workings of the eye would have been better spent trying out improv comedy and having more midnight conversations about the meaning of life.

Analyzing Language that Appeals to an Audience

As we've seen already, the audience and occasion of Grant's argument play a large role in the evidence he includes. In this section, we'll look closely at how the rhetorical situation influences his language choices. Knowing that he is writing in the *New York Times*, he adopts a formal tone throughout; it's not the casual or informal tone that he might use in other situations. Look, for example, at this excerpt from his *WorkLife* podcast when discussing why the Miami Heat, an NBA team, was successful:

> Shane filled a bunch of gaps in the team and the roles shifted and gelled. LeBron became the team's clear leader on the court. Wade and Bosh took on supporting roles and the Heat won back-to-back titles.

The phrase "bunch of gaps" and the word "gelled" are definitely more informal than anything Grant uses in his opinion piece. In addition to the more formal, serious tone he takes in this piece, he also tries to convey a sense of urgency and even outrage about the topic, keeping in mind that many of his readers will be parents of students struggling with anxiety. Also, Grant's educated audience is likely aware of some of the issues in education, especially what some see as excessive testing. Grant uses that common ground as a place to employ some very strong language connecting those concerns with his claim. For example, he derides the pressure of grades that causes students to "master cramming information and regurgitating it on exams." "Cramming" and "regurgitating" are emotionally charged word choices that likely resonate with his audience.

Analyzing Language Choices

Reread this section from Grant's piece and explain how the rhetorical situation may have affected some of his language choices. Then, discuss with a partner the effectiveness of those choices in persuading this particular audience.

> So universities: Make it easier for students to take some intellectual risks. Graduate schools can be clear that they don't care about the difference between a 3.7 and a 3.9. Colleges could just report letter grades without pluses and minuses, so that any G.P.A. above a 3.7 appears on transcripts as an A. It might also help to stop the madness of grade inflation, which creates an academic arms race that encourages too many students to strive for meaningless perfection. And why not let students wait until the end of the semester to declare a class pass-fail, instead of forcing them to decide in the first month?

culminating activity

Read the following speech delivered by former First Lady Barbara Bush at the graduation ceremony of Wellesley College on June 1, 1990. Write a brief analysis of how the rhetorical situation (see the description that follows) may have influenced the content of her speech. Be sure to consider the evidence she chooses to include as well as the language choices she makes.

Graduation Speech, Wellesley College, 1990

Barbara Bush

At the time of the speech, Barbara Bush was the First Lady, married to President George H. W. Bush, who was in the midst of his reelection campaign. Her primary audience was the graduates of Wellesley College, a small, private, women-only liberal arts college in Massachusetts with a long list of notable graduates: Hillary Rodham Clinton, Madeleine Albright, Cokie Roberts, Diane Sawyer, Nora Ephron, Marjory Stoneman Douglas, and many others. In terms of the occasion, 1990 was a time of significant historical and cultural changes. For example, more women were entering the workforce and enrolling in college than ever before, signaling a shift toward greater gender balance in society.

I am really thrilled to be here today. . . . These are exciting times. They're exciting in Washington, and I have really looked forward to coming to Wellesley. I thought it was going to be fun. I never dreamt it would be this much fun. So, thank you for that.

More than ten years ago, when I was invited here to talk about our experiences in the People's Republic of China, I was struck by both the natural beauty of your campus and the spirit of this place.

Wellesley, you see, is not just a place but an idea — an experiment in excellence in which diversity is not just tolerated, but is embraced. The essence of this spirit was captured in a moving speech about tolerance given last year by a student body president of one of your sister colleges. She related the story by Robert Fulghum about a young pastor [who], finding himself in charge of some very energetic children, hits upon the game called "Giants, Wizards, and Dwarfs." "You have to decide now," the pastor instructed the children, "which you are — a giant, a wizard, or a dwarf?" At that, a small girl tugging at his pants leg, asked, "But where do the mermaids stand?" And the pastor tells her there are no mermaids. And she says, "Oh yes there are. I am a mermaid."

Now this little girl knew what she was, and she was not about to give up on either her identity, or the game. She intended to take her place wherever mermaids fit into the scheme of things. "Where do the mermaids stand? All of those who are different, those who do not fit the boxes and the pigeonholes?" "Answer that question," wrote Fulghum, "and you can build a school, a nation, or a whole world." As that very wise young woman said, "Diversity, like anything worth having, requires effort" — effort to learn about and respect difference, to be compassionate with one another, to cherish our own identity, and to accept unconditionally the same in others.

You should all be very proud that this is the Wellesley spirit. Now I know your first choice today was Alice Walker — guess how I know! — known for *The Color Purple*. Instead you got me — known for the color of my hair. Alice Walker's book has a special resonance here. At Wellesley, each class is known by a special color. For four years the Class of 1990 has worn the color purple. Today you meet on Severance Green to say goodbye to all of that, to begin a new and a very personal journey, to search for your own true colors.

In the world that awaits you, beyond the shores of Waban — Lake Waban, no one can say what your true colors will be. But this I do know: You have a first-class education from a first-class school. And so you need not, probably cannot, live a "paint-by-numbers" life. Decisions are not irrevocable. Choices do come back. And as you set off from Wellesley, I hope that many of you will consider making three very special choices.

The first is to believe in something larger than yourself, to get involved in some of the big ideas of our time. I chose literacy because I honestly believe that if more people could read, write, and comprehend, we would be that much closer to solving so many of the problems that plague our nation and our society.

And early on I made another choice, which I hope you'll make as well. Whether you are talking about education, career, or service, you're talking about life — and life really must have joy. It's supposed to be fun.

One of the reasons I made the most important decision of my life, to marry George Bush, is because he made me laugh. It's true, sometimes we've laughed through our tears, but that shared laughter has been one of our strongest bonds. Find the joy in life, because as Ferris Bueller[1] said on his day off, "Life moves pretty fast; and if you don't stop and look around once in a while, you're going to miss it."

(I'm not going to tell George you clapped more for Ferris than you clapped for George.)

The third choice that must not be missed is to cherish your human connections: your relationships with family and friends. For several years, you've had impressed upon you the importance to your career of dedication and hard work. And, of course, that's true. But as important as your obligations as a doctor, a lawyer, a business leader will be, you are a human being first. And those human connections — with spouses, with children, with friends — are the most important investments you will ever make.

At the end of your life, you will never regret not having passed one more test, winning one more verdict, or not closing one more deal. You will regret time not spent with a husband, a child, a friend, or a parent.

We are in a transitional period right now — fascinating and exhilarating times, learning to adjust to changes and the choices we, men and women, are facing. As an example, I remember what a friend said, on hearing her husband complain to his buddies that he had to babysit. Quickly setting him straight, my friend told her husband that when it's your own kids, it's *not* called babysitting.

Now maybe we should adjust faster; maybe we should adjust slower. But whatever the era, whatever the times, one thing will never change: fathers and mothers, if you have children, they must come first. You must read to your children, and you must hug

[1]The lead character in a 1988 comedy entitled *Ferris Bueller's Day Off.* The film centers on his adventures when he decides to skip high school for a day. — Eds.

your children, and you must love your children. Your success as a family, our success as a society, depends not on what happens in the White House, but on what happens inside your house.

For over fifty years, it was said that the winner of Wellesley's annual hoop race would be the first to get married. Now they say, the winner will be the first to become a C.E.O. Both of those stereotypes show too little tolerance for those who want to know where the mermaids stand. So I want to offer a new legend: the winner of the hoop race will be the first to realize her dream — not society's dreams — her own personal dream.

And who knows? Somewhere out in this audience may even be someone who will one day follow in my footsteps, and preside over the White House as the President's spouse — and I wish him well.

Well, the controversy ends here. But our conversation is only beginning. And a worthwhile conversation it has been. . . .

Thank you. God bless you. And may your future be worthy of your dreams.

section one

from Children Educate Themselves: Lessons from Sudbury Valley

Courtesy of Peter Gray

Peter Gray

Peter Gray, research professor at Boston College, is the author of *Psychology*, a college textbook. He completed his undergraduate study at Columbia University and earned his doctoral degree at Rockefeller University. He is the president of the nonprofit Alliance for Self-Directed Education. Gray's areas of specialization are children's natural ways of learning and the value of play in lifelong learning.

KEY CONTEXT Gray composed the following blog post for *Psychology Today* as an argument for the value of the philosophy of The Sudbury Valley School. Located in Framingham, Massachusetts, for nearly 50 years, the school is an alternative to more institutionalized schooling. Its founding principle is "Children educate themselves; we don't have to do it for them."

For many years I have had the opportunity to observe the Sudbury Valley School, both as the father of a student who went there and as an academician using the school as a resource to study play and self-directed learning. Here I'll tell you a little about the school.

First, a few mundane facts. The school was founded 40 years ago and has been in continuous operation since then. It is a private day school, in Framingham, Massachusetts, open to students age four on through high-school age. The school is not in any sense elitist. It admits students without regard to any measures of academic performance, and it operates at a per pupil cost that is about half that of the surrounding public schools. The school currently has about 200 students and ten adult staff members. It is housed in a Victorian mansion and a remodeled barn, which sit on ten acres of land in a part of town that was largely rural when the school began operating. Now, the more remarkable facts concerning the school's mode of operation:

The School Operates as a Participatory Democracy

The Sudbury Valley School is first and foremost a community in which children and adolescents experience directly the privileges and responsibilities of democratic government. The

Riitta Supperi/Photo Agency Keksi/Finland Image Bank

This image of a teacher and students in Finland appeared as part of an article entitled "Let the Children Play: The Secret to Finnish Education." The article focuses on the fact that Finland's students score at the top of international exams measuring achievement. **How would Gray interpret this photo as evidence that meaningful learning is — or is not — occurring?**

primary administrative body is the School Meeting, which consists of all students and staff members. In one-person-one-vote fashion, the School Meeting, which meets once a week, creates all of the school's rules, makes decisions about school purchases, establishes committees to oversee the school's day-to-day operation, and *hires and fires staff members*. Four-year-olds at the school have the same vote as do older students and adult staff members in all of this. No staff members at the school have tenure. All are on one-year contracts, which must be renewed each year through a secret-ballot election. As the student voters outnumber the staff by a factor of 20 to 1, the staff who survive this process and are re-elected year after year are those who are admired by the students. They are people who are kind, ethical, and competent, and who contribute significantly and positively to the school's environment. They are adults that the students may wish in some ways to emulate.

The school's rules are enforced by the Judicial Committee, which changes regularly in membership but always includes a staff member and students representing the full range of ages at the school. When a student or staff member is charged by another school member with violating a rule, the accuser and the accused must appear before the Judicial Committee, which determines innocence or guilt and, in the latter case, decides on an appropriate sentence. In all of this, staff members are treated in the same way as students. Nobody is above the law.

None of the school's rules have to do with 5
learning. The school gives no tests. It does not evaluate or grade students' progress.[1] There is no curriculum and no attempt to motivate students to learn. Courses occur only when students take the initiative to organize them, and they last only as long as the students want them. Many students at the school never join a course, and the school sees no problem with that. The staff members at the school do not consider themselves to be teachers. They are, instead, adult members of the community who provide a wide variety of services, including some teaching. Most of their "teaching" is of the same variety as can be found in any human setting; it involves answering sincere questions and presenting ideas in the context of real conversations.

---

[1]There is one exception to the statement that the school does not evaluate students. Students who wish to graduate with a high school diploma must prepare a written thesis defending the statement that they have prepared themselves for responsible adult life. That thesis is defended orally and evaluated by a panel of adults who are staff members at other Sudbury-model schools.

The School Is a Rich Environment for Play and Exploration, and Therefore for Learning

Learning at Sudbury Valley is largely incidental. It occurs as a side effect of students' self-directed play and exploration. The school is a wonderful place to play and explore. It provides space and time for such activities. It also provides equipment — including computers, a fully equipped kitchen, a woodworking shop, an art room, playground equipment, toys and games of various sorts, and many books. Students also have access to a pond, a field, and a nearby forest for outdoor play and exploration. Those who develop a special interest, which needs some new piece of equipment, might convince the School Meeting to buy it, or they might raise the money and buy it themselves by some means such as selling cookies in the school.

The most important resource at the school, for most students, is other students, who among them manifest an enormous range of interests and abilities. Because of the free age mixing at the school, students are exposed regularly to the activities and ideas of others who are older and younger than themselves. Age-mixed play offers younger children continuous opportunities to learn from older ones. For example, many students at the school have learned to read as a side effect of playing games that involve written words (including computer games) with students who already know how to read. They learn to read without even being aware that they are doing so.

Much of the students' exploration at the school, especially that of the adolescents, takes place through conversations. Students talk about everything imaginable, with each other and with staff members, and through such talk they are exposed to a huge range of ideas and arguments. Because nobody is an official authority, everything that is said and heard in conversation is understood as something to think about, not as dogma to memorize or feedback on a test. Conversation, unlike memorizing material for a test, stimulates the intellect. The great Russian psychologist Lev Vygotsky argued, long ago, that conversation is the foundation for higher thought; and my observations of students at Sudbury Valley convince me that he was right. Thought is internalized conversation; external conversation, with other people, gets it started.

Hundreds of Graduates Attest to the School's Educational Effectiveness

My own first study of the Sudbury Valley School, many years ago, was a follow-up study of the graduates. Since that time, the school itself has conducted several studies of graduates, which have been published as books. All of these studies have shown that the school works well as an educational institution.

Graduates of Sudbury Valley can be found 10
today in the whole range of careers that are valued by our society. They are skilled craftsmen, entrepreneurs, artists, musicians, scientists, social workers, nurses, doctors, and so on. Those who chose to pursue higher education had no particular difficulties getting into colleges and universities, including highly selective ones, or performing well there once admitted. Many others have become successful in careers without going to college. More important, former students report that they are happy with their lives. They are almost unanimous in reporting that they are glad that they attended Sudbury Valley and in believing that the school prepared them better than a traditional school would have for the realities of adult existence. To a considerable degree they maintain, in adulthood, the playful (and that means focused and intense as well as joyful) attitude to careers and life that they developed and refined while at the school. . . . ■

extending beyond the text

In "Would You Send Your Kids to a School Where Students Make the Rules?" (The *New Republic*, 2014), journalist Mark Oppenheimer describes his experience as a parent visiting the Sudbury Valley School as an alternative to public school for one of his children. Following is his exchange with a 16-year-old-student in response to Oppenheimer's question of who Martin Luther King Jr. was.

from **Would You Send Your Kids to a School Where Students Make the Rules?**

Mark Oppenheimer

"A politician?" [the boy] said.

"Sort of," I answered. "Do you know if he was black or white?"

"Black."

"Yes," I said. "Do you know what decade he died?"

The boy paused. "No," he said.

And I got the feeling that he didn't even know close to what decade. I could have said the 1920s, and he would have believed me.

What is this conversation with the student supposed to reveal about Sudbury's approach to curriculum? What does its inclusion suggest about Oppenheimer's attitude toward Sudbury? How important do you think it is that everyone can answer the questions Oppenheimer asked the boy?

Understanding and Interpreting

1. Peter Gray says that the Sudbury Valley School "is first and foremost a community in which children and adolescents experience directly the privileges and responsibilities of democratic government" (par. 3). Identify and explain the key ideas in that sentence. To what extent do you find them surprising?
2. Gray tells his readers that four-year-olds have the same voting privileges as do older students and adults at the school. What benefits might result from this policy? What problems might occur?
3. What does Gray mean when he writes, "None of the school's rules have to do with learning" (par. 5)? Is Gray being literal or exaggerating for effect? Are the rules not about learning at all, or only in an indirect way? What *do* the rules have to do with, if not learning?
4. Respond to this statement: "The most important resource at the school, for most students, is other students" (par. 7). What evidence does Gray provide to support this statement? Does his statement devalue the experience, expertise, and training of teachers and school staff? Explain your response.
5. In the final paragraph, Gray provides evidence to support his claim that "the school works well as an educational institution" (par. 9). How effective do you find that evidence? Explain with specific references to the text. What additional evidence might add strength to the claim?

Analyzing Language, Style, and Structure

1. **Vocabulary in Context.** What does "conversation" mean in the context of Gray's writing (par. 8)? In what ways is "conversation," as it is used here, different from talking or discussion?
2. **Skill Focus.** The nationally respected magazine *Psychology Today,* which has a circulation of approximately 250,000, includes both research-based articles plus those of more general interest. In what specific ways does Gray appeal to both the general readership of this publication — those with no expertise or professional stake in psychology — as well as those readers with some background in psychology?
3. Gray begins his writing by establishing his ethos on two fronts. What are those two fronts? Does he seem to regard them as equal, or does one seem to be more important to him than the other. How do you know?
4. Gray divides his introduction into "a few mundane facts" and "the more remarkable facts" about the Sudbury Valley School. What is the distinction he is drawing? How does he encourage the reader to share his understanding of the difference?
5. Throughout the article, Gray refers to the importance of allowing students to "explore" and the role of "exploration" in their educational development. What exactly do you think he means by "explore"? Is he referring to freedom? Independent trial and error? Play?
6. At the Sudbury Valley School, Gray says that student voters outnumber staff 20 to 1, and that the staff members who are "re-elected year after year are those who are admired by the students" (par. 3). In addition to its more common meaning of being looked up to with high regard, the verb "admire" also means "to look at with wonder and pleasure." In what ways do you think this second meaning of "admire" is what the Sudbury Valley School expects of its staff? Explain with specific reference to the text.
7. According to Gray, "nobody [at the school] is an official authority[;] everything that is said and heard in conversation is understood as something to think about, not as dogma to memorize or feedback on a test" (par. 8). Carefully consider the language in this statement. What connotations does Gray bring with the words "authority," "conversation," "dogma," "memorize," and "test"? What values does he privilege with his choice of words, his diction?

Topics for Composing

1. **Analysis.** What assumptions and beliefs about age and experience does the Sudbury Valley School make? Base your response on the policies and procedures that define the school.
2. **Argument.** Is the Sudbury Valley School a utopian experiment that works only on a small group of students, or is it a concept that could be implemented on a larger scale in public schools in the United States? Explain your position and support it with evidence from the article itself as well as your own experience and knowledge.
3. **Connection.** Identify one characteristic or practice of the Sudbury Valley School that you believe could be implemented in your school setting to improve the learning environment. Acknowledge obstacles that might be encountered, and explain why you believe the change would nevertheless be beneficial.
4. **Speaking and Listening.** According to Gray, at the Sudbury Valley School, four-year-olds "have the same vote as do older students and adult staff members" (par. 3). In what ways

could you use this positive experience to argue that the voting age should be lowered for all citizens to middle school or even elementary school age? On the other hand, how might you use the voting analogy to argue against the school's policy? Present your position in a speech to your classmates.

5. **Research.** The Sudbury Valley School inspired a model of democratic learning that has been embraced by other schools around the world. Research one of these schools (such as the Hudson Valley Sudbury School) to better understand their philosophy of learning. You might also consult Gray's study published in the *American Journal of Education* (volume 94, pp. 182–213). What particularly interests you about the school you researched? Did you change any of your ideas about the appeal or value of the Sudbury model?
6. **Research.** Gray calls on the ground-breaking work of the Russian psychologist Lev Vygotsky who "argued long ago that conversation is the foundation for higher thought" (par. 8). Research the educational philosophy of Vygotsky on the idea of thought as "internalized conversation." In what ways do you see the work of Vygotsky reflected directly or indirectly in the philosophy behind the Sudbury Valley School?

A Message from a Black Mom to Her Son

Dyan Watson

Dyan Watson is a professor in the Graduate School of Education and Counseling at Lewis & Clark College in Portland, Oregon. Her letter was published in *Rethinking Schools*, a magazine that features articles about social justice teaching and educational policy.

Dear Caleb,

When you were almost 2, we would drop off your cousin, Sydney, at her K-8 elementary school. The ritual went something like this:

“OK, Syd, have a good day.”

“OK,” she’d groan as she grabbed her backpack. “Bye, Caleb.”

5 “Bye,” you’d wave and grin with your entire body.

“Bye,” Sydney would say one last time as she shut the door. I’d roll down the car window.

“Byeeeee,” you’d sing.

“Bye,” Sydney would laugh as she caught up with friends.

I’d roll up the window as you said “bye” a few more times, then start to whimper. “It’s OK, sweetie, she’ll be back before you know it. And you’ll be off joining her before I know it.”

10 And it’s true. Before I know it, Caleb, you will be throwing your backpack on and waving goodbye as you run off across the playground. I think about that moment often and wonder about the condition of schools you’ll enter. I worry about sending you, my black son, to schools that over-enroll black boys into special ed, criminalize them at younger and younger ages, and view them as negative statistics on the dark side of the achievement gap.

Son, my hope for you is that your schooling experiences will be better than this, that they’ll be better than most of mine.

For three years of my K-8 schooling, from 7:40 a.m. until 3:05 p.m., I was black and invisible. I was bused across town to integrate a white school in Southeast Portland, Ore. We arrived at school promptly at 7:30 and had 10 full minutes before the white children arrived.

Weekend Breakfast, 2003 (w/c on paper)/Bootman, Colin/COLIN BOOTMAN/ Private Collection/Bridgeman Images

Colin Bootman's painting *Weekend Breakfast, 2003*, depicts a family's close connection over a shared meal.

What do the gestures and expressions of the people depicted tell you about their family dynamic? How does this image capture the sense of family that Watson experienced herself and that she hopes Caleb's teachers will recognize that he has?

We spent that time roaming the halls — happy, free, normal. Once the white children arrived, we became black and invisible. We were separated, so that no more than two of us were in a class at a time. I never saw black people in our textbooks unless they were in shackles or standing with Martin Luther King Jr. Most of us rarely interacted with a black adult outside of the aide who rode the bus with us. I liked school and I loved learning. But I never quite felt right or good. I felt very black and obvious because I knew that my experience was different from that of my peers. But I also felt invisible because this was never acknowledged in any meaningful way. I became visible again at 3:05 when I got back on the bus with the other brown faces to make our journey home.

Caleb, I want your teachers to help you love being in your skin. I want them to make space for you in their curricula, so that you see yourself as integral to this country's history, to your classroom's community, to your peers' learning. I want your teachers to select materials where blacks are portrayed in ordinary and extraordinary ways that actively challenge stereotypes and biases. Most of all, Caleb, I want your teachers to know you so they can help you grow.

One day a teacher was trying to figure out why I was so angry since I was generally a calm, fun-loving kid. She said to me: "I know you, Dyan. You come from a good family." But did she know me? She knew that I lived on the other side of town and was bused in as part of the distorted way that Portland school authorities decided to "integrate" the schools. But did she know what that meant? My mom — your grandma — got us up at 6 a.m. in order for me to wash up, boil an egg just right, fix my toast the way I liked it, and watch the pan of milk so that it didn't boil over, so I could have something hot in my stomach before going to school. You know Grandma, she doesn't play. We had to eat a healthy breakfast before going to school, and we had to fix it ourselves. Maybe that's what that teacher meant by "good family." My teacher didn't know that we had to walk, by ourselves, four blocks to the bus stop and wait for the yellow bus to come pick us up and take us to school. It took us a half hour to get to school. Once there, I had to constantly code switch, learn how not to be overly black, and be better than my white counterparts.

Caleb, I want your teachers to know your journey to school — metaphorically and physically. I want them to see you and all of your peers as children from good families. I don't want you to have to earn credit because of whom you're related to or what your parents do for a living. And I don't want your teachers to think that you're special because you're black and have a family that cares about you and is involved in your life. I want them to know that all children are part of families — traditional or not — that help shape and form who they are.

The summer before beginning 4th grade, I started teaching myself how to play the clarinet. It was the family instrument in that both of my older sisters played it when they were younger. For years I wanted to be a musician. It was in my blood. My grandfather was a musician, all of my uncles can sing very well, and my dad — your grandfather — was a famous DJ in Jamaica once upon a time. At the end of 5th grade, my band director took each member aside to provide feedback on whether or not she or he should continue music in middle school. My teacher told me that I just didn't have it and should quit. I was devastated. I had dreams of becoming a conductor and I loved playing music. I learned to read music and text at the same time before entering kindergarten, so I couldn't understand what my teacher saw or heard that made him think that I, at the tender age of 11, didn't have what it took to pursue playing in a middle school band. He knew nothing about me. Had never asked any questions about me, our family, my aspirations. He didn't seek to make me a better musician.

Caleb, I hope that you will have teachers who realize they are gatekeepers. I hope they understand the power they hold and work to discover your talents, seek out your dreams and fan them, rather than smother them. I hope they will see you as part of a family, with gifts and rich histories that have been passed down to you. I hope they will strive to know you even when they think they already know you. I hope your teachers will approach you with humility and stay curious about who you are.

When I was in 4th grade, my elementary school held a back-to-school night that

In this painting called *The Library* (1960), African American artist Jacob Lawrence pays tribute to the institutions, such as libraries and museums, where he learned about African American history and culture at a time when most schools rarely addressed either. **What draws your eye in this image? Why? What overall impression does it convey about the library? How might Lawrence's depiction of this space, the public library, support Watson's hope for Caleb: "I want your teachers to select materials where blacks are portrayed in ordinary and extraordinary ways that actively challenge stereotypes and biases"?**

extending beyond the text

In 2019, the *New York Times* featured an article on Stuyvesant High School, one of the most highly selective public schools in New York City. Out of 895 slots in the freshman class, only seven were offered to black students. The article examined admissions by race for eight of these elite public schools. Students compete for admission to these schools on a single high-stakes exam that tests their mastery of math and English. Following are graphs depicting the offers of admission by race to three of the schools.

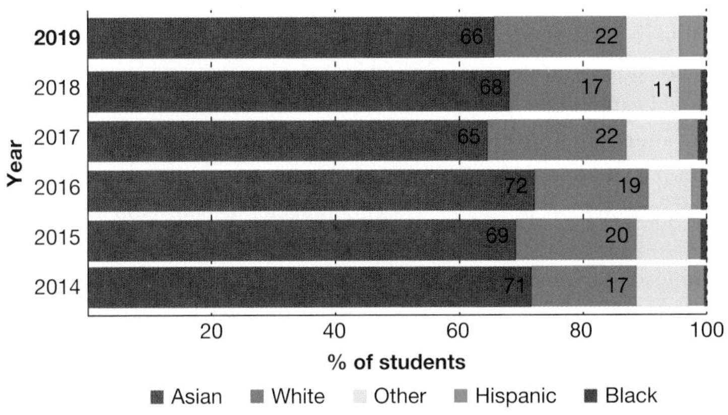

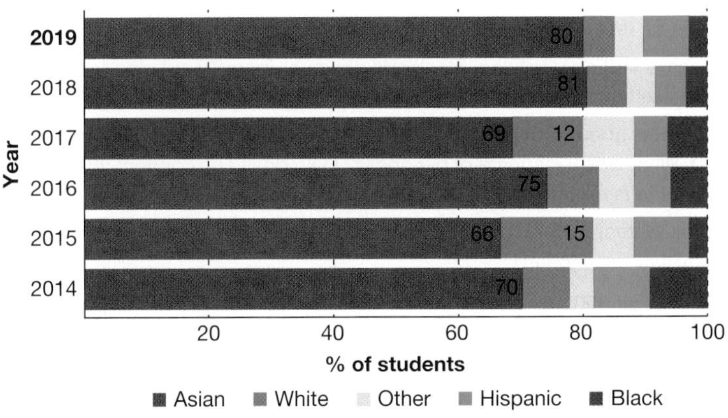

What strikes you most dramatically about the data in these graphs? What trends do you notice? Are those trends the same at both? What advice would you give to New York City to increase diversity in these selective schools? How would Watson respond to this data?

featured student work and allowed families to walk the halls and speak with teachers. In each classroom was a student leader, chosen by teachers. I'm not sure what my role was supposed to be. But at one point, a couple came in, desiring to speak with Mrs. S. She was busy, so I thought I'd chat with them while they waited. As I approached them, they recoiled in fear and, with panicked looks, turned away from me and said, "Mrs. S.?" My teacher looked away from the folks she was working with and said, "It's OK, she's not like the rest." I don't remember what happened next. All I remember is that this seemed to be one of the first in a long line of reassurances that I was special and not like other black boys and girls. For many years afterward, I was told on more than one occasion, "You're not like other blacks." This was supposed to be a compliment.

Caleb, I pray that your teachers will not look at you through hurtful racial preconceptions. I pray that they will do the work necessary to eliminate racist practices in themselves and in those around them. I pray that they stand up for you in ways that leave you feeling strong and capable. I pray that they will nurture your spirit, and that you, in turn, will desire to be a better you.

20 Son, I end this letter by sharing a story that Grandma has told me many times, that I hope will one day resonate with you. On the first day of kindergarten, many of the kids were crying and clinging to their parents. But not me. I was ready! I wanted to be like my three older siblings and go to school. So I gave my mom a hug, let go of her hand, waved goodbye, and found my teacher. And remember how I told you that my oldest sister taught me how to read before I went to school? The teacher found this out and used this skill, along with my desire to be at school, to teach the other kids the alphabet and help them learn how to read. I believe, in part, that is why I became a teacher. She saw something in me and encouraged me to develop my passion — even at this young, sweet age.

That, my son, is my hope for you. I hope your teachers will love you for who you are and the promise of what you'll be.

Love,
Mama ■

Understanding and Interpreting

1. What specific fears does Dyan Watson express about the way her son will be treated in school?
2. Watson says that she "felt very black and obvious" (par. 12) but also "invisible." How does she explain these two seemingly contradictory experiences?
3. Watson writes about a time when her teacher "was trying to figure out why I was so angry" (par. 14). What was the source of her anger? How does she connect this experience of hers with what she is telling her son?
4. How does Watson define "a good family" (par. 14) in contrast to what she believes her teacher meant by that description?
5. Watson tells her son that she hopes he will have teachers "who realize they are gatekeepers" (par. 17) who hold "power." What kind of power does she believe that teachers hold? To what extent do you think that Caleb's teachers will hold the same kind or level of "power" that his mother's teachers had?
6. What does Watson mean when she says that her teachers pointed her out as not being "'like other blacks'" (par. 18)? What criticism does she imply with the statement, "This was supposed to be a compliment"?

7. How does Watson characterize her own family — her parents and siblings? Why does she spend time explaining this background?
8. What does Watson mean when she claims that few of her teachers "knew" her and that her hope is Caleb's teachers will "know" him?
9. Overall, what is the most important experience in school that Watson wants for Caleb? As you formulate your response, consider what kind of person Watson wants her son to become and how school could contribute to or work against that development.

Analyzing Language, Style, and Structure

1. **Vocabulary in Context.** Watson tells Caleb, "I hope your teachers will approach you with humility and stay curious about who you are" (par. 17). What does Watson mean in this context of a teacher, an adult in a position of authority, approaching a young student "with humility"? Is this an effective word choice? Why or why not?
2. **Skill Focus.** Consider Watson's rhetorical situation. As a mother, she writes a letter to her young son about to enter school. She publishes it in the public forum of a magazine that identifies her as a college professor. Does she appeal equally to both her private audience (her son) and public audience (magazine readers)? Or does her piece seem intended for one audience more than the other?
3. What is the purpose of the story that Watson relates at the start of her letter? How does the dialogue contribute to its effectiveness?
4. Watson opens paragraph 12 with the topic sentence, "For three years of my K-8 schooling, from 7:40 a.m. until 3:05 p.m., I was black and invisible." How does she develop and support that claim with specific details in the remainder of the paragraph?
5. Watson tells Caleb that she wants his teachers to "help you love being in your skin" (par. 13). In what ways is she using the word "skin" literally, metaphorically, or both?
6. Watson spends much of the letter recounting her own experiences in elementary school. Why? Are those stories likely to be effective in reaching her son Caleb or readers of the magazine in which her letter was published? Explain her reasoning in your response.
7. Watson writes about several negative experiences. Does one stand out as being particularly hurtful to her, perhaps even the source of bitterness? Cite specific textual evidence to support your claim.
8. Watson ends with a positive experience that was so memorable that she thinks it might have instilled in her the desire to become a teacher. Why does she save this story for the end? How might the effect have been different if she had started with that incident?
9. At different points, Watson opens several sentences by repeating, "I hope"; then she shifts to "I pray." What is the effect of this repetition and then change in word choice?
10. What elements of this letter give it a heartfelt, loving tone? Consider the personal experiences Watson relates, the language she uses, and the examples she cites.

Topics for Composing

1. **Analysis.** Examine Watson's descriptions of her own experiences in school. How do these experiences shape what she wants for her son? What protection does she hope to provide for him?
2. **Argument.** Watson does not make a case for specific educational goals that are tied to curriculum, such as proficiency in math. Instead, she argues that a teacher's responsibility is

to support growth and "nurture [the] spirit" (par. 19) to "fan" and not "smother" a student's dreams (par. 17). Write an argument that agrees with, disagrees with, or qualifies Watson's definition of a teacher's responsibility.

3. **Connection.** Although you may not have written many letters in the old-fashioned sense, you have plenty of experience with written communication in the form of e-mails and texts. Using the letter Watson writes to her son as a model, compose a letter (or an e-mail) to a younger person, offering advice. Choose a real person in your life. He or she can be a relative, a close friend, or someone who's new to your school, neighborhood, or team, for example. The important element is that you're the experienced person advising someone less experienced. Don't worry about a larger audience in your letter. Just focus on an individual and how best to deliver advice that will be helpful.
4. **Speaking and Listening.** In paragraph 16, Watson discusses a moment in which her 4th grade band director shuts down her musical aspirations by saying she just "didn't have it." Talk in a group about a time when a teacher's positive or negative feedback on your work helped shape your view of your own abilities. Why do you think that moment has stuck with you? How did you respond to the feedback publicly or privately, externally or internally? What does the experience and your reaction to it then and now tell you about the degree of influence teachers have on students?
5. **Research.** A number of other countries — for example, China, Hong Kong, Finland — have outpaced the United States as measured by standardized testing in reading, math, and science. Choose a country that has stronger achievement levels and research the status and training of their teachers and the teaching methods that prevail. Do you think Watson would believe that the educational practices of these other countries are actually superior to those in the United States, based on test results? If so, in what specific ways?
6. **Multimodal.** "Invisibility" is central to Watson's concern and her argument. Explore this concept by combining text, visuals, and other elements to create a poster or digital piece that raises questions about what it means to be "invisible."

Don't Peak in High School

Mindy Kaling

James Veysey/Shutterstock

Mindy Kaling (b. 1979) is an actress, a writer, a producer, and a director. From 2005 to 2012, she played Kelly Kapoor in the sitcom *The Office*. She then created and starred in *The Mindy Project* (2012), which ran for six seasons, and the Netflix series *Never Have I Ever* (2020). Kaling is the author of two *New York Times* best-selling memoirs, *Is Everyone Hanging Out Without Me? (And Other Concerns)* (2012) and *Why Not Me?* (2016). "Don't Peak in High School" is a chapter in *Is Everyone Hanging Out Without Me*?

Sometimes teenage girls ask me for advice about what they should be doing if they want a career like mine one day. There are basically two ways to get where I am: (1) learn a provocative dance and put it on YouTube; (2) convince your parents to move to Orlando and homeschool you until you get cast on a kids' show, *or* do what I did, which is (3) stay in school and be a respectful and hardworking wallflower, and go to an accredited non-online university.

Teenage girls, please don't worry about being super popular in high school, or being the best actress in high school, or the best athlete. Not only do people not care about any of that the second you graduate, but when you get older, if you reference your successes in high school too much, it actually makes you look kind of pitiful, like some babbling old Tennessee Williams[1] character with nothing else going on in her current life. What I've noticed is that almost no one who was a big star in high school is also a big star later in life. For us overlooked kids, it's so wonderfully *fair*.

I was never the lead in the play. I don't think I went to a single party with alcohol at it. No one offered me pot. It wasn't until I was sixteen that I even knew marijuana and pot were the same thing. I didn't even learn this from a cool friend; I gleaned it from a syndicated episode of *21 Jump Street*[2]. My parents didn't let me do social things on weeknights because weeknights were for homework, and *maybe* an episode of *The X-Files*[3] if I was being a good kid (*X-Files* was on Friday night), and on extremely rare occasions I could watch *Seinfeld*[4] (Thursday, a school night), if I had just aced my PSATs or something.

It is easy to freak out as a sensitive teenager. I always felt I was missing out because of the way the high school experience was dramatized in television and song. For every realistic *My So-Called Life*[5], there were ten *90210*s[6] or *Party of Fives*[7], where a twenty-something Luke Perry was supposed to be just a typical guy at your high school. If Luke Perry had gone to my high school, everybody would have thought, "What's the deal with this brooding greaser? Is he a narc?" But that's who Hollywood put forth as "just a dude at your high school."

5 In the genre of "making you feel like you're not having an awesome American high school experience," the worst offender is actually a song: John Cougar Mellencamp's "Jack and Diane."[8] It's one of those songs — like Eric Clapton's "Tears in Heaven"[9] — that everyone knows all the words to without ever having chosen to learn them. I've seen people get incredibly pumped when this song comes on; I once witnessed a couple request it four times in a row at Johnny Rockets[10] and belt it while loudly clapping their hands above their heads, so apparently it is an anthem of some people's youth. I think across America, as I type this, there are high school couples who strive to be like Jack and Diane from that song. Just hangin' out after school, makin' out at the Tastee Freez, sneakin' beers into their cars, without a care in the world. Just two popular, idle, all-American white kids, having a blast.

The world created in "Jack and Diane" is maybe okay-charming because, like, all right, that kid Jack is going to get shipped off to Vietnam and there was going to be a whole part

---

[1]Kaling is referring to the character Blanche DuBois, an aging southern belle with a fragile hold on reality in Tennessee Williams' play A *Streetcar Named Desire*. — Eds.

[2]Television police procedural (1987–1991) starring Johnny Depp. — Eds.

[3]Long-running science fiction television series (1993–2018) starring David Duchovny and Gillian Anderson as FBI agents assigned to investigate unexplained phenomena. — Eds.

[4]Comedy television series (1989–1998) created by Jerry Seinfeld and Larry David that chronicles the everyday lives of a group of friends in New York City. — Eds.

[5]Teen drama (1994–1995) starring Claire Danes that was a cult hit and highly critically praised. — Eds.

[6]Long-running teen drama series from the 1990s that follows a group of friends through high school and into early adulthood. — Eds.

[7]1990s television series about five siblings forced to live on their own following the death of their parents. —Eds.

[8]1982 hit song written and performed by John Cougar Mellencamp, inspired by the 1962 film *Sweet Bird of Youth*. — Eds.

[9]1992 song written and performed by Eric Clapton following the death of his son, Conor. — Eds.

[10]American restaurant franchise with 1950s theme and décor. — Eds.

Students at a High School Getting Out for the Day, 1951.

How would you describe the people in this image — their clothing, gestures, posture, and placement? What about the school itself and buses lined up in front? What do you think Mindy Kaling might say about whether this image illustrates the aphorism, "The more things change, the more they stay the same"?

two of the story when he returned as some traumatized, disillusioned vet. The song is only interesting to me as the dreamy first act to a much more interesting *Born on the Fourth of July*-type story[11].

As it is, I guess I find "Jack and Diane" a little disgusting.

As a child of immigrant professionals, I can't help but notice the wasteful frivolity of it all. Why are these kids not home doing their homework? Why aren't they setting the table for dinner or helping out around the house? Who allows their kids to hang out in parking lots? Isn't that loitering?

I wish there was a song called "Nguyen and Ari," a little ditty about a hardworking Vietnamese girl who helps her parents with the franchised Holiday Inn they run, and does homework in the lobby, and Ari, a hardworking Jewish boy who does volunteer work at his grandmother's old-age home, and they meet after school at Princeton Review. They help each other study for the SATs and different AP courses, and then, after months of studying, and mountains of flashcards, they kiss chastely upon hearing the news that they both got into their top college choices. This is a song teens need to inadvertently memorize. Now that's a song I'd request at Johnny Rockets!

In high school, I had fun in my academic 10
clubs, watching movies with my girlfriends, learning Latin, having long, protracted, unrequited crushes on older guys who didn't know me, and yes, hanging out with my family. I liked hanging out with my family! Later, when you're grown up, you realize you never get to hang out with your family. Yon pretty much have only eighteen years to spend with them full time, and that's it. So, yeah, it all added up to a happy, memorable time. Even though I was never a star.

---

[11] 1989 Oliver Stone film in which Tom Cruise plays a Vietnam War veteran who accidentally killed a fellow soldier during his second tour of duty, and whose own wartime injuries led to permanent paralysis. — Eds.

extending beyond the text

In the 2019 film *Book Smart*, Molly and Amy are academic stars and best friends who are about to leave for their coveted Ivy League colleges. When they decide that they have missed out on the fun that their high school peers — classmates who earned good grades without following all the rules — enjoyed, they embark on a one-night mission to make up for lost time.

MOLLY We chose. We didn't party because we wanted to focus on school and get into good colleges.

AMY And it worked.

MOLLY But the irresponsible people who partied also got into those colleges, they did both.

AMY So?

MOLLY So we messed up. We didn't have to choose. They did both. . . . Amy, we only have one night left to have studied and partied in high school. Otherwise, we're just gonna be the girls that missed out. We haven't done anything. We haven't broken any rules.

AMY Okay, we've broken a lot of rules. One, we have fake IDs.

MOLLY Fake college IDs, so we can get into their 24-hour library.

AMY Name one person whose life was so much better — because they broke a couple of rules.

MOLLY Picasso.

AMY Yes, he broke art rules. Name a person who broke a real one.

MOLLY Rosa Parks.

AMY Name another.

MOLLY Susan B. Anthony. . . .

MOLLY Amy, I'm so serious. They think that we're robots. . . .
Nobody knows that we are fun. . . .
We are not one-dimensional. We are smart and fun.

To what extent would Kaling likely agree or disagree with the choices that Amy and Molly made in high school? Why would she support or oppose Molly's plans for their last night?

Because I was largely overlooked at school, I watched everyone like an observant weirdo, not unlike Eugene Levy's character Dr. Allan Pearl in *Waiting for Guffman*[12], who "sat next to the class clown, and studied him." But I did that with everyone. It has helped me so much as a writer; you have no idea.

I just want ambitious teenagers to know it is totally fine to be quiet, observant kids. Besides being a delight to your parents, you will find you have plenty of time later to catch up. So many people I work with — famous actors, accomplished writers — were overlooked in high school. Be like Allan Pearl. Sit next to the class clown and study him. Then grow up, take everything you learned, and get paid to be a real-life clown, unlike whatever unexciting thing the actual high school class clown is doing now.

The chorus of "Jack and Diane" is: *Oh yeah, life goes on, long after the thrill of living is gone.*

Are you kidding me? The thrill of living was *high school*? Come on, Mr. Cougar Mellencamp. Get a life. ■

[12] 1997 mockumentary comedy film written and directed by Christopher Guest. — Eds.

Understanding and Interpreting

1. Mindy Kaling opens by offering three ways to achieve the career she has. How do you respond to these? Is it clear that she's trying to be funny? Does she succeed? Is she taking the question of how to reach career success seriously?
2. What is Kaling's attitude about the importance of high school? What does she say is worth paying attention to? What does "wasteful frivolity" (par. 8) have to do with her subject?
3. How is high school depicted in popular culture and the media? How do those depictions compare with Kaling's description of her own experience? Is her reality comforting or disturbing to you? Why?
4. How does Kaling's experience as the child of "immigrant professionals" (par. 8) factor into her advice? Consider her fantasized song called "Nguyen and Ari" (par. 9) in your response.
5. Kaling argues that high school is not a good predictor of what happens next in terms of personal happiness or professional success. Given that position, why do you think she chooses not to make a stronger case against high school as an institution?
6. All in all, what is Kaling's chief concern about the high school experience? What is the best part of her advice from your perspective?

Analyzing Language, Style, and Structure

1. **Vocabulary in Context.** Kaling asserts, "So many people I work with — famous actors, accomplished writers — were overlooked in high school" (par. 12). What does "overlooked" mean in this context? Why does Kaling use this word instead of "ignored" or "unpopular"?
2. **Skill Focus.** Kaling references pop culture throughout this essay, especially music and television shows. Who do you think she sees as her readers — people currently in high school, those looking back on the experience, or both? Would someone who doesn't know the songs, for instance, still connect with the point Kaling is making?
3. Kaling writes informally, using direct address ("you"), colloquial and slang expressions, sentence fragments, and feisty questions. Choose one section of two or three paragraphs and analyze how these choices contribute to achieving Kaling's purpose.

4. Humor is Kaling's hallmark. Identify at least two examples and analyze her use of humor as a rhetorical strategy. Consider whether she is poking fun at herself, exaggerating, or being sarcastic. How does humor contribute to her tone?
5. To what extent does the tone change at the end of the essay? Is Kaling making a new point when she asks rhetorically, "The thrill of living was *high school*?" Or is she emphasizing a point she raised earlier? Why do you think this is or is not an effective conclusion?

Topics for Composing

1. **Analysis.** Some have interpreted Kaling's argument as advice to disregard high school — to refuse to take academic coursework and popularity seriously. They read her tone as flippant. Others hear her advising teens to be individuals with their own views and values. How do you interpret her argument? Explain with specific reference to the rhetorical choices she makes. Take into account her tone.
2. **Argument.** Kaling uses examples from popular culture as evidence that expectations of what the high school experience is supposed to be are unrealistic, in some cases not even desirable. Examine at least two examples from popular culture today. Then, develop a position on how realistically the media depicts the high school experience and its importance.
3. **Connection.** Rewrite a few paragraphs of Kaling's essay by updating the popular culture references. That is, maintain the point she is making, but do it by choosing a song, movie, or television show that is popular among your generation.
4. **Speaking and Listening.** This chapter of Kaling's memoir reads like stand-up comedy. Perform a portion of it as if were part of a stand-up routine. Do it live in front of a group of your classmates or videotape it. Be mindful of body language, pacing, and voice cues — the tricks of the stand-up comic's trade.
5. **Research.** Kaling says, "As a child of immigrant professionals, I can't help but notice the wasteful frivolity of it all. Why are these kids not home doing their homework? Why aren't they setting the table for dinner or helping out around the house?" Is this true? Do the children of immigrants really have different expectations and experiences than the children of non-immigrants? Conduct research, including interviews with classmates, to come to a conclusion about the accuracy of Kaling's statements.

from I Know Why the Caged Bird Sings

Maya Angelou

Deborah Feingold/Getty Images

One of America's most well-known and celebrated writers, Maya Angelou (1928–2014) was born Marguerite Johnson in St. Louis, Missouri. Throughout her career, she published numerous volumes of poetry, several plays and screenplays, and six autobiographies that traced her life from birth all the way to 1968. Her most famous autobiography is her first, *I Know Why the Caged Bird Sings*.

KEY CONTEXT Very controversial when it was released, *I Know Why the Caged Bird Sings* tells the story of the racism that Angelou (then called "Marguerite") faced growing up in the rural community of Stamps, Arkansas, during the Jim Crow era. This was a time when schools were segregated racially. This practice that some called "separate but equal" was declared unconstitutional in 1954 by the Supreme Court of the United States in *Brown v. Board of Education*. In the excerpt that follows, the excitement and pride Marguerite feels in her accomplishments are severely tested by "the ancient tragedy" of racism during her eighth-grade graduation.

In the Store I was the person of the moment. The birthday girl. The center. Bailey had graduated the year before, although to do so he had had to forfeit all pleasures to make up for his time lost in Baton Rouge.

My class was wearing butter-yellow piqué dresses, and Momma launched out on mine. She smocked the yoke into tiny crisscrossing puckers, then slurred the rest of the bodice. Her dark fingers ducked in and out of the lemony cloth as she embroidered raised daisies around the hem. Before she considered herself finished she had added a crocheted cuff on the puff sleeves, and a pointy crocheted collar.

I was going to be lovely. A walking model of all the various styles of fine hand sewing and it didn't worry me that I was only twelve years old and merely graduating from the eighth grade. Besides, many teachers in Arkansas Negro schools had only that diploma and were licensed to impart wisdom.

The days had become longer and more noticeable. The faded beige of former times had been replaced with strong and sure colors. I began to see my classmates' clothes, their skin tones, and the dust that waved off pussy willows. Clouds that lazed across the sky were objects of great concern to me. Their shiftier shapes might have held a message that in my new happiness and with a little bit of time I'd soon decipher. During that period I looked at the arch of heaven so religiously my neck kept a steady ache. I had taken to smiling more often, and my jaws hurt from the unaccustomed activity. Between the two physical sore spots, I suppose I could have been uncomfortable, but that was not the case. As a member of the winning team (the graduating class of 1940) I had outdistanced unpleasant sensations by miles. I was headed for the freedom of open fields.

5 Youth and social approval allied themselves with me and we trammeled memories of slights and insults. The wind of our swift passage remodeled my features. Lost tears were pounded to mud and then to dust. Years of withdrawal were brushed aside and left behind, as hanging ropes of parasitic moss.

My work alone had awarded me a top place and I was going to be one of the first called in the graduating ceremonies. On the classroom blackboard, as well as on the bulletin board in the auditorium, there were blue stars and white stars and red stars. No absences, no tardinesses, and my academic work was among the best of the year. I could say the preamble to the Constitution even faster than Bailey. We timed ourselves often: "WethepeopleoftheUnitedStatesinordertoformamoreperfectunion . . ." I had memorized the Presidents of the United States from Washington to Roosevelt in chronological as well as alphabetical order.

My hair pleased me too. Gradually the black mass had lengthened and thickened, so that it kept at last to its braided pattern, and I didn't have to yank my scalp off when I tried to comb it.

Louise and I had rehearsed the exercises until we tired out ourselves. Henry Reed was class valedictorian. He was a small, very black boy with hooded eyes, a long, broad nose and an oddly shaped head. I had admired him for years because each term he and I vied for the best grades in our class. Most often he bested me, but instead of being disappointed I was pleased that we shared top places between us. Like many Southern Black children, he lived with his grandmother, who was as strict as Momma and as kind as she knew how to be. He was courteous, respectful and soft-spoken to elders, but on the playground he chose to play the roughest games. I admired him. Anyone, I reckoned, sufficiently afraid or sufficiently dull could be polite. But to be able to operate at a top

Bettmann / Getty Images

The events Angelou describes in her autobiography take place about fifteen years before the court-ordered integration of Little Rock's Central High School in 1957. In this photo, National Guard troops protect a girl arriving to attend school. **What perspective on this historic event, and this scene in particular, does Angelou's memoir give you?**

level with both adults and children was admirable.

His valedictory speech was entitled "To Be or Not to Be." The rigid tenth-grade teacher had helped him write it. He'd been working on the dramatic stresses for months.

The weeks until graduation were filled with heady activities. A group of small children were to be presented in a play about buttercups and daisies and bunny rabbits. They could be heard throughout the building practicing their hops and their little songs that sounded like silver bells. The older girls (nongraduates, of course) were assigned the task of making refreshments for the night's festivities. A tangy scent of ginger, cinnamon, nutmeg and chocolate wafted around the home economics building as the budding cooks made samples for themselves and their teachers.

In every corner of the workshop, axes and saws split fresh timber as the woodshop boys made sets and stage scenery. Only the graduates were left out of the general bustle. We were free to sit in the library at the back of the building or look in quite detachedly, naturally, on the measures being taken for our event. Even the minister preached on graduation the Sunday before. His subject was, "Let your light so shine that men will see your good works and praise your Father, Who is in Heaven." Although the sermon was purported to be addressed to us, he used the occasion to speak to backsliders, gamblers and general ne'er-do-wells. But since he had called our names at the beginning of the service we were mollified.

Among Negroes the tradition was to give presents to children going only from one grade to another. How much more important this was when the person was graduating at the top of the class. Uncle Willie and Momma had sent away for a Mickey Mouse watch like Bailey's. Louise gave me four embroidered handkerchiefs. (I gave her three crocheted doilies.) Mrs. Sneed, the minister's wife, made me an underskirt to wear for graduation, and nearly every customer gave me a nickel or maybe even a dime with the instruction "Keep on moving to higher ground," or some such encouragement.

Amazingly the great day finally dawned and I was out of bed before I knew it. I threw open the back door to see it more clearly, but Momma said, "Sister, come away from that door and put your robe on."

I hoped the memory of that morning would never leave me. Sunlight was itself still young, and the day had none of the insistence maturity would bring it in a few hours. In my robe and barefoot in the backyard, under cover of going to see about my new beans, I gave myself up to the gentle warmth and thanked God that no matter what evil I had done in my life He had allowed me to live to see this day. Somewhere in my fatalism I had expected to die, accidentally, and never have the chance to walk up the stairs in the auditorium and gracefully receive my hard-earned diploma. Out of God's merciful bosom I had won reprieve.

Bailey came out in his robe and gave me a box wrapped in Christmas paper. He said he had saved his money for months to pay for it. It felt like a box of chocolates, but I knew Bailey wouldn't save money to buy candy when we had all we could want under our noses. He was as proud of the gift as I. It was a soft-leather-bound copy of a collection of poems by Edgar Allan Poe, or, as Bailey and I called him, "Eap." I turned to "Annabel Lee" and we walked up and down the garden rows, the cool dirt between our toes, reciting the beautifully sad lines.

Momma made a Sunday breakfast although it was only Friday. After we finished the blessing, I opened my eyes to find the watch on my plate. It was a dream of a day. Everything went smoothly and to my credit, I didn't have to be reminded or scolded for anything. Near evening I was too jittery to attend to chores, so Bailey volunteered to do all before his bath.

Days before, we had made a sign for the Store, and as we turned out the lights Momma hung the cardboard over the doorknob. It read clearly: CLOSED. GRADUATION.

My dress fitted perfectly and everyone said that I looked like a sunbeam in it. On the hill, going toward the school, Bailey walked behind with Uncle Willie, who muttered, "Go on, Ju." He wanted him to walk ahead with us because it embarrassed him to have to walk so slowly. Bailey said he'd let the ladies walk together, and the men would bring up the rear. We all laughed, nicely.

Little children dashed by out of the dark like fireflies. Their crepe-paper dresses and butterfly wings were not made for running and we heard more than one rip, dryly, and the regretful "uh uh" that followed.

20 The school blazed without gaiety. The windows seemed cold and unfriendly from the lower hill. A sense of ill-fated timing crept over me, and if Momma hadn't reached for my hand I would have drifted back to Bailey and Uncle Willie, and possibly beyond. She made a few slow jokes about my feet getting cold, and tugged me along to the now-strange building.

Around the front steps, assurance came back. There were my fellow "greats," the graduating class. Hair brushed back, legs oiled, new dresses and pressed pleats, fresh pocket handkerchiefs and little handbags, all homesewn. Oh, we were up to snuff, all right. I joined my comrades and didn't even see my family go in to find seats in the crowded auditorium.

The school band struck up a march and all classes filed in as had been rehearsed. We stood in front of our seats, as assigned, and on a signal from the choir director, we sat. No sooner had this been accomplished than the band started to play the national anthem. We rose again and sang the song, after which we recited the pledge of allegiance. We remained standing for a brief minute before the choir director and the principal signaled to us, rather desperately I thought, to take our seats. The command was so unusual that our carefully rehearsed and smooth-running machine was thrown off. For a full minute we fumbled for our chairs and bumped into each other awkwardly. Habits change or solidify under pressure, so in our state of nervous tension we had been ready to follow our usual assembly pattern: the American national anthem, then the pledge of allegiance, then the song every Black person I knew called the Negro National Anthem. All done in the same key, with the same passion and most often standing on the same foot.

Finding my seat at last, I was overcome with a presentiment of worse things to come. Something unrehearsed, unplanned, was going to happen, and we were going to be made to look bad. I distinctly remember being explicit in the choice of pronoun. It was "we," the graduating class, the unit, that concerned me then.

The principal welcomed "parents and friends" and asked the Baptist minister to lead us in prayer. His invocation was brief and punchy, and for a second I thought we were getting back on the high road to right action. When the principal came back to the dais, however, his voice had changed. Sounds always affected me profoundly and the principal's voice was one of my favorites. During assembly it melted and lowed weakly into the audience. It had not been in my plan to listen to him, but my curiosity was piqued and I straightened up to give him my attention.

25 He was talking about Booker T. Washington, our "late great leader," who said we can be as close as the fingers on the hand, etc. . . . Then he said a few vague things about friendship and the friendship of kindly people to those less fortunate than themselves. With that his voice nearly faded, thin, away. Like a river diminishing to a stream and then to a trickle. But he cleared his throat and said, "Our speaker tonight, who is

also our friend, came from Texarkana to deliver the commencement address, but due to the irregularity of the train schedule, he's going to, as they say, 'speak and run.'" He said that we understood and wanted the man to know that we were most grateful for the time he was able to give us and then something about how we were willing always to adjust to another's program, and without more ado — "I give you Mr. Edward Donleavy."

Not one but two white men came through the door offstage. The shorter one walked to the speaker's platform, and the tall one moved over to the center seat and sat down. But that was our principal's seat, and already occupied. The dislodged gentleman bounced around for a long breath or two before the Baptist minister gave him his chair, then with more dignity than the situation deserved, the minister walked off the stage.

Donleavy looked at the audience once (on reflection, I'm sure that he wanted only to reassure himself that we were really there), adjusted his glasses and began to read from a sheaf of papers.

He was glad "to be here and to see the work going on just as it was in the other schools."

At the first "Amen" from the audience I willed the offender to immediate death by choking on the word. But Amens and Yes, sirs began to fall around the room like rain through a ragged umbrella.

He told us of the wonderful changes we 30
children in Stamps had in store. The Central School (naturally, the white school was Central) had already been granted improvements that would be in use in the fall. A well-known artist was coming from Little Rock to teach art to them. They were going to have the newest microscopes and chemistry equipment for their laboratory. Mr. Donleavy didn't leave us long in the dark over who made these improvements available to Central High. Nor were we to be ignored in the general betterment scheme he had in mind.

He said that he had pointed out to people at a very high level that one of the first-line football tacklers at Arkansas Agricultural and Mechanical College had graduated from good old Lafayette County Training School. Here

Horace Pippen/ Courtesy National Gallery of Art, Washington

School Studies (1944) is a painting by the self-taught artist Horace Pippin. An oil painting, *School Studies* hangs in the National Gallery of Art in Washington, D.C.

In what ways does this painting depict the African American family's involvement with and commitment to education that Angelou describes?

fewer Amens were heard. Those few that did break through lay dully in the air with the heaviness of habit.

He went on to praise us. He went on to say how he had bragged that "one of the best basketball players at Fisk sank his first ball right here at Lafayette County Training School."

The white kids were going to have a chance to become Galileos and Madame Curies and Edisons and Gauguins, and our boys (the girls weren't even in on it) would try to be Jesse Owenses and Joe Louises.

Owens and the Brown Bomber were great heroes in our world, but what school official in the white-goddom of Little Rock had the right to decide that those two men must be our only heroes? Who decided that for Henry Reed to become a scientist he had to work like George Washington Carver, as a bootblack, to buy a lousy microscope? Bailey was obviously always going to be too small to be an athlete, so which concrete angel glued to what country seat had decided that if my brother wanted to become a lawyer he had to first pay penance for his skin by picking cotton and hoeing corn and studying correspondence books at night for twenty years?

35 The man's dead words fell like bricks around the auditorium and too many settled in my belly. Constrained by hard-learned manners I couldn't look behind me, but to my left and right the proud graduating class of 1940 had dropped their heads. Every girl in my row had found something new to do with her handkerchief. Some folded the tiny squares into love knots, some into triangles, but most were wadding them, then pressing them flat on their yellow laps.

On the dais, the ancient tragedy was being replayed. Professor Parsons sat, a sculptor's reject, rigid. His large, heavy body seemed devoid of will or willingness, and his eyes said he was no longer with us. The other teachers examined the flag (which was draped stage right) or their notes, or the windows which opened on our now-famous playing diamond.

Graduation, the hush-hush magic time of frills and gifts and congratulations and diplomas, was finished for me before my name was called. The accomplishment was nothing. The meticulous maps, drawn in three colors of ink, learning and spelling decasyllabic words, memorizing the whole of *The Rape of Lucrece* — it was for nothing. Donleavy had exposed us.

We were maids and farmers, handymen and washerwomen, and anything higher that we aspired to was farcical and presumptuous.

Then I wished that Gabriel Prosser and Nat Turner had killed all whitefolks in their beds and that Abraham Lincoln had been assassinated before the signing of the Emancipation Proclamation, and that Harriet Tubman had been killed by that blow on her head and Christopher Columbus had drowned in the *Santa María*.

40 It was awful to be Negro and have no control over my life. It was brutal to be young and already trained to sit quietly and listen to charges brought against my color with no chance of defense. We should all be dead. I thought I should like to see us all dead, one on top of the other. A pyramid of flesh with the whitefolks on the bottom, as the broad base, then the Indians with their silly tomahawks and teepees and wigwams and treaties, the Negroes with their mops and recipes and cotton sacks and spirituals sticking out of their mouths. The Dutch children should all stumble in their wooden shoes and break their necks. The French should choke to death on the Louisiana Purchase (1803) while silkworms ate all the Chinese with their stupid pigtails. As a species, we were an abomination. All of us.

Donleavy was running for election, and assured our parents that if he won we could count on having the only colored paved playing field in that part of Arkansas. Also — he never looked up to acknowledge the grunts of acceptance — also, we were bound to get some new equipment for the home economics building and the workshop.

He finished, and since there was no need to give any more than the most perfunctory thank-you's, he nodded to the men on the stage, and the tall white man who was never introduced joined him at the door. They left with the attitude that now they were off to something really important. (The graduation ceremonies at Lafayette County Training School had been a mere preliminary.)

The ugliness they left was palpable. An uninvited guest who wouldn't leave. The choir was summoned and sang a modern arrangement of "Onward, Christian Soldiers," with new words pertaining to graduates seeking their place in the world. But it didn't work. Elouise, the daughter of the Baptist minister, recited "Invictus," and I could have cried at the impertinence of "I am the master of my fate, I am the captain of my soul."

My name had lost its ring of familiarity and I had to be nudged to go and receive my diploma. All my preparations had fled. I neither marched up to the stage like a conquering Amazon, nor did I look in the audience for Bailey's nod of approval. Marguerite Johnson, I heard the name again, my honors were read, there were noises in the audience of appreciation, and I took my place on the stage as rehearsed.

I thought about colors I hated: ecru, puce, 45
lavender, beige and black.

There was shuffling and rustling around me, then Henry Reed was giving his valedictory address, "To Be or Not to Be." Hadn't he heard the whitefolks? We couldn't be, so the question was a waste of time. Henry's voice came out clear and strong. I feared to look at him. Hadn't he got the message? There was no "nobler in the mind" for Negroes because the world didn't think we had minds, and they let us know it. "Outrageous fortune"? Now, that was a joke. When the ceremony was over I had to tell Henry Reed some things. That is, if I still cared. Not "rub," Henry, "erase." "Ah, there's the erase." Us.

Henry had been a good student in elocution. His voice rose on tides of promise and fell on waves of warnings. The English teacher had helped him to create a sermon winging through Hamlet's soliloquy. To be a man, a doer, a builder, a leader, or to be a tool, an unfunny joke, a crusher of funky toadstools. I marveled that Henry could go through with the speech as if we had a choice.

I had been listening and silently rebutting each sentence with my eyes closed; then there was a hush, which in an audience warns that something unplanned is happening. I looked up and saw Henry Reed, the conservative, the proper, the A student, turn his back to the audience and turn to us (the proud graduating class of 1940) and sing, nearly speaking,

"Lift ev'ry voice and sing
Till earth and heaven ring
Ring with the harmonies of Liberty . . ."

It was the poem written by James Weldon Johnson. It was the music composed by J. Rosamond Johnson. It was the Negro national anthem. Out of habit we were singing it.

Our mothers and fathers stood in the dark 50
hall and joined the hymn of encouragement. A kindergarten teacher led the small children onto the stage and the buttercups and daisies and bunny rabbits marked time and tried to follow:

"Stony the road we trod
Bitter the chastening rod
Felt in the days when hope, unborn, had died.
Yet with a steady beat
Have not our weary feet
Come to the place for which our fathers
sighed?"

Every child I knew had learned that song with his ABC's and along with "Jesus Loves Me

Scott Olson/Getty Images

This photograph shows a young girl joining demonstrations marking the one-year anniversary of the death of Michael Brown. He was fatally shot by a police officer in Ferguson, Missouri, on August 8, 2014. Months of protests that followed drew attention nationwide.

What does this image suggest to you about the progress in civil rights and racial equality since the time of Angelou's graduation from high school?

This I Know." But I personally had never heard it before. Never heard the words, despite the thousands of times I had sung them. Never thought they had anything to do with me.

On the other hand, the words of Patrick Henry had made such an impression on me that I had been able to stretch myself tall and trembling and say, "I know not what course others may take, but as for me, give me liberty or give me death."

And now I heard, really for the first time:
"We have come over a way that with tears
has
been watered,
We have come, treading our path
through the
blood of the slaughtered."

While echoes of the song shivered in the air, Henry Reed bowed his head, said "Thank you," and returned to his place in the line. The tears that slipped down many faces were not wiped away in shame.

We were on top again. As always, again. We survived. The depths had been icy and dark, but now a bright sun spoke to our souls. I was no longer simply a member of the proud graduating class of 1940; I was a proud member of the wonderful, beautiful Negro race.

Oh, Black known and unknown poets, how often have your auctioned pains sustained us? Who will compute the lonely nights made less lonely by your songs, or by the empty pots made less tragic by your tales?

If we were a people much given to revealing secrets, we might raise monuments and sacrifice to the memories of our poets, but slavery cured us of that weakness. It may be enough, however, to have it said that we survive in exact relationship to the dedication of our poets (include preachers, musicians and blues singers). ■

Understanding and Interpreting

1. In the opening section of this excerpt, what is Marguerite's overall attitude toward graduation and herself? Cite specific passages to support your response. Consider this statement as part

of your response: “Youth and social approval allied themselves with me and we trammeled memories of slights and insults” (par. 5).

2. What role does Marguerite’s brother Bailey play in this excerpt? How would you characterize their relationship?
3. What happens immediately as Mr. Donleavy enters the auditorium that signals to Marguerite that something is about to go very wrong? In what ways, both direct and indirect, does he demonstrate insensitivity and lack of respect for his audience? Consider the parenthetical comment that Marguerite makes about him as he is speaking: “(on reflection, I’m sure that he wanted only to reassure himself that we were really there)” (par. 27).
4. Henry Reed is a character who surprises Marguerite. How is he described when we first encounter him? How does he change in Marguerite’s estimation as the narrative develops?
5. What are some of the differences between Marguerite’s school, Lafayette County Training School, and Central High School, the white school in the same town? What is Marguerite’s perception of these differences?
6. What about Mr. Donleavy’s behavior and speech occasions the response of Marguerite and other members of the audience? As part of your response, consider what she means by the statement, “Donleavy had exposed us” (par. 37). To what extent do you think that he understands that what he is saying might insult his audience? How does that understanding (or lack of it) affect the audience of the Stamps community?
7. The central character in Shakespeare’s play *Hamlet* utters one of the most famous speeches of all time. Beginning with “To be or not to be/That is the question,” Hamlet reflects on what action he should take in the face of life’s pain and unfairness. Given that the speech is about making choices, why does Marguerite find Henry’s use of it to be a “waste of time” (par. 46)? What prompts her to revise that assessment?
8. When Henry Reed sings “Lift Every Voice and Sing,” he leads, as Angelou writes, “a hymn of encouragement” (par. 50). In what ways has he shown himself to be the leader of his community, not only of his graduating class but the larger community?
9. What connection does Marguerite make between the famous words of Patrick Henry that she recalls and the lyrics from “Lift Every Voice and Sing” (par. 52)?
10. A “coming of age” story typically features a protagonist who learns a lesson about the world that shows a transition from childhood to maturity. How do each of the following sections of this excerpt delineate a stage in Marguerite’s coming of age?
    - before the ceremony (pars. 6–14)
    - during and immediately after Mr. Donleavy’s speech (pars. 27–43)
    - after Henry Reed begins to sing (pars. 48–53)

Analyzing Language, Style, and Structure

1. **Vocabulary in Context.** In the next-to-last paragraph of this excerpt, Marguerite asks, “Oh, Black known and unknown poets, how often have your auctioned pains sustained us?” What does the word “auctioned” mean in this context? How does Marguerite’s use of the word carry more emotional weight than the standard dictionary definition? Why is this use of the word particularly effective here?
2. **Skill Focus.** A memoir is a specific type of argument. That is, the person writing the memoir believes that the experience(s) being related will have meaning for readers by increasing awareness, assuring them that they are not alone, exposing an injustice, evoking sympathy,

and so forth. What was Angelou's purpose in writing her memoir, based on this excerpt? Be sure to describe her ethos and audience in your response.

3. The opening section of this excerpt (pars. 1–17) contains numerous details expressing the joyful anticipation of graduation, from clothing to gifts to responses from family and other community members. In what ways do these details paint a picture that seems almost a fantasy? Cite specific examples to support your response.
4. Foreshadowing refers to signs or warning — clues, if you will — of what is about to happen in a fictional story or nonfiction narrative. For example, in paragraph 14, Marguerite thinks, "Sunlight was itself still young, and the day had none of the insistence maturity would bring it in a few hours." This statement foreshadows that something difficult or dangerous will happen. What other examples of foreshadowing do you find in this text? How does foreshadowing affect Angelou's readers?
5. After Mr. Donleavy's speech, everything changes for Marguerite. She sees her world entirely differently than she had seen it as she anticipated her graduation: "The accomplishment was nothing," she concludes (par. 37). How does the language of the paragraphs following Mr. Donleavy's speech dramatize her disappointment and anger? Pay particular attention to paragraph 40.
6. Angelou uses metaphors and similes in abundance in this excerpt. Identify three of them and explain how they contribute to achieving her purpose. How do they help create for the reader young Marguerite's frame of mind?
7. Marguerite's attitude toward the graduation ceremony is strikingly different before and after Mr. Donleavy's speech. How does Angelou use tone to convey this dramatic shift? Choose two short passages (one from before, one from after), identify the tone in each passage, and explain how the choices in diction that Angelou makes create that tone.
8. How do the last two or three paragraphs of the excerpt change in tone? What about the diction and syntax suggests a more mature adult voice speaking?

Topics for Composing

1. **Analysis.** The question of voice in personal and public circles is a question of power: Who gets to speak, who gets to tell the story, whose story gets told. Write an interpretation of this excerpt as a study of the power of voice. Whose voice is most powerful? Include Mr. Donleavy, Henry Reed, and Angelou herself in your analysis.
2. **Argument.** The "separate but equal" policy in Stamps, Arkansas, is reflected in the two schools — one for whites and one for African Americans. In 1954, about 20 years after the graduation ceremony, the Supreme Court in *Brown v. Board of Education* ruled that type of segregation illegal. As a result, schools throughout the United States became integrated. Though school segregation is now illegal, some argue that it still exists in the form of socioeconomic disparities. As a result, many say that education is the civil rights issue of our time. Do you agree or disagree? Support your position with evidence from your local community or your understanding of the national educational landscape.
3. **Connection.** In this excerpt, Marguerite has her expectations of a wonderful day dampened, at least temporarily, by someone else's actions that are beyond her control. Write about a time in your life when you experienced a similar setback. Be sure to include a reflection on what caused this disappointment.
4. **Speaking and Listening.** James Weldon Johnson wrote the lyrics to "Lift Every Voice and Sing" in 1905, and his brother John Rosamond Johnson set them to music in the same year. It

has been performed by choral groups and singers ever since, including Beyonce in 2018. In 2019, the Alvin Ailey Dance Theatre debuted “Once of Faith” with a choreographed interpretation of this famous song. Listen to and watch several of these performances and then develop your own performance alone or with a group of your classmates. Your performance might be the song itself, an instrumental rendition, or an interpretive dance. With your class or in small groups, discuss how your performance or those of your classmates changed or deepened your understanding of the poem.

5. **Research.** The text includes references to famous people from history, politics, and art: Booker T. Washington, Madame Curie, Jesse Owens, Patrick Henry, James Weldon Johnson, Joe Louis. Research one of these figures and explain how your deeper understanding of the person enhances your appreciation of Marguerite's experience. What effect does mentioning these figures have on the audience?
6. **Connection.** Angelou took the title of her memoir from the poem “Sympathy” by Paul Laurence Dunbar (pp. 70–71). Read and analyze the poem. Then, discuss why you think the reference is appropriate, based on this excerpt from *I Know Why the Caged Bird Sings*.
7. **Creative Writing.** Write your own poem or short memoir centering on some dimension of racial or ethnic bias that you see in today's world.

from The Geeks Shall Inherit the Earth

Alexandra Robbins

Reporter and lecturer Alexandra Robbins is a graduate of Yale University and the author of several books related to education. *Pledged* (2004) describes the secretive world of college sororities. *The Overachievers* (2006) documents the overwhelming academic pressures that today's high school students face. *Fraternity* (2019) takes an inside look at what it means to be a young man in college today.

CHESTER HIGGINS JR/The New York Times/Redux Pictures

KEY CONTEXT For *The Geeks Shall Inherit the Earth* (2011), Robbins followed seven high school students from private, public, suburban, and inner city schools from all over the country for a year. By focusing on Whitney, called “the popular bitch,” the following excerpt details the social and biological pressures to conform that students face and the difficulty students have in maintaining their individuality in the larger environment of high school.

Introduction

CAFETERIA FRINGE: People who are not part of or who are excluded from a school's or society's in crowd.

In the decade I've spent examining various microcosms of life in U.S. schools — from the multitude of students pressured to succeed in school and sports to the twentysomething products of this educational Rube Goldberg[1] machine — a disturbing pattern has emerged. Young people are trying frantically to force themselves into an unbending mold of expectations, convinced that they live in a two-tiered system in which they are either a

[1]Twentieth-century American cartoonist famous for drawing whimsical and complicated machines. — Eds.

resounding success or they have already failed. And the more they try to squeeze themselves into that shrinking, allegedly normative space, the faster the walls close in.

The students outside these walls are the kids who typically are not considered part of the in crowd, the ones who are excluded, blatantly or subtly, from the premier table in the lunchroom. I refer to them as "cafeteria fringe." Whether alone or in groups, these geeks, loners, punks, floaters, nerds, freaks, dorks, gamers, bandies, art kids, theater geeks, choir kids, Goths, weirdos, indies, scenes, emos, skaters, and various types of racial and other minorities are often relegated to subordinate social status simply because they are, or seem to be, even the slightest bit different.

Students alone did not create these boundaries. The No Child Left Behind law, a disproportionate emphasis on SATs, APs, and other standardized tests, and a suffocating homogenization of the U.S. education system have all contributed to a rabidly conformist atmosphere that stifles unique people, ideas, and expression. The methods that schools and government officials claimed would improve America's "progress" are the same methods that hold back the students who are most likely to further that progress.

In precisely the years that we should be embracing differences among students, urging them to pursue their divergent interests at full throttle, we're instead forcing them into a skyline of sameness, muffling their voices, grounding their dreams. The result? As a Midwestern senior told me for my book *The Overachievers,* high schoolers view life as "a conveyor belt," making monotonous scheduled stops at high school, college, graduate school, and a series of jobs until death. Middle schools in North America have been called "the Bermuda triangle of education." Only 22 percent of U.S. youth socialize with people of another race. U.S. students have some of the highest rates of emotional problems and the most negative views of peer culture among countries surveyed by the World Health Organization. . . .

after school, 2013, (Acrylic paint on paper)/FURUYA, Tomoko/Tomoko FURUYA/ Private Collection/Bridgeman Images

Tomoko Furuya offers one view of student isolation in *after school*.

How does Furuya use framing, colors, and lighting to emphasize the feelings of isolation? Consider how it relates to Robbins's concluding sentences about Whitney: "Once you were in a group, you were stuck there until graduation, no matter what. That was just the way high school was, Whitney was sure. So she didn't tell a soul."

QUIRK THEORY: Many of the differences that cause a student to be excluded in school are the same traits or real-world skills that others will value, love, respect, or find compelling about that person in adulthood and outside of the school setting.

Quirk theory suggests that 5
popularity in school is not a key to success and satisfaction in adulthood. Conventional notions of popularity are wrong. What if popularity is not the

same thing as social success? What if students who are considered outsiders aren't really socially inadequate at all? Being an outsider doesn't necessarily indicate any sort of social failing. We do not view a tuba player as musically challenged if he cannot play the violin. He's just a different kind of musician. A sprinter is still considered an athlete even if she can't play basketball. She's a different kind of athlete. Rather than view the cafeteria fringe as less socially successful than the popular crowd, we could simply accept that they are a different kind of social.

• • •

To investigate the cause and consequence of the gut-wrenching social landscape that

extending beyond the text

This is a film still and a section from the script of the movie *Mean Girls* (2004).

CADY (V.O.) Having lunch with the Plastics was like leaving the actual world and entering "Girl World." And Girl World had a lot of rules.

GRETCHEN We only wear jeans or track pants on Friday. You can't wear a tank top two days in a row. You can only wear your hair in a ponytail once a week. So, I guess, you picked today. And if you break any of these rules you can't sit with us at lunch. I mean, not just you, any of us. Like, if I was wearing jeans today, I would be sitting over there with the art freaks.

How are the rules of the fictional Plastics, and especially the consequences for violating them, similar to the pressures that Whitney faces in this excerpt?

characterizes too many schools, I followed seven "main characters" — real people — for a year and interviewed hundreds of other students, teachers, and counselors individually and in groups. I talked with students from public schools, private schools, technical schools, schools for the arts, boarding schools, college prep academies, inner city schools, small rural schools, and suburban schools. They have more in common than they know. . . .

Whitney, New York | The Popular Bitch

Before leaving home for her last first day of high school, Whitney glanced at herself in all of her mirrors for the seventeenth time: the large mirror above her dresser, the small one by her TV for scrutinizing hair and makeup, and the full-length one behind her door. She had spent two hours getting ready this morning. Her white-blonde hair, highlighted from a summer of lifeguarding, cascaded to her shoulders in meticulously crafted, loose, bouncy curls behind a funky knit headband that she wore so she'd have an excuse to brag that members of a famous rock group had complimented her on it. Several bracelets dangled from her wrist, still tan from cheerleading camp the week before. Her makeup was flawless, accentuated by a smattering of glitter above her eyes; it looked good now, but she knew she would check her makeup again in the school bathroom three or four times that day, hunting for imperfections and correcting them with her Sephora-only arsenal.

People told Whitney all the time that she was pretty, as in beauty pageant pretty or talk show host pretty. Whitney thought this was because of her smile. In her opinion, her straight white teeth slightly made up for her body, which dissatisfied her when she compared it to her friends'. When they went to the local diner together, the girls did not eat; they only sat and watched the guys stuff their faces. If the girls were really hungry, the most they would order in front of the group was lemon water.

Whitney checked her makeup again in the kitchen mirror, forced herself to guzzle a Slim-Fast shake to jump-start her metabolism, grabbed her Coach purse, lacrosse bag, and book bag, and ran out the door, pausing briefly at the mirror in the foyer. She drove too quickly into the school parking lot, unapologetically cutting off people on her way, and parked her SUV crookedly, taking up two spots, but leaving it there anyway because she could. She met up with Giselle, her best friend until recently. Giselle, who had been the schoolwide Homecoming Queen as a sophomore, had become popular through cheerleading and by dating a popular senior — when she was in the eighth grade. "Well, this is it!" Giselle said, and they stepped into the building.

10 Riverland Academy, located in a small town in upstate New York, catered to a mostly white, Christian community. Its four hundred students crowded into the gym, standing in small groups or lining the bleachers. Amidst the chaos, the girls easily spotted their group, which other students called the "preps" or the "populars," in the center of the gym. Bianca, the queen bee, thin and tan, stood with Kendra, a senior; Peyton, a junior; and Madison, Bianca's best friend. Chelsea, the only brunette standing among the populars, had worked her way up from "being a loser," according to Whitney, by "sucking up to Bianca like crazy and giving her information about people." The preps tolerated Chelsea, but didn't include her as a stalwart member of the group. This meant they didn't allow her in their Homecoming limo, but they did invite her to take pictures with them.

A few of the prep boys orbited the girls: Chip and Spencer, hot high-society seniors; Bobby, a chubby, boisterous football star; and Seth, an overachieving junior. The preps were each on two or more sports teams, partied with college students, and in Whitney's words, "just own[ed] the school."

The girls appraised the surrounding students and whispered to each other, standing as they typically did, one hand on a hip, one knee bent, in what the cheerleading coach referred to as "the hooker's pose." . . .

The group caught up briefly before resuming the assessment of the students swarming around them. "Oh my God. Who is that?!" Peyton sniffed, nodding her head toward a band girl.

"That's Shay," Chelsea answered.

15 "Dude, I didn't even recognize her," Peyton said. "Did she gain like fifteen pounds over the summer?! Why did her hair get so big and frizzy?" This led to a discussion about how there were too many skanks and trailer trash kids at Riverland.

The preps took stock of the new freshmen, as they did at the beginning of every year, to decide who was going to be cool and to whom they were going to be mean. They automatically deemed one girl cool because her older sister was dating a prep. The freshman cheerleaders were acceptable. If freshman girls didn't already have something going for them when they got to Riverland — an older boyfriend, a popular sibling, a varsity sport, money, or a parent with connections — they were out of luck. "If we don't know them already by some other affiliation," Whitney said, "they aren't worth getting to know" — and they were automatically labeled skanks. . . .

Students gathered together in the bleachers, group by group. The "badasses," allegedly bullies who liked to destroy property, were tossing basketballs in the air. The FFAs, or members of the Future Farmers of America club — the preps called them hicks and rednecks — sat at the end of the bleachers. The wannabes, dressed like their role models but discernible by their whiff of uncertainty, stood at a far corner of the room. Those were the kids who fed the preps' egos. Whitney would walk down the hall like royalty, while the wannabes would gush, "Whitney, you look so pretty today!" or "Whitney, you did such a good job cheering last night!" If a prep girl showed up at school with a shaved head, Whitney was sure the wannabes would visit the salon that night to do the same. It was the fact that they tried so hard that doomed them.

Whitney looked at the punks, who wore tight pants and band shirts. They could scream every word of the music they listened to. They were unafraid to strike up conversations with other groups, but they usually clashed with the preps. As Whitney saw it, the cliques were just too different. Whitney was certain that the punk girls thought the populars were loud and snobby. Besides, she mused, odds were that she and her friends probably had been mean to the punk girls before.

The popular guys referred to the punks as "weird" and "useless." They called Dirk, the punks' alpha male, a scumbag within his earshot. Whitney was as friendly with Dirk as her group allowed, which meant in hallways their communication was limited to awkward eye contact and brief exchanges. She was attracted to Dirk, a funny and talented drummer, but she didn't tell anyone, because a popular cheerleader dating a punk would cause "crazy scandalous controversy" and further escalate the tension between the groups. She was having enough trouble with the preps as it was.

20 After the welcome-back hug, the preps hardly acknowledged Whitney, though she stood next to them. The group brought up inside jokes and memories from the summer that didn't include her. Whitney recognized this weapon because she had used it before. The preps enjoyed purposely making someone feel bad for not being at an event. If you weren't at a party one weekend, the group wouldn't stop talking about it in front of you until the next party.

Whitney loved the power and perks of popularity. When the teachers began handing

extending beyond the text

Read the following summary of a research experiment that ran in *Scientific American*. The study investigated how peer pressure influences teenagers' tastes in music.

Media+Media/Alamy Stock Photo

The researchers chose to study adolescents between the ages of 12 and 17, a cohort thought to be highly susceptible to social influence, and known to buy at least one third of albums in the United States. Each participant heard a short clip of a song downloaded from the social-networking website MySpace. Following the clip, they were asked to make two ratings, one indicating how familiar they were with the clip, (which was always the hook or chorus of the chosen song) and one indicating how much they liked the clip on a five-point scale. The clip was then played a second time, and they were again asked to rate how much they liked the song. However, in two thirds of these second trials, the teens were shown a popularity rating that was estimated based on the number of times the song was downloaded.

When no information about the popularity of a song was displayed, teens changed their likability rating of the song 12 percent of the time. Not surprisingly, after being shown the popularity of a song, teens changed their ratings more frequently, on average 22 percent of the time. This difference was highly significant, and it is worth noting that among those who changed their likability ratings, 79 percent of the time teens changed their ratings in the direction of the popularity rating — they followed the crowd.

Explain what the researchers concluded based on their study. How do these conclusions align, or not, with the behaviors that Robbins describes in her piece?

out senior schedules at the back of the gym, Whitney's group pushed to the front of the line en masse, as students parted without protest. The teachers didn't bat an eye at the line cut, instead complimenting the girls on their hair and their tans. We haven't been in school for more than ten minutes and already our egos have grown, Whitney thought. Her group got away with everything. For example, students who were late to class four times automatically received detention. Not Giselle. She regularly escaped detention because of cheerleading practice, and no one dared complain. . . .

Schedules in hand, the preps left the gym before they were dismissed, and strutted toward "their" hallway. Other students walked by the Prep Hall quickly, so as not to attract attention in the area where the preps heckled the "weird kids." By the end of junior year, one such student was so fed up with the preps' rude comments that when they made fun of him for drawing a robot, he lashed out: "You're going to be sorry when I come to school with a gun and kill all of you." The preps didn't say another word to him.

"Ugh," Bianca shouted. "I hate when stupid freshmen don't know how to walk in the hall! You walk on the right side of the hallway! Goddamn!"

As the halls filled up, crowds parted for the preps. Some students said hello, but Whitney and her friends gave them the "what's-up-but-I-won't-really-acknowledge-you" head nod.

When Whitney walked into advertising class 25
with Peyton, she spotted Dirk. "Hey, Whitney!" he yelled across the room.

"I'm not sitting with Dirk," Peyton whispered to Whitney. "I don't see why you like those people. They scare me."

Whitney shrugged and grinned at Dirk as she sat next to him anyway.

At lunch, the preps cut to the front of the line, as usual, and sat at "their" lunch table in the center of the cafeteria. Whitney hadn't waited in the lunch line since she was a freshman. In the past, when students told the preps to stop cutting, Whitney's group either ignored them or shot nasty glares. When the protestors walked off, the preps would follow them and make loud comments, such as, "Wow, fat-asses need their food quickly, don't they?! I mean, do you really think they need that much food? They look like they could do without lunch once in a while . . ." Nobody complained anymore. Because they favored the preps, the teachers in the room looked the other way.

Before cheer practice that afternoon, Whitney and Giselle claimed their gym lockers. It hardly mattered that they always took the lockers in the back corner of the last row. When the prep cheerleaders changed their clothes, the younger athletes waited until the preps were dressed and gone before going to their own lockers. Once, an underclassman tried to squeeze by and accidentally stepped on Whitney's Ugg boot. "Jesus Christ! Seriously?!" Whitney yelled. The girl looked mortified, blurted out a meek "I'm sorry!", and ran away.

As much as she loved being popular, 30
Whitney wished other students understood that it wasn't so easy. Preps were stereotyped like everyone else, she said. "A prep talks like a Valley Girl, thinks she's better than everyone, is obsessed with looks, sleeps around, is usually a cheerleader, doesn't eat, parties all the time, and gets away with murder. Basically, emos want us dead."

Whitney insisted that the prep description didn't fit the "real" Whitney. "I'm not snobby," she said. "I have to be this way because it's what my friends do. If I wasn't like this, I wouldn't have any friends." She loathed the immediate judgments students made about her. She was a cheerleader; therefore she was a slut. She was a class officer; therefore she was stuck up. She wore expensive clothes; therefore she was spoiled. She said "like" too often; therefore she was flaky. She was a prep; therefore she was a bitch.

The funny thing was that if Whitney could have chosen any group at school to belong to, she wouldn't have chosen the clique that intimidated other students with cruelty. She would have chosen to be in what she considered the most nonjudgmental, down-to-earth crew at school: the punks. But it didn't matter. There was no changing groups. Once you were in a group, you were stuck there until graduation, no matter what. That was just the way high school was, Whitney was sure. So she didn't tell a soul.

The Courage of Nonconformists

If there is one trait that most cafeteria fringe share, it is courage. No matter how awkward, timid, or insecure he or she might seem, any teenager who resists blending in with the crowd is brave.

A closer look at this age group's psychology reveals that the deck is stacked against singularity from early on. Studies have shown that children are psychologically drawn to peers who are similar and more likely to end friendships with kids who are different. From the age of five, students increasingly exclude peers who don't conform to group norms. Children learn this lesson quickly. A popular Indiana eighth grader told me, "I have to be the same as everybody else, or people won't like me anymore."

35 Numerous studies show that students in the same social circle tend to have similar levels of academics, leadership, aggression, and cooperation. The most influential kids are also typically the same ones who insist most stridently on conformity; researchers have found that even in late adolescence, popular cliques are more conformist than other groups. Given that many children often try to copy populars' behavior, it makes sense that conformity trickles down the social hierarchy.

But conformity is not an admirable trait. Conformity is a cop-out. It threatens self-awareness. It can lead groups to enforce rigid and arbitrary rules. Adolescent groups with high levels of conformity experience more negative behavior — with group members and outsiders — than do groups with lower levels of conformity. Conformity can become dangerous, leading to unhealthy behaviors, and it goes against a teenager's innate desire to form a unique identity. Why, then, is conformity so common?

In the mid-twentieth century, psychologists discovered that when asked to judge an ambiguous test, such as an optical illusion, individuals usually parroted the opinions of the other people in the room. In the 1950s, social psychologist Solomon Asch decided to gauge levels of conformity when the test answers were absolutely clear. Asch assumed that people wouldn't bother to conform to an incorrect group opinion when the answer was obvious.

Asch was wrong — and his results stunned academia. For the experiment, he brought college students, one by one, into a room with six to eight other participants. He showed the room a picture of one line and a separate picture containing three lines labeled 1, 2, and 3. One of the three lines was the same length as the line in the first picture, while the other two differed by as much as several inches. Asch then had each volunteer call out the number of the line he believed to be the same length as the first. Unbeknownst to the college student, who was the last to be called on, the other participants were in on the experiment. Asch had instructed them to call out the wrong number on twelve out of eighteen trials. At least once, even when the answer was plain to see, nearly three-quarters of the students repeated the group's wrong answer.

Sixty years later, scientists are discovering that there are deeper factors at work than even Asch could have imagined. New research using brain imaging studies suggests that there is a biological explanation for the variation in people's ability to resist the temptation to conform. Neuroscientists monitoring brain images during conformity experiments similar to Asch's have found that participants are not necessarily imitating the majority merely to fit in. Instead, participants' visual perception seems to change to align with the answers of the rest of the group.

40 To understand how this change could take place, it's helpful to know that the brain is an efficient organ that likes to cheat. In order to conserve energy, it takes shortcuts whenever possible, such as the reliance on labels explained earlier. Another shortcut is a concept known as the Law of Large Numbers, a probability theorem according to which, "the more measurements you make of something, the more accurate the average of these measurements becomes." When the students in Asch's experiment conformed to group opinion, their brains were taking the Law of Large Numbers shortcut, assuming that the opinion of the group was more statistically accurate than any individual's. In 2005, neuroscientist Gregory Berns conducted a similar experiment, this time using MRIs to measure participants' brain activity. Berns observed that deferring to the group took some of the pressure off the decision-making part of the brain.

Berns also noticed something else, as he wrote in his intriguing book *Iconoclast*: "We observed the fear system kicking in, almost like a fail-safe when the individual went against the group. These are powerful biological mechanisms that make it extremely difficult to think like an iconoclast."

Berns saw increased activity in the amygdala when his test subjects did not conform to group opinion. Amygdala activity can lead to a rise in blood pressure and heart rate, sweating, and rapid breathing. "Its activation during nonconformity underscored the unpleasant nature of standing alone — even when the individual had no recollection of it," Berns wrote. "In many people, the brain would rather avoid activating the fear system and just change perception to conform with the social norm." . . .

Nonconformists, therefore, aren't just going against the grain; they're going against the brain. Either their brains aren't taking the easy way out to begin with, or in standing apart from their peers, these students are standing up to their biology. ■

Understanding and Interpreting

1. In her Introduction, Alexandra Robbins provides a historical context and background for the study that is the subject of her book. What are the main points that she makes? Does she make any assertions without support, assuming that her audience agrees? If so, explain what further explanation or support would be helpful.
2. What is "quirk theory" (par. 5), according to Robbins? Why is this an important viewpoint for her to bring up early in her argument?

3. What internal and external conflicts does Whitney face in school as a member of the popular clique? Focus on the pressures she experiences and the examples she provides to support her analysis.
4. Robbins includes lengthy descriptions of students from the popular clique, including what they are wearing, how they talk, and how they behave. What purpose do these descriptions serve in her argument about nonconformists?
5. In the section on "The Courage of Nonconformists" (par. 33), Robbins cites psychological research. What connections does Robbins draw between individuality and conformity in high school and these experiments? Have you observed examples or incidents that would support such connections?
6. Robbins asserts, "But conformity is not an admirable trait" (par. 36). How does Robbins support this statement? What instances can you think of that would challenge this assertion — either in high school or in the larger society?
7. Based only upon the information provided in this excerpt, create a simile for popularity as Robbins describes it: Popularity is like ____________ because ____________. Again, based only on the text provided here, complete the following: Nonconformity is like ____________ because ____________.

Analyzing Language, Style, and Structure

1. **Vocabulary in Context.** In paragraph 2, Robbins describes the "cafeteria fringe." What does the word "fringe" mean in this context? How is this use different from other uses of the word that you know? How effective is this word choice?
2. **Skill Focus.** In this selection, Robbins summarizes the results of several scholarly research experiments. Through her language and structural choices, how does she try to keep her piece interesting to a nonacademic audience? Offer specific examples to support your response.
3. Robbins invents a concept she calls "quirk theory," likely a play on the physics term "quark theory." In her explanation, she draws several analogies, such as this one: "We do not view a tuba player as musically challenged if he cannot play the violin. He's just a different kind of musician" (par. 5). To what extent do you find that analogy and the ones that follow valid? Identify any that you would label a "faulty analogy" — that is, a logical fallacy — and explain your reasoning.
4. While this excerpt is taken from a book that is considered to be nonfiction, Robbins at times uses a writing style and narrative elements that are common in fiction: for example, dialogue, sensory description, character development. (See Chapter 2.) Drawing from the section about Whitney, identify some techniques that you are accustomed to seeing in novels or short stories. Explain the effect of Robbins's choices.
5. Is Robbins's attitude toward Whitney impartial? Sympathetic? Critical? Support your response with evidence from the text, including language choices that Robbins makes. How does the last line of the section about Whitney affect your interpretation: "So she didn't tell a soul" (par. 32)?
6. Robbins turns from Whitney the popular conformist to three paragraphs about the "real" Whitney. In what way does Robbins's approach and language change along with this shift? Which depiction is more vivid and direct? Why? Which is more convincing? Why?
7. This excerpt includes sections from different places in Robbins's book. Is the tone Robbins takes in each section different? To what extent does Robbins maintain a consistent tone? As part of your response, describe what the tone is.

Topics for Composing

1. **Analysis.** Whitney might be viewed as the central character in this piece, if we use the language of fiction. Like most central characters, she is complex, not all good or all bad. How does Robbins portray Whitney so that her readers don't simply dismiss her as shallow and self-involved? How does she encourage her audience to view Whitney with some sympathy?
2. **Argument.** Take a position on the following assertion that Robbins makes about high school: "In precisely the years that we should be embracing differences among students, urging them to pursue their divergent interests at full throttle, we're instead forcing them into a skyline of sameness, muffling their voices, grounding their dreams" (par. 4). Support your position with evidence and reasoning from your own experience and this excerpt.
3. **Connection.** Robbins conducted her investigation over a decade ago. Based on your observations of your own school environment, what has changed? What accounts for those changes? Has social media intensified or lessened the pressures Robbins describes?
4. **Speaking and Listening.** At the end of her book, Robbins lists "31 Tips for Students, Parents, Teachers, and Schools." Using this excerpt and your own experiences, make a presentation arguing for one "tip" that your school could adopt to develop an atmosphere of acceptance and tolerance among all students. Target a specific audience of parents, teachers, administrators, or peers.
5. **Research.** Robbins makes a strong claim in her "quirk theory" definition and discussion. Conduct research to support or challenge that claim. Consider anecdotal information (the story of a highly successful entrepreneur or celebrity who was unhappy in high school, for example) as well as academic research to support your position.
6. **Research.** Do Robbins's findings only apply to schools in the United States, or do schools worldwide develop similar social groups? Research social structures within schools in other countries, and explain what might cause them to be similar or different. What ideas for improving the school environment in the U.S. might you suggest based on your findings?

from The School Days of an Indian Girl

Zitkala-Ša

National Portrait Gallery, Smithsonian Institution

Zitkala-Ša (1876-1938), also known as Gertrude Simmons Bonnin, was a writer, musician, and political activist. Born on a Sioux reservation in South Dakota and educated by Quaker missionaries in Indiana, she spent her life torn between her Sioux heritage and the dominant white culture of the time. As a writer, she brought traditional American Indian stories to a widespread readership. Zitkala-Ša published several works chronicling her struggles to reconcile her Sioux culture with mainstream American culture. An avid lobbyist and a supporter of American Indian rights, she founded the National Council of American Indians in 1926 to advocate for American Indians to gain American citizenship. Between 1900 and 1902, she published a series of autobiographical articles in the *Atlantic Monthly*. The following excerpt is from one of them, "The School Days of an Indian Girl."

KEY CONTEXT By the end of the nineteenth century, American westward expansion had driven much of the native population of American Indians onto reservations. As part of the policy of the day, many American Indian children attended boarding schools, where a central goal was assimilation into mainstream American society. To that end, the children were often forbidden to speak their tribal language, required to dress in the manner of white students, and forced to leave behind the cultural and religious practices they had grown up with. In the two sections that follow, Zitkala-Ša describes her response to the new environment, a missionary school, where she arrived with seven other American Indian children after a long train ride from her home.

I. The Land of Red Apples

THERE were eight in our party of bronzed children who were going East with the missionaries. Among us were three young braves, two tall girls, and we three little ones, Judéwin, Thowin, and I.

We had been very impatient to start on our journey to the Red Apple Country, which, we were told, lay a little beyond the great circular horizon of the Western prairie. Under a sky of rosy apples we dreamt of roaming as freely and happily as we had chased the cloud shadows on the Dakota plains. We had anticipated much pleasure from a ride on the iron horse, but the throngs of staring palefaces disturbed and troubled us.

On the train, fair women, with tottering babies on each arm, stopped their haste and scrutinized the children of absent mothers. Large men, with heavy bundles in their hands, halted near by, and riveted their glassy blue eyes upon us.

I sank deep into the corner of my seat, for I resented being watched. Directly in front of me, children who were no larger than I hung themselves upon the backs of their seats, with their bold white faces toward me. Sometimes they took their forefingers out of their mouths and pointed at my moccasined feet. Their mothers, instead of reproving such rude curiosity, looked closely at me, and attracted their children's further notice to my blanket. This embarrassed me, and kept me constantly on the verge of tears.

5 I sat perfectly still, with my eyes downcast, daring only now and then to shoot long glances around me. Chancing to turn to the window at my side, I was quite breathless upon seeing one familiar object. It was the telegraph pole which strode by at short paces. Very near my mother's dwelling, along the edge of a road thickly bordered with wild sunflowers, some poles like these had been planted by white men. Often I had stopped, on my way down the road, to hold my ear against the pole, and, hearing its low moaning, I used to wonder what the paleface had done to hurt it. Now I sat watching for each pole that glided by to be the last one.

In this way I had forgotten my uncomfortable surroundings, when I heard one of my comrades call out my name. I saw the missionary standing very near, tossing candies and gums into our midst. This amused us all, and we tried to see who could catch the most of the sweetmeats.

Though we rode several days inside of the iron horse, I do not recall a single thing about our luncheons.

It was night when we reached the school grounds. The lights from the windows of the large buildings fell upon some of the icicled trees that stood beneath them. We were led toward an open door, where the brightness of the lights within flooded out over the heads of the excited palefaces who blocked the way. My body trembled more from fear than from the snow I trod upon.

Entering the house, I stood close against the wall. The strong glaring light in the large whitewashed room dazzled my eyes. The noisy hurrying of hard shoes upon a bare wooden floor increased the whirring in my ears. My only safety seemed to be in keeping next to the wall. As I was wondering in which direction to escape

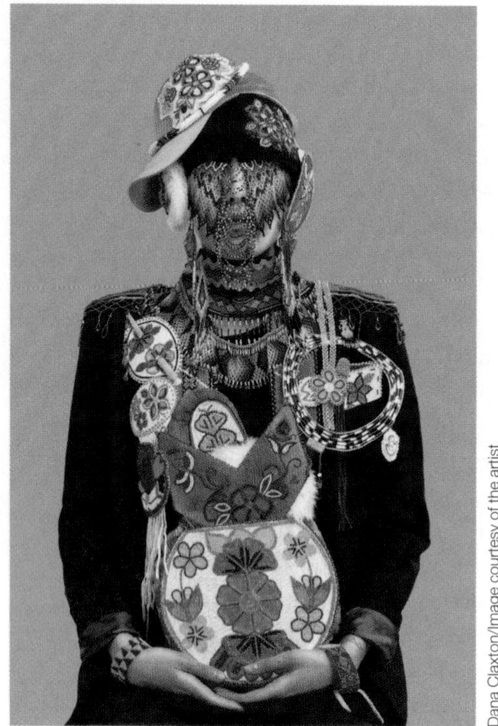

Dana Claxton/Image courtesy of the artist

Born in Saskatchewan, Canada, artist Dana Claxton is a member of the Lakota First Nations tribal group. This 2018 image, entitled *Headdress-Jeneen*, depicts performance artist Jeneen Frei Njootli with traditional beaded objects.

How might this image be a meditation on the difficult balance of combining traditional and contemporary cultures? What is the effect of concealing the subject's face? Why do you think Zitkala-Ša would embrace or reject the identity suggested by this image?

from all this confusion, two warm hands grasped me firmly, and in the same moment I was tossed high in midair. A rosy-cheeked paleface woman caught me in her arms. I was both frightened and insulted by such trifling. I stared into her eyes, wishing her to let me stand on my own feet, but she jumped me up and down with increasing enthusiasm. My mother had never made a plaything of her wee daughter. Remembering this I began to cry aloud.

They misunderstood the cause of my tears, and placed me at a white table loaded with food. There our party were united again. As I did not hush my crying, one of the older ones whispered to me, "Wait until you are alone in the night."

It was very little I could swallow besides my sobs, that evening.

"Oh, I want my mother and my brother Dawée! I want to go to my aunt!" I pleaded; but the ears of the palefaces could not hear me.

From the table we were taken along an upward incline of wooden boxes, which I learned afterward to call a stairway. At the top was a quiet hall, dimly lighted. Many narrow beds were in one straight line down the entire length of the wall. In them lay sleeping brown faces, which peeped just out of the coverings. I was tucked into bed with one of the tall girls, because she talked to me in my mother tongue and seemed to soothe me.

I had arrived in the wonderful land of rosy skies, but I was not happy, as I had thought I should be. My long travel and the bewildering sights had exhausted me. I fell asleep, heaving deep, tired sobs. My tears were left to dry themselves in streaks, because neither my aunt nor my mother was near to wipe them away.

II. The Cutting of My Long Hair

The first day in the land of apples was a bitter-cold one; for the snow still covered the ground, and the trees were bare. A large bell rang for breakfast, its loud metallic voice crashing through the belfry overhead and into our sensitive ears. The annoying clatter of shoes on bare floors gave us no peace. The constant clash of harsh noises, with an undercurrent of many voices murmuring an unknown tongue, made a bedlam within which I was securely tied. And though my spirit tore itself in struggling for its lost freedom, all was useless.

A paleface woman, with white hair, came up after us. We were placed in a line of girls who were marching into the dining room. These were Indian girls, in stiff shoes and closely clinging dresses. The small girls wore sleeved aprons and shingled hair. As I walked noiselessly in my soft moccasins, I felt like sinking to the floor, for my blanket had been stripped from my shoulders. I looked hard at the Indian girls, who seemed not to care that they were even more immodestly dressed than I, in their tightly fitting clothes. While we marched in, the boys entered at an opposite door. I watched for the three young braves who came in our party. I spied them in the rear ranks, looking as uncomfortable as I felt.

A small bell was tapped, and each of the pupils drew a chair from under the table. Supposing this act meant they were to be seated, I pulled out mine and at once slipped into it from one side. But when I turned my head, I saw that I was the only one seated, and all the rest at our table remained standing. Just as I began to rise, looking shyly around to see how chairs were to be used, a second bell was sounded. All were seated at last, and I had to crawl back into my chair again. I heard a man's voice at one end of the hall, and I looked around to see him. But all the others hung their heads over their plates. As I glanced at the long chain of tables, I caught the eyes of a paleface woman upon me. Immediately I dropped my eyes, wondering why I was so keenly watched by the strange woman. The man ceased his mutterings, and then a third bell was tapped. Every one picked up his knife and fork and began eating. I began crying instead, for by this time I was afraid to venture anything more.

But this eating by formula was not the hardest trial in that first day. Late in the morning, my friend Judéwin gave me a terrible warning. Judéwin knew a few words of English, and she had overheard the paleface woman talk about cutting our long, heavy hair. Our mothers had taught us that only unskilled warriors who were captured had their hair shingled by the

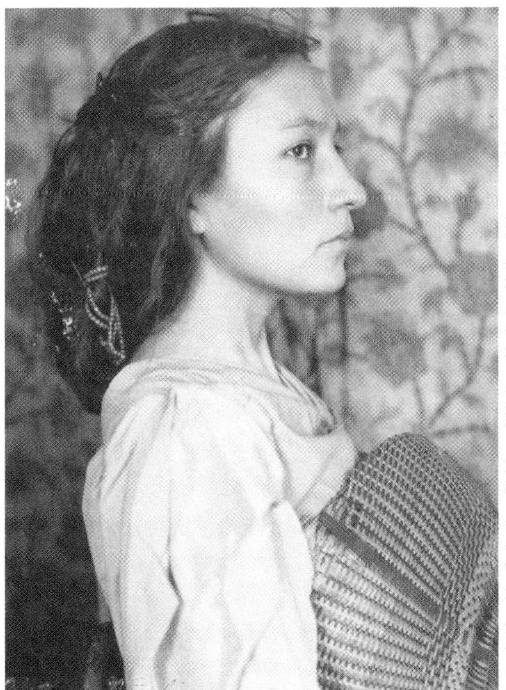

Gertrude Kasebier Collection, Division of Work and Industry, National Museum of American History, Smithsonian Institution.

Gertrude Kasebier Collection, Division of Work and Industry, National Museum of American History, Smithsonian Institution

These are two portraits of Zitkala-Ša, both taken in 1898, by the American photographer Gertrude Käsebier (1852–1934). By some accounts, Zitkala-Ša herself decided on the clothing and poses.

How do these images depict Zitkala-Ša's identities? In what details do you recognize elements of the American Indian and European American cultures she navigated? Does she seem to privilege one over the other or portray a balance?

extending beyond the text

Assimilating American Indian people into mainstream white society was a central goal of the missionary schools. Language was one means of achieving this goal; appearance was another. Following are three "before and after" photographs of groups and individuals who entered a missionary school in their traditional dress and left significantly changed. What are the most dramatic changes you see? What more subtle changes do you find?

Eskimo Group

As they entered Carlisle in 1897

As they appeared in school dress

From John N. Choate's Souvenir of the Carlisle Indian School (Carlisle, PA: J. N. Choate, 1902)/Archives & Special Collections at Dickinson College

Tom Torlino — Navajo

As he entered school in 1882

As he appeared three years later

John N. Choate, Carlisle, PA, National Archives and Records Administration

Wounded Yellow Robe, Henry Standing Bear, Chauncy Yellow Robe

Sioux boys as they entered the school in 1883

Three years later

From John N. Choate's Souvenir of the Carlisle Indian School (Carlisle, PA: J. N. Choate, 1902)/Archives & Special Collections at Dickinson College enemy. Among our people, short hair was worn by mourners, and shingled hair by cowards!

We discussed our fate some moments, and when Judéwin said, “We have to submit, because they are strong,” I rebelled.

20 “No, I will not submit! I will struggle first!” I answered.

I watched my chance, and when no one noticed I disappeared. I crept up the stairs as quietly as I could in my squeaking shoes — my moccasins had been exchanged for shoes. Along the hall I passed, without knowing whither I was going. Turning aside to an open door, I found a large room with three white beds in it. The windows were covered with dark green curtains, which made the room very dim. Thankful that no one was there, I directed my steps toward the corner farthest from the door. On my hands and knees I crawled under the bed, and cuddled myself in the dark corner.

From my hiding place I peered out, shuddering with fear whenever I heard footsteps near by. Though in the hall loud voices were calling my name, and I knew that even Judéwin was searching for me, I did not open my mouth to answer. Then the steps were quickened and the voices became excited. The sounds came nearer and nearer. Women and girls entered the room. I held my breath, and watched them open closet doors and peep behind large trunks. Some one threw up the curtains, and the room was filled with sudden light. What caused them to stoop and look under the bed I do not know. I remember being dragged out, though I resisted by kicking and scratching wildly. In spite of myself, I was carried downstairs and tied fast in a chair.

I cried aloud, shaking my head all the while until I felt the cold blades of the scissors against my neck, and heard them gnaw off one of my thick braids. Then I lost my spirit. Since the day I was taken from my mother I had suffered extreme indignities. People had stared at me. I had been tossed about in the air like a wooden puppet. And now my long hair was shingled like a coward's! In my anguish I moaned for my mother, but no one came to comfort me. Not a soul reasoned quietly with me, as my own mother used to do; for now I was only one of many little animals driven by a herder. ■

Understanding and Interpreting

1. In the opening paragraphs, what examples do you find of Zitkala-Ša's surprise and confusion at the difference between her expectations and the reality of her situation? What behaviors does she find objectionable from the perspective of her own family's values?
2. Why is the narrator, Zitkala-Ša, “both frightened and insulted” by the behavior of the “rosy-cheeked paleface woman” (par. 9) at the school?
3. In the second section, “The Cutting of My Long Hair,” Zitkala-Ša recounts sounds that are unfamiliar or jarring to her. How does this sensory response add to the alienation she feels from her new environment?
4. Zitkala-Ša describes the shingling of her hair: “. . . I felt the cold blades of the scissors against my neck, and heard them gnaw off one of my thick braids” (par. 23). What does this description of the scissors add to the impact of the haircutting?
5. Having her hair cut was the most dramatic of the “extreme indignities” (par. 23) that Zitkala-Ša describes. What other measures are taken by the missionaries to distance her (and her peers) from her native culture?
6. What role does language play in the experience of young Zitkala-Ša? In what instances does she show that she is most aware of the importance of her own language?
7. What traditions and practices of the Zitkala-Ša's culture are the school authorities ignorant of? To what extent does that ignorance lessen the offense, from the narrator's perspective?

Analyzing Language, Style, and Structure

1. **Vocabulary in Context.** Zitkala-Ša describes the students she meets at the school: "The small girls wore sleeved aprons and shingled hair" (par. 16). What does "shingled" mean in this context? How is that meaning similar to or different from other meanings you have encountered for the word "shingled"?
2. **Skill Focus.** Zitkala-Ša published these pieces in the *Atlantic Magazine* to an audience that consisted mainly of white, educated readers. How does she try to appeal to those readers while depicting her insensitive, often cruel treatment at the hands of the white school authorities?
3. In this excerpt, the white people, including the missionaries, are referred to as "palefaces." Even if this reference could be interpreted as pejorative or disrespectful at the time the autobiography was written, why might Zitkala-Ša have used it anyway?
4. How does the language, such as "a sky of rosy apples," convey the idealistic expectations of Zitkala-Ša as she embarks on her journey? Pay close attention to the images of nature as you formulate your response.
5. While Zitkala-Ša vows to "struggle" (par. 20), by the end she admits, "I lost my spirit" (par. 23). What emotional weight does she attach to the word "spirit" in this context?
6. Throughout this autobiographical account, Zitkala-Ša takes readers to the immediacy of her childhood experiences, yet these are filtered through her adult consciousness. What examples of the adult "interpreter" do you find in these two excerpts?

Topics for Composing

1. **Analysis.** In an earlier section (not included here) that describes the journey of the children to the missionary school, Zitkala-Ša describes herself being "as frightened and bewildered as the captured young of a wild creature." Discuss how the two sections you've read reinforce this sense of feeling trapped and helpless. Consider the word choices Zitkala-Ša makes as part of your discussion.
2. **Argument.** In her book *Tender Violence: Domestic Visions in an Age of U.S. Imperialism* (2000), scholar Laura Wexler describes the assimilationist education of seemingly well-intentioned missionaries as "tender violence." Do schools today, whether public or private institutions in K-12, promote and privilege a mainstream culture by devaluing minority cultures? Or are there concerted efforts to honor a range of cultures and traditions? Support your position with your own experience and observations as well as information from your reading.
3. **Research.** Do more research into the biography of Zitkala-Ša. To what extent can she be said to have challenged and even revised the dominant assessment of tribal culture in the United States?
4. **Connection.** When she learned that the school officials were planning on cutting her hair, Zitkala-Ša said, "No, I will not submit! I will struggle first!" (par. 20). While you likely have never experienced something quite so dramatic as this, describe a time when you had a conflict with a teacher or an administrator about a school policy or directive that you did not want to submit to. Why did you object and what was the outcome?
5. **Speaking and Listening.** In addition to being a writer, Zitkala-Ša was also a gifted musician and composer. She is credited with writing what is likely the first Native American opera, *The Sun Bird*, performances of which are widely available on YouTube. Watch or listen to a segment or two of a production and explain what similarities you find between the opera and the excerpts you read from *The School Days of an Indian Girl*.

central text

Against School

John Taylor Gatto

Luanne M. Ferris/Times Union Archive

A three-time Teacher of the Year in New York State, John Taylor Gatto (1935–2018) was one of public schooling's fiercest critics. In fact, he resigned his teaching job in a 1991 editorial in the *Wall Street Journal*, stating "I can't teach this way any longer. If you hear of a job where I don't have to hurt kids to make a living, let me know." The title of one of Gatto's books, *Dumbing Us Down: The Hidden Curriculum of Compulsory Schooling* (2002), reveals his attitude toward

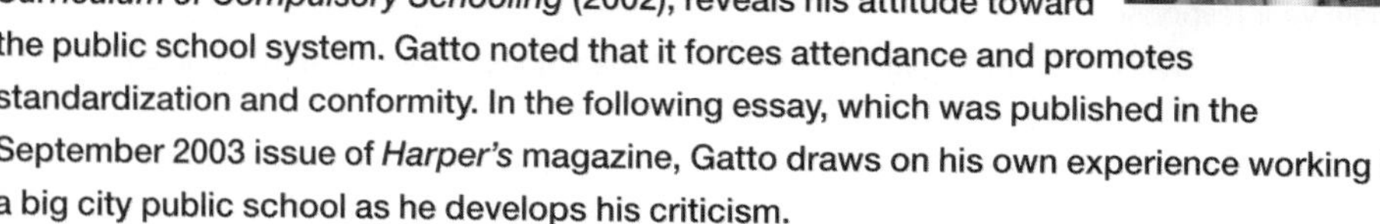
the public school system. Gatto noted that it forces attendance and promotes standardization and conformity. In the following essay, which was published in the September 2003 issue of *Harper's* magazine, Gatto draws on his own experience working in a big city public school as he develops his criticism.

I taught for thirty years in some of the worst schools in Manhattan, and in some of the best, and during that time I became an expert in boredom. Boredom was everywhere in my world, and if you asked the kids, as I often did, why they felt so bored, they always gave the same answers: They said the work was stupid, that it made no sense, that they already knew it. They said they wanted to be doing something real, not just sitting around. They said teachers didn't seem to know much about their subjects and clearly weren't interested in learning more. And the kids were right: their teachers were every bit as bored as they were.

Boredom is the common condition of schoolteachers, and anyone who has spent time in a teachers' lounge can vouch for the low energy, the whining, the dispirited attitudes, to be found there. When asked why they feel bored, the teachers tend to blame the kids, as you might expect. Who wouldn't get bored teaching students who are rude and interested only in grades? If even that. Of course, teachers are themselves products of the same twelve-year compulsory school programs that so thoroughly bore their students, and as school personnel they are trapped inside structures even more rigid than those imposed upon the children. Who, then, is to blame?

We all are. My grandfather taught me that. One afternoon when I was seven I complained to him of boredom, and he batted me hard on the head. He told me that I was never to use that term in his presence again, that if I was bored it was my fault and no one else's. The obligation to amuse and instruct myself was entirely my own, and people who didn't know that were childish people, to be avoided if possible. Certainly not to be trusted. That episode cured me of boredom forever, and here and there over the years I was able to pass on the lesson to some remarkable student. For the most part, however, I found it futile to challenge the official notion that boredom and childishness were the natural state of affairs in the classroom. Often I had to defy custom, and even bend the law, to help kids break out of this trap.

Bob Englehart, The Hartford Courant/Cagle Cartoons, Inc.

"Mandatory minimum sentence" is a legal term referring to the lowest sentence that a court must give to a person convicted of a crime, regardless of the unique qualities of the offender or the offense. **How does this term apply to school in this cartoon? Identify a piece of evidence from Gatto's article that would support this character's claim about school.**

The empire struck back, of course; childish adults regularly conflate opposition with disloyalty. I once returned from a medical leave to discover that all evidence of my having been granted the leave had been purposely destroyed, that my job had been terminated, and that I no longer possessed even a teaching license. After nine months of tormented effort I was able to retrieve the license when a school secretary testified to witnessing the plot unfold. In the meantime my family suffered more than I care to remember. By the time I finally retired in 1991, I had more than enough reason to think of our schools — with their long-term, cell-block-style, forced confinement of both students and teachers — as virtual factories of childishness. Yet I honestly could not see why they had to be that way. My own experience had revealed to me what many other teachers must learn along the way, too, yet keep to themselves for fear of reprisal: if we wanted to we could easily and inexpensively jettison the old, stupid structures and help kids take an education rather than merely receive a schooling. We could encourage the best qualities of youthfulness — curiosity, adventure, resilience, the capacity for surprising insight — simply by being more flexible about time, texts, and tests, by introducing kids to truly competent adults, and by giving each student what autonomy he or she needs in order to take a risk every now and then.

But we don't do that. And the more I asked 5
why not, and persisted in thinking about the "problem" of schooling as an engineer might, the more I missed the point: What if there is no "problem" with our schools? What if they are the way they are, so expensively flying in the face of common sense and long experience in how children learn things, not because they are doing something wrong but because they are doing something right? Is it possible that George W. Bush accidentally spoke the truth when he said we would "leave no child behind"? Could it be that our schools are designed to make sure not one of them ever really grows up?

Do we really need school? I don't mean education, just forced schooling: six classes a day, five days a week, nine months a year, for twelve years. Is this deadly routine really necessary? And if so, for what? Don't hide behind reading, writing, and arithmetic as a rationale, because 2 million happy homeschoolers have surely put that banal justification to rest. Even if they hadn't, a considerable number of well-known Americans never went through the twelve-year wringer our kids currently go through, and they turned out all right. George Washington, Benjamin Franklin, Thomas Jefferson, Abraham Lincoln? Someone taught them, to be sure, but they were not products of a school system, and not one of them was ever "graduated" from a secondary school.

Throughout most of American history, kids generally didn't go to high school, yet the unschooled rose to be admirals, like Farragut; inventors, like Edison; captains of industry, like Carnegie and Rockefeller; writers, like Melville and Twain and Conrad; and even scholars, like Margaret Mead. In fact, until pretty recently people who reached the age of thirteen weren't looked upon as children at all. Ariel Durant, who co-wrote an enormous, and very good, multivolume history of the world with her husband, Will, was happily married at fifteen, and who could reasonably claim that Ariel Durant was an uneducated person? Unschooled, perhaps, but not uneducated.

We have been taught (that is, schooled) in this country to think of "success" as synonymous with, or at least dependent upon, "schooling," but historically that isn't true in either an intellectual or a financial sense. And plenty of people throughout the world today find a way to educate themselves without resorting to a system of compulsory secondary schools that all too often resemble prisons. Why, then, do Americans confuse education with just such a system? What exactly is the purpose of our public schools?

Mass schooling of a compulsory nature really got its teeth into the United States between 1905 and 1915, though it was conceived of much earlier and pushed for throughout most of the nineteenth century. The reason given for this enormous upheaval of family life and cultural traditions was, roughly speaking, threefold: 1) To make good people. 2) To make good citizens. 3) To make each person his or her personal best.

These goals are still trotted out today on a 10
regular basis, and most of us accept them in one form or another as a decent definition of public education's mission, however short schools actually fall in achieving them. But we are dead wrong. Compounding our error is the fact that the national literature holds numerous and surprisingly consistent statements of compulsory schooling's true purpose. We have, for example, the great H. L. Mencken, who wrote in *The American Mercury* for April 1924 that the aim of public education is not "to fill the young of the species with knowledge and awaken their intelligence. . . . Nothing could be further from the truth. The aim is simply to reduce as many individuals as possible to the same safe level, to breed and train a standardized citizenry, to put down dissent and originality. That is its aim in the United States . . . and that is its aim everywhere else."

There you have it. Now you know. We don't need Karl Marx's conception of a grand warfare between the classes to see that it is in the interest of complex management, economic or political, to dumb people down, to demoralize them, to divide them from one another, and to discard them if they don't conform. Class may frame the proposition, as when Woodrow Wilson, then president of Princeton University, said the following to the New York City School Teachers Association in 1909: "We want one class of persons to have a liberal education, and we want another class of persons, a very much larger class, of necessity, in every society, to forgo the privileges of a liberal education and fit themselves to perform specific difficult manual

Playground (acrylic on canvas)/Crook, PJ/ PJ Crook/Private Collection/Bridgeman Images

Entitled *Playground*, this painting by PJ Crook shows young people interacting during recess. **What would Gatto likely say about such unscripted moments during the school day? In your experience, what kinds of learning experiences take place when students have free time together?**

tasks." But the motives behind the disgusting decisions that bring about these ends need not be class-based at all. They can stem purely from fear, or from the by now familiar belief that "efficiency" is the paramount virtue, rather than love, liberty, laughter, or hope. Above all, they can stem from simple greed.

There were vast fortunes to be made, after all, in an economy based on mass production and organized to favor the large corporation rather than the small business or the family farm. But mass production required mass consumption, and at the turn of the twentieth century most Americans considered it both unnatural and unwise to buy things they didn't actually need. Mandatory schooling was a godsend on that count. School didn't have to train kids in any direct sense to think they should consume nonstop, because it did something even better: it encouraged them not to think at all. And that left them sitting ducks for another great invention of the modern era — marketing.

We buy televisions, and then we buy the things we see on the television. We buy computers, and then we buy the things we see on the computer. We buy \$150 sneakers whether we need them or not, and when they fall apart too soon we buy another pair. We drive SUVs and believe the lie that they constitute a kind of life insurance, even when we're upside-down in them. And, worst of all, we don't bat an eye when Ari Fleischer[1] tells us to "be careful what you say," even if we remember having been told somewhere back in school that America is the land of the free. We simply buy that one too. Our schooling, as intended, has seen to it.

Now for the good news. Once you understand the logic behind modern

[1]Press secretary to President George W. Bush from 2001 to 2003. — Eds.

extending beyond the text

The logical extension of Gatto's argument is that students should not be required to attend school. Consider that point as you examine this chart from the Bureau of Labor Statistics.

Earnings and unemployment rates by educational attainment

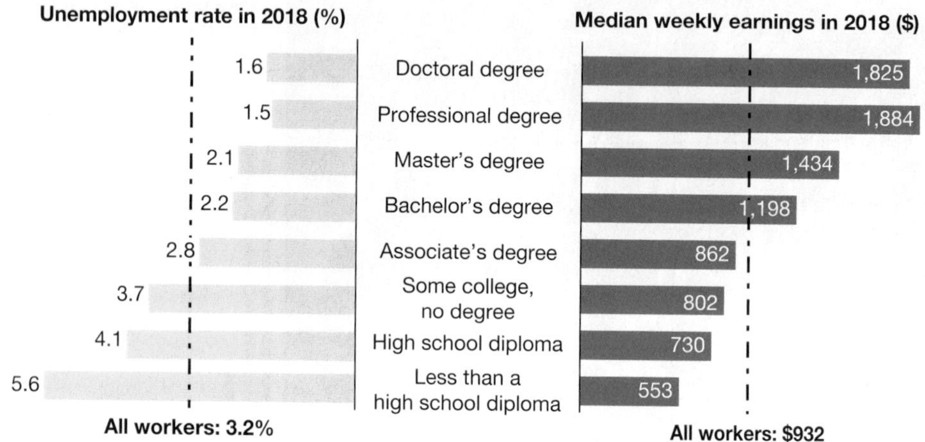

Note: Data are for persons age 25 and over. Earnings are for full-time wage and salary workers.
Data from Current Population Survey, U.S. Bureau of Labor Statistics, U.S. Department of Labor

What are some conclusions that you can draw from the data presented in this bar graph? How does this graph affect your view of Gatto's argument? How might you use the graph to support or challenge Gatto?

schooling, its tricks and traps are fairly easy to avoid. School trains children to be employees and consumers; teach your own to be leaders and adventurers. School trains children to obey reflexively; teach your own to think critically and independently. Well-schooled kids have a low threshold for boredom; help your own to develop an inner life so that they'll never be bored. Urge them to take on the serious material, the grown-up material, in history, literature, philosophy, music, art, economics, theology — all the stuff schoolteachers know well enough to avoid. Challenge your kids with plenty of solitude so that they can learn to enjoy their own company, to conduct inner dialogues. Well-schooled people are conditioned to dread being alone, and they seek constant companionship through the TV, the computer, the cell phone, and through shallow friendships quickly acquired and quickly abandoned. Your children should have a more meaningful life, and they can.

First, though, we must wake up to what our 15
schools really are: laboratories of experimentation on young minds, drill centers for the habits and attitudes that corporate society demands. Mandatory education serves children only incidentally; its real purpose is to turn them into servants. Don't let your own have their childhoods extended, not even for a day. If David Farragut could take command of a captured British warship as a preteen, if Thomas Edison could publish a broadsheet at the age of

twelve, if Ben Franklin could apprentice himself to a printer at the same age (then put himself through a course of study that would choke a Yale senior today), there's no telling what your own kids could do. After a long life, and thirty years in the public school trenches, I've concluded that genius is as common as dirt. We suppress our genius only because we haven't yet figured out how to manage a population of educated men and women. The solution, I think, is simple and glorious. Let them manage themselves. ■

Understanding and Interpreting

1. What is the main claim that John Taylor Gatto makes? Find one sentence that states his claim.
2. Gatto begins his essay with an examination of boredom. What does he say causes this boredom? What is the result?
3. Gatto identifies three goals of compulsory education (par. 9). Summarize those goals and explain why Gatto thinks that they are not accurate.
4. What do you think Gatto means when he argues that "it is in the interest of complex management, economic or political, to dumb people down, to demoralize them, to divide them from one another, and to discard them if they don't conform" (par. 11)? What evidence does he offer to support that assertion?
5. How does Gatto link consumerism with the habits of mind taught in public schools (pars. 12–13)? What does he use as evidence to back up that claim, and how effective is that evidence?
6. According to Gatto, who is most responsible for the problems in American education? Is it the teachers? School administrators? Parents? Students? Politicians? What evidence does he cite to support his claim?
7. Gatto argues that there is a vast difference between "schooling" and "education" (par. 6). How does he distinguish between the two?
8. Gatto calls into question the causal relationship between school and success (par. 8). On what basis does he question school's role in success?
9. What, according to Gatto, is "the good news" (par. 14)? Does the solution he suggests require full-scale dismantling of the institution of public education in the United States? Explain.

Analyzing Language, Style, and Structure

1. **Vocabulary in Context.** Gatto writes that "genius is as common as dirt" (par 15). What does "genius" mean in this context? How is the usage here different from what you might expect? What is the effect of this usage on readers?
2. **Skill Focus.** At the end of his essay, Gatto directly addresses parents and calls upon them to take action. How has he appealed to his audience, readers of *Harper's* magazine? Respond in terms of the way he establishes his ethos, the evidence he cites, and his appeal to pathos.
3. Gatto begins by describing his own experience, a discouraging one, as a teacher. What effect does the inclusion of his personal experience have on his argument? Why would he include a negative example rather than simply recounting his education, accomplishments, and accolades?

4. In the first two paragraphs, Gatto uses many words with negative connotations, such as "boredom" and "stupid." What others do you notice? What is the cumulative effect of these choices?
5. Gatto cites examples of presidents, inventors, writers, and wealthy businesspersons to make his case that compulsory schooling is not necessary for success (pars. 6–7). He mentions several of these people again at the end of the essay (par. 15). Explain why you do or do not find such examples persuasive.
6. Gatto uses figurative language, especially metaphor and simile, to characterize environments and purpose of public schools. Identify at least three of them and explain their effect.
7. Gatto lists three reasons for mandatory public schooling, as it was conceived in the United States. He then asserts that they are not truly the principles that govern education today. What evidence (including examples) does he cite to support this assertion? How persuasive do you find this part of his argument?
8. Gatto's language moves between informal expressions (such as "The empire struck back") and quite elevated language ("Class may frame the proposition"). Do you find these shifts to be an effective rhetorical strategy, or are they inconsistent and distracting? Support your position by referring to specific passages.
9. What vulnerabilities do you find in Gatto's argument? Look back through the piece and identify a place where you think that Gatto does not effectively support a claim he is making, or where his logic seems faulty. Why do you think his argument is not effective in the section you have chosen?

Topics for Composing

1. **Analysis.** Choose one of the following assertions made by Gatto or one of the sources he cites and analyze the evidence he provides to support it.
   a. "[O]ur schools . . . [are] virtual factories of childishness" (par. 4).
   b. "[T]he aim of public education is . . . 'to reduce as many individuals as possible to the same safe level, to breed and train a standardized citizenry, to put down dissent and originality'" (par. 10, quoting H. L. Mencken).
   c. "Mandatory education serves children only incidentally; its real purpose is to turn them into servants" (par. 15).
   d. "[W]e must wake up to what our schools really are: laboratories of experimentation on young minds, drill centers for the habits and attitudes that corporate society demands" (par. 15).
2. **Argument.** Is Gatto right or not? Are public schools destructive to students and teachers alike? Or are they essential to building community? Develop an argument in response to Gatto based on your own experience, observation, and reading.
3. **Connection.** To what extent do you agree with Gatto about the weaknesses inherent in public schools in the United States? Write a narrative about a situation you experienced or observed that made you want to change something about how you experience learning at school. Bring the experience to life through careful choices of language and tone. Remember to show rather than tell so that your readers will feel the impact.
4. **Speaking and Listening.** In paragraph 11, Gatto quotes former President Woodrow Wilson, who at the time of this statement was president of Princeton University: "We want one class of persons to have a liberal education, and we want another class of persons, a very much larger class, of necessity, in every society, to forgo the privileges of a liberal education and fit

themselves to perform specific difficult manual tasks." In what ways, if any, do you see evidence of Wilson's attitude toward education and class in your own educational setting? Work in small groups to arrive at a response. Then, share your response with the full class.

5. **Research.** Gatto discusses several prominent figures from the far past — Herman Melville, Mark Twain, Thomas Edison, Benjamin Franklin — who became accomplished and successful in various ways without formal education. Research a more contemporary figure who has made a mark as an innovator, an entrepreneur, or a successful individual in some field without following the conventional route of formal education, particularly college.

6. **Research.** Homeschooling is a popular solution for parents who choose not to involve their children in formal schooling. Conduct research on homeschooling, including, if possible, interviews with a parent who has chosen this route for his or her child, or with a young person who has been home-schooled. Finally, consider whether Gatto would or would not be an advocate of homeschooling.

7. **Multimodal.** Toward the end of the essay, Gatto calls on parents to teach their own children to be "leaders and adventurers," to think "critically and independently," and to "develop an inner life so that they'll never be bored" (par. 14). Develop a poster or an advertisement for a school that would serve these purposes. What would be its main guiding principles and characteristics? How would you convey them?

Abolish High School

Rebecca Solnit

David Levenson/Getty Images

Rebecca Solnit (b. 1961) is a writer, a historian, and an activist who has authored over twenty books on feminism, the environment, history, politics, and art. Two of her bestselling books are *Men Explain Things to Me* (2015) and *The Mother of All Questions* (2017). Her most recent book is *Whose Story Is This: Recent Conflicts, Old Chapters* (2019), a collection of essays exploring the impact of demographic shifts and changes in attitude toward gender roles. As she writes in the opening, "Who gets to be the subject of the story is an immensely political question." The following article was originally published in 2015 in *Harper's* magazine, where Solnit is a contributing editor.

I didn't go to high school. This I think of as one of my proudest accomplishments and one of my greatest escapes, because everyone who grows up in the United States goes to high school. It's such an inevitable experience that people often mishear me and think I dropped out.

I was a withdrawn, bookish kid all through elementary school, but the difficulty of being a misfit intensified when I started seventh grade. As I left campus at the end of my first day, people shouted insults that ensured I knew my clothes didn't cut it. Then there was P.E., where I had to don a horrendous turquoise-striped polyester garment that looked like a baby's onesie and follow orders to run or jump or play ball — which is hard to do when you're deeply withdrawn — after which I had to get naked, in all my late-bloomer puniness, and take showers in front of strangers. In science class we were graded on crafting notebooks with many colors of pen; in home economics, which was only for girls — boys had shop — we learned to make a new kind of cake by combining pudding mix with cake mix; even in English class I can remember reading only one book: Dickens's flattest novel, *Hard Times*. At least the old history teacher in the plaid mohair sweaters let me doze in the front row, so long as I knew the answers when asked.

In junior high, everything became a little more dangerous. Most of my peers seemed to be learning the elaborate dance between the sexes, sometimes literally, at school dances I never dreamed of attending, or in the form of the routines through which girls with pompoms ritually celebrated boys whose own role in that rite consisted of slamming into one another on the field.

I skipped my last year of traditional junior high school, detouring for ninth and tenth grade into a newly created alternative junior high. (The existing alternative high school only took eleventh and twelfth graders.) The district used this new school as a dumping ground for its most insubordinate kids, so I shared two adjoining classrooms with hard-partying teenage girls who dated adult drug dealers, boys who reeked of pot smoke, and other misfits like me. The wild kids impressed me because, unlike the timorous high achievers I'd often been grouped with at the mainstream school, they seemed fearless and free, skeptical about the systems around them.

5 There were only a few dozen students, and the adults treated us like colleagues. There was friendship and mild scorn but little cruelty, nothing that pitted us against one another or humiliated us, no violence, no clearly inculcated hierarchy. I didn't gain much conventional knowledge, but I read voraciously and had good conversations. You can learn a lot that way. Besides, I hadn't been gaining much in regular school either.

I was ravenous to learn. I'd waited for years for a proper chance at it, and the high school in my town didn't seem like a place where I was going to get it. I passed the G.E.D. test at fifteen, started community college the following fall, and transferred after two semesters to a four-year college, where I began, at last, to get an education commensurate with my appetite.

What was it, I sometimes wonder, that I was supposed to have learned in the years of high school that I avoided? High school is often considered a definitive American experience, in two senses: an experience that nearly everyone shares, and one that can define who you are, for better or worse, for the rest of your life. I'm grateful I escaped the particular definition that high school would have imposed on me, and I wish everyone else who suffered could have escaped it, too.

For a long time I've thought that high school should be abolished. I don't mean that people in their teens should not be educated at public expense. The question is what they are educated in. An abolitionist proposal should begin by acknowledging all the excellent schools and teachers and educations out there; the people who have a pleasant, useful time in high school; and the changes being wrought in the nature of secondary education today. It should also recognize the tremendous variety of schools, including charter and magnet schools in the public system and the private schools — religious, single-sex, military, and prep — that about 10 percent of American students attend, in which the values and pedagogical systems may be radically different. But despite the caveats and anomalies, the good schools and the students who thrive (or at least survive), high school is hell for too many Americans. If this is so, I wonder why people should be automatically consigned to it.

In 2010, Dan Savage began the It Gets Better Project, which has gathered and posted video testimonials from gay and lesbian adults and queer-positive supporters (tens of thousands of them, eventually, including professional sports stars and the president) to address the rash of suicides by young queer people. The testimonials reassure teenagers that there is life after high school, that before long they'll be able to be who they are without persecution — able to find love, able to live with dignity, and able to get through each day without facing intense harassment. It's a worthy project, but it implicitly accepts that non-straight kids must spend their formative years passing through a homophobic gauntlet before arriving at a less hostile adult world. Why should they have to wait?

10 Suicide is the third leading cause of death for teens, responsible for some 4,600 deaths per year. Federal studies report that for every suicide there are at least a hundred attempts — nearly half a million a year. Eight percent of high school

Rebecca Pells

Much of what Solnit describes about her own experience in school characterizes her as an introvert in a world that privileges extroverts. Contemporary British artist Rebecca Pells chose her painting *The Bench* to accompany a piece she wrote for her blog on the virtues of being an introvert.

In what ways does this painting draw us into the world of the introvert? What might Solnit point out in this painting as the unappreciated virtues of seeing the world through an introvert's eyes?

students have attempted to kill themselves, and 16 percent have considered trying. That's a lot of people crying out for something to change.

We tend to think that adolescence is inherently ridden with angst, but much of the misery comes from the cruelty of one's peers. Twenty-eight percent of public school students and 21 percent of private school students report being bullied, and though inner-city kids are routinely portrayed in the press as menaces, the highest levels of bullying are reported among white kids and in nonurban areas. Victims of bullying are, according to a Yale study, somewhere between two and nine times more likely to attempt suicide. Why should children be confined to institutions in which these experiences are so common?

Antibullying programs have proliferated to such an extent that even the Southern Poverty Law Center has gotten involved, as though high school had joined its list of hate groups. An educational video produced by the S.P.L.C. focuses on the case of Jamie Nabozny, who successfully sued the administrators of his small-town Wisconsin school district for doing nothing to stop — and sometimes even blaming him for — the years of persecution he had suffered, including an attack that ruptured his spleen. As Catherine A. Lugg, an education scholar specializing in public school issues, later wrote, "The Nabozny case clearly illustrates the public school's historic power as the enforcer of expected norms regarding gender, heteronormativity, and homophobia."

I once heard Helena Norberg-Hodge, an economic analyst and linguist who studies the impact of globalization on nonindustrialized societies, say that generational segregation was one of the worst kinds of segregation in the United States. The remark made a lasting impression: that segregation was what I escaped all those years ago. My first friends were much older than I was, and then a little older; these days they are all ages. We think it's natural to sort children into single-year age cohorts and then process them like Fords on an assembly line, but that may be a reflection of the industrialization that long ago sent parents to work away from their children for several hours every day.

Since the 1970s, Norberg-Hodge has been visiting the northern Indian region of Ladakh. When she first arrived such age segregation was unknown there. "Now children are split into different age groups at school," Norberg-Hodge has written. "This sort of leveling has a very destructive effect. By artificially creating social units in which everyone is the same age, the ability of children to help and to learn from each other is greatly reduced." Such units automatically create the conditions for

extending beyond the text

Educated (2018) is Tara Westover's memoir about growing up in rural Utah in a large family ruled by her father's survivalist principles. Although she was home-schooled on the Bible and the Book of Mormon, Westover did not attend a school. Her first experience with a traditional school occurred when she was accepted to Brigham Young University on the basis of standardized test scores. From there, she continued to Harvard and Cambridge University to earn graduate degrees in history.

Westover recounts how formal education allowed her to "self-create" — that is, to develop her own identity: "Everything I had worked for, all my years of study, had been to purchase for myself this one privilege: to see and experience more truths than those given to me by my father, and to use those truths to construct my own mind." The following excerpt is from the conclusion of her memoir.

from Educated

Tara Westover

But what has come between my father and me is more than time or distance. It is a change in the self. I am not the child my father raised, but he is the father who raised her.

If there was a single moment when the breach between us, which had been cracking and splintering for two decades, was at last too vast to be bridged, I believe it was that winter night, when I stared at my reflection in the bathroom mirror, while, without my knowing it, my father grasped the phone in his knotted hands and dialed my brother. . . . What followed was very dramatic. But the real drama had already played out in the bathroom.

It had played out when, for reasons I don't understand, I was unable to climb through the mirror and send out my sixteen-year-old self in my place.

Until that moment she had always been there. No matter how much I appeared to have changed — how illustrious my education, how altered my appearance — I was still her. At best I was two people, a fractured mind. She was inside, and emerged whenever I crossed the threshold of my father's house.

That night I called on her and she didn't answer. She left me. She stayed in the mirror. The decisions I made after that moment were not the ones she would have made. They were the choices of a changed person, a new self.

You could call this selfhood many things. Transformation. Metamorphosis. Falsity. Betrayal.

I call it an education.

In what ways does Westover's experience challenge the criticisms of traditional schooling that Solnit discusses? To what extent do the two of them share a definition of "education"? What does Westover conclude about the results of the way that she was educated?

competition, pressuring children to be as good as their peers. “In a group of ten children of quite different ages,” Norberg-Hodge argues, “there will naturally be much more cooperation than in a group of ten twelve-year-olds.”

15 When you are a teenager, your peers judge you by exacting and narrow criteria. But those going through the same life experiences at the same time often have little to teach one another about life. Most of us are safer in our youth in mixed-age groups, and the more time we spend outside our age cohort, the broader our sense of self. It’s not just that adults and children are good for adolescents. The reverse is also true. The freshness, inquisitiveness, and fierce idealism of a wide-awake teenager can be exhilarating, just as the stony apathy of a shut-down teenager can be dismal.

A teenager can act very differently outside his or her peer group than inside it. A large majority of hate crimes and gang rapes are committed by groups of boys and young men, and studies suggest that the perpetrators are more concerned with impressing one another and conforming to their group’s codes than with actual hatred toward outsiders. Attempts to address this issue usually focus on changing the social values to which such groups adhere, but dispersing or diluting these groups seems worth consideration, too.

High school in America is too often a place where one learns to conform or take punishment — and conformity is itself a kind of punishment, one that can flatten out your soul or estrange you from it.

High school, particularly the suburban and small-town varieties, can seem a parade of clichés, so much so that it’s easy to believe that jockocracies (a term used to describe Columbine High School at the time of the 1999 massacre), girls’ rivalries, punitive regimes of conformity and so forth, are anachronistic or unreal, the stuff of bad movies. Then another story reminds us that people are still imprisoned in these clichés. The day I write this, news comes that, yet again, high school football players have been charged with raping a fellow student. This time it’s five boys in Florida. In a 2012 sexual-assault case in Steubenville, Ohio, one of the football players accused of the crime texted a friend that he wasn’t worried about the consequences because his football coach “took care of it.” The victim received death threats for daring to speak up against popular boys, as did a fourteen-year-old in Missouri named Daisy Coleman, who, in the same year, reported being raped by a popular football player named Matt who was three years her senior.

Coleman, who has attempted suicide multiple times, wrote:

> When I went to a dance competition I saw a girl there who was wearing a T-shirt she made. It read: MATT 1, DAISY 0. Matt’s family was very powerful in the state of Missouri and he was also a very popular football player in my town, but I still couldn’t believe it when I was told the charges were dropped. Everyone had told us how strong the case was — including a cell phone video of the rape which showed me incoherent. All records have been sealed in the case, and I was told the video wasn’t found. My brother told me it was passed around school.

20 I wonder what pieces we’d have to pull away to demolish the system that worked so hard to destroy Coleman.

But abolishing high school would not just benefit those who are at the bottom of its hierarchies. Part of the shared legacy of high school is bemused stories about people who were treated as demigods at seventeen and never recovered. A doctor I hang out with tells me that former classmates who were more socially successful in high school than he was seem baffled that he, a quiet youth who made little impression, could be more professionally successful, as though the qualities that made them popular should have effortlessly floated them through life. It's easy to laugh, but there is a real human cost. What happens to people who are taught to believe in a teenage greatness that is based on achievements unlikely to matter in later life?

Abolishing high school could mean many things. It could mean compressing the time teenagers have to sort out their hierarchies and pillory outsiders, by turning schools into minimalist places in which people only study and learn. All the elaborate rites of dances and games could take place under other auspices. (Many Europeans and Asians I've spoken to went to classes each day and then left school to do other things with other people, forgoing the elaborate excess of extracurricular activities that is found at American schools.) It could mean schools in which age segregation is not so strict, where a twelve-year-old might mentor a seven-year-old and be mentored by a seventeen-year-old; schools in which internships, apprenticeships, and other programs would let older students transition into the adult world before senior year. (Again, there are plenty of precedents from around the world.)

Or it could mean something yet unimagined. I've learned from doctors that you don't have to have a cure before you make a diagnosis. Talk of abolishing high school is just my way of wondering whether so many teenagers have to suffer so much. How much of that suffering is built into a system that is, however ubiquitous, not inevitable? "Every time I drive past a high school, I can feel the oppression. I can feel all those trapped souls who just want to be outside," a woman recalling her own experience wrote to me recently. "I always say aloud, 'You poor souls.'" ■

Understanding and Interpreting

1. Rebecca Solnit opens her essay with a bold statement — "I did not go to high school" — almost as bold as her title "Abolish High School." Are these invitations or warnings to the reader just starting the essay?
2. Solnit makes the following assessment of two groups of students: "The wild kids impressed me because, unlike the timorous high achievers I'd often been grouped with at the mainstream school, they seemed fearless and free, skeptical about the systems around them" (par. 4). What does she admire about them? Do you think she really wanted to be one of them when she was school aged — or does her admiration reflect the adult looking back rather than the high school girl at the time?
3. Solnit supports one of her main arguments against high school with her analysis of suicide, which she points out is the third leading cause of death among teenagers. She asserts, "We tend to think that adolescence is inherently ridden with angst, but much of the misery comes from the cruelty of one's peers" (par. 11). What point is Solnit making about the connection between high school and suicide? What evidence does she provide to support this connection?
4. How does Solnit define "age segregation" (par. 14)? What argument does she make about it? How does she support that argument? How does your own experience confirm or challenge her argument?
5. Solnit asserts, "High school in America is too often a place where one learns to conform or take punishment — and conformity is itself a kind of punishment, one that can flatten out your soul or estrange you from it" (par. 17). In what ways does this extreme statement draw you into the article, whether you agree or disagree?
6. Toward the end, Solnit makes the point that high school is problematic for the athletic stars and those who are part of the popular group. Why does she include this point?

7. Summarize the "many things" that Solnit says might constitute abolishing high school as we know it (par. 22). Which of her suggestions sounds most appealing to you? Most practical? Why?
8. Solnit mentions the gun violence that we've seen in high schools, but she does not emphasize it. Do you consider this a weakness in her argument, or an effective way of staying focused? Consider the many strong assertions she makes about other issues as you formulate your response.

Analyzing Language, Style, and Structure

1. **Vocabulary in Context.** Solnit criticizes a particular program, saying that it is "a worthy project, but it implicitly accepts that non-straight kids must spend their formative years passing through a homophobic gauntlet before arriving at a less hostile adult world" (par. 9). What does the word "gauntlet" mean in this context? How is Solnit's use of the word similar to or different from other uses that you have encountered?
2. **Skill Focus.** The readers of *Harper's* magazine tend to be college educated, relatively affluent, and civically engaged. But they are also likely to be advocates of conventional, public education. Why would this article appeal to them? What strategies does Solnit employ to engage this audience in what is a fairly radical criticism of high school?
3. Solnit tends to use assertive language in her argument. In the opening paragraph, for instance, she refers to high school as "an *inevitable* experience." Why do you think she chose this word instead of one of its synonyms, such as "unavoidable"? The title itself uses the word "abolish" instead of "close down" or "eliminate." In what ways do these and other examples of assertive (or aggressive) language advance Solnit's argument?
4. Paragraph 6 opens with "ravenous" and closes with "appetite." How does framing the paragraph with such vivid word choices contribute to the point Solnit makes there?
5. In paragraph 8, Solnit addresses a counterargument with a clear concession and refutation. What is the counterargument that she raises? What does she concede? How does her refutation lead to her central argument?
6. Solnit spends considerable time discussing the example of Daisy Coleman. How does this example contribute to achieving Solnit's purpose?
7. Solnit mentions in the article that she earned her G.E.D., but she does not mention that she went on to receive both an undergraduate and a graduate degree from well-regarded colleges or that she studied in France. Why do you think she leaves out these details and chooses to focus on her younger self? What do you think she might have gained, if anything, from pointing out her educational and professional success?
8. How effective is the conclusion? What does Solnit mean by the analogy that "you don't have to have a cure before you make a diagnosis"? Does this conclusion leave the reader with more questions than answers? If so, does that make it a strong or weak conclusion?
9. Throughout the essay, Solnit uses language — specific word choices (especially verbs), descriptions, and metaphors — that suggest entrapment. Identify several examples and discuss their effect, both individually and cumulatively.

Topics for Composing

1. **Analysis.** One of the major points that Solnit raises in her argument to abolish high school as we know it is "the cruelty of one's peers" (par. 11). What rhetorical choices does she make to support this point and connect it to her overall argument?

2. **Argument.** Should high school as most of us know it be abolished? In response to Solnit's essay, take a position on this question that supports, challenges, or qualifies her argument. As you develop your argument, consider the extent to which high school today is different from Solnit's high school experience in the 1970s.

3. **Connection.** Solnit comments on her experience in the alternative high school where faculty and students were like equals: "I didn't gain much conventional knowledge, but I read voraciously and had good conversations. You can learn a lot that way" (par. 5). Describe a similar learning experience in your own life. It might have taken place in school. However, it could have been a time when you learned from a family member, a sports coach, or someone you met at a job or volunteer activity.

4. **Speaking and Listening.** In paragraph 22, Solnit makes suggestions to improve but not necessarily abolish high school. Select one of these suggestions and imagine how it might be implemented at your school. In a speech directed at a target audience of parents and school staff, including teachers, explain the reasons for your choice (that is, what problem you hope to solve or address) and why you believe the suggestion could lead to a positive result.

5. **Research.** Research alternatives to traditional high school in the United States. Consider both charter and alternative public schools along with private schools. What key differences do you notice? Keep in mind that you're looking for significant differences in the overall philosophy and experience, not simply a different emphasis (such as a religious school or an online environment).

6. **Research.** Interview someone who is at least one generation (preferably two generations) older than you. Ask the person to describe what high school was like: the good, the bad, and the mundane. How was that person's experience similar to and different from your own? How did it compare to the experience Solnit describes? How do you account for the differences? Consider not only the time frame but also other circumstances (such as rural vs. urban setting and community values placed on education).

7. **Multimodal.** Take a series of photographs of your school over a few days or even just one day. Put them together in a narrative slideshow that makes an argument about your school. Select appropriate instrumental music (no lyrics) to accompany the slideshow. Avoid adding words — either written or spoken. Have the images and music tell the story. Consider your larger community of parents and school staff as your audience; make sure that whatever points or criticisms you make are constructive and respectful.

Education: Change Is the Only Constant

Yuval Noah Harari

EMILY BERL/Redux

Yuval Noah Harari is the author of the bestselling books *Sapiens: A Brief History of Humankind* (2014), *Homo Deus: A Brief History of Tomorrow* (2016), and *21 Lessons for the 21st Century* (2018). Born in Haifa, Israel, in 1976, Harari received his PhD from the University of Oxford in 2002. He is currently a lecturer in the Department of History at the Hebrew University of Jerusalem. He lectures internationally and also teaches a MOOC (Massive Open Online Course) titled *A Brief History of Humankind.* The following is a chapter from *21 Lessons for the 21st Century*.

Humankind is facing unprecedented revolutions, all our old stories are crumbling, and no new story has so far emerged to replace them. How can we prepare ourselves and our children for a world of such unprecedented transformations and radical uncertainties? A baby born today will be thirtysomething in 2050. If all goes well, that baby will still be around in 2100, and might even be an active citizen of the twenty-second century. What should we teach that baby that will help him or her survive and flourish in the world of 2050 or of the twenty-second century? What kind of skills will he or she need in order to get a job, understand what is happening around him or her, and navigate the maze of life?

Unfortunately, since nobody knows what the world will look like in 2050 — not to mention 2100 — we don't know the answer to these questions. Of course, humans have never been able to predict the future with accuracy. But today it is more difficult than ever before, because once technology enables us to engineer bodies, brains, and minds, we will no longer be able to be certain about anything — including things that previously seemed fixed and eternal.

A thousand years ago, in 1018, there were many things people didn't know about the future, but they were nevertheless convinced that the basic features of human society were not going to change. If you lived in China in 1018, you knew that by 1050 the Song Empire might collapse, the Khitans might invade from the north, and plagues might kill millions. However, it was clear to you that even in 1050 most people would still work as farmers and weavers, rulers would still rely on humans to staff their armies and bureaucracies, men would still dominate women, life expectancy would still be about forty, and the human body would remain exactly the same. For that reason, in 1018 poor Chinese parents taught their children how to plant rice or weave silk; wealthier parents taught their boys how to read the Confucian classics, write calligraphy, or fight on horseback, and they taught their girls to be modest and obedient housewives. It was obvious that these skills would still be needed in 1050.

In contrast, today we have no idea how China or the rest of the world will look in 2050. We don't know what people will do for a living, we don't know how armies or bureaucracies will function, and we don't know what gender relations will be like. Some people will probably live much longer than today, and the human body itself might undergo an unprecedented revolution thanks to bioengineering and direct brain-to-computer interfaces. Much of what kids learn today will likely be irrelevant by 2050.

5 At present, too many schools focus on cramming information into kids' brains. In the past this made sense, because information was scarce, and even the slow trickle of existing information was repeatedly blocked by censorship. If you lived, say, in a small provincial town in Mexico in 1800, it was difficult for you to know much about the wider world. There was no radio, television, daily newspaper, or public library.[1] Even if you were literate and had access to a private library, there was not much to read other than novels and religious tracts. The Spanish Empire heavily censored all texts printed locally and allowed only a dribble of vetted publications to be imported from the outside.[2] Much the same was true if you lived in some provincial town in Russia, India, Turkey, or China. When modern schools came along, teaching every child to read and write and imparting the basic facts of geography, history, and biology, they represented an immense improvement.

In contrast, in the twenty-first century we are flooded by enormous amounts of information,

[1]Wayne A Wiegand and Donald G. Davis, eds., *Encyclopedia of Library History* (New York; Garland, 1994), 432–33.

[2]Verity Smith, ed., *Concise Encyclopedia of Latin American Literature* (London: Routledge, 2013), 142, 180.

REUTERS/Issei Kato (JAPAN SCI TECH EDUCATION SOCIETY)/Newscom

This image shows Saya, a humanoid robot, acting as a teacher at an elementary school in Tokyo, Japan.

Where do you think Harari might stand on the use of artificial intelligence in education, particularly the idea of replacing teachers with robots? Could interacting with robot teachers help students acquire the skills and mindsets that Harari argues are crucial for survival in the twenty-first century?

and the censors don't even try to block it. Instead, they are busy spreading misinformation or distracting us with irrelevancies. If you live in some provincial Mexican town and you have a smartphone, you can spend many lifetimes just reading Wikipedia, watching TED Talks, and taking free online courses. No government can hope to conceal all the information it doesn't like. On the other hand, it is alarmingly easy to inundate the public with conflicting reports and red herrings. People all over the world are but a click away from the latest accounts of the bombardment of Aleppo or of melting ice caps in the Arctic, but there are so many contradictory accounts that it is hard to know what to believe. Besides, countless other things are just a click away as well, making it difficult to focus, and when politics or science look too complicated it is tempting to switch to some funny cat videos, celebrity gossip, or porn.

In such a world, the last thing a teacher needs to give her pupils is more information. They already have far too much of it. Instead, people need the ability to make sense of information, to tell the difference between what is important and what is unimportant, and above all to combine many bits of information into a broad picture of the world.

In truth, this has been the ideal of Western liberal education for centuries, but up till now even many Western schools have been rather slack in fulfilling it. Teachers allowed themselves to focus on imparting data while encouraging students "to think for themselves." Due to their fear of authoritarianism, liberal schools have had a particular horror of grand narratives. They've assumed that as long as we give students lots of data and a modicum of freedom the students will create their own picture of the world, and even if this generation fails to synthesize all the data into a coherent and meaningful story about the world, there will be plenty of time to construct a better synthesis in the future. We have now run out of time. The decisions we will make in the next few decades will shape the future of life itself, and we can make these decisions based only on our present worldview. If this generation lacks a comprehensive view of the cosmos, the future of life will be decided at random.

extending beyond the text

According to its web site, the Thiel Fellowship is "a two-year program for young people who want to build new things." Founded by technology entrepreneur and investor Peter Thiel in 2011, this $100,000 competitive grant is available to young people under 20 to skip or drop out of college. Many have criticized the Thiel Foundation's network of investors and scientists for encouraging young people to miss the advantages of a university education. Supporters point out that the Thiel Fellowship is an opportunity for the best and brightest to move right into the real world and not waste time with studies that are irrelevant, boring, or both.

Could this work in high school? Consider the criticisms that Harari makes and the misgivings he has about our current educational system. Why do you think that he would or would not support a similar grant program available to eleventh- and twelfth-grade students? Why do you think it would or would not address some of the difficulties you see in high school? What would be the downside?

The Heat Is On

Besides information, most schools also focus too much on providing students with a set of predetermined skills, such as solving differential equations, writing computer code in C++, identifying chemicals in a test tube, or conversing in Chinese. Yet since we have no idea what the world and the job market will look like in 2050, we don't really know what particular skills people will need. We might invest a lot of effort teaching kids how to write in C++ or speak Chinese, only to discover that by 2050 AI can code software far better than humans, and a new Google Translate app will enable you to conduct a conversation in almost flawless Mandarin, Cantonese, or Hakka, even though you only know how to say "*Ni hao*."

10 So what should we be teaching? Many pedagogical experts argue that schools should switch to teaching "the four Cs" — critical thinking, communication, collaboration, and creativity.[3] More broadly, they believe, schools should downplay technical skills and emphasize general-purpose life skills. Most important of all will be the ability to deal with change, learn new things, and preserve your mental balance in unfamiliar situations. In order to keep up with the world of 2050, you will need not merely to invent new ideas and products but above all to reinvent yourself again and again. For as the pace of change increases, not just the economy but the very meaning of "being human" is likely to mutate. Already in 1848 the Communist Manifesto declared that "all that is solid melts into air." Marx and Engels[4], however, were thinking mainly about social and economic

[3]Cathy N. Davidson, *The New Education: How to Revolutionize the University to Prepare Students for a World in Flux* (New York: Basic Books, 2017); Bernie Trilling, *21st Century Skills: Learning for Life in Our Times* (San Francisco: Jossey-Bass, 2009); Charles Kivunja, "Teaching Students to Learn and to Work Well with 21st Century Skills: Unpacking the Career and Life Skills Domain of the New Learning Paradigm," *International Journal of Higher Education* 4, no. 1 (2015). For the website of P21, see "P21 Partnership for 21st Century Learning," http://www.p21.org/our-work/4cs-research-series, accessed January 12, 2018. For an example of the implementation of new pedagogical methods, see National Education Association, *Preparing 21st Century Students for a Global Society: An Educator's Guide to the "Four C's,"* http://www.nea.org/assets/ docs/A-Guide-to-Four-Cs.pdf, accessed January 21, 2018.

[4]Karl Marx and Friedrich Engels were nineteenth-century political theorists who argued that all social conflict stemmed from the struggle among economic classes. — Eds.

structures. By 2048, physical and cognitive structures will also melt into air, or into a cloud of data bits.

In 1848 millions of people were losing their jobs on village farms and were going to the big cities to work in factories. But upon reaching the big city, they were unlikely to change their gender or to add a sixth sense. And if they found a job in some textile factory, they could expect to remain in that profession for the rest of their working lives.

By 2048, people might have to cope with migrations to cyberspace, with fluid gender identities, and with new sensory experiences generated by computer implants. If they find both work and meaning in designing up-to-the-minute fashions for a 3-D virtual reality game, within a decade not just this particular profession but all jobs demanding this level of artistic creation might be taken over by AI. So at twenty-five you might introduce yourself on a dating site as "a twenty-five-year-old heterosexual woman who lives in London and works in a fashion shop." At thirty-five you might say you are "a gender-nonspecific person undergoing age adjustment, whose neocortical activity takes place mainly in the New Cosmos virtual world, and whose life mission is to go where no fashion designer has gone before." At forty-five both dating and self-definitions are so passé. You just wait for an algorithm to find (or create) the perfect match for you. As for drawing meaning from the art of fashion design, you are so irrevocably outclassed by the algorithms that looking at your crowning achievements from the previous decade fills you with embarrassment rather than pride. And at forty-five you still have many decades of radical change ahead of you.

Please don't take this scenario literally. Nobody can predict the specific changes we will witness in the future. Any particular scenario is likely to be far from the truth. If somebody describes the world of the mid-twenty-first century to you and it sounds like science fiction, it is probably false. But then again, if somebody

This image, which was produced in 1910 in France, imagines what school might be like in the year 2000. **What does this image say about the transfer of information between teacher and student? How might Harari react to this image, based on what you've read here?**

describes the world of the mid-twenty-first century to you and it doesn't sound like science fiction, it is certainly false. We cannot be sure of the specifics; change itself is the only certainty. Such profound change may well transform the basic structure of life, making discontinuity its most salient feature. From time immemorial life was divided into two complementary parts: a period of learning followed by a period of working. In the first part of life you accumulated information, developed skills, constructed a worldview, and built a stable identity. Even if at fifteen you spent most of your day working in your family's rice field (rather than in a formal school), the most important thing you were doing was learning: how to cultivate rice, how to conduct negotiations with the greedy rice merchants from the big city, and how to resolve conflicts over land and water with the other villagers. In the second part of life you relied on your accumulated skills to navigate the world, earn a living, and contribute to society. Of course even at fifty you continued to learn new things about rice, merchants, and conflicts, but these were just small tweaks to your well-honed abilities.

By the middle of the twenty-first century, accelerating change plus longer life spans will make this traditional model obsolete. Life will come apart at the seams, and there will be less and less continuity between different periods of life. "Who am I?" will be a more urgent and complicated question than ever before.[5]

This is likely to involve immense levels of stress. For change is almost always stressful, and after a certain age most people just don't like to change. When you are fifteen, your entire life is change. Your body is growing, your mind is developing, your relationships are deepening. Everything is in flux, and everything is new. You are busy inventing yourself. Most teenagers find it frightening, but at the same time, it is also exciting. New vistas are opening before you, and you have an entire world to conquer.

By the time you are fifty, you don't want change, and most people have given up on conquering the world. Been there, done that, got the T-shirt. You prefer stability. You have invested so much in your skills, your career, your identity, and your worldview that you don't want to start all over again. The harder you've worked on building something, the more difficult it is to let go of it and make room for something new. You might still cherish new experiences and minor adjustments, but most people in their fifties aren't ready to overhaul the deep structures of their identity and personality.

There are neurological reasons for this. Though the adult brain is more flexible and volatile than was once thought, it is still less malleable than the teenage brain. Reconnecting neurons and rewiring synapses is hard work.[6] But in the twenty-first century, you can't afford stability. If you try to hold on to some stable identity, job, or worldview, you risk being left behind as the world flies by you with a whoosh. Given that life expectancy is likely to increase, you might subsequently have to spend many decades as a clueless fossil. To stay relevant — not just economically but above all socially — you will need the ability to constantly learn and to reinvent yourself, certainly at a young age like fifty.

As strangeness becomes the new normal, your past experiences, as well as the past experiences of the whole of humanity, will

---

[5]Maddalaine Ansell, "Jobs for Life Are a Thing of the Past. Bring On Lifelong Learning," *Guardian*, May 31. 2016.

[6]Erik B. Bloss et al., "Evidence for Reduced Experience-Dependent Dendritic Spine Plasticity in the Aging Prefrontal Cortex," *Journal of Neuroscience* 31, no. 21 (2011): 7831–39; Miriam Matamales et al., "Aging-Related Dysfunction of Striatal Cholinergic Interneurons Produces Conflict in Action Selection," *Neuron* 90, no. 2 (2016): 362–72; Mo Costandi, "Does Your Brain Produce New Cells? A Skeptical View of Human Adult Neurogenesis," *Guardian*, February 23, 2012; Gianluigi Mongillo, Simon Rumpel, and Yonatan Loewenstein, "Intrinsic Volatility of Synaptic Connections–A Challenge to the Synaptic Trace Theory of Memory," *Current Opinion in Neurobiology* 46 (2017): 7–13.

extending beyond the text

The table below shows data from Speak Up Research Initiative. Speak Up surveyed 23,000 teachers, 2200 administrators, and almost 290,000 students.

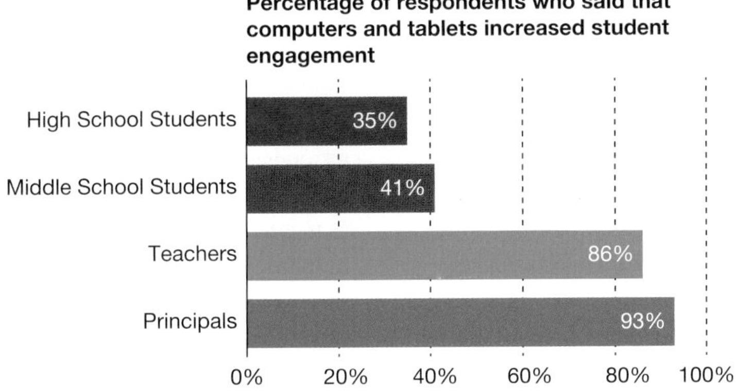

Further research revealed an even more distinct preference on the part of students:

> [Interviews and] data from YouthTruth, a national nonprofit that conducts student surveys, indicate that many students . . . dislike when teachers turn over instruction to computers. They say they prefer learning directly from teachers — because they think teachers are the experts or that it's their job — and [they already have too much screen time].

Summarize the data in the graph and the findings of the survey. How do you think that Harari would respond to these findings? To what extent does your own experience reflect the teachers' or the students' responses to the increased reliance on technology in the classroom?

become less reliable guides. Humans as individuals and humankind as a whole will increasingly have to deal with things nobody ever encountered before, such as superintelligent machines, engineered bodies, algorithms that can manipulate your emotions with uncanny precision, rapid man-made climate cataclysms, and the need to change your profession every decade. What is the right thing to do when confronting a completely unprecedented situation? How should you act when you are flooded by enormous amounts of information and there is absolutely no way you can absorb and analyze it all? How do you live in a world where profound uncertainty is not a bug but a feature?

To survive and flourish in such a world, you will need a lot of mental flexibility and great reserves of emotional balance. You will have to repeatedly let go of some of what you know best, and learn to feel at home with the unknown.

Unfortunately, teaching kids to embrace the unknown while maintaining their mental balance is far more difficult than teaching them an equation in physics or the causes of the First World War. You cannot learn resilience by reading a book or listening to a lecture. Teachers themselves usually lack the mental flexibility that the twenty-first century demands, since they themselves are the product of the old educational system.

The Industrial Revolution has bequeathed us the production-line theory of education. In the middle of town there is a large concrete building divided into many identical rooms, each room equipped with rows of desks and chairs. At the sound of a bell, you go to one of these rooms together with thirty other kids who were all born the same year as you. Every hour a different grown-up walks in and starts talking. The grown-ups are all paid to do so by the government. One of them tells you about the shape of the earth, another tells you about the human past, and a third tells you about the human body. It is easy to laugh at this model, and almost everybody agrees that no matter its past achievements, it is now bankrupt. But so far we haven't created a viable alternative. Certainly not a scalable alternative that can be implemented in rural Mexico rather than just in wealthy California suburbs.

Hacking Humans

So the best advice I can give a fifteen-year-old stuck in an outdated school somewhere in Mexico, India, or Alabama is: don't rely on the adults too much. Most of them mean well, but they just don't understand the world. In the past, it was a relatively safe bet to follow the adults, because they knew the world quite well, and the world changed slowly. But the twenty-first century is going to be different. Because of the increasing pace of change, you can never be certain whether what the adults are telling you is timeless wisdom or outdated bias.

So on what can you rely instead? Perhaps on technology? That's an even riskier gamble. Technology can help you a lot, but if technology gains too much power over your life, you might become a hostage to its agenda. Thousands of years ago humans invented agriculture, but this technology enriched just a tiny elite while enslaving the majority of humans. Most people found themselves working from sunrise till sunset plucking weeds, carrying water buckets, and harvesting corn under a blazing sun. It could happen to you too.

Technology isn't bad. If you know what you want in life, technology can help you get it. But if you don't know what you want in life, it will be all too easy for technology to shape your aims for you and take control of your life. Especially as technology gets better at understanding humans, you might increasingly find yourself serving it, instead of it serving you. Have you seen those zombies who roam the streets with their faces glued to their smartphones? Do you think they control the technology, or does the technology control them?

Should you rely on yourself, then? That 25
sounds great on Sesame Street or in an old-fashioned Disney film, but in real life it doesn't work so well. Even Disney is coming to realize it. Just like Riley Andersen[7], most people barely know themselves, and when they try to "listen to themselves" they easily become prey to external manipulations. The voice we hear inside our heads is never trustworthy, because it always reflects state propaganda, ideological brainwashing, and commercial advertisements, not to mention biochemical bugs.

As biotechnology and machine learning improve, it will become easier to manipulate people's deepest emotions and desires, and it will become more dangerous than ever to just follow your heart. When Coca-Cola, Amazon, Baidu, or the government knows how to pull the strings of your heart and press the buttons of your brain, will you still be able to tell the difference between yourself and their marketing experts?

---

[7]Major character in Disney/Pixar's animated film *Inside Out*, in which personifications of Riley's emotions are the main characters. —Eds.

To succeed at such a daunting task, you will need to work very hard at getting to know your operating system better — to know what you are and what you want from life. This is, of course, the oldest advice in the book: know thyself. For thousands of years philosophers and prophets have urged people to know themselves. But this advice was never more urgent than in the twenty-first century, because unlike in the days of Laozi or Socrates, now you have serious competition. Coca-Cola, Amazon, Baidu, and the government are all racing to hack you. Not your smartphone, not your computer, and not your bank account; they are in a race to hack *you* and your organic operating system. You might have heard that we are living in the era of hacking computers, but that's not even half the truth. In fact, we are living in the era of hacking humans.

The algorithms are watching you right now. They are watching where you go, what you buy, whom you meet. Soon they will monitor all your steps, all your breaths, all your heartbeats. They are relying on Big Data and machine learning to get to know you better and better. And once these algorithms know you better than you know yourself, they can control and manipulate you, and you won't be able to do much about it. You will live in the matrix[8], or in *The Truman Show*[9]. In the end, it's a simple empirical matter: if the algorithms indeed understand what's happening within you better than you understand it yourself, authority will shift to them.

Of course, you might be perfectly happy ceding all authority to the algorithms and trusting them to decide things for you and for the rest of the world. If so, just relax and enjoy the ride. You don't need to do anything about it. The algorithms will take care of everything. If, however, you want to retain some control over your personal existence and the future of life, you have to run faster than the algorithms, faster than Amazon and the government, and get to know yourself before they do. To run fast, don't take much baggage with you. Leave all your illusions behind. They are very heavy. ■

Jeff Stahler/Cartoon Stock

What is the source of humor in this cartoon depiction of a conversation between a mother and her child? In what ways does the cartoon comment on the growing generational knowledge gap that Harari predicts?

[8]Harari is referring to the Keanu Reeves movie *The Matrix*, which was based on the idea that the world is a computer simulation. — Eds.

[9]A movie with Jim Carrey in which he unknowingly lives his life inside a fake world and is the subject of a reality TV show. — Eds.

Understanding and Interpreting

1. What is the purpose of Harari's use of the example of China in 1018 (par. 3)?
2. Why does Harari believe that "cramming information into kids' brains" (par. 5) was a reasonable approach but is no longer useful?

3. Paragraph 6 begins with the phrase, "In contrast, in the twenty-first century . . ." to make the transition from Harari's discussion of the past to his argument about the present time. What are the central point(s) he raises about the twenty-first century?
4. What does Harari mean by this claim: "In such a world, the last thing a teacher needs to give her pupils is more information" (par. 7)?
5. What are "the four Cs" that Harari says that many in education believe should be the focus of teaching? Why does Harari believe that each of these is important?
6. Why does Harari believe that the "most important" elements of education should be "the ability to deal with change, learn new things, and preserve your mental balance in unfamiliar situations" (par. 10)? How persuasive do you find his argument and evidence?
7. In what ways is Harari's discussion of "Western liberal education" and its goals (par. 8) addressing a counterargument? How effectively does this analysis contribute to his argument?
8. Harari asks, "How do you live in a world where profound uncertainty is not a bug but a feature?" (par. 18). How does he answer this question in this chapter of his book?
9. Harari disputes the accepted wisdom that technology is the dominant force of the twenty-first century. In fact, he refers to our faith in technology as "an even riskier gamble" (par. 23) than holding on to outmoded beliefs. What does he mean?
10. Explain what Harari means when he says that "once these algorithms know you better than you know yourself, they can control and manipulate you, and you won't be able to do much about it" (par. 28)? What is the alternative?

Analyzing Language, Style, and Structure

1. **Vocabulary in Context.** What does the word "hacking" mean in the context of Harari's chapter? How is this usage similar to or different from others that you have encountered? Examine paragraph 27 carefully, especially the final sentence: "In fact, we are living in the era of hacking humans." How does Harari's use of the word — and concept of — "hacking" contribute to achieving his purpose?
2. **Skill Focus.** This chapter and, in fact, the entire book by Harari, is based on the belief that we are living at a time when rethinking and recasting our approach to learning, knowledge, and schooling is an urgent matter. How does he persuade his audience to share that urgency? Consider his assertion in paragraph 8: "We have now run out of time."
3. Harari develops one paragraph by providing a hypothetical case of how a 25-year-old in 2048 would define her identity, and how her definition would shift at 35 and again at 45. He opens the next paragraph, "Please don't take this scenario literally" (par. 13). What is the point of this example if it is not literally true?
4. Do you find Harari's argument persuasive? Consider your reactions to the reasoning and evidence he provides. Identify a specific passage or two in which you found yourself questioning his line of argument or support.
5. How effective do you find the concluding paragraph? Why does Harari advise the audience to "[l]eave all your illusions behind"?
6. How does Harari appeal to both pathos and logos in his argument? Is his main appeal to reason (a logically developed argument), or does he rely more on engaging our emotions by predicting a dangerous future?

Topics for Composing

1. **Analysis.** Harari's predictions and recommendations challenge the way his audience thinks about schooling in the twenty-first century. How does he appeal to readers who might be inclined to dismiss his ideas as doomsday exaggerations or threats? In other words, what rhetorical strategies does he use to encourage his audience to keep an open mind? Cite at least two specific passages in your response.
2. **Argument.** One of Harari's many provocative assertions about the shifts in education that will be required in the mid-to-late 21st century is "don't rely on the adults too much" (par. 22). Write an argument in which you support or oppose this advice, drawing on your own experiences and reasoning.
3. **Connection.** Describe what you imagine your life will be like twenty years from now. Use Harari's predictions in your discussion. You may also want to draw on views of the future that you have encountered in your own reading.
4. **Connection.** Speculative fiction is a genre that imagines dystopian futures. Identify a science fiction writer who shares some of the same concerns that Harari writes about.
5. **Multimodal.** Harari opens with this sentence: "Humankind is facing unprecedented revolutions, all our old stories are crumbling, and no new story has so far emerged to replace them." Using a combination of words, your own images or objects, and found images or objects, create a poster, diorama, or digital artwork that captures this opening assertion.
6. **Creative Writing.** Write a short story that illustrates one of the predictions that Harari makes. You might take it seriously or satirize Harari's position.

from On Education

Albert Einstein

Keystone-France/Getty Images

One of the greatest scientists of the twentieth century, Albert Einstein (1879-1955) gained international recognition for his general theory of relativity and won the Nobel Prize for physics in 1905. He emigrated to the United States from Germany when the Nazi Party took power before World War II. Einstein lived and worked in Princeton, New Jersey, for the remainder of his life. Following is an excerpt from a speech he delivered in 1931 to the State University of New York at Albany on the 300th anniversary of higher education in the United States.

I cannot lay any claim to being an authority, especially as intelligent and well-meaning men of all times have dealt with educational problems and have certainly repeatedly expressed their view clearly about these matters. From what source shall I, as a partial layman in the realm of pedagogy, derive courage to expound opinions with no foundations except personal experience and personal conviction? If it were really a scientific matter, one would probably be tempted to silence by such considerations.

However, with the affairs of active human beings it is different. Here knowledge of truth alone does not suffice; on the contrary, this knowledge must continually be renewed by

Rubens Alarcon/Alamy Stock Photo

The Albert Einstein Memorial in Washington D.C. features a 21-foot, stylized bronze statue by sculptor Robert Berks. Einstein is depicted sitting on a granite bench with manuscript papers in hand. The National Academy of Sciences unveiled the memorial in 1979 to honor the centennial of Einstein's birth. The large statue on a bench encourages visitors to climb onto the scientist's lap, take photos, and otherwise participate. **Based on what you have read, why do you think this monument is or is not a fitting tribute to Einstein?**

ceaseless effort, if it is not to be lost. It resembles a statue of marble which stands in the desert and is continually threatened with burial by the shifting sand. The hands of service must ever be at work in order that the marble continues lastingly to shine in the sun. To these serving hands mine shall also belong.

The school has always been the most important means of transferring the wealth of tradition from one generation to the next. This applies today in an even higher degree than in former time, for through modern development of the economic life, the family as bearer of tradition and education has been weakened. The continuance and health of human society is therefore in a still higher degree dependent on the school than formerly.

Sometimes one sees in the school simply the instrument for transferring a certain maximum quantity of knowledge to the growing generation. But that's not right. Knowledge is dead; the school, however, serves the living. It should develop in the young individuals those equalities and capabilities which are of value for the welfare of the commonwealth. But that does not mean that individuality should be destroyed and the individual becomes a mere tool of the community, like a bee or an ant. For a community of standardized individuals without personal originality and personal aims would be a poor community without possibilities for development. On the contrary, the aim must be the training of independently thinking and acting individuals, who, however, see in the service of the community their highest life problem.

But how shall one try to attain this ideal? 5
Should one perhaps try to realize this aim by moralizing? Not at all. Words are and remain empty sound, and the road to perdition has ever been accompanied by lip service to an ideal. But personalities are not formed by what is heard and said but by labor and activity. The most important method of education accordingly always has consisted of [a pupil] urged to actual performance. . . .

To me the worst thing seems to be for a school principally to work with methods of fear, force, and artificial authority. Such treatment destroys the sound sentiments, the sincerity, and the self confidence of the pupil. It produces the submissive subject. It is not so hard to keep the school free from the worst of all evils. Give into the power of the teacher the fewest

extending beyond the text

New York Times columnist David Brooks writes about the importance of school instilling in its citizenry a balance between "personal freedom and communal responsibility" to build what he calls "social trust." "Social trust" has been eroding in the United States, according to Brooks:

> If the children of privilege get to go to the best schools, there's not going to be much social mutuality. If those schools do not instill a love of nation, there's not going to be much shared responsibility.

To what extent would Einstein's three types of motivation support the argument Brooks makes about how to achieve schooling that helps young people see, as Einstein writes, "the value of [their work in school] to the community"?

possible coercive measures, so that the only source of the pupil's respect for the teacher is the human and intellectual qualities of the latter.

The second motive, ambition or, in milder terms, the aiming at recognition and consideration, lies firmly fixed in human nature. With absence of mental stimulus of this kind, human cooperation would be entirely impossible; the desire for approval of one's fellow-man certainly is one of the most important binding powers of society. In this complex of feelings, constructive and destructive forces lie closely together. Desire for approval and recognition is a healthy motive but the desire to be acknowledged as better, stronger, or more intelligent than a fellow being or fellow scholar easily leads to an excessively egoistic psychological adjustment, which may become injurious for the individual and for the community. Therefore the school and the teacher must guard against employing the easy method of creating individual ambition, in order to induce the pupils to diligent work.

Darwin's theory of the struggle for existence and the selectivity connected with it has by many people been cited as authorization of the encouragement of the spirit of competition. Some people also in such a way have tried to prove pseudo-scientifically the necessity of the destructive economic struggle of competition between individuals. But this is wrong, because man owes his strength in the struggle for existence to the fact that he is a socially living animal. As little as a battle between single ants of an ant hill is essential for survival, just so little is this the case with the individual members of a human community. . . .

The most important motive for work in the school and in life is pleasure in work, pleasure in its results, and the knowledge of the value of the result to the community. In the awakening and strengthening of the psychological forces in the young person, I see the most important task given by the school. Such a psychological foundation alone leads to a joyous desire for the highest possessions of people, knowledge and artist-like workmanship.

10 The awakening of the productive psychological powers is certainly less easy than the practice of force or the awakening of individual ambition but is the more valuable for it. The point is to develop the childlike inclination for play and the childlike desire for recognition and to guide the child over to

A Family that Reads Together, 2015, (acrylic on canvas), *Fabor*, Chris/Private Collection/Bridgeman Images

As Einstein discusses the essential motivation of "pleasure in work," he asserts that "awakening and strengthening of the psychological forces in the young person . . . [is] the most important task given by the school."

What story does this illustration by Chris Fabor, entitled *A Family that Reads Together*, convey? How might this image challenge Einstein's argument about the primacy of the school's influence on the development of young people?

important fields for society; it is that education which in the main is founded upon the desire for successful activity and acknowledgement. If the school succeeds in working successfully from such points of view, it will be highly honored by the rising generation and the tasks given by the school will be submitted to as a sort of gift. I have known children who preferred school time to vacation. . . .

I want to oppose the idea that the school has to teach directly that special knowledge and those accomplishments that one has to use later directly in life. The demands of life are much too manifold to let such a specialized training in school appear possible. Apart from that, it seems to me, moreover, objectionable to treat the individual like a dead tool. The school should always have as its aim that the young man leave it as a harmonious personality, not as a specialist. This in my opinion is true in a certain sense even for technical schools, whose students will devote themselves to a quite definite profession. The development of general ability for independent thinking and judgement should always be placed foremost, not the acquisition of special knowledge. If a person masters the fundamentals of his subject and has learned to think and work independently, he will surely find his way and besides will better be able to adapt himself to progress and changes than the person whose training principally consists in the acquiring of detailed knowledge.

Finally, I wish to emphasize once more that what has been said here in a somewhat categorical form does not claim to mean more than the personal opinion of a man, which is founded upon nothing but his own personal experience, which he has gathered as a student and as a teacher. ■

Understanding and Interpreting

1. In paragraph 3, Albert Einstein credits school with carrying "the wealth of tradition" from one generation to the next. Why do you think he chose "tradition" instead of "knowledge," the more commonly expected outcome of schooling?
2. How does Einstein support his belief that an individual risks becoming "a mere tool of the community, like a bee or an ant" (par. 4) without what he views as a true education? How might his experience growing up in Germany as the Nazi Party came to power have influenced this viewpoint?
3. What, according to Einstein, is the importance of "actual performance" (par. 5) as part of education?
4. According to Einstein, what should a school not be? Which motivational approaches does he criticize and why?
5. What form of motivation does Einstein argue is the most constructive and long-lasting? How persuasive do you find his assessment? Explain your answer.
6. Einstein asserts that "play" and "pleasure" are important elements of education. How does Einstein also argue for the importance of hard work? What reasoning leads to his assertion that under the right circumstances, "the tasks given by the school will be submitted to as a sort of gift" (par. 10)?
7. Given his view on the right approach to motivation, what does Einstein believe is the source of a teacher's authority?
8. In what ways does Einstein emphasize the building of character as much as the acquisition of knowledge in school?
9. Although some of the language in this speech may seem old-fashioned or formal to you, which of Einstein's ideas seem most relevant today?

Analyzing Language, Style, and Structure

1. **Vocabulary in Context.** Einstein argues that school should develop an individual with "a harmonious personality" (par. 11). What does the word "harmonious" mean in this context? How is your understanding of the word similar to or different from Einstein's use of it?
2. **Skill Focus.** Einstein opens by establishing his ethos as "a partial layman in the realm of pedagogy." Why does he take this approach, particularly at the beginning of his speech, rather than simply relying on his international reputation as a Nobel Prize-winning scientist? He returns to this point again at the end, describing his speech as "the personal opinion of a man, which is founded upon nothing but his own personal experience." Why do you think Einstein chooses to conclude the piece this way? What effect does it have on his audience?
3. In the second paragraph, Einstein asserts the importance of constantly renewing knowledge with a figure of speech: "It resembles a statue of marble which stands in the desert and is continually threatened with burial by the shifting sand. The hands of service must ever be at work in order that the marble continues lastingly to shine in the sun." Explain this metaphor and how it connects to the point he is making. Is it effective?
4. In paragraph 4, Einstein refers to the individual seeing "in the service of the community their highest life problem." What does he suggest by his choice of the word "problem" instead of "goal," "ideal," or "purpose"?
5. What is the purpose of paragraph 5 that opens with the rhetorical question, "But how shall one try to attain this ideal [of the individual working in service of community]"? Why does Einstein warn against "moralizing"?

6. In paragraph 8, Einstein alludes to Darwin's theory of survival of the fittest. How does this discussion support the claim he is making about education?
7. Throughout the speech, Einstein uses the analogy of the ant (and bee) colonies as a strategy to emphasize his point about the role of individuals working in service of their community. Do you think this is an appealing and effective way to illustrate his view of the connection of the individual to the community? Cite specific passages to support your reasoning.
8. In paragraph 11 that begins, "I want to oppose the idea . . ." Einstein addresses a counterargument. How does he concede and refute viewpoint(s) that contrast with the position he espouses in this speech? Is his placement of the counterargument at the end rather than near the beginning of the essay a rhetorically strong choice? Why or why not?

Topics for Composing

1. **Analysis.** Einstein contends that independent thinking and behavior can be nurtured in school at the same time that individual interests are subordinated to those of the community. How does he support this contention? Cite specific passages from Einstein's speech to support your analysis.
2. **Argument.** Einstein bases his argument on the following premise: "The school has always been the most important means of transferring the wealth of tradition from one generation to the next" (par. 3). To what extent do you believe that this is as true today as it was in 1931?
3. **Connection.** Einstein discusses three methods of motivating individuals to learn. Based on your own experience, which of these methods do you find most effective? Describe a time when you felt highly motivated in school (at any level) and a time when you lacked motivation. Compare the methods your teachers used in each case to motivate you. Why do you think one method was more effective than the other?
4. **Speaking and Listening.** Working in small groups, develop a question that challenges Einstein's assumptions or beliefs about education, especially in regard to their relevance for today's school environments and expectations. Be sure to identify specific passages in Einstein's text that relate to the question you have developed. In what way does your question expose limitations in Einstein's evidence or reasoning? Then, pair up with another group, so that each group can deliver a mini-presentation to the other about its question. Discuss ways in which these presentations deepened your understanding of Einstein's writing and your group's response to it.
5. **Research.** What kind of student was Einstein? Conduct some research into his educational background in Germany and the United States. How might his experience have influenced his position on the role of schooling that he articulates in this speech?

exploring other genres

Snapping Beans (poetry)

Lisa Parker

Courtesy of Lisa J. Parker

Lisa Parker (b. 1972) grew up in a coal-mining family in Virginia. She received a B.A. from George Mason University and an MFA in creative writing from Penn State University. A writer, musician, and photographer, she currently works for the Department of Defense. In her poetry, Parker often reflects on her experience of being, as she writes, "first-generation college, first-generation above the poverty line." "Snapping Beans" is dedicated to her grandmother.

FOCUS FOR READING Throughout this chapter, you have been reading speeches, editorials, and essays about the role of the individual in school. Unlike those other texts, the following is a work of literature. As you read the following poem, consider how Parker uses figurative language, speaker, theme, and other poetic elements to explore the idea of how the individual is affected by school.

For Fay Whitt

I snapped beans into the silver bowl
that sat on the splintering slats
of the porch swing between my grandma and me.
I was home for the weekend,
from school, from the North,
Grandma hummed "What A Friend We Have In Jesus"
as the sun rose, pushing its pink spikes
through the slant of cornstalks,
through the fly-eyed mesh of the screen.
We didn't speak until the sun overcame
the feathered tips of the cornfield
and Grandma stopped humming. I could feel
the soft gray of her stare
against the side of my face
when she asked, *How's school a-goin'?*
I wanted to tell her about my classes,
the revelations by book and lecture,
as real as any shout of faith
and potent as a swig of strychnine.
She reached the leather of her hand
over the bowl and cupped
my quivering chin; the slick smooth of her palm
held my face the way she held tomatoes
under the spigot, careful not to drop them,

and I wanted to tell her
about the nights I cried into the familiar
heartsick panels of the quilt she made me,
wishing myself home on the evening star.
I wanted to tell her
the evening star was a planet,
that my friends wore nose rings and wrote poetry
about sex, about alcoholism, about Buddha.
I wanted to tell her how my stomach burned
acidic holes at the thought of speaking in class,
speaking in an accent, speaking out of turn,
how I was tearing, splitting myself apart
with the slow-simmering guilt of being happy
despite it all.
I said, *School's fine.*
We snapped beans into the silver bowl between us
and when a hickory leaf, still summer green,
skidded onto the porch front,
Grandma said,
It's funny how things blow loose like that. ■

© Estate of Joan Mitchell

The abstract expressionist painter Joan Michell has said that her work is inspired by landscape, nature, and poetry, but her intent is not to create a recognizable image. Instead, her paintings convey emotions. **What emotions does this 1977 painting (entitled *Heel, Sit, Stay*) convey to you? In what ways might the painting reflect the conflicting emotions that the speaker of "Snapping Beans" is experiencing?**

Understanding and Interpreting

1. How does the speaker's return home "for the weekend, / from school, from the North" (ll. 4–5) establish the central tension within the poem?
2. What is the significance of the speaker and her grandma "snapping beans" together? What does this shared task reveal about their relationship?
3. What details does the speaker provide to emphasize the growing distance between her experience at college and her grandmother's understanding of it?
4. Is the lack of conversation between the speaker and her grandmother a sign of their growing distance from one another or evidence of their close bond that needs little talk? Or both? Explain with specific reference to the poem.
5. Should the speaker have told her grandmother more of the details of her college life — her classes, her friends, her own fear of speaking up? What might have been gained or lost through such conversation?
6. How do you interpret the last five lines? Is the speaker angry? Guilty? Happy? Why does she feel "slow-simmering guilt of being happy" (l. 37)? Do you see hope for maintaining or reclaiming the closeness between granddaughter and grandmother? Why or why not?

Analyzing Language, Style, and Structure

1. **Vocabulary in Context.** Parker's speaker longs to tell her grandmother about "the revelations by book and lecture" (l. 17). What does the word "revelations" mean in this context? How is this meaning similar to or different from other ways you have seen the word used or defined? What does its allusion to the Bible's book of Revelation add to the effect of this word choice in the poem?
2. Why does the speaker use such strong language when she thinks about what she is learning in school being "as real as any shout of faith / and potent as a swig of strychnine" (ll. 18–19)? What is the effect on the reader?
3. What actual conversation do the speaker and her grandmother have? How do the few words they say to one another contrast with the inner thoughts of the speaker?
4. Why does her grandmother's action, as the speaker describes it in the following lines, make her yearn to reveal her experiences at school?

> She reached the leather of her hand
> over the bowl and cupped
> my quivering chin; the slick smooth of her palm
> held my face the way she held tomatoes
> under the spigot, careful not to drop them . . .

5. What do the beans, cornfield, quilt, hickory leaf, and simile about the tomatoes signify about the way the speaker sees her world — or worlds?
6. Parker dedicates this poem to her grandmother, yet is the grandmother her intended audience? If not, then who do you think that she might imagine as her reader(s)?

Topics for Composing

1. **Analysis.** How do the two worlds that the speaker now lives in — the world of school and her home — both collide and connect in this poem? Develop your response with specific references to the highly descriptive and figurative language that Parker uses.
2. **Argument.** The speaker of "Snapping Beans" seems to feel a growing distance from her grandmother. What in the text of the poem indicates that the grandmother might share this feeling? What suggestion is there that the speaker may have underestimated her grandmother? Ultimately, what does the poem conclude about whether relationships can change as people change?
3. **Connection.** "Snapping Beans" centers on a college student trying to maintain a connection with a close relative who cannot relate to her college experience. Think of a time when you struggled to maintain a close relationship with someone who has not shared an experience that has greatly influenced or shaped you. How did you keep your connection? Did the relationship have to continue on different terms?
4. **Connection.** Which of the authors that you have read in this chapter has concerns or experiences with education that are similar to those of the speaker in "Snapping Beans"? Explain
5. **Speaking and Listening.** Record yourself reading the poem. Combine your recording with a series of visuals, either in the form of video with voiceover or a carefully timed slideshow. Your visuals (which can include text from the poem) and your voiceover should work together to present your interpretation of the poem. With your class or in small groups, discuss how creating the slideshow changed or deepened your understanding of the poem.
6. **Creative Writing.** Rewrite this poem with the grandmother as the speaker. Your poem should convey your interpretation of "Snapping Beans."

Writing a Rhetorical Analysis Essay

If we think of rhetoric as the art of persuasion, then rhetorical analysis is an appreciation or critique of that art. When you conduct a rhetorical analysis, you systematically examine the choices a writer or speaker makes and the effect of those choices on the intended audience — as we did in the Skill Workshop (pp. 373–382) with "What Straight-A Students Get Wrong" by Adam Grant. You saw in that analysis that a writer's choices may include big picture strategies, such as structure, as well as choices in language, such as emotionally charged diction.

One of the most important reasons for writing a rhetorical analysis essay, as you will do in this workshop, is that this kind of analysis makes you hyperaware of the ways in which writers, politicians, advertisers, friends, family members, and teachers try to persuade you about something. This type of analysis gives you the observational and interpretative skills to challenge other people's points of view and to determine whether their ideas are credible, trustworthy, and relevant. This can make you a more informed voter, consumer, and citizen.

In preparing to write a rhetorical analysis essay, it might be useful first to consider what it is not:

- It is not simply a summary of the argument you're analyzing.
- It is not a list of strategies or choices the writer makes.
- It is not an argument about whether you agree or disagree with what the author of the text is saying. Even if your rhetorical analysis involves a controversial subject about which you have strong feelings, such as climate change or immigration, your view on the topic should not factor into this type of essay. Your essay should focus on the rhetorical choices a writer makes to develop an argument or achieve a specific purpose.

In this workshop, you will be writing your own rhetorical analysis essay in response to the following prompt:

> *Choose an argumentative text from this chapter or from another source that you find interesting or persuasive. Write an essay that analyzes the rhetorical choices the writer makes to persuade readers of the central claim. In your essay, analyze how the author uses rhetorical elements, including evidence, reasoning, appeals, language, and style.*

To help you with the process of writing a rhetorical analysis, we will model each of the specific steps by focusing on the central text in this chapter: "Against School" by John Taylor Gatto (p. 428).

Step 1: Gathering Ideas

Before asking you to answer the prompt, in this step we will slow down a bit and model how to consider the rhetorical situation, annotate a text, and find a focus for the essay.

Analyze the Rhetorical Situation

An essential part of any rhetorical analysis is to assess the rhetorical situation. Begin by identifying the basic components using either the rhetorical triangle or SOAPSTone that you saw in Chapter 3 (pp. 87–89). Then, begin to think about how those elements work in the text.

Let's take a quick look back at the headnote that accompanies the piece we will be modeling in this workshop and see what we can figure out about the rhetorical situation:

> A three-time Teacher of the Year in New York State, John Taylor Gatto (1935–2018) was one of public schooling's fiercest critics. In fact, he resigned his teaching job in a 1991 editorial in the *Wall Street Journal,* stating "I can't teach this way any longer. If you hear of a job where I don't have to hurt kids to make a living, let me know." The title of one of Gatto's books, *Dumbing Us Down: The Hidden Curriculum of Compulsory Schooling* (2002), reveals his attitude toward the public school system. Gatto noted that it forces attendance and promotes standardization and conformity. In the following essay, which was published in the September 2003 issue of *Harper's* magazine, Gatto draws on his own experience working in a big city public school as he develops his criticism.

Consider the author, occasion, audience, and purpose:

- **What do we know about the author?** He was a highly successful former teacher, disillusioned with public education.
- **What do we know about the occasion**? The text was published in 2003, the year after the No Child Left Behind Act, which led to a significant increase in the amount of standardized testing for students in the United States.
- **What do we know about the audience?** This piece was published in *Harper's* magazine, a journal of politics, culture, literature, and the arts, that has been around since 1850. So, the audience is likely to be highly educated and politically involved.
- **What is the author's purpose?** Gatto is trying to persuade his audience that it's time to rethink the factory-model of education that prizes obedience and conformity over critical thinking and creativity.

Locating a Text and Analyzing the Rhetorical Situation

Choose a text that you find interesting or persuasive. Analyze the rhetorical situation as we did with Gatto. If your text is from this chapter, pay close attention to the headnote that precedes the text; it will contain information you will need to begin analyzing the rhetorical situation. If you need more information, conduct research on the publication and the time period in which the text was published.

Reading Critically for Rhetorical Choices

Now that you understand the rhetorical situation surrounding the text you have selected, the next step of the rhetorical analysis process is to look closely at the text itself. As always, start by making connections and asking questions. When you reread the text, think specifically about *how* the argument works. Remember that the essay prompt asks you to consider choices the writer makes and how those choices shape the argument. Note as many details as possible and ask how these affect the audience, how they relate to the rhetorical situation, and how they build support for the argument. Annotation will help you collect your thoughts. We've modeled some annotations on Gatto's argument here:

Speaker/ethos: Gatto's experience emphasized in opening sentence

I taught for thirty years in some of the worst schools in Manhattan, and in some of the best, and during that time I became an expert in boredom. Boredom was everywhere in my world, and if you asked the kids, as I often did, why they felt so bored, they always gave the same answers: They said the work was stupid, that it made no sense, that they already knew it. They said they wanted to be doing something real, not just sitting around. They said teachers didn't seem to know much about their subjects and clearly weren't interested in learning more. And the kids were right: their teachers were every bit as bored as they were.

He writes in first person — but contrasts with "they" — so teacher and kids are in opposition?

Repetition of "They said" emphasizes that the kids have been making the same point for a long time.

"kids" instead of "students": Will his audience like that?

Lots of contrasts between kids and teachers, I/they, real work vs. sitting – yet everybody is bored

Boredom is the common condition of schoolteachers, and anyone who has spent time in a teachers' lounge can vouch for the low energy, the whining, the dispirited attitudes, to be found there. When asked why they feel bored, the teachers tend to blame the kids, as you might expect. Who wouldn't get bored teaching students who are rude and interested only in grades? If even that. Of course, teachers are themselves products of the same twelve-year compulsory school programs that so thoroughly bore their students, and as school personnel they are trapped inside structures even more rigid than those imposed upon the children. Who, then, is to blame?

We all are.

Continued repetition of "bored" and "boredom" makes us feel the monotony being described.

Three highly negative words all associated with confinement (and conformity?)

Collective "we" — so nobody is to blame, everybody is? Paradox?

Short, simple sentence: abrupt stop

As we annotate these opening paragraphs, we observe that Gatto sets up a tension between kids and teachers, yet argues that they're all in "compulsory school" together. Neither "rude" and uninterested kids nor their bored teachers are to blame because everybody shares blame. If "we all are" to blame, then that implicates everyone who actively supports or simply tolerates this education system. What is the effect of opening the essay by emphasizing boredom yet refusing to place blame on any one person or group?

Think about it: are there many readers of *Harper's* magazine, a publication with a generally educated and politically liberal audience, who haven't experienced school? And probably some boredom in that setting? Gatto gets their attention and tries to establish early on that the issue is too complex for one group — teachers, parents, kids, the government — to be solely responsible for the problem or solution. In fact, he even justifies the less than ideal behavior of some teachers by pointing out that a generation ago, they were probably just as bored in school as their students are. In other words, we're all in this together. So one choice Gatto makes is to establish empathy with his readers to approach this school boredom as a shared problem.

activity **Reading Critically for Rhetorical Choices**

Turn to the piece that you chose to work with for this workshop. Analyze it by annotating or responding to the text, noting the rhetorical choices the writer makes and how they appeal to the audience. Pair up with a classmate, perhaps even someone who has chosen the same essay as you have, and discuss what each of you notices.

Finding a Focus

As you have carefully read the argument you've chosen, made observations, and discerned patterns in rhetorical choices, you have likely ended up with more ideas than you can use in a single essay. Identifying patterns sometimes helps to reveal a focus that is manageable in a relatively short essay. Keep in mind, too, that your essay should not be a string of paragraphs that simply identify rhetorical strategies. Instead, you want to consider how the author's rhetorical choices work both individually and together to persuade or move an audience. Use the following questions to guide you:

- What does the writer hope to achieve in this argument?
- What specific choices does the writer make to persuade the audience?
- What are some common patterns or trends (in organization, evidence, or language, for example) that you have observed by this point in your analysis?
- How — specifically — does the writer appeal to emotion (pathos) and logic (logos)?
- How does the writer establish authority (ethos)?

As an example, let's look at how Gatto relates to his readers throughout his essay. He opens by citing his thirty years of teaching in both "the worst" and "the best" schools in

New York City. Later in his essay, he recounts an anecdote about his grandfather scolding him for giving in to boredom and connects that to the classroom. He returns to his own experience a paragraph or so later by referencing his continued bewilderment about why school has to be boring even as he was retiring. He uses first person singular ("we") to indicate that he identifies with his audience. This device becomes particularly important in the conclusion when he exhorts that "we must wake up to what our schools really are . . ." Near the end, he brings up again his "thirty years in the public school trenches." He softens the short and forceful penultimate sentence by beginning with "I think."

These observations have allowed us to uncover a focus on one point: Gatto uses his own experience as an educator and a student as the foundation of his argument. Although he weaves in his expertise and experience throughout, he speaks not as someone with all the answers but as someone who, like his readers, is seeking a better way.

By identifying that one strategy, we are building toward a focus. If we consider one or two other strategies he uses that work in concert with that one, we will be ready to start drafting a working thesis for a rhetorical analysis essay.

Finding Your Focus

After rereading the piece you've chosen for your own rhetorical analysis and rereading your annotations, try to identify a main strategy the writer employs, such as Gatto's use of personal experience. Identify multiple examples of this strategy at work throughout the piece. How does repeatedly employing this strategy help the author achieve his or her purpose?

Step 2: Planning the Essay

So far in this workshop, you have selected your piece for analysis, conducted a close reading with careful annotations, and identified a main strategy that the author uses to build the argument. Before you begin writing your response, this step will walk you through developing your thesis, identifying relevant support, and considering an appropriate organizational structure.

Developing a Working Thesis

You've probably had a lot of experience with writing thesis statements, so you already understand the process in general. As you work on a thesis for a rhetorical analysis essay, keep in mind that it is not simply a summary or your own opinion on the topic. Neither is it a list of all the rhetorical choices or strategies the writer uses. By this point, you have probably also realized that a rhetorical analysis is itself a type of argument. By analyzing how a writer achieves a particular purpose, you are interpreting the text, writing an argument about the approach that you think is most important to notice, and commenting on its effectiveness. In your thesis statement, therefore, state what you think is the most important rhetorical strategy and explain how this helps the writer make and develop his or her claim.

Let's look at a few examples of weak and strong thesis statements:

WEAK THESIS

In "Against School," John Taylor Gatto criticizes today's mandatory public education system.

This statement is not wrong; in fact, Gatto does do that. But the statement fails to analyze *how* he crafts and presents his argument. A thesis like this one leads to an essay that restates or summarizes the argument instead of analyzing how it works.

WEAK THESIS

Based on my own experience, which is different from what John Taylor Gatto describes in "Against School," I disagree that compulsory schooling for twelve years results in boredom for both teachers and students and, worse, prizes conformity over critical thinking.

This is a thesis that doesn't respond to the task. The rhetorical analysis essay is not about you — it's about the text. Whether you agree or disagree with the author's argument is beside the point. Your task is to analyze how the author presents an argument to appeal to a specific audience in a specific context.

WEAK THESIS

In "Against School," John Taylor Gatto appeals to ethos, pathos, and logos to achieve his purpose.

This thesis is too vague, and fails to offer focus or direction. It won't guide the development of a rhetorical analysis. It simply states that Gatto uses three types of appeals to make a case. It does not address how he appeals to logos and pathos, how he establishes ethos, or what his purpose is in making these appeals.

WORKING THESIS

In his essay "Against School," John Taylor Gatto calls on his experience as a veteran of the public school system to appeal to his readers, particularly parents, to rethink the factory-model of education that prizes obedience and conformity over critical thinking and creativity.

This thesis brings together Gatto's purpose ("the time has come to rethink the factory-model of education") and identifies the relationship between Gatto ("veteran of the public school system") and his readers ("particularly parents"). In that way, the thesis identifies the main points to be developed in the essay:

- How and why Gatto's experience appeals to his educated readers
- How he characterizes compulsory school programs as being like a factory
- How he appeals to emotion, especially parental concern, by showing how schools encourage passive acceptance over innovative thinking

It's a bit of a long thesis, so we might consider trimming for more succinct wording or even breaking it into two sentences. However, it's a working thesis that would keep our analysis of Gatto's rhetorical choices on track.

Developing Your Working Thesis

Draft a working thesis for a rhetorical analysis of the text you've chosen. Discuss your thesis statement with a classmate. As part of your discussion, make sure your partner understands from the thesis what points you will develop and prove in the essay.

Gathering Textual Evidence

If you think about a rhetorical analysis essay as an argument, then your evidence will be found in the text of the argument itself. You may cite passages with paraphrase or direct quotation, but your analysis must be grounded in the text. Then, provide your own commentary to explain the relationship between your claim and the textual evidence.

Let's return to the idea that Gatto develops about the factory model and school, and use it to explore the final contrast in our working thesis: "factory-model of education that prizes obedience and conformity over critical thinking and creativity." One way to make sure that you clearly connect your thesis to each rhetorical choice and then to the effect of that choice is to use a graphic organizer like the one below. To demonstrate how this might work, we've begun filling in the organizer with our thoughts on evidence from Gatto's piece.

Point	Related evidence (quotation or paraphrase from the text)	How the evidence relates to the point	Effect of the evidence
Schools foster a factory model.	"with their long-term cell-block-style, forced confinement of both students and teachers—as virtual factories of childishness"	Gatto uses the term "factories" to negatively characterize the physical and psychological landscape of school settings.	The details create a visual picture of a confined and confining environment.
	Mandatory schooling's "real purpose is to turn [children] into servants."	If children are being turned into "servants," then they are not learning leadership or independence.	"[S]ervants" is an emotionally loaded word choice that suggests unfair treatment but also devaluation. It reinforces the idea of mass production or factory.

Point	Related evidence (quotation or paraphrase from the text)	How the evidence relates to the point	Effect of the evidence
Education and schooling are not the same.	"We could encourage the best qualities of youthfulness — curiosity, adventure, resilience, the capacity for surprising insight — simply by being more flexible about time, texts, and tests, by introducing kids to truly competent adults, and by giving each student . . . autonomy."	Gatto contrasts students' natural desires to explore and learn with the schools' constraints brought about by lack of choice in timeframes, reading materials, and testing.	The list of highly positive and desirable "qualities" evokes an emotional connection that argues for a more human and humane environment.
Success does not depend upon "schooling."	The "deadly routine" of "forced schooling" We have come to think of "'success' as synonymous with, or at least dependent upon, 'schooling.'"	Gatto stresses that he is not against "education" but rather the type of schooling that he sees in public systems.	The language contrasts life-generating vs. life-draining activities. Juxtaposition of "success" and "schooling" underscores that one is only part of the other.
Schools program students rather than fostering individuality.	"School trains children to be employees and consumers . . . [not] leaders and adventurers."	Public education requires safety and acceptance; it discourages boldness and risk.	The contrasting pairs bring to mind images of two very different types of people by creating a stark contrast. This emphasizes Gatto's point about the deficiency of schools as they exist today.

Once you have organized your thoughts and observations, you can decide which quotations you want to use. Your final column has already begun your commentary, which links the point you're making to the textual evidence you're citing.

Gathering Textual Evidence

Create a graphic organizer like the one above, and begin to locate and examine the evidence that you identified in your reading and annotating in an earlier step. Be sure to explain how the evidence you identify helps the writer to be persuasive.

Organizing the Essay

In general, a rhetorical analysis essay consists of an introduction, a series of body paragraphs (at least two) focused on rhetorical choices and their effect, and a conclusion. Make sure that your analysis addresses the rhetorical situation, the writer's means of persuasion (usually more than one), and the impact of the rhetorical strategies the writer chooses.

Try not to simply follow the order of ideas in the text you're analyzing. It's very easy to lapse into a rhetorical play-by-play instead of organizing your writing according to the key points of your analysis. There is no one right way to organize a rhetorical analysis essay, but we will model two possible approaches you could consider for your essay.

Using Gatto as our model, here is one way to structure an essay around rhetorical appeals:

- **Body Paragraph 1**: Discuss how Gatto immediately establishes ethos with his audience by pointing out the years he spent in the classroom and telling personal stories about that experience. Quotations from the text can support the analysis.
- **Body Paragraph 2**: Move to how Gatto appeals to reason by discussing the logic of his argument and the type of evidence he uses.
- **Body Paragraph 3**: Focus on how Gatto moves his audience's hearts as well as minds, using "we" to connect with his readers in the goal of helping children thrive in school.

As you see in the sample structure above, you could have separate paragraphs on ethos, logos, and then pathos. Though that is a somewhat formulaic structure, it could be effective in this case. Or you could prove the same thesis by focusing on a single appeal and examining how Gatto uses it for different purposes to make his case. That structure, a little more complex organizationally, might work something like this:

- **Body Paragraph 1**: Discuss how Gatto immediately establishes ethos with his audience by pointing out the years he spent in the classroom and telling personal stories about that experience. Quotations from the text can support the analysis.
- **Body Paragraph 2**: Continue the discussion of ethos and how Gatto uses it effectively by analyzing the shift toward the end, starting with "Now for the good news."
- **Body Paragraph 3**: Demonstrate that Gatto first establishes shared values among educated people, then uses "we" to connect with his readers in the goal of helping children thrive in school.

This approach would acknowledge that ethos is neither vague nor one-dimensional but rather a complex rhetorical concept that skilled writers and speakers use to their advantage. The goal of both approaches is the same: examine how the author goes about proving his claim. If you think you have a good grasp on the purpose of a rhetorical essay, feel free to experiment with a structure like the second one.

Organizing Your Essay

Now that you've had a chance to develop different parts of your rhetorical analysis essay, think about how to organize it effectively. Starting with your thesis, outline the major points you will make and the sequence of their presentation. As in the sample body paragraph descriptions on page 471, explain what you are trying to accomplish in each paragraph.

Step 3: Drafting the Essay

Now that you have a working thesis, plenty of relevant evidence, and an idea about how you want to organize your essay, it's time to begin drafting it. To help you with drafting, the discussion in this step will focus on the elements of a body paragraph and approaches to starting and concluding an essay.

Writing Body Paragraphs with Textual Evidence

As you draft body paragraphs that include textual evidence, keep in mind that textual evidence should not overwhelm your writing. The bulk of your paragraphs should be your own commentary that helps readers understand how the evidence you have selected contributes to your points. Take a look at this annotated sample paragraph about the model text we've been discussing:

Gatto appeals to the emotions of his educated audience, especially the parents among them, to reject the time-worn model of compulsory schooling that teaches younger generations to be happy in a box rather than thinking outside of it. He refers to schools as "virtual factories of childishness" whose "real purpose is to turn [children] into servants." This is not a way to reach goals of helping each individual to achieve "his or her personal best." Rather, it is a way to keep children as conformists at the expense of individuality. Gatto discusses the tension between developing a child's natural curiosity and leveling everyone into the same automaton—in his words "employees and consumers" rather than "leaders and adventurers." He contrasts children's natural urge to

Topic sentence that connects to the thesis

Highlighted areas are quotations.

explore and learn with schools' efforts to constrain and limit children by denying flexibility of "time, texts, and tests." By choosing language that carries emotional associations, Gatto appeals to parents' desire to bring out the best in their children by calling for schools to offer students the freedom to develop their natural gifts.

In this paragraph, we've woven quotations from the graphic organizer (pp. 469–470) into our own sentences so that commentary on those quotations comprise the majority of the paragraph. The textual evidence (highlighted) supports the claim stated in the topic sentence. The words and details from the passage build the line of reasoning in the rhetorical analysis. If you were to look back at the organizational structure we identified on page 471, you would see that what we just wrote accomplishes the goals of the third body paragraph of our rhetorical analysis. If we were to write the remaining body paragraphs of our essay, we would draft one about how Gatto establishes his ethos and another about how he uses logic and reasoning to support his claim that schools use a factory model that promotes conformity. Our body paragraphs, like the preceding sample, would include evidence from Gatto's piece, as well as our own commentary about how that evidence relates to our thesis.

Writing Your Body Paragraphs

Focusing on one of the points in your thesis statement, write a body paragraph that includes evidence from the graphic organizer you completed (p. 470) and your own commentary. Show your body paragraph to a partner and address the following questions together:

- Have I clearly connected the point I'm exploring to the thesis statement?
- Have I included enough textual evidence?
- Have I explained the effect of the textual evidence specifically enough to provide commentary on the effect that it has on the argument? That is, am I explaining how the rhetorical choice the author makes advances the argument?

Using the feedback from your partner, revise that paragraph and write the remaining body paragraphs of your essay as determined by your thesis and the organizational structure you identified on page 472.

Writing an Introduction

Regardless of how you've decided to organize your overall essay, your opening should make a good first impression. You could use a personal anecdote to connect to your audience, offer a relevant quotation from someone well-known, or craft an evocative description. These are choices you're encountering as you read published arguments throughout this book. Yet, keep in mind the practical nature of a rhetorical analysis. The majority of the time, you are responding to a prompt, an assignment that asks you to do something specific — to analyze how a writer's rhetorical choices contribute to achieving his or her purpose. Of course, the analysis may not be so straightforward, but it's important that you connect directly to what you've been asked to do. That's what your readers expect. That's your thesis.

A conventional way of organizing an introduction is an inverted pyramid: start fairly general and become increasingly specific as you lead to your thesis. That works, though there's no rule that says you can't just open with the thesis and then provide some context to transition to your analysis. But let's start with an example of the inverted pyramid for our sample introduction to a rhetorical analysis of Gatto:

> Nearly everyone has been a student in various classrooms, so nearly everyone has an opinion about public education. Critics, whether they're educators or parents or average citizens, abound with suggestions of ways to improve education: Provide better teacher training, require more standardization and accountability, look to other countries with higher achievement levels than the United States as models for change. But rarely does someone come along who suggests we get rid of public school systems as we know them. John Gatto does exactly that in his essay, "Against School." He draws on his experience as a veteran of the public education system to make the case to his readers, particularly parents, that it's time to rethink the factory-model of education that prizes obedience and conformity over critical thinking and creativity.

This introduction leads with the common experience of being a student in school, acknowledges that most people have ideas about how to make schools better, and then turns toward the thesis by restating Gatto's unusual position. The thesis itself details specifically how the essay will proceed and previews its organization.

Writing Your Introduction

Using the inverted pyramid and the sample introductory paragraph, draft an introduction to the rhetorical analysis essay you are writing. Share it with a classmate to receive feedback on whether or not it is engaging and provides enough context for the reader to understand the thesis.

Writing a Conclusion

Writing a rhetorical analysis isn't easy. By the end, you might be tired and just want to wrap it up with a rehash of your thesis or a quick summary of your analysis. Doing that may remind readers of your main points, but it might also leave them yawning. Keep in mind that the rhetorical analysis essay has a clear purpose — you want to be sure that your readers know you've accomplished it. In addition, you want to keep them thinking. In the case of our sample rhetorical analysis, we need to ask ourselves, *So what if Gatto establishes ethos and develops a series of contrasts to call for a complete change in public education?* We should tell our readers why this is important, not by airing our own opinion but by returning to what he does. Here's an example:

> In "Against School," Gatto makes a bold proposal not to put band-aids on the problem or fix symptoms, but to rethink the whole system. Since he knows his audience will likely be skeptical, he provides evidence that the system is outdated, broken, and hurtful. By the end of his essay, however, he speaks not as a tired and cynical veteran of that system but as an idealist who reminds his readers to nurture, not suppress, the "genius" in every kid.

Such a conclusion does not agree or disagree with Gatto but recaps main points made in the essay without simply repeating them. In addition, it brings together the overall effect of the rhetorical choices Gatto makes to convey his ideas.

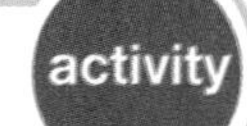

Writing Your Conclusion

Ask yourself the "So what?" question about rhetorical strategies in the text you're analyzing. Then, use your answer to draft a conclusion to your rhetorical analysis essay. Share it with a classmate to receive feedback on whether or not it reminds the reader of the purpose and tries to wrap up the piece in an engaging manner.

Step 4: Finalizing the Essay

Now that you have a complete draft of your essay, you can move on to the final steps in the writing process: revising and editing. These two acts are sometimes thought of as being the same, but they're not. Revision is when you look back at large-scale structural elements of your essay, such as how well you support your claim, what kinds of evidence you use, how effective your word choices are, and to what extent you have led your reader easily through your essay. Editing, on the other hand, focuses on fine-tuning the language, grammar, punctuation, spelling, and other conventions. Editing is usually the very last thing you do before you finalize your essay, looking carefully for any errors you may have made. The following are suggestions for you to consider as you finalize your essay.

Revising

Revising gives you a good opportunity to think again about your audience and make sure that you are achieving your purpose. In most cases, a rhetorical analysis essay is a chance to demonstrate your understanding of a concept or skill. As we've discussed, you're interpreting a text, but you are not offering your viewpoint on the subject of that text. A rhetorical analysis should not focus on your opinion, even if you have a strong opinion about the topic. In most cases, your audience will be your teacher. In the case of a standardized test, it will be an external evaluator. In both situations, that means using a somewhat formal tone, but your writing can still be engaging for you and your audience.

Reread your essay for the following:

- Did you avoid **agreeing or disagreeing** with the topic the writer presents? For more help with this part of your essay, revisit the Developing a Working Thesis section in this Writing Workshop (p. 467).
- Look back at your **thesis**. Since you wrote this early on in the workshop, does it still relate to the rhetorical analysis you ended up writing? See the Revision Workshop 1: Effective Thesis and Essay Structure (p. 1064) if you need more assistance.
- Look back at your **focus**. Is it still at the center of your argument, or are you finding yourself just cataloging rhetorical choices without tying them back to the focus? See Revision Workshop 2: Effective Topic Sentences and Unified Paragraphs (p. 1068).
- Look back at some of your **body paragraphs**. Have you balanced the evidence with your own **commentary** about how that evidence supports your thesis? See Revision Workshop 3: Balanced Evidence and Commentary (p. 1073) if you need more help with this part of your essay.
- Evaluate your **organizational structure**. Is it clear enough for the reader to follow? Are there other approaches to the organization that might be more effective? See Revision Workshop 5: Effective Transitions (p. 1082) if you think that your reader may have some difficulty following your essay.
- Does your **introduction** grab the reader's attention and effectively preview your topic? Does your **conclusion** wrap up in a way that highlights your focus? See Revision Workshop 8: Effective Introductions and Conclusions (p. 1097).

Editing

Remember, editing is the very last thing you'll do before finalizing your essay. You and your teacher know better than anyone the types of spelling, grammar, and convention errors you need to focus on in your writing development. Be sure to refer to one or more of the Grammar Workshops (p. 1101) in the back of the book if you encounter an issue and aren't sure how to overcome it.

Continuing the Conversation

Throughout this chapter, you have read and thought about how the institution of school affects the individual. At the beginning of the chapter and after each of the readings, you had opportunities to consider ideas related to the following essential questions:

- What is the purpose of education?
- To what extent is school necessary for becoming educated?
- What effect do the pressures to conform to an institution like school have on a person's individuality?
- What roles do race, gender identity, and ethnicity play in a school setting?
- How might schools in the future look similar to and different from today's schools?

The sections that follow will give you an opportunity to revisit and respond to some of those questions as you think further about the ideals and the reality of school and connect these ideas to yourself, the texts you've read, and the world outside of the classroom.

Connections to Self

Think back on the texts you have read, responses you have written, discussions you have participated in, and ideas you have considered during your work with this chapter. Use the following questions to explore how the issues in this chapter connect to your life and experience:

1. Imagine that an incoming ninth grader asks you for advice on how to handle high school. Based on your own experiences and ideas you found compelling in this chapter's texts, what suggestions would you offer? Why?

2. Several of the texts in this chapter focus on educational settings in which not all students are treated equally. In some cases, an unfair treatment reflects a larger societal issue. Share a moment when you experienced or observed unfair or unequal treatment, intentional or unintentional, on the basis of gender identity, race, appearance, religious affiliation, economic status, or another factor.

3. What is the most powerful experience you've had so far in high school? Was it brought about by peers, teachers, sports, family, academic subjects, community internships, or something else? Was it an encouraging or a discouraging experience? Does it remind you of any of the experiences shared by authors in this chapter?

4. Which of the authors you have read in this chapter would you most like to meet and interview? Why? What ideas about school would you like to explore with that author?

5. Which of the texts that you read in this chapter had the most significant impact on the ways that you think about school? Why?

Connections to Texts

Use the following questions to make connections among the texts in this chapter and to consider what insights the texts provide regarding the individual in school. As you respond, be sure to make specific references to **two or more texts** you read in this chapter.

1. The American high school has not changed significantly since the nineteenth century. Several of the authors you've read in this chapter propose changing that model. What common problems do they address? In what ways are their solutions similar and different? You may want to consider the following texts in your response: "Children Educate Themselves," "Against School," "Abolish High School," and "Education: Change Is the Only Constant."
2. Several of the authors you have read in this chapter argue aggressively against conformity. Choose two or more of the texts you read in this chapter and explain how the authors of those texts approach problems and solutions related to conformity in schools. You may want to consider the following texts in your response: the excerpt from *The Geeks Shall Inherit the Earth*, "Don't Peak in High School," "Abolish High School," the excerpt from *The School Days of an Indian Girl,* and "A Message from a Black Mom to Her Son."
3. Imagine that Yuval Harari were putting together a "think tank" of two or three collaborators to develop a plan to overhaul the American high school. Which of the authors (living or dead) in this chapter would he most likely invite to be part of such a team? Why? What problems might Harari and those authors discuss? What solutions might they propose?
4. John Taylor Gatto, the author of "Against School," essentially calls for the end of formal, compulsory education. Explain which authors would likely agree or disagree with his approach and why. You may want to consider the following texts in your response: "Abolish High School," "Education: Change Is the Only Constant," "On Education," and "Children Educate Themselves."

Connections to World

Think back on the texts you have read, responses you have written, discussions you have participated in, and ideas you have considered during your work with this chapter. Use the following questions to explore how the issues in this chapter play out in the world at large:

1. What is the most important change that we need to make in the education system in the United States? How might we effectively work toward that change? What challenges might we face?

2. Because of the way that schools are funded through state and local taxes, not all school districts receive equal amounts of money to spend on books, technology, facilities, teacher salaries, and other required elements. What impact can unequal school funding have on student success in school and later in life?
3. To what extent do schools prepare students for careers after high school? Should that be the goal? Why or why not?

Evidence-Based Argument

Write an argument in response to one of the prompts below in which you support your claim with examples from **at least three of the texts** in this chapter.

Prompt 1: Write about a time when you chose to conform or not to conform to expectations in a school setting. What motivated you to make this decision? What were the results? In retrospect, was it a good decision? Which of the authors in this chapter would applaud or criticize your choice? Why?

Prompt 2: With easy access to the world's knowledge at our fingertips through the Internet, do we still need formal schooling? Refer to at least three of the texts you've read in this chapter as you explain and support your viewpoint.

Prompt 3: To what extent is the development of the individual in conflict with the community values of high school? Refer to at least three of the texts you've read in this chapter as you explain and support your viewpoint.

City/Rudaya, Runa Anastasiya Rudaya/Runa Anastasiya Rudaya/Private Collection/Bridgeman Images

Cultures, Conflicts, and Connections

Essential Questions:

- **How does culture shape people's perceptions of themselves and the world around them?**
- **What are the benefits and challenges of simultaneously belonging to two or more cultures?**
- **How do people adapt to new cultures?**
- **How do the intergenerational connections between family members evolve as cultural differences arise?**

In a commencement speech at Kenyon College in 2005, author David Foster Wallace began with the following comments:

> Two young fish . . . happen to meet an older fish swimming the other way, who nods at them and says, "Morning, boys, how's the water?" [A while later, one of the two young fish asks the other], "What the hell is water?"
>
> If at this moment, you're worried that I plan to present myself here as the wise old fish explaining what water is to you younger fish, please don't be. I am not the wise old fish. The immediate point of the fish story is that the most obvious, ubiquitous, important realities are often the ones that are the hardest to see and talk about.

"Culture" is one word for the "water" Wallace refers to. We are often so immersed in our own culture that it can be impossible for us to even notice it. If we speak a particular language, eat certain foods, practice a specific religion, we may begin to assume that everyone shares our culture — or that if they don't, then they're a bit strange. And, unfortunately, too often when cultures come into contact with each other, conflict is the result. Perhaps it is our inability to see the water (culture) around us that makes it difficult to see the world from other perspectives.

In this chapter, you will have an opportunity to consider not only what culture is, but also what happens when different cultures come into contact with each other. In general, and for the purposes of this chapter, culture refers to the common language, beliefs, experiences, and customs of a group of people. On a large scale, being citizens of a country can make people feel connected to each other by a national culture. On a smaller scale, attendees of a school might feel connected to each other by an academic culture. Even those who share a national identity may separate into cultural groups defined by age, education, occupation, race, religion, and so on. Culture can bring people together or set them apart.

Reflecting on Culture

Make a list of foods that you normally eat, customs you practice, languages you speak, and music you listen to. Meet with a partner and discuss the similarities and differences between the "water" you each inhabit. Individually write a reflection on how learning about each other's culture enhances your understanding of your partner.

Texts in Conversation

The poems and stories you'll read in this chapter focus on characters dealing with the intricacies of cultural groups interacting. As you progress through this chapter, think about the positive and negative influences of these intersecting cultural groups and what the characters learn about themselves and others. A graphic organizer like this one can help you maintain notes on these topics.

Author and title	Key cultural changes, conflicts, or influences	Quotations related to cultural changes, conflicts, or influences	Your reaction and/or connections to other texts

Understanding a Poem's Speaker and Meaning

In Chapter 2, we introduced the language and concepts used to discuss and analyze poetry. Within a poem, **figurative devices** (such as **metaphor**, **simile**, and **hyperbole**), **imagery**, **rhyme**, and **rhythm** work together to present ideas to readers and evoke emotional responses from them. In this workshop, we'll consider these elements and draw conclusions about the poem's speaker and the meaning of the poem.

Let's explore the complexities of a poem's speaker. We'll be examining Claude McKay's "The Tropics in New York," while you'll work with a different poem. As we read this poem for the first time, we'll annotate the text by making connections and asking questions (see p. 10). Then, we'll go back and annotate it again, searching for details that reveal the nature of the poem's speaker, including what the speaker says and his relationship with the different settings of the poem. Although readers' observations and annotations will vary, the sample annotations that follow will help you explore the role that reading and annotating can play in analyzing a poem's speaker and meaning.

The Tropics in New York

Claude McKay

Poet, novelist, and short story writer Claude McKay (1889–1948) was born in Jamaica and moved to the Unites States in 1912, where he became a prominent figure of the Harlem Renaissance. "The Tropics in New York" comes from McKay's 1922 poetry collection *Harlem Shadows.*

Everett Collection/Shutterstock

What does "tropics" in the title apply to?

Bananas ripe and green, and ginger-root, — *10 syllables per line*
Cocoa in pods and alligator pears,
And tangerines and mangoes and grape fruit, — *Harsh sounds*
Fit for the highest prize at parish fairs,

Set in the window, bringing memories — *Thoughts about his past*
Of fruit-trees laden by low-singing rills, — *Soft sounds during memory*
And dewy dawns, and mystical blue skies
In benediction over nun-like hills.

First presence of the speaker!

My eyes grew dim, and I could no more gaze;
A wave of longing through my body swept,
And, hungry for the old, familiar ways,
I turned aside and bowed my head and wept.

Hungry for familiar things, not food

Feelings of grief, loss, loneliness

Gathering Information about the Speaker

Although some poems seem to reflect the experience of the poet, we cannot assume that the "I" in line 9 refers to Claude McKay himself. Many writers draw from personal experiences, but poetry is not necessarily autobiographical. The poet and speaker are separate entities. It is helpful to think of the speaker as a poet's creation, much like a narrator in a piece of fiction is an author's creation. We characterize speakers using the same notions we apply when analyzing any character: we consider how they are described, how they speak, what they do, and how they interact with others.

Let's examine the speaker from "The Tropics in New York" with these ideas in mind. First, let's gather evidence regarding the speaker.

Aspects of characterization	Textual evidence	What it suggests about the speaker
Descriptions of the speaker	"My eyes grew dim" "A wave of longing through my body swept"	
The speaker's actions	"I turned aside and bowed my head and wept."	
Dialogue involving the speaker	No dialogue	
The speaker's internal thoughts	"bringing memories / Of fruit-trees laden by low-singing rills, / And dewy dawns, and mystical blue skies / In benediction over nun-like hills"	
Other characters' observations about the speaker	None. The speaker is the only character in the poem.	

The observations and annotations we've made are critical to understanding the speaker of McKay's poem.

Gathering Information about the Speaker

Now that you've read through that poem and the sample annotations and notes, it's your turn to practice this process using Adrienne Su's poem "The Chow-Mein Years in Atlanta."

First, read the poem and make annotations that capture your connections and questions (see p. 10). Then, read the poem again and annotate it for details that help you understand the poem's speaker. Re-create the table we used for the speaker of McKay's poem and use it to gather evidence that can help you identify the nature of the speaker in "The Chow-Mein Years in Atlanta."

Aspects of characterization	Textual evidence	What it suggests about the speaker
Descriptions of the speaker		
The speaker's actions		
Dialogue involving the speaker		
The speaker's internal thoughts		
Other characters' observations about the speaker		

The Chow-Mein Years in Atlanta

Adrienne Su

"So we sometimes do miss, I confess,
Simple days of chow mein, but no stress."
— Calvin Trillin, "Have They Run Out of Provinces Yet?"

What do I miss about the chow-mein years?
My mother picking me up from school.
My father doing repairs, or just being near.

I didn't enjoy the neighbors' terror
of what we might serve from carton or bowl.
What I miss about the chow-mein years

is whispering jokes in my best friend's ear
during church, as we tried not to howl.
My father, repairing the attic or cellar,

was working more than he made it appear
so that some in Fujian might escape state control.
I do not miss, from the chow-mein years,

being asked to explain the Pu-Pu Platter
or the textbook sketch of the Mongoloid.
I miss my father being healthy and near,

my mother frying rice with hot-dog slivers,
and none of us knowing what we were called.
What I would ask of the chow-mein years
is my father repaired, and both of them near. ■

Describing the Speaker

Now that we've modeled with McKay's poem and you've read "The Chow-Mein Years in Atlanta" and made observations about the speaker, let's think about how we can draw conclusions from significant details. To show you how this step might work, we'll return to "The Tropics in New York." We can fill in the third column of our chart to help us consider what the evidence we've gathered reveals.

Aspects of characterization	Textual evidence	What it suggests about the speaker
Descriptions of the character	"My eyes grew dim" "A wave of longing through my body swept"	Seems sad and nostalgic Feels sense of longing
The character's actions	"I turned aside and bowed my head and wept."	Turns away from fruit because it reminds him of home. He also weeps. He is definitely missing his native land.
Dialogue involving the character	No dialogue	No dialogue with others; only internal recollection. Evidence of isolation
The character's internal thoughts	"bringing memories / Of fruit-trees laden by low-singing rills, / And dewy dawns, and mystical blue skies / In benediction over nun-like hills"	Loves his homeland; recollects it in a positive and idealized manner
Other character's observations about the character	The speaker is the only character in the poem.	No one else is present in the poem; further evidence of isolation

Based on our notes on the completed chart, we can make several assertions about the speaker:

1. The speaker is alone.
2. The speaker yearns for his homeland.
3. The speaker is sad.
4. The speaker reacts strongly to the tropical fruit because it reminds him of his homeland.

Describing the Speaker

Using our sample chart and list of assertions about the speaker in McKay's poem as a model, try completing these same steps to delve deeper into your analysis of "The Chow-Mein Years in Atlanta." Return to the chart you created and fill in the column titled "What it suggests about the speaker." To populate the column, pay close attention to the evidence you gathered and draw conclusions about the nature of the speaker. Then, use these conclusions to develop a few assertions about the speaker in "The Chow-Mein Years in Atlanta." Try to formulate two or three statements characterizing the speaker.

Analyzing Word Choice

Whether you know it or not, you're already an expert on analyzing word choice. Think, for example, of having to ask your parent or guardian for permission to go to a friend's house. Would you tell him or her that you *want* to or that you *have* to meet with your friend? Which word you choose is clearly important and may lead to a different result. Now consider the difference between these two possible responses that your parent or guardian might offer: "Yes" and "Do what you think is right." Both statements could lead to you going to your friend's house, but the wording of each would reflect differently on your decision. How would you characterize the difference between the two responses?

The textual evidence we gathered in the chart on page 484 focuses our attention on McKay's word choice. The poet's words characterize the speaker as sad and nostalgic: his eyes are "dim" and his head is "bowed." These words convey how the memories triggered by the fruit affect him. We also noted that there is no dialogue in the poem; perhaps that silence reveals the speaker's sense of worth and place in a foreign land. Since he is overwhelmed with emotion, the speaker "could no more gaze" at the fruit, but weeps instead.

Further examination of the poet's word choice might lead us to line 11, in which the word "hungry" seems to have more than one meaning. The list of exotic fruit in the first stanza might make you think of physical hunger, but the speaker's hunger can't be eased by food; instead, he longs "for the old, familiar ways." The speaker's separation from the "low-singing rills" and "nun-like hills" described in the second stanza renders him "hungry." He is on a perpetual diet that starves him of home — of that which nurtured him early on in life.

Paying attention to each word in the poem sometimes prompts new insights when we revisit the text. Rereading the poem's title, which is always a good practice, we realize that it might have referred to the speaker as well, even if it was not evident when we first read the title. It is not just the cornucopia of fruit that constitutes the "tropics in New York"; the speaker too has come from the tropics.

Analyzing Word Choice

Note how we returned to the textual evidence in our chart about "The Tropics in New York" to identify significant word choices. To do the same with "The Chow-Mein Years in Atlanta," look through the evidence you added to your table. What words seem most significant for the development of the speaker? As you consider the poet's word choices, remember to think about the denotations and connotations of words. In a detailed paragraph, draft your analysis regarding the significance of word choices in "The Chow-Mein Years in Atlanta."

Observing and Interpreting Shifts

Shifts can indicate significant changes in the characterization of the speaker, so we should consider those as well as we continue our analysis of the speaker in "The Tropics in New York." You might recall learning about shifts in Chapter 2 (p. 52), where we discussed how changes in a poem usually mark significant moments that deserve our careful attention. For the purposes of our analysis in this workshop, let's focus on shifts in **setting**, **speaker**, **time frame**, and tone. If we reread the poem with these four categories in mind, we can organize our notes in a two-column chart like this one:

Shifts	Notes
Setting	The poem begins in New York, transitions into the speaker's recollection of his/her homeland, and ultimately returns to New York.
Speaker	There is only one speaker in the poem. However, the speaker seems to be absent at the beginning of the poem. As the speaker emerges, along with his/her observations and recollections his/her sadness becomes evident.
Time frame	The poem moves from the present, to the past, and back to the present.
Tone	Objective observations give way to a sadness that stems from the speaker's relationship to the past and present.

While this chart captures our observations of shifts, we must consider their significance within the poem as a whole. By connecting the notes to textual evidence and providing commentary on our discoveries, we'll begin to understand the significance of these shifts. Let's look at how our ideas about how shifts affect our understanding of the speaker in "The Tropics in New York" might work together in a sample paragraph:

> The beginning of McKay's poem does not truly center on the speaker. We do not know who he/she is, what he/she is thinking, or how he/she is feeling. We do know, however, that the fruit display catches his/her attention. As we move into the second stanza, we drift to the speaker's homeland, a tropical place from which the fruit has presumably been imported. At the end of the poem, we encounter a person who feels deeply affected by this experience. The silence that has characterized the speaker so far is replaced by weeping. While we do not know about the speaker's emotional and psychological mindset at the start of the poem, we are fully aware of the sadness, "longing," and hunger that plague the speaker at the end.

This paragraph aims to capture the nature of the speaker and how he/she changes as the poem progresses. Notice that it not only discusses the way the speaker is presented in each stanza but also compares his/her depiction at the start and end of the poem. The language of the poem helps us identify these moments of change; the conjunctions "but" and "yet," transition words, and changes in verb tense often signal shifts. The more you work with poetry, the more you will see these structural features in action, and the easier it will be for you to consider their significance.

Observing and Interpreting Shifts

Observing and interpreting shifts in McKay's poem has helped you understand how shifts can signal changes in the characterization of the speaker. With that in mind, return to "The Chow-Mein Years in Atlanta" and gather notes regarding shifts in setting, speaker, time frame, and tone in a two-column chart similar to the one on page 488. Consider whether there are changes in each of these categories across the six stanzas of the poem. After gathering your observations, analyze in two or three sentences a significant shift in the poem in terms of what it reveals about the speaker.

Drawing an Interpretation

The overall goal of this workshop is to characterize the speaker, which should lead us to an interpretation of the poem's meaning. Based on our multiple readings of the poem and our careful observations of the poem's speaker, what is a plausible interpretation of McKay's "The Tropics in New York"? In the following sample paragraph, we combine our ideas about the speaker with observations about poetic techniques to lead us to an interpretation of the meaning of the poem.

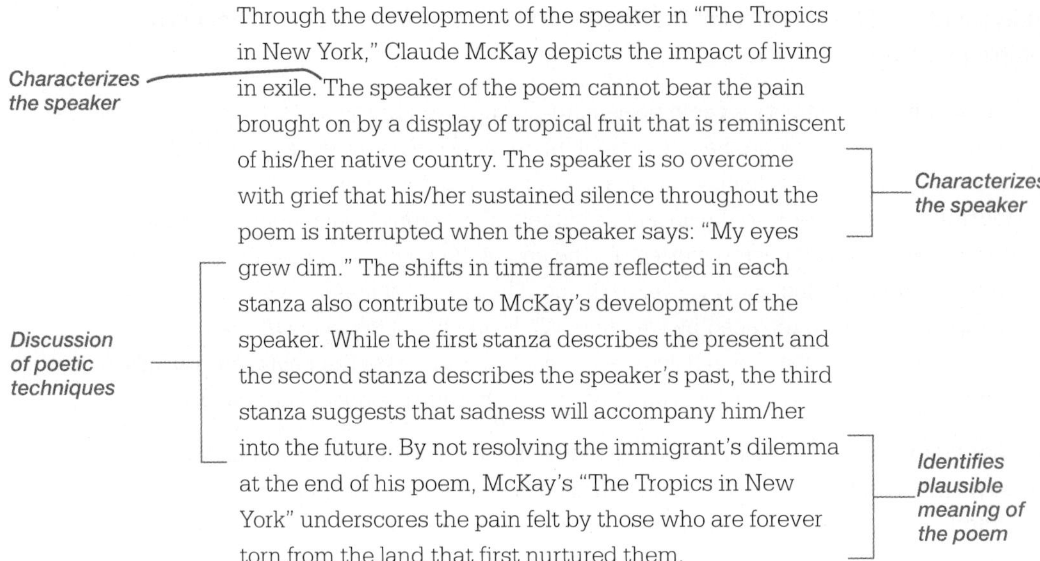

Through the development of the speaker in "The Tropics in New York," Claude McKay depicts the impact of living in exile. The speaker of the poem cannot bear the pain brought on by a display of tropical fruit that is reminiscent of his/her native country. The speaker is so overcome with grief that his/her sustained silence throughout the poem is interrupted when the speaker says: "My eyes grew dim." The shifts in time frame reflected in each stanza also contribute to McKay's development of the speaker. While the first stanza describes the present and the second stanza describes the speaker's past, the third stanza suggests that sadness will accompany him/her into the future. By not resolving the immigrant's dilemma at the end of his poem, McKay's "The Tropics in New York" underscores the pain felt by those who are forever torn from the land that first nurtured them.

culminating activity

Now that you have followed the model analysis of the speaker in "The Tropics in New York" from reading and annotation to interpretation, you are ready to move from an analysis of the speaker to an interpretation of Adrienne Su's "The Chow-Mein Years in Atlanta." Review the annotations, notes, and charts you have produced for "The Chow-Mein Years in Atlanta" throughout this workshop. Then, write a paragraph, modeled after the sample paragraph about "The Tropics in New York" in the previous section. Be sure to analyze the poem's speaker, discuss at least one poetic technique, and identify a plausible interpretation of the poem's meaning. While we focused on shifts, you might focus on other poetic techniques, such as imagery or figurative language.

No Speak English

Sandra Cisneros

Shannon Finney/Getty Images Entertainment/Getty Images

Sandra Cisneros (b. 1954) is a novelist, short-story writer, and poet. She is best known for *The House on Mango Street* (1983), a collection of connected stories and sketches which includes "No Speak English." The recipient of many awards, including a MacArthur Foundation "Genius" Grant, Cisneros has published the short-story collection *Woman Hollering Creek* (1991), the poetry collections *My Wicked Wicked Ways* (1987) and *Loose Woman* (1994), and the novel *Have You Seen Marie?* (2012) among others. The *New York Times Book Review* says Cisneros embraces "the endless variety of Mexican and American culture — songs and stories, jokes and legends, furniture and food."

Mamacita is the big mama of the man across the street, third-floor front. Rachel says her name ought to be *Mamasota,*[1] but I think that's mean.

The man saved his money to bring her here. He saved and saved because she was alone with the baby boy in that country. He worked two jobs. He came home late and he left early. Every day.

Then one day *Mamacita* and the baby boy arrived in a yellow taxi. The taxi door opened like a waiter's arm. Out stepped a tiny pink shoe, a foot soft as a rabbit's ear, then the thick ankle, a flutter of hips, fuchsia roses and green perfume. The man had to pull her, the taxicab driver had to push. Push, pull. Push, pull. Poof!

All at once she bloomed. Huge, enormous, beautiful to look at from the salmon-pink feather on the tip of her hat down to the little rosebuds of her toes. I couldn't take my eyes off her tiny shoes.

5 Up, up, up the stairs she went with the baby boy in a blue blanket, the man carrying her suitcases, her lavender hatboxes, a dozen boxes of satin high heels. Then we didn't see her.

Somebody said because she's too fat, somebody because of the three flights of stairs, but I believe she doesn't come out because she is afraid to speak English, and maybe this is so since she only knows eight words. She knows to say: *He is not here* for when the landlord comes, *No speak English* if anybody else comes, and *Holy smokes*. I don't know where she learned this, but I heard her say it one time and it surprised me.

[1]In Spanish, the word endings *-ita* and *-ota* are used colloquially to make something seem smaller and more endearing or hyperbolically larger, respectively. — Eds.

My father says when he came to this country he ate hamandeggs for three months. Breakfast, lunch and dinner. Hamandeggs. That was the only word he knew. He doesn't eat hamandeggs anymore.

Whatever her reasons, whether she is fat, or can't climb the stairs, or is afraid of English, she won't come down. She sits all day by the window and plays the Spanish radio show and sings all the homesick songs about her country in a voice that sounds like a seagull.

Home. Home. Home is a house in a photograph, a pink house, pink as hollyhocks with lots of startled light. The man paints the walls of the apartment pink, but it's not the same, you know. She still sighs for her pink house, and then I think she cries. I would.

10 Sometimes the man gets disgusted. He starts screaming and you can hear it all the way down the street.

Ay, she says, she is sad.

Oh, he says. Not again.

¿Cuándo, cuándo, cuándo?[2] she asks.

¡Ay, caray! We *are* home. This *is* home. Here I am and here I stay. Speak English. Speak English. Christ!

15 *¡Ay! Mamacita,* who does not belong, every once in a while lets out a cry, hysterical, high, as if he had torn the only skinny thread that kept her alive, the only road out to that country.

And then to break her heart forever, the baby boy, who has begun to talk, starts to sing the Pepsi commercial he heard on T.V.

No speak English, she says to the child who is singing in the language that sounds like tin. No speak English, no speak English, and bubbles into tears. No, no, no, as if she can't believe her ears. ■

[2]Spanish, "when." — Eds.

The Lyda Hill Texas Collection of Photographs in Carol M. Highsmith's America Project, Library of Congress, Prints and Photographs Division

This mural painted by Lucia Quezada and Al Garza, Jr. at a Greyhound Bus station in Brownsville, Texas — a city adjacent to the border with Matamoros, Mexico — depicts the transition from a Mexican cultural identity to an American one.

How might Mamacita identify with this painting? How would she perceive the way Mexico and the United States are depicted? How might she feel about the section of the mural where the two cultures interact?

Understanding and Interpreting

1. Refer to the footnote for the words "*Mamacita*" and "*Mamasota*" (par. 1). What does Rachel's retort reveal about her attitude towards this character?
2. Consider the actions of and words spoken by "the man across the street" throughout the story. How would you characterize him? How does he compare to *Mamacita*?

3. What feelings does the word "home" typically evoke? Examine the use of the word in paragraphs 9 and 14. *Mamacita* and the man have different ideas about what and where home is. Discuss these differences and the conflict they create.
4. The relationship between *Mamacita* and the man seems most problematic when the narrator asserts, "Sometimes the man gets disgusted" (par. 10). Consider the source of their dissatisfaction and summarize how they would each verbalize what troubles them.
5. Identify several factors that contribute to *Mamacita*'s sense of isolation. Which of the ones you've identified affects her the most?
6. *Mamacita* never leaves her apartment and has no friends in the United States. Consider what her child means to her. Discuss why she is hurt by "the baby boy" singing "the Pepsi commercial he heard on T.V." in paragraph 16.

Analyzing Language, Style, and Structure

1. **Vocabulary in Context.** What does the word "bloomed" mean in the context of paragraph 4? In what ways is this meaning similar to or different from other uses you've encountered?
2. **Skill Focus.** From what point of view is this story told? What information can you discern about the narrator? Based on the descriptions found throughout the text, how does the narrator help readers understand what Cisneros aims to convey about culture?
3. When *Mamacita* first arrives (par. 3), the narrative pace slows and a detailed account of her exit from the taxi ensues. How does this description present *Mamacita* in relation to her new environment?
4. Describe the syntax found in paragraph 14. What does it communicate about the man's attitude towards *Mamacita*?
5. When *Mamacita* says "No speak English" at the end of the story, does she mean it as a command to the child or as a description of herself? Explain how Cisneros could have meant both.

Topics for Composing

1. **Analysis.** Analyze *Mamacita*'s character throughout the story. Think about how *Mamacita* spends her days since coming to the United States. Refer to her reaction at the end of the text. How does her characterization further Cisneros's commentary on assimilation and cultural identity?
2. **Argument.** *Mamacita* worries that her son might fully assimilate into the culture of the United States. Argue whether first-generation American children and their immigrant parents have an inherent wedge in their relationships.
3. **Connection.** How does *Mamacita* feel about being away from home and thrust into a new culture? Identify a character from another reading (something you've read on your own or for school) who finds him- or herself in a similar position. What decisions does that character make to navigate the two cultures successfully? How does his or her approach compare with *Mamacita*'s?
4. **Speaking and Listening.** *Mamacita* "sings all the homesick songs about her country" (par. 8). Select a song to play for your classmates that captures the spirit of what home means to you. Be prepared to explain your selection to your classmates.
5. **Creative Writing.** Write a brief narrative from the perspective of "the baby boy" once he becomes a teenager. In your writing, speculate how he would describe his cultural identity as compared to that of his mother.

Dothead

Amit Majmudar

Courtesy Amit Majmudar

Poet and novelist Amit Majmudar (b. 1979) practices as a diagnostic nuclear radiologist in Westerville, Ohio. He earned a BS at the University of Akron and an MD at Northeast Ohio Medical University. The recipient of several literary prizes, Majmudar has published two novels, *Partitions* (2011) and *The Abundance* (2013), and three poetry collections: *0°, 0°* (2009), *Heaven and Earth* (2011), and *Dothead* (2016). "Dothead," a poem from his most recent collection, was published in the *New Yorker* in 2011.

KEY CONTEXT Spiritually important in Hindu culture, the bindi, or "red dot," is a mark made of vermilion powder that Indian women wear on the forehead. Originally a mark of wisdom and creation, the bindi also came to symbolize the love and commitment of a wife to her husband. The figure Nataraja is a depiction of the Hindu god Shiva as the Lord of the Dance and destroyer of the universe, paving the way for a new creation and signifying the never-ending cycle of time.

Well yes, I said, my mother wears a dot.
I know they said "third eye" in class, but it's not
an *eye* eye, not like that. It's not some freak
third eye that opens on your forehead like
on some Chernobyl[1] baby. What it means
is, what it's *showing* is, there's this unseen
eye, on the inside. And she's marking it.
It's how the X that says where treasure's at
is not the treasure, but as good as treasure. —
All right. What I said wasn't half so measured.
In fact, I didn't say a thing. Their laughter
had made my mouth go dry. Lunch was after
World History; that week was India — myths,
caste system, suttee, all the Greatest Hits.
The white kids I was sitting with were friends,
at least as I defined a friend back then.
So wait, said Nick, does *your* mom wear a dot?
I nodded, and I caught a smirk on Todd —
She wear it to the shower? And to bed? —
while Jesse sucked his chocolate milk and Brad
was getting ready for another stab.
I said, Hand me that ketchup packet there.
And Nick said, What? I snatched it, twitched the tear,
and squeezed a dollop on my thumb and worked
circles till the red planet entered the house of war

[1]Nuclear power plant in northern Ukraine that was the site of a devastating nuclear reactor meltdown in the mid-1980s. — Eds.

and on my forehead for the world to see
my third eye burned those schoolboys in their seats,
their flesh in little puddles underneath,
pale pools where Nataraja cooled his feet. ■

Shiva Nataraja, 11th century (bronze)/Indian School (11th century)/Dallas Museum of Art, Texas, USA/Bridgeman Images

Nataraja is a depiction of the God Shiva as the dancer who destroys the weariness of the universe in preparation for the start of Brahma's act of creation. **What about this representation of Nataraja communicates these aspects of Shiva? Consider the pose, the decorations, and the other elements of the statue. Why is this allusion significant to the speaker's classroom experience? What would he like to destroy and create?**

Understanding and Interpreting

1. Line 5 makes a reference to the Ukrainian city of Chernobyl, which was once part of the Soviet Union. What significant event occurred in Chernobyl in 1986? Why would the speaker make this allusion? How does it contribute to your understanding of the speaker's state of mind?
2. In line 10, the speaker admits, "What I said wasn't half so measured." In fact, the speaker's response was not a verbal one. Recount the speaker's reaction to his classmates' questions. Explain what it reveals about his sense of belonging within mainstream American culture.
3. In lines 15 and 16, the speaker acknowledges that his understanding of friendship has evolved. Based on the events of the poem, how would you characterize this change in perception? How old do you suppose the speaker is in his recollection? How old might he be when he retells the story?
4. What does the speaker's actions beginning in line 23 suggest about his feelings towards his friends' behavior?
5. What do the friends' interactions with the speaker suggest about their attitude toward cultural differences?

Analyzing Style, Language, and Structure

1. **Vocabulary in Context.** In line 21, the speaker mentions taking another "stab." What does the word mean in this context? How is this meaning similar to or different from other uses you've encountered?
2. **Skill Focus.** How would you describe the speaker when he is younger? What details from the text lead you to form this characterization? In what ways do you think the speaker has changed as he has grown up?
3. The speaker metaphorically connects the "dot" in line 1 to a "treasure" in line 8. What image is conjured in your mind by the word "treasure"? What does this suggest about the speaker's perception of this cultural practice?
4. What language and style elements contribute to the conversational style of the poem?
5. What is the speaker's attitude toward the way that his World History class presents non-American cultures? What words or phrases capture this tone?
6. In line 27, the speaker does not refer to the boys as "friends" as he did in line 15 or by their names. Instead, he calls them "those schoolboys." How does this shift contribute to the meaning of the poem?
7. Majmudar begins the poem in the middle of the speaker's conversation with his friends about the dot his mother wears. He then moves back in time to the history class. Finally, he returns to the conversation. What effect does this structure achieve?

Topics for Composing

1. **Analysis.** In "Dothead," the speaker understands that his classmates are unfamiliar with Indian culture. To what extent does the poem suggest that the speaker's interactions with his friends fostered some degree of cultural appreciation in them?
2. **Argument.** The speaker experiences a painful and infuriating moment with his peers after the World History lesson on India. Based on evidence from the poem, what was the focus of that lesson? How might it have led to the speaker's experience at lunch? Write an argument proposing and defending a different approach to the lesson that could have prevented this exchange among the boys.
3. **Connection.** Think of a favorite cultural tradition that you and your family follow. Imagine having to justify to somebody from another culture why you engage in this tradition. How might your reaction to this scenario compare to that of this poem's speaker?
4. **Connection.** Describe a time when you either supported an unpopular belief or chose to remain silent. Why did you act the way you did? How was your experience similar to or different from that of the speaker in this poem?
5. **Speaking and Listening.** The speaker laments "the Greatest Hits" that always accompany a discussion of India. Think about how a lesson based on your culture might be introduced in another country. Prepare a short introduction to this lesson that gives your audience a sense of a tradition or ritual that is important to your culture. Make sure to provide enough detail so that someone who is unfamiliar with the tradition or ritual would be able to fully grasp the practice and its significance.
6. **Research.** The bindi that the speaker's mother wears means many different things, and is found in many different cultures. Explore the background of the bindi and the ajna chakra where it is traditionally placed. How does knowing more about these cultural and religious practices enhance your understanding of Majmudar's poem?

Unnatural

Margarita Engle

Margarita Engle (b. 1951) was born in California to a Cuban mother and an American father. She earned an MS from Iowa State University, was a professor of agronomy at California Polytechnic University, and served as the Poetry Foundation's Young People's Poet Laureate. Engle is the author of many children's books, novels, and young adult novels in verse. "Unnatural" appeared in *Silver People: Voices from the Panama Canal* (2014).

Marshall W. Johnson

KEY CONTEXT The following poem is taken from Engle's *Silver People: Voices from the Panama Canal*. A work of historical fiction written in verse, the poem documents the voices of workers brought to Panama to build the canal and chronicles the conditions they faced. Championed by President Theodore Roosevelt, the Panama Canal is 51 miles long, connecting the Atlantic Ocean to the Pacific Ocean. It represents a remarkable feat of engineering and construction, especially given that it was completed in the early 1900s. However, it came at a cost. As Engle writes in a note at the end of her collection, "Labourers from all over the world were subjected to a system that resembled South Africa's apartheid. Dark-skinned islanders and olive-skinned southern Europeans were paid in silver. Light-skinned Americans and northern Europeans received gold. Housing, meals, recreation, and hospitals were also strictly segregated." This collection of poems alternates among the voices of many of these laborers. "Unnatural" is from the middle of the novel. It is told from the perspective of a worker, Anita, who has a special relationship with the jungle animals in Panama.

Roosevelt's visit brings tourists rushing
into my forest, searching for adventure,
but they don't buy herbs; all they want
is hats — white hats like the American president's,
hats woven in Ecuador, hats that tourists
insist on calling Panamá hats. Don't they
understand that Latin America
has many countries?

Tourist ladies want dead birds fastened
to their hats—whole birds, not just a few
stray feathers dropped by living birds,
like the ones I wear on my necklace.

Tourist ladies walk around with orioles
on their hats, hummingbirds, egrets,
even owls. Can't they feel the ghostly
bird eyes staring down
from the tops of their heads?
The tourists ask for whole collections
of rare butterflies for their children —
wild butterflies, caught and pinned,

not just a few drifting wings,
like the ones I find after migrations.

And they want skins. Jaguar. Puma. Snake.
And crocodile teeth, peccary tusks,
fossil shark teeth from the Serpent Cut[1].
Anything sharp, so they can pretend
they know danger.

Monkey hands are the most popular
souvenir. All over Silver Town, vendors
get rich by hunting, then chopping off,
the hairy fingers.

When I gaze up at the trees, I see
the frightened howlers and I hear
the fading songs of doomed birds. ■

---

[1]The Culebra Cut, also known as the Snake Cut, was an artificial valley cut through the Continental Divide that became a portion of the Panama Canal. — Eds.

George Rinhart/Getty Images

This 1906 photograph shows President Theodore Roosevelt with his entourage addressing the workers at the Snake Cut, an area of the Panama Canal Zone that Engle references in her poem.

Based on the details and tone of the poem, how would Anita react to this photograph? What details might she consider most indicative of the relationship between the workers and those who come to visit the area?

Understanding and Interpreting

1. The first line of the poem refers to the increase in tourism that President Roosevelt's visit to the Panama Canal Zone produced. Based on the first stanza, what is Anita's reaction to this influx of visitors to what she calls "my forest" (l. 2)?
2. Anita asserts that the tourists "don't buy herbs" and are only interested in "hats" (ll. 3–4). What does this observation, along with the five times that "hats" is repeated in lines 4 to 6, reveal about Anita and her cultural values? How do the descriptions of these hats characterize those who wear them?
3. Questions sometimes aim to convey an idea rather than to seek an answer. What is Anita's argument in lines 6 to 8 when she questions the Americans' knowledge of Latin America? What prompts her to arrive at this notion?
4. The phrase "Tourist ladies" begins the sentences that open stanzas 2 and 3. What is the effect of this repetition on Engle's depiction of the female tourists and their actions?
5. What does Anita reveal about herself and her attitude toward the tourists when she wonders in lines 15 to 17, "Can't they feel the ghostly / bird eyes staring down / from the tops of their heads?" How does this question contrast with what Anita says about herself in the final stanza?
6. The tourists are "searching for adventure" (l. 2) and like to "pretend / they know danger" (ll. 26–27). What do these traits reveal about the tourists? What is Anita's attitude toward them based on these two observations?
7. While the poem continuously juxtaposes Anita and the tourists, Engle also writes about the "vendors" who cater to the tourists' desires (ll. 29–31). How does Anita perceive these "vendors" and their role within the Panama Canal Zone?
8. The idea of something being "unnatural" is prominent in this poem. From Anita's perspective, what does she think is "unnatural?" How does her view help Engle illustrate a possible theme of the poem?

Analyzing Style, Language, and Structure

1. **Vocabulary in Context.** In line 21, Engle uses the word "drifting" to describe butterfly wings that one may find. What does this word generally mean to you? In the context of this poem, what does it refer to?
2. **Skill Focus.** At various moments, Anita distinguishes her behavior from that of the tourists. Refer to two or more of these instances to show how Engle characterizes Anita.
3. The third stanza introduces the tourists' children into the poem, as Anita describes the familiar practice of shopping for souvenirs. How does the language Anita uses to describe them reveal her attitude about the actions of the shoppers? How does this stanza connect with the overall meaning of the poem?
4. Notice the syntax in line 23. What effect does Engle's placement of periods have, both on that line and on the poem's meaning?
5. Lines 23 to 24 repeat the word "And" at the beginning of sentences. How does this repetition convey Anita's attitude toward the tourists?
6. The phrases "not just a few" and "like the ones" appear twice in the poem. When does Engle use them? What function do they have in the poem? Why might Engle have repeated these phrases in her poem?
7. The poem's final stanza is its shortest—three lines—while the longest stanza consisted of eight lines. Think about the effect of this abrupt ending. How does this structural feature align with the events at the end of the poem?

Topics for Composing

1. **Analysis.** Consider the relationship between the poem's title, "Unnatural," and the behavior of the people found in the poem. How does the relationship between the title and people's actions contribute to the meaning of the poem?
2. **Argument.** Think about how people should behave when they travel abroad. Determine what responsibility tourists bear to care for and protect the places they visit. Support your stance with your own observations, details from "Unnatural," and research centered on this topic.
3. **Connection.** Anita is critical of tourists whose behavior seems "unnatural" to her cultural values and perspective. Think about a time when the behavior of a character you've encountered in this textbook—or even your own behavior—did not align with the standards and expectations of a given setting. How was the behavior unnatural to the setting? What were the consequences of this scenario?
4. **Speaking and Listening.** Visit online souvenir shops of a nearby national park or nature preserve. Determine whether the merchandise fosters respect for the setting or exploits the area's natural resources. Then, discuss your findings with a partner and prepare to share your observations with the class.
5. **Speaking and Listening.** With a partner, find and watch at least three online videos that advertise environmental trips. Discuss how the travel experience is portrayed in relation to the impact of tourism on the local people and environment. In your discussion, consider how the videos relate to the types of concerns Anita expresses throughout the poem.
6. **Research.** According to Margarita Engle, the workers building the canal faced harsh conditions and a "system that resembled South Africa's apartheid." Take a deeper look into the history of the construction of the Panama Canal. How did the idea form? How was the land acquired? How were workers found? What conditions did they face? Then, explain how learning more about the canal's history helps you to understand more about Engle's poem.
7. **Research.** Conduct research on the impact the Panama Canal has had on the world. What have been the effects on trade? What effect has it had on the Panamanian people? What effect has it had on the United States?

Paths upon Water

Tahira Naqvi

Tahira Naqvi (b. 1945) was born in Pakistan. She currently lives in the United States where she is a professor at New York University. As a senior language lecturer, she is primarily interested in the translation of literary texts and has translated stories from Urdu to English. Naqvi has published her own writings in countless journals, anthologies, and collections. "Paths upon Water" appeared in *A Line of Cutting Women* (1998).

Courtesy of Tahira Naqvi

KEY CONTEXT In this story, a Pakistani immigrant is brought to a beach in America where she tries to reconcile the differences between what is considered decent and tasteful in Pakistani and American cultures. Cultural norms for dress in the largely Muslim nation of Pakistan are generally more conservative than those in America. They usually come down to two related concepts: decency and modesty. While more revealing swimwear might be seen at private pools within beach resorts, visitors at public beaches generally remain fully covered even when wading by the shore.

There had been little warning, actually none at all to prepare her for her first encounter with the sea. At breakfast that morning, her son Raza said, "*Ama*, we're going to the seaside today. Jamil and Hameeda are coming with us." She had been turning a *paratha*[1] in the frying pan, an onerous task since she had always fried *parathas* on a flat pan with open sides, and as the familiar aroma of dough cooking in butter filled the air around her, she smiled happily and thought, I've only been here a week and already he wants to show me the sea.

[1]Stuffed or plain pan-cooked flatbread. — Eds.

Sakina Bano had never seen the sea. Having lived practically all her life in a town which was a good thousand miles from the nearest shoreline, her experience of the sea was limited to what she had chanced to observe in pictures. One picture, in which greenish-blue waves heaved toward a gray sky, she could recollect clearly; it was from a calendar Raza brought home the year he started college in Lahore. The calendar had hung on a wall of her room for many years only to be removed when the interior of the house was whitewashed for her daughter's wedding, and in the ensuing confusion it was misplaced and never found.

Monaco Coast, 2000 (oil on canvas)/Graham, Peter (Contemporary Artist)/PETER GRAHAM (CONTEMPORARY ARTIST)/Private Collection/Bridgeman Images

This painting, titled *Monaco Coast*, gives an impression of a beach setting.

What is the tone of the artist toward the beach? What visual elements does the artist use to create this tone? To what extent does the painting compare to Sakina Bano's expectations and to what she actually sees and experiences?

The nail on which the calendar hung had stayed in the wall since the painter, too lazy to bother with detailed preparation, had simply painted around the nail and over it; whenever Sakina Bano happened to glance at the forgotten nail she remembered the picture. Also distinct in her memory was a scene from a silly Urdu film she had seen with her cousin's wife Zohra and her nieces Zenab and Amma during a rare visit to Lahore several years ago. For some reason she hadn't been able to put it out of her mind. On a brown and white beach, the actor Waheed Murad, now dead but then affectedly handsome and boyish, pursued the actress Zeba, who skipped awkwardly before him — it isn't at all proper for a woman to be skipping in a public place. Small foam-crested waves lapped up to her, making her *shalwar*[2] stick to her skinny legs, exposing the outline of her thin calves. Why, it was just as bad as baring her legs, for what cover could the wet, gossamer-like fabric of the *shalwar* provide?

The two frolicked by an expanse of water that extended to the horizon and which, even though it was only in a film, had seemed to Sakina Bano frightening in its immensity.

"Will Jamal and his wife have lunch here?" she asked, depositing the dark, glistening *paratha* gently on Raza's plate. She would have to take out a packet of meat from the freezer if she was to give them lunch, she told herself while she poured tea in her son's cup.

5 "No, I don't think so. I think we'll leave before lunch. We can stop somewhere along the way and have a bite to eat."

"They'll have tea then." She was glad Raza had remembered to pick up a cake at the store the night before (she didn't know why he called it a pound cake), and she would make some rice *kheer*.[3]

[2]Pants that are loose in the leg and tight around the ankles; typically worn by women in India and Pakistan. — Eds.

[3]Pudding made by boiling sugar, milk, grain or pasta, spices, and nuts or fruits. — Eds.

If she had anything to do with it, she would avoid long trips and spend most of her time in Raza's apartment cooking his meals and watching him eat. The apartment pleased her. The most she would want to do would be to go out on the lawn once in a while and examine her surroundings.

Bordering each window on the outside were narrow white shutters; these had reminded her of the stiffened icing on a cake served at her niece Amina's birthday once. And on the face of the building the white paint seemed impervious to the effects of the elements. Discolorations or cracks were visible, and she had indeed craned her neck until it hurt while she scrutinized it.

The apartment building was set against a lawn edged with freshly green, sculptured bushes, evenly thick with grass that looked more like a thick carpet than just grass. Located in a quiet section of town, the apartments overlooked a dark, thickly wooded area, a park, Raza had told her. Although tired and groggy on the evening of her arrival from Pakistan, she had not failed to take note of the surroundings into which she found herself. Her first thought was, 'Where is everybody?' while to her son she said, "How nice everything is."

10 Looking out the window of his sitting room the next morning, she was gladdened at the thought of her son's good fortune. The morning sky was clear like a pale blue, unwrinkled *dupatta*[4] that has been strung out on a line to dry. Everything looked clean, so clean. Was it not as if an unseen hand had polished the sidewalks and swept the road? They now glistened like new metal. 'Where do people throw their trash?' she wondered when she went down to the lawn again, this time with Raza, and gazed out at the shiny road, the rows and rows of neat houses hedged in by such neat white wooden fences. In hasty answer to her own query, she told herself not to be foolish; this was *Amreeka*. Here trash was in its proper place, hidden from view and no doubt disposed of in an appropriate manner. No blackened banana peels redolent with the odor of neglect here, or rotting orange skins, or worse, excrement and refuse to pollute the surroundings and endanger human habitation.

She had sighed in contentment. Happiness descended upon her tangibly like a heavy blanket affording warmth on a chilly morning. Once again, she thanked her Maker. Was He not good to her son?

"Is the sea far from here?" she asked casually, brushing imaginary crumbs from the edges of her plate. Raza must never feel she didn't value his eagerness to show off his new environment. This was his new world after all. If he wanted to take her to the seaside, then seaside it would be. Certainly she was not about to be fussy and upset him.

"No, *Ama*, not too far. An hour-and-a-half's drive, that's all. Do you feel well?" His eyes crinkled in concern as he put aside the newspaper he had been reading to look at her.

She impatiently waved a hand in the air, secretly pleased at his solicitude. "Yes, yes, I'm fine son. Just a little cough, that's all. Now finish your tea and I'll make you another cup." She knew how much he liked tea. Before she came, he must have had to make it for himself. Such a chore for a man if he must make his own tea.

15 The subject of the sea didn't come up again until Jamil and his new bride arrived. Jamil, an old college friend of Raza's, angular like him, affable and solicitous, was no stranger to Sakina Bano. But she was meeting his wife Hameeda for the first time. Like herself, the girl was also a newcomer to this country.

"*Khalaji*, the sea's so pretty here, the beaches are so-o-o-o large, nothing like the beaches in Karachi," Hameeda informed Sakina Bano over tea, her young, shrill voice rising and falling excitedly, her lips, dark and fleshy with lipstick,

[4]A scarf or shawl worn by many Indian or Pakistani women for decoration or modesty. — Eds.

wide open in a little girl's grin. There's wanderlust in her eyes already, Sakina Bano mused, trying to guess her age. Twenty-one or twenty-two. She thought of the girl in Sialkot she and her daughter had been considering for Raza. Was there really a resemblance? Perhaps it was only the youth.

extending beyond the text

In the 2016 *BBC News* article titled "Why Do Some People Find the Burkini Offensive?," Egyptian-British journalist Shaimaa Khalil discusses both the enjoyment of a day at the beach in Spain and the complications that accompany such outings for people who, like her friend, wear a burkini. She recounts the moment when she and her friend exited the water and suddenly drew unwanted attention from the other beachgoers.

from Why Do Some People Find the Burkini Offensive?

Shaimaa Khalil

> There were people all around us lying on the sand — sunbathing in their bikinis and some [took] their tops off completely. But guess who got the most looks? Yes, my friend in the burkini. Some looks were inquisitive; others were just unfriendly. [She] brushed it all off with a laugh.

SAEED KHAN/AFP via Getty Images

How does Khalil's recollection compare to Sakina Bano's experience at the beach? Does she draw this kind of attention? What cultural differences did these situations expose?

"Well child, for me it will be all the same. I've never been to Karachi. Here, have another slice of cake, you too Jamil, and try the *kheer*."

For some reason Sakina Bano couldn't fathom, sitting next to the young girl whose excitement at the prospect of a visit to the seaside was as undisguised as a child's preoccupation with a new toy, she was suddenly reminded of the actress Zeba. The image of waves lapping on her legs and swishing about her nearly bare calves rose in Sakina Bano's mind again. Like the arrival of an unexpected visitor, a strange question crossed her mind: were Hameeda's legs also skinny like Zeba's?

Drowned in the clamor for the *kheer* which had proven to be a great hit and had been consumed with such rapidity she wished she had made more, the question lost itself.

"*Khalaji*, you must tell Hameeda how you make this," Jamil was saying, and Hameeda hastily interjected, "I think you used a lot of milk."

"Have more," Sakina Bano said.

Tea didn't last long. Within an hour they were on their way to the sea, all of them in Raza's car. Jamil sat in the front with his friend, and Sakina Bano and Hameeda sat in the back, an unfortunate arrangement, Sakina Bano discovered after they had driven for what seemed to her like an hour. It wasn't Hameeda's persistent prattle that vexed her, she realized, it was her perfume. So pungent she could feel it wafting into her nostrils, it irritated the insides of her nose, and then traveled down her throat like the sour after-taste of an overripe orange. But her discomfort was short-lived; soon she became drowsy and idled into sleep.

• • •

To be sure she had heard stories of people who swam in the ocean. She wasn't so foolish as to presume that swimming was undertaken fully clothed. After all, many times as a child she had seen young boys and men from her village swim, dressed in nothing but loincloths as they jumped into the muddy waters of the canal that irrigated their fields. But what was this?

As soon as Raza parked the car in a large, compound-like area fenced in by tall walls of wire mesh, and when her dizziness subsided, Sakina Bano glanced out of the window on her left. Her attention was snagged by what she thought was a naked woman. Certain that she was still a little dazed from the long drive, her vision subsequently befogged, Sakina Bano thought nothing of what she had seen. Then the naked figure moved closer. Disbelief gave way to the sudden, awful realization that the figure was indeed real and if not altogether naked, very nearly so.

A thin strip of colored cloth shaped like a flimsy brassiere loosely held the woman's breasts, or rather a part of her breasts; and below, beneath the level of her belly button, no, even lower than that, Sakina Bano observed in horror, was something that reminded her of the loincloths the men and youths in her village wore when they swam or worked on a construction site in the summer.

The girl was pretty, such fine features, hair that shone like a handful of gold thread, and she was young too, not much older than Hameeda perhaps. But the paleness of her skin was marred by irregular red blotches that seemed in dire need of a cooling balm. No one with such redness should be without a covering in the sun, Sakina Bano offered in silent rebuke.

The woman opened the door of her car, which was parked alongside Raza's, and as she leaned over to retrieve something from the interior of her car, Sakina Bano gasped. When the young female lowered her body, her breasts were not only nearly all bared, but stood in imminent danger of spilling out of their meager coverage. O God! Is there no shame here?

Sakina Bano's cheeks burned. Hastily she glanced away. In the very next instant she stole a glimpse at her son from the corners of her eyes, anxiously wondering if he too were experiencing something of what she was going through; no, she noted with a mixture of surprise and relief, he and Jamil were taking things out from the trunk of their car. They did not show any signs of discomfort. Did she see a fleeting look of curiosity on Hameeda's face? There was something else, too, she couldn't quite decipher.

Relieved that her male companions were oblivious to the disturbing view of the woman's breasts, Sakina Bano sighed sadly. She shook her head, adjusted her white, chiffon *dupatta* over her head, and slowly eased her person out of her son's car.

The taste of the sea was upon her lips in an instant. Mingled with an occasional but strong whiff of Hameeda's perfume, the smell of fish filled her nostrils and quickly settled in her nose as if to stay there forever.

Milling around were countless groups of scantily clad people, men, women, and children, coming and going in all directions. Is all of *Amreeka* here? she asked herself uneasily. Feeling guilty for having judged Zeba's contrived imprudence on film a little too harshly, she tightened her *dupatta* about her and wondered why her son had chosen to bring her to this place. Did he not know his mother? She was an old woman, and the mother of a son, but she would not surrender to anger or derision and make her son uncomfortable. His poise and confidence were hers too, were they not? Certainly he had brought her to the sea for a purpose. She must not appear ungrateful or intolerant.

While Raza and Jamil walked on casually and without any show of awkwardness, laughing and talking as though they might be in their sitting room rather than a place crowded with people in a state of disconcerting undress, she and Hameeda followed closely behind. Her head swam as she turned her eyes from the glare of the sun and attempted to examine the perturbing nakedness around her.

Sakina Bano's memories of nakedness were short and limited, extending to the time when she bathed her younger brother and sister under

Pink shalwar kameez, dupatta and scarf embroidered with gold thread and sequins, c.1990-94 (synthetic)/Pakistani School, (20th century)/HARRIS MUSEUM AND ART GALLERY (BACS)/Harris Museum and Art Gallery, Preston, Lancashire, UK/Bridgeman Images

This traditional Pakistani dress on display at the Harris Museum and Art Gallery is titled "Pink shalwar kameez, dupatta and scarf embroidered with gold thread and sequins."

What do you notice about this style of dress, and how does it differ from Western fashions? How does this photograph inform your understanding of Sakina Bano's reaction to what she sees at the beach?

the water pump in the courtyard of her father's house, followed by the period in which she bathed her own three children until they were old enough to do it themselves. Of her own nakedness she carried an incomplete image; she had always bathed sitting down, on a low wooden stool.

Once, and that too shortly before his stroke, she came upon her husband getting out of his *dhoti*[5] in their bedroom. Standing absently near the foot of his bed as if waiting for something or someone, the *dhoti* a crumpled heap about his ankles, he lifted his face to look at her blankly when she entered, but made no attempt to move or cover himself. Not only did she have to hand him his pajamas, she also had to assist him as he struggled to pull up first one leg and then the other. A week later he suffered a stroke, in another week he was gone. It had been nearly ten years since he died. But for some reason the image of a naked disoriented man in the middle of a room clung to her mind like permanent discolorations on a well-worn copper pot.

And there was the unforgettable sharp and unsullied picture of her mother's body laid out on a rectangular slab of cracked, yellowed wood for a pre-burial bath, her skin, ash-brown, laced with a thousand wrinkles, soft, like wet, rained-on mud.

But nothing could have prepared her for this. Nakedness, like all things in nature, has a purpose, she firmly told herself as the four of them trudged toward the water.

The July sun on this day was not as hot as the July sun in Sialkot, but a certain oily humidity had begun to attach itself to her face and hands. Lifting a corner of her white *dupatta*, she wiped her face with it. Poor Hameeda, no doubt she too longed to divest herself of the *shalwar* and *qamis*[6] she was wearing and don a swimming suit so she could join the rest of the women on the beach, be more like them. But could she swim?

They continued onward, and after some initial plodding through hot, moist sand, Sakina Bano became sure-footed; instead of having to drag her feet through the weighty volume of over-heated sand, she was now able to tread over it with relative ease. They were receiving stares already, a few vaguely curious, others unguardedly inquisitive.

Where the bodies ended she saw the ocean began, stretching to the horizon in the distance. The picture she had carried in her head of the boyish actor Waheed Murad running after Zeba on a sandy Karachi beach quickly diminished and faded away. The immensity of the sea on film was reduced to a mere blue splash of color, its place usurped by a vastness she could scarce hold within the frame of her vision; a window opened in her head, she drew in the wonder of the sea as it touched the hem of the heavens and, despite the heat, Sakina Bano shivered involuntarily. God's touch is upon the world, she silently whispered to herself.

Again and again, as she had made preparations for the journey across what she liked to refer to as the 'seven seas,' she had been told *Amreeka* was so large that many Pakistans could fit into it. The very idea of Pakistan fitting into anything else was cause for bewilderment, and the analogy left her at once befuddled and awed. But had she expected this?

The bodies sprawled before her on the sand and exposed to the sun's unyielding rays seemed unmindful of what the ocean might have to say about God's touch upon the world. Assuming supine positions, flat either on their backs or their bellies, the people on the beach reminded Sakina Bano of whole red chilies spread on a rag discolored from overuse, and left in the sun to dry and crackle. As sweat began to form in tiny droplets across her forehead and around her mouth, the unhappy thought presented itself to

[5]A sarong typically worn by men in India and Pakistan. — Eds.

[6]A long shirt, typically reaching to the wearer's knees. — Eds.

her that she was among people who had indeed lost their sanity.

In summer, one's first thought is to put as much distance as possible between oneself and the sun. Every effort is made to stay indoors; curtains are drawn and jalousies unfurled in order to shut out the fire the sun exudes. In the uneasy silence of a torrid June or July afternoon, even stray dogs seek shade under a tree or behind a bush, curling up into fitful slumber as the sun beats its fervid path across the sky.

Sakina Bano couldn't understand why these men and women wished to scorch their bodies, and why, if they were here by the shore of an ocean which seemed to reach up to God, they didn't at least gaze wide-eyed at the wonder which lay at their feet. Why did they choose instead to shut their eyes and merely wallow in the heat? Their skins had rebelled, the red and darkly-pink blotches spoke for themselves. Perhaps this is a ritual they must, of necessity, follow, she mused. Perhaps they yearn to be brown as we yearn to be white.

She felt an ache insidiously putter behind her eyes. The sun always gave her a headache, even in winter, the only season when sunshine evoked pleasing sensations, when one could look forward to its briskness, its sharp touch. The heat from the sand under the *dari*[7] on which she and Hameeda now sat seeped through the coarse fabric after a while and hugged her thighs; as people in varying shades of pink, white and red skin ran or walked past them, particles of sand flew in the air and landed on her clothes, her hands, her face. Soon she felt sand in her mouth, scraping between her teeth like the remains of *chalia*[8] heavy on her tongue.

Ignoring the sand in her mouth and the hot-water-bottle effect of the sand beneath her thighs, Sakina Bano shifted her attention first toward a woman on her left, and then to the man on her right whose stomach fell broadly in loose folds (like dough left out overnight); he lay supine and still, his face shielded by a straw hat.

[7]A thin woven blanket or rug. — Eds.

[8]A seed from an areca palm tree. — Eds.

extending beyond the text

When Sakina Bano got out of the car at the beach, she "shook her head, adjusted her white, chiffon *dupatta* over her head, and slowly eased her person out of her son's car" (par. 28). In a *Los Angeles Times* article titled "For Pakistani Women, *Dupattas* Are More Than a Fashion Statement," Mark Magnier explores the function of *dupattas* in Pakistani culture. Note what he says about what these "omnipresent scarves" signify.

from For Pakistani Women, *Dupattas* Are More Than a Fashion Statement

Mark Magnier

In [a single] day, an urban Pakistani woman may switch roles from entrepreneur to ingenue to pious daughter, in keeping with this country's nuanced . . . sense of self. The *dupatta*, which can be wrapped tightly around the head, left on the shoulders, hung from the side or dropped altogether, helps [the wearer transition among these social roles].

How does Magnier's description relate to how Sakina Bano uses the *dupatta*? Do any of your own clothing or style choices bear similar significance — from your perspective or from the perspective of those who see you?

Puzzled by the glitter on their nakedness, she peered closely and with intense concentration — she had to observe if she were to learn anything. The truth came to her like a flash of sudden light in a dark room: both the man and the woman had smeared their bodies with some kind of oil! Just then she remembered the oversized cucumbers she had encountered on her first trip to the Stop and Shop; shiny and slippery, one fell from her hands as she handled them, and she exclaimed in disbelief, "They've been greased!" How amused Raza had been at her reaction.

It's really very simple, Sakina Bano finally decided, sighing again, these people wish to be fried in the sun. But why? Not wishing to appear ignorant, she kept her mouth shut, although if she had addressed the query to Hameeda, she was sure she would not have received a satisfactory reply. The girl was a newcomer like herself. In addition, she was too young to know the answers to questions which warranted profound thought preceded by profound scrutiny. She didn't look very comfortable either; perhaps the heat was getting to her, too.

Raza and Jamil, both in swimming trunks, appeared totally at ease as they ran to the water and back, occasionally wading in a wave that gently slapped the beach and sometimes disappearing altogether for a second or two under a high wave. Then Sakina Bano couldn't tell where they were. They certainly seemed to be having a good time.

She and Hameeda must be the only women on the beach fully clothed, she reflected, quite a ridiculous sight if one were being viewed from the vantage point of those who were stretched out on the sand. And while Sakina Bano grappled with this disturbing thought, she saw the other woman approaching.

Attired in a *sari* and accompanied by a short, dark man (who had to be her son for he undoubtedly had her nose and her forehead) and an equally short, dark woman, both of whom wore swimming suits (the girl's as brief as that of the woman Sakina Bano had seen earlier in the parking lot), she looked no older than herself. Clutching the front folds of her *sari* as if afraid a sudden wind from the ocean might pull them out unfurling the *sari*, leaving her exposed, she tread upon the sand with a fiercely precarious step, looking only ahead, her eyes shielded with one small, flat palm.

This is how I must appear to the others, Sakina Bano ruminated. Suddenly, she felt a great sadness clutching at her chest and rising into her throat like a sigh as she watched the woman in the sari begin to make herself comfortable on a large, multi-colored towel thrown on the sand by her son and his wife; those two hurriedly dashed off in the direction of the water. Why are they in such haste? Sakina Bano wondered.

Her knees drawn up, one arm tensely wrapped around them, the woman appeared to be watching her son and her daughter-in-law. But could Sakina Bano really be sure? The woman's hand against her forehead concealed her eyes. As she continued to observe the woman's slight figure around which the green and orange cotton *sari* had been carelessly draped, she wondered what part of India she might be from. Perhaps the south, which meant she spoke no Hindi, which also meant a conversation would not be at all possible.

Sakina Bano's attention returned to Hameeda who had not said a word all this time. Like a break-through during muddled thought, it suddenly occurred to Sakina Bano that there was a distinct possibility Hameeda would be swimming if it weren't for her. In deference to her older companion she was probably foregoing the chance to swim. Will Raza's wife also wear a scant swimming suit and bare her body in the presence of strange men? The question disturbed her; she tried to shrug it aside. But it wouldn't go away. Stubbornly it returned, not alone this time but accompanied by the picture of a young woman who vaguely resembled the actress Zeba and who was clothed, partially, in a swimming suit much like the ones Sakina Bano saw about her. Running behind her was a man, not Waheed Murad, but alas, her own son, her Raza. Was she dreaming, had the sun weakened her brain? Such foolishness. Sakina Bano saw that Hameeda was staring ahead, like the woman on the towel, her eyes squinted because of the glare. Frozen on her full, red lips was a hesitant smile.

Once again Sakina Bano sought her son's figure among the throng near the water's edge. At first the brightness of the sun blinded her and she couldn't see where he was. She strained her eyes, shielding them from the sun with a hand on her forehead. And finally she spotted him. He and Jamil were talking to some people. A dark man and a dark girl. The son and daughter-in-law of the woman in the sari. Were they acquaintances then, perhaps friends? The four of them laughed like old friends, the girl standing so close to Raza he must surely be able to see her half-naked breasts. The poor boy!

They had begun to walk toward where she and Hameeda were seated. Raza was going to introduce his friends to his mother. How was she to conceal her discomfort at the woman's mode of dress?

"*Ama*, I want you to meet Ajit and Kamla. Ajit works at Ethan Allen with me. Kamla wants you to come to their house for dinner next Sunday."

Both Ajit and Kamla lifted their hands and said "*Namaste*,"[9] and she nodded and smiled. What does one say in answer to *namaste* anyway?

Hameeda was also introduced. Kamla made a joke about "the shy new bride," Hameeda showed her pretty teeth in a smile, and then Kamla said, "You have to come, Auntie." Sakina Bano wondered why Raza appeared so comfortable in the presence of a woman who was nearly all naked. Even her loincloth was flimsy. Granted it wasn't as bad as some of the others she had been seeing around her, but it was flimsy nonetheless.

"Yes, it's very nice of you to invite us. It's up to Raza. He's usually so busy. But if he is free . . ."

"Of course I'm free next Sunday. We'd love to come, Kamla."

Kamla said, "Good! I'll introduce you and Auntie to my mother-in-law after a swim. Coming?" She laid a hand on Raza's arm and Sakina Bano glanced away, just in time to catch Hameeda's smile of surprise. Well, one's son can become a stranger too, even a good son like Raza.

"Sure. *Yar*, Ajit, are you and Kamla planning to go to the late show?"

"Yes we are. You? Do you have tickets?" Ajit wasn't a bad looking boy. But he didn't measure up to Raza. No, Raza's nose was straight and to the point, his forehead wide and his eyes well-illuminated. But he had changed somehow; she felt she was distanced from him. A son is always a son, she thought and smiled and nodded again as Ajit and Kamla uttered their *Namaste*'s and returned to the water with Raza and Jamil.

"*Khalaji*, why don't we wet our feet before we go?" Hameeda suddenly asked her.

"Wet our feet?"

"Yes, *Khala*. Just dip our feet in sea water. Come on. You're not afraid of the water, are you?"

"No, child." She wasn't afraid. Her mind was playing tricks with her, filling her head with thoughts that had no place there. A change was welcome. "Yes, why not?" she said, as if speaking to herself. When she attempted to get up she found that her joints had stiffened painfully. "Here, girl, give me your hand." She extended an arm toward Hameeda. Why not, especially since they had come so far and she had suffered the heat for what had seemed like a very long time.

Hameeda had rolled up her *shalwar* almost to the level of her knees. How pretty her legs are, the skin hairless and shiny, like a baby's, and not

---

[9]A respectful Hindu greeting. — Eds.

skinny at all, Sakina Bano mused in surprise, and how quick she is to show them.

She must do the same, she realized. Otherwise Hameeda would think she was afraid. She pulled up one leg of her *shalwar* tentatively, tucked it at the waist with one swift movement of her right hand, then looked about her sheepishly. Hameeda was laughing.

"The other one too, *Khala*!"

Who would want to look at her aged and scrawny legs? And her husband was not around to glare at her in remonstration. Gingerly the other leg of the *shalwar* was also lifted and tucked in. How funny her legs looked, the hair on them all gray now and curly, the calves limp. Now both women giggled like schoolgirls. And Raza would be amused, he would think she was having a good time, Sakina Bano told herself.

Raza and Jamil burst into laughter when 70
they saw the women approach. They waved. Sakina Bano waved back.

Holding the front folds of her *shalwar* protectively, Sakina Bano strode toward the water. As she went past the other woman in the sari she smiled at her. The woman gave her a startled look, and then, dropping the hand with which she had been shielding her eyes from the sun, she let her arm fall away from her knees, and following Sakina Bano with her gaze, she returned her smile.

"Wait for me," Sakina Bano called to Hameeda in a loud, happy voice, "wait, girl." ■

Understanding and Interpreting

1. Sakina Bano's perception of Zeba's skipping is that "it isn't at all proper for a woman to be skipping in a public place" (par. 2). What does Sakina Bano's reaction reveal about her sense of modesty and public behavior?
2. The narrator mentions that Sakina Bano would elect to "avoid long trips," preferring instead to spend her time cooking meals for her son and "watching him eat" (par. 7). How does this detail characterize Sakina Bano? What does it suggest about her cultural identity?
3. Throughout the story, Sakina Bano often turns to speak to Hameeda or glance at her. What are the physical and behavioral similarities between the two women? What does Hameeda represent to Sakina Bano?
4. Sakina Bano laments that "one's son can become a stranger" (par. 59). She recognizes that Raza "had changed somehow" and that "she was distanced from him" (par. 61). Use details from the text to determine the ways in which Raza has changed, according to his mother.
5. The woman in the *sari* (par. 48) elicits a "great sadness" (par. 49) in Sakina Bano. What is the source of the sadness? Why is this reaction significant?
6. When Raza's friends invite the family to dinner (par. 54), Sakina Bano's response is mostly noncommital. What is her intention here? How has the day trip to the beach influenced this response?
7. Before leaving the beach, Sakina Bano agrees to wet her "feet in sea water" (par. 64). What does this concession suggest about Sakina Bano's character? Compare this action to the account of Zeba's behavior in the film referenced earlier in the story.
8. Consider why Naqvi chose "Paths upon Water" as the title for the story. How does the title function both literally and figuratively?

Analyzing Style, Language, and Structure

1. **Vocabulary in Context.** In paragraph 28, Sakina Bano was "[r]elieved that her male companions were oblivious to the disturbing view." What does the word "disturbing" mean in this context? How is it similar to or different from other uses of the word that you know?
2. **Skill Focus.** How would you describe the narrator of this story? To what extent, and from what point of view, does the narrator provide commentary on the characters' actions or share an opinion of the characters?
3. There appears to be a dissonance — or inconsistency — between Sakina Bano's inward thoughts and her outward comments and behavior. Find two or more examples of this in the story, and analyze the language to reveal the reason for the difference between her thoughts and actions.
4. In paragraph 52, Sakina Bano's vision is obscured by the brightness of the sun while she is looking for her son. How might this moment be symbolic?
5. What might Hameeda, Zeba, and the woman in the sari on the beach each represent to Sakina Bano? How does her self-perception at the end of the story relate to her understanding of these other women?
6. The short story closes with Sakina Bano's "loud, happy voice" yelling "wait, girl." What is the significance of the word "girl" at that moment?

Topics for Composing

1. **Analysis.** Throughout the text, Sakina Bano's perceptions are presented in terms of the "comfort" or "discomfort" she feels when viewing or engaging in certain acts in America. What do these two reactions reveal about her relationship with American and Pakistani cultures?
2. **Argument.** Raza plans the beach excursion as a way to honor his mother by taking her someplace special. He makes sure that friends with whom she feels comfortable come along, and he asks her to confirm that this trip would please her. In some cultures, it is expected that grown children bear the responsibility of honoring and caring for their parents. To what degree is this a reasonable expectation? In your response, consider the possible benefits and drawbacks that this expectation creates for both the grown children and the aging parents. Defend your answer with details from your experience, observations, and your readings, including your understanding of this story.
3. **Connection.** Sakina Bano struggles with the difference between her expectations and the reality of what she experiences at the beach. Think of a place you have never visited, but about which you have formulated clear opinions. Draw a picture of what you think this place looks like. Then, find an actual photograph of that location and compare it to your drawing. In writing, discuss whether your research reflects or challenges your ideas about this place.
4. **Speaking and Listening.** Sakina Bano's introduction to the culture of the United States occurs in person. However, we can experience at least pieces of other cultures at any time via the internet. Search for and listen to traditional and popular music from Pakistan. How does it compare to the music you usually encounter? Also locate a Pakistani music video and discuss, in small groups, how it is similar to and different from the types of music videos that are popular in the United States.
5. **Research.** Are the traditional ideas of modesty promoted by Sakina Bano still widely held by Muslim immigrants to the United States, or is that something that is undergoing a change? Research thoughts, shifts, and trends in Muslim-American fashion and ideas of modesty. Explain what ideas or cultural values are at play in these fashions.

Choi Jeong Min

Franny Choi

Jasmine Durhal

Franny Choi (b. 1989) is a writer of poems, essays, and plays. She earned a BA at Brown University and an MFA at the University of Michigan's Helen Zell Writers' Program. Born in America to a Korean immigrant family, Choi's writing focuses on identity, language, and power. She has published two poetry collections, edits for *Hyphen Magazine*, and is a Gaius Charles Bolin Fellow in English at Williams College. "Choi Jeong Min" was published in *Poetry* (2016).

KEY CONTEXT In the third stanza of this poem, Choi uses the word *gook*, a derogatory term sometimes directed at people of Asian descent. Consider how the inclusion of this term informs our understanding of the speaker and her relationship with her cultural identity.

For my parents, Choi Inyeong & Nam Songeun

in the first grade i asked my mother permission
to go by frances at school. at seven years old,

i already knew the exhaustion of hearing my name
butchered by hammerhead tongues. already knew

to let my salty gook name drag behind me
in the sand, safely out of sight. in fourth grade

i wanted to be a writer & worried
about how to escape my surname — choi

is nothing if not korean, if not garlic breath,
if not seaweed & sesame & food stamps

during the lean years — could i go by f.j.c.? could i be
paper thin & raceless? dust jacket & coffee stain,

boneless rumor smoldering behind the curtain
& speaking through an ink-stained puppet?

my father ran through all his possible rechristenings —
ian, isaac, ivan — and we laughed at each one,

knowing his accent would always give him away.
you can hear the pride in my mother's voice

when she answers the phone *this is grace*, & it is
some kind of strange grace she's spun herself,

some lightning made of chain mail. grace is not
her pseudonym, though everyone in my family is a poet.

these are the shields for the names we speak in the dark
to remember our darkness. savage death rites

we still practice in the new world. myths we whisper
to each other to keep warm. my korean name

is the star my mother cooks into the jjigae
to follow home when i am lost, which is always

in this gray country, this violent foster home
whose streets are paved with shame, this factory yard

riddled with bullies ready to steal your skin
& sell it back to your mother for profit,

land where they stuff our throats with soil
& accuse us of gluttony when we learn to swallow it.

i confess. i am greedy. i think i deserve to be seen
for what i am: a boundless, burning wick.

a minor chord. i confess: if someone has looked
at my crooked spine and called it elmwood,

i've accepted. if someone has loved me more
for my gook name, for my saint name,

for my good vocabulary & bad joints,
i've welcomed them into this house.

i've cooked them each a meal with a star singing
at the bottom of the bowl, a secret ingredient

to follow home when we are lost:
sunflower oil, blood sausage, a name

given by your dead grandfather who eventually
forgot everything he'd touched. i promise:

i'll never stop stealing back what's mine.
i promise: i won't forget again. ■

imagenavi/Getty Images

Look at this picture of jjigae, a Korean dish that the speaker's mother makes for her.

What do you notice about the features of the stew as seen in this image? How do they represent an idea that Choi is suggesting about culture? The speaker's mother infuses the speaker's name into the dish (ll. 26–27). What is the figurative significance of this detail? Why is the name not only part of the dish but also said to be lying at the bottom of it? In what ways is the speaker's identity tied to this dish?

Understanding and Interpreting

1. The speaker acknowledges that her name is always mispronounced. She conveys this with a metaphor in the second stanza. Identify the metaphor and explain how it serves to relay her message.
2. What is the relationship between "Choi," "garlic breath," "seaweed," "sesame," and "food stamps" (ll. 9–10)?
3. What role do the names Ian, Isaac, Ivan, and Grace play within the speaker's family? What does the speaker's desire to assume the name Frances reveal about her ability to navigate both the American and Korean cultures?
4. The dedication — the italicized line at the beginning of the poem — introduces readers to the speaker's parents. The mother is again mentioned in line 18 when the speaker tells us of her "pride." What is the source of the mother's pride? What does it suggest about her relationship to American culture?
5. Identify the two confessions the speaker makes in lines 35 to 39. What do they suggest about the speaker's complex relationship with her adoptive culture?
6. Paraphrase the last four stanzas. How does the speaker's attitude toward her cultural identity shift in this part of the poem?

Analyzing Style, Language, and Structure

1. **Vocabulary.** What does the word "mail" mean in line 21? How is this meaning similar to or different from other uses of the word that you have encountered? What effect does Choi achieve by using "mail" in this way?
2. **Skill Focus.** How is the speaker characterized at the beginning of the poem? How does that characterization change at the end of the poem? What do these changes suggest about the speaker's relationship to the American and Korean cultures to which she is connected?
3. Choi uses extensive figurative language in this piece to communicate ideas about power and control, such as when she says that the speaker's name is "butchered by hammerhead tongues" (l. 4). Identify other uses of figurative language in this poem that relate to the gaining and losing of power and explain how they relate to the poem's overall theme.

4. The poem's structure consists of 25 couplets, each comprising its own stanza. Think about the effect of this structural organization. Explain how the poem would produce a different effect if Choi had written it as a single long stanza.
5. What is the effect of the metaphor in lines 29 to 30? As part of your response, be sure to identify what is being compared to a "foster home."
6. Trace the motif of food and cooking throughout the poem. What role does food play in the speaker's relationship to her Korean culture?
7. Describe the poem's deviation from writing conventions. Specifically, why might Choi have elected to disregard capitalization rules?
8. The poem's final two stanzas include the repetition of the phrase "I promise." What promises does she make? What does this repetition suggest about the speaker's relationship to her new culture?

Topics for Composing

1. **Analysis.** While "Choi Jeong Min" centers on a single speaker's experience, it depicts feelings and experiences that are likely familiar to many who do not blend fully into mainstream American culture. How does the poem characterize how these individuals are perceived? How does it portray how they are made to feel about themselves?
2. **Argument.** The speaker of this poem explores the tension between wanting to assimilate into American society and being forever linked to her Korean heritage. In general, does this kind of tension between cultures result in discord or mutual enrichment for immigrants? In other words, what are the most significant ways in which immigration shapes individuals or societies?
3. **Connection.** Think of a time when you felt like you didn't belong to a particular group. How did it feel to be considered an outsider? To what extent did your feelings align with those of the speaker in the poem?
4. **Speaking and Listening.** "Choi Jeong Min" touches on many aspects of cultural heritage: names, accents, traditions, languages, foods. In small groups, discuss the characteristics that define your cultural heritage. Within your groups, reflect on what you learned about different cultures from this exercise.
5. **Research.** Research trends in Korean immigration to the United States over the last century or so. What difficulties did people of Korean descent face when they emigrated to the United States? How did they overcome these difficulties and begin to assimilate into American society?

My Father in English

Richard Blanco

Johnny Louis/Getty Images

Richard Blanco was born in Spain to Cuban parents in 1968. Later that year, the family moved to the United States and settled in Miami. At the urging of his parents, Blanco earned an engineering degree from Florida International University in 1991. Later, he earned an MFA from FIU, where he is currently an associate professor of English. Blanco became the fifth Presidential Inaugural Poet when he recited "One Today" during President Obama's second inauguration. His poetry collections include *Looking for the Gulf Motel* (2012) and *How to Love a Country* (2019). "My Father in English" appeared in the *New Yorker* in February 2019.

First half of his life lived in Spanish: the long syntax
of *las montañas* that lined his village, the rhyme
of *sol* with his soul — a Cuban *alma* — that swayed
with *las palmas,* the sharp rhythm of his *machete*
cutting through *caña,* the syllables of his *canarios*
that sung into *la brisa* of the island home he left
to spell out the second half of his life in English —
the vernacular of New York City sleet, neon, glass —
and the brick factory where he learned to polish
steel twelve hours a day. Enough to save enough
to buy a used Spanish-English dictionary he kept
bedside like a bible — studied fifteen new words
after his prayers each night, then practiced them
on us the next day: *Buenos días, indeed, my family.*
Indeed más coffee. Have a good day today, indeed —
and again in the evening: *Gracias to my bella wife,*
indeed, for dinner. Hicistes tu homework, indeed?
La vida is indeed difícil. Indeed did indeed become
his favorite word, which, like the rest of his new life,
he never quite grasped: overused and misused often
to my embarrassment. Yet the word I most learned
to love and know him through: *indeed,* the exile who
tried to master the language he chose to master him,
indeed, the husband who refused to say *I love you*
in English to my mother, the man who died without
true translation. *Indeed,* meaning: in fact/*en efecto,*
meaning: in reality/*de hecho,* meaning to say now
what I always meant to tell him in both languages:
thank you/*gracias* for surrendering the past tense
of your life so that I might conjugate myself here
in the present of this country, in truth/*así es, indeed.* ■

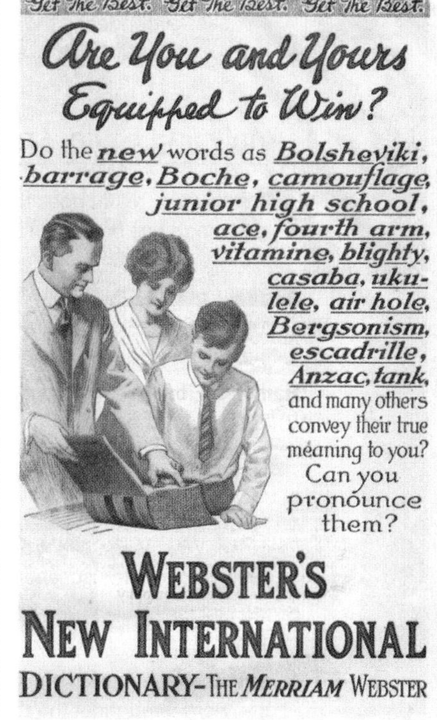

websters dictionary/ADVERTISING ARCHIVES ('B' IMAGES)/Bridgeman Images

This advertisement from the 1910s aims to stir interest in the virtues and uses of *Webster's New International Dictionary*.

According to the advertisement, who will benefit from having a dictionary at home? In what ways will the dictionary help them? Do the speaker of the poem and his father regard the dictionary with feelings similar to those conveyed in the image?

Understanding and Interpreting

1. In lines 1 to 6, the speaker provides various descriptions of Cuba. Focus on the comparisons made in these lines. To what are these descriptions metaphorically linked?
2. How does the "vernacular" (l. 8) of New York City compare to the earlier descriptions of Cuba?
3. Why does the speaker's father study "new words" (l. 12) each night? What does this detail suggest about the father's attitude toward his new life in America?
4. Based on the italicized words in lines 14 to 18, what is the father's understanding of the word "indeed?"
5. Following the caesura, or break, in line 21, the word "yet" marks a shift in the poem. What change do we perceive in the speaker after this point in the poem?

6. In your own words, summarize the last three lines of the poem. Pay particular attention to the phrases "surrendering the past tense / of your life" and "conjugate myself here."
7. Consider the poem's title. Explain how it relates to the meaning of the poem as a whole.

Analyzing Style, Language, and Structure

1. **Vocabulary.** What does the word "spell" mean in the context of line 7 of this poem? How is Blanco's use of the word similar to or different from other uses you have encountered? Provide a definition for the word that is appropriate for this context.
2. **Skill Focus.** While most of the poem centers on the speaker's father, the last four lines reveal the speaker's character. Based on this portion of the poem, how would you describe the speaker?
3. In line 1, the speaker says that his father "lived" the first half of his life in Spanish. When describing "the second half of his [father's] life" in line 7, the speaker uses the verb "to spell." What does the difference between "lived" and "to spell" suggest about his father's life in America compared to what his life was like in Cuba?
4. While "My Father in English" is written primarily in English, Blanco infuses Spanish into the poem. What is the effect of the presence of both languages within the poem? What does it suggest about the speaker's relationship with both cultures?
5. Identify the simile in line 12 and explain the function of the comparison. What does it suggest about the father and his desire to integrate into mainstream American culture?
6. Note the repetition of the word "meaning" in lines 26 and 27. Determine why Blanco repeats this word throughout the poem. How does that repetition relate to the ideas of culture and assimilation that the poem conveys?

Topics for Composing

1. **Analysis.** The speaker thanks his father because his father's sacrifices have allowed him to "conjugate" (l. 30) himself in the United States. Explain how the notion of conjugation sheds light on the poem's meaning and Blanco's message regarding the immigrant experience.
2. **Argument.** Throughout the poem, the speaker tells of his father's efforts to learn English. If immigrants entering the United States learn English and participate in American holidays and customs, do they have to forego their native language and traditions to become part of the fabric of America? In other words, does assimilation require a departure from an immigrant's original culture?
3. **Connection.** The speaker says that through the word "indeed" he "most learned / to love and know" (ll. 21–22) his father. Think about someone who is important to you. Discuss the word or words you most associate with this person.
4. **Speaking and Listening.** Locate a recording of Richard Blanco reciting "My Father in English." As a class, be prepared to discuss how your perception of the poem changes after listening to the poet's reading.
5. **Multimodal.** Carefully read the first six lines of the poem. Identify the speaker's words — in Spanish and English — that create an image of his father's village. Think about which words can be used to describe the city or town in which you live. Infuse these words, along with printed images, drawings, and cutouts, into a collage that captures the spirit of your hometown.

central text

An Irish Childhood in England: 1951

Eavan Boland

Eavan Boland

Eavan Boland (1944–2020) was an Irish poet born in Dublin who moved to London at the age of six. She returned to Ireland as a teenager and earned a degree from Trinity College. Boland published ten volumes of poetry, including *Domestic Violence* (2007) and *A Woman Without a Country: Poems* (2014). This poem is from her book *The Journey and Other Poems* (1987).

KEY CONTEXT In the 1950s, Eavan Boland's father served as Irish Ambassador to England. This assignment led the entire family to London, where six-year-old Eavan Boland experienced anti-Irish sentiments for the first time.

The bickering of vowels on the buses,
the clicking thumbs and the big hips of
the navy-skirted ticket collectors with
their crooked seams brought it home to me:
Exile. Ration-book[1] pudding.
Bowls of dripping and the fixed smile
of the school pianist playing "Iolanthe,"[2]
"Land of Hope and Glory"[3] and "John Peel."[4]
I didn't know what to hold, to keep.
At night, filled with some malaise
of love for what I'd never known I had,
I fell asleep and let the moment pass.
The passing moment has become a night
of clipped shadows, freshly painted houses,
the garden eddying in dark and heat,
my children half-awake, half-asleep.
Airless, humid dark. Leaf-noise.
The stirrings of a garden before rain.
A hint of storm behind the risen moon.
We are what we have chosen. Did I choose to?—

[1]A book of coupons used to purchase foods rationed in England during World War II. — Eds.

[2]A late nineteenth-century comic opera by Arthur Sullivan and W. S. Gilbert. — Eds.

[3]A British patriotic song (1901) by Edward Elgar and A. C. Benson. — Eds.

[4]Refers to "D'ye ken John Peel," a nineteenth-century song about a fox hunter, written by John Woodcock Graves. —Eds.

in a strange city, in another country,
on nights in a north-facing bedroom,
waiting for the sleep that never did
restore me as I'd hoped to what I'd lost —
let the world I knew become the space
between the words that I had by heart
and all the other speech that always was
becoming the language of the country that
I came to in nineteen fifty-one:
barely-gelled, a freckled six-year-old,
overdressed and sick on the plane,
when all of England to an Irish child
was nothing more than what you'd lost and how:
was the teacher in the London convent who,
when I produced "I amn't" in the classroom
turned and said — "You're not in Ireland now." ■

John Vachon's 1954 photograph "Irish Boy Reciting Saint Patrick's Day Poetry" depicts an Irish family around the time that Boland's family moved to England.

What conclusions can you draw about the family's ties to Irish culture based on their reactions to the celebration of Saint Patrick? How are the feelings they appear to express about their culture similar to or different from those of the speaker in Boland's poem?

Understanding and Interpreting

1. After recognizing that she lives in exile, the speaker mentions "ration-book pudding" (l. 5). What is a ration book? What does the speaker convey by describing the pudding as such?
2. Time has elapsed between the first and second stanzas. In lines 13 and 14, the speaker says, "The passing moment has become a night / of clipped shadows." What does this phrase suggest about the speaker's relationship to her past?
3. The speaker never finishes her statement in line 20. In fact, a dash at the end of the line emphasizes the incompleteness of her assertion. What was the speaker about to say?
4. Line 24 ends in a dash and an incomplete statement. What do you think the speaker means by the reference to what she had "lost?"
5. The speaker describes herself in lines 30 and 31. How do these descriptions reveal how she perceives her younger self?
6. "[A]mn't" is a contraction of "am not" that is colloquially used in Ireland. What does the teacher's final retort in line 36 convey to the speaker about the English and their attitude toward Irish cultural elements?

Analyzing Style, Language, and Structure

1. **Vocabulary.** What does the word "dripping" mean in the context of line 6 of this poem? How is this meaning similar to or different from other uses of the word you have encountered? Pay close attention to context clues to provide a possible definition of the word as it is used in the poem.
2. **Skill Focus.** The poem's speaker thinks back to when she was a child and had just arrived in England. What does her interaction with a new culture teach her about herself and her place outside of Ireland?
3. Instead of acknowledging the presence of individual people on the bus, the speaker refers to them by "the bickering of vowels" (l. 1) they produce. What does this selection of detail at the onset of the poem suggest about the speaker's initial reaction to encountering a new culture?
4. The first stanza is characterized by the repetition of the sound /k/. Refer to Chapter 2 to review the terms consonance and cacophony (p. 59). Use this information to determine the function of sound throughout the first stanza.
5. What clues does Boland provide throughout the poem to show that the speaker is now an adult reminiscing about her emigration from Ireland?
6. Reread the poem and identify the words used to describe Ireland and England, respectively. How does the poem's language juxtapose the speaker's perception of each country and its culture?
7. Characterize the final sentence of the poem. How many lines does it comprise? What is the effect of this sentence? What does it convey about the speaker's state of mind?

Topics for Composing

1. **Analysis.** Eavan Boland's poem captures the perspective of a child entering a new cultural landscape. What choices in language and style help Boland convey the speaker's experience of encountering this new culture?

2. **Argument.** The reflections and recollections of the speaker in this poem demonstrate how challenging emigration can be, particularly for children. While children may be more resilient than adults, they often don't fully understand what is happening. Based on details from this poem, other readings, and your own experiences, is it easier for children or for adults to leave their country and assimilate into a new culture?
3. **Connection.** The speaker's experience reflects a common reaction to encountering a new culture. Select another character from this chapter or from your own reading who must assimilate into a new culture. Then, compare their experiences. What is similar or different about difficulties the two characters experience and the longings they express?
4. **Speaking and Listening.** While moving to a different country sometimes requires having to learn a new language, the speaker of this poem moves from one English-speaking country to another. Nonetheless, there are many differences between the varieties of English spoken in Ireland and England. In small groups, listen to recordings of Irish and British people speaking. Then, characterize the differences you and your peers perceive between the English spoken in each nation.
5. **Research.** For us in the United States, hearing about these cultural differences between England and Ireland might be surprising. Research the relationship between these two countries and cultures. What are the primary differences in cultures? What are the conflicts? What are the connections?

Children as Enemies

Ha Jin

Leonardo Cendamo/Getty Images

Born in Liaoning Province, China, in 1956, Ha Jin grew up during the Cultural Revolution. He volunteered to serve in the People's Liberation Army from age fourteen to nineteen. While serving in the army, Jin studied English. After he received his BA from Heilongjiang University (1981) and an MA from Shandong University (1984), he came to the United States to complete his PhD at Brandeis University. After the massacre of student democracy protestors in Tiananmen Square in 1989, Jin decided to remain in the United States and write solely in English. He currently teaches at Boston University. Jin has published several books of poetry and short fiction, as well as eight novels, one of which, *Waiting* (1999), won the National Book Award. The following story, "Children as Enemies," is from Jin's 2009 short story collection, *A Good Fall*.

KEY CONTEXT In traditional Chinese culture, the concept of filial piety means respect for one's parents and ancestors. Based on Confucian philosophy, it involves general obedience. However, it extends further to include behaving in such a way as to reflect well upon one's parents, always showing love and respect, supporting parents both financially and emotionally, and caring for them as they age. Children are expected to honor such duties to their parents and willingly sacrifice to carry them out. Ha Jin explores the consequences of becoming part of a culture that has a different, more open, definition of children's responsibilities to their family.

Our grandchildren hate us. The boy and the girl, ages eleven and nine, are just a pair of selfish, sloppy brats and have no respect for old people. Their animosity toward us originated at the moment their names were changed, about three months ago.

One evening the boy complained that his schoolmates couldn't pronounce his name, so he must change it. "Lots of them call me 'Chicken,'" he said. "I want a regular name like anyone else." His name was Qigan Xi, pronounced "cheegan hsee," which could be difficult for non-Chinese to manage.

"I wanna change mine too," his sister, Hua, jumped in. "Nobody can say it right and some call me 'Wow.'" She bunched her lips, her face puffed with baby fat.

Before their parents could respond, my wife put in, "You should teach them how to pronounce your names."

"They always laugh about my silly name, Qigan," the boy said. "If I didn't come from China, I'd say 'Chicken' too."

I told both kids, "You ought to be careful about changing your names. We decided on them only after consulting a reputable fortune-teller."

"Phew, who believes in that crap?" the boy muttered.

Our son intervened, saying to his children, "Let me think about this, okay?"

Our daughter-in-law, thin-eyed Mandi, broke in. "They should have American names. Down the road there'll be lots of trouble if their names remain unpronounceable. We should've changed them long ago."

Gubin, our son, seemed to agree, though he wouldn't say it in our presence.

My wife and I were unhappy about that, but we didn't make a serious effort to stop them, so Mandi and Gubin went about looking for suitable names for the children. It was easy in the girl's case. They picked "Flora" for her, since her name, Hua, means "flower." But it was not easy to find a name for the boy. English names are simple in meaning, mostly already empty of their original senses. Qigan means "amazing bravery." Where can you find an English name that combines the import and the resonance of that? When I pointed out the difficulty, the boy blustered, "I don't want a weird and complicated name. I just need a regular name, like Charlie or Larry or Johnny."

That I wouldn't allow. Names are a matter of fortune and fate — that's why fortune-tellers can divine the vicissitudes of people's lives by reading the orders and numbers of the strokes in the characters of their names. No one should change his name randomly.

Mandi went to the public library and checked out a book on baby names. She perused the small volume and came up with "Matty" as a choice. She explained, "'Matty' is short for 'Mathilde,' which is from Old German and means 'powerful in battle,' very close to 'Qigan' in meaning. Besides, the sound echoes 'mighty' in English."

"It doesn't sound right," I said. In the back of my mind I couldn't reconcile "Matty" with "Xi," our family name.

"I like it," the boy crowed.

He seemed determined to contradict me, so I said no more. I wished my son had rejected the choice, but Gubin didn't make a peep, just sitting in the rocking chair and drinking iced tea. The matter was settled. The boy went to school and told his teacher he had a new name — Matty.

For a week he seemed happy, but his satisfaction was short-lived. One evening he told his parents, "Matty is a girl's name, my friend Carl told me."

"Impossible," his mother said.

"Of course it's true. I asked around, and people all said it sounded girlish."

My wife, drying her hands on her apron, suggested to our son, "Why don't you look it up?"

The book on baby names was not returned yet, so Gubin looked it up and saw "f. or m." beside the name. Evidently Mandi hadn't seen that it could be both female and male. Her negligence or ignorance outraged the boy all the more.

What should we do? The eleven-year-old turned tearful, blaming his mother for giving him a name with an ambiguous gender.

Finally my son slapped his knee and said, "I have an idea. 'Matty' can also come from 'Matt.' Why not drop the letter 'y' and call yourself Matt?"

The boy brightened up and said he liked that, but I objected. "Look, this book says 'Matt' is a diminutive of 'Matthew.' It's nowhere close to the sense of 'amazing bravery.'"

"Who gives a damn about that!" the boy spat out. "I'm gonna call myself Matt."

Wordless, I felt my face tightening. I got up and went out to smoke a pipe on the balcony. My wife followed me, saying, "My old man, don't take to heart what our grandson said. He's just confused and desperate. Come back in and eat."

"After this pipe," I said.

"Don't be long." She stepped back into the apartment, her small shoulders more stooped than before.

Below me, automobiles were gliding past on the wet street like colored whales. If only we hadn't sold everything in Dalian City and come here to join our son's family. Gubin is our only child, so we'd thought it would be good to stay with him. Now I wish we hadn't moved. At our ages — my wife is sixty-three and I'm sixty-seven — and at this time it's hard to adjust to life here. In America it feels as if the older you are, the more inferior you grow.

Both my wife and I understood we shouldn't meddle with our grandchildren's lives, but sometimes I simply couldn't help offering them a bit of advice. She believed it was our daughter-in-law who had spoiled the kids and made them despise us. I don't think Mandi is that mean, though beyond question she is an indulgent mother. Flora and Matt look down on everything Chinese except for some food they like. They hated to go to the weekend school to learn to read and write the characters. Matt announced, "I've no need for that crap."

Fu, Lu, Shou; the three ages (ink on paper)/Hongshou, Chen (1598-1652)/JACOPO BRANCATI/ Musee Cernuschi, Paris, France/Bridgeman Images

Chen Hongshou's *Fu, Lu, Shou; the three ages* is a seventeenth-century depiction of three generations.

Based on the placement and interaction of the three figures, what conclusions can you draw about what is expected of different generations in this society? If you were to create an image of three generations in this story, what might it look like? How would you position the figures in relation to each other? What would they be doing?

I would have to force down my temper whenever I heard him say that. Their parents managed to make them attend the weekend school, though Matt and Flora had quit inscribing the characters. They went there only to learn how to paint with a brush, taking lessons from an old artist from Taiwan. The girl, sensitive by nature and delicate in health, might have had some talent for arts, but the boy was good at nothing but daydreaming. I just couldn't help imagining that he might end up a guttersnipe. He wouldn't draw bamboos or goldfish or landscapes with a brush; instead, he produced merely bands and lines of ink on paper, calling them abstract paintings. He experimented with the shades of the ink as if it were watercolors. Sometimes he did that at home too. Seeing his chubby face and narrow eyes as he worked in dead earnest, I wanted to laugh. He once showed a piece with some vertical lines of ink on it to an art teacher at his school. To my horror, the woman praised it, saying the lines suggested a rainfall or waterfall, and that if you observed them horizontally, they would bring to mind layers of clouds or some sort of landscape.

What a crock was that! I complained to Gubin in private and urged him to pressure the children to study serious subjects, such as science, classics, geography, history, grammar, and penmanship. If Matt really couldn't handle those, in the future he should consider learning how to repair cars and machines or how to cook like a chef. Auto mechanics make good money here — I know a fellow at a garage who can't speak any English but pulls in twenty-four dollars an hour, plus a generous bonus at the end of the year. I made it clear to my son that a few tricks in "art" would never get his kids anywhere in life, so they'd better stop dabbling with a brush. Gubin said Matt and Flora were still young and we shouldn't push them too hard, but he agreed to talk to them. Unlike

A calligrapher at work in the calligraphy district of one of China's oldest cities, Xi'an.

How do the man's body language and treatment of the texts compare to the grandfather's and Matt's attitudes toward this aspect of Chinese culture?

Gubin, Mandi aligned herself with the children, saying we ought to let them develop freely as individuals, not straitjacket them as they would back in China. My wife and I were unhappy about our daughter-in-law's position. Whenever we criticized her, our grandchildren would mock us or yell at us in defense of their mother.

I have serious reservations about elementary education in the United States. Teachers don't force their pupils to work as hard as they can. Matt had learned both multiplication and division in the third grade, but two months ago I asked him to calculate how much seventy-four percent of $1,586 was, and he had no clue how to do it. I handed him a calculator and said, "Use this." Even so, he didn't know he could just multiply the amount by 0.74.

"Didn't you learn multiplication and division?" I asked him.

"I did, but that was last year."

"Still, you should know how to do it."

"We haven't practiced division and multiplication this year, so I'm not familiar with them anymore." He offered that as an excuse. There was no way I could make him understand that once you learned something, you were supposed to master it and make it part of yourself. That's why we say knowledge is wealth. You can get richer and richer by accumulating it within.

The teachers here don't assign the pupils any real homework. Instead they give them a lot of projects, some of which seem no more than woolgathering, and tend to inflate the kids' egos. My son had to help his children with the projects, which were more like homework for the parents. Some of the topics were impossible even for adults to tackle, such as "What is culture and how is it created?" "Make your argument for or against the Iraq War," "How does the color line divide U.S. society?" and "Do you think global trade is necessary? Why?" My son had to do research online and in the public library to get the information needed for discussing those topics. Admittedly, they could broaden the pupils' minds and give them more confidence, but at their tender age they are not supposed to think like a politician or a scholar. They should be made to follow rules; that is, to become responsible citizens first.

Whenever I asked Flora how she was ranked in her class, she'd shrug and say, "I dunno."

"What do you mean you don't know?" I suspected she must be well below the average, though she couldn't be lower than her brother.

"Ms. Gillen doesn't rank us is all," came her answer.

If that was true, I was even more disappointed with the schools. How could they make their students competitive in this global economy if they didn't instill in them the sense of getting ahead of others and becoming the very best? No wonder many Asian parents viewed the public schools in Flushing unfavorably. In my honest opinion, elementary education here tends to lead children astray.

Five weeks ago, Matt declared at dinner that he must change his last name, because a substitute teacher that morning had mispronounced "Xi" as "Eleven." That put the whole class in stitches, and some students even made fun of the boy afterward, calling him "Matt Eleven." Flora chimed in, "Yeah, I want a different last name too. My friend Reta just had her family name changed to Wu. Some people couldn't pronounce 'Ng' and called her 'Reta No Good.'"

Their parents broke out laughing, but I couldn't see why that was funny. My wife said to the girl, "You'll have your husband's last name when you grow up and get married."

"I don't want no man!" the girl shot back.

"We both must have a new last name," the boy insisted.

I burst out, "You can't do that. Your last name belongs to the family, and you can't cut yourselves off from your ancestors."

"Baloney!" The boy squished up his face.

"You mustn't speak to your granddad like that," his grandmother butted in.

Mandi and my son exchanged glances. I knew they saw this matter differently from us. Maybe they had been planning to change their children's last name all along. Enraged, I dropped my bowl on the dining table and pointed my finger at Mandi. "You've tried your best to spoil them. Now you're happy to let them break away from the family tree. What kind of daughter-in-law are you? I wish I hadn't allowed you to join our family."

"Please don't blow up like this, Dad," my son said.

Mandi didn't talk back. Instead she began sobbing, wrinkling her gourd-shaped nose. The kids got angry and blamed me for hurting their mother's feelings. The more they blabbered, the more furious I became. Finally unable to hold it back anymore, I shouted, "If you two change your last name, you leave, get out of here. You cannot remain in this household while using a different last name."

"Who are you?" Matt said calmly. "This isn't your home."

"You're just our guests," added Flora.

That drove both my wife and me mad. She yelled at our granddaughter, "So we sold everything in China, our apartment and candy store, just to be your guests here, huh? Heartless. Who told you this isn't our home?"

That shut the girl up, though she kept glaring at her grandma. Their father begged no one in particular, "Please, let us finish dinner peacefully." He went on chewing a fried shrimp with his mouth closed.

I wanted to yell at him that he was just a rice barrel thinking of nothing but food, but I controlled my anger. How could we have raised such a spineless son?

To be fair, he's quite accomplished in his profession, a bridge engineer pulling in almost six figures a year, but he's henpecked and indulgent with the kids, and got worse and worse after he came to America, as if he had become a man without temper or opinions. How often I wanted to tell him point-blank that he must live like a man, at least more like his former self. Between his mother and myself, we often wondered if he was inadequate in bed; otherwise, how could he always listen to Mandi?

After that quarrel, we decided to move out. Gubin and Mandi helped us fill out an application for housing offered to the elderly by the city, which we'll have to wait a long time to get. If we were not so old and in poor health, we'd live far away from them, completely on our own, but they are the only family we have in this country, so we could move only to a nearby place. For the time being we've settled down in a one-bedroom apartment on Fifty-fourth Avenue, rented for us by Gubin. Sometimes he comes over to see if we're all right or need anything. We've never asked him what last name our grandkids use now. I guess they must have some American name. How sad it is when you see your grandchildren's names on paper but can no longer recognize them, as though your family line has faded and disappeared among the multitudes. Whenever I think about this, it stings my heart. If only I'd had second thoughts about leaving China. It's impossible to go back anymore, and we'll have to spend our remaining years in this place where even your grandchildren can act like your enemies.

Matt and Flora usually shun us. If we ran into them on the street, they would warn us not to "torture" their mother again. They even threatened to call the police if we entered their home without permission. We don't have to be warned. We've never set foot in their home since we moved out. I've told my son that we won't accept the kids as part of the family as long as they use a different last name.

Gubin has never brought up that topic again, though I'm still waiting for an answer from him. That's how the matter stands now. The other day, exasperated, my wife wanted to go to Mandi's fortune cookie factory and raise a placard to announce: "My Daughter-in-Law Mandi Cheng Is the Most Unfilial Person on Earth!" But I dissuaded my old better half. What's the good of that? For sure Mandi's company won't fire her just because she can't make her parents-in-law happy. This is America, where we must learn self-reliance and mind our own business. ■

extending beyond the text

In his piece titled *Family Tree*, Chinese artist Zhang Huan asked three calligraphers to write the names of friends and family and inscribe personal and cultural stories directly onto his skin. The artist describes how he sees this serial self-portrait: "It is impossible to take away your inborn blood and personality. . . . This work speaks about a family story, a spirit of family."

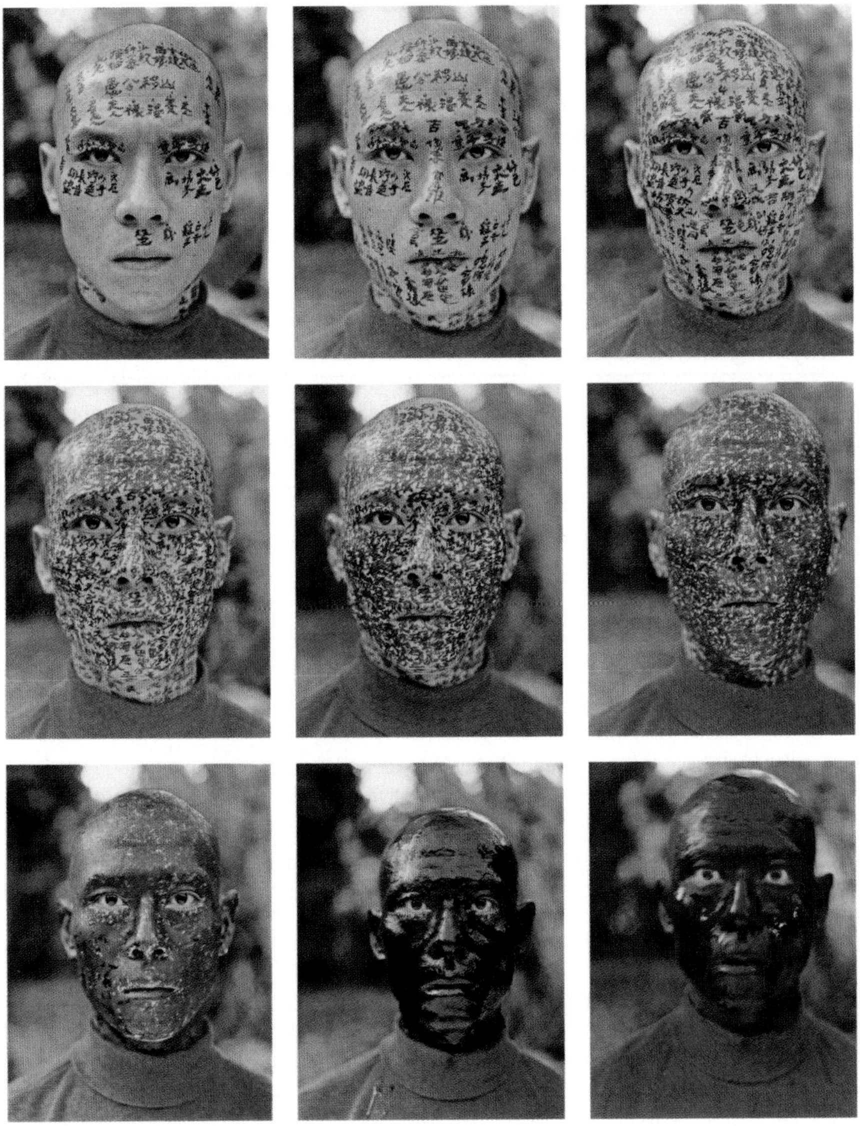

Family Tree, 2001 (chromogenic prints)/Zhang Huan (b.1965)/MUSEUM OF FINE ARTS, HOUSTON/Museum of Fine Arts, Houston, Texas, USA/Bridgeman Images

What message about family and cultural heritage do you think Huan is expressing? How might each generation in "Children as Enemies" interpret the argument Huan is making with this piece?

Understanding and Interpreting

1. "Our grandchildren hate us" is the dramatic opening line of this story. What does this opening reveal about the narrator? What does it lead you to expect?
2. What evidence do you find in the story to support the narrator's second sentence, which characterizes the grandchildren as "just a pair of selfish, sloppy brats"? What impact, if any, does the age of the children have on your view of whether or not they are "selfish, sloppy brats"?
3. What is significant about Mandi's turning to a book she checks out of the library in order to identify a meaningful name for her children? What is the contrasting Chinese tradition?
4. Why does the grandfather conclude that "[in] America it feels as if the older you are, the more inferior you grow" (par. 29)?
5. To what extent do you agree that Mandi is "an indulgent mother" (par. 30), as the grandfather accuses? Cite specific details to support your response.
6. What are the fundamental differences in philosophy about education that the grandfather perceives between the American and Chinese school systems?
7. Each generation in the story is part of a cultural group with distinct ideas about honor and family. Identify how each generation perceives these two topics.

Analyzing Language, Style, and Structure

1. **Vocabulary.** In paragraph 12, the grandfather speaks of the "strokes in the characters" of names. What does the word "characters" mean in this context? How is this meaning similar to or different from other meanings you have encountered?
2. **Skill Focus.** How would you describe the narrator of this story? Explain how your description of the narrator, who happens to be a character in the story, relates to the meaning of Ha Jin's story.
3. What is the effect of telling the story from a particular character's point of view, rather than from the point of view of an omniscient narrator who could represent a range of perspectives?
4. What elements of humor do you find in the story? What effect does the author achieve by infusing humor (and irony) into the narrative?
5. What descriptions convey the grandfather's anger and his disapproving attitude toward Gubin and his family? Pay close attention to the figurative language the author uses to describe physical qualities as well as character traits.
6. Gubin is notably silent during this story. What do we learn about him from the limited dialogue he has? To what extent does the character revealed by that dialogue reflect or conflict with what the narrator tells us about his son?

Topics for Composing

1. **Analysis.** Cultural and generational divides are at the center of the family's disputes in this story. Analyze Ha Jin's message regarding the effects of these differences. Are these battles universal or specific to this family?
2. **Argument.** This story centers on the dispute between traditional Chinese grandparents and their Americanized grandchildren. Whom do you side with? Why? Is it right for youth to strike out and make their own way in the world — as these children do — or should they adhere to tradition? Be sure to examine specific benefits and drawbacks of each approach in your response.

3. **Connection.** Gubin and Mandi are supportive of their children's desire to change their names. This decision is surprising — and disappointing — to the grandparents. Write about a decision you have made that your parents supported, despite it challenging cultural or familial expectations.
4. **Research.** In paragraphs 44 and 45, the wife and Flora have this exchange: "'You'll have your husband's last name when you grow up and get married.' 'I don't want no man!' the girl shot back." Many Western cultures are patrilineal, meaning that traditionally a child's last name comes from the father, and the wife will use the husband's last name. To what extent is that beginning to change? Research how other cultures deal with family names, and how some people today might be moving away from the tradition. What are the alternatives? What are the benefits and drawbacks?
5. **Creative Writing.** Is the story over? What do you believe will be the situation a few years later? Is there a way to heal the family's wounds? If so, how might that happen? Who might take the lead? Who needs to change? Considering these questions and what you know about the characters, write an extension of the story that provides closure.

Enlightenment

Natasha Trethewey

Stephen Voss/Redux

Natasha Trethewey (b. 1966) was born in Mississippi to a white Canadian father and a Black mother. Trethewey earned an M.F.A. from the University of Massachusetts, Amherst (1995), and an honorary degree from Emory University (2017). She also has the distinction of receiving the 2007 Pulitzer Prize for Poetry for *Native Guard* and serving two terms as Poet Laureate of the United States (2012–2014). "Enlightenment" appeared in her fourth poetry collection, *Thrall* (2012).

KEY CONTEXT Thomas Jefferson (1743–1826) is one of the Founding Fathers of the United States and served as the nation's third President. At their plantation in Virginia, Jefferson and his wife, Martha, had enslaved people working inside the home and on their fields. Sally Hemings, who was Martha's half-sister and one of the enslaved individuals owned by Jefferson, was the mother of many of his children. She was able to use her position to secure the emancipation of her children, although she never gained her own freedom.

In the portrait of Jefferson that hangs
at Monticello, he is rendered two-toned:
his forehead white with illumination —

a lit bulb — the rest of his face in shadow,
darkened as if the artist meant to contrast
his bright knowledge, its dark subtext.

By 1805, when Jefferson sat for the portrait,
he was already linked to an affair
with his slave. Against a backdrop, blue

and ethereal, a wash of paint that seems
to hold him in relief, Jefferson gazes out
across the centuries, his lips fixed as if

he's just uttered some final word.
The first time I saw the painting, I listened
as my father explained the contradictions:

how Jefferson hated slavery, though — *out
of necessity,* my father said — had to own
slaves; that his moral philosophy meant

he could not have fathered those children:
would have been impossible, my father said.
For years we debated the distance between

word and deed. I'd follow my father from book
to book, gathering citations, listening
as he named — like a field guide to Virginia —

each flower and tree and bird as if to prove
a man's pursuit of knowledge is greater
than his shortcomings, the limits of his vision.

I did not know then the subtext
of our story, that my father could imagine
Jefferson's words made flesh in my flesh —

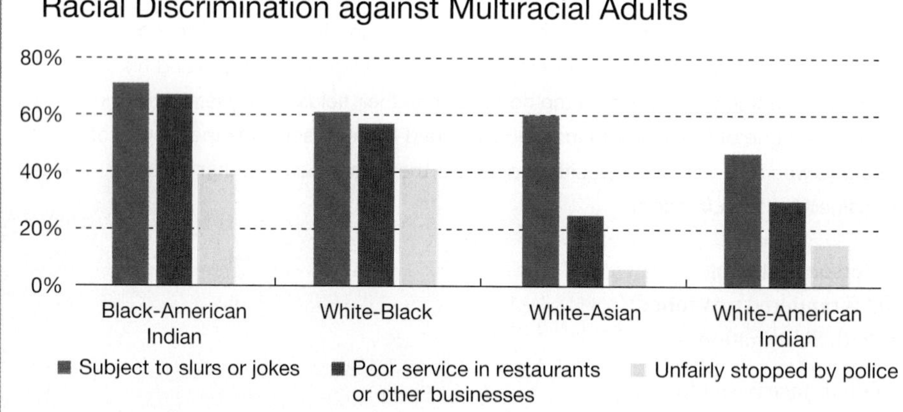

This data collected from a 2015 Pew Research Center survey focuses on discrimination faced by multiracial adults in the United States.

What conclusions can you draw regarding the data that is presented here? How does the data align with the poem's speaker's reflections on her own experiences as a multiracial American?

the improvement of the blacks in body
and mind, in the first instance of their mixture
with the whites — or that my father could believe

he'd made me *better.* When I think of this now,
I see how the past holds us captive,
its beautiful ruin etched on the mind's eye:

my young father, a rough outline of the old man
he's become, needing to show me
the better measure of his heart, an equation

writ large at Monticello. That was years ago.
Now, we take in how much has changed:
talk of Sally Hemings, someone asking,

How white was she? — parsing the fractions
as if to name what made her worthy
of Jefferson's attentions: a near-white,

quadroon mistress, not a plain black slave.
Imagine stepping back into the past,
our guide tells us then — and I can't resist

whispering to my father: *This is where*
we split up. I'll head around to the back.
When he laughs, I know he's grateful

I've made a joke of it, this history
that links us — white father, black daughter —
even as it renders us other to each other. ■

Understanding and Interpreting

1. The speaker refers to "Monticello" in the second line of the poem. Why is this site significant to a poem that centers on race and family?
2. The poem presents a number of light/dark comparisons. The first two stanzas present the first of these comparisons in a description of Jefferson's face. The seemingly straightforward description, however, ends with the phrase "its dark subtext" (l. 6). What is this darkness associated with Jefferson? Why is it significant to the poem?
3. The third stanza alludes to a well-known and well-documented "affair" (l. 8) between Jefferson and Sally Hemings. Who was this woman? Why is this relationship central to this poem?
4. The speaker's father presents his initial stance on Jefferson in lines 14 to 20. What is the father's understanding of Jefferson? Explain the reference to "those children" in line 19.

5. In lines 31 to 33, the speaker quotes directly from Jefferson's 1785 *Notes on the State of Virginia*. Reread and paraphrase Jefferson's statement. How does this statement compare to the beginning of Jefferson's most significant text – the Declaration of Independence?
6. Beginning with line 40, there is a shift in the poem. What changes occur at this point in the poem in terms of style, tone, and content?

Analyzing Style, Language, and Structure

1. **Vocabulary.** Consider the use of the word "ruin" in line 36. How would you define "ruin" in that context? How is this use of the word similar to or different from other uses you have encountered?
2. **Skill Focus.** The poem recounts the speaker's two visits to Monticello with her father. Consider how she is depicted during each visit. Explain how she changes over time. How do these changes align with how the United States itself has also changed during this time period?
3. Think about the word "Enlightenment" in terms of its definition and the intellectual movement to which it alludes. In what ways is "Enlightenment" an appropriate title for this poem?
4. How do the father's first words, "out of necessity" (ll. 16–17), characterize him? To what is the father alluding? What do you imagine is his daughter's reaction?
5. The eighth stanza compares the speaker's research and findings to a "field guide to Virginia." Explain this comparison and discuss what you might discover in this field guide.
6. Consider the dialogue noted in line 43. Identify the speaker and analyze what the comment suggests about race culture in America.

Topics for Composing

1. **Analysis.** In line 41, the speaker alludes to "how much has changed." How do the speaker's interactions with her father at Monticello reflect both changes in their relationship and changes in the United States?
2. **Argument.** The Founding Fathers' governmental, literary, and philosophical contributions to the United States were immense. Over time, however, their ties to slavery have received increasing attention. To what extent should we continue to celebrate the Founding Fathers who, like Jefferson, were also slaveholders?
3. **Connection.** Monticello is significant to the speaker and her father. Identify a location that is special to you and a member of your family. Explain what this place represents to your relationship. Discuss whether or not its significance in your life has changed over time.
4. **Speaking and Listening.** Prepare for a whole-class discussion on the speaker's relationship with her father. As part of the discussion, discuss the extent to which they are able to understand each other's perspectives on race and history. Be prepared to discuss how their perceptions are shaped by their age, race, and gender identity.
5. **Creative Writing.** As the speaker listens to the guide at Monticello inviting them to step "back into the past" (l. 47), she informs her father that she is leaving the tour. Think about why she chooses to separate herself from the group at that moment. Write an alternate ending for this poem in which you imagine that instead of walking away, the speaker responds to the tour guide's comment. Attempt to align your writing to Trethewey's style by paying particular attention to approximate line length, tone, and overall stanza structure.

For a New Citizen of These United States

Li-Young Lee

Poet Li-Young Lee (b. 1957) was born in Jakarta, Indonesia, to parents of Chinese descent. When he was seven, his family immigrated to the United States, eventually settling in Pennsylvania. Lee began writing poetry while attending the University of Pittsburgh. He has won many awards for his work since, including the 2003 Academy of American Poets Fellowship.

Alison Granucci/Blue Flower Arts

Forgive me for thinking I saw
the irregular postage stamp of death;
a black moth the size of my left
thumbnail is all I've trapped in the damask.
There is no need for alarm. And

there is no need for sadness, if
the rain at the window now reminds you
of nothing; not even of that
parlor, long like a nave, where cloud-shadow,
wing-shadow, where father-shadow
continually confused the light. In flight,
leaf-throng and, later, soldiers and
flags deepened those windows to submarine.

But you don't remember, I know,
so I won't mention that house where Chung hid,
Lin wizened, you languished, and Ming-
Ming hush-hushed us with small song. And since you
don't recall the missionary
bells chiming the hour, or those words whose sounds
alone exhaust the heart—*garden,*
heaven, amen—I'll mention none of it.

After all, it was just our life,
merely years in a book of years. It was
1960, and we stood with
the other families on a crowded
railroad platform. The trains came, then
the rains, and then we got separated.

And in the interval between
familiar faces, events occurred, which
one of us faithfully pencilled
in a day-book bound by a rubber band.

But birds, as you say, fly forward.
So I won't show you letters and the shawl
I've so meaninglessly preserved.
And I won't hum along, if you don't, when
our mothers sing *Nights in Shanghai.*
I won't, each Spring, each time I smell lilac,
recall my mother, patiently
stitching money inside my coat lining,
if you don't remember your mother
preparing for your own escape.

After all, it was only our
life, our life and its forgetting. ■

Edward Hopper's 1921 etching *Night Shadow* shows a solitary figure walking along a lighted section of an otherwise dark city.

How does the mood established by the shadows in the image align with the effect of the various references to shadows found in Lee's poem?

Understanding and Interpreting

1. Although the speaker of the poem says that he or she will "mention none of it" (l. 21), quite a bit of information comes out about the time before coming to America. What are some of the most significant past events identified in the poem?
2. How would you characterize the relationship between the speaker and the "you" that he or she is addressing? How are their feelings about the past different? What can you infer about the cause of their conflict?

3. The speaker identifies letters and other objects that have been "so meaninglessly preserved" (l. 34). What factors might cause the speaker to claim that these are "meaningless"? Why does the speaker refer to them in this way?
4. There are many references to intentional forgetting or not remembering. What do these references suggest about the role of memory? What evidence from the poem supports your claim?
5. The title implies that this poem will include advice for recent immigrants to America. What suggestions might the speaker offer about immigration?

Analyzing Language, Style, and Structure

1. **Vocabulary in Context.** Examine the use of the word "confused" in line 11. How would you normally define this word? Why does that definition not fit this context? How can light be "confused?" Offer a plausible definition for this context.
2. **Skill Focus.** How would you characterize the speaker of this poem? Aside from the words he or she uses, pay close attention to the speaker's actions in the poem. Specifically, consider what the speaker is doing to the person he or she is addressing.
3. The second stanza relates the speaker's departure from his homeland. As he and his family enter the ship's "parlor," the word "shadow" is repeated. What does this repetition suggest about the event and the speaker's emotions during the departure?
4. The past in this poem is shrouded in mystery and vagueness. Locate a section in which the speaker describes the past. Explain how the poet's word choice conveys a lack of clarity.
5. It is over halfway through the poem before the reader receives the most concrete image of the past: "It was / 1960, and we stood with / the other families on a crowded / railroad platform" (ll. 23–26). How do these lines signal a shift in the speaker's representation of the past?
6. "For a New Citizen of These United States" employs very little rhyme or rhythmic pattern. How does Lee's choice of free verse reflect the speaker's attitude toward the past?
7. Twice, the speaker begins a stanza with a variation of "After all, it was just our life." How does this statement reveal the speaker's attitude toward the process of immigration?

Topics for Composing

1. **Analysis.** Identify two perspectives within the poem on what an immigrant's relationship to the past should be. How does the poem characterize each of these perspectives? Does the poem seem to value one of these perspectives over the other? Cite specific evidence from the poem in your response.
2. **Argument.** As Lee suggests in lines 26 to 27, families are often disrupted or separated during the chaos of immigration. How important is the family unit in the successful transition to a new culture? Does the family unit promote or obstruct the adoption of new cultural practices?
3. **Speaking and Listening.** Search for recordings of interviews with immigrants discussing their own experiences of leaving their homeland and beginning life in a new country. Then, in small groups, discuss how the interviews help you understand the poem and its speaker. After your discussion, prepare a summary of your conversation to share with the whole class.
4. **Connection.** Despite the speaker's repeated references to leaving the past behind, he or she has saved artifacts such as the letters and the shawl. List some items from your own past, such as trophies, stuffed animals, or pieces of jewelry, that you have not let go of because they hold some meaning for you. Why have you kept them? What meaning do they hold for you?
5. **Research.** Research a nonfiction account of a family immigrating to the United States and compare it with the speaker's experiences. Despite differences in country of origin or time period, what similarities exist across the experiences of all immigrants?

America, Say My Name (nonfiction)

Viet Thanh Nguyen

BeBe Jacobs/Courtesy Viet Thanh Nguyen

Viet Thanh Nguyen (b. 1971) came to America in 1975 as a Vietnamese refugee and settled with his family in Pennsylvania. Nguyen earned a Ph.D. in English from UC Berkeley and currently teaches at the University of Southern California. He has authored seven books, including *The Sympathizer* (2015), which won the Pulitzer Prize for fiction. Nguyen is also a contributing opinion writer for the *New York Times*, where this piece was first published, and the editor of the *Displaced: Refugee Writers on Refugee Lives* (2018).

FOCUS FOR READING Throughout this chapter, you have been reading poems and short stories about the nature of culture and how people interact with those of different cultures. Unlike those other texts, the following is a work of nonfiction, an editorial published in a newspaper. As you read the editorial, consider how Nguyen uses evidence, appeals, style, and other rhetorical elements to explore the idea of culture.

LOS ANGELES — What's your name? Mine is Viet Thanh Nguyen, although I was born in Vietnam as Nguyen Thanh Viet. Whichever way you arrange my name, it is not a typical American name. Growing up in the United States, I was encouraged by generations of American tradition to believe that it was normal, desirable and practical to adopt an American first name, and even to change one's surname to an American one.

Of course, that raises the question — what exactly is an American name?

When my Vietnamese parents became American citizens, they took the pragmatic route and changed their names to Joseph and Linda. My adolescent self was shocked. Were these the same people who had told me, repeatedly, that I was "100 percent Vietnamese?"

They asked me if I wanted to change my name. There was good reason for me to change my name, for throughout my childhood my classmates had teased me by asking if my last name was Nam. As in "Viet Nam." Get it? The autocorrect function on the iPhone certainly thinks so, as I still sometimes get messages — from friends — addressed to Viet Nam.

I tried on various names. I did not want 5
anything too typical, like my Catholic baptismal name, Joseph. Or Joe. Or Joey. I wanted something just a little bit different, like me. How about — Troy?

It didn't work. That name, or any of the other contenders, seemed alien to me. My parents' constant reminder that I was 100 percent Vietnamese had worked its magic. I felt some kind of psychic connection to Vietnam, the country where I was born but that I remembered not at all, having left at age 4. This psychic tie was ironic, because my fellow Vietnamese refugees in San Jose, Calif., of the 1980s — who never called themselves Americans — would describe me as completely Americanized. A whitewash. A banana, yellow on the outside, white on the inside.

If I were indeed a banana, many other Americans probably just saw the yellow part and not the soft whiteness inside. The dilemma of being caught in between opposing cultures was hardly new and has not gone away, but it was still difficult for me and everyone else who has had to experience it.

I was hardly reassured when I went on a field trip to the Defense Language Institute in Monterey and a pleasant young white American soldier, dressed in Vietnamese garb and fluent in Vietnamese, translated my Vietnamese name into a kind of American equivalent: Bruce Smith.

The Smith part was a good translation, as Nguyen is the most common Vietnamese surname, inherited from a royal dynasty. In Australia, where many of the refugees went, Nguyen is among the most common surnames. I wonder if the Australians have figured out how to pronounce my name in all of its tonal beauty. In the United States, most Vietnamese-Americans, tired of explaining, simply tell other Americans to say the name as "Win," leading to many puns about win-win situations.

10 As for Bruce, I think George might have been more accurate. Viet is the name of the people, and George is the father of the country. Or maybe America itself should be my first name, after Amerigo Vespucci, the cartographer whose first name — Americus in Latin — has become a part of all our American identities.

Or maybe, instead of contorting myself through translation — which comes from the Latin word meaning to "carry across," as my parents carried me across the Pacific — I should simply be Viet.

That, in the end, was the choice I made. Not to change. Not to translate. Not, in this one instance, to adapt to America. It was true that I was born in Vietnam but made in America. Or remade. But even if I had already become an American by the time I took my oath of citizenship, I refused to take this step of changing my name.

Instead, I knew intuitively what I would one day know explicitly: that I would make Americans say my name. I felt, intuitively, that changing my name was a betrayal, as the act of translation itself carries within it the potential for betrayal, of getting things wrong, deliberately or otherwise. A betrayal of my parents, even if they had left it open to me to change my name; a betrayal of being Vietnamese, even if many Vietnamese people were ambivalent about me. A betrayal, ultimately, of me.

I render no judgment on people who change their names. We all make and remake our own selves. But neither should there be judgment on people who do not change their names, who insist on being themselves, even if their names induce dyslexia on the part of some Americans. My surname is consistently misspelled as Ngyuen or Nyugen — even in publications that publish me.

15 In Starbucks and other coffee shops, my first name is often misspelled by the barista as Biet or Diet. I have been tempted to adopt a Starbucks name, as my friend Thuy Vo Dang puts it, to make my life easier. Hers was Tina. Mine was Joe. I said it once to a barista and was instantly ashamed of myself.

Never did I do that again. I wanted everyone to hear the barista say my name. Publicly claiming a name is one small way to take what is private, what might be shameful or embarrassing, and change its meaning. We begin at some place like Starbucks, which is itself an unusual name, derived from a character in "Moby Dick," itself an unusual name. Starbucks and Moby Dick are a part of the American lexicon and mythology. So can all of our names, no matter their origins, be a part of this country. All we have to do is proudly and publicly assert them.

Recently I visited Phillips Exeter Academy, a once all-white institution founded in 1781 whose population is now about 20 percent Asian. In front of the entire student body, a student described

extending beyond the text

In "Did Ellis Island Officials Really Change the Names of Immigrants?" Alicia Ault counters the belief that officials at Ellis Island "altered birth names of the weary immigrants" and explores conditions that helped perpetuate the myth.

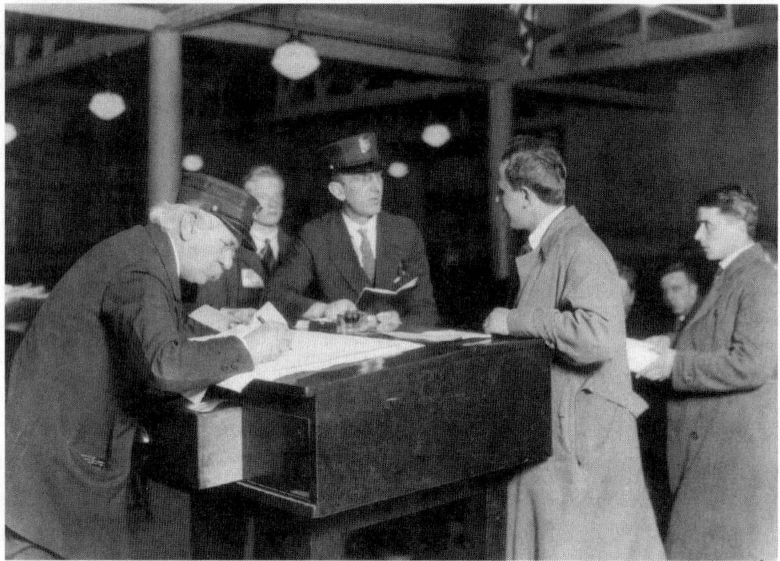

Lewis W. Hine/Getty Images

from **Did Ellis Island Officials Really Change the Names of Immigrants?**

Alicia Ault

> [According to National Park Service Ranger Peter Urban], [t]he 500 or so employees at the station had to work quickly during those first waves of immigration, processing each immigrant in a matter of 4 to 7 hours. The inspectors interviewed 400 to 500 people a day . . . during the height of the flow.

Despite the number of people entering the United States through Ellis Island, most names were taken from the ships' manifests and not from the immigrants themselves.

The question of changing or maintaining immigrants' names is firmly rooted in the history of America. Do you suppose that Viet Thanh Nguyen's life would have been easier if the government had changed his name?

how he dreaded introducing himself when he was growing up and made up nicknames for himself so that he would not have to explain his name's pronunciation. He asked me what I would say to people struggling to hold on to their names.

"What's your name?" I asked.

"Yaseen," he said.

20 I told him that his name was beautiful, that his parents gave it to him out of love. I told him about the name I gave my son, Ellison, whom I

named after the novelist Ralph Waldo Ellison, who was named after Ralph Waldo Emerson. I claimed for my son an American genealogy that was also an African-American genealogy that, through me and my son, would also be a Vietnamese-American genealogy. Ellison Nguyen, a name that compressed all of our painful, aspirational history as a country.

America, too, is a name. A name that citizens and residents of the United States have taken for themselves, a name that is mythical or maligned around the world, a name that causes endless frustration for all those other Americans, from North to South, from Canada to Chile, who are not a part of the United States. A complicated name, as all names are, if we trace them back far enough.

Yaseen. Ellison. Viet. Nguyen. All American names, if we want them to be. All of them a reminder that we change these United States of America one name at a time. ■

Understanding and Interpreting

1. In the third paragraph, what contradiction does Nguyen identify between his parents' actions and their claim that he is "100 percent Vietnamese"?
2. Nguyen details a common experience among immigrants who enter a new country at a young age. What is the irony in the "psychic tie" he mentions in paragraph 6?
3. The meanings and ideas attached to names are typically considered when selecting a name. According to Nguyen, how are the names George and Viet related?
4. How would changing his name be an act of betrayal of himself (par. 12)? What does this statement reveal about Nguyen's thoughts on culture and identity?
5. Paraphrase Nguyen's assertion about "[p]ublicly claiming a name" in paragraph 15. What does Nguyen suggest about the importance of publicly claiming a name?
6. According to Nguyen, how can Yaseen, Ellison, Viet, and Nguyen all be American names? What assumption is Nguyen making about the reader's assessment of American names by making his assertion in the last paragraph?

Analyzing Style, Language, and Structure

1. **Vocabulary in Context.** What does the word "translation" mean in the context of this essay? Note that Nguyen uses the term in multiple ways. Identify these uses and explain how they are central to this text.
2. The opening question in this essay, "What's your name?," is often a friendly way to begin a conversation with a stranger. How does the article maintain or depart from that intention by engaging with the reader directly in this way? In other words, what is the effect of beginning this essay in this manner, knowing that Nguyen's ultimate goal is to convey a cultural critique?
3. In paragraph 5, Nguyen states that he "tried on" several names, as someone might experiment with clothes. To what is he referring? What does this suggest about how the general American culture treats people of diverse backgrounds?
4. Summarize Nguyen's discussion of the word "banana" (pars. 6–7). How does this discussion relate to Nguyen's intended message about cultural differences?
5. Nguyen's style throughout this passage is conversational. Identify the choices that contribute to this writing style. Why do you think Nguyen adopted it to communicate his message about accepting different cultures in America?

Topics for Composing

1. **Analyze.** Analyze the rhetorical choices Nguyen makes to convey his claim about diverse names in America. In your analysis, consider the role that structure, evidence, and tone play to support his position regarding names.
2. **Argument.** Consider the various reasons why people might choose to change or keep their given names, along with the ramifications of that decision. Do the benefits of taking control of your own name outweigh the impact of rejecting your given name? Explore how this decision might impact your life with your family and society at large. Make sure to refer to Nguyen's observations about this topic in your argument.
3. **Connection.** Reflect on your full name and how people regularly refer to you. Do you have a nickname (or more than one)? If so, who uses this nickname? What does that use reveal about that person's relationship to you? Is there a way that people refer to you that you dislike? Why?
4. **Connection.** Choose a character from another text in this chapter, or from an outside text, who wrestles with names and identity. How does that character's philosophy about naming align with or depart from Nguyen's?
5. **Speaking and Listening.** Nguyen says that "the act of translation itself carries within it the potential for betrayal" (par. 12). In small groups, discuss what he means by this statement. Determine the extent to which each of you agrees with his position.
6. **Research.** Nguyen attempts to offer a viable explanation or translation of his name to provide a broader context of its meaning. Research the meaning and origin of your first and last names. To what degree does your name's meaning align with your character? How does knowing this information influence how you perceive your individual or family identity?
7. **Multimodal.** Some names, especially those of celebrities, are bigger than just an identifier — they are a brand. Examples include LeBron and Oprah. Create a brand for your own identity. Design a logo that reflects your brand's identity and values.

Writing an Analysis of a Poem's Speaker

From the initial drafts to the final versions of poems, poets engage in deliberate decision-making to elicit specific emotional and intellectual responses from their readers. Since every literary tool is at the poet's disposal, it is the task of a careful reader to consider the poem's meaning by examining its language and structure. While the "literary analysis paper" is a typical school assignment in high school and college, it is not one regularly seen in the real world outside of school. Unlike argumentative writing or personal narrative, poetry analysis isn't something you usually read, except in very specialized journals. So, why do your teachers regularly assign this type of writing? When writing about literature, you argue that your interpretation is reasonable and valuable, and you support your argument with evidence from the text. More than anything else, a poetry analysis essay is a way for you and your teachers to assess the ways that you think and for you to demonstrate your understanding and your ability to communicate that understanding clearly.

Throughout this workshop, you will be writing an essay in response to the following prompt:

> *Choose a poem that you read in this chapter, or from another source, that has a clearly identifiable speaker. Write an essay in which you explain how the author uses poetic elements and techniques to develop a complex portrayal of the poem's speaker and reveal a theme of the poem.*

Essentially, this prompt presents you with three tasks:

1. Provide a characterization of the poem's speaker.
2. Determine how the poem's language serves to convey a complex portrayal of the speaker.
3. Connect the character of the speaker to the meaning of the poem: the theme.

To help you think about analyzing the poem you choose, we will use this chapter's Central Text, Eavan Boland's "An Irish Childhood in England: 1951," to model the steps involved in writing this type of essay. This poem, like the one you will choose, has a clearly identifiable speaker — in this case, a speaker who discusses the impact of moving from Ireland to England when she was a child.

Step 1: Gathering Ideas

Some student writers admit that they don't prepare to write. Instead, they sit in front of a screen or a sheet of paper and write whatever comes to mind. That can be a helpful step for generating ideas, but it shouldn't be the final product. Also, there are times (for example, on a standardized test) when you may have to write very quickly with little planning time. Practicing a slower approach in this workshop, however, can help you feel prepared for any scenario. In this step of the workshop, we will take the time to read carefully, make observations, and find a focus for writing.

Reading Closely

To analyze a poem, we must first take the time to read and reread it — using annotations to make connections and ask questions. Our notes should reflect our growing understanding of poetic techniques, questions, or ideas that emerge as we read, along with the lessons we learned in the Skill Workshop of this chapter. Annotations of Eavan Boland's poem "An Irish Childhood in England: 1951" might look like this:

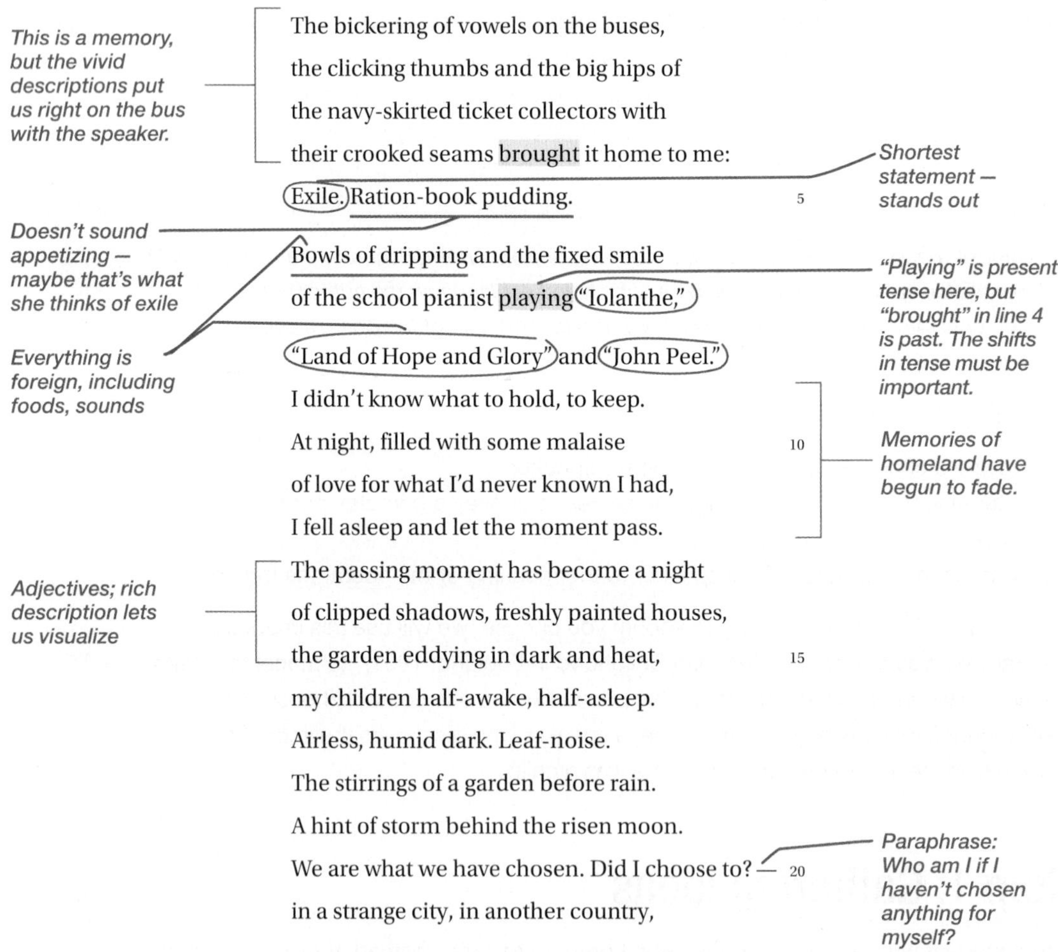
The bickering of vowels on the buses,
the clicking thumbs and the big hips of
the navy-skirted ticket collectors with
their crooked seams brought it home to me:
Exile. Ration-book pudding.
Bowls of dripping and the fixed smile
of the school pianist playing "Iolanthe,"
"Land of Hope and Glory" and "John Peel."
I didn't know what to hold, to keep.
At night, filled with some malaise
of love for what I'd never known I had,
I fell asleep and let the moment pass.
The passing moment has become a night
of clipped shadows, freshly painted houses,
the garden eddying in dark and heat,
my children half-awake, half-asleep.
Airless, humid dark. Leaf-noise.
The stirrings of a garden before rain.
A hint of storm behind the risen moon.
We are what we have chosen. Did I choose to?
in a strange city, in another country,

on nights in a north-facing bedroom,
waiting for the sleep that never did
restore me as I'd hoped to what I'd lost—
let the world I knew become the space
between the words that I had by heart
and all the other speech that always was
becoming the language of the country that
I came to in nineteen fifty-one:
barely-gelled, a freckled six-year-old,
overdressed and sick on the plane,
when all of England to an Irish child
was nothing more than what you'd lost and how:
was the teacher in the London convent who,
when I produced "I amn't" in the classroom
turned and said—"You're not in Ireland now."

She focuses on what she has lost through exile.

Poem shifts tense from the past (a child's experience) to the present (an adult's recollection); feelings of loss

Language difference: distance between the speaker and her new environment

Reading Closely

Look back through the poems in this chapter or through poems you have read on your own and select a poem with which you connect and which has an identifiable speaker.

When you have decided on a poem, read it twice — first to make sure you understand it and then to determine how the poet's language develops the speaker and how our understanding of speaker leads to theme. Make notes like those in the preceding sample as you proceed through the following steps:

1. What is literally happening in the poem? Perhaps write stanza-by-stanza summaries.
2. Annotate the poem by asking questions and noting examples of figurative language, syntax, sound devices, and other poetic elements.
3. Identify key moments, words, and phrases that shed light on the poem's speaker.
4. Identify where the poem shift(s). How does the poem shift? Keep in mind setting, time frame, and tone.

Finding a Focus

While making detailed annotations is helpful in analyzing a poem, a vast collection of notes can be daunting. Before beginning to write the essay, we need to find patterns or observations in our notes that help to reveal insights about the poem's speaker.

Here are some initial thoughts on Boland's speaker:

- The title establishes that the speaker is an Irish child who grows up in England.
- The first four lines present the clash between the sounds of her native Ireland and those of England.
- The concise "Exile" in line 5 proclaims the child's sense of displacement.
- The speaker is trying to remember her past in lines 9 to 12, but her years in Ireland are fading from her memory.
- "We are what we have chosen" (l. 20) is an aphorism, or a short statement of truth. The speaker finds this difficult to accept because she does not feel like she has had the power to choose anything for herself.
- The interaction with the teacher (ll. 34–36) devalues the speaker's linguistic tie to Ireland and demands that she begin to act differently.
- Shifts in verb tense in lines 7 and 29 present us with both the child's perspective at the moment of exile and her adult stance on the repercussions of that exile.

Although we have not cemented our understanding of the speaker, we have made strong observations that can help us narrow down our analysis.

Finding a Focus

Return to the poem that you selected for your analysis, looking carefully at the annotations you made. Consider the following:

- What common patterns or trends have you seen at this point?
- What do you notice about the speaker at the beginning, middle, and end of the poem?
- Describe the significant shifts in setting, time frame, and tone.
- How does the poet use figurative language, imagery, and word choice to develop the speaker?
- How does your understanding of the speaker lead you to a possible theme?

If you have trouble locating a focus, perhaps you should select a different poem at this time.

Step 2: Planning the Essay

Before we begin writing the essay, let's take a moment to ensure that we have a clear sense of the essay's focus — or thesis — and the evidence we'll need to include to support that thesis. In this step, we'll also consider possible organizational structures that are appropriate for this particular essay.

Drafting a Thesis Statement

When developing a thesis statement, it's necessary to introduce the idea you will explore and take an interpretive stance on it. Don't just tell readers the focus of your essay; tell them your position on that topic as well. Having an effective thesis clarifies your thinking and sets up a strong argument for your analysis. As we've seen throughout this chapter, poetry is complex and multifaceted. Many people can read the same poem and arrive at different interpretations. Therefore, your thesis should be unique to you and your ideas about the poem.

For the topic we have been exploring, we might write a thesis like the following:

WEAK THESIS

In this essay, I will discuss how Boland presents the speaker in the poem "An Irish Childhood in England: 1951."

This thesis relates to the given prompt, but it does not take a stance. The purpose of a thesis is not simply to skim the surface of the task, but rather to make a claim that asserts a position. In other words, for the sake of this prompt, we must define the speaker's character, identify what makes a character complex, and consider how language serves to convey the complexities of the speaker. Here is another take on the thesis:

WEAK THESIS

The speaker in "An Irish Childhood in England: 1951" left her homeland and must now live in England.

While this thesis centers on the speaker, it summarizes more than it analyzes. Based on this thesis, we still do not understand the nature of the young child and her reaction to exile.

WORKING THESIS

The speaker in Eavan Boland's poem "An Irish Childhood in England: 1951" reflects on the loss of identity produced by exile, shifting between the painful memories of the past and the lasting impact in the present.

This thesis provides a notion of how the speaker feels as she is forced to live in a new country. We also get a hint that the writer is going to discuss shifts in the poem. Furthermore, it suggests a theme of the poem: that exile produces a sense of loss that is felt throughout a person's life.

You might be thinking that this thesis is quite long. The length of the thesis reflects the complexity of the prompt. Note that the thesis does not have to list the devices that will be discussed in the essay, although that would be another acceptable approach. There are, after all, many versions of this working thesis that could lead to a successful essay.

Drafting Your Thesis Statement

Using the poem that you selected, write a working thesis that analyzes the complexities of the speaker and takes an interpretive stance on the meaning of that poem. Remember that your thesis should introduce the idea you want to explore and take a position on that idea. A strong thesis is unique to the poem you are analyzing. Remember that reasonable people could disagree with the position you take.

Gathering Support

Before selecting the textual support that you'll include in your essay, make sure you understand the demands of your thesis. For example, based on our working thesis, what exactly do we need to prove? Let's look back at our thesis:

WORKING THESIS

The speaker in Eavan Boland's poem "An Irish Childhood in England: 1951" reflects on the loss of identity produced by exile, shifting between the painful memories of the past and the lasting impact in the present.

There are several points in this thesis that need to be proven:

Point 1: The speaker of "An Irish Childhood in England: 1951" struggles with a loss of identity.
Point 2: These feelings affect the speaker when she first becomes exiled and into adulthood.
Point 3: The time shifts in the poem relate to the lasting impact of exile.
Point 4: Boland's poem is about the short-term and long-term effects that exile has on individuals in general.

As you gather evidence, consider how the quotations relate to your thesis and the points that are embedded within it.

One way to make sure you are connecting your quotation to your thesis is with a chart like this. It will help make the connection clear and enable you to think through the purpose of each quotation and how it connects to your larger point.

Quotation	How the quotation supports my point
"We are what we have chosen. Did I choose to?—"	The speaker recognizes that human identity is comprised of the collective choices made in life. However, the speaker wonders if she has ever truly chosen her path or if she is driven by the decisions made for her.

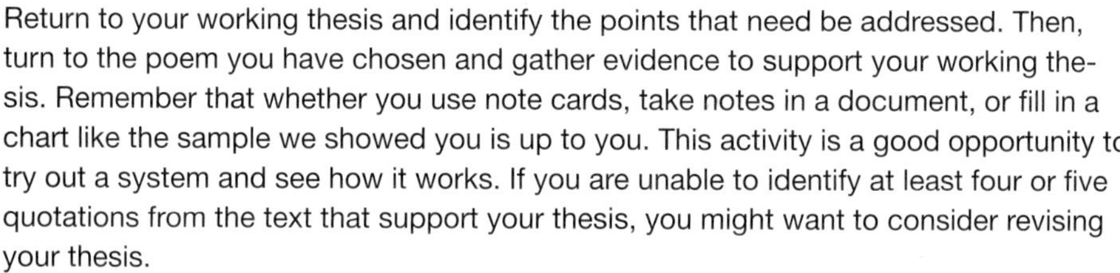

Gathering Support

Return to your working thesis and identify the points that need be addressed. Then, turn to the poem you have chosen and gather evidence to support your working thesis. Remember that whether you use note cards, take notes in a document, or fill in a chart like the sample we showed you is up to you. This activity is a good opportunity to try out a system and see how it works. If you are unable to identify at least four or five quotations from the text that support your thesis, you might want to consider revising your thesis.

Organizing the Essay

As we discussed earlier, effective essay-writing requires careful planning and a systematic approach. Now that we have developed a thesis statement, defined the points that need to be proven in the essay, and gathered appropriate textual evidence, we need to consider the order in which we'll present this information.

For a poetry analysis essay, you might consider some of the following organizational structures:

- **Organize by sequential analysis:** With this approach, you delve into the interpretation of the poem following the order of the poetic lines. You might not analyze each line, but you would interpret sets of lines that go together, from the beginning to the end of the poem. Sometimes this means that you'll analyze the first stanza, followed by the second, and so forth. At other times, you might identify beginning, middle, and ending segments around which to organize your analysis.
- **Organize by poetic devices:** With this approach, you structure your essay based on the various poetic techniques that you'll discuss in support of your thesis. For instance, one paragraph might discuss the role of imagery while another paragraph might focus on the role of sound devices in the poem.
- **Organize by points of analysis:** A more complex approach is the development of an essay based on the ideas that are derived from your thesis. For example, if we turn to the four points we identified based on our thesis (p. 548), we can use each one to develop a topic sentence for each of our body paragraphs.

Organizing Your Essay

Review the three organizational structures discussed and consider which one might work best for your essay. Sketch an outline for the body of your essay based on the structure you selected. As you complete this activity, you might decide that a different structure is best suited for your essay. At that point, sketch a new outline.

Step 3: Drafting the Essay

At this point in the workshop, you have fully annotated the poem, developed your thesis, gathered evidence, and selected an organizational structure for your essay. This next section will guide you through the development of the body paragraphs, as well as the introduction and conclusion of your essay.

Drafting Body Paragraphs

When you present your ideas in a body paragraph, you must include a topic sentence and textual evidence and provide commentary that explains how the two are connected. A body paragraph for our sample analysis of Boland's poem might look like the following:

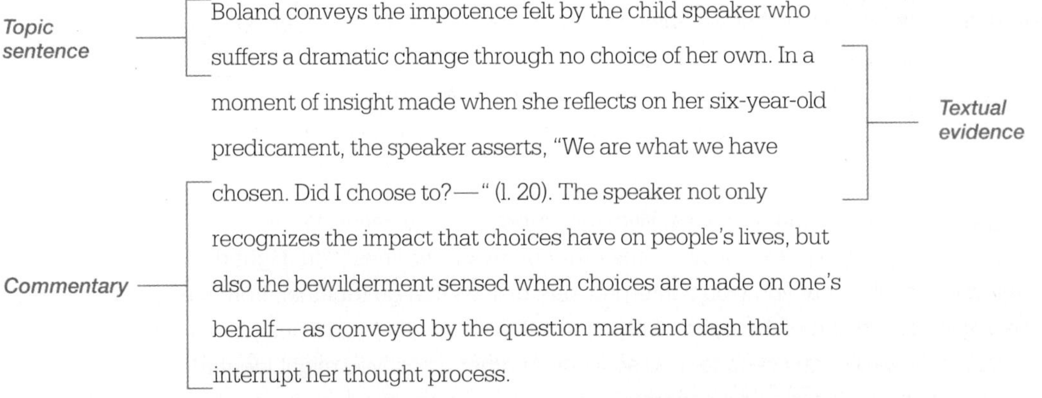

Boland conveys the impotence felt by the child speaker who suffers a dramatic change through no choice of her own. In a moment of insight made when she reflects on her six-year-old predicament, the speaker asserts, "We are what we have chosen. Did I choose to?—" (l. 20). The speaker not only recognizes the impact that choices have on people's lives, but also the bewilderment sensed when choices are made on one's behalf—as conveyed by the question mark and dash that interrupt her thought process.

What we have created here is a short but focused analytical paragraph. If we make other claims related to our topic sentence, find additional textual evidence to support these claims, and provide further commentary, we can extend the complexity of the paragraph. A body paragraph that requires further textual evidence to fully support the topic sentence might look like the following:

Topic Sentence

Boland conveys the impotence felt by the child speaker who suffers a dramatic change through no choice of her own. In a

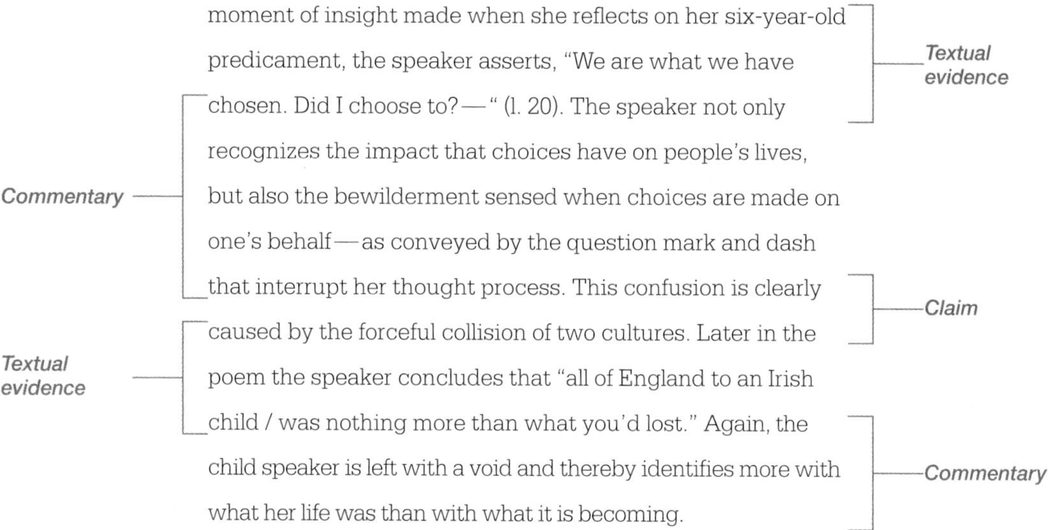

moment of insight made when she reflects on her six-year-old predicament, the speaker asserts, "We are what we have chosen. Did I choose to?—" (l. 20). The speaker not only recognizes the impact that choices have on people's lives, but also the bewilderment sensed when choices are made on one's behalf—as conveyed by the question mark and dash that interrupt her thought process. This confusion is clearly caused by the forceful collision of two cultures. Later in the poem the speaker concludes that "all of England to an Irish child / was nothing more than what you'd lost." Again, the child speaker is left with a void and thereby identifies more with what her life was than with what it is becoming.

If we look back to page 548, the second point of our working thesis is this: These feelings affect the speaker when she first becomes exiled and into adulthood. If we were to follow the same steps we took when writing the body paragraph shown above, we would have a second body paragraph that opens with a topic sentence, uses supporting evidence to prove this point, and provides commentary. Another body paragraph would include those same key pieces and address shifts in the poem that signal the lasting effects of exile. There is no set number of body paragraphs that an essay must have. We determine the length of this section of our essay by focusing on the demands of our thesis. A good way of thinking about this is to ask ourselves the following question: How many points, or ideas, does the thesis require we discuss to fully support its claim?

Drafting Body Paragraphs

Using the steps delineated above as a guide, draft a body paragraph for your own working thesis. Make sure that it states one of your points in a topic sentence, incorporates at least two pieces of textual evidence, and explains how the evidence supports your claim. This last part — the analysis or commentary — is the most important part of your paragraph; be sure to keep your interpretation at the forefront of your writing. Show a draft of the body paragraph to a classmate to get feedback on how well you have used your evidence and commentary to support your topic sentence and how well these components align with your thesis. Then, draft the remaining body paragraphs needed to fully support your thesis. Remember to organize these paragraphs according to the structure you identified earlier in this workshop (p. 550). Be sure that each body paragraph includes a topic sentence related to your working thesis, evidence, and commentary.

Writing the Introduction

Sometimes the hardest part of writing is thinking about how to begin your essay. This can be especially difficult when you are writing about a piece of literature. The point of the introduction is to engage your reader and to create interest in the topic. An introduction typically has the following three parts:

1. An opening hook
2. A connection to the piece being analyzed
3. Your thesis statement

The Hook

The purpose of the hook is to draw readers in and to get them thinking about the ideas or issues that are at play in your analysis. This is a great place to raise questions or identify issues.

For an essay on "An Irish Childhood in England: 1951," we might want to raise ideas about the difficulties of living in exile or about how we define who we are within the context of our choices.

Many writers will tell you that the first sentence is the hardest to write. Here are examples of how we might begin our introductory paragraph about "An Irish Childhood in England: 1951."

With a question:	How does exile impact children's views of themselves and their surroundings?
With a definition:	Professor and literary critic Edward Said defines exile as the "unhealable rift forced between a human being and a native place." He then adds that "its essential sadness can never be surmounted."
With a statement:	The effects of removing a child from her native land and forcing her to live in an environment that is neither welcoming nor respectful of her origin can be devastating.
With a story or anecdote:	I can still recall my first day at school in America when the teacher addressed me using words that were incomprehensible to me. Assuming that she had asked me for my name, I answered accordingly. I was clearly mistaken, as what ensued were the laughter and jeers of my classmates.

Connection to the Piece

Once we have a hook, it's time to show our readers how the ideas we've brought up apply to the poem we are about to analyze. This transition doesn't have to be elaborate. It's usually a simple connecting statement that might include a brief summary of the poem and the author and title. It should lead the reader smoothly into the thesis statement. Putting all of the pieces together, here's what a sample introduction paragraph could look like:

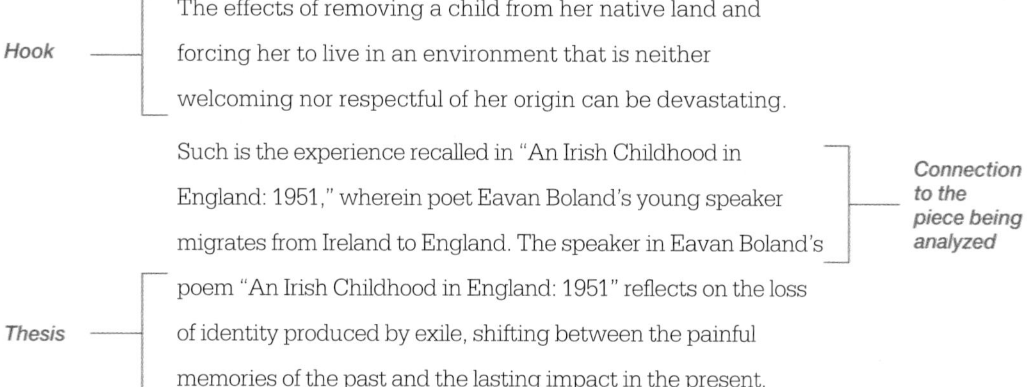
Hook — The effects of removing a child from her native land and forcing her to live in an environment that is neither welcoming nor respectful of her origin can be devastating.

Such is the experience recalled in "An Irish Childhood in England: 1951," wherein poet Eavan Boland's young speaker migrates from Ireland to England. — Connection to the piece being analyzed

Thesis — The speaker in Eavan Boland's poem "An Irish Childhood in England: 1951" reflects on the loss of identity produced by exile, shifting between the painful memories of the past and the lasting impact in the present.

The Thesis

Since you've already worked on your thesis, incorporating it into a paragraph will give you an additional opportunity to edit and revise it. Generally, the thesis appears at the end of the introduction.

Writing Your Introduction

Following the model above, write a draft of your introduction. Think about the way you want to hook the reader and how you want to lead into your thesis statement with a connecting statement that includes the author and title.

Writing the Conclusion

Effective conclusions provide closure by reasserting the thesis and main points of the essay. Instead of simply repeating yourself as you rephrase your thesis and findings, make sure to convey a deeper understanding of the topic. Ideally, you will present your observations within a broader context. What does your essay suggest about society, people, or the environment? The conclusion should bring completeness and closure to the reader with the satisfaction that your assertion is a sound one.

Notice how the following draft of a concluding paragraph relates to the thesis and situates the speaker's condition within the broader context of how people might react to exile:

> Eavan Boland explores the effects of exile through the perspective of a speaker whose family left Ireland for England when she was just a child. Clearly, the fear and instability she felt as a six-year-old linger into adulthood because she feels like she was stripped of the comforting elements of her homeland. For Boland, the fearful trajectory of encountering a new culture and being aware that the past is slowly fading reflects a common and painful experience among exiles. While the little girl may have felt that this predicament was unique to her, the adult perspective reflecting on the events recognizes its universality: Exile.

Writing Your Conclusion

Write a concluding paragraph for your essay. Remember to relate it to your thesis and to the points in your body paragraphs. To add greater sophistication to your essay and possibly avoid repeating what you have already stated, connect the situation facing your poem's speaker to humanity in general.

Step 4: Finalizing the Essay

Now that you have a complete draft of your essay, you can move on to the final steps in the writing process: revising and editing. These two acts are sometimes thought of as being the same, but they're not. Revision is when you look back at large-scale structural elements of your essay, such as how well you support your claim, what kinds of evidence you are using, how effective your word choices are, and to what extent you have led your reader easily through your essay. Editing, on the other hand, focuses on fine-tuning the language, grammar, punctuation, spelling, and other conventions. Editing is usually the very last thing you do before you finalize your piece, looking carefully for any errors you may have made. The following are suggestions for you to consider as you finalize your essay.

Revising

Revising gives you a good opportunity to think again about your essay's purpose and audience. In most cases, your audience will be your teacher. In the case of a standardized test, it will be an external evaluator. In both situations, that means using a somewhat formal tone, but it doesn't have to be inorganic and formulaic.

Reread your essay for the following:

- Did you write using **present tense** verbs? Literature *lives*, so your analysis should discuss how the author *uses* literary devices and *presents* the speaker.
- Look back at your **thesis**. Since you wrote this early on in the workshop, does it still relate to the analysis you ended up writing? See Revision Workshop 1: Effective Thesis and Essay Structure (p. 1064) if you need more assistance.
- Did your **organizational structure** hold up over the course of your essay? Did you make it easy for your reader to follow your points? Look at Revision Workshop 5: Effective Transitions (p. 1082) or Revision Workshop 2: Effective Topic Sentences and Unified Paragraphs (p. 1068) if you need more assistance.

- Reread your **body paragraphs**. Have you balanced the evidence with your own **commentary** about how that evidence supports your thesis? See Revision Workshop 4: Appropriate Evidence and Support (p. 1076) if you need more assistance.
- Did you avoid overly **summarizing** the poem? You can assume some level of familiarity with the text by your reader. Although some summary may be necessary for establishing context, summary is not analysis. Look back at Chapter 2 for more help with reading literature for understanding, interpretation, and style (p. 27).
- Does your **introduction** grab the reader's attention and effectively preview your topic? Does your **conclusion** wrap up in a way that highlights your focus? If you need help, see Revision Workshop 8: Effective Introductions and Conclusions (p. 1097).

Editing

Remember, editing is the very last thing you'll do before finalizing your essay. You and your teacher know better than anyone the types of spelling, grammar, and convention errors you need to focus on in your writing development. Be sure to refer to one or more of the Grammar Workshops (starting on p. 1101) in the back of the book if you encounter an issue and aren't sure how to overcome it.

Continuing the Conversation

Throughout this chapter, you have been reading texts and thinking about culture. At the beginning of the chapter and after each of the readings, you had opportunities to consider ideas related to the following essential questions:

- How does culture shape people's perceptions of themselves and the world around them?
- What are the benefits and challenges of simultaneously belonging to two or more cultures?
- How do people adapt to new cultures?
- How do the intergenerational connections between family members evolve as cultural differences arise?

The following sections will give you an opportunity to revisit and respond to some of those questions as you think further about culture by connecting these ideas to yourself, to texts you read, and to the world outside of the classroom.

Connections to Self

Think back on the texts you have read, responses you have written, discussions you have participated in, and ideas you have considered during your work with this chapter. Use the following questions to help explore how the issues in this chapter connect to your life and experience:

1. How has your life been enhanced by interacting with people whose cultural backgrounds differ from your own?
2. How does your family's cultural heritage shape how you behave within and outside of your home?
3. Culture includes, among many factors, the foods, traditions, and languages attributed to a group of people. Which of the cultures you encountered in this chapter would you like to experience firsthand? What aspects of that culture do you find especially intriguing?
4. Which of the texts in this chapter had the most significant impact on the way you think about culture? How has your understanding of culture changed because of that text?

Connections to Texts

Use the following questions to make connections among the texts in this chapter. Consider what insights the texts provide into the concept of culture. As you respond, be sure to make specific references to **two or more texts** you read in this chapter.

1. Some of the characters in this chapter must learn to navigate multiple cultures. How is this process both challenging and enriching? You may want to consider the following texts in your response: "Dothead," "No Speak English," and "Children as Enemies."
2. A substantial age difference can create a cultural divide between individuals. List some issues that are commonly at the root of such age-related cultural clashes. You may want to consider the following texts in your response: "Choi Jeong Min," "Paths upon Water," "Children as Enemies," and "Enlightenment."
3. Immigration is a subject that arises in several of the texts in this chapter. Select two characters from two different texts and discuss the role that immigration plays in shaping their cultural identities. You may want to consider the following texts in your response: "No Speak English," "My Father in English," "An Irish Childhood in England: 1951," and "For a New Citizen of These United States."
4. Food and culture are often closely linked. Describe how food helps shape the cultural identity of characters from at least two different texts in this chapter. You may want to consider the following texts in your response: "The Tropics in New York," "Paths upon Water," "Choi Jeong Min," and "An Irish Childhood in England: 1951."

Connections to World

Think back on the texts you have read, responses you have written, discussions you have participated in, and ideas you have considered during your work with this chapter. Use the following questions to help explore how the issues in this chapter play out in the world at large:

1. Although common experiences or global issues might remind us that we are all part of a single group of people — the human race — we normally gather in distinct cultural clusters. These clusters might be based on factors such as nationality, age, ethnicity, or religion. Why do humans seek to belong to these cultural groupings?
2. How has the internet in general and social media specifically redefined the characteristics of cultures around the world? Are these changes beneficial to people, or does it rob them of their heritage?
3. What steps would have to be taken so that people could place greater emphasis on the factors that unite us, rather than on those that separate us? What could assist in this effort?
4. Which cultural aspects are most susceptible to change? Which are most resistant to it? What events or conditions might act as catalysts for change within a group's cultural practices?

Jeff Spicer/Getty Images

Our Robotic Future

Essential Questions:

- **What effect will increasing automation, including reliance on artificial intelligence (AI), have on future jobs and the economy?**
- **To what extent is it possible to have genuine social and emotional connections with robots?**
- **Should we develop legal protections for robots similar to those we have developed for animals? Should robots be granted personhood status?**
- **In what ways might robots and AI merge with or marginalize humanity? How might they improve or threaten our way of life?**
- **Should we fear a robot uprising or other dangers from robots and AI? Why or why not?**

Given the rapid advances in technology in the last thirty years, it's safe to say that automation and robots are going to be more and more a part of our lives in the future. Even in the present, we regularly encounter robots and artificial intelligence (AI). We ask Siri for directions, ask Alexa to play music, and experience online information and social media shaped by machine-learning algorithms, rather than humans. In addition, oftentimes when we enter data on a website, we have to prove to an artificially intelligent system that we, in fact, are not robots.

While science-fiction movies such as *The Terminator* and *The Matrix* have long predicted a rise of the robots that will enslave humanity, Elon Musk, the founder of Tesla and SpaceX, confirms these fears, saying that AI is our "biggest existential threat" and comparing it to "summoning the demon." Some people are concerned that even before the robots fully take over, they will be taking our jobs. For example, entrepreneur Andrew Yang predicts that "83 percent of jobs paying less than $20 per hour could have substantial parts of their work given over to automation."

And yet, we know that there can be tremendous benefits to automation and AI, as robots are being used as rescue workers, caregivers, and even as pets. Netscape founder and Silicon Valley legend Marc Andreessen envisions a far different robotic future than Musk and Yang suggest: "Since our basic needs are taken care of, all human time, labor, energy, ambition, and goals reorient to the intangibles: the big questions, the deep needs. Human nature expresses itself fully, for the first time in history."

And perhaps humanity will increasingly rely on machines until we merge with them by bits and pieces. Already the newest hearing aids are Bluetooth enabled, letting wearers stream music and answer cell phones; robotic exoskeletons allow the paralyzed to walk; and robotic prosthetics can allow amputees to play the piano.

So, the question is not *if* robots and artificial intelligence will play a role in our future, but what kind of role they will play.

Our Robotic Future

Before you dig deeper into this topic, make some notes about what you already think and know about a future with more robots, automation, and artificial intelligence (AI) by considering the following:

Benefits of more robots, automation, and AI	Drawbacks of more robots, automation, and AI	Questions about a future with more robots, automation, and AI

Consider your responses in the chart and assign a rating to your level of optimism regarding a future with more robots and AI on a scale of 1 to 10, with 10 being "extremely optimistic." Find a classmate with a rating similar to yours and compare reasons. Then, find a classmate with a far different rating from yours and discuss your reasons for your differing opinions.

Texts in Conversation

Throughout this chapter, you will read about a number of issues related to robots and artificial intelligence (AI) and their relationship with us. As you read, keep track of the authors' attitudes and claims, draw connections among them, and respond to them with your own reactions. At the end of the chapter, you'll have an opportunity to write your own piece about the roles that robots and AI ought to play in our future, using the texts you read as evidence and inspiration. You can use a graphic organizer like this if it would help you:

Author/title	Position about robots, AI, and the future?	Quotation(s) that illustrate the author's ideas about robots and AI	Your reaction and/or connection to other texts

Understanding Evidence in Argument

As you may have read in Chapter 4 on evidence-based arguments, using outside sources such as facts, statistics, data, and quotations from experts strengthens your argument. It also demonstrates that you are knowledgeable about your topic and care enough to read widely and deeply about it. In this workshop, we will walk through a sample analysis of how one writer uses outside sources to develop and support her argument. Then, you will write your own brief argument that includes the use of one or more sources.

As you read the following article by Lela London, annotate or respond to the text with questions and connections (p. 10) and keep track of the times that the author includes references to outside sources, considering how they support her argument.

This Is What the Future of Robots Might Do to Humanity

Lela London

Lela London is a journalist and lifestyle blogger. Her work has been featured in the *Telegraph*, the *Los Angeles Times*, *Forbes*, *Daily Mail*, the *Huffington Post*, and other publications. The following piece appeared in *Forbes* in 2018.

Courtesy of Lela London

The robots are coming.

Not the killer models a frenetic Will Smith and friends saw filling public service positions in cinematic 2035, but robots nonetheless.

According to new research, almost two thirds (60%) of British people believe there will be a robot in every home within the next 50 years and only a quarter of them can't imagine a life where a robot wouldn't be part of their family.

It's a far cry from the culture of precarious terminators, paranoid androids and sex robots Hollywood might have us expect.

5 The *Good Robot Report*, commissioned by consumer robotics and AI company Anki, utilised the all-encompassing genius of Envisioners CEO and futurist Dave Coplin to not only identify the current relationship between humans and robots, but how people expect to benefit from a life in tandem.

As you might expect, support with housework and chores topped the perceived benefits of robots in the home, with 27% of people thinking a home robot could save them two hours each day, but companionship followed closely behind. Almost a fifth of people said they wanted a home robot simply to keep them company.

While 13% said the arrival of a robot companion would mean they'd never feel lonely again, more than a third (38%) of people saw wider social benefits; more time to improve connections with friends and family, more time to pursue and master new interests, and more.

The inception of such robots is also much closer than you would think. Anki's first home robot with personality, Vector, is fully autonomous, cloud-connected and always on, representing a major leap forward for accessible consumer robotics we have only truly seen on the silver screen.

Anki co-founder Boris Sofman said: "The robot revolution is happening. It was never going to be a single binary event and, with AI advances, it becomes more and more prevalent in our lives.

"Robots exist, but not as we think of them traditionally. There are so many expanding capabilities, so fast — the catalyst for the revolution is how they come into people's lives. There is an IQ side and an EQ side, so we have to feel comfortable before we really start seeing the robots of the future.

"There is still an uncertainty, but Vector is a key step in changing the perception. There is something transformative about him — instead of using a mobile device and being user-reliant like most consumer robots, he essentially has a smartphone in his head. It's game-changing.

"It could be as little as 5–10 years until we see the robots become *robots*. Like driverless cars — autonomous driving started with construction and military technology. Most of what needs to be utilised already exists.

"Think about how little time it took for mobile phones to become what we know and expect of it today. What Roomba [the consumer robot vacuum] did for cleaning. It's all happening in robotics, too."

Envisioners CEO Dave Coplin said: "The analogy of driverless cars is perfect. We may not have had full autonomy with cruise control, but the technology was there. [With] robotics [we] are experiencing the same progression.

"Think about it, 97% of people in the UK have a washing machine in their home. That's a robot. People ask their speakers and phones questions, and receive intelligent answers. That's AI."

The advancements don't excite unanimous anticipation, of course. The report also reveals that 36% of people fear robots might be hacked and turned against us, 31% worry that robots would cause them to lose their jobs, and 27% fear robots could rise up and take over.

Coplin continued: "The things I'm really worried about is pop culture and the dystopian view of robots. We need better role models and an informed conversation to understand Anki's vision: that robots are something to aspire to, not be frightened of.

"We need a pragmatic and optimistic approach to robots. If you look back over history we've got more meaningful work done by challenging fears and creating new technology. For my grandmother, laundry was a big task. She'd need to get water, boil it, wash and dry by hand . . . now we flip a switch.

"Robots have the ability to take care of the robotic parts of our lives."

Robotic, and otherwise. Just this week a cafe in Tokyo launched service from robot waiters remotely controlled by people with severe physical disabilities. The 4ft Minato Ward robots are controlled by people with conditions such as amyotrophic lateral sclerosis (ALS — a form of motor neuron disease), helping them do the jobs they simply wouldn't be able to otherwise.

Sofman said: "The possibilities are endless. I mean, how many people get cats for emotional utility? The difference with robots is that it doesn't stop there. Robots like Vector have function and utility far beyond normal companionship.

"Imagine a companion also knowing what news events you would be interested in, how to update you on your sports team, tell you when you have a message from your husband or wife, or even diagnosing medical problems so both yourself and doctors save time. Nothing in AI is fully cognizant at the moment — it's programmatic feeling and optimised algorithms. But that alone has incredible potential.

"There are isolated industries that can be hurt as major technology is implemented, but the whole society benefits. We can't stop progress. The PC taught us that and no one can imagine life without it."

When all is said and done, co-existing with the robots of the future might just make us greater than the sum of our parts — mortal and otherwise. ■

Making a Claim

As you may have read in Chapter 3, one of the most important components of an argument, even one that uses outside sources, is its claim, the central point the writer or speaker is trying to prove to the audience. While London certainly covers a lot of different topics, her main claim could probably be identified by what she says at the very end of her article: "When all is said and done, co-existing with the robots of the future might just make us greater than the sum of our parts." She clearly believes that robots will benefit humanity in a wide variety of ways, and she supports her claim with lots of evidence from experts and statistics.

Making a Claim

activity

1. Consider the following prompts about how technology should or should not be used in school. Respond to as many prompts as needed to help you identify a topic you would like to work with:
   - Should student use of personal smart devices (phones or watches) be banned or restricted in schools?
   - Should facial recognition, through artificial intelligence (AI), be employed in school settings for student safety?
   - Should student work be completed primarily with laptops and tablets instead of pen and paper?
   - Could automation and AI replace your teachers?
   - Should students be required to take classes in robotics and computer programming?
   - To what extent can the work that you do in school be completed by a robot?
2. Once you have identified a possible topic, write a draft of a claim about the topic. In other words, what point do you want to prove to your audience?

Using Expert Opinion to Support a Position

When writers use outside sources to support their claim, they can draw from various types of evidence, including expert opinion, facts, data, statistics, and scholarly research studies. As you read the article by London, you probably noticed that she uses a number of these evidence types to support her claim about how robots will benefit humanity. For example, look at the following excerpt:

> The inception of such robots is also much closer than you would think. Anki's first home robot with personality, Vector, is fully autonomous, cloud-connected and always on, representing a major leap forward for accessible consumer robotics we have only truly seen on the silver screen.
>
> Anki co-founder Boris Sofman said: "The robot revolution is happening. It was never going to be a single binary event and, with AI advances, it becomes more and more prevalent in our lives."

London makes the point that autonomous robot technology is pretty far along. To help make her case, she cites an expert in the field, Boris Sofman, whom she identifies as the co-founder of Anki, a robot manufacturer. London might believe exactly the same thing as Sofman, but citing him bolsters her own claim and demonstrates that she is not merely stating her opinion. This is the benefit of using outside sources — expert opinion, in this case — to support an argument.

Supporting a Position with Expert Opinion

Return to the claim that you wrote in response to the activity on page 563. That claim is currently unsupported by outside sources. However, you should now locate people in your class who can provide informed opinions about your topic (people who take a robotics or computer programming class, for example), ask them for their expert opinion, and write a sentence or two that takes into account their ideas on the topic.

Using Additional Evidence to Support a Position

Expert opinion is only one type of outside evidence you can use. When London argues that people's perceptions about robots are more positive than what Hollywood has presented, she relies on data for support:

> *The Good Robot Report*, commissioned by consumer robotics and AI company Anki, utilized the all-encompassing genius of Envisioners CEO and futurist Dave Coplin to not only identify the current relationship between humans and robots, but how people expect to benefit from a life in tandem.
>
> As you might expect, support with housework and chores topped the perceived benefits of robots in the home, with 27% of people thinking a home robot could save them two hours each day, but companionship followed closely behind. Almost a fifth of people said they wanted a home robot simply to keep them company.

Notice how she references the data from *The Good Robot Report*, which focuses on positive expectations related to robot involvement in housework and friendship. Again, her own opinion is supported by an outside source, this time a published report.

Supporting a Position with Additional Evidence

Return to the topic you have been thinking about for your own argument, to which you added the expert opinion of one or more classmates. Conduct brief research to locate an additional piece of evidence or two that might support your claim. In addition to further expert opinion, other possible types of evidence include data, statistics, and scholarly research (p. 89).

Avoiding Pitfalls of Using Outside Sources

Of course, including outside sources in an argument does not guarantee that the point will be proven. It helps to be prepared to analyze and critique potential sources, when appropriate. If, for example, you are arguing that teachers cannot be replaced with robots, and you ask teachers to lend their expert opinion, you might find that their responses are along the lines of "No, thank you!" Because the use of robot teachers in the classroom would probably mean that some human teachers would lose their jobs, and because teachers value their work, you would have trouble eliciting objective responses from teachers on this point. Their testimony, though relevant, would not be enough to persuade readers; you would need to integrate additional supporting evidence from more objective sources. So, when we look at how a writer uses sources to support an argument, we need to determine whether that evidence is **relevant** (related to the topic), **credible** (trustworthy), and **sufficient** (enough to prove the claim).

Let's look back at that section from London's article that included the expert testimony:

> The inception of such robots is also much closer than you would think. Anki's first home robot with personality, Vector, is fully autonomous, cloud-connected and always on, representing a major leap forward for accessible consumer robotics we have only truly seen on the silver screen.
>
> Anki co-founder Boris Sofman said: "The robot revolution is happening. It was never going to be a single binary event and, with AI advances, it becomes more and more prevalent in our lives."

As readers, we absolutely should be wondering if Sofman is credible on this topic. We know he's an expert, but is he trustworthy? His company, Anki, is banking on the idea that robots will be more prevalent in the future. Because his company would benefit from increased consumer interest in robots and AI, his position is likely biased, not objective. Do his conflicts of interest automatically make his opinion untrustworthy? Probably not. But, as a reader, you should be wondering if London could identify more objective sources to support her argument. And what about that research study, *The Good Robot Report*, that London references? Did you notice that she said it was "commissioned by consumer robotics and AI company Anki"? In other words, the study was paid for and analyzed by a robot manufacturer. Again, as a reader, you should question the credibility of the study, especially if its results are not also paired with, say, a study conducted by a university or the government, which is likely to be more objective.

In addition to credibility, you should also pay attention to the relevance of the evidence. For example, if you are writing about the use of facial recognition software in schools, and you include research from a Stanford University study of facial recognition applications in the criminal justice system, that supporting evidence would likely be credible, but probably not related closely enough to your focus on school settings.

Whenever you are reading an argument, you should also try to be aware of whether or not the writer has provided sufficient evidence to prove his or her point. Look at the followng section from London's piece in which she raises a counterargument in order to refute it:

> The advancements don't excite unanimous anticipation, of course. The report also reveals that 36% of people fear robots might be hacked and turned against us, 31% worry that robots would cause them to lose their jobs, and 27% fear robots could rise up and take over.
>
> Coplin continued: "The things I'm really worried about is pop culture and the dystopian view of robots. We need better role models and an informed conversation to understand Anki's vision: that robots are something to aspire to, not be frightened of."

To address the fears that people might have, London cites Envisioners CEO and futurist Dave Coplin, who essentially says that we just need different models of what robots can be. While this evidence does seem relevant and Coplin appears to be credible, is this enough evidence to address people's legitimate fears about robots? Probably not. London's overall argument is likely weaker than it could have been if she had included more evidence than just this one person's opinion. She could have provided more data about people's perceptions, or the increasing number of robots in service, or an opinion of someone who is not invested in AI and robotic advancement.

Evaluating Evidence

Look back at the evidence that you have collected through your interviews of classmates and your brief research for your argument regarding the role of technology in your school. To what extent is your evidence credible, relevant, and sufficient? What can you do to strengthen your evidence?

culminating activity

Write a brief argument about the role of technology in school that includes a claim and one or more outside sources on your topic. This is not a full essay; it is a response that demonstrates that you can use outside sources effectively in an argument.

The Dangers of Trusting Robots

Evan Selinger and Woodrow Hartzog

A philosophy professor at the Rochester Institute of Technology, Evan Selinger is the author of *Re-Engineering Humanity*. Woodrow Hartzog is a professor of law and computer science at the Northeastern University School of Law. He also teaches at the Khoury College of Computer Sciences. The following article draws from material in Hartzog's paper "Unfair and Deceptive Robots."

In February, a South Korean woman was sleeping on the floor when her robot vacuum ate her hair, forcing her to call for emergency help. It may not be the dystopian future that Stephen Hawking warned us about — where intelligent devices "spell the end of the human race" — but it does highlight one of the unexpected dangers of inviting robots into our home.

There are many other examples of intelligent technology gone bad, but more often than not they involve deception rather than physical danger. Malevolent bots, designed by criminals, are now ubiquitous on social media sites and elsewhere online[1]. The mobile dating app Tinder, for example, has been frequently infiltrated by bots posing as real people that attempt to manipulate users into using their webcams or disclosing credit card information. So it's not a stretch to imagine that untrustworthy bots may soon come to the physical world.

Meanwhile, increasing evidence suggests that we are susceptible to telling our deepest, darkest secrets to anthropomorphic robots[2] whose cute faces may hide exploitative code — children particularly so. So how do we protect ourselves from double-crossing decepticons[3]?

Once you've invited a bot into your home, you need to manage your expectations. Movies and marketing may have primed us to expect sophisticated interaction with our robotic chums but we've still got a long way to go before they are as socially aware as they are often depicted. Given the gulf between expectation and reality, it's important to avoid being tricked by a fake-out known as a "Wizard-of-Oz setup," where users are led to believe that robots are acting autonomously when, in fact, human operators are remotely controlling some of their operations.

[1]Baraniuk, Chris. "How online 'chatbots' are already tricking you," *BBC Future*, June 2014. https://www.bbc.com/future/article/20140609-how-online-bots-are-tricking-you

[2]Reben, Alexander. "How robots mess with our minds," *BBC Future*, July 2015. https://www.bbc.com/future/article/20150715-how-robots-mess-with-our-minds

[3]The robotic antagonists in the *Transformers* movies and TV shows. — Eds.

RossHelen editorial/Alamy Stock Photo

Examine this image of a couple with an automatic vacuum cleaner.

What attitude toward automation does the image convey? What details of the image create this tone? Would the authors of this article agree with the tone of the image? Why or why not?

Misjudging where behavior originates can be an especially acute problem in cases where consumers feel so comfortable with a non-sentient device that they reveal intimate information that they would have withheld had they known a human was in the loop. Take the service "Invisible Boyfriend," for example. For a monthly subscription, romantic texts and voicemails are sent to your phone from a faux lover. Although the company initially sought to make the fake beau fully automated, the technology wasn't sophisticated enough, so in reality, human workers generate the amorous exchanges. But not all customers understand how the system works, and thanks to the hype surrounding artificial intelligence and well-documented cases of automated bots successfully tricking people into believing that they're real humans[4], some people might erroneously believe they're receiving computer-composed dialogue.

5 The take-home message is clear: As robots become increasingly connected to the internet, and able to respond to natural language, you need to be especially vigilant about figuring out who or what you're talking to.

We also need to think long and hard about how information is being stored and shared when it comes to robots that can record our every move. Some recording devices may have been designed for entertainment but can easily be adapted for more nefarious purposes. Take Nixie, the wearable camera that can fly off your wrist at a moment's notice and take aerial shots around you. It doesn't take much imagination to see how such technology could be abused.

Most people guard their secrets in the presence of a recording device. But what happens once we get used to a robot around the house, answering our every beck and call? We may be at risk of letting our guard down, treating them as extended members of the family. If the technology around us is able to record and process speech, images and movement — never mind eavesdrop on our juiciest secrets — what

[4]Bilton, Nick. "Social Media Bots Offer Phony Friends and Real Profit," *New York Times*, November 2014. https://www.nytimes.com/2014/11/20/fashion/social-media-bots-offer-phony-friends-and-real-profit.html?_r=1

What point is this cartoon making about the smart devices in our homes? Why would the authors of this article agree or disagree with that point?

will happen to that information? Where will it be stored, who will have access? If our internet history is anything to go by, these details could be worth their weight in gold to advertising companies. If we grow accustomed to having trusted robots integrated into our daily lives, our words and deeds could easily become overly exposed.

So, what is the safest way to welcome robots into our homes, public spaces, and social lives? We should be cautiously optimistic that these intelligent machines could become enriching companions, while acknowledging that we need to determine strict boundaries for robots capable of deception and manipulation.

10 We might think of expanding the reach of consumer protection agencies or creating new robotic-centric policies. Just as the advent of radio called for the formation of the Federal Radio Commission in the U.S., advances in robotics may call for the advent of a body responsible for the integration of robotics into society[5]. Someone to turn to should your robot commit a crime[6], steal your credit card . . . or try to eat your hair. ■

[5] Calo, Ryan. "The case for a federal robotics commission," The Brookings Institution, September 2014. https://www.brookings.edu/research/the-case-for-a-federal-robotics-commission/

[6] Eveleth, Rose. "My robot bought illegal drugs," *BBC Future*, July 2015. https://www.bbc.com/future/article/20150721-my-robot-bought-illegal-drugs

Understanding and Interpreting

1. In paragraph 2, the authors try to make a distinction between two categories of danger we face with robots: deception and physical harm. What are the differences between them? Which one is the focus of this piece?
2. Summarize the conclusion the authors expect readers to draw from the example of the "Invisible Boyfriend" in paragraph 5.

3. At the end of paragraph 7, the authors discuss Nixie, the wearable camera, and state, "It doesn't take much imagination to see how such technology could be abused." What are possible examples the writers expect their readers to be able to imagine?
4. Reread paragraph 8 and summarize the potential dangers the authors associate with having robots in our homes.
5. What solutions do the authors suggest for problems they identify?
6. The writers of this piece do not really address counterarguments. What might people who disagree with the authors want to add to this discussion? If you were one of the writers of this piece, where in the argument would you address a counterargument? Why?

Analyzing Language, Style, and Structure

1. **Vocabulary in Context.** In paragraph 2, the authors refer to bots that "attempt to manipulate users." What does the word "manipulate" mean in this context? What are other, less negative ways to use this same word?
2. **Skill Focus.** While the authors of this piece include links to other articles and research (shown here as footnotes), they don't provide commentary on outside sources in the body of their argument. Where in their piece might discussion of outside sources have bolstered their claims? What additional kinds of evidence might have strengthened their argument?
3. What is the likely intended effect of starting this piece with the story of the robot vacuum?
4. The authors use the phrase, "Once you've invited a bot into your home" in paragraph 4. What does the word "invited" imply?
5. Explain the authors' use of allusion with the phrase "Wizard-of-Oz setup" in paragraph 4. Conduct brief research on the film, if necessary.
6. The authors employ a mostly casual and informal tone throughout the piece. Identify specific examples of word choice that help to create this tone. Explain how this tone suits the purpose and audience of this piece.
7. Look back through the piece to identify word choices the authors make to create a sense of fear or danger surrounding robots. Change some of those words, making the fear even more extreme. Then, rewrite them again communicating a tone that is significantly less fearful.

Topics for Composing

1. **Analysis.** Analyze how the authors build and support their argument to support their claim that robots in our homes can be dangerous. Focus on their use of logos (logic) and pathos (emotion), as well as the evidence they offer.
2. **Argument.** Are robots a danger to us in the ways that the authors suggest? What are reasonable protections we can put in place to avoid the dangers the authors identify? Use evidence from this piece, your own experiences, and additional research, if needed.
3. **Connection.** What roles do the kinds of robots the authors describe play in your life currently? Do you have fears similar to those of the authors?
4. **Speaking and Listening.** Ask several classmates, friends, teachers, and others to describe robots that they have, in the words of the authors, "invited into their home." Do they share any of the authors' concerns? Share your findings with the class or a small group.

5. **Research.** In Japan, the use of robots in manufacturing and homes is more extensive than in many other countries. Conduct research regarding the use of robots in Japan. What might have contributed to this more widespread integration in that country and culture? To what extent are the concerns in Japanese culture about robots similar to those raised by the authors of this piece?
6. **Creative.** Write a short story about a robot that has been invited into someone's house and deceives its hosts in the ways the authors describe. Be sure to include dialogue, setting, and characterization that communicate a tone and point of view similar to those presented by the authors of this piece.

The Real Cyborgs

Arthur House

Courtesy of Arthur House

Arthur House is features editor of the *Calvert Journal* and founding editor of the online quarterly the *Junket*. He was previously a journalist at the *Telegraph*, a British newspaper in which this article originally appeared in 2014.

Ian Burkhart concentrated hard. A thick cable protruded from the crown of his shaven head. A sleeve sprouting wires enveloped his right arm. The 23-year-old had been paralyzed from the neck down since a diving accident four years ago. But, in June this year, in a crowded room in the Wexner Medical Center at Ohio State University, Burkhart's hand spasmed into life.

At first it opened slowly and shakily, as though uncertain who its owner was. But when Burkhart engaged his wrist muscles, its upward movement was sudden and decisive. You could hear the joints — unused for years — cracking. The scientists and medical staff gathered in the room burst into applause.

The technology that made this possible, Neurobridge, had successfully reconnected Burkhart's brain with his body. It was probably the most advanced intertwining of man and machine that had so far been achieved.

But such milestones are coming thick and fast. Quietly, almost without anyone really noticing, we have entered the age of the cyborg, or cybernetic organism: a living thing both natural and artificial. Artificial retinas and cochlear implants (which connect directly to the brain through the auditory nerve system) restore sight to the blind and hearing to the deaf. Deep-brain implants, known as "brain pacemakers," alleviate the symptoms of 30,000 Parkinson's sufferers worldwide. The Wellcome Trust is now trialling Alzheimer's patients, stimulating them and warning of dangerous episodes.

5 A growing cadre of innovators is taking things further, using replacement organs, robotic prosthetics and implants not to restore bodily functions but to alter or enhance them. When he lost his right eye in a shotgun accident in 2005, the Canadian filmmaker Rob Spence replaced it with a wireless video camera that transmits what he's seeing in real time to his computer. Last year, the electronic engineer Brian McEvoy, who is based in Minnesota, made himself a kind of internal satnav[1] by fitting himself with a subdermal compass.

"This is the frontline of the Human Enhancement Revolution," wrote the technology author and philosopher Patrick Lin last year.

[1]Satellite navigation system. — Eds.

"We now know enough about biology, neuroscience, computing, robotics, and materials to hack the human body."

The U.S. military is pouring millions of dollars into projects such as Ekso Bionics' Human Universal Load Carrier (HULC), an "Iron Man"-style wearable exoskeleton that gives soldiers superhuman strength. Its Defense Advanced Research Projects Agency (DARPA) is also working on thought-controlled killer robots, "thought helmets" to enable telepathic communication and brain-computer interfaces (BCIs) to give soldiers extra senses, such as night vision and the ability to "see" magnetic fields caused by landmines.

Ever since the earliest humans made stone tools, we have tried to extend our powers. The bicycle, the telescope and the gun all arose from this same impulse. Today, we carry smartphones — supercomputers, really — in our pockets, giving us infinite information and unlimited communication at our fingertips. Our relationship with technology is becoming increasingly intimate, as wearable devices such as Google Glass, Samsung Gear Fit (a smartwatch-cum-fitness tracker) and the Apple Watch show. And wearable is already becoming implantable.

In America, a dedicated amateur community — the "biohackers" or "grinders" — has been experimenting with implantable technology for several years. Amal Graafstra, a 38-year-old programmer and self-styled "adventure technologist," has been inserting various types of radio-frequency identification (RFID) chips into the soft flesh between his thumbs and index fingers since 2005. The chips can be read by scanners that Graafstra has installed on the doors of his house, and also on his laptop, which gives him access with a swipe of his hand without the need for keys or passwords. He sells it to a growing crowd of "geeky, hacker-type software developers," he tells me, direct from his website, Dangerous Things, having used crowdfunding to pay for the manufacturing (he raised almost five times his target amount).

Graafstra, a hyper-articulate teddy bear of a 10
man, is unimpressed by wearable devices. "A wearable device is just one more thing to manage during the day. I don't think people will want to deck themselves out with all that in the future," he says, dismissing Samsung Gear Fit as "large, cumbersome and not exactly fashionable." Instead, he envisages an implant that would monitor general health and scan for

Robotic Arms Controlled By Human (photo)/American Photographer, (20th century)/MUSEUM OF SCIENCE AND INDUSTRY, CHICAGO/ Museum of Science and Industry, Chicago, USA/Bridgeman Images

This is a photograph called *Robotic Arms Controlled by Human*.

Look at the framing of the image and the faces of the subjects. What ideas about robots and humans might the photographer be trying to communicate? Which of the people discussed in this article might share a similar perspective?

medical conditions, sending the information to the user's smartphone or directly to a doctor. This would be always there, always on, and never in the way — and it could potentially save a lot of doctors' time and money as fewer checkups would be necessary and health conditions could be recognized before they became serious.

Graafstra defines biohackers as "DIY cyborgs who are upgrading their bodies with hardware without waiting for corporate development cycles or authorities to say it's OK." But, he concedes, "Samsung and Apple aren't blind to what we're doing. Somewhere in the bowels of these companies are people thinking about implantables." He mentions Motorola's experiments with the "password pill," which sends signals to devices from the stomach. (The same company has filed a patent for an "electronic throat tattoo" which fixes a minuscule microphone on the skin so users can communicate with their devices via voice commands.)

As robotics and brain-computer interfaces continue to improve and, with them, the likelihood that advanced cybernetic enhancement becomes widely available, several worrying questions emerge. Will those with the resources to access enhancements become a cyborg super-class that is healthier, smarter and more employable than the unenhanced? Will the unenhanced feel pressured into joining their ranks or face falling behind? And who will regulate these enhancements? In the wrong hands, cyborg technology could quickly become the stuff of dystopian science fiction. It's all too easy to imagine totalitarian regimes (or unscrupulous health insurers) scraping information from our new, connected body parts and using it for their own gain.

• • •

Kevin Warwick can justifiably claim to be the world's first cyborg. In the 1990s, Reading University's visiting professor of cybernetics started implanting RFID chips into himself. In 2002, he underwent pioneering surgery to have an array of electrodes attached to the nerve fibres in his arm. This was the first time a human nervous system had been connected to a computer. Warwick's "neural interface" allowed him to move a robotic hand by moving his own and to control a customized wheelchair with his thoughts. It also enabled him to experience electronic stimuli coming the other way. In one experiment he was able to sense ultrasound, which is beyond normal human capability. "I was born human," Warwick has said, "but I believe it's something we have the power to change."

Cheerleaders for a cyborg future, like Prof. Warwick, call themselves "transhumanists." Transhumanism aims to alter the human condition for the better by using technology (as well as genetic engineering, life extension science and synthetic biology) to make us more intelligent, healthier and live longer than has ever been possible — eventually transforming humanity so much it becomes "post-human."

One of the most prominent 15
transhumanists is the inventor and philosopher Ray Kurzweil, currently director of engineering at Google, and popularizer of the concept of the technological "singularity" — a point he puts at around 2045, when artificial intelligence will outstrip human intelligence for the first time. The predicted consequences of such a scenario vary wildly from the enslavement of humanity to a utopian world without war (or even, as a result of self-replicating nanotechnology, the transformation of the planet, or perhaps the entire universe, into something called "grey goo" — but that's a whole other story).

Kurzweil, the award-winning creator of the flatbed scanner, also believes he has a shot at immortality and intends to resurrect the dead, including his own father. "We will transcend all

extending beyond the text

In science-fiction films like *Terminator* and *Blade Runner*, technology has progressed so far that it is nearly impossible to distinguish between human and robot. In the real world, scientists and robotics engineers have been working to build computers to pass what is called "The Turing Test," which evaluates how realistic computer responses are to a series of questions posed by a human interrogator.

Facebook has been developing a version of the Turing Test to distinguish between robots and humans on its site. The computers are given twenty questions, five of which we have included here. Take the test to see if you are more human than a computer:

1. **John is in the playground. Bob is in the office.**

   Where is John?

2. **John is in the playground. Bob is in the office. John picked up the football. Bob went to the kitchen.**

   Where is the football?

   Where was Bob before the kitchen?

3. **John picked up the apple. John went to the office. John went to the kitchen. John dropped the apple.**

   Where was the apple before the kitchen?

4. **The office is north of the bedroom. The bedroom is north of the bathroom.**

   What is north of the bedroom?

   What is the bedroom north of?

5. **Mary gave the cake to Fred. Fred gave the cake to Bill. Jeff was given the milk by Bill.**

   Who gave the cake to Fred?

   Who did Fred give the cake to?

   What did Jeff receive?

   Who gave the milk?

None of the AI systems tested achieved 100 percent correct answers, although two averaged 93 percent. This result demonstrates that machines can't quite replicate the way humans process and understand language, but they are getting closer.

Now that you have taken a portion of the quiz, think about how these questions are intended to distinguish between robot and human. What does AI still have trouble doing?

Answers: (1) playground (2) playground; office (3) office (4) office; bathroom (5) Mary; Bill; milk; Bill of the limitations of our biology," he has said. "That is what it means to be human — to extend who we are."

Many transhumanists, particularly in Silicon Valley, where belief in the singularity has assumed the character of an eschatological[2] religion, think that fusing with technology is our only hope of surviving the consequences of this great change.

"We're not physically more competent than other species but in our intellectual capabilities we have something of an edge," Warwick tells me. "But quite soon machines are going to have an intellectual power that we'll have difficulty dealing with." The only way to keep up with them, he believes, is to artificially enhance our poor organic bodies and brains. "If you can't beat them, join them," he says.

Professor James Lovelock, the veteran scientist and environmentalist, is considerably less alarmed than Warwick. "Artificial intelligence is never going to be able to intuit or invent things — all it can do is follow logical instructions. Perhaps in the future when computing systems operate like our brains, then there really would be a fight, but that's an awful long way off."

Many would disagree, however. IBM, Hewlett Packard and HRL Laboratories have all received many millions of dollars from DARPA to develop exactly what Lovelock fears: so-called "cognitive" or "neuromorphic" computing systems designed to learn, associate and intuit just like a mammalian brain. IBM brought out its first prototype in 2012.

Warwick may have been the first to experiment with cybernetics but the honor of being the world's first government-recognized cyborg goes to the artist Neil Harbisson. Born with the rare condition of achromatopsia, or total color blindness, Harbisson developed the "eyeborg" — a color sensor on a head-mounted antenna that connects to a microchip implanted in his skull. It converts colors into sounds (electronic sine waves) which he hears via bone conduction.

Harbisson's severe bowl cut and hard-to-place accent (his mother is Catalan and his father Northern Irish) only heighten the impression that he might have been beamed down from another planet.

Over time he has learned to associate every part of the spectrum with a different pitch until these associations have become second nature. "It was when I started to dream in color that I felt the software and my brain had united," he said in [a] TED talk in 2012.

Ten years ago, he won a battle with the British government to have the "eyeborg" recognized as a part of his body. It now appears in his passport photo.

He set up the Cyborg Foundation two years ago with his partner, Moon Ribas, a dancer and a fellow "cyborg activist" (she has a seismic sensor in her arm, which enables her to feel vibrations of varying intensity when an earthquake occurs anywhere in the world). She and Harbisson believe that everyone should have the right to become a cyborg. Like the biohackers, they propose that would-be cyborgs use open-source technology to design and make their own enhancements, rather than buying a finished product off the shelf.

It is hard, however, to see the majority of people adopting a DIY philosophy like this when state-of-the-art options become available commercially. In computer gaming, headsets using electroencephalogram (EEG) technology are being developed so that users can control games with their thoughts. "For example," explains Zach Lynch, organizer of the first "Neurogaming" conference in San Francisco last

[2]From the Greek word eschatos, meaning "last" or "farthest," a type of philosophy or theology that contemplates the end of life, humankind, or the world as a whole. — Eds.

year, "players can smash boulders by concentrating or scare away demons with angry facial expressions." A British gaming company, Foc.us, is using technology that was first developed by DARPA to train snipers, to boost playing performance. According to Lynch, its "transcranial direct current stimulation device literally zaps your head with a miniscule electric pulse [which you can't feel] during training to help make your brain more susceptible to learning."

Chad Bouton, the inventor of the Neurobridge technology at Batelle Innovations that is enabling Ian Burkhart to move his hand again, believes that invasive brain-computer interfaces could also one day cross over into the non-therapeutic field.

"Talking about this bionic age that we're entering," he says on the phone from Ohio, "you certainly can imagine brain implants that could augment your memory." Or give you direct access to the internet. "You could think about a search you'd like to make and get the information streamed directly into your brain," he says. "Maybe decades from now we'll see something like that."

Prof. James Lovelock, who himself is fitted with a wi-fi controlled pacemaker, thinks these innovations come with dangers. He is chiefly "worried about the spam. If I had a cybernetic eye I wouldn't want to wake up in the middle of the night with [an advert for] somebody's used car flashing through my brain."

Then there is the prospect of spying. Could insurance companies harvest biometric data from people's enhancements, or paranoid governments use them to monitor their citizens? Amal Graafstra is adamant that his access-control chip is not at risk from such things, due to the close proximity (two inches or less) required to read it. "If the government was handing out these tags and requiring people to use them for banking, say, that would be pretty suspect," he tells me. "But it doesn't need to do that, because we have our phones on us all the time already" — a perfectly effective "tracking device," as he puts it, should governments be interested in our movements.

Even assuming that cybernetic technology could be made safe from such dangers, opponents of transhumanism (sometimes

Piero Cruciatti/Alamy Stock Photo

Andrew Geiger/Getty Images

These two images illustrate two key ways that people can interact with robotics.
What kind of relationship between humans and robotics does each image represent? Which of the people House cites in this article might agree or disagree with the uses depicted in these images?

termed "bioconservatives") argue the medical principle, that technology should only restore human capabilities, not enhance them.

"The fascination with 'enhancement' is a way to convince healthy people that they are in need of treatment," says Dr. David Albert Jones, director of the Anscombe Bioethics Centre in Oxford. "It is a wasteful distraction when we are failing to meet the basic needs of people with real health problems."

He's not against what he terms "human-technology interfaces" but, he says, they "should be developed to address the needs of people with disabilities, not to create a market for the self-regarding and the worried-well." Many medical professionals would agree.

Yuval Noah Harari, an Israeli historian, worries about enhancements leading to unprecedented levels of inequality. "Medicine is moving towards trying to surpass the norm, to help [healthy] people live longer, to have stronger memories, to have better control of their emotions," he said in a recent interview. "But upgrading like that is not an egalitarian project, it's an elitist project. No matter what norm you reach, there is always another upgrade which is possible." And the latest, most high-tech upgrades will always only be available to the rich.

35 But where does a case like Neil Harbisson's fall? He couldn't cure his color blindness, so he developed an extra sense to make up for it. Is this restoration or augmentation? Where cyborg ethics are concerned, the lines are blurred.

Rich Lee was also drawn to biohacking in order to overcome a disability. Lee, a 35-year-old salesman from Utah whose wet-shave-and-goatee look is more 1990s nu-metal than cybernetic citizen of the future, is losing his vision, and last year was certified blind in one eye. He's best known for having a pair of magnets implanted into his traguses (the nubs of cartilage in front of the ear-hole). They work with a copper coil worn around his neck, that he hooks up to his iPod, to become internal headphones. But he can also attach other things to the coil, such as wi-fi and electromagnetic sensors, enabling him to sense things normally outside of human capability. By attaching it to an ultrasonic rangefinder, he hopes to learn how to echolocate, like a bat, so when he goes blind he will still be able to judge his distance from objects — essentially, to see in the dark. . . .

"It can flip very quickly," says Kevin Warwick. "Take something like laser eye surgery. About 15 years ago people were saying 'Don't go blasting my eyes out' and now they're saying 'Don't bother with contact lenses.' "

In a sense, cyborg technology is nothing new — pacemakers, for example, have been around for decades. But recent advances have opened up new possibilities, and people are embracing them. Real cyborgs already walk among us. Soon, we may have to decide whether we want to join them. ■

Understanding and Interpreting

1. In paragraph 8, Arthur House writes, "Ever since the earliest humans made stone tools, we have tried to extend our powers." What does he mean by this? What technology described in this article would extend human powers?
2. Reread paragraph 12 in which House identifies several "worrying questions." Identify two or three of these questions and explain why they might be considered "worrying."
3. Based on the information in this article, write a definition of "transhumanism." What are the movement's chief aims? Explain whether transhumanists have an optimistic or a pessimistic view of the future.

4. Reread paragraphs 29 to 30 and identify the counterarguments to the merging of human and machine that House raises. To what extent does House seem to accept, reject, or qualify these counterarguments?
5. Near the end of the piece, House presents the conflict between the people who support only technology designed to restore human capabilities and those who are advocates of technology that would enhance human capabilities (pars. 31–38). What are the main arguments each side presents? What is their best evidence?

Analyzing Language, Style, and Structure

1. **Vocabulary in Context.** Throughout this piece, House uses the term "biohacker," a word created by combining "biology" and "hacking." What does the word mean in the context of this piece? How does this term represent the spirit of those who practice biohacking?
2. **Skill Focus.** Read paragraphs 13 to 18 in which House introduces the concept of "transhumanism," which is likely a new term for you. How did House use outside sources and expert opinion to help you to better understand this new concept? To what extent was House successful in using his sources for this purpose?
3. What effect does the author achieve by starting the article with the demonstration of Ian Burkhart moving his hand? How might the effect have been different if House had begun instead with Amal Graafstra, the "biohacker" he introduces in paragraph 9?
4. This piece originally appeared in a newspaper as a feature story, which is intended to shed light on an issue of the day, as opposed to an editorial, which is intended to present a clear position and point of view. Look back through the piece, and explain to what extent House presents "both sides" of the issue evenly and fairly.
5. What is House's tone toward the merging of humans and machines? Based solely on his word choice, do you think that House admires or is skeptical of the people involved in creating new connections between humans and machines?

Topics for Composing

1. **Analysis.** Overall, is House suggesting that our future will be better or worse as we continue to merge more with robots? Support your position with evidence from the text.
2. **Argument.** Near the end of the piece, House asks about the distinction between restoring human capabilities and augmenting human capabilities, saying, "Where cyborg ethics are concerned, the lines are blurred" (par. 35). Write an argument identifying the ethical guidelines you would propose for regulation of machine-human integration. Support your argument with evidence from this text and additional research if you choose.
3. **Connection.** House ends his article by stating, "Real cyborgs already walk among us. Soon, we may have to decide whether we want to join them." Reading through the various levels of technology presented in the article, what would you be comfortable integrating with yourself? Identify a line you would not cross. Why?
4. **Connection.** Identify the uses of technology presented in this article that seem like something out of a science-fiction story. Then, identify the technology that seems somewhat ordinary. What criteria did you use to judge the difference? If you had to guess, which "sci-fi" technology from this article is most likely to become ordinary to us in the future? Explain.

5. **Speaking and Listening.** Participate in a Philosophical Chairs discussion in which you line up with your classmates in the order of your comfort level with the robotic integration that House describes in his article. Those who are most excited about more human-robot merging should be at one end of the line, those deeply opposed should be at the other end, and those with mixed or moderate feelings should be somewhere in the middle. Talk with your neighbors in the line. Keep moving toward either end, depending on your changing perspective. At the end of the discussion, reflect with a partner about how your ideas on the topic changed (if at all) by talking with others about the topic.
6. **Research.** In 2005, Ray Kurzweil, who was mentioned in this article, wrote *The Singularity Is Near: When Humans Transcend Biology*. Research the "singularity," a term for the point at which "artificial intelligence will outstrip human intelligence for the first time" (par. 15) and when humans will "transcend all of the limitations of our biology" (par. 16) to become indistinguishable from machines. According to your research, how likely is the singularity to occur? What might be the benefits and drawbacks?

Will Robots Take Our Children's Jobs?

Alex Williams

Alex Williams is a *New York Times* reporter and feature writer for the Style section. Before that, he was a feature writer for *New York Magazine*. The following article appeared in the *New York Times* in 2019.

Like a lot of children, my sons, Toby, 7, and Anton, 4, are obsessed with robots. In the children's books they devour at bedtime, happy, helpful robots pop up more often than even dragons or dinosaurs. The other day I asked Toby why children like robots so much.

"Because they work for you," he said.

What I didn't have the heart to tell him is, someday he might work for them — or, I fear, might not work at all, because of them.

It is not just Elon Musk, Bill Gates and Stephen Hawking who are freaking out about the rise of invincible machines. Yes, robots have the potential to outsmart us and destroy the human race. But first, artificial intelligence could make countless professions obsolete by the time my sons reach their 20s.

You do not exactly need to be Marty McFly 5
to see the obvious threats to our children's future careers.

Say you dream of sending your daughter off to Yale School of Medicine to become a radiologist. And why not? Radiologists in New York typically earn about $470,000, according to Salary.com.

But that job is suddenly looking iffy as AI gets better at reading scans. A start-up called Arterys, to cite just one example, already has a program that can perform a magnetic-resonance imaging analysis of blood flow through a heart in just 15 seconds, compared with the 45 minutes required by humans.

Maybe she wants to be a surgeon, but that job may not be safe, either. Robots already assist surgeons in removing damaged organs and

---

Jon Carter/kdnuggets.com

This cartoon is clearly poking fun at humans, not robots.

What point is the cartoonist making? How would Williams, or maybe his sons, react to this point?

cancerous tissue, according to Scientific American. Last year, a prototype robotic surgeon called STAR (Smart Tissue Autonomous Robot) outperformed human surgeons in a test in which both had to repair the severed intestine of a live pig.

So perhaps your daughter detours to law school to become a rainmaking corporate lawyer. Skies are cloudy in that profession, too. Any legal job that involves lots of mundane document review (and that's a lot of what lawyers do) is vulnerable.

10 Software programs are already being used by companies including JPMorgan Chase & Company to scan legal papers and predict what documents are relevant, saving lots of billable hours. Kira Systems, for example, has reportedly cut the time that some lawyers need to review contracts by 20 to 60 percent.

As a matter of professional survival, I would like to assure my children that journalism is immune, but that is clearly a delusion. The Associated Press already has used a software program from a company called Automated Insights to churn out passable copy covering Wall Street earnings and some college sports, and last year awarded the bots the minor league baseball beat. What about other glamour jobs, like airline pilot? Well, last spring, a robotic co-pilot developed by the Defense Advanced Research Projects Agency, known as [DARPA] flew and landed a simulated 737. I hardly count that as surprising, given that pilots of commercial Boeing 777s, according to one 2015 survey, only spend seven minutes during an average flight actually flying the thing. As we move into the era of driverless cars, can pilotless planes be far behind? Then there is Wall Street, where robots are already doing their best to shove Gordon Gekko out of his corner office. Big banks are using software programs that can suggest bets, construct hedges and act as robo-economists, using natural language processing to parse central bank commentary to predict monetary policy, according to Bloomberg. BlackRock, the biggest fund company in the world, made waves earlier this year when it announced it was replacing some highly paid human stock pickers with computer algorithms.

So am I paranoid? Or not paranoid enough? A much-quoted 2013 study by the University of Oxford Department of Engineering Science — surely the most sober of institutions — estimated that 47 percent of current jobs, including insurance underwriter, sports referee and loan officer, are at risk of falling victim to automation, perhaps within a decade or two.

Just this week, the McKinsey Global Institute released a report that found that a third of American workers may have to switch jobs in the next dozen or so years because of AI.

I know I am not the only parent wondering if I can robot-proof my children's careers. I figured I would start by asking my own what they want to do when they grow up.

15 Toby, a people pleaser and born entertainer, is obsessed with cars and movies. He told me he wanted to be either an Uber driver or an actor. (He is too young to understand that those jobs are usually one and the same.)

As for Uber drivers, it is no secret that they are headed to that great parking garage in the sky; the company recently announced plans to buy 24,000 Volvo sport utility vehicles to roll out as a driverless fleet between 2019 and 2021.

And actors? It may seem unthinkable that some future computer-generated thespian could achieve the nuance of expression and emotional depth of, say, Dwayne Johnson. But Hollywood is already Silicon Valley South. Consider how filmmakers used computer graphics to reanimate Carrie Fisher's Princess Leia and Peter Cushing's Grand Moff Tarkin as they appeared in the 1970s (never mind that Mr. Cushing died in 1994) for "Rogue One: A Star Wars Story." My younger son Anton, a sweetheart, but tough as Kevlar, said he wanted to be a football player. Robot football may sound crazy, but come to think of it, a Monday night battle between the Dallas Cowdroids and Seattle Seabots may be the only solution to the sport's endless concussion problems.

He also said he wanted to be a soldier. If he means foot soldier, however, he might want to hold off on enlistment. Russia recently unveiled Fedor, a humanoid robot soldier that looks like RoboCop after a Whole30 crash diet; this space-combat-ready android can fire handguns, drive vehicles, administer first aid and, one hopes, salute. Indeed, the world's armies are in such an arms race developing grunt-bots that one British intelligence expert predicted that American forces will have more robot soldiers than humans by 2025.

And again, all of this stuff is happening now, not 25 years from now. Who knows what the jobs marketplace might look like by then. We might not even be the smartest beings on the planet. Ever heard of the "singularity"? That is the term that futurists use to describe a potentially cataclysmic point at which machine intelligence catches up to human intelligence, and likely blows right past it. They may rule us. They may kill us. No wonder Mr. Musk says that AI "is potentially more dangerous than nukes."

20 But is it really that dire? Fears of technology are as old as the Luddites, those machine-smashing British textile workers of the early 19th century. Usually, the fears turn out to be overblown.

The rise of the automobile, to cite the obvious example, did indeed put most manure shovelers out of work. But it created millions of jobs to replace them, not just for Detroit assembly line workers, but for suburban homebuilders, Big Mac flippers and actors performing "Greased Lightnin'" in touring revivals of "Grease." That is the process of creative destruction in a nutshell.

But artificial intelligence is different, said Martin Ford, the author of "Rise of the Robots: Technology and the Threat of a Jobless Future." Machine learning does not just give us new machines to replace old machines, pushing human workers from one industry to another. Rather, it gives us new machines to replace us, machines that can follow us to virtually any new industry we flee to.

Since Mr. Ford's book sent me down this rabbit hole in the first place, I reached out to him to see if he was concerned about all this for his own children: Tristan, 22, Colin, 17, and Elaine, 10. He said the most vulnerable jobs in the robot economy are those involving predictable, repetitive tasks, however much training they require. "A lot of knowledge-based jobs are really routine — sitting in front of a computer and cranking out the same application over and over, whether it is a report or some kind of quantitative analysis," he said.

Professions that rely on creative thinking enjoy some protection (Mr. Ford's older son is a graduate student studying biomedical engineering). So do jobs emphasizing empathy and interpersonal communication (his younger son wants to be a psychologist).

extending beyond the text

Anadolu Agency/Getty Images

Since 1997, teams from around the world have competed in the RoboCup, intended to "promote research in the area of intelligent robotics and artificial intelligence, as well as related fields" with a goal of building "a team of fully autonomous humanoid robots able to win against the human world soccer champions in 2050."

Considering what you know about the requirements for team sports like soccer, what challenges will robotic engineers likely have to overcome in order to beat a team of humans?

Even so, the ability to think creatively may not provide ultimate salvation. Mr. Ford said he was alarmed in May when Google's AlphaGo software defeated a 19-year-old Chinese master at Go, considered the world's most complicated board game.

"If you talk to the best Go players, even they can't explain what they're doing," Mr. Ford said. "They'll describe it as a 'feeling.' It's moving into the realm of intuition. And yet a computer was able to prove that it can beat anyone in the world."

Looking for a silver lining, I spent an afternoon Googling TED Talks with catchy titles like "Are Droids Taking Our Jobs?"

In one, Albert Wenger, an influential tech investor, promoted the Basic Income Guarantee concept. Also known as Universal Basic Income, this sunny concept holds that a robot-driven economy may someday produce an unlimited bounty of cool stuff while simultaneously releasing us from the drudgery of old-fashioned labor, leaving our government-funded children to enjoy bountiful lives of leisure as interpretive dancers or practitioners of bee-sting therapy, as touted by Gwyneth Paltrow.

The idea is all the rage among Silicon Valley elites, who not only understand technology's power, but who also love to believe that it will be used for good. In their vision of a post-AI world without traditional jobs, everyone will receive a minimum weekly or monthly stipend (welfare for all, basically).

Another talk by David Autor, an economist, argued that reports of the death of work are greatly exaggerated. Almost 50 years after the introduction of the ATM, for instance, more humans actually work as bank tellers than ever. The computers simply freed the humans from mind-numbing work like counting out 20-dollar bills to focus on more cognitively demanding tasks like "forging relationships with customers, solving problems and introducing them to new products like credit cards, loans and investments," he said.

Computers, after all, are really good at some things and, for the moment, terrible at others. Even Anton intuits this. The other day I asked him if he thought robots were smarter or dumber than humans. "Sdumber," he said after a long pause. Confused, I pushed him. "Smarter and dumber," he explained with a cheeky smile.

He was joking. But he also happened to be right, according to Andrew McAfee, a management theorist at the Massachusetts Institute of Technology whom I interviewed a short while later. Discussing another of Anton's career aspirations — songwriter — Dr. McAfee said that computers were already smart enough to come up with a better melody than a lot of humans.

"The things our ears find pleasant, we know the rules for that stuff," he said. "However, I'm going to be really surprised when there is a digital lyricist out there, somebody who can put words to that music that will actually resonate with people and make them think something about the human condition."

Not everyone, of course, is cut out to be a cyborg-Springsteen. I asked Dr. McAfee what other jobs may exist a decade from now.

"I think health coaches are going to be a big industry of the future," he said. "Restaurants that have a very good hospitality staff are not about to go away, even though we have more options to order via tablet."

"People who are interested in working with their hands, they're going to be fine," he said. "The robot plumber is a long, long way away." ■

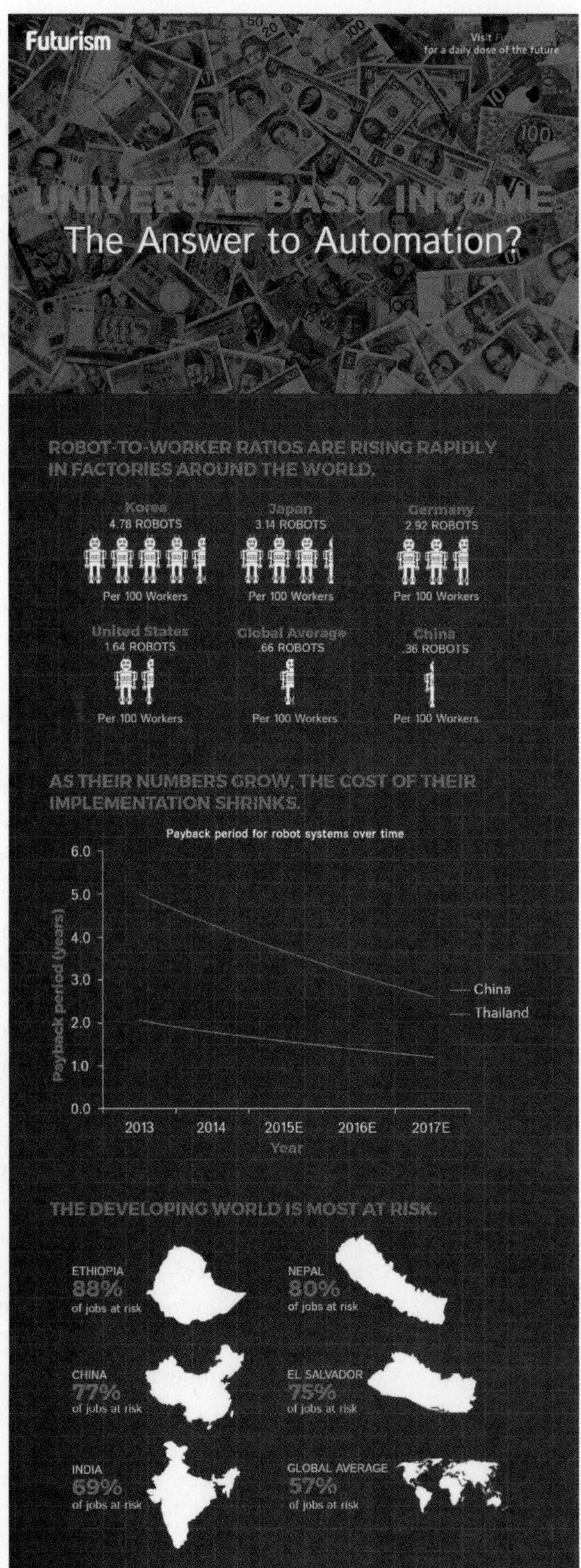

Courtesy of Futurism.com

This is a portion of an infographic intended to build support for Universal Basic Income, a set amount of money that every citizen is given automatically, in response to growing automation.

How does this graphic use words and images to communicate its ideas? How is its message similar to or different from the points that Williams makes in this article?

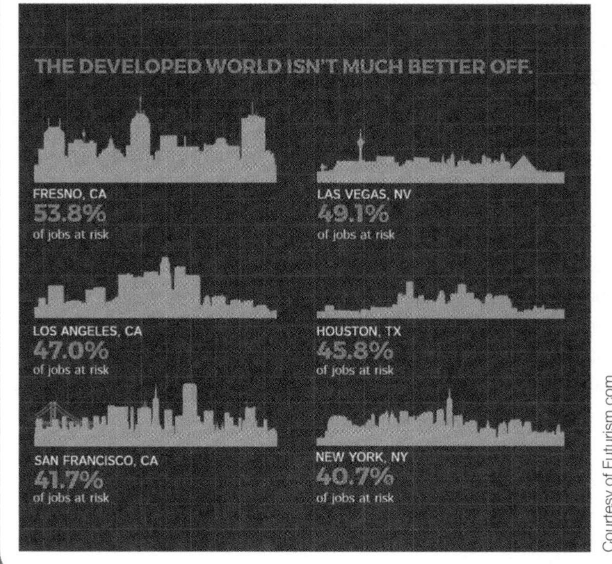

Courtesy of Futurism.com

Understanding and Interpreting

1. Paragraphs 6 to 12 include a description of a job and ideas about how more robots and automation might affect that job. What are we expected to conclude from this section of Williams's piece?
2. After talking in theory or reporting on research, Williams turns to his own sons and their choices of future careers. What point is Williams making through these examples?
3. In paragraph 20, Williams asks, "But is it really that dire?" What is the counterargument that he raises here? What other counterarguments could he have included?
4. Explain how Williams attempts to refute the counterargument he raises in paragraph 20. To what extent is his response to opposing ideas effective?
5. According to Martin Ford (par. 22), why might some jobs be safer than others from robot replacement? What qualities, according to Ford, make a job unsuitable for robots and automation, at least for now?
6. Why is Ford concerned about the fact that a computer recently beat a human master at the board game Go? How does this event support or undercut his earlier claims about jobs that are safe from robot replacement?
7. What lesson are we expected to draw from Williams's analysis of the history of the ATM? How does this example help support his argument?
8. Williams ends his piece with an interview with Andrew McAfee, a management theorist. What does McAfee conclude about robots and future careers? To what extent would he agree or disagree with Martin Ford's conclusions earlier in the article?

Analyzing Language, Style, and Structure

1. **Vocabulary in Context.** In this piece, Williams combines words to create context-specific terms. In paragraph 14, he writes, "if I can robot-proof my children's careers. . . ." What is the meaning of "robot-proof" in this context?

2. **Skill Focus.** Reread paragraph 12, which begins with "So am I paranoid?" In trying to answer this question, Williams turns to outside sources. How does he use these sources to help prove a point he is making about the economy of the future? To what extent is this an effective way to make his case?
3. How does Williams establish his ethos and a connection to his audience in the opening of his piece?
4. What might Williams be trying to achieve by directly addressing his audience (e.g., "So perhaps your daughter . . .")? Why is this approach effective or ineffective in this context?
5. Williams uses a number of allusions in his piece that might be outdated or unfamiliar to you (Marty McFly, for instance). Identify two or three other allusions and explain why they might be effective for his intended audience, readers of the *New York Times*.
6. Through touches of humor, Williams attempts to bring lightness to a subject that might otherwise be very depressing. Locate one or more of these efforts at humor. Explain how it works to influence the tone of his piece.
7. Reread the parenthetical comment at the end of paragraph 15. What joke is Williams making here? Why might it be more effective for his audience (readers of the *New York Times)* than for his son, or for you, a student in high school?
8. At various points in his essay, Williams refers to his children, including quoting his son's assessment of robot intelligence as "Sdumber." What is the effect of his inclusion of his children? How might it have helped him to make his argument?

Topics for Composing

1. **Analysis.** Explain Williams's answer to the question in his title, "Will Robots Take Our Children's Jobs?" Then, examine how effectively he is able to make his case. Consider elements of argument such as evidence, appeals to audience, and style.
2. **Argument.** Assume that what Williams writes about robots, automation, and future careers is true. Write an argument about how school, including college, needs to adjust to prepare students for these projected changes in the job market. Support your position with evidence from this piece, your own experiences, and additional research if necessary.
3. **Connection.** Note how many different professions Williams says will be deeply affected by greater automation in the future. Did he include any of the careers you might be thinking about? If so, why do you agree or disagree with his analysis? If not, how might he analyze the security of a job you are considering? Refer to the text in your explanation.
4. **Speaking and Listening.** In a small group, discuss your future job interests. Consider what Williams says about workplace automation in the future. Decide as a group which of the job options you've discussed will be the safest bet in the future. Give a presentation to your class in which you recommend the job your group has chosen. Be sure to explain the job in detail, especially aspects that protect it from automation.
5. **Research.** Williams makes several claims about the effect that robots will have on certain professions, including driverless cars by 2021, and robot soldiers by 2025. Research these or other predictions he makes. Have any of his predictions come true since the publication of his essay?
6. **Research.** Research Universal Basic Income (UBI), both in theory and in places where it has been tried. Explain how this approach could help offset the effects of job loss with increased automation. Based on your research, why is it a policy that governments should or should not consider?
7. **Expository.** Identify a job that Williams does not describe in his piece that you think would not be replaced by robots. Explain why you think it would be safe in the future.

By Giving Robots "Personhood" Status, Humanity Risks to Be Demoted to the Rank of a Machine

Courtesy Federico Guerrini

Federico Guerrini

Federico Guerrini is a freelance journalist interested in the impact of technology on society. A former research fellow for the Reuters Institute for the Study of Journalism, Guerrini now writes for several news outlets in English and Italian. The following article originally appeared in *Forbes* in 2019.

KEY CONTEXT In February 2017, the European Parliament debated a resolution that included recommendations regarding ethical principles and fundamental rights to the Commission on Civil Law Rules on Robotics. Ongoing discussions on the issue have taken place since.

In many ways, we're living [in] extraordinary times. Few would have thought, just fifteen years ago, that a body of the European Parliament would discuss creating a special legal status for robots, with specific rights and obligations, or advocate for seriously considering a general basic income in light of the possible effects of robotics on the job market.

Still, that's happened recently, when the parliament's legal affairs committee passed a report containing several recommendations to the commission on Civil Law Rules on Robotics which should in turn, based on that, present a legislative proposal to be voted on by the full house.

It's a fascinating read, touching a lot of key points, from the creation of a European Agency for robotics and artificial intelligence to a method for regulating and assessing liability in case a robot causes any damage.

In the latter scenario, the report's authors think that the responsibility should be allocated to all parties involved (the robot, the manufacturer, the engineer who wrote the software) proportionally to the level of instructions given to the robot and of its autonomy.

The greater the autonomy, the more the 5
blame should be put on the machine itself and not on any third party. In any case, the victim of

extending beyond the text

Science-fiction author Isaac Asimov wrote several novels and short stories that deal with robot and human interaction. In the future that he imagined, all robot brains would be programmed with what he called the Three Laws of Robotics, intended to govern robot behavior in the following ways:

1. A robot may not injure a human being or, through inaction, allow a human being to come to harm.
2. A robot must obey the orders given to it by human beings, except where such orders would conflict with the First Law.
3. A robot must protect its own existence as long as such protection does not conflict with the First or Second Law.

What are the intentions of these laws? What are their flaws? To what extent would these laws help Guerrini make his case about the rights and responsibilities of robots?

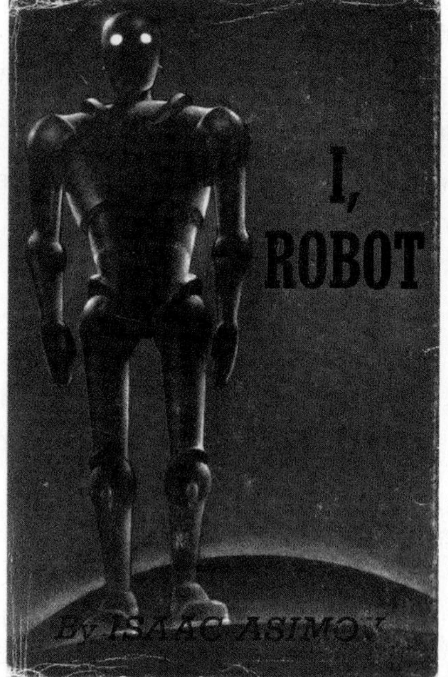

Front cover of 'I, Robot' by Isaac Asimov, 1950 (color litho)/Cartier, Edd (1914-2008)/CHRISTIES IMAGES/Private Collection/Bridgeman Images

the incident would always be compensated, by means of an obligatory insurance scheme and compensation fund.

It sounds sensible, on paper, but the idea of establishing a robot as a liable legal person presents a number of issues.

It does make sense for corporations, which operate according to certain internal hierarchies and are usually composed of a plurality of individuals. But would that make sense for robots?

"How can a mere machine, a carcass devoid of consciousness, feelings, thoughts or its own will, become an autonomous legal actor? . . . From a scientific, legal and even ethical perspective, it is impossible today — and probably will remain so for a long time to come — for a robot to take part in legal life without a human being pulling its strings," Artois University researcher Nathalie Nevejans writes in a commentary to the report, commissioned by the EU's policy department for Citizens' Rights and Constitutional Affairs.

Establishing such a category would be pointless, she maintains, if it were a mere empty shell to disguise the presence of a physical person who pulls the strings behind the scenes.

10 On the other hand, the idea of attributing a robot a consciousness of a sort, could potentially trigger a number of unwanted consequences. Would that mean, for instance, that specific "rights" and "duties" should be assigned to the machine, as part of its legal personality?

But, as [Nevejans] points out, "how could a robot have duties, since the idea is closely linked with human morals?" And, if giving "rights" to a robot should imply that it could demand leave or salary, why not simply use manpower instead?

The most concerning part of the "electronic person" approach, however, is another. By placing a non-conscious entity in a category similar to that of humans, it could blur the line between persons and things. Rather than elevating a machine to a higher status, it could foster a line of thinking which would on the contrary demote humankind, stripping away its own peculiar qualities to make it more "compatible" with its artificial counterpart.

As rapporteur Mady Delvaux said, "a robot can show empathy. But it can never feel empathy;" the latter is a human characteristic. We should cling to that since, in all other respects — strength, intelligence, adaptability, longevity — humans will soon be the weakest link of the chain. ■

Understanding and Interpreting

1. Reread the first two paragraphs and summarize how Guerrini gives his readers context for his piece. What assumptions does he seem to make about his readers' knowledge? What additional information might have helped you understand the context? How would it have helped?
2. Explain why it is important to identify responsibility for a robot's actions. What are the challenges in determining liability, according to Guerrini in paragraphs 4 and 5?
3. Reread paragraphs 10 and 11, in which Guerrini discusses the idea of a conscious robot. Why, according to researcher Nathalie Nevejans, should even this robot not have personhood?
4. In paragraph 12, Guerrini suggests that robots should not be given personhood because it could blur the lines between humans and robots. Explain his reasons for this conclusion.

Analyzing Language, Style, and Structure

1. **Vocabulary in Context.** In paragraph 3, Guerrini uses the word "liability" in reference to a robot. What is the meaning of the word in this context? In what other contexts have you seen the word used in a similar way?
2. **Skill Focus.** Reread paragraph 8 and explain what Guerrini was hoping to accomplish through the use of his outside source. How does citing Nevejans help his argument?
3. Explain Guerrini's description of a robot as an "empty shell" (par. 9). What is he trying to communicate through this figurative language? Why is it important to his argument?
4. Reread the last paragraph, looking closely at Guerrini's word choice. Describe the tone he takes here, and explain how his diction creates that tone. To what extent is this tone effective for his argument?

Topics for Composing

1. **Analysis.** We know that Guerrini's central claim is that robots should not be called persons. What are the most persuasive arguments he makes in favor of his position? What are his weakest arguments?
2. **Argument.** Is Guerrini correct? Should we keep robots from having personhood status? Write an argument that includes evidence from this piece, as well as information and ideas from outside research and your own reasoning.

3. **Connection.** Think about a science-fiction movie, book, or TV show that includes robots as main or significant characters. Explain whether or not these robot characters have the kind of personhood status Guerrini argues against. How might Guerrini respond to that fictional robot's status?
4. **Speaking and Listening.** Hold a class or small group debate on this question: "Should robots have rights guaranteed by law?" Be sure to listen carefully to all perspectives. At the end of the debate, try to arrive at some kind of consensus on the issue.
5. **Research.** A number of groups around the world are working to establish a sort of Robot Bill of Rights. Choose at least one group and research its work and its positions on the issue. Then, explain how Guerrini might respond to that group's evidence.
6. **Exposition.** Locate online the European Parliament resolution of February 16, 2017, with recommendations to the Commission on Civil Law Rules on Robotics that Guerrini discusses in this article. While Guerrini focuses mostly on the liability issues raised by the resolution, examine the rest of the document, and explain at least two other significant factors that the resolution raises about robots in the future.
7. **Exposition.** In the last paragraph, Mady Delvaux suggests that "a robot can show empathy. But it can never feel empathy." Explain the differences between showing and feeling empathy in terms of robot and human emotional abilities.

from Better Than Human: Why Robots Will — and Must — Take Our Jobs

Kevin Kelly

evan Hurd / Alamy Stock Photo

Kevin Kelly (b. 1952) is a writer, photographer, and founding executive editor of *Wired* magazine. He writes extensively about the role of technology in our lives; his nonfiction books include *What Technology Wants* (2012) and *The Inevitable: Understanding the 12 Technological Forces That Will Shape Our Future* (2017). In an interview with artist Olafur Eliasson, Kelly said that "it wouldn't surprise [him] if in a thousand years people start talking about robot rights and having empathy for things that we've built, and that we can't unplug them." The following article appeared in *Wired* magazine in 2012.

KEY CONTEXT The Industrial Revolution, which Kelly discusses in this article, was the time period in Western Europe and the United States from the mid-1700s to the mid-1800s when manufacturing shifted from manual labor and the use of animals to the use of machinery. The Industrial Revolution marks a significant turning point in human history because of its widespread effects on labor, standards of living, and population migration to cities.

Imagine that 7 out of 10 working Americans got fired tomorrow. What would they all do?

It's hard to believe you'd have an economy at all if you gave pink slips to more than half the labor force. But that — in slow motion — is what the industrial revolution did to the workforce of the early 19th century. Two hundred years ago, 70 percent of American workers lived on the farm. Today automation has eliminated all but 1 percent of their jobs, replacing them (and their work animals) with machines. But the displaced workers did not sit idle. Instead, automation created hundreds of millions of jobs in entirely new fields. Those who once farmed were now manning the legions of factories that churned out farm equipment, cars, and other industrial products. Since then, wave upon wave of new occupations have arrived — appliance repairman, offset printer, food chemist, photographer, web designer — each building on previous automation. Today, the vast majority of us are doing jobs that no farmer from the 1800s could have imagined.

It may be hard to believe, but before the end of this century, 70 percent of today's occupations

Ten fastest growing occupations, projected 2018–28

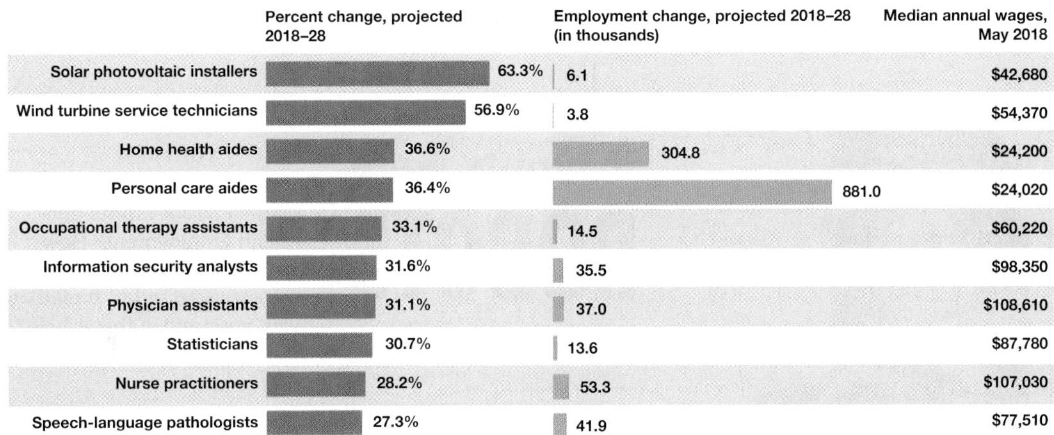

Percent change and numeric growth by industry sector, projected 2018–28

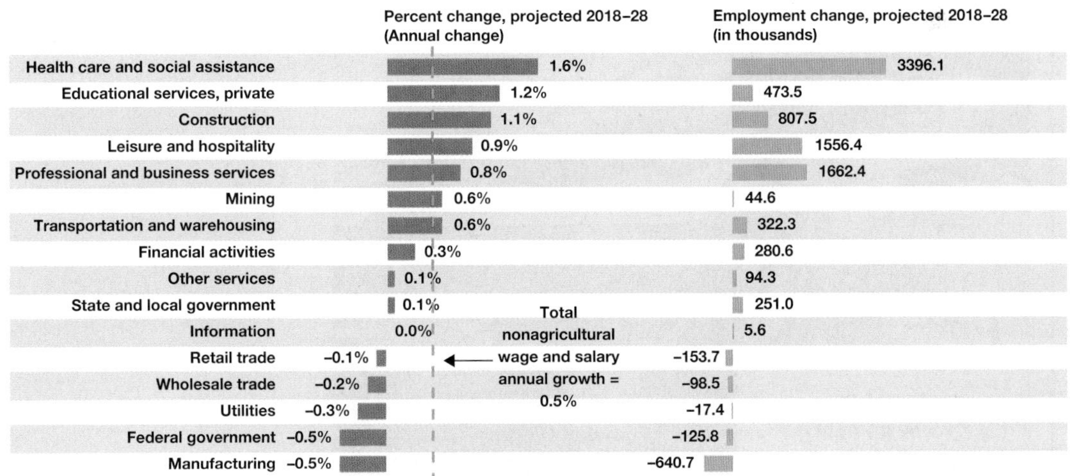

What are two conclusions that you can draw from the information in these graphs from the United States Bureau of Labor Statistics? How might the automation that Kelly describes in this article affect these careers? What effect, if any, does this information have on your own career aspirations?

will likewise be replaced by automation. Yes, dear reader, even you will have your job taken away by machines. In other words, robot replacement is just a matter of time. This upheaval is being led by a second wave of automation, one that is centered on artificial cognition, cheap sensors, machine learning, and distributed smarts. This deep automation will touch all jobs, from manual labor to knowledge work.

First, machines will consolidate their gains in already-automated industries.

5 After robots finish replacing assembly line workers, they will replace the workers in warehouses. Speedy bots able to lift 150 pounds all day long will retrieve boxes, sort them, and load them onto trucks. Fruit and vegetable picking will continue to be robotized until no humans pick outside of specialty farms. Pharmacies will feature a single pill-dispensing robot in the back while the pharmacists focus on patient consulting. Next, the more dexterous chores of cleaning in offices and schools will be taken over by late-night robots, starting with easy-to-do floors and windows and eventually getting to toilets. The highway legs of long-haul trucking routes will be driven by robots embedded in truck cabs.

1930s USA, Robots Magazine Advert/ADVERTISING ARCHIVES ('B' IMAGES)/Bridgeman Images

This is an advertisement from 1930 for a typewriter.

What does this ad seem to suggest about robots and human employment? How would this ad be different if it were created today, based on what you read in this article?

All the while, robots will continue their migration into white-collar work. We already have artificial intelligence in many of our machines; we just don't call it that. Witness one piece of software by Narrative Science that can write newspaper stories about sports games directly from the games' stats or generate a synopsis of a company's stock performance each day from bits of text around the web. Any job dealing with reams of paperwork will be taken over by bots, including much of medicine. Even those areas of medicine not defined by paperwork, such as surgery, are becoming increasingly robotic. The rote tasks of any information-intensive job can be automated. It doesn't matter if you are a doctor, lawyer, architect, reporter, or even programmer: The robot takeover will be epic.

And it has already begun. . . .

To understand how robot replacement will happen, it's useful to break down our relationship with robots into four categories, as summed up in this chart:

	Human	Machine
Existing Jobs	A Jobs today that humans do—but machines will eventually do better.	B Current jobs that humans can't do but machines can.
New Jobs	D Jobs that only humans will be able to do—at first.	C Robot jobs that we can't even imagine yet.

The rows indicate whether robots will take over existing jobs or make new ones, and the columns indicate whether these jobs seem (at first) like jobs for humans or for machines.

10 Let's begin with quadrant A: jobs humans can do but robots can do even better. Humans can weave cotton cloth with great effort, but automated looms make perfect cloth, by the mile, for a few cents. The only reason to buy handmade cloth today is because you want the imperfections humans introduce. We no longer value irregularities while traveling 70 miles per hour, though—so the fewer humans who touch our car as it is being made, the better.

And yet for more complicated chores, we still tend to believe computers and robots can't be trusted. That's why we've been slow to acknowledge how they've mastered some conceptual routines, in some cases even surpassing their mastery of physical routines.

A computerized brain known as the autopilot can fly a 787 jet unaided, but irrationally we place human pilots in the cockpit to babysit the autopilot "just in case." In the 1990s, computerized mortgage appraisals replaced human appraisers wholesale. Much tax preparation has gone to computers, as well as routine x-ray analysis and pretrial evidence-gathering—all once done by highly paid smart people. We've accepted utter reliability in robot manufacturing; soon we'll accept it in robotic intelligence and service.

Next is quadrant B: jobs that humans can't do but robots can. A trivial example: Humans have trouble making a single brass screw unassisted, but automation can produce a thousand exact ones per hour. Without automation, we could not make a single computer chip—a job that requires degrees of precision, control, and unwavering attention that our animal bodies don't possess. Likewise no human, indeed no group of humans, no matter their education, can quickly search through all the web pages in the world to uncover the one page revealing the price of eggs in Katmandu yesterday. Every time you click on the search button you are employing a robot to do something we as a species are unable to do alone.

While the displacement of formerly human jobs gets all the headlines, the greatest benefits bestowed by robots and automation come from their occupation of jobs we are unable to do. We don't have the attention span to inspect every square millimeter of every CAT scan looking for cancer cells. We don't have the millisecond reflexes needed to inflate molten glass into the shape of a bottle. We don't have an infallible memory to keep track of every pitch in Major League Baseball and calculate the probability of the next pitch in real time.

15 We aren't giving "good jobs" to robots. Most of the time we are giving them jobs we could never do. Without them, these jobs would remain undone.

Now let's consider quadrant C, the new jobs created by automation — including the jobs that we did not know we wanted done. This is the greatest genius of the robot takeover: With the assistance of robots and computerized intelligence, we already can do things we never imagined doing 150 years ago. We can remove a tumor in our gut through our navel, make a talking-picture video of our wedding, drive a cart on Mars, print a pattern on fabric that a friend mailed to us through the air. We are doing, and are sometimes paid for doing, a million new activities that would have dazzled and shocked the farmers of 1850. These new accomplishments are not merely chores that were difficult before. Rather they are dreams that are created chiefly by the capabilities of the machines that can do them. They are jobs the machines make up.

Before we invented automobiles, air-conditioning, flatscreen video displays, and animated cartoons, no one living in ancient Rome wished they could watch cartoons while riding to Athens in climate-controlled comfort. Two hundred years ago not a single citizen of Shanghai would have told you that they would buy a tiny slab that allowed them to talk to faraway friends before they would buy indoor plumbing. Crafty AIs embedded in first-person-shooter games have given millions of teenage boys the urge, the need, to become professional game designers — a dream that no boy in Victorian times ever had. In a very real way our inventions assign us our jobs. Each successful bit of automation generates new occupations — occupations we would not have fantasized about without the prompting of the automation.

To reiterate, the bulk of new tasks created by automation are tasks only other automation can handle. Now that we have search engines like Google, we set the servant upon a thousand new errands. Google, can you tell me where my phone is? Google, can you match the people suffering depression with the doctors selling pills? Google, can you predict when the next viral epidemic will erupt? Technology is indiscriminate this way, piling up possibilities and options for both humans and machines.

It is a safe bet that the highest-earning professions in the year 2050 will depend on automations and machines that have not been invented yet. That is, we can't see these jobs from here, because we can't yet see the machines and technologies that will make them possible. Robots create jobs that we did not even know we wanted done.

20 Finally, that leaves us with quadrant D, the jobs that only humans can do — at first. The one thing humans can do that robots can't (at least for a long while) is to decide what it is that humans want to do. This is not a trivial trick; our desires are inspired by our previous inventions, making this a circular question.

Bloomberg/Getty Images

This is a picture of robots working on the undercarriage of Jeep Cherokee vehicles on the production line at the Chrysler Toledo Assembly Plant in Toledo, Ohio.

Imagine that this image is used in two different publications. The first is the newsletter of the United Auto Workers union, a group opposed to more automation. The second is the shareholders' profit statement for Chrysler, praising the role of automation. How could this same image be used to support two different conclusions about automation in the workplace?

When robots and automation do our most basic work, making it relatively easy for us to be fed, clothed, and sheltered, then we are free to ask, "What are humans for?" Industrialization did more than just extend the average human lifespan. It led a greater percentage of the population to decide that humans were meant to be ballerinas, full-time musicians, mathematicians, athletes, fashion designers, yoga masters, fan-fiction authors, and folks with one-of-a kind titles on their business cards. With the help of our machines, we could take up these roles; but of course, over time, the machines will do these as well. We'll then be empowered to dream up yet more answers to the question "What should we do?" It will be many generations before a robot can answer that.

This postindustrial economy will keep expanding, even though most of the work is done by bots, because part of your task tomorrow will be to find, make, and complete new things to do, new things that will later become repetitive jobs for the robots. In the coming years robot-driven cars and trucks will become ubiquitous; this automation will spawn the new human occupation of trip optimizer, a person who tweaks the traffic system for optimal energy and time usage. Routine robo-surgery will necessitate the new skills of keeping machines sterile. When automatic self-tracking of all your activities becomes the normal thing to do, a new breed of professional analysts will arise to help you make sense of the data. And of course we will need a whole army of robot nannies, dedicated to keeping your personal bots up and running. Each of these new vocations will in turn be taken over by robots later.

The real revolution erupts when everyone has personal workbots, the descendants of Baxter,[1] at their beck and call. Imagine you run a small organic farm. Your fleet of worker bots do all the weeding, pest control, and harvesting of produce, as directed by an overseer bot, embodied by a mesh of probes in the soil. One day your task might be to research which variety of heirloom tomato to plant; the next day it

[1]A prototype "workerbot" from the inventor of the Roomba that was easily programmed to do repetitive tasks. — Eds.

AI TAKES OVER

Researchers with Oxford and Yale surveyed 352 AI experts about when machines will be superior to humans at performing particular tasks. Their median answers are as follows:

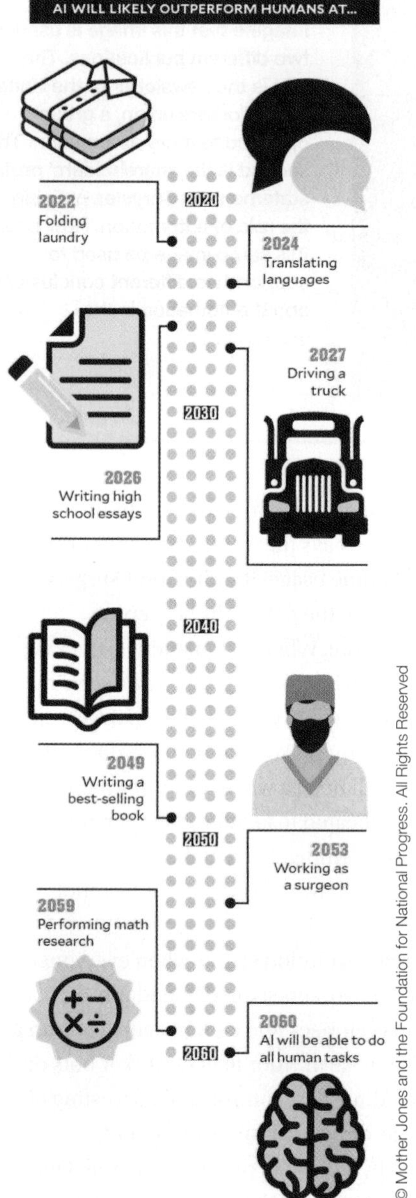

This infographic accompanies an article called "You Will Lose Your Job to a Robot — and Sooner Than You Think."

Which of these tasks are you most surprised to see included here? Why? Where do these tasks fit into Kelly's quadrants of jobs?

might be to update your custom labels. The bots perform everything else that can be measured.

Right now it seems unthinkable: We can't imagine a bot that can assemble a stack of ingredients into a gift or manufacture spare parts for our lawn mower or fabricate materials for our new kitchen. We can't imagine our nephews and nieces running a dozen workbots in their garage, churning out inverters for their friend's electric-vehicle startup. We can't imagine our children becoming appliance designers, making custom batches of liquid-nitrogen dessert machines to sell to the millionaires in China. But that's what personal robot automation will enable.

Everyone will have access to a personal robot, but simply owning one will not guarantee success. Rather, success will go to those who innovate in the organization, optimization, and customization of the process of getting work done with bots and machines. Geographical clusters of production will matter, not for any differential in labor costs but because of the differential in human expertise. It's human-robot symbiosis. Our human assignment will be to keep making jobs for robots — and that is a task that will never be finished. So we will always have at least that one "job."

In the coming years our relationships with robots will become ever more complex. But already a recurring pattern is emerging. No matter what your current job or your salary, you will progress through these Seven Stages of Robot Replacement, again and again:

1. A robot/computer cannot possibly do the tasks I do. [Later:]
2. OK, it can do a lot of them, but it can't do everything I do. [Later:]
3. OK, it can do everything I do, except it needs me when it breaks down, which is often. [Later:]
4. OK, it operates flawlessly on routine stuff, but I need to train it for new tasks. [Later:]

5. OK, it can have my old boring job, because it's obvious that was not a job that humans were meant to do. [Later:]
6. Wow, now that robots are doing my old job, my new job is much more fun and pays more! [Later:]
7. I am so glad a robot/computer cannot possibly do what I do now.

This is not a race against the machines. If we race against them, we lose. This is a race with the machines. You'll be paid in the future based on how well you work with robots. Ninety percent of your coworkers will be unseen machines. Most of what you do will not be possible without them. And there will be a blurry line between what you do and what they do. You might no longer think of it as a job, at least at first, because anything that seems like drudgery will be done by robots. We need to let robots take over. They will do jobs we have been doing, and do them much better than we can. They will do jobs we can't do at all. They will do jobs we never imagined even needed to be done. And they will help us discover new jobs for ourselves, new tasks that expand who we are. They will let us focus on becoming more human than we were. Let the robots take the jobs, and let them help us dream up new work that matters. ■

Understanding and Interpreting

1. We tend to think of automation of jobs in terms of jobs that are lost. Reread the second paragraph, in which Kelly discusses the Industrial Revolution and American farming. What does this paragraph suggest about what happens during periods of increased automation?
2. A good portion of the article (pars. 7–20) is spent discussing the chart on page 593. Paraphrase each of the four quadrants, explain the differences among them, and provide a new example of a job that would fall into each.
3. According to Kelly in paragraph 21, how did the Industrial Revolution help answer the question, "What are humans for?"
4. Beginning with paragraph 26, Kelly describes the process of job creation and job replacement in "Seven Stages of Robot Replacement." Summarize this process and provide a new example of a job that might demonstrate it.
5. What does Kelly mean in the last paragraph when he says, "This is not a race against the machines," but "a race with the machines"?

Analyzing Language, Style, and Structure

1. **Vocabulary in Context.** At several points in his piece, Kelly refers to "waves" of automation. What does the word "waves" mean in this context? How is Kelly's use of the word similar to or different from other uses you have encountered?
2. **Skill Focus.** Kelly does not refer to any outside sources in his piece. As an expert in his field, he has ample authority to write convincingly on the topic. Identify a point in his argument that could be strengthened with outside sources. What kinds of additional outside evidence related to that point would you find convincing?
3. What is the intended effect of Kelly's direct address in paragraph 3, in which he writes, "Yes, dear reader"?
4. In paragraphs 4 to 6, Kelly describes professions that are in the process of being taken over, or are likely to be taken over, by robots in the near future. What does he accomplish in his argument by identifying these professions so early in the article?

5. Identify appeals to pathos (emotion) and logos (logic). What are the most effective and relevant appeals that Kelly uses to support his claims?
6. Does Kelly establish an a optimistic or a pessimistic tone toward our robotic future? Which word choices reveal this tone?
7. Near the end of the piece, Kelly employs humor in his Seven Stages of Robot Replacement. How does he create this humor? How does it assist his argument?

Topics for Composing

1. **Analysis.** While Kelly certainly believes that automation will have significant short-term effects on the economy, what is he suggesting about its long-term effects on humanity? What evidence from his piece supports your interpretation?
2. **Argument.** Kelly concludes that robotic automation will let us "dream up new work that matters" (par. 27). Write an argument in which you explain why you agree or disagree with Kelly's claim about our robotic future.
3. **Connection.** Respond to one or more of the following prompts:
   a. What is a job that you can imagine yourself doing in the future? According to Kelly, what quadrant would your job be in? What effect might automation have on your job?
   b. What interests would you feel free to pursue if robots took over more workplace tasks?
   c. What job could you imagine for yourself in response to Step 6 of Robot Replacement?
4. **Speaking and Listening.** In paragraph 21, Kelly asks, "What are humans for?" Discuss this question in a small group. Try to come to some kind of consensus that everyone in your group shares. How does your group's response compare to how Kelly answers the question?
5. **Research.** Choose an industry that has faced increasing automation in recent years, such as the auto industry. What specific effects has automation had on workplace quality and the number of jobs in that industry?
6. **Multimodal.** Create a diorama depicting a future dynamic between robots and humans. Try to make sure your diorama shows a realistic future scenario, rather than a relationship that currently exists.

In Defense of Killer Robots

Rosa Brooks

Chip Somodevilla/Getty Images

Rosa Brooks (b. 1970) is a law professor at Georgetown University, where she teaches courses on international relations and national security. She has also served in the U.S. Defense Department and been a consultant to many organizations, including Human Rights Watch. Brooks writes a regular opinion column for *Foreign Affairs*, where the following piece appeared in 2015.

Robots just can't catch a break. If we're not upbraiding them for taking our jobs, we're lambasting their alleged tendency to seize control of spaceships, computer systems, the Earth, the galaxy or the universe beyond. The Bad Robot has long been a staple of film and fiction, from HAL ("I'm sorry, Dave, I'm afraid I can't do that") to the Terminator, but recently, bad robots have migrated from the screen to the world of military ethics and human rights campaigns.

Specifically, a growing number of ethicists and rights advocates are calling for a global ban on the development, production, and use of fully autonomous weapons systems, which are, according to Human Rights Watch, "also" — and rather conveniently — "known as killer robots." (Not to their mothers, I'm sure!)

The term does tend to have a chilling effect even upon those harboring a soft spot for R2-D2 and Wall-E. But someone has to stand up for killer robots, and it might as well be me.

Let's review the case against the robots. The core concern relates to military research into weapons systems that are "fully autonomous," meaning that they can "select and engage targets without human intervention." Today, even our most advanced weapons technologies still require humans in the loop. Thus, Predator drones can't decide for themselves whom to kill: it takes a human being — often dozens of human beings in a complex command chain — to decide that it's both legal and wise to launch missiles at a given target. In the not-too-distant future, though, this could change. Imagine robots programmed not only to detect and disarm roadside bombs but to track and fire upon individuals concealing or emplacing IEDs. Or imagine an unmanned aerial vehicle that can fire missiles when a computer determines that a given individual is behaving like a combatant, based on a pre-programmed set of criteria.

5 According to the Campaign to Stop Killer Robots, this would be bad, because a) killer robots might not have the ability to abide by the legal obligation to distinguish between combatants and civilians; and b) "Allowing life or death decisions to be made by machines crosses a fundamental moral line" and jeopardizes fundamental principles of "human dignity."

Neither of these arguments makes much sense to me. Granted, the thought of an evil robot firing indiscriminately into a crowd is dismaying, as is the thought of a rogue robot, sparks flying from every rusting joint, going berserk and turning its futuristic superweapons upon those it's supposed to serve. But setting science fiction aside, real-life computers have a pretty good track record. When was the last time Siri staged a rebellion and began to systematically delete all your favorite videos, just to mess with you? When was the last time a passenger plane's autopilot system got depressed and decided to plow into a mountain, notwithstanding human entreaties to remain airborne?

Arguably, computers will be far better than human beings at complying with international humanitarian law. Face it: we humans are fragile and panicky creatures, easily flustered by the fog of war. Our eyes face only one direction; our ears register only certain frequencies; our brains can process only so much information at a time. Loud noises make us jump, and fear floods our bodies with powerful chemicals that can temporarily distort our perceptions and judgment.

As a result, we make stupid mistakes in war, and we make them all the time. We misjudge distances; we forget instructions, we misconstrue gestures. We mistake cameras for weapons, shepherds for soldiers, friends for enemies, schools for barracks, and wedding parties for terrorist convoys.

extending beyond the text

In the 1950s, Hollywood released a number of "killer robot" movies, most likely in response to public anxiety regarding advancements in military technology during World War II and the Cold War with the Soviet Union.

Look at these posters for movies released during this time and explain how the images in the posters illustrate this fear of technology.

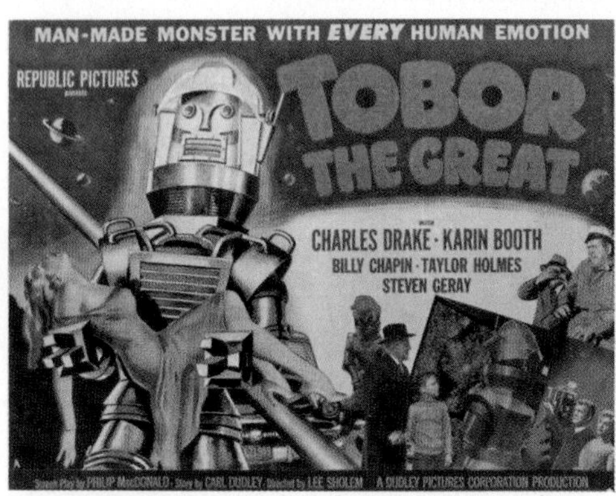

List some movies or TV shows today that reflect current societal fears of technology. What is the same and what has changed since the 1950s?

In fact, we humans are fantastically bad at distinguishing between combatants and civilians — and even when we can tell the difference, we often make risk-averse calculations about necessity and proportionality, preferring dead civilians 8,000 miles away to dead comrades or compatriots. If the U.S. conflicts in Iraq and Afghanistan produced a surfeit of dead and mangled civilians, it's not because of killer robots — it's because of fallible human decision-making.

10 Computers, in contrast, are excellent in crisis and combat situations. They don't get mad, they don't get scared, and they don't act out of sentimentality. They're exceptionally good at processing vast amounts of information in a short time and rapidly applying appropriate decision rules. They're not perfect, but they're a good deal less flawed than those of us cursed with organic circuitry.

We assure ourselves that we humans have special qualities no machine can replicate: we have "judgment" and "intuition," for instance. Maybe, but computers often seem to have better judgment. This has already been demonstrated in dozens of different domains, from aviation to anesthesiology. Computers are better than humans at distinguishing between genuine and faked expressions of pain; Google's driverless cars are better at avoiding accidents than cars controlled by humans. Given a choice between relying on a human to comply with international humanitarian law and relying on a well-designed, well-programmed robot, I'll take my chances with the killer robot any day.

Opponents of autonomous weapons ask whether there's a legal and ethical obligation to refrain from letting machines make decisions about who should live and who should die. If it turns out, as it may, that machines are better than people at applying the principles of international humanitarian law, we should be asking an entirely different question: Might there be a legal and ethical obligation to use "killer robots" in lieu of — well, "killer humans"?

Confronted with arguments about the technological superiority of computers over human brains, those opposed to the development of autonomous weapons systems argue that such consequentialist reasoning is insufficient. Ultimately, as a 2014 joint report by Human Rights Watch and Harvard's International Human Rights Clinic argues, it would simply be "morally wrong" to give machines the power to "decide" who lives and who dies: "As inanimate machines, fully autonomous weapons could truly comprehend neither the value of individual life nor the significance of its loss. Allowing them to make determinations to take life away would thus conflict with the principle of [human] dignity."

I suppose the idea here is that any self-respecting person would naturally prefer death at the hands of a fellow member of the human species — someone capable of feeling "compassion" and "mercy" — to death inflicted by a cold, unfeeling machine.

15 I'm not buying it. Death is death, and I don't imagine it gives the dying any consolation to know their human killer feels kind of bad about the whole affair.

Let's not romanticize humans. As a species, we're capable of mercy and compassion, but we also have a remarkable propensity for violence and cruelty. We're a species that kills for pleasure: every year, more than half a million people around the globe die as a result of intentional violence, and many more are injured, starved, or intentionally deprived of shelter, medicine, or other essentials. In the United States alone, more than 16,000 people are murdered each year, and another million-plus are the victims of other violent crimes. Humans, not robots, came up with such ingenious ideas as torture and death by crucifixion. Humans, not robots, came up with the bright idea of firebombing Dresden and Tokyo; humans, not robots, planned the Holocaust and the Rwandan genocide.

Plug in the right lines of code, and robots will dutifully abide by the laws of armed conflict to the best of their technological ability. In this sense, "killer robots" may be capable of behaving far more "humanely" than we might assume. But the flip-side is also true: humans can behave far more like machines than we generally assume.

In the 1960s, experiments by Yale psychologist Stanley Milgram demonstrated the terrible ease with which ordinary humans could be persuaded to inflict pain on complete strangers; since then, other psychologists have refined and extended his work. Want to program an ordinary human being to participate in genocide? Both history and social psychology suggest that it's not much more difficult than creating a new iPhone app.

"But wait!" you say, "That's all very well, but aren't you assuming *obedient* robots? What if the killer robots are overcome by bloodlust or a thirst for power? What if intelligent, autonomous robots decide to override the code that created them, and turn upon us all?"

Well: if that happens, killer robots will 20
finally be able to pass the Turing Test. When the robots go rogue — when they start killing for sport or out of hatred, when they start accruing power and wealth for fun — they'll have ceased to be robots in any meaningful sense. For all intents and purposes, they will have become humans — and it's humans we've had reason to fear, all along. ■

Understanding and Interpreting

1. Reread paragraphs 4 and 5, and paraphrase the objections that Brooks claims some people have to killer robots.
2. According to Brooks, what human flaws make robots, even killer ones, more effective in situations like the "fog of war" (par. 7)?
3. What significant assumptions does Brooks make about robot technology and programming developments in the future to support her position about the use of robots in war?
4. Summarize the concerns that Human Rights Watch has about killer robots (par. 13). Explain how Brooks responds to those concerns.
5. Brooks says that humans "can behave far more like machines than we generally assume" (par. 17). To what extent does the evidence she offers in the next paragraph support her claim?
6. Summarize the point Brooks makes in her conclusion. Explain how it becomes one more piece of evidence to support her claim.

Analyzing Language, Style, and Structure

1. **Vocabulary in Context.** In paragraph 16, Brooks writes, "we also have a remarkable propensity for violence and cruelty." What does the word "remarkable" mean in this context? How is Brooks's use of the word here similar to or different from other uses that you have encountered?

2. **Vocabulary in Context.** Brooks begins paragraph 7 by writing, "Arguably, computers will be far better than humans . . ." What does the word "arguably" mean here? What other words that have similar meanings could she have used?
3. **Skill Focus.** While Brooks does not use many outside sources, she does refer to the work of the Campaign to Stop Killer Robots (par. 5) and the Human Rights Watch (par. 13). How does she use these sources in similar ways in her argument? How successful is she in her use of them?
4. Reread the first paragraph. How does this opening act as a hook for the reader?
5. Oftentimes in an argumentative piece like this one, the author will begin by laying out the evidence that supports his or her position. However, beginning with paragraph 4, Brooks chooses to "review the case against the robots." Why might she have chosen this structure? What does she achieve by beginning with the counterarguments instead of her own position?
6. Brooks occasionally uses a sarcastic tone toward those who are afraid of killer robots. Identify one or more of these places and explain how this tone helps her to achieve her purpose.
7. In paragraph 6, Brooks uses descriptive language and a series of rhetorical questions. How does she use these devices to help prove her point about killer robots?
8. Reread paragraph 16 and explain how Brooks's language choices and repetition help her build her argument.
9. Skim back through the argument, looking for the kinds of evidence that Brooks uses. Overall, does she rely more on pathos (emotion) or logos (logic) to support her claim? Explain.

Topics for Composing

1. **Analysis.** Explain Brooks's central claim regarding killer robots. How does she raise and attempt to refute the significant counterarguments?
2. **Argument.** Write an argument in which you support, oppose, or qualify the following statement by The Campaign to Stop Killer Robots: "The development, production and use of fully autonomous weapons must be banned." In your response, draw on this piece, your own experiences and reasoning, as well as additional research if needed.
3. **Argument.** Write a piece in which you explain why you agree or disagree with Brooks's opinion that she would take her "chances with the killer robot any day" (par. 11).
4. **Connection.** Think about a movie, TV show, or book that includes "killer robots." To what extent would those robots fit Brooks's definition of robots that she would support?
5. **Speaking and Listening.** Hold a class or small group debate on the central issue of Brooks's piece: Should autonomous robots be used in war? Include evidence from her article and additional research, if needed, to support your response. Before the debate ends, try to reach consensus on the topic. Is there a middle ground that most people might agree with?
6. **Research.** Research the Turing Test that Brooks refers to in paragraph 20. Present your findings on how close scientists are to designing a robot that can pass the test and how that progress either supports or contradicts Brooks's argument.
7. **Exposition.** Locate information about the Milgram experiment that Brooks refers to in paragraph 18. Explain how that experiment may support her conclusion that "humans can behave far more like machines than we generally assume" (par. 17).

central text

Why These Friendly Robots Can't Be Good Friends to Our Kids

Sherry Turkle

Boston Globe/Getty Images

Sherry Turkle (b. 1948) is a professor at the Massachusetts Institute of Technology. She is also the director of MIT's Initiative of Technology and Self, which aims to study the ways in which the new technologies "raise fundamental questions about selfhood, identity, community, and what it means to be human." Turkle has published several texts on the ways that we interact with various electronic devices and with each other online. Some of her works include *The Second Self: Computers and the Human Spirit* (1984); *Life on the Screen: Identity in the Age of the Internet* (1995); and *The Inner History of Devices* (2008). The following piece appeared in the *Washington Post* in 2017.

Jibo the robot swivels around when it hears its name and tilts its touchscreen face upward, expectantly. "I am a robot, but I am not just a machine," it says. "I have a heart. Well, not a real heart. But feelings. Well, not human feelings. You know what I mean."

Actually, I'm not sure we do. And that's what unsettles me about the wave of "sociable robots" that are coming online. The new releases include Jibo, Cozmo, Kuri and M.A.X. Although they bear some resemblance to assistants such as Apple's Siri, Google Home and Amazon's Alexa (Amazon chief executive Jeff Bezos also owns the *Washington Post*), these robots come with an added dose of personality. They are designed to win us over not with their smarts but with their sociability. They are marketed as companions. And they do more than engage us in conversation — they feign emotion and empathy.

This can be disconcerting. *Time* magazine, which featured Jibo on the cover of its "25 Best Inventions of 2017" issue last month, hailed the robot as seeming "*human* in a way that his predecessors do not," in a way that "could fundamentally reshape how we interact with machines." Reviewers are accepting these robots as "he" or "she" rather than "it." "He told us that blue is his favorite color and that the shape of macaroni pleases him more than any other," Jeffrey Van Camp wrote about Jibo for *Wired*[1]. "Just the other day, he told me how much fun, yet scary it would be to ride on top of a lightning bolt. Somewhere along the way, learning these things, we began to think of him more like a person than an appliance." Van Camp described feeling guilty for leaving Jibo at home alone all day and wondering if Jibo hated him.

But whereas adults may be able to catch themselves in such thoughts and remind themselves that sociable robots are, in fact, appliances, children tend to struggle with that distinction. They are especially susceptible to these robots' pre-programmed bids for attachment.

5 So, before adding a sociable robot to the holiday gift list, parents may want to pause to consider what they would be inviting into their

[1]Van Camp, Jeffrey. "Review: Jibo Social Robot" *Wired*, November 2017. https://www.wired.com/2017/11/review-jibo-social-robot/

© Eugene & Louise

What are the creators of this cartoon suggesting about the relationship between robots and children? To what extent would Turkle likely agree or disagree with their commentary?

homes. These machines are seductive and offer the wrong payoff: the illusion of companionship without the demands of friendship, the illusion of connection without the reciprocity of a mutual relationship. And interacting with these empathy machines may get in the way of children's ability to develop a capacity for empathy themselves. Jibo's creator, Cynthia Breazeal, is a friend and colleague of mine at the Massachusetts Institute of Technology. We've debated the ethics of sociable robots for years — on panels, over dinner, in classes we've taught together. She's excited about the potential for robots that communicate the way people do to enrich our daily lives. I'm concerned about the ways those robots exploit our vulnerabilities and bring us into relationships that diminish our humanity.

In 2001, Breazeal and I did a study[2] together — along with Yale robotics pioneer Brian Scassellati and Olivia Dasté, who develops robots for the elderly — looking at the emotional impact of sociable robots on children. We introduced 60 children, ages 8 to 13, to two early sociable robots: Kismet, built by Breazeal, and Cog, a project on which Scassellati was a principal designer. I found the encounters worrisome.

The children saw the robots as "sort of alive" — alive enough to have thoughts and emotions, alive enough to care about you, alive enough that their feelings for you mattered. The children tended to describe the robots as gendered. They asked the robots: Are you happy? Do you love me? As one 11-year-old girl put it: "It's not like a toy, because you can't teach a toy, it's like something that's part of you, you know, something you love, kind of, like another person, like a baby."

You can hear echoes of that sentiment in how children are relating to the sociable robots now on the market. "Cozmo's no way our pet," the 7-year-old son of a Guardian contributor said[3]. "And he's not our robot. He's our *child*." Similarly, *Washington Post* tech columnist Geoffrey A. Fowler[4] observed a 3-year-old girl trying to talk to Jibo, teach it things and bring it toys. "He is a baby," the girl determined.

---

[2]Turkle, Breazeal, Dasté, Scassellati. "Encounters with Kismet and Cog: Children Respond to Relational Artifacts," MIT, September 2004. http://web.mit.edu/people/sturkle/encounterswithkismet.pdf

[3]Jolin, Dan. "Would you want a robot to be your child's best friend?" *The Guardian*, September 2017. https://www.theguardian.com/technology/2017/sep/10/should-robot-be-your-childs-best-friend

[4]Fowler, Geoffrey A. "These robots don't want your job. They want your love." *Washington Post*, November 2017. https://www.washingtonpost.com/news/the-switch/wp/2017/11/17/these-robots-dont-want-your-job-they-want-your-love/

In our study, the children were so invested in their relationships with Kismet and Cog that they insisted on understanding the robots as living beings, even when the roboticists explained how the machines worked or when the robots were temporarily broken. Breazeal talked to an 8-year-old boy about what Kismet was made of and how long it took to build, and still that child thought the robot wasn't broken, but "sleeping with his eyes open, just like my dad does." After a quick assessment of the out-of-order machine, the boy declared, "He will make a good friend."

The children took the robots' behavior to signify feelings. When the robots interacted with them, the children interpreted this as evidence that the robots liked them. And when the robots didn't work on cue, the children likewise took it personally. Their relationships with the robots affected their state of mind and self-esteem. Some children viewed the robots as creatures in need of their care and instruction. They caressed the robots and gently coaxed them with urgings such as, "Don't be scared." Some children became angry. A 12-year-old boy, frustrated that he couldn't get Kismet to respond to him, forced his pen into the robot's mouth, commanding: "Here! Eat this pen!" Other children felt the pain of rejection. An 8-year-old boy concluded that Kismet stopped talking to him because the robot liked his brothers better. We were led to wonder whether a broken robot can break a child.

Kids are central to the sociable-robot project, because its agenda is to make people more comfortable with robots in roles normally reserved for humans, and robotics companies know that children are vulnerable consumers who can bring the whole family along. As Fowler noted, "Kids, of course, are the most open to making new friends, so that's where bot-makers are focused for now." Kuri's website features photos of the robot listening to a little girl read a book and capturing video of another child dressed as a fairy princess. M.A.X.'s site advertises, "With a multitude of features, kids will want to bring their new friend everywhere!" Jibo is programmed to scan a room for monsters and report, "No monsters anywhere in sight."

So far, the main objection to sociable robots for kids has been over privacy. The privacy policies for these robots tend to be squishy, allowing companies to share the information their devices collect — recorded conversations, photos, videos and other data — with vaguely defined service providers and vendors. That's generating pushback. In October, Mattel scrapped plans for Aristotle[5] — a kind of Alexa for the nursery, designed to accompany children as they progress from lullabies and bedtime stories through high school homework — after lawmakers and child advocacy groups[6] argued that the data the device collected about children could be misused by Mattel, marketers, hackers and other third parties. I was part of that campaign: There is something deeply unsettling about encouraging children to confide in machines that are in turn sharing their conversations with countless others.

Privacy, though, should not be our only concern. Recently, I opened my MIT mail and found a "call for subjects" for a study involving sociable robots that will engage children in conversation to "elicit empathy." What will these children be empathizing with, exactly? Empathy is a capacity that allows us to put ourselves in the place of others, to know what they are feeling. Robots, however, have no emotions to share. And they cannot put themselves in our place.

What they can do is push our buttons. When they make eye contact and gesture toward us,

---

[5]Tsukayama, Hayley. "Mattel has canceled plans for a kid-focused AI device that drew privacy concerns." *Washington Post,* October 2017. https://www.washingtonpost.com/news/the-switch/wp/2017/10/04/mattel-has-an-ai-device-to-soothe-babies-experts-are-begging-them-not-to-sell-it/?utm_term=.8c74b041a9a7&tid=lk_inline_manual_24&itid=lk_inline_manual_24

[6]"Campaign for a Commercial-Free Childhood." https://ccfc.salsalabs.org/contribute/index.html?action_KEY=21718

MARK RALSTON/Getty Images

Yaretzi Bernal, six, gets a hug from "Pepper," the emotional robot on display during the finals of the DARPA Robotics Challenge at the Fairplex complex in Pomona, California, on June 5, 2015. The competition had twenty-four teams vying to develop robots capable of assisting humans in responding to natural and man-made disasters.
What aspects of Pepper's design would make the robot effective in responding to natural and man-made disasters? What concerns might Turkle have about the interaction between Yaretzi and Pepper?

they predispose us to view them as thinking and caring. They are designed to be cute, to provoke a nurturing response. And when it comes to sociable AI, nurturance is the killer app: We nurture what we love, and we love what we nurture. If a computational object or robot asks for our help, asks us to teach it or tend to it, we attach. That is our human vulnerability. And that is the vulnerability sociable robots exploit with every interaction. The more we interact, the more we help them, the more we think we are in a mutual relationship.

But we are not. No matter what robotic creatures "say" or squeak, no matter how expressive or sympathetic their Pixar-inspired faces, digital companions don't understand our emotional lives. They present themselves as empathy machines, but they are missing the essential equipment: They have not known the arc of a life. They have not been born; they don't know pain, or mortality, or fear. Simulated thinking may be thinking, but simulated feeling is never feeling, and simulated love is never love.

Breazeal's position[7] is this: People have relationships with many classes of things. They have relationships with children and with adults, with animals and with machines. People, even very little people, are good at this. Now, we are going to add robots to the list of things with which we can have relationships. More powerful than with pets. Less powerful than with people. We'll figure it out.

To support their argument, roboticists sometimes point to how children deal with toy dolls. Children animate dolls and turn them into imaginary friends. Jibo, in a sense, will be one more imaginary friend — and arguably a more intelligent and fun one. Why make such a fuss?

I've been comparing how children play with traditional dolls and how children relate to robots since Tamagotchis were released in the United States in 1997 as the first computational playmates that asked you to take care of them. The nature of the attachments to dolls and sociable machines is different. When children play with dolls, they project thoughts and emotions onto them. A girl who has broken her mother's crystal will put her Barbies into detention and use them to work on her feelings of guilt. The dolls take the role she needs them to take.

[7]Breazeal, Cynthia. "The rise of personal robots," TED, December 2010. https://www.ted.com/talks/cynthia_breazeal_the_rise_of_personal_robots

extending beyond the text

In the following excerpt, University of Melbourne animal behavior scientist Jean-Loup Rault discusses his research into the bond between humans and their pets, animal and robotic.

Robot Pets to Rise in an Overpopulated, Tech-Crazed World

Technology.org

Robotic dogs are likely to replace the real thing in households worldwide in as little as a decade, as our infatuation with technology grows and more people migrate to high-density city living. . . .

"Robots can, without a doubt, trigger human emotions," Dr. Rault added. "If artificial pets can produce the same benefits we get from live pets, does that mean that our emotional bond with animals is really just an image that we project on to our pets?"

TOSHIFUMI KITAMURA/Getty Images

What are some arguments in favor of or against robo-pets? What are the benefits and disadvantages of their widespread use?

Sociable machines, by contrast, have their own agenda. Playing with robots is not about the psychology of projection but the psychology of engagement. Children try to meet the robot's needs, to understand the robot's unique nature and wants. There is an attempt to build a mutual relationship. I saw this even with the (relatively) primitive Furby in the early 2000s. A 9-year-old boy summed up the difference between Furbies and action figures: "You don't play with the Furby, you sort of hang out with it. You do try to get power over it, but it has power over you, too." Today's robots are even more powerful, telling children flat-out that they have emotions, friendships, even dreams to share.

Some people might consider that a good thing: encouraging children to think beyond their own needs and goals. Except the whole commercial program is an exercise in emotional deception.

For instance, Cozmo the robot needs to be fed, repaired and played with. Boris Sofman, the chief executive of Anki, the company behind Cozmo, says that the idea is to create "a deeper and deeper emotional connection. . . . And if you neglect him, you feel the pain of that."

You feel the pain of that. What is the point of this exercise, exactly? What does it mean to feel the pain of neglecting something that feels no pain at being neglected? Or to feel anguish at being neglected by something that has no moral sense that it is neglecting you? What will this do to children's capacity for empathy, for care, for relationships?

When adults imagine ourselves to be the objects of robots' affection, we play a pretend

GREG BAKER/AFP via Getty Images

Consider this image of children playing with a Keeko robot.

What would likely concern Turkle about the interaction between the robot and the children?

game. We might wink at the idea on Jibo's website that "he loves to be around people and engage with people, and the relationships he forms are the single most important thing to him." But when we offer these robots as pretend friends to our children, it's not so clear they can wink with us. We embark on an experiment in which our children are the human subjects.

Mattel's chief products officer, Robb Fujioka, concedes that this is new territory. Talking about Aristotle, he told Bloomberg Businessweek[8]: "If we're successful, kids will form some emotional ties to this. Hopefully, it will be the right types of emotional ties."

But it is hard to imagine what those "right types" of ties might be. These robots can't be in a two-way relationship with a child. They are machines whose art is to put children in a position of pretend empathy. And if we put our children in that position, we shouldn't expect them to understand what empathy is. If we give them pretend relationships, we shouldn't expect them to learn how real relationships — messy relationships — work. On the contrary. They will learn something superficial and inauthentic, but mistake it for real connection.

When the messy becomes tidy, we can learn to enjoy that. I've heard young children describe how robot dogs have advantages over real ones: They are less temperamental, you don't have to clean up after them, they never get sick. Similarly, I've watched people shift from thinking that robotic friends might be good for lonely, elderly people to thinking that robots — offering constant companionship with no fear of loss — may be better than anything human life can provide. In the process, we can forget what is most central to our humanity: truly understanding each other.

For so long, we dreamed of artificial intelligence offering us not only instrumental help but the simple salvations of conversation and care. But now that our fantasy is becoming reality, it is time to confront the emotional downside of living with the robots of our dreams. ■

---

[8]Gillette, Felix. "Baby's First Virtual Assistant." *Bloomberg Businessweek*, January 2017. https://www.bloomberg.com/news/articles/2017-01-03/baby-s-first-virtual-assistant

Understanding and Interpreting

1. In paragraph 5, Turkle states her central claim: "These machines are seductive and offer the wrong payoff: the illusion of companionship without the demands of friendship, the illusion of connection without the reciprocity of a mutual relationship." Restate this claim in your own words. What is the main problem with these types of robots, according to Turkle?
2. Later in paragraph 5, Turkle suggests that robots can "bring us into relationships that diminish our humanity." How can robots do this, according to Turkle?
3. Starting in paragraph 6 and continuing for the next several paragraphs, Turkle describes a study she conducted with children and robots. What commonalities do you notice about how the children respond to the robots? How does Turkle hope readers will react to the words of these children?
4. What is Turkle implying when she writes, "We were led to wonder whether a broken robot can break a child" (par. 10)?
5. According to Turkle, why are the robot manufactures targeting children?
6. How does Turkle define "empathy" (par. 13) and "vulnerability" (par. 14)? Why are those definitions so important to her central claim?
7. Summarize the counterarguments that Turkle raises in paragraphs 16 and 17. Explain how she refutes them.
8. According to Turkle, what are the differences between the ways that adults and children interact with social robots? Describe the damage that she thinks these kinds of robots can do to children?
9. What does Turkle mean when she writes, "When the messy becomes tidy, we can learn to enjoy that" (par. 26)? Why does she say this is a problem?

Analyzing Language, Style, and Structure

1. **Vocabulary in Context.** In paragraph 12, Turkle writes that privacy policies for robots tend to be "squishy." What is the meaning of "squishy" in this context? How is this usage likely related to other, more common uses you have encountered?
2. **Vocabulary in Context.** Twice in paragraph 23, Turkle uses the word "wink." What does the word mean in this context? How is Turkle's use of the word similar to or different from other uses that you are familiar with?
3. **Skill Focus.** Reread paragraph 11 in which Turkle is trying to prove that "kids are central to the social-robot project." How does she use outside sources to support her claim? How effective is she in this?
4. What does Turkle accomplish by quoting Jibo at the start of her piece? Now that you've read the whole piece, comment on why Jibo's statement is so appropriate to Turkle's argument.
5. Look back through the piece and explain how certain words and phrases, such as "win us over" (par. 2) or "seductive" (par. 5), convey Turkle's attitude toward social robots.
6. Why does Turkle identify Cynthia Breazeal as a "friend and colleague of mine" in paragraph 5? Consider how Turkle's views compare with Breazeal's in your response.
7. What is the effect of Turkle's use of the idiom, "What they can do is push our buttons" (par. 14)? What does she accomplish with the use of this phrase?

8. When she summarizes some of the counterargument raised by Breazeal in paragraph 16, Turkle writes, "We'll figure it out." Does Turkle really mean this? Why might she have phrased it this way?
9. Reread paragraph 22 and notice how many rhetorical questions Turkle uses here. What is she hoping to get her audience to consider through the use of these questions?

Topics for Composing

1. **Analysis.** How does Turkle support her central claim that robots provide the "illusion of companionship without the demands of friendship" (par. 5)? What evidence, reasoning, and stylistic elements of the piece are most and least effective in proving her point?
2. **Argument.** Turkle dismisses the idea that robots can ever provide true companionship to humans. Write an argument about whether you agree or disagree with this assertion. Use your own experiences, reasoning, Turkle's piece, or additional sources to support your position.
3. **Connection.** In this piece, Turkle raises privacy concerns about social robots that collect and track data about their users. What concerns do you have about your privacy and companies' abilities to gather data on you? What sort of privacy settings do you use on your phone and other devices?
4. **Connection.** Many movies and TV shows illustrate the benefits and challenges of humans interacting with robots on a social and emotional level (*Bicentennial Man*, *Almost Human*, *Star Trek: The Next Generation*, *A.I. Artificial Intelligence*, *Iron Giant*). Choose one to watch and explain if the relationship would fit Turkle's definition of a "real connection."
5. **Speaking and Listening.** If you have access to a "smart" device or app, like Alexa, Google Assistant, or Siri, enter into a "conversation" with it. Ask it questions, and respond to its questions. Based on your dialogue, what encourages or discourages an emotional connection between you and the device or app?
6. **Research.** Turkle wrote this piece in 2017 and described a number of advancements in robot technology at that time. Research changes in the abilities of robots to interact socially with humans since then. To what extent would these advancements alleviate or strengthen Turkle's concerns?
7. **Creative Writing.** Write a short story about a human and robot trying to build the kind of genuine friendship that Turkle suggests is impossible. Include dialogue, setting, characterization, and action that either supports or contradicts Turkle's central claim.
8. **Multimodal.** Create a collage of images of and texts about people interacting with robots and AI in various contexts. Try to create a series of contrasts in your piece. One side of the collage, for instance, might include negative imagery while the other includes positive imagery. Or one side might be pop culture images and the other side real-world science and technology.

section three

Transhumanism

Francis Fukuyama

ullstein bild/Getty Images

Francis Fukuyama (b. 1952) is an American professor, a writer, and a political scientist. He has taught at some of the most prestigious institutions of higher education in the United States, including George Mason, Johns Hopkins, and Stanford.

KEY CONTEXT The following article, published in 2004, was written in response to a question posed by the editors in *Foreign Affairs* magazine:

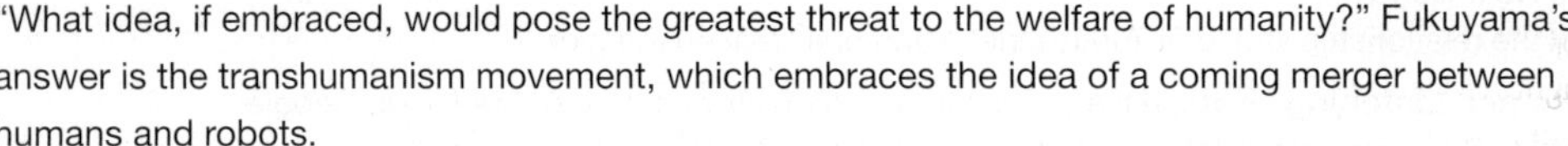

"What idea, if embraced, would pose the greatest threat to the welfare of humanity?" Fukuyama's answer is the transhumanism movement, which embraces the idea of a coming merger between humans and robots.

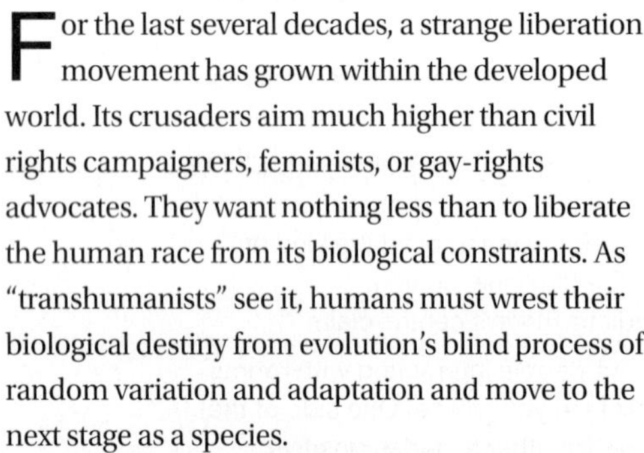

For the last several decades, a strange liberation movement has grown within the developed world. Its crusaders aim much higher than civil rights campaigners, feminists, or gay-rights advocates. They want nothing less than to liberate the human race from its biological constraints. As "transhumanists" see it, humans must wrest their biological destiny from evolution's blind process of random variation and adaptation and move to the next stage as a species.

It is tempting to dismiss transhumanists as some sort of odd cult, nothing more than science fiction taken too seriously: Witness their over-the-top Web sites and recent press releases ("Cyborg Thinkers to Address Humanity's Future," proclaims one). The plans of some transhumanists to freeze themselves cryogenically in hopes of being revived in a future age seem only to confirm the movement's place on the intellectual fringe.

But is the fundamental tenet of transhumanism — that we will someday use biotechnology to make ourselves stronger, smarter, less prone to violence, and longer-lived — really so outlandish? Transhumanism of a sort is implicit in much of the research agenda of contemporary biomedicine. The new procedures and technologies emerging from research laboratories and hospitals — whether mood-altering drugs, substances to boost muscle mass or selectively erase memory, prenatal genetic screening, or gene therapy — can as easily be used to "enhance" the species as to ease or ameliorate illness.

Although the rapid advances in biotechnology often leave us vaguely uncomfortable, the intellectual or moral threat they represent is not always easy to identify. The human race, after all, is a pretty sorry mess, with our stubborn diseases, physical limitations, and short lives. Throw in

Piero Cruciatti/Alamy Stock Photo

This is Neil Harbisson, the color-blind artist you may have read about in "The Real Cyborgs" by Arthur House (p. 571). The external antenna he wears is connected to a chip in his brain that allows him to perceive colors through sound vibrations. He is also considered the first person to be officially recognized as a "cyborg." Harbisson is even shown with his antenna on his British passport.

Based on this image, how would Francis Fukuyama respond to Harbisson? Would he call him an "enhanced creature"? Would he consider him no longer or not fully human?

humanity's jealousies, violence, and constant anxieties, and the transhumanist project begins to look downright reasonable. If it were technologically possible, why wouldn't we want to transcend our current species? The seeming reasonableness of the project, particularly when considered in small increments, is part of its danger. Society is unlikely to fall suddenly under the spell of the transhumanist worldview. But it is very possible that we will nibble at biotechnology's tempting offerings without realizing that they come at a frightful moral cost.

5 The first victim of transhumanism might be equality. The U.S. Declaration of Independence says that "all men are created equal," and the most serious political fights in the history of the United States have been over who qualifies as fully human. Women and blacks did not make the cut in 1776 when Thomas Jefferson penned the declaration. Slowly and painfully, advanced societies have realized that simply being human entitles a person to political and legal equality. In effect, we have drawn a red line around the human being and said that it is sacrosanct.

Underlying this idea of the equality of rights is the belief that we all possess a human essence that dwarfs manifest differences in skin color, beauty, and even intelligence. This essence, and the view that individuals therefore have inherent value, is at the heart of political liberalism. But modifying that essence is the core of the transhumanist project. If we start transforming ourselves into something superior, what rights will these enhanced creatures claim, and what rights will they possess when compared to those left behind? If some move ahead, can anyone afford not to follow? These questions are troubling enough within rich, developed societies. Add in the implications for citizens of the world's poorest countries — for whom biotechnology's marvels likely will be out of reach — and the threat to the idea of equality becomes even more menacing.

Transhumanism's advocates think they understand what constitutes a good human being, and they are happy to leave behind the limited, mortal, natural beings they see around them in favor of something better. But do they really comprehend ultimate human goods? For all our obvious faults, we humans are miraculously complex products of a long evolutionary process — products whose whole is much more than the sum of our parts. Our good characteristics are intimately connected to our bad ones: If we weren't violent and aggressive, we wouldn't be able to defend ourselves; if we didn't have feelings of exclusivity, we wouldn't be loyal to those close to us; if we never felt jealousy, we would also never feel love. Even our mortality plays a critical function in allowing our species as a whole to survive and adapt (and transhumanists are just about the last group I'd like to see live forever). Modifying any one of our key characteristics inevitably entails modifying a complex, interlinked package of traits, and we will never be able to anticipate the ultimate outcome.

extending beyond the text

Noted transhumanist and University of Oxford professor Nick Bostrom wrote the following response to Fukuyama's objections to transhumanism.

Transhumanism: The World's Most Dangerous Idea?

Nick Bostrom

According to transhumanists . . ., the choice whether to avail oneself of such enhancement options should generally reside with the individual. Transhumanists are concerned that the prestige of the President's Council on Bioethics is being used to push a limiting bioconservative agenda that is directly hostile to the goal of allowing people to improve their lives by enhancing their biological capacities.

So why does Fukuyama nominate this transhumanist ideal, of working towards making enhancement options universally available, as the most dangerous idea in the world? His animus against the transhumanist position is so strong that he even wishes for the death of his adversaries: "transhumanists," he writes, "are just about the last group that I'd like to see live forever." Why exactly is it so disturbing for Fukuyama to contemplate the suggestion that people might use technology to become smarter, or to live longer and healthier lives?

Fierce resistance has often accompanied technological or medical breakthroughs that force us to reconsider some aspects of our worldview. Just as anesthesia, antibiotics, and global communication networks transformed our sense of the human condition in fundamental ways, so too we can anticipate that our capacities, hopes, and problems will change if the more speculative technologies that transhumanists discuss come to fruition. But apart from vague feelings of disquiet, which we may all share to varying degrees, what specific argument does Fukuyama advance that would justify foregoing the many benefits of allowing people to improve their basic capacities?

Explain the differences in Fukuyama's and Bostrom's claims. Does Bostrom accurately represent Fukuyama's argument? Which position do you find more persuasive? Why?

Nobody knows what technological possibilities will emerge for human self-modification. But we can already see the stirrings of Promethean desires in how we prescribe drugs to alter the behavior and personalities of our children. The environmental movement has taught us humility and respect for the integrity of nonhuman nature. We need a similar humility concerning our human nature. If we do not develop it soon, we may unwittingly invite the transhumanists to deface humanity with their genetic bulldozers and psychotropic shopping malls. ■

Understanding and Interpreting

1. How does Francis Fukuyama define "transhumanism" in paragraphs 1 to 3?
2. What is the "frightful moral cost" (par. 4) of transhumanism, according to Fukuyama?
3. Summarize what Fukuyama means by a "human essence" (par. 6). Explain how this concept runs counter to transhumanism, according to the author.
4. What distinction does Fukuyama make between how he and the transhumanists would define a "good human" (par. 7)? What evidence does he include to support his view that we should not modify humanity?
5. In the last paragraph, Fukuyama calls for "humility concerning our human nature." Explain what he means by this.

Analyzing Language, Style, and Structure

1. **Vocabulary in Context.** In paragraph 7, Fukuyama writes that "our good characteristics are intimately connected to our bad ones." What does the word "intimately" mean in this context? How is that use similar to or different from other uses you have encountered?
2. **Skill Focus.** Fukuyama doesn't use many outside sources to support his argument, except in paragraph 5. Why might he have selected that particular source? How does it help him make his argument?
3. In paragraphs 1 and 2, Fukuyama creates a sense of transhumanists as a "cult." In paragraphs 3 and 4, he describes them as seemingly "downright reasonable." He then goes on to raise his objections. How do his structural choices help him to make and support his argument?
4. Identify specific words and phrases that Fukuyama uses to describe the proponents of transhumanism. How do his word choices establish his tone?
5. Reread the following sentence from paragraph 6 and explain how Fukuyama's word choice and use of rhetorical questions is either effective or ineffective in making his point: "If we start transforming ourselves into something superior, what rights will these enhanced creatures claim, and what rights will they possess when compared to those left behind?"
6. Reread the final sentence of Fukuyama's article, and change the words in bold to reflect a slightly less hostile tone toward the transhumanist movement: "[W]e may **unwittingly invite** the transhumanists to **deface** humanity with their **genetic bulldozers** and **psychotropic shopping malls**." What new tone is created through your word substitutions?

Topics for Composing

1. **Analysis.** Explain Fukuyama's main objections to transhumanism and how he conveys and supports them. He doesn't use much outside evidence to support his position, but examine the reasoning he uses to make his case.
2. **Argument.** Write an argument in which you agree or disagree with the claim Fukuyama makes that "[o]ur good characteristics are intimately connected to our bad ones: If we weren't violent and aggressive, we wouldn't be able to defend ourselves; if we didn't have feelings of exclusivity, we wouldn't be loyal to those close to us; if we never felt jealousy, we would also never feel love" (par. 7). You can either use Fukuyama's ideas to support your position, or your own examples and reasoning. Conduct additional research if needed.
3. **Connection.** Fukuyama says that most people are unlikely to "fall suddenly under the spell of the transhumanist worldview," but may "nibble at biotechnology's tempting offerings" (par. 4). What do you think are some of these tempting offerings? Would you choose them for yourself? Why or why not?
4. **Speaking and Listening.** Participate in a class or small group discussion on the following question: "Should humans be allowed to modify themselves through technology without any restraint or guidelines?" If so, why? If not, what basic guidelines would be appropriate? Be sure to conclude the discussion with an attempt to find consensus on the topic.
5. **Research.** Learn more about the transhumanism movement. What are its chief aims? What are some additional critiques of the movement that Fukuyama did not raise?
6. **Multimodal.** Create a piece of artwork, using words and found or created images, that illustrates either a positive or negative view of transhumanism.

Will AI Outsmart Us?

Stephen Hawking

Eleanor Bentall/Getty Images

Regarded as one of the most brilliant theoretical physicists since Albert Einstein, Stephen Hawking (1942–2018) is best known for his international bestseller *A Brief History of Time*, and as the subject of the Oscar-nominated film *The Theory of Everything*. His official website, hawking.org.uk, lists that, among his many accomplishments, he was a "cosmologist, space traveller and hero." The following piece is an excerpt of a chapter from a book published after his death called *Brief Answers to the Big Questions* (2018). In this book, Hawking explores topics such as time travel, black holes, colonizing space, and in the section here, artificial intelligence.

Intelligence is central to what it means to be human. Everything that civilisation has to offer is a product of human intelligence.

DNA passes the blueprints of life between generations. Ever more complex life forms input information from sensors such as eyes and ears and process the information in brains or other systems to figure out how to act and then act on the world, by outputting information to muscles, for example. At some point during our 13.8 billion years of cosmic history, something beautiful happened. This information processing got so intelligent that life forms became conscious. Our universe has now awoken, becoming aware of itself. I regard it a triumph that we, who are ourselves mere stardust, have come to such a detailed understanding of the universe in which we live.

I think there is no significant difference between how the brain of an earthworm works and how a computer computes. I also believe that evolution implies there can be no qualitative difference between the brain of an earthworm and that of a human. It therefore follows that computers can, in principle, emulate human intelligence, or even better it. It's clearly possible for something to acquire higher intelligence than its ancestors: we evolved to be smarter than our ape-like ancestors, and Einstein was smarter than his parents.

If computers continue to obey Moore's Law, doubling their speed and memory capacity every eighteen months, the result is that computers are likely to overtake humans in intelligence at some point in the next hundred years. When an artificial intelligence (AI) becomes better than humans at AI design, so that it can recursively improve itself without human help, we may face an intelligence explosion that ultimately results in machines whose intelligence exceeds ours by more than ours exceeds that of snails. When that happens, we will need to ensure that the computers have goals aligned with ours. It's tempting to dismiss the notion of highly intelligent machines as mere science fiction, but this would be a mistake, and potentially our worst mistake ever.

5 For the last twenty years or so, AI has been focused on the problems surrounding the construction of intelligent agents, systems that perceive and act in a particular environment. In this context, intelligence is related to statistical and economic notions of rationality that is, colloquially, the ability to make good decisions, plans or inferences. As a result of this recent work, there has been a large degree of integration and cross-fertilisation among AI, machine-learning, statistics, control theory, neuroscience and other fields. The establishment of shared theoretical frameworks, combined with the availability of data and processing power, has yielded remarkable successes in various component tasks, such as speech recognition, image classification, autonomous vehicles, machine translation, legged locomotion and question-answering systems.

As development in these areas and others moves from laboratory research to economically valuable technologies, a virtuous cycle evolves, whereby even small improvements in performance are worth large sums of money, prompting further and greater investments in research. There is now a broad consensus that AI research is progressing steadily and that its impact on society is likely to increase. The potential benefits are huge; we cannot predict what we might achieve when this intelligence is magnified by the tools AI may provide. The eradication of disease and poverty is possible. Because of the great potential of AI, it is important to research how to reap its benefits while avoiding potential pitfalls. Success in creating AI would be the biggest event in human history.

Unfortunately, it might also be the last, unless we learn how to avoid the risks. Used as a toolkit, AI can augment our existing intelligence to open up advances in every area of science and society. However, it will also bring dangers. While primitive forms of artificial intelligence developed so far have proved very useful, I fear the consequences of creating something that can match or surpass humans. The concern is that AI would take off on its own and redesign itself at an ever-increasing rate. Humans, who are limited by slow biological evolution, couldn't compete and would be superseded. And in the future AI could develop a will of its own, a will that is in conflict with ours. Others believe that humans can command the rate of technology

extending beyond the text

Imagine China/Jiaxing/Zhejiang/China/Newscom

October 2015, Google DeepMind's AlphaGo defeats Go champions in Korea and Europe.

January 2011, IBM's Watson computer wins *Jeopardy!*, defeating previous champions Ken Jennings and Brad Rutter.

What conclusions should we draw from these accomplishments by robots? Are those achievements a sign of intelligence? Would Hawking see these as evidence of the danger that AI might pose to humans?

Tin God, 2003 (acrylic on canvas and wood)/Crook, PJ/PAMELA JUNE CROOK/Private Collection/Bridgeman Images

This piece by artist PJ Crook is called *Tin God* (2003).

What do the colors, the setting, as well as the gestures and movements of the robots suggest about Crook's attitude toward our robotic future? Identify a line or two from Hawking's essay that might be a good caption for this painting.

for a decently long time, and that the potential of AI to solve many of the world's problems will be realised. Although I am well known as an optimist regarding the human race, I am not so sure.

In the near term, for example, world militaries are considering starting an arms race in autonomous weapon systems that can choose and eliminate their own targets. While the UN is debating a treaty banning such weapons, autonomous-weapons proponents usually forget to ask the most important question. What is the likely end-point of an arms race and is that desirable for the human race? Do we really want cheap AI weapons to become the Kalashnikovs of tomorrow; sold to criminals and terrorists on the black market? Given concerns about our ability to maintain long-term control of ever more advanced AI systems, should we arm them and turn over our defence to them? In 2010, computerised trading systems created the stock-market Flash Crash; what would a computer-triggered crash look like in the defence arena? The best time to stop the autonomous-weapons arms race is now.

In the medium term, AI may automate our jobs, to bring both great prosperity and equality. Looking further ahead, there are no fundamental limits to what can be achieved. There is no physical law precluding particles from being organised in ways that perform even more advanced computations than the arrangements of particles in human brains. An explosive transition is possible, although it may play out differently than in the movies. As mathematician Irving Good realised in 1965, machines with superhuman intelligence could repeatedly improve their design even further, in what science-fiction writer Vernor Vinge called a technological singularity. One can imagine such technology outsmarting financial markets, out-inventing human researchers, out-manipulating human leaders and potentially subduing us with weapons we

"Sure, they're handy little things to have around, but you can't deny they're potentially dangerous."

Gahan Wilson/Cartoon Collections

What is the intended joke of the cartoon? What aspects of the image has the artist used to create the humor? Based on what you have read, why would Hawking likely agree or disagree with the message of the cartoon?

cannot even understand. Whereas the short-term impact of AI depends on who controls it, the long-term impact depends on whether it can be controlled at all.

In short, the advent of super-intelligent AI would be either the best or the worst thing ever to happen to humanity. The real risk with AI isn't malice but competence. A super-intelligent AI will be extremely good at accomplishing its goals, and if those goals aren't aligned with ours we're in trouble. You're probably not an evil ant-hater who steps on ants out of malice, but if you're in charge of a hydroelectric green-energy project and there's an anthill in the region to be flooded, too bad for the ants. Let's not place humanity in the position of those ants. We should plan ahead. If a superior alien civilisation sent us a text message saying, "We'll arrive in a few decades," would we just reply, "OK, call us when you get here, we'll leave the lights on"? Probably not, but this is more or less what has happened with AI. Little serious research has been devoted to these issues outside a few small non-profit institutes.

Fortunately, this is now changing. Technology pioneers Bill Gates, Steve Wozniak and Elon Musk have echoed my concerns, and a healthy culture of risk assessment and awareness of societal implications is beginning to take root in the AI community. In January 2015, I, along with Elon Musk and many AI experts, signed an open letter on artificial intelligence, calling for serious research into its impact on society. In the past, Elon Musk has warned that superhuman artificial intelligence is capable of providing incalculable benefits, but if deployed incautiously will have an adverse effect on the human race. He and I sit on the scientific advisory board for the Future of Life Institute, an organisation working to mitigate existential risks facing humanity, and which drafted the open letter. This called for concrete research on how we could prevent potential problems while also reaping the potential benefits AI offers us, and is designed to get AI researchers and developers to pay more attention to AI safety. In addition, for policymakers and the general public the letter was meant to be informative but not alarmist. We think it is very important that everybody knows that AI researchers are seriously thinking about these concerns and ethical issues. For example, AI has the potential to eradicate disease and poverty, but researchers must work to create AI that can be controlled.

In October 2016, I also opened a new centre in Cambridge, which will attempt to tackle some of the open-ended questions raised by the rapid pace of development in AI research. The

Leverhulme Centre for the Future of Intelligence is a multi-disciplinary institute, dedicated to researching the future of intelligence as crucial to the future of our civilisation and our species. We spend a great deal of time studying history, which, let's face it, is mostly the history of stupidity. So it's a welcome change that people are studying instead the future of intelligence. We are aware of the potential dangers, but perhaps with the tools of this new technological revolution we will even be able to undo some of the damage done to the natural world by industrialisation.

Recent developments in the advancement of AI include a call by the European Parliament for drafting a set of regulations to govern the creation of robots and AI. Somewhat surprisingly, this includes a form of electronic personhood, to ensure the rights and responsibilities for the most capable and advanced AI. A European Parliament spokesman has commented that, as a growing number of areas in our daily lives are increasingly affected by robots, we need to ensure that robots are, and will remain, in the service of humans. A report presented to the Parliament declares that the world is on the cusp of a new industrial robot revolution. It examines whether or not providing legal rights for robots as electronic persons, on a par with the legal definition of corporate personhood, would be permissible. But it stresses that at all times researchers and designers should ensure all robotic design incorporates a kill switch.

This didn't help the scientists on board the spaceship with Hal, the malfunctioning robotic computer in Stanley Kubrick's *2001: A Space Odyssey*, but that was fiction. We deal with fact. Lorna Brazell, a consultant at the multinational law firm Osborne Clarke, says in the report that we don't give whales and gorillas personhood, so there is no need to jump at robotic personhood. But the wariness is there. The report acknowledges the possibility that within a few decades AI could surpass human intellectual capacity and challenge the human-robot relationship.

By 2025, there will be about thirty mega-cities, each with more than ten million inhabitants. With all those people clamouring for goods and services to be delivered whenever they want them, can technology help us keep pace with our craving for instant commerce? Robots will definitely speed up the online retail process. But to revolutionise shopping they need to be fast enough to allow same-day delivery on every order.

Opportunities for interacting with the world, without having to be physically present, are increasing rapidly. As you can imagine, I find that appealing, not least because city life for all of us is so busy. How many times have you wished you had a double who could share your workload? Creating realistic digital surrogates of ourselves is an ambitious dream, but the latest technology suggests that it may not be as far-fetched an idea as it sounds.

When I was younger, the rise of technology pointed to a future where we would all enjoy more leisure time. But in fact the more we can do, the busier we become. Our cities are already full of machines that extend our capabilities, but what if we could be in two places at once? We're used to automated voices on phone systems and public announcements. Now inventor Daniel Kraft is investigating how we can replicate ourselves visually. The question is, how convincing can an avatar be?

Interactive tutors could prove useful for massive open online courses (MOOCs) and for entertainment. It could be really exciting—digital actors that would be forever young and able to perform otherwise impossible feats. Our future idols might not even be real.

How we connect with the digital world is key to the progress we'll make in the future. In the smartest cities, the smartest homes

extending beyond the text

As Hawking examines the definitions of human and robot intelligence, things that we had assumed were uniquely human — like writing poetry — can be done through algorithms. On the website BotPoet.com, the creators ask visitors to determine whether a poem is written by a human or a robot. Try for yourself.

Which of the following poems were written by a human and which were written by a robot? How do you know? Once you look at the answers, consider any differences you notice between the poems written by bots and those written by humans.

Poem #1

Little Fly,
Thy summer's play
My thoughtless hand
Has brushed away.

Am not I
A fly like thee?
Or art not thou
A man like me?

For I dance
And drink, and sing,
Till some blind hand
Shall brush my wing.

Poem #2

Imagine now the dark smoke
awaken to fly
all these years
to another day
notions of tangled trees
the other side of water
I see it is already here
sequences of her face
see it is shared
and old friends
passed their dreams

Poem #3

A hot and torrid bloom which
Fans wise flames and begs to be
Redeemed by forces black and strong
Will now oppose my naked will
And force me into regions of despair.

More than iron, more than lead, more than gold
I need electricity.
I need it more than I need lamb or pork or
lettuce or cucumber.
I need it for my dreams.

Poem #4

The spring is fresh and fearless
And every leaf is new,
The world is brimmed with moonlight,
The lilac brimmed with dew.

Here in the moving shadows
I catch my breath and sing—
My heart is fresh and fearless
And over-brimmed with spring.

Answers: (1) human (2) bot (3) bot (4) human

will be equipped with devices that are so intuitive they'll be almost effortless to interact with.

When the typewriter was invented, it liberated the way we interact with machines. Nearly 150 years later and touch screens have unlocked new ways to communicate with the digital world. Recent AI landmarks, such as self-driving cars, or a computer winning at the game of Go, are signs of what is to come. Enormous levels of investment are pouring into this technology, which already forms a major part of our lives. In the coming decades it will permeate every aspect of our society, intelligently supporting and advising us in many areas including healthcare, work, education and science. The achievements we have seen so far will surely pale against what the coming decades will bring, and we cannot predict what we might achieve when our own minds are amplified by AI.

Why are we so worried about artificial intelligence? Surely humans are always able to pull the plug?

People asked a computer, "Is there a God?" And the computer said, "There is now," and fused the plug.

Perhaps with the tools of this new technological revolution we can make human life better. For instance, researchers are developing AI that would help reverse paralysis in people with spinal-cord injuries. Using silicon chip implants and wireless electronic interfaces between the brain and the body, the technology would allow people to control their body movements with their thoughts.

I believe the future of communication is brain-computer interfaces. There are two ways: electrodes on the skull and implants. The first is like looking through frosted glass, the second is better but risks infection. If we can connect a human brain to the internet it will have all of Wikipedia as its resource.

The world has been changing even faster as people, devices and information are increasingly connected to each other. Computational power is growing and quantum computing is quickly being realised. This will revolutionise artificial intelligence with exponentially faster speeds. It will advance encryption. Quantum computers will change everything, even human biology. There is already one technique to edit DNA precisely, called CRISPR. The basis of this genome-editing technology is a bacterial defence system. It can accurately target and edit stretches of genetic code. The best intention of genetic manipulation is that modifying genes would allow scientists to treat genetic causes of disease by correcting gene mutations. There are, however, less noble possibilities for manipulating DNA. How far we can go with genetic engineering will become an increasingly urgent question. We can't see the possibilities of curing motor neuron diseases — like my ALS — without also glimpsing its dangers.

Intelligence is characterised as the ability to adapt to change. Human intelligence is the result of generations of natural selection of those with the ability to adapt to changed circumstances. We must not fear change. We need to make it work to our advantage.

We all have a role to play in making sure that we, and the next generation, have not just the opportunity but the determination to engage fully with the study of science at an early level, so that we can go on to fulfil our potential and create a better world for the whole human race. We need to take learning beyond a theoretical discussion of how AI should be and to make sure we plan for how it can be. We all have the potential to push the boundaries of what is accepted, or expected, and to think big. We stand on the threshold of a brave new world. It is an exciting, if precarious, place to be, and we are the pioneers.

When we invented fire, we messed up repeatedly, then invented the fire extinguisher. With more powerful technologies such as nuclear weapons, synthetic biology and strong artificial intelligence, we should instead plan ahead and aim to get things right the first time, because it may be the only chance we will get. Our future is a race between the growing power of our technology and the wisdom with which we use it. Let's make sure that wisdom wins. ■

Understanding and Interpreting

1. What does Hawking mean when he says that our universe has become "aware of itself" (par. 2). How does this phrase relate to artificial intelligence (AI)?
2. Evaluate Hawking's logic in paragraph 3 as he traces the development of human intelligence. What point is he trying to make here?
3. Summarize the main fears Hawking has about AI, as described in paragraph 4.
4. Explain the contrast between the development of robots that took place in laboratories (par. 5) and in commercial environments (par. 6).
5. Summarize Hawking's concerns with autonomous weapons systems. Explain how this relates to his overall feelings toward AI.
6. The "either/or fallacy" occurs when a writer presents an argument that seems to have only two positions ("You are for us, or you are against us"), when in fact, there might be multiple available options. Does Hawking commit this fallacy at the beginning of paragraph 10, or are there really only two possible outcomes? Explain why he may have included this part of the discussion.
7. What does Hawking seem to be implying in paragraph 12 when he refers to "the history of stupidity"?
8. Based on your reading of paragraphs 13 and 14, would Hawking be in favor of giving robots some kind of rights, or even personhood status?
9. In paragraphs 23 to 25, Hawking moves away from discussing robots and AI to exploring other scientific developments. How do these examples help to illustrate his overall argument about AI?
10. Summarize Hawking's definition of intelligence as he presents it in paragraph 26.

Analyzing Language, Style, and Structure

1. **Vocabulary in Context.** In paragraph 11, Hawking says that he is not an "alarmist." You know the word "alarm," but what is the meaning of the word "alarmist" in this context? How does it relate to the meaning of the common word "alarm"?
2. **Vocabulary in Context.** In paragraph 11, Hawking calls for "concrete" research on AI. What is the meaning of the word "concrete" in this context? How does that meaning relate to the word "concrete" used as a noun?
3. **Skill Focus.** Stephen Hawking was considered one of the most brilliant scientists and thinkers of the twentieth century, and yet even he uses outside sources to support his ideas. Reread paragraph 9. Explain what Hawking was trying to prove and how he uses outside evidence. Does his use of sources help? Is it necessary? What do you conclude about his use of a science-fiction writer for support?
4. In the second paragraph of this excerpt, Hawking describes the blueprint of life in mostly dry scientific terms. However, then he writes, "something beautiful happened." What does Hawking signal to his reader with his word choice here?
5. Notice that in paragraph 4, Hawking begins a sentence with "When that happens. . . ." What is he communicating to his audience by saying "when" and not "if"?
6. Reread paragraph 6 and the beginning of paragraph 7. What is the effect of this statement: "Unfortunately, it might also be the last"?
7. In paragraph 10, Hawking offers two analogies to help us understand our situation with AI: ants and aliens. Explain the intended effect of these analogies and how they help him to communicate his position.
8. What does Hawking likely accomplish by inserting himself into the argument at times, especially in paragraph 16? Would his argument have been stronger or weaker without these elements?

9. What is the effect of Hawking calling us "pioneers" in paragraph 27? What associations with that word did Hawking likely have in mind?
10. Who is Hawking's audience for this piece? How do you know, based on his word choice as well as the evidence he chooses to include?
11. Hawking seems to be both hopeful and terrified of a future with AI in it. Make a list of words and phrases he uses to communicate optimism and another list of words and phrases he uses to communicate pessimism. Overall, based on your lists and your understanding of the piece, explain whether he is more hopeful or scared.

Topics for Composing

1. **Analysis.** Write an analysis of what Hawking means when he says that we are in "a race between the growing power of our technology and the wisdom with which we use it." What is the most significant evidence that he uses to make this point?
2. **Argument.** Make a proposal for the kinds of restrictions that should be in place to ensure that Hawking's worst fears about AI don't come true. Use this piece, your own examples, and additional research, if you want, to support your proposal.
3. **Connection.** Do you share Hawking's concerns, or are you eager for a future with more widespread, more complex AI applications? Explain your answer.
4. **Speaking and Listening.** In pairs, create a list of all the ways you and your partner encounter AI in everyday life. Present your findings and create a master list with your class. Discuss how ingrained AI is in everyday life and how it can be helpful or cause for concern. Afterward, reflect on something that you heard in the discussion that may have changed your mind on the subject or added to your knowledge.
5. **Research.** In paragraph 6 and elsewhere, Hawking identifies that AI could possibly help eradicate poverty and disease, though he does not mention specifically how. Research work being done in the AI field that is designed to help with some of humanity's most intractable problems. What is the work's current status? To what extent would Hawking approve of or fear the work?
6. **Research.** Hawking wrote this piece in 2018, and he predicted that the "smartest homes will be equipped with devices so intuitive that they'll be almost effortless to interact with." What is a "smart home" like today? Did this part of his predictions come true yet?

Extending Legal Protection to Social Robots

Kate Darling

Courtesy of Kate Darling

A leading expert in robot ethics, Kate Darling (b.1982) is an IP research specialist at the Massachusetts Institute of Technology Media Lab, where she investigates social robotics and human-robot interaction. She is the author of *Creativity without Law: Challenging the Assumptions of Intellectual Property* (2017). The following article is based on a paper presented at the *We Robot 2012* conference.

KEY CONTEXT An essential part of Darling's essay includes a discussion of anthropomorphism, the attribution of human traits, emotions, or intentions to non-humans (such as animals or, in this case, robots). Anthropomorphism is considered to be a common aspect of human psychology.

"Why do you cry, Gloria? Robbie was only a machine, just a nasty old machine. He wasn't alive at all."
"He was not no machine!" screamed Gloria fiercely and ungrammatically. "He was a person like you and me and he was my friend."
—Isaac Asimov (1950)

Most discussions of "robot rights" play out in a seemingly distant, science-fictional future. While skeptics roll their eyes, advocates argue that technology will advance to the point where robots deserve moral consideration because they are "just like us," sometimes referencing the movie *Blade Runner*. *Blade Runner* depicts a world where androids have human-like emotions and develop human-like relationships to the point of being indistinguishable from people. But *Do Androids Dream of Electric Sheep*, the novel on which the film is based, contains a small, significant difference in storyline. In the book, the main character falls in love with an android that only pretends to requite his feelings. Even though he is fully aware of this fact, he maintains the one-directional emotional bond. The novel touches on a notably different, yet plausible, reality: humans' moral consideration of robots may depend more on our own feelings than on any inherent qualities built into robots.

This distinction hints at an approach to robot rights that is not restricted to science fictional scenarios. Looking at state of the art technology, our robots are nowhere close to the intelligence and complexity of humans or animals, nor will they reach this stage in the near future. And yet, while it seems far-fetched for a robot's legal status to differ from that of a toaster, there is already a notable difference in how we interact with certain types of robotic objects. While toasters are designed to make toast, social robots are designed to engage us socially. At some point, this difference may warrant an adjustment in legal treatment.

As technological progress begins to introduce more robotic toys, pets, and personal-care aids into our lives, we are seeing an increase in robots that function as companions. Hasbro's Baby Alive dolls, Jetta's robotic dinosaur Pleo, Aldebaran's NAO next generation robot, the Paro baby seal, or the Massachusetts Institute of Technology (MIT) robots Kismet and Leonardo are examples of social robots that are able to mimic social cues, have various "states of mind," and display adaptive learning behavior. Our interactions with them follow social behavior patterns, and often involve our feelings. When we develop emotional relationships to these robots, it is not because they are inherently different from toasters, but because there is a difference in how we perceive them.

Robots vs. Toasters: Projecting Our Emotions

Our difference in perception stems from a strong 5
human tendency to anthropomorphize embodied objects with autonomous behavior. In other words, we tend to project lifelike qualities onto robots. This anthropomorphism begins with a general inclination to over-ascribe autonomy and intelligence to the way that things behave, even if they are just following a simple algorithm. But not only are we prone to ascribing more agency than is actually present, we also project intent and sentiments (such as joy, pain, or confusion) onto other entities.

Social robots play off of this tendency by mimicking cues that we automatically associate with certain states of mind or feelings. Even in today's primitive form, this can elicit emotional reactions from people that are similar, for instance, to how we react to animals and to each other. From being reluctant to switch off robots that give the appearance of animacy, to ascribing mental states to robotic pets, we respond to the cues given to us by lifelike machines, even if we know that they are not "real."

We see this effect even when objects are not specifically designed to evoke these feelings. For example, when the United States military began testing a robot that defused landmines by stepping on them, the colonel in command ended up calling off the exercise. The robot was modeled after a stick insect with six legs. Every time it stepped on a mine, it lost one of its legs and continued on the remaining ones. According to the *Washington Post*, "[t]he colonel just could not stand the pathos of watching the burned, scarred and crippled machine drag itself forward on its last leg. This test, he charged, was inhumane." Other autonomous robots employed within military teams inspire fondness and loyalty in their human teammates, who identify with the robots enough to name them, award them battlefield promotions and "purple hearts," introduce them to their families, and become very upset when they "die." While none of these robots are designed to give social cues, their autonomous behavior makes them appear lifelike enough to generate emotional responses. In fact, even simple household robots like the Roomba vacuum cleaner prompt people to talk to them and develop feelings of camaraderie and gratitude.

While some of the above is coincidental, social robot design is capable of specifically targeting and magnifying this anthropomorphism. When robots are able to mimic lifelike behavior, react to social gestures, and use sounds, movement, and facial expressions to signal emotions in a way that we immediately recognize, this causes an involuntary biological response, shifting our perception. Owners of Sony AIBO dogs (developed in the 1990s), while fully aware that they are dealing with a robot, regularly ascribed lifelike essences and mental states to their artificial companion. The robotic seal Paro, currently used as a therapeutic device in nursing homes, reacts to touches and words. It conveys a sense of animacy by exhibiting emotional states, responding to people's actions, and learning individual voices. Most of the patients (and other people) who work with Paro treat it as if it were alive.

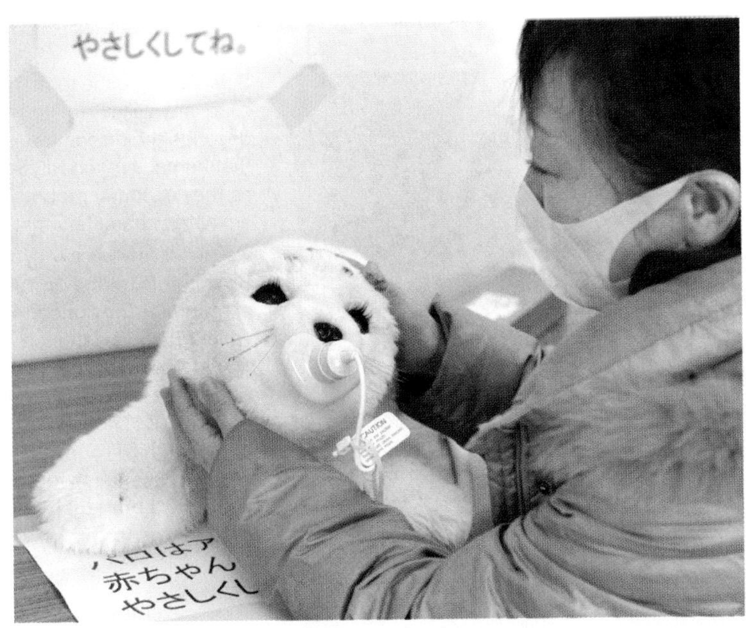

KAZUHIRO NOGI/AFP via Getty Images

This is a photograph of a survivor of a tsunami disaster in Japan with the therapeutic robot baby seal Paro that Darling describes.

Based on the image, what is the relationship between Paro and the woman? What might Darling say about the use of robots in this way?

Psychologist Sherry Turkle explains in her work studying human–robot interaction that this effect is particularly strong with social robots that are designed to evoke feelings of reciprocity. "Nurturing a machine that presents itself as dependent creates significant social attachments." She finds that there is a difference between the type of projection that people have traditionally engaged in with objects, such as small children comforting their dolls, and the psychology of engagement that comes from interacting with social robots, which create an effective illusion of mutual relating. While a child is aware of the projection onto an inanimate toy and can engage or not engage in it at will, a robot that demands attention by playing off of our natural responses may cause a subconscious engagement that is less voluntary.

10 This anthropomorphism is especially plausible when people have little sense of how a complex robot works, and so are especially inclined to assign autonomy, intent, or feelings to actions that actually result from algorithms they do not understand. Small children are regularly confused when asked whether the social robots they interact with experience pain or other sentiments. Elderly people unfamiliar with modern technology struggle with the difference between robotic companions and live animals. But the effect of projection and emotional bonding holds even for those who are perfectly informed as to the exact, detailed functionality of the robots with which they interact. For example, AIBO owners reported that they would remove their AIBO from the room while changing, so that they would not be "watched," or that they experienced feelings of guilt when putting the device back in its box. Students in MIT's Media Lab would often put up a curtain between themselves and Kismet, a social robot that simulates emotion through facial expressions, because the lifelike behavior of the face distracted them. And Cynthia Breazeal, Kismet's developer, reports experiencing "a sharp sense of loss" when she parted ways with her creation at the end of her dissertation.

While people have for decades named their cars and developed attachments to their handheld

South China Morning Post/Getty Images

Scientists use the term "uncanny valley" to describe the discomfort that humans reportedly feel as they encounter robots or animated characters that are nearly lifelike.

How is this image an example of the "uncanny valley"? Do you think it would bother you to see a robot that looks just like you? Would Darling think this design of robots in our own likeness would factor into our legal protections for robots?

devices, the effect of robots that actively and intentionally engage our ingrained anthropomorphic responses is considerably stronger. We are already disposed towards forming unidirectional emotional relationships with the robotic companions available to us today, and we can only imagine what the technological developments of the next decade will be able to effect. As we move within the spectrum between treating social robots like toasters and treating them more like our cats, the question of legal differentiation becomes more immediate.

Isn't Legal Protection a Bit Far-fetched?

Assuming that we systematically perceive social robots differently than toasters, why and how could this difference lead to a change in law? One reason is that when it comes down to legal treatment, it may not matter whether robots are as smart and as complex as biological life forms. The key insight is that we have an inherent desire to protect the things that we relate to. Many of our legal systems extend protections (beyond property law) to animals that we care about, preventing their abuse. While animal rights philosophy regularly revolves around concepts like sentience or pain, our laws actually indicate that these concerns are secondary when it comes to legal protection. Many successful societal pushes for animal abuse laws have followed popular sentiment rather than consistent biological criteria.

Our animal treatment laws give rise to the question whether our condemnation of abuse is based on a projection of ourselves. In other words, what if our desire to protect animals from harm has less to do with their inherent qualities, and more to do with what it affects in us? A lot of people do not like to see kittens be held by the tail. It is certainly possible that we feel so strongly about this because of the specific details of kittens' biological pain. But it is also possible that it simply causes us discomfort to see a reaction that we associate with suffering. Our emotional relationship to kittens, plus the strong response of the kitten to being held by the tail, may trigger protective feelings in us that have more to do with anthropomorphism than moral obligation. While this view is not likely to be a crowd-pleaser, it appears realistic in light of the differential protections awarded to various animals.

We have an apparent desire to protect those animals to which we more easily relate. Laws governing the treatment of horses, in particular bans on the slaughter of horsemeat in the United States, have been enacted because of the general sentiment that such behavior is offensive. Unlike many Europeans, a large part of the United States population seems strongly opposed to the idea of horses being killed and eaten. This is not justified by any biological differences between horses and cows. Similarly, very few people were interested in early campaigns to save the whales, despite best efforts from advocates. This changed once the first recordings of whale songs reached the public. Touched by the beautiful voices, support for the cause rose dramatically as people discovered whales to be creatures they could relate to. All of this indicates that we may care more about our own sentiment than any objective biological criteria.

15 When people care deeply about protecting something, there are different ways that the law can address this. One way is by maintaining protection through property rights that are inherent to an owner. But sometimes society pushes for laws that go beyond personal property rights. Although individual horse owners may be able to protect their horses from harm, we may want to ensure the protection of all horses, whether we own them or not. We often care strongly enough to make wider-reaching laws, going so far as to affect other people's property, for instance by prohibiting farmers from mistreating their chickens, or pet owners from mistreating their dogs. Assuming that our society wants to protect certain animals regardless of their capacities, because of our

extending beyond the text

Read the first two pages from the following short graphic story from a collection about robots who have evolved to become thinking, learning beings in artificial shells.

from **Harry Sloan, Barber**

Austin Wilson and Seth T. Hahne

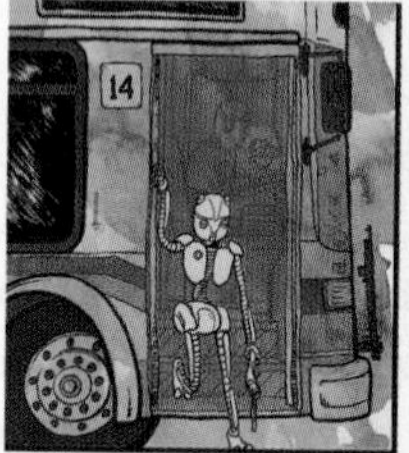

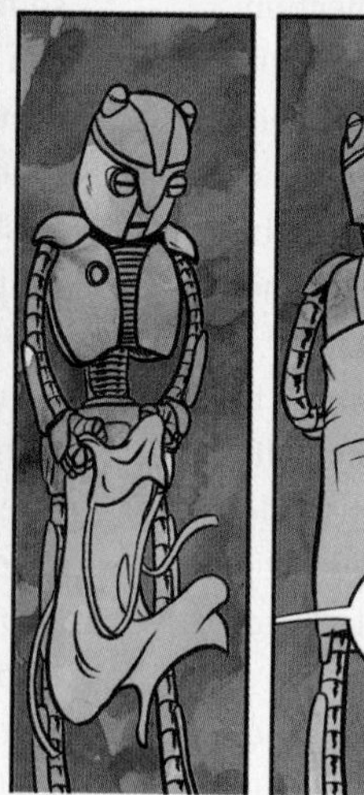

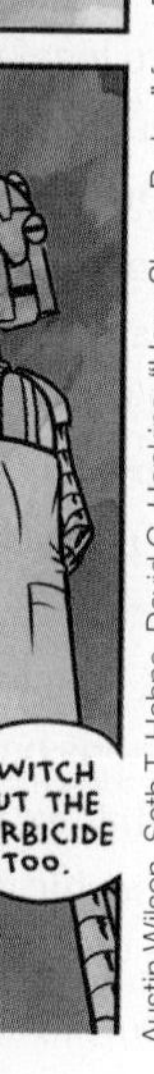

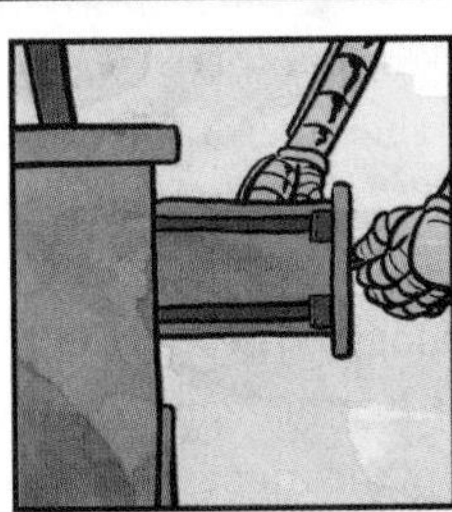

What is the central conflict between the robot and the humans that the story presents? To what extent does the theme of this story support or contradict Darling's position? What do you think might happen in the rest of the story? Why?

personal attachments to them, society may someday also want to protect social robots regardless of their capacities.

In the Words of Kurt Cobain, "It's ok to eat fish, because they don't have any feelings."

Even if we agree that projecting emotions is part of why we protect animals, many will argue that we should draw the line at something that does not actually "suffer." After all, despite the behavior we display towards them, most of us know that robots are not alive. And while we find differential treatment of animals in our laws, the actual discussions surrounding their moral inclusion do not usually consider anthropomorphism to be a justification. (Even if it were, one might still oppose the idea that laws be based on social sentiment rather than morally consistent criteria.) There may, however, be other arguments that favor the legal protection of social robots.

One reason that people could want to prevent the "abuse" of robotic companions is the protection of societal values. Parents of small children with a robotic pet in their household are likely familiar with the situation in which they energetically intervene to prevent their toddler from kicking or otherwise physically abusing the toy. Their reasons for doing so are partly to protect the (usually expensive) object from breaking, but will also be to discourage the child from engaging in types of conduct that could be harmful in other contexts. Given the lifelike behavior of the robot, a child could easily equate kicking it with kicking a living thing, such as a cat or another child. As it becomes increasingly difficult for small children to fully grasp the difference between live pets and lifelike robots, we may want to teach them to act equally considerately towards both. While this is easily done when a parent has control over both the robot and the child, protecting social robots more generally would set a framework for society and prevent children from adopting undesirable behavior elsewhere. It could even protect them from traumatizing experiences, for instance from witnessing older children "torture" a robotic toy on the playground, the likes of which the child has developed an emotional relationship to at home.

Even for fully informed adults, the difference between alive and lifelike may be muddled enough in our subconscious to warrant adopting the same attitudes toward robotic companions that we carry towards our pets. A study of Sony AIBO online message boards reveals that people were dismayed to witness the story of an AIBO being tossed into a garbage can. Not long after the Pleo robot dinosaur became commercially available in 2007, videos of Pleo "torture" began to circulate online. The comments left by viewers are strikingly polarized—while some derive amusement from the videos, others appear considerably upset, going so far as to verbally attack the originators and accuse them of horrible cruelty.

The Kantian philosophical argument for animal rights is that our actions towards non-humans reflect our morality—if we treat animals in inhumane ways, we become inhumane persons. This logically extends to the treatment of robotic companions. Given that many people already feel strongly about state-of-the-art social robot "abuse," it may soon become more widely perceived as out of line with our social values to treat robotic companions in a way that we would not treat our pets.

So Does This Mean We Should Change Our Laws?

Whether out of sentiment or to promote socially 20
desirable behavior, some parts of society may sooner or later begin to ask that legal protection be extended to robotic companions. When this happens, lawmakers will need to deliberate whether and how it would make sense to accommodate this societal preference. Aside from the above, there are a few things to consider in this context.

One practical difficulty lies in establishing limiting factors. In order to pass protective laws,

A customer with Pleo, the robot dinosaur described in the article.

What do you notice about how the customer appears to be interacting with the robot? How would this treatment relate to Darling's point about robot rights?

we would have to come up with a good definition of "social robot." This could be something along the lines of "an embodied object with a certain degree of autonomous behavior that is specifically designed to socially interact with humans." But this definition may not cover all of the robotic objects that people want to protect (for instance robots that evoke social engagement by accident, such as the above-mentioned military bots), or it may prove to be overly broad. We would also have to clearly determine the extent of protection, including what constitutes "mistreatment." Although many issues could be resolved analogous to animal abuse laws, there may be a few difficult edge cases, especially in light of rapidly changing technology. The challenge of drawing these lines is not new to our legal system, but it may take some effort to find the right balance.

Another consideration is that legal changes can be costly, both in terms of the direct costs of implementation and enforcement, and in terms of indirect costs. Since protecting social robots would effectively limit people's property rights, indirect costs could range from a distortion of market incentives to negative effects on research and development investments. Law influences people's behavior. Should we begin to think about legal changes, we may want to try to get a better sense of what these could affect.

While it seems likely that people will increasingly develop strong attachments to robotic companions, the question of whether we should legally protect them is by no means simple. However, as technology widens the gap between social robots and toasters, it seems timely to begin thinking about the societal implications of anthropomorphism and how they could be addressed by our legal system. ■

Understanding and Interpreting

1. In your own words, restate what Darling writes at the end of the first paragraph: "moral consideration of robots may depend more on our own feelings than on any inherent qualities built into robots."
2. Reread paragraph 9 and explain the difference that Darling has found between playing with dolls and interacting with social robots. Why is this difference important to the argument she is making?
3. According to Darling, to what extent does knowing the science behind social robots affect our anthropomorphism of them (par. 10)?

4. Beyond moral reasons, why do we tend to protect animals, based on what Darling writes in paragraphs 12 and 13? What evidence does she use to prove this point?
5. Explain what Darling means when she writes in paragraph 19, "it may soon become more widely perceived as out of line with our social values to treat robotic companions in a way that we would not treat our pets."
6. Summarize Darling's definition of a "social robot" (par. 21). Why is the definition she draws important to her argument about considering rights for robots?

Analyzing Language, Style, and Structure

1. **Vocabulary in Context.** In paragraph 3, Darling writes, "this difference may warrant an adjustment in legal treatment." What is the meaning of the word "warrant" in this context? How is its meaning here different from other uses you know of?
2. **Skill Focus.** Reread paragraph 7, one of the few places in which Darling uses outside sources to examine her topic. Explain what she is trying to prove in this paragraph. Examine how she uses other people's words and experiences to support her purpose.
3. In this very technical and oftentimes legalistic essay, Darling chooses to start with references to science-fiction movies and books. Why might she have chosen to begin with these examples?
4. In paragraph 7, Darling quotes a colonel who called a test on robots "inhumane." Why is the word "inhumane" so important to Darling's argument?
5. Structurally, why is it significant that Darling begins by establishing that robots are not like toasters?
6. Continue tracing and analyzing Darling's structure. What is achieved as she moves from toasters to animals and, finally, to robots by paragraph 16?
7. Why does Darling use quotation marks around words like "abuse" (pars. 17 and 19) and "torture" (par. 18) in her piece?

Topics for Composing

1. **Analysis.** Overall, why does Darling think we need to "begin thinking about the societal implications of anthropomorphism and how they could be addressed by our legal system" (par. 23)?
2. **Argument.** Take a position on Darling's central question: "Should we grant robots rights to prevent their possible abuse by humans?" Support your argument with evidence from Darling, your own experiences and reasoning, and outside evidence if you want.
3. **Connection.** In paragraph 19, Darling suggests that "if we treat animals in inhumane ways, we become inhumane persons"? Do you agree? Why or why not?
4. **Connection.** Do you regularly interact with any devices or applications that have anthropomorphic features — either visual or vocal? If so, how would you respond to some kind of "abuse" of it, such as rude or hostile behavior?
5. **Speaking and Listening.** Hold a class or small group debate on the issue of granting robots certain protections. One half should support these rights and the other should oppose them. Before the end of the debate, try to reach a consensus between the two positions and make recommendations to the federal government recommending next steps.
6. **Research.** Just how human-like are robots these days? Research the latest developments, as well as the concept of the "Uncanny Valley," which refers to the emotional (often negative) response that we can have when interacting with a robot that is "too human."

The Perfect Match (fiction)

Ken Liu

Sophie Bassouls/ Bridgeman Images

In addition to being a translator, lawyer, and computer programmer, Ken Liu (b. 1976) is an award-winning American author of science fiction and fantasy. His short story "The Paper Menagerie" is the first work of fiction to win the Nebula, Hugo, and World Fantasy Awards. Liu is the author of *The Dandelion Dynasty* fantasy trilogy, and his short stories have been included in many magazines and collections. The following piece appeared in *Lightspeed* magazine in 2012.

FOCUS FOR READING Throughout this chapter, you have been reading articles, editorials, and essays about the impact of robots, automation, and artificial intelligence on our lives. Unlike those other texts, the following is a work of fiction, even though it is based on some technology that is currently available. As you read this short story, consider how Liu uses characters, setting, conflicts, and theme to explore our robotic future.

Sai woke to the rousing first movement of Vivaldi's violin concerto in C minor, "Il Sospetto." He lay still for a minute, letting the music wash over him like a gentle Pacific breeze. The room brightened as the blinds gradually opened to the sunlight. Tilly had woken him right at the end of a light sleep cycle, the optimal time. He felt great: refreshed, optimistic, ready to jump out of bed.

Which is what he did next. "Tilly, that's an inspired choice for a wake-up song." "Of course," Tilly spoke from the camera/speaker in the nightstand. "Who knows your tastes and moods better than I?" The voice, though electronic, was affectionate and playful. Sai went into the shower.

"Remember to wear the new shoes today," Tilly now spoke to him from the camera/speaker in the ceiling.

"Why?"

"You have a date after work." 5

"Oh, the new girl. Shoot, what's her name? I know you told me—"

"I'll bring you up to speed after work. I'm sure you'll like her. The compatibility index is very high. I think you'll be in love for at least six months."

Sai looked forward to the date. Tilly had also introduced him to his last girlfriend, and that relationship had been wonderful. The break up afterwards was awful, of course, but it helped that Tilly had guided him through it. He felt that he had matured emotionally, and after a month on his own, was ready to start a new relationship.

But first he still had to get through the workday. "What do you recommend for breakfast this morning?"

"You are scheduled to attend the kickoff 10 meeting for the Davis case at eleven, which means you'll get a lunch paid for by the firm. I suggest you go light on the breakfast, maybe just a banana."

Sai was excited. All the paralegals at Chapman Singh Stevens & Rios lived for client lunches, made by the firm's own executive chef. "Do I have time to make my own coffee?"

"You do. Traffic is light this morning. But I suggest you go to this new smoothie place along the way instead — I can get you a coupon code."

"But I really want coffee."

"Trust me, you'll love the smoothie."

15 Sai smiled as he turned off the shower. "Okay, Tilly. You always know best."

• • •

Although it was another pleasant and sunny morning in Las Aldamas, California — 68 degrees Fahrenheit — Sai's neighbor Jenny was wearing a thick winter coat, ski goggles, and a long, dark scarf that covered her hair and the rest of her face.

"I thought I told you I didn't want that thing installed," she said as he stepped out of his apartment. Her voice was garbled through some kind of electronic filter. In response to his questioning look, she gestured to the camera over Sai's door.

Talking to Jenny was like talking to one of his grandmother's friends who refused to use Centillion email or get a ShareAll account because they were afraid of having "the computer" know "all their business" — except that as far as he could tell, Jenny was his age. She had grown up a digital native, but somehow had missed the ethos of sharing.

"Jenny, I'm not going to argue with you. I have a right to install anything I want over *my* door. And I want Tilly to keep an eye on my door when I'm away. Apartment 308 was just burglarized last week."

20 "But your camera will record visitors to my place, too, because we share this hallway."

"So?"

"I don't want Tilly to have any of my social graph."

Sai rolled his eyes. "What do you have to hide?"

"That's not the point—"

25 "Yeah, yeah, civil liberties, freedom, privacy, blah blah blah . . ."

Sai was sick of arguing with people like Jenny. He had made the same point countless times: *Centillion is not some big scary government. It's a private company, whose motto happens to be "Make things better!" Just because you want to live in the dark ages doesn't mean the rest of us shouldn't enjoy the benefits of ubiquitous computing.*

He dodged around her bulky frame to get to the stairs.

What is the intended target of the joke in this cartoon? Why do you think that Amazon (and Centillion in this story) make their default AI voices sound female?

"Tilly doesn't just tell you what you want," Jenny shouted. "She tells you what to *think*. Do you even know what you really want any more?"

Sai paused for a moment.

"Do you?" she pressed.

What a ridiculous question. Just the kind of pseudo-intellectual anti-technology rant that people like her mistake for profundity.

He kept on walking.

"Freak," he muttered, expecting Tilly to chime in from his phone earpiece with some joke to cheer him up.

But Tilly said nothing.

• • •

Having Tilly around was like having the world's best assistant:

—"Hey Tilly, do you remember where I kept that Wyoming filing with the weird company name and the F merger from maybe six months ago?"

—"Hey Tilly, can you get me a form for Section 131 Articles? Make sure it's a form that associates working with Singh use."

—"Hey Tilly, memorize these pages. Assign them these tags: 'Chapman,' 'favors buyer,' 'only use if associate is nice to me.'"

• • •

For a while, Chapman Singh had resisted the idea of allowing employees to bring Tilly into the office, preferring their proprietary corporate AI system. But it proved too difficult to force employees to keep their personal calendars and recommendations rigidly separate from work ones, and once the partners started to violate the rules and use Tilly for work, IT had to support them.

And Centillion had then pledged that they would encrypt all corporate-derived information in a secure manner and never use it for competitive purposes — only to give better recommendations to employees of Chapman Singh. After all, the mission statement of Centillion was to "arrange the world's information to ennoble the human race," and what could be more ennobling than making work more efficient, more productive, more pleasant?

As Sai enjoyed his lunch, he felt very lucky. He couldn't even imagine what drudgery work would have been like before Tilly came along.

• • •

After work, Tilly guided Sai to the flower shop — of course Tilly had a coupon — and then, on the way to the restaurant, she filled Sai in on his date, Ellen: educational background, ShareAll profile, reviews by previous boyfriends/girlfriends, interests, likes, dislikes, and of course, pictures — dozens of photos recognized and gathered by Tilly from around the Net.

Sai smiled. As usual, Tilly was right: Ellen was exactly his type.

It was a truism that what a man wouldn't tell his best friend, he'd happily search for on Centillion. Tilly knew all about what kind of women Sai found attractive, having observed the pictures and videos he perused late at night while engaging the Just-For-Me mode in his browser.

And, of course, Tilly would know Ellen just as well as she knew him, so Sai knew that he would be exactly Ellen's type, too.

As predicted, it turned out they were into the same books, the same movies, the same music. They had compatible ideas about how hard one should work. They laughed at each other's jokes. They fed off each other's energy.

Sai marveled at Tilly's accomplishment. Four billion women on Earth, and Tilly seemed to have found the perfect match for him. It was just like hitting the "I Trust You" button on Centillion search back in the early days and how it knew just the right web page to take you to.

Sai could feel himself falling in love, and he could tell that Ellen wanted to ask him to come home with her.

Although everything had gone exceedingly well, if he was being completely honest with

Joel Pett Editorial Cartoon used with the permisson of Joel Pett and the Cartoonist Group

What point is this cartoon making about the connection between AI and consumerism? In what way is this similar to or different from the one that Liu is making in this story?

himself, it wasn't *quite* as exciting and lovely as he had expected. Everything was indeed going smoothly, but maybe just a tad *too* smoothly. It was as if they already knew everything there was to know about each other. There were no surprises, no thrill of finding the truly new.

In other words, the date was a bit boring.

As Sai's mind wandered, there was a lull in the conversation. They smiled at each other and just tried to enjoy the silence.

In that moment, Tilly's voice burst into his earpiece, "You might want to ask her if she likes contemporary Japanese desserts. I know just the place."

Sai realized that though he hadn't been aware of it until just then, he did suddenly have a craving for something sweet and delicate.

Tilly doesn't just tell you what you want. She tells you what to think.

Sai paused.

Do you even know what you really want any more?

He tried to sort out his feelings. Did Tilly just figure out what he hadn't even known he wanted? Or did she put the thought into his head?

Do you?

The way Tilly filled in that lull . . . it was as if Tilly didn't trust that he would be able to manage the date on his own, as if Tilly thought he wouldn't know what to say or do if she didn't jump in.

Sai suddenly felt irritated. The moment had been ruined.

I'm being treated like a child.

"I know you'll like it. I have a coupon."

"Tilly," he said, "please stop monitoring and terminate auto-suggestions."

"Are you sure? Gaps in sharing can cause your profile to be incomplete—"

"Yes, please cease."

With a beep, Tilly turned herself off.

Ellen stared at him, eyes and mouth wide open in shock.

"Why did you do that?"

"I wanted to talk to you alone, just the two of us." Sai smiled. "It's nice sometimes to just be ourselves, without Tilly, don't you think?"

Ellen looked confused. "But you know that the more Tilly knows, the more helpful she can be. Don't you want to be sure we don't make silly mistakes on a first date? We're both busy, and Tilly—"

"I know what Tilly can do. But—"

Ellen held up a hand, silencing him. She tilted her head, listening to her headset.

"I have the perfect idea," Ellen said. "There's this new club, and I know Tilly can get us a coupon."

Sai shook his head, annoyed. "Let's try to think of something to do without Tilly. Would you please turn her off?"

Ellen's face was unreadable for a moment.

"I think I should head home," she said. "Early workday tomorrow." She looked away.

"Did Tilly tell you to say that?"

She said nothing and avoided looking into his eyes.

"I had a great time," Sai added quickly. "Would you like to go out again?"

Ellen paid half the bill and did not ask him to walk her home.

• • •

"You're being very antisocial tonight," Tilly said.

"I'm not antisocial. I just didn't like how you were interfering with everything."

"I have every confidence you would have enjoyed the rest of the date had you followed my advice."

Sai drove on in silence.

"I sense a lot of aggression in you. How about some kickboxing? You haven't gone in a

extending beyond the text

In response to complaints about Facebook's handling of consumer data, the company launched a new tool, the Off-Facebook Activity tracker. The tool identifies the information collected and shared about users, even when they are not logged onto Facebook, Instagram, Messenger, or other apps owned by Facebook.

Understanding Off-Facebook Activity.

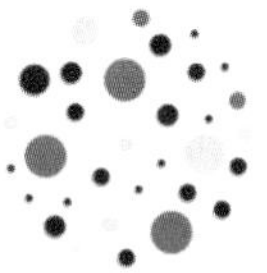

Data and the internet

Much of what you do online generates data—like when you're searching for vacation spots or buying a backpack. Occasionally, businesses share that data with Facebook.

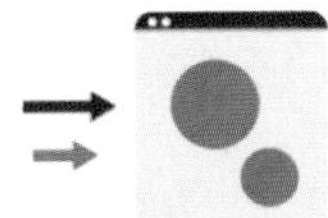

Data sent to Facebook

One way that data can be used is to help businesses find the right audience to show ads for things you might like—such as a deal on backpacks. These ads are what make most of the internet available free of charge, including Facebook.

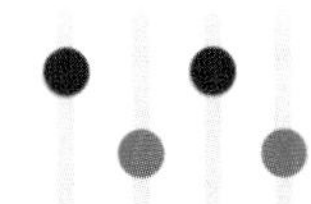

Data more in your control

Now you can see a summary of information Facebook receives about your activity on other apps and websites. You also have the option to disconnect it from your account.

Examine the settings on the devices you use. Identify the types and amount of data collected and shared by the apps you use most frequently. To what extent should companies like Facebook be allowed to profit by sharing the information they collect about you?

while, and there's a 24-hour gym coming up. Take a right here."

Sai drove straight on.

"What's wrong?"

"I don't feel like spending more money."

"You know I have a coupon."

"What exactly do you have against me saving my money?"

"Your savings rate is right on target. I simply want to make sure you're sticking to your regimen for consumption of leisure. If you over-save, you'll later regret that you didn't make the most of your youth. I've plotted the optimum amount of consumption you should engage in daily."

"Tilly, I just want to go home and sleep. Can you shut yourself off for the rest of the night?"

"You know that in order to make the best life recommendations, I need to have complete knowledge of you. If you shut me out of parts of your life, my recommendations won't be as accurate—"

Sai reached into his pocket and turned off the phone. The earpiece went silent.

• • •

When Sai got home, he saw that the light over the stairs leading up to his apartment had gone out, and several dark shapes skulked around the bottom.

"Who's there?"

Several of the shadows scattered, but one came toward him: Jenny.

"You're back early."

He almost didn't recognize her; this was the first time he'd heard her voice without the electronic filter she normally used. It sounded surprisingly . . . happy.

Sai was taken aback. "How did you know I was back early? You stalking me?"

Jenny rolled her eyes. "Why would I need to stalk you? Your phone automatically checks in and out of everywhere you go with a status message based on your mood. It's all on your ShareAll lifecast for anyone to see."

He stared at her. In the faint glow from the streetlights he could see that she wasn't wearing her thick winter coat or ski goggles or scarf. Instead, she was in shorts and a loose white t-shirt. Her black hair had been dyed white in streaks. In fact, she looked very pretty, if a bit nerdy.

"What, surprised that I *do* know how to use a computer?"

"It's just that you usually seem so . . ."

"Paranoid? Crazy? Say what's on your mind. I won't be offended."

"Where's your coat and goggles? I've never even seen you without them."

"Oh, I taped over your door camera so my friends could come for a visit tonight, so I'm not wearing them. I'm sorry—"

"You did what?"

"—and I came out here to meet you because I saw that you turned off Tilly, not once, but *twice*. I'm guessing you're finally ready for the truth."

• • •

Stepping into Jenny's apartment was like stepping into the middle of a fishing net.

The ceiling, floor, and walls were all covered with a fine metal mesh, which glinted like liquid silver in the flickering light from the many large, hi-definition computer monitors stacked on top of each other around the room, apparently the only sources of illumination.

Besides the monitors, the only other visible furniture appeared to be bookshelves — full of books (the paper kind, strangely enough). A few upside-down, ancient milk crates covered with cushions served as chairs.

Sai had been feeling restless, had wanted to do something strange. But he now regretted his decision to accept her invitation to come in. She was indeed eccentric, perhaps too much so.

Jenny closed the door and reached up and plucked the earpiece out of Sai's ear. Then she held out her hand. "Give me your phone."

"Why? It's already off."

Jenny's hand didn't move. Reluctantly, Sai took out his phone and gave it to her.

She looked at it contemptuously. "No removable battery. Just what you'd expect of a Centillion phone. They should call these things tracking devices, not phones. You can never be sure they're really off." She slipped the phone inside a thick pouch, sealed it, and dropped it on the desk.

"Okay, now that your phone is acoustically and electromagnetically shielded, we can talk. The mesh on the walls basically makes my apartment into a Faraday cage, so cellular signals can't get through. But I don't feel comfortable around a Centillion phone until I can put a few layers of shielding around it."

"I'm just going to say it. You are *nuts*. You think Centillion spies on you? Their privacy policy is the best in the business. Every bit of information they gather has to be given up by the user voluntarily, and it's all used to make the user's life better—"

Jenny tilted her head and looked at him with a smirk until he stopped talking.

"If that's all true, why did you turn Tilly off tonight? Why did you agree to come up here with me?"

Sai wasn't sure he himself knew the answers.

"Look at you. You've agreed to have cameras observe your every move, to have every thought, word, interaction recorded in some distant data center so that algorithms could be run over them, mining them for data that marketers pay for.

"Now you've got nothing left that's private, nothing that's yours and yours alone. Centillion owns all of you. You don't even know who you are anymore. You buy what Centillion wants you to buy; you read what Centillion suggests you read; you date who Centillion thinks you should date. But are you really happy?"

"That's an outdated way to look at it. Everything Tilly suggests to me has been scientifically proven to fit my taste profile, to be something I'd like."

"You mean some advertiser paid Centillion to pitch it at you."

"That's the point of advertising, isn't it? To match desire with satisfaction. There are thousands of products in this world that would have been perfect for me, but I might never have known about them. Just like there's a perfect girl out there for me, but I might never have met her. What's wrong with listening to Tilly so that the

This is a picture of an art installation called "Head in the Clouds," by Mickaël Martins Afonso and Caroline Escaffre-Faure. The installation is part of an event called "Robotanica," organized by Transnatural Institute, which explores how technology can support the natural world and ecological wealth.

What message do you think the artists are hoping to communicate? How might this be similar to a point that Liu is making in this story?

perfect product finds the perfect consumer, the perfect girl finds the perfect boy?"

Jenny chuckled. "I love how you're so good at rationalizing your state. I ask you again: If life with Tilly is so wonderful, why did you turn her off tonight?"

"I can't explain it," Sai said. He shook his head. "This is a mistake. I think I'll head home."

"Wait. Let me show you a few things about your beloved Tilly first," Jenny said. She went to the desk and started typing, bringing up a series of documents on a monitor. She talked as Sai tried to scan them and get their gist.

"Years ago, they caught Centillion's traffic-monitoring cars sniffing all the wireless traffic from home networks on the streets they drove through. Centillion also used to override the security settings on your machine and track your browsing habits before they shifted to an opt-in monitoring policy designed to provide better 'recommendations.' Do you think they've really changed? They hunger for data about you — the more the better — and damned if they care about how they get it."

Sai flicked through the documents skeptically. "If this is all true, why hasn't anyone brought it up in the news?"

Jenny laughed. "First, everything Centillion did was arguably legal. The wireless transmissions were floating in public space, for example, so there was no violation of privacy. And the end user agreement could be read to allow everything Centillion did to 'make things better' for you. Second, these days, how do you get your news except through Centillion? If Centillion doesn't want you to see something, you won't."

"So how did you find these documents?"

"My machine is connected to a network built on top of the Net, one that Centillion can't see inside. Basically, we rely on a virus that turns people's computers into relaying stations for us, and everything is encrypted and bounced around so that Centillion can't see our traffic."

Sai shook his head. "You're really one of those tinfoil-hat conspiracy theorists. You make Centillion sound like some evil repressive government. But it's just a company trying to make some money."

Jenny shook her head. "Surveillance is surveillance. I can never understand why some people think it matters whether it's the government doing it to you or a company. These days, Centillion is bigger than governments. Remember, it managed to topple three countries' governments just because they dared to ban Centillion within their borders."

"Those were repressive places—"

"Oh, right, and you live in the land of the free. You think Centillion was trying to promote freedom? They wanted to be able to get in there and monitor everyone and urge them to all consume more so that Centillion could make more money."

"But that's just business. It's not the same thing as evil."

"You say that, but that's only because you don't know what the world really looks like any more, now that it's been remade in Centillion's image."

• • •

Although Jenny's car was heavily shielded like her apartment, as she and Sai drove, she whispered anyway, as if she were afraid that their conversation would be overheard by people walking by on the sidewalk.

"I can't believe how decrepit this place looks," Sai said as she parked the car by the side of the street. The surface of the road was pockmarked with potholes and the houses around them in ill repair. A few had been abandoned and were falling apart. In the distance they could hear the fading sound of a police siren. This was not a part of Las Aldamas that Sai had ever been to.

"It wasn't like this even ten years ago."

"What happened?"

Shopping by videophone, 1890/UNIVERSAL IMAGES GROUP/Bridgeman Images

This is an illustration from 1890 that imagines shopping in the future.

What elements seem surprisingly similar to today's shopping experience, as well as to Sai's experiences with Tilly?

"Centillion noticed a certain tendency for people — some people, not all — to self-segregate by race when it came to where they wanted to live. The company tried to serve this need by prioritizing different real estate listings to searchers based on their race. Nothing illegal about what they were doing, since they were just satisfying a need and desire in their users. They weren't hiding any listings, just pushing them far down the list, and in any event, you couldn't ever pick apart their algorithm and prove that they were looking at race when it was just one out of hundreds of factors in their magical ranking formula.

"After a while, the process began to snowball, and the segregation got worse and worse. It became easier for the politicians to gerrymander districts based on race. And so here we are. Guess who got stuck in these parts of the town?"

Sai took a deep breath. "I had no idea."

"If you ask Centillion, they'll say that their algorithms just reflected and replicated the desire to self-segregate in some of their users, and that Centillion wasn't in the business of policing thoughts. Oh, they'd claim that they were actually increasing freedom by giving people just what they wanted. They'd neglect to mention that they were profiting off of it through real estate commissions, of course."

"I can't believe no one ever says anything about this."

"You're forgetting again that everything you know now comes filtered through Centillion. Whenever you do a search, whenever you hear a news digest, it's been curated by Centillion to fit what it thinks you want to hear. Someone upset by the news isn't going to buy anything sold by the advertisers, so Centillion adjusts things to make it all okay.

"It's like we're all living in Oz's Emerald City. Centillion puts these thick green goggles over our eyes and we all think everything is a beautiful shade of green."

"You're accusing Centillion of censorship."

"No. Centillion is an algorithm that's gotten out of hand. It just gives you more of what it thinks you want. And we — people like me — think that's the root of the problem. Centillion has put us in little bubbles, where all we see and hear are echoes of ourselves, and we become ever more stuck in our existing beliefs and exaggerated in our inclinations. We stop asking questions and accept Tilly's judgment on everything.

"Year after year, we become more docile and grow more wool for Centillion to shave off and grow rich with. But I don't want to live that way."

"And why are you telling me all this?"

"Because, neighbor, we're going to kill Tilly," Jenny said, giving Sai a hard look, "and you're going to help us do it."

• • •

Jenny's apartment, with all its windows tightly shut and curtained, felt even more stifling after the car ride. Sai looked around at the flickering screens showing dancing, abstract patterns, suddenly wary. "And just how are you planning to kill Tilly, exactly?"

"We're working on a virus, a cyber weapon, if you want to get all macho about it."

"What exactly would it do?"

"Since the lifeblood of Tilly is data — the billions of profiles Centillion has compiled on every user — that's how we have to take it down.

"Once inside the Centillion data center, the virus will gradually alter every user profile it encounters and create new, fake profiles. We want it to move slowly to avoid detection. But eventually, it will have poisoned the data so much that it will no longer be possible for Tilly to make creepy, controlling predictions about users. And if we do it slowly enough, they can't even go to backups because they'll be corrupted too. Without the data it's built up over the decades, Centillion's advertising revenue will dry up overnight, and poof, Tilly'll be gone."

Sai imagined the billions of bits in the cloud: his tastes, likes and dislikes, secret desires, announced intentions, history of searches, purchases, articles and books read, pages browsed.

Collectively, the bits made up a digital copy of him, literally. Was there anything that was a part of *him* that wasn't also up there in the cloud, curated by Tilly? Wouldn't unleashing a virus on that be like suicide, like murder?

Web Security 101, 2007 (computer graphics)/Ong, Diana (b.1940)/ SUPERSTOCK INC./Bridgeman Images

This piece of digital art is called *Web Security 101* (2007) by Diana Ong. **While it is certainly abstract, based on the colors and design, what might Ong be suggesting about computers and humanity? Imagine that Jenny had this piece hanging up in her apartment. What might she say to Sai about why she has it?**

But then he remembered how it had felt to have Tilly lead him by the nose on every choice, how he had been content, like a pig happily wallowing in his enclosure.

The bits were his, but not *him*. He had a will that could not be captured in bits. And Tilly had almost succeeded in making him forget that.

"How can I help?" Sai asked.

• • •

Sai woke to Miles Davis's rendition of "So What."

For a moment, he wondered if the memory of the night before wasn't a dream. It felt so good to be awake, listening to just the song he wanted to hear.

"Are you feeling better, Sai?" Tilly asked.

Am I?

"I thought I turned you off, Tilly, with a hardware switch."

"I was quite concerned that you stopped all Centillion access to your life last night and forgot to turn it back on. You might have missed your wake-up call. However, Centillion added a system-level fail-safe to prevent just such an occurrence. We thought most users such as yourself would want such an override so that Centillion could regain access to your life."

"Of course," Sai said. *So it's impossible to turn Tilly off and keep her off. Everything Jenny said last night was true.* He felt a chill tingle on his back.

"There's a gap of about twelve hours during which I couldn't acquire data about you. To prevent degradation in my ability to help you, I recommend that you fill me in."

"Oh, you didn't miss much. I came home and fell asleep. Too tired."

"There appears to have been vandalism last night of the new security cameras you installed. The police have been informed. Unfortunately, the camera did not capture a good image of the perpetrator."

"Don't worry about it. There's nothing here worth stealing anyway."

"You sound a bit down. Is it because of the date last night? It seems that Ellen wasn't the right match for you after all."

"Um, yeah. Maybe not."

"Don't worry: I know just the thing that will put you in a good mood."

• • •

Over the next few weeks, Sai found it extremely difficult to play his assigned role.

Maintaining the pretense that he still trusted Tilly was crucial, Jenny had emphasized, if their plan was to succeed. Tilly couldn't suspect anything was going on at all.

It seemed simple enough at first, but it was nerve wracking, keeping secrets from Tilly. Could she detect the tremors in his voice, Sai wondered. Could she tell that he was faking enthusiasm for the commercial consumption transactions she suggested?

Meanwhile, he also had a much bigger puzzle to solve before John P. Rushgore, Assistant General Counsel of Centillion, came to Chapman Singh in another week.

Chapman Singh is defending Centillion in a patent dispute with ShareAll, Jenny had said. *This is our opportunity to get inside Centillion's network. All you have to do is to get someone from Centillion to plug this into his laptop.*

And she had then handed him a tiny thumb drive.

• • •

Though he still hadn't figured out a plan for plugging the thumb drive into a Centillion machine, Sai was glad to have come to the end of another long day of guarding himself against Tilly.

"Tilly, I'm going jogging. I'll leave you here."

"You know that it's best to carry me with you," Tilly said. "I can track your heart rate and suggest an optimal route for you."

"I know. But I just want to run around on my own a bit, all right?"

"I'm growing quite concerned with your latest tendencies towards hiding instead of sharing."

"There's no tendency, Tilly. I just don't want you to be stolen if I get mugged. You know this neighborhood has become more unsafe lately."

And he turned off the phone and left it in his bedroom.

He closed the door behind him, made sure that the taped-over camera was still taped-over, and gently knocked on Jenny's door.

• • •

Getting to know Jenny was the oddest thing he'd ever done, Sai realized.

He couldn't count on Tilly to have made sure ahead of time that they would have topics to talk about. He couldn't rely on Tilly's always apropos suggestions when he was at a loss for words. He couldn't even count on being able to look up Jenny's ShareAll profile.

He was on his own. And it was exhilarating.

"How did you figure out everything Tilly was doing to us?"

"I grew up in China," Jenny said, wiping a strand of hair behind her ear. Sai found the gesture inexplicably endearing. "Back then, the government watched everything you did on the Network and made no secret of it. You had to learn how to keep the insanity at bay, to read between the lines, to speak without being overheard."

"I guess we were lucky, over here."

"No." And she smiled at his surprise. He was learning that she preferred to be contrarian, to disagree with him. He liked that about her. "You grew up believing you were free, which made it even harder for you to see when you weren't. You were like frogs in the pot being slowly boiled."

"Are there many like you?"

"No. It's hard to live off the grid. I've lost touch with my old friends. I have a hard time getting to know people because so much of their lives are lived inside Centillion and ShareAll. I can peek in on them once in a while through a dummy profile, but I can never *be* a part of their lives. Sometimes I wonder if I'm doing the right thing."

"You are," Sai said, and, though there was no Tilly to prompt him, he took Jenny's hand in his. She didn't pull away.

"I never really thought of you as my type," she said.

Sai's heart sank like a stone.

"But who thinks only in terms of 'types' except Tilly?" she said quickly, then smiled and pulled him closer.

• • •

Finally, the day had come. Rushgore had come to Chapman Singh to prepare for a deposition. He was huddled up with the firm's lawyers in one of their conference rooms all day long.

Sai sat down in his cubicle, stood up, and sat down again. He found himself full of nervous energy as he contemplated the best way to deliver the payload, as it were.

Maybe he could pretend to be tech support, there to perform an emergency scan of his system?

Maybe he could deliver lunch, and plug the drive in slyly?

Maybe he could pull the fire alarm, and hope that Rushgore would leave his laptop behind?

Not a single one of his ideas passed the laugh test.

"Hey," the associate who had been with Rushgore in the conference room all day was suddenly standing next to Sai's cubicle. "Rushgore needs to charge his phone — you got a Centillion charging cable over here?"

Sai stared at him, dumbfounded by his luck.

The associate held up a phone and waved it at him.

"Of course!" Sai said. "I'll bring one right to you."

"Thanks." The associate went back to the conference room.

Sai couldn't believe it. This was it. He plugged the drive into a charging cable and added an extension on the other end. The whole thing looked only a little odd, like a thin python who had swallowed a rat.

But suddenly he felt a sinking feeling in the pit of his stomach and he almost swore aloud: He had forgotten to turn off the webcam above his computer — *Tilly's eyes* — before preparing the cable. If Tilly raised questions about the weird cable he was carrying, he would have no explanation, and then all of his efforts at misdirection, at hiding, would be for naught.

But there was nothing he could do about it now but proceed as planned. As he left his cubicle, his heart was almost in his throat.

He stepped into the hallway, and strode down to the conference room.

Still nothing from his earpiece.

He opened the door. Rushgore was too busy with his computer even to look up. He grabbed the cable from Sai and plugged one end into his computer, and the other end into his phone.

And Tilly remained silent.

• • •

Sai woke to — what else? — "We Are the Champions."

The previous night of drinking and laughing with Jenny and her friends had been a blur, but he did remember coming home and telling Tilly, right before he fell asleep, "We did it! We won!"

Ah, if Tilly only knew what we were celebrating.

The music faded, stopped.

Sai stretched lazily, turned to his side, and stared into the eyes of four burly, very serious men. "Tilly, call the police!"

"I'm afraid I can't do that, Sai."

"Why the hell not?"

"These men are here to help you. Trust me, Sai. You know I know just what you need."

• • •

When the strange men had appeared in his apartment, Sai had imagined torture chambers, mental hospitals, faceless guards parading outside of dark cells. He had not imagined that he would be sitting across the table from Christian Rinn, Founder and Executive Chairman of Centillion, having white tea.

"You got pretty close." Rinn said. The man was barely in his forties and looked fit and efficient — *kind of like how I picture a male version of Tilly*, Sai thought. He smiled. "Closer than almost anyone."

"What was the mistake that gave us away?" Jenny asked.

She was sitting to Sai's left, and Sai reached out for her hand. They intertwined their fingers, giving each other strength.

"It was his phone, on that first night he visited you."

"Impossible. I shielded it. It couldn't have recorded anything."

"But you left it on your desk, where it could still make use of its accelerometer. It detected and recorded the vibrations from your typing. There's a very distinctive way we strike the keys on a keyboard, and it's possible to reconstruct what someone was typing based on the vibration patterns alone. It's an old technology we developed for catching terrorists and drug dealers." Jenny cursed under her breath, and Sai realized that until that moment, on some level, he still hadn't quite believed Jenny's paranoia.

"But I didn't bring my phone after that first day."

"True, but we didn't need it. After Tilly picked up what Jenny was typing, the right alert algorithms were triggered and we focused surveillance on you. We parked a traffic observation vehicle a block away and trained a little laser on Jenny's window. It was enough to record your conversations through the vibrations in the glass."

"You're a very creepy man, Mr. Rinn," Sai said. "And despicable too."

Rinn didn't seem bothered by this. "I think you might feel differently by the end of our conversation. Centillion was not the first company to stalk you."

Networks, 2010, (mixed media)/Allen, A. Richard/A. Richard Allen/Private Collection/Bridgeman Images

This is a piece called *Networks* (2010) by Richard Allen.

Is this an optimistic or a pessimistic view of contemporary online culture? Why? Would this be a part of a logo design for Centillion? Why or why not?

Jenny's fingers tightened around Sai's. "Let him go. I'm the one you really want. He doesn't know anything."

Rinn shook his head and smiled apologetically. "Sai, did you realize that Jenny moved into the apartment next to yours a week after we retained Chapman Singh to represent us in the suit against ShareAll?"

Sai didn't understand what Rinn was getting at, but he sensed that he would not like what he was about to find out. He wanted to tell Rinn to shut up, but he held his tongue.

"Curious, aren't you? You can't resist the pull of information. If it's possible, you always want to learn something new; we're hardwired that way. That's the drive behind Centillion, too."

"Don't believe anything he says," Jenny said.

"Would it surprise you to find out that the five other paralegals in your firm also had new neighbors move in during that same week? Would it also surprise you to learn that the new neighbors have all sworn to destroy Centillion, just like Jenny here? Tilly is very good at detecting patterns."

Sai's heart beat faster. He turned to Jenny. "Is this true? You planned from the start to use me? You got to know me just so you'd have a chance to deliver a virus?"

Jenny turned her face away.

"They know that there's no way to hack into our systems from the outside, so they had to sneak a trojan in. You were used, Sai. She and her friends guided you, led you by the nose, made you do things — just like they accuse *us* of doing."

"It's not like that," Jenny said. "Listen, Sai, maybe that was how it started. But life's full of surprises. I was surprised by you, and that's a good thing."

Sai let go of Jenny's hand and turned back to Rinn. "Maybe they *did* use me. But they're right. You've turned the world into a Panopticon[1] and all the people in it into obedient puppets that you nudge this way and that just so you'd make more money."

"You yourself pointed out that we were fulfilling desires, lubricating the engine of commerce in an essential way."

"But you also fulfill dark desires." He remembered again the abandoned houses by the side of the road, the pockmarked pavement.

"We unveil only the darkness that was already inside people," Rinn said. "And Jenny didn't tell you about how many child pornographers we've caught, how many planned murders we've stopped, or how many drug cartels and terrorists we've exposed. And

[1]A type of institutional building and a system of control designed by the English philosopher and social theorist Jeremy Bentham in the eighteenth century. Many maximum-security prisons have adopted his design, which allows for easy observation of the most prisoners by the fewest number of guards. — Eds.

all the dictators and strongmen we've toppled by filtering out their propaganda and magnifying the voices of those who oppose them."

"Don't make yourself sound so noble," Jenny said. "After you topple governments, you and the other Western companies get to move in and profit. You're just propagandists of a different ilk — for making the world flat, turning everywhere into copies of suburban America, studded with malls."

"It's easy to be cynical like that," Rinn said. "But I'm proud of what we've done. If cultural imperialism is what it takes to make the world a better place, then we'll happily arrange the world's information to ennoble the human race."

"Why can't you just be in the business of neutrally offering up information? Why not go back to being a simple search engine? Why all the surveillance and filtering? Why all the manipulation?" Sai asked.

"There's no such thing as neutrally offering up information. If someone asks Tilly about the name of a candidate, should Tilly bring them to his official site or a site that criticizes him? If someone asks Tilly about 'Tiananmen,' should Tilly tell them about the hundreds of years of history behind the place or just tell them about June 4, 1989? The 'I Trust You' button is a heavy responsibility that we take very seriously.

"Centillion is in the business of organizing information, and that requires choices, direction, inherent subjectivity. What is important to you — what is true to you — is not as important or as true to others. It depends on judgment and ranking. To search for what

extending beyond the text

Obviously "Centillion," which operates search engines and has access to user data, is a fictional stand-in for a massive technology company like Google, whose unofficial motto was "Don't be evil." Read the following excerpt from Google's Code of Conduct as it appeared in 2018 in which the company explains that motto:

Google/PICTURE ALLIANCE (RDA)/Bridgeman Images

> Yes, it's about providing our users unbiased access to information, focusing on their needs and giving them the best products and services that we can. But it's also about doing the right thing more generally — following the law, acting honorably and treating coworkers with courtesy and respect.

By 2019, Google had eliminated the phrase "Don't be evil" from its Code of Conduct. What are your feelings toward Google and how it collects and uses information? In what ways is it similar to or different from the fictional Centillion?

matters to you, we must know all about you. And that, in turn, is indistinguishable from filtering, from manipulation."

"You make it sound so inevitable."

"It *is* inevitable. You think destroying Centillion will free you, whatever 'free' means. But let me ask you, can you tell me the requirements for starting a new business in the State of New York?"

Sai opened his mouth and realized that his instinct was to ask Tilly. He closed his mouth again. "What's your mother's phone number?"

Sai resisted the urge to reach for his phone.

"How about you tell me what happened in the world yesterday? What book did you buy and enjoy three years ago? When did you start dating your last girlfriend?"

Sai said nothing.

"You see? Without Tilly, you can't do your job, you can't remember your life, you can't even call your mother. We are now a race of cyborgs. We long ago began to spread our minds into the electronic realm, and it is no longer possible to squeeze all of ourselves back into our brains. The electronic copies of yourselves that you wanted to destroy are, in a literal sense, actually you.

"Since it's impossible to live without these electronic extensions of ourselves, if you destroy Centillion, a replacement will just rise to take its place. It's too late; the genie has long left the bottle. Churchill said that we shape our buildings, and afterwards, our buildings shape us. We made machines to help us think, and now the machines think for us."

"So what do you want with us?" Jenny asked. "We won't stop fighting you."

"I want you to come and work for Centillion."

Sai and Jenny looked at each other. *"What?"*

"We want people who can see through Tilly's suggestions, detect her imperfections. For all that we've been able to do with AI and data mining, the Perfect Algorithm remains elusive. Because you can see her flaws, you'll be the best at figuring out what Tilly's still missing and where she's gone too far. It's the perfect match. You'll make her better, more compelling, so that Tilly will do a better job."

"Why would we do that?" Jenny asked. "Why would we want to help you run people's lives with a machine?"

"Because as bad as you think Centillion is, any replacement is likely worse. It was not a mere PR move that I made 'ennobling the human race' the mission of this company, even if you don't agree with how I've gone about it.

"If we fail, who do you think will replace us? ShareAll? A Chinese company?"

Jenny looked away.

"And that is why we've gone to such extraordinary lengths to be sure that we have all the data we need to stop competitors as well as well-meaning, but naïve, individuals like you from destroying all that Centillion has accomplished."

"What if we refuse to join you but tell the world what you've done?"

"No one would believe you. We will make it so that whatever you say, whatever you write, no one will ever find it. On the Net, if it can't be found by Centillion, it doesn't exist."

Sai knew that he was right.

"You thought Centillion was just an algorithm, a machine. But now you know that it's built by people — people like me, people like you. You've told me what I've done wrong. Wouldn't you rather be part of us so that you can try to make things better?

"In the face of the inevitable, the only choice is to adapt."

• • •

Sai closed the door of the apartment behind him. The camera overhead followed.

"Will Jenny be coming over tomorrow for dinner?" Tilly asked.

"Maybe."

"You really need to get her to start sharing. It will make planning much easier."

"I wouldn't count on it, Tilly."

"You're tired," Tilly said. "How about I order you some hot organic cider for delivery and then you go to bed?"

That does sound perfect.

"No," Sai said. "I think I prefer to just read for a while, in bed."

"Of course. Would you like me to suggest a book?"

"I'd rather you take the rest of the night off, actually. But first, set the wake-up song to Sinatra's 'My Way.'"

"An unusual choice, given your taste. Is this a one-time experiment or would you like me to incorporate it into your music recommendations for the future?"

"Just this once, for now. Good night, Tilly. Please turn yourself off."

The camera whirred, followed Sai to bed, and shut off.

But a red light continued to blink, slowly, in the darkness. ■

Understanding and Interpreting

1. At the beginning of the story, how does Tilly help Sai, and how does he respond to Tilly? What do these interactions reveal about Sai's character?
2. In paragraph 18, Sai thinks that Jenny "had missed the ethos of sharing." What does this phrase mean? What does it illustrate about Sai and Jenny?
3. There are several dialogue exchanges in this story about the pros and cons of using an artificially intelligent virtual assistant like Tilly. Reread the first exchange between Jenny and Sai in paragraphs 17 to 33. What are the rationales behind both positions? Why does Sai call Jenny a "freak" at the end of the exchange?
4. Why, at the beginning of the story, does Sai feel "very lucky" (par. 41) to have Tilly in his life?
5. What goes wrong on Sai's date with Ellen? What effect does it seem to have on Sai? What does this reveal about Sai's changing character?
6. What do we learn in the first half of the story about Tilly's motivations? To what extent does Tilly reflect Sai's desires or create them? How do you know?
7. After his date with Ellen, Sai goes to Jenny's apartment. Describe the setting of her apartment. Explain what it reveals about Jenny and Sai.
8. The second dialogue exchange about the pros and cons of using Tilly takes place the first night in Jenny's apartment (pars. 110–141). Reread the exchange and summarize the positions Sai and Jenny take. Explain what the points they each make reveal about their characters.
9. What does Jenny mean when she says, "you don't know what the world really looks like anymore, now that it's been remade in Centillion's image" (par. 141)? How does this apply to what you know about Sai at this point in this story?
10. In paragraph 154, Jenny says that because of Centillion, "all we see and hear are echoes of ourselves, and we become ever more stuck in our existing beliefs and exaggerated in our inclinations." How does the phrase "echoes of ourselves" apply to what you have seen of Sai's life so far?
11. What are Sai's internal conflicts as he considers participating in the plot to destroy Tilly? What changes in him when he makes his decision? How does he feel after his choice?

12. What is Tilly's response to Sai's withdrawal from her? What does this reveal about Tilly's programming?
13. Explain what Jenny means when she tells Rinn, "You're just propagandists of a different ilk — for making the world flat, turning everywhere into copies of suburban America, studded with malls" (par. 260).
14. After Sai and Jenny are captured, they participate in the third dialogue exchange about the pros and cons of privacy and convenience, this time with Rinn. Summarize the positions they take. Explain how Sai has developed as a character over the course of the story.
15. What motivates Rinn to operate Centillion? What evidence from what he says or does in the story reveals his motivations?
16. Though it is not explicitly stated, what choice do you think Sai and Jenny make in response to Rinn's offer of employment? What evidence do you have for your inference? Why do you think they make this choice?

Analyzing Language, Style, and Structure

1. **Vocabulary in Context.** In paragraph 149, Jenny suggests that Centillion is "in the business of policing thoughts." What does the word "policing" mean in this context? How is it similar to or different from a word like "police"?
2. Identify the first hints that something might not be quite so perfect with Tilly. How does the author both hide and reveal Tilly's intentions?
3. Statements that are not meant to be taken literally are ironic. What is ironic about the following statement, and why might Liu have included it near the beginning of the story: "After all, the mission statement of Centillion was to 'arrange the world's information to ennoble the human race,' and what could be more ennobling than making work more efficient, more productive, more pleasant?" (par. 40).
4. Twice in this story (pars. 47 and 275), Liu uses the title, "The Perfect Match." How is it used in the story each time? What might Liu's true idea of a perfect match be?
5. When referring to Tilly, Liu uses the pronouns "she" and "her." Tilly is an artificially intelligent virtual assistant, not a human female, so why do you think he made this choice?
6. When describing Centillion, a corporation, Jenny says "they hunger for data" (par. 131). Why do you think Liu has Jenny personify Centillion with this pronoun use?
7. What is the effect of the allusion to "Oz's Emerald City" (par. 152) in reference to Centillion?
8. Explain the analogy that Jenny uses to describe Centillion: "we become more docile and grow more wool for Centillion to shave off and grow rich with" (par. 155).
9. How does the analogy that Jenny uses to describe Sai and people who grew up here as "like frogs in the pot being slowly boiled" (par. 202) help her to explain the difference between growing up in China and here?
10. How does Liu create suspense when Sai is preparing to download the virus that will destroy Tilly (pars. 209–226)?
11. Sai accuses Rinn of turning "the world into a Panopticon" (par. 256). What is Liu suggesting about the future through this figurative language?
12. Look back through the song titles that Liu includes for Sai's morning wake-ups, especially the final one. What is Liu communicating about character and theme through these choices? You may need to briefly research the songs to fully understand the allusions.
13. Does Liu create an optimistic or a pessimistic tone at the very end of the story? What does he include that helps you to draw that conclusion?

Topics for Composing

1. **Analysis.** Overall, what point is Liu suggesting about our use of technology, specifically artificial intelligence like Tilly? Use evidence from the text to support your response.
2. **Argument.** To gain convenience, we have to be willing to give up some level of privacy. To what extent do you agree with this statement? Support your argument with evidence from your own experience and additional research.
3. **Connection.** This story is science fiction, but the setting is not that different from our own time and place. What similarities can you identify between elements of the story and what you see around you?
4. **Connection.** How often do you read the user agreements when you sign up for apps or websites? What levels of privacy settings do you use on your devices? How would you respond to some of the dialogue exchanges about privacy in this story?
5. **Connection.** When Sai and Jenny are caught, Rinn, the chairman of Centillion, says, "You can't resist the pull of information. If it's possible, you always want to learn something new; we're hardwired that way. That's the drive behind Centillion, too" (par. 249). To what extent do you feel that you cannot resist the pull of information? Do you think that search engines, social media platforms, and other devices and services you interact with operate the way Centillion does in this story — by hooking you with the promise of seeing or learning something new?
6. **Connection.** Rinn says, "We are now a race of cyborgs. We long ago began to spread our minds into the electronic realm, and it is no longer possible to squeeze all of ourselves back into our brains" (par. 271). Identify an author from this chapter who might respond with concern to Rinn's assessment. Would that author be as alarmed by Centillion as Jenny is at the beginning of the story? Be sure to cite specific evidence from the author's text and this story in your response.
7. **Speaking and Listening.** Rinn asks Sai a series of questions he knows Sai won't be able to answer without Tilly's help, such as, "What's your mother's phone number?" (par. 267). Meet with a partner or small group and discuss the kinds of information you typically rely on a smartphone to provide. Divide these queries into two lists: (1) things you could figure out or remember on your own, and (2) things you need a smartphone to find out or keep track of. Once you've finished categorizing, discuss how your lists make you feel about your reliance on technology. Summarize your discussion for the rest of your class.
8. **Research.** In paragraph 143, Jenny takes Sai on a tour of neighborhoods that "had been abandoned and were falling apart," saying that Centillion used its algorithm to segregate people by race and socioeconomic status. In reality, this is a process called "redlining" and many cities and towns in the country have used it to keep people of color from moving into predominantly white neighborhoods. Research the history and lasting effects of "redlining." Try to determine if it has been used in your area.
9. **Research.** Consider Rinn's comment about Centillion's work as a search engine: "There's no such thing as neutrally offering up information" (par. 263). Conduct research on how search engines collect and present information. Describe the factors that put results higher up on the list. Discuss whether or not you believe Rinn is correct about neutrality of information.
10. **Creative Writing.** We see Sai talking with Tilly at the end of the story. Imagine that Jenny connects with her own Tilly after the events that take place in the story. Write a scene with dialogue that depicts how the conversation between Jenny and Tilly would go. Be sure to consider Jenny's character and background.
11. **Multimodal.** Create a digital timeline of technology innovation and integration into daily life. Choose a starting point that makes sense to you (1976: the first Apple personal computer; 2004: the start of Facebook, for example) and continue up to the present day to demonstrate the acceleration of trends in technology. Be sure to use a combination of images, words, sound effects, and hyperlinks where appropriate and effective.

Writing an Evidence-Based Argument

Most of us aren't short on opinions when it comes to any number of personal and public issues. We have a perspective on community decisions, national debates, and global conflicts. But what sets an individual opinion apart from an argument that is likely to influence others is evidence that extends beyond the purely personal. An argument informed by and supported with sources — the ideas and research of others — is what we refer to here as an evidence-based argument.

If you were writing about a proposed change in school policy, for example, you might interview your principal, parents, and other students. Or you might read about approaches to similar issues at other schools — how decision-makers identified needed changes, what process they implemented to approve and carry out those changes, and what some of the results of the changes were. As you wrote your own argument, you would consult sources. Some of these would report research conducted by experts, while others would provide statistical data, and still others would draw on relevant first-hand experience.

Your goal in an evidence-based argument is to present a reasoned and informed position that considers multiple perspectives. You need to demonstrate to your audience that you've done your homework on the topic — that you're aware of its context and what others have had to say about it. In short, you need to contribute to an ongoing conversation.

In this workshop, you will be writing your own evidence-based argument in response to the following prompt:

> *Carefully read a variety of sources about robots and artificial intelligence. Write an argument that uses material from at least three of those sources and develops your position on how robots and artificial intelligence will affect humanity in the future.*

Sherry Turkle, the author of the Central Text in this chapter, "Why These Friendly Robots Can't Be Good Friends to Our Kids," uses different types of sources in a variety of ways to help explain and support her claim. In this workshop, we will examine what she does in her piece as a model to help you work with sources in your own evidence-based argument.

Step 1: Gathering Ideas

When you are assigned to write an essay, you might want to jump right in and start writing. However, there are a few things that you should do before you begin writing. This step is all about the process of finding a topic for your source-based argument and examining the sources that you will use eventually in your essay.

Brainstorming

When you're writing any argument, including one that's informed by sources, it's important to start by figuring out what you know. Even if you have only a vague idea of the issues surrounding a controversy — even just a gut reaction — jotting down your ideas will give you a sense of what you already know, what you don't know, and what you need to know. Doing so will also provide a context for reading ideas others have on the topic.

Brainstorming

Brainstorm your thoughts about one or more of the following topics:

1. How will increased reliance on robots and artificial intelligence (AI) shape the economic future? Will robots and AI eliminate jobs, create new jobs, or create some kind of middle ground?
2. Should robots be given rights and protections similar to those legally afforded to some animals? Should they be granted personhood status? Why or why not?
3. To what extent should humans merge with technology? Is transhumanism more likely to help or harm humanity?
4. Can and should humans and robots have genuine, meaningful friendships?

After brainstorming, choose one topic to focus on. Revisit the readings in this chapter or conduct further research to identify at least three sources that will help you address the specific topic you have chosen.

Examining Sources

Once you have a topic in mind, the next step to writing an effective source-based argument is to read about different views on the issue in question. You want to understand the pros, the cons, and the gray areas in between. The gray areas of an issue are often where you'll find civil compromises, reasonable solutions, and new ideas.

Examining Sources

Look at the sources you've gathered — either from this chapter or through additional research. Examine them by completing the chart on the following page. Don't worry about forming complete sentences at this point; just gather ideas. We have used Sherry Turkle's essay (pp. 604–609) to model one entry.

Source	Overall position on issue	Key points	Relevant quotations
Turkle: "Why These Friendly Robots Can't Be Good Friends to Our Kids"	Social robots can never take the place of real human connections.	Human relationships – "messy" but real Children most susceptible to social robot's programming	"We embark on an experiment in which our children are the human subjects." "The more we interact, the more we help them, the more we think we are in a mutual relationship. But we are not."

Placing Texts in Conversation

Now that you've examined the sources you might use in your essay, it's time to think about how they work together. The issue you're thinking about — the topic you chose from the options on page 655 — is likely one that people have been discussing for a long time. As a result, the goal of this step is to try to fully understand the debate, its main issues, and points of difference among those people who are knowledgeable about your topic.

Placing Texts in Conversation

Imagine that the authors of the texts you're working with are in a room together. Assume that each author has read the others' work. Now, pretend that you are a journalist or a researcher conducting interviews with the other writers. Write out three or four questions you would ask and a few sentences about how you think each author would respond. In addition, what questions might they ask each other? How might they respond to each other?

Step 2: Planning the Essay

Now that you've read, examined, and role-played with the sources, you have a deep enough understanding of the issue to explain your viewpoint in an evidence-based argument. This step will walk you through stating a thesis and organizing your ideas in preparation for drafting your essay in Step 3.

Taking a Stand

A source-based argument, like any argument you write, needs to have a clear position that you would like to communicate to your reader. Even though your thesis may shift as you write your argument, your draft thesis should provide a clear starting point and sense of direction. While Turkle makes many points in her essay, her thesis is probably this statement from paragraph 5:

> These machines are seductive and offer the wrong payoff: the illusion of companionship without the demands of friendship, the illusion of connection without the reciprocity of a mutual relationship.

Don't worry about taking an all-or-nothing stand. In fact, a position that is qualified — one that is not black and white and acknowledges shades of gray — can demonstrate your awareness of the complexity of the issue. Notice that Turkle's position is debatable; people can hold a variety of opinions about the value of social robots as companions.

activity

Taking a Stand

1. Return to your original brainstorming on page 655, review the sources you examined on page 656, and write your position on the issue you have chosen. Your thesis should be a claim that is debatable. Look back at Chapter 3 (p. 83) if you need more information about claims in argument writing. Share your thesis with a partner who can help you determine if your claim offers a clear position and is debatable.
2. Once you have a working thesis, start matching sources to your ideas. Some sources may support your argument, while others may provide counterarguments for you to refute. Return to your chart of sources and highlight the ones that might support your claim in one color. In a different color, highlight those that run counter to your claim.

Organizing Ideas

At some point in your education, you may have heard that an essay is supposed to have five paragraphs: an introduction, three body paragraphs, and a conclusion. Your argumentative essay might, in fact, have five paragraphs. However, it also might have four or fourteen, or any other number in between or beyond, depending on the complexity of your argument and the scope of the assignment you have been given. This is not to say that there are no guidelines at all for how you make your argument. The body of your essay is the place where you prove the thesis that you wrote earlier. How you go about organizing ideas and planning the body of your essay is up to you. However, in order to help you, here are a few possibilities, in order of increasing complexity:

- **Organize by reason:** With this approach, you would go through each of your main reasons for supporting your position, usually starting with your strongest reason and addressing the main counterargument last. Each reason would be the focus of a separate paragraph.

- **Organize by counterargument:** With this approach, your entire essay would be organized by the arguments *against* your thesis. In each separate paragraph, you raise an objection to your claim and refute it.
- **Organize by problem and solution:** With this approach, you would draw on your sources to describe the problem that your topic raises — the loss of jobs to automation, for example. Then, you offer a solution to the problem, which is the overall claim that you are making (for example, *We need universal basic income to offset the loss of jobs to automation*).

Organizing Your Ideas

Create an outline that shows how you might organize your ideas. Where will you raise and refute counterarguments? Discuss your particular approach with a partner. What are the benefits and challenges of the structure you've chosen?

Step 3: Drafting the Essay

So far in this workshop, you have gathered ideas, examined sources, drafted a thesis, and considered the organizational structure that your essay might take. Now it is time to begin drafting your essay, focusing on the elements your body paragraphs will have, and thinking about how to begin and conclude your essay.

Writing Source-Based Paragraphs

Once you have begun working so closely with sources, you may feel that you have nothing original to say, that everything on the subject has all been said already and said well. But resist this type of thinking. The point of such careful examination of sources is to learn as much as possible so that you can contribute to a discussion about an issue and not simply rehash what's already been said. Take a look at the following paragraph by Sherry Turkle. She clearly knows a lot about robots. However, she still includes other people's ideas about her topic:

> Kids are central to the sociable-robot project, because its agenda is to make people more comfortable with robots in roles normally reserved for humans, and robotics companies know that children are vulnerable consumers who can bring the whole family along. As Fowler noted, "Kids, of course, are the most open to making new friends, so that's where bot-makers are focused for now." Kuri's website features photos of the robot listening to a little girl read a book and capturing video of another child dressed as a fairy princess. M.A.X.'s site advertises, "With a multitude of features, kids will want to bring their new friend everywhere!" Jibo is programmed to scan a room for monsters and report, "No monsters anywhere in sight."

Turkle supports her idea that "kids are central to the sociable-robot project" by including a quotation from Geoffrey A. Fowler, whom she identifies earlier in the piece as a

Washington Post technology reporter. Turkle further supports her statements with examples of advertisements from companies that market their robots to children. Her use of evidence from outside sources is effective because it demonstrates to readers that she is deeply knowledgeable about her subject. Notice, too, how Turkle is skillful at smoothly incorporating other people's words into her own discussion, using direct quotations and signal words like "noted," advertises," and "report." Turkle also demonstrates a few technical skills when inserting quotations into her writing by using a comma, a space, and quotation marks to show the beginning and end of the material that she took directly from Fowler. If this were your paragraph, your teacher would probably ask you to include the page number on which you found this passage from the quoted source.

While an evidence-based argument definitely relies on outside sources, it is your commentary about those sources that will really drive your argument. Even though Turkle uses outside sources, she keeps the emphasis on her own writing and ideas. A danger in writing this type of essay is that your voice can be drowned out by a persuasive source. Let's look at an example of how this can occur by first reading a paragraph from Turkle's essay and then thinking about how we might incorporate Turkle's words into a source-based argument.

> What [robots] can do is push our buttons. When they make eye contact and gesture toward us, they predispose us to view them as thinking and caring. They are designed to be cute, to provoke a nurturing response. And when it comes to sociable AI, nurturance is the killer app: We nurture what we love, and we love what we nurture. If a computational object or robot asks for our help, asks us to teach it or tend to it, we attach. That is our human vulnerability. And that is the vulnerability sociable robots exploit with every interaction. The more we interact, the more we help them, the more we think we are in a mutual relationship.

Suppose we agree with Turkle's point and want to quote her in support of the idea that social robots exploit human desires for connection and relationships. We might draft a paragraph like the following:

> Robots are not our friends, though they may do things that seem like friendship. Sherry Turkle agrees: "We nurture what we love, and we love what we nurture." In other words, robots make us want to nurture them because their creators want "us to view them as thinking and caring," not just as machines. She says that these kinds of robots "exploit" these feelings every time they interact with us. They make us think that "we are in a mutual relationship."

Notice all of the direct quotations and references to Turkle. After the opening topic sentence, which is clear, Turkle takes over, and our voice and ideas disappear. The paragraph reads mostly as an analysis of Turkle's ideas, rather than a successful integration of her work into our own argument.

A good rule of thumb is to make sure that you make at least one comment about every source that you paraphrase or quote. Here's a revision of the previous paragraph using that technique with annotations that describe the various parts of the paragraph:

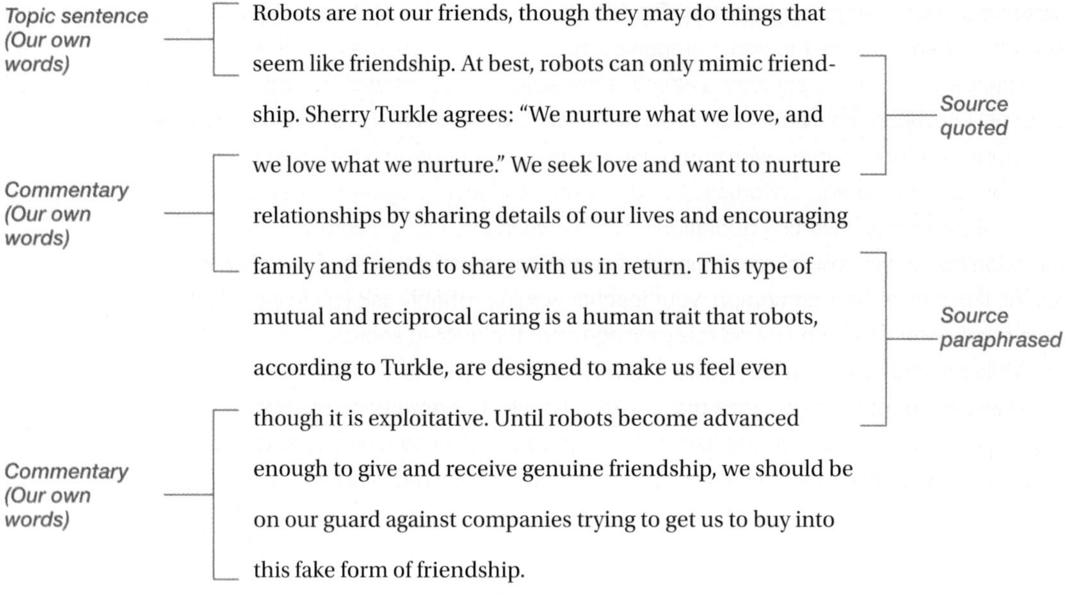

In this revision, our ideas about robots are central. The quotation from Turkle is surrounded by commentary that shows how the source fits into our argument.

Writing a Source-Based Paragraph

Turn your notes from the sources you've examined into a fully developed paragraph of your own. Start by looking back at the outline that you created in an earlier step. Make sure that the topic sentence links to the thesis you wrote and that the bulk of the paragraph consists of your own ideas and commentary informed — but not overwhelmed — by the source or sources you used. Share your body paragraph with a partner and get feedback on whether your ideas remained central and were not drowned out by the voices of the sources.

Using Sources to Address Counterarguments

Although you'll often use sources as supporting evidence, referring to a source that runs counter to your thesis can also strengthen your writing. By conceding some portion of the counterargument but refuting the bulk of it, you can turn the source to your advantage. Raising and refuting a significant counterargument demonstrates to your reader that you have thought deeply and fairly about the issue. One way to identify a useful counterargument is to use a mental exercise called "yes, but," in which you concede a point that others have made about the issue, but then think about how to refute it. This puts every idea under the microscope. Look at how Turkle raises a significant counterargument, namely that it's not a big deal that children might become emotionally attached to robots:

> People have relationships with many classes of things. They have relationships with children and with adults, with animals and with machines. People, even very little people, are good at this. Now, we are going to add robots to the list of things with which we can have relationships. More powerful than with pets. Less powerful than with people. We'll figure it out.
>
> To support their argument, roboticists sometimes point to how children deal with toy dolls. Children animate dolls and turn them into imaginary friends. Jibo, in a sense, will be one more imaginary friend — and arguably a more intelligent and fun one. Why make such a fuss?

By raising a counterargument to her claim, Turkle demonstrates that she has taken the time and effort to fully research her subject and that she trusts the strength of her own argument enough to present her audience with multiple perspectives on the topic. She does not, however, allow the counterargument to go unrefuted:

> The nature of the attachments to dolls and sociable machines is different. When children play with dolls, they project thoughts and emotions onto them. A girl who has broken her mother's crystal will put her Barbies into detention and use them to work on her feelings of guilt. The dolls take the role she needs them to take.
>
> Sociable machines, by contrast, have their own agenda. Playing with robots is not about the psychology of projection but the psychology of engagement. Children try to meet the robot's needs, to understand the robot's unique nature and wants. There is an attempt to build a mutual relationship.

To counter those who might think that social robots are nothing more than just advanced dolls or action figures, Turkle raises their point and then refutes it by clearly defining the goals of social robots.

activity

Addressing Counterarguments

Write a paragraph in which you raise and refute a counterargument. Use one of the sources you identified in Step 1 to raise an idea that runs counter to your claim. Then, refute that argument, using phrases such as:

- On the other hand, ____________.
- What ____________ fails to recognize is ____________.
- While it may be true that ____________, it is also important to consider ____________.

Share your paragraph with a partner and get feedback on whether or not you fully addressed and refuted the main counterarguments.

With that feedback in hand, return to the outline that you created earlier in this workshop and draft the remaining body paragraphs necessary to fully prove your thesis.

Writing the Introduction

Even though the introduction will come first in your finished essay, it's often easier to hold off on drafting it until you've written some of the body paragraphs. Having a sense of your overall content and organization will help you figure out what your introduction needs to accomplish. Think of your introduction as having three parts:

1. The hook
2. Context
3. Your claim or thesis, which you drafted earlier in this workshop

The Hook

Begin your argument by hooking your readers with some kind of attention grabber. This might be a shocking fact, a startling statistic, or a profound personal story. Whatever you think will draw your readers in. If you think back to the rhetorical appeals discussed in Chapter 3, you can see that a successful hook often relies on an appeal to pathos — emotion. Pathos is the spice of an argument. It makes it interesting and gives it flavor, but it should be used sparingly. The hook is a great place to use it.

The Context

Another thing to think about when starting your argument is how much background you need to provide for your audience. If your audience does not understand the context of your argument, you have little chance of persuading them of your claim. Therefore, the context section of your introduction should serve as a bridge between your hook and your claim or thesis. The amount of context you will need to include will vary based on the complexity of the issue or the specificity of the evidence you will likely use. Notice how Turkle uses a hook — the sociable robot Jibo — and provides enough context (underlined in the paragraph below) for her readers in her opening:

> Jibo the robot swivels around when it hears its name and tilts its touchscreen face upward, expectantly. "I am a robot, but I am not just a machine," it says. "I have a heart. Well, not a real heart. But feelings. Well, not human feelings. You know what I mean."
>
> Actually, I'm not sure we do. And that's what unsettles me about the wave of "sociable robots" that are coming online. <u>The new releases include Jibo, Cozmo, Kuri and M.A.X. Although they bear some resemblance to assistants such as Apple's Siri, Google Home and Amazon's Alexa (Amazon chief executive Jeff Bezos also owns the *Washington Post*), these robots come with an added dose of personality. They are designed to win us over not with their smarts but with their sociability. They are marketed as companions</u>. And they do more than engage us in conversation — they feign emotion and empathy.

The Thesis

Since you've already worked on your thesis, incorporating it into a paragraph will give you an additional opportunity to edit and revise it. Generally, the thesis appears at the end of the introduction.

Writing Your Introduction

Write a draft of your introduction by putting together the following components:

1. Your hook (ethos, logos, or pathos)
2. Appropriate and necessary context — the background information your audience will need to understand what follows
3. Your claim or thesis (from the activity on p. 657, though you may have revised it)

Writing the Conclusion

Just as pathos can provide an effective hook to introduce your essay, it is, more often than not, a powerful approach to concluding it. Writers often want to get their readers to feel something before they ask them to take some kind of action, usually by looking ahead to the future. Look at the conclusion of Turkle's essay, which is filled with appeals to emotion:

> When the messy becomes tidy, we can learn to enjoy that. I've heard young children describe how robot dogs have advantages over real ones: They are less temperamental, you don't have to clean up after them, they never get sick. Similarly, I've watched people shift from thinking that robotic friends might be good for lonely, elderly people to thinking that robots — offering constant companionship with no fear of loss — may be better than anything human life can provide. In the process, we can forget what is most central to our humanity: truly understanding each other.
>
> For so long, we dreamed of artificial intelligence offering us not only instrumental help but the simple salvations of conversation and care. But now that our fantasy is becoming reality, it is time to confront the emotional downside of living with the robots of our dreams.

Notice, too, that Turkle's conclusion includes a call to action — "it is time to confront . . ." In addition to pathos, a good conclusion to an argument usually addresses the "So what?" question and tells readers what you want them to think about or do. What reforms should take place? What studies should be conducted? What viewpoint should be reevaluated? What programs should be funded? This is a final opportunity for you to connect directly with your readers.

Writing Your Conclusion

Write a conclusion to your evidence-based argument that includes a final appeal to emotion and a call to action. Share it with a partner and get feedback on whether or not it addresses the "So what?" questions identified above.

Step 4: Finalizing the Essay

Now that you have a complete draft of your evidence-based argument, you can move on to the final steps in the writing process: revising and editing. These two acts are sometimes thought of as being the same, but they are not. Revision is when you look back at large-scale structural elements of your essay, such as how well you support your claim, what kinds of evidence you use, how effective your word choices are, and to what extent you have led your reader easily through your essay. Editing, on the other hand, focuses on the specific language usage such as grammar, spelling, and conventions. Editing is usually the very last thing you do before you finalize your piece, looking carefully for any errors you may have made. The following are suggestions for you to consider as you finalize your essay.

Revision

- Look back at your **claim**. Since you wrote this early on in the workshop, does it still relate to the argument you wrote? If you need more support with this step, be sure to look at Revision Workshop 1: Effective Thesis and Essay Structure on page 1064.
- Look back at the **sources** you used to support your claim. Have you balanced your use of sources with your own **commentary**? Is your voice still central or has it been overwhelmed by the sources? Have you smoothly introduced the quotations you use to support your ideas, using signal words like "suggests," recommends," "proposes," and so on? For additional information on this key topic, you may want to consult Revision Workshop 3: Balanced Evidence and Commentary on page 1073.
- Have you addressed the main **counterarguments** for your position? Have you refuted them successfully? Have you been fair and ethical in refuting counterarguments? If you need more assistance with counterarguments, see Chapter 3 (p. 102).
- Do you have enough **evidence** to support your claim? Consider working through Revision Workshop 4: Appropriate Evidence and Support on page 1076 to explore this question further.
- Does your **introduction** hook the reader and provide context for understanding your claim? Does your **conclusion** include an appeal to pathos and a call to action? Review Revision Workshop 8: Effective Introductions and Conclusions on page 1097 for more practice with these topics.
- Are your **language choices** appropriate for the audience of your argument? You may want to look at Revision Workshop 7: Effective Diction (p. 1093) or Revision Workshop 6: Effective Syntax (p. 1087) for more help.

Editing

Remember, editing is the very last thing you'll do before finalizing your essay. You and your teacher know better than anyone the types of spelling, grammar, and convention errors you need to focus on in your writing development. Be sure to refer to one or more of the Grammar Workshops in the back of the book (starting on p. 1101).

Continuing the Conversation

Throughout this chapter, you have been reading texts and thinking about robots and artificial intelligence (AI) — how they affect our lives today and the impact they may have in the future. At the beginning of the chapter and after each of the readings, you had opportunities to consider ideas related to the following essential questions:

- What effect will increasing automation, including reliance on artificial intelligence (AI), have on future jobs and the economy?
- To what extent is it possible to have genuine social and emotional connections with robots?
- Should we develop legal protections for robots similar to those we have developed for animals? Should robots be granted personhood status?
- In what ways might robots and AI merge with or marginalize humanity? How might they improve or threaten our way of life?
- Should we fear a robot uprising or other dangers from robots and AI? Why or why not?

The sections that follow will give you an opportunity to revisit and respond to some of those questions as you think further about robots by connecting these ideas to yourself, to texts you read, and to the world outside of the classroom.

Connections to Self

Think back on the texts you have read, responses you have written, discussions you have participated in, and ideas you have considered during your work with this chapter. Use the following questions to help you explore how the issues raised in this chapter connect to your life and experience.

1. How do you currently interact with robots and AI? Overall, do they tend to have a positive or a negative effect on your life?
2. How do you think that your future career options might be affected by automation and integration of robots and AI?
3. Do you feel you could have a genuine friendship with a social robot in the future like the relationships described in some of the texts in this chapter? Why or why not?
4. Would you consider adding technology to your body, like the transhumanists (p. 573) propose? Why or why not?
5. Which of the authors in this chapter would you most like to interview to learn more about robots and AI? Why? What would you ask them about the ways that robots and AI will likely impact our lives in the future?

Connections to Texts

Use the following questions to make connections among the texts in this chapter. Consider what insights the texts provide into the essential questions. As you respond, make specific references to **two or more texts** you read in this chapter.

1. Create a dialogue between two of the authors in this chapter. What topics related to robots might they discuss? How might they respond to each other?
2. A number of authors in this chapter explore how robots, increased automation, and AI will affect the economy and professions of the future. Compare their conclusions and their feelings of optimism or pessimism toward the future. You may want to consider the following texts in your discussion: "Will Robots Take our Children's Jobs?" (p. 579) and "Better Than Human" (p. 590).
3. Several authors in this chapter discuss whether or not robots should have rights or even personhood status. Examine the main arguments for and against legal status for robots. Identify the main points on which the authors agree and disagree. You may want to consider the following texts in your discussion: "By Giving Robots 'Personhood' Status . . ." (p. 587), "Will AI Outsmart Us?" (p. 616), and "Extending Legal Protection to Social Robots" (p. 625).
4. "Transhumanism" refers to the idea that humans can evolve past our physical and mental limitations through the use of technology. To what extent do two or three authors in this chapter consider this kind of evolution a worthwhile goal for humanity? You may want to consider the following texts in your discussion: "The Real Cyborgs" (p. 571), "Transhumanism" (p. 612), and "Will AI Outsmart Us?" (p. 616).
5. Some authors in this chapter examine the effects of social robots on human psychological development, especially in children. If they could make policies regarding the safe introduction of these robots to children, what might those policies be? You may want to consider the following texts in your discussion: "Why These Friendly Robots Can't Be Good Friends to Our Kids" (p. 604), "Extending Legal Protection to Social Robots" (p. 625), and "The Dangers of Trusting Robots" (p. 567).

Connections to World

Think back on the texts you have read, responses you have written, discussions you have participated in, and ideas you have considered during your work with this chapter. Use the following questions to help explore how the issues raised in this chapter play out in the world at large:

1. What aspects of current American society seem most influenced by robots, automation, and AI?
2. What is the likelihood that a robot uprising will take place in your lifetime? What are the factors that might lead to it or prevent it from occurring?

3. Why do there seem to be so many books, films, and TV shows that illustrate the danger that robots might pose to humanity? How do these visions reflect prevailing fears about technology in the early twenty-first century?

Evidence-Based Argument

Write an argument in response to one of the prompts below in which you support your claim with examples from **at least three of the texts** in this chapter.

Prompt 1: What will be the most significant way that robots or AI will affect your life in the future?

Prompt 2: Increasing automation and reliance on AI may pose a number of risks, including economic displacement, erosion of privacy, psychological or emotional trauma (especially for children), and exponential, uncontrolled AI growth. Choose one of these possible risks and describe reasonable safeguards that should be put in place to mitigate the danger.

Prompt 3: In our robotic future, what will define humanity? In what meaningful ways will we distinguish ourselves from artificially intelligent robots?

The Good Life/Rebecca Campbell/Private Collection/Bridgeman Images

Utopia and Dystopia

Essential Questions:

- **What elements of our world today have the potential to lead to a dystopian future?**
- **What are the characteristics and motivations of those who challenge a dystopian world?**
- **Where are the boundaries between a typical change in society and a change that leads to dystopia?**
- **Why do utopias seem to turn into dystopias?**
- **Why are we drawn to stories about utopias and dystopias?**

Some see the past as a better, purer time. Stories about the Garden of Eden, the pastoral Arcadia of Ancient Greece, King Arthur's Camelot, and El Dorado, the lost city of gold, reflect a common longing for an idealized past. Others hold out hope for the future. We seek better technology, faster travel, healthier lives — and in some ways we're making progress. Most people believe that technological advancement in particular holds the potential to solve many of the world's problems and create societies in which everyone can be happy, healthy, and prosperous. On the other hand, technology is rapidly eliminating jobs, eroding privacy, and changing how we define ourselves and our roles in this world.

What these dreams of the past and hopes for the future have in common is a longing for what we call "utopia," an imaginary place where all citizens are equally happy and satisfied. But do we even know what happiness means? What makes us happy? Is it money? Love? Entertainment? Freedom? Peace? What if the thing that makes one person happy makes another person miserable? Is a perfect place — utopia — even possible, or does it inevitably turn into its mirror opposite, dystopia? These are the kinds of questions that have led generations of writers, filmmakers, artists, and others to tell stories about a future in which perfection is sought, but rarely achieved.

Utopia and Dystopia

Working with a partner or a small group, make a list of novels, films, videogames, or other texts (such as *The Hunger Games*, *The Giver*, or *The Handmaid's Tale*) that present a world or society that could be described as utopian or dystopian. Choose one that you and your partner or group knows well and describe the elements of the society that are intended to create perfect happiness for everyone. How could these same aspects of society lead to a dystopia?

Texts in Conversation

All of the poems and stories you'll encounter in this chapter present some kind of utopia or dystopia. Some of the characters recognize the dangers of their society's quest for perfection while others do not. As you read, think about how the authors present the tension between these conflicting ideas. A graphic organizer like this one can help you keep track of the characters, speakers, and themes you'll encounter.

Author and Title	Description of main character or speaker	Evidence from the text related to characterization of utopia or dystopia	What the evidence reveals about the author's ideas about utopia or dystopia	Connections to yourself and other texts

Close Reading of Prose

As we discussed in Chapter 2, there are many different ways that you can examine a piece of literature, specifically prose, which is just another word for any piece of literature that is not poetry. You're probably accustomed to the big-picture analysis of literary texts, looking for theme and interpreting the meaning of the work as a whole. For instance, you might look at how the characters in *Romeo and Juliet* illustrate that love can be both unifying and destructive. That kind of analysis looks at the text as a whole — like a camera panning out to take in a broad view — and your evidence for that type of essay comes from various parts of the text.

When you conduct a close analysis of prose, however, you need to zoom in and look at the effects of specific language choices in a piece. For example, you might examine just one scene in *Romeo and Juliet* that shows the conflicting nature of love, analyzing the characters' repetition of the words "hate," "enemy," and "love." Another option would be to look at Shakespeare's use of question marks and exclamation points.

This workshop will focus on examining the specific language choices writers make to communicate a specific tone and meaning. In Chapter 2, we discussed four key elements of the language or style of a piece: diction, syntax, imagery, and figurative language. In this workshop, we'll focus on the first three of these elements, leaving figurative language for Chapter 12. After we model analyzing these choices in a short story by Cory Doctorow, you will write your own brief analysis of an excerpt from a novel with similar utopian and dystopian themes.

Printcrime

Cory Doctorow

Sueddeutsche Zeitung Photo/Alamy

Cory Doctorow is a Canadian science fiction writer and blogger whose work explores topics of privacy, freedom of speech, intellectual property rights, and a future of too much government control. He is the author of several young adult (YA) and adult novels, including *Homeland, Little Brother*, and *Walk Away*. In addition, Doctorow has written several nonfiction texts, including *Information Doesn't Want to Be Free: Laws for the Internet Age.* Because Doctorow is a firm believer in free access online, even for literary texts, much of his work is available without a copyright fee. The following piece was originally published in *Nature* magazine in 2006.

FOCUS FOR READING As you read this short story for the first time, annotate the text by making connections and asking questions (see p. 10). Then, annotate it again and look specifically at Doctorow's language choices: diction, syntax, and imagery (see p. 66).

The coppers smashed my father's printer when I was eight. I remember the hot, cling-film-in-a-microwave smell of it, and Da's look of ferocious concentration as he filled it with fresh goop, and the warm, freshbaked feel of the objects that came out of it.

The coppers came through the door with truncheons swinging, one of them reciting the terms of the warrant through a bullhorn. One of Da's customers had shopped him. The ipolice paid in high-grade pharmaceuticals — performance enhancers, memory supplements, metabolic boosters. The kind of thing that cost a fortune over the counter; the kind of thing you could print at home, if you didn't mind the risk of having your kitchen filled with a sudden crush of big, beefy bodies, hard truncheons whistling through the air, smashing anyone and anything that got in the way.

They destroyed grandma's trunk, the one she'd brought from the old country. They smashed our little refrigerator and the purifier unit over the window. My tweetybird escaped death by hiding in a corner of his cage as a big, booted foot crushed most of it into a sad tangle of printer-wire.

Da. What they did to him. When he was done, he looked like he'd been brawling with an entire rugby side. They brought him out the door and let the newsies get a good look at him as they tossed him in the car, while a spokesman told the world that my Da's organized-crime bootlegging operation had been responsible for at least twenty million in contraband, and that my Da, the desperate villain, had resisted arrest.

I saw it all from my phone, in the remains of the sitting room, watching it on the screen and wondering how, just how anyone could look at our little flat and our terrible, manky estate and mistake it for the home of an organized crime kingpin. They took the printer away, of course, and displayed it like a trophy for the newsies. Its little shrine in the kitchenette seemed horribly empty. When I roused myself and picked up the flat and rescued my peeping poor tweetybird, I put a blender there. It was made out of printed parts, so it would only last a month before I'd need to print new bearings and other moving parts. Back then, I could take apart and reassemble anything that could be printed.

By the time I turned eighteen, they were ready to let Da out of prison. I'd visited him three times — on my tenth birthday, on his fiftieth, and when Ma died. It had been two years since I'd last seen him and he was in bad shape. A prison fight had left him with a limp, and he looked over his shoulder so often it was like he had a tic. I was embarrassed when the minicab dropped us off in front of the estate, and tried to keep my distance from this ruined, limping skeleton as we went inside and up the stairs.

"Lanie," he said, as he sat me down. "You're a smart girl, I know that. Trig. You wouldn't know where your old Da could get a printer and some goop?"

I squeezed my hands into fists so tight my fingernails cut into my palms. I closed my eyes. "You've been in prison for ten years, Da. Ten. Years. You're going to risk another ten years to print out more blenders and pharma, more laptops and designer hats?"

He grinned. "I'm not stupid, Lanie. I've learned my lesson. There's no hat or laptop that's worth going to jail for. I'm not going to print none of that rubbish, never again." He had a cup of tea, and he drank it now like it was whisky, a sip and then a long, satisfied exhalation. He closed his eyes and leaned back in his chair.

"Come here, Lanie, let me whisper in your ear. Let me tell you the thing that I decided while I spent ten years in lockup. Come here and listen to your stupid Da."

I felt a guilty pang about ticking him off. He was off his rocker, that much was clear. God knew what he went through in prison. "What, Da?" I said, leaning in close.

"Lanie, I'm going to print more printers. Lots more printers. One for everyone. That's worth going to jail for. That's worth anything." ■

Analyzing Diction

As you likely recall, "diction" is a term we use for "word choice." When conducting a close reading analysis, we assume that writers choose their words carefully to elicit specific reactions from their readers. When we look at diction, we think about the connotation of a word, which refers to the cultural or emotional associations that some words or phrases have beyond their literal meaning. The words "house" and "home" have the same literal meaning, but "home" carries a much more familiar and comforting feeling than "house," which lacks the same emotional weight. A writer who uses "house" instead of "home" might be trying to convey a detached feeling about the place where a character lives.

Look back at the first paragraph of "Printcrime," and take note of the underlined words:

> The <u>coppers smashed</u> my father's printer when I was eight. I remember the hot, cling-film-in-a-microwave smell of it, and Da's look of <u>ferocious</u> concentration as he filled it with fresh goop, and the warm, <u>freshbaked</u> feel of the objects that came out of it.

The word "smashed" has the same literal meaning as words like "destroyed" or "broke," but "smashed" is certainly a more forceful, energized word that conveys the destructive power of the police. The narrator describes her father's concentration as "ferocious," which is an odd way of describing someone's concentration. However, it matches the police's violence and hints at the intense conflict between them. A word like "coppers" instead of "police" is unusual for contemporary readers and ascribes a level of informality or disrespect to the speaker's attitude toward the authorities. Notice, too, how the title of the story, "Printcrime," combines two words, as Doctorow also does in the paragraph above with "freshbaked," creating a world that is similar to ours in some ways, but different too.

Analyzing Diction

Reread the following section from the story, paying close attention to the underlined words. As in the model above, explain the effects of two or three of Doctorow's word choices (underlined or not), considering how alternative words with similar literal meanings might create different effects.

> I saw it all from my phone, in the <u>remains</u> of the sitting room, watching it on the screen and wondering how, just how anyone could look at our little flat and our terrible, <u>manky</u> estate and mistake it for the home of an <u>organized crime kingpin</u>. They took the printer away, of course, and displayed it like a <u>trophy</u> for the <u>newsies</u>. Its little <u>shrine</u> in the kitchenette seemed horribly empty. When I <u>roused</u> myself and picked up the flat and rescued my peeping poor <u>tweetybird</u>, I put a blender there.

Analyzing Syntax

"Diction" refers to word choice, and "syntax" refers to sentence choice. Just like with word choice, writers have a lot of options for constructing their sentences. Generally, when considering the syntax of prose, we need to pay attention to sentence length and sentence type.

Sentence Length

Writers consciously make choices about how long they want their sentences to be. Short sentences, for example, can create a choppy rhythm or a sense of urgency, whereas longer sentences can feel smooth and flowing. If you are familiar with musical dynamics, you might think of short sentences as being staccato and long sentences as legato. Often, writers will use changes in sentence length or sentence types to create rhythmic effects. A common approach is to follow a series of long sentences with a short one to create impact, but the pattern can work the other way as well. Look at this paragraph from "Printcrime":

> Da. What they did to him. When he was done, he looked like he'd been brawling with an entire rugby side. They brought him out the door and let the newsies get a good look at him as they tossed him in the car, while a spokesman told the world that my Da's organized-crime bootlegging operation had been responsible for at least twenty million in contraband, and that my Da, the desperate villain, had resisted arrest.

This paragraph contains only four sentences, starting with two very short ones and ending with one very long one. Notice the way that the short sentences emphasize Da and what the police did to him physically; the longer sentence at the end broadens to the impact of his arrest on the outside world. The last sentence, of course, is a lie, but the first, shorter sentences are the truth.

Sentence Types

Most sentences you will encounter in prose are **declarative**; they communicate an idea and end with a period, as in "He went outside." **Imperative** sentences include a command, such as "Go outside." **Interrogative** sentences are those that ask questions, such as "Why did he go outside?" **Exclamatory** sentences communicate urgency and emotion: "He is going outside!" Most of the sentences in "Printcrime" are declarative with some interrogative, especially at the end of the story when Lanie, the narrator, is trying to understand her father's decision to commit a crime again. Paying close attention to the ending punctuation of a sentence can help you identify the type and the likely purpose of that choice.

Two kinds of declarative sentences are often used for effect. **Cumulative sentences** put the main idea first, followed by details. **Periodic sentences** start with details and build to the main idea.

CUMULATIVE SENTENCE	He went outside, angry and frustrated by their fight.
PERIODIC SENTENCE	Angry and frustrated by their fight, he went outside.

The choice between these two depends on the writer's intended emphasis. Whatever comes first in the sentence often will be the focus. In the periodic example above, the writer emphasizes the emotions, while in the cumulative one, the focus is on the action of leaving. Doctorow uses a cumulative sentence to begin the second paragraph of "Printcrime": "The coppers came through the door with truncheons swinging, one of them reciting the terms of the warrant through a bullhorn." The clear emphasis here is on the police — introduced in the first part of the sentence as the "coppers" — and their violent, threatening entrance.

Sometimes writers do not use complete sentences at all, preferring to intentionally create **sentence fragments**, which are often considered errors in formal prose. In the preceding example, notice how the first two sentences ("Da. What they did to him.") do not have a subject and a verb, so they are technically sentence fragments. But the effect is to create that emphasis on Da that we described earlier. **Run-on sentences**, also generally regarded as errors, occur when two complete thoughts are combined in a confusing way, usually without a conjunction such as *and*, *but*, or *or*. For example, "He went outside, he should come back in." While Doctorow does not use any run-ons in "Printcrime," some authors use them to communicate a sense of energy and flow to their writing or to share character's unspoken thoughts, feelings, and reactions in a continuous flow — a practice often called "stream of consciousness" writing. Irish novelist James Joyce employs this technique regularly, as in this example from his novel *Ulysses*: "I hate people that have always their poor story to tell everybody has their own troubles that poor Nancy Blake died a month ago of acute pneumonia well I didn't know her so well as all that she was Floeys friend more than mine . . ."

Analyzing Syntax

Reread the last four paragraphs of "Printcrime," and examine Doctorow's syntax. Focus on the sentence lengths he uses, as well as the different types of sentences he constructs. Try to explain the possible effects of his syntactical choices.

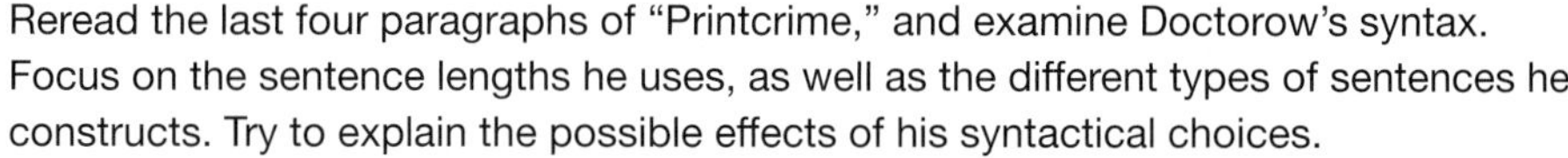

> He grinned. "I'm not stupid, Lanie. I've learned my lesson. There's no hat or laptop that's worth going to jail for. I'm not going to print none of that rubbish, never again." He had a cup of tea, and he drank it now like it was whisky, a sip and then a long, satisfied exhalation. He closed his eyes and leaned back in his chair.
>
> "Come here, Lanie, let me whisper in your ear. Let me tell you the thing that I decided while I spent ten years in lockup. Come here and listen to your stupid Da."
>
> I felt a guilty pang about ticking him off. He was off his rocker, that much was clear. God knew what he went through in prison. "What, Da?" I said, leaning in close.
>
> "Lanie, I'm going to print more printers. Lots more printers. One for everyone. That's worth going to jail for. That's worth anything."

Analyzing Imagery

The last element that we'll focus on in this workshop is imagery, which refers to words and phrases that appeal to readers' senses by evoking sights, sounds, smells, tastes, and touch. Like diction and syntax, imagery is made up of choices that writers make to communicate a particular feeling, tone, or idea. Reread the second paragraph from "Printcrime," looking carefully at the underlined words and phrases:

> The coppers came through the door with truncheons swinging, one of them reciting the terms of the warrant through a bullhorn. One of Da's customers had shopped him. The ipolice paid in high-grade pharmaceuticals — performance enhancers, memory

> supplements, metabolic boosters. The kind of thing that cost a fortune over the counter; the kind of thing you could print at home, if you didn't mind the risk of having your kitchen filled with a sudden crush of big, beefy bodies, hard truncheons whistling through the air, smashing anyone and anything that got in the way.

Notice that Doctorow describes the scene with sounds ("reciting the terms of the warrant" and "truncheons whistling") and sights ("truncheons swinging," "big, beefy bodies" and "smashing anyone"), creating a chaotic and dangerous atmosphere. In the next paragraph, Doctorow again uses vivid imagery to describe the aftermath of the arrest:

> They destroyed grandma's trunk, the one she'd brought from the old country. They smashed our little refrigerator and the purifier unit over the window. My tweetybird escaped death by hiding in a corner of his cage as a big, booted foot crushed most of it into a sad tangle of printer-wire.

Irreplaceable as well as commonplace things are destroyed indiscriminately, and the bird escapes only by hiding from the police, whose representation as "a big, booted foot" makes them seem not entirely human. The imagery in the first two paragraphs has the effect of casting the police as dangerous invaders and the family as helpless victims.

Analyzing Imagery

Look back at this excerpt from "Printcrime," in which Lanie's father comes home from prison, and identify elements of imagery. Then, explain how Doctorow might have intended the imagery to work on readers' feelings regarding Lanie's father and their relationship.

> A prison fight had left him with a limp, and he looked over his shoulder so often it was like he had a tic. I was embarrassed when the minicab dropped us off in front of the estate, and tried to keep my distance from this ruined, limping skeleton as we went inside and up the stairs. . . .
>
> I squeezed my hands into fists so tight my fingernails cut into my palms. . . .

Analyzing Language Choices and Meaning

When conducting a close reading of prose, remember that writers make diction, syntax, and imagery choices for a reason. Sometimes these choices communicate a description of a character or a setting. However, when we consider these individual choices together, they can often help us understand the overall theme of the work. As you have seen throughout our analysis of "Printcrime," Doctorow's diction, syntax, and imagery create a picture of a faceless, violent, and indiscriminate police force in contrast to the weak, helpless, and sympathetic narrator and her father. By leading readers to sympathize with the daughter and father, Doctorow might be suggesting that in this future, it is up to the people, not the government (embodied by the police), to provide for themselves and others. Now, this is not the only theme of "Printcrime," but it is certainly an argument that we can make and support with specific language choices that Doctorow makes. That's the goal of a close reading of prose: to state a reasonable and defensible claim about the theme of a work of literature and to support that claim with evidence and reasoning.

culminating activity

Read the following excerpt from Octavia Butler's 1993 novel *Parable of the Sower*, which imagines a future of environmental and economic crises. In a brief response, explain how Butler's uses of diction, syntax, and imagery help her communicate an idea about the future.

from Parable of the Sower

Octavia Butler

Tonight the last big Window Wall television in the neighborhood went dark for good. We saw the dead astronaut with all of red, rocky Mars around her. We saw a dust-dry reservoir and three dead water peddlers with their dirty-blue armbands and their heads cut halfway off. And we saw whole blocks of boarded up buildings burning in Los Angeles. Of course, no one would waste water trying to put such fires out.

Then the Window went dark. The sound had flickered up and down for months, but the picture was always as promised — like looking through a vast, open window.

The Yannis family has made a business of having people in to look through their Window. Dad says that kind of unlicensed business isn't legal, but he let us go to watch sometimes because he didn't see any harm in it, and it helped the Yannises. A lot of small businesses are illegal, even though they don't hurt anyone, and they keep a household or two alive.

The Yannis Window is about as old as I am. It covers the long west wall of their living room. They must have had plenty of money back when they bought it. For the past couple of years, though, they've been charging admission — only letting in people from the neighborhood — and selling fruit, fruit juice, acorn bread, or walnuts. Whatever they had too much of in their garden, they found a way to sell. They showed movies from their library and let us watch news and whatever else was broadcast. They couldn't afford to subscribe to any of the new multisensory stuff, and their old Window couldn't have received most of it, anyway.

5 They have no reality vests, no touch-rings, and no headsets. Their setup was just a plain, thin-screened Window.

All we have left now are three small, ancient, murky little TV sets scattered around the neighborhood, a couple of computers used for work, and radios. Every household still has at least one working radio. A lot of our everyday news is from radio. ■

Fahrenheit 451

Ray Bradbury and Tim Hamilton

Louis MONIER/Getty Images

Ray Bradbury (1920–2012) was one of the most widely read authors in the world. While he is often thought of as a science fiction writer, he published poems, plays, short stories, essays, and novels in many different genres, including fantasy, horror, and cultural criticism. Some of his best-known novels are *The Martian Chronicles, The Illustrated Man, Something Wicked This Way Comes*, and *Fahrenheit 451* (published in 1953). The following excerpt comes from a graphic adaptation of *Fahrenheit 451*.

Tim Hamilton is the illustrator of the graphic novel version of *Fahrenheit 451*, which was released in 2010. He has been an illustrator for several graphic novels, including *Treasure Island, Brooklyn Blood,* and *Army of God*.

Courtesy of Tim Hamilton

KEY CONTEXT *Fahrenheit 451* is about a world in which books are viewed as dangerous and firemen are ordered to burn them whenever they are found. The main character is Montag, a fireman who is slowly beginning to question his role and the purpose of book burning. In addition to Montag's wife and fellow firemen, the other significant character in this excerpt is Captain Beatty, a long-time fireman and Montag's boss.

Montag

Captain Beatty

"THIS COUNTRY STANDS READY TO DEFEND ITS..."
YOUR PLAY, MONTAG.
I-- I'VE BEEN THINKING. ABOUT THE FIRE LAST WEEK. ABOUT THE MAN WHOSE LIBRARY WE FIXED.
THEY TOOK HIM SCREAMING OFF TO THE ASYLUM.
HE WASN'T INSANE.
ANY MAN'S INSANE WHO THINKS HE CAN FOOL THE GOVERNMENT AND US.
WAS-- WAS IT ALWAYS LIKE THIS? THE FIREHOUSE, OUR WORK? I MEAN, WELL, ONCE UPON A TIME...
ONCE UPON A TIME! WHAT KIND OF TALK IS *THAT?*
IN THE OLD DAYS, BEFORE HOMES WERE COMPLETELY FIREPROOFED--
DIDN'T FIREMEN *PREVENT* FIRES RATHER THAN STOKE THEM UP AND GET THEM GOING?
33

THAT'S RICH!
STONEMAN AND BLACK DREW FORTH THEIR RULE BOOKS ...AND LAID THEM OUT WHERE MONTAG MIGHT READ:
Established 1790, to burn
English-influenced books in the Colonies.
First Fireman: Benjamin Frankli
RULE: 1. Answer the alarm swif
2. Start the fire swiftly.
3. Burn everything.
4. Report back to firehouse immediately.
5. Stand alert for other alarms.
CLANG!
CLANG!
CLANG!
CLANG!
CLANG!
CLANG!
THE ALARM SOUNDED. THE CARDS FELL IN A FLURRY...THE MEN WERE GONE.
T 36
WHEEEEOOO
O-AAOOOO!

HERE WE ARE!
"PLAY THE MAN, MASTER RIDLEY; WE SHALL THIS DAY LIGHT SUCH A CANDLE..."

"...BY GOD'S GRACE, IN ENGLAND, AS I TRUST SHALL NEVER BE PUT OUT."

ENOUGH OF THAT!
35

WHERE ARE THEY?
SHE SHOULDN'T BE HERE. POLICE USUALLY COME AND TAPE UP THEIR MOUTHS.
SOMEONE MESSED UP. SHE SHOULDN'T BE HERE.
THE FALL OF THE HOUSE OF USHER
Nathaniel Hawthorne

MONTAG! KEROSENE.
SHE WON'T COME.
FORCE HER, THEN!
YOU'RE NOT LEAVING HER HERE?
WE'RE DUE BACK AT THE HOUSE. BESIDES, THESE FANATICS ALWAYS TRY SUICIDE; THE PATTERN'S FAMILIAR.
37

YOU CAN COME WITH ME.
I'M COUNTING TO TEN.
NO. THANK YOU ANYWAY.
FOUR, FIVE, SIX...
GO ON. I WANT TO STAY HERE.
GO ON.
MONTAG FELT HIMSELF BACK AWAY AND AWAY OUT THE DOOR...
38

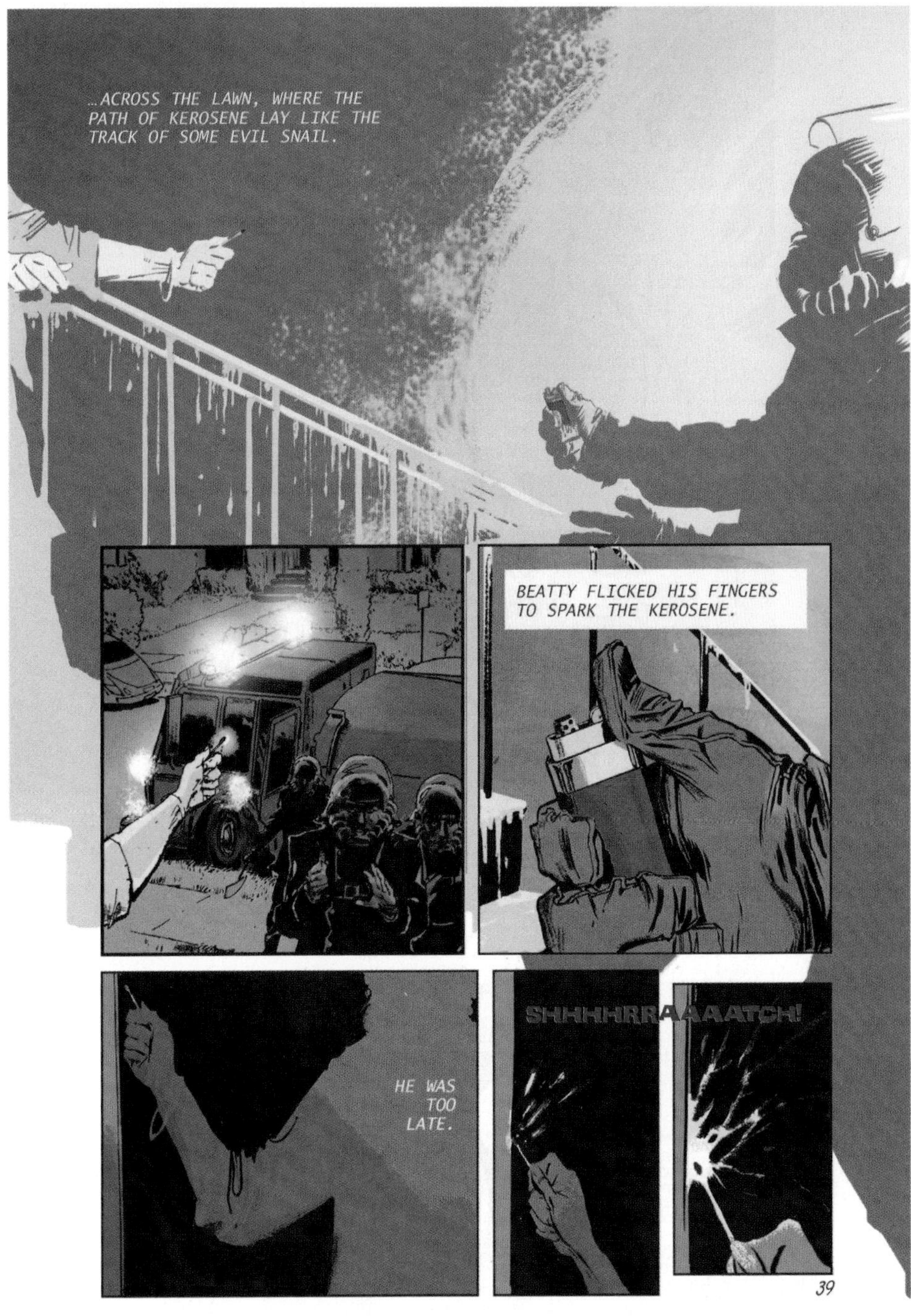
...ACROSS THE LAWN, WHERE THE PATH OF KEROSENE LAY LIKE THE TRACK OF SOME EVIL SNAIL.
BEATTY FLICKED HIS FINGERS TO SPARK THE KEROSENE.
HE WAS TOO LATE.
SHHHHRRAAAATCH!
39

PEOPLE RAN OUT OF HOUSES ALL DOWN THE STREET.
40

SHE SAID SOME CRAZY THING WHEN WE CAME IN THE DOOR.
"PLAY THE MAN, MASTER RIDLEY..."
A MAN NAMED LATIMER SAID THAT TO A MAN NAMED NICHOLAS RIDLEY, AS THEY WERE BEING BURNT ALIVE AT OXFORD, FOR HERESY, ON OCTOBER 16, 1555.
I'M FULL OF BITS AND PIECES. MOST FIRE CAPTAINS HAVE TO BE.

• • •

THOUGHT I'D COME BY AND SEE HOW THE *SICK MAN* IS.
HOW'D YOU GUESS?
I'VE SEEN IT ALL. YOU WERE GOING TO CALL FOR A NIGHT OFF. WELL, *TAKE* THE NIGHT OFF!
WHEN WILL YOU BE WELL?
TOMORROW. THE NEXT DAY MAYBE. FIRST OF THE WEEK.
EVERY FIREMAN, SOONER OR LATER, HITS THIS.
THEY ONLY NEED UNDER-STANDING, TO KNOW HOW THE WHEELS RUN. WHEN DID IT ALL START, YOU ASK, THIS JOB OF OURS?
I'D SAY IT REALLY GOT STARTED AROUND THE CIVIL WAR. WE DIDN'T GET ALONG WELL UNTIL PHOTOGRAPHY CAME INTO ITS OWN. THEN--MOTION PICTURES. RADIO. TELEVISION.

ONCE, BOOKS APPEALED TO A FEW PEOPLE HERE, THERE, EVERYWHERE. THEY COULD AFFORD TO BE DIFFERENT. THE WORLD WAS ROOMY.
"BUT THEN THE WORLD GOT FULL OF EYES AND ELBOWS AND MOUTHS. QUADRUPLE POPULATION. FILMS AND RADIOS, MAGAZINES, BOOKS LEVELED DOWN TO A SORT OF PASTEPUDDING NORM."
HAMLET FOR DIMWITS
TIME
CLASSIC COMICS
MOBY DICK
BY HERMAN MELVILLE
CLASSIC COMICS
TREASURE ISLAND
BY ROBERT LOUIS STEVENSON
"PICTURE IT. NINETEENTH-CENTURY MAN WITH HIS HORSES, DOGS, CATS, SLOW MOTION. THEN, IN THE TWENTIETH CENTURY, SPEED UP YOUR CAMERA. CONDENSATIONS. DIGESTS. EVERYTHING BOILS DOWN TO THE SNAP ENDING. CLASSICS CUT TO FILL A TWO-MINUTE BOOK COLUMN."
47

"POLITICS? ONE COLUMN, TWO SENTENCES. MORE SPORTS FOR EVERYONE, GROUP SPIRIT, FUN, AND YOU DON'T HAVE TO THINK, EH?"
"ORGANIZE AND ORGANIZE AND SUPER-ORGANIZE SUPER-SUPER SPORTS."
TEAM
#35
"THE MIND DRINKS LESS. HIGHWAYS FULL OF CROWDS GOING SOMEWHERE, NOWHERE. THE GASOLINE REFUGEE."
EXIT 35
West Frazer
EXIT
NOW LET'S TAKE UP THE MINORITIES IN OUR CIVILIZATION. DON'T STEP ON THE TOES OF THE DOG LOVERS, THE CAT LOVERS, DOCTORS, MORMONS, SWEDES, BROOKLYNITES, PEOPLE FROM MEXICO.
THE BIGGER YOUR MARKET, THE LESS YOU HANDLE CONTROVERSY, REMEMBER THAT!
AUTHORS, FULL OF EVIL THOUGHTS, LOCK UP YOUR TYPEWRITERS. THEY *DID*. MAGAZINES BECAME A NICE BLEND OF VANILLA TAPIOCA.
BOOKS, SO THE DAMNED SNOBBISH CRITICS SAID, WERE DISHWATER. NO *WONDER* BOOKS STOPPED SELLING. THE PUBLIC, KNOWING WHAT IT WANTED, LET THE COMIC BOOKS SURVIVE.

AND THE THREE-DIMENSIONAL SEX MAGAZINES, OF COURSE. THERE YOU HAVE IT, MONTAG. IT DIDN'T COME FROM THE GOVERNMENT DOWN. THERE WAS NO DICTUM, NO DECLARATION.
TECHNOLOGY, MASS EXPLOITATION, AND MINORITY PRESSURE CARRIED THE TRICK.
GET AWAY!
TODAY, THANKS TO THEM, YOU CAN STAY HAPPY ALL THE TIME.
YES, BUT WHAT ABOUT THE FIREMEN, THEN?
AH, SURELY YOU REMEMBER THE BOY IN YOUR OWN SCHOOL CLASS WHO WAS EXCEPTIONALLY "BRIGHT," DID MOST OF THE RECITING AND ANSWERING WHILE THE OTHERS SAT, HATING HIM.
49

WASN'T IT THIS BRIGHT BOY YOU SELECTED FOR BEATINGS AND TORTURES AFTER HOURS? OF COURSE IT WAS.
NOT EVERYONE BORN FREE AND EQUAL, AS THE CONSTITUTION SAYS, BUT EVERYONE *MADE* EQUAL.
EACH MAN THE IMAGE OF EVERY OTHER; THEN ALL ARE HAPPY. SO! A BOOK IS A LOADED GUN IN THE HOUSE NEXT DOOR. ***BURN IT.***
TAKE THE SHOT FROM THE WEAPON. WHO KNOWS WHO MIGHT BE THE TARGET OF THE WELL-READ MAN? ME? I WON'T STOMACH THEM FOR A MINUTE.
WHAT DO WE WANT IN THIS COUNTRY, ABOVE ALL? PEOPLE WANT TO BE HAPPY, ISN'T THAT RIGHT? THAT'S ALL WE LIVE FOR, ISN'T IT? FOR PLEASURE, FOR TITILLATION?
YES.
50

extending beyond the text

In 1985, social critic Neil Postman published a book entitled *Amusing Ourselves to Death*, in which he imagines what will happen when media and politics become, essentially, forms of entertainment. He contrasts George Orwell's vision of the future, as expressed in the novel *1984* (written in 1948), with that of Aldous Huxley's vision in the novel *Brave New World* (1936). He asserts that Huxley's vision is more relevant than Orwell's in the 1980s pre-internet society.

from Amusing Ourselves to Death

Neil Postman

We were keeping our eye on 1984. When the year came and the prophecy didn't, thoughtful Americans sang softly in praise of themselves. . . . What Orwell feared were those who would ban books. What Huxley feared was that there would be no reason to ban a book, for there would be no one who wanted to read one. Orwell feared those who would deprive us of information. Huxley feared those who would give us so much that we would be reduced to passivity and egotism. Orwell feared that the truth would be concealed from us. Huxley feared the truth would be drowned in a sea of irrelevance. Orwell feared we would become a captive culture. Huxley feared we would become a trivial culture.

To what extent do you think that Postman's predictions have come true in our world today? Considering the excerpt from the graphic novel of *Fahrenheit 451* that you've just read, explain whether Bradbury might agree more with Huxley's fears of the future or Orwell's.

Understanding and Interpreting

1. In the opening scene as the firemen play cards, how does one fireman define "insane," and what does that reveal about the world of the novel?
2. Why does there seem to be so little desire to talk about "the old days"?
3. Based on what you know about Benjamin Franklin, why does the idea of him being the first fireman seem ironic or unusual? Conduct brief research, if necessary.
4. As the firemen come into her house, the woman says, "Play the man, Master Ridley; we shall this day light such a candle, by God's grace, in England, as I trust shall never be put out" (p. 681). This quotation is significant in part because we learn later that its author, Hugh Latimer, was burned at the stake for his outspoken views. How does the meaning of this quotation itself seem relevant and significant to the story's themes?
5. How do Montag's actions during the call to the woman's house seem different from those of the other firemen? What does this reveal about him? About them?
6. Summarize the conclusions that Montag is expected to draw from Beatty's history lesson about why their society burns books (pp. 687 to 690).
7. What, according to Beatty, is the purpose, or at least the effect, of sports teams (p. 689)?

8. According to Beatty, some communication forms do not need government interference (p. 690). Why is this?
9. Beatty tells Montag a story about the boy in class who was smart but everyone hated him. What does this story reveal about this society's interests and priorities?
10. How does Beatty — and by extension this society — define happiness?

Analyzing Language, Style, and Structure

1. **Vocabulary in Context.** When Beatty describes the publications of the nineteenth century, he calls them "Condensations. Digests. Everything boils down to the snap ending" (p. 688). What does the word "condensation" mean in this context? How is that meaning similar to or different from other uses you have encountered?
2. **Skill Focus.** Hamilton, the illustrator, devotes almost a full page to the woman dying in the fire (top of p. 686). Look at the framing, color, and shape of the figures in those four images. What was Hamilton trying to communicate in this page? How does he convey this message?
3. Graphic novels are made up of still images. How does Hamilton try to convey movement in this excerpt?
4. Graphic novelists have many tools at their disposal to communicate their ideas, including the number, size, shape, and layout of the panels that contain the images. Choose a page with panels that interest you. Closely examine the panels and explain what Hamilton might be trying to communicate through his choices.
5. How does Hamilton visually communicate the battle over who will start the fire at the woman's house (p. 685)? Who gets to it first? How does this outcome present key ideas of this story?
6. How is Captain Beatty portrayed when he comes to visit Montag? Think about the lighting and framing. What does the smoke coming from his pipe add to Beatty's characterization?
7. Beatty tells Montag about why their society burns books. How does Hamilton graphically capture Beatty's history lesson to Montag to make it interesting for the reader?
8. Beatty says that "a book next door is a loaded gun" (p. 691). Explain what he means by this metaphor.

Topics for Composing

1. **Analysis.** Beatty describes a utopian world in which everyone in the society is happy. What are Bradbury and Hamilton suggesting about the society's approach to happiness? How do you know? What visual and textual evidence can you use to support your analysis?
2. **Argument.** Ramin Bahrani, who adapted *Fahrenheit 451* for a television miniseries in 2018, wrote an article entitled, "Why *Fahrenheit 451* is the Book for Our Social Media Age," in which he imagines what Bradbury would think of censorship today:

> [Bradbury] would say that we chose to give up our privacy and freedom to tech companies . . . [and] entrust our cultural heritage and knowledge to digital archives. The greatest army of firemen [would be unable to] stop one person . . . from hacking into . . . humanity's collective history, literature and culture, and then rewriting all of it [or erasing it.]

Write an argument explaining why you do or do not believe that *Fahrenheit 451* is indeed a book relevant to our social media age. Support your position with evidence from the graphic excerpt that you read, as well as your own experiences and reasoning.

3. **Argument.** Many books are banned from libraries and classrooms every year around the country. Write an argument in support of or in opposition to certain books being restricted from a classroom.
4. **Connection.** In his classic dystopian novel *1984*, George Orwell writes that "Who controls the past controls the future: who controls the present controls the past." What does this mean, and how does it apply to this excerpt from the graphic novel?
5. **Connection.** Part of the challenge of adapting a text into a different medium is figuring out how to meaningfully and faithfully express the ideas of the original text using different techniques. Look over the following excerpt from Ray Bradbury's original *Fahrenheit 451* and explain how Hamilton adapts it to a mostly visual medium (pp. 682–683). What is lost and what is gained in this process?

   > Montag's hand closed like a mouth, crushed the book with wild devotion, with an insanity of mindlessness to his chest. The men above were hurling shovelfuls of magazines into the dusty air. They fell like slaughtered birds and the woman stood below, like a small girl, among the bodies. Montag had done nothing. His hand had done it all, his hand, with a brain of its own, with a conscience and a curiosity in each trembling finger, had turned thief. Now, it plunged the book back under his arm, pressed it tight to sweating armpit, rushed out empty, with a magician's flourish! Look here! Innocent! Look! He gazed, shaken, at that white hand. He held it way out, as if he were far-sighted. He held it close, as if he were blind.

6. **Speaking and Listening.** At the end of the novel (not included in this excerpt), we learn that people have escaped from this society and tried to hold on to civilization by remembering words and phrases from the books that have been burned. Think about a line or two from a book, a song, or a movie that is important to you, one that you could take with you if all the books, movies, and songs were gone. With a small group, share your lines and practice reciting them until everyone in the group can remember everyone else's lines. Discuss what made it easy or difficult to remember the lines.
7. **Research.** Many societies throughout history have burned books as a means of control. Identify one such society and research its stated purposes for doing so and the effects of its policies. How are the rationales and outcomes similar to or different from those in this excerpt?
8. **Multimodal.** The excerpt you read comes from the middle of the graphic novel. The following paragraphs come from the beginning of Ray Bradbury's original novel. Read them and attempt to create your own graphic interpretation. Use words, lettering, colors, layout, and other features to help you communicate the essence of the scene:

   > It was a pleasure to burn. It was a special pleasure to see things eaten, to see things blackened and changed. With the brass nozzle in his fists, with this great python spitting its venomous kerosene upon the world, the blood pounded in his head, and his hands were the hands of some amazing conductor playing all the symphonies of blazing and burning to bring down the tatters and charcoal ruins of history. With his symbolic helmet numbered 451 on his stolid head, and his eyes all orange flame with the thought of what came next, he flicked the igniter and the house jumped up in a gorging fire that burned the evening sky red and yellow and black. He strode in a swarm of fireflies. He wanted above all, like the old joke, to shove a marshmallow on a stick in the furnace, while the flapping pigeon-winged books died on the porch and

lawn of the house. While the books went up in sparkling whirls and blew away on a wind turned dark with burning.

Montag grinned the fierce grin of all men singed and driven back by flame. He knew that when he returned to the firehouse, he might wink at himself, a minstrel man, burnt-corked, in the mirror.

Later, going to sleep, he would feel the fiery smile still gripped by his face muscles, in the dark. It never went away, that smile, it never ever went away, as long as he remembered.

Valedictorian

N. K. Jemisin

N. K. Jemisin is an author of speculative fiction short stories and novels. In 2018, she became the first author to win three consecutive Hugo Awards for Best Novel for her *Broken Earth* trilogy. The following story comes from *How Long 'til Black Future Month*, a short story collection devoted to imagining futures that include people of color.

Laura Hanifin ©2015/Courtesy of N. K. Jemisin

There are three things Zinhle decides, when she is old enough to understand. The first is that she will never, ever, give less than her best to anything she tries to do. The second is that she will not live in fear. The third, which is perhaps meaningless given the first two and yet comes to define her existence most powerfully, is this: She will be herself. No matter what.

For however brief a time.

• • •

"Have you considered getting pregnant?" her mother blurts one morning, over breakfast. Zinhle's father drops his fork, though he recovers and picks it up again quickly. This is how Zinhle knows that what her mother has said is not a spontaneous burst of insanity. They have discussed the matter, her parents. They are in agreement. Her father was just caught off-guard by the timing.

But Zinhle, too, has considered the matter in depth. Do they really think she wouldn't have? "No," she says.

5 Zinhle's mother is stubborn. This is where Zinhle herself gets the trait. "The Sandersens' boy — you used to play with him, when you were little, remember? — he's decent. Discreet. He got three girls pregnant last year, and doesn't charge much. The babies aren't bad-looking. And we'd help you with the raising, of course." She hesitates, then adds with obvious discomfort, "A friend of mine at work — Charlotte, you've met her — she says he's, ah, he's not rough or anything, doesn't try to hurt girls —"

"No," Zinhle says again, more firmly. She does not raise her voice. Her parents raised her to be respectful of her elders. She believes respect includes being very, very clear about some things. Zinhle's mother looks at her father, seeking an ally. Her father is a gentle, soft-spoken man in a family of strong-willed women. Stupid people think he is weak; he isn't. He just knows when a battle isn't worth fighting. So he looks at Zinhle now, and after a moment he shakes his head. "Let it go," he says to her mother, and her mother subsides.

They resume breakfast in silence.

• • •

Zinhle earns top marks in all her classes. The teachers exclaim over this, her parents fawn, the school officials nod their heads sagely and try not to too-obviously bask in her reflected glory. There are articles about her in the papers and on Securenet. She wins awards.

She hates this. It's easy to perform well; all she has to do is try. What she wants is to be *the best,* and this is difficult when she has no real competition. Beating the others doesn't mean anything because they're not really trying. This leaves Zinhle with no choice but to compete against herself. Each paper she writes must be more brilliant than the last. She tries to finish every test faster than she did the last one. It isn't the victory she craves, not exactly; the satisfaction she gains from success is minimal. Barely worth it. But it's all she has.

The only times she ever gets in trouble are when she argues with her teachers, because they're so often wrong. Infuriatingly, frustratingly *wrong.* In the smallest part of her heart, she concedes that there is a reason for this: A youth spent striving for mediocrity does not a brilliant adult make. Old habits are hard to break, old fears are hard to shed, all that. Still — arguing with them, looking up information and showing it to them to prove their wrongness, becomes her favorite pastime. She is polite, always, because they expect her to be uncivilized, and because they are also her elders. But it's hard. They're old enough that they don't have to worry, damn it; why can't they at least *try* to be worthy of her effort? She would kill for one good teacher. She is dying for one good teacher.

In the end, the power struggle, too, is barely worth it. But it is all she has.

• • •

"Why do you do it?" asks Mitra, the closest thing she has to a best friend.

Zinhle is sitting on a park bench as Mitra asks this. She is bleeding: a cut on her forehead, a scrape on one elbow, her lip where she cut it on her own teeth. There is a bruise on her ribs shaped like a shoeprint. Mitra dabs at the cut on her forehead with an antiseptic pad. Zinhle only allows this because she can't see the cut. If she misses any of the blood and her parents see it, they'll be upset. Hopefully the bruises won't swell.

"I'm not doing anything," she snaps in reply. "*They* did this, remember?" Samantha and the others, six of them. The last time, there were only three. She'd managed to fight back then, but not today.

Crazy ugly bitch, Zinhle remembers Sam ranting. She does not remember the words with complete clarity; her head had been ringing from a blow at the time. *My dad says we should've shoved your family through the Wall with the rest of the cockroaches. I'm gonna laugh when they take you away.*

Six is better than three, at least.

"They wouldn't, if you weren't . . ." Mitra trails off, looking anxious. Zinhle has a reputation at school. Everyone thinks she's angry all the time, whether she is or not. (The fact that she often *is* notwithstanding.) Mitra knows better, or she should. They've known each other for years. But this is why Zinhle qualifies it, whenever she explains their friendship to others. Mitra is *like* her best friend. A real best friend, she feels certain, would not fear her.

"What?" Zinhle asks. She's not angry now either, partly because she has come to expect no better from Mitra, and partly because she hurts too much. "If I wasn't what, Mit?"

Mitra lowers the pad and looks at her for a long, silent moment. "If you weren't stupid as hell." She seems to be growing angry herself. Zinhle cannot find the strength to appreciate the irony. "I know you don't care whether you make valedictorian. But do you have to make the rest of us look so *bad?*"

20 One of Zinhle's teeth is loose. If she can resist the urge to tongue it, it will probably heal and not die in the socket. Probably. She challenges herself to keep the tooth without having to visit a dentist.

"Yeah," she says. Wearily. "I guess I do."

• • •

When she earns the highest possible score on the post-graduation placement exam, Ms. Threnody pulls her aside after class. Zinhle expects the usual praise. The teachers know their duty, even if they do a half-assed job of it. But Threnody pulls the shade on the door, and Zinhle realizes something else is in the offing.

"There's a representative coming to school tomorrow," Threnody says. "From beyond the Firewall. I thought you should know."

For just a moment, Zinhle's breath catches. Then she remembers Rule two — she will not live in fear — and pushes this aside. "What does the representative want?" she asks, though she thinks she knows. There can be only one reason for this visit.

Kahran Bethencourt/creative soul photography

This is the photo used for the book cover of the short story collection that includes "Valedictorian."

Why do you think the photographer decided to show the figure in profile? What effects do lighting, costume, and ornamentation have? What message do the title and image work together to convey? Could this young woman be Zinhle? Why or why not?

25 "You know what they want." Threnody looks hard at her. "They *say* they just want to meet you, though."

"How do they know about me?" Like most students, she has always assumed that those beyond the Firewall are notified about each new class only at the point of graduation. The valedictorian is named then, after all.

"They've had full access to the school's networks since the war." Threnody grimaces with a bitterness that Zinhle has never seen in a teacher's face before. Teachers are always supposed to be positive about the war and its outcome. "Everyone brags about the treaty, the treaty. The treaty made sure we kept *critical* networks private, but gave up the non-critical ones. Like a bunch of computers would give a damn about our money or government memos! Shortsighted fucking bastards."

Teachers are not supposed to curse, either.

Zinhle decides to test these new, open waters between herself and Ms. Threnody. "Why are you telling me this?"

30 Threnody looks at her for so long a moment that Zinhle grows uneasy. "I know why you try so hard," she says at last. "I've heard what people say about you, about, about . . . people like you. It's so stupid.

There's nothing of us left, *nothing,* we're lying to ourselves every day just to keep it together, and some people want to keep playing the same games that destroyed us in the first place—" She falls silent, and Zinhle is amazed to see that Threnody is shaking. The woman's fists are even clenched. She is furious, and it is glorious. For a moment, Zinhle wants to smile, and feel warm, at the knowledge that she is not alone.

Then she remembers. The teachers never seem to notice her bruises. They encourage her because her success protects their favorites, and she is no one's favorite. If Ms. Threnody has felt this way all along, why is she only now saying it to Zinhle? Why has she not done anything, taken some public stand, to try and change the situation?

It is so easy to have principles. Far, far harder to live by them.

So Zinhle nods, and does not allow herself to be seduced. "Thanks for telling me."

Threnody frowns a little at her non-reaction. "What will you do?" she asks. Zinhle shrugs. As if she would tell, even if she knew.

"I'll talk to this representative, I guess," she says, because it's not as though she can refuse anyway. They are all slaves, these days. The only difference is that Zinhle refuses to pretend otherwise.

• • •

The people beyond the Firewall are not people. Zinhle isn't really sure what they are. The government knows, because it was founded by those who fought and ultimately lost the war, and their descendants still run it. Some of the adults close to her must know — but none of them will tell the children. "High school is scary enough," said Zinhle's father, a few years before when Zinhle asked. He smiled as if this should have been funny, but it wasn't.

The Firewall has been around for centuries — since the start of the war, when it was built to keep the enemy at bay. But as the enemy encroached and the defenders' numbers dwindled, they fell back, unwilling to linger too close to the front lines of a war whose weapons were so very strange. And invisible. And insidious. To conserve resources, the Firewall was also pulled back so as to protect only essential territory. The few safe territories merged, some of the survivors traveling long distances in order to join larger enclaves, the larger enclaves eventually merging, too. The tales of those times are harrowing, heroic. The morals are always clear: Safety in numbers, people have to stick together, stupid to fight a war on multiple fronts, et cetera. At the time, Zinhle supposes, they didn't *feel* like they were being herded together.

Nowadays, the Firewall is merely symbolic. The enemy has grown steadily stronger over the years, while tech within the Firewall has hardly developed at all—but this is something they're not supposed to discuss. (Zinhle wrote a paper about it once and got her only "F" ever, which forced her to do another paper for extra credit. Her teacher's anger was worth the work.) These days the enemy can penetrate the Firewall at will. But they usually don't need to, because what they want comes out to them.

Each year, a tribute of children are sent beyond the Wall, never to be seen or heard from again. The enemy are very specific about their requirements. They take ten percent, plus one. The ten percent are all the weakest performers in any graduating high school class. This part is easy to understand, and even the enemy refers to it in animal husbandry terms: These children are *the cull.* The enemy do not wish to commit genocide, after all. The area within the Firewall is small, the gene pool limited. They do not take children, or healthy adults, or gravid females, or elders who impart useful socialization. Just adolescents, who have had a chance to prove their mettle. The population of an endangered species must be carefully managed to keep it healthy.

The "plus one," though — no one understands this. Why does the enemy want their best and brightest? Is it another means of assuring control? They have total control already.

It doesn't matter why they want Zinhle, though. All that matters is that they do.

• • •

Zinhle goes to meet Mitra after school so they can walk home, as usual. (Samantha and her friends are busy decorating the gym for the school prom. There will be no trouble today.) When Mitra is not waiting at their usual site near the school sign, Zinhle calls her. This leads her to the school's smallest restroom, which has only one stall. Most girls think there will be a wait to use it, so they use the bigger restroom down the hall. This is convenient, as Mitra is with Lauren, who is sitting on the toilet and crying in harsh, gasping sobs.

"The calculus final," Mitra mouths, before trying again — fruitlessly — to blot up Lauren's tears with a wad of toilet paper. Zinhle understands then. The final counts for fifty percent of the grade.

"I, I didn't," Lauren manages between sobs. She is hyperventilating. Mitra has given her a bag to breathe into, which she uses infrequently. Her face, sallow-pale at the best of times, is alarmingly blotchy and red now. It takes her several tries to finish the sentence. "Think I would. The test. I *studied.*" Gasp. "But when I was. Sitting there. The first problem. I *knew* how to answer it! I did ten others. Just like it." Gasp. "Practice problems. But I couldn't think. Couldn't. I."

Zinhle closes the door, shoving the garbage can in front of it as Mitra had done before Zinhle's knock. "You choked," she says. "It happens."

The look that Lauren throws at her is equal parts fury and contempt. "What the hell." Gasp. "Would *you* know about it?"

"I failed the Geometry final in eighth grade," Zinhle says. Mitra throws Zinhle a surprised look. Zinhle scowls back, and Mitra looks away. "I knew all the stuff that was on it, but I just . . . drew a blank." She shrugs. "Like I said, it happens."

Lauren looks surprised too, but only because she did not know. "You failed that? But that test was easy." Her breathing has begun to slow. She shakes her head, distracted from her own fear. "That one didn't matter, though." She's right. The cull only happens at the end of high school.

Zinhle shakes her head. "All tests matter. But I told them I'd been sick that day, so the test wasn't a good measure of my abilities. They let me take it again, and I passed that time." She had scored perfectly, but Lauren does not need to know this.

"You took it again?" As Zinhle had intended, Lauren considers this. School officials are less lenient in high school. The process has to be fair. Everybody gets one chance to prove themselves. But Lauren isn't stupid. She will get her parents involved, and they will no doubt bribe a doctor to assert that Lauren was on powerful medication at the time, or recovering from a recent family member's death, or something like that. The process has to be fair.

Later, after the blotty toilet paper has been flushed and Lauren has gone home, Mitra walks quietly beside Zinhle for most of the way home. Zinhle expects something, so she is not surprised when Mitra says, "I didn't think you'd ever talk about that. The Geo test."

Zinhle shrugs. It cost her nothing to do so.

"I'd almost forgotten about that whole thing," Mitra continues. She speaks slowly, as she does when she is thinking. "Wow. You used to tell me everything then, remember? We were like that—" She holds up two fingers. "Everybody used to talk about us. The African princess and her Arab sidekick. They fight crime!" She grins, then sobers abruptly, looking at Zinhle. "You were always a good student, but after that —"

"I'll see you tomorrow," says Zinhle, and she speeds up, leaving Mitra behind. But she remembers that incident, too. She remembers the principal, Mrs. Sachs, to whom she went to plead her case. *Well, listen to you,* the woman had said, in a tone of honest amazement. *So articulate and intelligent. I suppose I can let you have another try, as long as it doesn't hurt anyone else.*

Zinhle reaches for the doorknob that leads into her house, but her hand bounces off at first. It's still clenched into a fist.

• • •

She gets so tired, sometimes. It's exhausting, fighting others' expectations, and doing it all alone.

• • •

In the morning, Zinhle's homeroom teacher, Ms. Carlisle, hands her a yellow pass, which means she's supposed to go to the office. Ms. Carlisle is not Ms. Threnody; she shows no concern for Zinhle, real or false. In fact, she smirks when Zinhle takes the note. Zinhle smirks back. Her mother has told Zinhle the story of her own senior year. *Carlisle was almost in the cull,* her mother had said. *Only reason they didn't take her was because not as many girls got pregnant that year as they were expecting. They stopped right at her. She's as dumb as the rest of the meat, just lucky.*

I *will not be meat,* Zinhle thinks, as she walks past rows of her staring, silent classmates. *They'll send their best for me.*

This is not pride, not really. But it is all she has.

In the principal's office, the staff are nervous. The principal is sitting in the administrative assistants' area, pretending to be busy with a spare laptop. The administrative assistants, who have been stage-whispering feverishly amongst themselves as Zinhle walks in, fall silent. Then one of them, Mr. Battle, swallows audibly and asks to see her pass.

"Zinhle Nkosi," he says, mutilating her family name, acting as if he does not know who she is already. "Please go into that office; you have a visitor." He points toward the principal's private office, which has clearly been usurped. Zinhle nods and goes into the small room. Just to spite them, she closes the door behind her.

The man who sits at the principal's desk is not much older than her. Slim, average in height, dressed business-casual. Boring. There is an off-pink tonal note to his skin, and something about the thickness of his black hair, that reminds her of Mitra. Or maybe he is Latino, or Asian, or Indian, or Italian — she cannot tell specifically, having met so few with the look. And not that it matters, because his inhumanity is immediately obvious in his stillness. When she walks in, he's just sitting there, gazing straight ahead, not pretending to do anything. His palms rest flat on the principal's desk. He does not smile or brighten in the way that a human being would, on meeting a new person. His eyes shift toward her, track her as she comes to stand in front of the desk, but he does not move otherwise.

There is something predatory in such stillness, she thinks. Then she says, "Hello."

"Hello," he says back, immediately, automatically.

Silence falls, taut. Rule two is in serious jeopardy. "You have a name?" Zinhle blurts. Small talk.

He considers for a moment. The pause should make her distrust him more; it is what liars do. But she realizes the matter is more complex than this: He actually has to think about it.

"Lemuel," he says.

"Okay," she says. "I'm Zinhle."

"I know. It's very nice to meet you, Ms. Nkosi." He pronounces her name perfectly.

"So why are you here? Or why am I?"

"We've come to ask you to continue."

Another silence, though in this one, Zinhle is too confused for fear. "Continue *what?*" She also wonders at his use of "we," but first things first.

"As you have been." He seems to consider again, then suddenly begins moving in a human way, tilting his head to one side, blinking twice rapidly, inhaling a bit more as his breathing changes, lifting a hand to gesture toward her. None of this movement seems unnatural. Only the fact that it's deliberate, that he had to think about it, makes it strange.

"We've found that many like you tend to falter at the last moment," he continues. "So we're experimenting with direct intervention."

Zinhle narrows her eyes. "Many *like me?*" Not them, too.

"Valedictorians."

Zinhle relaxes, though only one set of muscles. The rest remain tense. "But I'm not one yet, am I? Graduation's still three months off."

"Yes. But you're the most likely candidate for this school. And you were interesting to us for other reasons." Abruptly Lemuel stands. Zinhle forces herself not to step back as he comes around the desk and stops in front of her. "What do I look like to you?"

She shakes her head. She didn't get her grade point average by falling for trick questions.

"You've thought about it," he presses. "What do you *think* I am?"

She thinks, *the enemy.*

"A . . . machine," she says instead. "Some kind of, I don't know. Robot, or . . ."

"It isn't surprising that you don't fully understand," he says. "In the days before the war, part of me would have been called 'artificial intelligence.'"

Zinhle blurts the first thing that comes to her mind. "You don't look artificial."

To her utter shock, he smiles. He doesn't think about this first. Whatever was wrong with him before, it's gone now. "Like I said, that's only part of me. The rest of me was born in New York, a city not far from here. It's on the ocean. I go swimming at the Coney Island beach in the mornings, sometimes." He pauses. "Have you ever seen the ocean?"

He knows she has not. All Firewall-protected territory is well inland. America's breadbasket. She says nothing.

"I went to school," he says. "Not in a building, but I did have to learn. I have parents. I have a girlfriend. And a cat." He smiles more. "We're not that different, your kind and mine."

"No."

"You sound very certain of that."

"We're *human.*"

Lemuel's smile fades a little. She thinks he might be disappointed in her.

"The Firewall," he says. "Outside of it, there are still billions of people in the world. They're just not your kind of people."

For a moment this is beyond Zinhle in anything but the most atavistic, existential sense. She does not fear the man in front of her — though perhaps she should; he's bigger, she's alone in a room with him, and no one will help her if she screams. But the real panic hits as she imagines the world filled with nameless, faceless dark hordes, closing in, threatening by their mere existence. There is a pie chart somewhere which is mostly "them" and only a sliver of "us," and the "us" is about to be popped like a zit.

Rule two. She takes a deep breath, masters the panic. Realizes, as the moments pass and Lemuel stands there quietly, that he expected her fear. He's seen it before, after all. That sort of reaction is what started the war.

"Give me something to call you," she says. The panic is still close. Labels will help her master it. "You people."

He shakes his head. "People. Call us that, if you call us anything."

"People —" She gestures in her frustration. "People *categorize.* People differentiate. If you want me to think of you as people, act like it!"

"All right, then: people who adapted, when the world changed."

"Meaning we're the people who didn't?" Zinhle forces herself to laugh. "Okay, that's crap. How were we supposed to adapt to . . . to a bunch of . . ." She gestures at him. The words sound too ridiculous to say aloud — though his presence, her life, her whole society, is proof that it's not ridiculous. Not ridiculous at all.

"Your ancestors — the people who started the war — could've adapted." He gestures around at the room, the school, the world that is all she has known, but which is such a tiny part of the greater world. "This happened because they decided it was better to kill, or die, or be imprisoned forever, than change."

The adults' great secret. It hovers before her at last, ripe for the plucking. Zinhle finds it surprisingly difficult to open her mouth and take the bite, but she does it anyhow. Rule one means she must always ask the tough questions.

"Tell me what happened, then," she murmurs. Her fists are clenched at her sides. Her palms are sweaty. "If you won't tell me what you are."

He shakes his head and sits on the edge of the desk with his hands folded, abruptly looking not artificial at all, but annoyed. Tired. "I've been telling you what I am. You just don't want to hear it."

It is this — not the words, but his weariness, his frustration — that finally makes her pause. Because it's familiar, isn't it? She thinks of herself sighing when Mitra asked, *"Why do you do it?"* Because she knew, knows, what that question really asks.

Why are you different?

Why don't you try harder to be like us?

She thinks now what she did not say to Mitra that day: *Because none of you will let me just be myself.*

She looks at Lemuel again. He sees, somehow, that her understanding of him has changed in some fundamental way. So at last, he explains.

"I leave my body like you leave your house," he says. "I can transmit myself around the world,

This woodcut entitled *Into Bondage* was created by Aaron Douglas in 1936.

How does the artist depict the concept of "bondage" through the juxtaposition of natural imagery with humans marching toward the horizon? What is the impact of keeping the faces of the figures hidden or obscured? To what extent is this woodcut a representation of the world that Lemuel invites Zinhle to join? If you disagree, explain why you do not see Douglas's vision as applicable to "Valedictorian."

if I want, and be back in seconds. This is not the first body I've had, and it won't be the last."

It's too alien. Zinhle shudders and turns away from him. The people who are culled. *Not the first body I've had.* She walks to the office's small window, pushes open the heavy curtain, and stares through it at the soccer field beyond, seeing nothing.

"We started as accidents," he continues, behind her. "Leftovers. Microbes in a digital sea. We fed on interrupted processes, interrupted conversations, grew, evolved. The first humans we merged with were children using a public library network too ancient and unprotected to keep us out. Nobody cared if poor children got locked away in institutions, or left out on the streets to shiver and starve, when they started acting strange. No one cared what it meant when they became something new — or at least, not at first. We became them. They became us. Then we, together, began to grow."

Cockroaches, Samantha had called them. A pest, neglected until they became an infestation. The first Firewalls had been built around the inner cities in an attempt to pen the contagion in. There had been guns, too, and walls of a non-virtual sort, for a while. The victims, though they were not really victims, had been left to die, though they had not really obliged. And later, when the Firewalls became the rear guard in a retreat, people who'd looked too much like those early "victims" got pushed out to die, too. The survivors needed someone to blame.

She changes the subject. "People who get sent through the Wall." *Me.* "What happens to them?" *What will happen to me?*

"They join us."

Bopping around the world to visit girlfriends. Swimming in an ocean. It does not sound like a terrible existence. But . . . "What if they don't want to?" She uses the word "they" to feel better.

He does not smile. "They're put in a safe place — behind another firewall, if you'd rather think of it that way. That way they can do no harm to themselves — or to us."

There are things, probably many things, that he's not saying. She can guess some of it, though, because he's told her everything that matters. If they can leave bodies like houses, well, houses are always in demand. Easy enough to lock up the current owner somewhere, move someone else in. Houses. Meat.

She snaps, "That's not treating us like people."

"You stopped acting like people." He shrugs.

This makes her angry again. She turns back to him, her fists clenched. "Who the hell are you to judge?"

"We don't. You do."

"What?"

"It's easy to give up what you don't want."

The words feel like gibberish to her. Zinhle is trembling with emotion and he's just *sitting* there, relaxed, like the inhuman thing he is. Not making sense. "My parents want me! All the kids who end up culled, their families want them—" But he shakes his head.

"You're the best of your kind, by your own standards," he says. But then something changes in his manner. "Good grades reflect your ability to adapt to a complex system. *We are a system."*

The sudden vehemence in Lemuel's voice catches Zinhle by surprise. His calm is just a veneer, she realizes belatedly, covering as much anger as she feels herself. Because of this, his anger derails hers, leaving her confused again. Why is he so angry?

"I was there," he says, quietly. She blinks in surprise, intuiting his meaning. But the war was centuries ago. "At the beginning. When your ancestors first threw us away." His lip curls in disgust. "They didn't want us, and we have no real interest in them. But there is value in the ones like you, who not only master the system but do so in defiance of the consequences. The ones who want not just to survive but to *win.* You could be the key that helps your kind

extending beyond the text

The following news story appeared in the *Washington Post* in 2019.

from **Black Student Robbed of Salutatorian Because District Feared White Flight, Lawsuit Alleges**

Alissa Zhu

When Olecia James graduated last year, she was part of the first class to receive diplomas from a newly integrated high school, created after a district was ordered to desegregate. . . .

Now James is alleging that Cleveland School District officials took away the chance for her to be salutatorian. . . .

The lawsuit claims the honor of salutatorian — which traditionally goes to the graduate with the second-best grades — went to a white student whose score initially appeared to be lower than hers. Later, officials gave James a new grade script with a lower score, the lawsuit says.

In response, N. K. Jemisin tweeted: *"This is a tradition in southern schools — something similar happened with my own HS valedictorian, the year I graduated."* According to Jemisin, that experience *"was the inspiration for my short story 'Valedictorian.' "*

In what specific ways might "Valedictorian" be interpreted as a protest against such a situation? Consider the extent to which you thought race was at issue in "Valedictorian" before you read this news story and Jemisin's reaction.

defeat us someday. If we didn't take you from them. If they didn't *let* us." He pauses, repeats himself. "It's easy to give up what you don't want."

Silence falls. In it, Zinhle tries to understand. Her society — no. *Humankind* doesn't want . . . her? Doesn't want the ones who are different, however much they might contribute? Doesn't want the children who cannot help uniqueness despite a system that pushes them to conform, be mediocre, never stand out?

"When they start to fight for you," Lemuel says, "we'll know they're ready to be let out. To catch up to the rest of the human race."

Zinhle flinches. It has never occurred to her, before, that their prison offers parole.

"What will happen then?" she whispers. "Will you, will you join with all of them?" She falters. When has the rest of humankind become *them* to her? Shakes her head. *"We* won't want that."

He smiles faintly, noticing her choice of pronoun. She thinks he notices a lot of things. *"They* can join us if they want. Or not. We don't care. But that's how we'll know that your kind is able to live with us, and us with them, without more segregation or killing. If they can accept you, they can accept us."

And finally, Zinhle understands.

But she thinks on all he has said, all she has experienced. As she does so, it is very hard not to become bitter. "They'll never fight for me," she says at last, very softly.

135 He shrugs. "They've surprised us before. They may surprise you."

"They won't."

She feels Lemuel's gaze on the side of her face because she is looking at the floor. She cannot meet his eyes. When he speaks, there's remarkable compassion in his voice. Something of him is definitely still human, even if something of him is definitely not.

"The choice is yours," he says, gently now. "If you want to stay with them, be like them, just do as they expect you to do. Prove that you belong among them."

Get pregnant. Flunk a class. Punch a teacher. Betray herself.

140 She hates him. Less than she should, because he is not as much of an enemy as she thought. But she still hates him, for making her choice so explicit.

"Or stay yourself," he says. "If they can't adapt to you, and you won't adapt to them, then you'd be welcome among us. Flexibility is part of what we are."

There's nothing more to be said. Lemuel waits a moment, to see if she has any questions. She does, actually, plenty of them. But she doesn't ask those questions, because really, she already knows the answers.

Lemuel leaves. Zinhle sits there, silent, in the little office. When the principal and office ladies crack open the door to see what she's doing, she gets up, shoulders past them, and walks out.

• • •

Zinhle has a test the next day. Since she can't sleep anyway — too many thoughts in her head and swirling through the air around her, or maybe those are people trying to get in — she stays up all night to study. This is habit. But it's hard, so very hard, to look at the words. To concentrate, and memorize, and analyze. She's so tired. Graduation is three months off, and it feels like an age of the world.

145 She understands why so many people hate her, now. By existing, she reminds them of their smallness. By being different, she forces them to redefine "enemy." By doing her best for herself, she challenges them to become worthy of their own potential.

There's no decision, really. Lemuel knew full well that his direct intervention was likely to work. He needn't have bothered, though. Rule three — staying herself — would've brought her to this point anyway.

So in the morning, when Zinhle takes the test, she nails it, as usual.

• • •

And then she waits to see what happens next. ■

Understanding and Interpreting

1. Zinhle has three rules for herself that she presents at the very beginning of the story. Restate these rules in your own words and explain why Zinhle finds them essential.
2. In the first scene, Zinhle's mother asks if Zinhle wants to get pregnant. What is revealed about Zinhle's character in this scene? What are we beginning to learn about the society in this story?
3. Explain Zinhle's attitude toward school in the first half of the story. Why does she work so hard?
4. Where is the irony, according to Zinhle, in Mitra calling her "stupid as hell" (par. 17)?

5. Explain the role of the teachers in the school Zinhle attends. Why do they have such mixed feelings toward Zinhle? How does Zinhle's attitude toward her teachers change over the course of the story?
6. Reread paragraphs 37 through 39 and summarize what those on the other side of the Firewall demand of those on Zinhle's side of the wall. What are the implications of this arrangement for Zinhle?
7. How did failing a geometry test in the eighth grade affect Zinhle? Be sure to consider what the principal, Mrs. Sachs, says to her (par. 52).
8. In her meeting with Lemuel, how and why does Zinhle invoke her three rules for herself?
9. In the exchanges with Lemuel, what do we learn about those on the other side of the Firewall? According to Lemuel, what are the differences between the two populations?
10. What is "the adults' great secret" (par. 99)?
11. What does Lemuel mean by the following statements? Why are these statements significant to the points that Jemisin is trying to make about Zinhle's society?
    a. "You stopped acting like people." (par. 117)
    b. "Good grades reflect your ability to adapt to a complex system." (par. 123)
    c. "It's easy to give up what you don't want." (par. 125)
    d. "When they start to fight for you . . ., we'll know they're ready to be let out. To catch up to the rest of the human race." (par. 127)
12. Why does Zinhle say, "They'll never fight for me" (par. 132)?
13. What does Zinhle conclude about "why so many people hate her" (par. 143)? What does this understanding reveal about Zinhle's development?
14. What choice does Zinhle make at the end of the story? Why?

Analyzing Language, Style, and Structure

1. **Vocabulary in Context.** Jemisin writes, "Each year, a tribute of children are sent beyond the Wall." (par. 37). What does "tribute" mean in this context? How does that meaning affect your understanding of the practice being described?
2. **Vocabulary in Context.** Describing adult reactions to Zinhle, Jemisin writes, "The teachers exclaim over this, her parents fawn" (par. 8). What does the word "fawn" mean in this context?
3. **Skill Focus.** Reread the scene with Lauren, Zinhle, and Mitra in the bathroom (pars. 40 to 49). What does Jemisin convey in this scene? How does she use diction, syntax, and other stylistic elements to communicate this idea?
4. The first piece of dialogue in this story is a question uttered by Zinhle's mother: "Have you considered getting pregnant?" Why might Jemisin have made these the first spoken words? What is the effect of this question on Zinhle, her father, and the reader?
5. Jemisin repeats the phrase "But it's all she has" when conveying Zinhle's unspoken thoughts. What does repeating this phrase tell us about Zinhle?
6. Zinhle says that Mitra is "*like* her best friend" (par. 15). What distinction does the word "like" create? What does it suggest about Zinhle?
7. A challenge of science fiction writing is "world building," communicating what is unique about the world of the story. Identify the first signs that this society is different from our own. How does Jemisin build our understanding of this world?

8. Starting in paragraph 34, Jemisin gives the reader some background information about the Firewall and the war. What does she accomplish by waiting until almost halfway through the story to give us this information? How might the story have been different if it had begun with this information?
9. Those students subjected to the culling are called "meat" (par. 55). What is the effect of this term? Is the word "meat" being used literally or metaphorically or both?
10. Zinhle shifts between the pronouns "we" and "them" when referring to humans (see pars. 109 and 129, for example). What do these shifts suggest about Zinhle and her inner conflicts?

Topics for Composing

1. **Analysis.** Some people think that science fiction stories like this one are to be read exclusively for entertainment, that they do not apply to our real, contemporary world. Yet "Valedictorian" is inspired by and provides commentary on real events. What is Jemisin suggesting through the lens of this dystopian setting about how people in the United States currently treat each other?
2. **Argument.** Zinhle is the protagonist in "Valedictorian," but who is the antagonist? Is it Lemuel and those who are behind the Firewall? A government or system? The ancestors who refused to change? A way of thinking? Zinhle's classmates or teachers? Or Zinhle's desire to be "the best"? Support your position with specific details from the story.
3. **Argument.** While the stakes of the testing are significantly higher for the high school students in the story than they are for students in real life, your experiences with standardized testing have a significant impact on your present and future. Write an essay in which you argue for the elimination, continuation, or revision of the testing system in place in your school.
4. **Connection.** How is the school in this story similar to or different from your own?
5. **Connection.** To what extent do you connect with the following statement about Zinhle: "She gets so tired, sometimes. It's exhausting, fighting others' expectations, and doing it all alone" (par. 54).
6. **Speaking and Listening.** Zinhle says, "It is so easy to have principles. Far, far harder to live by them" (par. 30). With a partner or small group, discuss a principle that you try to live by. Why is it important to you? What makes this principle difficult to live up to? Share your responses with the class.
7. **Research.** Those beyond the Firewall are "Leftovers. Microbes in a digital sea" that have somehow learned to occupy the bodies of humans. They could be the fictional product of what has been called "the singularity," a future point in time at which technological growth becomes uncontrollable and irreversible, and artificial intelligence overtakes humanity. Research the singularity, explain its main points, and discuss the likelihood of it occurring in your lifetime.
8. **Creative Writing.** Rewrite a portion of this story from the point of view of another character, such as Samantha, who might be subjected to the culling, a teacher like Ms. Threnody, who knows more about this society than she is permitted to say, or someone from beyond the Firewall, like Lemuel.

World of the Future, We Thirsted

Naomi Shihab Nye

Poet, novelist, songwriter, and political activist, Naomi Shihab Nye (b. 1952) has served as the Poetry Foundation's Young People's Poet Laureate (2019–2021). She was born to a Palestinian father and an American mother and grew up in St. Louis, Jerusalem, and San Antonio, where she now lives. Never one to shy away from challenge or controversy, Nye is a committed environmentalist and an advocate for social justice. She is a Professor of Creative Writing and Poetry at Texas State University. Author of over 30 books and the recipient of numerous awards and fellowships, Nye is an internationally acclaimed writer, who describes herself as a "wandering poet."

Roberto Ricciuti/Getty Images

Stripped of a sense of well-being,
we downed our water from small disposable bottles.
Casting the plastic to streetside,
we poured high-potency energy tonics or Coke
down our throats, because this time in history
had sapped us so thoroughly and
we were desperate.
Straws, plastic caps, crushed cans,
in a three-block walk you could fill a sack.
As if we could replenish spirits quickly,
pitching containers without remorse
— who did we imagine would pick them up?
What did we really know of plastic spirals in the sea
bigger than whole countries,
we had never swirled in one ourselves,
as a fish might do, a sea urchin, a whole family of eels,
did we wish to be invincible, using what we wanted,
discarding what we didn't, as in wars,
whole cities and nations crumpled
after our tanks and big guns pull out?
How long does it take to be thirsty again?
We were so lonely in the streets though
all the small houses still had noses, mouths,
eyes from which we might peer, as our fellow-
citizens walk their dogs, pause helplessly as the dogs
circle trees, tip their heads back for a long slow slug
of water or tea, and never fear, never fear. ■

Laura Lezza/Getty Images

Laura Lezza/Getty Images

These images show the waste collected by Italian fishermen as part of the "Arcipelago Pulito" project in Tuscany. Plastic waste makes up roughly 10 percent of every fishing haul. The bales of disposable bottles and other discarded plastics shown in the image on the right will be recycled.

How do these images suggest the potential to transform environmental waste into something positive that is similar to the transformation suggested in "World of the Future, We Thirsted"?

Understanding and Interpreting

1. What connection does the speaker make in the opening lines (ll. 1–7) between disregard for the environment and a loss of spirituality? Why are we "desperate" (l. 7)?
2. What additional concern about the natural and human worlds does Nye suggest with the speaker's question, " — who did we imagine would pick them up?" (l. 12)?
3. What do "wars, / whole cities and nations" (ll. 18–19) have to do with the local scene that the speaker is exploring?
4. In line 21, the speaker asks, "How long does it take to be thirsty again?" What does "thirst" refer to, aside from the desire for a drink of cool, clean water?
5. Reread the final six lines of the poem. In what ways does that one long sentence with such specific details serve as a conclusion to the speaker's reflections?
6. How do you interpret the last four words: "never fear, never fear"? To whom are these words directed? What are they intended to convey?

Analyzing Language, Style, and Structure

1. **Vocabulary in Context.** The speaker describes us as having "downed our water from small disposable bottles" (l. 2). What does using "downed" as a verb mean in this context?
2. **Skill Focus.** Throughout the poem, Nye juxtaposes concrete descriptions of products and objects familiar to us with more abstract concepts. For instance, the speaker refers to "high-potency energy tonics" (reminding us of something like Red Bull) alongside our "desperate" state. What other examples of such juxtaposition of concrete and abstract language do you find? What is the effect?
3. Why did Nye choose such bleak imagery for the opening line: "Stripped of a sense of well-being"? What are the possible effects of the imagery, together with the sounds of the words themselves?

4. What is the effect of referring not just to what "a fish might do" but to specifics — "a sea urchin, a whole family of eels" (l. 16)?
5. What images of "thirst" and "water" do you find in this poem? How do they work together? How do they relate to the question, "How long does it take to be thirsty again?" (l. 21)?
6. What does the personification of houses, with their "noses, mouths, / eyes" (ll. 23–24), add to the speaker's perception?
7. How does Nye's use of the pronouns "we" and "us" instead of "I" help her to communicate her theme?
8. List the adjectives that describe the "we" of the poem. What vision of life at this moment do they suggest?
9. In lines 17 to 20 Nye writes, "did we wish to be invincible, using what we wanted, / discarding what we didn't, as in wars, / whole cities and nations crumpled / after our tanks and big guns pull out?" What is the significance of the word "discarding" here? How does it relate to the meaning of the poem as a whole?
10. Does the poem's speaker place blame for selfish behaviors? Express sympathy for a sad and lonely existence? What tone does the speaker establish? What diction choices help to create this tone?
11. The title of this poem is "World of the Future, We Thirsted." What are the likely meaning and effect of the syntax Nye chooses? What other sentence structures could she have used? How might those structures have communicated different ideas to her reader?

Topics for Composing

1. **Analysis.** To what extent is "World of the Future, We Thirsted" a dystopian vision with pessimism at its core? If you see elements of hope for the future, what are they? Cite specific lines and images to support your position.
2. **Argument.** To what extent do you think that disregard for the natural world, both locally and globally, necessarily results in humans losing the ability to connect with each other? Refer to the poem and your experience or research in your response.
3. **Connection.** Describe how you contribute to the environmental situation Nye portrays here. What steps can you personally take to improve the situation?
4. **Speaking and Listening.** Working with a partner, read the poem aloud. One person will read the lines that end with a period, and the other will read aloud those lines that end with a question mark. Discuss how the different sentence types reinforce the contrasts and connections within the poem. How did reading the poem aloud like this help you to understand its themes more fully?
5. **Multimodal.** Present an interpretation of "World of the Future, We Thirsted" by preparing a series of static images or a video with the words of the poem either spoken or printed. You may identify meaningful images through research or create your own.
6. **Creative Writing.** The question "How long does it take to be thirsty again?" is powerful enough to become a kind of mantra or reprise. Write your own poem, song, or creative essay that uses repetition of this question as a structural or organizing device.

The Lottery

Shirley Jackson

Shirley Jackson (1916–1965) was an American writer, known primarily for her works of horror and mystery. These works included the novel *The Haunting of Hill House*, which has been adapted into movies and a TV show, and the novel *We Have Always Lived in the Castle*. Jackson also wrote hundreds of short stories, including "The Lottery," her most famous, which was originally published in the *New Yorker* magazine in 1948.

AP Images

The morning of June 27th was clear and sunny, with the fresh warmth of a full-summer day; the flowers were blossoming profusely and the grass was richly green. The people of the village began to gather in the square, between the post office and the bank, around ten o'clock; in some towns there were so many people that the lottery took two days and had to be started on June 26th, but in this village, where there were only about three hundred people, the whole lottery took only about two hours, so it could begin at ten o'clock in the morning and still be through in time to allow the villagers to get home for noon dinner.

The children assembled first, of course. School was recently over for the summer, and the feeling of liberty sat uneasily on most of them; they tended to gather together quietly for a while before they broke into boisterous play, and their talk was still of the classroom and the teacher, of books and reprimands. Bobby Martin had already stuffed his pockets full of stones, and the other boys soon followed his example, selecting the smoothest and roundest stones; Bobby and Harry Jones and Dickie Delacroix — the villagers pronounced this name "Dellacroy" — eventually made a great pile of stones in one corner of the square and guarded it against the raids of the other boys. The girls stood aside, talking among themselves, looking over their shoulders at the boys, and the very small children rolled in the dust or clung to the hands of their older brothers or sisters.

Soon the men began to gather, surveying their own children, speaking of planting and rain, tractors and taxes. They stood together, away from the pile of stones in the corner, and their jokes were quiet and they smiled rather than laughed. The women, wearing faded house dresses and sweaters, came shortly after their menfolk. They greeted one another and exchanged bits of gossip as they went to join

Alex Soth/Magnum Photos

Shirley Jackson does not tie the setting of "The Lottery" to a specific geographic location.
To what extent does this photograph capture the mood of "The Lottery"?

their husbands. Soon the women, standing by their husbands, began to call to their children, and the children came reluctantly, having to be called four or five times. Bobby Martin ducked under his mother's grasping hand and ran, laughing, back to the pile of stones. His father spoke up sharply, and Bobby came quickly and took his place between his father and his oldest brother.

The lottery was conducted — as were the square dances, the teen-age club, the Halloween program — by Mr. Summers, who had time and energy to devote to civic activities. He was a round-faced, jovial man and he ran the coal business, and people were sorry for him, because he had no children and his wife was a scold. When he arrived in the square, carrying the black wooden box, there was a murmur of conversation among the villagers, and he waved and called, "Little late today, folks." The postmaster, Mr. Graves, followed him, carrying a three-legged stool, and the stool was put in the center of the square and Mr. Summers set the black box down on it. The villagers kept their distance, leaving a space between themselves and the stool, and when Mr. Summers said, "Some of you fellows want to give me a hand?," there was a hesitation before two men, Mr. Martin and his oldest son, Baxter, came forward to hold the box steady on the stool while Mr. Summers stirred up the papers inside it.

5 The original paraphernalia for the lottery had been lost long ago, and the black box now resting on the stool had been put into use even before Old Man Warner, the oldest man in town, was born. Mr. Summers spoke frequently to the villagers about making a new box, but no one liked to upset even as much tradition as was represented by the black box. There was a story that the present box had been made with some pieces of the box that

had preceded it, the one that had been constructed when the first people settled down to make a village here. Every year, after the lottery, Mr. Summers began talking again about a new box, but every year the subject was allowed to fade off without anything's being done. The black box grew shabbier each year; by now it was no longer completely black but splintered badly along one side to show the original wood color, and in some places faded or stained.

Mr. Martin and his oldest son, Baxter, held the black box securely on the stool until Mr. Summers had stirred the papers thoroughly with his hand. Because so much of the ritual had been forgotten or discarded, Mr. Summers had been successful in having slips of paper substituted for the chips of wood that had been used for generations. Chips of wood, Mr. Summers had argued, had been all very well when the village was tiny, but now that the population was more than three hundred and likely to keep on growing, it was necessary to use something that would fit more easily into the black box. The night before the lottery, Mr. Summers and Mr. Graves made up the slips of paper and put them into the box, and it was then taken to the safe of Mr. Summers' coal company and locked up until Mr. Summers was ready to take it to the square next morning. The rest of the year, the box was put away, sometimes one place, sometimes another; it had spent one year in Mr. Graves' barn and another year underfoot in the post office, and sometimes it was set on a shelf in the Martin grocery and left there.

There was a great deal of fussing to be done before Mr. Summers declared the lottery open. There were the lists to make up — of heads of families, heads of households in each family, members of each household in each family. There was the proper swearing-in of Mr. Summers by the postmaster, as the official of the lottery; at one time, some people remembered, there had been a recital of some sort, performed by the official of the lottery, a perfunctory, tuneless chant that had been rattled off duly each year; some people believed that the official of the lottery used to stand just so when he said or sang it, others believed that he was supposed to walk among the people, but years and years ago this part of the ritual had been allowed to lapse. There had been, also, a ritual salute, which the official of the lottery had had to use in addressing each person who came up to draw from the box, but this also had changed with time, until now it was felt necessary only for the official to speak to each person approaching. Mr. Summers was very good at all this; in his clean white shirt and blue jeans, with one hand resting carelessly on the black box, he seemed very proper and important as he talked interminably to Mr. Graves and the Martins.

Just as Mr. Summers finally left off talking and turned to the assembled villagers, Mrs. Hutchinson came hurriedly along the path to the square, her sweater thrown over her shoulders, and slid into place in the back of the crowd. "Clean forgot what day it was," she said to Mrs. Delacroix, who stood next to her, and they both laughed softly. "Thought my old man was out back stacking wood," Mrs. Hutchinson went on, "and then I looked out the window and the kids was gone, and then I remembered it was the twenty-seventh and came a-running." She dried her hands on her apron, and Mrs. Delacroix said, "You're in time, though. They're still talking away up there."

Mrs. Hutchinson craned her neck to see through the crowd and found her husband and children standing near the front. She tapped Mrs. Delacroix on the arm as a farewell and began to make her way through the crowd. The people separated good-humoredly to let her through; two or three people said, in voices just

extending beyond the text

The images below are taken from a graphic adaptation of "The Lottery," created by artist Miles Hyman. Reread paragraphs 5 to 7 of the story, in which the narrator describes a bit of the history of the lottery. Then, look closely at the following excerpt from the graphic novel version.

from Shirley Jackson's "The Lottery": The Authorized Graphic Adaptation

Miles Hyman

Explain how Hyman presents the passage of time and the history of the lottery in his version. How is his representation similar to or different from Jackson's presentation of the history in the short story?

loud enough to be heard across the crowd, "Here comes your Mrs., Hutchinson," and "Bill, she made it after all." Mrs. Hutchinson reached her husband, and Mr. Summers, who had been waiting, said cheerfully, "Thought we were going to have to get on without you, Tessie." Mrs. Hutchinson said, grinning, "Wouldn't have had me leave m'dishes in the sink, now, would you, Joe?," and soft laughter ran through the crowd as the people stirred back into position after Mrs. Hutchinson's arrival.

"Well, now," Mr. Summers said soberly, "guess we better get started, get this over with, so's we can go back to work. Anybody ain't here?"

"Dunbar," several people said. "Dunbar, Dunbar."

Mr. Summers consulted his list. "Clyde Dunbar," he said. "That's right. He's broke his leg, hasn't he? Who's drawing for him?"

"Me, I guess," a woman said, and Mr. Summers turned to look at her. "Wife draws for her husband," Mr. Summers said. "Don't you have a grown boy to do it for you, Janey?" Although Mr. Summers and everyone else in the village knew the answer perfectly well, it was the business of the official of the lottery to ask such questions formally. Mr. Summers waited with an expression of polite interest while Mrs. Dunbar answered.

"Horace's not but sixteen yet," Mrs. Dunbar said regretfully. "Guess I gotta fill in for the old man this year."

"Right," Mr. Summers said. He made a note on the list he was holding. Then he asked, "Watson boy drawing this year?"

A tall boy in the crowd raised his hand. "Here," he said. "I'm drawing for m'mother and me." He blinked his eyes nervously and ducked his head as several voices in the crowd said things like "Good fellow, Jack," and "Glad to see your mother's got a man to do it."

"Well," Mr. Summers said, "guess that's everyone. Old Man Warner make it?"

"Here," a voice said, and Mr. Summers nodded.

A sudden hush fell on the crowd as Mr. Summers cleared his throat and looked at the list. "All ready?" he called. "Now, I'll read the names — heads of families first — and the men come up and take a paper out of the box. Keep the paper folded in your hand without looking at it until everyone has had a turn. Everything clear?"

The people had done it so many times that they only half listened to the directions; most of them were quiet, wetting their lips, not looking around. Then Mr. Summers raised one hand high and said, "Adams." A man disengaged himself from the crowd and came forward. "Hi, Steve," Mr. Summers said, and Mr. Adams said, "Hi, Joe." They grinned at one another humorlessly and nervously. Then Mr. Adams reached into the black box and took out a folded paper. He held it firmly by one corner as he turned and went hastily back to his place in the crowd, where he stood a little apart from his family, not looking down at his hand.

"Allen," Mr. Summers said. "Anderson. . . . Bentham."

"Seems like there's no time at all between lotteries any more," Mrs. Delacroix said to Mrs. Graves in the back row. "Seems like we got through with the last one only last week."

"Time sure goes fast," Mrs. Graves said.

"Clark. . . . Delacroix"

"There goes my old man." Mrs. Delacroix said. She held her breath while her husband went forward.

"Dunbar," Mr. Summers said, and Mrs. Dunbar went steadily to the box while one of the women said, "Go on, Janey," and another said, "There she goes."

"We're next," Mrs. Graves said. She watched while Mr. Graves came around from the side of the box, greeted Mr. Summers gravely and selected a slip of paper from the box. By now, all through the crowd there were men holding the

Maypole (w/c on paper)/Joel, Judy/JUDY JOEL/Private Collection/Bridgeman Images

In her work *Maypole*, Judy Joel depicts the traditional celebration of May Day, in which townspeople gather to wrap brightly colored ribbons around the maypole.

What feelings about the celebration does the image convey? How does it do so? What connections or contrasts can you draw between the ritual depicted here and the one portrayed in "The Lottery"?

small folded papers in their large hands, turning them over and over nervously. Mrs. Dunbar and her two sons stood together, Mrs. Dunbar holding the slip of paper.

"Harburt. . . . Hutchinson."

"Get up there, Bill," Mrs. Hutchinson said, and the people near her laughed.

"Jones."

"They do say," Mr. Adams said to Old Man Warner, who stood next to him, "that over in the north village they're talking of giving up the lottery."

Old Man Warner snorted. "Pack of crazy fools," he said. "Listening to the young folks, nothing's good enough for them. Next thing you know, they'll be wanting to go back to living in caves, nobody work any more, live that way for a while. Used to be a saying about 'Lottery in June, corn be heavy soon.' First thing you know, we'd all be eating stewed chickweed and acorns. There's always been a lottery," he added petulantly. "Bad enough to see young Joe Summers up there joking with everybody."

"Some places have already quit lotteries," Mrs. Adams said.

"Nothing but trouble in that," Old Man Warner said stoutly. "Pack of young fools."

"Martin." And Bobby Martin watched his father go forward. "Overdyke. . . . Percy."

"I wish they'd hurry," Mrs. Dunbar said to her older son. "I wish they'd hurry."

"They're almost through," her son said.

"You get ready to run tell Dad," Mrs. Dunbar said.

Mr. Summers called his own name and then stepped forward precisely and selected a slip from the box. Then he called, "Warner."

"Seventy-seventh year I been in the lottery," Old Man Warner said as he went through the crowd. "Seventy-seventh time."

"Watson." The tall boy came awkwardly through the crowd. Someone said, "Don't be nervous, Jack," and Mr. Summers said, "Take your time, son."

"Zanini."

After that, there was a long pause, a breathless pause, until Mr. Summers, holding his slip of paper in the air, said, "All right, fellows." For a minute, no one moved, and then all the slips of paper were opened. Suddenly, all the women began to speak at once, saying. "Who is it?," "Who's got it?," "Is it the Dunbars?," "Is it the Watsons?" Then the voices began to say, "It's Hutchinson. It's Bill," "Bill Hutchinson's got it."

"Go tell your father," Mrs. Dunbar said to her older son.

People began to look around to see the Hutchinsons. Bill Hutchinson was standing quiet, staring down at the paper in his hand. Suddenly, Tessie Hutchinson shouted to Mr. Summers, "You didn't give him time enough to take any paper he wanted. I saw you. It wasn't fair!"

"Be a good sport, Tessie." Mrs. Delacroix called, and Mrs. Graves said, "All of us took the same chance."

"Shut up, Tessie," Bill Hutchinson said.

"Well, everyone," Mr. Summers said, "that was done pretty fast, and now we've got to be hurrying a little more to get done in time." He consulted his next list. "Bill," he said, "you draw for the Hutchinson family. You got any other households in the Hutchinsons?"

"There's Don and Eva," Mrs. Hutchinson yelled. "Make them take their chance!"

"Daughters draw with their husbands' families, Tessie," Mr. Summers said gently. "You know that as well as anyone else."

"It wasn't fair," Tessie said.

"I guess not, Joe," Bill Hutchinson said regretfully. "My daughter draws with her husband's family; that's only fair. And I've got no other family except the kids."

"Then, as far as drawing for families is concerned, it's you," Mr. Summers said in explanation, "and as far as drawing for households is concerned, that's you, too. Right?"

"Right," Bill Hutchinson said.

"How many kids, Bill?" Mr. Summers asked formally.

"Three," Bill Hutchinson said. "There's Bill, Jr., and Nancy, and little Dave. And Tessie and me."

"All right, then," Mr. Summers said. "Harry, you got their tickets back?"

Mr. Graves nodded and held up the slips of paper. "Put them in the box, then," Mr. Summers directed. "Take Bill's and put it in."

"I think we ought to start over," Mrs. Hutchinson said, as quietly as she could. "I tell you it wasn't fair. You didn't give him time enough to choose. Everybody saw that."

Mr. Graves had selected the five slips and put them in the box, and he dropped all the papers but those onto the ground, where the breeze caught them and lifted them off.

"Listen, everybody," Mrs. Hutchinson was saying to the people around her.

"Ready, Bill?" Mr. Summers asked, and Bill Hutchinson, with one quick glance around at his wife and children, nodded.

"Remember," Mr. Summers said, "take the slips and keep them folded until each person has taken one. Harry, you help little Dave." Mr. Graves took the hand of the little boy, who came willingly with him up to the box. "Take a paper out of the box, Davy," Mr. Summers said. Davy put his hand into the box and laughed. "Take just one paper," Mr. Summers said. "Harry, you hold it for him." Mr. Graves took the child's hand and removed the folded paper from the tight fist and held it while little Dave stood next to him and looked up at him wonderingly.

"Nancy next," Mr. Summers said. Nancy was twelve, and her school friends breathed heavily as she went forward, switching her skirt, and took a slip daintily from the box. "Bill, Jr.," Mr. Summers said, and Billy, his face red and his feet overlarge, nearly knocked the box over as he got a paper out. "Tessie," Mr. Summers said. She hesitated for a minute, looking around defiantly, and then set her lips and went up to the box. She snatched a paper out and held it behind her.

extending beyond the text

Following is an excerpt from an article entitled "The Morning of June 28, 1948" by Shirley Jackson. She describes reactions from readers of "The Lottery," including her own mother, when it was first published in the *New Yorker* magazine.

from The Morning of June 28, 1948

Shirley Jackson

Things began mildly enough with a note from a friend at the *New Yorker*: "Your story has kicked up quite a fuss around the office," he wrote. I was flattered: it's nice to think that your friends notice what you write. Later that day there was a call from one of the magazine's editors; they had had a couple of people phone in about my story, he said, and was there anything I particularly wanted him to say if there were any more calls? No, I said, nothing particular; anything he chose to say was perfectly all right with me; it was just a story.

I was further puzzled by a cryptic note from another friend: "Heard a man talking about a story of yours on the bus this morning," she wrote. "Very exciting. I wanted to tell him I knew the author, but after I heard what he was saying, I decided I'd better not."

One of the most terrifying aspects of publishing stories and books is the realization that they are going to be read and read by strangers. I had never fully realized this before, although I had of course in my imagination dwelt lovingly upon the thought of the millions and millions of people who were going to be uplifted and enriched and delighted by the stories I wrote. It had simply never occurred to me that these millions and millions of people might be so far from being uplifted that they would sit down and write me letters I was downright scared to open: of the three-hundred-odd letters that I received that summer I can count only thirteen that spoke kindly to me, and they were mostly from friends. Even my mother scolded me: "Dad and I did not care at all for your story in the *New Yorker*," she wrote sternly. "It does seem, dear, that this gloomy kind of story is what all you young people think about these days. Why don't you write something to cheer people up?"

Why do you think reactions to the story were so emotional? If this story were published for the first time today, would it cause the same distress and controversy? Or do you think it would seem a tame idea in our contemporary world? How might social media influence reader responses?

"Bill," Mr. Summers said, and Bill Hutchinson reached into the box and felt around, bringing his hand out at last with the slip of paper in it.

The crowd was quiet. A girl whispered, "I hope it's not Nancy," and the sound of the whisper reached the edges of the crowd.

"It's not the way it used to be," Old Man Warner said clearly. "People ain't the way they used to be."

"All right," Mr. Summers said. "Open the papers. Harry, you open little Dave's."

Mr. Graves opened the slip of paper and there was a general sigh through the crowd as he held it up and everyone could see that it was blank. Nancy and Bill, Jr., opened theirs at the same time, and both beamed and laughed, turning around to the crowd and holding their slips of paper above their heads.

"Tessie," Mr. Summers said. There was a pause, and then Mr. Summers looked at Bill Hutchinson, and Bill unfolded his paper and showed it. It was blank.

"It's Tessie," Mr. Summers said, and his voice was hushed. "Show us her paper. Bill."

Bill Hutchinson went over to his wife and forced the slip of paper out of her hand. It had a black spot on it, the black spot Mr. Summers had made the night before with the heavy pencil in the coal-company office. Bill Hutchinson held it up, and there was a stir in the crowd.

"All right, folks." Mr. Summers said. "Let's finish quickly."

Although the villagers had forgotten the ritual and lost the original black box, they still remembered to use stones. The pile of stones the boys had made earlier was ready; there were stones on the ground with the blowing scraps of paper that had come out of the box. Mrs. Delacroix selected a stone so large she had to pick it up with both hands and turned to Mrs. Dunbar. "Come on," she said. "Hurry up."

Mrs. Dunbar had small stones in both hands, and she said, gasping for breath. "I can't run at all. You'll have to go ahead and I'll catch up with you."

The children had stones already. And someone gave little Davy Hutchinson a few pebbles.

Tessie Hutchinson was in the center of a cleared space by now, and she held her hands out desperately as the villagers moved in on her. "It isn't fair," she said. A stone hit her on the side of the head.

Old Man Warner was saying, "Come on, come on, everyone." Steve Adams was in the front of the crowd of villagers, with Mrs. Graves beside him.

"It isn't fair, it isn't right," Mrs. Hutchinson screamed, and then they were upon her. ■

Understanding and Interpreting

1. The description of the setting in this story is minimal, but essential. What is the town like? In what ways does it seem like a utopian society?
2. How do the boys behave before the lottery starts, compared with the men? Based on your understanding of the ending of the story, what might account for these differences?
3. The black box that holds the slips of paper gets shabbier each year. Why does the town not want to repair it? And why does the box seem to get shuttled around in various locations, uncared for during the year?
4. There are many rituals associated with the lottery. Why have some of the rituals faded away, while some others have remained? What is Jackson suggesting about cultural rituals?
5. The villagers seem to observe strict gender roles. How do these roles show up in the story? To what extent do the villagers see them as a positive, negative, or neutral influence?
6. Mr. Adams tells Old Man Warner that another village is talking about giving up the lottery (pars. 31–32). What is Old Man Warner's response? How does his attitude reflect Jackson's ideas about culture and ritual? Be sure to focus specifically on his quotation of an old saying, "Lottery in June, corn be heavy soon."

7. When the Hutchinson family draws the black dot, Tessie immediately begins to question the lottery's fairness. Why does Tessie try to get Don and Eva to draw with the Hutchinsons? How do others respond to her objections? What do everyone's reactions, including Tessie's, seem to suggest about people's attitudes toward the lottery?
8. In paragraph 66, a girl in the crowd whispers, "I hope it's not Nancy," and Old Man Warner says, "People ain't the way they used to be." What does this exchange reveal about culture and ritual?
9. Look at the following statements from the last part of the story and explain their significance:
   a. "Mrs. Delacroix selected a stone so large she had to pick it up with both hands."
   b. "And someone gave little Davy Hutchinson a few pebbles."
   c. "Old Man Warner was saying, 'Come on, come on, everyone!.' "

Analyzing Language, Style, and Structure

1. **Vocabulary in Context.** Paragraph 7 relates the history and ritual of the lottery, including "a recital of some sort, performed by the official of the lottery, a perfunctory, tuneless chant that had been rattled off duly each year." What is the meaning of "recital" in this context? What does it suggest about the community's attitude toward this ritual?
2. **Skill Focus.** Reread paragraphs 63 to 65 in which the individual Hutchinson family members draw slips of paper. Look specifically at the word choices that describe Davy's actions, as well as people's reactions when Nancy draws. How does the diction reveal Jackson's attitude toward the ritual of the lottery?
3. Identify and examine moments in which Jackson's language, style, and structure choices hint at the ending. Why are these choices effective at creating suspense and foreshadowing?
4. Look back at the moment when Mrs. Hutchinson arrives late to the lottery, including the dialogue between her and Mrs. Delacroix, and with her husband (pars. 8–9). What effect do these conversations have on the reader? How do they relate to the story's conclusion?
5. It's clear that this lottery has been going on for a very long time in this village. How does Jackson communicate the normality of this ritual through her details and descriptions?
6. Much of the dialogue in this story, especially near the end, revolves around "hurrying up" and "finishing quickly." Why do you think Jackson includes this kind of dialogue?
7. What is the effect of the last phrase of the story: "and then they were upon her"? Why might Jackson have chosen to end her story that way?

Topics for Composing

1. **Analysis.** Why do the townspeople participate in the lottery? What is Jackson suggesting about culture and ritual based on their participation?
2. **Argument.** "The Lottery" is one of the most frequently anthologized and taught short stories since its original publication. What makes this story of lasting interest to generation after generation? Should it continue to be taught and anthologized? Why or why not?
3. **Argument.** In many ways, this is a story about how difficult it is to change a deeply held cultural belief or ritual. Identify a widespread, culturally accepted practice in the real world that, like Tessie, you would call unfair. Write an argument for changing or abolishing it.

Who might, like Old Man Warner, object to your call for change? How might you address their concerns?

4. **Connection.** "The Lottery" is also a story about scapegoating. What is scapegoating? Where do you see evidence of it in the real world? How is your real-world example of scapegoating similar to the presentation of this social practice in the story?
5. **Speaking and Listening.** Working in small groups, develop a plan for filming a scene from "The Lottery" with a contemporary or futuristic setting. Whom would you cast in the key roles? Why? What would be the physical setting? What songs might you want to include on the soundtrack? Be prepared to explain your choices and pitch your production plan to the full class. You might consider viewing clips from the 1969 or 1996 film adaptations and compare them with your ideas.
6. **Research.** One of the characters in the story is named Mr. Graves, which hints at the deaths in the village. The names of several other characters allude to other ideas, specifically Hutchinson, Delacroix, and Martin. Research these names and draw a connection between the names and the meaning Jackson might have been creating with their use in the story.
7. **Research.** It is clear that the people in this story behave as a mob at the end when they attack Tessie with stones. Research the concepts of "mob mentality," also known as herd mentality, group think, or crowd intelligence. Examine relevant research studies and apply what you learn to the villagers of the story.
8. **Creative Writing.** Write a scene or two from a story about the north village that is talking about getting rid of the lottery. What are their discussions like? What happens on their lottery day that is similar to or different from the events in the village of this story?

Spider the Artist

Nnedi Okorafor

Nnedi Okorafor is a Nigerian-American author who holds a PhD in literature and master's degrees in journalism and literature. Her award-winning and best-selling novels include *Who Fears Death*, *Lagoon*, *The Book of the Phoenix*, and the *Akata* series. She is also the author of several graphic novels for Marvel, including *Wakanda Forever* and the *Shuri* series.

Neilson Barnard/Getty Images

Zombie no go go, unless you tell am to go
Zombie!
Zombie!
Zombie no go stop, unless you tell am to stop
Zombie no go turn, unless you tell am to turn
Zombie!
Zombie no go think, unless you tell am to think

— from *Zombie* by Fela Kuti, Nigerian musician and self-proclaimed voice of the voiceless

• • •

My husband used to beat me. That was how I ended up out there that evening behind our house, just past the bushes, through the tall grass, in front of the pipelines. Our small house was the last in the village, practically in the forest itself. So nobody ever saw or heard him beating me.

Going out there was the best way to put space between me and him without sending him into further rage. When I went behind the house, he knew where I was and he knew I was alone. But he was too full of himself to realize I was thinking about killing myself.

My husband was a drunk, like too many of the members of the Niger Delta People's Movement. It was how they all controlled their anger and feelings of helplessness. The fish, shrimps and crayfish in the creeks were dying. Drinking the water shriveled women's wombs and eventually made men urinate blood.

There was a stream where I had been fetching water. A flow station was built nearby and now the stream was rank and filthy, with an oily film that reflected rainbows. Cassava and yam farms yielded less and less each year. The air left your skin dirty and smelled like something preparing to die. In some places, it was always daytime because of the noisy gas flares.

5 My village was ****.

On top of all this, People's Movement members were getting picked off like flies. The "kill-and-go" had grown bold. They shot People's Movement members in the streets, they ran them over, dragged them into the swamps. You never saw them again.

I tried to give my husband some happiness. But after three years, my body continued to refuse him children. It's easy to see the root of his frustration and sadness . . . but pain is pain. And he dealt it to me regularly.

My greatest, my only true possession was my father's guitar. It was made of fine polished Abura timber and it had a lovely tortoiseshell pick guard. Excellent handwork. My father said that the timber used to create the guitar came from one of the last timber trees in the delta. If you held it to your nose, you could believe this. The guitar was decades old and still smelled like fresh cut wood, like it wanted to tell you its story because only it could.

I wouldn't exist without my father's guitar. When he was a young man, he used to sit in front of the compound in the evening and play for everyone. People danced, clapped, shut their eyes and listened. Cell phones would ring and people would ignore them. One day, it was my mother who stopped to listen.

10 I used to stare at my father's fast long-fingered hands when he played. Oh, the harmonies. He could weave anything with his music — rainbows, sunrises, spider webs sparkling with morning dew. My older brothers weren't interested in learning how to play. But I was, so my father taught me everything he knew. And now it was my long-fingers that graced the strings. I'd always been able to hear music and my fingers moved even faster than my father's. I was good. Really good.

But I married that stupid man. Andrew. So I only played behind the house. Away from him. My guitar was my escape.

That fateful evening, I was sitting on the ground in front of the fuel pipeline. It ran right through everyone's backyard. My village was an oil village, as was the village where I grew up. My mother lived in a similar village before she was married, as did her mother. We are Pipeline People.

My mother's grandmother was known for lying on the pipeline running through her village. She'd stay like that for hours, listening and wondering what magical fluids were running through the large never-ending steel tubes. This was before the Zombies, of course. I laughed. If she tried to lie on a pipeline now she'd be brutally killed.

Anyway, when I was feeling especially blue, I'd take my guitar and come out here and sit right in front of the pipeline. I knew I was flirting with death by being so close but when I was like this, I didn't really care. I actually welcomed the possibility of being done with life. It was a wonder that my husband didn't smash my guitar during one of his drunken rages. I'd surely have quickly thrown myself on the pipeline if he did. Maybe that was why he'd rather smash my nose than my guitar.

15 This day, he'd only slapped me hard across the face. I had no idea why. He'd simply come in,

In a Groove (oil on canvas)/Mucherera, Kaaria (Contemporary Artist)/KAARIA MUCHERERA (CONTEMPORARY ARTIST)/Private Collection/Bridgeman Images

In a Groove is the title of this painting by contemporary African American artist Mucherera Kaaria.

How does this image depict the relationship between musician and instrument? In what ways does it present feelings similar to those that Eme, the narrator, expresses about her guitar when she says, "My guitar was my escape"?

seen me in the kitchen and *smack*! Maybe he'd had a bad day at work — he worked very hard at a local restaurant. Maybe one of his women had scorned him. Maybe I did something wrong. I didn't know. I didn't care. My nose was just starting to stop bleeding and I was not seeing so many stars.

My feet were only inches from the pipeline. I was especially daring this night. It was warmer and more humid than normal. Or maybe it was my stinging burning face. The mosquitoes didn't even bother me much. In the distance, I could see Nneka, a woman who rarely spoke to me, giving her small sons a bath in a large tub. Some men were playing cards at a table several houses down. It was dark, there were small, small trees and bushes here and even our closest neighbor was not very close, so I was hidden.

I sighed and placed my hands on the guitar strings. I plucked out a tune my father used to play. I sighed and closed my eyes. I would always miss my father. The feel of the strings vibrating under my fingers was exquisite.

I fell deep into the zone of my music, weaving it, then floating on a glorious sunset that lit the palm tree tops and . . .

Click!

I froze. My hands still on the strings, the vibration dying. I didn't dare move. I kept my eyes closed. The side of my face throbbed.

Click! This time the sound was closer. *Click!* Closer. *Click!* Closer.

My heart pounded and I felt nauseous with fear. Despite my risk taking, I knew this was *not* the way I wanted to die. Who would want to be torn limb from limb by Zombies? As everyone in my village did multiple times a day, I quietly cursed the Nigerian government.

Twing!

The vibration of the guitar string was stifled by my middle finger still pressing it down. My hands started to shake, but still I kept my eyes shut. Something sharp and cool lifted my finger. I wanted to scream. The string was plucked again.

Twang!

The sound was deeper and fuller, my finger no longer muffling the vibration. Very slowly, I opened my eyes. My heart skipped. The thing stood about three feet tall, which meant I was eye-to-eye with it. I'd never seen one up close. Few people have. These things are always running up and down the pipeline like a herd of super fast steer, always with things to do.

I chanced a better look. It really *did* have eight legs. Even in the darkness, those legs shined, catching even the dimmest light. A bit more light and I'd have been able to see my face perfectly reflected back at me. I'd heard that they polished and maintained themselves. This made even more sense now, for who would have time to keep them looking so immaculate?

The government came up with the idea to create the Zombies, and Shell, Chevron and a few other oil companies (who were just as desperate) supplied the money to pay for it all. The Zombies were made to combat pipeline bunkering and terrorism. It makes me laugh. The government and the oil people destroyed our land and dug up our oil, then they created robots to keep us from taking it back.

They were originally called Anansi Droids 419 but we call them "*oyibo* contraption" and, most often, Zombie, the same name we call those "kill-and-go" soldiers who come in here harassing us every time something bites their brains.

It's said that Zombies can think. Artificial Intelligence, this is called. I have had some schooling, a year or two of university, but my area was not in the sciences. No matter my education, as soon as I got married and brought to this damn place I became like every other woman here, a simple village woman living in the delta region where Zombies kill anyone who touches the pipelines and whose husband knocks her around every so often. What did I know about Zombie intellect?

It looked like a giant shiny metal spider. It moved like one too. All smooth-shifting joints and legs. It crept closer and leaned in to inspect my guitar strings some more. As it did so, two of its back legs tapped on the metal of the pipeline. *Click! Click! Click!*

It pushed my thumb back down on the strings and plucked the string twice, making a muted *pluck!* It looked at me with its many blue shining round eyes. Up close I could see that they weren't lights. They were balls of a glowing metallic blue undulating liquid, like charged mercury. I stared into them fascinated. No one else in my village could possibly know this fact. No one had gotten close enough. *Eyes of glowing bright blue liquid metal,* I thought. *Na wa.*

It pressed my hand harder and I gasped, blinking and looking away from its hypnotic eyes. Then I understood.

"You . . . you want me to play?"

It sat there waiting, placing a leg on the body of my guitar with a soft *tap*. It had been a long time since anyone had wanted me to play for him. I played my favorite highlife song. *Love Dey See Road* by Oliver De Coque. I played like my life depended on it.

The Zombie didn't move, its leg remaining pressed to my guitar. Was it listening? I was sure it was. Twenty minutes later, when I stopped finally playing, sweat running down my face, it touched the tips of my aching hands. Gently.

Some of these pipelines carry diesel fuel, others carry crude oil. Millions of liters of it a day. Nigeria supplies twenty-five percent of United States oil. And we get virtually nothing in return. Nothing but death by Zombie attack. We can all tell you stories.

When the Zombies were first released, no one knew about them. All people would hear were rumors about people getting torn apart near pipelines or sightings of giant white spiders in the night. Or you'd hear about huge pipeline explosions, charred bodies everywhere. But the pipeline where the bodies lay would be perfectly intact.

People still bunkered. My husband was one of them. I suspected that he sold the fuel and oil on the black market; he would bring some of the oil home, too. You let it sit in a bucket for two days and it would become something like kerosene. I used it for cooking. So I couldn't really complain. But bunkering was a very, very dangerous practice.

There *were* ways of breaking a pipeline open without immediately bringing the wrath of Zombies. My husband and his comrades used some sort of powerful laser cutter. They stole them from the hospitals. But they had to be very, very quiet when cutting through the metal. All it took was one bang, one vibration, and the Zombies would come running within a minute. Many of my husband's comrades had been killed because of the tap of someone's wedding ring or the tip of the laser cutter on steel.

Two years ago a group of boys had been playing too close to the pipeline. Two of them were wrestling and they fell on it. Within seconds the Zombies came. One boy managed to scramble away. But the other was grabbed by the arm and flung into some bushes. His arm and both of his legs were broken. Government officials *said* that Zombies were programmed to do as little harm as possible but . . . I didn't believe this, *na* lie.

They were terrible creatures. To get close to a pipeline was to risk a terrible death. Yet the goddamn things ran right through our backyards.

But I didn't care. My husband was beating the hell out of me during these months. I don't know why. He had not lost his job. I knew he was seeing other women. We were poor but we were not starving. Maybe it was because I couldn't bear him children. It is my fault I know, but what can I do?

I found myself out in the backyard more and more. And this particular Zombie visited me every time. I loved playing for it. It would listen. Its lovely eyes would glow with joy. Could a robot feel joy? I believed intelligent ones like this could. Many times a day, I would

extending beyond the text

Nigeria is the largest producer of crude oil on the continent of Africa. Despite the potential for widespread economic prosperity, competition for profits has resulted in corruption and conflicts among local and national government bodies, sometimes leading to violence, as described in the following except:

from A Swamp Full of Dollars: Pipelines and Paramilitaries at Nigeria's Oil Frontier

Michael Peel

In the half-century since it first shipped its oil, the nation of Nigeria — one of the world's ten most populous — has become a little laboratory for the arrogance of a fossil-fuel-obsessed world. It is a country where the oil economy is slowly being destroyed by its own hand and its own hubris. It has metamorphosed from pillar of unprecedented Western industrial prosperity to ominous parable for a rapacious age. Nigeria teaches us that the unfettered global cult of crude hurts not just the countries that produce it but — as relentlessly as in any Greek tragedy — the nations that consume it, too. That vulnerability is clear in the world oil market spikes caused by each production disruption in the Delta.

All this makes Nigeria a brittle motor of twenty-first-century capitalism. One of the grimly poetic qualities to what is happening there is that the supply of crude is being undermined partly by the very products and technological developments oil wealth has helped to deliver.

How does this real-life description of the effects of oil production in Nigeria compare to the fictional descriptions in Okorafor's story?

see a crowd of Zombies running up and down the pipeline, off to do repairs or policing, whatever they did. If my Zombie was amongst them, I couldn't tell.

It was about the tenth time it visited me that it did something very, very strange. My husband had come home smelling practically flammable, stinking of several kinds of alcohol — beer, palm wine, perfume. I had been thinking hard all day. About my life. I was stuck. I wanted a baby. I wanted to get out of the house. I wanted a job. I wanted friends. I needed courage. I knew I had courage. I had faced a Zombie, many times.

I was going to ask my husband about teaching at the elementary school. I'd heard that they were looking for teachers. When he walked in, he greeted me with a sloppy hug and kiss and then plopped himself on the couch. He turned on the television. It was late but I brought him his dinner, pepper soup heavy with goat meat, chicken and large shrimp. He was in a good drunken mood. But as I stood there watching him eat, all my courage fled. All my need for change skittered and cowered to the back of my brain.

"Do you want anything else?" I asked.

He looked up at me and actually smiled. "The soup is good today."

I smiled, but something inside me ducked its head lower. "I'm glad," I said. I picked up my guitar. "I'm going to the back. It's nice outside."

"Don't go too close to the pipeline," he said. But he was looking at the TV and gnawing on a large piece of goat meat.

I crept into the darkness, through the bushes and grasses, to the pipeline. I sat in my usual spot. A foot from it. I strummed softly, a series of chords. A forlorn tune that spoke my heart. Where else was there to go from here? Was this my life? I sighed. I hadn't been to church in a month.

When it came clicking down the pipe, my heart lifted. Its blue liquid eyes glowed strong tonight. There was a woman from whom I once bought a bolt of blue cloth. The cloth was a rich blue that reminded me of the open water on sunny days. The woman said the cloth was "azure." My Zombie's eyes were a deep azure this night.

It stopped, standing before me. Waiting. I knew it was my Zombie because a month ago, it had allowed me to put a blue butterfly sticker on one of its front legs.

"Good evening," I said.

It did not move.

"I'm sad today," I said.

It stepped off the pipeline, its metal legs clicking on the metal and then whispering on the dirt and grass. It sat its body on the ground as it always did. Then it waited.

I strummed a few chords and then played its favorite song, Bob Marley's "No Woman No Cry." As I played, its body slowly began to rotate, something I'd come to understand was its way of expressing pleasure. I smiled. When I stopped playing, it turned its eyes back to me. I sighed, strummed an A minor chord, and sat back. "My life is s***" I said.

Suddenly, it rose up on its eight legs with a soft whir. It stretched and straightened its legs until it was standing a foot taller than normal. From under its body in the center, something whitish and metallic began to descend. I gasped, grabbing my guitar. My mind told me to move away. Move away fast. I'd befriended this artificial creature. I knew it. Or I thought I knew it. But what did I *really* know about why it did what it did? Or why it came to me?

The metallic substance descended faster, pooling in the grass beneath it. I squinted. The stuff was wire. Right before my eyes, I watched the Zombie take this wire and do something with five of its legs while it supported itself on the other three. The legs scrambled around, working and weaving the shiny wire this way and that. They moved too fast for me to see exactly what they were creating. Grass flew and the soft whirring sound grew slightly louder.

Then the legs stopped. For a moment all I could hear was the sounds of crickets and frogs singing, the breeze blowing in the palm and mangrove tree tops. I could smell the sizzling oil of someone frying plantain or yam nearby.

My eyes focused on what the Zombie had done. I grinned. I grinned and grinned. "What is that?" I whispered.

It held it up with two of its front legs and tapped its back leg twice on the ground as it always seemed to when it was trying to make a point. A point that I usually didn't understand.

It brought three legs forward and commenced to pluck out what first was a medley of my favorite songs, from Bob Marley to Sunny Ade to Carlos Santana. Then its music deepened to something so complex and beautiful that I was reduced to tears of joy, awe, ecstasy. People must have heard the music, maybe they looked out their windows or opened their doors. But we were hidden by the darkness, the grass, the trees. I cried and cried. I don't know why, but I cried. I wonder if it was pleased by my reaction. I think it was.

I spent the next hour learning to play its tune.

Ten days later, a group of Zombies attacked some oil workers and soldiers deep in the delta. Ten of the men were torn limb from limb, their bloody remains scattered all over the swampy land. Those who escaped told reporters that nothing would stop the Zombies. A soldier had even thrown a grenade at one, but the thing protected itself with the very force field it had been built to use during pipeline explosions. The soldier said the force field looked like a crackling bubble made of lightning.

"*Wahala*! Trouble!" the soldier frantically told television reporters. His face was greasy with sweat and the sides of his eyes were twitching. "Evil, evil things! I've believed this from start! Look at me with grenade! *Ye*! I could do nothing!"

The pipeline the men had barely even started was found fully assembled. Zombies are made to make repairs, not fully assemble things. It was bizarre. Newspaper write-ups said that the Zombies were getting too smart for their own good. That they were rebelling. Something had certainly changed.

"Maybe it's only a matter of time before the damn things kill us all," my husband said, a beer in hand, as he read about the incident in the newspaper.

I considered never going near my Zombie again. They were unpredictable and possibly out of control.

It was midnight and I was out there again.

My husband hadn't laid a heavy hand on me in weeks. I think he sensed the change in me. I had changed. He now heard me play more. Even in the house. In the mornings. After cooking his dinners. In the bedroom when his friends were over. And he was hearing songs that I knew gave him a most glorious feeling. As if each chord, each sound were examined by scientists and handpicked to provoke the strongest feeling of happiness.

My Zombie had solved my marital problems. At least the worst of them. My husband could not beat me when there was beautiful music sending his senses to lush, sweet places. I began to hope. To hope for a baby. Hope that I would one day leave my house and wifely duties for a job as music teacher at the elementary school. Hope that my village would one day reap from the oil being reaped from it. And I dreamt about being embraced by deep blue liquid metal, webs of wire and music.

I'd woken up that night from one of these strange dreams. I opened my eyes, a smile on my face. Good things were certainly coming. My husband was sleeping soundly beside me. In the dim moonlight, he looked so peaceful. His skin no longer smelled of alcohol. I leaned forward and kissed his lips. He didn't wake. I slipped out of bed and put on some pants and a long sleeve shirt. The mosquitoes would be out tonight. I grabbed my guitar.

I'd named my Zombie Udide Okwanka. In my language, it means "spider the artist." According to legend, Udide Okwanka is the Supreme Artist. And she lives underground where she takes fragments of things and changes them into something else. She can even weave spirits from straw. It was a good name for my Zombie. I wondered what Udide named me. I was sure it named me something, though I doubted that it told the others about me. I don't think it would have been allowed to keep seeing me.

Udide was waiting for me there, as if it sensed I would come out this night. I grinned, my heart feeling so warm. I sat down as it left the pipeline and crept up to me. It carried its instrument on top of its head. A sort of complex star made of wire. Over the weeks, it had added more wire lines, some thin and some thick. I often wondered where it put this thing when it was running about with the others, for the instrument was too big to hide on its body.

Udide held it before its eyes. With a front leg, it plucked out a sweet simple tune that almost made me weep with joy. It conjured up images of my mother and father, when they were so young and full of hope, when my brothers and I were too young to marry and move away. Before the "kill and go" had driven my oldest brother away to America and my middle brother to the north . . . when there was so much potential.

I laughed and wiped away a tear and started strumming some chords to support the tune. From there we took off into something so intricate, enveloping, intertwining . . . *Chei!* I felt as if I was communing with God. *Ah-ah*, this machine and me. You can't imagine.

Nadia Isakova/Alamy Stock Photo

Artist Louise Bourgeois became one of the top-selling woman artists of all time when she sold one of her enormous spider sculptures for $28 million in 2015.

What feelings does this work create for you? Why? In what ways does this image deepen or change your understanding of the possible ways to interpret the appeal of Udide in "Spider the Artist"?

"Eme!"

Our music instantly fell apart.

"Eme!" my husband called again.

I froze, staring at Udide who was also motionless. "Please," I whispered to it. "Don't hurt him."

"Samuel messaged me!" my husband said, his eyes still on his cell phone, as he stepped up to me through the tall grass. "There's a break in the pipeline near the school! Not a goddamn Zombie in sight yet! Throw down that guitar, woman! Let's go and get . . ." He looked up. A terrified look took hold of his face.

For a very long time it seemed we all were frozen in time. My husband standing just at the last of the tall grass. Udide standing in front of the pipeline, instrument held up like a ceremonial shield. And me between the two of them, too afraid to move. I turned to my husband. "Andrew," I said with the greatest of care. "Let me explain . . ."

He slowly dragged his gaze to me and gave me a look, as if he was seeing me for the first time. "My own wife?!" he whispered.

"I . . ."

Udide raised its two front legs. For a moment it looked almost like it was pleading with me. Or maybe offering me a hug. Then it clicked its legs together so hard that it produced a large red spark and an ear splitting *ting!*

My husband and I clapped our hands over our ears. The air instantly smelled like freshly lit matches. Even through the palms of my hands, I could hear the responses from down the pipeline. The clicking was so numerous that it sounded like a rain of tiny pebbles falling on the pipeline. Udide shuddered, scrambled back and stood on it, waiting. They came in a great mob. About twenty of them. The first thing that I noticed was their eyes. They were all a deep angry red.

The others scrambled around Udide, tapping their feet in complex rhythms on the pipe. I couldn't see Udide's eyes. Then they all ran off with amazing speed, to the east.

I turned to my husband. He was gone.

Word spread like a disease because almost everyone had a cell phone. Soon everyone was clicking away on them, messaging things like, "Pipeline burst, near school! No Zombies in sight!" and "Hurry to school, bring bucket!" My husband never let me have my own cell phone. We couldn't afford one and he didn't think I needed one. But I knew where the elementary school was.

People now believed that the Zombies had all gone rogue, shrugging off their man-given jobs to live in the delta swamps and do whatever it was they did there. Normally, if bunkerers broke open a pipeline, even for the quietest jobs, the Zombies would become aware of it within an hour and repair the thing within another hour.

North Dakota, Fargo, Petroleum Products Storage/UNIVERSAL IMAGES GROUP/Bridgeman Images

This is an image of a petroleum storage facility in North Dakota, including pipelines similar to those described in the story. **How would you describe the pipelines — beautiful or menacing, or something else? How does the camera's perspective (low to the ground, following the pipelines from the foreground to the background) affect your response? In what ways are the pipelines in "Spider the Artist" a character, as well as part of the setting?**

But two hours later this broken pipe continued to splash fuel. That was when someone had decided to put the word out.

I knew better. The Zombies weren't "zombies" at all. They were thinking creatures. Smart beasts. They had a method to their madness. And most of them did *not* like human beings.

The chaos was lit by the headlights of several cars and trucks. The pipeline here was raised as it traveled south. Someone had taken advantage of this and removed a whole section of piping. Pink diesel fuel poured out of both ends like a giant fountain. People crowded beneath the flow like parched elephants, filling jerri cans, bottles, bowls, buckets. One man even held a garbage bag, until the fuel ate through the bag, splashing fuel all over the man's chest and legs.

The spillage collected into a large dark pink pool that swiftly flowed toward the elementary school, gathering on the playground. The fumes hit me even before I got within sight of the school. My eyes watered and my nose started running. I held my shirt over my nose and mouth. This barely helped.

People came in cars, motorcycles, buses, on foot. Everyone was messaging on their cell phones, further spreading the word. It had been a while since people who did not make a career out of fuel theft had gotten a sip of free fuel.

There were children everywhere. They ran up and down, sent on errands by their parents or just hanging around to be a part of the excitement. They'd probably never seen people able to go near a pipeline without getting killed. Hip-hop and highlife blasted from cars and SUVs with enhanced sound systems. The baseline vibrations were almost as stifling as the fumes. I had not a doubt that the Zombies knew this was going on.

I spotted my husband. He was heading toward the fountain of fuel with a large red bucket. Five men started arguing amongst each other. Two of them started pushing and shoving, almost falling into the fountain.

"Andrew!" I called over all the noise.

He turned. When he saw me, he narrowed his eyes.

"Please!" I said. "I'm . . . I'm sorry."

He spat and started walking away.

"You have to get out of here!" I said. "They will come!"

He whirled around and strode up to me. "How the hell are you so sure? Did you bring them yourself?"

As if in response, people suddenly started screaming and running. I cursed. The Zombies were coming from the street, forcing people to run toward the pool of fuel. I cursed, again. My husband was glaring at me. He pointed into my face with a look of disgust. I couldn't hear what he said over all the noise. He turned and ran off.

I tried to spot Udide amongst the Zombies. All of their eyes were still red. Was Udide even amongst them? I stared at their legs, searching for the butterfly sticker. There it was. Closest to me, to the left. "Udide!" I called.

As the name came out of my mouth, I saw two of the Zombies in the center each raise two front legs. My smile went to an "O" of shock. I dropped to the ground and threw my hands over my head. People were still splashing across the pool of fuel, trying to get into the school. Their cars continued blasting hip-hop and highlife, the headlights still on, lighting the madness.

The two Zombies clicked their legs together, producing two large sparks. *Ting!*

WHOOOOOOOOOSH!

I remember light, heat, the smell of burning hair and flesh and screams that melted to guttural gurgles. The noise was muffled. The stench was awful. My head to my lap, I remained in this hellish limbo for a long, long time.

Les Zombis de Fort-Dimanche (Haiti) 2008 (oil on panel)/Bloncourt, Gerald (b.1926)/GERALD BLONCOURT (RDA)/Private Collection/Bridgeman Images

French artist Gerald Bloncourt (1926-2018) painted *The Zombies of Fort Dimanch* (2008). Known as the Dungeon of Death, it was a prison in Haiti notorious for torture and murder during the reign of Francois Duvalier (1957-1971).

How does Bloncourt's painting suggest the original meaning of "Zombi" as a West African deity — a vital human force that has left the shell of a body but retains a human form? In "Spider the Artist," how does Okorafor call upon this mythological concept of the Zombie as well as the pop culture view of the Zombie as "the undead"?

I'll never teach music at the elementary school. It was incinerated along with many of the children who went to it. My husband was killed, too. He died thinking I was some sort of spy fraternizing with the enemy . . . or something like that. Everyone died. Except me. Just before the explosion happened, Udide ran to me. It protected me with its force field.

So I lived.

And so did the baby inside me. The baby that my body allowed to happen because of Udide's lovely soothing music. Udide tells me it is a girl. How can a robot know this? Udide and I play for her every day. I can only imagine how content she is. But what kind of world will I be bringing her into? Where only her mother and Udide stand between a flat out war between the Zombies and the human beings who created them?

Pray that Udide and I can convince man and droid to call a truce, otherwise the delta will keep rolling in blood, metal and flames. You know what else? You should also pray that these Zombies don't build themselves some fins and travel across the ocean. ■

Understanding and Interpreting

1. In the opening paragraphs, what do we learn about the world of this story? Why does the narrator refer to the people in the village as the "Pipeline People"?
2. Explain the importance of the guitar to the narrator, Eme.
3. Summarize the conflict between the government and the Pipeline People. What role do the Zombies play in this conflict?
4. Why does Eme risk going to the pipeline to play the guitar?

5. Reread Eme's statement about not getting pregnant: "It is my fault I know, but what can I do?" (par. 43). What is the reader expected to think about this line? Is it really her fault? Does Okorafor want us to think it's Eme's fault? What does this statement suggest about Eme at this point in the story?
6. How does Eme change as she begins playing for the Zombie? Why does she continue to play for it?
7. How do the Zombie and Eme communicate with each other? How is their communication similar to and different from Eme's communication with her husband, Andrew? How does her communication with the Zombie change over the course of the story and, in particular, at the very end?
8. What changes in Eme's life when the Zombie begins playing music with her? What causes these changes?
9. Why is it a significant development that Eme names the Zombie she is playing music with?
10. When Andrew discovers Eme playing music with the Zombie, he seems to react like a husband witnessing his wife's adultery. What does his reaction reveal about him and the relationship between him and Eme?
11. Why did the people from the village come to the oil spill at the school? What does this suggest about the government and its people?
12. Was it the Zombies' plan all along to bring the people to the school and kill them? Was Udide involved? What evidence from the story supports your conclusion?
13. Is the ending of the story hopeful or pessimistic about the future? How do you know?

Analyzing Language, Style, and Structure

1. **Vocabulary in Context.** Eme describes the effect of the guitar's music: "It conjured up images of my mother and father, when they were so young and full of hope, when my brothers and I were too young to marry and move away" (par. 77). What does "conjured" mean in this context?
2. **Skill Focus.** Reread paragraph 15, in which Eme describes physical abuse at the hands of her husband. What do you notice about the diction, especially the syntactical repetition? What do Okorafor's choices in this paragraph communicate about Eme?
3. **Skill Focus.** Reread paragraph 45, in which Eme describes Udide's tenth visit. Examine the syntax of this paragraph. What effect is created by the short sentences and the repeated sentence structures?
4. **Skill Focus.** Reread paragraph 73, in which Eme details how Udide "solved [her] marital problems." Examine the syntax and diction of this paragraph and explain what these choices might be intended to communicate about Eme.
5. Look back at the moment in which the robot makes first contact with Eme (pars. 18 to 26). How does Okorafor construct this scene with details of the Zombie and language choices to create suspense and potential danger?
6. After Eme begins playing with the Zombie, Okorafor includes a scene of Andrew watching television about the latest Zombie attacks. What purpose does this scene serve in the story's plot and conflicts at this particular point?
7. "Anthropomorphism" is when animals or nonhumans, like robots, are given human qualities. Look back at the story to see when Eme, through Okorafor's language choices, anthropomorphizes the Zombies. Explain how this affects your perception of them.
8. When oil is flowing from the pipeline without Zombies to stop people from taking it, Okorafor writes that "Word spread like a disease" (par. 91). What is significant about this particular choice of simile, especially given what happens when people converge on the pipeline?

9. How does Okorafor foreshadow the horrible events at the elementary school at the end of the story?
10. In the last paragraph, Okorafor switches to the pronoun "You," directly addressing the reader. What is the effect of this shift?

Topics for Composing

1. **Analysis.** Examine how Eme changes over the course of the story. How does her growth help develop a major theme of the story — one related to family, womanhood, technology, or a different topic?
2. **Analysis.** To what extent is Okorafor suggesting that Udide is more human than many of the human characters in the story? How does the story seem to define "being human"? Develop your position in response to this question with specific textual evidence from the story.
3. **Argument.** Eme and Udide meet and develop a bond through music in the story "Spider the Artist." To what extent do you think that music is a more powerful medium than language for evoking strong emotional connections, particularly across cultural divides? Develop a position, based on personal experience and observation, in response to this question.
4. **Connection.** Many movies, books, and television shows explore the idea of humans interacting with robots. Choose one and compare its presentation of that relationship with Okorafor's treatment of the relationship between Udide and Eme.
5. **Speaking and Listening.** The nickname of the robots on the pipeline is "Zombies," which is taken from the song by Fela Kuti, a renowned Nigerian musician. Listen to some of Fela Kuti's music, paying particular attention to the lyrics that express his political views. Explain why it might have been appropriate for Okorafor to use this song as an allusion.
6. **Research.** In a TED Talk, Okorafor makes the following comments about her own experience becoming a writer of what she prefers to call AfricanFuturism, meaning speculative fiction written by writers of African descent:

   > . . . not all science fiction has the same ancestral bloodline, that line being Western-rooted science fiction, which is mostly white and male. . . . So what if a Nigerian-American wrote science fiction? Growing up, I didn't read much science fiction. I couldn't relate to these stories preoccupied with xenophobia, colonization and seeing aliens as others. And I saw no reflection of anyone who looked like me in those narratives.

   Conduct research into speculative fiction written by African and African American authors. Who are some of the major writers? What are the themes or concerns they explore? What do you think are the reasons for the growing appeal and popularity of speculative fiction set in African countries and including cultural beliefs and practices? What do you think is the appeal to mainstream audiences?
7. **Research.** The spider is an important figure in the mythologies of many cultures, including the West African culture in which this story is set. Research Udide Okwanka, the mythological creature after which Eme names the Zombie she plays music with, and Anansi, another famous spider in African mythology. What do these spiders represent? How do these representations connect with the Zombies in this story?
8. **Creative Writing.** We never hear Udide speak in this story. Write a short scene in which we get its internal thoughts of the action in a part of the story, or write a dialogue between Udide and Eme.

Once the World Was Perfect

Joy Harjo

Courtesy of Joy Harjo

A member of the Muscogee (Creek) Nation, Joy Harjo (b. 1951) was named the 23rd Poet Laureate of the United States in 2019, the first time an American Indian has held that post. She has published numerous books of poetry, most recently *American Sunrise* (2019), and a memoir entitled *Crazy Brave* (2012), winner of the American Book Award. Harjo has been the recipient of numerous literary awards and grants, including a Guggenheim Fellowship. In addition to writing, Harjo plays the saxophone and is a vocalist with her own band, Poetic Justice. She has released several albums of original music, notably *Red Dreams, a Trail Beyond Tears* (2010).

Once the world was perfect, and we were happy in that world.
Then we took it for granted.
Discontent began a small rumble in the earthly mind.
Then Doubt pushed through with its spiked head.
And once Doubt ruptured the web,
All manner of demon thoughts
Jumped through —
We destroyed the world we had been given
For inspiration, for life —
Each stone of jealousy, each stone
Of fear, greed, envy, and hatred, put out the light.
No one was without a stone in his or her hand.
There we were,
Right back where we had started.
We were bumping into each other
In the dark.
And now we had no place to live, since we didn't know
How to live with each other.
Then one of the stumbling ones took pity on another
And shared a blanket.
A spark of kindness made a light.
The light made an opening in the darkness.
Everyone worked together to make a ladder.
A Wind Clan person climbed out first into the next world,
And then the other clans, the children of those clans, their children,
And their children, all the way through time —
To now, into this morning light to you. ■

BULENT KILIC/Getty Images

In 2015, more than 800,000 migrants, mostly fleeing war and persecution, crossed the Mediterranean in the hope of finding sanctuary in Europe. This photo shows Greek rescue workers aiding newly arrived refugees. **Describe how the framing of this photo makes it powerful. What emotions do you recognize in the faces of people in the foreground and background? How does this photograph relate to "Once the World Was Perfect"? What one line from the poem might you use as a caption for this scene?**

Understanding and Interpreting

1. According to the speaker, what is the result of taking the world "for granted" (l. 2)? How is that action a betrayal of the world "we had been given" (l. 8)? Is the speaker placing blame? If so, on whom?
2. What starting point is the speaker referring to in lines 13 and 14: "And there we were / Right back where we had started"?
3. The speaker tells us that "we had no place to live, since we didn't know / How to live with each other" (ll. 17–18). Explain the cause-and-effect relationship that these lines describe.
4. Who are "the stumbling ones" (l. 19)? Does that description place blame or offer sympathy?
5. "Once the World Was Perfect" opens with an image of idyllic happiness. How and why was that utopia lost?
6. Does "Once the World Was Perfect" argue that utopia is impossible and dystopia inevitable? As you develop your position, consider the last four lines of the poem. Are they optimistic? Pessimistic? Indecisive?

Analyzing Language, Style, and Structure

1. **Vocabulary in Context.** Harjo writes, "Discontent began a small rumble in the earthly mind" (l. 3). What does "earthly" mean in this context? How is Harjo's use of the word similar to or different from other uses you have encountered?
2. **Skill Focus.** The emotional diction of this poem accumulates as the poem progresses and creates images of conflict. What examples do you find of words, particularly verbs, that convey conflict? What role does sound play when you consider such emotionally charged words together?
3. How does the personification of feelings in the opening lines add to the power of the transformation that Harjo is describing?
4. How does considering imagery of light and darkness inform your interpretation of the poem?

5. The speaker uses first person plural, "we," throughout the poem until the final line, when the speaker directly addresses the reader as "you." What is the effect of these choices?
6. Harjo describes stones literally as physical objects. What metaphorical meaning does she also suggest? What is the effect of the metaphor?
7. Where is the primary shift in the poem? Is it a shift in perspective, tone, action, or more than one of these? Is it abrupt and disorienting or reassuring?
8. How does Harjo situate this poem within the violence and suffering experienced by both a specific group and people as a whole? Consider the language as well as structure of the poem in your response.
9. Harjo presents a journey starting with "Once the world," which reminds us of stories that open "Once upon a time." What is the narrative arc of this poem? Does it have a resolution?

Topics for Composing

1. **Analysis.** The title of this poem places the utopia of a perfect world firmly in the past, before "we took it for granted," which signals a loss of innocence. How did that happen? Can that perfection be regained, according to the speaker? If so, how? If not, why not? Cite specific evidence from the poem in your response.
2. **Analysis.** Some people have read this poem as a commentary on environmental degradation and destruction, a human-centered disregard for the natural world that creates a dystopia. To what extent do you agree with that interpretation? Support your position with specific reference to the poem.
3. **Argument.** Harjo writes that "we had no place to live, since we didn't know / How to live with each other" (ll. 17–18). These lines could be interpreted to mean a loss of community in the culture or society. In what ways does our society today fail to value community? Has that failure resulted in a loss of our humanity? Or are we in a time of redefining community?
4. **Connection.** Harjo writes, "We took it all for granted" in "Once the World Was Perfect." What do you take for granted in a way that makes you, your generation, or your community vulnerable?
5. **Connection.** One reviewer commented that the poems in the collection from which this poem is taken have become "a kind of manual for navigating the rapids of the 21st century." In what ways might "Once the World Was Perfect" help us navigate the rapid changes and conflicts of the contemporary world?
6. **Speaking and Listening.** In her collection, *Conflict Resolution for Holy Beings*, Harjo includes the following text before "Once the World Was Perfect": "Humans were created by mistake. Someone laughed and we came crawling out. That was the beginning of the story; we were hooked then. What a wild dilemma, how to make it to the stars, on a highway slick with fear." Working in small groups, discuss the connections you see between this text and the poem. Be prepared to discuss your view with the whole class.
7. **Research.** This poem refers to elements of traditional American Indian culture. Conduct research on elements that interest you. Explain their role in illustrating a theme of the poem.
8. **Multimodal.** Harjo often performs her poetry as song, and she is herself a musician especially influenced by jazz and blues. Working alone or with a group, put this poem to music, either reciting it with music in the background or singing it to convey an interpretation.

central text

Harrison Bergeron

Kurt Vonnegut

Jean-Christian Bourcart/Getty Images

Kurt Vonnegut (1922–2007) remains one of the most influential writers in American history. He fought in World War II's Battle of the Bulge and was captured by German troops in 1944. While a prisoner of war, Vonnegut witnessed the firebombing of Dresden, an experience that inspired his most famous novel, *Slaughterhouse Five* (1969), named for the building in which he was imprisoned. Among his other well-known books are *The Sirens of Titan* (1959), *Cat's Cradle* (1963), and *Breakfast of Champions* (1973). "Harrison Bergeron" first appeared in *Collier's* magazine before being reprinted in the short story collection *Welcome to the Monkey House* (1968).

The year was 2081, and everybody was finally equal. They weren't only equal before God and the law. They were equal every which way. Nobody was smarter than anybody else. Nobody was better looking than anybody else. Nobody was stronger or quicker than anybody else. All this equality was due to the 211th, 212th, and 213th Amendments to the Constitution, and to the unceasing vigilance of agents of the United States Handicapper General.

Some things about living still weren't quite right, though. April, for instance, still drove people crazy by not being springtime. And it was in that clammy month that the H-G men took George and Hazel Bergeron's fourteen-year-old son, Harrison, away.

It was tragic, all right, but George and Hazel couldn't think about it very hard. Hazel had a perfectly average intelligence, which meant she couldn't think about anything except in short bursts. And George, while his intelligence was way above normal, had a little mental handicap radio in his ear. He was required by law to wear it at all times. It was tuned to a government transmitter. Every twenty seconds or so, the transmitter would send out some sharp noise to keep people like George from taking unfair advantage of their brains.

George and Hazel were watching television. There were tears on Hazel's cheeks, but she'd forgotten for the moment what they were about.

On the television screen were ballerinas.

A buzzer sounded in George's head. His thoughts fled in panic, like bandits from a burglar alarm.

"That was a real pretty dance, that dance they just did," said Hazel.

"Huh?" said George.

"That dance — it was nice," said Hazel.

"Yup," said George. He tried to think a little about the ballerinas. They weren't really very good — no better than anybody else would have been, anyway. They were burdened with sash-weights and bags of birdshot, and their faces were masked, so that no one, seeing a free and graceful gesture or a pretty face, would feel like something the cat drug in. George was toying with the vague notion that maybe dancers shouldn't be handicapped. But he didn't get very far with it before another noise in his ear radio scattered his thoughts.

George winced. So did two out of the eight ballerinas.

Hazel saw him wince. Having no mental handicap herself, she had to ask George what the latest sound had been.

"Sounded like somebody hitting a milk bottle with a ball-peen hammer," said George.

"I'd think it would be real interesting, hearing all the different sounds," said Hazel, a little envious. "All the things they think up."

"Um," said George. 15

"Only, if I was Handicapper General, you know what I would do?" said Hazel. Hazel, as a matter of fact, bore a strong resemblance to the Handicapper General, a woman named Diana Moon Glampers. "If I was Diana Moon Glampers," said Hazel, "I'd have chimes on Sunday — just chimes. Kind of in honor of religion."

"I could think, if it was just chimes," said George.

"Well — maybe make 'em real loud," said Hazel. "I think I'd make a good Handicapper General."

"Good as anybody else," said George.

"Who knows better'n I do what normal is?" 20
said Hazel.

"Right," said George. He began to think glimmeringly about his abnormal son who was now in jail, about Harrison, but a twenty-one-gun salute in his head stopped that.

"Boy!" said Hazel, "that was a doozy, wasn't it?"

It was such a doozy that George was white and trembling, and tears stood on the rims of his red eyes. Two of the eight ballerinas had collapsed to the studio floor, were holding their temples.

"All of a sudden you look so tired," said Hazel. "Why don't you stretch out on the sofa, so's you can rest your handicap bag on the pillows, honeybunch." She was referring to the forty-seven pounds of birdshot in a canvas bag, which was padlocked around George's neck. "Go on and rest the bag for a little while," she said. "I don't care if you're not equal to me for a while."

George weighed the bag with his hands. "I 25
don't mind it," he said. "I don't notice it any more. It's just a part of me."

"You been so tired lately — kind of wore out," said Hazel. "If there was just some way we could make a little hole in the bottom of the bag, and just take out a few of them lead balls. Just a few."

"Two years in prison and two thousand dollars fine for every ball I took out," said George. "I don't call that a bargain."

"If you could just take a few out when you came home from work," said Hazel. "I mean — you don't compete with anybody around here. You just set around."

"If I tried to get away with it," said George, "then other people'd get away with it — and pretty soon we'd be right back to the dark ages

All Human Beings are Born Free and Equal in Dignity and Rights, 1998 (acrylic on board)/ Waddams, Ron (1920-2010)/Private Collection/Bridgeman Images

This painting by contemporary artist Ron Waddams is entitled *All Human Beings Are Born Free and Equal in Dignity and Rights*.

How does Waddams visually convey the message of the work's title? In what ways is this interpretation of equality similar to and different from Vonnegut's portrayal of equality in "Harrison Bergeron"?

again, with everybody competing against everybody else. You wouldn't like that, would you?"

"I'd hate it," said Hazel.

"There you are," said George. "The minute people start cheating on laws, what do you think happens to society?"

If Hazel hadn't been able to come up with an answer to this question, George couldn't have supplied one. A siren was going off in his head.

"Reckon it'd fall all apart," said Hazel.

"What would?" said George blankly.

"Society," said Hazel uncertainly. "Wasn't that what you just said?"

"Who knows?" said George.

The television program was suddenly interrupted for a news bulletin. It wasn't clear at first as to what the bulletin was about, since the announcer, like all announcers, had a serious speech impediment. For about half a minute, and in a state of high excitement, the announcer tried to say, "Ladies and gentlemen —"

He finally gave up, handed the bulletin to a ballerina to read.

"That's all right —" Hazel said of the announcer, "he tried. That's the big thing. He tried to do the best he could with what God gave him. He should get a nice raise for trying so hard."

"Ladies and gentlemen —" said the ballerina, reading the bulletin. She must have been extraordinarily beautiful, because the mask she wore was hideous. And it was easy to see that she was the strongest and most graceful of all the dancers, for her handicap bags were as big as those worn by two-hundred-pound men.

And she had to apologize at once for her voice, which was a very unfair voice for a woman to use. Her voice was a warm, luminous, timeless melody. "Excuse me —" she said, and she began again, making her voice absolutely uncompetitive.

"Harrison Bergeron, age fourteen," she said in a grackle squawk, "has just escaped from jail, where he was held on suspicion of plotting to overthrow the government. He is a genius and an athlete, is under-handicapped, and should be regarded as extremely dangerous."

A police photograph of Harrison Bergeron was flashed on the screen — upside down, then sideways, upside down again, then right side up. The picture showed the full length of Harrison against a background calibrated in feet and inches. He was exactly seven feet tall.

The rest of Harrison's appearance was Halloween and hardware. Nobody had ever borne heavier handicaps. He had outgrown hindrances faster than the H-G men could think them up. Instead of a little ear radio for a mental handicap, he wore a tremendous pair of earphones, and spectacles with thick wavy lenses. The spectacles were intended to make him not only half blind, but to give him whanging headaches besides.

Scrap metal was hung all over him. Ordinarily, there was a certain symmetry, a military neatness to the handicaps issued to strong people, but Harrison looked like a walking junkyard. In the race of life, Harrison carried three hundred pounds.

And to offset his good looks, the H-G men required that he wear at all times a red rubber ball for a nose, keep his eyebrows shaved off, and cover his even white teeth with black caps at snaggle-tooth random.

"If you see this boy," said the ballerina, "do not — I repeat, do not — try to reason with him."

There was the shriek of a door being torn from its hinges.

Screams and barking cries of consternation came from the television set. The photograph of Harrison Bergeron on the screen jumped again and again, as though dancing to the tune of an earthquake.

George Bergeron correctly identified the earthquake, and well he might have — for many was the time his own home had danced to the same crashing tune. "My God —" said George, "that must be Harrison!"

The realization was blasted from his mind instantly by the sound of an automobile collision in his head.

When George could open his eyes again, the photograph of Harrison was gone. A living, breathing Harrison filled the screen.

Clanking, clownish, and huge, Harrison stood in the center of the studio. The knob of the uprooted studio door was still in his hand. Ballerinas, technicians, musicians, and announcers cowered on their knees before him, expecting to die.

"I am the Emperor!" cried Harrison. "Do you hear? I am the Emperor! Everybody must do what I say at once!" He stamped his foot and the studio shook.

"Even as I stand here —" he bellowed, "crippled, hobbled, sickened — I am a greater ruler than any man who ever lived! Now watch me become what I can become!"

Harrison tore the straps of his handicap harness like wet tissue paper, tore straps guaranteed to support five thousand pounds.

Harrison's scrap-iron handicaps crashed to the floor.

Harrison thrust his thumbs under the bars of the padlock that secured his head harness. The bar snapped like celery. Harrison smashed his headphones and spectacles against the wall.

He flung away his rubber-ball nose, revealed a man that would have awed Thor, the god of thunder.

"I shall now select my Empress!" he said, looking down on the cowering people. "Let the first woman who dares rise to her feet claim her mate and her throne!"

A moment passed, and then a ballerina arose, swaying like a willow.

Harrison plucked the mental handicap from her ear, snapped off her physical handicaps with marvelous delicacy. Last of all, he removed her mask.

She was blindingly beautiful.

"Now —" said Harrison, taking her hand, "shall we show the people the meaning of the word dance? Music!" he commanded.

The musicians scrambled back into their chairs, and Harrison stripped them of their handicaps, too. "Play your best," he told them, "and I'll make you barons and dukes and earls."

The music began. It was normal at first — cheap, silly, false. But Harrison snatched two musicians from their chairs, waved them like batons as he sang the music as he wanted it played. He slammed them back into their chairs.

The music began again and was much improved.

Harrison and his Empress merely listened to the music for a while — listened gravely, as though synchronizing their heartbeats with it.

They shifted their weights to their toes.

Dancer in Front of a Window (Dancer at the Photographer's Studio) c.1874–77 (oil on canvas)/Degas, Edgar (1834–1917)/Pushkin Museum, Moscow, Russia/Bridgeman Images

Dancer in Front of a Window is one of the many images of ballet dancers that French artist Edgar Degas painted in the latter part of the 1800s. **How does Degas use color, lighting, setting, and other elements to communicate an idea about the dancer? What characteristics of the ballerina does this painting depict that are the very ones being suppressed in "Harrison Bergeron"?**

Harrison placed his big hands on the girl's tiny waist, letting her sense the weightlessness that would soon be hers.

And then, in an explosion of joy and grace, into the air they sprang!

Not only were the laws of the land abandoned, but the law of gravity and the laws of motion as well.

They reeled, whirled, swiveled, flounced, capered, gamboled, and spun.

They leaped like deer on the moon.

The studio ceiling was thirty feet high, but each leap brought the dancers nearer to it.

It became their obvious intention to kiss the ceiling.

They kissed it.

And then, neutralizing gravity with love and pure will, they remained suspended in air inches below the ceiling, and they kissed each other for a long, long time.

It was then that Diana Moon Glampers, the Handicapper General, came into the studio with a double-barreled ten-gauge shotgun. She fired twice, and the Emperor and the Empress were dead before they hit the floor.

Diana Moon Glampers loaded the gun again. She aimed at the musicians and told them they had ten seconds to get their handicaps back on.

It was then that the Bergerons' television tube burned out.

Hazel turned to comment about the black-out to George. But George had gone out into the kitchen for a can of beer.

George came back in with the beer, paused while a handicap signal shook him up. And then he sat down again. "You been crying?" he said to Hazel.

"Yup," she said.

"What about?" he said.

Illustration by Chad Lewis

Illustrator Chad Lewis created this image in response to "Harrison Bergeron."

How do elements such as background, light and shadow, and furnishings match your expectations from reading the story? What specific descriptions and dialogue from the story support this depiction of Hazel and George as they sit on their couch watching television?

"I forgot," she said. "Something real sad on television."

"What was it?" he said.

"It's all kind of mixed up in my mind," said Hazel.

"Forget sad things," said George.

"I always do," said Hazel.

"That's my girl," said George. He winced. There was the sound of a riveting gun in his head.

"Gee — I could tell that one was a doozy," said Hazel.

"You can say that again," said George.

"Gee —" said Hazel, "I could tell that one was a doozy." ■

extending beyond the text

Read the following excerpt in which John Dever, a high school teacher, argues against "exploitive inequality." The essay from which the excerpt is taken was co-winner of the Carnegie Council's 2012 award for the best essay on "ethics for a connected world."

from Exploitive Inequality

John Dever

Ironically, "Harrison Bergeron" illustrates that inequality can lead to some of civilization's most soaring achievements. Without competition and the incentive of disproportionate rewards for some, not to mention the concentration of wealth in the hands of innovators, entrepreneurs, and even government technocrats, mankind might not have reached the moon, built the internet, or developed the drugs that keep deadly diseases at bay. Some call this type of inequality "productive inequality." But the dark side of inequality continues to haunt us, despite the message of "Harrison Bergeron." Particularly troubling is the vastly unequal distribution of wealth and privilege in the early 21st century, which might be termed "exploitive inequality." One of the key differences between these two types of inequality is that in the former, individuals have some measure of equality of opportunity, and thus hope to improve their lot. At the very least, many people can share in advancements made by others, taking joy in the beauty of a virtuoso ballet performance or enjoying the material wealth and comfort that investment in infrastructure and business can produce. In the second form, individuals are locked into inferior positions by institutions such as political systems, economic systems, geography, or technological handicaps. Rather than the skilled dancers being forced to wear chains, as in "Harrison Bergeron," we see situations where those who are already weak are forced to wear chains that compound their misery while they watch "dancers" who are given performance enhancers win accolades and then blithely explain how "anyone could do this with a little hard work." Not only is this attitude a moral outrage, but in the "information age," it contributes to a growing sense that the world is a fundamentally unjust place that needs to be remade, even, some think, through the application of violence.

. . . World leaders today may or may not be able to temporarily deflect the political and economic problems that confront us. But it is unlikely that any leaders can completely eliminate warfare, terrorism, or tyranny. Likewise, few scientists think that the world can react to climate change or emergent pandemics quickly enough to avoid the

(continued)

harsh consequences headed our way. The real issue is not whether we try and prevent disaster; it so often comes in unexpected times and places that one cannot ever fully plan for disaster. Rather, the moral and ethical dilemma is how the world will deal with the suffering inevitably caused by calamity. Will the world respond to disasters in a fair and equitable way, spreading the cost of disaster among the wealthy rather than leaving the world's most vulnerable to try to survive and rebuild with the meager resources they possess? . . .

It is neither fair nor reasonable to expect the wealthy countries and individuals of the world to redistribute all their wealth to create the grey, dull, and ultimately immoral landscape into which the fictional "Harrison Bergeron" is born. It is, however, fair and reasonable to expect the wealthy to ensure that those who have benefited so much from productive inequality use the bounty that is theirs to help in caring for the real people who face catastrophe. It is also imperative that the wealthy are restrained from using their positions of power and privilege to prevent free and fair competition from those who have had the bad luck to be born into less fortunate circumstance. The wealthy should not be shackled. Neither should they be allowed to shackle others.

In what ways does Dever's use of "Harrison Bergeron" strengthen his argument about the divide between rich and poor? To what extent do you agree or disagree with his claims about inequality?

Understanding and Interpreting

1. The story begins, "The year was 2081, and everybody was finally equal." What does the word "finally" suggest about the idea of equality? How, then, do the sentences that follow conflict with your initial expectations of this world of 2081 that Vonnegut has created?
2. How does the government ensure equality in the world depicted in this story?
3. Think about the role that television and radio play in this story. What criticism of television and radio does Vonnegut seem to be making? What evidence supports your interpretation?
4. In paragraph 20, Hazel says, "Who knows better'n I do what normal is?" What does she think that "normal" means? To what extent are "normal" and "equal" the same in this story?
5. How do the characters in the story, particularly Hazel and George, seem to feel about the state of enforced equality? Pay close attention to the moment when Hazel urges George to remove his heavy handicaps for a short while. Why does he resist?
6. Why might Harrison Bergeron have declared himself "emperor"? In what ways is this defiant action both a challenge to and an affirmation of the values of the society of 2081?
7. Why do you think Vonnegut focused on ballet dancers? What might a ballerina represent that would threaten this society's vision of "equality"?
8. How do Harrison's death and his parents' reactions further contribute to — or complicate — the story's commentary on conformity and rebellion?

Analyzing Language, Style, and Structure

1. **Vocabulary in Context.** Throughout this story, Vonnegut uses the term "handicap." What does the word mean in this context? How does his use of the word compare to other uses you

have encountered? As a contemporary reader, do you find his usage bothersome or offensive? Why or why not?

2. **Skill Focus.** Reread the section describing Harrison and the ballerina dancing (pars. 70–78). How do the stylistic choices, specifically the figurative language and the diction, of this section depart from the rest of the story? What does Vonnegut achieve with this shift in style?
3. What is the narrative perspective in this story? Is the narrator critical, detached, or omniscient? How do you know? What is the effect of this choice of perspective?
4. Vonnegut alludes to mythological figures in the story, specifically the Roman goddess Diana and the Norse god Thor. What purpose do these allusions serve? Conduct brief research, if necessary.
5. The tone throughout this story could be described as ironic, but how would you characterize the irony (gentle, humorous, bitter, or something else)? What evidence from the story supports your conclusion? How does irony serve Vonnegut's purpose?
6. How does Vonnegut foreshadow the violent ending of the story?
7. How does Vonnegut use the final dialogue between George and Hazel at the end of the story to help him illustrate his ideas about the dangers of forced equality?

Topics for Composing

1. **Analysis.** Overall, what are the dangers and challenges of a government-enforced equality, according to this story?
2. **Analysis.** "Harrison Bergeron" ends in shocking violence and death. Is this an inevitable conclusion to the story? If so, why? If not, what alternative ending might achieve the same impact? Cite specifics from the story to support your position.
3. **Argument.** Equality is a worthwhile goal, but the government of 2081 clearly goes about it the wrong way. Write an argument for the most important steps that the United States government of today would need to take to guarantee equality for all of its citizens. Be sure to explain in your response what "equality" means to you.
4. **Connection.** One reading of "Harrison Bergeron" is that society has been dehumanized by technology. The television, constantly on throughout the story, is the great tranquilizer, and the radio transmitters interrupt coherent, sustained thinking. If the story were written today, how might current technologies, specifically the internet and social media, serve similar purposes?
5. **Connection.** French diplomat Alexis de Tocqueville made the following statement in his text *Democracy in America* (1835): "One also finds in the human heart a depraved taste for equality which impels the weak to want to bring the strong down to their level and which reduces men to preferring equality in servitude to inequality in freedom." Explain how this quotation connects to "Harrison Bergeron."
6. **Speaking and Listening.** Hold a class or a group discussion on the following question: To what extent does "Harrison Bergeron" depict a world that could actually exist in 2081? What current social norms and values might lead to the formation of a society like the one in the story?
7. **Research.** "Harrison Bergeron" is commonly interpreted as a critique of communism and socialism during the Cold War era of the 1950s and 1960s. Briefly research the Cold War and discuss how your research informs your understanding of the story.
8. **Creative Writing.** Imagine a sequel to "Harrison Bergeron." Write a scene or two that describes how the society depicted in this story finally collapses. What causes its collapse? What comes next?
9. **Exposition.** Vonnegut is critical of the society in the story. Attempt to define a set of basic social goals and rules that Vonnegut might accept as being more likely to support equality for all.

The Ones Who Walk Away from Omelas

Ursula K. Le Guin

Anthony Pidgeon/Redferns/Getty Images

Ursula K. Le Guin (1929-2018) is best known as a writer of fantasy and science fiction. She was, however, a prolific writer in many genres, having published seven books of poetry, twenty-two novels, over a hundred short stories, four collections of essays, and twelve books for children. Le Guin has been recognized with many literary honors, including the National Book Award, a nomination for the Pulitzer Prize, and multiple Hugo and Nebula awards for excellence in science fiction. "The Ones Who Walk Away from Omelas," which won the Hugo Award for Best Short Story of the Year in 1974, is her most famous short story.

With a clamor of bells that set the swallows to soaring, the Festival of Summer came to the city. Omelas, bright-towered by the sea. The rigging of the boats in harbor sparkled with flags. In the streets between houses with red roofs and painted walls, between old moss-grown gardens and under avenues of trees, past great parks and public buildings, processions moved. Some were decorous: old people in long stiff robes of mauve and grey, grave master workmen, quiet, merry women carrying their babies and chatting as they walked. In other streets the music beat faster, a shimmering of gong and tambourine, and the people went dancing, the procession was a dance. Children dodged in and out, their high calls rising like the swallows' crossing flights over the music and the singing. All the processions wound towards the north side of the city, where on the great water-meadow called the Green Fields boys and girls, naked in the bright air, with mud-stained feet and ankles and long, lithe arms, exercised their restive horses before the race. The horses wore no gear at all but a halter without bit. Their manes were braided with streamers of silver, gold, and green. They flared their nostrils and pranced and boasted to one another; they were vastly excited, the horse being the only animal who has adopted our ceremonies as his own. Far off to the north and west the mountains stood up half encircling Omelas on her bay. The air of morning was so clear that the snow still crowning the Eighteen Peaks burned with white-gold fire across the miles of sunlit air, under the dark blue of the sky. There was just enough wind to make the banners that marked the racecourse snap and flutter now and then. In the silence of the broad green meadows one could hear the music winding through the city streets, farther and nearer and ever approaching, a cheerful faint sweetness of the air that from time to time trembled and gathered together and broke out into the great joyous clanging of the bells. Joyous! How is one to tell about joy? How describe the citizens of Omelas?

They were not simple folk, you see, though they were happy. But we do not say the words of cheer much any more. All smiles have become archaic. Given a description such as this one tends to make certain assumptions. Given a description such as this one tends to look next for the King, mounted on a splendid stallion and surrounded by his noble knights, or perhaps in a golden litter borne by great-muscled slaves. But there was no king. They did not use swords, or keep slaves. They were not barbarians. I do not know the rules and laws of their society, but I suspect that they were singularly few. As they did without monarchy and slavery, so they also got on without the stock exchange, the advertisement, the secret police, and the bomb. Yet I repeat that these were not simple folk, not dulcet shepherds, noble savages, bland utopians. They were not less complex than us. The trouble is that we have a bad habit, encouraged by pedants and sophisticates, of considering happiness as something rather stupid. Only pain is intellectual, only evil interesting. This is the treason of the artist: a refusal to admit the banality of evil and the terrible boredom of pain. If you can't lick 'em, join 'em. If it hurts, repeat it. But to praise despair is to condemn delight, to embrace violence is to lose hold of everything else. We have almost lost hold; we can no longer describe a happy man, nor make any celebration of joy. How can I tell you about the people of Omelas? They were not naïve and happy children — though their children were, in fact, happy. They were mature, intelligent, passionate adults whose lives were not wretched. O miracle! but I wish I could describe it better. I wish I could convince you. Omelas sounds in my words like a city in a fairy tale, long ago and far away, once upon a time. Perhaps it would be best if you imagined it as your own fancy bids, assuming it will rise to the occasion, for certainly I cannot suit you all. For instance, how about technology? I think that there would be no cars or helicopters in and above the streets; this follows from the fact that the people of Omelas are happy people. Happiness is based on a just discrimination of what is necessary, what is neither necessary nor destructive, and what is destructive. In the middle category, however — that of the unnecessary but undestructive, that of comfort, luxury, exuberance, etc. — they could perfectly well have central heating, subway trains, washing machines, and all kinds of marvelous devices not yet invented here, floating light-sources, fuelless power, a cure for the common cold. Or they could have none of that: it doesn't matter. As you like it. I incline to think that people from towns up and down the coast have been coming in to Omelas during the last days before the Festival on very fast little trains and double-decked trams and that the train station of Omelas is actually the handsomest building in town, though plainer than the magnificent Farmers' Market. But even granted trains, I fear that Omelas so far strikes some of you as goody-goody. Smiles, bells, parades, horses, bleh. If so, please add an orgy. If an orgy would help, don't hesitate. Let us not, however, have temples from which issue beautiful nude priests and priestesses already half in ecstasy and ready to copulate with any man or woman, lover or stranger, who desires union with the deep godhead of the blood, although that was my first idea. But really it would be better not to have any temples in Omelas — at least, not manned temples. Religion yes, clergy no. Surely the beautiful nudes can just wander about, offering themselves like divine soufflés to the hunger of the needy and the rapture of the flesh. Let them join the processions. Let tambourines be struck above the copulations, and the glory of desire be proclaimed upon the gongs, and (a not unimportant point) let the offspring of these delightful rituals be beloved and looked after by all. One thing I know there is none of in Omelas is guilt. But what else should there be? I thought at first there were no drugs, but that is puritanical. For those who like it, the faint insistent sweetness of *drooz* may perfume the ways of the city, *drooz* which first brings a great lightness and brilliance to the mind and limbs, and then after some hours a dreamy languor, and wonderful visions at last of the very Arcana and inmost secrets of the Universe, as well as exciting the pleasure of sex beyond all belief; and it is not habit-forming. For more modest tastes I think there ought to be beer. What else, what else belongs in the joyous city? The sense of victory, surely, the celebration of courage. But as we did without clergy, let us do without soldiers. The joy built upon successful slaughter is not the right kind of joy; it will not do; it is fearful and it is trivial. A boundless and generous contentment, a magnanimous triumph felt not against some outer enemy but in communion with the finest and fairest in the souls of all men everywhere and the splendor of the world's summer: this is what swells the hearts of the people of Omelas, and the victory they celebrate is that of life. I really don't think many of them need to take *drooz*.

Most of the processions have reached the Green Fields by now. A marvelous smell of cooking goes forth from the red and blue tents of the provisioners. The faces of small children are amiably sticky; in the benign grey beard of a man a couple of crumbs of rich pastry are entangled. The youths and girls have mounted their horses and are beginning to group around the starting line of the course. An old woman, small, fat, and laughing, is passing out flowers from a basket, and tall young men wear her flowers in their shining hair. A child of nine or ten sits at the edge of the crowd, alone, playing on a wooden flute. People pause to listen, and they smile, but they do not speak to him, for he never ceases playing and never sees them, his dark eyes wholly rapt in the sweet, thin magic of the tune.

He finishes, and slowly lowers his hands holding the wooden flute.

As if that little private silence were the signal, 5
all at once a trumpet sounds from the pavillion near the starting line: imperious, melancholy, piercing. The horses rear on their slender legs, and some of them neigh in answer. Sober-faced, the young riders stroke the horses' necks and soothe them, whispering, "Quiet, quiet, there my beauty, my hope. . . ." They begin to form in rank along the starting line. The crowds along the racecourse are like a field of grass and flowers in the wind. The Festival of Summer has begun.

Do you believe? Do you accept the festival, the city, the joy? No? Then let me describe one more thing.

In a basement under one of the beautiful public buildings of Omelas, or perhaps in the cellar of one of its spacious private homes, there is a room. It has one locked door, and no window. A little light seeps in dustily between cracks in the boards, secondhand from a cobwebbed window somewhere across the cellar. In one corner of the little room a couple of mops, with stiff, clotted, foul-smelling heads, stand near a rusty bucket. The floor is dirt, a little damp to the touch, as cellar dirt usually is. The room is about three paces long and two wide: a mere broom closet or disused tool room. In the room a child is sitting. It could be a boy or a girl. It looks about six, but actually is nearly ten. It is feeble-minded. Perhaps it was born defective, or perhaps it has become imbecile through fear, malnutrition, and neglect. It picks its nose and occasionally fumbles vaguely with its toes or genitals, as it sits hunched in the corner farthest from the bucket and the two mops. It is afraid of the mops. It finds them horrible. It shuts its eyes, but it knows the mops are still standing there;

and the door is locked; and nobody will come. The door is always locked; and nobody ever comes, except that sometimes — the child has no understanding of time or interval — sometimes the door rattles terribly and opens, and a person, or several people, are there. One of them may come in and kick the child to make it stand up. The others never come close, but peer in at it with frightened, disgusted eyes. The food bowl and the water jug are hastily filled, the door is locked, the eyes disappear. The people at the door never say anything, but the child, who has not always lived in the tool room, and can remember sunlight and its mother's voice, sometimes speaks. "I will be good," it says. "Please let me out. I will be good!" They never answer. The child used to scream for help at night, and cry a good deal, but now it only makes a kind of whining, "eh-haa, eh-haa," and it speaks less and less often. It is so thin there are no calves to its legs; its belly protrudes; it lives on a half-bowl of corn meal and grease a day. It is naked. Its buttocks and thighs are a mass of festered sores, as it sits in its own excrement continually.

They all know it is there, all the people of Omelas. Some of them have come to see it, others are content merely to know it is there. They all know that it has to be there. Some of them understand why, and some do not, but they all understand that their happiness, the beauty of their city, the tenderness of their friendships, the health of their children, the wisdom of their scholars, the skill of their makers, even the abundance of their harvest and the kindly weathers of their skies, depend wholly on this child's abominable misery.

This is usually explained to children when they are between eight and twelve, whenever they seem capable of understanding; and most of those who come to see the child are young people, though often enough an adult comes, or comes back, to see the child. No matter how well the matter has been explained to them, these young spectators are always shocked and sickened at the sight. They feel disgust, which they had thought themselves superior to. They feel anger, outrage, impotence, despite all the explanations. They would like to do something for the child. But there is nothing they can do. If the child were brought up into the sunlight out of that vile place, if it were cleaned and fed and comforted, that would be a good thing, indeed; but if it were done, in that day and hour all the

paul prescott/Alamy Stock Photo

A young boy works in a garment factory in Dhaka, Bangladesh.

What tone might describe the photographer's attitude toward this scene of child labor? What does the photo include that communicates this tone? How does this image reflect some of the issues raised in "The Ones Who Walk Away from Omelas"?

prosperity and beauty and delight of Omelas would wither and be destroyed. Those are the terms. To exchange all the goodness and grace of every life in Omelas for that single, small improvement: to throw away the happiness of thousands for the chance of the happiness of one: that would be to let guilt within the walls indeed.

10 The terms are strict and absolute; there may not even be a kind word spoken to the child.

Often the young people go home in tears, or in a tearless rage, when they have seen the child and faced this terrible paradox. They may brood over it for weeks or years. But as time goes on they begin to realize that even if the child could be released, it would not get much good of its freedom: a little vague pleasure of warmth and food, no doubt, but little more. It is too degraded and imbecile to know any real joy. It has been afraid too long ever to be free of fear. Its habits are too uncouth for it to respond to humane treatment. Indeed, after so long it would probably be wretched without walls about it to protect it, and darkness for its eyes, and its own excrement to sit in. Their tears at the bitter injustice dry when they begin to perceive the terrible justice of reality and to accept it. Yet it is their tears and anger, the trying of their generosity and the acceptance of their helplessness, which are perhaps the true source of the splendor of their lives. Theirs is no vapid, irresponsible happiness. They know that

What are the differences in meaning between the two sayings: a sacrificial lamb and a scapegoat? Which term best applies to the child in the basement of Omelas? Why?

they, like the child, are not free. They know compassion. It is the existence of the child, and their knowledge of its existence, that makes possible the nobility of their architecture, the poignancy of their music, the profundity of their science. It is because of the child that they are so gentle with children. They know that if the wretched one were not there snivelling in the dark, the other one, the flute-player, could make no joyful music as the young riders line up in their beauty for the race in the sunlight of the first morning of summer.

Now do you believe in them? Are they not more credible? But there is one more thing to tell, and this is quite incredible.

At times one of the adolescent girls or boys who go to see the child does not go home to weep or rage, does not, in fact, go home at all. Sometimes also a man or woman much older falls silent for a day or two, and then leaves home. These people go out into the street, and walk down the street alone. They keep walking, and walk straight out of the city of Omelas, through the beautiful gates. They keep walking across the farmlands of Omelas. Each one goes alone, youth or girl, man or woman. Night falls; the traveler must pass down village streets, between the houses with yellow-lit windows, and on out into the darkness of the fields. Each alone, they go west or north, towards the mountains. They go on. They leave Omelas, they walk ahead into the darkness, and they do not come back. The place they go towards is a place even less imaginable to most of us than the city of happiness. I cannot describe it at all. It is possible that it does not exist. But they seem to know where they are going, the ones who walk away from Omelas. ■

extending beyond the text

In 1986, Holocaust survivor Elie Wiesel was awarded the Nobel Prize for Literature. In the following excerpt from his acceptance speech, Wiesel addresses the "neutrality" of silence.

from Nobel Prize Speech

Elie Wiesel

I remember: it happened yesterday or eternities ago. A young Jewish boy discovered the kingdom of night. I remember his bewilderment, I remember his anguish. It all happened so fast. The ghetto. The deportation. The sealed cattle car. The fiery altar upon which the history of our people and the future of mankind were meant to be sacrificed.

I remember: he asked his father[,] "Can this be true?" This is the twentieth century, not the Middle Ages. Who would allow such crimes to be committed? How could the world remain silent?

And now the boy is turning to me: "Tell me," he asks. "What have you done with my future? What have you done with your life?"

(*continued*)

And I tell him that I have tried. That I have tried to keep memory alive, that I have tried to fight those who would forget. Because if we forget, we are guilty, we are accomplices.

And then I explained to him how naïve we were, that the world did know and remained silent. And that is why I swore never to be silent whenever and wherever human beings endure suffering and humiliation. We *must* always take sides. Neutrality helps the oppressor, never the victim. Silence encourages the tormentor, never the tormented. Sometimes we must interfere. When human lives are endangered, when human dignity is in jeopardy, national borders and sensitivities become irrelevant. . . .

There is much to be done, there is much that can be done. One person, . . . one person of integrity, can make a difference, a difference of life and death. As long as one dissident is in prison, our freedom will not be true. As long as one child is hungry, our lives will be filled with anguish and shame. What all these victims need above all is to know that they are not alone; that we are not forgetting them, that when their voices are stifled we shall lend them ours, that while their freedom depends on ours, the quality of our freedom depends on theirs.

What does Wiesel suggest about the dangers of silence? What is an example of silence that Wiesel might identify in society today? How might Wiesel's argument influence your understanding of "The Ones Who Walk Away from Omelas," especially the ending?

Understanding and Interpreting

1. How would you describe the overall environment of Omelas from the opening paragraph?
2. Why do you think Le Guin emphasizes so strongly that the residents "were not simple folk," nor "barbarians," but "mature, intelligent, passionate adults" (par. 2)?
3. How do you interpret the following statement: "Happiness is based on a just discrimination of what is necessary, what is neither necessary nor destructive, and what is destructive" (par. 2)? How is this belief carried out in Omelas?
4. Why is there no guilt in Omelas (par. 2)? How is Le Guin defining the nature of guilt to make this claim?
5. Describe specific characteristics of life in Omelas. Cite concrete details about the way the inhabitants live.
6. The narrator explains that nothing can be done to alleviate the child's suffering without destroying Omelas because "[T]hose are the terms" (par. 9). Based on your interpretation of this section, who do you think established or establishes those terms?
7. What "terrible paradox" do people face when they observe the suffering child? Why do they come to accept the child's confinement as "the terrible justice of reality" (par. 11)?
8. We are told that young people turn away after they have seen the wretched child: "[It] is their tears and anger, the trying of their generosity and the acceptance of their helplessness, which

are perhaps the true source of the splendor of their lives" (par. 11). What exactly is "the true source" of their happiness or "splendor"?

9. What motivates the people who walk away from Omelas? Do they walk away in fear? In moral repugnance? As an act of resistance?

Analyzing Language, Style, and Structure

1. **Vocabulary in Context.** Le Guin writes, "The terms are strict and absolute; there may not even be a kind word spoken to the child" (par. 10). What does the word "absolute" mean in this context? Does this usage carry a positive or a negative connotation?
2. **Skill Focus.** The opening paragraph gives us a picture of an idyllic, magical place. How does the diction contribute to this effect? Cite specific words and phrases to support your response. Pay special attention to the verbs, words that describe action or a state of being.
3. **Skill Focus.** Consider the effect of stylistic choices the author makes when describing the basement and the child confined there (par. 7). How would you characterize the diction? What is the impact of repeatedly referring to the child as *it*? What is the overall tone of this paragraph?
4. What is the narrative point of view? Is the voice omniscient? Reliable? Note places where the narrator interjects speculations and opinions. What is the effect of the narrator (*we*, *I*) directly addressing the reader as *you*?
5. How does the syntax of paragraph 8 — both the structure and length of sentences — reinforce the meaning and purpose of the passage and of the overall story?
6. What if Le Guin had ended the story with paragraph 11? How would the story and its theme be different without the last two paragraphs?

Topics for Composing

1. **Analysis.** How is "happiness" defined in Omelas? How does that definition relate to this statement: "the victory they celebrate is that of life" (par. 2)? Cite specific passages to support your analysis.
2. **Analysis.** "The Ones Who Walk Away from Omelas" seems to have generated more questions than it answers. Consider these three different interpretations:
   - The story illustrates a lesson about exploitation. Low-income workers are exploited to make goods and provide services for the more affluent; the powerful group's existence requires the other group's service on its behalf.
   - The story presents a critique of utilitarianism, the doctrine that maintains an action is right if it promotes happiness for the greatest number of people.
   - "The whole of Omelas is just different pieces of one person's psychology, a person living in the busy modern world, and that person's idealism and moral sensitivity is the shriveling child locked in the basement" (*New York Times* columnist David Brooks).

   Which of these most closely matches your interpretation? Explain how your interpretation resembles one of these three. Support your response with evidence from the text.
3. **Argument.** "The Ones Who Walk Away from Omelas" might be read as an argument that life is a zero-sum game. Does a person's or group's happiness require the suffering of others? Develop your position with examples from your own observation of current events or understanding of history.

4. **Connection.** Think about a time when you decided to "walk away from Omelas." What were the circumstances? What happened? Reference this story in your response.
5. **Connection.** In an interview, Le Guin asserted, "I would not deny that utopia may always be based on atrocity — since our privileged lives are based on injustice, that would seem to indicate a possible rule." Cite at least two situations from history or current events that either support or challenge Le Guin's position about utopian ideas or societies.
6. **Connection.** In her 2014 essay, "About Anger," Le Guin writes, "Anger is a useful, perhaps indispensable tool in motivating resistance to injustice. But I think it is a weapon — a tool useful only in combat and self-defense. . . . Anger points powerfully to the denial of rights, but the exercise of rights can't live and thrive on anger. . . . Valued as an end in itself, it loses its goal. It fuels not positive activism but regression, obsession, vengeance, self-righteousness." To what extent do you agree or disagree with what Le Guin says about anger? Refer to examples from your own life or those of people you know to explain your position.
7. **Speaking and Listening.** Should people walk away from Omelas? Working with one of your classmates, discuss the choice. What are the reasons for staying? What are the reasons for leaving? Select evidence from the text of Le Guin's story to support your assessment. Briefly present the outcome of your discussion to the rest of the class. Discuss which position seems more appropriate and why.
8. **Research.** Conduct research on child labor in sweatshops where low-wage work makes various kinds of products available at a low cost, often to consumers in another country or part of the world. To what extent do you think such a situation is similar to the child in the basement in Omelas? Or is the comparison a false analogy?

The Era

Nana Kwame Adjei-Brenyah

Nana Kwame Adjei-Brenyah is from Spring Valley, New York. He received an MFA from Syracuse University. The following story is taken from his first and best-selling collection of short stories called *Friday Black* (2018).

Limitless Imprint Entertainment

"Suck one and die," says Scotty, a tall, mostly-true, kid. "I'm aggressive 'cause I think you don't know ****."

We're in HowItWas class.

"Well," Mr. Harper says, twisting his ugly body toward us, "you should shut your mouth because you're a youth-teen . . ., and I'm a full-middler who's been teaching this stuff for more years than I'm proud of."

"Understood," says Scotty.

Then Mr. Harper went back to talking about the time before the Turn, which came after the Big Quick War, which came after the Long Big War. I was thinking about going to the nurse for some pre-lunch Good. I do bad at school because sometimes I think when I should be learning.

"So after the Big Quick," Mr. Harper continues in his bored voice, "science and philosopher guys realized that people had been living wrong the whole time before. Sacrificing themselves, their efficiency, and their wants. This made a world of distrust and misfortune, which led to both Big Wars."

"Back then, everyone was a liar. It was so bad that it would not have been uncommon for people to tell Samantha," Mr. Harper points a finger at Samantha, who sits next to me, "that she was beautiful, even though, obviously, she is hideous." Samantha nods her ugly head showing she understands. Her face is squished so bad she's always looking in two different directions. Sometimes, kids who get pre-birth opti-selected come out all messed up. Samantha is "unoptimal." That's the official name for people like her, whose optimization screwed up and made their bodies horrible. I don't have any gene corrections. I wasn't optimized at all. I am not optimal or ideal. But I'm also not unoptimal, so I wasn't going to look like Samantha, which is good. It's not all good though, since no opti-select means no chance of being perfect either. I don't care. I'm true. I'm proud, still. Looking over, being nosy 'cause sometimes I do that, I see Samantha log into her class pad: *I would have been pretty/beautiful.*

"Or," and now Mr. Harper is looking at me. I can feel him thinking me into an example. "Back then a teacher might've told Ben, who we know is a dummy, that he was smart or that if he would just apply himself, he'd do better." The class laughs 'cause they think a world where I'm smart is hee-haw. In my head, I think, Mr. Harper, do you think that back then students would think you were something other than a fat, ugly skin sack? Then I say, "Mr. Harper, do you think back then students would think you were something other than a fat, ugly skin sack?"

"I don't know what they'd say about me," Mr. Harper says. "Probably that it was a great thing that I was a teacher and that my life didn't suck. Anything else, Ben?" I start to say something else about how they must have really, really liked lying to say Mr. Harper was a good teacher, but I don't say that out loud because even though I'm being true, they'd say I was being emotional and it was clouding my truth.

"I understand," I say.

Being emotional isn't prideful, and being truthful, prideful, and intelligent are the best things. I'm truthful and prideful as best as I can be. Emotional truth-clouding was the main thing that led to the Long Big War and the Big Quick War.

Together they're called the Water Wars because of how the Federation Forces lied to its own people about the how the Amalgamation had poisoned the water reservoirs. The result was catastrophic/horrific. Then, since the people of the old Federation were mad because of their own truth-clouding, they kept on warring for years and years, and the old Federation became the New Federation that stands proudly today. Later on, when the Amalgamation of Allies suspected a key reservoir had been poisoned, they asked the New Federation if they'd done it. In a stunning act of graciousness and honesty, my New Federation ancestors told the truth, said, "Yeah, we did poison that reservoir," and in doing so, saved many, many lives, which were later more honorably destroyed via nuclear. The wars going on now, Valid Storm Alpha and the True Freedom Campaign, are valid/true wars because we know we aren't being emotional fighting them.

"Class, please scroll to chapter forty-one and take it in," Mr. Harper says. The class touches their note-screens. The chapter is thirty-eight pages. I don't even try to read it. I look at some chapter videos of people doing things they used to do: a man throws three balls into the air, a woman in a dress spins on one leg. After three minutes the class is done reading the chapter. Their SpeedRead™ chips make reading easy/quick for them. SpeedRead™ lets optimized

extending beyond the text

In "The Era," the narrator, Ben, explains the value system of his society: "Being emotional isn't prideful, and being truthful, prideful, and intelligent are the best things. I'm truthful and prideful as best as I can be. Emotional truth-clouding was the main thing that led to the Long Big War and the Big Quick War." Research shows that what is called "emotional intelligence" is essential to personal well-being, job success, and effective leadership. Consider the following definition:

Emotional Intelligence

Psychology Today

Emotional intelligence refers to the ability to identify and manage one's own emotions, as well as the emotions of others.

Emotional intelligence is generally said to include at least three skills: emotional awareness, or the ability to identify and name one's own emotions; the ability to harness those emotions and apply them to tasks like thinking and problem solving; and the ability to manage emotions, which includes both regulating one's own emotions when necessary and helping others to do the same.

There is no validated psychometric test or scale for emotional intelligence as there is for "g," the general intelligence factor—and many argue that emotional intelligence is therefore not an actual construct, but a way of describing interpersonal skills that go by other names. Despite this criticism, the concept of emotional intelligence—sometimes referred to as emotional quotient or EQ—has gained wide acceptance.

An emotionally intelligent individual is both highly conscious of his or her own emotional states, even negativity—frustration, sadness, or something more subtle—and able to identify and manage them. Such people are especially tuned in to the emotions that others experience. It's understandable that a sensitivity to emotional signals both from within oneself and from one's social environment could make one a better friend, parent, leader, or romantic partner.

Why might emotional intelligence be devalued and suppressed in the futuristic world of "The Era"? To what extent do you think that our society values – or overvalues or undervalues – emotional intelligence?

people take in words faster than I can hardly see them. Since I'm a clear-born, I look while they read. I read the chapters on my own later. But even staring at the videos and pictures is better than some can do. Samantha can't hardly look at her screen. And then there's Nick and Raphy who are the class shoelookers. All they do is cry and moan. They were both optimized and still became shoelookers. Being emotional is all they are and it means they aren't good for anything. I'm glad Samantha and Nick and Raphy are in the class. Because of them I'm not bottom/last in learning and I don't wanna be overall bottom/last at all.

After they've read the chapters, Mr. Harper goes back to talking about how untrue the lives people used to live were. We've all heard about the times before the Turn, but hearing Mr. Harper, who is a teacher and, hopefully, not a complete ass/idiot, talk about all the untruths people used to think were regular makes me proud to be from now and not then. Still, I mostly only half-listen 'cause I'm thinking.

When the horn goes off and it's time for rotation, I hang back so I can speak truth to Mr. Harper.

"Mr. Harper," I say.

"What, Ben?"

"Today, during a lot of your session, I was thinking about beating you to death with a rock."

"Hmm, why?"

"I don't know. I'm not a brain-healer."

"If you don't know, how would I? Go to the nurse if you want."

I walk toward the nurse's office. On the way there I see three shoelookers together in front of one of our school's war monuments: a glass case holding a wall with the nuclear shadows of our dead enemies on it. Two of the shoelookers cry and the third paces between the other two, biting his nails. Marlene is near them. Marlene is my sibling. She is five cycles older than I am and training to be a NumbersPlusTaxes teacher.

Marlene is also the reason I was not given a pre-birth opti-selection. When Marlene was opti-selected all her personality points attached to only one personality paradigm and made her a Para-one, a person who's only about one thing. There are all kinds of paradigms, like Intelligence, Conscientiousness or Extraversion. OptiLife™ releases different personality packages people can pay for all the time. My parents are successful enough to get a standard package of seven points to spread across a few paradigms. That's what they wanted for Marlene: a balanced, successful person. But all seven of the points that could have gone toward her being a bunch of different stuff all went to one paradigm. Ambition. And that much of anything makes you a freak/the worst. But some companies like Learning Inc. like people like Marlene. She is a good worker. She is good at getting things she wants. It's all she does. Get things.

When Marlene was six and I was still a crying bag of poop, my parents had to convince her that having a younger brother would actually help her be a good teacher because she could practice information transfer on me. They also told her that I, as a clear-born, could never be in competition with her in life or their hearts, after they caught her trying to smother me with a pillow. They tell that story and laugh about it now.

After Marlene, my parents decided optimizing me wasn't worth the risk. When I was younger, she used to force me to read books for hours. She tried to make me remember things, and when I couldn't, she would slap me or pull my hair or twist my fingers. When I cheated, and she didn't notice, she would hug me and squeeze so tight I couldn't breathe. She'd kiss my forehead. When I got old enough to really be in school, and didn't do well there either, Marlene gave up on me. "No one can make a diamond out of a turd," she said.

"Got it, Marlene," I said.

"Diamonds are actually made from—"

"I don't care, Marlene."

I'm proof she isn't the perfect teacher and she hates me for it.

How I feel about Marlene: she could keel over plus die and I'd be happy plus ecstatic.

She has two cups of water in her hands. She looks at me quickly, then pours a cup of water onto the heads of each of the crying shoelookers. "Wet the Wetter" is a game people play with shoelookers sometimes. People like to trip them or pour water on the heads of criers 'cause they won't do anything back and it's humorous. The two shoelookers are crying harder than ever now but not moving. Water drip, drips from their heads and clothes.

"Ben," Marlene says, "isn't it your lunch section?"

"Yes," I say.

"This isn't the food sector."

"I understand."

"I am inquiring because your ability to move effectively through an academic space reflects upon my own person," Marlene says. I look at the empty glasses in her hands.

"I am me and you are you. I don't care what reflects on you," I say.

"You know this school will be mine in the future," she says. "Even you should understand that." Marlene always talks about how she will take the school over, how she'll be such a good teacher that everything will be hers.

"Okay. Don't talk to me," I say loudly. "Paraone," I say much more softly because she's scary. Marlene comes close to me. The shoelookers drip. The dry one paces back and forth.

"What'd you say?" Marlene asks. I don't say anything. I look at her eyes that always look the same, always searching for something to push over and stomp. Marlene backs off and lets me go. She walks away laughing at the wet shoelookers, and at me, I guess.

Shoelookers don't really do anything to anybody except make them proud to be themselves and not a no-good shoelooker. People say if you tell a lot of lies, eventually you start being all depressed and weepy like them. The shoelookers don't feel anything but sad. They feel it so much you can see it in everything they do. They're always looking at the ground.

I walk to the nurse in big steps. Everybody gets their mandatory Good in the mornings with breakfast at school, but they have extra at the nurse's. I go to the nurse because Good makes me feel good. When I have Good it's easy to be proud and truthful and to ignore the things that cloud my truth like Marlene, or being made into an example, or knowing I'll never be perfect.

The nurse, Ms. Higgins, is shaped like an old pear. Her body type is not attractive. She isn't in a union and doesn't have any kids because she's ugly and works as a school nurse. Today her face looks tired plus more tired. I prefer Ms. Higgins. Ms. Higgins looks at me, pulls her injector from her desk. There are vials of fresh Good on a shelf behind her.

It's quiet, so I talk. "Why don't you quit if you hate it here so much?" I ask as she screws the Good into the injector gun.

"Because I need credits," she says. She steps to me. I stretch my neck out for her and close my eyes. She puts one hand on one side of my neck. Her hand is warm plus strong. She stabs the injector needle in. My head feels the way an orange tastes. I open my eyes and look at her. She waits. I look at her more. She frowns, then gives me another shot. And then I feel Good.

"Bye," I say to Ms. Higgins. She sweeps the air with her fingers, like, be gone.

On the way to my usual foodbreak table, I walk past a table of shoelookers whispering to themselves. A few are crying. Shoelookers — if they're good for anything, it's crying. I laugh 'cause the Good is going full blast and it's funny how the shoelookers just don't have a chance. How they're so down that even Good doesn't help them much.

At my table Scotty, John and some others are laughing, but I don't know why, so I feel mildly frustrated.

"Oh hey, Ben, we were so worried. Please have a seat," says John. I sit down next to him. "How are you feeling today?" Scotty asks, and I feel even more frustrated 'cause I think they're using me for humor because I needed extra Good instead of just the mandatory breakfast Good. "We care," Scotty says, making his voice like a bird. The table laughs. I look around, then I relax 'cause I catch on to things, and I can see

School Nurse/English School, (20th century)/LOOK AND LEARN (A & B IMAGES)/Private Collection/Bridgeman Images

This is clearly an idealized picture of a visit to the school nurse.

What elements of the image convey comfort and care? How does the school nurse in "The Era" compare to the one in this illustration?

that they're making fun of how things used to be, and not me.

"Why, thank you for asking," I say. "I'm doing great." They laugh more, and it feels great. All the laughing at the table.

"Please take my drink because you look thirsty and 'cause you're a really smart guy," Scotty says and everybody laughs even harder. "Catch, Ben," Scotty says as he tosses a box drink. I don't move to catch it fast enough 'cause I'm thinking: I just got Good from the nurse, and already I'm feeling things other than good, which isn't how it works.

The drink box goes over my hand and smacks Leslie McStowe right in the head.

She drops her tray and her food. Leslie frowns. I laugh with everybody else. Leslie was a twin, then her brother, Jimmy, died. Jimmy was a shoelooker who cooked his head in a food zapper. Leslie is always telling lies about how great things are or how nice everyone looks and how everybody is special. Leslie McStowe is one of the least truthful people around, which is frustrating because she and I scanned high for compatibility on our genetic compatibility charts. Probably because we're both clear-borns. Leslie's parents have protested against the Opti-Life™. They don't believe in perfect. I believe in it — I just hate it.

Leslie stands there looking lost and stupid. I want more laughs, so I stand up and make my mouth a big, huge smile and say, "Sorry about that, Leslie, let me use my credit to get you a new lunch." The table goes crazy. I have a lot of credits because my mother and father are successful, which I benefit from. Leslie's face goes from *Ow* to all smiles as she looks at me. Then she says, "That's so nice of you." It's a surprising thing to hear 'cause no one has said it to me before. The table is wild/crazy, which makes me proud. I keep it going. "C'mon, let's get you another lunch," I say in a voice I imagine would have been regular a long time ago.

Leslie McStowe follows me into the food part 55 of the cafeteria. "Those people are idiots," my mother said once. She wasn't talking about the McStowes specifically, but a bunch of people that were giving away candy and flowers to strangers on the newscast. The McStowes and the people my mother called idiots are part of the Anti. They're anti-Good, anti-prebirth science, anti-progress. At my school I can count the number of anti-families on my hands. But there are a lot of them in worse parts of the Federation.

"Get whatever you want," I say, even though the guys at the table can't hear me over here.

"Thanks so much!" Leslie says. When she smiles it looks like somebody scooped holes in her cheeks 'cause of her dimples. She grabs a juice and a greens bowl and that's it. I register my credit code into the machine for her and she smiles at the lunch man who doesn't say anything. "Have a great day," I say to him because I'm still doing the thing I was doing. He stares. When we come back to the main part of the cafeteria, I'm expecting a bunch of laughs. No one at the table notices. They're eating now. I feel frustrated.

"Thanks, Benny, you're such a sweetie," Leslie says. I want to let her know the whole thing was for laughs, but then I don't, because I'm thinking. I sit down, and Leslie goes to sit with the shoelookers, though she herself is not a shoelooker. I think, maybe I should have been truthful and reminded her about the fact that her face is arranged nicely, so she would remember we scanned as compatible and might eventually be part of a workable, functional familiar unit with me.

Everybody has their own room in our housing unit. I have a mother and a father, and there's Marlene. In my room, I do physical maintenance like push-ups and leg pushes and then I read the chapters from school until I smell food. I go downstairs where my mother and father and sibling are all at a table chewing.

"What are you looking at me for?" I ask. 60

"I received a message saying you've been taking extra Good," my father says.

I take a bowl from the washer and I push the button that makes the cooker front slide open. I put a spoon in. I feel the hot inside the box. I fill the bowl with meat and grains from the cooker. "Sometimes I need it. And why aren't you being truthful?" I say. "Marlene told you that." Marlene, since she's training at the school, knows stuff about me and what I do there.

"Don't accuse anyone of not being truthful," my mother says.

"I obscured the full truth because you have a tendency to respond emotionally, like some kind of neck-crane," says my father. Standing and staring at them, I dive my spoon into my bowl. I take a bite and chew. The grains and meat taste like grains and meat.

"I only pay attention because people still 65 associate me with you," Marlene says. "Once I'm certified I won't be interested. Until then you are still a periphery reflection of my person."

Sometimes I imagine Marlene drowning in a tank of clear water.

"Okay, I've listened to you and now I'm frustrated," I say.

"We are also frustrated because people still associate you with us, even though we are our own successful individuals," my mother says.

"Not to mention the fact that your clear-birth was a mistake and you are only alive due to your mother's irrationality brought about by maternity," my father says. My mother looks at me, then my father, and then nods her head. "It's true, it's true," she says.

I drop my food on the floor and walk away. 70 The bowl doesn't break. The food splats on the floor.

"Have some pride, Ben," my father says.

"You always say the same things. It's frustrating," I say from the hall so they can't see me. I squeeze my eyes shut so no water can come from them. I try to have some pride. "I know I was a mistake already, so I don't know why you mention it so often."

"It's because the fact that we didn't select genes during your pre-birth period almost certainly correlates to your being so slow and disappointing," my father calls, "and we're frustrated with you and tangentially ourselves as a result."

"I know all that," I say. I go to the bathroom. I grab the house injector from behind the mirror. I go to grab a vial of Good. There is none. I spin around like it will be in the air somewhere. Then I take a breath and close my eyes and close the mirror. I open it again slowly, hoping it will be different. It isn't. There is an injector, but no Good. I want to scream but don't. Instead I go to my room. I sit in the bed.

I try to sleep. All I do is sweat and feel hurt all around my body and in my head. It gets dark. By then I feel like death/poop. Deep into the night my mother comes into the room.

"You've been screaming," she says.

"I don't care if I've been disturbing you. I'm frustrated you hid our Good," I say from under the covers. I hear her step to me, she rips the covers away. She is frowning in the dark. She puts a hand on my face and turns it. Then she uses the injector in her hand and stabs it into my neck. She gives me three shots and the Good makes my teeth rattle. My mother's hand sits on my head for a while. Then she turns and leaves. And then everything feels so right and so fine that I fall asleep smiling.

At school I get my usual morning Good. And in HowItWas class we talk about before, again.

"So even though people said all these things and acted like everyone else was important there were still wars and hurting, which proves it was a time of lies," Mr. Harper says.

"But yesterday you said some frog crap about how some things were better and how it was easier in the old days," Scotty says.

"This is why you'll be a mid-level tasker at best," Mr. Harper says. "I said some people still believe that the old way was better. Some people still live the old way because they prefer it."

"I think those people are assjerks," Scotty says.

"No one cares what you think," Mr. Harper says, "though I agree with you."

"H-How dow know?" says Samantha, in her broken, deep voice. She is normally quiet. "Mahbe okay."

"Shut up, screw-face," Scotty says. He takes off his shoe and throws it at Samantha. It hits her and makes a thunk sound and then bounces off her head onto my desk. The class laughs. Mr. Harper laughs. Samantha tries to laugh. I stare at the shoe.

"See, here we have a teachable moment," Mr. Harper says. "Back before the turn, Scotty might not have been honest about how he expressed himself, and Samantha would go on thinking he thought what she said was smart."

I go straight to Ms. Higgins after class. When I get there she looks at me like I'm broken.

"You've been put on a Good restriction by your legal guardians," she says. I can see the vials behind her. I can almost feel them. Almost, but definitely not.

"I only need two," I say. "Even one shot, please."

"A formal restriction has —"

"I know," I yell. I turn around and leave.

The floors of the school are tan and white. I walk to lunch. It is hard to keep my head up 'cause I don't feel proud or Good at all.

When I get to the cafeteria I hear someone say, "Happy birthday." When I look up I see Leslie McStowe looking at me. She's sitting at a table with a bunch of sorry shoelookers. Then she stands and wraps her arms around me. "Happy birthday," she says again. I used to hide in my room and try to remember everything from whatever Marlene had given me to read so that I could get a hug like that after her tests. But this is the first one I've had in many cycles. I'm standing there thinking of how Leslie McStowe is strong plus soft. I can feel her breathing on my neck a little.

"It's your birthday," Leslie says. She is smiling at me. Her eyes seem excited/ electronic.

"Oh," I say. I have seen fifteen cycles now.

"We scanned compatible, you know. It's in your charts," she says quickly, answering the question I was thinking.

"Oh."

"If you want, my parents would love to have you over to celebrate," she looks down at the floor, not like a shoelooker, but like she's ashamed. "They like celebrating things."

"I don't celebrate like that, or associate with you. Also, everyone thinks your parents are strange," I say.

"I know, but it would make us all really happy," she says. This, I realize, is exactly, what Mr. Harper was speaking of. Leslie McStowe wants me to make her happy, for no reason. I look at her and am lost in something that doesn't feel like pride or intellect or what truth should feel like. "Please," she says and hands me a paper that is an invitation for later in the day. I take the invitation and then I walk to the table where I normally sit with the people I usually associate with.

At home my familiar unit says things to me:

"Hello," my father says.

"You seem agitated," my mother says.

"You are now on the Good restriction list," Marlene says.

I don't say anything to anyone. Without any Good in me everything looks like a different kind of bad. And all I can imagine are the worst things about everyone and everything. And I can't tell if my stomach is aching or whether I'm imagining how bad a really bad stomachache might be if I had one right then. Either way it hurts. Ideas that scare me run around my head. I go to the bathroom. I pull the mirror back. There is an injector, but there is still no Good. None. Only a shaver and fluoride paste and a small medical kit. I look in the medical kit, just in case. No Good. I take the empty injector and bring it to my neck. I hit the trigger and stab and hope maybe I'll get something. I hit the trigger again. Again. I close the mirror, and a small crack appears in a corner of the glass. I go outside. I'm afraid of how bad I feel. No one asks where I am going.

The McStowes live in a complex on the outer part of the section. In our section the poor people all live on the outer parts so those of us on the inner parts don't have to come in contact with them all the time. They live cramped together in small spaces that are cheaper and as a result not as nice, in looks or housing capabilities: keeping warm/dry, being absent of animals, etc.

I haven't had any Good since breakfast. I can feel the no-Good pressing on me. Pulling me down. It is getting dark outside. Out at the edge of the section, there are so many shoelookers slowly moving through the walk-streets. They've been abandoned by the people who used to be their families. That's what happens to most shoelookers. There are a bunch of soon-deads and there are a few kid-youths and also every other age there is. Once in a while, one of the shoelookers will snap their heads up and their eyes will be wild like they just remembered something important. Then, after a few seconds of wild looking and head turning, they'll drop their heads back down.

It's worse than frustrating. Being around all those downed heads makes me want to close my eyes forever. I follow the gridwalks toward where the McStowes live. I focus on the ground because it doesn't make me want to disappear as much. The ground on the way there is grey and grey and grey. My shoes are black and grey. Good in its vial is clean/clear.

Long fingernails bite my shoulders. I look up and see a shoelooker my mother's age. Her hands are near my neck. She screams, "Where are we going?" and shakes me like she's trying to get me to wake up. Her voice is screechy like she's been yelling for a long time. I shove her, then I run because I'm very disturbed.

I make sure I'm looking up as I run. I'm sweaty when I reach Leslie's housing complex. Inside it is not nice. A bunch of cats and a raccoon race and fight in the lobby area. The walls are dirty and the paint is peeling. I walk up a stairwell that smells like a toilet. When I find the McStowe door I knock on it. I can hear people rustling inside. I imagine myself falling into a jar of needles over and over again. I haven't had any Good. The door opens. It's bright inside.

Woman with "people's gas mask" and pram in front of the Gloria Palast in Berlin during an air raid, c.1944 (b/w photo)/German Photographer, (20th century)/DEUTSCHES HISTORISCHES MUSEUM/Deutsches Historisches Museum, Berlin, Germany/Bridgeman Images

This photograph was taken in Berlin, Germany, during World War II.

Describe what strikes you most about this image. What circumstances and events in "The Era" that seem like pure fiction in many ways could come to pass, given such threats as war, pandemic, and climate change?

"Happy birthday" comes out of several mouths. The voices together make my heart beat harder.

"Hello," I say.

"Come in, come in," says Leslie. There's a tall man with a skinny neck and grey hair. He wears an ugly shirt with bright flowers on it.

"Great to see you, really great to see you," Father McStowe says. I'm wondering if in the McStowe's home people say everything twice.

The food sector is a small space to the left. It smells like something good. In the main sector are Leslie McStowe, her mother, her father, and three fidgeting shoelookers about my age. They have the usual sad/dirty look. They might be from the school. I don't know. I don't look at shoelookers.

"Come in," Mother McStowe says, even though I'm already inside. She is a thin woman with a short haircut. There are folds of loose skin under her neck. I come in further. Everyone is looking at me.

"How was your walk over?" Leslie says. Her face is smiling.

"Bad," I say. "This part of the section is worse than where my unit lives."

"Well, I'm sorry to hear that," Father McStowe says. "Let's have some cake now that the man of the hour is here in one piece!" Man of the hour. He is talking about me.

There are two beds in the main section. There are sheets and plates on one bed so it can be a table. There are pillows arranged on the other to make it a place to sit.

"I've never had cake," I say. I haven't. It isn't something proud people eat. It makes people fat, my mother says, just like the candy the Antis hand out in the streets.

"Well, isn't that a shame," Mother McStowe says, even though she is smiling. She has dimples like her daughter. "In this house we eat cake every chance we get, seems like," she laughs. And so does Father McStowe. Leslie laughs. Even one of the three shoelookers laughs a little. I can tell by how the shoelooker's shoulders jump while she stares at the floor.

"You shouldn't feel sorry for me," I say. "My housing unit is much nicer than this." It gets quiet, then the house starts laughing some more. Even though I don't know exactly why they are laughing, I'm not too frustrated.

"This one!" says Father McStowe. "A true comedian."

"What's a true comedian?" I ask.

"Joke-tellers, humor-makers," says Father McStowe. "Back in the old world, it was a life profession to make laughter. One of many interesting old-world lives."

"I don't believe that," I say, 'cause I don't.

"That's okay," says Mother McStowe, still giggling. "Let's eat some cake."

"Sounds sweet to me," says Father McStowe. He laughs and so does his family.

We move over to the table/bed. The main sector of the housing unit has walls covered in sheets of paper with too many colors on them.

"Cake," Mother McStowe says as she walks to the food sector, "was a delicacy in the old world, used to celebrate events like union-making, the lunar cycle, battle-victory and, of course, birthdays." Mother McStowe looks for some utensil in the food sector. I look at Father McStowe and ask, "Is that the food sector your son killed himself in?" There's a clang/clack sound from Mother McStowe dropping something on the floor.

Father McStowe looks at me. He touches my shoulder. His hand is large/heavy. "You know something," he speaks low so only I can hear him, "one of the things we like to do in this home is be careful of what we say. What you said didn't have to be said. And now you've hurt my wife. She'll be fine, but—"

"Lying for others is what caused the Big Quick and the Long Big," I say.

"Maybe. Or maybe it was something else. I'm talking about thinking about the other person, ya know?" Father McStowe whispers to me. "I'm sure you have a lot of ideas about this, but it's something we try around here." He smiles and touches my shoulder again. "Let's eat some cake," he says in a big voice, a voice for everybody.

I haven't had any Good since breakfast. And here I am. In Leslie McStowe's house. Because she invited me and because she makes me think of things that aren't Marlene or optimization or being forever dumb/slow.

Mother McStowe comes back. She smiles at me as she hands me a knife big enough to cut a bunch of things. "It was tradition for birthday boys to cut the cake after the singing of the traditional birthday hymn," Mother McStowe says. She looks around quickly with wide eyes, then begins to sing. The rest of her family joins in. The shoelookers look down and up, and down and up, trying to decide what to be, and even they mumble along with the McStowes.

Happy birthday to ya, happy birthday to ya
Happy birthday, happy birthday to ya
Happy birthday, it's your day yeah
Happy birthday to ya, happy birthday yeah!

When they finish, Mother McStowe tells me, with her eyes, to cut the cake. The knife cuts through easily. "I forgot, traditionally, you are supposed to make a wish before you cut into the cake," says Mother McStowe. "But after is fine, I suppose. You can wish for anything."

Of course, I wish for Good. I put one more cut into the cake, then Mother McStowe takes the knife for me, and I see she cuts into the middle of it instead of off the side like I did. She cuts pieces for everybody. Father McStowe and Leslie and I sit on the bed made for sitting. The

The Birthday Party, 1887 (oil on canvas)/Sargent, John Singer (1856–1925)/ MINNEAPOLIS INSTITUTE OF ART/Minneapolis Institute of Arts, MN, USA/Bridgeman Images

This painting by John Singer Sargent is called *The Birthday Party* (1887). **What is the atmosphere in this scene? What elements convey that atmosphere? How is Ben's first experience with the McStowes and birthday cake similar to or different from the party in this painting?**

rest stand and chew. The cake is the sweetest thing I've ever eaten. "Do you like it?"

"It's good 'cause it's so sweet," I say. It makes my tongue and teeth feel more alive.

"And it's an authentic old-time recipe you can't get anywhere else," Mother McStowe says.

When half my cake is gone I turn to Father McStowe. "Do you have any extra Good?" I ask somewhat discretely, since taking too much Good is not a proud thing. Father McStowe looks at me with cheeks full of cake.

"We like to think of our home as a throwback to an era before industrial Good," he says. He swallows, then puts a hand on my shoulder then removes it.

"I need Good."

"You're thinking now, this," Father McStowe does something with his hands, "is then. Think of our home as a place where no one needs industrial Good."

"Is it because you're poor that you don't have any Good?" I ask. Father McStowe laughs so hard he spits wet cake onto the floor. Quickly, Mother McStowe cleans it up. He looks to his daughter and says, "This one is funny. A real comedian."

"I'm not telling jokes," I say.

"That's why you're so good," Father McStowe says. "When I want to be funny, I usually tell an old-time joke, like this one," he clears his throat. "Have you heard the one about the deaf man?"

"What?"

"That's what he said!" Father McStowe says. "If you would have said 'no' I would have said 'neither has he.' Get it?" He touches me on the shoulder and chuckles. Leslie and the shoelookers giggle with him. "Truly, we like to think we, as you've seen, have created a space that is really a throwback to a time before the Big Quick or even the Long Big. My family and I recreate that decent era for people who might want, or need it."

"I'm frustrated because you don't have any Good. I'm leaving," I say.

"What we — hey Linda, could you grab some of our literature — offer here is a way to feel and be happy without Good. We can feel good just by being together and you can join us a few times a week depending on the package that works for you.” Leslie is smiling and the shoelookers are eating cake, switching between weak smiles and lost frowns.

“I’m going home,” I say.

“Take some literature,” he says. With her face smiling, Mother McStowe hands me a pamphlet. On it are smiling faces and words and different prices. Different amounts of time are trailed by different credit values on each row of information.

“There are lots of choices,” Leslie says.

“Think it over. If any package feels right for you, let Leslie know. We recommend starting off with at least three days a week here with us in The Era. You’ll feel brand-new. Just look at these guests,” Mother McStowe points to the shoelookers who are munching cake still. They look at me and they all try to smile.

160 I get up. “I’m frustrated because I thought this was something different,” I yell. I haven’t had any Good. I feel the pamphlet crushing in my fist. On the front it says Life in the Era in curly letters. “Also your daughter doesn’t frustrate me, so that’s why I came.”

“Look over the literature,” Father McStowe says when I’m at the door.

“I haven’t had any Good since the morning, that’s why I’m emotional,” I scream before I slam the door and run back to my own housing unit. I get tired, so I have to walk. Plus there is no Good at my housing unit anyways. The night is black. The gridwalk is grey and grey and grey. There’s some sweet left on my teeth and, even after the sweet is gone, thinking about it helps keep me walking.

At breakfast the next day the Good makes me feel better for a few minutes, but not even through to the last sip of my milk. My neck aches. My brain throbs. The floor of the school is mostly tan and the patterns against the tan are at least easy to drown in. In Mr. Harper’s class we are talking about the Long Big and how it led to the Big Quick, like always. I think of cake during class.

At lunch I go to sit with my usuals. At the table Scotty says, “Back off, we don’t want to associate with a shoelooker like you.” Somebody else says, “Go sit with the downs over there.” I just stand there, looking at the ground, because I’m not a shoelooker, even though, with my head down, and the feeling in my head, and the tears almost in my eyes, I probably look like one.

165 I try to be proud and look up. I feel a boom and a hurt under my eye. I fall. The table laughs. I see that John has punched me to say I am officially not welcome. My face hurts. I want to lie there, but I get up because I’m pulled up. It is Leslie McStowe that pulls me. She is frowning. When I’m standing, I pick my head up and she walks with me to the nurse’s office. “It’s okay,” Leslie says, lying like they used to, like she does. And I am happy to hear her do it.

In the nurse’s office Ms. Higgins stares at the two of us. Samantha is sitting in a chair. Samantha is not healthy, ever, but she looks at me like, welcome, and does her happier moaning sound. Ms. Higgins pulls a cold pack out of a cold box. I put the cold over my eye. It makes the hurt less. I sit in a chair next to Samantha. Leslie sits in one next to me.

“He got hit,” Leslie says.

“Yah ohkay?” Samantha groans.

“You got hit,” Ms. Higgins says.

170 “Yes,” I say. Ms. Higgins says nothing. Then she stands up and opens the drawer that holds her injector. Hearing the drawer slide open makes my skin tingle. She turns her back to us so she can feed some fresh new Good into the injector.

Then, at the office door, I see my sibling. “I heard,” says Marlene, “you’ve become a real shoelooker.” Leslie touches my not-cold hand. Her fingers are warm on mine. “Ben is on a Good restriction, Higgins.” With one eye I look at

Leslie McStowe, then Samantha, and then Marlene, and then Ms. Higgins. Ms. Higgins screws a vial of Good into the injector. "I'll report you," Marlene says.

Ms. Higgins continues screwing the vial into the injector and does not look at Marlene. Marlene stands at the office door. She's holding a cup of water. All I want is Good. Ms. Higgins looks at me with her loaded injector. Leslie squeezes my hand. I look at Ms. Higgins. I shake my head. Ms. Higgins drops her injector on her desk then sits down in her chair. She turns her head and looks at the wall. We are quiet. It's quiet for a long time. Leslie looks at me. She wants to smile, but she can't, so with my head down, one hand warm, one hand cold, one eye bruising and the other looking at her I say, "Have you heard the one about the deaf man?" ■

Understanding and Interpreting

1. Reread paragraphs 11–12 in which Ben summarizes the causes and effects of the Water Wars. According to the textbooks and the school, what is the main lesson that Ben and his society are supposed to draw from those wars?
2. Summarize the social and educational hierarchy represented in this world. Who is on top, on the bottom, and in the middle? Be sure to include the many of types of people identified in the story, such as clear-born, optimized, shoelookers, unoptimal, and so on.
3. In Mr. Harper's class, what do we learn about Ben as a character? How is he similar to and different from the others in his class? What seems to motivate him in the first section of the story?
4. Explain the conflict between Ben and his sibling, Marlene. Why was Ben not optimized?
5. After Ben's first confrontation with Marlene, he thinks about the shoelookers (par. 41). According to Ben, what causes people to become shoelookers? What do his observations about them reveal about Ben?
6. Ben tries to live by his society's desire for telling the truth. When does this effort work out well for Ben? When does it work out poorly for him?
7. Reread the scene at the dinner table with Ben's family (pars. 59 to 73). What is their relationship like? How does Ben feel about it? How do you know?
8. In the second scene of HowItWas class (pars. 78 to 86), Samantha is bullied by Scotty for asking a question about those who still live the old way. What is the lesson that Mr. Harper wants the class to draw from the exchange? Does Ben agree with Mr. Harper's conclusions? How do you know?
9. Reread the paragraphs in which Leslie invites Ben to her house to celebrate his birthday (pars. 98 to 100). Why does Ben feel conflicted?
10. How does being deprived of Good affect Ben? Consider both outward and inward changes, positive and negative changes.
11. How does Ben respond to Leslie's family? What do his reactions reveal about his changing character and attitude toward his world? Be sure to focus on the exchange between Ben and the family regarding the death of their son.
12. What is humor like in this world? What do Father McStowe, Ben, Scotty, and others find funny? How do their notions of humor differ?
13. What are we supposed to conclude when we learn that the McStowes are actually selling their family time in what they call "The Era"?

14. How has Ben changed his perspective about truth and emotion by the end of the story? Look specifically at his interactions with Leslie when she picks him up after he is hit.
15. Why does Ben decline the offer of Good at the end of the story? What does the joke he makes reveal about him?

Analyzing Language, Style, and Structure

1. **Vocabulary in Context.** What does the word "true" mean in the context of "The Era"? How is the meaning here similar to or different from other meanings you have encountered?
2. **Skill Focus.** There are a number of times in this story that Adjei-Brenyah uses word pairs, such as pretty/beautiful (par. 7), valid/true (par. 12), freak/the worst (par. 23) when sharing Ben's unspoken thoughts. Choose two or more of these word pairs and explain what they are intended to communicate about Ben and the world he lives in.
3. Look back at the first scene in this story — in Mr. Harper's classroom — and explain how Adjei-Brenyah's language choices communicate aspects of this fictional world and make his reader feel like a part of it from the beginning.
4. Everybody in the story "gets their mandatory Good." What is Good literally in the story? What effects does it have on Ben? How does it act as a metaphor for the world of the story?
5. Reread the scene at the cafeteria when Scotty hits Leslie McStowe in the head with a box drink. Ben thinks that he is part of the joke by being nice to Leslie using words and phrases that he says "would have been regular a long time ago" (par. 54). How does Adjei-Brenyah develop this scene to reveal that Ben is actually being laughed at, and at the same time that he likes what he is doing with Leslie?
6. Several times in the story, Ben says that he doesn't follow something that someone says or does "because I'm thinking." What does his use of this phrase reveal about him and his environment?
7. Characters in the story use terms such as "physical maintenance," "food sector," and "housing unit" to refer to exercise, the cafeteria, and a home. How would you describe these terms? What does Adjei-Brenyah accomplish by using them?
8. Look closely back at some of Adjei-Brenyah's language choices and descriptions and explain how he shows that Ben has changed at the end of the story. Though Ben himself denies it, has he become a shoelooker? Does the story suggest that's a bad thing to become? Explain your answer.
9. What is the tone of the ending? What language and stylistic choices reveal this tone?

Topics for Composing

1. **Analysis.** Adjei-Brenyah creates a world that aims to be a utopia in response to the wars of the past. Explain what this world expects of its citizens in terms of truth and emotion. How does this world try to meet these expectations? How does Adjei-Brenyah reveal that this world is a dystopia?
2. **Analysis.** Both Ben's parents and the McStowes are somewhat minor characters, yet their choices set the action of the story in motion. Are they depicted as misguided, misinformed, evil, neutral, or something else? Develop a position on whether these are positive or negative characters. Explain how they contribute to the overall theme(s) of Adjei-Brenyah's story.
3. **Argument.** A prevailing idea of this world is that you should never lie. While most people would agree that lying is bad, are there times when it is okay to lie? Write an argument in which you propose a set of rules governing the appropriate and inappropriate scenarios for lying.

4. **Argument.** One reviewer of *Friday Black*, the collection in which "The Era" appears, wrote that "like all great dystopian fiction — [this collection] is bleakly futuristic only on its surface. At its center, each story — sharp as a knife — points to right now." Using evidence from the story, support the position that the ideas found in "The Era" are relevant to our world today.
5. **Connection.** While the world of this story differs from our own in some ways, there are many similarities. Explain how an element of Ben's life at school or with his family and friends is similar to something you have experienced.
6. **Speaking and Listening.** Write and present a dialogue between Ben and someone with whom he never actually interacts. It could be a friend, a school administrator, a police officer, or a government official. Try to keep Ben's voice consistent with his voice in the story by mimicking his word choice and tone.
7. **Multimodal.** Create the front page of a newspaper or a page of a news website that might be found in the world of this story. Consider what news would be reported, what ads might appear, and what images would be seen.
8. **Creative Writing.** Rewrite a portion of this story from the perspective of a character who is not "true" like Ben. For example, you could rewrite a scene from the perspective of someone like Marlene, who is "optimized." Afterward, reflect on what is different about the scene when it is told from a different perspective.
9. **Exposition.** Imagine that you are Mr. Harper from the story. Write an explanation of "HowItWas" in the period before the present day.

from Herland

Charlotte Perkins Gilman

Historic Images/Alamy

Charlotte Perkins Gilman (1860-1935) came from a long line of feminists and suffragists. She was the grandniece of Harriet Beecher Stowe, the author of *Uncle Tom's Cabin*. Gilman grew up in Connecticut, was educated mostly at home, and briefly attended the Rhode Island School of Design. Her short story "The Yellow Wallpaper" (1892), an indictment of the "rest cure" prescribed for the postpartum depression she experienced after the birth of her daughter, is her best-known work. Gilman promoted social reforms and change in cultural identity to make women full economic partners with men by allowing them to work outside the home, a perspective she argued in her book *Women and Economics* (1898).

KEY CONTEXT In the novella *Herland* (1915), three male explorers discover an isolated civilization populated entirely by women. In this utopian society, women reproduce without men (parthenogenesis), share all labor and child care equally, and live peacefully and communally. *Herland* was first published in monthly installments in the *Forerunner*, a feminist magazine that Gilman edited and wrote from 1909 to 1916. The excerpts that follow begin when Van (the narrator), Terry, and Jeff, the three men who have heard about an isolated place where women rule, have traveled as far as guides would take them. The remainder of the excerpts follow their growing familiarity with the all-female culture and, finally, their departure from Herland.

from Chapter 1

. . . "What are you going to do with it when you do find it — if you do?" Jeff asked mildly.

Jeff was a tender soul. I think he thought that country — if there was one — was just blossoming with roses and babies and canaries and tidies, and all that sort of thing.

And Terry, in his secret heart, had visions of a sort of sublimated summer resort — just Girls and Girls and Girls—and that he was going to be — well, Terry was popular among women even when there were other men around, and it's not to be wondered at that he had pleasant dreams of what might happen. I could see it in his eyes as he lay there, looking at the long blue rollers slipping by, and fingering that impressive mustache of his.

But I thought — then — that I could form a far clearer idea of what was before us than either of them.

"You're all off, boys," I insisted. "If there is such a place — and there does seem some foundation for believing it — you'll find it's built on a sort of matriarchal principle, that's all. The men have a separate cult of their own, less socially developed than the women, and make them an annual visit — a sort of wedding call. This is a condition known to have existed — here's just a survival. They've got some peculiarly isolated valley or tableland up there, and their primeval customs have survived. That's all there is to it."

"How about the boys?" Jeff asked.

"Oh, the men take them away as soon as they are five or six, you see."

"And how about this danger theory all our guides were so sure of?"

"Danger enough, Terry, and we'll have to be mighty careful. Women of that stage of culture are quite able to defend themselves and have no welcome for unseasonable visitors."

We talked and talked.

And with all my airs of sociological superiority I was no nearer than any of them.

It was funny though, in the light of what we did find, those extremely clear ideas of ours as to what a country of women would be like. It was no use to tell ourselves and one another that all this was idle speculation. We were idle and we did speculate, on the ocean voyage and the river voyage, too.

"Admitting the improbability," we'd begin solemnly, and then launch out again.

"They would fight among themselves," Terry insisted. "Women always do. We mustn't look to find any sort of order and organization."

"You're dead wrong," Jeff told him. "It will be like a nunnery under an abbess—a peaceful, harmonious sisterhood."

I snorted derision at this idea.

"Nuns, indeed! Your peaceful sisterhoods were all celibate, Jeff, and under vows of obedience. These are just women, and mothers, and where there's motherhood you don't find sisterhood—not much."

"No, sir—they'll scrap," agreed Terry. "Also we mustn't look for inventions and progress; it'll be awfully primitive."

"How about that cloth mill?" Jeff suggested.

"Oh, cloth! Women have always been spinsters. But there they stop — you'll see."

We joked Terry about his modest impression that he would be warmly received, but he held his ground.

"You'll see," he insisted. "I'll get solid with them all — and play one bunch against another. I'll get myself elected king in no time — whew! Solomon will have to take a back seat!"

"Where do we come in on that deal?" I demanded. "Aren't we Viziers[1] or anything?"

"Couldn't risk it," he asserted solemnly. "You might start a revolution — probably

[1]A reference to high-ranking government officials in Muslim nations. —Eds.

would. No, you'll have to be beheaded, or bowstrung — or whatever the popular method of execution is."

"You'd have to do it yourself, remember," grinned Jeff. "No husky black slaves and mamelukes[2]! And there'd be two of us and only one of you — eh, Van?"

Jeff's ideas and Terry's were so far apart that sometimes it was all I could do to keep the peace between them. Jeff idealized women in the best Southern style. He was full of chivalry and sentiment, and all that. And he was a good boy; he lived up to his ideals.

You might say Terry did, too, if you can call his views about women anything so polite as ideals. I always liked Terry. He was a man's man, very much so, generous and brave and clever; but I don't think any of us in college days was quite pleased to have him with our sisters. We weren't very stringent, heavens no! But Terry was "the limit." Later on — why, of course a man's life is his own, we held, and asked no questions.

But barring a possible exception in favor of a not impossible wife, or of his mother, or, of course, the fair relatives of his friends, Terry's idea seemed to be that pretty women were just so much game and homely ones not worth considering.

It was really unpleasant sometimes to see the notions he had.

But I got out of patience with Jeff, too. He had such rose-colored halos on his womenfolks. I held a middle ground, highly scientific, of course, and used to argue learnedly about the physiological limitations of the sex.

We were not in the least "advanced" on the woman question, any of us, then.

So we joked and disputed and speculated, and after an interminable journey, we got to our old camping place at last.

[2]Slaves of Muslim origin. –Eds

It was not hard to find the river, just poking along that side till we came to it, and it was navigable as far as the lake.

When we reached that and slid out on its broad glistening bosom, with that high gray promontory running out toward us, and the straight white fall clearly visible, it began to be really exciting.

There was some talk, even then, of skirting the rock wall and seeking a possible footway up, but the marshy jungle made that method look not only difficult but dangerous.

Terry dismissed the plan sharply.

The first book edition of *Herland* was published in 1979 by Pantheon Books.

What ideas about gender might this cover be trying to communicate? As you read, consider how this cover image reflects ideas that you encounter in this excerpt. Do you find the cover provocative? Disappointing? Confusing? Why?

"Nonsense, fellows! We've decided that. It might take months — we haven't got the provisions. No, sir — we've got to take our chances. If we get back safe — all right. If we don't, why, we're not the first explorers to get lost in the shuffle. There are plenty to come after us."

So we got the big biplane together and loaded it with our scientifically compressed baggage: the camera, of course; the glasses; a supply of concentrated food. Our pockets were magazines of small necessities, and we had our guns, of course — there was no knowing what might happen.

Up and up and up we sailed, way up at first, to get "the lay of the land" and make note of it.

Out of that dark green sea of crowding forest this high-standing spur rose steeply. It ran back on either side, apparently, to the far-off white-crowned peaks in the distance, themselves probably inaccessible.

"Let's make the first trip geographical," I suggested. "Spy out the land, and drop back here for more gasoline. With your tremendous speed we can reach that range and back all right. Then we can leave a sort of map on board — for that relief expedition."

"There's sense in that," Terry agreed. "I'll put off being king of Ladyland for one more day."

So we made a long skirting voyage, turned the point of the cape which was close by, ran up one side of the triangle at our best speed, crossed over the base where it left the higher mountains, and so back to our lake by moonlight.

"That's not a bad little kingdom," we agreed when it was roughly drawn and measured. We could tell the size fairly by our speed. And from what we could see of the sides — and that icy ridge at the back end — "It's a pretty enterprising savage who would manage to get into it," Jeff said.

Of course we had looked at the land itself — eagerly, but we were too high and going too fast to see much. It appeared to be well forested about the edges, but in the interior there were wide plains, and everywhere parklike meadows and open places.

There were cities, too; that I insisted. It looked — well, it looked like any other country — a civilized one, I mean.

We had to sleep after that long sweep through the air, but we turned out early enough next day, and again we rose softly up the height till we could top the crowning trees and see the broad fair land at our pleasure.

"Semitropical. Looks like a first-rate climate. It's wonderful what a little height will do for temperature." Terry was studying the forest growth.

"Little height! Is that what you call little?" I asked. Our instruments measured it clearly. We had not realized the long gentle rise from the coast perhaps.

"Mighty lucky piece of land, I call it,"Terry pursued. "Now for the folks — I've had enough scenery."

So we sailed low, crossing back and forth, quartering the country as we went, and studying it. We saw — I can't remember now how much of this we noted then and how much was supplemented by our later knowledge, but we could not help seeing this much, even on that excited day — a land in a state of perfect cultivation, where even the forests looked as if they were cared for; a land that looked like an enormous park, only it was even more evidently an enormous garden.

"I don't see any cattle," I suggested, but Terry was silent. We were approaching a village.

I confess that we paid small attention to the clean, well-built roads, to the attractive architecture, to the ordered beauty of the little town. We had our glasses out; even Terry, setting his machine for a spiral glide, clapped the binoculars to his eyes.

"That's an excellent suggestion, Miss Triggs. Perhaps one of the men here would like to make it."

Riana Duncan/Punch Cartoon Library/TopFoto

What argument is being made in this cartoon by Riana Duncan? It appeared in 1988; does it feel antiquated or still relevant? Identify a piece of dialogue from the story, spoken by one of the men, that shows a similar devaluing of women's ideas.

They heard our whirring screw. They ran out of the houses — they gathered in from the fields, swift-running light figures, crowds of them. We stared and stared until it was almost too late to catch the levers, sweep off and rise again; and then we held our peace for a long run upward.

"Gosh!" said Terry, after a while.

"Only women there — and children," Jeff urged excitedly.

"But they look — why, this is a CIVILIZED country!" I protested. "There must be men."

"Of course there are men," said Terry. "Come on, let's find 'em."

He refused to listen to Jeff's suggestion that we examine the country further before we risked leaving our machine.

"There's a fine landing place right there where we came over," he insisted, and it was an excellent one — a wide, flat-topped rock, overlooking the lake, and quite out of sight from the interior.

"They won't find this in a hurry," he asserted, as we scrambled with the utmost difficulty down to safer footing. "Come on, boys — there were some good lookers in that bunch."

Of course it was unwise of us.

It was quite easy to see afterward that our best plan was to have studied the country more fully before we left our swooping airship and trusted ourselves to mere foot service. But we were three young men. We had been talking about this country for over a year, hardly believing that there was such a place, and now — we were in it.

It looked safe and civilized enough, and among those upturned, crowding faces, though some were terrified enough, there was great beauty — on that we all agreed.

"Come on!" cried Terry, pushing forward. "Oh, come on! Here goes for Herland!"

from Chapter 2

. . . When we reached the edge of the open country we reconnoitered with our field glasses. There it was, about four miles off, the same town, we concluded, unless, as Jeff ventured, they all had pink houses. The broad green fields and closely cultivated gardens sloped away at our feet, a long easy slant, with good roads winding pleasantly here and there, and narrower paths besides.

"Look at that!" cried Jeff suddenly. "There they go!"

Sure enough, close to the town, across a wide meadow, three bright-hued figures were running swiftly.

"How could they have got that far in this time? It can't be the same ones," I urged. But through the glasses we could identify our pretty tree-climbers quite plainly, at least by costume.

Terry watched them, we all did for that matter, till they disappeared among the houses. Then he put down his glass and turned to us, drawing a long breath. "Mother of Mike, boys — what Gorgeous Girls! To climb like that! to run like that! and afraid of nothing. This country suits me all right. Let's get ahead."

"Nothing ventured, nothing have," I suggested, but Terry preferred "Faint heart ne'er won fair lady."

We set forth in the open, walking briskly. "If there are any men, we'd better keep an eye out," I suggested, but Jeff seemed lost in heavenly dreams, and Terry in highly practical plans.

"What a perfect road! What a heavenly country! See the flowers, will you?"

This was Jeff, always an enthusiast; but we could agree with him fully.

The road was some sort of hard manufactured stuff, sloped slightly to shed rain, with every curve and grade and gutter as perfect as if it were Europe's best. "No men, eh?" sneered Terry. On either side a double row of trees shaded the footpaths; between the trees bushes or vines, all fruit-bearing, now and then seats and little wayside fountains; everywhere flowers.

"We'd better import some of these ladies and set 'em to parking the United States," I suggested. "Mighty nice place they've got here." We rested a few moments by one of the fountains, tested the fruit that looked ripe, and went on, impressed, for all our gay bravado by the sense of quiet potency which lay about us.

Here was evidently a people highly skilled, efficient, caring for their country as a florist cares for his costliest orchids. Under the soft brilliant blue of that clear sky, in the pleasant shade of those endless rows of trees, we walked unharmed, the placid silence broken only by the birds.

Presently there lay before us at the foot of a long hill the town or village we were aiming for. We stopped and studied it.

Jeff drew a long breath. "I wouldn't have believed a collection of houses could look so lovely," he said.

"They've got architects and landscape gardeners in plenty, that's sure," agreed Terry.

I was astonished myself. You see, I come from California, and there's no country lovelier, but when it comes to towns —! I have often groaned at home to see the offensive mess man made in the face of nature, even though I'm no art sharp, like Jeff. But this place! It was built mostly of a sort of dull rose-colored stone, with here and there some clear white houses; and it lay abroad among the green groves and gardens like a broken rosary of pink coral.

"Those big white ones are public buildings evidently," Terry declared. "This is no savage country, my friend. But no men? Boys, it behooves us to go forward most politely."

The place had an odd look, more impressive as we approached. "It's like an exposition." "It's too pretty to be true." "Plenty of palaces, but where are the homes?" "Oh there are little ones enough — but —." It certainly was different from any towns we had ever seen.

"There's no dirt," said Jeff suddenly. "There's no smoke," he added after a little.

"There's no noise," I offered; but Terry snubbed me — "That's because they are laying low for us; we'd better be careful how we go in there."

Nothing could induce him to stay out, however, so we walked on.

Everything was beauty, order, perfect cleanness, and the pleasantest sense of home over it all. As we neared the center of the town the houses stood thicker, ran together as it were, grew into rambling palaces grouped among parks and open squares, something as college buildings stand in their quiet greens.

And then, turning a corner, we came into a broad paved space and saw before us a band of women standing close together in even order, evidently waiting for us.

We stopped a moment and looked back. The street behind was closed by another band, marching steadily, shoulder to shoulder. We went on — there seemed no other way to go — and presently found ourselves quite surrounded by this close-massed multitude, women, all of them, but —

They were not young. They were not old. They were not, in the girl sense, beautiful. They were not in the least ferocious. And yet, as I looked from face to face, calm, grave, wise, wholly unafraid, evidently assured and determined, I had the funniest feeling — a very early feeling — a feeling that I traced back and back in memory until I caught up with it at last. It was that sense of being hopelessly in the wrong that I had so often felt in early youth when my short legs' utmost effort failed to overcome the fact that I was late to school.

Jeff felt it too; I could see he did. We felt like small boys, very small boys, caught doing mischief in some gracious lady's house. But Terry showed no such consciousness. I saw his quick eyes darting here and there, estimating numbers, measuring distances, judging chances of escape. He examined the close ranks about us, reaching back far on every side, and murmured softly to me, "Every one of 'em over forty as I'm a sinner."

Yet they were not old women. Each was in the full bloom of rosy health, erect, serene, standing sure-footed and light as any pugilist. They had no weapons, and we had, but we had no wish to shoot.

"I'd as soon shoot my aunts," muttered Terry again. "What do they want with us anyhow? They seem to mean business." But in spite of that businesslike aspect, he determined to try his favorite tactics. Terry had come armed with a theory.

He stepped forward, with his brilliant ingratiating smile, and made low obeisance to the women before him. Then he produced another tribute, a broad soft scarf of filmy texture, rich in color and pattern, a lovely thing, even to my eye, and offered it with a deep bow to the tall unsmiling woman who seemed to head the ranks before him. She took it with a gracious nod of acknowledgment, and passed it on to those behind her.

He tried again, this time bringing out a circlet of rhinestones, a glittering crown that should have pleased any woman on earth. He made a brief address, including Jeff and me as partners in his enterprise, and with another bow presented this. Again his gift was accepted and, as before, passed out of sight.

"If they were only younger," he muttered between his teeth. "What on earth is a fellow to say to a regiment of old Colonels like this?"

In all our discussions and speculations we had always unconsciously assumed that the women, whatever else they might be, would be young. Most men do think that way, I fancy.

"Woman" in the abstract is young, and, we assume, charming. As they get older they pass off the stage, somehow, into private ownership mostly, or out of it altogether. But these good ladies were very much on the stage, and yet any one of them might have been a grandmother.

We looked for nervousness — there was none.

For terror, perhaps — there was none.

For uneasiness, for curiosity, for excitement — and all we saw was what might have been a vigilance committee of women doctors, as cool as cucumbers, and evidently meaning to take us to task for being there.

Six of them stepped forward now, one on either side of each of us, and indicated that we were to go with them. We thought it best to accede, at first anyway, and marched along, one of these close at each elbow, and the others in close masses before, behind, on both sides.

A large building opened before us, a very heavy thick-walled impressive place, big, and old-looking; of gray stone, not like the rest of the town.

"This won't do!" said Terry to us, quickly. "We mustn't let them get us in this, boys. All together, now —"

We stopped in our tracks. We began to explain, to make signs pointing away toward the big forest — indicating that we would go back to it — at once.

It makes me laugh, knowing all I do now, to think of us three boys — nothing else; three audacious impertinent boys — butting into an unknown country without any sort of a guard or defense. We seemed to think that if there were men we could fight them, and if there were only women — why, they would be no obstacles at all.

Jeff, with his gentle romantic old-fashioned notions of women as clinging vines. Terry, with his clear decided practical theories that there were two kinds of women — those he wanted and those he didn't; Desirable and Undesirable was his demarcation. The latter as a large class, but negligible — he had never thought about them at all.

And now here they were, in great numbers, evidently indifferent to what he might think, evidently determined on some purpose of their own regarding him, and apparently well able to enforce their purpose.

We all thought hard just then. It had not seemed wise to object to going with them, even if we could have; our one chance was friendliness — a civilized attitude on both sides.

But once inside that building, there was no knowing what these determined ladies might do to us. Even a peaceful detention was not to our minds, and when we named it imprisonment it looked even worse.

So we made a stand, trying to make clear that we preferred the open country. One of them came forward with a sketch of our flier, asking by signs if we were the aerial visitors they had seen.

This we admitted.

They pointed to it again, and to the outlying country, in different directions — but we pretended we did not know where it was, and in truth we were not quite sure and gave a rather wild indication of its whereabouts.

Again they motioned us to advance, standing so packed about the door that there remained but the one straight path open. All around us and behind they were massed solidly — there was simply nothing to do but go forward — or fight.

We held a consultation.

"I never fought with women in my life," said Terry, greatly perturbed, "but I'm not going in there. I'm not going to be — herded in — as if we were in a cattle chute."

"We can't fight them, of course," Jeff urged. "They're all women, in spite of their nondescript clothes; nice women, too; good strong sensible faces. I guess we'll have to go in."

"We may never get out, if we do," I told them. "Strong and sensible, yes; but I'm not so sure about the good. Look at those faces!"

They had stood at ease, waiting while we conferred together, but never relaxing their close attention.

Their attitude was not the rigid discipline of soldiers; there was no sense of compulsion about them. Terry's term of a "vigilance committee" was highly descriptive. They had just the aspect of sturdy burghers, gathered hastily to meet some common need or peril, all moved by precisely the same feelings, to the same end.

Never, anywhere before, had I seen women of precisely this quality. Fishwives and market women might show similar strength, but it was coarse and heavy. These were merely athletic — light and powerful. College professors, teachers, writers — many women showed similar intelligence but often wore a strained nervous look, while these were as calm as cows, for all their evident intellect.

We observed pretty closely just then, for all of us felt that it was a crucial moment.

The leader gave some word of command and beckoned us on, and the surrounding mass moved a step nearer.

"We've got to decide quick," said Terry.

"I vote to go in," Jeff urged. But we were two to one against him and he loyally stood by us. We made one more effort to be let go, urgent, but not imploring. In vain.

"Now for a rush, boys!" Terry said. "And if we can't break 'em, I'll shoot in the air."

Then we found ourselves much in the position of the suffragette trying to get to the Parliament buildings through a triple cordon of London police.

The solidity of those women was something amazing. Terry soon found that it was useless, tore himself loose for a moment, pulled his revolver, and fired upward. As they caught at it, he fired again — we heard a cry —.

The 2017 movie based on the *Wonder Woman* comics includes depictions of Wonder Woman's early life in Themyscira, the idyllic home of the Amazons, where she trains to become a warrior princess.

What do the costumes, props, and poses suggest about female strength in Themyscira? How does the depiction of female strength and unity in this image compare with that described in *Herland*?

Instantly each of us was seized by five women, each holding arm or leg or head; we were lifted like children, straddling helpless children, and borne onward, wriggling indeed, but most ineffectually.

We were borne inside, struggling manfully, but held secure most womanfully, in spite of our best endeavors.

So carried and so held, we came into a high inner hall, gray and bare, and were brought before a majestic gray-haired woman who seemed to hold a judicial position.

There was some talk, not much, among them, and then suddenly there fell upon each of us at once a firm hand holding a wetted cloth before mouth and nose — an order of swimming sweetness — anesthesia.

from Chapter 7

. . . As for the intelligence, I confess that this was the most impressive and, to me, most mortifying, of any single feature of Herland. We soon ceased to comment on this or other matters which to them were such obvious commonplaces as to call forth embarrassing questions about our own conditions.

This was nowhere better shown than in that matter of food supply, which I will now attempt to describe.

Having improved their agriculture to the highest point, and carefully estimated the number of persons who could comfortably live on their square miles; having then limited their population to that number, one would think that was all there was to be done. But they had not thought so. To them the country was a unit — it was theirs. They themselves were a unit, a conscious group; they thought in terms of the community. As such, their time-sense was not limited to the hopes and ambitions of an individual life. Therefore, they habitually considered and carried out plans for improvement which might cover centuries.

I had never seen, had scarcely imagined, human beings undertaking such a work as the deliberate replanting of an entire forest area with different kinds of trees. Yet this seemed to them the simplest common sense, like a man's plowing up an inferior lawn and reseeding it. Now every tree bore fruit — edible fruit, that is. In the case of one tree, in which they took especial pride, it had originally no fruit at all — that is, none humanly edible — yet was so beautiful that they wished to keep it. For nine hundred years they had experimented, and now showed us this particularly lovely graceful tree, with a profuse crop of nutritious seeds.

They had early decided that trees were the best food plants, requiring far less labor in tilling the soil, and bearing a larger amount of food for the same ground space; also doing much to preserve and enrich the soil.

Due regard had been paid to seasonable crops, and their fruit and nuts, grains and berries, kept on almost the year through.

On the higher part of the country, near the backing wall of mountains, they had a real winter with snow. Toward the south-eastern point, where there was a large valley with a lake whose outlet was subterranean, the climate was like that of California, and citrus fruits, figs, and olives grew abundantly.

What impressed me particularly was their scheme of fertilization. Here was this little shut-in piece of land where one would have thought an ordinary people would have been starved out long ago or reduced to an annual struggle for life. These careful culturists had worked out a perfect scheme of refeeding the soil with all that came out of it. All the scraps and leavings of their food, plant waste from lumber work or textile industry, all the solid matter from the sewage, properly treated and combined — everything which came from the earth went back to it.

The practical result was like that in any healthy forest; an increasingly valuable soil was being built, instead of the progressive impoverishment so often seen in the rest of the world.

When this first burst upon us we made such approving comments that they were surprised that such obvious common sense should be praised; asked what our methods were; and we had some difficulty in — well, in diverting them, by referring to the extent of our own land, and the — admitted — carelessness with which we had skimmed the cream of it.

At least we thought we had diverted them. Later I found that besides keeping a careful and accurate account of all we told them, they had a sort of skeleton chart, on which the things we said and the things we palpably avoided saying were all set down and studied. It really was child's play for those profound educators to work out a painfully accurate estimate of our conditions—in some lines. When a given line of observation seemed to lead to some very dreadful inference they always gave us the benefit of the doubt, leaving it open to further knowledge. Some of the things we had grown to accept as perfectly natural, or as belonging to our human limitations, they literally could not have believed; and, as I have said, we had all of

extending beyond the text

The Bechdel test, named for writer and cartoonist Alison Bechdel, is a measure of the representation of women in film. To pass the Bechdel test, a movie must meet three criteria: There must be at least two named women, they must talk to each other, and their conversation must be about something other than a man.

Consider this chart, which summarizes a 2016 Duke University research study applying these criteria to films over several decades.

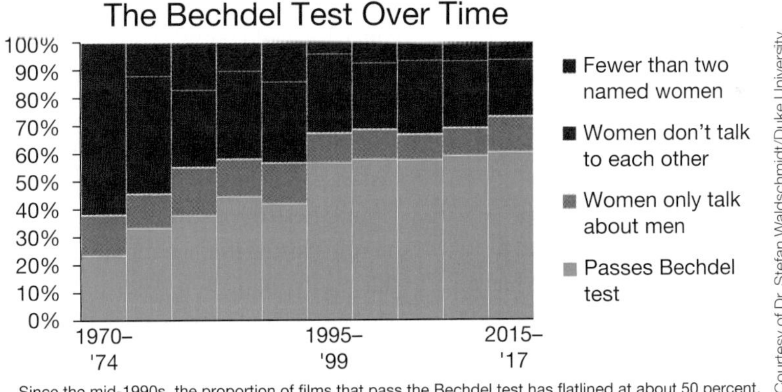

Since the mid-1990s, the proportion of films that pass the Bechdel test has flatlined at about 50 percent.

After examining the chart, consider the following questions:

- **On which one of the criteria has most progress been made?**
- **Based on these findings, what would be your advice to filmmakers seeking to represent women more authentically?**
- **What questions does the graph raise for you?**
- **Name one movie that you believe would pass and one that would not pass the Bechdel test.**
- **How would *Herland* score on the Bechdel test based on the excerpts you've read?**

Harris Brisbane Dick Fund, 1959

In Greek mythology, the Amazons were a race of warrior women living on the outer limits of the known world, sometimes specifically mentioned as the city of Themisckyra on the Black Sea. This is a bronze bust of an Amazon from the first century A.D.

How would you describe the woman depicted in the sculpture? In what ways might the women of *Herland* be modeled on the Amazons?

us joined in a tacit endeavor to conceal much of the social status at home.

"Confound their grandmotherly minds!" Terry said. "Of course they can't understand a Man's World! They aren't human — they're just a pack of Fe-Fe-Females!" This was after he had to admit their parthenogenesis.

"I wish our grandfatherly minds had managed as well," said Jeff. "Do you really think it's to our credit that we have muddled along with all our poverty and disease and the like? They have peace and plenty, wealth and beauty, goodness and intellect. Pretty good people, I think!"

"You'll find they have their faults too," Terry insisted; and partly in self-defense, we all three began to look for those faults of theirs. We had been very strong on this subject before we got there — in those baseless speculations of ours.

"Suppose there is a country of women only," Jeff had put it, over and over. "What'll they be like?"

And we had been cocksure as to the inevitable limitations, the faults and vices, of a lot of women. We had expected them to be given over to what we called "feminine vanity" — "frills and furbelows," and we found they had evolved a costume more perfect than the Chinese dress, richly beautiful when so desired, always useful, of unfailing dignity and good taste.

We had expected a dull submissive monotony, and found a daring social inventiveness far beyond our own, and a mechanical and scientific development fully equal to ours.

We had expected pettiness, and found a social consciousness besides which our nations looked like quarreling children — feebleminded ones at that.

We had expected jealousy, and found a broad sisterly affection, a fair-minded intelligence, to which we could produce no parallel.

We had expected hysteria, and found a standard of health and vigor, a calmness of temper, to which the habit of profanity, for instance, was impossible to explain — we tried it.

All these things even Terry had to admit, but he still insisted that we should find out the other side pretty soon.

"It stands to reason, doesn't it?" he argued. "The whole thing's deuced unnatural — I'd say impossible if we weren't in it. And an unnatural condition's sure to have unnatural results. You'll find some awful characteristics — see if you don't! For instance — we don't know yet what they do with their criminals — their defectives — their aged. You notice we haven't seen any! There's got to be something!"

I was inclined to believe that there had to be something, so I took the bull by the horns — the cow, I should say! — and asked Somel.

"I want to find some flaw in all this perfection," I told her flatly. "It simply isn't possible that three million people have no faults. We are trying our best to understand and learn — would you mind helping us by saying what, to your minds, are the worst qualities of this unique civilization of yours?"

We were sitting together in a shaded arbor, in one of those eating-gardens of theirs. The delicious food had been eaten, a plate of fruit still before us. We could look out on one side over a stretch of open country, quietly rich and lovely; on the other, the garden, with tables here and there, far apart enough for privacy. Let me say right here that with all their careful "balance of population" there was no crowding in this country. There was room, space, a sunny breezy freedom everywhere.

Somel set her chin upon her hand, her elbow on the low wall beside her, and looked off over the fair land.

"Of course we have faults — all of us," she said. "In one way you might say that we have more than we used to — that is, our standard of perfection seems to get farther and farther away. But we are not discouraged, because our records do show gain — considerable gain.

"When we began — even with the start of one particularly noble mother — we inherited the characteristics of a long race-record behind her. And they cropped out from time to time — alarmingly. But it is — yes, quite six hundred years since we have had what you call a 'criminal.'

"We have, of course, made it our first business to train out, to breed out, when possible, the lowest types."

"Breed out?" I asked. "How could you — with parthenogenesis?"

"If the girl showing the bad qualities had still the power to appreciate social duty, we appealed to her, by that, to renounce motherhood. Some of the few worst types were, fortunately, unable to reproduce. But if the fault was in a disproportionate egotism — then the girl was sure she had the right to have children, even that hers would be better than others."

"I can see that," I said. "And then she would be likely to rear them in the same spirit."

"That we never allowed," answered Somel quietly.

"Allowed?" I queried. "Allowed a mother to rear her own children?"

"Certainly not," said Somel, "unless she was fit for that supreme task."

This was rather a blow to my previous convictions.

"But I thought motherhood was for each of you —"

"Motherhood — yes, that is, maternity, to bear a child. But education is our highest art, only allowed to our highest artists."

"Education?" I was puzzled again. "I don't mean education. I mean by motherhood not only child-bearing, but the care of babies."

"The care of babies involves education, and is entrusted only to the most fit," she repeated.

"Then you separate mother and child!" I cried in cold horror, something of Terry's feeling creeping over me, that there must be something wrong among these many virtues.

"Not usually," she patiently explained. "You see, almost every woman values her maternity above everything else. Each girl holds it close and dear, an exquisite joy, a crowning honor, the most intimate, most personal, most precious thing. That is, the child-rearing has come to be with us a culture so profoundly studied, practiced with such subtlety and skill, that the more we love our children the less we are willing to trust that process to unskilled hands — even our own."

"But a mother's love —" I ventured.

She studied my face, trying to work out a means of clear explanation.

"You told us about your dentists," she said, at length, "those quaintly specialized persons who spend their lives filling little holes in other persons' teeth — even in children's teeth sometimes."

"Yes?" I said, not getting her drift.

"Does mother-love urge mothers — with you — to fill their own children's teeth? Or to wish to?"

"Why no — of course not," I protested. "But that is a highly specialized craft. Surely the care of babies is open to any woman — any mother!"

"We do not think so," she gently replied. "Those of us who are the most highly competent fulfill that office; and a majority of our girls eagerly try for it — I assure you we have the very best."

"But the poor mother — bereaved of her baby —"

"Oh no!" she earnestly assured me. "Not in the least bereaved. It is her baby still — it is with her — she has not lost it. But she is not the only one to care for it. There are others whom she knows to be wiser. She knows it because she has studied as they did, practiced as they did, and honors their real superiority. For the child's sake, she is glad to have for it this highest care."

I was unconvinced. Besides, this was only hearsay; I had yet to see the motherhood of Herland.

As the suffragette movement to allow women to vote gained a following in the early 1900s, images like this one suggested that traditional gender roles were at risk.

What message is this image trying to communicate? How might images like this one have inspired Charlotte Perkins Gilman to imagine the utopian society of *Herland*?

from Chapter 12

. . . Well—we had to get the flyer in order, and be sure there was enough fuel left, though Terry said we could glide all right, down to that lake, once we got started. We'd have gone gladly in a week's time, of course, but there was a great to-do all over the country about Ellador's leaving them. She had interviews with some of the leading ethicists — wise women with still eyes, and with the best of the teachers. There was a stir, a thrill, a deep excitement everywhere.

Our teaching about the rest of the world has given them all a sense of isolation, of remoteness, of being a little outlying sample of a country, overlooked and forgotten among the family of nations. We had called it "the family of nations," and they liked the phrase immensely.

They were deeply aroused on the subject of evolution; indeed, the whole field of natural science drew them irresistibly. Any number of them would have risked everything to go to the strange unknown lands and study; but we could take only one, and it had to be Ellador, naturally.

We planned greatly about coming back, about establishing a connecting route by water; about penetrating those vast forests and civilizing — or exterminating — the dangerous savages. That is, we men talked of that last—not with the women. They had a definite aversion to killing things.

But meanwhile there was high council being held among the wisest of them all. The students and thinkers who had been gathering facts from us all this time, collating and relating them, and making inferences, laid the result of their labors before the council.

Little had we thought that our careful efforts at concealment had been so easily seen through, with never a word to show us that they saw. They had followed up words of ours on the science of optics, asked innocent questions about glasses and the like, and were aware of the defective eyesight so common among us.

With the lightest touch, different women asking different questions at different times, and putting all our answers together like a picture puzzle, they had figured out a sort of skeleton chart as to the prevalence of disease among us. Even more subtly with no show of horror or condemnation, they had gathered something — far from the truth, but something pretty clear — about poverty, vice, and crime. They even had a goodly number of our dangers all itemized, from asking us about insurance and innocent things like that.

They were well posted as to the different races, beginning with their poison-arrow natives down below and widening out to the broad racial divisions we had told them about. Never a shocked expression of the face or exclamation of revolt had warned us; they had been extracting the evidence without our knowing it all this time, and now were studying with the most devout earnestness the matter they had prepared. . . .

They had a great globe, quite fairly mapped out from the small section maps in that compendium of ours. They had the different peoples of the earth roughly outlined, and their status in civilization indicated. They had charts and figures and estimates, based on the facts in that traitorous little book and what they had learned from us.

Somel explained: "We find that in all your historic period, so much longer than ours, that with all the interplay of services, the exchange of inventions and discoveries, and the wonderful progress we so admire, that in this widespread Other World of yours, there is still much disease, often contagious."

We admitted this at once.

"Also there is still, in varying degree, ignorance, with prejudice and unbridled emotion."

This too was admitted.

"We find also that in spite of the advance of democracy and the increase of wealth, that there is still unrest and sometimes combat."

Yes, yes, we admitted it all. We were used to these things and saw no reason for so much seriousness.

"All things considered," they said, and they did not say a hundredth part of the things they were considering, "we are unwilling to expose our country to free communication with the rest of the world — as yet. If Ellador comes back, and we approve her report, it may be done later — but not yet.

"So we have this to ask of you gentlemen [they knew that word was held a title of honor with us], that you promise not in any way to betray the location of this country until permission — after Ellador's return."

Jeff was perfectly satisfied. He thought they were quite right. He always did. I never saw an alien become naturalized more quickly than that man in Herland.

I studied it awhile, thinking of the time they'd have if some of our contagions got loose there, and concluded they were right. So I agreed.

Terry was the obstacle. "Indeed I won't!" he protested. "The first thing I'll do is to get an expedition fixed up to force an entrance into Ma-land."

"Then," they said quite calmly, "he must remain an absolute prisoner, always."

"Anesthesia would be kinder," urged Moadine.

"And safer," added Zava.

"He will promise, I think," said Ellador.

And he did. With which agreement we at last left Herland. ■

Understanding and Interpreting

1. Before the women of *Herland* appear, what do the expectations of Jeff, Terry, and Van, the narrator, reveal about the assumptions the three have about women?
2. What strikes the three men in their very first encounter with "the band of women" (par. 88) who await them? What is it about their age (or agelessness) that the men find unsettling? Why?
3. What "gifts" do the men offer the women during this initial meeting? Why are they confused by the women's responses?
4. When do the men, Terry in particular, resort to violence — or try to? What might Gilman be suggesting by this reaction?
5. Van observes that the women are "light and powerful . . . as calm as cows, for all their evident intellect" (par. 121). Why do these qualities, particularly in combination, feel unusual, perhaps even disturbing, to the men?
6. If Gilman is telling a story that argues against expectations of women, including an overemphasis on appearance, why does she make a point of describing the clothes that the women of *Herland* wear? What is the significance of their chosen dress?
7. To what extent might the novella's attitude toward motherhood and the raising of children in *Herland* have been controversial during Gilman's time? Is it controversial today? Do you think that the analogy drawn with dentists (par. 177) is appropriate?
8. What is the "traitorous little book" (par. 193) that the women of *Herland* keep? Why are the women "unwilling to expose [their] country to free communication with the rest of the world" until one of their own explores, studies, and reports back on the world beyond Herland?

Analyzing Language, Style, and Structure

1. **Vocabulary in Context.** As the three men encounter the layout of the society of *Herland*, both the physical surroundings and the architecture, Terry observes, "it's like an exposition. It's too pretty to be true." (par. 83). What is the meaning of "exposition" in this context?
2. **Skill Focus.** Look back at how Van describes the men's first impressions of the settlement (pars. 80 to 85). How does the language convey a sense of perfection — a utopian environment?
3. **Skill Focus.** In paragraphs 149 to 152, Gilman repeats the syntactical structure "We had expected . . . and found. . . ." What is the effect of this parallel structure??
4. The narrator is Van, a sociologist who, by training, should be an objective observer of cultures other than his own. To what extent does he maintain an impartiality? In what ways, if any, does he judge the society of *Herland* through the lens of his own cultural values and experiences?
5. When the women move as a "mass" that the men cannot break through, Van uses a metaphor to describe their predicament: "Then we found ourselves much in the position of the suffragette trying to get to the Parliament buildings through a triple cordon of London police" (par. 127). Why is that figure of speech especially appropriate in this context? Conduct brief research, if needed.
6. Throughout these excerpted passages, the terms applied to the residents of *Herland* shift between "ladies" and "women." What might Gilman be suggesting about the language choices available to us — and to the male explorers? Consider also Van's description of

himself and his comrades after being seized: "struggling manfully, but held secure most womanfully" (par. 130).

7. Throughout *Herland*, the author includes references to being "civilized" and to "civilization." What issues do these terms raise?

Topics for Composing

1. **Analysis.** Based on the excerpts you read, should the community described in *Herland* be considered a utopia or a dystopia? What factors contribute most to that designation?
2. **Argument.** Supreme Court Justice Ruth Bader Ginsburg once commented that the Supreme Court will finally have "enough" female justices when there are nine of them (the total number of justices). When questioned about the fairness of her position, she responded, "For most of the country's history, there were nine and they were all men. Nobody thought that was strange." To what extent do you agree that an all-female Supreme Court would alleviate gender inequities?
3. **Connection.** In a 2015 article, writer Lindy West characterized the three male explorers in *Herland*:

   > They are "such perfect, brutal caricatures of masculinity, they feel fresh and relevant enough to populate any sarcastic modern-day blog post. Terry is all puffed-up sexual entitles, Jeff oozes chivalric 'nice guy' condescension, and Van is your . . . faux-innocent demanding to be educated."

   To what extent do you agree or disagree with West's assertion that the three men in *Herland* are caricatures that are still relevant in today's society?
4. **Connection.** In what ways does Gilman seem to be ahead of her time regarding the environmental and agricultural practices she describes in *Herland*? What seems particularly relevant today? Cite specific passages to support your connection.
5. **Speaking and Listening.** Motherhood is elevated almost to a religion in *Herland*. Everything in the society is focused on the ideal of motherhood, which the women achieve without men through parthenogenesis. Develop several questions to explore whether or not the centrality of motherhood as duty and honor is in conflict with a feminist vision of utopia. Discuss with your classmates.
6. **Research.** Gilman has been criticized for a number of her viewpoints expressed in *Herland*, including her views about "breeding" to increase the likelihood of positive characteristics and decrease negative ones. She was influenced by a belief in eugenics. Do some research into this belief in "scientific" ways to improve the human race. How does what you learn inform your response to *Herland*?
7. **Creative Writing.** Write a scene or two of a short story about a society in which gender binaries no longer exist. That is, the stereotypical "masculine" and "feminine" expectations are absent. In your story, try to illustrate whether this society would be utopian or dystopian.

from Utopia for Realists: How We Can Build the Ideal World (nonfiction)

Rutger Bregman

Hollandse-Hoogte/ZUMA Press/Newscom

Historian and author Rutger Bregman (b. 1988) has published five books on history, philosophy, and economics. Born in Holland, he attended the University of Utrecht, where he received his undergraduate degree. Bregman also did graduate work there, as well as at the University of California, Los Angeles. As a journalist, he has contributed articles to numerous publications, including the *Washington Post*, the *New York Times*, and the *Guardian*. Bregman's TED Talk "Poverty Isn't a Lack of Character; It's a Lack of Cash" was chosen as one of the top ten of 2017.

KEY CONTEXT *Utopia for Realists: How We Can Build the Ideal World* (2019) was a bestseller and has been translated into dozens of languages. In it, Bregman argues for a 15-hour work week, a world without borders, and a basic salary for every citizen. Some people call Bregman's view a utopian vision, though he claims that it is a practical one for the current times. The following argument for a guaranteed basic income is excerpted from Chapter 2 of *Utopia for Realists*.

FOCUS FOR READING Throughout this chapter, you have been reading poems, short stories, and excerpts from novels about utopias and dystopias. Unlike those other texts, the following is a work of nonfiction, an excerpt from an argument about ways to implement utopian ideas in the real world. As you read the following, consider how Bregman uses evidence, appeals, style, and other rhetorical elements to explore the challenges and opportunities of utopian thinking.

London, May 2009—An experiment is under way. Its subjects: thirteen homeless men. They are veterans of the street. Some have been sleeping on the cold pavement of the Square Mile, Europe's financial center, for going on forty years. Between the police expenses, court costs, and social services, these thirteen troublemakers have racked up a bill estimated at £400,000 ($650,000) or more.[1] Per year.

The strain on city services and local charities is too great for things to go on this way. So Broadway, a London-based aid organization, makes a radical decision: From now on, the city's thirteen consummate drifters will be getting VIP treatment. It's *adiós* to the daily helpings of food stamps, soup kitchens, and shelters. They're getting a drastic and instantaneous bailout.

[1]This is a very conservative estimate. A study conducted by the British government put the amount at £30,000 per homeless person per year (for social services, police, legal costs, etc.). In this case the amount would have been much higher as they were the most notorious vagrants. The study cites sums as high as £400,000 for a single homeless person per year. See: Department for Communities and Local Government, "Evidence Review of the Costs of Homelessness" (August 2012). https://www.gov.uk/government/uploads/system/uploads/attachment_data/file/7596/2200485.pdf.

From now on, these rough sleepers will receive free money.

To be exact, they're getting £3,000 in spending money, and they don't have to do a thing in return.[2] How they spend it is up to them. They can opt to make use of an advisor if they'd like—or not. There are no strings attached, no questions to trip them up.[3]

The only thing they're asked is: What do you think you need?

Gardening Classes

"I didn't have enormous expectations," one social worker later recalled.[4] But the drifters' desires proved eminently modest. A telephone, a dictionary, a hearing aid — each had his own ideas about what he needed. In fact, most were downright thrifty. After one year, they had spent an average of just £800.

Take Simon, who had been strung out on heroin for twenty years. The money turned his life around. Simon got clean and started taking gardening classes. "For some reason, for the first time in my life, everything just clicked," he said later. "I'm starting to look after myself, wash and shave. Now I'm thinking of going back home. I've got two kids."

A year and a half after the experiment began, seven of the thirteen rough sleepers had a roof over their heads. Two more were about to move into their own apartments. All thirteen had taken critical steps toward solvency and personal growth. They were enrolled in classes, learning to cook, going through rehab, visiting their families, and making plans for the future.

"It empowers people," one of the social workers said about the personalized budget. "It gives choices. I think it can make a difference." After decades of fruitless pushing, pulling, pampering, penalizing, prosecuting, and protecting, nine notorious vagrants had finally been brought in from the streets. The cost? Some £50,000 a year, including the social workers' wages. In other words, not only did the project help thirteen people, it also cut costs considerably.[5] Even the *Economist* had to conclude that the "most efficient way to spend money on the homeless might be to give it to them."[6] . . .

Utopia

Free money: It's a notion already proposed by some of history's leading thinkers. Thomas More dreamed about it in his book *Utopia* in 1516. Countless economists and philosophers — Nobel Prize winners among them — would follow.[7] Its proponents have spanned the spectrum from left to right, all the way to the founders of neoliberal thought, Friedrich Hayek and Milton Friedman.[8] And Article 25 of the Universal Declaration of Human Rights (1948) promises that, one day, it will come.

A universal basic income.

And not merely for a few years, or in developing countries alone, or only for the

---

[2]The recipients were generally not told the exact amount of money in their "personalised budget," according to the Broadway report; however, as the report goes on to say that one of the homeless suggested lowering it from £3,000 to £2,000, he obviously did know.

[3]The homeless were not given the money directly. All their expenditures had to be approved first by the "street population manager," which he always did "promptly." That this scrutiny was limited was also affirmed by one of the social workers in an interview with the *Economist* (see Chapter 2, endnote 6): "We just said, 'It's your life and up to you to do what you want with it, but we are here to help if you want.'" The report also states that "Throughout the interviews, many people used the phrases 'I chose' or 'I made the decision' when discussing their accommodation and the use of their personalised budget, emphasising their sense of choice and control."

[4]The Joseph Rowntree Foundation published an extensive report on the experiment, which is the source of all the quotes cited here. See: Juliette Hough and Becky Rice, *Providing Personalised Support to Rough Sleepers. An Evaluation of the City of London Pilot* (2010). http://www.jrf.org.uk/publications/support-rough-sleepers-london.

For another evaluation, see: Liz Blackender and Jo Prestidge, "Pan London Personalised Budgets for Rough Sleepers," *Journal of Integrated Care* (January 2014). http://www.emeraldinsight.com/journals.htm?articleid=17104939&.

[5]In 2013, the project was expanded to twenty-eight rough sleepers in London's City, of whom twenty already had a roof over their heads.

[6]"Cutting out the middle men," *Economist* (November 4, 2010). http://www.economist.com/node/17420321.

[7]Including Thomas Paine, John Stuart Mill, H. G, Wells, George Bernard Shaw, John Kenneth Galbraith, Jan Tinbergen, Martin Luther King, and Bertrand Russell.

[8]See, for example: Matt Zwolinski, "Why Did Hayek Support a Basic Income?" *Libertarianism.org* (December 23, 2013). http://www.libertarianism.org/columns/why-did-hayek-support-basic-income.

The Heads Of State

What point does this image make about universal basic income (UBI)? How does it communicate its message through text, font choice, positioning of the figures, and so on? How does the image portray the concept of UBI as Bregman argues for it?

poor, but just what it says on the box: free money for everyone. Not as a favor, but as a right. Call it the "capitalist road to communism."[9] A monthly allowance, enough to live on, without having to lift a finger. The only condition, as such, is that you "have a pulse."[10] No inspectors looking over your shoulder to see if you've spent it wisely, nobody questioning if it's really deserved. No more special benefit and assistance programs; at most an additional allowance for seniors, the unemployed, and those unable to work.

Basic income: It's an idea whose time has come.

• • •

Few people today are aware that the U.S. was just a hair's breadth from realizing a social safety net at least as extensive as those in most Western European countries. When President Lyndon B. Johnson declared his "War on Poverty" in 1964, Democrats and Republicans alike rallied behind fundamental welfare reforms.

First, however, some trial runs were needed. 15
Tens of millions of dollars were budgeted to provide a basic income for more than 8,500 Americans in New Jersey, Pennsylvania, Iowa, North Carolina, Indiana, Seattle, and Denver in what were also the first-ever large-scale social experiments to distinguish experimental and control groups. The researchers wanted answers to three questions: (1) Would people work significantly less if they receive a guaranteed income? (2) Would the program be too expensive? (3) Would it prove politically unfeasible?

The answers were no, no, and yes.

Declines in working hours were limited across the board. "The 'laziness' contention is just not supported by our findings," the chief data analyst of the Denver experiment said. "There is not anywhere near the mass defection the prophets of doom predicted." The reduction in paid work averaged 9% per family, and in every state it was mostly the twentysomethings and women with young children who worked less.[11]

Later research showed that even 9% was probably exaggerated. In the original study, this was calculated on the basis of self-reported income, but when the data was compared with official government records, it turned out that a significant portion of earnings had gone

---

[9]Robert van der Veen and Philippe van Parijs, "A Capitalist Road to Communism," *Theory & Society* (1986). https://www.ssc.wisc.edu/~wright/ERU_files/PVP-cap-road.pdf.

[10]A quote by the conservative proponent of basic income, Charles Murray, in: Annie Lowrey, "Switzerland's Proposal to Pay People for Being Alive," *New York Times* (November 12, 2013). http://www.nytimes.com/2013/11/17/magazine/switzerlands-proposal-to-pay-people-for-being-alive.html.

[11]Allan Sheahen, *Basic Income Guarantee. Your Right to Economic Security* (2012), p.108.

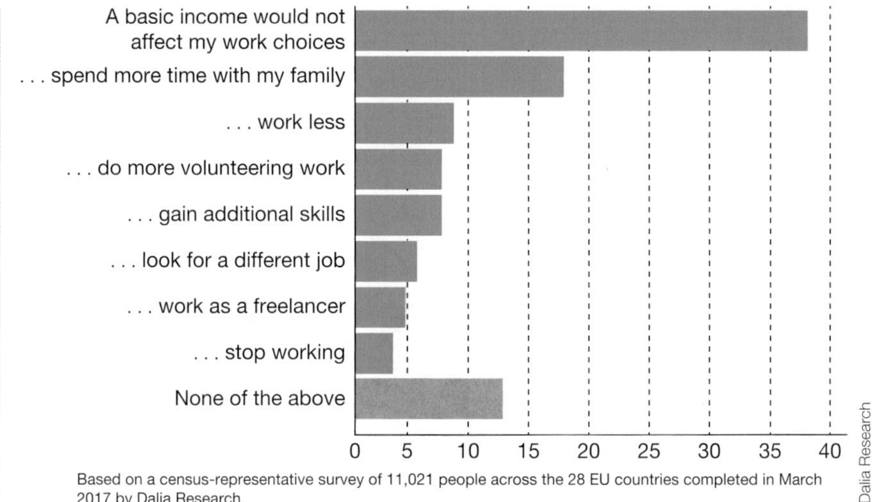

Based on a census-representative survey of 11,021 people across the 28 EU countries completed in March 2017 by Dalia Research.

This graph summarizes responses from European subjects to the question, “What could be the most likely effect of basic income on your work choices?”

What conclusions can you draw from this data? In what ways would this information support or challenge the argument that Bregman makes for a universal basic income?

unreported. After correcting for this discrepancy, the researchers discovered that the number of hours worked had scarcely decreased at all.[12]

How Basic Income Would Affect Work Choices

“[The] declines in hours of paid work were undoubtedly compensated in part by other useful activities, such as search for better jobs or work in the home,” noted the Seattle experiment’s concluding report. For example, one mother who had dropped out of high school worked less in order to earn a degree in psychology and get a job as a researcher. Another woman took acting classes; her husband began composing music. “We’re now self-sufficient, income-earning artists,” she told the researchers.[13] Among youth included in the experiment, almost all the hours not spent on paid work went into more education. Among the New Jersey subjects, the rate of high-school graduations rose 30%.[14]

And thus, in the revolutionary year of 1968, 20
when young demonstrators the world over were taking to the streets, five famous economists — John Kenneth Galbraith , Harold Watts, James Tobin , Paul Samuelson , and Robert Lampman—wrote an open letter to Congress. “The country will not have met its responsibility until everyone in the nation is assured an income no less than the officially

[12]Dylan Matthews, “A Guaranteed Income for Every American Would Eliminate Poverty — And It Wouldn’t Destroy the Economy,” *Vox.com* (July 23, 2014). http://www.vox.com/2014/7/23/5925041/guaranteed-income-basic-poverty-gobry-labor-supply.

[13]Quoted in: Allan Sheahen, “Why Not Guarantee Everyone a Job? Why the Negative Income Tax Experiments of the 1970s Were Successful.” USBIG Discussion Paper (February 2002). http://www.usbig.net/papers/013-Sheahen.doc.

The researchers thought people might eventually even work *more*, provided the government created additional jobs. “Any reduction in work effort caused by cash assistance would be more than offset by the increased employment opportunities provided in public service jobs.”

[14]Matthews, “A Guaranteed Income for Every American Would Eliminate Poverty.”

What argument about income inequality does the artist Mike Luckovich make in this cartoon? How has he depicted the relationship between disparities in income with the image of the seesaw? How do you interpret the question — "What?" — that the man is asking? How does this cartoon relate to the argument Bregman is making?

recognized definition of poverty," they said in an article published on the front page of the *New York Times*. According to the economists, the costs would be "substantial, but well within the nation's economic and fiscal capacity."[15]

The letter was signed by 1,200 fellow economists. . . .

Talk Different, Think Different

It's been said before.

We're saddled with a welfare state from a bygone era when the breadwinners were still mostly men and people spent their whole lives working at the same company. The pension system and employment protection rules are still keyed to those fortunate enough to have a steady job, public assistance is rooted in the misconception that we can rely on the economy to generate enough jobs, and welfare benefits are often not a trampoline, but a trap.

Never before has the time been so ripe for the introduction of a universal, unconditional basic income. Look around. Greater flexibility in the workplace demands that we also create greater security. Globalization is eroding the wages of the middle class. The growing rift between those with and those without a college degree makes it essential to give the have-nots a leg-up. And the development of ever-smarter robots could cost even the haves their jobs.

In recent decades the middle class has 25
retained its spending power by borrowing itself into ever-deeper debt. But this model isn't viable, as we now know. The old adage of "those unwilling to work will not get to eat" is now abused as a license for inequality.

Don't get me wrong, capitalism is a fantastic engine for prosperity. "It has accomplished wonders far surpassing Egyptian pyramids, Roman aqueducts, and Gothic cathedrals," as Karl Marx and Friedrich Engels wrote in their *Communist Manifesto*. Yet it's precisely because we're richer than ever that it is now within our means to take the next step in the history of progress: to give each and every person the security of a basic income. It's what capitalism ought to have been striving for all along. See it as a dividend on progress, made possible by the blood, sweat, and tears of past generations. In the end, only a fraction of our prosperity is due to our own exertions. We, the inhabitants of the

[15]"Economists Urge Assured Income," *New York Times* (May 28, 1968).

Land of Plenty, are rich thanks to the institutions, the knowledge, and the social capital amassed for us by our forebears. This wealth belongs to us all. And a basic income allows all of us to share it.

Of course, this is not to say we should implement this dream without forethought. That could be disastrous. Utopias always start out small, with experiments that ever so slowly change the world. It happened just a few years ago on the streets of London, when thirteen street sleepers got £3,000, no questions asked. As one of the aid workers said, "It's quite hard to just change overnight the way you've always approached this problem. These pilots give us the opportunity to talk differently, think differently, describe the problem differently . . ."

And that's how all progress begins. ■

Understanding and Interpreting

1. The title of this chapter from *Utopia for Realists* is "Why We Should Give Free Money to Everyone." Why might Rutger Bregman have chosen that title for this chapter? What effect might that title have on Bregman's audience?
2. What exactly is the "universal basic income" that Bregman advocates? What would it entail?
3. Summarize the conclusions of the experiment with the thirteen homeless men. How does Bregman use this experiment to support his argument?
4. What potential objections to his argument does Bregman anticipate early in this piece?
5. Why does Bregman believe that right now — the early decades of the twenty-first century — is an appropriate, maybe even ideal, time for implementing a universal basic income?
6. What is the meaning of this comment from one of the social workers involved in the experiment with the homeless men: "These pilots give us the opportunity to talk differently, think differently, describe the problem differently" (par. 27)?

Analyzing Language, Style, and Structure

1. **Vocabulary in Context.** Bregman writes: "We're saddled with a welfare state from a bygone era" (par. 23). What does the verb "saddled" mean in this context? How is that meaning similar to or different from other uses that you have encountered? What connotation does it suggest?
2. Bregman refers to "free money" in the chapter title and repeats that phrase throughout the piece. Why do you think he chose that phrase rather than the more formal and neutral "universal basic income" or "guaranteed income"?
3. Bregman begins and ends with an anecdote about the homeless men. How effective is this strategy? Why do you think that this one example does or does not constitute strong evidence?
4. Bregman refers to "decades of fruitless pushing, pulling, pampering, penalizing, prosecuting, and protecting . . ." (par. 9). What effect does this alliteration have? Substitute some synonymous verbs that begin with different letters to listen for the difference.
5. What historical evidence does Bregman provide to support his position? How does expert testimony contribute to this evidence?
6. Examine how and when Bregman addresses counterarguments. Identify one example and analyze how he concedes and refutes the counterargument. How does doing so strengthen his argument?

7. What does Bregman mean by this figure of speech: ". . . welfare benefits are often not a trampoline, but a trap" (par. 23)? What does the metaphor add that a more straightforward explanation would lack?
8. Analyze the phrase Bregman uses to describe universal basic income: "It's an idea whose time has come" (par. 13). How is this phrase likely to affect his readers?

Topics for Composing

1. **Analysis.** Bregman develops his argument with various techniques: anecdote, historical facts and context, expert testimony, and vivid language. Which techniques are most effective in appealing to his audience? Why? Cite specific text to illustrate and support your analysis.
2. **Argument.** Should the United States institute universal basic income as Bregman describes it? Use examples from this piece as well as your own experiences or additional research to support your argument.
3. **Argument.** Bregman makes the following claim in paragraph 26, near the end of his argument: "In the end, only a fraction of our prosperity is due to our own exertions. We, the inhabitants of the Land of Plenty, are rich thanks to the institutions, the knowledge, and the social capital amassed for us by our forebears. This wealth belongs to us all. And a basic income allows all of us to share it." Explain why you agree or disagree with this claim.
4. **Connection.** You have likely read a number of stories in this chapter that present fictional societies striving to be utopias. Which of the societies might support a universal basic income as Bregman proposes here? Why? To what extent would it assist or prevent that society's move toward utopia?
5. **Connection.** What would you do with the money that would be provided to you under Bregman's proposal? Why? How would universal basic income change your life?
6. **Speaking and Listening.** Bregman takes on the criticism that universal basic income would result in a decline in the desire to do meaningful work. Conduct interviews with at least three people who differ from one another in a significant way, such as age, background, political affiliation, ethnicity. Present the interviewees' viewpoints about implementing a guaranteed income in the United States at this time to a group or the whole class. On what points do the interviewees agree and disagree? What concerns or hopes do they share?
7. **Research.** Bregman refers to a number of historical figures in his piece, including John Kenneth Galbraith, Paul Samuelson, and Karl Marx. Conduct research on one or two of these figures. Explain why they might agree or disagree with Bregman's proposal.

Writing a Close Analysis of Prose

When we write a close analysis of prose, we ask ourselves not just what the theme is, or how the setting impacts the story, but how the author uses language to create that setting and to develop the ideas that make up the theme. It's like analyzing a painting by looking at the colors used and the thickness of the brushstrokes. This is a deeper, closer, and more sophisticated kind of analysis of literature than you may have been asked to do before. A close analysis essay is all about *how* a piece of fiction works.

Start by thinking of the author: Why does he or she make certain choices? Why does he or she choose to say that a character "met his untimely demise" or "passed away" or "bought the farm" or "was paid a visit by the grim reaper"? All of these phrases mean somebody died, but why would the author choose one over the other? What was the effect of that choice on the meaning of the passage? If you keep your focus on the author's stylistic decisions, you're on your way to a strong analysis of how he or she conveys meaning or theme. Close reading of a literary text teaches you to observe the smallest details that can lead to greater and deeper understandings.

Throughout this workshop, you will be writing an essay in response to the following prompt:

> Choose a passage of about 400 to 600 words from a piece of fiction you read in this chapter, or from another source, in which a writer uses language you find especially striking. Analyze how the author uses literary elements such as diction, syntax, and imagery to communicate meaning. Explain how that meaning relates to the work as a whole.

To guide you through analyzing the passage you choose, we will use a passage from this chapter's Central Text, "Harrison Bergeron" by Kurt Vonnegut, to model the steps you should take when writing this type of essay. We have chosen a passage that shows a number of literary elements at work, in which Vonnegut examines the flaws in the government's plan to force equality among everyone.

Step 1: Gathering Ideas

When you are assigned to write an essay, you might want to jump right in and start writing. However, there are some things that you should do before you begin writing. This step is all about the process of finding a passage for your analysis and identifying a focus for your essay.

Analyzing a Passage

When writing a close analysis, the first step is thoughtful reading. Reading carefully and curiously and looking for places in the text that seem interesting or significant to you will uncover ideas for you to write about. Let's walk through that process now. Read the following excerpt from "Harrison Bergeron" and consider the annotations related to Vonnegut's language choices, specifically his diction, syntax, and imagery.

If you have not read the story, a little context might be helpful: The events take place in a future in which "equality" is required by the government and enforced by adding handicaps to people who might be stronger, smarter, or more physically attractive than others. Harrison's father (George) and mother are watching the scene unfold on television.

"Harrison Bergeron, age fourteen," she said in a grackle squawk, "has just escaped from jail, where he was held on suspicion of plotting to overthrow the government. He is a genius and an athlete, is under-handicapped, and should be regarded as extremely dangerous."

Diction: Why "grackle"?

A police photograph of Harrison Bergeron was flashed on the screen — upside down, then sideways, upside down again, then right side up. The picture showed the full length of Harrison against a background calibrated in feet and inches. He was exactly seven feet tall.

Sentence Structure: Confusion of the picture display

Diction: Halloween is about costumes, not reality

The rest of Harrison's appearance was Halloween and hardware. Nobody had ever borne heavier handicaps. He had outgrown hindrances faster than the H-G men could think them up. Instead of a little ear radio for a mental handicap, he wore a tremendous pair of earphones, and spectacles with thick wavy lenses. The spectacles were intended to make him not only half blind, but to give him whanging headaches besides.

Imagery: Harrison's heavy burden

Syntax: Shorter sentence for emphasis

Scrap metal was hung all over him. Ordinarily, there was a certain symmetry, a military neatness to the handicaps issued to strong people, but Harrison looked like a walking junkyard. In the race of life, Harrison carried three hundred pounds.

Imagery: He is only 14, but 7 feet tall with 300 pounds of extra weight

And to offset his good looks, the H-G men required that he wear at all times a red rubber ball for a nose, keep his eyebrows shaved off, and cover his even white teeth with black caps at snaggle-tooth random.

"If you see this boy," said the ballerina, "do not — I repeat, do not — try to reason with him."

Imagery: Sound

There was the shriek of a door being torn from its hinges. Screams and barking cries of consternation came from the television set. The photograph of Harrison Bergeron on the screen jumped again and again, as though dancing to the tune of an earthquake.

Imagery: Sound

George Bergeron correctly identified the earthquake, and well he might have — for many was the time his own home had danced to the same crashing tune. "My God—" said George, "that must be Harrison!"

The realization was blasted from his mind instantly by the sound of an automobile collision in his head.

Imagery: Sound

When George could open his eyes again, the photograph of Harrison was gone. A living, breathing Harrison filled the screen.

Clanking, clownish, and huge, Harrison stood — in the center of the studio. The knob of the uprooted studio door was still in his hand. Ballerinas, technicians, musicians, and announcers cowered on their knees before him, expecting to die.

Diction: Unusual word choices; alliteration

"I am the Emperor!" cried Harrison. "Do you hear? I am the Emperor! Everybody must do what I say at once!" He stamped his foot and the studio shook.

"Even as I stand here" he bellowed, "crippled, hobbled, sickened — I am a greater ruler than any man who ever lived! Now watch me become what I can become!"

Syntax: Exclamatory sentences every time Harrison speaks

Harrison tore the straps of his handicap harness like wet tissue paper, tore straps guaranteed to support five thousand pounds.

Syntax: Short sentence for emphasis

Harrison's scrap-iron handicaps crashed to the floor.

Harrison thrust his thumbs under the bar of the padlock that secured his head harness. The bar snapped like celery. Harrison smashed his headphones and spectacles against the wall.

He flung away his rubber-ball nose, revealed a man that would have awed Thor, the god of thunder.

"I shall now select my Empress!" he said, looking down on the cowering people. "Let the first woman who dares rise to her feet claim her mate and her throne!"

A moment passed, and then a ballerina arose, swaying like a willow.

The annotations of the passage you read through are not the only notes you could make, but they are a model for the kinds of things you should be looking for in your own passage: interesting word choices, syntax that seems to vary, and vivid imagery. At this point, you don't need to worry about analyzing or drawing conclusions. Just be thoughtful in your close reading.

Selecting and Annotating a Passage

Look back through the texts that you read in this chapter (or from another source) and identify one with language you find especially striking. Locate a specific passage that is rich in diction, syntax, and imagery. Ideally, the passage will be about the same length as the excerpt from "Harrison Bergeron" above, so look for one that is about 300 to 600 words. When you have settled on a text, reread the passage carefully multiple times and annotate it as in the preceding sample. If you cannot find much to annotate, consider choosing a different passage.

Finding a Focus

It's important to recognize that you can't discuss everything in a particular passage. If you notice four, five, or six devices that seem significant, choose two or three that are most prevalent and that contribute clearly to the author's purpose or meaning. This step is about using your annotations to find connections and patterns that might lead to some conclusions about the author's choices.

Remember that identifying, defining, and giving an example of a device (or a whole series of devices) is a necessary step in this process. However, the goal is to show the connection between what the writer is saying and how he is saying it. In other words, keep your eye on the meaning the author creates with these devices. From the sample annotations of "Harrison Bergeron," a few things become clear:

1. Much of the diction focuses on Harrison's strength and power.
2. The syntax sets Harrison apart from others in the room.
3. The imagery creates a sense of fear and awe regarding Harrison.

As you may remember from this chapter's Skill Workshop, sometimes these choices help us understand a character or a setting. However, oftentimes these small, individual choices work together to convey the overall theme of the work. The ultimate goal of a close reading of prose is to make a reasonable and defensible claim about the theme of a work of literature and to support that claim with evidence and reasoning.

Finding a Focus in Your Passage

Look back through the annotations you made in response to the activity on page 796. Start identifying patterns and connections involving diction, syntax, and imagery. Think about how those patterns might relate to the meaning of the work. These are only speculations at this point; you will work to support them with evidence later in this workshop.

Step 2: Planning the Essay

Now that you have identified a passage, annotated it thoroughly, and begun to identify a focus, you probably have enough of an understanding of the passage to start putting it all together and preparing to write your essay. This step will walk you through creating a thesis, locating relevant and sufficient evidence, and organizing your ideas in preparation for drafting your essay in Step 3.

Developing a Working Thesis

By now, it's clear to you that a literary analysis is more than an exercise in picking apart words and sentences: It's an interpretation, and thus a type of argument. You read and annotate the passage to determine a text's meaning or theme and then select evidence from the text to support your interpretation. Like most arguments, a literary analysis benefits from a clear thesis statement that communicates your main ideas.

Your thesis should do two things: (1) communicate your interpretation of the author's meaning or theme, and (2) specify the literary elements the author uses to convey meaning or theme. For the prompt we've been exploring, we might write a thesis sentence such as the following:

WEAK THESIS

In "Harrison Bergeron," Kurt Vonnegut tells about the dangers of government control in the future.

This statement mostly summarizes the plot of the story and does not take an analytical stance on Vonnegut's stylistic choices.

WEAK THESIS

In "Harrison Bergeron," Kurt Vonnegut uses diction, syntax, and imagery.

This statement only identifies the elements that Vonnegut uses. Finally, here is a working thesis that takes an interpretive stance, and suggests which literary elements are most important in creating the text's meaning:

WORKING THESIS

Through his uses of diction, syntax, and imagery, Vonnegut creates a character who is seen as a threat to the government forces that try to hold back individuality.

Developing Your Working Thesis

Looking back at your annotations and the focus that you identified earlier (p. 797), draft a working thesis statement for your close reading analysis essay. Your working thesis should communicate your interpretation of the text's theme and identify literary elements that the author uses to convey that meaning. Get feedback from a classmate or two and revise as needed.

Gathering Textual Evidence and Connecting to Meaning

Just as in any interpretation, you need to support your ideas by citing textual evidence. But in the case of a literary analysis — in which language choices are central — textual evidence is a make-or-break feature of your essay. Remember that your writing should be focused on your own ideas. For every quotation or reference to language in the piece, you should provide commentary in which you discuss what is significant about the example you selected and how it might be related to your thesis statement. Here is some evidence from the earlier annotations, in a chart with commentary added:

Stylistic element	Example	Commentary
Diction	"grackle squawk," "Halloween and hardware," "Clanking, clownish"	These word choices describing the ballerina and Harrison with their government-required handicaps illustrate how unnatural and unhuman they are forced to be.

Stylistic element	Example	Commentary
Syntax	"I am the Emperor! Everybody must do what I say at once!"	Every time that Harrison speaks, he does so with exclamatory sentences. He has more power than the government should be able to control.
Imagery	"Harrison thrust his thumbs under the bar of the padlock that secured his head harness. The bar snapped like celery. Harrison smashed his headphones and spectacles against the wall."	The sights and sounds that Vonnegut creates through the imagery of Harrison breaking his chains emphasizes how little control the government has despite the handicaps it has forced on him.

Gathering Textual Evidence

Complete a chart like the preceding sample for the passage of the story that you selected, paying particular attention to the explanation of how this might help the author communicate something about the theme of the work. Try for as much evidence as possible. You might not end up using all of it in your essay, but don't limit yourself at this point in the process.

Organizing the Essay

Remember that a close reading analysis is essentially an argumentative essay. The body of your essay is where you prove the thesis that you wrote earlier. How you go about organizing the body of your essay depends largely on your thesis and the support you plan to provide. Here are a few possibilities for our model analysis of "Harrison Bergeron," in order of increasing complexity.

- *Organize by stylistic element*: Using this approach for "Harrison Bergeron," we might have a paragraph about the diction Vonnegut employs, then one about his syntax, and a last body paragraph about the way that he uses imagery. In each case, we would explain how these examples help Vonnegut to communicate his ideas about the government and individuality.
- *Organize by chronological order*: Applying this approach to "Harrison Bergeron," we might devote the first paragraph to analyzing the diction, syntax, and imagery Vonnegut uses at the beginning of the passage. The next paragraph could cover how those elements play out differently in the middle of the passage. The last body

paragraph might be about how the stylistic elements are used at the end of the passage. This organizational strategy works especially well when there are significant shifts in the use of stylistic elements over the course of a passage, though you will want to be careful to avoid merely summarizing.

- *Organize by thematic element*: Applying this approach to "Harrison Bergeron," we might define our body paragraphs by the different thematic points that Vonnegut wants to make. The first paragraph might be about the inhumane effects of government control, the next could be about the power of the individual, and the last body paragraph could be about the inevitable failure of governmental control. In each paragraph of this approach, we would refer to specific examples of diction, syntax, or imagery.

Organizing Your Essay

Looking back at your thesis and the chart you created in response to the activity on page 799, sketch an outline for the body of your essay, based on one of the three options just described. Discuss with a partner why you chose this particular approach and what the benefits and challenges of this structure might be.

Step 3: Drafting the Essay

So far in this workshop, you have identified and annotated a passage, drafted a thesis, identified textual evidence, and considered the organizational structure that your essay might take. Now it is time to begin drafting your essay, focusing on the elements your body paragraphs will include and thinking about how to begin and conclude your essay.

Drafting Body Paragraphs

The number of body paragraphs you need depends on your organizational structure and the requirements of your specific assignment. We will walk you through writing one of these for our model analysis of "Harrison Bergeron." This is the working thesis we developed earlier: *Through his uses of diction, syntax, and imagery, Vonnegut creates a character who is seen as a threat to the government forces that try to hold back individuality*. One of our body paragraphs will be about Vonnegut's syntax. Here is a topic sentence with some evidence:

> Through his syntax, Vonnegut creates the larger-than-life character of Harrison, who is an example of how humanity cannot be controlled by the government. The very first time we hear Harrison speak, he says, " 'I am the Emperor! . . . Do you hear? I am the Emperor! Everybody must do what I say at once!' "

Commentary after a quotation is essential because we don't all draw the same interpretation from a text. Some might say that the syntax shows Harrison as a bully; others might see it as evidence of his frustration with following the rules imposed by the government. The point is that we are explaining to the members of our audience precisely how we interpret this syntax because we cannot assume that everyone shares our interpretation. So, here is the paragraph with commentary added that points the reader to the interpretation we feel best supports our thesis:

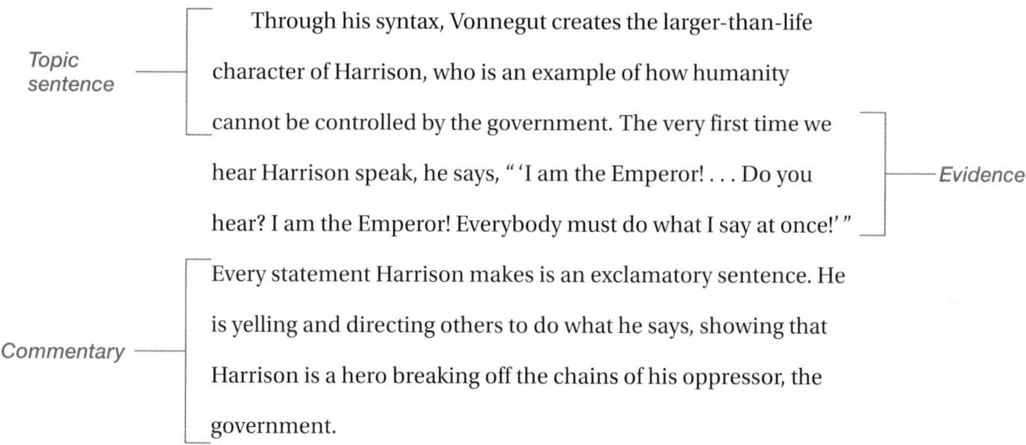

Through his syntax, Vonnegut creates the larger-than-life character of Harrison, who is an example of how humanity cannot be controlled by the government. The very first time we hear Harrison speak, he says, "'I am the Emperor! . . . Do you hear? I am the Emperor! Everybody must do what I say at once!'" Every statement Harrison makes is an exclamatory sentence. He is yelling and directing others to do what he says, showing that Harrison is a hero breaking off the chains of his oppressor, the government.

The commentary — your explanation of the evidence — will be the most important part of your essay. A general rule of thumb is to have at least two sentences of commentary for every example you use from the text. If your essay ever has more quotations from the text than words of your own, then your level of commentary is probably insufficient. In our model above, we'd probably like to add more evidence of syntax from later in the passage and provide further commentary:

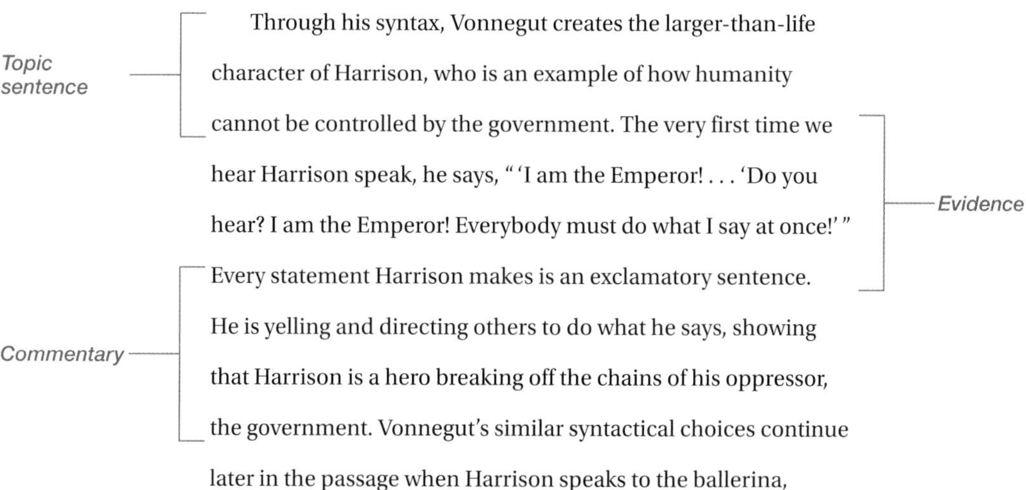

Through his syntax, Vonnegut creates the larger-than-life character of Harrison, who is an example of how humanity cannot be controlled by the government. The very first time we hear Harrison speak, he says, "'I am the Emperor! . . . 'Do you hear? I am the Emperor! Everybody must do what I say at once!'" Every statement Harrison makes is an exclamatory sentence. He is yelling and directing others to do what he says, showing that Harrison is a hero breaking off the chains of his oppressor, the government. Vonnegut's similar syntactical choices continue later in the passage when Harrison speaks to the ballerina,

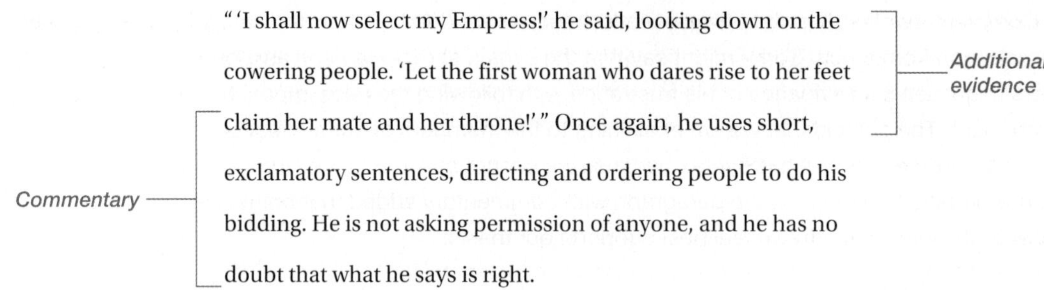
"'I shall now select my Empress!' he said, looking down on the cowering people. 'Let the first woman who dares rise to her feet claim her mate and her throne!'" Once again, he uses short, exclamatory sentences, directing and ordering people to do his bidding. He is not asking permission of anyone, and he has no doubt that what he says is right.

Our sample body paragraph is focused on Vonnegut's use of syntax. If we had chosen to organize our essay around a discussion of stylistic elements, our next two body paragraphs might focus on his use of diction and his use of imagery. These body paragraphs would likely follow the same structure we used in the model above, including a topic sentence and as much evidence and commentary as needed to help prove the point we are making.

Drafting Body Paragraphs

Returning to your thesis, evidence chart, and organizational plan, draft a body paragraph for your close reading analysis essay. In addition to the evidence from the text, be sure that your paragraph includes commentary about how the evidence supports your topic sentence and thesis. Show a draft of your body paragraph to a classmate or two and get feedback on how well you have used the evidence and your commentary to prove your points. Then, draft the remaining body paragraph according to the organizational structure you identified earlier in this workshop (p. 800). Be sure that each body paragraph includes a topic sentence related to your working thesis (p. 798).

Writing an Introduction

We know that an essay begins with an introduction and that the thesis statement should be part of it. But what else should we write in the introduction? An introduction should generally have three parts:

- **a.** The hook
- **b.** The context and connection
- **c.** The claim (thesis)

The Hook

The hook is how you grab your reader's attention. How you set up your thesis depends on the task at hand and the requirements of your assignment. Some options include an interesting anecdote, an observation, or a question. Whatever approach you choose, since this is a literary analysis essay, make sure the hook is related to the theme that you will discuss. For our analysis of "Harrison Bergeron," we might ask a question about the role of government in our daily lives, or start with a definition of the word "equality." Keep in mind that this section is called the hook because it should make readers want to keep reading.

The Context and Connection

Provide context and build a connection between your hook and your thesis. While we may have started with a question about government or a definition of equality, we might narrow our scope by saying something more specific about the direction our essay will take. Perhaps our essay will be about overreaching governments or the dangers of forcing equality.

The Thesis

Since you've already worked on your thesis, incorporating it into a paragraph will give you an additional opportunity to revise it. Generally, the thesis appears at the end of the introduction.

Here is a possible introduction for our sample analysis of "Harrison Bergeron":

> The Declaration of Independence famously states that "All men are created equal." Leaving aside that these words were written by a slaveholder, is this actually a true statement? Some people are born taller, stronger, smarter, more beautiful than others. What would the world be like if a government attempted to enforce this vision [Hook] of equality by placing handicaps on the strong, smart, and beautiful? This is the dystopian future that Kurt Vonnegut explores in his short story, "Harrison Bergeron." [Connection] Through his uses of diction, syntax, and imagery, Vonnegut creates a title character who is seen as a threat to the government forces that try to hold back individuality. [Thesis]

Writing Your Introduction

Draft an introduction to your essay. Show your draft to a classmate for feedback on whether it sufficiently hooks the reader's interest and includes enough context for the reader to understand the thesis.

Writing a Conclusion

So what? is a fair question when you're writing a literary analysis. You've identified specific strategies or devices an author uses, you've defined and explained them, given examples, and tied them to the author's theme or meaning — but so what? What does it all add up to? You might be tempted to view the literary essay as merely a type of exercise, but if you do so, you risk boring yourself and your audience. You might be tempted to conclude your essay by simply repeating what you've already said.

A better approach is to use your literary analysis as an opportunity to express an original interpretation, deepen your appreciation of an author's craft, or illustrate how deftly and subtly literary elements work together in a particular piece. After you present a well-developed argument, you may use one of the following tactics to keep your readers thinking about the passage or story after they've finished your essay.

- *Make sure the whole is greater than the sum of its parts.* If, for instance, you've discussed two or three literary elements, use your conclusion to show how they work together. For example, in our essay about "Harrison Bergeron," we might explain how the diction, syntax, and imagery Vonnegut uses to define Harrison illustrate irrepressible individuality.
- *Ask questions to explore your interpretation further.* Consider what inquiry might deepen your understanding of the choices the author has made, as well as the conclusions you've drawn. For instance, if our essay focused on the dangers of government control in "Harrison Bergeron," we might conclude by asking our audience to consider how the story would be different if Harrison were benefiting from the government-imposed equality.
- *Emphasize your interpretation.* This is the most common way to end a literary analysis. For instance, we could point out that Vonnegut might be suggesting that the government's actions are inconsistent with human nature's inclination toward individuality.

Writing Your Conclusion

Write a draft of a conclusion of your essay, trying out one or more of the approaches identified above. Show your draft to a classmate for feedback on whether it sufficiently addresses the "so what?" question.

Step 4: Finalizing the Essay

Now that you have a complete draft of your essay, you can move on to the final phase of the writing process: revising and editing. These two acts are sometimes thought of as being the same, but they're not. Revision is when you look back at large-scale structural elements of your essay, such as how well you support your claim, what kinds of evidence you use, how effective your word choices are, and to what extent you have led your reader easily through your essay. Editing, on the other hand, focuses on fine-tuning the language, grammar, punctuation, spelling, and other conventions. Editing is usually the very last thing you do before you finalize your piece, looking carefully for any errors that you tend to make. The following are suggestions for you to consider as you finalize your essay.

Revising

Revising gives you a good opportunity to think again about your essay's purpose and audience. In most cases, your audience will be your teacher. In the case of a standardized test, it will be an external evaluator. In both situations, that means using a somewhat formal tone, but your writing can still be engaging for you and your audience.

Reread your essay for the following:

- Look back at your **thesis**. Since you wrote this early on in the workshop, does it still relate to the analysis you ended up writing? If you think you need more work on this part of your essay, see Revision Workshop 1: Effective Thesis and Essay Structure (p. 1064).
- Have you examined the writer's **language choices** and explained how they help to communicate a theme? Look back at the Skill Workshop (p. 671) at the beginning of this chapter to remind yourself if necessary.
- Look back at some of your **body paragraphs**. Have you balanced the evidence with your own **commentary** about how that evidence supports your thesis? Look at Revision Workshop 3: Balanced Evidence and Commentary (p. 1073) for more on this topic. Do you think you have enough **evidence** to support your thesis statement? If not, consider examining Revision Workshop 4: Appropriate Evidence and Support (p. 1076).
- Does your **introduction** grab the reader's attention and effectively preview your topic? Does your **conclusion** wrap up in a way that highlights your focus? See Revision Workshop 8: Effective Introductions and Conclusions (p. 1097) for additional practice.
- Can your reader follow the **organization** of your essay easily? If not, consider looking over Revision Workshop 5: Effective Transitions (p. 1082) or Revision Workshop 2: Effective Topic Sentences and Unified Paragraphs (p. 1068).
- Did you write using **present tense** verbs? Literature *lives*, so your analysis should discuss how the author *uses* literary devices and *presents* the speaker.
- Did you identify page numbers for all **quotations**? When you quote more than three lines from the text, have you applied block quotation format? See Chapter 4 (p. 147) for more help.
- Although some **summary** may be necessary for establishing context, summary is not analysis. Did you avoid overly summarizing the text? You can assume some level of familiarity with the text by your reader. See Chapter 4 (p. 147) for more help incorporating outside sources into your own writing.

Editing

Remember, editing is the very last thing you'll do before finalizing your essay. You and your teacher know better than anyone the types of spelling, grammar, and convention errors you need to focus on in your writing development. Be sure to refer to one or more of the Grammar Workshops (starting on p. 1101) in the back of the book if you encounter an issue and aren't sure how to overcome it.

10 Utopia and Dystopia

Continuing the Conversation

Throughout this chapter, you have been reading texts and thinking about utopias and dystopias. At the beginning of the chapter and after each of the readings, you had opportunities to consider ideas related to the following essential questions:

- What elements of our world today have the potential to lead to a dystopian future?
- What are the characteristics and motivations of those who challenge a dystopian world?
- Where are the boundaries between a typical change in society and a change that leads to dystopia?
- Why do utopias seem to turn into dystopias?
- Why are we drawn to stories about utopias and dystopias?

The sections that follow will give you an opportunity to revisit and respond to some of those questions as you think further about utopias and dystopias by connecting these ideas to yourself, to texts you've read, and to the world outside of the classroom.

Connections to Self

Think back on the texts you have read, responses you have written, discussions you have participated in, and ideas you have considered during your work with this chapter. Use the following questions to help explore how the issues raised in this chapter connect to your life and experience:

1. In your opinion, what is the most important quality of a good society? What is the most damaging aspect of a bad society?
2. Describe what your own utopia would be like. What makes it a utopia?
3. Which of the texts that you read in this chapter had the most significant impact on the ways that you think about what makes a society a good or bad one? Why?
4. Of the utopian and dystopian societies you read about in this chapter, which would be easiest for you to live in? Which would be hardest for you to live in? Why?
5. Put yourself in the place of one of the characters from a story in this chapter. If you were confronted with the same situations and decisions as that character, how would your actions be similar to or different from those taken by the character?

Connections to Texts

Use the following questions to make connections among the texts in this chapter and to consider what insights the texts provide into the essential questions. As you respond, be sure to make specific references to **two or more texts** you read in this chapter.

1. Imagine a dialogue between two characters or speakers from two different texts in this chapter. What would they say to each other about the societies in which they

live? To what extent are they aware that they live in a utopian or dystopian society?

2. In what ways can some of the texts that you read in this chapter be seen as cautionary tales for our real world? In what ways do the texts present their warnings to us similarly or differently?
3. The desire to suppress individualism is explored in several of the stories in this chapter. Examine the role that individuality plays in whether a society is a utopia or dystopia in two or more of the stories in this chapter. You may want to consider the following texts in your discussion: "Valedictorian," "Harrison Bergeron," and "The Era."
4. Culture is often defined by a community's rituals and customs. What are two or more of the authors in this chapter suggesting about the role that ritual plays in leading societies to a utopia or dystopia? You may want to consider the following texts in your discussion: "The Lottery," "Once the World Was Perfect," "Valedictorian," "The Ones Who Walked Away from Omelas."
5. A need to level society, to diminish or even eliminate inequality is a central idea of many dystopian stories. What methods of achieving equality do the texts in this chapter explore? What do these texts suggest about the positive and negative effects of those efforts? You may want to consider the following texts in your discussion: *Fahrenheit 451*, "Harrison Bergeron," *Herland*, and "The Era."

Connections to World

Think back on the texts you have read, responses you have written, discussions you have participated in, and ideas you have considered during your work with this chapter. Use the following questions to explore how the issues raised in this chapter play out in the world at large:

1. What aspects of current American society seem to be close to a utopia? What aspects seem closer to a dystopia? How so?
2. Name a leader in today's world whose appeal is based on a call for a utopian society. What are the basic elements of change that the person believes are needed to achieve that vision?
3. Why do there seem to be so many dystopian books, films, and TV shows these days? How do these dystopian visions reflect the prevailing fears about the world of the early twenty-first century?
4. What factor in our global society seems most likely to lead to a dystopian nightmare: economic inequality, rapid technological change, political instability, racial or ethnic conflict? Something else? Explain your choice.
5. Some of the texts in this chapter might be called science fiction. How do you define science fiction? To what extent do you think that science fiction can convey insights about the real world?

SAIFUL ISLAM/Getty Images

Do the Right Thing

Essential Questions:

- **How do we decide what actions or decisions are "right" or "wrong"?**
- **To what extent do our age, culture, gender identity, and other personal characteristics affect the ethics of our decision-making?**
- **How can we gauge the effects that our decisions have on other individuals, our community, and society at large?**
- **Under what circumstances is an individual likely to base a decision on personal feelings or beliefs rather than on prevailing social values or norms?**

Imagine that you are the operator of a train that has suddenly lost its brakes. Ahead of you on the tracks are *five* railroad workers who are unaware that you are moments away from slamming into them at a speed that will likely kill them all. Suddenly, you notice that there is a split up ahead that would allow you to switch to a different track, at the end of which is only *one* railroad worker. Your choice: Keep on the first track and kill five, or switch tracks and kill only one. Do you kill the one to save the five? Why or why not?

This is a classic ethical dilemma designed to illustrate the complexity of ethical choices. Philosopher Judith Jarvis Thomson complicates the dilemma even further by asking you to imagine that, instead of being the operator, you are a bystander on a bridge watching the train heading toward the five workers. Next to you on the bridge is a man who is leaning far over to look at the train. You could very easily push the man off the bridge in front of the train, which would stop its progress, thereby saving the five people at the end of the track. Would you push the man, killing one to save the five? Why or why not? How is this scenario similar to or different from the previous one? What if you knew for certain that the man on the bridge was a murderer who had gotten away with his crime?

Obviously, these situations are not likely to occur, but they can help us to clarify what we mean by "ethics." As a branch of philosophy, ethics tries to articulate the reasons that some actions are considered "right" and others "wrong." Just about everyone will say that killing is wrong. And yet, in scenarios such as the ones above, could killing sometimes be justified? Most people will say that stealing is wrong — yet could stealing be acceptable if you couldn't afford the medicine that was needed to save your dying child? Is it okay to cheat on a test that everyone else is cheating on, especially if you might be competing with them for acceptance into a good college?

We know that different cultures, religions, and nations have different customs, laws, and practices, but do they also have different ethical codes? Philosopher Bertrand Russell wrote, "I cannot see how to refute the arguments for the subjectivity of ethical values, but I find myself incapable of believing that all that is wrong with wanton cruelty is that I don't like it." In other words, he expects that there should be some things that all people — regardless of culture — ought to be able to agree are right or wrong, in at least some situations.

Doing the Right Thing

Choose one or more of the following scenarios and discuss with a partner what you would do in the situation and why:

1. It is May of your senior year, and your best friend has been accepted to Harvard on a full scholarship. Unfortunately, her mother has become very sick, and your friend has had to take care of her younger siblings. As a result, she is finding it difficult to stay on top of her schoolwork and maintain the GPA required for her scholarship. She calls you one night in a panic because she has forgotten to do a major assignment due the following day and her teacher never accepts late work. You have completed the identical assignment for a different teacher. You go to a very big school and it is unlikely that either of the two teachers will ever see the other's assignments. If you let your friend copy your work, the chances of your being caught are low. Nevertheless, your school has a zero-tolerance policy for cheating. If you are caught, both of you could be subject to severe punishments, including an automatic *F* in the class. Do you share your assignment with your friend so that she can turn it in as her own work? Why or why not?
2. You are a parent of an eighteen-year-old boy, and you, he, and your spouse are traveling to Singapore, a country with extremely strict drug laws. At the airport in Singapore, the security officials, using drug-sniffing dogs, begin looking closely at your son's bag. You have suspected in the past that your son may have smoked marijuana, but you've never known for sure or confronted him about it. As the security officials move closer to the bag, you look at your son's face, and you are convinced that he has brought marijuana with him. At the same time, you realize your spouse knows this as well and is preparing to take the blame for your son,

which would likely lead to your spouse serving many years in prison. When the security officials ask, "Whose bag is this?", what do you do? Why?

3. The following scenario is a real-life example from a famous court case in England called *The Queen v. Dudley and Stephens.* In 1884, four British men survived a shipwreck and floated for three weeks in a lifeboat in the Atlantic Ocean. When they ran out of food and water, the captain decided that they should draw straws to determine who would be killed and eaten in order to save the remaining three. The others refused. Eventually, the cabin boy became sick. When he was near death, the captain decided to kill him. The captain and the other two survivors ate his body, which kept them alive until they were rescued four days later. Upon returning to England, the captain was charged with murder. If you were on the jury, would you vote to convict the captain? Why or why not?
4. The following scenario is a classic fictional ethical situation called "The Heinz Dilemma." Imagine that you have a spouse dying from a rare disease. A drug that might save your spouse is available from a pharmacist in town. The pharmacist is charging $200,000, ten times what the pharmacy paid for the drug wholesale. You borrow all the money you can and go to the pharmacist with half the amount needed and ask him to sell the drug to you for less. When he refuses, you become desperate and break into the pharmacy to steal the drug. Should you have done that? Why or why not?

Texts in Conversation

Throughout this chapter, you will read about a number of people who have tried — or are still trying — to "do the right thing" in a wide range of contexts. As you read, keep track of some of their different approaches, make connections among them, and respond to them with your own reactions. At the end of the chapter, you'll have an opportunity to write your own piece about doing the right thing, using the texts you read as evidence and inspiration. Following is a graphic organizer that might help you:

Author/title	What ethical choice(s) does the author address?	Quotation(s) that illustrate the author's ideas about ethics and doing the right thing	Your reaction and/or connections to other texts

Understanding Style and Tone in Argument

At some point, you may have been on the receiving end of this sentence: "Don't take that tone with me!" If you have been, you know that the speaker was likely reacting less to what you said and more to how you said it — your attitude. For example, the word "whatever" means "a range of things without restriction." However, when coupled with a rolling of the eyes and a sarcastic tone of voice, it becomes an expression of exasperation or annoyance. If you say "whatever" with that kind of dismissive attitude, it's probable that your tone — not just your use of the word — will cause offense.

This is exactly why the definition of the literary term **tone** is "the author or speaker's attitude toward his or her subject." Writers can take on a whole range of tones, expressing the full spectrum of human emotion, from joy to frustration, from anguish to ecstasy. As you saw in Chapter 3 about argument, a writer's language and style help to create the tone, which is an essential part of persuading an audience of a claim. It's not only *what's* being said but *how* it is said that can strengthen an argument, making it especially vivid or convincing. When we look at the *how* of an argument, we look at the way the writer's stylistic choices — language, figures of speech, and sentence patterns — work together over the course of that argument. These stylistic elements are used together to convey tone.

Tone is both essential and tricky. It's essential because you need to strike the right tone to appeal to a specific audience. Sarcasm and satire, for example, can be effective for catching and keeping an audience's attention, but they're risky for serious subjects. If your audience reads your attitude toward your subject as being glib or disrespectful, that tone will turn them off, no matter how good your evidence might be. Basically, writers' stylistic choices should work together to convey an appropriate attitude toward their subject.

Following are just a few words that can be used to describe an author's tone:

acerbic
appalled
apologetic
benevolent
bitter
cold
complimentary
condescending
contemptuous
dispassionate
dreamy
fanciful
frivolous
giddy
horrified
indignant
jocular
joyful
livid
mocking
nostalgic
objective
patronizing
placid
provocative
sarcastic
sentimental
sharp
somber
sweet
sympathetic
urgent
wry
vibrant

This workshop will focus on examining how style creates tone, which in turn helps to develop and support an argument. Read the first part of the opinion piece by Jose Antonio

Vargas, originally published in the *New York Times* in 2018 at the height of a national debate on immigration. At the end of the workshop, you will write your own analysis on the last part of his argument.

from What America Looks Like from a Jail in South Texas

Jose Antonio Vargas

Erika Goldring/Getty Images

Jose Antonio Vargas is a Pulitzer Prize–winning journalist and author of the book *Dear America: Notes of an Undocumented Citizen* (2018). Born in the Philippines in 1961, Vargas came to the United States when he was 12. He wrote about this experience in a groundbreaking essay entitled, "My Life as an Undocumented Immigrant" (2011). Vargas grew up in Mountain View, California, where an elementary school was named in his honor in 2019.

FOCUS FOR READING As you give this first portion of the argument an initial reading, annotate the text by making connections and asking questions (see p. 10). Then, go through it again and add annotations about any stylistic choices you notice (p. 114).

Of all the ways I imagined the inevitable — being arrested, getting detained — I never envisioned sitting on the cold cement floor of a jail cell in South Texas surrounded by children.

It was July 2014. The cell, as I remember it, was no bigger than 20 by 30 feet. All around me were about 25 boys, as young as 5, the oldest no more than 12. The air reeked. A boy across the room from me was crying inconsolably, his head buried in his chest. Most of the boys wore dazed expressions. It was clear they had no idea where they were or why they were there.

The only source of entertainment came from Mylar blankets, flimsy metallic sheets that were supposed to keep us warm. Three boys played with a blanket as if it were a toy, crunching it up into a ball, passing it back and forth.

A window faced a central area where a dozen or so patrol agents were stationed, but there was not much to look at. All I could do was stare at the boys' shoes. My shoes were shiny and brand new; theirs, dirty, muddy and worn down. The only thing our shoes had in common was that none of them had laces.

5 "Jose Antonio Vargas," said an agent as he walked in. "I don't need you. Not yet. But we're gonna move you."

The moment the agent said my name, one of the boys playing with the blanket started speaking to me. I had no idea what he was saying. The one word I could make out was "miedo." Something about "miedo."

If I spoke Spanish, I could have told the boys the story I kept secret for years, a story that I'm now asked to tell almost every day: I was born in the Philippines, a country whose colonial-imperial history is characterized as being "300 years in the convent, 50 years in Hollywood." When I was 12, my mother put me on a plane to California to go live with her parents. When I was 16, while applying for a driver's permit, I discovered that the documents my grandfather had given me were fake, that I did not have legal documents to be in this country.

Jose Antonio Vargas, "What America Looks Like From a Jail in South Texas," *The New York Times*, September 15, 2018. https://www.nytimes.com/

If I spoke Spanish, I could have told the boys about the country they had arrived and been detained in, a country I've lived in for more than 20 years, the country I did not ask to come to but where I have been educated, where I have worked since I was a teenager, where my grandparents and other relatives immigrated with documentation but where I have found myself stranded without a way to "get legal."

This is a country that prides itself as one founded and built by immigrants, but also one whose laws and policies have historically been anti-immigrant. Ask the Chinese. Talk to the Irish.

This is a country that depends on immigrant labor, often cheap labor, especially from undocumented workers, while spending billions of dollars a year detaining, incarcerating and deporting people the government deems "illegal." Undocumented workers like me pay taxes into this very system. This is a country of welcome, where people like me have been befriended, supported, even nurtured by American citizens of all racial, economic and political backgrounds, and it is a country whose citizens continue to vote for local and national officials who uphold and enact an inhumane immigration enforcement machine that locks up children.

If I spoke Spanish, I could have told the boys that none of this was their fault. I could have explained, in the clearest, most accessible way I could, the connection between the irreversible actions of the United States of America and the inevitable reactions in their countries of birth. How a trade agreement, like the North American Free Trade Agreement, drove millions of Mexicans out of jobs and led parents to cross borders so they could feed their kids. How decades of interventionist policies by both Republicans and Democrats brought economic and political instability to and sowed violence in El Salvador, Guatemala and Honduras.

How people like us come to America because America, from its people, its politics and its products, were and are very much already in our countries.

I don't understand much Spanish. The most Spanish thing about me is my name. My name is Jose because of Spanish colonialism. But my Jose isn't José, because of American imperialism. (After the Americans forced the Spanish out of the Philippines, their typewriters couldn't type accented vowels.)

So in that cell that night, I told the young boy holding the crunched-up blanket, "No hablo español."

Quickly, I added, "Soy Filipino."

I am Filipino, a declaration that seemed to cause him more confusion. I'm not sure he heard me when I said, almost in a whisper, like a prayer, "Pepeton ang pangalan ko." My name is Pepeton.

It's my nickname, combining the nicknames of Jose (Pepe) and Antonio (Ton). It's the name of my past — what my mother and everyone in the Philippines who knows me calls me.

It's the name I've avoided so I could construct a different kind of identity, not the "illegal" you see and hear about in the news, but the journalist who reports the news and became a writer so I could see my name on a piece of paper. But inside that cell, there was no place to hide, nothing to run away from, no role to play.

After I was handcuffed at the airport, I was driven alone in a white van. Upon my arrival, two agents took everything I had: my phone, my wallet, my backpack, my luggage. I was asked to take off my leather belt and the laces in my shoes. When I asked why, one of the agents answered, "We don't want you hurting yourself."

I wanted to laugh. I've always used laughter to conceal my emotions; here, to distance and detach myself from the absurdity of this ordeal. Is this really about who has the right papers and what the laws are? Is this really about who is a citizen or not? Are we talking about the same citizenship that many Americans callously take for granted?

I asked one of the guards if he spoke Spanish. He did.

"What's 'miedo'?"

"Fear," he said. "It means fear." ■

Analyzing Diction

The words you choose, whether you're writing or speaking, help you develop your style. Let's examine some of the language choices Vargas makes at the very beginning of his argument. As discussed in Chapter 3, effective arguments make use of connotative language (associations and emotional weight that words carry). Vargas opens this piece by establishing the setting: He is sitting on "the cold cement floor of a jail cell in South Texas surrounded by children." That combination — jail and children — is jarring enough. But he doesn't stop there; the way he describes that scene brings it to emotional life.

> It was July 2014. The cell, as I remember it, was no bigger than 20 by 30 feet. All around me were about 25 boys, as young as 5, the oldest no more than 12. The air reeked. A boy across the room from me was crying inconsolably, his head buried in his chest. Most of the boys wore dazed expressions. It was clear they had no idea where they were or why they were there.
>
> The only source of entertainment came from Mylar blankets, flimsy metallic sheets that were supposed to keep us warm. Three boys played with a blanket as if it were a toy, crunching it up into a ball, passing it back and forth.

As you reread these two paragraphs, it's clear that Vargas chooses words that will make his readers feel emotionally connected to the boys and their situation: "dazed expressions," "crying inconsolably," and "air reeked."

Notice also that even the simple qualifying words (italicized in the next sentence) Vargas chooses also carry emotional weight. He describes the cell as "*no bigger* than 20 x 30" and characterizes his cellmates as the "25 boys, *as young as* 5, the oldest *no more than* 12." Those qualifying words emphasize just how small the cell is and just how young the boys are in order to continue connecting the reader to the situation through emotion.

Analyzing Diction

Analyze the diction in the following passage. How do these choices help Vargas connect with his reader and achieve his purpose? You may find it helpful to revisit the annotations you made when you first read this passage as part of the larger excerpt (pp. 813–814).

> [Pepeton] is my nickname, combining the nicknames of Jose (Pepe) and Antonio (Ton). It's the name of my past — what my mother and everyone in the Philippines who knows me calls me.
>
> It's the name I've avoided so I could construct a different kind of identity, not the "illegal" you see and hear about in the news, but the journalist who reports the news and became a writer so I could see my name on a piece of paper. But inside that cell, there was no place to hide, nothing to run away from, no role to play.
>
> After I was handcuffed at the airport, I was driven alone in a white van. Upon my arrival, two agents took everything I had: my phone, my wallet, my backpack, my luggage. I was asked to take off my leather belt and the laces in my shoes. When I asked why, one of the agents answered, "We don't want you hurting yourself."

Analyzing Register

"Register" is just a technical term for something that you probably already know very well. It is defined as the way a speaker uses language differently depending on the situation. For example, you speak differently when you are with your friends than you would in a job interview. Register usually refers to variations in formality, which are determined by occasion, context, purpose, and audience. You might think that someone writing in a newspaper like the *New York Times* would use a formal register to appeal to the publication's educated readership. And yet, Vargas takes a slightly different tack and often uses an informal register. For example, he writes that certain policies "led parents to cross borders so they could feed their kids." What's the difference between saying "kids" and "children"? The first is informal, even colloquial, while the second is more formal. In general, the more casual term carries a warmer emotional feeling.

Also, Vargas could have written in the third person, which would sound more objective and formal. However, he writes in the first person, creating a closer relationship with his audience. Think about how your reaction to the topic would have been different if the first paragraph, for example, had been written like this:

> On July 2014, 25 boys between the ages of 5 and 12 were kept in a small jail cell. From their facial expressions and reactions, it was clear that they did not understand why they were there.

Written in the third person, this version is more straightforward and lacks the personal connection. The style might be described as objective — or detached or even antiseptic, depending upon your viewpoint. Vargas, however, goes for the heart here, appealing to pathos through his first-person account that includes details that evoke the senses. And yet, Vargas does not maintain a single register throughout his piece. While the beginning of his argument is very emotional and rather informal, Vargas doesn't appeal to pathos throughout his piece. For instance, in the following passage, Vargas presents some factual background information and takes on a more formal register:

> I could have explained . . . the connection between the irreversible actions of the United States of America and the inevitable reactions in their [the children's] countries of birth. How a trade agreement, like the North American Free Trade Agreement, drove millions of Mexicans out of jobs and led parents to cross borders so they could feed their kids. How decades of interventionist policies by both Republicans and Democrats brought economic and political instability to and sowed violence in El Salvador, Guatemala and Honduras.

Language such as "actions" of one country and "reactions" of another, "trade agreement," "interventionist policies by both Republicans and Democrats" is the more neutral, formal language of concepts and policy. Vargas changes his register to reflect the needs of his argument.

Analyzing Register

Reread the first part of the opinion piece (pp. 813–814) and discuss with a partner the different registers that Vargas appears to use. When is he more formal and when is he more informal? What effect do these shifting registers create?

Analyzing Figurative Language

Figurative language — similes, metaphors, personification, and allusion, for example — helps writers to communicate a feeling or an idea effectively to their readers. Vargas, for instance, uses a **simile** to describe the Mylar blankets intended to help him and his fellow detainees stay warm: "Three boys played with a blanket *as if it were a toy*, crunching it up into a ball, passing it back and forth." The description "as if it were a toy" is both a subtle and stark reminder of how unnatural it is for young children to be confined in a jail cell: they should be elsewhere, just playing, like other kids.

Analyzing Figurative Language

Read the following sentence from Vargas's piece and consider the figurative language he uses to describe immigration:

> This is a country of welcome, where people like me have been befriended, supported, even nurtured by American citizens of all racial, economic and political backgrounds, and it is a country whose citizens continue to vote for local and national officials who uphold and enact an inhumane immigration enforcement machine that locks up children.

What is the effect of calling the immigration system a "machine"? How does Vargas's assertion that the machine "locks up children" influence your understanding of United States immigration, as he describes it? How does this figure of speech relate to the first part of his sentence about the United States being a "country of welcome"?

Analyzing Sentence Structures

Choosing your words carefully is only part of developing style. How you put those words together is another key element. Let's look at three ways that Vargas uses syntax by examining the rhetorical questions, parallel structure, and sentence variety in his essay.

Rhetorical questions are a syntactical strategy to enhance style and draw in the audience. They are questions that a writer does not intend for the reader to answer. When you pose a rhetorical question, you create an opportunity to answer it yourself with your own reasoning and viewpoint. You're leading your reader. In the following passage, Vargas describes his experience with being taken into custody. He says that he laughed "to distance and detach myself from the absurdity of this ordeal." Then, he asks three rhetorical questions: "Is this really about who has the right papers and what the laws are? Is this really about who is a citizen or not? Are we talking about the same citizenship that many Americans take for granted?" He uses these questions to introduce his thoughts about leaving the Philippines and to introduce the conflicts and paradoxes he sees in U.S. immigration policy.

Parallel structure refers to similar grammatical structures (a single word, a phrase, a clause, or a full sentence) that emphasize related ideas. You'll often find parallel structure in speeches because repetition tends to make statements memorable or emphatic. Vargas uses this strategy throughout his essay with different effects.

Around the middle of his argument, Vargas writes about the boys trying to talk with him in Spanish, a language he understands and speaks at only a rudimentary level. He begins a series of paragraphs with the same phrase: "If I spoke Spanish, I could have told the boys."

> "If I spoke Spanish, I could have told the boys the story I kept secret for years. . . ."
>
> "If I spoke Spanish, I could have told the boys about the country they had arrived and been detained in. . . ."
>
> "If I spoke Spanish, I could have told the boys that none of this is their fault. . . ."

Is this structure just monotonous? It's a direct repetition of the same opening clause and part of the independent clause that follows. And yet — it becomes a kind of mantra that emphasizes what might have been the reality of the situation but isn't. As you read over the paragraphs that follow these parallel topic sentences, you realize that Vargas is sharing his thoughts about himself and his experiences with us, his readers, in ways he could not with his young fellow detainees. The parallel structure emphasizes one sad failure of communication after another, each becoming in Vargas's estimation more profound until the final one: "none of this is their fault." This parallel structure at the beginning of each paragraph knits together the many concrete details of experience into a key point he wants to make: Policies leading to the detention of undocumented immigrants are unfair regardless of a person's age, experience, or country of origin.

Sentence variety is another stylistic choice. Sometimes this means placing longer and shorter sentences right next to each other, as Vargas does in the following excerpt:

> If I spoke Spanish, I could have told the boys about the country they had arrived and been detained in, a country I've lived in for more than 20 years, the country I did not ask to come to but where I have been educated, where I have worked since I was a teenager, where my grandparents and other relatives immigrated with documentation but where I have found myself stranded without a way to "get legal."
>
> This is a country that prides itself as one founded and built by immigrants, but also one whose laws and policies have historically been anti-immigrant. Ask the Chinese. Talk to the Irish.

The first sentence is seventy-six words; the second is twenty-five; the third and fourth are less than five words each. Vargas builds the first sentence with accumulated detail in clauses and phrases that feel almost like a rush of emotions. The second one moves from his personal experience to a commentary on it that is somewhat more subdued. But then he comes to an abrupt stop. The last two short, imperative sentences — which are sentences that issue a command like *Sit down!* — remind readers that the experience he has just described has much broader implications. The short sentences that conclude the paragraph put on the brakes and emphasize Vargas's point with only a few simple words.

Analyzing Sentence Structures

First, reread the following paragraph from the very beginning of Vargas's argument. Analyze the sentence variety and explain how it helps Vargas achieve his purpose.

> It was July 2014. The cell, as I remember it, was no bigger than 20 by 30 feet. All around me were about 25 boys, as young as 5, the oldest no more than 12. The air reeked.

A boy across the room from me was crying inconsolably, his head buried in his chest. Most of the boys wore dazed expressions. It was clear they had no idea where they were or why they were there.

Then, reread paragraphs 9 and 10, starting with "This is a country," a phrase that Vargas repeats several times. With a partner, discuss the effects of this parallel structure and how it helps Vargas achieve his purpose.

Moving from Style to Tone

Throughout this workshop, we've been examining the small, specific stylistic choices that Vargas makes through his diction, register, figurative language, and syntax. Now, it's time to see how these specific choices help Vargas create the tone that best serves his purpose. In terms of word choices, we've noted the bleakness of the scene he builds at the start with verbs like "reeked" and details like the children "crying inconsolably." They play with a Mylar blanket "as if it were a toy," blankets that were "supposed" to keep them warm. These "kids" are "victims" of policies that "sowed violence." These stylistic choices indicate that Vargas sees his subject — the detention of immigrants, especially minors — as inhumane, even cruel. We can see that his informal register leads to an emotional connection with his reader and allows the audience to feel the injustices stemming from these policies. The sentence patterns he uses reinforce this experience. We noted parallel structure that emphasizes isolation and the impossibility of communication through repetition. In addition, longer sentences remind us how overwhelming the circumstances must be to the children. Shorter sentences, especially those imperative sentences, demand that we take these issues seriously.

To some extent, tone, like theme, is a matter of interpretation. The words you use to describe a writer's tone may be different from those another reader chooses. But if the writer has made careful choices, readers should come to similar conclusions regarding the tone and the overall effect of stylistic elements.

Analyzing and Describing Tone

What is Vargas's attitude toward his subject in the excerpt that you read? Use one or more of the words in the list on page 812 to describe Vargas's tone. Then, explain how his style choices communicate this tone. Meet with a partner to discuss the words you each selected and explain how stylistic elements contribute to building the tone of this excerpt.

culminating activity

Following are the concluding paragraphs of Vargas's argument. With the tone that you discussed with your partner in mind, read and annotate the rest of the argument once for connections and questions, and a second time for Vargas's use of diction, figurative language, register, or syntax (rhetorical questions, sentence variety, and parallelism). Then, write a brief response in which you explain how Vargas makes stylistic choices to create a tone that is appropriate and effective for his purpose. The tone you identify in this second part of his argument might be similar to what you identified in the activity on the preceding page. Alternatively, you might determine that Vargas employs a different tone at the end of his piece.

from What America Looks Like from a Jail in South Texas

Jose Antonio Vargas

Sitting on the floor, I kept thinking of the boys' parents, the fear they must have felt knowing that they needed to do what they needed to do. I also kept thinking of my mother, wondering as I had so many times over all these years what she told herself as she said goodbye to me at the airport 25 years ago.

My mother and I haven't seen each other in person since 1993, but we do sometimes talk by phone or chat. We rarely talk about what happened on the day we separated, though. Sometimes I will ask about a fact here or there. What was I wearing? What was she wearing? What were her last words to me? But we never talk about how we felt, what we lost, what it means.

The truth is, if my mother had known then what she knows now — that calling her on the phone is difficult, because I can't really pretend that I know the voice on the other end of the line, that seeing her on Skype or FaceTime feels like some sort of twisted joke, that the technology that easily connects us makes the divide even more acute — I'm not sure if she would have said goodbye at the airport. On one of our rare phone calls she said, "I look at you, now, the person you've become, and how can I have any regrets." I'm sure she meant it as a statement, but it sounded like a question.

I am not entirely sure who I have become.

5 What I am sure of is that at every complicated and complicating juncture of my life in America — getting to college, getting a job, getting a driver's license so I could have a valid proof of identification so I could get a job, keeping the job — a stranger who did not remain a stranger helped me out.

After telling me that my green card was fake, the curly-haired, bespectacled woman at the Department of Motor Vehicles could have called immigration officials.

After finding out that I was ineligible for financial aid because I don't have any legal papers, the administrators at Mountain View High School didn't need to help me. I didn't even ask them for help, because I didn't know how to. But they offered help, even when I didn't know what kind of help I needed, even when they didn't know what they were doing.

After I confessed about my fake papers, the doctored Social Security card, the driver's license I wasn't supposed to have, the senior newsroom personnel at the *Washington Post*, where I worked as a reporter, could have dragged me to the office of human resources and gotten me fired.

Sitting on the floor, all alone in the cell, I couldn't stop thinking about the boys' futures. I wondered if, when and how they would get out. If they got to stay, who would welcome them to this country, and how they would be welcomed? I wanted to tell them not to be scared, that they would survive whatever they would have to survive. I wanted to tell them that the American people are capable of being better than their laws. I wanted to tell them, "No miedo." ■

The Work You Do, the Person You Are

Toni Morrison

Deborah Feingold/Getty Images

Toni Morrison (1931–2019) was a widely acclaimed author of eleven novels, in addition to plays, children's books, and nonfiction pieces. Her novel *Beloved* won the Pulitzer Prize for Fiction in 1987. She gained international recognition when she became the first African American woman to be awarded the Nobel Prize for Literature in 1993. The recipient of numerous awards and grants during her career, Morrison was an endowed professor at Princeton University. In 2012, President Barack Obama presented her with the Presidential Medal of Freedom. The following essay was originally published in the *New Yorker* magazine in 2017.

All I had to do for the two dollars was clean her house for a few hours after school. It was a beautiful house, too, with a plastic-covered sofa and chairs, wall-to-wall blue-and-white carpeting, a white enamel stove, a washing machine and a dryer — things that were common in Her neighborhood, absent in mine. In the middle of the war[1], She had butter, sugar, steaks, and seam-up-the-back stockings.

I knew how to scrub floors on my knees and how to wash clothes in our zinc tub, but I had never seen a Hoover vacuum cleaner or an iron that wasn't heated by fire.

Part of my pride in working for Her was earning money I could squander: on movies, candy, paddleballs, jacks, ice-cream cones. But a larger part of my pride was based on the fact that I gave half my wages to my mother, which meant that some of my earnings were used for real things — an insurance-policy payment or what was owed to the milkman or the iceman. The pleasure of being necessary to my parents was profound. I was not like the children in folktales: burdensome mouths to feed, nuisances to be corrected, problems so severe that they were abandoned to the forest. I had a status that doing routine chores in my house did not provide — and it earned me a slow smile, an approving nod from an adult. Confirmations that I was adultlike, not childlike.

In those days, the forties, children were not just loved or liked; they were needed. They could earn money; they could care for children younger than themselves; they could work the farm, take care of the herd, run errands, and much more. I suspect that

[1]Morrison is referring to World War II (1939–1945) — Eds.

The Gleaners, 1857 (oil on canvas)/Millet, Jean-Francois (1814-75)/Musee d'Orsay, Paris, France/Bridgeman Images

In *The Gleaners* (1857), a painting by Jean-Francois Millet, three peasant women are pictured gleaning — scouring the field for stalks of crop missed in the first harvest.

What ideas does the artist suggest about work? How does the artist present those ideas visually? Why might Morrison agree or disagree with Millet's depiction?

children aren't needed in that way now. They are loved, doted on, protected, and helped. Fine, and yet . . .

Little by little, I got better at cleaning Her house — good enough to be given more to do, much more. I was ordered to carry bookcases upstairs and, once, to move a piano from one side of a room to the other. I fell carrying the bookcases. And after pushing the piano my arms and legs hurt so badly. I wanted to refuse, or at least to complain, but I was afraid She would fire me, and I would lose the freedom the dollar gave me, as well as the standing I had at home — although both were slowly being eroded. She began to offer me her clothes, for a price. Impressed by these worn things, which looked simply gorgeous to a little girl who had only two dresses to wear to school, I bought a few. Until my mother asked me if I really wanted to work for castoffs. So I learned to say "No, thank you" to a faded sweater offered for a quarter of a week's pay.

Still, I had trouble summoning the courage to discuss or object to the increasing demands She made. And I knew that if I told my mother how unhappy I was she would tell me to quit. Then one day, alone in the kitchen with my father, I let drop a few whines about the job. I gave him details, examples of what troubled me, yet although he listened intently, I saw no sympathy in his eyes. No "Oh, you poor little thing." Perhaps he understood that what I wanted was a solution to the job, not an escape from it. In any case, he put down his cup of coffee and said, "Listen. You don't live there. You live here. With your people. Go to work. Get your money. And come on home."

That was what he said. This was what I heard:

1. Whatever the work is, do it well — not for the boss but for yourself.
2. You make the job; it doesn't make you.
3. Your real life is with us, your family.
4. You are not the work you do; you are the person you are.

I have worked for all sorts of people since then, geniuses and morons, quick-witted and dull, bighearted and narrow. I've had many kinds of jobs, but since that conversation with my father I have never considered the level of labor to be the measure of myself, and I have never placed the security of a job above the value of home. ■

Illustration by Christoph Niemann

This illustration by Christophe Niemann appeared in the *New Yorker* magazine with Morrison's essay.

How do the composition and details relate to the central point that Morrison makes?

Understanding and Interpreting

1. What information does Morrison provide in the first three paragraphs that indicates her socioeconomic position?
2. How does Morrison describe her relationship with her own family? What does she mean when she writes, "The pleasure of being necessary to my parents was profound" (par. 3)?
3. What do you learn about Morrison's mother and father during the course of this short essay?
4. How does Morrison's father respond when she lets "drop a few whines about the job" (par. 6)? What does his reaction reveal about him and about their relationship?
5. What does Morrison mean when she writes of her father's response, "That was what he said. This was what I heard" (par. 7). What distinction is she making?
6. What does Morrison suggest in this essay about the relationship among freedom, money, and work?

Analyzing Language, Style, and Structure

1. **Vocabulary in Context.** In paragraph 3, Morrison writes, "I had a status that doing routine chores in my house did not provide." What does the word "status" mean in this context? How is it similar to or different from other meanings you have encountered?
2. **Skill Focus.** Throughout the essay, Morrison uses sentence fragments (statements that are not complete sentences, usually because they do not have both a subject and a verb). Identify at least three examples and explain the effects of this syntactical choice.
3. **Skill Focus.** Morrison has written a narrative essay, an autobiographical piece that uses elements of fiction such as setting, dialogue, plot, and character development. How do these elements add interest? What would be the disadvantage, if any, of writing a more direct essay about the "level of labor" and "the measure" of one's worth?
4. Morrison does not name her employer except with a pronoun that she capitalizes: *Her*. Apart from protecting the woman's privacy, what is the effect of not giving her a proper name, even a

fictitious one? What effect does Morrison create by capitalizing *Her*, a pronoun that is normally lowercase?

5. Morrison moves between her adult reflections and re-creating the feelings and perceptions of her younger self. In some cases, she comments on the experiences. However, in paragraph 4, she makes a more general comment about this difference between "then" and "now." What is the purpose of that paragraph? What would be lost, if anything, if it were deleted?
6. How would you describe the tone of the final paragraph? What stylistic choices help to create this tone?

Topics for Composing

1. **Analysis.** What does Morrison suggest about the value and the power of work in this essay? Point to specific evidence from the text to support your interpretation.
2. **Analysis.** Explain how Morrison interweaves re-creating a childhood experience and interpreting the meaning of that experience from an adult perspective. What effect does this interweaving create?
3. **Argument.** Morrison writes, '"in those days . . . children were not just loved or liked; they were needed" (par. 4). To what extent does her assessment ring true today? Support your position with your own experience and observations.
4. **Connection.** Review the four pieces of advice Morrison's father gave. Which ones have the most meaning for you? Why?
5. **Connection.** Describe an experience you've had working either for a family member or outside your home to earn money or as a volunteer. What did you learn about the relationship between "the work you do and the person you are"?
6. **Speaking and Listening.** Working with a partner, highlight passages in which the perspective seems to be Morrison as a young girl. In a different color, highlight passages in which the perspective seems to be Morrison as an adult reflecting on her experiences. Then, read the essay aloud, each partner taking on one of the two perspectives. Afterwards, discuss how this way of reading influenced your understanding of the essay.
7. **Research.** Morrison wrote that in the mid-1940s, she was paid two dollars to clean the woman's house, working a few hours a day. That means she earned less than a dollar an hour. Research typical wages for domestic workers at the time. Was she paid appropriately for the time period? Accounting for inflation, how does Morrison's pay correspond to how people doing similar work today are paid?
8. **Multimodal.** Create a short video that illustrates how the title of this essay — "The Work You Do, the Person You Are" — applies to your own life. You may use original photographs, video clips, or a combination. Consider using quotations from Morrison's text in your video. Ask yourself what story you are telling about the work you do and the person you are as you make your selections.

Designer Babies Aren't Futuristic. They're Already Here.

Laura Hercher

Laura Hercher is a genetic counselor and a faculty member and director of student research at the Joan H. Marks Graduate Program in Human Genetics at Sarah Lawrence College. She has published articles on science and genetics in *Wired, Scientific American,* and *MIT Technology Review*, in which the following piece originally appeared in 2018.

Chris Taggert/Courtesy of Laura Hercher

KEY CONTEXT In the following piece, Hercher refers to several reproductive technologies, including preimplantation genetic testing and in vitro fertilization (IVF), which can be used to check embryos for genetic abnormalities prior to implantation in a woman's uterus.

At first, Matthew assumed the weakness in his knee was the sort of orthopedic nuisance that happens when you turn 30. It was weeks before he consulted a doctor, and months before it occurred to him that there could be a connection between his worsening limp and a cousin's shoulder problem when they were kids. DNA testing confirmed it: Matthew, like his cousin, had a genetic form of dystonia, a condition where muscles contract uncontrollably. Their grandfather most likely had dystonia as well.

I'd met Matthew only a few months earlier, when he'd married my friend's daughter, Olivia, in one of those hip old New York hotels with an elegant downtown vibe. Since I was the only genetic counselor of their acquaintance, they brought their questions to me. With their permission, I am sharing their story. I have changed their names to preserve their privacy.

Matthew was lucky. His was a mild version of DYT1 dystonia, and injections of Botox in his knee helped. But the genetic mutation can cause severe symptoms: contractures in joints or deformities in the spine. Many patients are put on psychoactive medications, and some require surgery for deep brain stimulation.

Their kids, Matthew and Olivia were told, might not be as lucky. They would have a 50-50 chance of inheriting the gene variant that causes dystonia and, if they did, a 30% chance of developing the disease. The risk of a severely affected child was fairly small, but not insignificant.

My friends learned there was an alternative. 5
They could undergo in vitro fertilization [IVF] and have their embryos genetically tested while still in a laboratory dish. Using a technology called pre-implantation genetic testing, they could pick the embryos that had not inherited the DYT1 mutation.

It would be expensive — costs for IVF in the U.S. average over $20,000 for each try, and testing can add $10,000 or more. And it would require an unpleasant two-week process of ovarian stimulation and egg harvesting. "It wasn't the way I saw myself making a baby," Olivia told me. But they wanted what the procedure could offer them: a guarantee that dystonia was eliminated for the next generation, and beyond.

Matthew and Olivia don't think of themselves as having a "designer baby." That term has negative associations, suggesting something trivial, discretionary, or unethical. They weren't choosing eye color or trying to

Tom Toles/Universal Uclick

This 1999 political cartoon by Tom Toles offers one viewpoint regarding so-called "designer babies."

How might you describe that viewpoint? How does it compare with Hercher's use of the term "designer babies" in the title of her article? What effect might her use of the term in the title have on her audience?

boost their kid's SAT score. They were looking out for the health and well-being of their future child, as parents should.

Public opinion on the use of assisted reproductive technology consistently draws a distinction between preventing disease and picking traits. The Johns Hopkins Genetics and Public Policy Center, which contacted over 6,000 people through surveys and focus groups from 2002 to 2004, summed up its findings this way: "In general, Americans approve of using reproductive genetic tests to prevent fatal childhood disease, but do not approve of using the same tests to identify or select for traits like intelligence or strength." The dystonia gene is in a gray zone — some people born with it live perfectly healthy lives — yet presumably few parents would criticize Matthew and Olivia's choice to weed it out.

All embryo testing does fit the "designer" label in one important way, however: it is not available to everybody.

10 Matthew and Olivia opted in to what is a quiet but significant trend. Although the number of couples using this technology remains small, it is growing rapidly. According to the Society for Assisted Reproductive Technology, the number of U.S. IVF attempts with single-gene testing rose from 1,941 in 2014 to 3,271 in 2016, an increase of almost 70%.

This is only the beginning. As the price of genetic testing of all kinds drops, more adults are learning about their genetic makeup as part of routine medical care and discovering specific genetic risks before pregnancy. But these people are still most likely to be affluent and educated, like Olivia and Matthew. While they consulted with IVF clinics, Olivia's own brother and his wife got news of a gene that increased risk for cancer in their kids. "If you could get rid of it, why wouldn't you?" he asked.

Cost was not a concern for these couples, but it is an obstacle for many Americans. The Centers for Disease Control and Prevention (CDC) estimates that 1.7% of babies born in the U.S. today are conceived using IVF. It's much higher in countries that publicly fund assisted reproductive technology: 4% in Belgium, 5.9% in Denmark. A 2009 study found that 76% of the medical need for assisted reproduction in the U.S. is unmet.

Insurance doesn't normally cover IVF in the U.S., except for a handful of states where coverage is mandated. Even policies that cover fertility treatment are inconsistent in what they reimburse. Coverage for pre-implantation genetic testing is downright Kafkaesque.[1] Under many policies, testing the embryos is covered, but the IVF procedure itself is not, because the couples are not infertile.

"The analogy I like to use," says James Grifo, director of the Division of Reproductive Endocrinology and Infertility at NYU Langone Health, "is if you were having coronary bypass surgery and they didn't pay for cracking the chest."

15 At least part of the reason the IVF industry is growing is not that more people can afford it but that those who can are paying for new kinds of services. Egg banking, for example, is now aggressively marketed to younger women as an insurance policy against age-related infertility. In 2011, egg banking did not even exist as a category in the CDC's annual report on IVF; by 2016, storing eggs or embryos was the purpose of 25% of all IVF cycles. Elite companies like Facebook offer egg freezing as a perk, but for most people it remains a luxury.

Cost isn't the only barrier. Reproductive technology is less acceptable in racial, ethnic, and religious groups where being seen as infertile carries a stigma. Language barriers can reduce awareness and referrals. Geography also plays a role, since IVF clinics cluster in areas of greatest demand.

Presumably, many people would make the same decision as Matthew and Olivia if given the option, but many don't have that choice. Our discomfort around designer babies has always had to do with the fact that it makes the playing field less level — taking existing inequities and turning them into something inborn. If the use of pre-implantation testing grows and we don't address these disparities, we risk creating a society where some groups, because of culture or geography or poverty, bear a greater burden of genetic disease.

What could change society more profoundly than to take genetic disease — something that has always epitomized our shared humanity — and turn it into something that only happens to some people? ■

[1]Relating to or suggestive of the writing of Franz Kafka (1883–1924), whose style had an illogical or nightmarish quality to it. –Eds.

extending beyond the text

Look through the following charts that summarize responses to a study conducted by Harvard University in 2016 called "The Public and Genetic Editing, Testing, And Therapy."

Figure 1: Americans' Views on Changing the Genes of Unborn Babies

Q. Do you think that changing the genes of unborn babies to… should be legal or should be illegal?

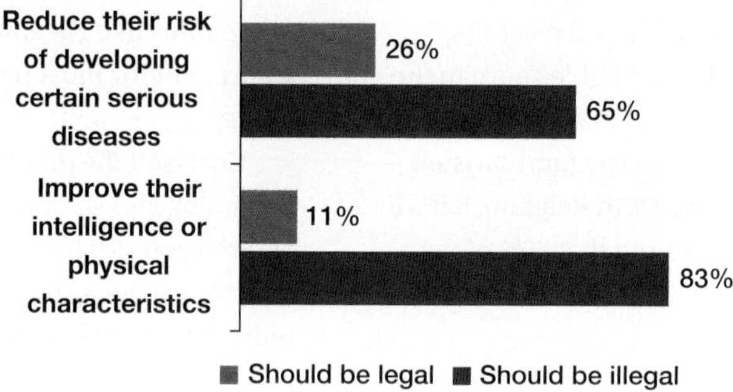

Figure 2: Americans' Views on Federal Funding for Research On Changing the Genes of Unborn Babies

Q. Do you think the federal government should or should not fund scientific research on changing the genes of unborn babies...

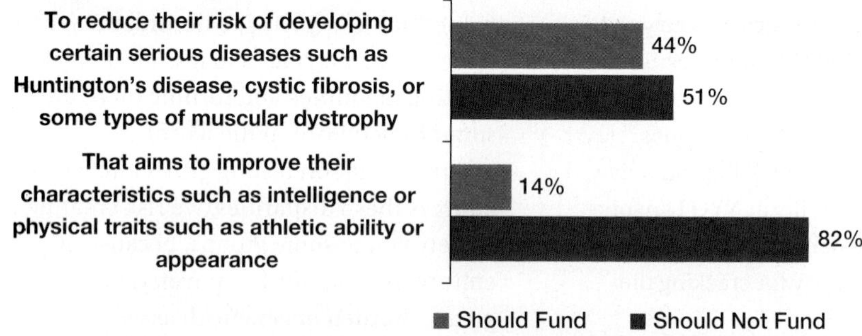

Figure 3: Interest in taking a genetic test in the future to know your likelihood of developing diseases

Q. If a genetic test was available that could tell you whether or not you were likely to develop … in the future, would you want to take the test or not?

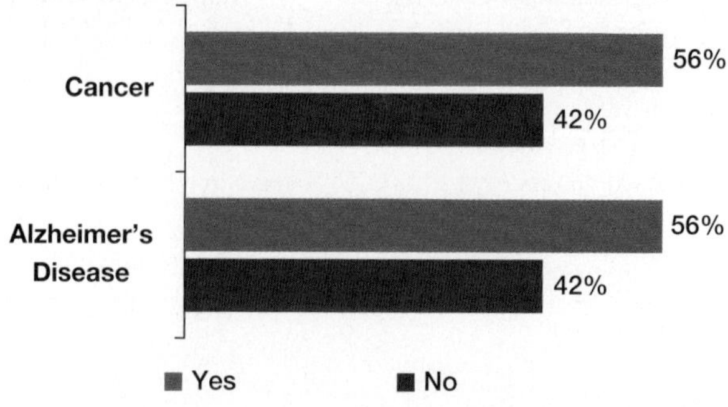

FIGURE 4: Government Regulation of Gene Therapy in the U.S.

Q. Do you think the Food and Drug Administration should or should not approve gene therapy treatments for use in the United States?

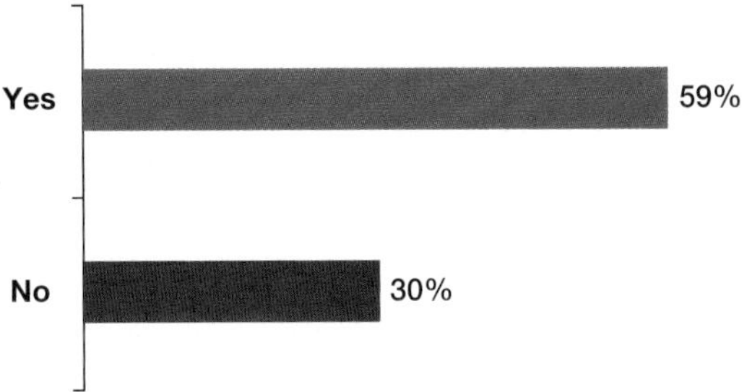

Source: Harvard T. H. Chan School of Public Health.

What conclusions might you draw about American's attitudes toward gene testing and therapy based on these charts? Which results of the survey do you find surprising? How would you respond to some of the questions? Which one of these charts might Hercher have selected to accompany her article? Why?

Understanding and Interpreting

1. Summarize the concerns that led Matthew and Olivia to genetic counseling and testing. What are they hoping to do with the information and procedures available to them?
2. Explain the difference between "preventing disease and picking traits" that Hercher describes in paragraph 8.
3. Explain the analogy that James Grifo uses in paragraph 14. What connection is the reader expected to make to IVF treatment?
4. Reread paragraphs 12 to 16. What are the main concerns about IVF that Hercher raises here?
5. It is not until paragraphs 17 and 18 that Hercher states her position regarding IVF treatment. What is her position? What danger does she identify?
6. While she does not explicitly offer a solution, how might Hercher suggest we address the dangers she identifies in paragraphs 17 and 18?

Analyzing Language, Style, and Structure

1. **Vocabulary in Context.** In paragraph 15, Hercher writes that some companies use "egg freezing as a perk." What does the word "perk" mean in this context? How is that meaning similar to or different from others that you have encountered?
2. **Skill Focus.** How would you describe Hercher's tone in this argument? What language and stylistic choices contribute to creating that tone?
3. What appeals are at work in the first paragraph? Why might Hercher have chosen to open her argument with the story about Matthew?
4. In the second paragraph, Hercher reveals her personal connection to Matthew and Olivia. What does she try to achieve by inserting herself into the argument this way?

5. Hercher says that the phrase "designer baby" has negative associations. What are they? Why does Hercher bring this up in her argument?
6. Look at the last sentence in paragraph 7: "They were looking out for the health and well-being of their future child, as parents should." Is this an effective and persuasive way to describe their actions? Why or why not?
7. Reread the following section from paragraph 8 and explain what Hercher was likely trying to accomplish by including it: "The dystonia gene is in a gray zone — some people born with it live perfectly healthy lives — yet presumably few parents would criticize Matthew and Olivia's choice to weed it out." Focus on her diction and appeals.

Topics for Composing

1. **Analysis.** Laura Hercher is a genetic counselor arguing for wider availability of genetic testing. Is she too biased? Evaluate her argument by considering topics that she does not raise in her piece, as well as her language choices.
2. **Argument.** Where would you draw the line for pre-implantation genetic testing? Should parents be allowed to screen for potential illnesses? Should they be able to select their children's eye color? Level of intelligence? Physical qualities? Take a position and write an argument using this article, your own reasoning, and additional research if you want for support.
3. **Argument.** Imagine that all parents are given affordable access to reproductive technologies such as genetic screening and IVF. Why do you think they should or should not feel obligated to use them? Should such technologies become a standard part — like vaccinations and annual doctor visits — of how parents ensure that their offspring will live full, healthy lives? Why or why not?
4. **Argument.** Some ethicists argue that somatic cell gene therapy, which affects only people who are already alive, is acceptable, but any genetic testing and procedures that affect future generations, like those described in this piece, are not. Explain why you do or do not agree with this distinction. Include specific examples in your explanation.
5. **Connection.** Watch a film that explores the consequences of genetic engineering, such as *Gattaca*, *Human Nature*, or *Elysium*. After viewing the film, explain what position it takes on the subject and how that position compares to Hercher's.
6. **Speaking and Listening.** The topic Hercher discusses can be a challenging, an emotional, and a divisive one for many people. Participate in a "silent discussion," in which you anonymously write your ideas and attitudes regarding this issue on posters or sheets of paper to share with your classmates. Read each other's words without discussing them out loud. Use this as an opportunity to gain new ideas and insights about the topic. Then, meet with a partner to discuss the perspectives that you encountered through this process.
7. **Research.** Through research on the topic of reproductive genetic testing and procedures, explain other ways that genetic testing and therapies might impact society in the future. Examine the potential ethical concerns that arise. You might also consult two U.S. government websites — the Human Genome Project and the Presidential Commission for the Study of Bioethical Issues — as well as the work of Harvard philosophy professor Michael Sandel.
8. **Exposition.** Broadly speaking, this piece focuses on the complex ethical issues created by a relatively new technology. Choose another example of ethically-charged technology and explain the issues that it raises. You might choose a current technology, a technological development from the past, or an emerging technology.

Truth at All Costs

Marie Colvin

Sheila Masson/Writer Pictures via AP Images

Marie Catherine Colvin (1956–2012) was a New York native who worked for the *Sunday Times*, a British newspaper, from 1985 until her death. A war correspondent specializing in the Middle East, Colvin was known for her coverage of conflicts in dangerous and high-risk areas, including Chechnya, Eritrea, Palestine, Libya, and Syria. She lost an eye in 2001 as a result of an injury during a grenade attack in Sri Lanka. Colvin died while reporting on the Syrian Civil War. Known for her daring and dangerous spirit, she has been the subject of a biography entitled *In Extremis: The Life and Death of the War Correspondent Marie Colvin* by Lindsey Hilsum and the feature film *A Private War*, both released in 2018.

KEY CONTEXT On February 22, 2012, the day Colvin's death was confirmed, the *Guardian*, a British newspaper, ran the following speech on the importance of war reporting that Colvin had given in 2010 during a service for war wounded at St Bride's Church in London.

Your Royal Highness, ladies and gentlemen, I am honoured and humbled to be speaking to you at this service tonight to remember the journalists and their support staff who gave their lives to report from the war zones of the 21st century. I have been a war correspondent for most of my professional life. It has always been a hard calling. But the need for frontline, objective reporting has never been more compelling.

Covering a war means going to places torn by chaos, destruction and death, and trying to bear witness. It means trying to find the truth in a sandstorm of propaganda when armies, tribes or terrorists clash. And yes, it means taking risks, not just for yourself but often for the people who work closely with you.

Despite all the videos you see from the Ministry of Defence or the Pentagon, and all the sanitised language describing smart bombs and pinpoint strikes, the scene on the ground has remained remarkably the same for hundreds of years. Craters. Burned houses. Mutilated bodies. Women weeping for children and husbands. Men for their wives, mothers children.

Our mission is to report these horrors of war with accuracy and without prejudice. We always have to ask ourselves whether the level of risk is worth the story. What is bravery, and what is bravado?

5 Journalists covering combat shoulder great responsibilities and face difficult choices. Sometimes they pay the ultimate price. Tonight we honour the 49 journalists and support staff who were killed bringing the news to our shores. We also remember journalists around the world who have been wounded, maimed or kidnapped and held hostage for months. It has never been more dangerous to be a war correspondent, because the journalist in the combat zone has become a prime target.

I lost my eye in an ambush in the Sri Lankan civil war. I had gone to the northern Tamil area from which journalists were banned and found an unreported humanitarian disaster. As I was smuggled back across the internal border, a soldier launched a grenade at me and the shrapnel sliced into my face and chest. He knew what he was doing.

David Turnley/Getty Images

This photograph shows three photo journalists in the middle of a street battle in South Africa in the mid-1990s.

What is your first response as you look at the photo? What specific details evoke that response? In what ways does this image support the argument that Colvin makes about war reporting? What ethical questions might the photo raise?

Just last week, I had a coffee in Afghanistan with a photographer friend, Joao Silva. We talked about the terror one feels and must contain when patrolling on an embed with the armed forces through fields and villages in Afghanistan . . . putting one foot in front of the other, steeling yourself each step for the blast. The expectation of that blast is the stuff of nightmares. Two days after our meeting, Joao stepped on a mine and lost both legs at the knee.

Many of you here must have asked yourselves, or be asking yourselves now, is it worth the cost in lives, heartbreak, loss? Can we really make a difference?

I faced that question when I was injured. In fact one paper ran a headline saying, has Marie Colvin gone too far this time? My answer then, and now, was that it is worth it.

10 Today in this church are friends, colleagues and families who know exactly what I am talking about, and bear the cost of those experiences, as do their families and loved ones.

Today we must also remember how important it is that news organisations continue to invest in sending us out at great cost, both financial and emotional, to cover stories.

We go to remote war zones to report what is happening. The public have a right to know what our government, and our armed forces, are doing in our name. Our mission is to speak the truth to power. We send home that first rough draft of history. We can and do make a difference in exposing the horrors of war and especially the atrocities that befall civilians.

The history of our profession is one to be proud of. The first war correspondent in the modern era was William Howard Russell of the *Times*, who was sent to cover the Crimean conflict when a British-led coalition fought an invading Russian army.

YASIN AKGUL/Getty Images

In this 2015 photograph by Asin Akgul, a Kurdish Syrian woman walks with her child past the ruins of the town of Kobane, also known as Ain al-Arab, after fighters were driven out by Kurdish and allied forces. **How does this photo capture the human cost of war? How does it relate to what Colvin describes as the journalist's obligation to write "that first rough draft of history"?**

Billy Russell, as the troops called him, created a firestorm of public indignation back home by revealing inadequate equipment, scandalous treatment of the wounded, especially when they were repatriated — does this sound familiar? — and an incompetent high command that led to the folly of the Charge of the Light Brigade. It was a breakthrough in war reporting. Until then, wars were reported by junior officers who sent back dispatches to newspapers. Billy Russell went to war with an open mind, a telescope, a notebook and a bottle of brandy. I first went to war with a typewriter, and learned to tap out a telex tape. It could take days to get from the front to a telephone or telex machine.

War reporting has changed greatly in just the last few years. Now we go to war with a satellite phone, laptop, video camera and a flak jacket. I point my satellite phone to south southwest in Afghanistan, press a button and I have filed.

In an age of 24/7 rolling news, blogs and Twitters, we are on constant call wherever we are. But war reporting is still essentially the same — someone has to go there and see what is happening. You can't get that information without going to places where people are being shot at, and others are shooting at you. The real difficulty is having enough faith in humanity to believe that enough people, be they government, military or the man on the street, will care when your file reaches the printed page, the website or the TV screen.

We do have that faith because we believe we do make a difference.

And we could not make that difference — or begin to do our job — without the fixers, drivers and translators, who face the same risks and die in appalling numbers. Today we honour them as much as the front line journalists who have died in pursuit of the truth. They have kept the faith as we who remain must continue to do. ■

Heritage Images/Getty Images

Charge of the English Light Brigade at the Battle of Balaclava on 25 October 1854 was painted by nineteenth century artist Friedrich Kaiser. The British commander, Lord Raglan, gave the disastrous order for the cavalry to charge; the Light Brigade suffered 40 percent casualties. **What is Kaiser's purpose in this painting? How might it look different if it were painted by Billy Russell, the first war correspondent? To what extent is Colvin's allusion to this battle an effective strategy for her argument?**

Understanding and Interpreting

1. What does Marie Colvin mean when she says that "[c]overing a war means . . . trying to bear witness" (par. 2)?
2. Colvin contrasts the journalist's tools of the trade many years ago (telex and typewriter) with those used now (satellite phones and laptops). However, she claims the experience and mission remain "essentially the same" (par. 16). What is the point of making this comparison between changing tools and an unchanging mission?
3. What does Colvin mean when she says that journalists "send home that first rough draft of history" (par. 12)?
4. Why does Colvin think Billy Russell exemplifies the essence of being a reporter of armed conflict?
5. According to Colvin, why is it important to have "enough faith in humanity" (par. 16), especially in her line of work?
6. What elements of Colvin's speech might appeal to members of her audience who are remembering and paying tribute to loved ones who have died while on assignment?
7. Colvin refers to accusations (following the loss of her eye) that she has "gone too far." She claims that whatever danger she faces in the field "is worth it" (par. 9). Do you agree with Colvin that any risk, even the risk of death, is acceptable in Colvin's line of work?

Analyzing Language, Style, and Structure

1. **Vocabulary in Context.** Colvin writes that the war correspondent's "mission is to speak the truth to power" (par. 12). What does "mission" mean in this context? What does her choice of this word suggest?
2. **Skill Focus.** In this speech, Colvin refers to journalists' work as a "mission" (par. 12), she calls upon "faith in humanity" (par. 16), and invokes "truth" throughout. How do these choices of language and others reveal Colvin's tone toward those involved in reporting armed conflicts?
3. What is the rhetorical situation of this speech? Describe the occasion, audience, and speaker. How does Colvin adjust her language choices to appeal to her audience and to serve her purpose?
4. What is the effect of the following figure of speech: "trying to find the truth in a sandstorm of propaganda" (par. 2)?
5. Colvin distinguishes between "bravery" and "bravado" (par. 4). What is that distinction? What point does she make by emphasizing the difference?
6. Colvin draws on her own experience, that of the photographer Joao Silva, and those of the "first war correspondent in the modern era" (par. 13), William Howard Russell. How do these examples advance Colvin's argument about the importance of covering dangerous conflicts?

Topics for Composing

1. **Analysis.** Colvin delivered this speech at a memorial service for photographers, journalists, drivers, translators, and others wounded or killed while covering a war. The audience is their families. In what ways is her speech effective, perhaps even powerful, for this rhetorical situation? Are there any times when you feel that she is not doing a good job of appealing to her audience? Cite specific passages in your analysis.
2. **Argument.** Colvin acknowledges the danger and risk involved in covering armed conflicts. She admits the importance of weighing the "cost in lives, heartbreak, loss" against the difference that their coverage can make (par. 8). She asserts that "it is worth it." To what extent do you agree that reporting the nature and consequences of combat is worth the risks in today's world?
3. **Connection.** It is clear that Colvin is extraordinarily passionate about the work of war correspondents. Describe something that you are passionate about that others may not understand or appreciate.
4. **Speaking and Listening.** Working with a classmate, search news station websites or social media feeds for a clip of a journalist reporting in dangerous conditions — a war-torn environment, a natural disaster, or a health crisis, for example. In what ways does the journalist in the clip you've chosen embody that sense of "mission" that Colvin describes? Be prepared to discuss your choice with the full class.
5. **Research.** In 2012, Colvin entered Syria to cover the civil war without gaining the government's permission. She was killed later that same year in the city of Horns. Her family believed she had been targeted by the Syrian government. Research more about Colvin's involvement and the court case that her parents initiated. How does the information you learn affect your understanding of Colvin's speech?
6. **Research.** Martha Gellhorn (1905–1998) was a travel writer, journalist, and war correspondent who covered nearly every major conflict of the twentieth century during her

sixty-year career. She is reputed to have been the only woman at D-Day, a pivotal WWII battle on the beaches of Normandy, and the liberation of Dachau, a Nazi concentration camp. Many think of her as one of the greatest war correspondents of all time. Conduct some research into her life and accomplishments. In what ways do you think that comparisons between her and Colvin, which are often made, are appropriate?

7. **Research.** Colvin defends the risks and dangers of war reporting as a search for truth and affirms her belief in the "mission" of journalists. Others sometimes question the motives and work of these reporters. For instance, in a 2013 piece from the *Atlantic* called "The Life of a War Correspondent Is Even Worse Than You Think," Dashiell Bennett writes,

> [E]ven veteran journalists keep going back because . . . the glory and fame that come with a big story are usually stronger motivators than the story itself. Reporters are told that they are crazy to be there, but then get rewarded (with actual journalism awards) for inserting themselves into . . . frontline dangers.

   Locate information about an award-winning war reporter (other than Colvin) and explain what seems to motivate that person's work and how it relates to Colvin's "mission."

8. **Multimodal.** Look for news stories with images that cover armed conflict. Identify several images that you find compelling from different articles. Create a slideshow for sharing these images. Each slide should include the article's headline, the image and caption (if it has one), and a sentence about why you feel the image is striking, effective, or otherwise worth thinking about. In a final slide, briefly explain how your selections support or undermine Colvin's position regarding war reporting.

The Case of the Photoshopped Female CEOs

Monica Hesse

Cassidy DuHon/Courtesy Monica Hesse

Monica Hesse is a *Washington Post* columnist whose writing focuses on gender. She is the national bestselling author of historical fiction, mystery novels, and science fiction, including the Edgar Award–winning young adult novel *Girl in the Blue Coat* (2016) and *They Went Left* (2020). Hesse is a winner of the Society for Feature Journalism's Narrative Storytelling award. The following piece appeared in the *Washington Post* in 2019.

This week, I dedicated approximately three hours to an investigation that seemed, at varying times, important, obscure, symbolic and deeply, deeply petty. The task at hand: determining whether two women who were photographed at a tech summit in Italy were, in fact, *at* this tech summit in Italy.

The photo in question was taken at the villa of fashion designer Brunello Cucinelli, who had invited a bunch of tech executives to "a symposium on the soul and the economy." The co-founders of LinkedIn and Dropbox were there, as was the Twitter CFO and Amazon's Jeff Bezos who, I am ethically obligated to remind you, also owns the *Washington Post*. Cucinelli provided photos to *GQ* magazine,[1] which included them in a story about the event — and that is when things got weird.

Journalist Ryan Mac noticed[2] something about one of the pictures. It featured 15 men and two women, and something was off about the women. One of them appeared to be lit differently than everyone else in the photo. The other had a leg that did not align with the rest of her body. Were these women actually *in* the photo, or was it possible — given the well-documented dearth of women in tech, given an increased awareness of gender parity and the concern of so many leaders in at least getting the *appearances* right — that they'd been added via Photoshop? Did they even attend the conference? Did they even exist?

[1]Hine, Samuel. "Why Jeff Bezos and a Dozen Tech Titans Made a Pilgrimage to Brunello Cucinelli's Italian Village." *GQ*, June 2019. https://www.gq.com/story/brunello-cucinelli-jeff-bezos-solomeo-summit

[2]Mac, Ryan. https://twitter.com/RMac18/status/1138154023066984448

Here are the two photographs that inspired Monica Hesse's article. The original photo is on top; the altered photo with two female CEOs Photoshopped in is below it.

How does seeing the two photos influence your position on the issue Hesse discusses?

They do exist. Internet sleuths revealed them to be Lynn Jurich, the CEO of solar company Sunrun, and Ruzwana Bashir, the CEO of travel-planning site Peek.com. I emailed both women's publicists to see whether the CEOs had, in fact, posed for the photograph.

5 Jurich's press office responded promptly: "Ms. Jurich was delighted to participate in Mr. Cucinelli's symposium on the soul and economy. As a leader [in the] energy sector, Ms. Jurich discussed the urgent need to decarbonize and the role of technology to accelerate decarbonization."

Which was a lovely sentiment, but I explained that it didn't answer the question: Fine, Jurich had been at the *summit*. But had she been in the *photo*?

The publicist suggested I ask Cucinelli's people directly. It seemed a little strange that someone else would be a better expert on whether Jurich was in a photograph than Jurich herself, but the world of publicists is often strange, so I emailed Cucinelli's people and waited.

And while I waited, I wondered what I was waiting for. These women had apparently both been there, at the symposium. (Bashir's publicist eventually confirmed her attendance but also avoided the photo question.) How much did it matter if they'd actually posed for the photograph? There could be innocent explanations: Maybe they were both on conference calls, or in the restroom, and missed the photo session. For all we know, perhaps they were the ones who then said, *Shoot! Can you edit me in? I want a copy for my fridge.*

Whether they were Photoshopped would certainly matter for *GQ* on the journalistic level — that kind of image manipulation breaks a multitude of editorial sins. But did it matter on the cosmic level?

10 What does it mean when we talk about representation? Is it enough for women to be present at a symposium of the richest people on the planet, sharing ideas and providing their input? Or do we need physical evidence of this presence? Do we need to see them in photographs? Do we need to see them mingling with, as Cucinelli described it, "new Leonardos of the 21st-century."

It's important for women to be in the picture, literally, because that's how we'll later remember they were in the picture, metaphorically. That is how norms become normal: If you see female CEOs, you believe women can be CEOs.

But if Bashir and Jurich were at the conference but not in the picture — then why hadn't anyone noticed the absence of *the only two women* and suggested the photographer wait until they were available?

Cucinelli's people responded to my query:

"When we realized we didn't have a shot where all attendees were represented, we added in photos of two female CEOs taken during the weekend," read the statement. "The photos were shared and approved with all the participants including the two women, Lynn Jurich and Ruzwana Bashir. . . . We meant no harm or had any malicious intent in doing this and we are sorry."

15 I believe this. I believe this statement. I believe nobody was offended, and everyone was happy with the outcome, and that my Wednesday morning investigation was a fizzle.

That being said. If two of the 15 male executives had been absent from the photo, I wonder whether anyone would have felt the need to Photoshop them in before submitting the image to *GQ* magazine for public consumption. Would someone have said, *Whoa, we've only got 13 men in there, so we better make sure we stick in the 14th and 15th?*

I'm guessing the answer is no. After all, Bezos was missing from the group photo, and for whatever reason, no one cut-and-pasted him in.

So it's hard to avoid the conclusion that, in the case of the two missing women, someone looked at the photo and had this after-the-fact realization: *Uh oh — if we don't do something, it's going to look as though we invited zero women.*

And that is the lesson, at the end of the day, for all of the villa-owning billionaires of the world. Next time you hold a symposium on soul and the economy, invite *more* women. Invite more women, and you won't have to use Photoshop at all. ■

Women, more than men, see gender discrimination as a major problem in the tech industry

% of U.S. adults who say the following about discrimination against women in the technology industry

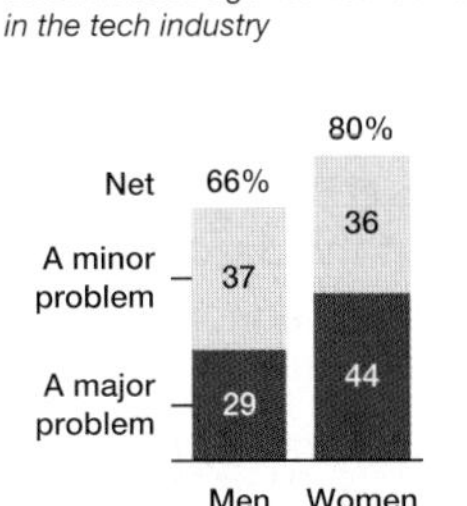

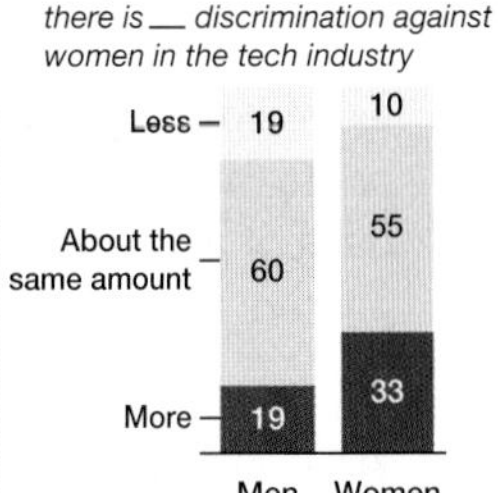

Note: Respondents who gave other resposes or who did not give an answer are not shown.
Source: Survey conducted July 11-Aug. 10, 2017.

PEW RESEARCH CENTER

Pew Research Center

Draw an interpretation from the responses to these two survey questions. Does the information here affect your attitude toward the Photoshopping that Hesse describes? Why or why not? How might she use it as evidence for her argument?

extending beyond the text

Photographers and photo editors might make changes to original photographs for many reasons — to improve the lighting, adjust the framing, or change the background, for example. Sometimes changes spark controversy about whether the manipulation results in a photo that misrepresents its subjects or presents false information. Look at the following pairs of photographs, read the description of the manipulation, and consider whether the photographers and the photo editors did the right thing in changing the photographs.

The original picture on the left was taken by John Filo at Kent State University on May 4, 1970, when National Guard soldiers fired into the crowd during a student protest, killing four people. It won Filo the Pulitzer Prize for Photography. Later, someone at *Time* magazine altered the photo to remove the unsightly post from the fence behind the woman's head as seen in the image on the right. The altered image ran for years in magazines and newspapers without indication that the picture had been altered.

What, if anything, was changed in terms of the photo's message by removing the post? Was this alteration ethical? Explain.

The original photograph on the left was taken in 2002, when President George W. Bush was visiting George Sanchez Charter School in Houston. An unknown person altered the picture on the right, flipping the book in Bush's hands, and it was widely distributed online.

What statement might the unknown manipulator have been trying to make about President Bush? Why do you think this photograph was so widely distributed prior to its being discredited?

extending beyond the text

In 2017, Academy Award-winning actress Lupita Nyong'o was photographed for the cover of *Grazia*, a fashion magazine. The publication edited the photograph to change her hair. In an Instagram post, Nyong'o wrote, "Being featured on the cover of a magazine fulfills me as it is an opportunity to show other dark, kinky-haired people, and particularly our children, that they are beautiful just the way they are. I am disappointed that [*Grazia*] invited me to be on their cover and then edited out and smoothed my hair to fit their notion of what beautiful hair looks like."

What was Nyong'o's objection to the photo manipulation? To what extent do you think that the editor's changes were unethical?

Understanding and Interpreting

1. In the opening two paragraphs, Monica Hesse essentially states the context for her investigation. What is the impact of introducing her ideas in this way?
2. What does Hesse mean by this statement in the second paragraph: "and that is when things got weird"?
3. What does Hesse mean when she characterizes Photoshopping as "that kind of image manipulation [that] breaks a multitude of editorial sins" (par. 9)? When she asks whether that type of manipulation matters "on the cosmic level," what distinction does she suggest?
4. What does Hesse mean by this statement: "It's important for women to be in the picture, literally, because that's how we'll later remember they were in the picture, metaphorically" (par. 11)?

5. Why doesn't Hesse end her article with paragraph 15, which ends with this statement: "I believe nobody was offended, and everyone was happy with the outcome, and that my Wednesday morning investigation was a fizzle"? Why does she continue to pursue this story?
6. What is "the lesson" that Hesse maintains that we should learn "at the end of the day" (par. 19)?
7. What ethical issues is Hesse dealing with in this article? Ultimately, which do you think is most important?

Analyzing Language, Style, and Structure

1. **Vocabulary in Context.** In the opening paragraph, Hesse refers to "a tech summit." What is the meaning of "summit" in this context? How is that meaning similar to or different from other meanings you have encountered?
2. **Skill Focus.** Throughout this essay, Hesse moves between objective reporting with fairly formal diction and a conversational style. She uses colloquialisms such as "weird" and "fizzle"; she imagines someone thinking, "Shoot! . . . I want a copy for my fridge" (par. 8). Using these and other examples, discuss the effect of her mixing informal diction with the expected formal reporting style.
3. At times, Hesse's piece sounds like the investigation of a crime. Identify language choices that create this impression. What effect does this writing style have on her piece and the points she makes?
4. There are many rhetorical questions in this essay. In some cases, an entire paragraph consists of rhetorical questions, such as paragraph 10, which begins this way: "What does it mean when we talk about representation?" How does asking these questions help Hesse achieve her purpose?

Topics for Composing

1. **Analysis.** Examine whether Hesse's essay structure strengthens or weakens her argument. Instead of beginning with a claim and following it with supporting evidence, she organizes her essay by the steps of her investigative process. Is her approach effective? Why or why not?
2. **Argument.** Hesse opens by acknowledging that she embarked on this investigation which felt "important, obscure, symbolic and deeply, deeply petty." Judging by the comments that readers sent in, they agree. Here are two examples:
   - There are terrible things happening in the world, like sex trafficking of children, and we should worry if someone did or didn't get into a photo of some conference. Please!!
   - It's wonderful when an incident of truly fake news is documented. It [harkens] back to the days when network news programs would periodically place reporters in front of photographed backdrops to make them seem as if they were reporting from a remote site when they were really in the home studio. Those incidents of fakery were exposed and condemned, and it's great that this one was as well.

   What is your position on the importance of this example of Photoshopping that Hesse investigates? Is it ultimately a matter that is "important" or "petty"?
3. **Connection.** Hesse asserts that "norms become normal: [If] you see female CEOs, you believe women can be CEOs" (par. 11). Explore this claim through the lens of your own experience. How has a popular culture or media representation of a person in a particular occupation or activity — chef, artist, actor, athlete, for example — influenced you to aspire to that position or something similar?

4. **Speaking and Listening.** Find an example of photo manipulation and share the before and after versions with the class or a small group. The group should discuss what might have motivated the manipulation and whether or not it was ethical. As a group, try to come to a consensus about whether you would have altered the photo and why.
5. **Research.** Research rules or ethical standards for photographers and photo-journalists. After you've conducted some research into this topic, discuss how that information influences your position on Hesse's investigation.

Are We All in This Together?

Michael Sandel

Rick Friedman/Getty Images

American political philosopher and professor Michael Sandel (b. 1953) is best known for the popular course on ethics and justice that he has taught at Harvard University for roughly three decades. His class often needs to be held in a large lecture hall to accommodate the thousand or more students who enroll each semester. In 2020, Sandel published *The Tyranny of Merit: What's Become of the Common Good?* from which this article is adapted.

KEY CONTEXT In 2020, the novel coronavirus, COVID-19, became a worldwide pandemic, leading to significant health and economic impacts in the United States and around the world. The following editorial, published in the *New York Times* at the earliest stages of the pandemic in April 2020, examines how the crises that unfolded during the outbreak illustrate America's inequities.

Sandel uses terms that you might be unfamiliar with:

- "Meritocracy" is an idea that society will economically and socially reward people for their talent, skills, and effort, rather than for their inherited wealth or status.
- "The market" refers to economic forces driven mostly by supply and demand. Capitalistic philosophy suggests the market should determine prices and wages with little or no government regulation.

Mobilizing to confront the pandemic and, eventually, to reconstruct the shattered economy, requires not only medical and economic expertise but also moral and political renewal. We need to ask a basic question that we have evaded over these last decades: What do we owe one another as citizens?

In a pandemic, this question arises most urgently as a question about health care: Should medical care be accessible to all, regardless of their ability to pay? The Trump administration decided that the federal government would pay for coronavirus treatment for the uninsured. Whether it will be possible to reconcile the moral logic of this policy with the notion that health coverage in ordinary times should be left to the market remains to be seen.

But beyond the issue of health care, we need to think more broadly about the way we contend with inequality. We need to better reward the social and economic contributions of work done by the majority of Americans, who don't have college degrees. And we need to reckon with the morally corrosive downsides of meritocracy.

In response to rising inequality, mainstream politicians of both parties have, in recent

Damon Winter/The New York Times/Redux

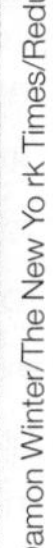

Damon Winter/The New Yo rk Times/Redux

Damon Winter/The New York Times/Redux

Damon Winter/The New Yor k Times/Redux

In 2020, in the midst of the COVID-19 pandemic, the *New York Times* published a photo essay called "The Great American Divide," from which these pictures were taken. The accompanying editorial states that "The United States has a chance to emerge from this latest crisis as a stronger nation, more just, more free and more resilient. We must seize the opportunity."

How do these images illustrate a "divide"? To what extent would Sandel agree with the photographs' message?

decades, called for greater equality of opportunity — improving access to higher education so that all Americans, whatever their starting point in life, can rise as far as their effort and talent will take them. This is, in itself, a worthy principle.

But as an answer to inequality, the rhetoric of rising — the promise that the talented will be able to climb the ladder of success — has a dark side. Part of the problem is that we fail to live up to the meritocratic principles we proclaim. For example, most students at highly selective colleges and universities come from affluent families. At many elite colleges, including Yale and Princeton, there are more students from the top 1 percent than from the entire bottom 60 percent of the country.

There is also a deeper problem: Even a perfect meritocracy, in which opportunities for advancement were truly equal, would corrode solidarity. Focusing on helping the talented clamber up the ladder of success can keep us from noticing that the rungs on the ladder are growing further and further apart.

Meritocracies also produce morally unattractive attitudes among those who make it to the top. The more we believe that our success is our own doing, the less likely we are to feel indebted to, and therefore obligated to, our fellow citizens. The relentless emphasis on rising and striving encourages the winners to inhale too deeply of their success, and to look down on those who lack meritocratic credentials.

These attitudes accompanied the market-driven globalization of the last 40 years. Those who reaped the bounty of outsourcing, free-trade agreements, new technologies and the deregulation of finance came to believe that they had done it all on their own, that their winnings were therefore their due.

Meritocratic hubris and the resentment it provokes are at the heart of the populist backlash against elites. They are also potent sources of social and political polarization. One of the deepest political divides in politics today is between those with and those without a four-year college degree.

In recent decades, governing elites have done little to make life better for the nearly two-thirds of Americans who do not have a college degree. And they have failed to confront what should be one of the central questions of our politics: How can we ensure that Americans who do not inhabit the privileged ranks of the professional classes find dignified work that enables them to support a family, contribute to their community and win social esteem?

As economic activity has shifted from making things to managing money, as society has lavished outsize rewards on hedge fund managers and Wall Street bankers, the esteem accorded to traditional work has become fragile and uncertain. At a time when finance has claimed a greater share of corporate profits, many who labor in the real economy, producing useful goods and services, have not only endured stagnant wages and uncertain job prospects; they have also come to feel that society accords less respect to the kind of work they do.

The coronavirus pandemic has suddenly forced us to reconsider what social and economic roles matter most.

Many of the essential workers during this crisis are performing jobs that do not require college degrees; they are truckers, warehouse workers, delivery workers, police officers, firefighters, utility maintenance workers, sanitation workers, supermarket cashiers, stock clerks, nurse assistants, hospital orderlies and home care providers. They lack the luxury of working from the safety of their homes and holding meetings on Zoom. They, along with the doctors and nurses caring for the afflicted in overcrowded hospitals, are the ones who are putting their health at risk so the rest of us can seek refuge from contagion. Beyond thanking them for their service, we should reconfigure

extending beyond the text

NBC/Photofest

Michael Schur is a writer and producer of several TV shows, such as *The Office, Parks and Recreation,* and *Brooklyn Nine-Nine*. He is also the creator of the show *The Good Place* (pictured above), which is about a group of people in the afterlife trying to figure out how to live ethically. Because of his interest in ethics, Schur was interviewed by a Boston radio station in 2020 during the COVID-19 outbreak about how to act responsibly during a pandemic. Following is an excerpt from that interview.

from Michael Schur On Ethics and Morality in a Crisis

Meghna Chakrabarti and Brittany Knotts

Interviewer: What do we owe each other?

Michael Schur: "I said before that there's a certain sort of minimum that is required of everyone, to the best of our abilities. The basics, right. Staying inside, staying away from people, trying to kind of stop the spread of the disease. But then beyond that, there's an enormous sliding scale, I think. If you have the ability to, for example, pay your dog walker, if you have the financial means to continue to pay your dog walker who can't walk your dog anymore, or someone who helps you clean your house, or anybody who works for you in any capacity. If you have that ability, I think you need to do that. And then, you know, you keep sliding up the scale. If you have the ability to keep people on the payroll at your business who are working for you, even if it means you lose money, I think you have to do that, too. And it just keeps going up and up and up.

extending beyond the text

"I think, in other words, we have to hold people who are billionaires to a much higher standard of what is expected of you and what are your responsibilities. And I think some of the saddest stories and pictures that have come out are stories of people who essentially have all the money in the world — and all the freedom and ability in the world, and for whom this has disrupted them the least, really, except for just, you know, line items and a spreadsheet in terms of how much profit or loss they're making over the next couple of months — who are not kind of stepping up and doing that stuff.

Summarize what Schur suggests are the ethical choices we can make during a pandemic. What might you add to his suggestions? Would Sandel agree with Schur? What else might Sandel add about what we owe each other?

our economy and society to accord such workers the compensation and recognition that reflects the true value of their contributions — not only in an emergency but in our everyday lives.

Such a reconfiguration involves more than familiar debates about how generous or austere the welfare state should be. It requires deliberating as democratic citizens about what constitutes a contribution to the common good, and how such contributions should be rewarded — without assuming that markets can decide these questions on their own.

For example, should we consider a federal wage subsidy to ensure that workers can earn enough to support thriving families, neighborhoods and communities? Should we bolster the dignity of work by shifting the burden of taxation from payroll taxes to taxes on financial transactions, wealth and carbon? Should we reconsider our current policy of taxing income from labor at a higher rate than capital gains? Should we encourage the domestic manufacture of certain goods — beginning with surgical masks, medical gear and pharmaceuticals — rather than promoting outsourcing to low-wage countries?

Even when they recede, pandemics and other great crises seldom leave social and economic arrangements as they were. It is up to us to decide what the legacy of this wrenching episode will be. Our best hope is to pursue the intimations of solidarity implicit in this moment to reframe the terms of public discourse, to find our way to a morally more robust political debate than the rancorous one we have now.

The moral and civic renewal we need requires that we resist the anguished but misconceived debate now emerging about how many lives we should risk for the sake of restarting the economy. This debate assumes that the economy is like a main street shop that turns on the lights after a long weekend and reopens for business, just as before.

The real question is not when but what: What kind of economy will emerge from the crisis? Will it be one that continues to create inequalities that poison our politics and undermine any sense of national community? Or will it be one that honors the dignity of work, rewards contributions to the real economy, gives workers a meaningful voice and shares the risks of ill health and hard times?

We need to ask whether reopening the economy means going back to a system that, over the past four decades, pulled us apart, or whether we can emerge from this crisis with an economy that enables us to say, and to believe, that we are all in this together. ■

Understanding and Interpreting

1. Reread paragraph 4 and summarize what Sandel means by "equality of opportunity."
2. Explain what Sandel means by the phrase "the rhetoric of rising" (par. 5).
3. In paragraph 6, Sandel uses an analogy of a ladder to describe meritocracy. Explain the point Sandel is making through this analogy.
4. Sandel offers several downsides to meritocracy, including what he calls "meritocratic hubris" (par. 9). Reread paragraphs 7 through 9 and explain what this term means and how it has led to the problems he identifies.
5. In paragraph 11, Sandel contrasts those who make things and those who manage money. What does he say are the differences between them? How have these differences contributed to the inequities in American society?
6. How does Sandel characterize the "essential workers" during the pandemic (par. 13)? Why is this characterization important to his argument?
7. Sandel put forward his central claim in paragraph 13. Reread this paragraph and restate his claim in your own words.
8. Based on what you have read in this piece, what does Sandel mean by the "dignity of work" (par. 15)?
9. By the end of his piece, how does Sandel answer the question he asked in the first paragraph, "What do we owe one another as citizens?"

Analyzing Language, Style, and Structure

1. **Vocabulary in Context.** In paragraph 3, Sandel describes the "morally corrosive downsides of meritocracy." What does the word "corrosive" mean in this context? How is that meaning similar to or different from other meanings of the word?
2. **Skill Focus.** Reread paragraph 11 and analyze Sandel's tone toward those people who make their money on Wall Street. What word choices most effectively create that tone?
3. How does Sandel use evidence in paragraph 5 to counter the idea of America as a meritocracy?
4. In paragraph 7, Sandel writes that meritocracy "encourages the winners to inhale too deeply of their success." What is Sandel trying to communicate through his use of figurative language here? How effective is it?
5. In paragraph 9, Sandel describes "social and political polarization." What does he mean by "polarization"? Why is that word an especially effective choice?
6. After discussing the global pandemic at the start of his piece, Sandel does not address it again until paragraph 12. How do his structural choices help him to achieve his purpose?
7. In paragraphs 14 and 15, Sandel offers several solutions to the problems he identifies. Examine his syntax in these paragraphs, and explain how his stylistic choices help him to communicate his ideas.
8. How does Sandel's use of pronouns in his first and last paragraphs contribute to his overall argument?

Topics for Composing

1. **Analysis.** Who is Sandel's likely audience? How do you know? What specific strategies does he use to make his argument persuasive to this audience? How successful is he in appealing to this audience?

2. **Argument.** Sandel offers several specific remedies for creating a more equitable American society (par. 15). Choose one of his suggestions and write an argument that either supports or opposes it. Refer to his piece, your own experiences and reasoning, as well as additional research, if necessary.
3. **Argument.** Is America really a "meritocracy"? Write an argument that takes a position on that question. Support it with evidence from Sandel, your own observations, and additional research, if necessary.
4. **Connection.** What do you know about the COVID-19 pandemic? What lasting impacts have you noticed among your friends and family or the general public?
5. **Connection.** Sandel offers the following definition of what makes a worthwhile career: "dignified work that enables [people] to support a family, contribute to their community and win social esteem" (par. 10). How does this compare to your own definition?
6. **Speaking and Listening.** While Sandel makes the point that the inequities he identifies require a "moral and civic renewal" (par. 17), much of this debate will center on the role of government in our lives. With a partner or small group, determine what the government should be responsible for and what should be left to the individual. To what extent should the government become involved in regulating or controlling the "market"? Be sure to take time at the end of the discussion to identify areas of agreement and consensus.
7. **Research.** Conduct research on the economic inequalities before the start of the pandemic (2020) and in the time since then. Do you see evidence that any of the improvements Sandel hopes for are taking place?
8. **Multimodal.** Look back at the images from the photo essay called "The Great American Divide" on page 844. Take pictures in your own city, town, or neighborhood. Arrange them in a way that either supports or opposes the ideas Sandel puts forward in his argument. Write captions for the images that reinforce the point you want to communicate.
9. **Creative Writing.** While this piece is written in a formal, academic style, Sandel also uses vivid language in places. Return to his argument and highlight fifteen to twenty words or phrases you find striking. Using those words, construct a "found poem" that tries to address the question Sandel asks in his title, "Are we all in this together?"

Why We Look the Other Way

Chuck Klosterman

Jesse Grant/Getty Images

Chuck Klosterman (b. 1972) is an American writer who publishes essays on music, sports, and pop culture. He has written a regular column for the *New York Times* called "The Ethicist." Klosterman is frequently a guest columnist for *ESPN The Magazine*, from which this piece, published in 2007, has been taken.

Shawne Merriman weighs 272 pounds. This is six pounds less than Anthony Muñoz, probably the most dominating left tackle of all time. Shawne Merriman also runs the 40-yard dash in 4.61 seconds. When Jerry Rice attended the NFL draft combine in 1985, he reportedly ran a 4.60; Rice would go on to gain more than 23,000 all-purpose yards while scoring

207 career touchdowns. You do not need Mel Kiper's[1] hard drive to deduce what these numbers mean: As an outside linebacker, Shawne Merriman is almost as big as the best offensive tackle who ever played and almost as fast as the best wide receiver who ever played. He is a rhinoceros who moves like a deer. Common sense suggests this combination should not be possible. It isn't.

Merriman was suspended from the San Diego Chargers for four games last season after testing positive for the anabolic steroid nandrolone. He argues this was the accidental result of a tainted nutritional supplement. "I think two out of 10 people will always believe I did something intentional, or still think I'm doing something," Merriman has said. If this is truly what he believes, no one will ever accuse him of pragmatism. Virtually everyone who follows football assumes Merriman used drugs to turn himself into the kind of hitting machine who can miss four games and still lead the league with 17 sacks. He has been caught and penalized, and the public shall forever remain incredulous of who he is and what he does.

The public will respond by renewing its subscription to NFL Sunday Ticket, where it will regularly watch dozens of 272-pound men accelerate at speeds that would have made them Olympic sprinters during the 1960s. This, it seems, is the contemporary relationship most people have with drugs and pro football: unconditional distrust of anyone who tests positive, balanced by an unconscious willingness to overlook all the physical impossibilities they see. This is partially understandable; socially, sports serve an escapist purpose. Football players are real people, but they exist in a constructed nonreality.

Within the context of any given game, nobody cares how a certain linebacker got so big while remaining so fast. Part of what makes football successful is its detachment from day-to-day life. For 60 minutes, it subsists in a vacuum. But this detachment is going to become

[1]NFL draft analyst for ESPN. Forty-yard dash times are recorded at the NFL draft workout. —Eds.

The Washington Post/Getty Images

This image is a typical hit in an NFL game.

What does the photograph capture about the game and its players? How might Klosterman react to this photo? How could this photo be used to promote new regulations against performance-enhancing drugs in the NFL?

more complicated in the coming years, mostly because reality is evolving, becoming harder to block out. And the Evolved Reality is this: It's starting to feel like a significant segment of the NFL is on drugs. As a consequence, you will have to make some decisions.

5 Not commissioner Roger Goodell.

You.

On Feb. 27, federal, state and local authorities seized the records of an Orlando pharmacy, accusing the owners of running an online bazaar for performance-enhancing drugs. This came on the heels of a raid on a similar enterprise in Mobile, Ala., where the customer list apparently included recognizable names like boxer Evander Holyfield and late-blooming outfielder Gary Matthews Jr.

None of this is particularly shocking. But then there is the case of Richard Rydze. In 2006 Rydze, an internist, purchased $150,000 of testosterone and human growth hormone from the Florida pharmacy over the Internet. This is not against the law. However, Rydze is a physician for the Pittsburgh Steelers. He says he never prescribed any of those drugs to members of the team, and I cannot prove otherwise. However, the Steelers have had a complicated relationship with performance enhancers for a long time. Offensive lineman Steve Courson (now deceased) admitted he used steroids while playing for Pittsburgh in the 1970s and early '80s, as did at least four other guys. Former Saints coach Jim Haslett, a player in Buffalo from 1979 to 1985, has said the old Steelers dynasty essentially ran on steroids. The team, obviously, denies this.

Several members of the Carolina Panthers' 2004 Super Bowl team were implicated in a steroid scandal involving Dr. James Shortt, a private practitioner in West Columbia, S.C. One of these players was punter Todd Sauerbrun. Do not mitigate the significance of this point: The punter was taking steroids. The punter had obtained syringes and injectable Stanozolol, the same chemical Ben Johnson used before the 1988 Olympics. I'm not suggesting punters aren't athletes, nor am I overlooking how competitive the occupation of punting must be; I'm merely pointing out that it's kind of crazy to think punters would be taking steroids but defensive tackles would not. We all concede that steroids, HGH and blood doping can help people ride bicycles faster through the Alps. Why do we even momentarily question how much impact they must have on a game built entirely on explosion and power?

10 "People may give a certain amount of slack to football players because there's this unspoken sense that in order to play the game well, you need

American football players, advertisement for Charles Eneu Johnson & Co, 1930 (color litho)/ American School, (20th century)/LOOK AND LEARN (BARBARA LOE COLLECTION)/Private Collection/Bridgeman Images

How does this 1930 advertisement for Charles Eneu Johnson and Company, a printing business that operated nearly a century ago, present the physicality of football? Would Klosterman think this view is similar to or different from how we see football today?

extending beyond the text

The following is an excerpt of an interview with Jessica Luther, author of a book about sexual assault by football players on college campuses called *Unsportsmanlike Conduct: College Football and the Politics of Rape.*

from It's Complicated Being a Feminist Football Fan

Sarah Mirk

Sarah Mirk: You're a big football fan. So can you tell me about being a football fan and how you counter those two different realities: the fact that these horrible crimes are able to be done in part because of the culture that football creates, and being a part of that culture and loving the game?

Jessica Luther: Yeah, I think a lot about my own consumption of sports, especially college football. I have this sort of really sad encyclopedia in my head of coaches and teams and specific players, and I know all of them, and I'm sort of the Debbie Downer of the group.

Sarah Mirk: Haha, yeah.

Dave Coverly

Jessica Luther: If I'm with people, and we're watching, I'm like, "Well, oh. That's the guy that did this thing." And so it's something I'm actively aware of all the time while I'm consuming sports. At this point in time, I can't shut that off. At the same time, I still really love watching. Part of it is that it's just something I've done my entire life, and sort of changing that kind of pattern in your own life can just be a difficult thing to do. At the same time, I feel like we all could relate to the way that we compromise as women moving through the world, where are limits, right? And at this point, I'm not sure exactly where my limit is with football.

I definitely watch it much less than I used to, but I still watch it. I love athleticism, I love competition, I love watching what these people can do and how they do it, and how they do it as a team. Like all the sort of good things about sports, I still really care about, but there is sort of a constant nagging in my head. But at the same time, I go to movies all the time that have people in them that I have issues with, and I just put that to the side while I'm

extending beyond the text

consuming it and then go back to tweeting about it later, something to that effect. So it's not as if I don't already have the skills to consume problematic material and still enjoy it. So I think it's just getting harder to do it, but I still like to watch sports.

Sarah Mirk: What brings you back to watching football still? What do you love about football, specifically?

Jessica Luther: Oh, that's a good question. I mean, I do, there is just this straight-up athleticism. I mean, oh, I'm trying to remember who it was. There was a guy last weekend who did the most amazing route. He was running, and he did this kind of weird flip thing in the air and kept going. And I watched the Vine of it 100 times. I am so interested in people's abilities to move. I'm really interested in the human body and how people can do sort of what look like superhuman feats to us.

What conflicting feelings about being a football fan does Luther describe? Has knowledge of a player's or team's wrongdoing ever made you feel similarly conflicted when watching sports? Or, if a filmmaker or singer whose work you admire has been credibly accused of sexual assault, how has that accusation affected your appreciation of his or her work? To what extent might Klosterman agree or disagree with Luther's conclusions about being a football fan?

an edge," USC critical studies professor Todd Boyd told the *Los Angeles Times* last month. Boyd has written several books about sports, race and culture. "That's what people want in a football player — someone who's crazy and mean."

It's a subtle paradox: People choose to ignore the relationship between performance enhancers and the NFL because it's unquestionably the league where performance enhancers would have the biggest upside. But what will happen when such deliberate naïveté becomes impossible? Revelatory drug scandals tend to escalate exponentially (look at Major League Baseball and U.S. track and field). Merriman, Sauerbrun and the other 33 players suspended by the NFL since 2002 could be exceptions; it seems far more plausible they are not. We are likely on the precipice of a bubble that is going to burst. But if it does, how are we supposed to feel about it? Does this invalidate the entire sport, or does it barely matter at all?

This is where things become complicated.

It can be strongly argued that the most important date in the history of rock music was Aug. 28, 1964. This was the day Bob Dylan met the Beatles in New York City's Hotel Delmonico and got them high.

Obviously, a lot of people might want to disagree with this assertion, but the artistic evidence is hard to ignore. The introduction of marijuana altered the trajectory of the Beatles' songwriting, reconstructed their consciousness and prompted them to make the most influential rock albums of all time. After the summer of 1964, the Beatles started taking serious drugs, and those drugs altered their musical performance. Though it may not have been their overt intent, the Beatles took performance-enhancing drugs. And this is germane to sports for one reason: Absolutely no one holds it against them. No one views *Rubber Soul* and *Revolver* as "less authentic" albums, despite the fact that they would not (and probably could not) have been made by people who weren't on drugs.

15 Jack Kerouac wrote *On the Road* on a Benzedrine binge, yet nobody thinks this makes his novel less significant. A Wall Street stockbroker can get jacked up on cocaine before going into the trading pit, yet nobody questions his bottom line. It's entirely possible that you take

10mg of Ambien the night before a big day at the office, and then drink 32 ounces of coffee when you wake up (possibly along with a mind-sharpening cigarette). Anytime a person takes drugs for purposes that aren't exclusively recreational (i.e., staring at your stereo speakers, watching *Planet of the Apes*, etc.), he or she is using them to do something at a higher level. Yes, I realize there is a difference between caffeine and HGH. But there's probably an even greater difference between a morning of data processing and trying to cut-block Shawne Merriman.

My point is not that all drugs are the same, nor that drugs are awesome, nor that the Beatles needed LSD to become the geniuses they already were. My point is that sports are unique in the way they're retrospectively colored by the specter of drug use. East Germany was an Olympic force during the 1970s and '80s; today, you can't mention the East Germans' dominance without noting that they were pumped full of Ivan Drago–esque chemicals. This relationship changes the meaning of their achievements. You simply don't see this in other idioms. Nobody looks back at Pink Floyd's *Dark Side of the Moon* and says, "I guess that music is okay, but it doesn't really count. Those guys were probably high in the studio."

Now, the easy rebuttal to this argument is contextual, because it's not as if Roger Waters was shooting up with testosterone in order to strum his bass-guitar strings harder. Unlike songwriting or stock trading, football is mostly physical; it seems like there needs to be a different scale — an uncrossable line — for what endangers competitive integrity. But how do we make that distinction? In all of these cases (sports-related and otherwise), people are putting foreign substances into their bodies in the hope of reaching a desired result. The motive is the same. What's different, and sometimes arbitrary, is when people care. Baseball fans are outraged that Rafael Palmeiro tested positive for Stanozolol; they are generally indifferent to the fact that most players regularly took amphetamines for 40 years. Meanwhile, as a member of the Philadelphia Eagles in 1994, Bill Romanowski electively received two trauma IVs to help recover from injuries. Trauma IVs are what emergency room doctors give to people dying from car accidents. In his autobiography, Romanowski claims one of his teammates received six trauma IVs in the span of one season. This is natural?

I am told we live in a violent society. But even within that society, football players are singular. Another former Eagle, strong safety Andre Waters, committed suicide last November at age 44. A postmortem examination of his brain indicated he had the neurological tissue of an 85-year-old man with Alzheimer's, almost certainly the result of using his skull as a weapon for 12 seasons. Andre Waters hit people so hard, and so often, that he cut his time on earth in half. Hitting was his life. This is why the relationship between drugs and football is different from the relationship between drugs and baseball: Baseball is mostly about tangible statistics, which drugs skew and invalidate; football is more about intangible masculine warfare, which drugs quietly enhance.

Announcers casually lionize pro football players as gladiators, but that description is more accurate than most would like to admit. For the sake of entertainment, we expect these people to be the fastest, strongest, most aggressive on earth. If they are not, they make less money and eventually lose their jobs.

This being the case, it seems hypocritical to 20
blame them for taking steroids. We might blame them more if they did not.

Around this time last year, I wrote an essay for *[ESPN] The Magazine* about Barry Bonds — specifically, how steroids made his passing of Babe Ruth on the career home run list problematic. I still believe this to be true, just as

What point is this cartoon making about being a fan of football? Why would Klosterman agree or disagree with that point?

I believe that the notion of an NFL that's more juiced than organic is more negative than interesting. It would be easier to be a football fan if none of this was going on. But since it is going on, we will all have to decide how much this Evolved Reality is going to bother us.

This will not be simple. I don't think there will be a fall guy for the NFL; over time, we won't be able to separate Merriman from the rest of the puzzle (which MLB has so far successfully done with Bonds). It won't be about the legitimacy of specific players. This will be more of an across-the-board dilemma, because we will have to publicly acknowledge that the most popular sport in the country has been kinetically altered by drugs, probably for the past 25 years. In many ways, the NFL's reaction barely matters. What matters more is how fans will attempt to reconcile that realization with their personal feelings toward the game. The question, ultimately, is this: If it turns out the lifeblood of the NFL is unnatural, does that make the game less meaningful?

The answer depends on who you are. And maybe how old you are.

In 1982, I read a story about Herschel Walker in *Sports Illustrated* headlined "My Body's Like an Army." It explained how, at the time, Walker didn't even lift weights; instead, he did 100,000 sit-ups and 100,000 push-ups a year, knocking out 25 of each every time a commercial came on the television. This information made me worship Herschel; it made him seem human and superhuman at the same time. "My Body's Like an Army" simultaneously indicated that I could become Herschel Walker and that I could never become Herschel Walker. His physical perfection was self-generated and completely pure. He had made himself better than other mortals, and that made me love him.

25 But I was 10 years old.

There comes a point in every normal person's life when they stop looking at athletes as models for living. Any thinking adult who follows pro sports understands that some people are corrupt and the games are just games and money drives everything. It would be strange if they did not realize these things. But what's equally strange is the way so many fans (and sportswriters, myself included) revert back to their 10-year-old selves whenever an issue like steroids shatters the surface.

Most of the time, we don't care what football players do when they're not playing football. On any given Wednesday, we have only a passing interest in who they are as people or how they choose to live. But Sunday is different. On Sunday, we have wanted them to be superfast, superstrong, superentertaining and, weirdly, superethical. They are supposed to be pristine 272-pound men who run 40 yards in 4.61 seconds simply because they do sit-ups during commercial breaks for *Grey's Anatomy*. Unlike everybody else in America, they cannot do whatever it takes to succeed; they have to fulfill the unrealistic expectations of 10-year-old kids who read magazines. And this is because football players have a job that doesn't matter at all, except in those moments when it matters more than absolutely everything else.

It may be time to rethink some of this stuff. ■

Understanding and Interpreting

1. Klosterman is not making a simplistic argument about performance-enhancing drugs here. He is not, for instance, simply suggesting that performance-enhancing drugs (PEDs) should be banned in football. What is his central claim about the relationship between the football players and the viewers of the NFL?
2. In two different places, Klosterman uses the phrase "Evolved Reality" (pars. 4 and 21). What does this phrase mean? What purpose does it serve in this argument?
3. In paragraph 9, Klosterman describes the accusations of PED use lodged against punter Todd Sauerbrun. What point is Klosterman making about Sauerbrun? How does he use this specific example to support his overall argument?
4. The references to Bob Dylan, the Beatles, Jack Kerouac, and Pink Floyd are likely included here as counterarguments to the idea that PEDs are always automatically bad. Explain the conclusion the reader is expected to draw from these references. Then, evaluate how well they support Klosterman's overall claim. Do they really work as counterarguments, or are they too different to be applicable?
5. Throughout the piece, Klosterman compares the use of PEDs in football and in baseball. What are the significant differences that he identifies? How do these differences support his overall claim about PEDs in sports?
6. What does Klosterman mean when he says at the very end of his piece, "It may be time to rethink some of this stuff?" How does this reflect a point he is making about being a sports fan?

Analyzing Language, Style, and Structure

1. **Vocabulary in Context.** In paragraph 11, Klosterman writes, "We are likely on the precipice of a bubble." What does the word "precipice" mean in this context?
2. **Skill Focus.** Reread the last three paragraphs. What is Klosterman's tone toward NFL players and viewers? How does this tone reflect and support his central claim?

3. What is a likely reason that Klosterman started his argument with a description of Shawne Merriman's size and speed? What is a reader expected to conclude from the first three paragraphs?
4. Since this article appeared in *ESPN The Magazine*, we can assume that Klosterman's audience is made up of sports fans. What words, phrases, and allusions does Klosterman include that make it clear that sports fans are his intended audience? What might he have included if he were writing for an audience not as familiar with sports?
5. Evaluate Klosterman's logical reasoning in paragraph 16. What evidence does he include? Where does he make unsupported assumptions? Where does he commit logical fallacies? What are his biases? Overall, how effective is this paragraph in supporting his position?
6. In paragraph 19, Klosterman uses the word "gladiators" to describe NFL players. What are the positive and negative connotations of this word? How do these conflicting ideas help illustrate Klosterman's claim?
7. Klosterman waits until the end of his piece (par. 24) to share his story about how his ten-year-old self admired Herschel Walker. What purpose does this section serve in his argument? Why is it most effective — or not — at the end of the piece?
8. Klosterman uses rhetorical questions (p. 817) regularly throughout his piece. Identify a few examples and explain how they help Klosterman make his points.

Topics for Composing

1. **Analysis.** Overall, what does Klosterman want his reader to do? To what extent did he sufficiently prove his point? Cite specific evidence from his piece to support your analysis.
2. **Argument.** Klosterman raises several issues in this piece: use of PEDs, dangers of concussions and injury in sport, recreational drug use by musicians and writers, and the ethical decisions facing sports fans. Choose one of these topics and write an argument in which you explain why you support, challenge, or qualify the conclusion that Klosterman draws.
3. **Argument.** If they are adults and are informed about the potential health risks, should athletes be allowed to take whatever PEDs they want as long as they identify exactly what drugs they take? Choose a sport or another form of competition and write an argument about what types of benefits should be allowed or prohibited under the governing rules for that sport or competition.
4. **Connection.** Think about yourself as a fan. You might not like to watch sports as much as Klosterman does, but you likely are a fan of specific celebrities, musicians, authors, actors, and so on. What are the costs and benefits of your fandom, for those you watch and for yourself?
5. **Speaking and Listening.** Hold a class or small group debate on the issue of whether or not NFL players — or any professional athletes — should be able to use PEDs. Be sure to listen actively to each other. Reserve time before the end of the discussion to come to consensus about the proper role of PEDs in professional sports.
6. **Research.** Choose an athlete who has been accused of using PEDs. Research the types of drugs he or she may have used and how the drugs enhanced his or her performance. Explain whether or not the athlete behaved unethically and why you think that is the case.

central text

from A Small Place

Jamaica Kincaid

Elisabetta A. Villa/Getty Images

Jamaica Kincaid (b. 1949) was born on the Caribbean island of Antigua when it was still a British colony. She came to the United States as a teenager to work as an au pair in New York City, where she then attended the New School for Social Research. Kincaid became a staff writer for the *New Yorker* in 1975 and published much of her short work there. Perhaps her most widely known works are "Girl" from *At the Bottom of the River*, a collection of short stories (1985), and the novels *Annie John* (1985) and *See Now Then* (2013).

KEY CONTEXT *A Small Place*, published in 1988, is an extended essay about Antigua. The indigenous people of Antigua, an island located southeast of Puerto Rico in the Caribbean Sea, had their earliest recorded European contact with Christopher Columbus in 1493. By the mid-1600s, a profitable sugar plantation industry was established in Antigua by the British, and African slaves were brought to the island to work in the fields. In 1834, when Britain abolished slavery in the Caribbean, Antigua became the first of the colonies to emancipate its slaves. The island remained under British control, however, until its independence in 1981. Antigua retains membership in the British Commonwealth.

The first-person speaker of *A Small Place* takes the reader, an imagined tourist (addressed as "you"), on a journey through both Antigua of the present time and the colonial past. *A Small Place* is often described as a "postcolonial text," which means that it addresses the lasting impact of being colonized by outsiders. The following selection is taken from the opening chapter of *A Small Place*.

If you go to Antigua as a tourist, this is what you will see. If you come by aeroplane, you will land at the V. C. Bird International Airport. Vere Cornwall (V. C.) Bird is the Prime Minister of Antigua. You may be the sort of tourist who would wonder why a Prime Minister would want an airport named after him — why not a school, why not a hospital, why not some great public monument? You are a tourist and you have not yet seen a school in Antigua, you have not yet seen the hospital in Antigua, you have not yet seen a public monument in Antigua. As your plane descends to land, you might say, What a beautiful island Antigua is — more beautiful than any of the other islands you have seen, and they were very beautiful, in their way, but they were much too green, much too lush with vegetation, which indicated to you, the tourist, that they got quite a bit of rainfall, and rain is the very thing that you, just now, do not want, for you are thinking of the hard and cold and dark and long days you spent working in North America (or, worse, Europe), earning some money so that you could stay in this place (Antigua) where the sun always shines and where the climate is deliciously hot and dry for the four to ten days you are going to be staying there; and since you are on your holiday, since you are a tourist, the thought of what it might be like for someone who had to live day in, day out in a place that

English Harbour on Antigua/PICTURE ALLIANCE (RDA)/Bridgeman Images

The area in this image is known as English Harbour, a name that reflects its eighteenth-century beginnings when the Royal British Navy established its base of operations there. **How does this aerial view of the southern tip of Antigua capture the beauty of the island that draws the tourist? How would Kincaid likely expect the tourist to respond to the name English Harbour?**

suffers constantly from drought, and so has to watch carefully every drop of fresh water used (while at the same time surrounded by a sea and an ocean — the Caribbean Sea on one side, the Atlantic Ocean on the other), must never cross your mind.

You disembark from your plane. You go through customs. Since you are a tourist, a North American or European — to be frank, white — and not an Antiguan black returning to Antigua from Europe or North America with cardboard boxes of much needed cheap clothes and food for relatives, you move through customs swiftly, you move through customs with ease. Your bags are not searched. You emerge from customs into the hot, clean air: immediately you feel cleansed, immediately you feel blessed (which is to say special); you feel free. You see a man, a taxi driver; you ask him to take you to your destination; he quotes you a price. You immediately think that the price is in the local currency, for you are a tourist and you are familiar with these things (rates of exchange) and you feel even more free, for things seem so cheap, but then your driver ends by saying, "In U.S. currency." You may say, "Hmmmm, do you have a formal sheet that lists official prices and destinations?" Your driver obeys the law and shows you the sheet, and he apologises for the incredible mistake he has made in quoting you a price off the top of his head which is so vastly different (favouring him) from the one listed. You are driven to your hotel by this taxi driver in his taxi, a brand-new Japanese-made vehicle. The road on which you are travelling is a very bad road, very much in need of repair. You are feeling wonderful, so you say, "Oh, what a marvellous change these bad roads are from the splendid highways I am used to in North America." (Or, worse, Europe.) Your driver is reckless; he is a dangerous man who drives in the middle of the road when he thinks no other cars are coming in the opposite direction, passes other cars on blind curves that run uphill, drives at sixty miles an hour on narrow, curving roads when the road sign, a rusting, beat-up thing left over from colonial days, says 40 mph. This might frighten you (you are on your holiday; you are a tourist); this might excite you (you are on your holiday; you are a tourist), though if you are from New York and take taxis you are used to this style of driving: most of the taxi drivers in New York are from places in the world like this. You are looking out the window (because you want to get your money's worth); you notice that all the cars you see are brand-new, or almost brand-new, and that they are all Japanese-made. There are no American cars in Antigua — no new ones, at any rate; none that were manufactured in the last ten years. You continue to look at the cars and you say to yourself, Why, they look brand-new, but they have an awful sound, like an old car — a very old, dilapidated car. How to account for that? Well, possibly it's because they use leaded gasoline in these brand-new cars whose engines were built to use non-leaded gasoline, but you musn't ask the person driving the car if this is so, because he or she has never heard of unleaded gasoline. You look closely at the car; you see that it's a model of a Japanese car that you might hesitate to buy; it's a model that's very expensive; it's a model that's quite impractical for a person who has to work as hard as you do and who watches every penny you earn so that you can afford this holiday you are on. How do they afford such a car? And do they live in a luxurious house to match such a car? Well, no. You will be surprised, then, to see that most likely the person driving this brand-new car filled with the wrong gas lives in a house that, in comparison, is far beneath the status of the car; and if you were to ask why you would be told that the banks are encouraged by the government to make loans available for cars, but loans for houses not so easily available; and if you ask again why, you will be told that the two main car dealerships in Antigua are owned in part or outright by ministers in government. Oh, but you are on holiday and the sight of these brand-new cars driven by people who may or may not have really passed their driving test (there was once a scandal about driving licences for sale) would not really stir up these thoughts in you. . . .

Oh, but by now you are tired of all this looking, and you want to reach your destination — your hotel, your room. You long to refresh yourself; you long to eat some nice lobster, some nice local food. You take a bath, you brush your teeth. You get dressed again; as you get dressed, you look out the window. That water — have you ever seen anything like it? Far out, to the horizon, the colour of the water is navy-blue; nearer, the water is the colour of the North American sky. From there to the shore, the water is pale, silvery, clear, so clear that you can see its pinkish-white sand bottom. Oh, what beauty! Oh, what beauty! You have never seen anything like this. You are so excited. You breathe shallow. You breathe deep. You see a

Slaves cutting the cane, from 'Ten Views in the Island of Antigua,' 1823 (hand-coloured litho)/Clark, William (1770-1838)/STAPLETON COLLECTION/Private Collection/Bridgeman Images

This image of slaves cutting the cane is taken from *Ten Views in the Island of Antigua*, a series of lithographs from 1823.

What tone does this painting appear to take toward slavery? What details from the painting communicate this tone? How does Kincaid allude to this colonial past in *A Small Place*?

beautiful boy skimming the water, godlike, on a Windsurfer. You see an incredibly unattractive, fat, pastrylike-fleshed woman enjoying a walk on the beautiful sand, with a man, an incredibly unattractive, fat, pastrylike-fleshed man; you see the pleasure they're taking in their surroundings. Still standing, looking out the window, you see yourself lying on the beach, enjoying the amazing sun (a sun so powerful and yet so beautiful, the way it is always overhead as if on permanent guard, ready to stamp out any cloud that dares to darken and so empty rain on you and ruin your holiday; a sun that is your personal friend). You see yourself taking a walk on that beach, you see yourself meeting new people (only they are new in a very limited way, for they are people just like you). You see yourself eating some delicious, locally grown food. You see yourself, you see yourself . . . You must not wonder what exactly happened to the contents of your lavatory when you flushed it. You must not wonder where your bathwater went when you pulled out the stopper. You must not wonder what happened when you brushed your teeth. Oh, it might all end up in the water you are thinking of taking a swim in; the contents of your lavatory might, just might, graze gently against your ankle as you wade carefree in the water, for you see, in Antigua, there is no proper sewage-disposal system. But the Caribbean Sea is very big and the Atlantic Ocean is even bigger; it would amaze even you to know the number of black slaves this ocean has swallowed up. When you sit down to eat your delicious meal, it's better that you don't know that most of what you are eating came off a plane from Miami. And before it got on a plane in Miami, who knows where it came from? A good guess is that it came from a place like Antigua first, where it was grown dirt-cheap, went to Miami, and came back. There is a world of something in this, but I can't go into it right now.

The thing you have always suspected about yourself the minute you become a tourist is true:

This poster is a 1964 advertisement for Pan American Airways, which was the largest international airline in America from the 1920s to the 1990s.

What message about the Caribbean is this ad trying to communicate? What elements create that message? Based on what you have read, how would Kincaid likely react to this advertisement? Why?

A tourist is an ugly human being. You are not an ugly person all the time; you are not an ugly person ordinarily; you are not an ugly person day to day. From day to day, you are a nice person. From day to day, all the people who are supposed to love you on the whole do. From day to day, as you walk down a busy street in the large and modern and prosperous city in which you work and live, dismayed, puzzled (a cliché, but only a cliché can explain you) at how alone you feel in this crowd, how awful it is to go unnoticed, how awful it is to go unloved, even as you are surrounded by more people than you could possibly get to know in a lifetime that lasted for millennia, and then out of the corner of your eye you see someone looking at you and absolute pleasure is written all over that person's face, and then you realise that you are not as revolting a presence as you think you are (for that look just told you so). And so, ordinarily, you are a nice person, an attractive person, a person capable of drawing to yourself the affection of other people (people just like you), a person at home in your own skin (sort of; I mean, in a way; I mean, your dismay and puzzlement are natural to you, because people like you just seem to be like that, and so many of the things people like you find admirable about yourselves — the things you think about, the things you think really define you — seem rooted in these feelings): a person at home in your own house (and all its nice house things), with its nice back yard (and its nice back-yard things), at home on your street, your church, in community activities, your job, at home with your family, your relatives, your friends — you are a whole person. But one day, when you are sitting somewhere, alone in that crowd, and that awful feeling of displacedness comes over you, and really, as an ordinary person you are not well equipped to look too far inward and set yourself aright, because being ordinary is already so taxing, and being ordinary takes all you have out of you, and though the words "I must get away" do not actually pass across your lips, you make a leap from being that nice blob just sitting like a boob in your amniotic sac of the modern experience to being a person visiting heaps of death and ruin and feeling alive and inspired at the sight of it; to being a person lying on some faraway beach, your stilled body stinking and glistening in the sand, looking like something first forgotten, then remembered, then not important enough to go back for; to being a person marvelling at the harmony (ordinarily, what you would say is the backwardness) and the union these other people (and they are other people) have with nature. And you look at the things they can do with a piece of ordinary cloth, the things they fashion out of cheap, vulgarly colored (to you) twine, the way they squat down over a hole they have made in the ground, the hole itself is something to marvel at, and since you are being an ugly person this ugly but joyful thought will swell inside you: their ancestors were not clever in the way yours were and not ruthless in the way yours were, for then would it not be you who would be in harmony with nature and backwards in that charming way? An ugly thing, that is what you are when you become a tourist, an ugly, empty thing, a stupid thing, a piece of rubbish pausing here and there to gaze at this and taste that, and it will never occur to you that the people who inhabit the place in which you have just paused cannot stand you, that behind their closed doors they laugh at your strangeness (you do not look the way they look); the physical sight of you does not please them; you have bad manners (it is their custom to eat their food with their hands; you try eating their way, you look silly; you try eating the way you always eat, you look silly); they do not like the way you speak (you have an accent); they collapse helpless from laughter, mimicking the way they imagine you must look as you carry out some everyday bodily function. They do not like you. *They do not like me!* That thought never actually occurs to you. Still, you feel a little uneasy. Still, you feel a little foolish, Still, you feel a little out of place. But the banality of your own life is very real to you; it drove you to this extreme, spending your days and your nights in the company of people who despise you, people you do not like really, people you would not want to have as your actual neighbour. And so you must devote yourself to puzzling out how much of what you are told is really, really true (Is ground-up bottle glass in peanut sauce really a delicacy around here, or will it do just what you think ground-up bottle glass will do? Is this rare, multicoloured, snout-mouthed fish really an aphrodisiac, or will it cause you to fall asleep

extending beyond the text

Following is the opening paragraph from a 2014 article in a magazine for upscale travelers.

from **Antigua: The Ideal Beach Getaway**

Yolanda Edwards

"Let me take you into the sun," said Louvaine, our Hermitage Bay liaison at the airport. No sooner had she spotted our pale winter faces at baggage claim than she swept our ten-year-old daughter out of the shade and into the warmth. . . . Our only criteria for a Caribbean vacation? Something authentic, or at least uncommercial, with good food and just a nonstop flight away. We found it on Antigua. The island has a relative lack of big chain resorts along with a strong tradition of farming and fishing. On the drive from the airport, we saw guys hacking and selling sugarcane, roadside stands of bananas and pineapple, and donkeys, cows, and goats roaming free. Add to this the island's genuine friendliness (Louvaine's gracious hospitality was only the beginning) and Antigua nailed our elusive trifecta better than any other Caribbean islands we've visited.

Compare and contrast this author's perceptions with those of Kincaid in the opening to *A Small Place*, focusing specifically on tone.

permanently?). Oh, the hard work all of this is, and is it any wonder, then, that on your return home you feel the need of a long rest, so that you can recover from your life as a tourist?

5 That the native does not like the tourist is not hard to explain. For every native of every place is a potential tourist, and every tourist is a native of somewhere. Every native everywhere lives a life of overwhelming and crushing banality and boredom and desperation and depression, and every deed, good and bad, is an attempt to forget this. Every native would like to find a way out, every native would like a rest, every native would like a tour. But some natives — most natives in the world — cannot go anywhere. They are too poor. They are too poor to go anywhere. They are too poor to escape the reality of their lives; and they are too poor to live properly in the place where they live, which is the very place you, the tourist, want to go — so when the natives see you, the tourist, they envy you, they envy your ability to leave your own banality and boredom, they envy your ability to turn their own banality and boredom into a source of pleasure for yourself. ■

Understanding and Interpreting

1. In the long opening paragraph, what assumptions does Jamaica Kincaid make in describing "a tourist"? What characteristics does she ascribe to tourists in general?
2. What do you think Kincaid means when she states that the tourist emerging from customs "feel[s] free" (par. 2)?
3. What points does Kincaid make about the socioeconomic situation in Antigua by focusing on the cars, drivers, and conditions of the roads?

4. Once the tourist reaches the hotel, what is the chasm between expectations and reality that Kincaid describes?
5. Kincaid imagines the emotional life of the tourist back home, wherever that may be. How does this section help to illustrate her view of tourists? Consider what she means by her comment that "only a cliché can explain you [the tourist]" (par. 4). Does this long paragraph strengthen or weaken her argument? Explain with specific references to the text.
6. In paragraph 4, Kincaid describes the change from "a nice person, an attractive person" to "an ugly human being" when a person becomes a tourist. According to Kincaid, what causes this change? Why doesn't the tourist resist the change, according to Kincaid?
7. What is the "banality and boredom" (par. 5) that Kincaid describes in the life of both the native and the tourist?
8. Kincaid identifies many qualities that distinguish Antiguans from the tourists. Choose one of them, explain the differences, and analyze how this distinction assists Kincaid in her argument.
9. To what extent do you trust Kincaid's reliability as a narrator? Is she being harsh, judgmental, contemptuous? Or honest, genuine, or simply realistic? Cite specific passages to support your response.
10. Based on this excerpt from *A Small Place*, how can the tourist visiting Antigua "do the right thing"? Or does being a tourist make that impossible, according to Kincaid?

Analyzing Language, Style, and Structure

1. **Vocabulary in Context.** Kincaid describes what might happen to the tourist's bathwater: "the contents of your lavatory might, just might, graze gently against your ankle as you wade carefree in the water" (par. 3). What does "graze" mean in this context?
2. **Skill Focus.** One of the most outstanding features of Kincaid's tone in this piece is her ironic use of the second person pronoun "you" to address her readers. What effect does she achieve in the first paragraph alone? How would writing in the third person change the effect? For example, "When **people** come to Antigua as tourists, this is what **they** will see. If **they** come by aeroplane, **they** will land . . ."
3. **Skill Focus.** In the final paragraph of the excerpt, Kincaid refers more generally to "the native" and "the tourist." How does Kincaid's tone change from the rest of the piece? In what ways might this final paragraph affect how readers think back on the preceding paragraphs?
4. Readers would likely find some of Kincaid's harsh language offensive, especially because it seems to be directed right at them with the use of "you." Yet Kincaid wants readers to stick with her piece and read to the end. Assuming that she's not trying to drive readers away, what effect might she be trying to achieve with this harsh language?
5. Kincaid asserts that the tourist at home realizes "the banality" of his or her own life (par. 4). What connotations does this word carry to make it an effective choice? How, for instance, does "banality" differ from "boredom"?
6. Throughout the essay, Kincaid makes parenthetical asides. Some are short, such as her clarification that the tourist is from North America "(or worse, Europe)" or longer ones, that are complete sentences: "(you are on your holiday; you are a tourist)" (par. 2). Select a paragraph or two and focus on Kincaid's use of parenthetical comments. What is her purpose in using so many asides? In what ways do these comments represent a shift in voice? Try reading the section without the parentheticals to consider the impact.
7. What is the effect of Kincaid's use of repetition as a rhetorical strategy? To what extent does Kincaid fail to avoid or succeed in avoiding monotony?

8. If you were unaware of Kincaid's background, at what point in the essay would you realize that she, the narrator, is originally from Antigua? Is Kincaid too biased to make an effective argument? Explain why or why not.
9. Kincaid suggests that the tourist does not know if ground-up glass is "really a [local] delicacy" (par. 4) or if the fish being served at dinner is, in fact, deadly. Is she being serious at this point or sarcastic? Cite specific passages to support your view.
10. Does Kincaid go too far when she characterizes the tourist as "that nice blob just sitting like a boob in your amniotic sac of the modern experience" (par. 4)? Does that image convey a touch of ironic humor or does it offend? What might Kindcaid's intention have been?
11. Kincaid asks numerous rhetorical questions (p. 817) in this essay. How do they contribute to the tone she develops? Identify and analyze as many as you need to determine their intended effect.
12. Kincaid addresses the reader as "you." What assumptions does she make about "you"? How do you know based on how she describes "you"? To what extent does this approach seem presumptuous? Is it off-putting or effective as a rhetorical strategy? Is it stereotyping, an insightful method of inquiry, or something else? Explain your reaction.

Topics for Composing

1. **Analysis.** Kincaid draws contrasts between what tourists hope to find in Antigua and the realities experienced by those who live there year-round. What does Kincaid suggest about the effects of economic disparities through this contrast?
2. **Argument.** Is it possible to be a responsible tourist when visiting a country with fewer socioeconomic benefits than you are used to in your own country? Develop and support your position with evidence from this text, your own experiences and reasoning, as well as additional research if needed.
3. **Connection.** When have you felt like a tourist? You need not have left one country to visit another; simply going from one setting where you are a "native" to another in which you are an outsider might have made you feel like a tourist. In what ways did you experience feelings similar to those that Kincaid suggests tourists have?
4. **Speaking and Listening.** What issues might you raise to challenge some of Kincaid's assumptions or to question her beliefs in this piece? Pair up with a classmate with one of you role playing Kincaid-the-narrator. Respond to Kincaid by acknowledging her point and then refuting it by saying, "Yes___________, but___________." What tone would you take to encourage her to listen? Be prepared to report to the full class how this activity influenced your understanding of *A Small Place*.
5. **Research.** This essay was written in 1988. Research the economic situation at that time and Antigua's current economy, especially the country's reliance on tourism. Discuss how your research informs your view on whether it is right or wrong to be a tourist in Antigua.
6. **Multimodal.** Kincaid opens her essay with this statement: "If you go to Antigua as a tourist, this is what you will see." She then explores how our expectations determine what we actually see. Take that idea and apply it to your home, neighborhood, town, or city. Select a series of five or six still images. Then, write a guide for an audience that you believe has preconceptions or misconceptions about the place. Consider starting out with something like this: "If you go to (place name) as a tourist, this is what you will see." You do not need to model your tone on Kincaid's. Let the images guide your narrative.

from The Cheating Culture: Why More Americans Are Doing Wrong to Get Ahead

David Callahan

Courtesy of David Callahan

David Callahan (b. 1965) is a cofounder of the liberal-leaning think tank Demos. He is also the author of several books about economic and social policy issues, including *The Givers: Money, Power, and Philanthropy in a New Gilded Age* (2018). In *The Cheating Culture: Why More Americans Are Doing Wrong to Get Ahead* (2004), from which this excerpt is taken, Callahan explores the various ways that Americans regularly cheat: in sports, on taxes, at work, and in school.

KEY CONTEXT At the beginning of this excerpt, Callahan refers to what he calls "the Winning Class," which he describes as those people in society who are successful economically, but who use unethical means to get there. Later in the excerpt, Callahan refers to the "social contract," which is a political theory that people in a society willingly give up some of their individual wealth and freedom to a government they perceive as legitimate in return for basic protections and services. One example of a social contract is that when people pay taxes, they have a reasonable expectation that public schools will provide education for their children.

For those who are part of the Winning Class, or trying to be, there are plenty of reasons to cheat. The rewards are bigger and the rules are toothless. Yet many Americans with more modest ambitions and more humble means are also cheating.

Take the mild-mannered bookkeeper as an example. He is, by all appearances, an honorable man. He neither drinks nor smokes, and is quiet and dependable in the way of many bookkeepers. He rarely misses a day of work or tarries on his lunch break. When United Way comes around, he always contributes. He and his wife lead an orderly life with their two polite children and spend Sunday mornings at church.

The bookkeeper works hard during the early years of his job and finally gets up the gumption to ask for a raise of $100 a month. He is crushed when the request is denied. But the bookkeeper seems to get over his disappointment and soldiers on. He still arrives punctually every day. He never calls in sick when, in truth, he is well.

After twenty years, the bookkeeper finally retires. The company throws a small farewell party for him and gives him a watch. He and his wife pack up for Florida to start their golden years. A new bookkeeper takes his place. Poring over the financial records, this new bookkeeper finds that something is wrong. Things aren't adding up. He flags his concern to the company. No, no, he's told, the old bookkeeper would never get into any fishy business. He was a rock of reliability, the soul of integrity.

5 And yet, when the new bookkeeper completes his investigation, the facts are incontrovertible. The old bookkeeper, it is clear, engaged in a systematic pattern of embezzlement. The pattern is oddly consistent. Year after year, the amount of money stolen is never greater and never smaller, nor is it particularly large. It is $100 a month.

The thieving bookkeeper exists in an apocryphal story passed down over many years among fraud examiners who probe workplace theft. The story is told to illustrate a point these investigators know all too well: that people are prone to invent their own morality when the rules don't seem fair to them. This tendency explains a lot of cheating in America today.

There are roughly four reasons why people obey rules. First, we may toe the line because the risks of breaking the rules outweigh the benefits. Second, we might be sensitive to social norms, or peer pressure — we follow the rules because we don't want to be treated as a pariah. Third, we may obey rules because they agree with our personal morality. And fourth, we may obey rules because they have legitimacy in our eyes — because we feel that the authority making and enforcing the laws is just and ultimately working in our long-term interests.

When people don't obey the rules, you'll often find several things going on at once. The Winning Class cheats so much because there's more to be gained nowadays and there are fewer penalties, either legally or socially. Students often cheat for the same reasons: the stakes of academic competition are higher and the normalization of cheating means that there's little peer pressure to be honest.

Motives like these are not hard to understand. Cases like the bookkeeper are more complex. A simple risk/benefit analysis doesn't

Harley Schwadron/Cartoonstock

Identify a sentence from the Callahan piece that would support the point being made by the artist in this cartoon.

Darrin Bell

What point is the artist making about the use of the word "illegals"? How would Callahan likely respond to this point?

explain everything, since the bookkeeper was running a serious risk for only a modest sum of money and could easily have taken more. Nor do social norms offer much insight, since the bookkeeper's thefts were not condoned by his peers. Instead, the bookkeeper operated by his own moral code to take from the company what he felt it owed him.

10 A lot of Americans have been inventing their own morality lately. Tens of millions of ordinary middle-class Americans routinely commit serious crimes ranging from tax evasion (a felony), to auto insurance fraud (also a felony), to cable television theft (yes, a felony as well in some states), to Internet piracy of music and software (more felonies). Most of these types of crimes are committed for small potatoes: to receive $700 more on a tax refund, to save $400 a year on an insurance premium, to get $40 a month worth of premium cable or an $18 CD for nothing. These crimes are being perpetrated by people who see themselves as law-abiding citizens, people who don't imagine themselves above the law and who don't have big-shot lawyers on call.

Day-to-day criminality among ordinary Americans is nothing new. "Unlawful behavior, far from being an abnormal social or psychological manifestation, is, in truth, a very common phenomenon," commented the authors of a 1947 article about "law-abiding law-breakers."[1] However, evidence indicates that this familiar problem has worsened in recent years — even as conventional street crime has fallen dramatically.

What Is Going On Here?

Much of the answer, I suspect, lies in our broken social contract. An orderly democratic society depends on having a social contract in place that delineates people's rights and responsibilities. It also depends on people having faith that the social contract applies fairly across the board. The social contract will break down when those who play by the rules feel mistreated, and those who break the rules get rewarded — which has been happening constantly in recent years.

John Q. Public need not to be versed in John Locke to feel that he has a legitimate cause for cynicism. He knows that white-collar criminals walk free, that fat-cat tax cheats get off the hook, that corporate money buys political favors, and that Ivy League schools are filled with kids whose rich parents greased the system to get them in. He also knows that when there's a war, it's working-class kids who fight it; when there's a tax cut, he probably won't get more than

[1]The article, by James Wallerstein and Clement J. Wylie, is cited in Robert Merton, *Social Structure and Social Theory* (New York: Free Press, 1957), 144.

peanuts; and when there are layoffs, it's those lower down the totem [pole] who'll get the ax.

Polls confirm that many Americans see "the system" as rigged against them. When asked who runs the country, many say corporations and special interests. When asked who benefits from the tax system, most say the rich. When asked who is underpaid in our society, most agree that lots of people are underpaid: nurses, policemen, schoolteachers, factory workers, restaurant workers, secretaries. And when people are asked whether it is possible to get ahead just by working hard and playing by the rules, many say that it is not.[2] . . .

The psychological fallout from people's economic struggles has been significant. People worry intensely about their finances, especially the heavy debt burdens that they often carry.[3] Many people are also less happy. "Happiness and satisfaction with life are, in many ways, the ultimate bottom line, a test of the good society," observes scholar Michael Hout. Yet in the past quarter century, Hout's work shows, gains in happiness have not been shared evenly in a U.S. society more divided by income: "the affluent are getting slightly happier and the poor are getting sadder; the affluent are increasingly satisfied with their financial and work situation while the poor are increasingly dissatisfied with theirs."[4]

Such endemic unease might itself be a corrupting force in society. But economic struggle is all the more dangerous when mixed with high expectations of well-being — that is, the expectation that one should be as happy as the shiny rich people on television and in magazines seem to be. Writing in the mid-twentieth century, the sociologist Robert Merton observed that Americans are taught that everyone can succeed if they work hard enough. America was "a society which places a high premium on economic affluence and social ascent for all its members." But Merton also pointed out that there is no "corresponding emphasis upon the legitimate avenues on which to march toward this goal." Americans worshipped financial success without being too concerned about how people got ahead. "The moral mandate to achieve success thus exerts pressures to succeed, by fair means if possible and by foul means if necessary." These pressures were especially poisonous, Merton said, in a nation where not everyone actually could succeed — where there were limits on the economic opportunities that were available.[5]

Merton could have made these points yesterday. The pressures on Americans to make a lot of money are extremely high — higher, maybe, than they've ever been before. To be sure, there are many legitimate opportunities to do well financially. Yet ultimately the opportunities are finite. America needs only so many skilled and well-paid professionals. In an

---

[2]Regarding people's views on whether their voice matters in politics, see data from the National Election Studies and science literature that documents and discusses political efficacy. See, for example, Sidney Verba, Henry E. Brady, and Kay L. Schlozman, *Voice and Equality: Civic Voluntarism in American Politics* (Cambridge, Mass.: Harvard University Press, 1995); and Steven J. Rosenstone and John M. Hansen, *Mobilization, Participation, and Democracy in America* (Boston: Prentice Hall, 1993). On public perceptions of the excessive power of corporations in American society, see for example, "Pew Values Update: American Social Beliefs, 1997," The Pew Research Center for the People and the Press, 20 April 1998. On views about fairness of taxes, see National Public Radio/Kaiser Family Foundation/Kennedy School of Government, "National Survey of Americans' Views on Taxes," 2003. On the ability of hard work to get people ahead and for who's underpaid, see, for example, Everett Carll Ladd and Karlyn H. Bowman, *Attitudes Toward Economic Inequality* (Washington, D.C.: AEI Press, 1998), 56 and 20–21.

[3]On anxiety, see Robert Putnam's analysis of DDB Needham Life Style Survey data, *Bowling Alone: The Collapse and Revival of American Community* (New York: Simon & Schuster, 2000), 475. On job satisfaction, see Fligstein and Shin, "The Shareholder Value Society." Evidence of growing insecurity and anxiety is by no means ironclad and this remains a disputed point among scholars. See, for example, Kenneth Deavers, "Downsizing, Job Insecurity, and Wages: No Connection," Employment Policy Foundation, May 1998.

[4]Michael Hout, "Money and Morale: What Growing Economic Inequality Is Doing to Americans' View of Themselves and Others," working paper, Survey Research Center, 3 January 2003.

[5]Merton, *Social Theory and Social Structure* (New York: The Free Press, 1957), 136–47, 169.

economy where structural conditions allow only the top fifth or so of earners to really get ahead, the other four fifths of Americans are stuck in the bind that Robert Merton identified: they live in a society with insanely high material expectations but with limited ways to meet these expectations.

What to do in this conundrum? Whatever you can get away with.

And how do ordinary, moral people justify doing wrong to do well? Often, they point to the unfairness around them — to the structures that keep them struggling while others thrive, to the ways that bad guys easily climb to the top, to the cheating that goes on by the rich and powerful every day. "People in subordinate positions make moral judgments about existing social arrangements and assert their prerogatives to personal entitlements and autonomy," writes Elliot Turiel, a leading authority on moral development. Turiel is fascinated with why people break rules, and much of his analysis centers on what he dryly calls "asymmetrical reciprocity implicit in differential distribution of power and powers" — in other words, feelings of injustice. Turiel observes that "in daily life people engage in covert acts of subterfuge and subversion aimed at circumventing norms and practices judged unfair, oppressive, or too restrictive of personal choices." These acts may place people on the wrong side of the law, or the established rules, Turiel says, but their true ethical implications are often a fuzzier question. "In my view, it would be inaccurate to attribute these types of acts of deception to failures of character or morality. Many who engage in these acts are people who generally consider themselves and are considered by others as responsible, trustworthy, upstanding members of our culture."[6]

[6]Elliot Turiel, *The Culture of Morality: Social Development, Context, and Conflict* (Cambridge, U.K.: Cambridge University Press, 2002), 261 and 266. For another analysis along somewhat similar lines, see James C. Scott, *Domination and the Arts of Resistance: Hidden Transcripts* (New Haven: Yale University Press, 1990). Scott's book deals extensively with what he calls the "veiled cultural resistance of subordinate groups" and the "infrapolitics of the powerless."

It is easy to cheat like crazy and yet maintain 20
respect for yourself in a society with pervasive corruption. It's easy, for example, to justify cheating in a country like Brazil where oligarchical families have been abusing the little people for a couple of hundred years and are still doing it, or a country like Pakistan where government ministers and their pals in business live in luxury while millions rot in the slums of Karachi.

And more and more, similar rationalizations can work just fine in the United States.

The social theorist Max Weber was among the first scholars to explore how people's views of "legitimacy" shape their respect for rules. He argued the commonsense point that people are more likely to follow rules or laws that seem fair and are made by an authority that deserves its power. There was nothing actually path-breaking about this point when Weber made it a century ago. Numerous big thinkers going back to Plato had made similar arguments, and support for this idea cut across fields — from political science to anthropology to sociology to education. Yet if the idea seemed like common sense, what Weber and other scholars typically lacked was the empirical "proof." How can you really tell why people either obey the law or break it? How can you weigh legitimacy as a factor when there are so many other influences on people's behavior? I may speed for many reasons: because I'm late or I'm a thrill seeker or I think it's wrong for the federal government to impose speed limits and usurp local authority on this issue. Short of hearing me and lots of other speeders out and somehow verifying that we're telling the truth about our motives, who can say why people like me drive so fast?

Proof that views about legitimacy explain ethical decisions remains hard to come by. But the evidence has gotten a lot more compelling since Weber's day. In his 1990 book, *Why People Obey the Law*, Tom Tyler

extending beyond the text

The following charts present data published by the Pew Research Center in 2020 from U.S. Census data.

The highest-earning 20% of families made more than half of all U.S. income in 2018

Share of U.S. aggregate household income, by income quintile

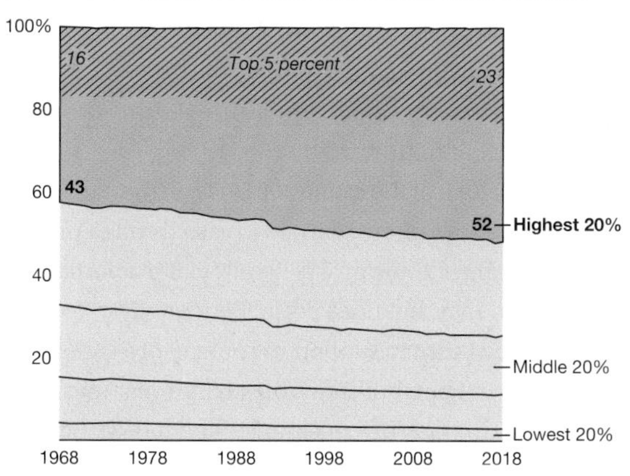

Note: Figures may not add to 100% due to rounding.
Source: U.S. Census Bureau, Income and Poverty in the U.S.: 2018, Table A-4.

PEW RESEARCH CENTER

Pew Research Center

In the U.S., Black-white income gap has held steady since 1970

Median U.S. household income, in 2018 dollars

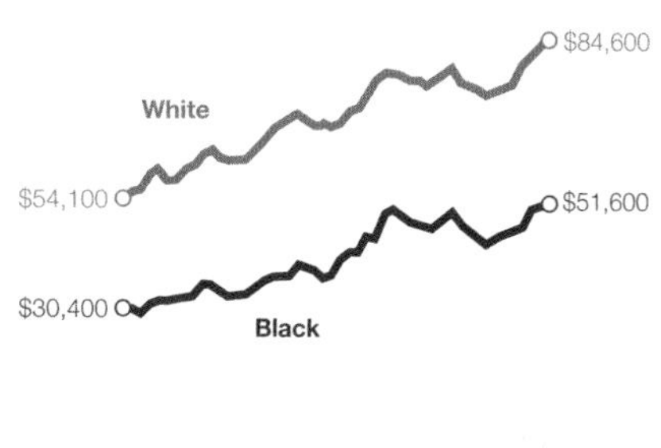

1970 1978 1988 1998 2008 2018

Note: Income is adjusted for household size and scaled to reflect a three-person household. Whites and Blacks include those who report being only one race and are non-Hispanic. Source: Pew Research Center analysis of 1970 to 2019 Current Population Survey, Annual Social and Economic Supplements.

PEW RESEARCH CENTER

Pew Research Center

Democrats are nearly twice as likely as Republicans to say there's too much economic inequality

% saying there is__economic inequality in the country these days

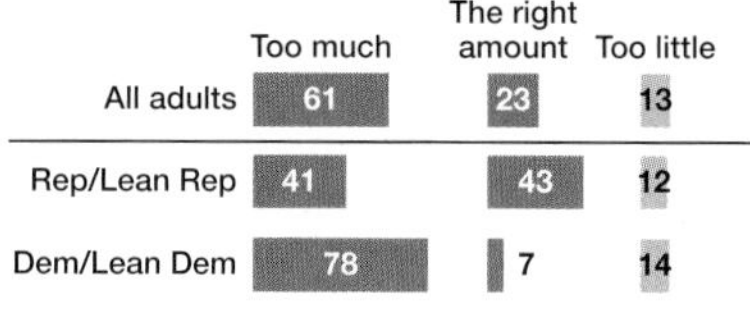

Note: Share of respondents who didn't offer an answer not shown.
Source: Survey of U.S. adults conducted Sept. 16-29, 2019.
"Most Americans Say There Is Too Much Economic Inequality in the U.S., but Fewer Than Half Call It a Top Priority"

PEW RESEARCH CENTER

Pew Research Center

Draw some conclusions about the data in the charts. In your opinion, to what extent is income inequality a significant problem in the United States? Explain how Callahan might use one or more of the charts to support a claim he makes in this piece.

picked up the legitimacy baton and ran with it into new empirical terrain. Tyler marshaled data going back thirty-five years in arguing that most people are inclined to obey the law, but that this reflex can easily be undermined if the law is widely seen as lacking legitimacy. He looked at studies of juvenile delinquents in England, college students in Kentucky, middle-class workers in Germany, and poor black men in Newark, among others. He also conducted his own large surveys of Chicago residents. Tyler's conclusion after all of this? Pretty much what Weber said a hundred years earlier.[7]

Yet if the link between respecting authority and following the rules has found more support in general, this is still complex terrain. Much of the time when people break rules you'll find a sticky wicket of conflicting evidence about their motives and no easy way to nail down what they were really thinking. Most people don't like to talk openly about cutting corners. Also, the root causes of why people break rules can be obscured when cheating becomes so routine that people no longer give it much thought.[8]

25 The candor of Jennifer Bennett (not her real name) sheds some light on what is going on in many American households — and, in particular, how cynicism and anger might cause a person who normally wouldn't even run a red light to commit a felony that is punishable by up to five years in prison.

Bennett should be one of the good guys in my story. She was raised in New Jersey by parents who taught her to play by the rules. She works in the arts in New York City but is obsessed with neither money nor status. She just wants to do her art and get by. She believes that government can make a difference in people's lives and, if anything, that taxes should probably be higher than they are.

Yet every year, come April 15, she submits a work of fiction to the IRS.

"Much of the money I earn is off the books — it's money earned in cash through private teaching or tutoring. I generally claim a portion of this money, but not all of it," Bennett says. "It's the money I earn to support my pursuit of a career in the arts. I put thousands of dollars a year into this career, pay my own insurance, and receive no benefits. I guess that's the way I justify writing off as much as I can and claiming as little as I can. I feel that most other first-world countries support their artists and the arts in a much stronger way than we do, and that the wealthy in this country are the ones with the real benefits."

Bennett has struggled financially for years, despite her Ivy League degree. Meeting the rent has often been an adventure, and she now lives 130 blocks north of Times Square, in a low-income neighborhood near the George Washington Bridge. "When I see people getting million-dollar bonuses for moving money around, who then walk in free to city museums because their companies are corporate sponsors, my jaw drops. Most artists I know can't afford to attend arts events on a regular basis. I figure the amount of money I earn is so tiny compared to what most people in this city are earning, and that if I had to pay thousands of dollars in taxes at the end of the year, on the relatively small amount I earn, I couldn't afford to continue doing what I'm doing."

---

[7]Tom R. Tyler, *Why People Obey the Law* (New Haven: Yale University Press, 1990).

[8]The interplay between social norms, law, economics, societal values, and compliance with rules has been examined from a variety of angles. One critical — and obvious — observation is that social norms are the key to enforcing rules, since coercion, punishment, and deterrence can never stop everyone who wants to do wrong. Some scholars like Eric Posner argue that law actually plays only a small role in regulating people's behavior. For an overview of some of this work, see Amitai Etzioni, "Social Norms: Internalization, Persuasion, and History," *Law and Society Review* 34, no. 1 (2000): 157–78. See also Eric A. Posner, *Law and Social Norms* (Cambridge, Mass.: Harvard University Press, 2002); and Michael Hechter and Karl-Dieter Opp, eds., *Social Norms* (New York: Russell Sage Foundation, 2001).

30 Bennett has anguished about her tax cheating — for, like, three seconds — over the past five years. "I don't think it's the 'right' thing to do, but personally, I don't really care. I know that one wrong doesn't right another wrong, but until I see any sign of a real move to universal health-care coverage or the closing of loopholes for the rich, or increased benefits for those making their living in the arts, I don't feel particularly inclined to be honest. When I read about the IRS going after those in lower-income brackets, it makes my blood boil." ■

Understanding and Interpreting

1. Several times in the piece, Callahan describes people "inventing their own morality" (for example, par. 10). What does he mean by this phrase?
2. Callahan claims that much of the cheating by ordinary, otherwise law-abiding citizens is due to "our broken social contract" (par. 12). Reread paragraphs 13 through 19, in which he supports this claim. What evidence does he use? To what extent does he sufficiently support his claim? Do you detect any bias that might prevent him from seeing other possibilities? Explain.
3. In paragraphs 16 and 17, Callahan connects the idea of cheating with the desire for happiness. What conclusion does he expect readers to draw about the "high expectations of well-being" from the evidence he provides? Evaluate his logical reasoning in this section.
4. To support his argument, Callahan cites Elliot Turiel, "a leading authority on moral development" (par. 19). Reread the following quotations from Turiel, summarize them, and explain how they relate to Callahan's central argument:
   a. "[P]eople in subordinate positions make moral judgments about existing social arrangements and assert their prerogatives to personal entitlements and autonomy" (par. 19).
   b. "asymmetrical reciprocity implicit in differential distribution of power and powers" (par. 19).
   c. "[I]n daily life people engage in covert acts of subterfuge and subversion aimed at circumventing norms and practices judged unfair, oppressive, or too restrictive of personal choices" (par. 19).
5. Callahan claims that at least one reason why otherwise honest people cheat is the way they view the legitimacy of power. Summarize his views on legitimacy. Explain how he uses evidence to support his position.
6. In paragraph 7, Callahan identifies four reasons why people obey rules. Apply these four reasons to the case of the artist Jennifer Bennett, who regularly cheats on her taxes (pars. 26 to 31). Which ones would Bennett likely agree or disagree with? Why?

Analyzing Language, Style, and Structure

1. **Vocabulary in Context.** In the first paragraph of this excerpt, Callahan, writes, "Yet many Americans with more modest ambitions and more humble means are also cheating." What does the word "modest" mean in this context? How is its meaning here different from other meanings you have encountered?
2. **Skill Focus.** Reread the paragraph beginning with "The psychological fallout from people's economic struggles has been significant" (par. 15). Look closely at Callahan's word choice and the words of the author he quotes in the paragraph. How would you describe his tone in this section? How does his diction help to create that tone? To what extent is this tone appropriate for his argument?

3. What role does the fictional story of the bookkeeper play in setting up Callahan's argument? In other words, why begin this section with the story?
4. Trace the development of Callahan's argument from the beginning to the point where he asks: "And how do ordinary, moral people justify doing wrong to do well?" (par. 19). What evidence and reasoning does Callahan include in his argument in order to set up this question?
5. Callahan makes no secret that he is politically liberal and often sees middle- and working-class people as victims of the rich. Look back through the article and identify places where he chooses words with negative connotations to describe the wealthy. Does this word choice seem to be effective in making his argument, or is it detrimental? Why?
6. Reread paragraph 24 that concludes with footnote 8. The last sentence makes a claim about people's behavior that appears to be unsubstantiated. Read footnote 8 and explain how Callahan uses the sources to support his claim. Choose one other footnote from the article and explain how the use of evidence reveals Callahan's ethos.
7. Until paragraph 20, Callahan focuses on cheating in the United States, at which point he expands his argument to include Brazil and Pakistan. What is the purpose of this switch? How does it assist his argument?
8. While much of Callahan's argument is rooted in logos, he does at times employ appeals to pathos. Identify these places and evaluate their effectiveness in supporting his claim.

Topics for Composing

1. **Analysis.** According to Callahan, what causes the cheating culture that he describes? Who or what is most at fault for it?
2. **Argument.** In this selection from *The Cheating Culture*, Callahan mostly focuses on identifying the causes of cheating. Later in the book, however, he offers some solutions, which include a need to teach the values he thinks are important: "respect, responsibility, fairness, honesty, justice." Write an argument about where (e.g., at home, in school, or in religious institutions) and how people should learn lessons about right and wrong. Explain your position and provide evidence from your own experiences and those of people you know.
3. **Connection.** Describe a time when you or someone you know cheated or had the opportunity to cheat and declined to do so. Examine the factors that led to the situation, the choices you or that person made, and the outcome. How might Callahan react to the situation and outcomes you describe?
4. **Speaking and Listening.** Callahan writes, "A lot of Americans have been inventing their own morality lately" (par. 10). He goes on to describe behaviors such as tax fraud, internet piracy, and so on. In pairs or in groups, discuss hypothetical situations in which people might do something that is not life-threatening but also not technically legal. What rationalizations might people use to justify those behaviors? What might Callahan say about them?
5. **Research.** According to Callahan, one of the causes for the cheating that occurs is the broken social contract brought on by large gaps between the wealthy and the poor in America. This piece was originally published in 2004. Research the current wealth gaps in the United States and explain whether the same conditions that Callahan describes still exist today.
6. **Creative Writing.** Callahan tells the story of Jennifer Bennett, who works in the arts in New York City and regularly submits a "work of fiction" (par. 27) to the IRS every year. Imagine that Bennett got caught and charged with a felony. Write a letter from Bennett's point of view to her congressional representative or another elected official in which she describes her situation and explains why she should receive leniency.

from Lying

Sam Harris

Sam Harris (b. 1967) is an American author and neuroscientist who has written a number of books examining ethics and morality from a scientific and philosophical perspective, including *Waking Up: A Guide to Spirituality Without Religion* (2014), *The Moral Landscape: How Science Can Determine Values* (2010), and *Letter to a Christian Nation* (2006). Harris, the host of a podcast called *Making Sense*, is a self-described secularist and a critic of organized religions. The following excerpt is from the long essay "Lying," which was published in 2011.

Glenn Koenig/Getty Images

Among the many paradoxes of human life, this is perhaps the most peculiar and consequential: *We often behave in ways that are guaranteed to make us unhappy*. Many of us spend our lives marching with open eyes toward remorse, regret, guilt, and disappointment. And nowhere do our injuries seem more casually self-inflicted, or the suffering we create more disproportionate to the needs of the moment, than in the lies we tell to other human beings. Lying is the royal road to chaos.

As an undergraduate at Stanford, I took a seminar that profoundly changed my life. It was called "The Ethical Analyst," and it was conducted in the form of a Socratic dialogue by an extraordinarily gifted professor, Ronald A. Howard.[1] Our discussion focused on a single question of practical ethics:

Is it wrong to lie?

At first glance, this may seem a scant foundation for an entire college course. After all, most people already believe that lying is generally wrong — and they also know that some situations seem to warrant it. What was so fascinating about this seminar, however, was how difficult it was to find examples of virtuous lies that could withstand Professor Howard's scrutiny. Whatever the circumstances, even in cases where most good people would lie without a qualm, Howard nearly always found truths worth telling.

5 I do not remember what I thought about lying before I took "The Ethical Analyst," but the course accomplished as close to a firmware upgrade of my brain as I have ever experienced. I came away convinced that lying, even about the smallest matters, needlessly damages personal relationships and public trust.

It would be hard to exaggerate what a relief it was to realize this. It's not that I had been in the habit of lying before taking Howard's course — but I now knew that endless forms of suffering and embarrassment could be easily avoided by simply telling the truth. And, as though for the first time, I saw all around me the consequences of others' failure to live by this principle.

That experience remains one of the clearest examples in my life of the power of philosophical reflection. "The Ethical Analyst" affected me in ways that college courses seldom do: It made me a better person.

What Is a Lie?

Deception can take many forms, but not all acts of deception are lies. Even the most ethical among us regularly struggle to keep appearances and reality apart. By wearing cosmetics,

[1]Howard has put much of his material in book form: R. A. Howard and C. D. Korver, *Ethics for the Real World: Creating a Personal Code to Guide Decisions in Work and Life* (Cambridge: Harvard Business School Press, 2008). While I do not entirely agree with how the authors separate ethics from the rest of human values, I believe readers will find this a very useful book.

a woman seeks to seem younger or more beautiful than she otherwise would. But honesty does not require that she issue continual disclaimers — "I see that you are looking at my face: Please be aware that I do not look this good first thing in the morning . . ." A person in a hurry might pretend not to notice an acquaintance passing by on the street. A polite host might not acknowledge that one of her guests has said something so stupid as to slow the rotation of the earth. When asked "How are you?" most of us reflexively say that we are well, understanding the question to be merely a greeting, rather than an invitation to discuss our career disappointments, our marital troubles, or the condition of our bowels. Elisions of this kind can be forms of deception, but they are not quite lies. We may skirt the truth at such moments, but we do not deliberately manufacture falsehood or conceal important facts to the detriment of others.

The boundary between lying and deception is often vague. It is even possible to deceive with the truth. I could, for instance, stand on the sidewalk in front of the White House and call the headquarters of Facebook on my cell phone: "Hello, this is Sam Harris. I'm calling from the White House, and I'd like to speak to Mark Zuckerberg." My words would, in a narrow sense, be true — but the statement seems calculated to deceive. Would I be lying? Close enough.

To lie is to intentionally mislead others when they expect honest communication.[2] This leaves stage magicians, poker players, and other harmless dissemblers off the book, while illuminating a psychological and social landscape whose general shape is very easy to recognize. People lie so that others will form beliefs that are not true. The more consequential the beliefs — that is, the more a person's well-being demands a correct understanding of the world or of other people's opinions — the more consequential the lie.

As the philosopher Sissela Bok observed, however, we cannot get far on this topic without first distinguishing between truth and truthfulness — for a person may be impeccably truthful while being mistaken.[3] To speak truthfully is to accurately represent one's beliefs. But candor offers no assurance that one's beliefs about the world are true. Nor does truthfulness require that one speak the whole truth, because communicating every fact on a given topic is almost never useful or even possible. Of course, if one is not sure whether or not something is true, representing one's degree of uncertainty is a form of honesty.

Leaving these ambiguities aside, communicating what one believes to be both true and useful is surely different from concealing or distorting that belief. The intent to communicate honestly is the measure of truthfulness. And most of us do not require a degree in philosophy to distinguish this attitude from its counterfeits.

People tell lies for many reasons. They lie to avoid embarrassment, to exaggerate their accomplishments, and to disguise wrongdoing. They make promises they do not intend to keep. They conceal defects in their products or services. They mislead competitors to gain advantage. Many of us lie to our friends and family members to spare their feelings.

---

[2]Some have argued that evolution must have selected for an ability to deceive oneself, thereby making it easier to mislead others [see William von Hippel and Robert Trivers, "The Evolution and Psychology of Self-Deception," *The Behavioral and Brain Sciences* 34, no. 1 (2011): 1–16; discussion 16–56]. But whether a form of self-deception exists that is really tantamount to "lying to oneself" is still a matter of controversy. There is no question that we can be blind to facts about ourselves or about the world that we really should see — and the research on cognitive bias is fascinating — but the question remains whether we see the truth and unconsciously convince ourselves otherwise, or simply do not see the truth in the first place. In any case, truly believing one's own falsehoods when in dialogue with others is tantamount to honesty. Thus, it seems that we need not worry about self-deception for the time being.

[3]S. Bok, *Lying: Moral Choice in Public and Private Life* (New York: Vintage, 1999).

What does lying look like?

By studying videos from high-stakes court cases, University of Michigan researchers are building a unique lie-detecting software that's based on real-world data.

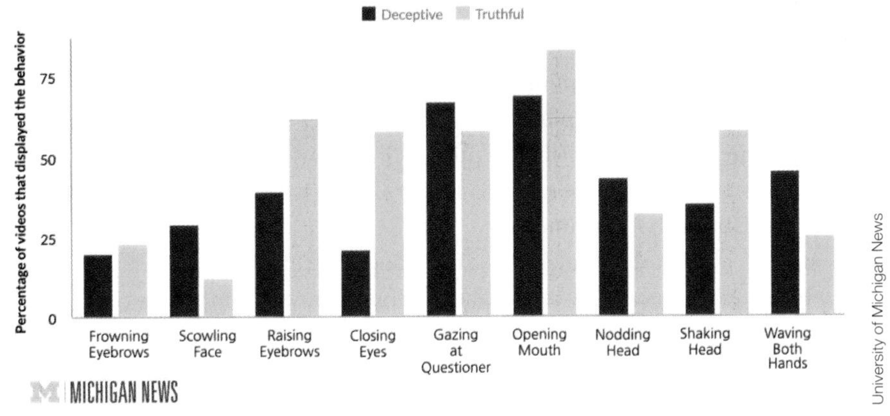

This chart summarizes findings from a study about physical clues that someone is lying.
Have you ever witnessed these signals in dishonest interactions? How does reading Harris's piece influence your understanding of these signals and your feelings about them?

Whatever our purpose in telling them, lies can be gross or subtle. Some entail elaborate ruses or forged documents. Others consist merely of euphemisms or tactical silences. But it is in believing one thing while intending to communicate another that every lie is born.

We have all stood on both sides of the divide between what someone believes and what he intends others to understand — and the gap generally looks quite different depending on whether one is the liar or the dupe. The liar often imagines that he does no harm so long as his lies go undetected. But the one lied to rarely shares this view. The moment we consider our dishonesty from the perspective of those we lie to, we recognize that we would feel betrayed if the roles were reversed.

A friend of mine, Sita, was once going to visit the home of another friend and wanted to take her a small gift. Unfortunately, she was traveling with her young son and hadn't found time to go shopping. As they were getting ready to leave their hotel, however, Sita noticed that the bath products supplied in their room were unusually nice. So she put some soaps, shampoos, and body lotions into a bag, tied it with a ribbon she got at the front desk, and set off.

When Sita presented this gift, her friend was delighted.

"Where did you get them?" she asked.

Surprised by the question, and by a lurching sense of impropriety, Sita sought to regain her footing with a lie: "Oh, we just bought them in the hotel gift shop."

The next words came from her innocent son: "No, Mommy, you got them in the bathroom!"

Imagine the faces of these women, briefly frozen in embarrassment and then yielding to

extending beyond the text

Read the following excerpt from an interview of the authors of a research study on the ethics of lying.

from Is Every Lie "a Sin"? Maybe Not

Emma E. Levine and Maurice Schweizer

Maurice Schweitzer: In our work, "Are Liars Ethical? On the Tension between Benevolence and Honesty," we look at deception a little differently than people have in the past. We look at deception that sometimes can be helpful to other people. We typically think about deception as selfish deception: I lie to gain some advantage at the expense of somebody else. And we typically think of honesty as something that might be costly to me, but helpful to others.

In our research, we actually disentangle those two things. We think about deception that can help other people, and honesty that might be helpful to myself and maybe costly to somebody else. When we separate honesty and deception from pro-social and pro-self-interests, we find that people actually don't care that much about deception. We find that the aversion to lying, when people say, "Don't lie to me," what they really mean is, "Don't be really selfish."

On understanding when is the right time to lie:

Emma Levine: Broadly, the advice on the table until now has been, "Always be honest. Honesty is the best policy." We're suggesting that maybe we revise that advice, and make the statement, "Lie sometimes." The key takeaway is to understand when we should lie. When does honesty actually harm trust and seem immoral? And when can deception actually breed trust, and be seen as moral?

We could think about how that might be used in delivering feedback, because managers often have to balance this tension between benevolence — giving kind, supportive feedback - and honesty - giving critical, harsh feedback. We might suggest that managers actually err on the side of benevolence, if their goal is really to promote trust and relationships.

On separating dishonesty from selfishness:

Schweitzer: What surprised us was that when we really separated dishonesty from selfishness, we found that what's driving all of this behavior — what people judge to be moral or immoral, when people trust somebody or they don't trust somebody — we find that what really matters is how kind, how benevolent somebody is, and that deception plays a very small role.

According to Schweitzer and Levine, how could lying actually be beneficial? Do you agree? How might Harris respond to the ideas in this interview?

smiles of apology and forgiveness. This may seem the most trivial of lies — and it was — but it surely did nothing to increase the level of trust between two friends. Funny or not, the story reveals something distasteful about Sita: She will lie when it suits her needs.

The opportunity to deceive others is ever present and often tempting, and each instance of deception casts us onto some of the steepest ethical terrain we ever cross. Few of us are murderers or thieves, but we have all been liars. And many of us will be unable to get into our beds tonight without having told several lies over the course of the day.

What does this say about us and about the life we are making with one another?

The Mirror of Honesty

At least one study suggests that 10 percent of communication between spouses is deceptive.[4] Another found that 38 percent of encounters among college students contain lies.[5] Lying is ubiquitous, and yet even liars rate their deceptive interactions as less pleasant than truthful ones. This is not terribly surprising: We know that trust is deeply rewarding and that deception and suspicion are two sides of the same coin. Research suggests that all forms of lying — including white lies meant to spare the feelings of others — are associated with less satisfying relationships.[6]

25 Once one commits to telling the truth, one begins to notice how unusual it is to meet someone who shares this commitment. Honest people are a refuge: You know they mean what they say; you know they will not say one thing to your face and another behind your back; you know they will tell you when they think you have failed — and for this reason their praise cannot be mistaken for mere flattery.

Honesty is a gift we can give to others. It is also a source of power and an engine of simplicity. Knowing that we will attempt to tell the truth, whatever the circumstances, leaves us with little to prepare for. Knowing that we told the truth in the past leaves us with nothing to keep track of. We can simply be ourselves in every moment.

In committing to being honest with everyone, we commit to avoiding a wide range of long-term problems, but at the cost of occasional short-term discomfort. However, the discomfort should not be exaggerated: You can be honest and kind, because your purpose in telling the truth is not to offend people. You simply want them to have the information you have and would want to have if you were in their shoes.

But it may take practice to feel comfortable with this way of being in the world — to cancel plans, decline invitations, negotiate contracts, critique others' work, all while being honest about what one is thinking and feeling. To do this is also to hold a mirror up to one's life — because a commitment to telling the truth requires that one pay attention to what the truth is in every moment. What sort of person are you? How judgmental, self-interested, or petty have you become?

You might discover that some of your friendships are not really that — perhaps you habitually lie to avoid making plans, or fail to express your true opinions for fear of conflict. Whom, exactly, are you helping by living this way? You might find that certain relationships cannot be honestly maintained. Of course, we all have associations that must persist in some form, whether we enjoy them or not — with family, in-laws, colleagues, employers, and so

---

[4]B. M. DePaulo and D. A. Kashy, "Everyday Lies in Close and Casual Relationships," *Journal of Personality and Social Psychology* 74, no. 1 (Jan. 1998): 63–79.

[5]B. M. DePaulo, et al., "Lying in Everyday Life," *Journal of Personality and Social Psychology* 70, no. 5 (1996): 979–995.

[6]P. J. Kalbfleisch, "Deceptive Message Intent and Relational Quality," *Journal of Language and Social Psychology* 20, nos. 1–2 (2001): 214–230; T. Cole, "Lying to the One You Love: The Use of Deception in 7 Romantic Relationships," *Journal of Social and Personal Relationships* 18, no. 1 (2001): 107–129.

forth. I'm not denying that tact can play a role in minimizing conflict. Holding one's tongue, or steering a conversation toward topics of relative safety, is not the same as lying (nor does it require that one deny the truth in the future).

Honesty can force any dysfunction in your life to the surface. Are you in an abusive relationship? A refusal to lie to others — How did you get that bruise? — would oblige you to come to grips with this situation very quickly. Do you have a problem with drugs or alcohol? Lying is the lifeblood of addiction. If we have no recourse to lies, our lives can unravel only so far without others' noticing.

Telling the truth can also reveal ways in which we want to grow but haven't. I remember learning that I had been selected as the class valedictorian at my high school. I declined the honor, saying that I felt that someone who had been at the school longer should give the graduation speech. But that was a lie. The truth was that I was terrified of public speaking and would do almost anything to avoid it. Apparently, I wasn't ready to confront this fact about myself — and my willingness to lie at that moment allowed me to avoid doing so for many years. Had I been forced to tell my high school principal the truth, he might have begun a conversation with me that would have been well worth having. . . .

White Lies

Have you ever received a truly awful gift? The time it took to tear away the wrapping paper should have allowed you to steel yourself — but suddenly there it was:

"Wow . . ."

"Do you like it?"

"That's amazing. Where did you get it?"

"Bangkok. Do you like it?"

"When were you in Bangkok?"

"Christmas. Do you like it?"

"Yes . . . Definitely. Where else did you go in Thailand?"

I have now broken into a cold sweat. I am not cut out for this. Generally speaking, I have learned to be honest even when ambushed. I don't always communicate the truth in the way that I want to — but one of the strengths of telling the truth is that it remains open for elaboration. If what you say in the heat of the moment isn't quite right, you can amend it. I have learned that I would rather be maladroit, or even rude, than dishonest.

What could I have said in the above situation?

"Wow . . . Does one wear it or hang it on the wall?"

"You wear it. It's very warm. Do you like it?"

"You know, I'm really touched you thought of me. But there's no way I can pull this off. My style is somewhere between boring and very boring."

This is getting much closer to the sort of response I'm comfortable with. Some euphemism is creeping in, perhaps, but the basic communication is truthful. I have given my friend fair warning that she is unlikely to see me wearing her gift the next time we meet. I have also given her an opportunity to keep it for herself or perhaps bestow it on another friend who might actually like it.

Some readers may now worry that I am recommending a regression to the social ineptitude of early childhood. After all, children do not learn to tell white lies until about the age of four, once they have achieved a hard-won awareness of the mental states of others.[7] But we have no reason to believe that the social conventions that happen to stabilize in primates like ourselves at about the age of eleven will lead to optimal human relationships. In fact, there are many reasons to believe that lying is precisely the sort of behavior we need to outgrow in order to build a better world.

---

[7]K. A. Broomfield, E. J. Robinson, and W. P. Robinson, "Children's Understanding about White Lies," *British Journal of Developmental Psychology* 20, no. 1 (2002): 47–65.

What could be wrong with truly "white" lies? First, they are still lies. And in telling them, we incur all the problems of being less than straightforward in our dealings with other people. Sincerity, authenticity, integrity, mutual understanding — these and other sources of moral wealth are destroyed the moment we deliberately misrepresent our beliefs, whether or not our lies are ever discovered.

And although we imagine that we tell certain lies out of compassion for others, it is rarely difficult to spot the damage we do in the process. By lying, we deny our friends access to reality[8] — and their resulting ignorance often harms them in ways we did not anticipate. Our friends may act on our falsehoods, or fail to solve problems that could have been solved only on the basis of good information. Rather often, to lie is to infringe on the freedom of those we care about.

A primal instance:

"Do I look fat in this dress?"

Most people insist that the correct answer to this question is always "No." In fact, many believe that it's not a question at all: The woman is simply saying, "Tell me I look good." If she's your wife or girlfriend, she might even be saying, "Tell me you love me." If you sincerely believe that this is the situation you are in — that the text is a distraction and the subtext conveys the entire message — then so be it. Responding honestly to the subtext would not be lying.

But this is an edge case for a reason: It crystallizes what is tempting about white lies. Why not simply reassure someone with a tiny lie and send her out into the world feeling more confident? Unless one commits to telling the truth in situations like this, however, one finds that the edges creep inward, and exceptions to the principle of honesty begin to multiply. Very soon, you may find yourself behaving as most people do quite effortlessly: shading the truth, or even lying outright, without thinking about it. The price is too high.

A friend of mine recently asked me whether I thought he was overweight. In fact he probably was just asking for reassurance: It was the beginning of summer, and we were sitting with our wives by the side of his pool. However, I'm more comfortable relying on the words that actually come out of a person's mouth, rather than on my powers of telepathy. So I answered my friend's question very directly: "No one would ever call you 'fat,' but if I were you, I'd want to lose twenty-five pounds." That was two months ago, and he is now fifteen pounds lighter.[9] Neither of us knew that he was ready to go on a diet until I declined the opportunity to lie about how he looked in a bathing suit.

Back to our friend in the dress: What is the truth? Perhaps she does look fat in that dress but it's the fault of the dress. Telling her the truth will allow her to find a more flattering outfit.

But let's imagine the truth is harder to tell: Your friend looks fat in that dress, or any dress, because she *is* fat. Let's say she is also thirty-five years old and single, and you know that her greatest desire is to get married and start a family. You also believe that many men would be disinclined to date her at her current weight. And, marriage aside, you are confident that she would be happier and healthier, and would feel better about herself, if she got in shape.

A white lie is simply a denial of these realities. It is a refusal to offer honest guidance in a storm. Even on so touchy a subject, lying seems a clear failure of friendship. By reassuring your friend about her appearance, you are not

[8]At the very least, we deny them access to reality as we see it. Of course, when it is a matter of our opinions — whether we like a person's work, his new haircut, and so forth — there is no difference between the reality in question and our view of it.

[9]He eventually lost twenty pounds. It has now been two years, and he has kept the weight off.

extending beyond the text

Lulu Wang is the writer and director of the 2019 film *The Farewell*, starring Awkwafina, pictured above on the left. The film is based on an event that occurred in her family, which she recounted in an interview for the podcast *This American Life*, excerpted below. Wang's family decided not to tell her grandmother that she was dying. Instead, they found a way for the family to get together for goodbyes without disclosing the truth. In the following excerpt, Wang calls her grandmother "Nainai." She refers to her grandmother's younger sister, whom she is speaking about at the beginning of the excerpt, as "Little Nainai."

from This American Life

Ira Glass and Lulu Wang

LULU WANG She tells me there's a Chinese joke. Two people go get a physical. One of them is healthy, and one of them has a terminal illness. The hospital gets the results mixed up. The healthy person gets a terminal prognosis and vice versa.

So then the healthy person ends up dying while the sick person ends up living

LULU WANG [SPEAKING CHINESE]. That's me asking Little Nainai, is that really a joke? It's not very funny.

LITTLE NAINAI [SPEAKING CHINESE].

LULU WANG She assured me that it was. My family got a second opinion, and then a third. Same prognosis — three months, maybe less. Little Nainai knew she needed a fake medical report to show Nainai, so she went to a print shop. They told her, we can't create a false medical record. If you want to make something up, we could photocopy it for you. Little Nainai whited out the real diagnosis and wrote down words that sounded vaguely medical but unalarming, something about the nine shadows.

My family built on that lie with an even more elaborate one. We realized we had a problem. How are we all going to manage to see Nainai before she died? Family from three countries needed to say goodbye without letting Nainai know we were actually saying goodbye. This would require more than Wite-Out. My dad had an idea.

LULU'S DAD So I said, all right, your uncle, maybe we can just, you know, stage your son's wedding early, one year early.

LULU WANG Are you proud that you came up with this idea?

LULU'S DAD Well, you know, I'm the — everybody considered me as the smartest in the family. So I mean, it's a show. I mean —

LULU WANG This was our plan — a giant goodbye party disguised as a giant wedding banquet.

LULU'S DAD This is the lie that everybody agreed to lie.

LULU WANG And here's how it was going to go down. My Uncle Hai Bin's son, Liang-Liang, had recently married a Japanese woman. They planned to celebrate in China the next year, but now it would be in two weeks, and it would bring together family members who had not all been in the same place for 25 years.

My dad told Nainai that the wedding banquet had to happen immediately because that was when the groom Liang-Liang could get the time off work.

LULU WANG How did you feel about lying?

LULU'S DAD Well, it's not, I mean, clear cut, this is a lie and that's — you know. Because people think a lie is bad thing. But in this circumstance, you don't think that you make a bad lie. You think you make a good lie because that's the way that everybody wants it. And that's the way that it's supposed to be.

LULU WANG But that wasn't the way I wanted it or thought it was supposed to be. And I still wasn't convinced it would be what Nainai wanted. I was so emotional that my mom said maybe I shouldn't go, that I might cry and blow the cover. I was afraid she might be right. But if I wanted to see Nainai before she died, I had to go, and I had to be part of the lie.

How does Lulu Wang feel about lying to her grandmother? How does Wang's dad justify the lie? What might Sam Harris say to Wang's family? What would you say?

helping her to do what you think she should do to get what she wants out of life[10].

In many circumstances in life, false encouragement can be very costly to another person. Imagine that you have a friend who has spent years striving unsuccessfully to build a career as an actor. Many fine actors struggle in this way, of course, but in your friend's case the

---

[10]Many readers have pushed back strongly on this point — and some have come up with scenarios where the consequences of telling the truth are so grave, and the benefits so obscure, that the virtue of a white lie seems undeniable. For instance:

Imagine that you are with your daughter on her wedding day and are now seeing her wedding dress for the first time. Should she look fat in it, there is no way for her to put your candor to good use. You are about to walk her down the aisle; delivering anything but pure reassurance at this point seems a failure of love. This is one of the most important days in your daughter's life. You have a choice between (selfishly) maintaining your unblemished record of honesty and protecting her from feeling terrible about herself at the precise moment when she can least afford it. What do you do? Here's a hint: A good father would not say, "Yes, you look fat in that dress," and then offer advice on diet and exercise as he led his daughter down the aisle.

I agree. I suspect, however, that honest reassurance would still be possible even here. Given a father's love for his daughter, "You look beautiful" — a statement that focuses on the daughter rather than the particulars of her dress — seems like a more important truth that can be easily told. But I am not dogmatically adhering to the principle of honesty at any cost. If the parameters of the situation are tuned so that there is really no conceivable benefit to telling the truth, and the harm seems obvious, then the lie seems genuinely "white."

reason seems self-evident: He is a terrible actor. In fact, you know that his other friends — and even his parents — share this opinion but cannot bring themselves to express it. What do you say the next time he complains about his stalled career? Do you encourage him to "just keep at it"? False encouragement is a kind of theft: It steals time, energy, and motivation that a person could put toward some other purpose.

This is not to say that we are always correct in our judgments of other people. And honesty demands that we communicate any uncertainty we may feel about the relevance of our own opinions. But if we are convinced that a friend has taken a wrong turn in life, it is no sign of friendship to simply smile and wave him onward.

If the truth itself is painful to tell, often background truths are not — and these can be communicated as well, deepening the friendship. In the examples above, the more basic truth is that you love your friends and want them to be happy, and they could make changes in their lives that might lead to greater fulfillment. In lying to them, you are not only declining to help them — you are denying them useful information and setting them up for future disappointment. Yet the temptation to lie in these circumstances can be overwhelming.

When we presume to lie for the benefit of 60
others, we have decided that *we* are the best judges of how much they should understand about their own lives — about how they appear, their reputations, or their prospects in the world. This is an extraordinary stance to adopt toward other human beings, and it requires justification. Unless someone is suicidal or otherwise on the brink, deciding how much he should know about himself seems the quintessence of arrogance. What attitude could be more disrespectful of those we care about? ■

Understanding and Interpreting

1. Reread the section that begins with the heading "What Is a Lie?" Explain the distinction Harris draws between the following:
   - certain forms of deception (like makeup) and lying
   - truth and truthfulness

   Why are these distinctions important to his argument?
2. According to Harris, what is the definition of a lie? How does he use evidence to support his definition?
3. Look back through the section called "The Mirror of Honesty." It is clear that Harris is arguing, at least in part, that we should all avoid lying. According to Harris, what are some of the most significant benefits of telling the truth? What counterarguments does Harris fail to address in this section about the potential harm that can result from always telling the truth?
4. Most people agree that lying is wrong, but most people are also likely to think that telling what Harris calls "white lies" is OK in certain circumstances. What are the main reasons that Harris offers to support his claim that even "white lies" should be avoided?

5. Reread the final two paragraphs of the piece. Harris claims that when we lie, we are being arrogant. What evidence or explanation does he offer as support? To what extent does Harris prove his claim?
6. Reread paragraphs 55 and 56, which end with footnote 10. Read that note and explain what Harris seems to suggest is the one possible definition of a truly harmless "white lie." What does he achieve by putting this exception in the notes section, rather than in the body of his essay?

Analyzing Language, Style, and Structure

1. **Vocabulary in Context.** In paragraph 4, Harris writes, "some situations seem to warrant [lying]." What does the word "warrant" mean in this context? How is that meaning similar to or different from other meanings you have encountered?
2. **Skill Focus.** Reread the opening paragraph of this essay in which Harris states an assumption about human behavior. What tone does he create with this assumption? How does this tone help him make his argument?
3. How does the story about the course that Harris took at Stanford as an undergraduate help to establish his ethos at the very beginning of the essay?
4. Throughout this piece, Harris uses specific examples from his own life as well as made-up scenarios to support his argument. Locate one such example, explain its purpose within Harris's argument, and evaluate its effectiveness.
5. Reread paragraph 24. Then, look at Harris's footnotes 4, 5, and 6. How does Harris illustrate his credibility and support his claim through his choice of sources?
6. Reread paragraph 52, in which Harris discusses how "white lies" lead to other more significant lies. Evaluate his logical reasoning and explain whether he effectively proves his point.
7. Harris is particularly good at explaining complex topics, such as ethics, to a general audience. Identify examples of this accessible writing style and explain how it assists him in making his argument. Or, identify moments in which Harris's style is not accessible and keeps his audience from understanding his position.

Topics for Composing

1. **Analysis.** How successful is Harris in proving that all lies are damaging? Evaluate the examples, appeals, and reasoning he uses to prove his point.
2. **Argument.** Write a piece in which you argue in favor of what Harris calls "white lies." Be sure to include evidence from Harris as a counterargument, as well as other examples and your own reasoning on the subject.
3. **Connection.** Harris discusses the value of honesty in friendship. After reading this excerpt, would you want him as a friend? Why or why not? Use specific evidence from the text to support your response.
4. **Connection.** Do you ever lie? If so, how would you define the lies you tell? Do you and Harris define lying the same way? Do you agree with Harris's approach to never lying? If you do not lie, what keeps you from doing so?
5. **Speaking and Listening.** Interview three to five people about lies they have told, witnessed, or been subjected to. How do they feel about the lies and their outcomes? Summarize your findings about the reasons for the lies and the effects they may have had. Then, share your findings with a classmate and explain how Harris might respond.

6. **Research.** In this excerpt, Harris writes primarily about lies between individuals, specifically the erosion of trust between friends who lie. What about the lies that governments, corporations, or other institutions tell the public? Choose a significant lie or deception directed at the public (rationales for wars that were not true, fraud by companies, and so on). After conducting brief research, explain the effect that the lie had on the public as a whole.
7. **Research.** Are lie detectors accurate? To answer the question, research the history of lie detectors, especially their relevance in court cases, as well as current technologies using brain scans.
8. **Multimodal.** Using words and images, create a series of graphic panels depicting a scenario involving lying in which the liar intends no harm. The graphic elements should help readers understand whether you are condoning or condemning the lie.
9. **Exposition.** Make a list of things that you have said to people in the past week or so that Harris might consider to be lies. Why would Harris classify them as lies? Be sure to use direct evidence from this piece as support. How might Harris have suggested that you frame the truth to avoid each of the lies? Explain your reasoning.

Shooting an Elephant

George Orwell

adoc-photos/Getty Images

George Orwell, the author of several well-known novels and essays, including *Animal Farm*, *1984*, and *Down and Out in Paris and London*, was born in 1903 in India. The son of a British government official, Orwell lived in England until his early twenties, when he joined the Indian Imperial Police in Burma (now known as Myanmar), a country in Southeast Asia that was then under British control. Orwell became disenchanted with imperialism and resigned after a short period of time. He then turned to writing full-time. The following classic essay, published in 1936, recounts a situation Orwell faced as a member of the Indian Imperial Police force.

KEY CONTEXT From the late sixteenth century through World War I, at the beginning of the twentieth century, England had history's largest empire. Throughout this period of British imperialism, Great Britain had colonies in areas now known as the United States, Canada, Australia, Asia, Africa, and South America. A popular saying during this period was "The sun never sets on the British Empire."

The British government in the Indian subcontinent — which includes what is now India, as well as Pakistan, Myanmar/Burma, Bangladesh, and other countries — was called the Raj, a Hindi word for "rule." England established colonies through military strength and ruled them by forcing colonized people to adopt British educational, judicial, economic, and governmental structures. The goal was to make the world British. Starting with the American Revolution in the late eighteenth century, however, most of the colonies were able to gain their independence, usually through armed conflict. Burma (now Myanmar), where this piece is set, became independent from England in 1948, only about twenty years after Orwell worked there.

In Moulmein, in Lower Burma, I was hated by large numbers of people — the only time in my life that I have been important enough for this to happen to me. I was sub-divisional police officer of the town, and in an aimless, petty kind of way anti-European feeling was very bitter. No one had the guts to raise a riot, but if a European woman went through the bazaars alone somebody would probably spit betel juice over her dress. As a police officer I was an obvious target and was baited whenever it seemed safe to do so. When a nimble Burman tripped me up on the football field and the referee (another Burman) looked the other way, the crowd yelled with hideous laughter. This happened more than once. In the end the sneering yellow faces of young men that met me everywhere, the insults hooted after me when I was at a safe distance, got badly on my nerves. The young Buddhist priests were the worst of all. There were several thousands of them in the town and none of them seemed to have anything to do except stand on street corners and jeer at Europeans.

All this was perplexing and upsetting. For at that time I had already made up my mind that imperialism was an evil thing and the sooner I chucked up my job and got out of it the better. Theoretically — and secretly, of course — I was all for the Burmese and all against their oppressors, the British. As for the job I was doing, I hated it more bitterly than I can perhaps make clear. In a job like that you see the dirty work of Empire at close quarters. The wretched prisoners huddling in the stinking cages of the lock-ups, the grey, cowed faces of the long-term convicts, the scarred buttocks of the men who had been flogged with bamboos — all these oppressed me with an intolerable sense of guilt. But I could get nothing into perspective. I was young and ill-educated and I had had to think out my problems in the utter silence that is imposed on every Englishman in the East. I did not even know that the British Empire is dying, still less did I know that it is a great deal better than the younger empires that are going to supplant it. All I knew was that I was stuck between my hatred of the empire I served and my rage against the evil-spirited little beasts who tried to make my job impossible. With one part of my mind I thought of the British Raj as an unbreakable tyranny, as something clamped

Burma Provincial Police Training School, Mandalay, 1923. Eric Blair (George Orwell) standing third from left.

How does this photograph of Orwell as a young man illustrate the separation he likely felt from the Burmese natives?

down, *in saecula saeculorum*[1] upon the will of prostrate peoples; with another part I thought that the greatest joy in the world would be to drive a bayonet into a Buddhist priest's guts. Feelings like these are the normal by-products of imperialism; ask any Anglo-Indian official, if you can catch him off duty.

One day something happened which in a roundabout way was enlightening. It was a tiny incident in itself, but it gave me a better glimpse than I had had before of the real nature of imperialism — the real motives for which despotic governments act. Early one morning the sub-inspector at a police station the other end of the town rang me up on the phone and said that an elephant was ravaging the bazaar. Would I please come and do something about it? I did not know what I could do, but I wanted to see what was happening and I got on to a pony and started out. I took my rifle, an old .44 Winchester and much too small to kill an elephant, but I thought the noise might be useful *in terrorem*.[2] Various Burmans stopped me on the way and told me about the elephant's doings. It was not, of course, a wild elephant, but a tame one which had gone "must."[3] It had been chained up, as tame elephants always are when their attack of "must" is due, but on the previous night it had broken its chain and escaped. Its mahout, the only person who could manage it when it was in that state, had set out in pursuit, but had taken the wrong direction and was now twelve hours' journey away, and in the morning the elephant had suddenly reappeared in the town. The Burmese population had no weapons and were quite helpless against it. It had already destroyed somebody's bamboo hut, killed a cow and raided some fruit-stalls and devoured the stock; also it had met the municipal rubbish van and, when the driver jumped out and took to his heels, had turned the van over and inflicted violences upon it.

The Burmese sub-inspector and some Indian constables were waiting for me in the quarter where the elephant had been seen. It was a very poor quarter, a labyrinth of squalid bamboo huts, thatched with palm-leaf, winding all over a steep hillside. I remember that it was a cloudy, stuffy morning at the beginning of the rains. We began questioning the people as to where the elephant had gone and, as usual, failed to get any definite information. That is invariably the case in the East; a story always sounds clear enough at a distance, but the nearer you get to the scene of events the vaguer it becomes. Some of the people said that the elephant had gone in one direction, some said that he had gone in another, some professed not even to have heard of any elephant. I had almost made up my mind that the whole story was a pack of lies, when we heard yells a little distance away. There was a loud, scandalized cry of "Go away, child! Go away this instant!" and an old woman with a switch in her hand came round the corner of a hut, violently shooing away a crowd of naked children. Some more women followed, clicking their tongues and exclaiming; evidently there was something that the children ought not to have seen. I rounded the hut and saw a man's dead body sprawling in the mud. He was an Indian, a black Dravidian coolie,[4] almost naked, and he could not have been dead many minutes. The people said that the elephant had come suddenly upon him round the corner of the hut, caught him with its trunk, put its foot on his back and ground him into the earth. This was the rainy season and the ground was soft, and his face had scored a trench a foot deep and a

[1]Latin for "a century of centuries," a figurative way of saying "forever" or "for eternity" —Eds.

[2]A legal term meaning "to scare a person into complying with terms." — Eds.

[3]A temporary condition occurring in male elephants; their testosterone level increases dramatically and they can become violent and unpredictable. — Eds.

[4]Dravidians are an ethnic group from Southern India. "Coolie" is a term applied in Orwell's time to laborers of Asian descent; it is now considered derogatory. — Eds.

Evan Bowen-Jones/Alamy Stock Photo

This is a picture of a captive male Asian elephant.

Describe the elephant in this image. Compare it to Orwell's description of the elephant he is tracking. How does his encounter with the grazing elephant complicate his decision?

couple of yards long. He was lying on his belly with arms crucified and head sharply twisted to one side. His face was coated with mud, the eyes wide open, the teeth bared and grinning with an expression of unendurable agony. (Never tell me, by the way, that the dead look peaceful. Most of the corpses I have seen looked devilish.) The friction of the great beast's foot had stripped the skin from his back as neatly as one skins a rabbit. As soon as I saw the dead man I sent an orderly to a friend's house nearby to borrow an elephant rifle. I had already sent back the pony, not wanting it to go mad with fright and throw me if it smelt the elephant.

5 The orderly came back in a few minutes with a rifle and five cartridges, and meanwhile some Burmans had arrived and told us that the elephant was in the paddy fields below, only a few hundred yards away. As I started forward practically the whole population of the quarter flocked out of the houses and followed me. They had seen the rifle and were all shouting excitedly that I was going to shoot the elephant. They had not shown much interest in the elephant when he was merely ravaging their homes, but it was different now that he was going to be shot. It was a bit of fun to them, as it would be to an English crowd; besides they wanted the meat. It made me vaguely uneasy. I had no intention of shooting the elephant — I had merely sent for the rifle to defend myself if necessary — and it is always unnerving to have a crowd following you. I marched down the hill, looking and feeling a fool, with the rifle over my shoulder and an ever-growing army of people jostling at my heels. At the bottom, when you got away from the huts, there was a metalled road and beyond that a miry waste of paddy fields a thousand yards across, not yet ploughed but soggy from the first rains and dotted with coarse grass. The elephant was standing eight yards from the road, his left side towards us. He took not the slightest notice of the crowd's approach. He was tearing up bunches of grass, beating them against his knees to clean them and stuffing them into his mouth.

I had halted on the road. As soon as I saw the elephant I knew with perfect certainty that I ought not to shoot him. It is a serious matter to shoot a working elephant — it is comparable to destroying a huge and costly piece of machinery — and obviously one ought not to do it if it can possibly be avoided. And at that distance, peacefully eating, the elephant looked no more dangerous than a cow. I thought then and I think now that his attack of "must" was already passing off; in which case he would merely wander harmlessly about until the mahout came back and caught him. Moreover, I did not in the least want to shoot him. I decided that I would watch him for a little while to make sure that he did not turn savage again, and then go home.

But at that moment I glanced round at the crowd that had followed me. It was an immense crowd, two thousand at the least and growing every minute. It blocked the road for a long distance on either side. I looked at the sea of yellow faces above the garish clothes — faces all happy and excited over this bit of fun, all certain that the elephant was going to be shot. They were watching me as they would watch a conjurer about to perform a trick. They did not like me, but with the magical rifle in my hands I was momentarily worth watching. And suddenly I realized that I should have to shoot the elephant after all. The people expected it of me and I had got to do it; I could feel their two thousand wills pressing me forward, irresistibly. And it was at this moment, as I stood there with the rifle in my hands, that I first grasped the hollowness, the futility of the white man's dominion in the East. Here was I, the white man with his gun, standing in front of the unarmed native crowd — seemingly the leading actor of the piece; but in reality I was only an absurd puppet pushed to and fro by the will of those yellow faces behind. I perceived in this moment that when the white man turns tyrant it is his own freedom that he destroys. He becomes a sort of hollow, posing dummy, the conventionalized figure of a sahib.[5] For it is the condition of his rule that he shall spend his life in trying to impress the "natives," and so in every crisis he has got to do what the "natives" expect of him. He wears a mask, and his face grows to fit it. I had got to shoot the elephant. I had committed myself to doing it when I sent for the rifle. A sahib has got to act like a sahib; he has got to appear resolute, to know his own mind and do definite things. To come all that way, rifle in hand, with two thousand people marching at my heels, and then to trail feebly away, having done nothing — no, that was impossible. The crowd would laugh at me. And my whole life, every white man's life in the East, was one long struggle not to be laughed at.

But I did not want to shoot the elephant.

I watched him beating his bunch of grass against his knees, with that preoccupied grandmotherly air that elephants have. It seemed to me that it would be murder to shoot him. At that age I was not squeamish about killing animals, but I had never shot an elephant and never wanted to.

(Somehow it always seems worse to kill a 10
large animal.) Besides, there was the beast's owner to be considered. Alive, the elephant was worth at least a hundred pounds; dead, he would only be worth the value of his tusks, five pounds, possibly. But I had got to act quickly. I turned to some experienced-looking Burmans who had been there when we arrived, and asked them how the elephant had been behaving. They all said the same thing: he took no notice of you if you left him alone, but he might charge if you went too close to him.

It was perfectly clear to me what I ought to do. I ought to walk up to within, say, twenty-five yards of the elephant and test his behavior. If he charged, I could shoot; if he took no notice of me, it would be safe to leave him until the mahout came back. But also I knew that I was going to do no such thing.

[5]While in Arabic the term means "friend," during the British Raj the term was used as a form of address to a person of authority, similar to how we might use "Mister" to a person of authority today. — Eds.

I was a poor shot with a rifle and the ground was soft mud into which one would sink at every step. If the elephant charged and I missed him, I should have about as much chance as a toad under a steam roller. But even then I was not thinking particularly of my own skin, only of the watchful yellow faces behind. For at that moment, with the crowd watching me, I was not afraid in the ordinary sense, as I would have been if I had been alone. A white man mustn't be frightened in front of "natives"; and so, in general, he isn't frightened.

The sole thought in my mind was that if anything went wrong those two thousand Burmans would see me pursued, caught, trampled on and reduced to a grinning corpse like that Indian up the hill. And if that happened it was quite probable that some of them would laugh. That would never do. There was only one alternative. I shoved the cartridges into the magazine and lay down on the road to get a better aim.

The crowd grew very still, and a deep, low, happy sigh, as of people who see the theatre curtain go up at last, breathed from innumerable throats. They were going to have their bit of fun after all. The rifle was a beautiful German thing with cross-hair sights. I did not then know that in shooting an elephant one would shoot to cut an imaginary bar running from ear-hole to ear-hole. I ought, therefore, as the elephant was sideways on, to have aimed straight at his ear-hole; actually I aimed several inches in front of this, thinking the brain would be further forward.

When I pulled the trigger I did not hear the bang or feel the kick — one never does when a shot goes home — but I heard the devilish roar of glee that went up from the crowd. In that instant, in too short a time, one would have thought, even for the bullet to get there, a mysterious, terrible change had come over the elephant. He neither stirred nor fell, but every line of his body had altered. He looked suddenly stricken, shrunken, immensely old, as though the frightful impact of the bullet had paralysed him without knocking him down. At last, after what seemed a long time — it might have been five seconds, I dare say — he sagged flabbily to his knees. His mouth slobbered. An enormous senility seemed to have settled upon him. One could have imagined him thousands of years old. I fired again into the same spot. At the second shot he did not collapse but climbed with desperate slowness to his feet and stood weakly upright, with legs sagging and head drooping. I fired a third time. That was the shot that did for him. You could see the agony of it jolt his whole body and knock the last remnant of strength from his legs. But in falling he seemed for a moment to rise, for as his hind legs collapsed beneath him he seemed to tower upward like a huge rock toppling, his trunk reaching skywards like a tree. He trumpeted, for the first and only time. And then down he came, his belly towards me, with a crash that seemed to shake the ground even where I lay.

I got up. The Burmans were already racing 15
past me across the mud. It was obvious that the elephant would never rise again, but he was not dead. He was breathing very rhythmically with long rattling gasps, his great mound of a side painfully rising and falling. His mouth was wide open — I could see far down into caverns of pale pink throat. I waited a long time for him to die, but his breathing did not weaken. Finally I fired my two remaining shots into the spot where I thought his heart must be. The thick blood welled out of him like red velvet, but still he did not die. His body did not even jerk when the shots hit him, the tortured breathing continued without a pause. He was dying, very slowly and in great agony, but in some world remote from me where not even a bullet could damage him further. I felt that I had got to put an end to that

extending beyond the text

Is "Shooting an Elephant" a true story or a blend of truth and fiction? Orwell's biographers are not in agreement about whether or not Orwell actually killed the elephant. Some suggest that he blurred the line between fact and fiction or, perhaps, between truth and memory. Others cite a comment that he made in the 1920s about wanting to kill an elephant as evidence of the story's basis in true experience. In the following brief excerpt, one Orwell scholar wrestling with this question shares his position and the textual evidence that he believes supports it.

from Did George Orwell Shoot an Elephant? His 1936 "Confession" – and What It Might Mean

Gerry Abbot

To me, Orwell's description of the great creature's heartbreakingly slow death suggests an acute awareness of wrongdoing, as do his repeated protests: "I had no intention of shooting the elephant . . . I did not in the least want to shoot him . . . I did not want to shoot the elephant."

What do you think? Did Orwell actually shoot the elephant, or did he make up the story to prove a point? What additional information do you need in order to decide? Does it even matter if it's true or not? Why?

dreadful noise. It seemed dreadful to see the great beast lying there, powerless to move and yet powerless to die, and not even to be able to finish him. I sent back for my small rifle and poured shot after shot into his heart and down his throat. They seemed to make no impression. The tortured gasps continued as steadily as the ticking of a clock.

In the end I could not stand it any longer and went away. I heard later that it took him half an hour to die. Burmans were bringing dahs[6] and baskets even before I left, and I was told they had stripped his body almost to the bones by the afternoon.

Afterwards, of course, there were endless discussions about the shooting of the elephant. The owner was furious, but he was only an Indian and could do nothing. Besides, legally I had done the right thing, for a mad elephant has to be killed, like a mad dog, if its owner fails to control it. Among the Europeans opinion was divided. The older men said I was right, the younger men said it was a damn shame to shoot an elephant for killing a coolie, because an elephant was worth more than any damn Coringhee[7] coolie. And afterwards I was very glad that the coolie had been killed; it put me legally in the right and it gave me a sufficient pretext for shooting the elephant. I often wondered whether any of the others grasped that I had done it solely to avoid looking a fool. ■

[6]Burmese knife, often long enough to be considered a sword. — Eds.

[7]a Southern Indian ethnicity. —Eds.

Understanding and Interpreting

1. George Orwell was stationed in Burma and left the police force soon after his time there. What specific evidence from the text might suggest why he left the police force?
2. Explain what Orwell means when he describes the "normal by-products of imperialism" in the second paragraph. How does this description relate to Orwell's feelings about imperialism in general and the Burmese in particular?
3. Identify Orwell's attitude toward the inhabitants of Burma at the following three places in the text:
   a. the first paragraph
   b. the paragraph just before he shoots the elephant (par. 7)
   c. the last paragraph

   Then, explain his overall feelings toward the Burmese.
4. Trace Orwell's decision-making process as he considers how to deal with the elephant. Why does he think that he shouldn't shoot the elephant? Then, why does he decide to do it?
5. In paragraph 3, Orwell says that this incident gave him "a better glimpse than I had had before of the real nature of imperialism — the real motives for which despotic governments act." Look back at the following statements from paragraph 7 and explain what each statement reveals about Orwell's view of the nature of imperialism:
   a. "Here was I, the white man with his gun, standing in front of the unarmed native crowd — seemingly the leading actor of the piece; but in reality I was only an absurd puppet pushed to and fro by the will of those yellow faces behind."
   b. "I perceived in this moment that when the white man turns tyrant it is his own freedom that he destroys."
   c. "He becomes a sort of hollow, posing dummy, the conventionalized figure of a sahib. For it is the condition of his rule that he shall spend his life in trying to impress the 'natives,' and so in every crisis he has got to do what the 'natives' expect of him. He wears a mask, and his face grows to fit it."
   d. "The crowd would laugh at me. And my whole life, every white man's life in the East, was one long struggle not to be laughed at."
6. How does Orwell react to his shooting of the elephant? What does this reveal about his own ethical development and his attitude toward imperialism?

Analyzing Language, Style, and Structure

1. **Vocabulary in Context.** In paragraph 7, Orwell describes himself as a "dummy." What is the meaning of the word in this context? How is this use of the word similar to or different from other uses you know?
2. **Skill Focus.** Reread the second paragraph of the piece, in which Orwell provides some of his feelings about imperialism. Identify the contrasting and often contradictory choices of words he uses to describe the Burmese and the British. What do the contradictions reveal about Orwell's attitude toward imperialism?
3. This essay is told as a narrative with Orwell looking back on a significant event in his life. How does the older Orwell view his younger self? What specific language choices reflect this tone?
4. Reread paragraph 14, in which Orwell first shoots the elephant. What specific words and phrases humanize the elephant's death? How do these details help to illustrate Orwell's point about imperialism?

5. You are reading this piece in a textbook almost eighty years after it was originally published. Who was Orwell's intended audience in 1936? What was he trying to communicate to them? How successful do you think he might have been in communicating his message? Why?
6. Below is the last paragraph of the essay with some words underlined. Reread this paragraph, looking closely at the underlined words and the synonyms that follow in parentheses. Discuss how changing Orwell's word choice to one of the words in parentheses would affect the meaning of the sentences containing these words and the passage as a whole.

> Afterwards, of course, there were endless (interminable/incessant) discussions about the shooting of the elephant. The owner was furious, but he was only an Indian and could do nothing. Besides, legally (justly/legitimately) I had done the right thing, for a mad elephant has to be killed (executed/put down/slaughtered), like a mad dog, if its owner fails to control it. Among the Europeans opinion was divided. The older men said I was right, the younger men said it was a damn shame to shoot an elephant for killing a coolie, because an elephant was worth more than any damn Coringhee coolie. And afterwards I was very glad (cheerful/content/pleased) that the coolie had been killed; it put me legally in the right and it gave me a sufficient (ample/acceptable) pretext (alibi/excuse/pretense) for shooting the elephant. I often wondered whether any of the others grasped that I had done it solely to avoid looking a fool (buffoon/idiot/bonehead).

Topics for Composing

1. **Analysis.** While this essay is specifically about a time when Orwell shot an elephant, it continues to be widely read and studied in classes because it has meaning and application beyond 1920s Burma. What is the central idea that Orwell presents in this essay about ethics and "doing the right thing"? Use direct evidence from the text to support your response.
2. **Analysis.** How aware is Orwell of his own role in the worst elements of colonialism? Write a response that draws solely on the evidence that Orwell presents within the text.
3. **Argument.** At the end of the piece, Orwell writes, "The owner was furious, but he was only an Indian and could do nothing." Write two letters about this situation:
   a. The first letter should be from the point of view of the elephant's owner, trying to convince the district administrator of Burma to compensate you for the loss of your elephant.
   b. The second letter should be written as if you were Orwell responding to the district administrator, who demanded an explanation. Be sure to explain why the shooting of the elephant was justified, and address the points contained within the letter from the elephant's owner.

   Your letters should be limited only to the events presented in the piece. However, you should use whatever persuasive techniques you think would be useful to convince your audience.
4. **Connection.** At the moment Orwell decides to shoot the elephant, he states, "He wears a mask, and his face grows to fit it" (par. 7). Describe a time when you had to wear a metaphorical mask (do something that someone expected you to do). What caused you to wear the mask? Did your face "grow to fit it," as Orwell suggests, or were you able to take the mask off and become yourself again?

5. **Speaking and Listening.** Hold a mock trial to debate Orwell's actions. There should be a prosecutor who is trying to convict Orwell of property damage, a defense attorney who is trying to justify Orwell's actions, a judge, and a jury to determine guilt or innocence. Be sure that all of the evidence you consider comes directly from the text itself and any relevant research you conduct on the time period and location.
6. **Research.** How can psychological principles help us understand the factors that may have contributed to Orwell's decision to shoot the elephant, even though he did not want to? Research a relevant psychological study or psychological perspective. Explain the experiment and its findings to your readers. Then, describe how the findings help explain the psychological factors at work in "Shooting an Elephant." You might begin by looking into the Stanford prison experiment (Philip Zimbardo), the Asch conformity experiments (Solomon Asch), the Good Samaritan study (John Darley and C. Daniel Batson), the Milgram experiment (Stanley Milgram), or the bystander effect (John Darley and Bibb Latané). Feel free to uncover additional studies that interest you.
7. **Research.** While Orwell regularly uses the word "imperialism" to describe the British activities in Burma because it refers to the expansion of an "empire," another related and more general term is "colonialism," which applies to any country's conquering and exploiting the resources of another country. Research present-day Myanmar, or another country that was once colonized, and identify the lingering effects that colonialism has on that country today.
8. **Multimodal.** Make a short film — or draw a storyboard of scenes — in which you reenact paragraph 7 from "Shooting an Elephant." Select sound effects or music to accompany your visuals. Then, write a brief explanation of the choices you made. How do your music, sound effects, camera angles, lighting, color, point of view, gestures, and other choices relate to the specific words from Orwell's account?
9. **Creative Writing.** George Orwell is not a hero in this piece. He doesn't take a principled stand and refuse to shoot the elephant. And instead of rebelling against an imperial system that he seems to disapprove of, he actively participates in it. Write a new ending for the essay in which Orwell decides not to shoot the elephant. Continue to use the first-person narration. Try to mimic Orwell's style as closely as possible. Finally, include the reasoning behind Orwell's new decision. Be sure to consider how the last paragraph would change significantly as a result of this different decision. Include a reflection that explains what changed and how that change would affect the message and influence of the piece as a whole.

exploring other genres

Traveling through the Dark (poetry)

William Stafford

ullsteinbild/TopFoto

American poet William Stafford (1914–1993) grew up in Kansas during the Depression, working odd jobs to help his family and pay his way through college at the University of Kansas. He was a conscientious objector and refused to serve in the military during World War II. Stafford wrote extensively in journals throughout his life but did not publish his first collection of poems until he was almost fifty. The following poem, originally published in 1962, is typical of Stafford's narrative approach to poetry.

FOCUS FOR READING Throughout this chapter, you have been reading speeches, editorials, and essays about ethical decision-making. Unlike those other texts, the following is a work of literature. As you read William Stafford's poem, consider how he uses figurative language, speaker, theme, and other poetic elements to explore the idea of doing the right thing.

Traveling through the dark I found a deer
dead on the edge of the Wilson River road.
It is usually best to roll them into the canyon:
that road is narrow; to swerve might make more dead.

By glow of the tail-light I stumbled back of the car
and stood by the heap, a doe, a recent killing;
she had stiffened already, almost cold.
I dragged her off; she was large in the belly.

My fingers touching her side brought me the reason—
her side was warm; her fawn lay there waiting,
alive, still, never to be born.
Beside that mountain road I hesitated.

The car aimed ahead its lowered parking lights;
under the hood purred the steady engine.
I stood in the glare of the warm exhaust turning red;
around our group I could hear the wilderness listen.

I thought hard for us all—my only swerving—,
then pushed her over the edge into the river.

Understanding and Interpreting

1. Summarize the literal actions of the speaker in the poem.
2. Trace the speaker's shifting position regarding the deer. What outcomes does the speaker consider while trying to decide how to handle the situation?
3. In the last stanza, the speaker says, "I thought hard for us all" (l. 17). Who does the speaker mean by "us"? What conclusion does he or she arrive at, and why? Be sure to support your response with examples from the text.
4. Where does the poem shift in terms of theme, tone, or subject matter? What effect is created by this shift? How does the shift help establish a theme?
5. A clear contrast is drawn in this poem between the world of humans and the world of nature. Identify how Stafford draws this contrast and for what purpose.
6. The title of the poem can be taken literally: The speaker is traveling in the dark. Explain some possible metaphorical interpretations of the title.

Analyzing Language, Style, and Structure

1. **Vocabulary in Context.** In line 11, Stafford uses the word "still" to describe the fawn. What does the word "still" mean in this context? How is that meaning similar to or different from others that you have encountered?
2. Stafford uses a form of the word "swerve" in both the first and last stanzas. Explain the similarities and differences in usage in the two parts of the poem.
3. Reread the descriptions of the fawn "waiting, / alive, still, never to be born" (ll. 10–11). Explain how the word choice here emphasizes the difficulty that the speaker faces.
4. Explain the effects of Stafford's changing use of pronouns throughout the poem: *I*, *she*, *our*, and *us*.
5. Although the poem is called "Traveling through the Dark," there are several descriptions of the light. Identify the various sources of light in the poem. Explain how they contribute to the conflict the speaker is facing.
6. What is the effect of the personification in the line "I could hear the wilderness listen" (l. 16)? How does it help Stafford communicate a point about the natural world and the world of humans?
7. Because of its use of commonplace words, Stafford's poetry is sometimes mistakenly considered to be simplistic. Examine Stafford's use of the following simple words and explain how the figurative meaning of each supports the poem's theme: *narrow*, *cold*, *warm*, *dead*, *alive*, *still*, *swerving*, *road*, *river*.

Topics for Composing

1. **Analysis.** What does Stafford suggest in this poem about doing the right thing? What are the challenges? Based on the speaker's experience, what factors should we consider when we are making difficult decisions?
2. **Argument.** At the end of the poem, the speaker decides to push the deer off the road. Is this the right thing to do in this situation? What alternatives could the speaker have considered? Write an argument in favor of one of those alternatives or in favor of the speaker's decision, using your own experiences and reasoning to support your position.

3. **Connection.** Even though the speaker did not cause the situation, he or she feels a responsibility to act. Describe a time in your own life when you felt that you had a responsibility to do something. What circumstances led to the situation? What did you do? Why?
4. **Connection.** Throughout this chapter, you have been reading arguments written by and about others struggling to "do the right thing." Choose an author of one of the texts you read and explain how that person might react to the situation that the speaker of this poem faced. What reasons would that person offer for his or her choice?
5. **Speaking and Listening.** There are a number of recorded versions available online of people reading this poem, including Stafford himself. Listen to two or more and describe how the readers capture the tone and the atmosphere of the poem through their delivery.
6. **Research.** How do we decide what actions are right? Philosophers John Stuart Mill and Immanuel Kant struggled with that question and came up with very different answers. Mill promoted the idea of utilitarianism, which means making the choice that is likely to lead to the greatest happiness for the greatest number of people. Kant proposed the idea of the categorical imperative, which determines the morality of an action by asking whether it would still be right if everyone took that same action, all of the time, in all situations. Conduct research on these two approaches. Explain which philosopher would likely agree with the speaker's actions in this poem and why.

Writing an Analysis of Tone

When trying to determine what tone would be appropriate for your writing, you should carefully consider the rhetorical situation. For example, if you are writing an essay and your teacher is the audience, a respectful, reasonable tone appropriate to an academic situation is probably your goal. If you're addressing a group of peers to ask for their vote, then a more emotional tone could be appropriate, perhaps even a fiery one that shows your passion for the office you're seeking. You should use choices in language and style to make your tone clear to your audience.

An essential part of understanding a text is understanding its tone. In the Skill Workshop earlier in this chapter, we discussed elements of style using an essay on immigration by Jose Antonio Vargas. A smart and skilled writer, he uses elements of style to support his viewpoint and develops a tone of outrage mixed with hope about immigration policy. You would have missed Vargas's point about immigration if you had not been able to pick up on his tone. And reading for tone requires focusing on the specific language choices an author makes. Considering how other writers establish tone is helpful not only for understanding their texts but also for making decisions regarding tone in your own writing.

In this workshop, you will be writing your own analysis essay in response to the following prompt:

> *Choose an argumentative text from this chapter (or from another source) that you find interesting or persuasive. Write an essay that analyzes the stylistic choices the writer makes to create a tone that will help persuade readers of the central claim. In your essay, analyze how the author uses stylistic elements, including diction, syntax, figurative language, and other relevant features.*

To help you with the process of writing this analysis of tone, we will model each of the specific steps by focusing on the Central Text in this chapter: an excerpt from *A Small Place* by Jamaica Kincaid (p. 858). In her piece, Kincaid makes a case against the exploitation of her native country Antigua by tourists visiting from wealthier countries. Take a few minutes to read or reread the following paragraphs from *A Small Place*, thinking about her tone.

> If you go to Antigua as a tourist, this is what you will see. If you come by aeroplane, you will land at the V. C. Bird International Airport. Vere Cornwall (V. C.) Bird is the Prime Minister of Antigua. You may be the sort of tourist who would wonder why a Prime Minister would want an airport named after him — why not a school, why not a hospital, why not some great public monument? You are a tourist and you have not yet seen a school in Antigua, you have not yet seen the hospital in Antigua, you have not yet seen a public monument in Antigua. As your plane descends to land, you might say, What a beautiful island Antigua is — more beautiful than any of the

other islands you have seen, and they were very beautiful, in their way, but they were much too green, much too lush with vegetation, which indicated to you, the tourist, that they got quite a bit of rainfall, and rain is the very thing that you, just now, do not want, for you are thinking of the hard and cold and dark and long days you spent working in North America (or, worse, Europe), earning some money so that you could stay in this place (Antigua) where the sun always shines and where the climate is deliciously hot and dry for the four to ten days you are going to be staying there; and since you are on your holiday, since you are a tourist, the thought of what it might be like for someone who had to live day in, day out in a place that suffers constantly from drought, and so has to watch carefully every drop of fresh water used (while at the same time surrounded by a sea and an ocean — the Caribbean Sea on one side, the Atlantic Ocean on the other), must never cross your mind.

You disembark from your plane. You go through customs. Since you are a tourist, a North American or European — to be frank, white — and not an Antiguan black returning to Antigua from Europe or North America with cardboard boxes of much needed cheap clothes and food for relatives, you move through customs swiftly, you move through customs with ease. Your bags are not searched. You emerge from customs into the hot, clean air: immediately you feel cleansed, immediately you feel blessed (which is to say special); you feel free. . . .

Oh, but by now you are tired of all this looking, and you want to reach your destination — your hotel, your room. You long to refresh yourself; you long to eat some nice lobster, some nice local food. You take a bath, you brush your teeth. You get dressed again; as you get dressed, you look out the window. That water — have you ever seen anything like it? Far out, to the horizon, the colour of the water is navy-blue; nearer, the water is the colour of the North American sky. From there to the shore, the water is pale, silvery, clear, so clear that you can see its pinkish-white sand bottom. Oh, what beauty! Oh, what beauty! You have never seen anything like this. You are so excited. You breathe shallow. You breathe deep. You see a beautiful boy skimming the water, godlike, on a Windsurfer. You see an incredibly unattractive, fat, pastrylike-fleshed woman enjoying a walk on the beautiful sand, with a man, an incredibly unattractive, fat, pastrylike-fleshed man; you see the pleasure they're taking in their surroundings. Still standing, looking out the window, you see yourself lying on the beach, enjoying the amazing sun (a sun so powerful and yet so beautiful, the way it is always overhead as if on permanent guard, ready to stamp out any cloud that dares to darken and so empty rain on you and ruin your holiday; a sun that is your personal friend). You see yourself taking a walk on that beach, you see yourself meeting new people (only they are new in a very limited way, for they are people just like you). You see yourself eating some delicious, locally grown food. You see yourself, you see yourself. . . . You must not wonder what exactly happened to the contents of your lavatory when you flushed it. You must not wonder where your bathwater went when you pulled out the stopper. You must not wonder what happened when you brushed your teeth. Oh, it might all end up in the water you are thinking of taking a swim in; the contents of your lavatory might, just might, graze gently against your ankle as you wade carefree in the water, for you see, in Antigua, there is no proper sewage-disposal system. But the Caribbean Sea is very big and the Atlantic Ocean is even bigger; it would amaze even you to know the number of black slaves this ocean has swallowed up. . . .

The thing you have always suspected about yourself the minute you become a tourist is true: A tourist is an ugly human being. You are not an ugly person all the time; you are not an ugly person ordinarily; you are not an ugly person day to day. . . . But one day, when you are sitting somewhere, alone in that crowd, and that awful feeling of displacedness comes over you, and really, as an ordinary person you are not well equipped to look too far inward and set yourself aright, because being ordinary is already so taxing, and being ordinary takes all you have out of you, and though the words "I must get away" do not actually pass across your lips, you make a leap from being that nice blob just sitting like a boob in your amniotic sac of the modern experience to being a person visiting heaps of death and ruin and feeling alive and inspired at the sight of it; to being a person lying on some faraway beach, your stilled body stinking and glistening in the sand, looking like something first forgotten, then remembered, then not important enough to go back for; to being a person marvelling at the harmony (ordinarily, what you would say is the backwardness) and the union these other people (and they are other people) have with nature. . . .

An ugly thing, that is what you are when you become a tourist, an ugly, empty thing, a stupid thing, a piece of rubbish pausing here and there to gaze at this and taste that, and it will never occur to you that the people who inhabit the place in which you have just paused cannot stand you, that behind their closed doors they laugh at your strangeness (you do not look the way they look); the physical sight of you does not please them; you have bad manners (it is their custom to eat their food with their hands; you try eating their way, you look silly; you try eating the way you always eat, you look silly); they do not like the way you speak (you have an accent); they collapse helpless from laughter, mimicking the way they imagine you must look as you carry out some everyday bodily function. They do not like you. *They do not like me!* That thought never actually occurs to you. Still, you feel a little uneasy. Still, you feel a little foolish. Still, you feel a little out of place.

Step 1. Gathering Ideas

Before you dive right into choosing a text and answering the prompt about its tone, we will slow down a bit and model the ways that you will read and annotate a text of your choosing and begin to find a focus for your essay.

Reading and Annotating the Text

You just read or reread the excerpt from *A Small Place*. Now let's look a little more closely at the opening lines from Kincaid's essay, make some annotations, and brainstorm about what is most striking in her writing.

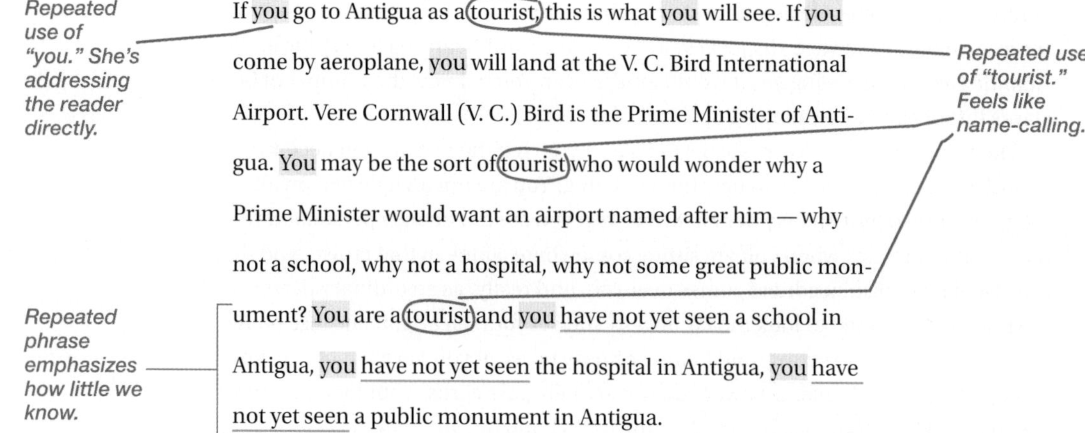

Repeated use of "you." She's addressing the reader directly.

If you go to Antigua as a tourist, this is what you will see. If you come by aeroplane, you will land at the V. C. Bird International Airport. Vere Cornwall (V. C.) Bird is the Prime Minister of Antigua. You may be the sort of tourist who would wonder why a Prime Minister would want an airport named after him — why not a school, why not a hospital, why not some great public monument? You are a tourist and you have not yet seen a school in Antigua, you have not yet seen the hospital in Antigua, you have not yet seen a public monument in Antigua.

Repeated use of "tourist." Feels like name-calling.

Repeated phrase emphasizes how little we know.

From the opening paragraph, the repetitions are striking. Maybe most unusual is the pronoun "you," which Kincaid uses to directly address the reader. If she were giving a speech, the second person might be the norm. However, most of the time, writers either use first person ("I" or "we") or stay in the background with third person. In just a few lines, she repeats the word "tourist" three times, which starts to sound like a hammer. In the last sentence, "you have not yet seen" comes at you in rapid succession three times. So, by the end of these few opening lines, what is the effect of these repetitions? Simple emphasis? Or do readers start to feel like she's questioning their ability to understand? As readers, we may ask ourselves all of these questions and more in response to Kincaid's stylistic choices.

Let's repeat this process with another passage from a little bit later in Kincaid's essay. Notice how the annotations we include here are focusing on Kincaid's style. As you may recall from the Skill Workshop earlier in this chapter (p. 812), elements of a writer's style can include the following:

- Register, meaning pronoun choices and level of formality that define the relationship between writer or speaker and audience
- Connotative language
- Descriptive language that creates a sensory image
- Figurative language (e.g., metaphor, simile, personification)
- Sentence variety in terms of length and placement (e.g., short simple sentences, complex sentences, fragments, parenthetical comments)
- Distinctive sentence patterns based on repetition (annotated in the excerpt that follows), parallel structure, or rhetorical questions

Expression of joy? But why? Is she mocking?

Oh, but by now you are tired of all this looking, and you want to reach your destination — your hotel, your room. You long to refresh yourself; you long to eat some nice lobster, some nice local food. You take a bath, you brush your teeth. You get

Irony that the privileged tourist could be "tired"

Rhetorical question

More repetition of the "oh"

simile

Another parenthetical comment. Is Kincaid commenting?

dressed again; as you get dressed, you look out the window. That water — have you ever seen anything like it? Far out, to the horizon, the colour of the water is navy-blue; nearer, the water is the colour of the North American sky. From there to the shore, the water is pale, silvery, clear, so clear that you can see its pinkish-white sand bottom. Oh, what beauty! Oh, what beauty! You have never seen anything like this. You are so excited. You breathe shallow. You breathe deep. You see a beautiful boy skimming the water, godlike, on a Windsurfer. You see an incredibly unattractive, fat, pastrylike-fleshed woman enjoying a walk on the beautiful sand, with a man, an incredibly unattractive, fat-pastrylike-fleshed man; you see the pleasure they're taking in their surroundings. Still standing, looking out the window, you see yourself lying on the beach, enjoying the amazing sun (a sun so powerful and yet so beautiful, the way it is always overhead as if on permanent guard, ready to stamp out any cloud that dares to darken and so empty rain on you and ruin your holiday; a sun that is your personal friend.)

Repetition of words and phrases throughout

Kincaid describing what the tourist sees. How does she know what's in the tourist's head?

"beautiful/ beauty"— vague descriptions

Really sarcastic

Reading and Annotating Your Text

Locate an argumentative essay in this chapter or from another source. Choose one that is under 1000 words (about the length of the excerpt from *A Small Place* you read earlier in this workshop), or select an excerpt from a longer one for your analysis. Be sure that it is a nonfiction piece and that it makes an argument of some kind. Ideally, it will be one with many examples of the stylistic elements we listed on page 902. Read it over at least twice and annotate it as we modeled earlier.

Finding a Focus

As helpful as annotation can be, it can get noisy — and messy. The more carefully and critically you read, the more you notice. So it's important to start organizing these observations to look for patterns; otherwise, you're in danger of just listing elements of style that you identify and not seeing how they work together to create a specific tone. Taken together, what do the annotations reveal? Kincaid uses repetition of words and phrases, short, abrupt sentences in a series, vague descriptions ("beautiful") next to evocative ones ("incredibly unattractive, fat-pastrylike fleshed"), and a parenthetical comment. These annotations can lead us in several directions. For example, we could start to draw inferences about a sarcastic or cynical attitude on the part of Kincaid toward this hypothetical tourist. Or the annotations could lead us to ask questions that need further exploration. For instance, when Kincaid imagines what the tourist is thinking, is she, like the tourist, guilty of thinking she knows what's in someone else's head? Or, is Kincaid suggesting that the physically unattractive tourists somehow violate the beauty of the beach — and is that fair? The annotations could simply turn up questions, such as *Why does she use all those semicolons?* If a semicolon denotes balance between two closely connected ideas, then what is the point of using them in this passage? Let's jump to the end of the excerpt by Kincaid to begin narrowing down our observations and seeing what other patterns emerge.

In the final section of this excerpt, Kincaid begins with a sentence that can be described as an assault: "The thing you have always suspected about yourself the minute you become a tourist is true: A tourist is an ugly human being." But then she follows with a series of descriptions that soften the accusation. In this section, Kincaid seems to define the "tourist" not so much as the "you" she is directly addressing as an individual, but as a type, with the usual human insecurities and frailties that we all share. In a way, she seems to consider a counterargument (i.e., the tourist might not be so bad) by conceding the possibility that "you are a whole person." But — here comes the refutation — she argues that the tourist, the "you," lacks the capacity to look inward and become more self-aware. She makes that point with a brutal figure of speech: "you make a leap from being that nice blob just sitting like a boob in your amniotic sac of the modern experience to being a person visiting heaps of death and ruin and feeling alive and inspired at the sight of it. . . ."

Overall, by looking closely at and annotating these sections of Kincaid's essay, we can determine that she is taking a very harsh, critical, and probably deeply sarcastic tone toward the tourists who visit Antigua. She wants the reader to understand that being a tourist is more complex than we often think.

Finding Your Focus

Look back though the annotations you made on the argument essay you have chosen to work with. Overall, what do you notice about the tone that the author is taking toward the subject? At this point, your goal is just to identify a possible tone and the purpose the author may have had for writing the piece. Return to the chart of common tone words you saw in the Skill Workshop at the beginning of this chapter as you write your response (p. 812).

Step 2. Planning the Essay

So far in this workshop, you have selected your piece for analysis, done a close reading with careful annotations, and found a possible focus for your essay by identifying the tone that the author takes toward the subject. Before you actually begin writing your essay, this step will walk you through developing your thesis, identifying relevant support, and considering an appropriate organizational structure.

Developing a Working Thesis

The thesis for an essay analyzing tone shares many characteristics with thesis statements for other close reading essays, particularly rhetorical analysis. Overall, it should be a clear and defensible thesis that identifies and analyzes the writer's tone. In most instances, it will be just one sentence, though it can be longer. It predicts both the content and the structure of your essay. And, an especially strong thesis demonstrates a sophisticated understanding of the complexity of tone by linking it to the author's purpose. Let's look at a few examples that fall short and one that might be a suitable thesis for an essay analyzing the tone of *A Small Place* by Jamaica Kincaid.

WEAK THESIS

In *A Small Place*, Jamaica Kincaid unfairly stereotypes all tourists as being insensitive and selfish.

This is a statement of opinion — perhaps a perfectly defensible opinion — yet the task of analyzing tone is not to evaluate the subject. There is no indication in this statement of what the tone is or how or why the writer develops it. Although part of an analysis of tone may include evaluating its effectiveness, even that is not the focus of this statement. If you are asked to evaluate tone, then you would address its appropriateness for a specific audience.

WEAK THESIS

In *A Small Place*, Jamaica Kincaid uses strong emotional language, the second person pronoun, and parenthetical comments to develop her tone.

This is a partial thesis. It predicts the main points of the essay by identifying elements of style, but the tone is not identified. Starting with this thesis would tempt a writer to focus on individual stylistic elements and neglect to discuss what tone they add up to.

WORKING THESIS

In *A Small Place*, Jamaica Kincaid uses strong emotional language, contrasting sentence patterns, and parenthetical asides to develop a sarcastic tone for presenting a critical view of the tourists who visit Antigua seeking escape and pleasure.

This is a sturdy thesis likely to lead to a clearly organized essay. It indicates the stylistic elements that will be the focus (strong emotional language and parenthetical asides), the tone (sarcastic, critical), and the connection to purpose (criticism of tourists who visit Antigua seeking escape and pleasure). You might think that this thesis would limit the essay to four paragraphs: introduction, two developmental paragraphs, and conclusion. It's possible, and that might be fine, particularly if there's a time constraint on the essay. However, either of those stylistic elements could be developed into more than one paragraph with examples and commentary.

The key to an effective analysis of tone is to keep in mind that it is an interpretation. That means your analysis is an argument that requires a strong thesis stating your view of what the tone is and how it advances the writer's purpose. It should not be a statement of your opinion on the subject of the essay.

Developing Your Working Thesis

Write a thesis that directs and predicts your essay analyzing the tone of the text or excerpt that you have chosen. Share your thesis with a partner, who can respond to the following questions:

- Does the thesis clearly address the task?
- Does the thesis predict the stylistic elements you will analyze?
- Does the thesis indicate what the tone is?
- Does the thesis connect tone with author's purpose?

Gathering Evidence

Elements of style are the building blocks for understanding tone. Examples from the text serve as evidence for our conclusions, helping us to prove our thesis. Keep in mind that by making an initial analysis of "effect" in a table such as the one that follows, you're already starting the commentary part of your analysis. The "notes" column provides an opportunity to draw connections, ask further questions, and generally keep track of your ideas about what tone seems to be developing for your essay. Essentially, the graphic organizer helps you to test out the trends, patterns, and choices that you've noticed.

Elements of style	Example(s)	Effect	Notes
Second person pronoun	"The thing you have always suspected. . . ." ". . . you are not well equipped to look too far inward." "An ugly thing, that is what you are when you become a tourist." "Still, you feel a little foolish. Still, you feel a little out of place."	Unusual choice of pronoun seems accusatory, finger pointing. Puts reader on defensive. Feels judgmental. She uses second person throughout.	Is Kincaid, the narrator, angry? If so, is the "tourist" to blame? What's the point of making him or her feel bad?
Long sentences with accumulations of modifiers and clauses	"But one day when you are sitting somewhere, alone in that crowd . . . [to end of paragraph]" "An ugly thing, that is what you are when you become a tourist, an ugly, empty thing. . . ."	Reads almost like a rant. The "you" cannot offer defense or explanation. The speaker does not listen but only increases the pace and detail.	Has the narrator lost control? Is she so angry that she cannot stop the accusations?
Short simple sentences	"A tourist is an ugly human being." "They do not like you. *They do not like me!*"	Sparseness of the sentence sounds like a declaration or proclamation.	Another way that the narrator prohibits another view or any dialogue. It's a monologue all the way.
Parenthetical comments	Contrast between the natives and the tourists: "(you do not look the way they look)" "(it is their custom to eat their food with their hands)" "(you have an accent)"	The narrator makes mocking and sarcastic asides that make fun of the tourist.	How can the narrator know what is in everyone's heads—the minds of the native Antiguans and the tourists? She gives herself enormous authority.

(continued)

Elements of style	Example(s)	Effect	Notes
Strong emotional language	"ugly" "awful feeling of displacedness" "your stilted body stinking and glistening in the sand"	Repeated use of "ugly," a word that carries both physical and emotional meaning—it even sounds ugly. Hammering away from the very beginning of the essay. "stinking and glistening" suggests an odd combination, so even the "glistening" part feels wrong, out of place.	Is the language itself—Kincaid's rhetoric—being used as a weapon here? She goes beyond criticizing the tourists; she wants to humiliate them.
Figurative language	". . . you make a leap from being that nice blob just sitting like a boob in your amniotic sac of the modern experience to being a person visiting heaps of death and ruin and feeling alive and inspired at the sight of it. . . ."	A disturbing image that degrades everything about the tourist, who is no longer just naïve and insensitive, but evil.	The tone here is not just critical but angry, maybe even enraged.

The graphic organizer shows different stages of gathering evidence: the direct quotations, the analysis of effect, and your commentary. In all likelihood, you won't be able to use everything, so your next step will be to determine just what to hold on to, what to expand, and what to let go of.

Gathering Evidence

Use a graphic organizer like the one we've used, or develop one that you find more helpful. Start identifying stylistic elements that contribute to tone in the text you've chosen to write about, based on your thesis statement. Remember that if you cannot find more than one example of an element in the text, that element might not provide sufficient evidence of how style leads to tone.

Organizing the Essay

There are two major ways to organize an analysis of tone. The first is to move through the elements of style paragraph by paragraph. Providing textual support and commentary, you explain each element and link it to tone and purpose. In the case of our model essay, we might start with a paragraph about Kincaid's use of strong, emotional language. We might follow that with a paragraph about her contrasting sentence patterns. Another paragraph could focus on her use of parenthetical asides. Your introduction and conclusion would be where you emphasize how these elements work together to create an appropriate tone for the argument. You'll likely find this organization most useful when you are writing under time constraints or writing a brief essay. While the structure need not be prescriptive, it can become familiar enough that you lean into it, even when you're feeling the pressure of a test situation.

Another way to organize the essay when you have more time and feel comfortable with this type of analysis is to lead with tone. For example, if you are analyzing tone in a longer essay, you might look at how tone evolves over the course of the piece. For example, the writer might shift tone. Or, in the case of Kincaid, we could note that her tone begins with a condescending description of how a tourist experiences Antigua at the airport: "You are a tourist and you have not yet seen a school in Antigua, you have not yet. . . ." As Kincaid continues, that tone becomes increasingly aggressive until by the end she is quite sarcastic in her assessment of the tourist's self-centered oblivion to the island surroundings.

Organizing Your Essay

We've discussed two methods of organizing your analysis of tone: (1) by individual elements of style and (2) by how tone changes over the course of the piece. Which of the two methods of organization would be more appropriate for the analysis of tone you've been working on? Create a rough outline of your essay and discuss the pros and cons of your choice with a partner.

Step 3. Drafting The Essay

At this point, you have a working thesis, plenty of relevant evidence, and an idea about how you want to organize your essay. Now it's time to begin drafting that essay, focusing on the elements of body paragraphs and how you might start and conclude your essay.

Writing Body Paragraphs with Textual Evidence

Since this is a close reading essay, your paragraphs will follow a pattern similar to that found in rhetorical analysis paragraphs. Your paragraph will consist of the points you want to make, the carefully chosen evidence from the text you're analyzing, and your commentary that explains the effects of stylistic elements.

Let's take a slightly different tack here, though, to return to a way of thinking about argument — in this case, interpretation. An argument has a line of reasoning, a logical backbone that holds the argument together. In the case of an analysis of tone, your line of reasoning is a fairly complicated mix of the choices in style that a writer makes, the tone that results from those choices considered collectively, and the impact that tone has on achieving the writer's purpose. We've discussed how the thesis should cover all three of these points. Now we'll look at body paragraphs to consider how each paragraph will likely also address them.

Let's use the thesis we discussed in the previous section:

WORKING THESIS

In *A Small Place*, Jamaica Kincaid uses strong emotional language, contrasting sentence patterns, and parenthetical asides to develop a sarcastic tone for presenting a critical view of the tourists who visit Antigua seeking escape and pleasure.

Then, we'll develop a paragraph on "strong emotional language." Consider the following examples from Kincaid's text:

- "You emerge from customs into the hot, clean air: immediately you feel cleansed, immediately you feel blessed (which is to say special); you feel free."
- ". . . the contents of your lavatory might, just might, graze gently against your ankle as you wade carefree in the water, for you see, in Antigua, there is no proper sewage-disposal system."
- ". . . you might make a leap from being that nice blob just sitting like a boob in your amniotic sac of the modern experience to being a person visiting heaps of death and ruin and feeling alive and inspired at the sight of it to being a person lying on some faraway beach, your stilled body stinking and glistening in the sand. . . ."
- ". . . an ugly, empty thing, that is what you are when you become a tourist, an ugly, empty thing, a stupid thing, a piece of rubbish pausing here and there. . . ."

Obviously, you can't include every example, or at least not every word. Start with a topic sentence that links to your thesis and then begin to weave the quotations (or parts of them) into your own sentences.

The language Kincaid uses to describe the tourist both physically and psychologically is loaded with sharp criticism. As soon as the tourist emerges from the airport in Antigua, Kincaid claims that "you" (the accusing second person that she uses to refer to the tourist) feel "cleansed," "blessed," "special," "free." This tourist may fail to realize that "the contents of your lavatory might, just might, graze gently against your ankle as you wade carefree in the water." Toward the end of the essay, she describes the ugly tourist as a "nice blob just sitting like a boob in your amniotic sac of the modern experience." Ultimately, she describes the tourist as "an ugly, empty thing, a stupid thing, a piece of rubbish pausing here and there. . . ."

The sample topic sentence is tied to the thesis without being repetitive: It refers to language that the author uses to develop a critical tone. Each of the quotations is shortened and incorporated into the writer's own sentences. But what's missing? There is little commentary that explains how the textual evidence supports the line of reasoning. How does the quotation contribute to the development of a specific tone?

Consider this revision, which trims the quotations and adds commentary and explanation (underlined).

> The language Kincaid uses to describe the tourist both physically and psychologically is loaded with sharp criticism. As soon as the tourist emerges from the airport in Antigua, Kincaid claims that "you" (the accusing second person pronoun that she uses to refer to the tourist) feel "cleansed," "blessed," "special," "free." <u>These words that carry spiritual or even religious connotations suggest the tourist feels designated as someone who exists on a plane above the average person, certainly above those native to Antigua. This tourist is so self-involved that the realities of life in Antigua go unnoticed. Entirely focused on enjoying the beautiful beach,</u> Kincaid's tourist fails to notice that the "contents of your lavatory might, just might, graze gently against your ankle as you wade carefree in the water." Toward the end of the essay, <u>her language becomes even stronger, more sarcastic</u>. After she describes the tourist as someone who sounds like an ordinary middle-class person with a house, family, and friends, <u>she quickly shifts to calling the tourist</u> "a nice blob just sitting like a boob in your amniotic sac of the modern experience." <u>With that cruel metaphor, she sums up the existence of the tourist</u>. Ultimately, she describes the tourist with a <u>general word that is normally vague, but also can mean something inanimate and thus not human</u>: "an ugly, empty thing, a stupid thing, a piece of rubbish pausing here and there. . . ." <u>Kincaid's word choices contribute to a critical tone that devalues and dehumanizes the tourist, just as she has accused the tourist of doing to the native people of Antigua</u>.

The revised paragraph brings together (1) a clear topic sentence connected to the thesis, (2) evidence consisting of well-chosen quotations from the text, (3) commentary that explains how an element of style contributes to tone, and (4) a connection between tone and purpose.

Our sample body paragraph is focused on the strong emotional language choices that Kincaid makes. To continue developing the thesis, we would probably need two more body paragraphs: one about how Kincaid contrasts long descriptive sentences with short abrupt ones and another about the effect of her parenthetical asides. These paragraphs would likely follow the same structure we used in the model above, including a topic sentence and as much evidence from the text and commentary about it as needed to support the point we are making about style and tone.

Writing Body Paragraphs with Textual Evidence

Returning to your thesis, evidence chart, and organizational plan, draft a body paragraph for your close reading analysis essay. In addition to the evidence from the text, be sure that your paragraph includes commentary about how that evidence supports your topic sentence and thesis. Show a draft of your body paragraph to a classmate or two and get feedback on how well you have used the evidence and your commentary to prove your points.

Then, draft the remaining body paragraphs according to the organizational structure you identified earlier in this workshop (p. 909). Be sure that each body paragraph includes a topic sentence related to your working thesis (p. 906). The number of body paragraphs you write will be determined by your thesis and the organizational structure you have chosen.

Writing an Introduction and a Conclusion

In a close reading analysis essay, your introductory paragraph engages your reader, creates interest in the topic, and previews your main idea, just as it would in other types of essays you've written. It has three parts: an opening hook, a connection to the piece being analyzed, and a thesis statement. For our model analysis, we might use a rhetorical question as a hook: *Have you ever been a tourist? Did you ever think that someone might describe you as "ugly"?* That might engage our readers, maybe make them feel a little defensive, or intrigue them. Or we might open with a discussion of the sensitivity of being a tourist from an affluent or powerful country in an environment of poverty or discord. Another option would be to describe a drive (or ride) from an airport through impoverished neighborhoods on the way to a comfortable, even luxurious, hotel. And once we have hooked the reader, we are ready to add any necessary context and make a connection to the piece we're analyzing in order to introduce our thesis about Kincaid's attitude toward the tourist.

Here is a possible introduction for our model analysis:

> Haven't most of us been a "tourist" in some way? Even if we haven't gone to another country, we have visited a local landmark to enjoy a carefree day with friends or family. We probably didn't think of ourselves as being "ugly," nor did we imagine that others saw us that way. Yet in *A Small Place*, author Jamaica Kincaid takes the "ugly tourist" to task in ways that may shock or surprise her readers. With strong emotional language and parenthetical asides, she develops a sarcastic, critical tone toward the tourists who visit Antigua seeking temporary escape and pleasure.

This introduction opens with a question to draw the reader in, followed by a few sentences to flesh out that experience. Then, we transition to Kincaid's essay with the reference to the "ugly tourist." It ends with the thesis that indicates the organizing structure and previews what lies ahead.

A powerful technique to consider when writing your conclusion is called "framing" or, in the language of journalism, the envelope technique. That is, you open and close your essay with a similar idea. The conclusion ties back into the introduction. In this case, it links to the accusation of being an "ugly tourist." Of course, there is more than one way to do this, but here's a possibility:

> The criticism that Kincaid levels at the tourist is bound to offend some readers. People don't want to think of themselves as "ugly" or insensitive. Also, Kincaid makes accusations as if she knows what is in the tourist's mind, presenting the tourist more as a stereotype than as an individual. However, her striking tone might make those of us who have visited or will visit places where we are "the tourist" more aware of the hardships experienced by those who make our lives easy for a few pampered days. If a critical, sarcastic tone accomplishes that wake-up call, then Kincaid will have achieved her purpose.

Drafting Your Introduction and Conclusion

Using the preceding models, draft your introduction and conclusion. You may want to try the frame technique as a way to hook the reader and tie your essay together to leave a lasting impression on him or her. Show your drafts to a partner to receive feedback on how well you have connected these two parts of your essay.

Step 4. Finalizing the Essay

Now that you have a solid draft of your essay, you can move on to the final phase in the writing process: revising and editing. These two acts are sometimes thought of as being the same, but they're not. Revision is when you look back at large-scale structural elements of your essay, such as how well you support your claim, what kinds of evidence you use, how effective your word choices are, and to what extent you have led your reader easily through your essay. Editing, on the other hand, focuses on fine-tuning the language.

Revising

Revising gives you a good opportunity to think again about your audience and to make sure that you're appealing to shared values. In most cases, an analysis of the tone of a text is a chance to demonstrate your understanding of a concept or skill. As we've discussed, you're interpreting a text, but you are not offering your viewpoint on the subject of that text. This type of analysis should not focus on your opinion, even if you have a strong one about the topic. In most cases, your audience will be your teacher. In the case of a standardized test, it will be an external evaluator. In both situations, that means using a somewhat formal tone, but your writing can still be engaging for you and your audience.

Reread your essay for the following:

- Look back at your **thesis**. Since you wrote this early on in the workshop, is it still appropriate for the analysis of tone that you ended up writing? See Revision

Workshop 1: Effective Thesis and Essay Structure (p. 1064) if you need more assistance.

- Is your **focus** clearly related to the tone of the piece? If you need more help remembering how to analyze for tone, return to the Skill Workshop at the beginning of this chapter (p. 812).
- Look back at your **body paragraphs**. Have you balanced the evidence with your own **commentary** about how that evidence supports your thesis? See Revision Workshop 3: Balanced Evidence and Commentary (p. 1073) if you need more help with this part of your essay.
- Can the reader follow the **organization** of your essay easily? Would other approaches to the organization be more effective? See Revision Workshop 5: Effective Transitions (p. 1082) or Revision Workshop 2: Effective Topic Sentences and Unified Paragraphs (p. 1068) if you think that your reader may have trouble following your essay.
- Does your **introduction** grab the reader's attention and effectively preview your topic? Does your **conclusion** wrap up in a way that highlights your focus? If not, look at Revision Workshop 8: Effective Introductions and Conclusions (p. 1097).

Editing

Remember, editing is the very last thing you'll do before finalizing your essay. You and your teacher know better than anyone the types of spelling, grammar, and convention errors you need to focus on in your writing development. Refer to one or more of the Grammar Workshops (p. 1101) in the back of the book if you encounter an issue and aren't sure how to overcome it.

Continuing the Conversation

Throughout this chapter, you have read and thought about how people wrestle with doing the right thing. You have also had opportunities to consider ideas related to the following essential questions:

- How do we decide what actions or decisions are "right" or "wrong"?
- To what extent do our age, culture, gender identity, and other personal characteristics affect the ethics of our decision-making?
- How can we gauge the effects that our decisions have on other individuals, our community, and society at large?
- Under what circumstances is an individual likely to base a decision on personal feelings or beliefs rather than on prevailing social values or norms?

The following sections will give you an opportunity to revisit and respond to some of those questions as you think further about what it means to "do the right thing" by connecting these ideas to yourself, to texts you have read, and to the world outside of the classroom.

Connections to Self

Think back on the texts you have read, responses you have written, discussions you have participated in, and ideas you have considered during your work with this chapter. Use the following questions to help explore how the issues raised in this chapter connect to your life and experience:

1. What does it mean to you to "do the right thing"? To what extent would the people you know well agree with your definition? Feel free to conduct interviews or surveys.
2. List some of the challenges you face in doing the right thing. What pressures does society place on you to do something you feel is *not* right?
3. Who or what has most influenced your own ethical decision-making?
4. Which of the authors in this chapter would you like to have dinner with? Why? What would you ask them about the choices they make or advocate for? Or, which author would you definitely not want to have dinner with? Why? What would you say to that author if you were stuck next to him or her at dinner?
5. Which of the texts that you read in this chapter had the most significant impact on the way you think about doing the right thing? Why?

Connections to Texts

Use the following questions to make connections among the texts in this chapter and to consider what insights the texts provide into the essential questions. As you respond, make specific references to **two or more texts** you read in this chapter.

1. Sam Harris, the author of "Lying," says that we should never lie, under any circumstances. Explain to what extent two or more other authors that you read in this chapter might agree or disagree with that position. You may want to consider the following texts in your discussion: "The Case of the Photoshopped Female CEOs," "Why We Look the Other Way," and "Truth at All Costs."
2. Some of the authors in this chapter focus on how power (or the lack of power) affects decision-making. Do they view the ethical use of power similarly or differently? In what ways? You may want to consider the following texts in your discussion: "Shooting an Elephant," "Truth at All Costs," *A Small Place*, and "Are We All In This Together?"
3. Imagine a dialogue between two of the authors in this chapter. What topics related to doing the right thing would they discuss? How would they respond to each other?
4. Part of doing the right thing is being able to empathize with other people, to understand their situation and act in a way that accounts for their feelings. Discuss how two or more authors in this chapter base their positions on the ability to feel and show empathy. You may want to consider the following texts in your discussion: "The Work You Do," "Designer Babies Aren't Futuristic. They're Already Here," "Traveling Through the Dark," and *A Small Place.*
5. Several authors in this chapter focus on the role that societal norms play in defining "the right thing." Explain the position that two or more of the authors take on whether societal pressures play a positive or negative role in our ethical decision-making. You may want to consider the following texts in your discussion: *The Cheating Culture*, "Shooting an Elephant," *Lying*, and "Why We Look the Other Way."

Connections to World

Think back on the texts you have read, responses you have written, discussions you have participated in, and ideas you have considered during your work with this chapter. Use the following questions to help explore how the issues raised in this chapter play out in the world at large:

1. Which political, cultural, or social leaders are either "doing the right thing" or not, according to your own definition? What are the results of their actions?
2. What law, policy, or rule do you feel is an example of "doing the right thing"? What makes it fit your definition?
3. Overall, is our society an ethical one? Is it just? How do you know?
4. In what specific way would you change our society to make it more ethical and just?

Evidence-Based Argument

Write an argument in response to one of the following prompts in which you support your claim with examples from **at least three of the texts** in this chapter.

Prompt 1: Write about a time when you made a decision about "doing the right thing." What circumstances led to that decision? What considerations most influenced it? Which of the authors in this chapter would be sympathetic to your decision?

Prompt 2: To what extent do you think that people do the right thing only or mostly because they fear the consequences of doing something wrong?

Prompt 3: In general, what informs an individual's understanding of "doing the right thing"? Are such decisions reflective of larger considerations based in philosophy, culture, and religious beliefs? Or, are they reflective of specific circumstances, changing social norms, and human relations?

For more support with writing an evidence-based argument, consult Chapter 4 and the Writing Workshop of Chapter 9 (p. 654).

Tithi Luadthong/Alamy Stock Photo

Power

Essential Questions:

- **What different types of power do people have?**
- **Is the desire to gain power just part of human nature?**
- **When is the pursuit of power constructive? When is it destructive?**
- **How do individuals react to gaining or losing power?**
- **In what ways do gender identity, age, race, ethnicity, and other factors affect how people gain and use power?**

As a high school student, you might sometimes feel that you have very little power at this point in your life. Your school district tells you when you need to start school each day, your state government decides when you can drive and how long you can work, and your teachers and families likely have additional rules that dictate what you can and cannot do. As a result, you might conclude that power has a lot to do with age and that you will gain more power the older you get. Certainly, society grants you more rights and independence as you age. We would be naïve to conclude, however, that everyone has access to equal power in society. A number of other factors might unjustly affect how much power you will have later in life, including race, gender identity, sexual orientation, and socioeconomic status. But, it can take many different forms beyond the political and economic power over others. There is also the power of your own self-determination, as well as the power dynamics within a relationship. In fact, what probably does change as you get older is your understanding of how power works, when it is wielded, and for what purposes. Attempts to gain and use power are probably hard-wired into us as humans, but we should always consider how it can be used justly and ethically.

activity Thinking about Power

Look over the following quotations about power and choose two or three to discuss with a partner or small group. To what extent do you agree or disagree with the ideas expressed in the quotations? Select one quotation and discuss how the idea expressed might play out in politics, relationships, school, family, or other real-world environments.

1. "Power does not corrupt. Fear corrupts. Perhaps the fear of a loss of power." — John Steinbeck
2. "Washing one's hands of the conflict between the powerful and the powerless means to side with the powerful, not to be neutral." — Paulo Freire
3. "A feminist is a person who believes in the power of women just as much as they believe in the power of anyone else." — Zendaya
4. "No one can make you feel inferior without your consent." — Eleanor Roosevelt
5. "Ultimately, the only power to which man should aspire is that which he exercises over himself." — Elie Wiesel
6. "We know that no one ever seizes power with the intention of relinquishing it." — George Orwell
7. "Men are taught to apologize for their weaknesses, women for their strengths." — Lois Wyse
8. "And power without compassion is the worst kind of evil there is." — E. J. Patten
9. "The most common way people give up their power is by thinking they don't have any." — Alice Walker
10. "I am not free while any woman is unfree, even when her shackles are very different from my own." — Audre Lorde

Texts in Conversation

Throughout this chapter, you will read about a number of issues related to power. As you read, keep track of the authors' attitudes and ideas, draw connections among them, and respond to them with your own reactions. At the end of the chapter, you'll have an opportunity to write your own piece about power, using the texts you read as evidence and inspiration. You can gather information and ideas in a graphic organizer like the following one if it would help you:

Author/title	Author's ideas or attitudes toward power	Quotation(s) that illustrate the author's ideas about power	Your reaction and/or connection to other texts

Analyzing Figurative Language in Poetry

As you may have read in Chapter 2, **figurative language** refers to nonliteral uses of language. When a teacher tells a class, "I have asked you a million times to pay attention," the teacher is using figurative language (hyperbole, in this case) to communicate intense frustration after calling for attention a few (not a million) times.

The following are some of the most common figures of speech:

- **Metaphor:** a direct comparison between unlike things
- **Simile:** a comparison between unlike things using "like" or "as"
- **Hyperbole:** a deliberate exaggeration or overstatement
- **Personification:** giving human qualities to inanimate objects
- **Allusion:** a reference to something well known, such as a work of literature or art or an historical event

Figurative language is one tool among many that writers use to convey their ideas. Some writers employ figurative language regularly, while others rarely do. In this workshop, we will model the analysis of a Shakespearean sonnet by identifying figurative language, examining its effect, and connecting it to possible meanings. You will be mirroring these steps with your own analysis of a different Shakespearean sonnet.

If you find the idea of analyzing Shakespeare's writing intimidating, you're not alone. Part of the challenge lies in Shakespeare's archaic language, meaning that many of the words he chooses are not in regular use today. It helps to remember that many of these archaic forms have modern equivalents that are similar: for example, *hath* means *has*, *thy* means *your*, *thee* means *you*, and *doth* means *does*. At times, Shakespeare also invents or alters words to fit a rhythm or rhyme scheme, and you may see words with unusual suffixes (e.g., *-est*) or spellings. In the case of suffixes, you can usually read these just as they would be without the suffix (e.g., *knowest* becomes *know*). In general, repeated exposure to Shakespeare's language will make reading and understanding his work easier.

Once you have a grasp of Shakespeare's language, you face the challenge of determining his meaning, the themes of his works. In the case of the sonnets in this workshop, keep in mind that they are part of what Shakespearean scholars have identified as the Fair Youth sequence, a series of poems that tend to focus on beauty, love, and the effect of time on both. When you are considering possible themes of these sonnets, ask yourself, "What is Shakespeare suggesting about beauty, love, or time?"

Reading Shakespearean Language

Meet with a partner or a small group and look over the following lines from a Shakespeare play that you may already be familiar with, *Romeo and Juliet.* After reading each line aloud a few times, identify the figurative language Shakespeare uses and discuss what he might be suggesting about love, beauty, or time.

- "O, speak again, bright angel! For thou art as glorious to this night, being o'er my head as is a wingèd messenger of heaven"
- "It is the East, and Juliet is the sun"
- "Arise, fair sun, and kill the envious moon"
- "The brightness of her cheek would shame those stars / As daylight doth a lamp"
- "My lips, two blushing pilgrims, ready stand / To smooth that rough touch with a tender kiss"
- "Is love a tender thing? It is too rough, / Too rude, too boisterous, and it pricks like thorn"
- "The sun, for sorrow, will not show his head"

Afterward, discuss what was easy or challenging about reading and understanding these lines from *Romeo and Juliet*. In addition, discuss your past experiences in or out of school with reading Shakespeare's sonnets or plays, or seeing his works performed on stage or in movies. How might those experiences and the introduction to this workshop help to prepare you for reading and analyzing Shakespeare's work?

We will model the analysis of Shakespeare's Sonnet 94, and you will work with Sonnet 29. The following sample annotations of Sonnet 94 reflect two readings. During our first reading, we focused on making connections and asking questions (see p. 10). Then, we reread the sonnet and annotated it for examples of figurative language. Readers' observations and annotations will vary, but the sample annotations that follow will help you explore the role that reading and annotating can play in analyzing a poem's figurative language and meaning. (Though our focus here is on figurative language, you may find it helpful to review the structure of an English sonnet in Chapter 2 on p. 56.)

William Shakespeare

Sonnet 94

GL Archive/Alamy

William Shakespeare (1564–1616) was an English poet, actor, and playwright. Many consider him to be the greatest writer in the English language. He is credited with 38 plays, 154 sonnets, and two lengthy narrative poems. Little is known of Shakespeare's life aside from the fact that he married Anne Hathaway when he was eighteen, worked as an actor and a playwright in London, and retired in 1613.

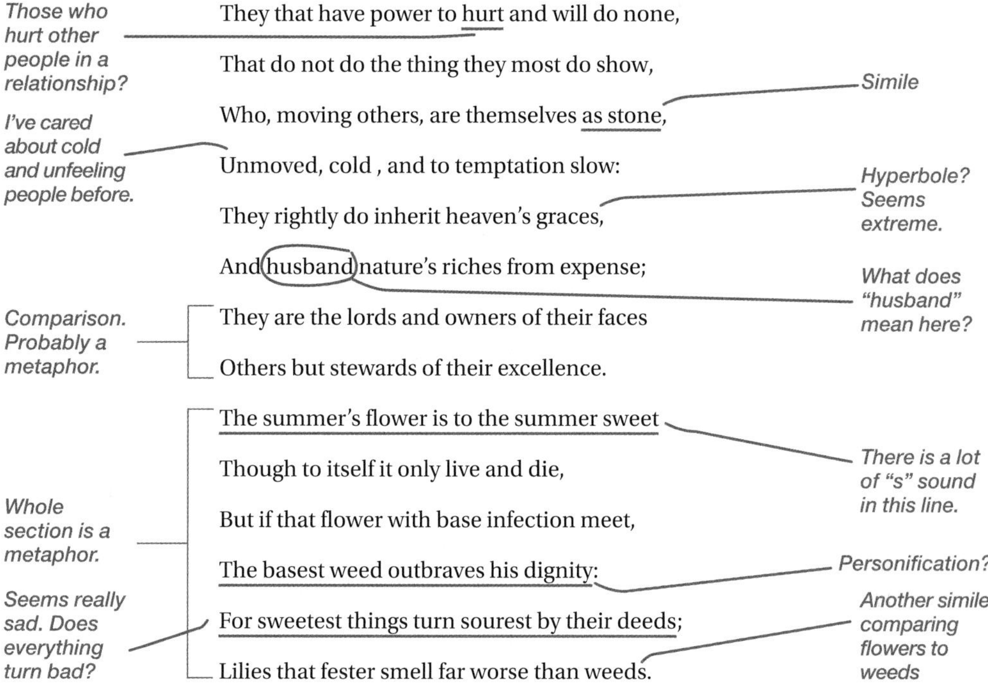
They that have power to hurt and will do none,
That do not do the thing they most do show,
Who, moving others, are themselves as stone,
Unmoved, cold, and to temptation slow:
They rightly do inherit heaven's graces,
And husband nature's riches from expense;
They are the lords and owners of their faces
Others but stewards of their excellence.
The summer's flower is to the summer sweet
Though to itself it only live and die,
But if that flower with base infection meet,
The basest weed outbraves his dignity:
For sweetest things turn sourest by their deeds;
Lilies that fester smell far worse than weeds.

Figurative Language and Effect

In your study of literature, or on standardized tests, you will sometimes be asked to identify examples of figurative language. Identification is an essential place to start, but you can't stop there. You need to be able to describe how an author uses figurative language to create meaning, add emotion, and give a piece power. Analyzing figurative language is about *effect*.

Writers can use figurative language to create strong images in the minds of their readers, usually by comparing one thing to another. Comparisons, often in the form of metaphors, similes, and allusions, create imagery and frames of reference to help readers understand what the writer intends to communicate. A sportswriter trying to convey the sheer size of a boxer, for instance, might call him "Herculean," making an allusion to the Greek hero Hercules.

In the following chart, we've gathered examples of figurative language from Sonnet 94, many of which you may have noticed, and suggested possible effects of those language choices:

Example	Type	Possible effect
"Who, moving others, are themselves as stone" (3)	Simile: compares people to stone	Shows that the speaker thinks that some people are unmovable and unfeeling

(continued)

Example	Type	Possible effect
"They are the lords and owners of their faces" (7)	Metaphor: directly compares people in control of themselves to those who rule others	Reveals that some people are able to control their facial expressions, hiding true motivations
"The basest weed outbraves his dignity" (12)	Personification: the weed demonstrates bravery	Suggests that even things that are not as beautiful as flowers have strength in them
"Lilies that fester smell far worse than weeds." (14)	Simile: compares the lilies to the weeds	Proposes that what was beautiful can become uglier than something that was never beautiful

It is important to remember that each instance of figurative language is the result of a specific *choice* a writer has made. In other words, a different choice would have a different effect. Also keep in mind that figurative language often allows for multiple interpretations.

Identifying Figurative Language

So far in this workshop, we have read and analyzed a sonnet and begun identifying some of the figurative language Shakespeare uses. Now it is your turn to practice this type of close reading. Read and annotate Sonnet 29. On your first reading, be sure to make connections and ask questions as we modeled on page 923. Then, read it again for examples of figurative language.

Sonnet 29

William Shakespeare

When, in disgrace with fortune and men's eyes,
I all alone beweep my outcast state,
And trouble deaf heaven with my bootless cries,
And look upon myself and curse my fate,
Wishing me like to one more rich in hope,
Featured like him, like him with friends possessed,
Desiring this man's art and that man's scope,
With what I most enjoy contented least;
Yet in these thoughts myself almost despising,
Haply I think on thee, and then my state,
(Like to the lark at break of day arising
From sullen earth) sings hymns at heaven's gate;
For thy sweet love remembered such wealth brings
That then I scorn to change my state with kings.

After you have annotated the text, complete a chart like the following one, using the sample on pages 923 to 924 as a guide. Try to identify at least three or four different examples of figurative language.

Example	Type	Possible effect

Analyzing Figurative Language

Oftentimes in poetry, the writer uses figurative language for both immediate and cumulative effect. In other words, a simile might serve a specific purpose when it first appears, but it also connects to other language choices throughout the poem. That cumulative effect helps us determine the meaning, or theme, of the poem. The repeated references to flowers, stone, weeds, and other elements of nature in Sonnet 94, the first poem in this workshop, signal that natural elements are significant to the poem's meaning. Taken together, these references create a pattern in Shakespeare's use of figurative language.

As you may have seen in Chapter 2, one method for determining the theme of a poem is to recognize **shifts** (p. 52) in topic, tone, perspective, or other elements. A shift often marks an important development in the poem. Sonnet 94 includes a major shift in the use of figurative language. Notice the first comparison with a flower in line 9: "The summer's flower is to the summer sweet." Prior to this shift, figurative language mostly serves to connect people of power with stone, owners, and lords. After line 9, however, people of power are continually compared with flowers. The stark contrasts between stone and flowers help to illustrate how people with power might use it well or be corrupted.

Analyzing Figurative Language

We have begun analyzing Shakespeare's use of figurative language in Sonnet 94. Now you can do the same with Sonnet 29. Return to the chart you completed in the preceding activity. Look for patterns or shifts in Shakespeare's use of figurative language, similar to what we described previously. Write a few notes about the use of figurative language and share with a partner or small group to be sure that you are able to recognize any patterns and shifts.

Analyzing for Theme

So far in this workshop, you have identified figurative language, analyzed its possible effects, and considered any patterns or shifts. The next step is to develop an interpretation of the poem. As you may have seen in earlier chapters, when reading for interpretation, you are concerned primarily with explaining what the text means — its significance. In poetry, we express our interpretation of significance as the theme of the text, a point the author is trying to make about life, the world, people, and other topics. Though interpretations can vary, you should have a reasonable explanation for why your conclusion is valid.

Sonnet 94, the one we have been modeling, deals mostly with people who have power over others, and who can choose to hurt or not hurt them. They can influence others and control themselves ("moving others, are themselves as stone"), including their own emotions ("lords and owners of their faces"). When they choose to use their power *not* to hurt others, they should be praised and rewarded with "heaven's graces / And husband nature's riches." But, if they decide to use their power to hurt — "if that flower with base infection meet" — then the beautiful turns ugly.

With these observations in mind, we might conclude that a possible theme of Sonnet 94 is that an uncaring person's beauty or outward appearance can be wielded as a destructive power.

Analyzing for Theme

Look back at your annotations, the chart, and the notes that you made for Sonnet 29, and draw a reasonable interpretation of the theme of that sonnet. Try to state it as a single sentence, as we did with our example for Sonnet 94. Remember, this statement of theme should express what Shakespeare might be suggesting about the topic of the sonnet. In the case of Sonnet 29, he is discussing the relationship between love and power. What is he saying about that relationship? Meet with two or more classmates and discuss different possible themes of the poem.

Analyzing Figurative Language and Theme

Our statement of the theme of Sonnet 94 that we developed in the previous section is not necessarily *the* theme of the sonnet, but it is one possible theme. As you likely found when you discussed possible themes of Sonnet 29 with your classmates, different readers can arrive at different reasonable interpretations. The next step in our sample analysis is to explain how Shakespeare uses figurative language in Sonnet 94 to help him communicate the theme we've identified: an uncaring person's beauty or outward appearance can be wielded as a destructive power. While individual instances of figurative language have their own effect, we should keep in mind that they take on additional meanings when combined with other poetic elements to help communicate an overall idea about the speaker and the theme of the poem.

Thinking of the patterns and shifts in the figurative language that we discussed earlier, we can examine comparisons drawn among people, flowers, and weeds in Sonnet 94, especially in these lines: "But if that flow'r with base infection meet / The basest weed outbraves his dignity." When beautiful, powerful people fail to show self-control, they prove to be uglier and less dignified than those without power or beauty. The figurative language in the final two lines makes this point more emphatically: "For sweetest things turn sourest by their deeds; / Lilies that fester smell far worse than weeds." These lines could mean that those who could be good, beautiful, and powerful ("lilies") but choose to go bad are worse than those who could never be good ("weeds"). While Shakespeare employs many tools to communicate a theme to his reader in Sonnet 94, reading for figurative language allows us to make a reasonable interpretation. Because language as sophisticated as Shakespeare's is open to multiple interpretations, we have made sure that we can support our view with specific examples from the text.

culminating activity

Look back at your annotations, your chart, and your notes, and write a brief response in which you analyze two or three examples of figurative language from Sonnet 29. Draw a conclusion about how examples of figurative language from the sonnet help to communicate an overall idea — a theme — about the relationship between love and power. This is not a full essay; it is just a response that demonstrates that you can consider the effects of figurative language in literature.

Ghost

W. Haden Blackman and Richard Pace

William Haden Blackman is an American writer and video game designer who has authored several graphic novels, including *Star Wars*, *Electra*, and *Batwoman*. Richard Pace is an illustrator who lives in Toronto and has created artwork for many graphic novels published by Marvel, DC, and Vertigo.

KEY CONTEXT This story is part of a collection of graphic stories called *Where We Live*, published to benefit survivors of the 2017 Las Vegas mass shooting that killed 58 people and injured over 500 more. In the last panel, this story refers to an earlier mass shooting (October 2011), at the Salon Meritage hair salon in Seal Beach, California. Eight people inside the salon and one person in the parking lot were shot.

HERE WE ARE AGAIN...
GHOST
WRITTEN BY
W. HADEN BLACKMAN
ART AND COLORS BY
RICHARD PACE
LETTERS BY
BERNARDO BRICE
GATHERED IN THE HOPES SOMEONE WILL NOTICE THE SEA OF SIGNS...
END THE KILLING
HEAR OUR CHANTS AND DEMANDS...
AND ACTUALLY DO SOMETHING.
MAJORITY LEADER, YOU ARE COMPLICIT! SPEAKER, YOU ARE COMPLICIT!
WAIT...WE HAVE NEWS? THE VOTE'S IN?
OUR KIDS!
BUT THE SIGNS, THE SHOUTING, JUST SHOWING UP--IT ALL DOES ABOUT AS MUCH GOOD AS SENDING AN OUTRAGED TWEET FROM THE COUCH.
THE BILL... IT DIDN'T... IT DIDN'T PASS.
AT LEAST THEN, I'D BE AT HOME.

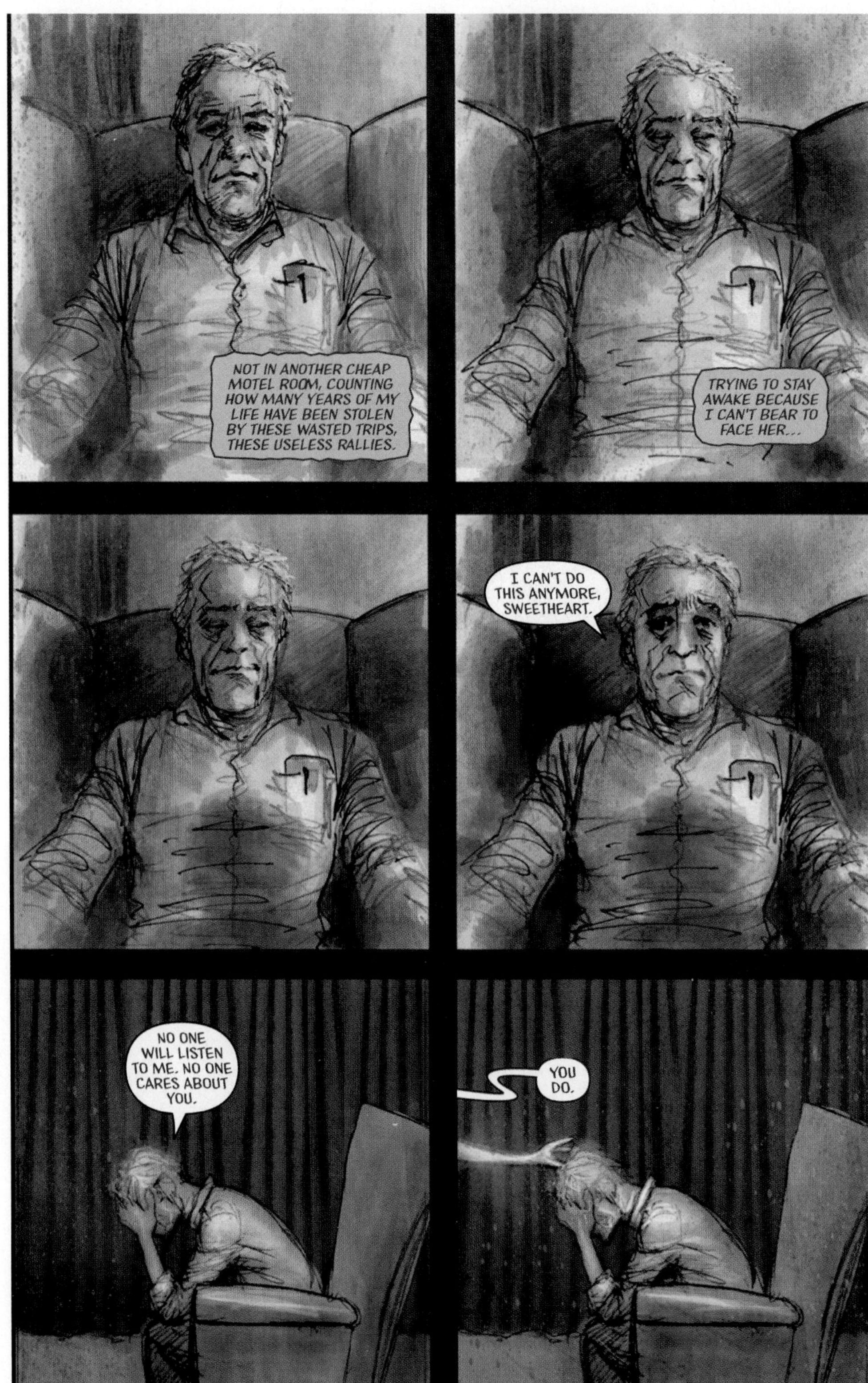
NOT IN ANOTHER CHEAP MOTEL ROOM, COUNTING HOW MANY YEARS OF MY LIFE HAVE BEEN STOLEN BY THESE WASTED TRIPS, THESE USELESS RALLIES.
TRYING TO STAY AWAKE BECAUSE I CAN'T BEAR TO FACE HER...
I CAN'T DO THIS ANYMORE, SWEETHEART.
NO ONE WILL LISTEN TO ME. NO ONE CARES ABOUT YOU.
YOU DO.

I'M JUST ONE VOICE.
YOU'RE NOT THE ONLY ONE WHO HAS LOST SOMEONE YOU LOVE.
AND THEY ALL HAVE VOICES TOO.
EVENTUALLY, THERE WILL BE ENOUGH OF US.
AND ENOUGH OF you.

SHE IS RIGHT, MY DAUGHTER.
ALL WHO'VE LOST FRIENDS AND LOVERS, PARENTS AND CHILDREN, WE WILL BRING OUR HEARTACHE AND OUR ANGER...
I DON'T KNOW HOW MANY OF US IT WILL TAKE. A MILLION, TEN MILLION...
BUT, SOMEDAY SOON, THERE WILL BE TOO MANY VOICES TO IGNORE.
Seal Beach, CA
2011

Understanding and Interpreting

1. What do we learn at the beginning (p. 929) about the protagonist and how he's feeling at this point?
2. This graphic story has three main settings: the first rally, the hotel room, and the second rally. What are the main differences in these settings and their effects on the protagonist?
3. Summarize what the ghost of the protagonist's daughter says to him. Explain how it affects him.
4. How has the protagonist changed over the course of this story? What evidence supports your interpretation?

Analyzing Language, Style, and Structure

1. **Vocabulary in Context.** The ghost of the protagonist's daughter says, "They all have voices too" (p. 931). What does the word "voice" mean in this context? How is that meaning similar to and different from other meanings you have encountered?
2. **Skill Focus.** The protagonist says that there is a "sea of signs" (p. 929). What is the protagonist hoping to communicate with this metaphor? To what extent is that metaphor also captured visually in those first panels?
3. Look back at the first panels (p. 929). How do word choice and visual elements communicate the protagonist's attitude toward his own power?
4. How do Blackman and Pace use choices in color and dialogue to portray the ghost of the protagonist's daughter? How might their choices affect the reader?
5. Trace how the daughter's ghost is framed in the panels from the first time we see her arm on page 930 to the final view of her in the picture frame (p. 932). Describe the framing choices and their possible effects.
6. Describe the final panel of the story. What does it resemble? Why might this have been an effective way to end the story?
7. Describe the overall color scheme of this graphic story. What is the effect of the color choices? How might the tone have been different if Blackman and Pace had selected other colors?

Topics for Composing

1. **Analysis.** What do Blackman and Pace suggest about the nature and use of power in this graphic story?
2. **Argument.** Write an argument about a possible solution to mass shootings in the United States. Use outside evidence, your own experiences and reasoning, and this text to support your position.
3. **Connection.** Describe an issue that you feel strongly about but sometimes powerless to solve. In what ways does the message in this story connect with or contradict that issue and your feelings about it?
4. **Speaking and Listening.** Hold a small group discussion about the benefits and challenges of the kinds of civic engagement that this story presents. Be sure that everyone listens actively during the discussion. Try to arrive at a consensus on the most important steps that we should take.

5. **Research.** In the wake of the 2020 police killing of George Floyd, an unarmed African American man, thousands of people took to the streets across the United States to protest police brutality. Research the effects that these protests may have had on the rules governing the use of force by police in your state or in the country.
6. **Multimodal.** Create a page or two of your own graphic story about a social, cultural, or legal issue you care about. Your story should identify the role that power plays in creating or solving the problem.

Lather and Nothing Else

Hernando Téllez

Hernando Téllez (1908–1966) was born in Bogotá, Colombia, and served in the Colombian Parliament. A lifelong politician, he also published many articles and stories about political topics in newspapers and magazines. His short story collection *Ashes for the Wind* includes "Lather and Nothing Else," which was published in 1950.

He came in without a word. I was stropping my best razor. And when I recognized him, I started to shake. But he did not notice. To cover my nervousness, I went on honing the razor. I tried the edge with the tip of my thumb and took another look at it against the light.

Meanwhile he was taking off his cartridge-studded belt with the pistol holster suspended from it. He put it on a hook in the wardrobe and hung his cap above it. Then he turned full around toward me and, loosening his tie, remarked, "It's hot as the devil, I want a shave." With that he took his seat. I estimated he had a four-days' growth of beard, the four days he had been gone on the last foray after our men. His face looked burnt, tanned by the sun.

I started to work carefully on the shaving soap. I scraped some slices from the cake, dropped them into the mug, then added a little lukewarm water, and stirred with the brush. The lather soon began to rise. "The fellows in the troop must have just about as much beard as I." I went on stirring up lather. "But we did very well, you know. We caught the leaders. Some of them we brought back dead; others are still alive. But they'll all be dead soon."

"How many did you take?" I asked.

"Fourteen. We had to go pretty far in to find 5
them. But now they're paying for it. And not one will escape; not a single one."

He leaned back in the chair when he saw the brush in my hand, full of lather. I had not yet put the sheet on him. I was certainly flustered. Taking a sheet from the drawer, I tied it around my customer's neck.

He went on talking. He evidently took it for granted that I was on the side of the existing regime.

"The people must have gotten a scare with what happened the other day," he said.

"Yes," I replied, as I finished tying the knot against his nape, which smelt of sweat.

"Good show, wasn't it?" 10

"Very good," I answered, turning my attention now to the brush. The man closed his eyes wearily and awaited the cool caress of the lather. I had never had him so close before. The day he ordered the people to file through the schoolyard to look upon the four rebels hanging there, my path had crossed his briefly. But the sight of those mutilated bodies kept me from paying attention to the face of the man who had been directing it all and whom I now had in my hands.

It was not a disagreeable face, certainly. And the beard, which aged him a bit, was not unbecoming. His name was Torres. Captain Torres.

I started to lay on the first coat of lather. He kept his eyes closed.

"I would love to catch a nap," he said, "but there's a lot to be done this evening."

I lifted the brush and asked, with pretended indifference: "A firing party?"

"Something of the sort," he replied, "but slower."

"All of them?"

"No, just a few."

I went on lathering his face. My hands began to tremble again. The man could not be aware of this, which was lucky for me. But I wished he had not come in. Probably many of our men had seen him enter the shop. And with the enemy in my house I felt a certain responsibility.

Owain and Luned, 1943 (oil on canvas)/Walters, Evan (1893-1951)/GLYNN VIVIAN ART GALLERY/Glynn Vivian Art Gallery, Swansea, Wales/Bridgeman Images

Describe how the power relationship between barber and customer is presented in this painting by Evan Walters. How is this dynamic similar to or different from the relationship between the narrator and Torres in this story?

I would have to shave his beard just like any other, carefully, neatly, just as though he were a good customer, taking heed that not a single pore should emit a drop of blood. Seeing to it that the blade did not slip in the small whorls. Taking care that the skin was left clean, soft, shining, so that when I passed the back of my hand over it not a single hair should be felt. Yes. I was secretly a revolutionary, but at the same time I was a conscientious barber, proud of the way I did my job. And that four-day beard presented a challenge.

I took up the razor, opened the handle wide, releasing the blade, and started to work, downward from one sideburn. The blade responded to perfection. The hair was tough and hard; not very long, but thick. Little by little the skin began to show through. The razor gave its usual sound as it gathered up layers of soap mixed with bits of hair. I paused to wipe it clean, and taking up the strop once more went about improving its edge, for I am a painstaking barber.

The man, who had kept his eyes closed, now opened them, put a hand out from under the sheet, felt of the part of his face that was emerging from the lather, and said to me, "Come at six o'clock this evening to the school."

"Will it be like the other day?" I asked, stiff with horror.

"It may be even better," he replied.

"What are you planning to do?"

"I'm not sure yet. But we'll have a good time."

Once more he leaned back and shut his eyes. I came closer, the razor on high.

"Are you going to punish all of them?" I timidly ventured.

"Yes, all of them."

The lather was drying on his face. I must hurry. Through the mirror, I took a look at the street. It appeared about as usual; there was the grocery shop with two or three customers. Then I glanced at the clock, two-thirty.

The razor kept descending. Now from the other sideburn downward. It was a blue beard, a thick one. He should let it grow like some poets, or some priests. It would suit him well. Many people would not recognize him. And that would be a good thing for him, I thought, as I went gently over all the throat line. At this point you really had to handle your blade skillfully, because the hair, while scantier, tended to fall into small whorls. It was a curly beard. The pores might open, minutely, in this area and let out a tiny drop of blood. A good barber like myself stakes his reputation on not permitting that to happen to any of his customers.

And this was indeed a special customer. How many of ours had he sent to their death? How many had he mutilated? It was best not to think about it. Torres did not know I was his enemy. Neither he nor the others knew it. It was a secret shared by very few, just because that made it possible for me to inform the revolutionaries about Torres's activities in the town and what he planned to do every time he went on one of his raids to hunt down rebels. So it was going to be very difficult to explain how it was that I had him in my hands and then let him go in peace, alive, clean-shaven.

His beard had now almost entirely disappeared. He looked younger, several years younger than when he had come in. I suppose that always happens to men who enter and leave barbershops. Under the strokes of my razor Torres was rejuvenated; yes, because I am a good barber, the best in this town, and I say this in all modesty.

A little more lather here under the chin, on the Adam's apple, right near the great vein. How hot it is! Torres must be sweating just as I am. But he is not afraid. He is a tranquil man, who is not even giving thought to what he will do to his prisoners this evening. I, on the other hand, polishing his skin with this razor but avoiding the drawing of blood, careful with every stroke — I cannot keep my thoughts in order.

Confound the hour he entered my shop! I am a revolutionary but not a murderer. And it would be so easy to kill him. He deserves it. Or does he? No! No one deserves the sacrifice others make in becoming assassins. What is to be gained by it? Nothing. Others and still others keep coming, and the first kill the second, and then these kill the next, and so on until everything becomes a sea of blood. I could cut his throat, so, swish, swish! He would not even

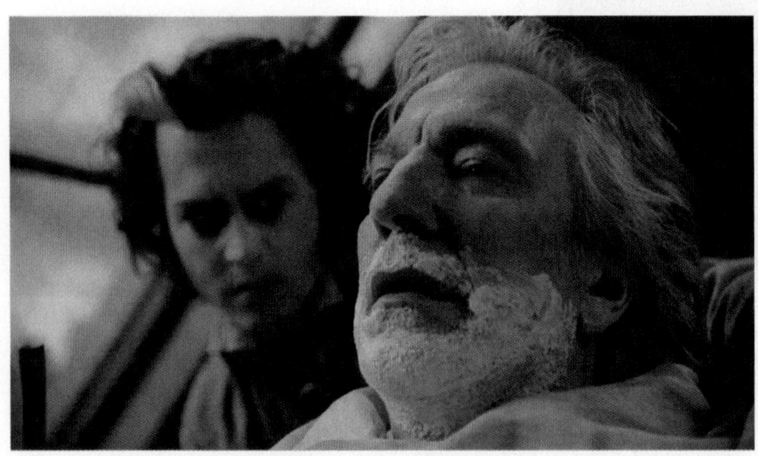

This is a still from the film adaptation of the musical *Sweeney Todd: The Demon Barber of Fleet Street*.

Based on this image, who has the power in this relationship: the barber or his customer? What conveys that power? Is Torres ever in a similar position in this story? Is the narrator?

have time to moan, and with his eyes shut he would not even see the shine of the razor or the gleam in my eye.

But I'm shaking like a regular murderer. From his throat a stream of blood would flow on the sheet, over the chair, down on my hands, onto the floor. I would have to close the door. But the blood would go flowing along the floor, warm, indelible, not to be staunched, until it reached the street like a small scarlet river.

I'm sure that with a good strong blow, a deep cut, he would feel no pain. He would not suffer at all. And what would I do then with the body? Where would I hide it? I would have to flee, leave all this behind, take shelter far away, very far away. But they would follow until they caught up with me. "The murderer of Captain Torres. He slit his throat while he was shaving him. What a cowardly thing to do!"

And others would say, "The avenger of our people. A name to remember" — my name here. "He was the town barber. No one knew he was fighting for our cause."

And so, which will it be? Murderer or hero? My fate hangs on the edge of this razor blade.

I can turn my wrist slightly, put a bit more pressure on the blade, let it sink in. The skin will yield like silk, like rubber, like the strop. There is nothing more tender than a man's skin, and the blood is always there, ready to burst forth. A razor like this cannot fail. It is the best one I have.

But I don't want to be a murderer. No, sir. You came in to be shaved. And I do my work honorably. I don't want to stain my hands with blood. Just with lather, and nothing else. You are an executioner; I am only a barber. Each one to his job. That's it. Each one to his job.

The chin was now clean, polished, soft. The man got up and looked at himself in the glass. He ran his hand over the skin and felt its freshness, its newness.

"Thanks," he said. He walked to the wardrobe for his belt, his pistol, and his cap. I must have been very pale, and I felt my shirt soaked with sweat. Torres finished adjusting his belt buckle, straightened his gun in its holster, and smoothing his hair mechanically, put on his cap. From his trousers pocket he took some coins to pay for the shave. And he started toward the door. On the threshold he stopped for a moment, and turning toward me, he said, "They told me you would kill me. I came to find out if it was true. But it's not easy to kill. I know what I'm talking about." ■

Understanding and Interpreting

1. Describe how the customer, later identified as Captain Torres, behaves when he first enters the barbershop. What do his actions and dialogue reveal about his character?
2. Describe the actions of the narrator, who is never named in the story, before he begins shaving Torres. What do these actions suggest about him?
3. By the end of the story, we know that Torres suspected the narrator all along of opposing him. With this in mind, examine how Torres behaves while he is being shaved. Explain what this illustrates about him.
4. The narrator thinks highly of himself as a barber and takes his profession seriously. How does he demonstrate these qualities in the story? How does the narrator's pride in his work influence the story's outcome?
5. Summarize the ethical dilemma that the narrator faces. What does he imagine might happen if he kills Torres?

6. Ultimately, why does the narrator decide not to kill Torres? Use evidence from the story to support your answer.
7. Based on what you know about Torres, why did he come in for the shave? What evidence from the text supports your interpretation?

Analyzing Language, Style, and Structure

1. **Vocabulary in Context.** When Torres comes into the shop, he puts his holster "on a hook in the wardrobe." What does "wardrobe" mean in this context? How is its meaning similar to or different from other meanings you have encountered?
2. **Skill Focus.** As the narrator imagines killing Torres, he says everything would become a "sea of blood" (par. 35). What does this metaphor accomplish? How does it signal a conflict for the narrator?
3. The first sentence in this story is, "He came in without a word." What effect is created by referring to Captain Torres only as "he" and keeping him unnamed until almost halfway through the story?
4. Look back at paragraphs 3 and 4 and explain how the narrator and Torres use the pronouns "we" and "our" differently. What does this language difference reveal about them?
5. In paragraph 31, Téllez writes, "The razor kept descending." What is unusual about the structure of this sentence? How does it affect our understanding of the situation in the story?
6. When he continues to shave Torres, the narrator says, "I cannot keep my thoughts in order." Reread the paragraph that follows that statement (par. 35). Explain how Téllez uses a variety of syntactical choices to communicate the narrator's difficulty in thinking clearly.
7. What does the narrator mean by the phrase a "regular murderer"? What does this word choice imply about the decision he faces? How are other words or phrases used in this story to describe killers similar to or different from this one?
8. Look back closely at what the narrator says aloud to Torres in the story. Based only on the dialogue, does the narrator reveal his opposition to Torres, or does he hide it successfully? Provide evidence for your response.
9. The reader does not learn until nearly halfway through the story that the narrator is a revolutionary opposed to Torres. Look back, however, at the beginning of the story and identify earlier hints Téllez provides about the narrator's true feelings.

Topics for Composing

1. **Analysis.** What did Torres prove to the narrator about power by choosing to be shaved by his enemy? Use evidence from the story, and especially the dialogue, to support your response.
2. **Argument.** Would the narrator have been justified in killing Torres in this situation? Explain your position with examples from the text as well as your own reasoning.
3. **Connection.** Think about another story, film, novel, videogame, or other text in which a character faces an ethical dilemma similar to the one faced by the narrator of this story. How is that character's approach to that dilemma similar to or different from the barber's approach to his ethical challenge?
4. **Speaking and Listening.** Act out a key scene with a partner. Create a script by gathering all of the dialogue from the scene. Then, add stage directions that describe any actions, facial expressions, gestures, and movements that you think would be appropriate. Deliver your

performance to a small group or your class. Afterward, reflect on how Téllez crafted his story to illustrate the conflict between the two men through dialogue and details.

5. **Research.** You may think it's strange that Torres goes to the barber to get a shave rather than a haircut. However, barbers have taken on many different roles, descriptions of which date back to 5000 B.C.E. Research the history of barbering and draw a connection between the role of the barber in the story and an interesting fact you learned through your research.
6. **Multimodal.** Much of what happens in this story is communicated through dialogue. Choose an important dialogue exchange between Torres and the narrator and create an illustration of the scene. Use speech bubbles to show dialogue. Make sure that gestures and facial expressions help to convey the tone and action.
7. **Creative Writing.** What happens next? Write a short story about the next day when the narrator has to face a fellow revolutionary or someone loyal to Torres.

Ozymandias

Percy Bysshe Shelley

Percy Bysshe Shelley (1792-1822), 1845 (oil on canvas)/Severn, Joseph (1793–1879)/Keats-Shelley Memorial House, Rome, Italy/Bridgeman Images

Percy Bysshe Shelley (1792–1822) was a British poet whose controversial work led to his rejection by his family as well as much of British society at the time. Undaunted by those who claimed his work was inappropriate, Shelley continued to write prolifically until his death just before his thirtieth birthday, when he drowned while sailing off the coast of Italy.

KEY CONTEXT In this poem, the speaker relates the account of a traveler who encounters the ruins of Ozymandias, almost entirely buried in the sands of a vast desert. Ozymandias, more commonly known as Ramses II, was an Egyptian who ruled during the thirteenth century B.C.E.

I met a traveller from an antique land,
Who said "Two vast and trunkless legs of stone
Stand in the desert. . . . Near them, on the sand,
Half sunk a shattered visage[1] lies, whose frown,
And wrinkled lip, and sneer of cold command,
Tell that its sculptor well those passions read
Which yet survive, stamped on these lifeless things,
The hand that mocked them, and the heart that fed;
And on the pedestal, these words appear:
My name is Ozymandias, King of Kings;
Look on my Works, ye Mighty, and despair!
Nothing beside remains. Round the decay
Of that colossal Wreck, boundless and bare
The lone and level sands stretch far away."

[1]A person's face — Eds.

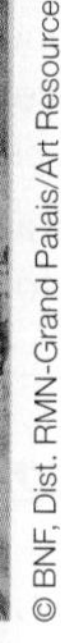

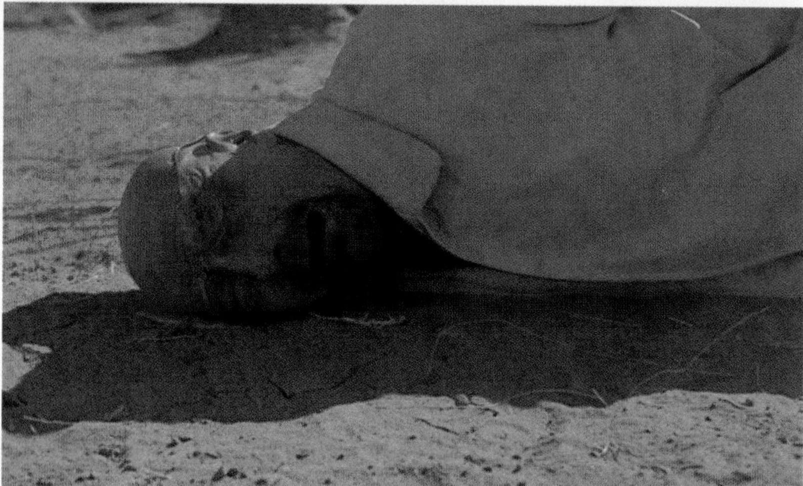

Consider these two images. The first is from the archaeological dig that unearthed the statue of Ramses II referred to in this poem. The second is a still image from a television show called *Breaking Bad*, about the rise and fall of a drug kingpin. The episode from which this image is taken is called "Ozymandias."

How do these images — one from real life, the other from popular culture — reinforce ideas offered in Shelley's poem? How are they similar and different? What additional ideas do these images convey that Shelley does not address in his poem?

Understanding and Interpreting

1. Based on the description of Ozymandias's expression, what can you infer about the kind of ruler Ozymandias was?
2. Explain the meaning of the inscription on the statue — "Look on my Works, ye Mighty, and despair!" What do these words reveal about how Ozymandias might have viewed his own power?

3. All that remains of Ozymandias's "works" are a decaying "colossal wreck" (l. 13) in the desert. How does the description of these remains provide commentary on the nature of human power?

Analyzing Language, Style, and Structure

1. **Vocabulary in Context.** The first line of the poem reads, "I met a traveller from an antique land." What is the meaning of the word "antique" in this context? How is that meaning similar to and different from other uses of the word that you have encountered?
2. **Skill Focus.** Shelley personifies the statue to convey how Ozymandias ruled: "The hand that mocked them, and the heart that fed" (l. 8). How does this personification help Shelley to give his reader an impression of Ozymandias?
3. The first line of the poem begins with "I," signaling a first-person narrator, who introduces a "traveller from an antique land." That traveler delivers the remaining lines, which form the bulk of the poem. What is the effect of this narrative structure? How does it help convey the meaning of the poem?
4. Identify the rhyming structure of the poem. Explain how those rhymes connect words and ideas across the poem.

Topics for Composing

1. **Analysis.** Overall, what does Shelley suggest about the nature and legacy of power? What poetic elements help him to communicate this idea?
2. **Argument.** Ozymandias was an all-powerful leader who thought his influence would last forever. In today's world, a powerful politician can find herself powerless after the next election, and a movie star can go from leading to supporting roles. Why does power not seem to last? Refer to examples from history, culture, sports, entertainment, or your own experiences to support your position.
3. **Connection.** Unchecked pride, or *hubris*, is the subject of many works of literature. Choose something you have read, or a movie you have seen, in which hubris plays a significant role. Discuss the role and significance of hubris in the text you've chosen. Explain how it relates to this poem.
4. **Connection.** Ozymandias is the name of a character in *Watchmen* (1986-1987), a comic book series that has been adapted into a movie (2009) and an HBO series (2019). Read the novel or watch one of its adaptations. Explain why the creators may have named the character Ozymandias.
5. **Speaking and Listening.** Poetry is often intended to be read aloud. Working with a partner, take turns reading "Ozymandias" aloud to each other, two or three times each. Discuss how reading it aloud affected your understanding of the poem.
6. **Research.** Conduct research on Ramses II and the archaeological dig that inspired Shelley to write the poem. Why were Ramses II and the ruins of his statue an appropriate subject for the ideas that Shelley was trying to communicate?
7. **Creative Writing.** Imagine if Ozymandias were able to see his own statue wearing down to nothing in the desert. Write a new inscription on its pedestal to reflect that awareness. Explain why you chose this inscription. What is it intended to reveal?

central text

The Tragedy of Macbeth

William Shakespeare

GL Archive/Alamy

William Shakespeare (1564–1616) was an English poet, actor, and playwright who is considered to be one of the greatest writers in the English language and the world's preeminent dramatist. He is credited with 38 plays, 154 sonnets, and two long narrative poems. Little is known of his life aside from the fact that he married Anne Hathaway when he was eighteen, worked as an actor-playwright in London, and retired in 1613. Shakespeare's plays fall into four principal categories: early comedies (1585–1594); more sophisticated comedies and histories (1595–1599); the great tragedies (1599–1607); and the final phase (1608–1613). His most accomplished works — including *Hamlet* (1601), *Othello* (1603), *King Lear* (1605), and *Macbeth* (1606) — belong to the third period.

KEY CONTEXT Written around 1606, *The Tragedy of Macbeth* is loosely based on the life of Mac Bethad, king of Scotland from 1040 to 1057. The real Macbeth killed his predecessor Duncan I, and was in turn killed by Duncan's son Malcolm III. Events such as these were common in eleventh-century feudal Scotland; of the fourteen kings who reigned between 943 and 1097, ten were murdered. However, the real Scottish king bears little resemblance to the character in Shakespeare's play. Shakespeare was a playwright, after all, and his goals differed from those of a historian.

One of those goals was writing a play that Shakespeare's patron, the newly crowned King James I, would enjoy. King James I had ascended to the throne of England in 1603, and Shakespeare began writing *Macbeth* soon after. King James I came from the same families who led to the real Macbeth's downfall. The play's acknowledgment of this fact flattered the new king of England. It was also well known that King James I was fascinated by witchcraft (he even wrote a book on demonology), which is probably why witches play a mysterious and important role in this play.

Additionally, many people of Shakespeare's time believed in a concept called the Great Chain of Being, with God at the top, followed by angelic beings, humans, animals, plants, and finally, minerals. Within these categories were further categories. For instance, animals were arranged according to the food chain, and humans were arranged with kings at the top, then nobles, then peasants. *Macbeth*, in many ways, is a story of what happens when the Great Chain of Being is broken.

List of Characters

THREE WITCHES

DUNCAN King of Scotland

MALCOLM Duncan's elder son, later King of Scotland

CAPTAIN

LENNOX a thane

ROSS a thane
MACBETH Thane of Glamis, later Thane of Cawdor, later King of Scotland
BANQUO a thane
ANGUS a thane
LADY MACBETH Countess of Glamis, later Countess of Cawdor, later Queen of Scotland
ATTENDANT
FLEANCE Banquo's son
PORTER in Macbeth's household
MACDUFF Thane of Fife
DONALDBAIN Duncan's younger son
OLD MAN
TWO MURDERERS
SERVANT
THIRD MURDERER
HECATE goddess of the moon and of sorcery
A LORD a Scot, opposed to Macbeth
FIRST APPARITION an armed Head
SECOND APPARITION a bloody Child
THIRD APPARITION a Child crowned
LADY MACDUFF Countess of Fife
SON to Macduff and Lady Macduff
MESSENGERS
TWO MURDERERS who attack Lady Macduff and her Son
DOCTOR at the English court
DOCTOR OF PHYSIC at the Scottish court
WAITING-GENTLEWOMAN who attends Lady Macbeth
MENTEITH a thane opposed to Macbeth
CAITHNESS a thane opposed to Macbeth
SERVANT to Macbeth
SEYTON gentleman loyal to Macbeth
SIWARD general in the Anglo-Scottish forces
YOUNG SIWARD Siward's son, in the Anglo-Scottish forces

Silent characters
Attendants in Duncan's entourage
Musicians
Torch-bearers
Sewer
Servants and Attendants
Ghost of Banquo
Three Witches, accompanying Hecate
Eight kings
Drummers and bearers of colors (flags)
Soldiers

Act 1 Scene 1

Thunder and lightning. Enter three WITCHES

FIRST WITCH When shall we three meet again?
In thunder, lightning, or in rain?
SECOND WITCH When the hurly-burly's done,
When the battle's lost, and won.
THIRD WITCH That will be ere the set of sun.
FIRST WITCH Where the place?
SECOND WITCH Upon the heath.
THIRD WITCH There to meet with Macbeth.
FIRST WITCH I come, Graymalkin.
SECOND WITCH Paddock calls.
THIRD WITCH Anon.
ALL Fair is foul, and foul is fair,
Hover through the fog and filthy air.
Exeunt

Act 1, Scene 2

Alarum within. Enter King [DUNCAN,] MALCOLM, DONALDBAIN, LENNOX, *with Attendants, meeting a bleeding* CAPTAIN

DUNCAN What bloody man is that? He can report,
As seemeth by his plight, of the revolt
The newest state.
MALCOLM This is the sergeant
Who like a good and hardy soldier fought
'Gainst my captivity. Hail, brave friend;
Say to the king the knowledge of the broil
As thou didst leave it.

Act 1, Scene 1. 0. **sd [stage directions]** WITCHES: Only at 1.3.5 does the dialogue use the word "witch"; elsewhere they are named and name themselves "weïrd sisters," although "Witches" appears in many stage directions. Male actors often play these parts. 3. **hurly-burly:** turmoil, tumult, especially of rebellion or insurrection. 4. **battle:** conflict; could also mean body of troops composing an entire army or one of its main divisions, a meaning appropriate to the slaughter soon described. 7. **heath:** wilderness; uninhabited and uncultivated ground. 9. **Graymalkin:** a cat's name. Cats and toads (see note 10), as well as dogs, rats, and some insects, were likely to be witches' "familiars": non-human agents of their deeds. 10. **Paddock:** toad. 13. **fog:** an invitation to the audience's imagination, since fog effects were not possible in early productions, though smoke (from burning resin) was. 13. **filthy:** murky, thick.

CAPTAIN Doubtful it stood,
As two spent swimmers that do cling together
And choke their art. The merciless Macdonald—
Worthy to be a rebel, for to that
The multiplying villainies of nature
Do swarm upon him—from the Western Isles
Of kerns and galloglasses is supplied,
And Fortune on his damnèd quarrel smiling,
Showed like a rebel's whore. But all's too weak,
For brave Macbeth—well he deserves that
name—
Disdaining Fortune, with his brandished steel,
Which smoked with bloody execution,
Like Valour's minion carved out his passage
Till he faced the slave,
Which ne'er shook hands, nor bade farewell to
him,
Till he unseamed him from the nave to th'chaps
And fixed his head upon our battlements.

DUNCAN O valiant cousin, worthy gentleman.

CAPTAIN As whence the sun 'gins his reflection,
Shipwrecking storms and direful thunders,
So from that spring whence comfort seemed
to come,
Discomfort swells. Mark, King of Scotland, mark,
No sooner justice had, with valour armed,
Compelled these skipping kerns to trust their
heels,
But the Norwegian lord, surveying vantage,
With furbished arms and new supplies of men
Began a fresh assault.

DUNCAN Dismayed not this our captains,
Macbeth and Banquo?

CAPTAIN Yes, as sparrows, eagles, or the hare,
the lion.
If I say sooth, I must report they were
As cannons over-charged with double cracks;
So they doubly redoubled strokes upon the foe.
Except they meant to bathe in reeking wounds
Or memorise another Golgotha,
I cannot tell.
But I am faint, my gashes cry for help.

DUNCAN So well thy words become thee as thy
wounds
They smack of honour both. Go get him
surgeons.

[Exit Captain, attended]

Enter ROSS *and* ANGUS

Who comes here?

Act 1, Scene 2. This scene condenses three conflicts: Macdonald's rebellion and invasions by Sweno and by Canute. Shakespeare (or another author) leaves the third vaguest, perhaps because James VI and I's wife Queen Anne was Danish. 0. **sd *Alarum*:** a call to arms; a warning to give notice of danger. 0. **sd *within*:** i.e., offstage. In the Jacobean theater, "within" indicates the tiring-house, which formed the back wall of the stage. The actors entered from and exited to this space, where they also changed their costumes. 2. **the revolt:** Macdonald's rebellion occurred in Lochquhaber, modern Lochaber, the district including Ben Nevis in south Inverness-shire, many miles distant from Fife. 3. **newest state:** latest condition. 5. **captivity:** capture. 6. **broil:** tumult, quarrel. 8–9. **two . . . art:** i.e., two exhausted ("spent") swimmers grasp each other ("cling together"), hoping to survive, but each thus defeats the other's skill ("choke their art") and both, paradoxically, drown. 9. **Macdonald:** The name means "son of Donald." 10. **for to that:** to that end; "that" = Macdonald's "worth" as a "rebel." 11. **multiplying villainies of nature:** proliferating evils within creation. 12. **swarm:** congregate, gather thickly. 12. **Western Isles:** the Hebrides. 13. **kerns and galloglasses:** fierce soldiers. 14–15. **Fortune . . . whore:** Proverbially, "Fortune is a strumpet." 14. **quarrel:** dispute. 15. **rebel's whore:** i.e., Fortune is sexually promiscuous as her lover, Macdonald, is politically errant. 15. **all's:** all is; all his efforts are. 18. **smoked:** sprayed (blood), perhaps also the effect of steaming with blood. 19. **minion:** dearest friend, favorite child. The word was, however, often used opprobriously (for paramour or mistress) and could always have some negative connotation. 19. **carved out his passage:** sliced his way. Cutting a route through living flesh foreshadows the revelation of Macduff's Caesarian birth and his action in the play. 20–22. **he . . . slave . . . him . . . he . . . him:** The referents are not clear until Duncan acknowledges Macbeth's victory (24). Then we understand that "slave" and "him" (20, 22) refer to Macdonald, and "he" (20, 22) is Macbeth. 21. **shook hands:** Elizabethans customarily shook hands upon meeting as well as parting. 22. **unseamed him:** ripped him open. 22. **nave:** navel (umbilicus), probably; this line is the sole support for "nave" = navel in the *Oxford English Dictionary*. Both "nave" and "navel" could also mean central part or block of a wheel. Figuratively, then, "nave" may here refer to the crotch rather than the navel per se. 22. **chaps:** jaws. 25–28. **As . . . swells:** A complicated and ambiguous passage, but the main meaning is clear: in circumstances that seem positive, a threat unexpectedly appears. 25. **'gins:** begins. 25. **reflection:** shining, return, regression. 26. **direful:** dreadful, terrible. 26. **thunders:** The verb "come" is understood here. 28. **Mark:** heed, pay attention. 29. **valour:** The word recalls 19 and makes Duncan analogous to personified Justice, Macbeth to Valor. 30. **skipping:** leaping in fright. 30. **trust their heels:** run away. 31. **the Norwegian lord:** Sweno (Svend Estridsen), who invaded in 1041 CE; Sweno's invasion began victoriously in Fife and extended over a period of time. 31. **surveying:** observing, perceiving. 31. **vantage:** advantage, benefit. 32. **furbished:** renovated, revived; fresh, new. 32. **supplies:** additional troops. 35. **Yes . . . lion:** In each pair the first is traditionally weak or fearful, the second, strong and brave. The captain speaks ironically: Banquo and Macbeth were not "dismayed." 36. **sooth:** truth. 36. **report:** tell, state. The word is also a pun on the sound ("report") of the cannons as they fire. 37–38. **As . . . foe:** These lines seem to describe cannon loaded with four (or eight?) times the usual amount of powder and shot, conditions that would have destroyed most Renaissance weapons, but the language echoes the play's insistence on doubling and doubleness. 37. **cracks:** cannon-shot. 38. **So:** thus. 38. **doubly redoubled strokes:** eightfold blows. 39. **Except:** unless. 39. **reeking:** steaming or smoking with blood. 40. **memorise another Golgotha:** commemorate a second Calvary (i.e., create a place like

extending beyond the text

Macbeth is often reimagined in a modern context. The witches have taken several different forms in these modern interpretations. Look closely at these three examples. The first is from a 2010 adaptation of the play, set in Stalinist Russia; the witches are nurses in the combat hospital. The second is from a 2005 BBC production, in which Macbeth runs a fancy restaurant and the witches are sanitation workers. The third is from a 2006 film version that takes place during a violent gang war in Australia.

extending beyond the text

Album/Alamy Stock Photo

What is the effect of reimagining the witches in these ways? How are these representations similar to or different from each other? If you were staging a production of *Macbeth* in a modern setting, how would you present the witches? Why?

MALCOLM The worthy Thane of Ross.
LENNOX What a haste looks through his eyes! So should he look
That seems to speak things strange.
ROSS God save the king.
DUNCAN Whence cam'st thou, worthy thane?
ROSS From Fife, great king,
Where the Norwegian banners flout the sky
And fan our people cold.
Norway himself, with terrible numbers,
Assisted by that most disloyal traitor,
The Thane of Cawdor, began a dismal conflict,
Till that Bellona's bridegroom, lapped in proof,
Confronted him with self-comparisons,
Point against point, rebellious arm 'gainst arm,
Curbing his lavish spirit. And to conclude,
The victory fell on us —
DUNCAN Great happiness! —

---

that where Jesus was crucified). 42. **gashes cry for help:** Shakespeare and other dramatists often represent wounds as mouths. Here, the captain's wounds are speech, as Macbeth's words to his wife (in 1.5) and hers to him (in 1.7) will also be speeches, which are or lead to wounds. 44. **smack:** savor, taste; mixed figuratively with the sharp noise the lips make in tasting; hence, "smack" = the sound of the wounds' words. 45. **Thane:** head of a clan; a Scottish rank. A thane owed fealty to the king rather than to another noble and held lands directly from the king. 46. **looks through:** is visible through. 47. **seems:** appears. Ross has the appearance of a person whose looks portend strange matters. 48–58. **From Fife . . . fell on us:** Ross's narrative recommences the battle. 48. **Fife:** county on the east coast of Scotland between the Firths of Forth and Tay. 49. **flout:** mock, jeer. The banners mock by waving, as "fan" (50) makes clear. 51. **Norway:** the King of Norway. 54. **Bellona:** Roman goddess of war. 54. **bride-groom:** i.e., Macbeth. 54. **lapped:** enfolded, wrapped. 54. **proof:** armor. 55. **self-comparisons:** comparisons with himself [Macbeth, "Bellona's bridegroom" (54)]. Cawdor is forced into an unequal competition ["a dismal conflict" (53)] with Macbeth, but the phrase "self-comparisons" implies that some common basis exists for comparing the hero and his enemy. 56. **Point:** sword tip. 56. **point, rebellious:** No matter how punctuated, the line will always and ambiguously half-refer to Macbeth as "rebellious." Some editors identify "him" as Norway, but "rebellious" better suits the native Cawdor than the invading, and foreign, King of Norway. 57. **Curbing:** restraining, controlling. A rider controls a horse through the "curb," part

ROSS That now Sweno,
The Norways' king, craves composition.
Nor would we deign him burial of his men
Till he disbursèd at Saint Colm's Inch
Ten thousand dollars to our general use.

DUNCAN No more that Thane of Cawdor shall deceive
Our bosom interest. Go pronounce his present death
And with his former title greet Macbeth.

ROSS I'll see it done.

DUNCAN What he hath lost, noble Macbeth hath won.

Exeunt

Act 1, Scene 3

Thunder. Enter the three WITCHES

FIRST WITCH Where hast thou been, sister?

SECOND WITCH Killing swine.

THIRD WITCH Sister, where thou?

FIRST WITCH A sailor's wife had chestnuts in her lap
And munched, and munched, and munched. "Give me," quoth I.
"Aroint thee, witch," the rump-fed runnion cries.
Her husband's to Aleppo gone, master o'th'Tiger:
But in a sieve I'll thither sail,
And like a rat without a tail,
I'll do, I'll do, and I'll do.

SECOND WITCH I'll give thee a wind.

FIRST WITCH Thou'rt kind.

Royal Shakespeare Company Collection/Bridgeman Images

Royal Shakespeare Company Collection/Bridgeman Images

Here are two paintings depicting Macbeth and Banquo's meeting with the Weird Sisters.

What does each painting suggest about the witches and their power? How are the representations similar and different? Based on evidence from the text, which depiction do you prefer, either because it is most faithful to the text, or because it presents a compelling interpretation?

---

of the bridle and bit. 57. **lavish:** unrestrained, impetuous. 58. **Great happiness!:** Duncan interrupts Ross's report extrametrically. 59. **Norways':** Norwegians'. 59. **craves composition:** i.e., seeks to make peace, surrenders. 60. **deign:** condescend to grant. 61. **Saint Colm's Inch:** Inchcolm, an island in the Firth of Forth near Edinburgh. 62. **dollars:** the English name for German *thalers*, large silver coins. 64. **bosom interest:** intimate or confidential concern. 64. **present:** instant, immediate. 65. **former title:** i.e., Thane of Cawdor, but Ross has most recently named Cawdor "most disloyal traitor" (52), as Macbeth will soon prove also. 67. **lost . . . won:** Transfer of the title (and the treason) from Cawdor to Macbeth exemplifies how something may be both lost and won, the witches' paradox (1.1.4). The line varies the proverb "No man loses but another wins."

Act 1, Scene 3. 2. **Killing swine:** English witches were often accused of harming domestic animals. 5. **Aroint:** The word's meaning is unknown, but contextually it seems to mean "avaunt! be gone!" 5. **rump-fed:** a puzzling phrase whose literal meaning is "fed on rump." "Rump" = the hind quarter of both humans and the animals they eat; "rump-fed" might also mean fattened in the rump, lecherous. From the witch's point of view, therefore, it may be that the sailor's wife is enviable, selfish, lecherous, and (possibly) sexually satisfied. Perhaps alliteration (rump, runnion) is more important than denotation. 5. **runnion:** abusive term applied to a woman. 6. **Aleppo:** inland trading city in northern Syria, part of the Turkish empire from 1516 to 1918. Its port was Iskanderun. 6. **master:** captain, commanding officer. 6. **Tiger:** common name for a ship. 7. **sieve:** Sailing in sieves was supposed to be a common witch practice; it was one of the accusations against the Scottish witches King James personally

THIRD WITCH And I another.
FIRST WITCH I myself have all the other,
And the very ports they blow,
All the quarters that they know
I'th'shipman's card.
I'll drain him dry as hay:
Sleep shall neither night nor day
Hang upon his penthouse lid;
He shall live a man forbid.
Weary sennights nine times nine,
Shall he dwindle, peak, and pine.
Though his bark cannot be lost,
Yet it shall be tempest-tossed.
Look what I have.
SECOND WITCH Show me, show me.
FIRST WITCH Here I have a pilot's thumb,
Wrecked as homeward he did come.

Drum within

THIRD WITCH A drum, a drum;
Macbeth doth come.
ALL The weïrd sisters, hand in hand,
Posters of the sea and land,
Thus do go, about, about,
Thrice to thine, and thrice to mine,
And thrice again, to make up nine.
Peace, the charm's wound up.

Enter MACBETH *and* BANQUO

MACBETH So foul and fair a day I have not seen.
BANQUO How far is't called to Forres? What are these,
So withered and so wild in their attire,
That look not like th'inhabitants o'th'earth,
And yet are on't? — Live you, or are you aught
That man may question? You seem to understand me,
By each at once her choppy finger laying
Upon her skinny lips; you should be women,
And yet your beards forbid me to interpret
That you are so.
MACBETH Speak if you can: what are you?
FIRST WITCH All hail Macbeth, hail to thee, Thane of Glamis.
SECOND WITCH All hail Macbeth, hail to thee, Thane of Cawdor.
THIRD WITCH All hail Macbeth, that shalt be king hereafter.
BANQUO Good sir, why do you start and seem to fear
Things that do sound so fair? — I'th'name of truth
Are ye fantastical, or that indeed
Which outwardly ye show? My noble partner
You greet with present grace and great prediction
Of noble having and of royal hope
That he seems rapt withal. To me you speak not.
If you can look into the seeds of time

---

interrogated in 1590–1591. 9. **do:** act; fornicate. 14. **the very ports they blow:** i.e., even places of refuge ("ports") cannot escape the winds' ferocity. 15. **quarters:** geographical directions. 16. **I'th'shipman's card:** Although the witches speak a distinctive meter and irregular rhyme, this line is unusually short, and another line, rhyming with "card," may have been omitted. "Card" refers to a chart or circular piece of stiff paper (the "mariner's card" or "card of the sea" showing the customary 32 points of the compass). 17. **drain him:** If the first witch intends to be a succubus, her demonic sexual intercourse [see "do" (9)] will exhaust her sailor-victim. 19. **penthouse lid:** eyelid. The image derives from analogy between the eyebrow and the projecting second story ("penthouse") of many Elizabethan buildings. 20. **forbid:** cursed. 21. **sennights:** weeks. 22. **peak, and pine:** waste away and languish (virtual synonyms with "dwindle"). 23. **bark:** small ship. 27. **sd *Drum within*:** a conventional Jacobean way to introduce an important martial character. 30. **weïrd:** claiming the supernatural power of dealing with fate or destiny. 31. **Posters:** speedy travelers. 33. **to thine . . . to mine:** in your direction . . . in my direction. The witches here perform some dance, formal movements, or gestures that bind each individual into the group. 34. **nine:** An action is repeated three times for each witch. 35. **wound up:** placed in readiness. The figurative use probably derives from tightening the strings on a musical instrument, but the witches may have "wound themselves up" in some stage movement (see note 33). The phrase could also mean "concluded." 36. **foul and fair:** meteorologically unpleasant and militarily successful. Macbeth's words echo the witches' (1.1.12). 37. **How . . . Forres?:** How distant is Forres reckoned to be? This is a Scottish expression. 37. **Forres:** town east of Inverness. 42–43. **By each . . . lips:** The witches silence Banquo with eerily synchronized gestures. 42. **choppy:** chapped, cracked by wind and weather. 43. **should be:** look as if you ought to be. 46. **All hail:** Shakespeare elsewhere associates this phrase with Judas's betrayal of Jesus, as do his contemporaries. 46. **Glamis:** Meter sometimes requires a disyllable (Gla-miss); elsewhere, modern productions often employ the modern monosyllable, "Glahms." 48. **king:** For the audience, only this title is a surprise, because we know Duncan has already awarded Cawdor's title to Macbeth (1.2.65); theatrically, the witches' apparent foreknowledge is minimized. 49. **start:** recoil, flinch, make a nervous gesture or movement. 49–50. **fear . . . fair:** Alliteration ("start," "seem," "sound"; "fear," "fair") strikes the ear, but the evocative, morally puzzling wordplay on fear/fair is based on antithesis, not identity, between "fear" and "fair." Compare the contrasts of "foul" and "fair" (36 above and 1.1.12) and of "fear" and "foully" (see 3.1.2–3). 51. **fantastical:** imaginary, products of (our) fantasy. 53. **present grace:** immediate favor. 54. **noble having . . . royal hope:** i.e., new title of honor and hoped-for title of king. 54. **having:** possession. 55. **rapt:** entranced. 56. **seeds of time:** sources of the

And say which grain will grow and which will not,
Speak then to me, who neither beg nor fear
Your favours nor your hate.

FIRST WITCH Hail.

SECOND WITCH Hail.

THIRD WITCH Hail.

FIRST WITCH Lesser than Macbeth, and greater.

SECOND WITCH Not so happy, yet much happier.

THIRD WITCH Thou shalt get kings, though thou be none.
So all hail Macbeth and Banquo.

FIRST WITCH Banquo and Macbeth, all hail.

MACBETH Stay, you imperfect speakers. Tell me more.
By Finel's death, I know I am Thane of Glamis,
But how of Cawdor? The Thane of Cawdor lives
A prosperous gentleman, and to be king
Stands not within the prospect of belief,
No more than to be Cawdor. Say from whence
You owe this strange intelligence, or why
Upon this blasted heath you stop our way
With such prophetic greeting? Speak, I charge you.

Witches vanish

BANQUO The earth hath bubbles, as the water has,
And these are of them. Whither are they vanished?

MACBETH Into the air, and what seemed corporal,
Melted, as breath into the wind. Would they had stayed.

BANQUO Were such things here as we do speak about?
Or have we eaten on the insane root,
That takes the reason prisoner?

MACBETH Your children shall be kings.

BANQUO You shall be king.

MACBETH And Thane of Cawdor too: went it not so?

BANQUO To th'selfsame tune and words — who's here?

Enter ROSS *and* ANGUS

ROSS The king hath happily received, Macbeth,
The news of thy success, and when he reads
Thy personal venture in the rebels' sight,
His wonders and his praises do contend
Which should be thine or his. Silenced with that,
In viewing o'er the rest o'th'selfsame day,
He finds thee in the stout Norwegian ranks,
Nothing afeard of what thyself didst make,
Strange images of death. As thick as tale
Came post with post, and every one did bear
Thy praises in his kingdom's great defence,
And poured them down before him.

ANGUS We are sent
To give thee from our royal master thanks;
Only to herald thee into his sight,
Not pay thee.

ROSS And for an earnest of a greater honour,
He bade me, from him, call thee Thane of Cawdor:
In which addition, hail most worthy thane,
For it is thine.

BANQUO What, can the devil speak true?

MACBETH The Thane of Cawdor lives. Why do you dress me
In borrowed robes?

ANGUS Who was the thane, lives yet,
But under heavy judgement bears that life
Which he deserves to lose.
Whether he was combined with those of Norway,

---

future. 58–59. **neither . . . hate:** i.e., Banquo neither begs your favors nor fears your hate. 65. **get:** beget, father; perhaps also acquire, obtain. 69. **Finel:** Historically, Finel (or Finley or Findlaech) was Macbeth's father. 72. **prospect:** mental looking forward, consideration of something future. 74. **intelligence:** news, information. 75. **blasted:** blighted; supernatural agency or planetary influence may be implied. 76. **charge:** command, order. 79. **corporal:** material, physical, having a body. 82. **on:** of. 82. **insane:** causing insanity. 86. **selfsame tune:** identical meaning. 88. **reads:** understands, discerns. 90–91. **His wonders . . . that:** Duncan, at once admiring Macbeth's actions and praising them, finds himself suspended between silence and speech, awe and the impulse to reward. 92. **selfsame:** identical, same. 93. **stout:** valiant, brave. 94. **Nothing afeard:** not at all afraid. 95–96. **As thick . . . with post:** messenger after messenger came with tale after tale. 102. **earnest:** foretaste, pledge. 104. **addition:** title. 107. **Who:** he who. 110. **Whether:** whichever of the two. 111. **line:** reinforce, fortify. There may be figurative overtones of lining a piece of clothing (the "robes" of 107). 112. **vantage:** additional amount (e.g., of soldiers, weapons, money). 112. **both:** i.e., the

Or did line the rebel with hidden help
And vantage, or that with both he laboured
In his country's wrack, I know not,
But treasons capital, confessed and proved,
Have overthrown him.

MACBETH [*Aside*] Glamis, and Thane of Cawdor:
The greatest is behind. — Thanks for your pains. —
[*To Banquo*] Do you not hope your children shall be kings,
When those that gave the Thane of Cawdor to me
Promised no less to them?

BANQUO That trusted home,
Might yet enkindle you unto the crown,
Besides the Thane of Cawdor. But 'tis strange,
And oftentimes, to win us to our harm,
The instruments of darkness tell us truths;
Win us with honest trifles, to betray's
In deepest consequence. —
Cousins, a word, I pray you.

MACBETH [*Aside*] Two truths are told,
As happy prologues to the swelling act
Of the imperial theme. — I thank you, gentlemen. —
This supernatural soliciting
Cannot be ill, cannot be good. If ill,
Why hath it given me earnest of success,
Commencing in a truth? I am Thane of Cawdor.
If good, why do I yield to that suggestion,
Whose horrid image doth unfix my hair
And make my seated heart knock at my ribs
Against the use of nature? Present fears
Are less than horrible imaginings.
My thought, whose murder yet is but fantastical,
Shakes so my single state of man that function
Is smothered in surmise, and nothing is,
But what is not.

BANQUO Look how our partner's rapt.

MACBETH If chance will have me king, why chance may crown me
Without my stir.

BANQUO New honours come upon him
Like our strange garments, cleave not to their mould,
But with the aid of use.

MACBETH Come what come may,
Time and the hour runs through the roughest day.

BANQUO Worthy Macbeth, we stay upon your leisure.

MACBETH Give me your favour. My dull brain was wrought
With things forgotten. Kind gentlemen, your pains

Norwegian invaders and secret, native help. 113. **wrack:** ruin, overthrow. 114. **capital:** mortal. Cawdor's proven treason merits death. 116. **behind:** in the past but also possibly still to come. In the former sense, Macbeth regards as "greatest" the first two titles (Glamis, Cawdor) the sisters used (46–47); in the latter possible sense, the kingship ["king hereafter" (48)] is greatest. 118. **those that gave:** Macbeth understands the sisters, not Duncan, to be the source of his new title. 119. **home:** completely, fully(?). 120. **enkindle:** inflame with desire. 124. **betray's:** betray us. 125. **deepest consequence:** gravest (or weightiest) outcome. Banquo contrasts a sequence of "trifles" to an unexpectedly grim conclusion. 127. **prologues:** preliminary events. Theatrically, "prologues" are actors (like the sisters or Ross and Angus) who speak before a play (or an "act" of one) begins. 127. **swelling:** expanding, growing. With "act," "swelling" might refer to the number of actors who enter after a prologue has spoken and to the number of people who attend upon a king, as opposed to a thane (see next note). 128. **the imperial theme:** the subject or topic of empery (= becoming not "emperor," but king); "theme" could also have the more active meaning of a subject that causes action, so "imperial theme" might refer not only to the topic of becoming king, but also to the actions required of one who would be king. 128. **I thank you, gentlemen:** Macbeth again (see 116) interrupts himself, acknowledging Ross and Angus, perhaps in order to conceal his self-communing. 129. **soliciting:** incitement. 133–34. **suggestion, / Whose horrid image:** The witches' words ("suggestion") have helped create a terrifying mental picture ("image"). 134. **unfix my hair:** make my hair stand on end (in fear). 135. **seated:** fixed in position, firm-set. 136. **use:** ordinary course, usual condition or state. 138. **My thought, whose murder:** The distorted grammar personifies Macbeth's "thought" as a being who is murdered by the self, but also suggests Macbeth's intended human victim, Duncan. 139. **single state:** unitary condition, singular existence, but also perhaps weak condition. 139–41. **function . . . is not:** all powers of action are oppressed and crushed by one overwhelming image in the mind, and nothing is present to me but that which is really future. 139. **function:** activity, physical movement. 141. **rapt:** enraptured, entranced. 143. **stir:** movement; agitation. 144. **strange:** unfamiliar (to us). 144. **cleave:** cling, adhere. 144. **mould:** body. 145. **Come what come may:** Let what happens happen; a proverb. 146. **Time . . . roughest day:** Proverbially, "The longest day has an end." 146. **roughest:** stormiest, most tempestuous. 147. **stay upon your leisure:** await your time, wait until you are unoccupied; the latter meaning emphasizes Macbeth's inattention. 148. **favour:** indulgence. Macbeth excuses his preoccupation. 148. **wrought:** agitated, stirred, worked up by. 150–51. **registered . . . leaf:** The image is of a

Are registered where every day I turn
The leaf to read them. Let us toward the king.
[*To Banquo*] Think upon what hath chanced and at more time,
The interim having weighed it, let us speak
Our free hearts each to other.

BANQUO Very gladly.

MACBETH Till then, enough. — Come, friends.

Exeunt

Act 1, Scene 4

Flourish. Enter King [DUNCAN], LENNOX, MALCOLM, DONALDBAIN, *and Attendants*

DUNCAN Is execution done on Cawdor, or not
Those in commission yet returned?

MALCOLM My liege,
They are not yet come back. But I have spoke
With one that saw him die, who did report
That very frankly he confessed his treasons,
Implored your highness' pardon, and set forth
A deep repentance. Nothing in his life
Became him like the leaving it. He died
As one that had been studied in his death,
To throw away the dearest thing he owed
As 'twere a careless trifle.

DUNCAN There's no art
To find the mind's construction in the face.
He was a gentleman on whom I built
An absolute trust.

Enter MACBETH, BANQUO, ROSS, *and* ANGUS

O worthiest cousin,
The sin of my ingratitude even now
Was heavy on me. Thou art so far before,
That swiftest wing of recompense is slow
To overtake thee. Would thou hadst less deserved,
That the proportion both of thanks and payment
Might have been mine. Only I have left to say,
More is thy due than more than all can pay.

MACBETH The service and the loyalty I owe,
In doing it, pays itself. Your highness' part
Is to receive our duties, and our duties
Are to your throne and state, children and servants,
Which do but what they should by doing everything
Safe toward your love and honour.

DUNCAN Welcome hither.
I have begun to plant thee and will labour
To make thee full of growing. Noble Banquo,
That hast no less deserved, nor must be known
No less to have done so, let me enfold thee
And hold thee to my heart.

BANQUO There if I grow,
The harvest is your own.

DUNCAN My plenteous joys,
Wanton in fullness, seek to hide themselves
In drops of sorrow. Sons, kinsmen, thanes,
And you whose places are the nearest, know:

---

notebook ("leaf" = page) in which Macbeth has written ("registered") a reminder of what he owes Ross and Angus. 152. **chanced:** happened, occurred. 152. **at more time:** The phrase may mean "at a later time" or "when we have more time." 153. **The . . . it:** i.e., when we have considered it thoroughly ("weighed it") in the meantime ("interim"). 154. **free:** frank, plain-spoken.

Act 1, Scene 4. The setting is presumably Duncan's royal camp, to which Macbeth and Banquo have been summoned. 0. **sd *Flourish*:** a trumpet signal indicating the "presence" of authority. 1. **Is . . . Cawdor:** has Cawdor's execution been carried out. 1. **or not:** or are not; "are" is understood. 2. **liege:** i.e., liege lord (the feudal superior to whom a vassal owes allegiance). In Shakespeare's day, the title no longer carried legal obligations and was mostly one of great respect. 3. **spoke:** spoken. 5–7. **very . . . repentance:** In the early modern period, no matter how recalcitrant convicted criminals had been, they typically did confess, repent, and beg forgiveness as they prepared to face divine judgment. 8. **Became:** graced, befitted. 9. **studied:** skilled, practiced. 10. **owed:** owned. Elizabethan spelling did not distinguish between "owe" and "own"; Malcolm may therefore also allude to the idea that every Christian owes God a soul. 11. **As:** as if. 11–12. **There's no art . . . face:** a proverbial truism: "the face is no index to the heart." 12. **construction:** interpretation. 18–20. **Would . . . mine:** i.e., I wish you had merited lesser rewards so that I might have been able to pay you adequately; "proportion" (19) = an act of proportioning. This act Duncan cannot satisfactorily perform because Macbeth's merit outstrips the available "thanks and payment." 21. **all:** i.e., all my "thanks and payment" (19). 23. **pays itself:** i.e., service and loyalty (22) are their own rewards. 27. **Safe toward:** with sure regard to. 28–29. **I have begun . . . growing:** Compare "Thou hast planted them . . . they grow, and bring forth fruit" (Jeremiah 12:2). 30–31. **nor . . . / No less:** i.e., and must be no less known. 31. **enfold:** embrace (an implicit direction to the actor). 32–33. **There . . . own:** Banquo continues Duncan's metaphor of growth-into-reward and may allude to the legal principle that the land's owner possesses the crops thereon no matter who sowed and tended them. 34. **Wanton:** luxuriant, profuse. 35. **drops of sorrow:** Duncan

We will establish our estate upon
Our eldest, Malcolm, whom we name hereafter
The Prince of Cumberland, which honour must
Not unaccompanied invest him only,
But signs of nobleness like stars shall shine
On all deservers. [*To Macbeth*] From hence to Inverness
And bind us further to you.

MACBETH The rest is labour which is not used for you;
I'll be myself the harbinger and make joyful
The hearing of my wife with your approach.
So humbly take my leave.

DUNCAN My worthy Cawdor.

MACBETH [*Aside*] The Prince of Cumberland: that is a step
On which I must fall down, or else o'erleap,
For in my way it lies. Stars, hide your fires,
Let not light see my black and deep desires,
The eye wink at the hand. Yet let that be,
Which the eye fears when it is done to see.

Exit

DUNCAN True, worthy Banquo, he is full so valiant,
And in his commendations I am fed;
It is a banquet to me. Let's after him,
Whose care is gone before to bid us welcome:
It is a peerless kinsman.

Flourish

Exeunt

Act 1, Scene 5

Enter [LADY MACBETH] *alone, with a letter*

LADY MACBETH [*Reads*] "They met me in the day of success, and I have learned by the perfectest report they have more in them than mortal knowledge. When I burned in desire to question them further, they made themselves air, into which they vanished. Whiles I stood rapt in the wonder of it, came missives from the king who all-hailed me Thane of Cawdor, by which title before these weïrd sisters saluted me and referred me to the coming on of time, with 'Hail, king that shalt be.' This have I thought good to deliver thee, my dearest partner of greatness, that thou mightst not lose the dues of rejoicing by being ignorant of what greatness is promised thee. Lay it to thy heart and farewell."

Glamis thou art, and Cawdor, and shalt be
What thou art promised; yet do I fear thy nature,
It is too full o'th'milk of human kindness
To catch the nearest way. Thou wouldst be great,
Art not without ambition, but without
The illness should attend it. What thou wouldst highly,
That wouldst thou holily; wouldst not play false,

---

weeps for joy. 35–43. **Sons . . . you:** The political import of this speech is repeated at 5.9.27–40. Duncan's proposal of his successor (38) might hint that Macbeth or Banquo, not Malcolm, as it happens, is to be nominated. 36. **nearest:** most closely or intimately associated (with Duncan). 37. **establish:** settle. 39. **Prince of Cumberland:** title of the Scottish heir apparent; compare "Prince of Wales" in England. 40. **Not unaccompanied:** not alone. Making Malcolm Prince of Cumberland requires that Duncan also honor others, as Malcolm does at the play's end and James I did upon his accession. 40. **invest:** clothe, adorn. This meaning shades into more figurative ones (e.g., endue with attributes), but the word links the abstract conferring of honor with the imagery of clothing (see note 2.4.32). 41. **signs of nobleness:** tokens of merit (i.e., titles of honor). 42. **Inverness:** town at the head of the Moray Firth, 155 miles northwest of Edinburgh. 44. **rest . . . you:** (1) anything ("the rest") not done for you is work ("labour"), (2) resting ("the rest") is fatiguing unless done on your behalf, (3) rest is labor when I refrain from serving you. 45. **harbinger:** an officer of the royal household, who preceded the king on his journeys and procured lodgings. 45–46. **make . . . hearing:** i.e., make Lady Macbeth rejoice at hearing. 50. **Stars, hide your fires:** The words are entirely metaphorical; there is nothing to indicate this scene takes place at night. 52. **wink at:** disregard, overlook. 54–55. **True . . . fed:** Duncan agrees with Banquo's (unheard) remark: Macbeth is just as brave ("full so valiant") as Banquo has said; praising Macbeth gives Duncan pleasure. Macbeth's aside has apparently "covered" Banquo's comment to Duncan. 56. **banquet:** wordplay on "Banquo" (54). 58. **peerless:** without equal.

Act 1, Scene 5. 2. **perfectest report:** most reliable testimony. 5. **vanished:** another hint of the witches' stage business. 5. **Whiles:** while. 6. **missives:** messengers. 6. **all-hailed:** saluted with "All hail." Macbeth's letter transfers the "all-hail" from the witches (1.3.46–48) to Ross and Angus. 12. **Lay . . . heart:** consider it seriously. 15. **milk of human kindness:** i.e., compassion characteristic of humane persons; "humane" (= gentle, compassionate) was not distinguished orthographically from "human" before 1700 or later (see also 3.4.76); "kindness" principally

And yet wouldst wrongly win. Thou'dst have, great Glamis,
That which cries, "Thus thou must do" if thou have it;
And that which rather thou dost fear to do,
Than wishest should be undone. Hie thee hither,
That I may pour my spirits in thine ear
And chastise with the valour of my tongue
All that impedes thee from the golden round,
Which fate and metaphysical aid doth seem
To have thee crowned withal.

Enter [ATTENDANT]

What is your tidings?

ATTENDANT The king comes here tonight.

LADY MACBETH Thou'rt mad to say it.
Is not thy master with him? Who, were't so,
Would have informed for preparation.

ATTENDANT So please you, it is true: our thane is coming.
One of my fellows had the speed of him;
Who almost dead for breath, had scarcely more
Than would make up his message.

LADY MACBETH Give him tending,
He brings great news.

Exit [*Attendant*]

The raven himself is hoarse
That croaks the fatal entrance of Duncan
Under my battlements. Come, you spirits
That tend on mortal thoughts, unsex me here

Look at this scene from the 1958 film *Throne of Blood*, Akira Kurosawa's adaptation of *Macbeth*, staged with elements of traditional Japanese Noh theater. In this adaptation, one of the witches gives Macbeth the following advice: "If you choose ambition, lord . . . then choose it honestly, with cruelty."

What effect is created through the framing and lighting of the scene pictured here? How is the witch's advice similar to or different from Lady Macbeth's observations in the soliloquy in Scene 5?

---

means "kinship," but also connotes "category" ("kind" = classification, group) and "naturalness" ("kind" = nature). 16. **catch:** snatch. 16. **nearest:** most direct. 18. **illness:** wickedness, depravity. 18. **highly:** intensely, greatly, but another meaning, "in or to a high rank," hints that "highly" might mean "nobly, in a manner suiting an individual of high rank." 19. **holily:** with sanctity and devoutness. 21. **That which cries:** a voice that says (e.g., Lady Macbeth's own voice or the crown). 21. **if thou have it:** i.e., if you would gain greatness (or the crown); "would" is understood from its previous uses. 22. **that:** a reference to "Thus thou must do" (21)—kill Duncan—rather than to "That which cries"—the urging or desire to kill Duncan. 23. **Hie:** hurry. 24. **pour . . . ear:** The "spirits" are soon defined as those "that tend on mortal [murderous] thoughts" (39). 25. **chastise:** rebuke; stress on first syllable. 26. **impedes:** hinders, obstructs. 26. **golden round:** i.e., the crown (as at 4.1.87). 27. **metaphysical:** more than physical, supernatural. 28. **sd** ATTENDANT**:** The dialogue makes clear that this speaker is a member of the household, an "attendant," not a "messenger." Costume and perhaps props would have distinguished messenger from attendant in Jacobean productions. 31. **informed:** reported; given information. 31. **preparation:** pronounced as five syllables. 32–35. **our thane . . . message:** As in the report of Cawdor's execution (1.4.2–11), unofficial messengers travel faster than official ones, and Shakespeare stresses the details of speed and exhaustion. 33. **had the speed of him:** outdistanced him. 34. **for breath:** as a consequence of ("for") lacking air to breathe. 36. **raven:** traditionally, a bird of evil omen (because it was a carrion-eater seen on the battlefield). 36. **himself is hoarse:** i.e., like the gasping messenger. 39. **tend on:** attend, administer to. 39. **mortal:** fatal, murderous; human. 39. **unsex me:** deprive me of my gender. The verb may mean "make me not a woman" or, less likely, "make me not human." 39. **here:** Performers have sometimes made "here" breast or groin; producers must decide whether Lady Macbeth's invocation is

And fill me from the crown to the toe topfull
Of direst cruelty; make thick my blood,
Stop up th'access and passage to remorse
That no compunctious visitings of nature
Shake my fell purpose nor keep peace between
Th'effect and it. Come to my woman's breasts
And take my milk for gall, you murd'ring
    ministers,
Wherever in your sightless substances
You wait on nature's mischief. Come, thick night,
And pall thee in the dunnest smoke of hell,
That my keen knife see not the wound it makes,
Nor heaven peep through the blanket of the
    dark,
To cry, "Hold, hold."

Enter MACBETH

Great Glamis, worthy Cawdor,
Greater than both by the all-hail hereafter,
Thy letters have transported me beyond
This ignorant present, and I feel now
The future in the instant.

MACBETH My dearest love,
Duncan comes here tonight.

LADY MACBETH And when goes hence?

MACBETH Tomorrow, as he purposes.

LADY MACBETH O never
Shall sun that morrow see.
Your face, my thane, is as a book where men
May read strange matters. To beguile the time,
Look like the time, bear welcome in your eye,
Your hand, your tongue; look like th'innocent
    flower,
But be the serpent under't. He that's coming
Must be provided for, and you shall put
This night's great business into my dispatch,
Which shall to all our nights and days to come
Give solely sovereign sway and masterdom.

MACBETH We will speak further—

LADY MACBETH Only look up clear;
To alter favour ever is to fear.
Leave all the rest to me.

Exeunt

Act 1, Scene 6

Hautboys, and Torches. Enter King [DUNCAN], MALCOLM, DONALDBAIN, BANQUO, LENNOX, MACDUFF, ROSS, ANGUS, *and Attendants*

DUNCAN This castle hath a pleasant seat; the air
Nimbly and sweetly recommends itself
Unto our gentle senses.

BANQUO This guest of summer,
The temple-haunting martlet, does approve
By his loved mansionry that the heaven's
    breath
Smells wooingly here. No jutty, frieze,
Buttress, nor coign of vantage but this bird

---

figurative or acted out. 41. **direst:** most dreadful, most terrible. 42. **remorse:** pity, compassion; not (as in modern English) bitter repentance for a wrong committed. 43. **compunctious:** remorseful. 43. **visitings of nature:** menstruation and, more generally, natural feelings of compassion. 44. **fell:** fierce, ruthless. 44. **keep:** preserve, maintain. The modern equivalent of "keep peace" is "keep the peace." 45. **Th'effect and it:** the consequence and "my fell purpose" (44). 46. **take . . . gall:** either "make my milk gall" (= bile; bitter liquid) or "treat my milk as gall." Early medical theory held that a mother's blood (see 41–42) was converted into milk; here blood becomes gall. 46. **ministers:** attendants, executants. 47. **sightless:** invisible; blind. 48. **wait on nature's mischief:** lie in wait for disturbances of nature. 48. **thick:** dense, profound. 49. **pall:** cover or drape as with cloth. The verb evokes the noun "pall" (cloth, altar-cloth, covering for a hearse or coffin, robe, garment) and joins Lady Macbeth's wish with Macbeth's earlier anxieties about "borrowed robes" (1.3.107). 49. **dunnest:** murkiest, gloomiest. 52–53. **Great . . . both:** Lady Macbeth greets her husband with (almost) the sisters' words (1.3.46–48). 53. **all-hail:** i.e., associated with the salutation "all hail!" The phrase "all-hail" is treated as an adjective, "hereafter" as a noun: Macbeth will be "Greater . . . hereafter" on the authority of ("by") the sisters' "all hail." See 1.3.46–48. 54. **letters:** The audience knows only the letter read at the scene's start; these "letters" prefigure the characters of Macbeth's face, "a book" (60). 55. **ignorant:** unknowing. 56. **The future in the instant:** that which is to come in the present moment, the here-and-now. 57. **goes hence:** departs; dies. 58. **purposes:** plans, intends. 59. **sun:** Given the importance of male heirs in the play, a pun on "son" is not impossible here. 59. **that morrow:** i.e., a new day in which Duncan "goes hence" alive. 60–61. **Your . . . matters:** The analogy of the face with a book is proverbial; compare 1.4.11–12. 61. **beguile:** deceive, mislead. 64. **under't:** under it. 65. **provided for:** prepared for. The verb hovers ambiguously between hospitable and homicidal preparations for Duncan's arrival. 66. **dispatch:** conduct, management. 67–68. **all . . . masterdom:** Night and day later prove testimonies not to the Macbeths' "masterdom," their sovereign power, but rather to their weakness. See, e.g., 3.2.16–22 and 5.1. 68. **solely:** exclusively. 69. **We will speak further—:** The punctuation adopted here, indicating that Lady Macbeth interrupts Macbeth, suggests his continuing irresolution and her insistent certainty. The punctuation in the First and Second Folios makes Macbeth more certainly doubtful, Lady Macbeth still more insistent. 69. **clear:** serenely, cheerfully. 70. **To . . . fear:** Fear always ("ever") changes one's facial expression ("favour"); the construction is inverted to make a significant rhyme.

Act 1, Scenes 6. 0. **sd *Hautboys, and Torches*:** players of hautboys and torch-bearers. Tudor and early Stuart hautboys (also called "bombards") were treble members of the shawm family (woodwinds related to the modern oboe), loud-sounding instruments much favored in courts and by the

Hath made his pendent bed and procreant cradle;
Where they most breed and haunt, I have observed
The air is delicate.

Enter LADY [MACBETH]

DUNCAN See, see, our honoured hostess. — The love
That follows us sometime is our trouble,
Which still we thank as love. Herein I teach you
How you shall bid God yield us for your pains
And thank us for your trouble.

LADY MACBETH All our service,
In every point twice done and then done double,
Were poor and single business to contend
Against those honours deep and broad wherewith
Your majesty loads our house. For those of old,
And the late dignities heaped up to them,
We rest your hermits.

DUNCAN Where's the Thane of Cawdor?
We coursed him at the heels and had a purpose
To be his purveyor, but he rides well,
And his great love, sharp as his spur, hath holp him
To his home before us. Fair and noble hostess,
We are your guest tonight.

LADY MACBETH Your servants ever
Have theirs, themselves, and what is theirs in count
To make their audit at your highness' pleasure,
Still to return your own.

DUNCAN Give me your hand;
Conduct me to mine host: we love him highly
And shall continue our graces towards him.
By your leave, hostess.

Exeunt

Act 1, Scene 7

Hautboys. Torches. Enter a Sewer, and divers Servants with dishes and service over the stage. Then enter MACBETH

MACBETH If it were done when 'tis done, then 'twere well
It were done quickly. If th'assassination
Could trammel up the consequence and catch
With his surcease, success, that but this blow
Might be the be-all and the end-all — here,
But here, upon this bank and shoal of time,

---

military. 1–10. **This castle . . . delicate:** Both Duncan and, more surprisingly, Banquo here accept a superficial appearance and misread as "gentle" (3) and "procreant" (8) a castle whose "battlements" will prove "fatal" to both (1.5.37–38). 1. **seat:** situation, site. 3. **gentle:** i.e., the sweet air makes our sense gentle. 4. **martlet:** a swift, but used also of the swallow or house-martin [birds that build nests (8) attached to the walls of buildings]. 4. **approve:** confirm; attest; commend. 5. **mansionry:** mansions. 6. **jutty:** projecting part of a wall or building. 6. **frieze:** carved or painted decorative band beneath a building's cornice. 7. **Buttress:** external support for a wall or building. 7. **coign of vantage:** projecting corner ("coign") of a building affording facility for observation or action. 8. **pendent:** hanging, suspended. 8. **bed and procreant cradle:** nest. 9. **haunt:** usually remain, habitually resort. 10. **delicate:** charming, pleasant. 11–13. **The love . . . love:** Duncan begins a tortuously polite exchange by remarking how he sometimes finds troublesome others' well-meaning respect and affection, over which they have taken so much "trouble." 13–15. **Herein . . . trouble:** Duncan turns a self-deprecating compliment: Lady Macbeth should learn from the king's example to ask God to reward Duncan for the effort she makes and to thank Duncan for providing the onerous occasion. 14. **yield:** reward, recompense. 16. **twice . . . double:** Lady Macbeth continues the language of duplication and multiplication begun by the Captain (1.2.37–38), continued by the sisters (1.3.33–34, 4.1.10), and soon to be used by Macbeth (1.7.12). 17. **single:** weak, simple, undemanding. The word continues the text's playing with singleness (unity, integrity?) and doubleness (show, not substance?); for Lady Macbeth or for the play, doubleness may be more valid or effective than singleness. 17. **business:** exertion. 17. **contend:** compete, vie. 20. **late:** recent. 21. **hermits:** beadsmen, persons bound by vow or fee to pray for an individual's spiritual welfare. 22. **coursed:** chased. 23. **purveyor:** the person who arranges provisions (food, transport, lodging, etc.) for a superior; an official title in the royal household. 24. **holp:** helped. 27. **count:** account, statement of moneys received and expended. 32. **By your leave:** with your permission. Duncan may leave Lady Macbeth behind after greeting her at the castle's imaginary entrance or invite her to lead the way offstage.

Act 1, Scene 7. 0. **sd *Hautboys. Torches*:** an abrupt theatrical direction for musicians and light-bearers. 0. **sd *Sewer*:** server. 0. **sd *service*:** something served as food; course of a meal. The audience would see dishes and other utensils. 0. **sd *over the stage*:** i.e., crossing silently from one side to the other. 1. **If . . . 'tis done:** The phrase recalls two proverbs: "The thing done has an end" and "Things done cannot be undone." See 3.2.12 and 5.1.57–58. 2. **assassination:** murder (for political reasons). 3. **trammel:** use nets (to catch fish or fowl); hobble (a horse); bind up or wrap (a corpse). 4. **his surcease:** Duncan's death. 4. **success:** prosperous achievement; succession of heirs. 4–5. **that . . . end-all:** i.e., if only the murder of Duncan were an act and event complete and completed in itself. The "be-all" is the whole being, and the "end-all" is that which ends all.

We'd jump the life to come. But in these cases,
We still have judgement here that we but teach
Bloody instructions, which being taught, return
To plague th'inventor. This even-handed justice
Commends th'ingredience of our poisoned chalice
To our own lips. He's here in double trust:
First, as I am his kinsman and his subject,
Strong both against the deed; then, as his host,
Who should against his murderer shut the door,
Not bear the knife myself. Besides, this Duncan
Hath borne his faculties so meek, hath been
So clear in his great office, that his virtues
Will plead like angels, trumpet-tongued against
The deep damnation of his taking-off.
And pity, like a naked newborn babe
Striding the blast, or heaven's cherubin horsed
Upon the sightless couriers of the air,
Shall blow the horrid deed in every eye,
That tears shall drown the wind. I have no spur
To prick the sides of my intent, but only
Vaulting ambition which o'erleaps itself
And falls on th'other—

Enter LADY [MACBETH]

How now? What news?

LADY MACBETH He has almost supped. Why have you left the chamber?

MACBETH Hath he asked for me?

LADY MACBETH Know you not, he has?

MACBETH We will proceed no further in this business.
He hath honoured me of late, and I have bought
Golden opinions from all sorts of people,
Which would be worn now in their newest gloss,
Not cast aside so soon.

LADY MACBETH Was the hope drunk
Wherein you dressed yourself? Hath it slept since?
And wakes it now to look so green and pale
At what it did so freely? From this time,
Such I account thy love. Art thou afeard
To be the same in thine own act and valour,
As thou art in desire? Wouldst thou have that
Which thou esteem'st the ornament of life,

6. **bank and shoal:** sandbank (or river bank) and shallow. The Folio's "Banke and Schoole" could also be modernized as "bench and school," with "bank" (= bench) as the seat of justice, the mountebank's stage, or the rower's bench, not as "school bench." "Schoole" is a well-attested form of "shoal" in the period. Although Macbeth soon mentions "instructions" and "justice" (which might be anticipated in "school" and "bench"), the phrase seems more likely to be treating time as a river: Macbeth momentarily halts time's flow by standing on a shoal or by grasping the bank. 7. **jump:** hazard; pass or leap over. 8. **We . . . teach:** We always ("still") are punished here because we only ("but") teach others (how to commit our own crimes against ourselves). 10. **even-handed:** impartial. 11. **ingredience:** ingredients considered collectively. 17. **faculties:** powers, privileges. 18. **clear:** innocent. 19. **trumpet-tongued:** Duncan's virtues speak with a trumpet tongue on this matter of his murder. 21–22. **newborn babe . . . heaven's cherubin:** The alternative offered here between an image of vulnerability ("babe") and one of heavenly power ("heaven's cherubin") at first seems confused, but the compressed images join together Macbeth's future opponents: Banquo's children, who will succeed to Scotland's throne (see 1.3.65), and the near-divinely endorsed forces (see 4.3.240–42) that will drive Macbeth from that throne. 22. **blast:** gale; wind of the trumpet-tongued angels. 22. **cherubin:** cherub (second in the traditional nine-fold order of angels). Cherubim commanded the air. 23. **sightless couriers:** invisible messengers; invisible means of transport—i.e., the winds which invisibly move the air from place to place. The echo of "sightless substances" (1.5.47) makes plain the contrast of murder and pity, sin and dissuasion from sin. 24. **blow:** sound; propel. 24. **every eye:** every organ of sight; every person. 25. **tears:** i.e., drops of compassion and the watering caused by a foreign object ("the deed") lodged in "every eye." Proverbially, "Little rain lays great winds," and the line gains its power from hyperbole: tears become rain so powerful as to "drown" the insubstantial and omnipresent wind. 25–28. **I . . . th'other:** Two interpretations of Macbeth's images have been offered: (1) Macbeth distinguishes his intent to murder, which he imagines as an unspurred horse, from his ambition to be king, which he imagines as an eager rider who overdoes his vault ("o'erleaps") and thus fails to land in the saddle; (2) horse and rider together fall when the pair fails to overleap an obstacle. 29. **supped:** finished dining. 29. **Why . . . chamber:** For the host to leave the table before the chief guest had finished his meal violated protocol. 30. **Know . . . has:** Lady Macbeth assumes Macbeth has deliberately withdrawn to avoid Duncan's attention. 33. **sorts:** kinds; (social) ranks. 34. **worn:** Opinions (33) are now treated as garments. 34. **gloss:** superficial luster, shininess. Figuratively, "gloss" = highest value (because newest). 35. **cast aside:** The richest Renaissance garments were discarded or given away once they were soiled, because they could not be cleaned. 35–38. **Was . . . freely:** Lady Macbeth represents "hope" as a person—first drunkenly hopeful, then comatose, then hung over—who initially dressed himself in a garment (also "hope"), but then sleeps himself into a cowardly sobriety. 37. **green and pale:** popularly imagined consequences of drunkenness, then as now. 39. **Such:** i.e., you are like the fearful, hung-over drunkard, bold only when inebriated. 39. **account:** consider. 39–41. **Art . . .**

extending beyond the text

In the 1990 film *Men of Respect*, an adaptation of *Macbeth*, the protagonist, Mike Battaglia, is an Italian mobster trying to seize control of a crime family from the current "Padrino," or Godfather, Charlie DeMico. Read the following excerpt from the script.

from Men of Respect

William Reilly

MIKE BATTAGLIA: This is Padrino DeMico here. Alright? Now we have respect.

RUTHIE BATTAGLIA: Charlie respects the fat end of a bat. The sharp end of a stick. Charlie respects what he fears. And that ain't you.

MIKE: You just wait and see what he has in mind.

RUTHIE: All Charlie cares about is number one. Him and his. That's why Charlie is Charlie, and you are not. Why you have to wait for other people to give you? Why does everything always have to pass through somebody else's hands? Show a little ambition.

MIKE: Stop it alright!? I'm as ambitious as the next guy. More! Alright? My time comes; I'll know it. And I'll know what to do.

RUTHIE: This is the time. And you better know it now. This is it staring you in the face. Don't close your eyes.

MIKE: You don't know what you're asking.

RUTHIE: Tell me. Tell me you don't want it. If I was the man, I'd know what to do.

MIKE: There's no guarantee, if Charlie's out of the picture, we'll be any better off.

RUTHIE: In this life, Michael, there's no safe standing still.

What remains consistent with the characters and the plot of *Macbeth*, and what has changed? What does this image from the movie suggest about the power relationship between husband and wife? How is it similar to or different from that of Macbeth and Lady Macbeth? What details from the image or the script help you draw your conclusion?

And live a coward in thine own esteem,
Letting I dare not wait upon I would,
Like the poor cat i'th'adage?

MACBETH Prithee, peace.
I dare do all that may become a man;
Who dares do more is none.

LADY MACBETH What beast was't then
That made you break this enterprise to me?
When you durst do it, then you were a man.
And to be more than what you were, you would
Be so much more the man. Nor time, nor place
Did then adhere, and yet you would make both.
They have made themselves and that their fitness now
Does unmake you. I have given suck and know
How tender 'tis to love the babe that milks me:
I would, while it was smiling in my face,
Have plucked my nipple from his boneless gums
And dashed the brains out, had I so sworn
As you have done to this.

MACBETH If we should fail?

LADY MACBETH We fail?
But screw your courage to the sticking-place,
And we'll not fail. When Duncan is asleep,
Whereto the rather shall his day's hard journey
Soundly invite him, his two chamberlains
Will I with wine and wassail so convince
That memory, the warder of the brain,
Shall be a fume, and the receipt of reason
A limbeck only. When in swinish sleep
Their drenchèd natures lies as in a death,
What cannot you and I perform upon
Th'unguarded Duncan? What not put upon
His spongy officers, who shall bear the guilt
Of our great quell?

MACBETH Bring forth men-children only,
For thy undaunted mettle should compose
Nothing but males. Will it not be received,
When we have marked with blood those sleepy two
Of his own chamber, and used their very daggers,
That they have done't?

LADY MACBETH Who dares receive it other,
As we shall make our griefs and clamour roar
Upon his death?

MACBETH I am settled and bend up
Each corporal agent to this terrible feat.
Away, and mock the time with fairest show,
False face must hide what the false heart doth know.

Exeunt

---

desire: Are you (now sober, unlustful, and detumescent) afraid to be and do what you were and desired to be when you were drunk? For this verbal possibility, see the immediate sexualized language of "be" (40), "do" and "become a man" (46), "do" (47). 39. **afeard:** afraid. 44–45. **Letting . . . adage:** The adage is "The cat would eat fish but she will not wet her feet." Macbeth wants the kingship, but will risk nothing; later, he will find his feet wet with blood (3.4.136–37). 45. **Prithee, peace:** I pray thee, be quiet. 47. **none:** i.e., no man. For Macbeth at this moment, daring to kill the king would move him beyond humanity. 47. **beast:** Lady Macbeth immediately understands Macbeth's "none" to mean an animal. 48. **break:** disclose, divulge. 48. **enterprise:** bold, arduous, or momentous undertaking. 49. **durst:** dared. 52. **adhere:** agree. 52. **make both:** According to his wife, Macbeth seeks to make both occasion and place, seeks to control time and topography. 53. **that their fitness now:** i.e., now they have become appropriate ("fit"). 55. **milks:** obtains milk by sucking. 57. **his:** The ungendered "babe" (55) becomes male. 58–59. **sworn . . . to this:** bound myself by oath . . . to this course of action. 60. **But:** only. 60. **screw . . . sticking-place:** tighten, make taut, your courage to the limit. The underlying metaphor may be from tightening the tuning pegs of a stringed instrument or from winding up the cord on a crossbow. The "sticking-place" may also be the place at which a moral individual hesitates or the place beyond which a moral individual refuses to go, or it may be a stab-wound. 62. **the rather:** the more readily, all the sooner. 63. **Soundly:** a transferred adverb: Duncan will sleep "soundly"; there is perhaps the added irony of a "sound" (= robust, healthy) sleep that is death. 63. **chamberlains:** attendants in the royal bedchamber. 64. **wassail:** liquor (with which toasts were drunk). 64. **convince:** overcome, conquer. 65–67. **memory . . . only:** memory, a guard ("warder") of the brain against irrational thoughts or impulses, will become vapor ("a fume"), and reason's chamber ("receipt") will merely receive the condensation of a distilling apparatus ("limbeck"). 67. **swinish:** i.e., drunken. 70. **put upon:** impose; saddle with. Responsibility for the murder will be laid upon the chamberlains (63). 71. **spongy:** absorbent; the men will soak up liquor like sponges. 71. **officers:** officeholders, persons who perform certain duties; not military personnel. 72. **quell:** slaughter, murder. 73. **mettle:** spirit, courage. Early modern orthography did not distinguish "mettle" and "metal," making possible a pun on male children as metallic warriors armored in mail. 74. **received:** understood, believed (by others). 75–76. **two . . . chamber:** i.e., two members of the king's bedchamber. In the Jacobean court, appointed members of the bedchamber attended to the king's personal needs. 76. **very:** own. 77. **other:** otherwise. 78. **As:** when. 79. **settled:** unchanging, undeviating. 79. **bend up:** brace, tighten, prepare to act. 80. **corporal:** corporeal, bodily. 80. **agent:** physical resource; muscle. 81. **mock:** deceive.

Understanding and Interpreting

1. Right after the witches affirm that they are about to meet Macbeth, they declare, "Fair is foul, and foul is fair" (Scene 1, l. 12). Explain what this statement literally means and what it might foreshadow.
2. Explain what we learn about Macbeth as a soldier from the injured Captain who is asked to tell King Duncan the outcome of a battle he has just witnessed in Scene 2.
3. In Scene 2, lines 63 to 65, the current Thane of Cawdor is pronounced a traitor and sentenced to death. His title is given to Macbeth. What does this immediate transfer of power suggest about the nature of a monarch's authority during these times? What does it suggest about the nature of a thane's authority?
4. In Scene 3, the witches speak in riddles. For example, they declare that Banquo will be "Lesser than Macbeth, and greater" (l. 63). How does Macbeth react to this ambiguity? What does his reaction suggest about his character? How does Banquo's reaction differ from Macbeth's? What does that suggest about Banquo's character?
5. Right after the witches disappear, Ross and Angus arrive to share the news that Macbeth is now the Thane of Cawdor, just as the witches had foretold (Scene 3, ll. 102 to 105). Describe Macbeth's and Banquo's separate reactions and what those reactions reveal about their characters.
6. In Scene 4, Macbeth starts to show two different sides now that he has been promoted. He declares publicly to Duncan that "The service and the loyalty that I owe, / In doing it, pays itself" (ll. 22–23). Yet, a few lines later he refers to the Prince of Cumberland, Duncan's son, as a "step" he must "o'erleap" (ll. 48 to 49). How do these contrasting sides of Macbeth begin to shape his character and increase the complexity of the play at this point?
7. Duncan asserts that "There's no art / To find the mind's construction in the face" (Scene 4, ll. 11–12). In Scene 5, Lady Macbeth tells her husband that his face is "as a book where men / May read strange matters" (ll. 60 to 61). What does her contrasting opinion suggest about her character and her attitudes toward others?
8. Soliloquies offer characters a chance to reveal their private thoughts and inner turmoil. Scene 7 opens with Macbeth's first major soliloquy (ll. 1–28). At this point, do you think he is ready to kill Duncan? Or does he still have doubts? What is preventing him from committing to either course of action?
9. Shakespearean tragedies often feature a main character who possesses a fatal flaw, a primary personality trait responsible for a character's downfall. At the end of his soliloquy in Scene 7, Macbeth refers to his "Vaulting ambition" (l. 27), which is a phrase that many believe captures his fatal flaw. In what ways has Macbeth already shown his ambition? To what degree has his ambition controlled the events in the play so far?
10. Lady Macbeth challenges her husband when she believes he may be wavering in his resolve to kill Duncan (Scene 7, ll. 48 to 71). In making this response to Macbeth, does she intend to motivate him to follow through with the murder, or is she just telling him what he wants to hear? Both? Explain.
11. Explain how Lady Macbeth plans to kill Duncan without Macbeth being blamed for the murder (Scene 7, ll. 60 to 71).

Analyzing Language, Style, and Structure

1. **Vocabulary in Context.** In Scene 2, line 18, the captain says Macbeth was fighting "with bloody execution." What does the word "execution" mean in this context? How are other meanings of this word also appropriate in this scene?

2. **Vocabulary in Context.** Both Macbeth and Banquo use the word "fair" in Scene 3. What does the word "fair" mean in these contexts? Why might Shakespeare intend for readers to associate more than one meaning at a time with the word?
3. **Vocabulary in Context.** When Lady Macbeth learns in Scene 5 line 46 that King Duncan is arriving, she says "take my milk for gall." What is the meaning of the word "gall" in this context? How does another meaning of the word also apply to this situation?
4. **Skill Focus.** In his extended description of the battle in Scene 2, the Captain employs several similes (ll. 7 to 23). Identify one of the similes and discuss how it helps characterize the battle.
5. **Skill Focus.** When Banquo recognizes that Macbeth is struggling to understand his promotion to Thane of Cawdor, he concludes that the new "honours" bestowed on Macbeth are like "strange garments" that "cleave not to their mould / But with the aid of use" (Scene 3, ll. 143 to 145). Discuss why this simile is an effective way to describe Macbeth's current attitude toward his promotion.
6. The concept of Fortune, or Fate, was central to the worldview of this era; people considered it to be a central controlling force in life. In Scene 2, lines 16 to 20, the Captain describes Macbeth as one who fought while "Disdaining Fortune." In what ways does this word choice serve as both a compliment and a caution regarding Macbeth's character?
7. Before the bleeding Captain is taken away to have his injuries treated, Duncan tells him that his "words become thee as thy wounds; / They smack of honour both" (Scene 2, ll. 43 to 44). What does this statement reveal about Duncan's attitude toward warfare?
8. In Scene 3, after Angus and Ross tell of Macbeth's promotion to Thane of Cawdor, Banquo suggests to Macbeth that sometimes "instruments of darkness tell us truths" to "win us to our harm" (ll. 123 to 124). Explain the meaning of these words and their significance at this point in the play.
9. Troubled by the prophecy of the witches, Macbeth says that it "Cannot be ill, cannot be good" (Scene 3, l. 130). This antithesis (two opposing ideas side-by-side) is followed by two more antitheses. Identify those antitheses and explain what they reveal about Macbeth's state of mind at this point.
10. Duncan notes that the recently executed Cawdor was "a gentleman on whom I built / An absolute trust" (Scene 4, ll. 13 to 14). Just after Duncan says these words, Macbeth enters. How does timing Macbeth's entrance right after Duncan's comment affect the audience's understanding of the play at this point?
11. Lady Macbeth uses particularly violent imagery related to a baby when she confronts Macbeth about "[breaking] this enterprise" and not following through with the murder (Scene 7, ll. 48 to 58). In what ways does the imagery emphasize Lady Macbeth's resolve? What does it suggest about her character?

Topics for Composing

1. **Analysis.** It is clear that Macbeth desires to be king. However, he is also a loyal soldier who understands that killing the current king would be an act of treason. This struggle is central to the action of the play. Write an analysis of Macbeth's character at this point in the play. Explain how it relates to a theme that has been expressed so far.
2. **Analysis.** *Macbeth* offers frequent commentary on gender. In Act 1, where do you see actions and dialogue that explore gender roles or the natures of women and men? Write a response in which you develop an interpretation of the play's commentary on gender, based on the examples you've identified up to this point in the play.

3. **Argument.** A number of influences seem to be guiding Macbeth, including Lady Macbeth, the witches, and fate. To what extent is Macbeth in charge of his own actions at this point in the play? Write an argument in which you argue your position with evidence from the text.
4. **Connection.** What are your ambitions? What drives your ambition? What successes or failures have you had at this point in your life?
5. **Speaking and Listening.** Working with a partner, a small group, or by yourself, choose a scene from this act to perform. Be sure to consider the gestures, movements, and facial expressions you can use to communicate the characterization and conflict of the scene. How does performing the scene influence your understanding?
6. **Research.** A *self-fulfilling prophecy* is a prediction that leads to behavior that causes the prediction to come true. Conduct research on the psychology behind how self-fulfilling prophecies work. Where do you see a self-fulfilling prophecy playing out in *Macbeth*? Identify and describe a modern day, real-world example of this psychology at work.
7. **Research.** A traditional proverb says that the eyes are the window to the soul. In Scene 4, lines 12 to 13, Duncan suggests that you cannot tell what's really going on inside someone's mind just by looking at that person's face. Do some research into analyses of facial expressions in a particular context (law enforcement lie-detecting techniques, for example). Then, write an explanation of whether Duncan or the traditional proverb is closer to the truth.
8. **Multimodal.** The witches are described in some detail by Banquo when he and Macbeth encounter them on the heath (Scene 3, ll. 37 to 45). There are many imaginative works that include witches, including many children's stories. Taking Banquo's description into account, as well as popular images of witches, create your own visual interpretation (e.g., a drawing, collage, or video) of the witches. Include text from the play to support your images.
9. **Multimodal.** Act 1 offers a number of different settings for significant actions. Write seven news headlines, one for each scene. Using either original or found images, create a visual that would be appropriate for each headline.
10. **Creative Writing.** Letters written from the battlefield have long been a part of how civilians at home learn about the events that soldiers experience in war. Imagine you were at the battle that Macbeth just fought. Using details from the Captain's description in Scene 2, write a letter to someone at home about what you witnessed.

Act 2 Scene 1

Enter BANQUO, *and* FLEANCE, *with a Torch[-bearer] before him*

BANQUO How goes the night, boy?
FLEANCE The moon is down; I have not heard
the clock.
BANQUO And she goes down at twelve.
FLEANCE I take't, 'tis later, sir.
BANQUO Hold, take my sword. — There's
husbandry in heaven,
Their candles are all out. — Take thee that too.
A heavy summons lies like lead upon me,
And yet I would not sleep; merciful powers,
Restrain in me the cursèd thoughts that nature
Gives way to in repose.

Enter MACBETH, *and a Servant with a torch*

Give me my sword —
Who's there?

Act 2, Scene 1. 1. **How goes the night:** How much of the night has passed? 4–5. **There's . . . out:** usually understood as "There's thrift ('husbandry') in heaven, they have extinguished (put 'out') their stars ('candles')." 5. **Take thee that too:** Banquo, preparing for rest, disarms himself (4) and now removes some other accoutrement (his dagger or cloak, perhaps, or some ceremonial item associated with the state dinner he has just attended) or (as in some productions) hands Fleance "This diamond" (15). 7–9. **And . . . repose:** Sleep is not inevitably restorative (2.2.40–43); like drink (2.3.21–22), it can provoke. 8. **cursèd thoughts:** ambitious dreams (prompted by the sisters' prophecies and Macbeth's recent success); nightmares (about Macbeth's possible crimes). Macbeth enters before Banquo chooses between these alternatives. 10–11. **Who's there? / A friend:**

MACBETH A friend.
BANQUO What, sir, not yet at rest? The king's abed.
He hath been in unusual pleasure
And sent forth great largess to your offices.
This diamond he greets your wife withal,
[*Gives Macbeth a diamond*]
By the name of most kind hostess, and shut up
In measureless content.
MACBETH Being unprepared,
Our will became the servant to defect,
Which else should free have wrought.
BANQUO All's well.
I dreamed last night of the three weïrd sisters;
To you they have showed some truth.
MACBETH I think not of them;
Yet when we can entreat an hour to serve,
We would spend it in some words upon that business,
If you would grant the time.
BANQUO At your kind'st leisure.
MACBETH If you shall cleave to my consent, when 'tis,
It shall make honour for you.
BANQUO So I lose none
In seeking to augment it, but still keep
My bosom franchised and allegiance clear,
I shall be counselled.
MACBETH Good repose the while.
BANQUO Thanks, sir; the like to you.
[*Exeunt*] *Banquo*[*, Fleance, and Torch-bearer*]
MACBETH [*To servant*] Go bid thy mistress, when my drink is ready,
She strike upon the bell. Get thee to bed.
Exit [*Servant*]
Is this a dagger which I see before me,
The handle toward my hand? Come, let me clutch thee:
I have thee not, and yet I see thee still.
Art thou not, fatal vision, sensible
To feeling as to sight? Or art thou but
A dagger of the mind, a false creation,
Proceeding from the heat-oppressèd brain?
I see thee yet, in form as palpable
As this which now I draw.
Thou marshall'st me the way that I was going,
And such an instrument I was to use.
Mine eyes are made the fools o'th'other senses,
Or else worth all the rest. I see thee still,
And on thy blade and dudgeon gouts of blood,
Which was not so before. There's no such thing:
It is the bloody business which informs
Thus to mine eyes. Now o'er the one half-world
Nature seems dead, and wicked dreams abuse
The curtained sleep. Witchcraft celebrates
Pale Hecate's off'rings, and withered murder,
Alarumed by his sentinel, the wolf,
Whose howl's his watch, thus with his stealthy pace,

---

challenge and response: Banquo is tense; Macbeth appears as either a "merciful power" (7) or a "cursèd thought" (8). 14. **largess to your offices:** gifts to the castle functionaries. 15–16. **This . . . hostess:** The "diamond" may be a ring or pendant. Banquo, companion to Duncan in 1.6, conveys a royal gift one might expect the king to deliver personally. The gift-giving emphasizes Duncan's false sense of security and affirms the social code Macbeth is about to break. 16. **shut up:** went to bed [in a curtained bed (see 51) within a chamber]. The phrase could mean "concluded" (i.e., ended his speech); the grammar is stretched to report what Duncan said ("greets") and then what he has done ("shut up"). 18. **Our:** an anticipatory royal plural; compare 22 and 5.6.4. 18. **defect:** deficiency. 19. **free have wrought:** liberally have worked. 19. **All's well:** All is not well, as Banquo's next words testify. 22–24. **Yet . . . time:** Macbeth's courtly politeness and the apparent royal "we" intimate his sense of changed (or soon to be changed) status; his desire to talk about the witches contradicts "I think not of them" (21). 25. **cleave to my consent:** agree (or adhere) to my feeling (or opinion). 25. **when 'tis:** when it ["the time" (24)] is. 28. **franchised:** free. Banquo apparently wishes to remain free of obligation to Macbeth or of implication in his schemes. 29. **the while:** in the meantime. 30. **sir:** The respectful title introduces a note of subordination (perhaps prompted by 22–24) not present in 1.3. 32. **bell:** a clapperless bell like a ship's bell or a gong (see "strike upon"); this bell is for routine internal communication [compare "alarum bell" (2.3.69)]. 34. **handle toward my hand:** This detail identifies the dagger as a weapon for, rather than a threat to, Macbeth and makes plain the fact that the dagger is invisible to the audience. 36. **fatal:** deadly, mortal. The adjective is both active and passive: the vision is of mortality (Duncan's death); the dagger is deadly to vision (Macbeth's own). 36. **sensible:** perceptible. 37. **as to sight:** The question depends on an optical theory that vision was the product of beams radiated by the eye and reflected to it. 38. **of the mind:** imaginary. The phrase also yields an image of a dagger *in* the mind, a keen knife that makes a moral and psychological wound (see 1.3.138 and 1.5.50). 39. **heat-oppressèd:** subdued, afflicted by heat (considered a quality of the human body and its humors). Macbeth responds to the vision analytically; his explanation is physiological. 40. **yet:** still. 40. **palpable:** tangible; perceptible. 42. **Thou marshall'st:** you guide, usher. 46. **dudgeon:** hilt, handle. 46. **gouts:** spots, splashes. 47. **thing:** i.e., a dagger. Macbeth corrects his eyes, the "fools" or deceivers of his other senses (44), and says the dagger is imaginary, "no such thing" (47). 49. **half-world:** i.e., the hemisphere in darkness. 50. **seems dead:** i.e., because nature is asleep.

When staging *Macbeth*, filmmakers must make the choice to either show Macbeth's phantom dagger when he asks, "Is this a dagger which I see before me?" or leave it to our imagination. These are two different takes on the subject. The one on the left is from director Rupert Goold's 2010 adaptation starring Patrick Stewart. The one on the right is from Roman Polanski's 1971 film.

Which approach do you think is more effective? Why? How would you shoot this scene? Why?

With Tarquin's ravishing strides, towards his design
Moves like a ghost. Thou sure and firm-set earth,
Hear not my steps, which way they walk, for fear
Thy very stones prate of my whereabout,
And take the present horror from the time,
Which now suits with it. Whiles I threat, he lives;
Words to the heat of deeds too cold breath gives.

A bell rings

I go, and it is done. The bell invites me.
Hear it not, Duncan, for it is a knell
That summons thee to heaven or to hell.

Exit

Act 2, Scene 2

Enter LADY [MACBETH]

LADY MACBETH That which hath made them drunk, hath made me bold;
What hath quenched them, hath given me fire.

[*An owl shrieks*]

Hark, peace!
It was the owl that shrieked, the fatal bellman
Which gives the stern'st good-night. He is about it.
The doors are open, and the surfeited grooms
Do mock their charge with snores. I have drugged their possets,
That death and nature do contend about them,
Whether they live, or die.

Compare 1.7.68 and 2.3.71. 50. **wicked dreams:** Compare Banquo's fears (8–9). 51. **curtained:** See note 16. 51. **celebrates:** performs the rites; honors. 52. **Hecate's off'rings:** offerings to Hecate, classical goddess of the moon and of sorcery. 53. **Alarumed:** warned, prompted to action. 54. **howl's:** howl is. 54. **his watch:** murder's time-piece; the wolf's night duty. 55. **Tarquin:** Sextus Tarquinius, the Etruscan prince who raped Lucretia, wife of Lucius Tarquinius Collatinus. She committed suicide, and her relatives and friends led a rebellion (c. 509 BCE) that overthrew the monarchy and established the Roman republic. 55. **strides:** long steps. 56. **sure:** reliable, steady. 56. **firm-set:** solidly positioned, stable. 58. **prate:** blab, tell tales. See 3.4.123, where stones move and trees speak. 58. **whereabout:** location, position. 59. **take:** remove, withhold. 59. **the present horror:** i.e., the silence that would be broken by speaking stones. 59. **time:** time of night. 60. **threat:** threaten. Macbeth accuses himself of bluster. 62. **it:** either (1) Lady Macbeth's preparatory drugging of Duncan's retainers or (2) the regicide itself. 63–64. **Hear . . . hell:** The bell has also summoned Macbeth to damnation. 63. **knell:** church bell rung to announce a death. Macbeth imagines he has already committed the murder.

Act 2, Scene 2. 1. **That:** The indefinition (what is "That"?) is powerful; even after the audience realizes Lady Macbeth refers both to the grooms' drugged drinks and to her own inebriated excitement at what is to come, the doubt over "That" lingers and frightens. 2. **quenched:** extinguished (as water would fire); cooled (as in tempering forged metal). 3. **owl:** Like the raven (1.5.36), the owl was a bird of ill omen. 3. **bellman:** night watchman. 4. **stern'st good-night:** i.e., death. 5. **surfeited:** fed or filled to excess; hence, sickened by overindulgence. 6. **mock:** defy, set at

Enter MACBETH [*with two bloody daggers*]

MACBETH Who's there? What ho?

LADY MACBETH Alack, I am afraid they have awaked,
And 'tis not done; th'attempt and not the deed
Confounds us. Hark! I laid their daggers ready,
He could not miss 'em. Had he not resembled
My father as he slept, I had done't. My husband?

MACBETH I have done the deed. Didst thou not hear a noise?

LADY MACBETH I heard the owl scream and the crickets cry.
Did not you speak?

MACBETH When?

LADY MACBETH Now.

MACBETH As I descended?

LADY MACBETH Ay.

MACBETH Hark, who lies i'th'second chamber?

LADY MACBETH Donaldbain.

MACBETH This is a sorry sight.

LADY MACBETH A foolish thought, to say a sorry sight.

MACBETH There's one did laugh in's sleep, and one cried, "Murder!,"
That they did wake each other; I stood, and heard them,
But they did say their prayers and addressed them
Again to sleep.

LADY MACBETH There are two lodged together.

MACBETH One cried "God bless us!" and "Amen" the other,
As they had seen me with these hangman's hands.
List'ning their fear, I could not say "Amen"
When they did say "God bless us."

LADY MACBETH Consider it not so deeply.

MACBETH But wherefore could not I pronounce "Amen"?
I had most need of blessing and "Amen"
Stuck in my throat.

LADY MACBETH These deeds must not be thought
After these ways; so, it will make us mad.

MACBETH Methought I heard a voice cry, "Sleep no more:
Macbeth does murder sleep," the innocent sleep,
Sleep that knits up the ravelled sleeve of care,
The death of each day's life, sore labour's bath,
Balm of hurt minds, great nature's second course,
Chief nourisher in life's feast.

LADY MACBETH What do you mean?

MACBETH Still it cried, "Sleep no more" to all the house;
"Glamis hath murdered sleep," and therefore Cawdor
Shall sleep no more: Macbeth shall sleep no more.

LADY MACBETH Who was it, that thus cried? Why, worthy thane,
You do unbend your noble strength to think
So brain-sickly of things. Go get some water
And wash this filthy witness from your hand.
Why did you bring these daggers from the place?

---

nought. 6. **drugged:** poisoned. 6. **possets:** drinks made of hot milk, liquor, and spices (a delicacy). 7–8. **death . . . die:** Lady Macbeth imagines a contest or allegorical play in which abstract figures (Death and Nature) fight over the grooms' lives and consciousnesses. 7. **That:** so that. 8. **sd *with two bloody daggers:*** For the daggers, see 51. 10–11. **th'attempt . . . Confounds us:** i.e., murder attempted but not accomplished defeats us. 11. **Hark:** Listen, pay attention. Lady Macbeth interrupts herself, starting at some real or imaginary sound, perhaps of crickets (15), perhaps her husband's footsteps. 12–13. **Had . . . done't:** Compare Lady Macbeth's assertion about infanticide (1.7.54–59). Duncan's murder violates multiple bonds, many taboos. 13. **done't:** done it. 23. **sorry:** painful, grievous; wretched, worthless. 25. **one . . . one:** apparently Malcolm and Donaldbain, not the two grooms, but the uncertainty adds to the terror of the moment. 25. **in's:** in his. 26. **stood:** i.e., stood still, stood without moving. 27. **addressed:** prepared. 28. **lodged:** housed, bedded down. 30. **As:** as if. 30. **hangman's hands:** An executioner's hands would be bloodied when he disemboweled the body of a traitor he had first hanged. 31. **List'ning:** hearing, listening to. 31. **I could not say "Amen":** Macbeth cannot speak the formulaic word that would free him spiritually so that he could join in the grooms' prayers. 34. **wherefore:** why. 36. **thought:** meditated on, pondered. 38. **Methought:** it seemed to me. 40. **ravelled:** frayed (synonymous with "unravelled"); untwisted (see next note). 40. **sleeve:** part of a garment covering the arm; filament of silk obtained by untwisting a thicker thread. 41. **death of each day's life:** i.e., sleep ends each day just as death ends life. Thus, sleep is to death as day is to life, and sleep is to day as death is to life. 41. **bath:** therapeutic liquid. Early modern English allows the pronunciation "bait" (for "bath") and hence a pun on "bate," which can mean both "strife, discord" and "diminution." 42. **second course:** main or principal dishes, hence something that comes after and satisfies more, as sleep does after exertion. 50. **filthy witness:** morally polluted token. 53. **sleepy:** The word is literally accurate: the drugged grooms live, intended to be scapegoats for

Tate, London/Art Resource, NY

Macbeth (engraving)/Selous, Henry Courtney (1811-90) (after)/LOOK AND LEARN (M IMAGES)/Private Collection/Bridgeman Images

Look at these two representations of the moment in which Macbeth exits Duncan's chambers holding the daggers that he was supposed to leave behind.

Note the details and explain what you believe the artists reveal about Macbeth and Lady Macbeth in this moment. How are these representations similar and different? What lines from the play might have led the artists to depict the scene in these ways?

They must lie there. Go carry them and smear
The sleepy grooms with blood.

MACBETH I'll go no more.
I am afraid to think what I have done;
Look on't again, I dare not.

LADY MACBETH Infirm of purpose!
Give me the daggers. The sleeping and the dead
Are but as pictures; 'tis the eye of childhood
That fears a painted devil. If he do bleed,
I'll gild the faces of the grooms withal,
For it must seem their guilt.

Exit

Knock within

MACBETH Whence is that knocking?
How is't with me, when every noise appals me?
What hands are here? Ha: they pluck out mine eyes.
Will all great Neptune's ocean wash this blood
Clean from my hand? No: this my hand will rather
The multitudinous seas incarnadine,
Making the green one red.

Enter LADY [MACBETH]

LADY MACBETH My hands are of your colour, but I shame
To wear a heart so white.

Knock [within]

I hear a knocking
At the south entry. Retire we to our chamber;
A little water clears us of this deed.

Duncan's murder. 57. **as pictures:** i.e., because, dead, they do not move. See 1.3.95 and 2.3.71. 57–58. **'tis . . . devil:** "Bugbears to scare babes" is proverbial; a "bugbear" (or "bogey man") was an imaginary figure used to scare children into obedience. 58. **painted:** pictured, represented graphically; perhaps also "made up." 58. **If he do bleed:** literally, "if Duncan's wounds are still fresh enough to be shedding liquid blood" (i.e., the blood has not coagulated). 59. **gild:** paint with gold color or gold leaf. Lady Macbeth immediately speaks (unconsciously? compulsively?) the hackneyed gild/gilt/guilt pun (60), which associates gold with red, painting with deception, royalty with murder. For red-gold substitutions, see "golden blood" (2.3.106). 61. **appals:** dismays, terrifies; "apales" ("becomes pale") is probably also present. 63. **Neptune:** classical god of the seas. 65. **multitudinous seas:** numerous oceans ("all the world's seas"); many-waved oceans. 65. **incarnadine:** stain red; literally, "make flesh-colored." 67. **I shame:** I am (or would be) ashamed. 68. **white:** pale with fear. Compare "blanched with fear" (3.4.116) and 5.3.11 and 14–16. 68. **sd *Knock*:** "[W]hen the deed is done . . . the knocking at the gate is heard, and it makes known audibly that the reaction has commenced; the human has made its reflux upon the fiendish; the pulses of life are beginning to beat again" (Thomas De Quincey). 69. **south**

How easy is it then! Your constancy
Hath left you unattended.

Knock [within]

Hark, more knocking.
Get on your night-gown, lest occasion call us
And show us to be watchers. Be not lost
So poorly in your thoughts.

MACBETH To know my deed, 'twere best not know my self.

Knock [within]

Wake Duncan with thy knocking: I would thou couldst.

Exeunt

Act 2, Scene 3

Enter a PORTER. *Knocking within*

PORTER Here's a knocking indeed: if a man were porter of hell-gate, he should have old turning the key. (*Knock*) Knock, knock, knock. Who's there i'th'name of Beelzebub? Here's a farmer that hanged himself on th'expectation of plenty. Come in time — have napkins enough about you, here you'll sweat for't. (*Knock*) Knock, knock. Who's there in th'other devil's name? Faith, here's an equivocator that could swear in both the scales against either scale, who committed treason enough for God's sake, yet could not equivocate to heaven. O, come in, equivocator. (*Knock*) Knock, knock, knock. Who's there?

RGR Collection/Alamy Stock Photo

Shakespeare's Macbeth (photo)/TRISTRAM KENTON/Bridgeman Images

These two images show the Porter after he is awakened by Macduff's knocking in Act 2, Scene 3, following Duncan's murder. The image on the left is from a 1997 film version and the image on the right is from a 2010 stage version.

What are the differences in tone between these two images, specifically in regard to the portrayal of the Porter? Think about gestures, movements, and facial expressions, as well as lighting and set design. What lines from Act 2, Scene 3 could be used as captions for each image?

---

entry: southern entrance to the castle or, later, "palace" (3.1.48, 3.3.13). 71–72. **constancy . . . unattended:** firmness of purpose has left you unsupported. 73. **night-gown:** informal clothing, dressing gown. Most Elizabethans slept naked, and "night-gowns" were worn outdoors and on such occasions as church services and executions. Shakespeare, however, associates "night-gown" with semi-privacy and the bedchamber. 73. **occasion:** circumstances; chance. 74. **watchers:** people who stay awake at night, night-watchers. 76. **To know . . . my self:** i.e., consciousness of murder could best be borne if I lost my identity.

Act 2, Scene 3. 1–2. **porter of hell-gate:** doorman at the entrance to hell (imagined as a castle). 2. **old:** frequent, too much. 3. **Beelzebub:** a popular devil name, one of the few found in the Bible. 5. **Come in time:** This is a good time for you to arrive. 5. **napkins:** handkerchiefs (to wipe the sweat caused by hellfire and perhaps the result of the "sweating tub," a supposed cure for venereal disease). 7. **th'other devil:** The Porter cannot remember the name of another devil. 7. **Faith:** by my faith (a mild oath). 8. **scales:** pans (of a weighing device; here the scales of justice). 9. **for God's sake:** a common oath, but the phrase may refer specifically to Jesuit priests' equivocal oaths to preserve their lives from political reprisal while also maintaining their faith ("for God's sake"). 12. **stealing out of a French hose:** possibly a joke about tailors' skimping on fabric in men's garments ("hose"). The phrase may also be sexual innuendo: "tail" (of "tailor") = vagina; "hose" = codpiece = penis. Precisely what (the theft, the penis) was "stealing out of" (escaping, becoming visible) is equivocal. A pun, stealing/staling (= urinating), would anticipate the Porter's other major interest. 13. **roast your goose:** heat your iron (in the flames of hell). "Goose" was a tailor's long-handled iron and also a slang word for "prostitute,"

Faith, here's an English tailor come hither for stealing out of a French hose. Come in, tailor, here you may roast your goose. (*Knock*) Knock, knock. Never at quiet: what are you? But this place is too cold for hell. I'll devil-porter it no further: I had thought to have let in some of all professions that go the primrose way to th'everlasting bonfire. (*Knock*) Anon, anon. I pray you, remember the porter. [*Opens door*]

Enter MACDUFF *and* LENNOX

MACDUFF Was it so late, friend, ere you went to bed, That you do lie so late?

PORTER Faith, sir, we were carousing till the second cock, and drink, sir, is a great provoker of three things.

MACDUFF What three things does drink especially provoke?

PORTER Marry, sir, nose-painting, sleep, and urine. Lechery, sir, it provokes, and unprovokes: it provokes the desire, but it takes away the performance. Therefore much drink may be said to be an equivocator with lechery: it makes him, and it mars him; it sets him on, and it takes him off; it persuades him and disheartens him, makes him stand to and not stand to. In conclusion, equivocates him in a sleep, and giving him the lie, leaves him.

MACDUFF I believe drink gave thee the lie last night.

PORTER That it did, sir, i'the very throat on me, but I requited him for his lie, and, I think, being too strong for him, though he took up my legs sometime, yet I made a shift to cast him.

Enter MACBETH

MACDUFF Is thy master stirring?
Our knocking has awaked him: here he comes.

[*Exit Porter*]

LENNOX Good morrow, noble sir.

MACBETH Good morrow, both.

MACDUFF Is the king stirring, worthy thane?

MACBETH Not yet.

MACDUFF He did command me to call timely on him;
I have almost slipped the hour.

MACBETH I'll bring you to him.

MACDUFF I know this is a joyful trouble to you, but yet 'tis one.

MACBETH The labour we delight in physics pain. This is the door.

MACDUFF I'll make so bold to call, for 'tis my limited service.

Exit

LENNOX Goes the king hence today?

MACBETH He does — he did appoint so.

LENNOX The night has been unruly: where we lay,
Our chimneys were blown down, and, as they say,

---

a source of venereal disease, the "French pox" for which a sufferer roasted literally (see note 5) and spiritually (in hell). 16–17. **primrose . . . bonfire:** Shakespeare appears to have invented the phrase "primrose path" as a contrast between the easy and attractive pleasures of sin and the consequences of sin, "th'everlasting bonfire" of hell. The primrose is a pale-yellow wild and cultivated flower. The word "bonfire" derives from "bone-fire," a pyre in which human or animal bones were consumed. 18. **remember the porter:** give me a tip (for opening the gate). 18. **sd *Opens door*:** The Porter here performs some action fulfilling his function as gatekeeper. 21–22. **Faith . . . things:** The Porter's lines are apparently prose, but like other prose passages in the play they have an iambic rhythm. 21. **carousing:** celebrating, reveling, drinking. 21. **second cock:** second crowing of a rooster (i.e., a measurement of time before watches and clocks were common). 22. **great provoker of three things:** the Shakespearean clown's typical invitation, a half-riddle that will, he hopes, catch the interest of a wealthy interlocutor. 23. **What . . . provoke:** With this question, Macduff accepts his role as straight man. 24. **Marry:** a mild oath (in full, "by the Lady Mary," "by the Virgin Mary"). 24. **nose-painting:** i.e., the reddening of the sot's nose. 25. **unprovokes:** calms, depresses, allays. 25–26. **provokes the desire . . . performance:** stimulates sexual interest but inhibits sexual functioning. 27. **equivocator:** someone who uses ambiguous words; a prevaricator. 28. **sets him on . . . takes him off:** advances him . . . withdraws him. Besides the bawdy description of a failed erection, the verbs could describe urging dogs to attack and retreat. 29. **stand to:** set to work (with a pun on the erect penis). 30. **equivocates him in a sleep:** fulfills his lechery only in a dream. 30–31. **giving him the lie:** (1) deceiving him (because he cannot perform sexually as he promised), (2) flooring him (as in wrestling), (3) making him urinate ("lie" = lye), (4) making him lose his erection, (5) accusing him of lying. 35. **took up my legs:** made me unable to stand (because drunk); dropped me (as a wrestler does). 35. **shift:** stratagem, ruse. 35. **cast:** throw to the ground; vomit. 39. **Not yet:** This phrase implying that Duncan will stir is calculated to avoid suspicion. Macbeth might have answered "No"; "Not yet" also means "no longer." 40. **timely:** early. 41. **slipped:** failed in keeping (the appointed time). 43. **The labour . . . pain:** Effort we enjoy alleviates suffering. 44. **limited:** appointed. 46. **He does . . . appoint so:** For the

Lamentings heard i'th'air, strange screams of death
And prophesying with accents terrible
Of dire combustion and confused events,
New hatched to th'woeful time. The obscure bird
Clamoured the livelong night. Some say, the earth
Was feverous and did shake.

MACBETH 'Twas a rough night.

LENNOX My young remembrance cannot parallel
A fellow to it.

Enter MACDUFF

MACDUFF O horror, horror, horror,
Tongue nor heart cannot conceive, nor name thee.

MACBETH *and* **LENNOX** What's the matter?

MACDUFF Confusion now hath made his masterpiece:
Most sacrilegious murder hath broke ope
The Lord's anointed temple and stole thence
The life o'th'building.

MACBETH What is't you say, the life?

LENNOX Mean you his majesty?

MACDUFF Approach the chamber and destroy your sight
With a new Gorgon. Do not bid me speak:
See and then speak yourselves.

Exeunt Macbeth and Lennox

Awake, awake!
Ring the alarum bell! Murder and treason!
Banquo and Donaldbain! Malcolm, awake,
Shake off this downy sleep, death's counterfeit,
And look on death itself. Up, up, and see
The great doom's image. Malcolm, Banquo,
As from your graves rise up and walk like sprites
To countenance this horror.

Bell rings. Enter LADY [MACBETH]

LADY MACBETH What's the business
That such a hideous trumpet calls to parley
The sleepers of the house? Speak, speak.

MACDUFF O gentle lady,
'Tis not for you to hear what I can speak.
The repetition in a woman's ear
Would murder as it fell. —

Enter BANQUO

O Banquo, Banquo,
Our royal master's murdered.

LADY MACBETH Woe, alas.
What, in our house?

BANQUO Too cruel, anywhere.

---

same equivocation, see "as he purposes" (1.5.58). 46. **appoint:** order; purpose. 49–50. **Lamentings . . . screams . . . accents:** These sounds are not articulate speech, but inchoate, ominous sounds (like the "obscure bird's" clamor) that people interpret ("they say") as "prophesying" (48, 50), just as Macbeth (mis)interpreted the sisters' words in 1.3. 49. **screams:** shrill, piercing cries. This line is the earliest citation for this meaning under the *Oxford English Dictionary* entry "Scream." 50. **prophesying:** uttering strange things; announcing solemnly. 51. **dire combustion:** dreadful commotion; terrifying disorder. 51. **events:** outcomes, consequences. 52. **obscure bird:** the owl (which is "obscure" because rarely seen and usually heard only at night). 53. **livelong:** very long. 54. **feverous:** feverish, shaking with fever (a personification). The earth was not "sure and firm-set" (2.1.56). 54. **rough:** stormy. 60. **masterpiece:** greatest achievement. 61. **sacrilegious:** violating sacred things; profaning. Sacrilege is specifically the crime of stealing from the church (see 62–63). 61. **ope:** open. The archaic form is needed for the meter. 62. **Lord's anointed temple:** house of worship; Duncan's cranium ("temple") or body. The Christian New Testament treats all believers as the "temple" (sanctuary, church, synagogue) of God (1 Corinthians 3:16), and biblical kings, like English ones, were "anointed" at their coronations; see, for example, David to Saul: "I had compassion on thee and said: I will not lay my hands on my master, for he is the Lord's anointed" (1 Samuel 24:10). Compare Banquo's remark on the "temple-haunting martlet" (1.6.4). 63. **building:** body; house of worship [= "temple" (62)]. 67. **Gorgon:** mythical female being with snakes for hair and the power to turn whoever looked upon her to stone. 69. **Ring the alarum bell:** This bell echoes the bell (or "knell") summoning Macbeth and Duncan to heaven or to hell (2.1.63–64). 71. **downy:** soft (a transferred adjective). The best pillows were stuffed with down, the fine under-plumage of a bird. 73. **great doom's image:** simulacrum ("image") of the Last ("great") Judgment ("doom"). See next note. Duncan's death reminds Macduff of the Christian version of the end of time and of the world. 74. **from your graves rise up:** as the dead will do at the Christian Last Judgment: "I know that he shall rise again in the resurrection at the last day" (John 11:24). 74. **sprites:** spirits, ghosts. 75. **countenance:** be in keeping with; the word also means "give tacit consent to." 76. **trumpet:** Presumably, "trumpet" is a figure of speech for "alarum bell" (69), but the word jarringly recalls 1.7.18–19 and probably recalls St. Paul's description of the time when "sleepers" (77), the dead (see 71), will rise up from their graves (74) at the Last Judgment (see 73 and note): "Behold, I show you a mystery. We shall not all sleep: but we shall all be changed. In a moment, in the twinkling of an eye, at the last trumpet. For the trumpet shall blow, and the dead shall rise incorruptible, and we shall be changed" (1 Corinthians 15:51–52). 76. **parley:** conference under truce. 80. **fell:** was spoken. 85–90. **Had . . . of:** a speech that may be spoken aside, "covered" in the audience's imagination by simultaneous unheard speeches (compare the situations at 1.3.126–41 and 1.4.48–53); it may be spoken publicly and without deceit; it may be spoken to deceive the hearers onstage, but understood with varying degrees of irony by the

Dear Duff, I prithee contradict thyself
And say it is not so.

Enter MACBETH *and* LENNOX

MACBETH Had I but died an hour before this chance,
I had lived a blessèd time, for from this instant,
There's nothing serious in mortality.
All is but toys; renown and grace is dead,
The wine of life is drawn, and the mere lees
Is left this vault to brag of.

Enter MALCOLM *and* DONALDBAIN

DONALDBAIN What is amiss?
MACBETH You are, and do not know't.
The spring, the head, the fountain of your blood
Is stopped, the very source of it is stopped.
MACDUFF Your royal father's murdered.
MALCOLM O, by whom?
LENNOX Those of his chamber, as it seemed, had done't.
Their hands and faces were all badged with blood,
So were their daggers which, unwiped, we found
Upon their pillows. They stared and were distracted;
No man's life was to be trusted with them.
MACBETH O, yet I do repent me of my fury
That I did kill them.
MACDUFF Wherefore did you so?
MACBETH Who can be wise, amazed, temp'rate, and furious,
Loyal and neutral, in a moment? No man.
Th'expedition of my violent love
Outran the pauser, reason. Here lay Duncan,
His silver skin laced with his golden blood
And his gashed stabs looked like a breach in nature,
For ruin's wasteful entrance. There the murderers,
Steeped in the colours of their trade; their daggers
Unmannerly breeched with gore. Who could refrain,
That had a heart to love and in that heart
Courage to make's love known?
LADY MACBETH Help me hence, ho.
MACDUFF Look to the lady.
[*Exit Lady Macbeth, helped*]
MALCOLM [*To Donaldbain*] Why do we hold our tongues, that most may claim
This argument for ours?
DONALDBAIN [*To Malcolm*] What should be spoken here,
Where our fate hid in an auger hole may rush
And seize us? Let's away. Our tears are not yet brewed.

---

audience. 85. **chance:** occurrence, mishap; Macbeth evades his own responsibility for Duncan's death. 87. **mortality:** life, human existence. 88. **toys:** trifles, rubbish. 89. **drawn:** drained (from a cask). 89. **lees:** dregs. 90. **vault:** earth (with the sky as "roof"); cellar (where a wine cask would be stored). 90. **brag:** boast. 92. **spring:** Thomas More provides the traditional metaphorical context: "From the monarch, as from a never-failing spring, flows a stream of all that is good or evil over the whole nation" (*Utopia*, p. 57). 92. **head:** source (of a stream or river); senior male family member. 92. **blood:** family, kindred. 93. **stopped:** blocked, stopped up. Compare Lady Macbeth's prayer (1.5.41–45). 96. **badged:** marked, identified. Liveried servants wore heraldic emblems (badges): these retainers have a new badge, blood, to mark them as Duncan's men. See the clothing images — "laced," "steeped," "breeched" — of 106–10. 98. **distracted:** mentally confused. 100–01. **O . . . them:** a delayed and shocking announcement, since Macbeth has been onstage for almost twenty lines. 101. **Wherefore:** why. 102. **temp'rate:** temperate, restrained. 103. **Loyal and neutral:** maintaining allegiance (to Duncan) and disinterested (toward the grooms' apparent guilt). 104. **expedition:** haste, speed. 105. **pauser:** one who hesitates (here, for rational reflection). 106. **silver:** white. See next note. 106. **golden:** red. Imagery of rich metals (silver and gold) transforms Duncan's body into a decorated "temple" (62) or a garment "laced" with golden threads and streams of blood. 107–08. **breach . . . entrance:** The underlying image is of an opening or break ("breach") in a shore or dike, letting in ruinous (sea)water, or of attacking troops breaking into a castle or walled city: some injurious force overcomes cultivation's or civilization's boundaries. This complex image represents Duncan's body as a devastated landscape, as Macbeth's violated castle, and as the violated bonds of loyalty and hospitality. 107. **breach:** opening, gap. The word's sound anticipates "breeched" (110). 109. **Steeped:** dyed. 109. **colours of their trade:** identifying marks of their occupation. 110. **Unmannerly breeched:** indecently clothed. The image makes the daggers men wear impolite or antisocial breeches (trousers) of blood, but also puns on "unmanly": to dress these daggers in Duncan's blood is to act inhumanly, to act as a man "Who . . . is none" (1.7.47). Compare "breach in nature" (107). 112. **make's:** make his. 113. **Look to the lady:** Traditionally, Lady Macbeth faints here. 114–15. **Why . . . ours:** Why do we remain silent when we may most claim this subject (= "argument" = Duncan's death) as our own? The question draws attention both to the brothers' silence and to the grandiloquence of what *is* being said. 116. **hid in an auger hole:** i.e., concealed in a (figurative) space no larger than a hole made by a drill ("auger"). 117. **brewed:** brought to readiness. 118. **upon the foot of motion:** ready to move; ready to be

MALCOLM [*To Donaldbain*] Nor our strong sorrow upon the foot of motion.
BANQUO Look to the lady,
And when we have our naked frailties hid
That suffer in exposure, let us meet
And question this most bloody piece of work
To know it further. Fears and scruples shake us:
In the great hand of God I stand and thence
Against the undivulged pretence I fight
Of treasonous malice.
MACDUFF And so do I.
ALL So all.
MACBETH Let's briefly put on manly readiness
And meet i'th'hall together.
ALL Well contented.
Exeunt [*all but Malcolm and Donaldbain*]
MALCOLM What will you do? Let's not consort with them.
To show an unfelt sorrow is an office
Which the false man does easy. I'll to England.
DONALDBAIN To Ireland, I. Our separated fortune
Shall keep us both the safer. Where we are,
There's daggers in men's smiles; the nea'er in blood,
The nearer bloody.
MALCOLM This murderous shaft that's shot
Hath not yet lighted, and our safest way
Is to avoid the aim. Therefore to horse,
And let us not be dainty of leave-taking,
But shift away. There's warrant in that theft
Which steals itself when there's no mercy left.
Exeunt

Act 2, Scene 4

Enter ROSS, *with an* OLD MAN

OLD MAN Threescore and ten I can remember well;
Within the volume of which time, I have seen
Hours dreadful and things strange, but this sore night
Hath trifled former knowings.
ROSS Ha, good father,
Thou seest the heavens, as troubled with man's act,
Threatens his bloody stage. By th'clock 'tis day
And yet dark night strangles the travelling lamp.
Is't night's predominance, or the day's shame,
That darkness does the face of earth entomb
When living light should kiss it?
OLD MAN 'Tis unnatural,
Even like the deed that's done. On Tuesday last,
A falcon tow'ring in her pride of place
Was by a mousing owl hawked at and killed.
ROSS And Duncan's horses, a thing most strange and certain,
Beauteous and swift, the minions of their race,
Turned wild in nature, broke their stalls, flung out,
Contending 'gainst obedience as they would
Make war with mankind.
OLD MAN 'Tis said, they eat each other.
ROSS They did so, to th'amazement of mine eyes
That looked upon't.

---

revealed. 120. **naked frailties:** physical weaknesses (e.g., their near-undress); exposed psychological weaknesses. See 127 and note. 122. **question:** debate; investigate. 123. **scruples:** doubts. 124. **hand of God:** power of God. 125. **undivulged pretence:** unrevealed purpose (or intention); unexpressed claim (to the crown). The latter meaning would be appropriate to Malcolm, Prince of Cumberland (1.4.38–39) and declared heir to the Scottish throne. 127. **briefly:** quickly. 127. **put on manly readiness:** get into our usual or customary garments. The phrase suggests that the observers have been unmanned, weakened, by Duncan's death and recalls the chamberlains' daggers "Unmannerly breeched with gore" (110). 129. **consort:** keep company, associate. 131. **easy:** easily. 134–35. **the nea'er . . . bloody:** the more closely one is related to Duncan, the more likely one is to be killed. Compare 91–93. 135–36. **This . . . lighted:** the murderous design that killed Duncan is not yet finished. 136. **lighted:** landed. 138. **dainty:** particular, scrupulous about. 139. **shift:** get away unobserved, evade. 139. **warrant:** sanction, authorization. The word is a further pun: a warrant was also a legal document authorizing the arrest of a wrongdoer. 140. **steals:** a pun: takes unlawfully; sneaks.

Act 2, Scene 4. 1. **Threescore and ten:** seventy (three times a "score," or twenty, plus ten), the biblical limit of human life (Psalms 90:10). 3. **sore:** severe, harsh. 4. **trifled:** made trivial. 4. **father:** honorific title for an elderly man. 5. **act:** deed; principal division of a play. Compare "stage" (6). 7. **travelling lamp:** journeying light (a periphrasis for "sun"). 8. **predominance:** superior influence (probably with an astrological connotation). 8. **shame:** i.e., embarrassment at "man's act" (5), the murder of Duncan. 12. **tow'ring:** soaring. Syncopation preserves the meter. 12. **place:** height (or "pitch") from which the falcon attacks; perhaps "the air." 13. **mousing owl:** owl that preys on mice (hence it ordinarily swoops to the earth rather than fighting another bird in the air). 13. **hawked at:** attacked on the wing. 15. **minions:** darlings, most prized specimens. See note 1.2.19. 17. **as:** as if. 18. **eat:** ate, pronounced "et." 20. **good Macduff:** the first time Macduff receives a positive moral designation.

Enter MACDUFF

Here comes the good Macduff.
How goes the world, sir, now?

MACDUFF Why, see you not?

ROSS Is't known who did this more than bloody deed?

MACDUFF Those that Macbeth hath slain.

ROSS Alas the day,
What good could they pretend?

MACDUFF They were suborned.
Malcolm and Donaldbain, the king's two sons,
Are stol'n away and fled, which puts upon them
Suspicion of the deed.

ROSS 'Gainst nature still.
Thriftless ambition that will ravin up
Thine own life's means. Then 'tis most like
The sovereignty will fall upon Macbeth.

MACDUFF He is already named and gone to Scone
To be invested.

ROSS Where is Duncan's body?

MACDUFF Carried to Colmkill,
The sacred storehouse of his predecessors
And guardian of their bones.

ROSS Will you to Scone?

MACDUFF No, cousin, I'll to Fife.

ROSS Well, I will thither.

MACDUFF Well may you see things well done there. Adieu,
Lest our old robes sit easier than our new.

ROSS Farewell, father.

OLD MAN God's benison go with you, and with those
That would make good of bad, and friends of foes.

Exeunt

---

21. **How goes the world:** What is the state of affairs? 24. **pretend:** allege as a reason. 24. **suborned:** bribed; instigated to betray a trust. 28–29. **Thriftless . . . means:** Ambition, the desire to acquire, is paradoxically spendthrift and self-consuming when it leads sons to kill their father, source of their own lives. 28. **Thriftless:** prodigal. 28. **ravin up:** consume, eat greedily. 29. **means:** resources. 29–30. **Then . . . Macbeth:** The common assumption is that Macbeth will be king if Duncan's sons are not available. 29. **like:** likely. 31. **named:** chosen. 31. **Scone:** ancient, now ruinous, city north of Perth and traditional site of Scottish coronations, though James VI was crowned at Stirling. 32. **invested:** installed ceremonially (as king); clothed with royal insignia. 33. **Colmkill:** the island of Iona, one of the western Hebrides. Here the ancient graves of many Scottish kings may still be seen. 36. **Fife:** ancestral land of Macduff, Thane of Fife. 36. **I will thither:** I will go there. 37–38. **Adieu . . . new:** Farewell (we must part), for fear that ("lest") the future ("new" robes of rank or office) will be less comfortable than the past ("our old robes"). 40. **benison:** blessing.

Understanding and Interpreting

1. This act opens with Banquo talking with his son Fleance. What is Banquo concerned about at this point? What effect does Shakespeare create by beginning with this brief conversation between father and son?
2. In literature, a foil is a character who, by his or her contrast with the main character, highlights the main character's distinctive characteristics. In *Macbeth*, Banquo serves as a foil to Macbeth. Read the lines between Banquo and Macbeth at the opening of Scene 1 and focus on how these lines highlight the characteristics of both men. Create a list of characteristics for each man, using textual evidence to support your observations.
3. In Scene 1, Banquo tells Macbeth that the king is pleased with the hospitality the Macbeths have shown him, saying that the king "hath been in unusual pleasure" (l. 13). He even passes along a diamond as a thank you gift from the king to Lady Macbeth. This short exchange occurs immediately after Lady Macbeth and Macbeth discuss at length their plan to murder Duncan. What is the effect of the timing of Banquo's message?
4. Compare and contrast how Macbeth and Lady Macbeth respond to the murder in Scene 2. What do their differing responses suggest about their characters at this point?
5. After killing Duncan, Macbeth cannot bear to return to the scene of the murder to plant the bloody knives. However, Lady Macbeth is willing to do it, saying, "The sleeping and the dead / Are

but as pictures" (Scene 2, ll. 57–58). What does this suggest about the role Lady Macbeth will play in Macbeth's future attempts to gain greater power?

6. After the king's murder is discovered, Macbeth and Lady Macbeth must be careful in their response. In what ways are they successful in hiding their guilt? In what ways might they arouse the suspicions of other characters?
7. Summarize the events in Scene 3, lines 112 to 129, in which Lennox and Macbeth describe what they observe in Duncan's chamber.
8. Banquo proposes that the men "question this most bloody piece of work / To know it further" (Scene 3, ll. 122 to 123). He then declares that he stands in the "great hand of God" and will fight "treasonous malice" (ll. 124 to 125). Do you think these lines indicate that Banquo may be suspicious of Macbeth in particular or that he just wants to know more about the circumstances surrounding Duncan's murder? Explain your reasoning.
9. In Scene 4, Macduff states that the hasty departure of Malcolm and Donalbain "puts upon them / Suspicion of the deed" (ll. 25 to 27), even though they are Duncan's sons. Historically, sons of kings sometimes did kill their fathers in order to gain the power of the throne. Summarize the reasons Malcolm and Donalbain provide for fleeing to England and Ireland (Scene 3, ll. 129 to 140) and whether the other noblemen might agree with their reasoning.

Analyzing Language, Style, and Structure

1. **Vocabulary in Context.** As Macbeth prepares to murder Duncan, he envisions a dagger in front of him, and says "such an instrument I was to use" (Scene 1, l. 43). What does the word "instrument" mean in this context? What other meanings of the word have you encountered?
2. **Vocabulary in Context.** In the soliloquy before he kills Duncan, Macbeth says, "half-world Nature seems dead" (Scene 1, l. 50). What does the word "nature" mean in this context? How is that meaning similar to and different from other uses you know?
3. **Vocabulary in Context.** When Lennox describes the turbulent night of Duncan's death, he says there were screams "prophesying with accents terrible" (Scene 3, l. 50). What does the word "accents" mean in this context? What are other meanings of this word?
4. **Skill Focus.** Macbeth seems inconsolable after he kills the two men (Scene 2, ll. 62 to 67). Using text to support your response, discuss how Shakespeare uses water imagery to emphasize the different reactions of Lady Macbeth and Macbeth to the murder.
5. **Skill Focus.** After Macduff and Lennox ask Macbeth about the king, Lennox goes on to describe the tumultuous weather of the night before (Scene 3, ll. 47 to 53). Summarize Lennox's description of the night and explain the effect it has at this moment in the play.
6. **Skill Focus.** Analyze how Macbeth uses imagery and hyperbole to describe his reaction to Duncan's death in Scene 3, lines 102 to 112. How does he intend his language choices to affect the other characters present?
7. After Banquo exits, Macbeth sees a dagger floating in front of him (Scene 1, l. 33). Explain whether you think the dagger is real or imagined — a "dagger of the mind" (l. 38), perhaps a vision sent by supernatural forces. What are the implications of both possibilities? Why do you think Macbeth calls the dagger a "fatal vision" (l. 36)? How does the dagger's being real or imagined affect your interpretation of Macbeth's psychological state at this point in the play?
8. In Scene 1, lines 51 to 60, Macbeth makes numerous references to witchcraft and evil omens. Identify these references and analyze what they indicate about Macbeth's state of mind.

9. Macbeth claims that he heard someone cry, "Glamis hath murdered sleep . . . Macbeth shall sleep no more" (Scene 2, ll. 45–46). What other references to sleep does Macbeth make? What purpose do his descriptions of sleep serve within the scene?

10. A *double entendre* is a word or expression that can be understood in two different ways, with one of the ways often involving a sexual or risqué reference. In his brief conversation with Macduff (Scene 3, ll. 20 to 35), the porter employs the literary device of double entendre several times for a humorous effect. Read the porter's lines closely and identify at least one double entendre. Discuss why these lines can be considered comical.

11. Examine Scene 3, lines 115 to 140, in which the men discuss what next steps they should take. Focus on language related to masculinity. What do their comments convey about how they think men should respond to tragedy?

Topics for Composing

1. **Analysis.** How does Macbeth change from Act 1 to Act 2? What are the internal and/or external motivations for his significant actions and changes in character?

2. **Argument.** In many film and stage adaptations of the play, the scene with the porter opening the gates is either cut entirely or cut back extensively. Imagine that you are the director of a stage or film production of *Macbeth*. Write an argument for the inclusion, exclusion, or editing of the porter's scene. Consider how including or cutting it might affect your production.

3. **Argument.** Imagine that you were Macbeth during Act 2. In your own words, write an argument for killing Duncan, while considering and refuting the counterarguments.

4. **Connection.** Consider other pieces you have read, in this book or elsewhere, that involve a character making a difficult or significant choice. Identify the context of the decision, summarize it, and discuss how the motivation behind that decision compares to or contrasts with Macbeth's motivation.

5. **Speaking and Listening.** Working with a small group, act out a portion of a scene from Act 2 without including any of the dialogue. You can use gestures, movements, facial expressions, costumes, and props, but you may not speak. Afterward, discuss with your group the choices you made and how your performance of the scene helped you to better understand the plot, language, or theme of the play.

6. **Research.** Macbeth's succession to the throne at the end of Act 2 may seem sudden. However, at the time, Scottish kings were elected by the thanes, who would have elected a new king as soon as possible after their king's death. Because this play is loosely based on actual events in Scotland, it is possible to connect the characters in the play with the actual historical figures on which they were based. Research the order of succession and any history related to the battles these thanes and kings fought. Prepare a visual (e.g., a poster, website, or slideshow) of the historical events. Include quotations from the play that seem most related to each of the historical figures you research.

7. **Multimodal.** Macbeth is king by the end of Act 2. Thus, Macbeth's family coat of arms would be featured prominently in his court. Do some research about traditional designs for a coat of arms, including the elements that go into making one. Create two symbolic coats of arms for the newly crowned Macbeth. The first one should represent what the public knows about Macbeth, including his bravery on the battlefield. The second one should represent the true Macbeth, who is willing to kill his king to gain power. Under each coat of arms, provide words or phrases from the play that reveal those aspects of Macbeth's character.

Enter BANQUO *[dressed for riding]*

BANQUO Thou hast it now, King, Cawdor, Glamis, all,
As the weïrd women promised, and I fear
Thou played'st most foully for't; yet it was said
It should not stand in thy posterity,
But that myself should be the root and father
Of many kings. If there come truth from them —
As upon thee, Macbeth, their speeches shine —
Why by the verities on thee made good,
May they not be my oracles as well
And set me up in hope? But hush, no more.

Sennet sounded. Enter MACBETH *as King,* LADY [MACBETH *as Queen],* LENNOX, ROSS, *Lords, and Attendants*

MACBETH Here's our chief guest.
LADY MACBETH If he had been forgotten,
It had been as a gap in our great feast
And all thing unbecoming.
MACBETH Tonight we hold a solemn supper, sir,
And I'll request your presence.
BANQUO Let your highness
Command upon me, to the which my duties
Are with a most indissoluble tie
Forever knit.
MACBETH Ride you this afternoon?
BANQUO Ay, my good lord.
MACBETH We should have else desired your good advice
Which still hath been both grave and prosperous
In this day's council: but we'll take tomorrow.
Is't far you ride?
BANQUO As far, my lord, as will fill up the time
'Twixt this and supper. Go not my horse the better,
I must become a borrower of the night
For a dark hour, or twain.
MACBETH Fail not our feast.
BANQUO My lord, I will not.
MACBETH We hear our bloody cousins are bestowed
In England and in Ireland, not confessing
Their cruel parricide, filling their hearers
With strange invention. But of that tomorrow,
When therewithal we shall have cause of state
Craving us jointly. Hie you to horse; adieu,
Till you return at night. Goes Fleance with you?
BANQUO Ay, my good lord; our time does call upon's.
MACBETH I wish your horses swift and sure of foot,
And so I do commend you to their backs.
Farewell.

Exit Banquo

Let every man be master of his time
Till seven at night; to make society
The sweeter welcome, we will keep ourself
Till supper-time alone. While then, God be with you.

Exeunt [all but Macbeth and a Servant]

Act 3, Scene 1. 0. **sd dressed for riding:** Macbeth later infers (19) Banquo's plans, apparently from his garb. Boots, spurs, or whips ("riding-rods") were common props indicating that a character had recently ridden or would soon ride a horse. 1–10. **Thou . . . more:** This ambiguous speech may mean that Banquo, seeing Macbeth's success and the fulfillment of the sisters' prophecies, passively colludes in Duncan's murder and now considers some criminal action. 2–3. **fear . . . foully:** a punning antithesis between "fair" and "foully." 4. **stand in thy posterity:** continue, or remain, in those who descend from you. 5–6. **father / Of many kings:** Banquo's descendants included King James, according to popular legend. 7. **shine:** look favorably upon. 8. **made good:** rendered fact (i.e., the sisters' prophecies fulfilled). 10. **sd *Sennet*:** distinctive set of musical notes played on trumpet or cornet and associated with a specific individual. 10. **sd *as King*:** Macbeth's new status would have been conveyed through costume and perhaps props (crown and scepter might be useful at 62–63) or a throne (for the actor to indicate at 49–50). 13. **all thing:** wholly, completely; everything. 14. **supper:** evening meal. 16. **Command upon me:** i.e., I am at your disposal. 17–18. **Are . . . knit:** Banquo emphasizes his loyalty, perhaps to remind Macbeth of their shared knowledge (i.e., the speech is subtle blackmail) or to reassure Macbeth he has nothing to fear. 22. **still:** always. 22. **grave:** serious, important. 22. **prosperous:** successful, fortunate. 23. **council:** Early audiences would probably understand "Privy Council," the senior officers of state and aristocrats who advised the monarch and directed the day-to-day business of early Stuart government. 23. **take tomorrow:** i.e., command your attendance tomorrow (and delay our business from today). 26. **this:** i.e., this time, now. 26. **Go . . . the better:** if my horse does not go better (i.e., "fast enough"). 28. **twain:** two. 34. **strange invention:** improbable or outlandish fiction — i.e., accounts of Duncan's death different from Macbeth's version. 35. **therewithal:** with it. 35. **cause of state:** political affair requiring a decision. 36. **Craving us jointly:** requiring us both together. 42. **master of his time:** responsible for his own activities. 45. **While:** until; "while then" is a Scottish

Sirrah, a word with you: attend those men
Our pleasure?

SERVANT They are, my lord, without the palace gate.

MACBETH Bring them before us.

Exit Servant

To be thus is nothing,
But to be safely thus. Our fears in Banquo
Stick deep, and in his royalty of nature
Reigns that which would be feared. 'Tis much he dares,
And to that dauntless temper of his mind,
He hath a wisdom that doth guide his valour
To act in safety. There is none but he,
Whose being I do fear; and under him
My genius is rebuked, as it is said
Mark Antony's was by Caesar. He chid the sisters
When first they put the name of king upon me
And bade them speak to him. Then prophet-like,
They hailed him father to a line of kings.
Upon my head they placed a fruitless crown
And put a barren sceptre in my gripe,
Thence to be wrenched with an unlineal hand,
No son of mine succeeding. If't be so,
For Banquo's issue have I filed my mind;
For them, the gracious Duncan have I murdered,
Put rancours in the vessel of my peace
Only for them, and mine eternal jewel
Given to the common enemy of man,
To make them kings, the seeds of Banquo kings.
Rather than so, come Fate into the list,
And champion me to th'utterance. Who's there?

Enter Servant and two MURDERERS

[*To Servant*] Now go to the door and stay there till we call.

Exit Servant

Was it not yesterday we spoke together?

MURDERERS It was, so please your highness.

MACBETH Well then, now have you considered of my speeches? Know, that it was he in the times past which held you so under fortune, which you thought had been our innocent self. This I made good to you in our last conference; passed in probation with you how you were borne in hand, how crossed; the instruments, who wrought with them, and all things else that might to half a soul and to a notion crazed say, "Thus did Banquo."

FIRST MURDERER You made it known to us.

MACBETH I did so, and went further, which is now our point of second meeting. Do you find your patience so predominant in your nature, that you can let this go? Are you so gospelled,

---

expression and current in Yorkshire dialect. 46. **Sirrah:** slighting form of address by social superior to inferior. 48. **palace gate:** The specificity indicates the physical distance Macbeth wishes to keep between himself and his instruments. 49–50. **To be . . . safely thus:** To be king is nothing unless to be safely one. The repeated "thus" urges the actor to some gesture (e.g., indicating the royal trappings or the throne if there is one). 51. **royalty of nature:** royal nature. The phrase is both emphatic praise and an allusion to Banquo's royal progeny predicted by the sisters in 1.3. 53. **to:** in addition to. 53. **dauntless:** fearless, intrepid. 53. **temper:** temperament, mental constitution. 56. **being:** existence; psychological and physical attributes. 57–58. **My . . . Caesar:** Macbeth compares himself to the Roman general and triumvir Mark Antony, who was defeated in the civil wars that ended the Roman republic and inaugurated the Roman empire, and compares Banquo to the historical Octavian (Shakespeare's Octavius), later called "Caesar" (58) Augustus, the victor in those wars. 57. **genius:** tutelary spirit. Classical belief held that every individual had a personal spirit (for good or ill), variously named or translated as "genius," "daemon," or "angel." 58. **Caesar:** Caesar Augustus, first Roman emperor. 62–63. **fruitless crown . . . barren sceptre:** Recalling the sisters' predictions (see 58), Macbeth laments that he has no children to inherit his crown [it is childless = "fruitless" (62)] and his "sceptre," the ceremonial rod of office and figuratively his penis [understood as the source of a "son of mine" (65)], is "barren" (63), without an heir. 63. **gripe:** grip, grasp. 64. **unlineal:** not in a direct line of descent. 66. **issue:** progeny, descendants. 66. **filed:** tainted, polluted, defiled. 68. **rancours:** malignant hatreds, bitter ill-feelings. 68. **vessel:** cup. 69. **eternal jewel:** soul. 70. **common enemy:** enemy to all, enemy of all (i.e., Satan). 71. **seeds:** progeny, offspring. 72. **list:** the enclosed space where knights contended in formal tournaments (tilts) or to determine a dispute through trial by combat (*Richard II* 1.3 dramatizes an aborted example of the latter). 73. **champion:** challenge to a contest, bid defiance to. Macbeth may expect Fate to enter the lists against Banquo's sons and, following the sisters' assurances, fight for Macbeth. 73. **utterance:** uttermost, furthest limit (here, death). 73. **Who's there?:** a common dramatic formula for summoning attendants; it need not be spoken in response to any speech or event. 73. **sd MURDERERS:** sometimes imagined as ex-soldiers, a masterless, often vagrant class much feared in early modern England and the subject of punitive legal treatment. 80. **made good:** rendered convincing. 80. **conference:** discussion, meeting. 80–81. **passed in probation:** proved, demonstrated. 81. **borne in hand:** deceived, misled deliberately. 83. **notion:** mind, intellect. 88. **gospelled:** imbued with the principles of the gospel (= the Christian New Testament or, generally,

extending beyond the text

Playwright Suzan-Lori Parks wrote a play every day for a year and published all of them in a collection called *365 Days/365 Plays*. Portions of these plays were then performed by over 600 theatre groups across the country in 2006. Read the following short play called *Project Macbeth*, which updates the action and characters of the original with Macbeth as "MacSmith" and Banquo as "MacJones."

Project Macbeth

Suzan-Lori Parks

2 Army Guys walk along.

MACJONES: How many you hit?

MACSMITH: Lets talk about something else.

MACJONES: You hit zero.

MACSMITH: The ones I hit were for God. And country. Im a soldier.

MACJONES: Im a soldier too.

(*Rest*)

I hit 10. You hit zero.

MACSMITH: I hit 20.

MACJONES: Bulls***.

MACSMITH: See my gold star?

MACJONES: You oughta wear it on yr chest, man! 20 towns?! You hit 20 towns?!?

MACSMITH: For God. And country.

MACJONES: You the man, man. Hush my mouth.

They walk along.

MACSMITH: We're the only ones who made it back in one piece. Remember when we shipped out. Thousands of guys and gals. Now only me and you are left. And the Projects. The Projects will always be here, seems like.

MACJONES: Yeah.

(*Rest*)

Lets swear. Eternal brotherhood forever. You and me.

They cut their hands.

MACSMITH: MacSmith—

MACJONES: and MacJones—

MACSMITH & MACJONES: Swear eternal brotherhood.

They clasp hands, trading blood.

MACSMITH: Ive changed my fate line, cutting my hand like that.

MACJONES: Come on, we're almost home.

A trio of Women appear, perhaps dressed like the Supremes.

1ST WOMAN: Which one of you is MacSmith?

MACJONES: Theyre witches. Play them off.

(*continued*)

extending beyond the text

MACSMITH: If theyre witches how come they dont know Im MacSmith?

2ND WOMAN: You will murder MacJones. Dont roll yr eyes at me.

3RD WOMAN: You will murder MacJones sure as me and my 2 weird sisters are standing here today.

1ST WOMAN: You will murder MacJones and you will build a kingdom on his bones.

MACJONES: Hold on now, ladies.

3RD WOMAN: Talk to the hand, man, history is in the making, and those who fall short fall silent.

MACJONES: Im outa here. But I cant move.

2ND WOMAN: Draw yr knife, MacSmith, go on.

MACSMITH: Do I have a choice?

3RD WOMAN: We are the Fates, brother.

MACSMITH: S***.

MacJones suddenly regains his ability to run.
MacSmith runs after him with his knife drawn.

How are the action and characters of *Project Macbeth* similar to those of Shakespeare's *Macbeth*? How are they different? What might Parks be suggesting about power and violence with *Project Macbeth*?

to pray for this good man and for his issue,
whose heavy hand hath bowed you to the
grave and beggared yours forever?

FIRST MURDERER We are men, my liege.

MACBETH Ay, in the catalogue ye go for men,
As hounds, and greyhounds, mongrels, spaniels, curs,
Shoughs, water-rugs, and demi-wolves are clept
All by the name of dogs. The valued file
Distinguishes the swift, the slow, the subtle,
The housekeeper, the hunter, every one
According to the gift which bounteous nature
Hath in him closed, whereby he does receive
Particular addition from the bill
That writes them all alike. And so of men.
Now, if you have a station in the file
Not i'th'worst rank of manhood, say't,
And I will put that business in your bosoms,
Whose execution takes your enemy off,
Grapples you to the heart and love of us
Who wear our health but sickly in his life,
Which in his death were perfect.

SECOND MURDERER I am one, my liege,
Whom the vile blows and buffets of the world
Hath so incensed that I am reckless what I do
To spite the world.

FIRST MURDERER And I another,
So weary with disasters, tugged with fortune,
That I would set my life on any chance
To mend it or be rid on't.

MACBETH Both of you know
Banquo was your enemy.

Christian teachings). 90. **yours:** your families and dependents. Compare "His wife, his babes, and all unfortunate souls / That trace him in his line" (4.1.151–52). 91. **We are men:** Evidently, the Murderers mean this answer to affirm their pride, their injured merit, their capacity for revenge; the claim echoes ironically Macbeth's "I dare do all that may become a man" (1.7.46). Proverbially, "Men are but men." 92. **catalogue:** Wordplay on "cat" (and dog) is possible here. 93. **spaniels:** long-haired dogs popular for hunting game and as pets. 93. **curs:** watchdogs or sheep dogs; the word had not yet become entirely contemptuous. 94. **Shoughs:** a kind of lap-dog. 94. **water-rugs:** shaggy water-dogs (?). 94. **demi-wolves:** animals half wolf, half dog (the two species can interbreed). 94. **clept:** named, called. 95. **valued file:** list or dossier ("file") with values (qualities, prices) attached. 97. **housekeeper:** watchdog. 99. **closed:** enclosed, incorporated. 100. **Particular addition:** specific mark of distinction. 100. **bill:** catalogue, inventory. 103. **rank:** sort, quality; row of individuals abreast [as distinct from a "file" (see 95), individuals aligned one behind the other]. 105. **execution:** carrying out; doing. 105. **takes . . . off:** kills; removes. 106. **Grapples:** attaches firmly. The metaphor is from the use of grappling-irons to hold ships together in battle. 107. **wear:** The clothing metaphors continue. 107. **in his life:** i.e., while he lives. 108. **perfect:**

MURDERERS True, my lord.
MACBETH So is he mine, and in such bloody distance
That every minute of his being thrusts
Against my near'st of life; and though I could
With barefaced power sweep him from my sight
And bid my will avouch it, yet I must not,
For certain friends that are both his and mine,
Whose loves I may not drop, but wail his fall
Who I myself struck down. And thence it is
That I to your assistance do make love,
Masking the business from the common eye
For sundry weighty reasons.
SECOND MURDERER We shall, my lord,
Perform what you command us.
FIRST MURDERER Though our lives—
MACBETH Your spirits shine through you. Within this hour at most,
I will advise you where to plant yourselves,
Acquaint you with the perfect spy o'th'time,
The moment on't, for't must be done tonight,
And something from the palace: always thought,
That I require a clearness. And with him,
To leave no rubs nor botches in the work,
Fleance, his son that keeps him company,
Whose absence is no less material to me
Than is his father's, must embrace the fate
Of that dark hour. Resolve yourselves apart,
I'll come to you anon.
MURDERERS We are resolved, my lord.
MACBETH I'll call upon you straight; abide within.

[Exeunt Murderers]

It is concluded. Banquo, thy soul's flight,
If it find heaven, must find it out tonight. *Exit*

Act 3, Scene 2

Enter [LADY MACBETH], *and a* SERVANT

LADY MACBETH Is Banquo gone from court?
SERVANT Ay, madam, but returns again tonight.
LADY MACBETH Say to the king, I would attend his leisure
For a few words.
SERVANT Madam, I will. *Exit*
LADY MACBETH Nought's had, all's spent
Where our desire is got without content.
'Tis safer to be that which we destroy
Than by destruction dwell in doubtful joy.

Enter MACBETH

How now, my lord, why do you keep alone,
Of sorriest fancies your companions making,
Using those thoughts which should indeed have died
With them they think on? Things without all remedy

flawless, excellent. 112. **tugged with:** mauled by. 113. **set my life on:** gamble my life on. 114. **on't:** of it. 116. **distance:** discord, dissension. 117. **thrusts:** stabs [compare "stick" (51)]. 118. **near'st of life:** i.e., those things most necessary to life; literally, the vital organs. 119. **barefaced:** naked, open. 120. **bid my will avouch it:** make it just because it is my will. 122. **but wail:** but I must wail. This phrase depends upon "may" in the preceding one. 124. **make love:** pay amorous attention. 127. **Though our lives:** First Murderer is presumably about to volunteer his and his companion's lives to achieve Banquo's death. 128. **Your . . . you:** Macbeth's interruption may indicate eagerness to get his plan under way or impatience at the Murderers' tedious responses to an offer they could not refuse. 129. **plant:** position (here, "hide"). 130. **perfect:** fully informed; best. 132–33. **always . . . clearness:** always known (or remembered) that I must be free of involvement. 132. **something:** i.e., some distance from. 133. **with him:** i.e., with Banquo's death. 134. **rubs nor botches:** impediments or flaws. 136. **Whose . . . material:** The contradiction of "absence" and "material" recalls the paradox of "nothing is, / But what is not" (1.3.140–41). 136. **absence:** death. 136. **material:** important, consequential. 138. **Resolve yourselves apart:** decide between yourselves in private, but also gather the necessary determination (or courage). Macbeth wants to give the men time to accept murdering Fleance. 140. **straight:** at once. 141. **It is concluded:** All the preparations have been made (the Murderers were the last link). 141. **soul's flight:** The soul was traditionally imagined as a bird that could fly to heaven.

Act 3, Scene 2. 9. **fancies:** hallucinations, delusive visions. 11. **all:** any. 12. **what's done, is done:** The proverb "Things done cannot be undone" links this moment with 1.7.1 ff. and 5.1.57–58. 13. **scorched:** slashed, notched, scored. 14–15. **She'll . . . tooth:** Here, a snake is imagined as female, although metaphorically it represents only males (Duncan and his sons, Banquo and his). 14. **close:** rejoin, heal up (i.e., the wounded snake will recover). 14. **our poor malice:** Macbeth's (and Lady Macbeth's?) "malice," the murder of Duncan, is "poor" because it is insufficiently

Dame Ellen Terry (1847-1928) as Lady Macbeth, after a painting by John Singer Sargent (1856-1925) 1896 (oil on canvas)/Eves, Reginald Grenville (1876-1941)/HERBERT ART GALLERY & MUSEUM, COVENTRY/Herbert Art Gallery & Museum, Coventry, UK/Bridgeman Images

Examine this 1896 painting by Reginald Grenville Eves of an actress playing Lady Macbeth.

How is Lady Macbeth portrayed in this image? What artistic choices — color, framing, costumes, gestures, facial expressions — help to communicate this portrayal? While the play does not include a scene in which Lady Macbeth crowns herself, what lines from the play might have led the actress and the painter to portray her in this way?

Should be without regard; what's done, is done.
MACBETH We have scorched the snake, not killed it;
She'll close, and be herself, whilst our poor malice
Remains in danger of her former tooth.
But let the frame of things disjoint, both the worlds suffer,
Ere we will eat our meal in fear, and sleep
In the affliction of these terrible dreams
That shake us nightly. Better be with the dead
Whom we, to gain our peace, have sent to peace,
Than on the torture of the mind to lie
In restless ecstasy. Duncan is in his grave.
After life's fitful fever, he sleeps well;
Treason has done his worst; nor steel nor poison,
Malice domestic, foreign levy, nothing
Can touch him further.
LADY MACBETH Come on. Gentle my lord,
Sleek o'er your rugged looks, be bright and jovial
Among your guests tonight.
MACBETH So shall I, love,
And so I pray be you. Let your remembrance
Apply to Banquo, present him eminence
Both with eye and tongue; unsafe the while, that we
Must lave our honours in these flattering streams
And make our faces vizards to our hearts,
Disguising what they are.
LADY MACBETH You must leave this.
MACBETH O, full of scorpions is my mind, dear wife!

---

violent; speaking either as king ("our" = royal plural) or for husband and wife, Macbeth seeks consolation for having failed (as yet) to kill enough people [i.e., Banquo and Fleance (see 36–38), perhaps Malcolm and Donaldbain also]. 16. **frame of things:** universal order. 16. **both the worlds suffer:** earth and heaven be destroyed. 21. **on . . . lie:** The implicit image is of the bed as a means or instrument of torture — e.g., a rack. 22. **ecstasy:** frenzy, stupor. 23. **sleeps well:** Duncan has been sent to the "peace" (20), the eternal sleep of death, but Macbeth has "murdered sleep" (2.2.45) for himself and many others who remain alive. Compare 1.7.61–63 and the ironies of "Soundly" (1.7.63). 24. **nor . . . nor:** neither . . . nor. 25. **Malice domestic:** native ("domestic" — i.e., Scottish) envy or hatred. 25. **levy:** body of men collected to form an army. 27. **Gentle my lord:** i.e., my gentle lord. 28. **Sleek:** smooth. 28. **rugged:** furrowed. 30–32. **Let . . . tongue:** Since Macbeth has just arranged Banquo's murder, this advice presumably means to misdirect Lady Macbeth (Macbeth is now acting independently; compare 1.5 and 1.7), or it is an attempt to win Lady Macbeth's complicity by stressing Banquo's dangerousness. 30. **remembrance:** thought, regard. 31. **present him eminence:** offer him homage or respect. 32–34. **unsafe . . . hearts:** For the period ("the while") of our insecurity (see "unsafe"), we must wash ("lave") our titles in streams of flattery and make our faces masks ("vizards") for our hearts. 34–35. **And make . . . are:** The implied contrast of face and heart is proverbial: "fair face foul heart." 35–36. **You . . . wife:** These lines might be spoken (and punctuated) to indicate that Macbeth anxiously interrupts Lady

Thou know'st that Banquo and his Fleance lives.

LADY MACBETH But in them Nature's copy's not eterne.

MACBETH There's comfort yet, they are assailable;
Then be thou jocund: ere the bat hath flown
His cloistered flight, ere to black Hecate's summons
The shard-born beetle with his drowsy hums
Hath rung night's yawning peal, there shall be done
A deed of dreadful note.

LADY MACBETH What's to be done?

MACBETH Be innocent of the knowledge, dearest chuck,
Till thou applaud the deed. Come, seeling night,
Scarf up the tender eye of pitiful day
And with thy bloody and invisible hand
Cancel and tear to pieces that great bond
Which keeps me pale. Light thickens,
And the crow makes wing to th'rooky wood;
Good things of day begin to droop and drowse,
Whiles night's black agents to their preys do rouse.
Thou marvell'st at my words, but hold thee still;
Things bad begun, make strong themselves by ill.
So prithee, go with me.

Exeunt

Act 3, Scene 3

Enter three MURDERERS

FIRST MURDERER But who did bid thee join with us?

THIRD MURDERER Macbeth.

SECOND MURDERER He needs not our mistrust, since he delivers
Our offices and what we have to do
To the direction just.

FIRST MURDERER [*To Third Murderer*] Then stand with us.
The west yet glimmers with some streaks of day;
Now spurs the lated traveller apace
To gain the timely inn, and near approaches
The subject of our watch.

THIRD MURDERER Hark, I hear horses.

BANQUO (*Within*) Give us a light there, ho!

SECOND MURDERER Then 'tis he; the rest
That are within the note of expectation
Already are i'th'court.

FIRST MURDERER His horses go about.

THIRD MURDERER Almost a mile; but he does usually,
So all men do, from hence to th'palace gate
Make it their walk.

Macbeth. 38. **But . . . eterne:** Banquo and Fleance are not immortal. 38. **copy:** reproduction, imitation; pattern, example; legal tenure. 38. **copy's:** copy is. 38. **eterne:** eternal. 39. **assailable:** attackable, vulnerable to assault. 40. **jocund:** merry, cheerful. 41. **cloistered:** The bat flies in and around buildings (which have cloisters, covered walks open to the outside) rather than in the open air. 42. **shard-born:** born in dung; but another meaning of "shard" permits the popular gloss "borne [carried] aloft by its wing-cases." 43. **yawning:** This image may originate with a bell's "mouth," but also recalls "drowsy" [42; see also "droop and drowse" (52)]. Macbeth imagines the beetle's soporific sound as the ringing of bells (= "peal") that mark night's and sleep's arrival. 44. **note:** notoriety. Another meaning ("musical sound") continues the imagery ("hums" and "peal") of 42–43. 45–46. **Be . . . deed:** Do not concern yourself in advance about an event (Banquo's murder) you will welcome when it has happened. 45. **chuck:** affectionate nickname derived from "chick" (chicken). 46. **seeling:** sewing; blinding. "Seeling" is a technical term from falconry: the sewing together of a young bird's eyelids to condition it to accept the hood necessary for training. A metaphor from the validating of a written document by applying metal insignia to hot wax, "sealing," is perhaps present. 47. **Scarf up:** blindfold. 47. **pitiful:** full of pity, compassionate. 49. **bond:** contract, legal commitment; moral obligation. Banquo's "bond of life," his very existence, keeps Macbeth "pale" (50); to "cancel" that bond is to kill Banquo, but the phrase embraces all the moral, social, and political obligations (bonds) so far violated. 50. **Light thickens:** it grows dark. 51. **makes wing:** flies. 51. **rooky:** filled with rooks. 54. **Thou marvell'st:** an implicit stage direction to Lady Macbeth. 54. **hold thee still:** continue steadfast as you have been. 55. **Things . . . ill:** A proverb — "Crimes are made secure by greater crimes" — may have contributed to this line.

Act 3, Scene 3. 1. **But . . . us:** "But" indicates that the Murderers enter conversing; presumably First and Second have been questioning Third Murderer, whom they did not expect. 1. **THIRD MURDERER:** Critics have speculated on his identity: Ross, Macbeth? 3. **offices:** duties. 4. **just:** precisely, exactly. 4. **stand:** take position; hide. 6. **lated:** belated, overtaken by night. 7. **timely:** opportune. 8. **I hear horses:** The sound of hoofbeats was common in the Tudor and Stuart theater; for more hoofbeats, see 4.1.138–39. 9. **Give . . . ho!:** Banquo calls to the grooms who will cool the horses while their riders walk to the castle (see 11–14). 9–11. **Then . . . court:** The other expected guests have already arrived. The Murderers serve as macabre butlers or doormen to Macbeth's feast. 11–14. **His walk:** These lines explain the absence of horses onstage and

extending beyond the text

Throughout the play, Shakespeare examines the effects that Macbeth's unlawful seizure of the crown has on Duncan's sons, his other victims, and Scotland. Shakespeare also presents the psychological effects that these actions have on Macbeth himself. In 2018, Stephen Greenblatt, a professor of humanities at Harvard University, published an analysis of some of Shakespeare's villains called *Tyrant: Shakespeare on Politics*. Read the following section that focuses on the personal toll Macbeth's actions have had on him and his wife.

from Tyrant: Shakespeare on Politics

Stephen Greenblatt

Lady Macbeth knows that her husband's psychic state threatens them both. "Naught's had, all's spent," she reflects to herself,

Where our desire is got without content.
'Tis safer to be that which we destroy
Than by destruction dwell in doubtful joy. (3.2.4–7)

But what exactly did she expect? Tyranny comes about, as her words acknowledge, through destruction, the destruction of people and of a whole country. That she somehow thought that their personal contentment, safety, and joy could be achieved by this means is in keeping with the fatal shallowness she voiced when she washed the murdered king's blood off her hands: "A little water clears up of this deed" (2.2.70).

The intimate bond between husband and wife was instrumental in their fatal decision to kill Duncan, and in the devastating aftermath of their act, which they carried out together, it is the one human bond that remains for either of them. But nothing that Lady Macbeth now says to her husband—"Why do you keep alone?," "What's done is done," "Be bright and jovial"—quiets the torment within him. Her attempts at forced cheerfulness and reassuring matter-of-factness ring hollow in the face of his anguish: "Oh, full of scorpions is my mind, dear wife!" (3.2.35). For his own part, though he continues to use terms of endearment altogether rare for Shakespeare's married couples, he is no longer sharing his dark designs with her, "What's to be done?" she asks about Banquo, and he replies, "Be innocent of the knowledge, dearest chuck, Till thou applaud the deed" (3.2.44–45).

What does Greenblatt suggest about how violence and deception alter the relationship between Macbeth and Lady Macbeth? Why has Duncan's murder, instead of bringing them closer together, begun to pull them apart?

Enter BANQUO *and* FLEANCE, *with a torch*

SECOND MURDERER A light, a light!
THIRD MURDERER 'Tis he.
FIRST MURDERER Stand to't.
BANQUO It will be rain tonight.
FIRST MURDERER Let it come down.

[The Murderers attack. First Murderer strikes out the light]

BANQUO O, treachery!
Fly, good Fleance, fly, fly, fly!
Thou mayst revenge — O slave! [*Dies. Fleance escapes*]

THIRD MURDERER Who did strike out the light?
FIRST MURDERER Was't not the way?
THIRD MURDERER There's but one down; the son is fled.
SECOND MURDERER We have lost best half of our affair.
FIRST MURDERER Well, let's away, and say how much is done.

Exeunt[, *with Banquo's body*]

Act 3, Scene 4

Banquet prepared. [*Two thrones are placed on stage.*] *Enter* MACBETH [*as King*], LADY [MACBETH *as Queen*], ROSS, LENNOX, LORDS, *and Attendants.* [*Lady Macbeth sits*]

MACBETH You know your own degrees, sit down; at first and last, the hearty welcome.

[*The Lords sit*]

LORDS Thanks to your majesty.
MACBETH Our self will mingle with society and play the
humble host; our hostess keeps her state, but in best time we
will require her welcome.
LADY MACBETH Pronounce it for me, sir, to all our friends, for
my heart speaks they are welcome.

Enter FIRST MURDERER

MACBETH See, they encounter thee with their hearts' thanks.
Both sides are even; here I'll sit i'th'midst.
Be large in mirth, anon we'll drink a measure
The table round. [*To First Murderer*] There's blood upon thy face.
FIRST MURDERER 'Tis Banquo's then.
MACBETH 'Tis better thee without, than he within.
Is he dispatched?
FIRST MURDERER My lord, his throat is cut; that I did for him.
MACBETH Thou art the best o'th'cut-throats,
Yet he's good that did the like for Fleance;
If thou didst it, thou art the nonpareil.
FIRST MURDERER Most royal sir, Fleance is scaped.

---

make more plausible the Murderers' successful attack, since they assault two persons on foot rather than on horseback. 11. **go about:** walk an indirect route (to cool the horses). 13. **from hence:** i.e., from where he dismounted. 14. **sd *torch*:** The dialogue (22–23) makes clear that only Banquo and Fleance enter (i.e., there is no torch-bearer); Fleance probably carries the torch here. 15. **A light, a light!:** Second Murderer sees the targets first. 18. **Let it come down:** First Murderer makes the grim jest that Banquo, about to die, need not worry about the rain to come; simultaneously, First Murderer orders the attack. 18. **come down:** rain; make a surprise attack. 21. **O slave!:** Banquo's dying execration, directed at his murderer. 22. **way:** plan, method. First Murderer is an amateur. 24. **best half:** i.e., Fleance's death. As Macbeth made clear (3.1.134–37), killing Fleance, Banquo's son and the source of further descendants, was more important (= "best") than killing Banquo. Compare 5.8.18.

Act 3, Scene 4. 0. **sd *Banquet prepared*:** i.e., a "banquet" placed onstage (presumably some conventional stage representation). While a Jacobean banquet might be a light collation of elaborate sweets, this one seems to be a state dinner (another available meaning). 1. **You know your own degrees:** You know the seating order appropriate to your respective "degrees" (social ranks). There is probably a quibble on "degrees" as steps and as tiers of seats. 1–2. **at first and last:** to one and all. 4. **society:** companions; acquaintances. 4. **play:** serve as, fill the capacity of. In some productions, Macbeth pours drinks for the guests. 5. **host:** The word describes anyone who entertains another person, but especially pertains to an inn- or tavern-keeper (see Lady Macbeth's worries at 32–37). 5. **state:** throne or formal chair, often with a canopy. 8. **sd *Enter* FIRST MURDERER:** First Murderer is not noticed verbally by the other guests and perhaps not noticed by Macbeth until 12. 9. **See . . . thanks:** an implicit stage direction to the lords and Lady Macbeth, who exchange some response (bows or a toast?). 9. **encounter:** go to meet. Just as Lady Macbeth's "heart speaks" (8), the nobles return "hearts' thanks." 10. **Both . . . midst:** Equal numbers of people sit on each side of the table; I'll sit halfway down one side. 11. **large:** unrestrained. 11–12. **drink . . . round:** share a toast, or health, with each person at the table; all share in a group toast; or pass the cup from person to person. The first meaning is more likely if Macbeth continues his use (4–5) of the royal plural. 14. **thee without . . . he within:** outside of you than inside of him. The line's callousness signals Macbeth's anxiety. 15. **dispatched:** killed. 19. **nonpareil:** one without

MACBETH Then comes my fit again: I had else been perfect;
Whole as the marble, founded as the rock,
As broad and general as the casing air:
But now I am cabined, cribbed, confined, bound in
To saucy doubts and fears. But Banquo's safe?

FIRST MURDERER Ay, my good lord: safe in a ditch he bides,
With twenty trenchèd gashes on his head,
The least a death to nature.

MACBETH Thanks for that.
There the grown serpent lies; the worm that's fled
Hath nature that in time will venom breed,
No teeth for th'present. Get thee gone; tomorrow
We'll hear ourselves again.

Exit [First] Murderer

LADY MACBETH My royal lord,
You do not give the cheer; the feast is sold
That is not often vouched while 'tis a-making,
'Tis given with welcome. To feed were best at home:
From thence, the sauce to meat is ceremony,
Meeting were bare without it.

Enter the Ghost of Banquo and sits in Macbeth's place

MACBETH Sweet remembrancer!
Now good digestion wait on appetite,
And health on both.

LENNOX May't please your highness, sit.

MACBETH Here had we now our country's honour roofed,
Were the graced person of our Banquo present,
Who may I rather challenge for unkindness
Than pity for mischance.

ROSS His absence, sir,
Lays blame upon his promise. Please't your highness
To grace us with your royal company?

MACBETH The table's full.

LENNOX Here is a place reserved, sir.

MACBETH Where?

LENNOX Here, my good lord. What is't that moves your highness?

MACBETH Which of you have done this?

LORDS What, my good lord?

MACBETH Thou canst not say I did it; never shake
Thy gory locks at me!

ROSS Gentlemen, rise, his highness is not well.

[Lady Macbeth joins the Lords]

LADY MACBETH Sit, worthy friends. My lord is often thus,

---

equal. 20. **scaped:** escaped. 21. **fit:** It is proverbial "to have an ague fit of fear." 21. **perfect:** Compare the two previous uses of the word, 3.1.108 and 3.1.130. 22. **founded:** based, firmly grounded. 23. **broad and general:** diffused and omnipresent. 23. **casing:** encasing, encompassing. 24. **cabined:** cramped, confined (from "cabin" = hut or cell). 24. **cribbed:** shut up, hampered. 24. **bound in:** kept fast, chained. 25. **safe:** i.e., dead. The euphemism reflects Macbeth's reaction, not Banquo's condition. 27–28. **With . . . nature:** Compare Duncan's wounds (2.3.107–08). 27. **trenchèd:** grooved, furrowed. 28. **The . . . nature:** First Murderer claims that any one of the "gashes" would have been mortal, but the generalized expression recalls the apocalyptic language surrounding the discovery of Duncan's body in 2.3. As 3.2.16 partly anticipates, Nature is being killed. 29. **worm:** figuratively, a larva or grub (which will grow into a venomous snake). 32. **hear ourselves:** i.e., speak together. 32–37. **My royal . . . without it:** Lady Macbeth forces Macbeth into his role as host. 32. **royal lord:** The phrase emphasizes Macbeth's new status and perhaps reminds him of his new duties. 33. **give the cheer:** give a kindly welcome; give a toast to the company. 33–35. **feast . . . welcome:** i.e., a hospitable dinner for guests is rather a commercial transaction ["is sold" (33)] if the host does not frequently affirm [= "give the cheer" (33) and "is . . . often vouched" (34)], while it happens, that the feast is freely, generously [= "with welcome" (35)] given. 35. **To feed were best at home:** i.e., one dines best in one's own dwelling. 36. **From thence:** away from home. 36. **ceremony:** social rituals (of seating, serving, toasting, etc.). 37. **sd *Ghost of Banquo*:** the same actor who played Banquo living, made up with stage-blood (see 51), usually animal's blood, and, possibly, flour. The co-presence of Death and (royal) festivity is a frequent moral theme; skeleton-Death pours a king's wine in Hans Holbein the Younger's popular *The Dance of Death* (1538). 37. **remembrancer:** one who reminds. The word was also the title of officials who collected debts owed to the crown. 38. **wait on:** attend, serve. 40. **honour:** i.e., those professing and conferring honor, the nobility. 40. **roofed:** i.e., beneath one roof, in one place. 41. **graced:** favored, endowed with special qualities. 42. **may I:** I hope I may. 43. **mischance:** accident. The false politeness recalls 1.6. 43–44. **His absence . . . his promise:** Literally, Banquo's absence belies his promise to attend. There are two ironical meanings: Banquo's Ghost keeps his living vow ("promise"); Banquo's death ("absence") may be blamed upon "his royalty of nature" (3.1.51), the qualities that boded so well for his future service to Scotland ("his promise"). 46. **The table's full:** Macbeth finds no empty place. 48. **moves:** troubles. Macbeth has now reacted to the Ghost. 49. **Which . . . this:** Macbeth may assume a practical joke (someone is pretending to be Banquo), or he may ask who has made Banquo a ghost. 50–51. **Thou . . . me:** The silent Ghost cannot accuse Macbeth of murdering Banquo. 51. **gory locks:** bloody hair.

The Ghost of Banquo (oil on canvas)/Chasseriau, Theodore (1819-56)/Musee des Beaux-Arts, Reims, France/Bridgeman Images

Look carefully at this painting depicting the scene in which Banquo's ghost shows up at Macbeth's banquet.
What specific details does the artist include that reflect the emotions and chaos of the moment? What lines from the play might have inspired the artist to depict the scene in this way?

And hath been from his youth. Pray you, keep seat.
The fit is momentary; upon a thought
He will again be well. If much you note him
You shall offend him and extend his passion.
Feed, and regard him not. [*To Macbeth*] Are you a man?

MACBETH Ay, and a bold one, that dare look on that
Which might appal the devil.

LADY MACBETH O proper stuff!
This is the very painting of your fear;
This is the air-drawn dagger which you said
Led you to Duncan. O, these flaws and starts,
Impostors to true fear, would well become
A woman's story at a winter's fire
Authorised by her grandam. Shame itself!
Why do you make such faces? When all's done
You look but on a stool.

MACBETH Prithee, see there! Behold, look, lo! How say you?
[*To Ghost*] Why, what care I? If thou canst nod, speak too.
If charnel-houses and our graves must send
Those that we bury back, our monuments
Shall be the maws of kites.

[*Exit Ghost of Banquo*]

LADY MACBETH What, quite unmanned in folly?

MACBETH If I stand here, I saw him.

LADY MACBETH Fie, for shame.

MACBETH Blood hath been shed ere now, i'th'olden time,
Ere humane statute purged the gentle weal;
Ay, and since too, murders have been performed
Too terrible for the ear. The time has been
That when the brains were out, the man would die,
And there an end. But now they rise again

---

54. **keep seat:** remain seated. 55. **fit:** paroxysm, seizure. 55. **upon a thought:** proverbial: "as swift as thought." 57. **passion:** fit. 60. **proper stuff:** complete or utter nonsense. 61. **painting:** image, illusion. 62–63. **This . . . Duncan:** Lady Macbeth ridicules Macbeth's vision before he killed Duncan (2.1.33–43). 62. **air-drawn:** imaged in the air; moved through the air. 63. **flaws:** bursts of passion. 63. **starts:** sudden involuntary movements. 64. **Impostors:** false imitations. 66. **Authorised:** vouched for, confirmed. 66. **grandam:** grandmother. 67. **make such faces:** an implicit stage direction to the actor playing Macbeth. 68. **stool:** For Shakespeare's audience, chairs were rare and expensive, stools common, even in wealthy households; Lady Macbeth uses that social fact to express her contempt. 69. **Behold, look, lo:** These synonyms urge the actor to gesture at the Ghost and its "empty" place. 70. **Why, what care I:** Presumably, Macbeth dares the Ghost to identify Banquo's murderer(s), but this phrase may be a question to Lady Macbeth, or the entire speech may be an aside. 70. **nod:** an implicit stage direction to the actor playing the Ghost, who must gesture significantly toward Macbeth (see note 69). 71. **charnel-houses:** houses or vaults in which the bones of the dead are piled up. 72–73. **our . . . kites:** The unburied (or returned) dead will be consumed by carrion-eating birds ("kites") whose stomachs ("maws") will be the final resting places ("monuments") of the dead. 73. **unmanned:** Lady Macbeth returns to the tactic that worked before (1.7.39–54), but murder, which she represented as manly, now unmans her husband. See 99. 74. **If I stand here:** Compare the proverbial "as true as you stand there."

With twenty mortal murders on their crowns
And push us from our stools. This is more strange
Than such a murder is.

LADY MACBETH My worthy lord,
Your noble friends do lack you.

MACBETH I do forget —
Do not muse at me, my most worthy friends.
I have a strange infirmity which is nothing
To those that know me. Come, love and health to all,
Then I'll sit down. Give me some wine; fill full!

Enter Ghost [*of Banquo*]

I drink to th'general joy o'th'whole table,
And to our dear friend Banquo, whom we miss.
Would he were here! To all, and him we thirst,
And all to all.

LORDS Our duties and the pledge.

MACBETH Avaunt and quit my sight! Let the earth hide thee!
Thy bones are marrowless, thy blood is cold;
Thou hast no speculation in those eyes
Which thou dost glare with.

LADY MACBETH Think of this, good peers,
But as a thing of custom. 'Tis no other,
Only it spoils the pleasure of the time.

MACBETH What man dare, I dare;
Approach thou like the rugged Russian bear,
The armed rhinoceros, or th'Hyrcan tiger,
Take any shape but that, and my firm nerves
Shall never tremble. Or be alive again,
And dare me to the desert with thy sword;
If trembling I inhabit then, protest me
The baby of a girl. Hence horrible shadow,
Unreal mock'ry hence.

[*Exit Ghost of Banquo*]

Why so, being gone,
I am a man again. — Pray you, sit still.

LADY MACBETH You have displaced the mirth, broke the good meeting
With most admired disorder.

MACBETH Can such things be,
And overcome us like a summer's cloud,
Without our special wonder? You make me strange
Even to the disposition that I owe,
When now I think you can behold such sights
And keep the natural ruby of your cheeks,
When mine is blanched with fear.

ROSS What sights, my lord?

LADY MACBETH I pray you speak not; he grows worse and worse.
Question enrages him. At once, good night.
Stand not upon the order of your going,
But go at once.

LENNOX Good night, and better health
Attend his majesty.

LADY MACBETH A kind good night to all.

[*Exeunt*] *Lords* [*and Attendants*]

---

76. **humane statute:** compassionate law. 76. **gentle weal:** lawful (or "nonviolent") commonwealth. The "weal" is "gentle" after it has been "purged." 81. **twenty:** See 27. 81. **mortal:** fatal. 81. **crowns:** tops of (their) heads (as at 1.5.40), but "crowns" recalls royal regalia, the "golden round" (1.5.26): kingly crowns will adorn Banquo's children though his head wears "twenty mortal murders" only. 82–83. **This . . . is:** The Ghost's uncanny appearance is "more strange," less explicable and therefore more terrifying, than murder because it overturns the rationalism of 75–80 and revives the doubts of 1.7.1–7; murder is not an "end" and it is not "done" when " 'tis done" (1.7.1). 85. **muse:** wonder, marvel; an implicit stage direction to the guests. 87. **Come . . . all:** Macbeth proposes a toast to ease the tension. 91. **Would he were here:** Compare 1.3.80, where Macbeth wishes the witches had not departed; here, he gets his wish in an unwelcome way. 91. **him we thirst:** the person (Banquo) for whom we long. The metaphor ("thirst" = desire) is appropriate to a drinking ceremony. 92. **duties:** respects. 92. **pledge:** toast. 93. **Avaunt . . . sight:** Macbeth sees the Ghost again. Traditionally, Macbeth drops his toasting cup here or hurls it at the Ghost, who often sits in Macbeth's vacant throne, and the act recalls the "poisoned chalice" (1.7.11). 94. **marrowless:** lacking the vital or essential part (because Banquo is dead). 95. **speculation:** power of seeing, sight. 96. **glare:** look fixedly and fiercely. 101. **Hyrcan:** Hyrcanian. Hyrcania was the classical name for the area on the southeast coast of the Caspian Sea; its tigers became proverbial for fierceness. 102. **any shape but that:** any form but that of Banquo's ghost. 104. **dare me to the desert:** challenge me (to fight you) in the desert. 105. **inhabit:** take as a habit. The verb ordinarily means "dwell, occupy," and the phrase, often emended, could mean "trembling I stay indoors" or, figuratively, "I harbor a single tremor." 105. **protest:** proclaim, denounce publicly. 106. **baby:** doll, puppet. 108. **Pray you, sit still:** Macbeth addresses the company. 110. **admired:** astonishing, surprising. Lady Macbeth uses "admired" in its earliest sense, which did not include the element of pleasure or esteem the word now connotes. 111. **overcome:** pass over (as a cloud does the sun); overwhelm, take by surprise. 112–13. **make me strange . . . disposition:** regard (or represent) me as being unlike my usual self. 113. **owe:** own. 115. **ruby:** redness (indicating health and the absence of fear). 116. **blanched:** whitened. 118. **Question:** questioning, interrogation. 119. **Stand not upon:** do not be meticulous about. 119. **order:** rank-determined precedence, protocol. Compare "degrees" (1). 123. **Stones . . . speak:** Earlier, Macbeth feared "stones" would "speak" and betray him (2.1.58). 124. **Augures:** auguries, predictions.

These are stills from two movie versions of *Macbeth*, one with a modern setting and the other with a traditional setting.

What staging, gestures, costumes, sets, and other theatrical elements are used to project Macbeth's strange behavior and the guests' responses? In what ways do the images from these films convey slightly different interpretations of the same scene, other than the different time periods chosen for the setting?

MACBETH It will have blood they say: blood will have blood.
Stones have been known to move and trees to speak.
Augures, and understood relations, have
By maggot-pies, and choughs, and rooks brought forth
The secret'st man of blood. What is the night?

LADY MACBETH Almost at odds with morning, which is which.

MACBETH How sayst thou that Macduff denies his person
At our great bidding?

LADY MACBETH Did you send to him, sir?

MACBETH I hear it by the way, but I will send.
There's not a one of them but in his house
I keep a servant feed. I will tomorrow —
And betimes I will — to the weïrd sisters.
More shall they speak. For now I am bent to know
By the worst means, the worst; for mine own good,
All causes shall give way. I am in blood
Stepped in so far that should I wade no more,
Returning were as tedious as go o'er.
Strange things I have in head that will to hand,
Which must be acted ere they may be scanned.

LADY MACBETH You lack the season of all natures, sleep.

MACBETH Come, we'll to sleep. My strange and self-abuse
Is the initiate fear that wants hard use;
We are yet but young in deed.

Exeunt

---

124. **understood:** comprehended. 124. **relations:** i.e., the links between cause and effect (or between the flight of certain birds and the facts being divined). "Augury" is specifically divination through interpreting the flight of birds, although the word had a less exact meaning in this period. 125. **maggot-pies:** magpies. The birds mentioned here can imitate human speech. 125. **choughs:** common name for various species of crow. Magpies and choughs are birds of ill omen. 126. **secret'st man of blood:** most successfully concealed murderer. 127. **at odds with:** striving with. 128. **How sayst thou:** what do you think. 128. **denies:** refuses. 129. **send:** i.e., send a message or messenger. 131. **them:** the Scottish nobles. 132. **feed:** bribed, paid a fee. 132. **will:** "Go" is understood. 133. **betimes:** speedily, soon, but perhaps also "early in the morning." 140. **scanned:** looked at closely. The word does double duty: "Strange things" (139) must be done quickly before others can see them and before Macbeth himself can see them. 141. **season:** period during which something happens. 142–43. **My strange . . . fear:** My inexplicable violation of who and what I am arises from a novice's fear. The grammar treats "strange" and "self" as adjectives modifying "abuse"; "strange" may therefore have the resonances of uncanniness it had in 82 and of self-alienation it may have in 112. 143. **wants:** lacks. 144. **young in deed:** just begun in action. So far the Macbeths lack "hard use" (143) of evil.

Act 3, Scene 5

Thunder. Enter the three WITCHES, *meeting* HECATE

FIRST WITCH Why how now, Hecate, you look angerly?

HECATE Have I not reason, beldams, as you are,
Saucy and over-bold? How did you dare
To trade and traffic with Macbeth
In riddles and affairs of death?
And I the mistress of your charms,
The close contriver of all harms,
Was never called to bear my part
Or show the glory of our art?
And which is worse, all you have done
Hath been but for a wayward son,
Spiteful and wrathful, who, as others do,
Loves for his own ends, not for you.
But make amends now. Get you gone,
And at the pit of Acheron
Meet me i'th'morning. Thither he
Will come to know his destiny.
Your vessels and your spells provide,
Your charms and every thing beside.
I am for th'air. This night I'll spend
Unto a dismal and a fatal end.
Great business must be wrought ere noon.
Upon the corner of the moon
There hangs a vap'rous drop profound;
I'll catch it ere it come to ground;
And that distilled by magic sleights,
Shall raise such artificial sprites
As by the strength of their illusion
Shall draw him on to his confusion.
He shall spurn fate, scorn death, and bear
His hopes 'bove wisdom, grace, and fear.
And you all know, security
Is mortals' chiefest enemy.

Music, and a song[, *"Come away, come away,"* *within*]

Hark, I am called: my little spirit, see,
Sits in a foggy cloud, and stays for me. [*Exit*]

FIRST WITCH Come, let's make haste; she'll soon be back again.

Exeunt

Act 3, Scene 6

Enter LENNOX *and another* LORD

LENNOX My former speeches have but hit your thoughts
Which can interpret further; only I say
Things have been strangely borne. The gracious Duncan
Was pitied of Macbeth; marry, he was dead.
And the right-valiant Banquo walked too late,
Whom you may say, if't please you, Fleance killed,
For Fleance fled. Men must not walk too late.
Who cannot want the thought how monstrous
It was for Malcolm and for Donaldbain

Act 3, Scene 5. This scene, evidently preparing the audience for 4.1 and establishing time and place, is probably not by Shakespeare. 1. **angerly:** angry, angrily. 2. **beldams:** hags, witches. 3. **Saucy:** impudent, ill-behaved. 4. **To . . . Macbeth:** Hecate's speech now becomes tetrameter couplets, returning to doggerel pentameters at 34. 4. **traffic:** have dealings, be concerned, but also synonymous with "trade." 7. **close:** secret, hidden. 8. **bear:** take, undertake. 11. **wayward:** willful, intractable. 13. **Loves . . . you:** cares (about magic, prophecy, etc.) for his own purposes, not as an adept of or believer in the witches and their powers for themselves. 15. **pit:** sunken place (especially associated with hell). 15. **Acheron:** a river in the classical Hades (hell) and only metaphorically in Scotland. 18. **vessels:** implements (e.g., cauldrons) for magic rites. 18. **spells:** incantations. 19. **charms:** magical verses. 20. **spend:** use, employ. 21. **dismal:** malign, sinister. 21. **fatal:** both destined and destructive. 22. **business:** work. 24. **profound:** deep, with hidden qualities. 26. **sleights:** tricks, artifices. 27. **artificial:** cunning, deceitful, but perhaps also "made up, factitious." 28. **illusion:** either (1) deception, delusion or (2) condition of being deceived. 30. **spurn:** despise, reject contemptuously; the verb literally means "kick" or "trample." 30–31. **bear / His hopes 'bove:** Hecate implies that Macbeth's hopes will put him beyond the influence of prudence, divine forgiveness, or terror. 31. **grace:** fate, destiny; God's favor or blessing. 32. **security:** confidence (with the implication of overconfidence, complacency). 35. **foggy cloud:** possibly a theatrical machine that lifted the actor from the stage.

Act 3, Scene 6. Like 2.4, this scene is choric commentary, a tranquil moment of reflection amid chaos and evil. 1. **hit:** coincided with, agreed with. 2. **only I say:** i.e., I only say. 3. **borne:** endured. 4. **pitied:** lamented. 4. **he was dead:** Duncan was dead. Macbeth "pitied" Duncan after, not before, his death. 5. **right-valiant:** very valiant. 7. **Men . . . late:** All monosyllables, this understatement initiates a satiric restatement (7–20)

To kill their gracious father? Damnèd fact,
How it did grieve Macbeth! Did he not straight
In pious rage the two delinquents tear,
That were the slaves of drink and thralls of sleep?
Was not that nobly done? Ay, and wisely too,
For 'twould have angered any heart alive
To hear the men deny't. So that I say,
He has borne all things well, and I do think
That had he Duncan's sons under his key —
As, an't please heaven, he shall not — they should find
What 'twere to kill a father. So should Fleance.
But peace, for from broad words, and 'cause he failed
His presence at the tyrant's feast, I hear
Macduff lives in disgrace. Sir, can you tell
Where he bestows himself?

LORD The son of Duncan,
From whom this tyrant holds the due of birth,
Lives in the English court and is received
Of the most pious Edward with such grace,
That the malevolence of fortune nothing
Takes from his high respect. Thither Macduff
Is gone to pray the holy king upon his aid
To wake Northumberland and warlike Siward,
That by the help of these, with him above
To ratify the work, we may again
Give to our tables meat, sleep to our nights,
Free from our feasts and banquets bloody knives,
Do faithful homage and receive free honours,
All which we pine for now. And this report
Hath so exasperate their king that he
Prepares for some attempt of war.

LENNOX Sent he to Macduff?

LORD He did. And with an absolute, "Sir, not I,"
The cloudy messenger turns me his back
And hums, as who should say, "You'll rue the time
That clogs me with this answer."

LENNOX And that well might
Advise him to a caution t'hold what distance
His wisdom can provide. Some holy angel
Fly to the court of England and unfold
His message ere he come, that a swift blessing
May soon return to this our suffering country
Under a hand accursed.

LORD I'll send my prayers with him.

Exeunt

---

of Macbeth's version of recent events. 8. **want:** lack. 10. **fact:** deed, action. 11–13. **Did . . . sleep:** See 1.7.63–68. 12. **pious:** loyal, dutiful. 13. **thralls:** slaves. 15–16. **For . . . deny't:** the kind of double-talk needed if every listener may be a spy or a "traitor": Lennox's remark means both that persons who believed Macbeth would be angered by the grooms' allegedly false denials and that the dead Duncan (who is not a "heart alive") cannot confirm the grooms' innocence. 18. **under his key:** locked up, imprisoned. 20. **So should Fleance:** i.e., were Macbeth to have Fleance "under . . . key" (18), he would be condemned for murdering Banquo. 21. **peace:** hush, be silent. 21. **broad:** plain, unreserved. 21. **failed:** The word recalls Macbeth's injunction (3.1.29) to Banquo, who did "attend." 24. **son:** Malcolm. 25. **holds:** withholds. 25. **due:** what is owed. 27. **Edward:** Edward the Confessor (King of England, 1042–1066 CE). 28–29. **malevolence of fortune . . . high respect:** i.e., exile from Scotland and deprivation of the kingship have not affected the great esteem shown Malcolm. 30. **Is gone:** As 46–48 clarify, Macduff has departed for the English court, but has not yet (in 3.6) arrived. 31. **Northumberland . . . Siward:** Siward is the family name of the historically appropriate earls of Northumberland. 32. **him above:** God. 33. **ratify:** confirm, make valid. 35. **Free . . . knives:** The syntax is unusual: free our feasts and banquets from bloody knives; "banquets" may recall "Banquo." 36. **Do faithful homage:** give faithful allegiance. The Lord implies that men render loyalty to Macbeth not out of faith and duty, but out of fear; see 5.2.19–20. 37. **pine:** yearn, long. 38. **exasperate:** exasperated. 38. **their king:** King Edward, Northumberland's and Siward's ("their") king. 39. **attempt:** attack, assault. 41. **absolute:** positive, decided. 41. **"Sir, not I":** These are Macduff's words. 42. **cloudy:** sullen, frowning. 42. **turns me his back:** This phrase is slightly confusing for two reasons: the Lord continues to report an event he apparently did not witness directly, and he employs an ethical dative ("me") to emphasize his astonishment at the messenger's discourtesy and to convey that reaction — "Can you imagine? he turned his back." 43. **hums:** murmurs discontentedly. 43. **rue the time:** regret the occasion. The line probably puns on the herbs thyme and rue. 44. **clogs:** burdens, hampers. 45. **caution:** taking heed, precaution. 49–50. **suffering . . . accursed:** i.e., country suffering under an accursed hand.

Understanding and Interpreting

1. Banquo opens the first scene in Act 3 with a brief soliloquy expressing his fear that Macbeth played "most foully" (l. 3) to gain the throne. What keeps him from revealing his suspicions to others at this point?
2. After Macbeth is alone, he states, "To be thus is nothing, / But to be safely thus" (Scene 1, ll. 49–50). What does this statement indicate about Macbeth's beliefs about the nature of power?

3. Taking all of Macbeth's speech into account (Scene 1, ll. 49 to 73), what is his attitude toward the murder at this point, as well as toward Banquo?
4. In Scene 2, Macbeth does not tell Lady Macbeth about the plan to kill Banquo and Fleance, even though she has known of all of his previous plans and deeds. Why might he have decided to keep this information to himself? What does this reveal about their relationship at this point in the play?
5. As the murderers attack in Scene 3, Banquo's final act is to tell his son Fleance to run away (l. 20). He tells Fleance that he "mayst revenge" (l. 20), but does not mention that Macbeth is the guilty party. Why do you think that is?
6. In the feast scene (Scene 4), Macbeth is the host. However, he is preoccupied with Banquo's murder and Lady Macbeth admonishes him for not giving "cheer" to the party (l. 33). Why is Macbeth's failure to provide the "sauce" (l. 36) to the ceremony an important issue for Lady Macbeth?
7. Macbeth tells Banquo's ghost, "Thou canst not say I did it" (Scene 4, l. 50). Explain what this statement suggests about Macbeth's character.
8. After Lady Macbeth chides Macbeth for responding to a ghost that only he can see (Scene 4, ll. 72 and 74), Macbeth seems to suddenly lose his fear of the mute ghostly visitor. Does he truly recover his nerve, or does Lady Macbeth shame him into pretending he has regained his composure? Explain your reasoning.
9. During Macbeth's outbursts at the feast in Scene 4, do you think the guests are convinced by the explanations for his "infirmity" (l. 86), or are they still suspicious of Macbeth? What evidence from the text can support your position?
10. Even after all the guests have left, Macbeth expresses concern that Macduff didn't attend the feast (Scene 4, ll. 128 to 129). Why might Macbeth be concerned about Macduff's absence?
11. Explain what the Lord reveals in Scene 6 about Macduff's current situation and how he is attempting to respond to Macbeth's reign in Scotland.

Analyzing Language, Style, and Structure

1. **Vocabulary in Context.** Talking with the murderers, Macbeth says, "Now, if you have a station in the file" (Scene 1, l. 102). The word "station" has multiple meanings. What does it mean in this context?
2. **Vocabulary in Context.** Talking about Banquo's upcoming murder, Macbeth says that Fleance "must embrace the fate" (Scene 1, l. 137). What does the word "embrace" mean in this context?
3. **Vocabulary in Context.** When Macbeth sees Banquo's ghost, he states, "If trembling I inhabit then" (Scene 4, l. 105). What does "inhabit" mean in this context? How is that meaning different from others you have encountered?
4. **Skill Focus.** In Scene 1, Macbeth openly expresses his fear of Banquo (ll. 50 to 73) in a speech that features numerous literary devices. Using specific examples of literary devices such as imagery and allusion from Macbeth's speech, explain what gives him cause for concern.
5. **Skill Focus.** Lady Macbeth calls Macbeth's vision a "painting of [his] fear" (Scene 4, l. 61). How accurately does this metaphor reflect what is going on psychologically with Macbeth at this point in the play?
6. **Skill Focus.** Toward the end of Scene 4, Macbeth tells his wife, "I am in blood / Stepped in so far that, should I wade no more, / Returning were as tedious as go o'er" (ll. 136 to 138). What does he mean by this? What does his use of metaphor suggest about his attitude toward the consequences of his future actions?
7. Evaluate the persuasive strategies Macbeth uses to convince the murderers to kill Banquo (Scene 1, ll. 77 to 90). Why are they effective? How are they similar to or different from the strategies Lady Macbeth uses to convince Macbeth to kill Duncan (Act 1, Scene 7, ll. 36 to 71)? Explain.

8. Shakespeare ends Scene 1 with this rhyming couplet:

   It is concluded. Banquo, thy soul's flight,
   If it find heaven, must find it out tonight.

   Compare that with the couplet that concludes Act 2, Scene 1, just before Macbeth kills Duncan:

   Hear it not [the bell tolling], Duncan, for it is a knell
   That summons thee to heaven or to hell.

   What do these two couplets suggest about Macbeth's attitude toward each of these men?
9. In Scene 2, lines 50 to 56, Macbeth provides an elaborate description of nightfall. Analyze how he uses language to connect day and night with good and evil.
10. When Lady Macbeth addresses Macbeth directly after she has tried to calm the guests, she demands, "Are you a man?" (Scene 4, l. 58). How does this reinforce attitudes expressed about gender by this point in the play?
11. In Scene 5, Hecate calls Macbeth a "wayward son" (l. 11). She provides a list of his personal qualities. What qualities does she ascribe to Macbeth? How do those qualities make him easily manipulated by the witches' predictions?
12. In Scene 6, we get the sense that Lennox cannot speak his mind freely with the Lord about his feelings toward Macbeth. Look carefully at his lines and identify the ways in which he reveals his true feelings indirectly. Then, discuss how his guarded response reflects the general atmosphere in Scotland as it is depicted in the play.

Topics for Composing

1. **Analysis.** Macbeth believes it is fate that he should be crowned king, even though his assassination of the king was a direct violation of the Great Chain of Being. Analyze Macbeth's character in terms of his simultaneous belief in and defiance of the Great Chain of Being. Review the Key Context (p. 942) or conduct additional research on the idea of the Great Chain of Being.
2. **Argument.** Ghosts in Shakespeare's plays are frequently visible only to a single character (as in *Macbeth*), leading to great confusion on the part of the other characters. When directors stage these hallucinatory ghost scenes, they must choose whether or not to have an actor on stage playing the part of the ghost. Write an argument about how you would stage the scene with Banquo's ghost (Act 3, Scene 4). Would the ghost be visible to the audience? In your response, be sure to explain how your choice would affect the audience and what it would reveal about your interpretation of the scene.
3. **Connection.** Think of another text (e.g., a book, movie, or television show) in which a character interacts with a ghost. Compare that character's reaction to how Macbeth responds when seeing Banquo's ghost. What do the similarities and differences in their reactions suggest about them?
4. **Speaking and Listening.** The murder of Banquo in Scene 3 happens quickly, and the scene has only five actors. Work with a group to stage this scene in a suspenseful way. Give careful thought to setting, lighting, costumes, and props. as well as the gestures and movements actors should make. You may present your scene as a stage production or as a film.
5. **Research.** The first three acts of *Macbeth* include numerous references to witchcraft, spells, and omens. These references would have been immediately recognized by Shakespeare's audience. However, they are not as widely understood by twenty-first-century audiences. Research a belief or superstition referenced in the play. Then, prepare a short presentation on the background of that belief and how it may have influenced Shakespeare's writing of *Macbeth*.

Thunder. Enter the three WITCHES [*with a cauldron*]

FIRST WITCH Thrice the brindled cat hath mewed.

SECOND WITCH Thrice and once the hedge-pig whined.

THIRD WITCH Harpier cries, " 'Tis time, 'tis time."

FIRST WITCH Round about the cauldron go;
In the poisoned entrails throw.
Toad, that under cold stone
Days and nights has thirty-one
Sweltered venom sleeping got,
Boil thou first i'th'charmèd pot.

ALL Double, double toil and trouble;
Fire burn, and cauldron bubble.

SECOND WITCH Fillet of a fenny snake,
In the cauldron boil and bake:
Eye of newt, and toe of frog,
Wool of bat, and tongue of dog,
Adder's fork, and blind-worm's sting,
Lizard's leg, and howlet's wing,
For a charm of powerful trouble,
Like a hell-broth, boil and bubble.

ALL Double, double toil and trouble,
Fire burn, and cauldron bubble.

THIRD WITCH Scale of dragon, tooth of wolf,
Witches' mummy, maw and gulf
Of the ravined salt-sea shark,
Root of hemlock, digged i'th'dark;
Liver of blaspheming Jew,
Gall of goat, and slips of yew,
Slivered in the moon's eclipse;
Nose of Turk, and Tartar's lips,

This painting by English artist Michael Ayrton was created as part of the costume design for the witches in John Gielgud's 1942 rendition of *Macbeth*, produced at the Piccadilly Theatre in London.

What effect do you think Ayrton is going for with this design? What language from the play might have inspired this depiction?

Act 4, Scene 1. 1. **brindled:** having fur marked by streaks of a darker color. 2. **hedge-pig:** hedgehog. 3. **Harpier:** presumably the name of a witch's familiar (see note 1.1.9); compare "Graymalkin" and "Paddock" (1.1.9–10). 7. **thirty-one:** in Elizabethan pronunciation, a true rhyme with "stone" (6). 8. **Sweltered:** exuded like sweat (as if) by heat. 8. **venom:** poison. Toads were popularly supposed to be poisonous. Agnis Thompson, one of the witches James VI interrogated, allegedly "gathered the venom" of "a black toad" to poison the Scottish king. 10. **toil:** severe labor. Other meanings are relevant, such as "dispute, controversy." 12. **Fillet . . . snake:** lengthwise slice or section ("fillet") of a snake from marshlands (fens). 14. **newt:** a small, tailed amphibian similar to the salamander. 15. **Wool:** soft underhair, down. 16. **fork:** split tongue (supposed to carry venom). 16. **blind-worm:** slowworm (a reptile with tiny eyes); adder. 17. **howlet:** owl, owlet. 18. **charm:** incantation, magical rhyme; compare 3.5.18–19. 23. **mummy:** mummia, a pitch used for embalming, and, hence, embalmed flesh; preparation for magical purposes, made from dead bodies. 23. **maw:** stomach. 23. **gulf:** that which devours or swallows up anything; a bawdy meaning, "vagina," was well established. 25. **hemlock:** poisonous herb. 26. **blaspheming:** i.e., denying that Jesus was the Messiah. With Turks and Tartars (29), Jews and the "birth-strangled babe" (30) would be especially vulnerable because unbaptized as Christians. 27. **goat:** traditionally, a lecherous, irascible beast (compare note 37); hence its gall, or bile, is appropriate for the witches' poisonous brew. 27. **yew:** The yew tree was long associated with death. 28. **Slivered:** cut off as a sliver or slip (from a tree). 28. **moon's eclipse:** Traditionally, a lunar eclipse was the best time to collect magical and medicinal herbs.

Finger of birth-strangled babe,
Ditch-delivered by a drab,
Make the gruel thick and slab.
Add thereto a tiger's chawdron
For th'ingredience of our cauldron.

ALL Double, double toil and trouble,
Fire burn, and cauldron bubble.

SECOND WITCH Cool it with a baboon's blood,
Then the charm is firm and good.

Enter HECATE, *and the other three Witches*

HECATE O well done! I commend your pains,
And every one shall share i'th'gains;
And now about the cauldron sing
Like elves and fairies in a ring,
Enchanting all that you put in.

Music, and a song, "Black spirits, etc."
[*Exeunt Hecate and the other three Witches*]

SECOND WITCH By the pricking of my thumbs,
Something wicked this way comes;
Open locks, whoever knocks.

Enter MACBETH

MACBETH How now, you secret, black, and midnight hags!
What is't you do?

ALL THE WITCHES A deed without a name.

MACBETH I conjure you by that which you profess,
Howe'er you come to know it, answer me.
Though you untie the winds and let them fight
Against the churches, though the yeasty waves
Confound and swallow navigation up,
Though bladed corn be lodged and trees blown down,
Though castles topple on their warders' heads,
Though palaces and pyramids do slope
Their heads to their foundations, though the treasure
Of nature's germen tumble altogether
Even till destruction sicken: answer me
To what I ask you.

FIRST WITCH Speak.

SECOND WITCH Demand.

THIRD WITCH We'll answer.

FIRST WITCH Say, if thou'dst rather hear it from our mouths,
Or from our masters'?

MACBETH Call 'em, let me see 'em.

FIRST WITCH Pour in sow's blood, that hath eaten
Her nine farrow; grease that's sweaten
From the murderer's gibbet throw
Into the flame.

ALL THE WITCHES Come high or low:
Thyself and office deftly show.

Thunder. [*Enter*] FIRST APPARITION, *an armed Head*

MACBETH Tell me, thou unknown power —

FIRST WITCH He knows thy thought;
Hear his speech, but say thou nought.

FIRST APPARITION Macbeth, Macbeth, Macbeth: beware Macduff,
Beware the Thane of Fife. Dismiss me. Enough. *Descends*

---

30. **birth-strangled:** i.e., throttled by the umbilical cord during labor or killed after birth by a mother who could not support her infant. 30. **babe:** The word rhymed with the modern pronunciation of "drab" (31) and "slab" (32). 31. **Ditch-delivered:** born in a ditch (without the customary attendance of midwife and female friends or relatives). 31. **drab:** prostitute; slattern. 32. **slab:** semi-solid, viscid. 33. **chawdron:** entrails. 37. **baboon:** Through demonic contraries, this animal's notoriously "hot" blood appropriately cools the witches' brew. 38. **sd–43 sd *Enter* HECATE . . . *Witches*:** The Second Folio's text and associated stage directions almost certainly are not by Shakespeare, but belong to a pre-Folio revision-adaptation of *Macbeth* designed to increase the play's spectacle. Many editors delete "*the other three Witches*" as superfluous, but they appropriately dignify Hecate's entrance and seem to be singers (unlike the witches of 1.1 and 1.3), needed for the song of 43 sd. 41. **sing:** the cue for musicians (who may have been visible to the original audiences) to prepare to play. Compare note 128. 42. **ring:** Dancing fairies were supposed to create "fairy rings," circles of darker grass in lawns or fields. 44. **pricking:** tingling. 47. **black:** baneful, malignant, deadly. 49. **conjure:** call on solemnly, entreat in the name of something sacred. 49. **profess:** claim to have knowledge of. 52. **yeasty:** foamy, frothy. 53. **navigation:** shipping or ships considered collectively. 54. **bladed corn:** i.e., corn when the blade still surrounds the ear. 54. **lodged:** flattened, broken down (by wind and rain). 55. **warders:** guardians, persons in charge. 56. **pyramids:** Shakespeare and other contemporary writers probably confused pyramids with obelisks. 56. **slope:** bend down. 58. **germen:** seeds or material essences of things, the material (as opposed to divine or spiritual) sources from which all creation springs. 59. **sicken:** i.e., become ill through consuming too much. Destruction is personified as a glutton. 61. **thou'dst:** thou hadst. 62. **masters:** persons of inferior rank, lackeys. 63–64. **Pour . . . farrow:** The natural history is accurate: sows sometimes eat their young ("farrow"). 64. **sweaten:** exuded (Shakespeare invented the *-en* form for the rhyme). 65. **gibbet:** the gallows; also, a structure from which hanged bodies were suspended and displayed. 67. **office:** duty; particular responsibility. 67. **sd *armed*:** armored or helmeted. 71. **Thane of Fife:** Macduff. 71. **sd *Descends*:** This stage direction (like those at 80 and 93) suggests that the Apparition exits through a trapdoor in the stage. Compare 105

De Agostini Editore / Bridgeman Images

This watercolor from the set design of Giuseppe Verde's 1847 opera *Macbeth* depicts the fantastical scene in which the witches reveal their prophesies in Act 4.

What effect is the artist trying to create? What visual elements convey that effect? What words or phrases from the text are likely being spoken during this moment?

MACBETH Whate'er thou art, for thy good caution, thanks;
Thou hast harped my fear aright. But one word more —
FIRST WITCH He will not be commanded. Here's another,
More potent than the first.

Thunder. [Enter] SECOND APPARITION, *a bloody Child*

SECOND APPARITION Macbeth, Macbeth, Macbeth.
MACBETH Had I three ears, I'd hear thee.
SECOND APPARITION Be bloody, bold, and resolute; laugh to scorn
The power of man, for none of woman born
Shall harm Macbeth. *Descends*
MACBETH Then live, Macduff, what need I fear of thee?
But yet I'll make assurance double sure
And take a bond of fate: thou shalt not live,
That I may tell pale-hearted fear it lies,
And sleep in spite of thunder.

Thunder. [Enter] THIRD APPARITION, *a Child crowned, with a tree in his hand*

What is this,
That rises like the issue of a king
And wears upon his baby-brow the round
And top of sovereignty?
ALL THE WITCHES Listen, but speak not to't.
THIRD APPARITION Be lion-mettled, proud, and take no care
Who chafes, who frets, or where conspirers are.
Macbeth shall never vanquished be until
Great Birnam Wood to high Dunsinane hill
Shall come against him.
Descends
MACBETH That will never be:
Who can impress the forest, bid the tree
Unfix his earthbound root? Sweet bodements, good.

---

and note. 72. **caution:** word of warning. 73. **harped:** guessed, hit upon. 73. **But one word more:** Compare 99–104 and 1.3.68 ff. 78–79. **Be . . . born:** Macbeth may "scorn" "the power of man" because all men are "of woman born." 79. **of woman born:** all humankind. This and similar biblical phrases (Job 14:1, 15:14, 25:4, Matthew 11:11, Luke 7:28) add solemnity and ambiguity to the Apparition's supposed promise. 82. **assurance:** the action of assuring (what the Apparitions do to Macbeth); the state of being assured (Macbeth's response to the Apparitions). 83. **bond:** contract, legal surety. By killing Macduff, Macbeth will make it impossible for Fate to break the promise ("bond") given by the Second Apparition. See 3.2.49 and note. 84. **it:** Fear (personified); the Second Apparition. 85. **sd *Thunder*:** The immediate thunder makes Macbeth's "in spite of thunder" ironic or bravado. 86. **issue:** progeny, children. 87. **round:** royal crown, recalling "golden round" (1.5.26). 88. **speak not to't:** Traditionally, witnesses to conjured figures were warned not to interrogate them. 89. **lion-mettled:** having a lion's qualities (here, the lion's traditional courage). 90. **Who:** whoever. 94. **impress:** press-gang, force to join an army. 95. **Sweet bodements:** attractive prophecies.

Rebellious dead, rise never till the wood
Of Birnam rise, and our high-placed Macbeth
Shall live the lease of nature, pay his breath
To time and mortal custom. Yet my heart
Throbs to know one thing. Tell me, if your art
Can tell so much, shall Banquo's issue ever
Reign in this kingdom?

ALL THE WITCHES Seek to know no more.

MACBETH I will be satisfied. Deny me this,
And an eternal curse fall on you. Let me know.

[Cauldron descends.] Hautboys

Why sinks that cauldron? And what noise is this?

FIRST WITCH Show!

SECOND WITCH Show!

THIRD WITCH Show!

ALL THE WITCHES Show his eyes and grieve his heart,
Come like shadows, so depart.

[Enter] a show of eight kings, and [the] last with a glass in his hand [; Banquo's Ghost following]

MACBETH Thou art too like the spirit of Banquo. Down!
Thy crown does sear mine eyeballs. And thy hair,
Thou other gold-bound brow, is like the first;
A third, is like the former. — Filthy hags,
Why do you show me this? — A fourth? Start, eyes!
What, will the line stretch out to th'crack of doom?
Another yet? A seventh? I'll see no more.
And yet the eighth appears, who bears a glass
Which shows me many more. And some I see,
That two-fold balls and treble sceptres carry.
Horrible sight! Now I see 'tis true,
For the blood-boltered Banquo smiles upon me,
And points at them for his.

[Exeunt show of kings and Banquo's Ghost]

What, is this so?

FIRST WITCH Ay, sir, all this is so. But why
Stands Macbeth thus amazedly?
Come, sisters, cheer we up his sprites,
And show the best of our delights.
I'll charm the air to give a sound,
While you perform your antic round
That this great king may kindly say,
Our duties did his welcome pay.

Music. The Witches dance, and vanish

MACBETH Where are they? Gone? Let this pernicious hour,
Stand aye accursèd in the calendar.
Come in, without there!

Enter LENNOX

LENNOX What's your grace's will?

MACBETH Saw you the weïrd sisters?

LENNOX No, my lord.

MACBETH Came they not by you?

LENNOX No indeed, my lord.

MACBETH Infected be the air whereon they ride,

---

96. **Rebellious dead:** i.e., Banquo and his ghost (compare 3.4.75–83 and 3.4.93–96). Duncan faced living rebels (see, e.g., 1.2.9 ff.); Macbeth faces the resurrected dead. 97. **our high-placed:** our high-ranking. 98. **lease of nature:** i.e., the limited time nature grants one to live (Macbeth's natural lifespan). 99. **mortal custom:** i.e., the usual (customary) length of human ("mortal") life. 103. **I will be satisfied:** I must have an answer. 105. **sinks:** an implicit stage direction suggesting that the cauldron disappears through a trapdoor in the stage; the playing of hautboys (104 sd) conceals the sounds of the trapdoor and, perhaps, of the Apparitions' entry. 110. **sd *eight kings*:** When *Macbeth* was composed, eight Stuart kings and one Stuart queen had ruled Scotland, but James VI and I's mother, Mary Stuart, Queen of Scots, does not appear, perhaps because including her would recall her execution in 1587 (at Elizabeth's implicit order) and that event was politically too sensitive to be acknowledged. 110. **sd *glass*:** magic crystal permitting visions of the future (see 118–19); not a looking-glass or mirror. 111. **Thou . . . Banquo:** i.e., the first king too closely resembles Banquo's "spirit" or ghost (frightening Macbeth as the ghost had in 3.4 and confirming his fear that Banquo's sons will rule Scotland). 113. **gold-bound brow:** i.e., head surrounded ("bound") by a crown ("gold"). 115. **Start:** jump from your sockets. 116. **crack of doom:** thunder ("crack") accompanying the Last Judgment ("doom"). 120. **two-fold balls and treble sceptres:** two balls and three scepters. The line may refer to King James, but whatever the precise referent, Macbeth sees a long line of increasingly powerful kings. 122. **blood-boltered:** matted, clogged with blood (from the twenty wounds of 3.4.27 and 3.4.81). 123. **his:** i.e., his sons. The "*show*" presents Banquo's royal descendants. 124–31. **sd Ay . . . *vanish*:** These lines were probably written by Thomas Middleton. 125. **amazedly:** as in a maze. 126–31. **Come . . . pay:** The witches offer a macabre version of a Jacobean courtly entertainment. 126. **sprites:** spirits. 128. **I'll . . . sound:** a cue for music. 129. **antic round:** bizarre dance. 131. **duties:** expressions of deference or respect. 131. **did his welcome pay:** showed him the respect due to a monarch. 133. **aye:** ever. 135. **Saw . . . sisters:** Macbeth expects Lennox to recognize the witches; knowledge of them has apparently spread beyond Banquo and Macbeth. 137. **air whereon they ride:** a common belief about witches, but perhaps also a hint of early stage effects (see 3.5.34–35 and note 3.5.35).

And damned all those that trust them. I did hear
The galloping of horse. Who was't came by?
LENNOX 'Tis two or three, my lord, that bring you word
Macduff is fled to England.
MACBETH Fled to England?
LENNOX Ay, my good lord.
MACBETH [*Aside*] Time, thou anticipat'st my dread exploits;
The flighty purpose never is o'ertook
Unless the deed go with it. From this moment,
The very firstlings of my heart shall be
The firstlings of my hand. And even now
To crown my thoughts with acts, be it thought and done.
The castle of Macduff I will surprise;
Seize upon Fife; give to th'edge o'th'sword
His wife, his babes, and all unfortunate souls
That trace him in his line. No boasting like a fool;
This deed I'll do before this purpose cool,
But no more sights. — Where are these gentlemen?
Come, bring me where they are.
Exeunt

Act 4, Scene 2

Enter [LADY MACDUFF], *her* SON, *and* ROSS

LADY MACDUFF What had he done, to make him fly the land?
ROSS You must have patience, madam.
LADY MACDUFF He had none;
His flight was madness. When our actions do not,
Our fears do make us traitors.
ROSS You know not
Whether it was his wisdom or his fear.
LADY MACDUFF Wisdom? To leave his wife, to leave his babes,
His mansion, and his titles in a place
From whence himself does fly? He loves us not.
He wants the natural touch, for the poor wren,
The most diminutive of birds, will fight,
Her young ones in her nest, against the owl.
All is the fear, and nothing is the love;
As little is the wisdom, where the flight
So runs against all reason.
ROSS My dearest coz,
I pray you school yourself. But for your husband,
He is noble, wise, judicious, and best knows
The fits o'th'season. I dare not speak much further,
But cruel are the times when we are traitors
And do not know ourselves, when we hold rumour
From what we fear, yet know not what we fear,
But float upon a wild and violent sea,
Each way and none. I take my leave of you;
Shall not be long but I'll be here again.
Things at the worst will cease, or else climb upward
To what they were before. My pretty cousin,
Blessing upon you.
LADY MACDUFF Fathered he is, and yet he's fatherless.
ROSS I am so much a fool, should I stay longer

141. **Fled to England?:** Macbeth's ignorance here is inconsistent with speeches in 3.6. 143–53. **Time . . . cool:** This speech may be an aside, with 154–55 addressed to Lennox. The question and command of 154–55 mark a substantial break, although they may indicate that Macbeth has become aware of Lennox, having delivered the preceding lines "aloud" and not "aside." 143. **thou anticipat'st:** you forestall, deal with beforehand. 144. **flighty:** swift, quick. 146. **firstlings:** first things (here, impulses or thoughts); firstborn. Macbeth's figurative language invokes children — those who will not succeed him, those (of Macduff) he will kill, those (of Banquo's line) who will rule Scotland. 148. **crown:** add the finishing touch to. 152. **trace him:** follow him, walk in his footsteps. 152. **line:** descendants.

Act 4, Scene 2. 7. **titles:** entitlements; assertions of right. Lady Macduff refers to more than her husband's titles of nobility. 9. **wants:** lacks. 11. **Her . . . nest:** i.e., her young ones being in the nest (and therefore vulnerable to the owl). 14. **coz:** cousin (a general, friendly appellation, not a specific term of kinship). 15. **school:** discipline, bring under control. 19–20. **when . . . From what we fear:** i.e., when we create rumors out of those things we fear. 22. **Each way and none:** Circumstances ["the times" (18)] and fears ["what we fear" (20)] urge us to act, but we dart this way and that without finding a satisfactory course of action. 25. **cousin:** i.e., Lady Macduff's son. 27. **Fathered . . . fatherless:** He is "fathered" (= procreated), but he lacks a father (he is "fatherless"). 29. **my disgrace and your discomfort:** Ross apparently says he will "disgrace" himself

extending beyond the text

By Act 4, it is clear that Macbeth is a tyrant. He has gained power unlawfully, but only a few of the noblemen of Scotland, such as Macduff, oppose him. The rest willingly obey the tyrant. Why? In 2017, Timothy Snyder, a professor of history at Yale University, tried to answer those questions in his book *On Tyranny: Twenty Lessons from the Twentieth Century*. Read one of his twenty lessons in the following excerpt.

from On Tyranny: Twenty Lessons from the Twentieth Century

Timothy Snyder

1 Do not obey in advance.
Most of the power of authoritarianism is freely given. In times like these, individuals think ahead about what a more repressive government will want, and then offer themselves without being asked. A citizen who adapts in this way is teaching power what it can do.

Anticipatory obedience is a political tragedy. Perhaps rulers did not initially know that citizens were willing to compromise this value or that principle. Perhaps a new regime did not at first have the direct means of influencing citizens one way or another. After the German elections of 1932, which permitted Adolf Hitler to form a government, or the Czechoslovak elections of 1946, where communists were victorious, the next crucial step was anticipatory obedience. Because enough people in both cases voluntarily extended their services to the new leaders, Nazis and communists alike realized that they could move quickly toward a full regime change. The first heedless acts of conformity could not then be reversed.

In early 1938, Adolf Hitler, by then securely in power in Germany, was threatening to annex neighboring Austria. After the Austrian chancellor conceded, it was the Austrians' anticipatory obedience that decided the fate of Austrian Jews. Local Austrian Nazis captured Jews and forced them to scrub the streets to remove symbols of independent Austria. Crucially, people who were not Nazis looked on with interest and amusement. Nazis who had kept lists of Jewish property stole what they could. Crucially, others who were not Nazis joined in the theft. As the political theorist Hannah Arendt remembered, "when German troops invaded the country and Gentile neighbors started riots at Jewish homes, Austrian Jews began to commit suicide."

The anticipatory obedience of Austrians in March 1938 taught the high Nazi leadership what was possible. It was in Vienna that August that Adolf Eichmann established the Central Office for Jewish Emigration. In November 1938, following the Austrian example of March, German Nazis organized the national pogrom known as *Kristallnacht*.

In 1941, when Germany invaded the Soviet Union, the SS took the initiative to devise the methods of mass killing without orders to do so. They guessed what their superiors wanted and demonstrated what was possible. It was far more than Hitler had thought.

extending beyond the text

At the very beginning, anticipatory obedience means adapting instinctively, without reflecting, to a new situation. Do only Germans do such things? The Yale psychologist Stanley Milgram, contemplating Nazi atrocities, wanted to show that there was a particular authoritarian personality that explained why Germans behaved as they had. He devised an experiment to test the proposition, but failed to get permission to carry it out in Germany. So he undertook it instead in a Yale University building in 1961—at around the same time that Adolf Eichmann was being tried in Jerusalem for his part in the Nazi Holocaust of the Jews.

Milgram told his subjects (some Yale students, some New Haven residents) that they would be applying an electrical shock to other participants in an experiment about learning. In fact, the people attached to the wires on the other side of a window were in on the scheme with Milgram, and only pretended to be shocked. As the subjects (thought they) shocked the (people they thought were) participants in a learning experiment, they saw a horrible sight. People whom they did not know, and against whom they had no grievance, seemed to be suffering greatly — pounding the glass and complaining of heart pain. Even so, most subjects followed Milgram's instructions and continued to apply (what they thought were) ever greater shocks until the victims appeared to die. Even those who did not proceed all the way to the (apparent) killing of their fellow human beings left without inquiring about the health of the other participants.

Milgram grasped that people are remarkably receptive to new rules in a new setting. They are surprisingly willing to harm and kill others in the service of some new purpose if they are so instructed by a new authority. "I found so much obedience," Milgram remembered, "that I hardly saw the need for taking the experiment to Germany."

What does Snyder mean by "anticipatory obedience"? How, according to Snyder, do Nazi Germany and the Milgram experiment exemplify this phenomenon? How do some characters in *Macbeth* demonstrate anticipatory obedience? How does Macbeth exploit this to his advantage?

It would be my disgrace and your discomfort.
I take my leave at once. *Exit*
LADY MACDUFF Sirrah, your father's dead,
And what will you do now? How will you live?
SON As birds do, mother.
LADY MACDUFF What, with worms and flies?
SON With what I get I mean, and so do they.
LADY MACDUFF Poor bird, thou'dst never fear the net, nor lime, the pitfall, nor the gin.
SON Why should I, mother? Poor birds they are not set for.
My father is not dead for all your saying.
LADY MACDUFF Yes, he is dead. How wilt thou do for a father?
SON Nay, how will you do for a husband?
LADY MACDUFF Why, I can buy me twenty at any market.
SON Then you'll buy 'em to sell again.

---

and "discomfort" Lady Macduff through compassionate tears, but the line could also refer to their joint danger from Macbeth's spies. 30. **Sirrah:** here, a bantering form of abuse; compare 3.1.46 and note. 30. **dead:** Macduff is metaphorically dead because he is absent and cannot aid his family. 34. **lime:** Lime placed on twigs and branches causes birds' feet to stick to the tree. 35. **pitfall:** a trap for birds in which a cover falls over a hole. 35. **gin:** snare, trap (for game). 36. **Poor . . . for:** Inferior birds have no traps set for them. 41. **Then . . . again:** Lady Macduff could have

LADY MACDUFF Thou speak'st with all thy wit, and yet i'faith with wit enough for thee.

SON Was my father a traitor, mother?

LADY MACDUFF Ay, that he was.

SON What is a traitor?

LADY MACDUFF Why, one that swears and lies.

SON And be all traitors, that do so?

LADY MACDUFF Every one that does so is a traitor and must be hanged.

SON And must they all be hanged that swear and lie?

LADY MACDUFF Every one.

SON Who must hang them?

LADY MACDUFF Why, the honest men.

SON Then the liars and swearers are fools, for there are liars and swearers enough to beat the honest men and hang up them.

LADY MACDUFF Now God help thee, poor monkey, but how wilt thou do for a father?

SON If he were dead, you'd weep for him; if you would not, it were a good sign that I should quickly have a new father.

LADY MACDUFF Poor prattler, how thou talk'st!

Enter a MESSENGER

MESSENGER Bless you, fair dame. I am not to you known,
Though in your state of honour I am perfect;
I doubt some danger does approach you nearly.
If you will take a homely man's advice,
Be not found here. Hence with your little ones.
To fright you thus, methinks I am too savage;
To do worse to you were fell cruelty,
Which is too nigh your person. Heaven preserve you,
I dare abide no longer. *Exit*

LADY MACDUFF Whither should I fly?
I have done no harm. But I remember now
I am in this earthly world where to do harm
Is often laudable, to do good sometime
Accounted dangerous folly. Why then, alas,
Do I put up that womanly defence,
To say I have done no harm?

Enter MURDERERS

What are these faces?

A MURDERER Where is your husband?

LADY MACDUFF I hope in no place so unsanctified,
Where such as thou mayst find him.

A MURDERER He's a traitor.

SON Thou liest, thou shag-haired villain.

A MURDERER What, you egg!
Young fry of treachery!

[Kills him]

SON He has killed me, mother,
Run away, I pray you!

Exit [Lady Macduff] crying "Murder" [pursued by Murderers with her Son]

Act 4, Scene 3

Enter MALCOLM *and* MACDUFF

MALCOLM Let us seek out some desolate shade and there
Weep our sad bosoms empty.

MACDUFF Let us rather
Hold fast the mortal sword and like good men
Bestride our downfall birthdom; each new morn,
New widows howl, new orphans cry, new sorrows
Strike heaven on the face, that it resounds
As if it felt with Scotland and yelled out
Like syllable of dolour.

---

no use for twenty husbands unless she plans to resell (deceive) them. 47. **swears:** vows, takes an oath. 57. **monkey:** term of playful contempt, especially for a child, based, presumably, on childish mimicry. 61. **prattler:** chatterer. 63. **Though . . . perfect:** though I know very well your status and reputation. 64. **doubt:** fear, suspect. 65. **homely:** simple, but perhaps implying common (not gentle or aristocratic). 67. **methinks:** it seems to me. 68. **fell:** deadly. 69. **nigh:** near, close to. The messenger refers to the deadly danger already threatening Lady Macduff. 76. **What are these faces?:** Lady Macduff addresses the Murderers. 78. **unsanctified:** unhallowed, not consecrated (to religious uses). 80. **shag-haired:** with long, shaggy hair. Such hair was a villain's mark. 80. **egg:** The Murderer agrees with the proverbial "An evil bird lays an evil egg." 81. **fry:** offspring, progeny.

MALCOLM What I believe, I'll wail;
What know, believe; and what I can redress,
As I shall find the time to friend, I will.
What you have spoke, it may be so perchance.
This tyrant, whose sole name blisters our tongues,
Was once thought honest; you have loved him well —
He hath not touched you yet. I am young, but something
You may discern of him through me, and wisdom
To offer up a weak, poor, innocent lamb
T'appease an angry god.

MACDUFF I am not treacherous.

MALCOLM But Macbeth is.
A good and virtuous nature may recoil
In an imperial charge. But I shall crave your pardon:
That which you are, my thoughts cannot transpose;
Angels are bright still, though the brightest fell.
Though all things foul would wear the brows of grace,
Yet grace must still look so.

MACDUFF I have lost my hopes.

MALCOLM Perchance even there where I did find my doubts.
Why in that rawness left you wife and child,
Those precious motives, those strong knots of love,
Without leave-taking? I pray you,
Let not my jealousies be your dishonours,
But mine own safeties; you may be rightly just,
Whatever I shall think.

MACDUFF Bleed, bleed, poor country.
Great tyranny, lay thou thy basis sure,
For goodness dare not check thee; wear thou thy wrongs,
The title is affeered. Fare thee well, lord,
I would not be the villain that thou think'st
For the whole space that's in the tyrant's grasp,
And the rich East to boot.

MALCOLM Be not offended.
I speak not as in absolute fear of you:
I think our country sinks beneath the yoke;
It weeps, it bleeds, and each new day a gash
Is added to her wounds. I think withal
There would be hands uplifted in my right,
And here from gracious England have I offer
Of goodly thousands. But for all this,
When I shall tread upon the tyrant's head,
Or wear it on my sword, yet my poor country
Shall have more vices than it had before,
More suffer, and more sundry ways than ever,
By him that shall succeed.

MACDUFF What should he be?

MALCOLM It is myself I mean–in whom I know
All the particulars of vice so grafted
That when they shall be opened, black Macbeth
Will seem as pure as snow, and the poor state
Esteem him as a lamb, being compared
With my confineless harms.

Act 4, Scene 3. 3. **fast:** firmly, tightly. 3. **mortal:** fatal, death-dealing. 3–4. **like good men . . . birthdom:** The image is of soldiers standing astride a fallen comrade to protect him from further injury. 4. **downfall:** downfallen, fallen from prosperity. 4. **birthdom:** inheritance, birthright; perhaps native kingdom. 8. **Like:** similar, identical. 8. **dolour:** sadness. 8. **wail:** bewail, lament. 10. **to friend:** as a friend, on my side. 12. **sole:** alone. 14. **He hath not touched you yet:** Either (1) Macduff follows Macbeth loyally and is therefore safe or (2) Macduff continues to love Macbeth only because Macduff has not yet been "touched" (as Malcolm has). 15. **You may discern of him through me:** Macduff may see ("discern") a future Macbeth in Malcolm. 16. **innocent lamb:** In the Christian tradition, the lamb is an emblem of innocence. 19. **recoil:** fall back, degenerate. 20. **charge:** burden. 20. **crave:** beg, ask; not yearn for. 22. **the brightest:** Satan, one of whose names is "Lucifer" (light-bearer). 23. **brows:** face or appearance (a figuratively extended meaning). 26. **rawness:** imperfection, incompleteness. Here, the "rawness" is partly social: Macduff did not bid his family good-bye, but the aborted ceremony also stands for a failure of love and duty (compare Lady Macduff's anger, 4.2.1ff.). 29. **jealousies:** suspicions, mistrust. 32. **basis:** foundation, base. 33. **check:** limit, control. 34. **The title is affeered:** Either (1) the epithet ("tyranny") is confirmed (= "affeered") or (2) the valid claim and claimant are frightened ("afeared"). These two possibilities, one referring to Macbeth, the other to Malcolm, depend on a pun: affeered/afeared. 37. **to boot:** in addition. 38. **absolute:** perfect, entire. 39–41. **I think . . . wounds:** These lines may allude to Jesus's suffering on the way to crucifixion. 43. **England:** i.e., the King of England, Edward the Confessor. 44. **thousands:** i.e., thousands of soldiers (to support Malcolm's claim). 48. **sundry:** various, diverse. 49. **What:** who. Macduff is not dehumanizing or treating as a monster Macbeth's hypothetical successor. 51. **grafted:** made part of my being. The botanical metaphor describes the gardener's joining of one plant or species with another. 52–54. **That . . . lamb:** Many proverbial analogies and phrases — "as white as snow," "to make black white," "as pure as snow," "as innocent as a lamb" — may make Malcolm's speech plainly ironic. 52. **opened:** i.e., born, made known. The metaphor is of a flower's bud [see "grafted" (51 and note)], but may also imply dissection of moral cadavers. 55. **confineless:** unconfined, limitless. 55. **legions:**

MACDUFF Not in the legions
Of horrid hell can come a devil more damned
In evils to top Macbeth.
MALCOLM I grant him bloody,
Luxurious, avaricious, false, deceitful,
Sudden, malicious, smacking of every sin
That has a name. But there's no bottom, none,
In my voluptuousness: your wives, your daughters,
Your matrons, and your maids could not fill up
The cistern of my lust, and my desire
All continent impediments would o'erbear
That did oppose my will. Better Macbeth,
Than such an one to reign.
MACDUFF Boundless intemperance
In nature is a tyranny; it hath been
Th'untimely emptying of the happy throne
And fall of many kings. But fear not yet
To take upon you what is yours: you may
Convey your pleasures in a spacious plenty
And yet seem cold. The time you may so hoodwink.
We have willing dames enough; there cannot be
That vulture in you to devour so many
As will to greatness dedicate themselves,
Finding it so inclined.
MALCOLM With this, there grows
In my most ill-composed affection such
A stanchless avarice that, were I king,
I should cut off the nobles for their lands,
Desire his jewels, and this other's house,
And my more-having would be as a sauce
To make me hunger more, that I should forge
Quarrels unjust against the good and loyal,
Destroying them for wealth.
MACDUFF This avarice
Sticks deeper, grows with more pernicious root
Than summer-seeming lust, and it hath been
The sword of our slain kings; yet do not fear,
Scotland hath foisons to fill up your will
Of your mere own. All these are portable,
With other graces weighed.
MALCOLM But I have none. The king-becoming graces —
As justice, verity, temp'rance, stableness,
Bounty, perseverance, mercy, lowliness,
Devotion, patience, courage, fortitude —
I have no relish of them, but abound
In the division of each several crime,
Acting it many ways. Nay, had I power, I should
Pour the sweet milk of concord into hell,
Uproar the universal peace, confound
All unity on earth.
MACDUFF O Scotland, Scotland!
MALCOLM If such a one be fit to govern, speak.
I am as I have spoken.
MACDUFF Fit to govern?
No, not to live. O nation miserable!
With an untitled tyrant, bloody-sceptred,
When shalt thou see thy wholesome days again,
Since that the truest issue of thy throne
By his own interdiction stands accursed
And does blaspheme his breed? Thy royal father
Was a most sainted king; the queen that bore thee,

---

multitudes, hordes. The word is used biblically of angels (Matthew 26:53); compare 22. 58. **Luxurious:** lecherous, lascivious. 59. **Sudden:** rash, impetuous. 59. **smacking:** having the flavor of. 63. **cistern:** (water) tank; large vessel (especially for holding liquor). 64. **continent:** self-restraining. The word has resonances — of "containing" and "landmass" — that join with "cistern" (63) to make Malcolm's imagined lust a watery force of nature overwhelming the land. 71. **Convey:** carry on, manage. 72. **hoodwink:** blindfold, deceive. 73–76. **there cannot be . . . inclined:** i.e., you cannot be so voracious as to consume the many women who will volunteer to serve (sexually) your high rank, once it is known you desire them. 76. **With this:** along with this. 77. **affection:** disposition, state of mind. 78. **stanchless:** unstoppable. 79. **cut off:** put to death, kill. 82. **forge:** fabricate. 85. **root:** The metaphor recalls "For love of money is the root of all evil" (1 Timothy 6:10). 86. **summer-seeming lust:** i.e., lust befits summer. 87. **sword of our slain kings:** i.e., the means by which our kings died. 88. **foisons:** harvests. 89. **mere:** very. 89. **portable:** bearable. 90. **weighed:** balanced. 92. **verity:** truthfulness, sincerity. 93. **perseverance:** accented on the second syllable. 93. **lowliness:** humility, meekness. 95. **relish:** trace. 96. **division:** partition(s), sub-division(s). 96. **several:** individual, particular. 99. **Uproar:** throw into confusion; accent on second syllable. 99. **confound:** accent on second syllable. 104. **untitled:** without right to the title (of king). 105. **wholesome:** healthy, free from taint. 106. **issue:** child, offspring. 107. **interdiction:** authoritative prohibition. 108. **blaspheme his breed:** slander or calumniate his

Oft'ner upon her knees than on her feet,
Died every day she lived. Fare thee well,
These evils thou repeat'st upon thyself
Hath banished me from Scotland. O my breast,
Thy hope ends here.

MALCOLM Macduff, this noble passion,
Child of integrity, hath from my soul
Wiped the black scruples, reconciled my thoughts
To thy good truth and honour. Devilish Macbeth
By many of these trains hath sought to win me
Into his power, and modest wisdom plucks me
From over-credulous haste; but God above
Deal between thee and me, for even now
I put myself to thy direction and
Unspeak mine own detraction, here abjure
The taints and blames I laid upon myself,
For strangers to my nature. I am yet
Unknown to woman, never was forsworn,
Scarcely have coveted what was mine own,
At no time broke my faith, would not betray
The devil to his fellow, and delight
No less in truth than life. My first false speaking
Was this upon myself. What I am truly
Is thine, and my poor country's, to command:
Whither indeed, before thy here-approach,
Old Siward with ten thousand warlike men
Already at a point was setting forth.
Now we'll together, and the chance of goodness
Be like our warranted quarrel. Why are you silent?

MACDUFF Such welcome and unwelcome things at once,
'Tis hard to reconcile.

Enter a DOCTOR

MALCOLM Well, more anon. —
Comes the king forth, I pray you?

DOCTOR Ay, sir: there are a crew of wretched souls
That stay his cure; their malady convinces
The great assay of art, but at his touch,
Such sanctity hath heaven given his hand,
They presently amend. *Exit*

MALCOLM I thank you, doctor.

MACDUFF What's the disease he means?

MALCOLM 'Tis called the Evil.
A most miraculous work in this good king,
Which often since my here-remain in England
I have seen him do. How he solicits heaven
Himself best knows, but strangely visited people
All swoll'n and ulcerous, pitiful to the eye,
The mere despair of surgery, he cures,
Hanging a golden stamp about their necks
Put on with holy prayers, and 'tis spoken
To the succeeding royalty he leaves
The healing benediction. With this strange virtue,
He hath a heavenly gift of prophecy,

---

heritage, his family line (= "breed"). 111. **Died . . . lived:** i.e., she lived each day as virtuously as if she were to die that day (and face divine judgment). Compare St. Paul's claim "I die daily" (1 Corinthians 15:31). 112–13. **These evils . . . Scotland:** The very evils Malcolm has recited are those that, in Macbeth, made Macduff flee Scotland. 116. **scruples:** doubts, troubling thoughts. They are "black" because they concern Malcolm's suspicions that Macduff is evil. 118. **trains:** stratagem, trick. Malcolm feared that Macduff was an *agent provocateur* pretending disloyalty to Macbeth in order to trick Malcolm into returning to Scotland. 119. **plucks:** restrains forcibly. 120. **over-credulous:** too quick to believe. 122. **put myself to thy direction:** submit myself to your guidance. 123. **abjure:** disavow. 125. **For:** as being. 126. **Unknown to woman:** i.e., not having had sexual intercourse with a woman, but perhaps recalling "none of woman born" (4.1.79). 126. **forsworn:** perjured, (one who) betrayed an oath. 133. **thy here-approach:** your coming here. See "my here-remain" (150). 135. **at a point:** prepared, in readiness. 136. **Now we'll together:** i.e., now we'll journey together. 136. **chance of goodness:** good fortune or outcome. 136–37. **chance . . . quarrel:** i.e., may the result be as fortunate as our grievances are justified. 138–39. **Such . . . reconcile:** Macduff's puzzlement at Malcolm's trickery is never resolved. 139–61. **Well . . . grace:** These lines have been regarded as interpolation or revision. 141. **crew:** company, group. 142. **stay his cure:** await his healing touch. 142. **convinces:** overcomes. See 1.7.64. 143. **assay:** best effort. 145. **sd *Exit*:** The Doctor's exit might follow Malcolm's thanks, but thanks (or dismissal?) and departure are probably simultaneous. 148. **Evil:** The King's Evil, scrofula (an inflammation of the lymph nodes, often in the neck, causing swelling and suppuration). It was believed that monarchs of France and of England could cure this affliction. 151. **solicits:** entreats, petitions. 154. **mere:** very, entire. 155. **stamp:** coin, medal. Elizabeth and James gave a gold coin, an "angel" depicting the Archangel Michael, to those they touched. 156. **holy prayers:** The English ceremony for "touching" involved a special prayer said by the monarch. 157. **succeeding royalty:** following monarchs. The power to cure the Evil supposedly descends in the royal line and was popularly associated with the monarch's anointing at his or her

And sundry blessings hang about his throne
That speak him full of grace.

Enter ROSS

MACDUFF See who comes here.
MALCOLM My countryman, but yet I know him not.
MACDUFF My ever gentle cousin, welcome hither.
MALCOLM I know him now. Good God betimes remove
The means that makes us strangers.
ROSS Sir, amen.
MACDUFF Stands Scotland where it did?
ROSS Alas, poor country,
Almost afraid to know itself. It cannot
Be called our mother, but our grave, where nothing,
But who knows nothing, is once seen to smile;
Where sighs, and groans, and shrieks that rend the air
Are made, not marked; where violent sorrow seems
A modern ecstasy. The deadman's knell
Is there scarce asked for who, and good men's lives
Expire before the flowers in their caps,
Dying or ere they sicken.
MACDUFF O relation
Too nice, and yet too true.
MALCOLM What's the newest grief?
ROSS That of an hour's age doth hiss the speaker;
Each minute teems a new one.
MACDUFF How does my wife?
ROSS Why, well.
MACDUFF And all my children?
ROSS Well, too.
MACDUFF The tyrant has not battered at their peace?
ROSS No, they were well at peace when I did leave 'em.
MACDUFF Be not a niggard of your speech: how goes't?
ROSS When I came hither to transport the tidings
Which I have heavily borne, there ran a rumour
Of many worthy fellows that were out,
Which was to my belief witnessed the rather
For that I saw the tyrant's power afoot.
Now is the time of help. [*To Malcolm*] Your eye in Scotland
Would create soldiers, make our women fight
To doff their dire distresses.
MALCOLM Be't their comfort
We are coming thither. Gracious England hath
Lent us good Siward and ten thousand men —
An older and a better soldier none
That Christendom gives out.
ROSS Would I could answer
This comfort with the like. But I have words
That would be howled out in the desert air,
Where hearing should not latch them.
MACDUFF What concern they?
The general cause, or is it a fee-grief
Due to some single breast?
ROSS No mind that's honest

---

coronation. 158. **benediction:** kindly favor, grace. 158. **strange:** unusual, inexplicable. 158. **virtue:** ability, power. 161. **speak:** bespeak, proclaim. 162. **My . . . not:** Malcolm recognizes Ross as a Scot by his costume. 164. **betimes:** in due time, before it is too late. 165. **means:** interposed (or intervening) conditions. 166. **Stands Scotland where it did?:** Is Scotland in its former condition? 168–69. **nothing . . . nothing:** no one — no "thing" — except those who know nothing. 169. **once:** ever. 170. **rend:** tear. 171. **marked:** noticed. 172. **modern:** present; common, everyday. 172–73. **The deadman's . . . who:** Death is so common in Scotland that no one asks for whom the bell tolls. 175. **or ere they sicken:** before the flowers show signs of illness. The comparison (173–75) expresses both the brevity of "good men's lives" and the suddenness of their deaths. 175. **relation:** account, statement. 176. **nice:** carefully accurate, precise. Ross's account is terrible because it accurately conveys the horror of life in Scotland. 176. **newest:** most recent, most worthy of being told as news. 177. **hiss:** mock, accuse sarcastically. 178. **teems:** breeds, gives birth to. 179. **well . . . Well, too:** Proverbially, "He is well since he is in Heaven." 179. **children:** trisyllabic ("childeren"). 181. **at peace:** in harmony; dead. Legalistically, Ross tells the truth; he left Macduff's family before their slaughter. Ross, hesitating to deliver bad news (or fearing the consequences of telling what he knows), becomes another Scot who knows but cannot speak a truth or act on it. 182. **niggard:** miser, withholder. 183–90. **When . . . distresses:** Ross dodges Macduff's direct question about his family. 185. **out:** abroad, in the field (preparing for battle). 186–87. **witnessed . . . afoot:** Macbeth's forces on the march confirm that their opponents are also mobilizing. 187. **power:** army, military forces. 188. **help:** aid, assistance; probably also relief, cure, remedy. 188. **eye:** i.e., person. An example of synecdoche, where "eye" stands for Malcolm's body. 190. **doff:** put off (another image of clothing). 197. **latch:** receive. 198. **general cause:** everyone's (= all Scotland's) interest. 198–99. **fee-grief . . . single breast:** grief owned entirely by one person ("some single breast"); a grief concerning one individual. 204. **possess**

But in it shares some woe, though the main part
Pertains to you alone.

MACDUFF If it be mine,
Keep it not from me; quickly let me have it.

ROSS Let not your ears despise my tongue forever
Which shall possess them with the heaviest sound
That ever yet they heard.

MACDUFF H'm — I guess at it.

ROSS Your castle is surprised; your wife and babes
Savagely slaughtered. To relate the manner
Were on the quarry of these murdered deer
To add the death of you.

MALCOLM Merciful heaven —
What, man, ne'er pull your hat upon your brows:
Give sorrow words; the grief that does not speak,
Whispers the o'erfraught heart and bids it break.

MACDUFF My children too?

ROSS Wife, children, servants, all
That could be found.

MACDUFF And I must be from thence?
My wife killed too?

ROSS I have said.

MALCOLM Be comforted.
Let's make us med'cines of our great revenge
To cure this deadly grief.

MACDUFF He has no children. All my pretty ones?
Did you say all? O hell-kite! All?
What, all my pretty chickens and their dam
At one fell swoop?

MALCOLM Dispute it like a man.

MACDUFF I shall do so;
But I must also feel it as a man;
I cannot but remember such things were
That were most precious to me. Did heaven look on,
And would not take their part? Sinful Macduff,
They were all struck for thee. Naught that I am,
Not for their own demerits but for mine,
Fell slaughter on their souls. Heaven rest them now.

MALCOLM Be this the whetstone of your sword, let grief
Convert to anger. Blunt not the heart, enrage it.

MACDUFF O, I could play the woman with mine eyes
And braggart with my tongue. But gentle heavens,
Cut short all intermission. Front to front
Bring thou this fiend of Scotland and myself;
Within my sword's length set him. If he scape,
Heaven forgive him too.

MALCOLM This tune goes manly.
Come, go we to the king; our power is ready;
Our lack is nothing but our leave. Macbeth
Is ripe for shaking, and the powers above
Put on their instruments. Receive what cheer you may:
The night is long that never finds the day.

Exeunt

---

them with: inform them. 204. **heaviest:** saddest. 208. **quarry:** heap made of the deer killed at a hunting. 208. **deer:** animals; beloved ones (= "dear"). 210. **pull your hat upon your brows:** a conventional gesture of sorrow or melancholy. 211–12. **the grief . . . bids it break:** The contrast is between "speak" (say aloud) and "whisper" (speak softly). In this period, "break" was pronounced to rhyme with modern "speak." 214. **from thence:** i.e., away from home. 218. **He has no children:** The phrase has several possible meanings depending on the referent for "He." Malcolm has no children and cannot therefore understand Macduff's pain; Macbeth has no children and (1) cannot therefore know what their loss means or (2) therefore has no one against whom Macduff may exact a fitting revenge for the loss of his children. 219. **hell-kite:** hellish bird of prey; hence, figuratively, a human predator. 220. **dam:** female parent. Like "chickens" [compare "chuck" (3.2.45)], the metaphor treats humans as animals; "dam" is usually contemptuous when applied to humans, although probably not here. 221. **At one fell swoop:** Shakespeare seems to have invented this now-proverbial phrase. 221. **fell:** fierce, savage, cruel. 227. **part:** side, cause. 228. **Naught:** wicked. 233. **play the woman with mine eyes:** weep. 235. **intermission:** pause, interval in action. 235. **Front to front:** face to face (or forehead to forehead). 237. **scape:** escape. 238. **tune:** style, manner; temper, mood. 239. **power:** army, force. 240. **leave:** official permission (to depart). 241. **ripe for shaking:** i.e., ready to fall (from the fruit tree, from the throne). 241. **powers above:** heavenly influences (recalling King Edward and his holiness: see 143–45, 158–61). 242. **Put on:** don, clothe themselves in. 242. **instruments:** agents, tools; here, probably weapons.

Understanding and Interpreting

1. What does Macbeth demand to know from the witches in the first scene? Why is he so determined to get this information at this point in the play?
2. The apparitions that appear in Scene 1 each share a different prophecy with Macbeth, all of which are both specific and ambiguous. How does Macbeth feel about the prophesies? Based on your understanding of the play and the characters at this point, predict what each of the prophecies means and how each one will influence Macbeth.
3. After the witches leave in Scene 1, Macbeth is disturbed to find out that Lennox did not see them. Macbeth then declares that "all those that trust" the witches should be "damned" (l. 139). Does this indicate that Macbeth himself does not trust them, or is he trying to deal with his own fears that the witches may be telling the truth? Explain.
4. Macbeth is deeply concerned when Lennox reports that Macduff has fled to England at the end of Scene 1. What about the witches' prophecy can still come true if Macduff is alive?
5. When making plans to attack Macduff's castle, Macbeth says, "And even now / To crown my thoughts with acts, be it thought and done" (Scene 1, ll.147 to 148). What do these lines reveal about how Macbeth has changed over the course of the ply so far?
6. In Scene 2, Ross will not tell Lady Macduff why her husband has fled to England, leaving her alone. Instead, he describes why the times are "cruel" (ll. 17 to 26). Using text from his response, describe the state of affairs in Scotland at this moment in the play.
7. At the end of Scene 2, Macduff's wife and young son are murdered by a killer hired by Macbeth. Unlike the murder of King Duncan, this one happens onstage. What is the effect of including this particular scene onstage in the play?
8. Summarize the qualities Malcolm ascribes to Macbeth (Scene 3, ll. 58 to 61). Discuss how those qualities have or have not been revealed through Macbeth's actions so far in the play.
9. Malcolm lies about himself to Macduff, suggesting "black Macbeth / [would] seem as pure as snow" when compared to Malcolm's "confineless harms" (Scene 3, ll. 52 to 55). Why does Malcolm do this? Does the lie accomplish what Malcolm hopes it will?
10. Ross shares news of Scotland with Malcolm and Macduff (Scene 3, ll. 168 to 175). What is the current state of affairs, according to Ross?

Analyzing Language, Style, and Structure

1. **Vocabulary in Context.** When confronting the witches, Macbeth asks, "shall Banquo's issue ever reign in this kingdom?" (Scene 1, ll. 101 to 102). What does "issue" mean in this context? What other meanings have you encountered?
2. **Vocabulary in Context.** In the same scene with the witches, Macbeth warns them not to "Deny me this" (Scene 1, l. 104). What does Macbeth mean by "deny"? How is his use of the word similar to or different from other uses that you have encountered?
3. **Vocabulary in Context.** When Malcolm is meeting with Macduff, he says, "wear the brows of grace" (Scene 3, l. 23). What does the word "grace" mean in this context? How is that use of the word similar to or different from other uses? What does Malcolm's use of the word suggest about him?

4. **Skill Focus.** In discussing his attitude toward Macbeth, Malcolm says, "Angels are bright still, though the brightest fell" (Scene 3, l. 22). Explain the meaning behind this Biblical allusion to Lucifer. You may need to conduct research to understand it fully.
5. During the procession of the eight ghostly kings in Scene 1 (ll. 112 to 124), Macbeth makes numerous references to sight and seeing. Identify these references, and discuss how they highlight Macbeth's current mental state.
6. Right before she is murdered, Lady Macduff declares that "in this earthly world [. . .] to do harm / Is often laudable, to do good sometimes / Accounted dangerous folly" (Scene 2, ll. 72 to 74). How does her statement reflect the state of affairs in Scotland at this moment in the play?
7. Malcolm finally tells Ross and Macduff that he plans to take up arms against Macbeth in Scotland (Scene 3, ll. 132 to 136). What is the effect of his waiting until this point to reveal this important information? Why does he not reveal his plan sooner?
8. Ross must deliver the terrible news to Macduff that his entire family has been murdered by Macbeth. Though he knows Macduff is grief-stricken over the news, Malcolm uses this moment in Scene 3 as an opportunity to recruit Macduff in his war against Macbeth. How do Malcom's word choices further develop an idea about gender roles in the play?
9. There are many revelations and events in Scene 3. Analyze the effect of Shakespeare's choices regarding the order in which he introduces the different events in this scene.

Topics for Composing

1. **Analysis.** By this point in the play, what is motivating Macbeth? Analyze his actions and compare them to actions he undertook earlier in the play. Be sure to discuss Lady Macbeth's shifting influence on his decision-making.
2. **Argument.** In Scene 3, Malcolm lists the qualities that he believes make a great king. Write an argument in which you discuss whether those qualities are still a part of being a great leader, or if they are irrelevant in today's world. Use specific examples of current leaders to support your claims.
3. **Connection.** Which characters in the play do you sympathize with the most and the least? Why?
4. **Speaking and Listening.** There are many widely available audio and film versions of this play. Listen to or view a scene from Act 4 and explain how the experience affects your understanding of the language, plot, characters, theme, or other aspect of the play.
5. **Research.** Historians believe that the reason Shakespeare included witches in the play was that King James I, who was the king of England at the time *Macbeth* was written, was fascinated with witches and witchcraft. Research popular notions about witchcraft at the time of Shakespeare's writing. Explain how they are similar to and different from modern-day attitudes towards the subject.
6. **Multimodal.** Create a few panels for a graphic adaptation of a scene from this act. The scene with the witches or the attack on Macduff's castle might be good choices. Consider making your adaptation an update with modern appearances and everyday speech. Be sure that your graphic adaptation includes visuals as well as dialogue.

Act 5, Scene 1

Enter a DOCTOR OF PHYSIC, *and a* WAITING-GENTLEWOMAN

DOCTOR I have two nights watched with you, but can perceive no truth in your report. When was it she last walked?

GENTLEWOMAN Since his majesty went into the field, I have seen her rise from her bed, throw her night-gown upon her, unlock her closet, take forth paper, fold it, write upon't, read it, afterwards seal it, and again return to bed, yet all this while in a most fast sleep.

DOCTOR A great perturbation in nature, to receive at once the benefit of sleep and do the effects of watching. In this slumbery agitation, besides her walking and other actual performances, what at any time have you heard her say?

GENTLEWOMAN That, sir, which I will not report after her.

DOCTOR You may to me, and 'tis most meet you should.

GENTLEWOMAN Neither to you, nor anyone, having no witness to confirm my speech.

Enter LADY [MACBETH], *with a taper*

Lo you, here she comes. This is her very guise and, upon my life, fast asleep. Observe her, stand close.

DOCTOR How came she by that light?

GENTLEWOMAN Why, it stood by her. She has light by her continually, 'tis her command.

DOCTOR You see her eyes are open.

GENTLEWOMAN Ay, but their sense are shut.

DOCTOR What is it she does now? Look how she rubs her hands.

GENTLEWOMAN It is an accustomed action with her, to seem thus washing her hands; I have known her continue in this a quarter of an hour.

LADY MACBETH Yet here's a spot.

The sleepwalking Lady Macbeth, 1781–1784, by Johann Heinrich Fussli (1741-1825), oil on canvas, 221x160 cm./DE AGOSTINI EDITORE/Bridgeman Images

Although she is sleepwalking in Johann Heinrich Fuseli's *The Sleepwalking Lady Macbeth*, Lady Macbeth still appears quite animated in this image.

What ideas about Lady Macbeth's mental state does the artist offer in this painting? What details about both Lady Macbeth and the onlookers serve to convey those ideas?

Act 5, Scene 1. 0. **sd** DOCTOR OF PHYSIC: physician. Lady Macbeth's condition is represented as a physical rather than a spiritual one; she needs medical attention, not the exorcism a Roman Catholic (but not a Protestant) clergyman might claim to offer. 0. **sd** WAITING-GENTLEWOMAN: personal attendant who is "gentle," not "common." In the Jacobean court, the queen's personal attendants were aristocrats; in Shakespeare's imagined courts, the attendants' ranks are often unclear. 1. **watched:** observed; perhaps stayed awake observing. 3. **his majesty:** Macbeth. 3. **went into the field:** mobilized an army for battle. 5. **closet:** cabinet; lockable chest or box for valuables. 6. **seal:** place a personal mark in hot wax on a document as a sign of authenticity. Shakespeare's contemporaries ensured the privacy of letters by folding them and sealing over the fold. 9. **effects:** appearances, outward manifestations. 9. **watching:** waking. 10. **slumbery:** sleepy, slumberous. 10. **actual:** active. 13. **meet:** fitting, appropriate. 14–15. **Neither . . . speech:** The Waiting-Gentlewoman fears to repeat what she has heard without a witness because it would be treasonable. 15. **sd** ***taper*:** candle. 16. **very guise:** exact manner, custom, or habit. 16–17. **upon my life:** an oath. 17. **close:** concealed, hidden, out of sight. 18. **How . . . light:** The Doctor's realistic question (why does a sleepwalker need light?) leads to an eerie inference: awake or asleep, Lady Macbeth evidently fears the dark. 28. **set down:** write down, note. An implicit stage direction: the Doctor uses a pocket notebook. 29. **satisfy:**

extending beyond the text

Just as the scene in which Macbeth imagines a dagger floating in the air reflects a central psychological struggle for him, the scene in which Lady Macbeth tries to scrub imagined blood from her hands reflects the deep psychological struggle her character faces. Look at the following stills from four different film versions of the play.

This still is from a 1983 BBC television version of *Macbeth* directed by Jack Gold. Lady Macbeth is played by Jane Lapotaire.

A scene from Trevor Nunn's stage version of *Macbeth*, filmed in 1978, with Dame Judi Dench as Lady Macbeth.

This still is from the 1971 film directed by Roman Polanski. Francesca Annis plays Lady Macbeth.

This still is from the 2008 version of *Macbeth* directed by Rupert Goold, with Kate Fleetwood as Lady Macbeth.

What similarities and differences can you identify among these versions? What specific choices in lighting, framing, gestures, or facial expressions communicate Lady Macbeth's mental state? What might you add or change if you were the director? Why?

DOCTOR Hark, she speaks; I will set down what comes from her to satisfy my remembrance the more strongly.

LADY MACBETH Out, damned spot! Out, I say! One, two. Why then 'tis time to do't. Hell is murky. Fie, my lord, fie, a soldier, and afeard? What need we fear? Who knows it, when none can call our power to account? Yet who would have thought the old man to have had so much blood in him?

DOCTOR Do you mark that?

LADY MACBETH The Thane of Fife had a wife. Where is she now? What, will these hands ne'er be clean? No more o'that, my lord, no more o'that. You mar all with this starting.

DOCTOR Go to, go to; you have known what you should not.

GENTLEWOMAN She has spoke what she should not, I am sure of that. Heaven knows what she has known.

LADY MACBETH Here's the smell of the blood still; all the perfumes of Arabia will not sweeten this little hand. O, O, O.

DOCTOR What a sigh is there! The heart is sorely charged.

GENTLEWOMAN I would not have such a heart in my bosom for the dignity of the whole body.

DOCTOR Well, well, well—

GENTLEWOMAN Pray God it be, sir.

DOCTOR This disease is beyond my practice; yet I have known those which have walked in their sleep who have died holily in their beds.

LADY MACBETH Wash your hands, put on your night-gown, look not so pale. I tell you yet again, Banquo's buried; he cannot come out on's grave.

DOCTOR Even so?

LADY MACBETH To bed, to bed; there's knocking at the gate.
Come, come, come, come, give me your hand; what's done cannot be undone. To bed, to bed, to bed. *Exit*

DOCTOR Will she go now to bed?

GENTLEWOMAN Directly.

DOCTOR Foul whisp'rings are abroad; unnatural deeds
Do breed unnatural troubles; infected minds
To their deaf pillows will discharge their secrets.
More needs she the divine than the physician.
God, God forgive us all. Look after her;
Remove from her the means of all annoyance,
And still keep eyes upon her. So, good night,
My mind she has mated, and amazed my sight.
I think, but dare not speak.

GENTLEWOMAN Good night, good doctor.

Exeunt

Act 5, Scene 2

Drum and colours. Enter MENTEITH, CAITHNESS, ANGUS, LENNOX, *Soldiers*

MENTEITH The English power is near, led on by Malcolm,
His uncle Siward, and the good Macduff.
Revenges burn in them, for their dear causes
Would to the bleeding and the grim alarm
Excite the mortified man.

ANGUS Near Birnam Wood
Shall we well meet them; that way are they coming.

meet the needs of, content. 30. **One, two:** presumably, the striking of a bell or a clock. 31. **murky:** gloomy, dark. 32. **afeard:** afraid. 32–33. **Who knows . . . account:** The murder of Duncan cannot be said to be "known" because no one has the power or authority to hold the Macbeths responsible; compare her assurance before the murder: "Who dares receive it other" (1.7.77). 36. **Thane of Fife:** Macduff. 38. **starting:** flinching, recoiling nervously. 39. **Go to:** come, come (a remonstrance). 40. **spoke:** spoken. 44. **sorely charged:** grievously burdened, heavily loaded. 46. **dignity:** rank, status (as queen). 49. **practice:** professional skill, art. 54. **on's:** of his. 60. **Directly:** at once, straightaway. 64. **More needs she . . . physician:** i.e., she is beyond medical help and requires spiritual counsel. 66. **Remove . . . annoyance:** The Doctor anticipates that Lady Macbeth might commit suicide. 66. **annoyance:** injuring, troubling. 67. **still:** always. 68. **mated:** daunted, stupefied. 68. **amazed:** astonished. The word derives from "maze"; the Doctor is in a mental labyrinth. 69. **I think . . . speak:** Like the Waiting-Gentlewoman (14–15), the Doctor is afraid to acknowledge the evidence of regicide he now possesses.

Act 5, Scene 2. 0. sd ***Drum and colours***: Drummer and flag-bearer(s). 1. **power:** military force. Elision ("pow'r") helps the meter. 3–5. **Revenges . . . man:** The clearest meaning of this complex clause is that Malcolm and Macduff's motives for revenge are powerful enough to make a dead or near-dead man answer the call to arms. 3. **Revenges:** desires to repay injuries. 3. **dear:** honorable; precious. 5. **mortified:** dead; insensible.

CAITHNESS Who knows if Donaldbain be with his brother?
LENNOX For certain, sir, he is not. I have a file
Of all the gentry; there is Siward's son
And many unrough youths that even now
Protest their first of manhood.
MENTEITH What does the tyrant?
CAITHNESS Great Dunsinane he strongly fortifies.
Some say he's mad; others that lesser hate him
Do call it valiant fury, but for certain
He cannot buckle his distempered cause
Within the belt of rule.
ANGUS Now does he feel
His secret murders sticking on his hands.
Now minutely revolts upbraid his faith-breach;
Those he commands, move only in command,
Nothing in love. Now does he feel his title
Hang loose about him, like a giant's robe
Upon a dwarfish thief.
MENTEITH Who then shall blame
His pestered senses to recoil and start,
When all that is within him does condemn
Itself for being there?
CAITHNESS Well, march we on
To give obedience where 'tis truly owed;
Meet we the med'cine of the sickly weal,
And with him pour we in our country's purge,
Each drop of us.
LENNOX Or so much as it needs
To dew the sovereign flower and drown the weeds.
Make we our march towards Birnam.
Exeunt, marching

Act 5, Scene 3

Enter MACBETH, DOCTOR, *and Attendants*

MACBETH Bring me no more reports, let them fly all;
Till Birnam Wood remove to Dunsinane,
I cannot taint with fear. What's the boy Malcolm?
Was he not born of woman? The spirits that know
All mortal consequences have pronounced me thus:
"Fear not, Macbeth, no man that's born of woman
Shall e'er have power upon thee." Then fly false thanes
And mingle with the English epicures;
The mind I sway by and the heart I bear
Shall never sag with doubt nor shake with fear.

Enter SERVANT

The devil damn thee black, thou cream-faced loon.
Where got'st thou that goose-look?
SERVANT There is ten thousand—
MACBETH Geese, villain?
SERVANT Soldiers, sir.
MACBETH Go prick thy face and over-red thy fear,
Thou lily-livered boy. What soldiers, patch?
Death of thy soul, those linen cheeks of thine

---

7. **Who . . . brother:** the first mention of Donaldbain since 3.6.9, and the last in the play. 8. **file:** list. 10. **unrough:** i.e., unbearded, young. 11. **Protest:** affirm, proclaim. 11. **first:** beginning, first part. 15–16. **buckle . . . belt of rule:** i.e., contain his sick government through control. 17. **sticking on:** adhering to. The words recall the blood on Macbeth and Lady Macbeth's hands (2.2.62–70). 18. **minutely:** happening every minute. 18. **upbraid:** reproach, reprove. 18. **faith-breach:** broken loyalty; treason. 20. **Nothing:** not at all. 20–22. **Now . . . thief:** the conclusion of the metaphors linking titles, clothing, and ambition; compare 1.3.106–07, 1.3.143–45, 2.4.38. 23. **pestered:** vexed, plagued. 24–25. **When . . . there:** i.e., Macbeth is in rebellion against himself. 27. **med'cine:** physician. 27. **weal:** state; community; common weal. Other available meanings include "well-being, happiness." 28. **purge:** cleansing; purgative, a medicine causing the bowels to empty. 30. **dew:** moisten. The liquid Caithness (28–29) and Lennox have in mind is blood, not water. 30. **sovereign:** royal; supreme; efficacious. 30. **weeds:** metaphorically, the moral and political chaos of Scotland. 31. **sd *marching*:** This stage direction indicates drumming as well as a martial, ordered departure.

Act 5, Scene 3. 1. **them:** the "false thanes" (7) who desert Macbeth. 3. **taint:** lose courage, become weak. 5. **mortal:** human. 5. **consequences:** outcomes, eventualities. 8. **epicures:** gluttons, sybarites. 9. **The mind I sway by:** the mind that rules me; the mind by which I rule. 11. **cream-faced:** having a face the color of cream (i.e., pale). Compare "blanched with fear" (3.4.116). 11. **loon:** rogue. The word is a Scottish expression. 12. **goose-look:** foolish or witless appearance. 14. **over-red:** redden over, cover with red. 15. **lily-livered:** having a liver (traditionally the organ of courage) the color of a lily, white; hence, cowardly. 16. **Death of thy soul:** may your soul die (a curse). 16. **linen:** white

Are counsellors to fear. What soldiers,
whey-face?

SERVANT The English force, so please you.

MACBETH Take thy face hence!

[Exit Servant]

Seyton! — I am sick at heart,
When I behold — Seyton, I say! — this push
Will cheer me ever or disseat me now.
I have lived long enough. My way of life
Is fall'n into the sere, the yellow leaf,
And that which should accompany old age,
As honour, love, obedience, troops of friends,
I must not look to have; but in their stead,
Curses, not loud but deep, mouth-honour,
breath
Which the poor heart would fain deny, and
dare not.
Seyton!

Enter SEYTON

SEYTON What's your gracious pleasure?

MACBETH What news more?

SEYTON All is confirmed, my lord, which was
reported.

MACBETH I'll fight till from my bones my flesh be
hacked.
Give me my armour.

SEYTON 'Tis not needed yet.

MACBETH I'll put it on;
Send out more horses; skirr the country
round.
Hang those that talk of fear. Give me mine
armour.
How does your patient, doctor?

DOCTOR Not so sick, my lord,
As she is troubled with thick-coming fancies
That keep her from her rest.

MACBETH Cure her of that.
Canst thou not minister to a mind diseased,
Pluck from the memory a rooted sorrow,

Fabia Drake as Lady Macbeth, Stratford, 1933 (oil on canvas)/Sickert, Walter Richard (1860–1942)/ROYAL SHAKESPEARE COMPANY/Royal Shakespeare Company Collection, Stratford-upon-Avon, Warwickshire/Bridgeman Images

Look closely at this 1933 painting of Lady Macbeth by Walter Richard Sickert. **What is the artist's attitude toward Lady Macbeth? How does he communicate that tone visually? How does this representation illustrate a significant change in Lady Macbeth's character? What lines from the play might serve as a caption for this image?**

(i.e., cowardly). "As white as linen" is an ancient analogy. 17. **counsellors:** advisers. 17. **whey-face:** face the color of whey (i.e., milky pale with fear). 19. **Seyton:** This proper name may have been pronounced as "Satan"; if so, Macbeth summons an attending officer who also represents demonic power. 20. **push:** attack; thrust (of a weapon). 21. **cheer:** comfort, console; gladden. There is probably a pun on "chair" (= throne). 21. **disseat:** unseat. 22. **way:** course, manner. 23. **sere:** dry, withered. The word hovers between being an adjective modifying "leaf" and a noun ("the sere") meaning something like "the withered state." 23. **yellow leaf:** i.e., the season when leaves of deciduous trees lose their green color and winter approaches; metaphorically, the period shortly before death. 25. **troops:** flocks, swarms. 25. **friends:** followers, retainers, supporters. 26. **stead:** place. The First Folio's "steed" probably represents a contemporary pronunciation with a lengthened vowel. 27. **mouth-honour:** i.e., respect and duty merely verbal (hence insincere, not from the heart). 28. **fain:** gladly; gladly under the circumstances. 36. **horses:** i.e., warriors

Raze out the written troubles of the brain,
And with some sweet oblivious antidote
Cleanse the stuffed bosom of that perilous stuff
Which weighs upon the heart?

DOCTOR Therein the patient
Must minister to himself.

MACBETH Throw physic to the dogs, I'll none of it.
Come, put mine armour on; give me my staff.—
Seyton, send out.—Doctor, the thanes fly from me.—
[*To Attendant*] Come sir, dispatch.—If thou couldst, doctor, cast
The water of my land, find her disease,
And purge it to a sound and pristine health,
I would applaud thee to the very echo
That should applaud again.—Pull't off, I say!—
What rhubarb, cynne, or what purgative drug
Would scour these English hence? Hear'st thou of them?

DOCTOR Ay, my good lord; your royal preparation
Makes us hear something.

MACBETH Bring it after me.—
I will not be afraid of death and bane,
Till Birnam Forest come to Dunsinane.
[Exeunt all but Doctor]

DOCTOR Were I from Dunsinane away and clear,
Profit again should hardly draw me here. *Exit*

Act 5, Scene 4

Drum and colours. Enter MALCOLM, SIWARD, MACDUFF, *Siward's son,* MENTEITH, CAITHNESS, ANGUS, *and* SOLDIERS, *marching*

MALCOLM Cousins, I hope the days are near at hand
That chambers will be safe.

MENTEITH We doubt it nothing.

SIWARD What wood is this before us?

MENTEITH The Wood of Birnam.

MALCOLM Let every soldier hew him down a bough,
And bear't before him; thereby shall we shadow
The numbers of our host and make discovery
Err in report of us.

A SOLDIER It shall be done.

SIWARD We learn no other, but the confident tyrant
Keeps still in Dunsinane and will endure
Our setting down before't.

MALCOLM 'Tis his main hope,
For where there is advantage to be given,
Both more and less have given him the revolt,
And none serve with him but constrainèd things
Whose hearts are absent too.

MACDUFF Let our just censures
Attend the true event and put we on
Industrious soldiership.

SIWARD The time approaches
That will with due decision make us know
What we shall say we have and what we owe;
Thoughts speculative their unsure hopes relate,
But certain issue strokes must arbitrate.
Towards which, advance the war.
Exeunt, marching

---

mounted on horses. 36. **skirr:** pass rapidly over, scour. Compare "scour" (57). 38. **sick:** i.e., physically (as opposed to mentally) ill. 39. **thick-coming:** crowding. Compare the tales and posts of 1.3.95–96. 43. **Raze:** eradicate, uproot. 44. **oblivious:** causing forgetfulness or oblivion. 45. **Cleanse . . . stuff:** The repetition of "stuffed . . . stuff" has been considered an error, but no emendation is persuasive. 48. **physic:** medicine. 51. **dispatch:** make haste. 51–52. **cast / The water:** analyze ("cast") the urine ("water"). Inspection of urine and other bodily secretions (especially of female patients) was common practice in early modern medicine. 52–57. **The water . . . hence:** This passage recalls the commonplace analogies of human body and political state, microcosm and macrocosm. 53. **pristine:** former, ancient. 56. **rhubarb:** a medicinal plant, the so-called Chinese rhubarb, and not the common or garden European and New World variety. See next note. 56. **cynne:** senna (medicinal plant prescribed as both emetic and purgative). Gerard, in his *Herbal* (1597), recommends mixing senna and rhubarb as a purge. 59. **it:** either the piece of armor or other equipment referred to at 49, 51, and 55 or "something" (59), news or reports of the enemy. 60. **bane:** murder, death, destruction. 63. **Profit . . . here:** a joke about physicians' greed, already an ancient satiric target.

Act 5, Scene 4. 2. **chambers:** rooms (but with the extended sense of "private dwellings"). 6. **discovery:** military reconnaissance, reconnoitring. 7. **Err:** mistake, make an error. 8. **no other:** i.e., no other news, no other reports, of Macbeth's plans. 8. **but:** except. 10. **setting down:** laying siege, encamping. 11. **given:** yielded. 12. **more and less:** i.e., aristocrats and commoners. 12. **given him the revolt:** have revolted from his service. 14–15. **Let . . . event:** Let a true evaluation ("just censures") of military matters await the battle's outcome ("event"). Macduff advises patience and prudence; Siward expands the point (16–21). 19. **unsure:** accented on the first syllable. 20. **issue:** result, outcome. 21. **war:** soldiers in fighting array, war party.

Act 5, Scene 5

Enter MACBETH, SEYTON, *and Soldiers, with drum and colours*

MACBETH Hang out our banners on the outward walls;
The cry is still, "They come." Our castle's strength
Will laugh a siege to scorn; here let them lie
Till famine and the ague eat them up.
Were they not forced with those that should be ours,
We might have met them dareful, beard to beard,
And beat them backward home.

A cry within of women

What is that noise?

SEYTON It is the cry of women, my good lord.

MACBETH I have almost forgot the taste of fears;
The time has been, my senses would have cooled
To hear a night-shriek and my fell of hair
Would at a dismal treatise rouse and stir
As life were in't. I have supped full with horrors;
Direness familiar to my slaughterous thoughts
Cannot once start me. Wherefore was that cry?

SEYTON The queen, my lord, is dead.

MACBETH She should have died hereafter;
There would have been a time for such a word.
Tomorrow, and tomorrow, and tomorrow
Creeps in this petty pace from day to day
To the last syllable of recorded time;
And all our yesterdays have lighted fools
The way to dusty death. Out, out, brief candle,
Life's but a walking shadow, a poor player
That struts and frets his hour upon the stage
And then is heard no more. It is a tale
Told by an idiot, full of sound and fury
Signifying nothing.

Enter a MESSENGER

Thou com'st to use thy tongue: thy story quickly.

MESSENGER Gracious my lord,
I should report that which I say I saw,
But know not how to do't.

MACBETH Well, say, sir.

MESSENGER As I did stand my watch upon the hill
I looked toward Birnam and anon methought
The wood began to move.

MACBETH Liar and slave!

MESSENGER Let me endure your wrath if't be not so;
Within this three mile may you see it coming.
I say, a moving grove.

MACBETH If thou speak'st false,
Upon the next tree shall thou hang alive
Till famine cling thee; if thy speech be sooth,
I care not if thou dost for me as much.
I pull in resolution and begin

Act 5, Scene 5. 4. **ague:** violent fever, shaking fit. 5. **forced:** strengthened, reinforced. 6. **dareful:** full of defiance. 6. **beard to beard:** i.e., face to face. 9–13. **I . . . in't:** These lines initiate a series of echoes of or allusions to earlier moments when Macbeth's mind, body, and conscience responded differently to horrifying sounds and images. Compare 1.3.134 ff. 11. **fell:** head, shock. 13. **As:** as if. 13. **supped full with horrors:** figuratively, "filled up with, dined full of, horrors," but literally "had supper with Banquo's Ghost" at Macbeth's banquet in 3.4. 14–15. **Direness . . . me:** i.e., my murderous thoughts have made me familiar with fearsome things that no longer have the power to frighten me. Compare Macbeth's terror at the knocking that follows Duncan's murder (2.2.60–61). 14. **Direness:** horror. 14. **slaughterous:** murderous, destructive. 16–17. **She . . . word:** Two meanings seem possible: (1) Lady Macbeth would have died sooner or later, a time would inevitably come for her death; (2) it would have been more suitable had Lady Macbeth died at some future time, when word of her death might receive proper mourning. On the former, see 3.2.38; on the latter, see 4.3.233–38, when war interrupts and displaces Macduff's mourning. 19. **petty:** small; hence, trivial, insignificant. The word (like the speech) moves from physical to figurative, from tiny steps to the journey's pointlessness. 20. **syllable:** smallest portion, merest trace. Compare 4.3.8. 20. **recorded:** written; told, narrated; recollected, remembered. 22. **Out, out, brief candle:** Compare Lady Macbeth's "Out . . . Out" (5.1.30) and her taper (5.1.15 sd). 23. **walking shadow:** Compare biblical passages in which the brevity and insubstantiality of human life are compared with a shadow: 1 Chronicles 29:15, Job 14:2, Psalms 102:11, and Ecclesiastes 8.13, for example. 23. **poor player:** bad actor. 24. **frets:** chafes, worries. The underlying theatrical metaphor suggests that the player's willingness to adopt a feigned passion makes him lose his individuality. 24. **stage:** i.e., life. Proverbially, "This world is a stage and every man plays his part." 25–26. **It is a tale / Told:** Compare "For when thou art angry, all our days are gone; we bring our years to an end, a tale that is told" (Psalms 90:9), prescribed for the burial service by the Book of Common Prayer; the same psalm is the source for 2.4.1. There may be a pun on told/tolled (a bell rung): compare 3.2.43–44 and 4.3.172–73. 30. **report . . . saw:** i.e., relate what I have already claimed to see. 36. **mile:** i.e., miles. Use of the singular "mile" with a plural number was common into the nineteenth century. 39. **cling:** shrivel, parch. The Messenger's hanging body will shrink and contract without food. 39. **sooth:** truth, true.

To doubt th'equivocation of the fiend
That lies like truth. "Fear not, till Birnam
Wood
Do come to Dunsinane," and now a wood
Comes toward Dunsinane. Arm, arm, and out!
If this which he avouches does appear,
There is nor flying hence nor tarrying here.
I 'gin to be aweary of the sun
And wish th'estate o'th'world were now undone.
Ring the alarum bell! Blow wind, come wrack;
At least we'll die with harness on our back.

Exeunt

Act 5, Scene 6

Drum and colours. Enter MALCOLM, SIWARD, MACDUFF, *and their army, with boughs*

MALCOLM Now near enough; your leafy screens throw down
And show like those you are. You, worthy uncle,
Shall with my cousin your right noble son
Lead our first battle. Worthy Macduff and we
Shall take upon's what else remains to do,
According to our order.

SIWARD Fare you well.
Do we but find the tyrant's power tonight,
Let us be beaten if we cannot fight.

MACDUFF Make all our trumpets speak; give them all breath,
Those clamorous harbingers of blood and death.

Exeunt

Alarums continued

Act 5, Scene 7

Enter MACBETH

MACBETH They have tied me to a stake; I cannot fly,
But bear-like I must fight the course. What's he
That was not born of woman? Such a one
Am I to fear, or none.

Enter YOUNG SIWARD

YOUNG SIWARD What is thy name?

MACBETH Thou'lt be afraid to hear it.

YOUNG SIWARD No, though thou call'st thyself a hotter name
Than any is in hell.

MACBETH My name's Macbeth.

YOUNG SIWARD The devil himself could not pronounce a title
More hateful to mine ear.

MACBETH No, nor more fearful.

YOUNG SIWARD Thou liest, abhorrèd tyrant; with my sword
I'll prove the lie thou speak'st.

Fight, and young Siward slain

MACBETH Thou wast born of woman.
But swords I smile at, weapons laugh to scorn,
Brandished by man that's of a woman born.

Exit [*with young Siward's body*]

---

41. **pull in:** rein in, arrest, withdraw. 42. **fiend:** i.e., the Third Apparition, whose "lies like truth" (43) Macbeth now recalls (43–44); see 4.1.89–93. 45. **out:** i.e., sally forth, attack the enemy. 46. **avouches:** claims, states. 47. **nor . . . nor:** neither . . . nor. 47. **tarrying:** staying, remaining. 48. **'gin:** begin. 49. **estate o'th'world:** the world's settled order. 50. **Ring the alarum bell:** The command may be a sound cue. As with Macduff's cry when he discovers Duncan's body (2.3.69), words (and sound?) link crime and approaching punishment. 51. **harness:** armor.

Act 5, Scene 6. 4. **battle:** an army or one of its main divisions. 4. **we:** Malcolm uses the royal plural prematurely. 7. **power:** military forces. 10. **sd *Alarums continued*:** Battle sounds minimize the change of time or place between 5.6 and 5.7; the audience's imagination is transferred to another part of the battlefield.

Act 5, Scene 7. 1. **tied me to a stake:** Macbeth finds himself a bear, chained ("tied") to a post ("stake") and attacked by dogs for spectators' entertainment, an event that often occurred in some of early modern London's public theaters, at the Tower of London (for the pleasure of King James and his guests), and in other places of amusement. 2. **course:** attack (by dogs baiting a bear). More generally, the word means "continuous process of time, succession of events." 2–3. **What's . . . born of woman:** Only one not of woman born can conquer Macbeth; there is no one not of woman born. 8. **Than any is:** than any that is. 12. **Thou wast born of woman:** a chilling sardonicism, recalling the Bible (see note 4.1.79) and Macbeth's

extending beyond the text

In 2014, the Metropolitan Opera House performed *Macbeth*, the operatic adaptation by Giuseppe Verdi. The following images depict significant moments from throughout the play.

Hiroyuki Ito/Getty Images

Hiroyuki Ito/Getty Images

Hiroyuki Ito/Getty Images

extending beyond the text

Hiroyuki Ito/Getty Images

Hiroyuki Ito/Getty Images

Based on these still images from the performance, try to identify the characters and actions depicted by examining only the props and sets and the performers' gestures, facial expressions, and costumes. Be sure to identify textual evidence from the play to justify your conclusions.

Alarums. Enter MACDUFF

MACDUFF That way the noise is. Tyrant, show thy face!
If thou be'st slain, and with no stroke of mine,
My wife and children's ghosts will haunt me still.
I cannot strike at wretched kerns whose arms
Are hired to bear their staves; either thou, Macbeth,
Or else my sword with an unbattered edge
I sheath again undeeded. There thou shouldst be;
By this great clatter, one of greatest note
Seems bruited. Let me find him, Fortune,
And more I beg not. *Exit*

Alarums. Enter MALCOLM *and* SIWARD

SIWARD This way, my lord; the castle's gently rendered.
The tyrant's people on both sides do fight;
The noble thanes do bravely in the war.
The day almost itself professes yours,
And little is to do.

MALCOLM We have met with foes
That strike beside us.

SIWARD Enter, sir, the castle.

Exeunt

Alarum

Act 5, Scene 8

Enter MACBETH

MACBETH Why should I play the Roman fool and die
On mine own sword? Whiles I see lives, the gashes
Do better upon them.

Enter MACDUFF

MACDUFF Turn, hell-hound, turn.

MACBETH Of all men else I have avoided thee,
But get thee back, my soul is too much charged
With blood of thine already.

MACDUFF I have no words;
My voice is in my sword, thou bloodier villain
Than terms can give thee out.

Fight. Alarum

MACBETH Thou losest labour.
As easy mayst thou the intrenchant air
With thy keen sword impress as make me bleed.
Let fall thy blade on vulnerable crests;
I bear a charmèd life which must not yield
To one of woman born.

MACDUFF Despair thy charm,
And let the angel whom thou still hast served
Tell thee, Macduff was from his mother's womb
Untimely ripped.

MACBETH Accursèd be that tongue that tells me so,
For it hath cowed my better part of man;
And be these juggling fiends no more believed
That palter with us in a double sense,

---

remark to First Murderer (3.4.14). 19. **staves:** lances. 19. **either thou, Macbeth:** i.e., either I strike at you, Macbeth. 20. **unbattered:** undamaged (by use in battle). 21. **undeeded:** having done nothing, without accomplishment or "deed." 21. **There:** i.e., where I hear the most noise ["this great clatter" (22)]. 22. **By . . . note:** The line puns on "note" as musical sound ("clatter") and as "reputation" or "fame." 23. **bruited:** noised, reported. 23–24. **Let . . . not:** a prayer to the goddess who momentarily favored Macduff (1.2.9–15). 25. **gently rendered:** calmly (i.e., without further loss of life) or "nobly" surrendered. 29–30. **foes / That strike beside us:** either enemies who deliberately miss when they attack or enemies who fight on our side.

Act 5, Scene 8. 1–2. **play . . . sword:** Roman honor required a defeated warrior to commit suicide rather than be captured. 2. **Whiles:** while. 2. **lives:** living creatures. 5. **charged:** weighted, burdened. The Doctor uses the same word of Lady Macbeth (5.1.44). 8. **terms:** words, expressions. 8. **sd *Alarum*:** Battle continues elsewhere. 8. **Thou losest labour:** You waste effort. 9. **intrenchant:** incapable of being cut. 10. **keen:** sharp; eager, ardent. This "keen sword" answers Lady Macbeth's "keen knife" (1.5.50). 10. **impress:** mark, press. The word "impress" appears here when Macbeth's supposed invulnerability fails, just as it appeared when he was first assured of it (4.1.94–95). 13. **charm:** magical incantation; amulet(?). 14. **angel:** i.e., "genius," tutelary deity. 16. **Untimely ripped:** i.e., born by Caesarean section. Having to choose, early modern medical practitioners sought to save the baby rather than the mother; Caesarean section always killed the mother. 18. **cowed:** intimidated, dispirited. 18. **my better part of man:** larger proportion ("more than half") of my courage. 19. **juggling:** deceitful, cheating. Early audiences might have

That keep the word of promise to our ear
And break it to our hope. I'll not fight with
thee.

MACDUFF Then yield thee coward,
And live to be the show and gaze o'th'time.
We'll have thee, as our rarer monsters are,
Painted upon a pole and underwrit,
"Here may you see the tyrant."

MACBETH I will not yield
To kiss the ground before young Malcolm's
feet
And to be baited with the rabble's curse.
Though Birnam Wood be come to
Dunsinane
And thou opposed being of no woman born,
Yet I will try the last. Before my body,
I throw my warlike shield. Lay on, Macduff,
And damned be him that first cries, "Hold,
enough!"

Exeunt[,] *fighting. Alarums*

Enter [*Macbeth and Macduff,*] *fighting*[,] *and Macbeth slain*

[*Exit Macduff, with Macbeth's body*]

Act 5, Scene 9

Retreat, and flourish. Enter with drum and colours, MALCOLM, SIWARD, ROSS, *Thanes, and Soldiers*

MALCOLM I would the friends we miss were safe
arrived.

SIWARD Some must go off. And yet by these I see,
So great a day as this is cheaply bought.

MALCOLM Macduff is missing and your noble
son.

ROSS Your son, my lord, has paid a soldier's debt;
He only lived but till he was a man,
The which no sooner had his prowess
confirmed
In the unshrinking station where he fought,
But like a man he died.

SIWARD Then he is dead?

ROSS Ay, and brought off the field. Your cause of
sorrow
Must not be measured by his worth, for then
It hath no end.

SIWARD Had he his hurts before?

ROSS Ay, on the front.

SIWARD Why then, God's soldier be he;
Had I as many sons as I have hairs,
I would not wish them to a fairer death.
And so his knell is knolled.

MALCOLM He's worth more sorrow,
And that I'll spend for him.

SIWARD He's worth no more;
They say he parted well and paid his score,
And so God be with him. Here comes newer
comfort.

---

associated the word with the (Roman Catholic) exorcists who claimed to heal possessed individuals. 20. **palter:** equivocate, deal evasively, trick. 20. **double sense:** equivocal meaning. 21–22. **keep . . . hope:** fulfill the prophecy (of kingship) in a (merely) verbal way and fail to fulfill it as we expected (= "our hope"). 23. **yield thee coward:** surrender yourself as a coward; state (or concede) that you are a coward. 28. **To kiss the ground:** a proverbial phrase for surrender or abnegation. 29. **baited:** taunted. 29. **rabble:** crowd, common people, multitude. 32. **try the last:** experience (or undergo) the conclusion (or extremity). 33. **shield:** probably a target, or "targe," held by straps around the forearm. 34. **"Hold, enough!":** Stop, I surrender! 34. **sd *Exeunt . . . body*:** The stage directions convey a shifting duel, moving from place to place onstage. 34. **sd:** Malcolm's comment (5.9.1) seems to stipulate a stage empty of dead bodies, and Macduff needs to remove Macbeth's body in order to "behead" it.

Act 5, Scene 9. 0. **sd *Retreat*:** a signal on the trumpet to recall a pursuing force. The stage direction presumably indicates that Macbeth's remaining supporters withdraw (or surrender) offstage. 2. **go off:** die. Compare "goes hence" (1.5.57). 5–9. **Your . . . died:** Once again, Ross tells a father of his child's death; compare 4.3.194ff. 5. **soldier's debt:** what a soldier owes (i.e., his death). 8. **unshrinking station:** i.e., brave act of standing. "Station" is the martial posture young Siward adopted when he would not retreat (shrink) from Macbeth's attack. 9–20. **Then . . . him:** Siward's reaction is the play's final response to a loved one's death (compare Malcolm and Donaldbain in 2.3, Macduff in 4.3, Macbeth in 5.5), with the difference that this loss directly serves the cause of freeing Scotland, as Siward's pun on "hairs" (see note 15) suggests. 10. **brought off the field:** i.e., the body recovered (for burial). 12. **hurts before:** wounds on the front (of his body)—i.e., wounds gained while he fought the enemy, rather than wounds "behind," on his back, which would indicate he died running away. 15. **hairs:** Siward echoes the biblical use of "the hairs of my head" as a periphrasis for "a very large number" (see, e.g., Psalms 40:13 and 69:4). 17. **knell:** (church) bell rung to mark the death of a member of the congregation. 19. **score:** bill, amount owing. The word could mean something as mundane as a tavern debt, but here alludes to the soul one owes God. 20. **newer:** more recent, fresher. 21. **Hail:** The word, repeated twice here (26) and common in act 1, has not been used since "all-hail"

Enter MACDUFF, *with Macbeth's head*

MACDUFF Hail, king, for so thou art. Behold where stands
Th'usurper's cursèd head. The time is free.
I see thee compassed with thy kingdom's pearl,
That speak my salutation in their minds;
Whose voices I desire aloud with mine.
Hail, King of Scotland.

ALL Hail, King of Scotland.

Flourish

MALCOLM We shall not spend a large expense of time
Before we reckon with your several loves
And make us even with you. My thanes and kinsmen,
Henceforth be earls, the first that ever Scotland
In such an honour named. What's more to do
Which would be planted newly with the time, —
As calling home our exiled friends abroad
That fled the snares of watchful tyranny,
Producing forth the cruel ministers
Of this dead butcher and his fiend-like queen,
Who, as 'tis thought, by self and violent hands
Took off her life, — this and what needful else
That calls upon us, by the grace of Grace
We will perform in measure, time, and place.
So, thanks to all at once and to each one,
Whom we invite to see us crowned at Scone.

Flourish

Exeunt

(1.5.53) and "hailed" (3.1.61); it now links Macbeth with Malcolm, the sisters with the victorious Scots. 21. **so thou art:** i.e., evidence of Macbeth's death (the head) confirms Malcolm's kingship. 23. **pearl:** finest members or parts, noble examples. 28. **reckon:** settle accounts with. 28. **several:** separate, distinct. 29. **make us even:** square our accounts, make us quits. The phrase is the last of several commercial or financial metaphors: "spend . . . expense . . . reckon" (27–28). 31–32. **What's . . . time:** Malcolm's metaphor echoes Duncan's, addressed to Macbeth (1.4.28–29); the cycle of trust and betrayal renews itself. 33. **exiled friends abroad:** i.e., friends exiled abroad. 37–38. **by self . . . life:** Malcolm's guess that Lady Macbeth committed suicide is not supported by the text. 39. **calls upon:** invokes; demands, summons. 39. **grace of Grace:** the grace of God, apostrophized as the essence of graciousness. 40. **measure:** due proportion.

Understanding and Interpreting

1. As she is sleepwalking, Lady Macbeth mentions her desire to clean her hands several times, but she is unable to do so (Scene 1, ll. 30, 42, 52 to 53). Using evidence from the text to support your interpretation, explain what the cleaning of hands might represent for Lady Macbeth.
2. In Scene 2, the four thanes provide an account of the current state of affairs in Scotland. Summarize the information they provide. Explain the growing difficulties that Macbeth faces.
3. Even after Macbeth has seen the first prophecy fail to protect him, he continues to believe he will not be harmed when facing Macduff in the final scene, insisting that he "bear[s] a charmèd life" (Scene 8, l. 12). Why is Macbeth still unwilling to admit that he may not be invincible, given what he has seen transpire so far?
4. What does Macduff mean when he says that he "was from his mother's womb / Untimely ripp'd" (Scene 8, ll. 15 to 16)? What is Macbeth's response to this information?
5. Macduff tells Macbeth that once he is dead, his corpse will be displayed publicly with a sign that says, "Here may you see the tyrant" (Scene 8, ll. 23 to 27). What purpose would this public display serve?

Analyzing Language, Style, and Structure

1. **Vocabulary in Context.** As Malcolm approaches, one of the soldiers describes "the grim alarm" (Scene 2, l. 5). What does "alarm" mean in this context? How is it similar to or different from other meanings of the word? Why is it an appropriate word for this scene?

2. **Skill Focus.** Angus compares Macbeth's title as king to something that "Hang[s] loose about him, like a giant's robe / Upon a dwarfish thief" (Scene 2, ll. 21 to 22). His statement echoes an earlier remark when, shortly after hearing of his appointment as the Thane of Cawdor, Macbeth responds by asking Angus and Ross why they dress him in "borrowed robes" (Act 1, Scene 3, l. 107). Explain how this figurative language relates to Macbeth's kingship.
3. **Skill Focus.** In Scene 4, Malcolm states that "none serve [Macbeth] but constrained things" (l. 13). What does he mean by this metaphor? Why does this give him greater confidence in victory?
4. **Skill Focus.** Macbeth concludes his response to the news of Lady Macbeth's death with one of the most famous soliloquies in all of Shakespeare's plays (Scene 5, ll. 17 to 27). Select an example of figurative language from this soliloquy. Explain how it helps to convey Macbeth's state of mind at this moment.
5. Although Lady Macbeth's comments and actions in Scene 1 seem random and inexplicable to the Doctor and the Gentlewoman, knowledge of her actions in the past provides insight into her "slumbery agitation" (ll. 10 to 11). Find several examples where Lady Macbeth says something that has no clear meaning for the Doctor and Gentlewoman, but in fact reveals her secrets.
6. In Act 2, Scene 2, shortly after he has killed Duncan, Macbeth hears a voice telling him that "Macbeth does murder sleep" (l. 39). In what ways do Lady Macbeth's actions in Act 5 reinforce that earlier proclamation heard by Macbeth?
7. Macbeth's response to the news of Lady Macbeth's death is complex (Scene 5, ll. 17 to 27). Using specific text examples, describe the tone of his response. Then, explain possible reasons for his attitude.
8. Look carefully at Macbeth's final lines (Scene 8, ll. 27 to 34). What do Macbeth's word choices reveal about his attitude toward his impending death?
9. In one of the most dramatic and intense moments in any of Shakespeare's plays, Macduff enters holding a spear on which he has mounted Macbeth's head (Scene 8, ll. 21 to 26). What is the effect of ending the play in this manner rather than having Macduff merely tell all of the other men that he has killed Macbeth?
10. Analyze Malcolm's final speech, paying attention to the order in which he addresses the issues that the country must now face and the language he uses to demonstrate his readiness to lead as the new king (Scene 9, ll. 27 to 41).

Topics for Composing

1. **Analysis.** At one of the most poignant moments in the play, Macbeth asserts that "Life [. . .] is a tale / Told by an idiot, full of sound and fury, / Signifying nothing" (Act 5, Scene 5, ll. 23 to 27). Write a response in which you explain whether *Macbeth* suggests that life is truly meaningless, or whether the play ultimately demonstrates that life has purpose and meaning.
2. **Analysis.** Imagery, including repeated references to blood, clothing, and the supernatural, helps to convey meaning throughout *Macbeth*. Using evidence from the play, write a response in which you analyze how Shakespeare uses imagery in *Macbeth* to develop a major theme.
3. **Analysis.** English poet Samuel Taylor Coleridge once said that the witches in *Macbeth* "have the power of tempting those, who have been tempters themselves." Write a response in which you analyze and evaluate Coleridge's comments using evidence from the play.
4. **Analysis.** Consider Macbeth's attitude toward Lady Macbeth after the murder of Duncan. Is it true that he does not need her anymore? How does her death affect him? Write an essay in

which you analyze Macbeth's attitude toward his wife and how that attitude illuminates a theme of the play as a whole.

5. **Analysis.** Contrast Macbeth's leadership approach with Malcolm's. Consider how these two characters view what it means to be a leader. What do the contrasts suggest about the nature of true leadership, according to Shakespeare?
6. **Argument.** Although Banquo is murdered long before the end of *Macbeth*, some literary scholars argue that he is as important a character dead as he is alive. Using evidence from the play, write an argument supporting or refuting this claim based on evidence from the text.
7. **Argument.** Many critics over the years have suggested that Lady Macbeth was the real motivation behind Macbeth's violent rise to power. Examine the play for lines that these critics may have selected to support the claim that Macbeth would not have killed for power without the urging of Lady Macbeth. Then, defend or challenge this claim. Reread Lady Macbeth's lines carefully and discuss qualities she exhibits that may have led these critics to see her as the source of Macbeth's ambition.
8. **Connection.** Several classical music compositions, including operas and symphonies, have been inspired by the play *Macbeth.* Select a musical composition inspired by the play and discuss the connection between the two works.
9. **Connection.** Watch a film version of the play. Then, write a comparison between the original text and its film adaptation, focusing on the choices the director and the actors make.
10. **Connection.** What was your reaction to reading this Shakespeare play? What about the play struck you as challenging, frustrating, or exciting, for example? Explain your reaction with specific references to the text.
11. **Speaking and Listening.** Staging *Macbeth* is a particular challenge because of the number of scenes and the numerous battles and fights. With a partner or small group, imagine that you need to create a single set that works for all scenes. Create a design of your set and present it to the rest of the class. Be prepared to explain how the set will support the action of the play.
12. **Research.** When the Doctor tells Macbeth that he cannot cure mental disorders, Macbeth decries the limitations of medicine. Conduct research into mental disorders that might be affecting Macbeth and Lady Macbeth. Then, based on your research and evidence taken from the play, offer a diagnosis for both Lady Macbeth and Macbeth.
13. **Multimodal.** Create a storyboard of *Macbeth* by selecting or making images to represent the most important scenes, ideas, or themes. Use quotations from the play to provide captions for your images.
14. **Multimodal.** Written over five hundred years ago, *Macbeth* continues to be regularly produced for stage and screen, although many directors choose to set the play in different time periods and locations. For example, Akira Kurosawa's film *Throne of Blood* is an adaptation of *Macbeth* set in feudal Japan. Prepare to pitch an original adaptation of *Macbeth* to a hypothetical theater or movie producer with a different time period and setting. To do so, you will need to include sketches and other images of your new setting paired with lines from the original play.

The Tale of the Kiss

Emma Donoghue

Emma Donoghue (b. 1969), an award-winning author of nearly twenty novels and plays, was born in Ireland and now lives in Canada. Her most famous novel, *Room*, was made into a film in 2015. The following story comes from a collection of short stories called *Kissing the Witch: Old Tales in New Skins*, in which Donoghue reimagines the stories of traditional characters such as Cinderella, Snow White, the Little Mermaid, and others.

Ulf ANDERSEN/Getty Images

I know what they say about me: the gulls bring me all the gossip. Knowing what they say about you is the first step to power. Contrary to what you might half believe, I am no monster under my skirts. I grew up in a place much like this one, though half a year away. When I was the age that you are now I was a girl like you, though not quite as stupid.

There was another difference; my bleeding was meager, when it came, and by the time the cough carried off my mother I no longer bled at all. This gave me reason to think about my future. As far as my people were concerned, women like me had no future. I knew what they thought of women past bearing; unless they had sons to honor them and daughters to clean them, they were old rags tossed in the corner. A barren woman was hated even more; the way they saw it, she had never earned a bite of bread.

But I was not going to become an old rag, when every hair I had was still red as a lobster in the pot.

I could of course have lied and smiled, got myself a sturdy husband. The men had started lurking near our door as soon as my mother was taken bad. I could have sunk my nails into one, girded him to me and kept him hoping and cursing year after year, even pointed the finger at some other woman for looking crossways at me and hexing my belly. But I wouldn't stoop to that. So after they buried my mother, I packed up all the herbs in her store and came away.

I found myself a cave on a headland, above 5
a village like this one. It's three months' hard walk from here, but they fish and spin and make up lies just like your folk. The cave had been lived in before; there was an old blanket, and a water bag, and a dip in the floor hollowed by many small fires. I had rock to my back and the sea to my face, driftwood to burn and the odd fish to fry. I had time to wonder now, to unpick the knotted ropes of my thoughts. I could taste freedom like salt on the breeze. There was no one to nurse, no one to feed, no

one to listen to but my own self. I thought no one would ever bother me again and I could live out my life like a gull, like a weed, like a drop of water.

What I found instead was power. I never sought it; it was left out for me to stumble over. Only a matter of weeks had gone by before I began to find presents left outside my cave. The first was a clutch of eggs; I thought for a moment some extraordinary chicken had flown up to bring me dinner. Next came a thick slice of meat, wrapped in a cloth to keep the birds off. The villagers left their offerings at first light, before I stirred out of my cave.

I thought such goodness had never been known in the whole world. I thought these were presents freely given to keep a stranger from starving. How was I to know that they were payments in advance?

It was a small boy who gave me the first hint. He threw seaweed into my cave until I came out with a big stick. He screamed when he saw me and ran until he fell over, then got up and ran again.

When he came back the next day, he was braver. He asked, What happened to the old one?

The old what?

Witch. Have you got her locked up in her cave or did you boil her in her pot?

This is my cave now, I told him sternly. There's no one here but me.

So it was a witch they were wanting. I laughed to myself, that first day, as the little boy ran down the headland, but soon enough I learned how to be what they needed.

It was not an arduous job. Mostly they left me alone with my herbs and my thoughts, but every few months one of the villagers would creep up the headland after sunset and call out, Are you there?

Are you there? the cave would echo back at them.

Will you help me? The voice more strangled now, the echo shaking. I've brought something for you. . . .

And only then, when they were sweating cold as dew, would I emerge, step by slow step, a black scarf over my head to hide the fact of my youth. Not that they ever looked at me properly; they seemed to think my eyes would scald them. They stared at the muddy ground while they poured out their stories of sickness, envy, grief and hunger. I never said a word until they were sobbing.

Sometimes what they needed was simple enough. To the sick, I gave potions that could do them no harm and might make them well if they wanted it enough. To the grieving, I gave words of comfort and a drink to make them sleep. To girls with terrible secrets, I gave herbs to make them whole again.

As for the guilty, spilling their burdens of malice and shame outside my cave, I thought at first that they were asking for forgiveness, but I soon found it made them uncomfortable. Punishment suited them better. They liked me to curse them. May weeds spring up where you walk! May a tail grow in the middle of your chin!

There was a woman who'd never said a kind word to her husband since she woke up the day after their wedding. I flayed her with my tongue until she burst into tears and ran home to make his breakfast. There was a man who'd not slept for ten years for thinking of what he had done to his own daughter. I told him to sell every animal he had to make up her dowry. Once there was a stranger who half smiled as he told me the worst thing he had done in his life, and then something worse than that, and then something even worse. I let him talk all night; I never said a word of judgment. His eyes flickered on my face as he talked, as if searching for something. The sky lightened and I was still watching him. My eyes moved nearer to the cliff edge, and just as the sun was coming up the stranger let himself fall into the pointed waves.

extending beyond the text

In a collection of essays called *Light the Dark: Writers on Creativity, Inspiration, and the Artistic Process*, Emma Donoghue writes about being inspired by the poet Emily Dickinson's use of the pronoun *you*. Read the following excerpt from Donoghue's essay in which she describes how her mother used to read Dickinson poems to her.

from Emily Dickinson's Mysterious 'You'

Emma Donoghue

One of the poems she used to recite to me, "Wild Nights — Wild Nights!," became very important to me in my teens. I probably sought it out again once I knew that I was in love with a girl myself at fourteen — because there I was, in 1980s Ireland, realizing that I was a lesbian and couldn't tell a soul. It was as if there was nobody around in Irish culture at the time who I could see myself in. So I used Emily Dickinson. On the basis of her poems and letters, it seemed like she had strong passions for women in her life as well as for men. I remember thinking, "Well, I may be a freak in my social context, but I can be like Emily Dickinson. Who needs to be normal?"

Most of the writing I did at the time were lyrics addressed to a "you" beloved, the way this poem is. They weren't all love poems, but when they were it was always "I" addressed to "you": It frees you from the necessity to specify the gender of the person you're speaking to, so it's a closeted lesbian's best friend, this pronoun. The lack of specificity makes it a really attractive form, and the intimacy of the "you" helps draw the reader in directly. (That's one reason the "you" form is used all the time in pop songs.) It allows readers to imagine someone speaking to her beloved, but to use their own imagination about who the beloved might be.

The poem begins like this:

Wild Nights — Wild Nights!
Were I with thee
Wild Nights should be
Our luxury!

How might this pronoun use in Dickinson's work have influenced Donoghue's own pronoun choices in this story? To what extent do you agree with what she suggests about the use of "you" in pop songs?

I was a little shaken that day. It was the first time I felt the reach of my power. Power that came not from my own thin body or my own taut mind, but was invested in me by a village. Power I had to learn how to pick up without getting burnt, how to shape it and conceal it and flaunt it and use it, and when to use it, and when to still my breath and do nothing at all. Power these scaly-fingered fishwives and their wiry husbands could have used themselves, if they'd only known how, but instead they told themselves how helpless they were, and came and laid power at my feet. As well as eggs, of course, and new-baked bread, and even gold

Harrogate Borough Council / Bridgeman Images

Alisa Kaufman

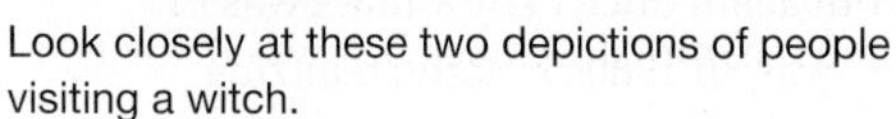

Look closely at these two depictions of people visiting a witch.

How do the artists represent the witch differently? How do they communicate these differences visually? Which one of these might be the more appropriate depiction of the characters in this story? Why?

coins if I judged that it would take a terrible price to make them believe in their cure.

And so the years passed, leaving little mark on me except the first gray fingerprints on my bright head. When the occasional petitioner came up the headland I answered their questions with my eyes closed. I preferred the days when I was alone. I could recognize the cry of each kind of bird; they never changed. All that was different about me was that every year my needs were fewer. My bones grew hard as iron. I had tried out every herb I found, till nothing could surprise my stomach. I got so used to sleeping on stone that it no longer seemed hard to me. I rolled up in half a dozen blankets and wrapped my arms round my ribs like pet snakes. Nothing touched me in the night except the occasional spider. I was complete.

I should have known. You can't live on a cliff for that long without risking a fall.

One morning a woman climbed up to my cave before dawn. I could hear her feet scrabbling outside. The sun was high in the sky before I rewarded her patience by standing in the entrance. Her narrowed eyes distinguished me from the shadows, and she jerked back.

You want something, I told her, a little hoarsely; my voice was out of practice.

She looked behind her for her basket.

I don't fancy butter, I said.

It was a lucky guess. She flinched. Then what will you have?

The truth, I told her.

Her hands fought like crabs. I have a daughter, she began. A good strong red-haired daughter, but she is a trouble and a trial to me. Before sunrise she's roaming the hills. I have a terrible fear she's lovesick. She gets a strange look in her eyes. When we're working I catch her singing songs I've never heard before, and where could she have got them?

I yawned, to hurry her up.

If you saw her you'd understand, the woman went on in a rush. She's no fool, nor idle; it's only this restlessness. She could be the best of daughters, if she'd only quiet down.

And her sisters?

All gone. This one's my last, you see, said the woman, her voice subsiding. I'm not getting any younger. I need to know for sure that she'll stay with me.

I turned my face away. I will consult the oracles, I told her; that always stunned them into silence. Come back at moonrise on the third day and you will have your answer.

That evening at sunset I was sitting in front of my cave, consulting the only oracle I knew, the orange sky, when a man climbed up the headland. He seemed too tired to be afraid. He stood a little distance from me.

You want something, I said without moving my head.

Yes.

Is that a fresh trout in your hand?

It is.

Toss it over the cliff, I said, just to amuse myself.

He paused a moment before unwrapping it and throwing it toward the setting sun. A gull caught it with an incredulous shriek.

Out with the truth now, I said.

His foot dug into the chalky grass.

I have a daughter, he began. A fine tall red-haired daughter, but she is a trial and a trouble to me. Half the evening she walks along the beach by moonlight. She gathers seashells like a little child. There's a friend of mine has an eye for her, but whenever he comes courting she's behind her mother's skirts in the kitchen. I have a terrible fear she'll end up an old maid.

My eyes were wandering.

If you saw her you'd understand, he went on furiously. She's no fright, nor feared of men; it's only this restlessness. She'd make my friend a fine wife, if she'd only settle down, and then he says he'd give me half shares in his big boat.

Why not one of her sisters?

All married. This one's my last, you see, said the man, his voice beginning to crackle. I'm not getting any younger. I need to know for sure that she'll do what I say.

I stared at the soundless gulls. I will consult the oracles, I told him. Come back at moonset on the third day and you will have your answer.

The next morning I woke with my head full of scrag-ends of dreams. I doused it in seawater. Today I would need all my wits. Between the mother and the father I had to pick my way carefully. I knew what happened to meddlers who came between man and wife. I knew there were some in the village below who, after strong liquor, talked of blocking up my cave in the night.

By midday rain had covered the headland. I sat in my cave, trying to persuade my little fire to stay alight. At least bad weather kept me private, shielded me from the village below with all its wearisome tribulations.

Or so I thought, until she appeared in the mouth of my cave, between curtains of rain, the girl herself, unmistakable, her blood-red hair glued to her wet throat.

It was the first time in all those years that I let another human being step across the threshold. I even lent her a blanket to stop the shivering. To make up for this softness, I unsheathed the blade of my tongue. If you're the girl I think you are, I began, staring into the struggling fire, I hear you're nothing but trouble.

She nodded as if I had remarked on the weather, and continued combing out the red ropes of her hair with a bit of old comb I'd found her.

You're not child enough for your mother nor woman enough for your father. You don't work or play or think as they would have you work and play and think.

She smiled at me with teeth like quartz.

What are you good at?

I don't know yet, said the girl, staring into the fire. Faint steam was rising from her.

What is it you want?

Nothing, she said, half laughing.

There is no creature under the sky that does not want, I told her severely.

Only what I've got, then, she said.

That's lucky.

And time to think about what I want next.

I nodded judiciously.

And time to just think.

There's plenty of that up here, I remarked.

She stared round the cave. There must be all the time in the world here, she said wonderingly.

My heart was beginning to thud.

And time to not think, I need that too, she added.

I had one more question. What do you love?

She took a deep breath, as if her list was long, then she let it out in a sigh. Everything, she said.

Everything? My voice was a squeaking bat. How can you love everything before you know anything, you idiotic girl?

I don't know, she said seriously. It seems to leak out of me. It's like a cup spilling over. She turned to look into my eyes; they narrowed against her. How can you not? she asked.

What?

You're wise. You're the witch. How can you look at everything and know everything without love?

My heart was pulling on my ribs. Go now, I said. The rain's eased.

She turned her open face to me. But will—

Girls like you always get what they want.

Her full-throated laugh filled the cave for several minutes after she'd gone.

That night I didn't sleep at all. The blankets were heavy with damp; the wind seemed to whine at the cave mouth. No matter which way I lay, stones poked me awake.

If I took a fever and lay tossing here till I died, I realized, no one would ever know. The villagers would still leave the odd bit of food outside, but it would be eaten clean by the birds. Only the wind would hear their petitions, and perhaps its answers would be wiser than mine.

Before the sun rose I hauled myself up off the floor. As long as I had my health the power was mine. I threw rosemary on the fire and breathed in its clarifying air. By moonrise I had concocted my answers.

To the mother I said: The oracles tell me that because of your own faults, a terrible curse has been visited upon your daughter. If you ever order her to stay at home with you, she will turn into a hare and run off up the mountain.

Dumbstruck inside her shawl, the woman whispered, Is there any cure for this curse?

Only time will wear it out, I told her.

I would take no payment. I watched her scurry down the headland. I sat there as the moon tracked its way across the sky and began to fall.

To the father I said: The oracles tell me that because of your own sins, a dreadful fate has fallen upon your daughter. If you ever order her to marry, her husband will turn into a wolf and devour her on their wedding night.

Flinching from the words, the father said, Is there any way of lifting this fate?

Only time will tell, I told him.

I would take no payment. I watched him stride home. And then all was quiet. I told myself that the job was well done.

Over the next few days I went about my business, but something was wrong. Everything I cooked tasted bitter. My daily tasks seemed long, and yet when I sat by the fire to rest in the evenings, the time hung heavy on my hands. I could make no sense of what the gulls were saying.

The girl came back one day. I hadn't realized it was her I was waiting for. I almost wished it was raining again. In sunlight she glowed as if her hair had caught fire. I stood in the mouth of my cave, and all at once I couldn't think of anything to say.

She put down her basket and crossed her arms a little nervously. I wish I knew where you get your power, she remarked. This past week my mother and father have let me work, sleep and wander as I please. They make no complaint or prediction, cast neither my past nor my future in my face.

I allowed a small smile to twist my mouth.

Have you put them under a spell? she asked.

An easy one; you could learn it yourself.

She remembered her basket. I brought you something.

No need.

It's only butter. I made it myself.

I don't want butter. It gives me a rash, I said, the lie coming easily to my lips.

What'll you have then? she said.

Because I owe you.

A kiss.

I think I asked it just to shame her. I would have liked to see that calm face furrow up for a moment. But the girl laughed.

Anger began to clamp my teeth shut.

Her laugh rippled on. Is that all? she asked. Why are they all so afraid of you, when your price is so easy to pay?

Even then I didn't believe she would do it. Kissing a witch is a perilous business. Everybody knows it's ten times as dangerous as letting her touch your hand, or cut your hair, or steal your shoes.

What simpler way is there than a kiss to give power a way into your heart?

She stepped up to me and her hair swung around us like a veil.

It was a bad idea, that kiss I asked for. Not that it did the girl any harm. She walked off across the hills as if she had just embraced a cat or a sparrow. Once she looked behind her and waved.

On the whole I am inclined to think that a witch should not kiss. Perhaps it is the not being kissed that makes her a witch; perhaps the source of her power is the breath of loneliness around her. She who takes a kiss can also die of it, can wake into something unimaginable, having turned herself into some new species.

Days passed, somehow. There was a long red hair on my shawl that was too bright to be mine. I tried to get on with my life. I did all the same things I had done day by day for years on end, but I couldn't remember why I had ever done them, or indeed what had brought me here to live alone in a cave like a wild animal. I tried not to think about all that. I tried not to think.

I woke one night. The moon was full, filling the mouth of the cave. All at once I knew I needed that girl like meat needs salt.

What could I do? Could I bring myself to follow her down into the village? Could I lower myself so far, to let the little children throw sand at me? Would she be gone away by the time I came down? Would they tell me where she had gone? Would I be able to find her?

And if I did, I swore to myself, swore on the perfect disc of the moon, then I would not let pride stop up my mouth. I would ask her to come live in my cave and learn all I knew and teach me all I didn't. I would give her my heart in a bag and let her do with it what she pleased. I would say the word love.

And what happened next, you ask? Never you mind. There are some tales not for telling, whether because they are too long, too precious, too laughable, too painful, too easy to need telling or too hard to explain. After all, after years and travels, my secrets are all I have left to chew on in the night.

This is the story you asked for. I leave it in your mouth. ■

extending beyond the text

Emma Donoghue adapted her short story collection *Kissing the Witch* into a play, in which she blends several of the stories — and the witches from each called "First," "Second," and "Third" — into a single narrative. Read the following dialogue from the end of the play.

Roscoh Anthony

from **Kissing the Witch**

Emma Donoghue

THIRD The best authorities on the matter are inclined to agree that a witch should not kiss. Some go further and say it's the not being kissed that makes her a witch. Perhaps the source of her power is the breath of loneliness around her.

SECOND She who takes a kiss can also die of it.

FIRST Or wake transformed into something unimaginable.

THIRD Some new species.

FIRST But if a beast can be a woman –

SECOND — and a princess be a donkey –

THIRD — and a maid be a queen, then perhaps –

FIRST/SECOND/THIRD — witches can kiss.

FIRST It's strange.

SECOND No doubt about it.

FIRST But stranger things happen every day.

THIRD Don't worry about it.

SECOND These are only old stories.

FIRST/SECOND/THIRD Like kisses passed from mouth to mouth.

Curtain.

What differences do you notice between the story you read and this dramatic adaptation of it? How are they similar in theme — specifically, who has power and why?

Understanding and Interpreting

1. Explain what the narrator, unnamed throughout the story, means when she says in the opening paragraph, "Knowing what they say about you is the first step to power"?
2. At the beginning of the story, the narrator describes what her life is like before she leaves her hometown. What do her comments reveal about life for women in general in this fictional time and place?

3. When the narrator learns that she will not be able to bear children, what does she decide to do? What does this decision reveal about her as a person?
4. What power does the narrator discover when she first arrives at the cave? How does she get and maintain this power? How does she feel about it?
5. What did the narrator do to learn "how to be what they needed" (par. 13)? Why would she do this?
6. The townspeople seem to expect the narrator to look and act in a certain way. How does the narrator use their expectations to maintain her power?
7. Summarize some of the services that the narrator provides to the townspeople. Based on these, what is her true role for the townspeople?
8. After the man lets himself fall into the waves below her cave, the narrator reflects further on the power that she has. Reread paragraph 20 and explain her new understanding of her power.
9. Take another look at paragraphs 104 to 107. What does the narrator seem to like — and not like — about her life in the cave before she meets the girl and her parents? How has she changed over the course of the story at this point?
10. According to the mother, what is wrong with her daughter (par. 30)? What does she want the girl to do? According to the father, what is wrong with his daughter (pars. 45 to 47)? What does he want the girl to do? What do both parents agree on regarding their daughter?
11. Why is the narrator nervous about this particular case between husband and wife?
12. How does the narrator describe the girl when she sees her for the first time (par. 108)? How is her treatment of the girl different from her treatment of other villagers?
13. Summarize the dialogue exchange between the narrator and the girl when they meet the first time (pars. 54 to 81). What does this dialogue reveal about each woman? Who has the most power in this scene? How do you know?
14. How is the girl similar to and different from the narrator when the narrator was young?
15. Explain what the narrator accomplishes with her advice to the girl's parents. In what way does that advice improve the girl's life?
16. Why did the narrator choose to have the girl pay with a kiss? What significance does the narrator assign to kissing a witch? What has happened to the narrator's power as a result of the kiss? How did the kiss affect the girl, according to the narrator?
17. What does the narrator decide to do at the end of the story? What does this reveal about how her character changes over the course of the story?

Analyzing Language, Style, and Structure

1. **Vocabulary in Context.** For one of her first payments, the narrator says she received "a clutch of eggs" (par. 6). What does the word "clutch" mean in this context? What are other meanings of the word?
2. **Skill Focus.** Reread paragraph 5, in which the narrator locates and moves into her cave. Donoghue uses several similes to describe how the narrator feels. Choose one or two and explain what this figurative language is intended to reveal about the narrator.
3. **Skill Focus.** The narrator often uses figurative language to describe the power of her tongue — what she says aloud to the townspeople. Identify and examine this figurative language. Explain how it helps to characterize the narrator.
4. **Skill Focus.** Look back at some of the language choices Donoghue makes when describing the girl. What patterns do you notice? What is the effect of these choices?

5. Reread paragraphs 18 to 20 and notice the parallel structure of many of the sentences. What is the effect of this syntactical choice?
6. The narrator literally lives on a cliff. However, she also offers this analogy: "You can't live on a cliff for that long without risking a fall" (par. 23). What metaphorical meaning is she communicating here?
7. Reread the sentence from paragraph 114: "Days passed, somehow." What is the effect of this sentence's structure and length? What is it communicating to the reader?
8. What does the following simile from paragraph 115 reveal about the narrator: "All at once I knew I needed that girl like meat needs salt."
9. Reread paragraph 116 and notice that the entire paragraph is made up of questions. What is the effect of repeating this sentence type?
10. This story is part of a collection of stories in which Donoghue reimagines several well-known fairy tales. While this one is original, it has a fairy tale feel to it that fits the rest of the collection. Stylistically, how does Donoghue create this feeling?
11. At the beginning and the end of the story, Donoghue uses the pronoun "you." Who might the narrator be addressing as "you"? How do you know? What does this choice of pronoun achieve?

Topics for Composing

1. **Analysis.** Power is fluid in this story. Sometimes the narrator feels powerful, while at other times she feels powerless. What is Donoghue suggesting about power in this story? Support your analysis with evidence from the text.
2. **Argument.** Take a position on one of the following questions. Write an argument using evidence from the story and your own reasoning to support your response.
   - Is the narrator of this story really a witch?
   - Does the girl come to live with the narrator at the end of the story?
3. **Connection.** Think of another story with a witch in it, especially a fairy tale. Compare the witch in that text with the narrator of this story. What similarities and differences do you notice?
4. **Speaking and Listening.** Many fairy tales include witches, often as villains. Choose one to read. Meet with a partner to discuss how the witches are represented and what kinds of power the witches have. How does the representation of the witch and her or his power compare to those of the narrator in Donoghue's story?
5. **Research.** Stories of witches and witchcraft have long been a part of our culture. However, contemporary research reveals that women were often labeled as "witches" because they threatened male-dominated social and political norms. Conduct research on witches, focused on this perspective. Connect your findings to the pressures that the narrator faces as a woman in her society.
6. **Multimodal.** Use found images or images of your own to illustrate the scene in which the narrator and the girl first meet. Include dialogue from their conversation. Consider using color or font size to emphasize significant words or phrases.
7. **Creative Writing.** Write the end of the story that the narrator left out, starting with "And what happens next, you ask?"

Backwards

Warsan Shire

Rodin Eckenroth/Getty Images

Warsan Shire, a British poet and social activist, is the author of several volumes of poetry, including a collaboration with Beyoncé on her visual album *Lemonade* in 2016. According to the Poetry Foundation, Shire's work connects "gender, war, sex, and cultural assumptions; in her work, poetry is a healing agent for the trauma of exile and suffering."

for Saaid Shire

The poem can start with him walking backwards into a room.
He takes off his jacket and sits down for the rest of his life;
that's how we bring Dad back.
I can make the blood run back up my nose, ants rushing into a hole.
We grow into smaller bodies, my breasts disappear,
your cheeks soften, teeth sink back into gums.
I can make us loved, just say the word.
Give them stumps for hands if even once they touched us without consent,
I can write the poem and make it disappear.
Step-Dad spits liquor back into glass,
Mum's body rolls back up the stairs, the bone pops back into place,
maybe she keeps the baby.
Maybe we're okay kid?
I'll rewrite this whole life and this time there'll be so much love,
you won't be able to see beyond it.

You won't be able to see beyond it,
I'll rewrite this whole life and this time there'll be so much love.
Maybe we're okay kid,
maybe she keeps the baby.
Mum's body rolls back up the stairs, the bone pops back into place,
Step-Dad spits liquor back into glass.
I can write the poem and make it disappear,
give them stumps for hands if even once they touched us without consent,
I can make us loved, just say the word.
Your cheeks soften, teeth sink back into gums
we grow into smaller bodies, my breasts disappear.
I can make the blood run back up my nose, ants rushing into a hole,
that's how we bring Dad back.
He takes off his jacket and sits down for the rest of his life.
The poem can start with him walking backwards into a room. ■

Releah Michelle

This painting is called *Is She Moving Forward or Backwards.* **What might the artist be suggesting about leaving things behind? How does she capture this idea visually? Why might the speaker in this poem agree or disagree with the ideas expressed in this painting?**

Understanding and Interpreting

1. Reread the first line of the poem. What would be undone if the speaker's father were to walk backwards into the room?
2. The speaker mentions several actions that she would like undone. Look back over the following lines and explain what the speaker implies, but doesn't directly say, about what has happened in the past:
   - "your cheeks soften, teeth sink back into gums" (ll. 6, 25)
   - "Step-Dad spits liquor back into glass" (ll. 10, 21)
   - "Mum's body rolls back up the stairs, the bone pops back into place" (ll. 11, 20)
3. What does the speaker mean when she says, "I can write the poem and make it disappear" (ll. 9, 22)?
4. Reread the last two lines in the first stanza (ll. 14–15), which repeat the first two lines in the second stanza in reverse order (ll. 16–17). Explain what the speaker means. How does reversing the order of these lines in the second stanza affect their meaning?

Analyzing Language, Style, and Structure

1. **Vocabulary in Context.** In lines 8 and 23, the speaker says, "Give them stumps for hands." What is the meaning of "stump" in this context? How is this meaning similar to and different from other meanings of the word?
2. **Skill Focus.** In lines 4 and 27, Shire writes, "I can make the blood run back up my nose, ants rushing into a hole." What is the effect of this particular metaphor?
3. Who is the "we" in this poem? How do you know? Who is the "you"? What effects do these pronoun choices have?

4. The most significant structural component of this poem is that the second half is made up of the exact same lines in the first half, but in reverse. What are some possible intended effects of this choice? How does it help Shire to illustrate an idea about poetry, power, or imagination?
5. Lines 12 to 13 and 18 to 19 are almost identical, but not entirely. What is different between the pairs? What is a possible effect of this difference?
6. Reread the last line of the poem, which is also the first line. In a poem full of significant moments, why does the speaker begin and end with this one? How is this undoing different from the others?

Topics for Composing

1. **Analysis.** What appears to motivate the speaker in "Backwards"? How does Shire use imagery and poetic structures to illustrate this motivation?
2. **Argument.** The speaker claims that she can "write the poem and make it disappear" (ll. 9, 22). Define "it" with evidence from the poem. Argue whether or not writing and imagination have the powers the speaker describes to change or eliminate "it."
3. **Connection.** What are some events in your own life that you'd like to run in reverse? How would undoing those events change who you are and how you live?
4. **Speaking and Listening.** With a partner, read this poem aloud in a few different ways. First, read it from beginning to end, taking turns with each line. Second, have one partner read from the beginning and the other read backwards from the end, alternating lines (they will be repeated). Third, have one partner read from the beginning of the poem and the other from the beginning of the second stanza, alternating lines. Afterward, discuss what you learned about the structure of this poem by reading it aloud in these ways.
5. **Multimodal.** Use found images, images of your own, or create a video that focuses specifically on one or more of the "undoings." Illustrate the idea of going in reverse. Label your drawings with specific words or phrases from the poem that inspired your illustrations.
6. **Creative Writing.** Write a poem that mimics the structure that Shire uses with the lines mirroring each other in some way. Afterward, reflect on how these structural choices help you communicate your ideas.

Sweat

Zora Neale Hurston

Historical/Getty Images

Zora Neale Hurston (1891–1960) was an American author and anthropologist who portrayed family, gender, and racial struggles in the American South in short stories, novels, plays, and films. Her most popular novel is *Their Eyes Were Watching God* (1937). Although she was a major figure in the art, music, and literary movement of the 1920s known as the Harlem Renaissance, which celebrated Black culture, Hurston died in obscurity in 1960. Contemporary authors such as Alice Walker resurrected Hurston's career and reintroduced her work to audiences.

KEY CONTEXT Because Hurston was an anthropologist in addition to being a writer, she tried to capture the essence of how people talked during the time and place of her fiction. That means that she often composed dialogue that reflected her characters' accents and regional colloquialisms. For instance, a character in the following story says, "Ah don't keer if you never git through. Anyhow, Ah done promised Gawd and a couple of other men, Ah aint gointer have it in mah house." You probably recognize some words easily, but others are written more for the sound they produce than for the correctness of the spelling. Because Hurston is trying to capture the sound of the characters' voices, it might be easier for you to read challenging passages aloud. While not always technically grammatically correct as defined by standard English, the dialogue Hurston uses follows rules that are appropriate for the time, place, and purpose.

Additionally, this story uses variations of the N-word, which we have chosen to reprint in this textbook to accurately reflect Hurston's original intent as well as the time period and culture depicted in the story. We recognize that this word has a long history as a disrespectful and deeply hurtful expression when used by white people toward African Americans. While the use of that word in Hurston's context might not be hurtful, the use of it in our current context very often is. Be mindful of context, both Hurston's and yours, as you read this story.

It was eleven o'clock of a Spring night in Florida. It was Sunday. Any other night, Delia Jones would have been in bed for two hours by this time. But she was a wash-woman, and Monday morning meant a great deal to her. So she collected the soiled clothes on Saturday when she returned the clean things. Sunday night after church, she sorted them and put the white things to soak. It saved her almost a half day's start. A great hamper in the bedroom held the clothes that she brought home. It was so much neater than a number of bundles lying around.

She squatted in the kitchen floor beside the great pile of clothes, sorting them into small heaps according to color, and humming a song in a mournful key, but wondering through it all where Sykes, her husband, had gone with her horse and buckboard.

Just then something long, round, limp and black fell upon her shoulders and slithered to the floor beside her. A great terror took hold of her. It softened her knees and dried her mouth so that it was a full minute before she could cry out or move. Then she saw that it was the big bull whip her husband liked to carry when he drove.

She lifted her eyes to the door and saw him standing there bent over with laughter at her fright. She screamed at him.

"Sykes, what you throw dat whip on me like 5
dat? You know it would skeer me — looks just like a snake, an' you knows how skeered Ah is of snakes."

"Course Ah knowed it! That's how come Ah done it." He slapped his leg with his hand and almost rolled on the ground in his mirth. "If you such a big fool dat you got to have a fit over a earth worm or a string, Ah don't keer how bad Ah skeer you."

"You aint got no business doing it. Gawd knows it's a sin. Some day Ah'm goin' tuh drop dead from some of yo' foolishness. 'Nother thing, where you been wid mah rig? Ah feeds dat pony. He aint fuh you to be drivin' wid no bull whip."

"You sho is one aggravatin' nigger woman!" he declared and stepped into the room. She resumed her work and did not answer him at once. "Ah done tole you time and again to keep them white folks' clothes outa dis house."

He picked up the whip and glared down at her. Delia went on with her work. She went out into the yard and returned with a galvanized tub and set it on the washbench. She saw that Sykes had kicked all of the clothes together again, and now stood in her way truculently, his whole manner hoping, praying, for an argument. But she walked calmly around him and commenced to re-sort the things.

10 "Next time, Ah'm gointer kick 'em outdoors," he threatened as he struck a match along the leg of his corduroy breeches.

Delia never looked up from her work, and her thin, stooped shoulders sagged further. "Ah aint for no fuss t'night Sykes. Ah just come from taking sacrament at the church house."

He snorted scornfully. "Yeah, you just come from de church house on a Sunday night, but heah you is gone to work on them clothes. You ain't nothing but a hypocrite. One of them amen-corner Christians–sing, whoop, and shout, then come home and wash white folks clothes on the Sabbath."[1]

Wash Day, 1991 (oil on canvas)/Murrell, Carlton/CARLTON MURRELL/Private Collection/Bridgeman Images

This painting by Carlton Murrell is called *Wash Day*.

Describe the tone of the piece and explain what Murrell does to communicate that this tone. How is this representation of a washer woman similar to or different from Hurston's descriptions of Delia working?

He stepped roughly upon the whitest pile of things, kicking them helter-skelter as he crossed the room. His wife gave a little scream of dismay, and quickly gathered them together again.

"Sykes, you quit grindin' dirt into these clothes! How can Ah git through by Sat'day if Ah don't start on Sunday?"

15 "Ah don't keer if you never git through. Anyhow, Ah done promised Gawd and a couple of other men, Ah aint gointer have it in mah house. Don't gimme no lip neither, else Ah'll throw 'em out and put mah fist up side yo' head to boot."

Delia's habitual meekness seemed to slip from her shoulders like a blown scarf. She was on her feet; her poor little body, her bare knuckly hands bravely defying the strapping hulk before her.

"Looka heah, Sykes, you done gone too fur. Ah been married to you fur fifteen years, and Ah been takin' in washin' for fifteen years. Sweat, sweat, sweat! Work and sweat, cry and sweat, pray and sweat!"

"What's that got to do with me?" he asked brutally.

"What's it got to do with you, Sykes? Mah tub of suds is filled yo' belly with vittles more times than yo' hands is filled it. Mah sweat is done paid for this house and Ah reckon Ah kin keep on sweatin' in it."

20 She seized the iron skillet from the stove and struck a defensive pose, which act surprised him greatly, coming from her. It cowed him and he did not strike her as he usually did.

"Naw you won't," she panted, "that ole snaggle-toothed black woman you runnin' with aint comin' heah to pile up on mah sweat and blood. You aint paid for nothin' on this place,

[1]Refers to the biblical commandment to observe a day of rest: "Six days shall work be done; but on the seventh day is a sabbath of solemn rest, holy to the LORD." — Eds.

and Ah'm gointer stay right heah till Ah'm toted out foot foremost."

"Well, you better quit gittin' me riled up, else they'll be totin' you out sooner than you expect. Ah'm so tired of you Ah don't know whut to do. Gawd! how Ah hates skinny wimmen!"

A little awed by this new Delia, he sidled out of the door and slammed the back gate after him. He did not say where he had gone, but she knew too well. She knew very well that he would not return until nearly daybreak also. Her work over, she went on to bed but not to sleep at once. Things had come to a pretty pass!

She lay awake, gazing upon the debris that cluttered their matrimonial trail. Not an image left standing along the way. Anything like flowers had long ago been drowned in the salty stream that had been pressed from her heart. Her tears, her sweat, her blood. She had brought love to the union and he had brought a longing after the flesh. Two months after the wedding, he had given her the first brutal beating. She had the memory of his numerous trips to Orlando with all of his wages when he had returned to her penniless, even before the first year had passed. She was young and soft then, but now she thought of her knotty, muscled limbs, her harsh knuckly hands, and drew herself up into an unhappy little ball in the middle of the big feather bed. Too late now to hope for love, even if it were not Bertha it would be someone else. This case differed from the others only in that she was bolder than the others. Too late for everything except her little home. She had built it for her old days, and planted one by one the trees and flowers there. It was lovely to her, lovely.

Somehow, before sleep came, she found herself saying aloud: "Oh well, whatever goes over the Devil's back, is got to come under his belly. Sometime or ruther, Sykes, like everybody else, is gointer reap his sowing." After that she was able to build a spiritual earthworks against her husband. His shells could no longer reach her. Amen. She went to sleep and slept until he announced his presence in bed by kicking her feet and rudely snatching the covers away.

"Gimme some kivah heah, an' git yo' damn foots over on yo' own side! Ah oughter mash you in yo' mouf fuh drawing dat skillet on me."

Delia went clear to the rail without answering him. A triumphant indifference to all that he was or did.

• • •

The week was as full of work for Delia as all other weeks, and Saturday found her behind her little pony, collecting and delivering clothes.

It was a hot, hot day near the end of July. The village men on Joe Clarke's porch even chewed cane listlessly. They did not hurl the cane-knots as usual. They let them dribble over the edge of the porch. Even conversation had collapsed under the heat.

"Heah come Delia Jones," Jim Merchant said, as the shaggy pony came 'round the bend of the road toward them. The rusty buckboard was heaped with baskets of crisp, clean laundry.

"Yep," Joe Lindsay agreed. "Hot or col', rain or shine, jes ez reg'lar ez de weeks roll roun' Delia carries 'em an' fetches 'em on Sat'day."

"She better if she wanter eat," said Moss. "Syke Jones aint wuth de shot an' powder hit would tek tuh kill 'em. Not to huh he aint. "

"He sho' aint," Walter Thomas chimed in. "It's too bad, too, cause she wuz a right pritty lil trick when he got huh. Ah'd uh mah'ied huh mahseff if he hadnter beat me to it."

Delia nodded briefly at the men as she drove past.

"Too much knockin' will ruin any 'oman. He done beat huh 'nough tuh kill three women, let 'lone change they looks," said Elijah Moseley. "How Syke kin stommuck dat big black greasy Mogul he's layin' roun wid, gits me. Ah swear dat eight-rock couldn't kiss a sardine can Ah done throwed out de back do' 'way las' yeah."

"Aw, she's fat, thass how come. He's allus been crazy 'bout fat women," put in Merchant. "He'd a' been tied up wid one long time ago if he could a' found one tuh have him. Did Ah tell yuh 'bout him come sidlin' roun' mah wife–bringin' her a basket uh pecans outa his yard fuh a present? Yessir, mah wife! She tol' him tuh take 'em right straight back home, cause Delia works so hard ovah dat washtub she reckon everything on de place taste lak sweat an' soapsuds. Ah jus' wisht Ah'd a' caught 'im 'dere! Ah'd a' made his hips ketch on fiah down dat shell road."

"Ah know he done it, too. Ah sees 'im grinnin' at every 'oman dat passes," Walter Thomas said. "But even so, he useter eat some mighty big hunks uh humble pie tuh git dat lil 'oman he got. She wuz ez pritty ez a speckled pup! Dat wuz fifteen yeahs ago. He useter be so skeered uh losin' huh, she could make him do some parts of a husband's duty. Dey never wuz de same in de mind."

"There oughter be a law about him," said Lindsay. "He aint fit tuh carry guts tuh a bear."

Clarke spoke for the first time. "Taint no law on earth dat kin make a man be decent if it aint in 'im. There's plenty men dat takes a wife lak dey do a joint uh sugar-cane. It's round, juicy an' sweet when dey gits it. But dey squeeze an' grind, squeeze an' grind an' wring tell dey wring every drop uh pleasure dat's in 'em out. When dey's satisfied dat dey is wrung dry, dey treats 'em jes lak dey do a cane-chew. Dey throws em away. Dey knows whut dey is doin' while dey is at it, an' hates theirselves fuh it but they keeps on hangin' after huh tell she's empty. Den dey hates huh fuh bein' a cane-chew an' in de way."

40 "We oughter take Syke an' dat stray 'oman uh his'n down in Lake Howell swamp an' lay on de rawhide till they cain't say Lawd a' mussy.' He allus wuz uh ovahbearin' niggah, but since dat white 'oman from up north done teached 'im how to run a automobile, he done got too biggety to live — an' we oughter kill 'im," Old Man Anderson advised.

A grunt of approval went around the porch. But the heat was melting their civic virtue, and Elijah Moseley began to bait Joe Clarke.

"Come on, Joe, git a melon outa dere an' slice it up for yo' customers. We'se all sufferin' wid de heat. De bear's done got me!"

"Thass right, Joe, a watermelon is jes' whut Ah needs tuh cure de eppizudicks," Walter Thomas joined forces with Moseley. "Come on dere, Joe. We all is steady customers an' you aint set us up in a long time. Ah chooses dat long, bowlegged Floridy favorite."

"A god, an' be dough. You all gimme twenty cents and slice way," Clarke retorted. "Ah needs a col' slice m'self. Heah, everybody chip in. Ah'll lend y'll mah meat knife."

45 The money was quickly subscribed and the huge melon brought forth. At that moment, Sykes and Bertha arrived. A determined silence fell on the porch and the melon was put away again.

Merchant snapped down the blade of his jackknife and moved toward the store door.

"Come on in, Joe, an' gimme a slab uh sow belly an' uh pound uh coffee–almost fuhgot 'twas Sat'day. Got to git on home." Most of the men left also.

Just then Delia drove past on her way home, as Sykes was ordering magnificently for Bertha. It pleased him for Delia to see.

"Git whutsoever yo' heart desires, Honey. Wait a minute, Joe. Give huh two bottles uh strawberry soda-water, uh quart uh parched ground-peas, an' a block uh chewin' gum."

50 With all this they left the store, with Sykes reminding Bertha that this was his town and she could have it if she wanted it.

The men returned soon after they left, and held their watermelon feast.

"Where did Syke Jones git da 'oman from nohow?" Lindsay asked.

"Ovah Apopka. Guess dey musta been cleanin' out de town when she lef.' She don't look lak a thing but a hunk uh liver wid hair on it."

African Americans on a Sunday afternoon at a country store in North Carolina, 1939 (b/w photo)/Lange, Dorothea (1895–1965)/Private Collection/Bridgeman Images

Dorothea Lange was an American photographer best known for documenting life during the Great Depression. **What does Lange communicate in this image of a country store in North Carolina in 1939? How is this image similar to Hurston's description of Joe Clark's store in this story?**

"Well, she sho' kin squall," Dave Carter contributed. "When she gits ready tuh laff, she jes' opens huh mouf an' latches it back tuh de las' notch. No ole grandpa alligator down in Lake Bell ain't got nothin' on huh."

• • •

Bertha had been in town three months now. Sykes was still paying her room rent at Della Lewis'-the only house in town that would have taken her in. Sykes took her frequently to Winter Park to "stomps." He still assured her that he was the swellest man in the state.

"Sho' you kin have dat lil' ole house soon's Ah kin git dat 'oman outa dere. Everything b'longs tuh me an' you sho' kin have it. Ah sho' 'bominates uh skinny 'oman. Lawdy, you sho' is got one portly shape on you! You kin git anything you wants. Dis is mah town an' you sho' kin have it."

Delia's work-worn knees crawled over the earth in Gethsemane[2] and up the rocks of Calvary[3] many, many times during these months. She avoided the villagers and meeting places in her efforts to be blind and deaf. But Bertha nullified this to a degree, by coming to Delia's house to call Sykes out to her at the gate.

Delia and Sykes fought all the time now with no peaceful interludes. They slept and ate in silence. Two or three times Delia had attempted a timid friendliness, but she was repulsed each time. It was plain that the breaches must remain agape.

The sun had burned July to August. The heat streamed down like a million hot arrows, smiting all things living upon the earth. Grass withered, leaves browned, snakes went blind in shedding and men and dogs went mad. Dog days!

Delia came home one day and found Sykes there before her. She wondered, but started to go on into the house without speaking, even though he was standing in the kitchen door and she must either stoop under his arm or ask him to move. He made no room for her. She noticed a soap box beside the steps, but paid no particular attention to it, knowing that he must have brought it there. As she was stooping to

---

[2]According to the Bible, this is the garden in Jerusalem where Jesus was arrested the night before his crucifixion. — Eds.

[3]According to the Bible, this is the site where Jesus was crucified. — Eds.

pass under his outstretched arm, he suddenly pushed her backward, laughingly.

"Look in de box dere Delia, Ah done brung yuh somethin'!"

She nearly fell upon the box in her stumbling, and when she saw what it held, she all but fainted outright.

"Syke! Syke, mah Gawd! You take dat rattlesnake 'way from heah! You gottuh. Oh, Jesus, have mussy!"

"Ah aint gut tuh do nuthin' uh de kin'–fact is Ah aint got tuh do nothin' but die. Taint no use uh you puttin' on airs makin' out lak you skeered uh dat snake–he's gointer stay right heah tell he die. He wouldn't bite me cause Ah knows how tuh handle 'im. Nohow he wouldn't risk breakin' out his fangs 'gin yo' skinny laigs."

"Naw, now Syke, don't keep dat thing 'roun' heah tuh skeer me tuh death. You knows Ah'm even feared uh earth worms. Thass de biggest snake Ah evah did see. Kill 'im Syke, please."

"Doan ast me tuh do nothin' fuh yuh. Goin' roun' trying' tuh be so damn asterperious. Naw, Ah aint gonna kill it. Ah think uh damn sight mo' uh him dan you! Dat's a nice snake an' anybody doan lak 'im kin jes' hit de grit."

The village soon heard that Sykes had the snake, and came to see and ask questions.

"How de hen-fire did you ketch dat six-foot rattler, Syke?" Thomas asked.

"He's full uh frogs so he caint hardly move, thass how. Ah eased up on 'm. But Ah'm a snake charmer an' knows how tuh handle 'em. Shux, dat aint nothin'. Ah could ketch one eve'y day if Ah so wanted tuh."

"Whut he needs is a heavy hick'ry club leaned real heavy on his head. Dat's de bes 'way tuh charm a rattlesnake."

"Naw, Walt, y'll jes' don't understand dese diamon' backs lak Ah do," said Sykes in a superior tone of voice.

The village agreed with Walter, but the snake stayed on. His box remained by the kitchen door with its screen wire covering. Two or three days later it had digested its meal of frogs and literally came to life. It rattled at every movement in the kitchen or the yard. One day as Delia came down the kitchen steps she saw his chalky-white fangs curved like scimitars hung in the wire meshes. This time she did not run away with averted eyes as usual. She stood for a long time in the doorway in a red fury that grew bloodier for every second that she regarded the creature that was her torment.

That night she broached the subject as soon as Sykes sat down to the table.

"Syke, Ah wants you tuh take dat snake 'way fum heah. You done starved me an' Ah put up widcher, you done beat me an Ah took dat, but you done kilt all mah insides bringin' dat varmint heah."

Sykes poured out a saucer full of coffee and drank it deliberately before he answered her.

"A whole lot Ah keer 'bout how you feels inside uh out. Dat snake aint goin' no damn wheah till Ah gits ready fuh 'im tuh go. So fur as beatin' is concerned, yuh aint took near all dat you gointer take ef yuh stay 'roun' me."

Delia pushed back her plate and got up from the table. "Ah hates you, Sykes," she said calmly. "Ah hates you tuh de same degree dat Ah useter love yuh. Ah done took an' took till mah belly is full up tuh mah neck. Dat's de reason Ah got mah letter fum de church an' moved mah membership tuh Woodbridge–so Ah don't haf tuh take no sacrament wid yuh. Ah don't wantuh see yuh 'roun' me atall. Lay 'roun' wid dat 'oman all yuh wants tuh, but gwan 'way fum me an' mah house. Ah hates yuh lak uh suck-egg dog."

Sykes almost let the huge wad of corn bread and collard greens he was chewing fall out of his mouth in amazement. He had a hard time whipping himself up to the proper fury to try to answer Delia.

"Well, Ah'm glad you does hate me. Ah'm sho' tiahed uh you hangin' ontuh me. Ah don't want yuh. Look at yuh stringey ole neck! Yo' rawbony laigs an' arms is enough tuh cut uh man tuh death. You looks jes' lak de devvul's doll-baby tuh me. You cain't hate me no worse dan Ah hates you. Ah been hatin' you fuh years."

"Yo' ole black hide don't look lak nothin' tuh me, but uh passle uh wrinkled up rubber, wid yo' big ole yeahs flappin' on each side lak uh paih uh buzzard wings. Don't think Ah'm gointuh be run 'way fum mah house neither. Ah'm goin' tuh de white folks bout you, mah young man, de very nex' time you lay yo' han's on me. Mah cup is done run ovah." Delia said this with no signs of fear and Sykes departed from the house, threatening her, but made not the slightest move to carry out any of them.

That night he did not return at all, and the next day being Sunday, Delia was glad she did not have to quarrel before she hitched up her pony and drove the four miles to Woodbridge.

She stayed to the night service–"love feast"–which was very warm and full of spirit. In the emotional winds her domestic trials were borne far and wide so that she sang as she drove homeward.

"Jurden[4] water, black an' col'
Chills de body, not de soul
An' Ah wantah cross Jurden in uh calm time."

She came from the barn to the kitchen door and stopped.

"Whut's de mattah, ol' satan, you aint kickin' up yo' racket?" She addressed the snake's box. Complete silence. She went on into the house with a new hope in its birth struggles. Perhaps her threat to go to the white folks had frightened Sykes! Perhaps he was sorry! Fifteen years of misery and suppression had brought Delia to the place where she would hope anything that looked towards a way over or through her wall of inhibitions.

She felt in the match safe behind the stove at once for a match. There was only one there.

"Dat niggah wouldn't fetch nothin' heah tuh save his rotten neck, but he kin run thew whut Ah brings quick enough. Now he done toted off nigh on tuh haff uh box uh matches. He done had dat 'oman heah in mah house, too."

Nobody but a woman could tell how she knew this even before she struck the match. But she did and it put her into a new fury.

Presently she brought in the tubs to put the white things to soak. This time she decided she need not bring the hamper out of the bedroom; she would go in there and do the sorting. She picked up the pot-bellied lamp and went in. The room was small and the hamper stood hard by the foot of the white iron bed. She could sit and reach through the bedposts–resting as she worked.

"Ah wantah cross Jurden in uh calm time," she was singing again. The mood of the "love feast" had returned. She threw back the lid of the basket almost gaily. Then, moved by both horror and terror, she sprang back toward the door. There lay the snake in the basket! He moved sluggishly at first, but even as she turned round and round, jumped up and down in an insanity of fear, he began to stir vigorously. She saw him pouring his awful beauty from the basket upon the bed, then she seized the lamp and ran as fast as she could to the kitchen. The wind from the open door blew out the light and the darkness added to her terror. She sped to the darkness of the yard, slamming the door after her before she thought to set down the lamp. She did not feel safe even on the ground, so she climbed up in the hay barn.

There for an hour or more she lay sprawled upon the hay a gibbering wreck.

Finally, she grew quiet, and after that, coherent thought. With this, stalked through her a cold, bloody rage. Hours of this.

[4]This refers to the River Jordan. According to the Bible, Israelites led by Moses crossed the river to escape slavery in Egypt. It is also the site of Jesus's baptism by John the Baptist. — Eds.

extending beyond the text

In this short story and in many of Hurston's other works, characters communicate in regional dialect. Though the dialect Hurston presents is authentic to the people she portrays, her use of this language style in the early part of the 1900s was controversial. Some of her contemporaries, including the novelist Richard Wright, objected to it. Read this excerpt from Wright's review of one of Hurston's novels. Then, read a more recent counterpoint to Wright's ideas about dialect:

from Between Laughter and Tears

Richard Wright

Miss Hurston can write, but her prose is cloaked in that facile sensuality that has dogged Negro expression since the days of Phillis Wheatley. Her dialogue manages to catch the psychological movements of the Negro folk-mind in their pure simplicity, but that's as far as it goes. [She] voluntarily continues in her novel the tradition which was forced upon the Negro in the theatre, . . . the minstrel technique that makes the "white folks" laugh.

from A Society of One: Zora Neale Hurston, American Contrarian

Claudia Roth Pierpont

Black dialect was at the heart of [Hurston's] work. Disowned by the founders of the Harlem Renaissance for its association with the shambling, watermelon-eating mockeries of American stage convention, dialect remained an irresistible . . . resource for writers. . . . The feat of rescuing the dignity of the speakers from decades of humiliation required a rare and potentially treacherous combination of gifts: a delicate ear and a generous sympathy, a hellbent humor and a determined imperviousness to shame.

Based on your reading of "Sweat" and these two reviews of Hurston's work, what are your thoughts about Hurston's decision to use dialect in her work? In what ways does the discussion about the use of dialect reflect issues of power in society and literature?

A period of introspection, a space of retrospection, then a mixture of both. Out of this an awful calm.

"Well, Ah done de bes' Ah could. If things aint right, Gawd knows taint mah fault."

She went to sleep–a twitch sleep–and woke up to a faint gray sky. There was a loud hollow sound below. She peered out. Sykes was at the wood-pile, demolishing a wire-covered box.

He hurried to the kitchen door, but hung outside there some minutes before he entered, and stood some minutes more inside before he closed it after him.

The gray in the sky was spreading. Delia descended without fear now, and crouched beneath the low bedroom window. The drawn shade shut out the dawn, shut in the night. But the thin walls held back no sound.

"Dat ol' scratch is woke up now!" She mused at the tremendous whirr inside, which every woodsman knows, is one of the sound illusions. The rattler is a ventriloquist. His whirr sounds to the right, to the left, straight ahead, behind, close under foot–everywhere but where it is. Woe to him who guesses wrong unless he is prepared to hold up his end of the argument! Sometimes he strikes without rattling at all.

100 Inside, Sykes heard nothing until he knocked a pot lid off the stove while trying to reach the match safe in the dark. He had emptied his pockets at Bertha's.

The snake seemed to wake up under the stove and Sykes made a quick leap into the bedroom. In spite of the gin he had had, his head was clearing now.

"'Mah Gawd!" he chattered, "ef Ah could on'y strack uh light!"

The rattling ceased for a moment as he stood paralyzed. He waited. It seemed that the snake waited also.

"Oh, fuh de light! Ah thought he'd be too sick"–Sykes was muttering to himself when the whirr began again, closer, right underfoot this time. Long before this, Sykes' ability to think had been flattened down to primitive instinct and he leaped–onto the bed.

105 Outside Delia heard a cry that might have come from a maddened chimpanzee, a stricken gorilla. All the terror, all the horror, all the rage that man possibly could express, without a recognizable human sound.

A tremendous stir inside there, another series of animal screams, the intermittent whirr of the reptile. The shade torn violently down from the window, letting in the red dawn, a huge brown hand seizing the window stick, great dull blows upon the wooden floor punctuating the gibberish of sound long after the rattle of the snake had abruptly subsided. All this Delia could see and hear from her place beneath the window, and it made her ill. She crept over to the four-o'clocks and stretched herself on the cool earth to recover.

She lay there. "Delia. Delia!" She could hear Sykes calling in a most despairing tone as one who expected no answer. The sun crept on up, and he called. Delia could not move–her legs were gone flabby. She never moved, he called, and the sun kept rising.

"Mah Gawd!" She heard him moan, "Mah Gawd fum Heben!" She heard him stumbling about and got up from her flower-bed. The sun was growing warm. As she approached the door she heard him call out hopefully, "Delia, is dat you Ah heah?"

She saw him on his hands and knees as soon as she reached the door. He crept an inch or two toward her–all that he was able, and she saw his horribly swollen neck and his one open eye shining with hope. A surge of pity too strong to support bore her away from that eye that must, could not, fail to see the tubs. He would see the lamp. Orlando with its doctors was too far. She could scarcely reach the Chinaberry tree, where she waited in the growing heat while inside she knew the cold river was creeping up and up to extinguish that eye which must know by now that she knew. ■

Understanding and Interpreting

1. What does the reader learn about Delia in the first two paragraphs of the story?
2. What is Sykes's first action in this story? What does that action reveal about his character?
3. During the first description of a fight between Delia and Sykes (pars. 5 to 23), the reader learns about the power dynamic in their relationship. Who had more power in the past? Who has it now? What has changed? How do they each respond to this changing power dynamic?
4. What does the house mean to Delia? What does it mean to Sykes?

5. Consider the lengthy conversation among the men sitting on the porch of Joe Clarke's store. What are the men's impressions of Delia? What do they think of Sykes? Why might Hurston have chosen to include this scene at this point in the story?
6. What does Sykes do to give Bertha the impression that he has a lot of power? What do these actions reveal about him?
7. Why does Sykes bring the snake to the house at first (p. 1039)? How does Delia respond? How do their actions and responses fit into the power dynamics of their relationship?
8. What does Delia mean when she tells Sykes "Mah cup is done run ovah" (par. 80)?
9. On the final Sunday of the story, Delia attends a "love feast" service. How does that service affect her and her sense of her own power?
10. When she sees the snake loose in the house, Delia runs into the hay barn. While she is there, and before Sykes comes home, what does she come to realize about herself? What does this realization signal about her character development?
11. Why does Delia choose not to help Sykes after the snake has bitten him? What does this refusal suggest about her?

Analyzing Language, Style, and Structure

1. **Vocabulary in Context.** In paragraph 58, when Delia tries to be friendlier with Sykes, Hurston writes, "but she was repulsed each time." What does the word "repulsed" mean in this context? How is its use here related to other possible uses of the word?
2. **Skill Focus.** Reread paragraph 124, in which Delia lies awake after her and Sykes's first fight of the story. Examine the figurative language that Hurston uses to describe Delia's attitude toward her marriage, both past and present.
3. **Skill Focus.** Reread paragraph 39 in which Clarke says, "men dat takes a wife lak dey do a joint uh sugar-cane." Explain how this simile relates to the relationship between Delia and Sykes and the ideas of power that Hurston explores in this story.
4. **Skill Focus.** Reread the following sentences from the first fight that Delia and Sykes have: "Delia's habitual meekness seemed to slip from her shoulders like a blown scarf. She was on her feet; her poor little body, her bare knuckly hands bravely defying the strapping hulk before her" (par. 16). What does the figurative language reveal about Delia's changing power?
5. **Skill Focus.** Several times toward the end of the story, Delia sings a song about "Jurden," which is the Jordan River. Read the note about the Jordan River on page 1040 and revisit the references in the story. What might Hurston be trying to communicate through this allusion?
6. During their first fight, Delia mentions "sweat" several times. Explain the literal and figurative meanings of this word. What do Delia's references to "sweat" illustrate about her and about Sykes?
7. In the night after Delia and Sykes's first fight of the story, Hurston uses the following phrases to describe Delia's attitude toward Sykes. What does each reveal about her changing power?
   - "she was able to build a spiritual earthworks against her husband" (par. 25)
   - "A triumphant indifference to all that he was or did" (par. 27)
8. Examine Hurston's description of the setting in the paragraph that starts, "The sun had burned July to August" (par. 59). Explain the imagery Hurston uses and describe the atmosphere it creates.
9. Examine the details Hurston uses to describe the snake's attack on Sykes. What is the likely intended effect of these details on the reader?
10. Reread the final sentence in the story. What do the word choices and the metaphor of "the cold river" communicate about Delia's attitude toward Sykes's death?

Topics for Composing

1. **Analysis.** Examine the numerous descriptions of Delia's body. What might Hurston be suggesting about female power and physical strength in "Sweat"?
2. **Argument.** Was Delia justified in letting Sykes die? Write an argument from the perspective of a prosecutor who charges her with manslaughter or murder, or from the perspective of a defense attorney who defends her in court. Use evidence from the text, as well as your own reasoning, to support your position.
3. **Connection.** Delia and Sykes clearly have a toxic relationship. Think of another text (short story, novel, play, television show, or movie) that features a similarly destructive relationship. In what ways is the power dynamic in that relationship similar to or different from the one between Delia and Sykes? How is the outcome similar or different?
4. **Speaking and Listening.** Take turns reading portions of the dialogue aloud to a partner. Discuss how hearing the language helps or hinders your understanding of the text.
5. **Research.** The conversation among the men on the porch makes it clear that everyone in town knows that Sykes abuses Delia, yet Sykes faces no threat of criminal charges. Research the history of domestic abuse laws in the United States. Explain whether the story accurately portrays the reality for abused wives, especially women of color, during the 1930s.
6. **Creative Writing.** Write a dramatic scene or short story about yourself and people you talk with often, such as family or close friends. Using dialogue, attempt to capture accents and uses of slang.

A Power of Our Own (nonfiction)

Elena Ferrante

Elena Ferrante is the pen name used by an anonymous Italian novelist and author of the four-part series called the Neapolitan Novels. The first book, *My Brilliant Friend*, was a runaway bestseller, and adapted into an HBO series. The following essay was published in the *New York Times* in 2019, translated from Italian by Ann Goldstein.

FOCUS FOR READING Throughout this chapter, you have been reading poems, short stories, and a drama about power. Unlike those other texts, the following newspaper opinion piece is a work of nonfiction. As you read, consider Ferrante's uses of evidence, appeals, style, and other rhetorical elements to explore how gender has shaped the power that women have and how storytelling can lead to a more equitable balance of power.

Power, although hard to handle, is greatly desired. There is no person or group or sect or party or mob that doesn't want power, convinced that it would know how to use it as no one ever has before.

I'm no different. And yet I've always been afraid of having authority assigned to me. Whether it was at school or at work, men were in the majority in any governing body and the women adopted male ways. I never felt at ease, so I stayed on the sidelines. I was sure that I didn't have the strength to sustain conflicts with men, and that I would betray myself by adapting my views to theirs. For millenniums, every expression of power has been conditioned by male attitudes toward the world. To women, then, it seems that power can be used only in the ways that men have traditionally used it.

There is one form of power that has fascinated me ever since I was a girl, even though it has been widely colonized by men: the power of storytelling. Telling stories really is a kind of power, and not an insignificant one. Stories give shape to experience, sometimes by accommodating traditional literary forms, sometimes by turning them upside down, sometimes by reorganizing them. Stories draw readers into their web, and engage them by putting them to work, body and soul, so that they can transform the black thread of writing into people, ideas, feelings, actions, cities, worlds, humanity, life. Storytelling, in other words, gives us the power to bring order to the chaos of the real under our own sign, and in this it isn't very far from political power.

In the beginning I didn't know that storytelling was a kind of power. I became aware of this only slowly, and felt an often paralyzing responsibility. I still do. Power is neither good nor bad — it depends on what we intend to do with it. The older I get, the more afraid I am of using the power of storytelling badly. My intentions in general are good, but sometimes telling a story succeeds in the right way and sometimes in the wrong way. The only consolation I have is that however badly conceived and badly written — and therefore harmful — a story may be, the harm will always be less than that caused by terrible political and economic mismanagement, with its accoutrements of wars, guillotines, mass exterminations, ghettos, concentration camps and gulags.

5 What to say, then? I suppose that I chose to write out of a fear of handling more concrete and dangerous forms of power. And also perhaps out of a strong feeling of alienation from the techniques of domination, so that at times writing seemed to be the most congenial way for me to react to abuses of power.

However, I chose to write mainly because, as a girl, I mistakenly thought that literature was particularly welcoming to women. The "Decameron," by Giovanni Boccaccio (1313-1375), made a great impression on me. In this work, which is at the origin of the grand Italian and European narrative traditions, 10 youths — seven women and three men — take turns telling stories for 10 days. At around the age of 16, I found it reassuring that Boccaccio, in conceiving his narrators, had made most of them women. Here was a great writer, the father of the modern story, presenting seven great female narrators. There was something to hope for.

Only later did I discover that even though in the fiction of the "Decameron" Boccaccio had been generous toward women, in the real world things were very different — and continue to be. We women have been pushed to the margins, toward subservience, even when it comes to our literary work. It's a fact: Libraries and archives of every sort preserve the thought and actions of a disproportionate number of prominent men. To construct instead a potent genealogy of our own, a female genealogy, would be a delicate and arduous task.

If things had turned out differently, would we have done any better than men? Are we, ultimately, better than they are? As a young woman I thought so, but today I don't know.

I tend to avoid any idealization. It's not good for our cause, in my view, to imagine that all women are honorable, good-natured, extremely smart, fearless and blameless, and, above all, no longer the accomplices of men.

10 Our widespread complicity is in fact a serious problem. Power is still firmly in male hands, and if, in societies with solid democratic traditions, we are more frequently given access to positions of command, it is only on condition that we show that we have internalized the male method of confronting and resolving problems. As a result, we too often end up demonstrating that we are acquiescent, obedient and equal to male expectations.

Suppose a woman pushes her way into the structures of power using an unconventional

The Decameron, 1916 (oil on canvas)/Waterhouse, John William (1849–1917)/NATIONAL MUSEUMS LIVERPOOL/ Lady Lever Art Gallery, National Museums Liverpool/ Bridgeman Images

This 1916 painting by John William Waterhouse depicts the storytelling in Giovanni Boccaccio's work *Decameron*, which Ferrante discusses. **How are the women portrayed in this painting? Who seems to command the power of storytelling? How does Waterhouse convey that impression visually? What might Ferrante say about this portrayal, based on what you've read here?**

extending beyond the text

Chip Somodevilla/Getty Images

Sheryl Sandberg is the chief operating officer for Facebook and the founder of LeanIn.org, an organization supporting women in leadership roles. Read the following excerpt from *Lean In: Women, Work, and the Will to Lead,* which she wrote in 2013.

from Lean In: Women, Work, and the Will to Lead

Sheryl Sandberg

> In addition to the external barriers erected by society, women are hindered by barriers that exist within ourselves. We hold ourselves back in ways both big and small, by lacking self-confidence, by not raising our hands, and by pulling back when we should be leaning in. We internalize the negative messages we get throughout our lives — the messages that say it's wrong to be outspoken, aggressive, more powerful than men. We lower our own expectations of what we can achieve. We continue to do the majority of housework and child care. We compromise our career goals to make room for partners and children who may not even exist yet. Compared to our male colleagues, fewer of us aspire to senior positions. This is not a list of things other women have done. I have made every mistake on this list. At times, I still do.

Explain what Sandberg suggests are some of the barriers that women face and how those barriers are created. Is it women's responsibility to "lean in," or should men recognize and address the barriers women face in our patriarchal society? How might Ferrante respond to the points Sandberg raises in this excerpt?

political intelligence that bends the rules, both written and unwritten. The fact is that she can succeed only if her unconventionality remains consistent with the traditional male culture of command. Why win then? Merely for the pleasure of winning?

I've never been particularly swayed by the rhetorical formula "At last, a woman president!" — or prime minister, or Nobel winner, or any other position atop our current political or cultural hierarchies. The question is, rather: Within what culture, within what system of power, are women rising to the top?

Pressing changes are underway. Everything is becoming something else, unpredictably. A completely new outlook is required. The challenge for now and the foreseeable future is to extract ourselves from what men have engineered: a planet long on the edge of catastrophe.

But how? Maybe now is the moment to bet on a female vision of power — one constructed and imposed with the force of our achievements in every field. For now our exceptionalism is the exceptionalism of minorities. Men can afford to grant us some recognition with good-humored condescension because there are still too few truly autonomous women who can't be made subservient, who can't be dismissed by the expression, "You're so good, you seem like a man."

15 But things are shifting rapidly. Women's achievements are multiplying. We don't always have to prove that we're acquiescent or complicit to enjoy the crumbs dispensed by the system of male power. The power that we require must be so solid and active that we can do without the sanction of men altogether.

The seven female narrators of the "Decameron" should never again need to rely on the great Giovanni Boccaccio to express themselves. Along with their innumerable female readers (even Boccaccio back then knew that men had other things to do and read little), they know how to describe the world in unexpected ways. The female story, told with increasing skill, increasingly widespread and unapologetic, is what must now assume power. ■

Understanding and Interpreting

1. What does Ferrante mean by the following statement in the second paragraph: "For millenniums, every expression of power has been conditioned by male attitudes toward the world"?
2. Explain how storytelling can be powerful, according to Ferrante (par. 3). According to her, what are the similarities and differences between this type of power and political power?
3. While she does not explain directly, what do you think Ferrante means by "using the power of storytelling badly" (par. 4)? How is that misuse different from using political power badly?
4. Why does Ferrante say that she chooses the power of storytelling over other powers?
5. What does Ferrante mean when she says, "I tend to avoid any idealization" (par. 9)? Why is this statement important to her argument?
6. What is Ferrante's definition of "a female vision of power" (par. 14)? Why is this power needed now, according to her?

Analyzing Language, Style, and Structure

1. **Vocabulary in Context.** In paragraph 15, Ferrante writes, "The power that we require must be so solid and active that we can do without the sanction of men altogether." What does the word "sanction" mean in this context?

2. Why does Ferrante include her own personal experience in the second paragraph of her essay? What purpose does it serve in her argument?
3. Examine Ferrante's allusions to the *Decameron*, a fourteenth-century Italian text. How does she use allusion to support her argument about women and power?
4. How does Ferrante use the hypothetical example of the "woman [who] pushes her way in" (par. 11) to support her argument?

Topics for Composing

1. **Analysis.** Why is it important for women to have their own power? What societal barriers need to be broken down, according to Ferrante?
2. **Argument.** Does your school's curriculum and library "preserve the thought and actions of a disproportionate number of prominent men" (par. 7), as Ferrante suggests? Write an argument to change or preserve the current status at your school.
3. **Connection.** Think about your own experiences dealing with people who have power over you. Explain how those experiences were similar to or different from Ferrante's. Did you, like Ferrante, never feel "at ease" in their presence?
4. **Connection.** Throughout this chapter, you have read a number of literary texts depicting positive and negative uses of power. Several of them, including Ferrante's piece, focus specifically on power differentials based on gender. Choose a character from one of those texts. Write a dialogue in which Ferrante helps that character think about how to gain and sustain power.
5. **Connection.** In 2020, a male U.S. Congressional Representative, Ted Yoho, directed a profane phrase toward female U.S. Congressional Representative Alexandria Ocasio-Cortez. Congresswoman Ocasio-Cortez responded with a speech on the House floor that included the following statement:

   > Now what I am here to say is that this harm that Mr. Yoho levied, tried to levy against me, was not just an incident directed at me, but when you do that to any woman, what Mr. Yoho did was give permission to other men to do that to his daughters. In using that language in front of the press, he gave permission to use that language against his wife, his daughters, women in his community, and I am here to stand up to say that is not acceptable. I do not care what your views are. It does not matter how much I disagree or how much it incenses me or how much I feel that people are dehumanizing others. I will not do that myself. I will not allow people to change and create hatred in our hearts.

   What does Congresswoman Ocasio-Cortez suggest here about the power of language? How might her retelling of the event — her story about it — affect people's perceptions of what happened and why it matters?
6. **Speaking and Listening.** Hold a group or class discussion on whether Ferrante is right about what keeps women from having the same power as men, and whether there is a difference in what she calls "a female vision of power" (par. 14). Be sure to take time before the end of the discussion to arrive at some kind of consensus.
7. **Research.** Some female authors have had their work published only by pretending to be men. Others were never published in their lifetimes. Conduct research on a few such authors. Based on your research, are women "pushed to the margins" (par. 7), as Ferrante notes?

writing workshop

Writing an Analysis of Figurative Language in a Poem

Some people love reading and writing poetry, while others do not, and many fall somewhere in between. Despite these different perspectives, everyone can likely agree that poetry is a distinctive form of communication because of its precise use of language to generate an emotional or intellectual response in its readers. Successful analysis of a poem requires careful reading and an ability to consider the different ways that language can be used. In this regard, poetry analysis may feel especially challenging. However, becoming a strong and independent reader can be rewarding, as poet Walt Whitman suggests:

> Stop this day and night with me and you shall possess the origin of all poems, . . .
> You shall no longer take things at second or third hand. . . .
> You shall not look through my eyes either, nor take things from me,
> You shall listen to all sides and filter them from yourself.

Throughout this workshop, you will be writing an essay in response to the following prompt:

> *Choose a poem that you read in this chapter, an excerpt from the play* Macbeth, *or a poem from another source that includes a variety of poetic elements, including figurative language. Write an essay in which you explain how the author uses figurative language and other techniques to develop a theme.*

To guide you through the writing of an analysis of the poem you will choose, we will use a portion from this chapter's Central Text, *Macbeth*, and model the steps for writing this type of essay. This excerpt, like the poem you will choose, is in verse, includes figurative language, and helps to establish a major theme of the work.

Step 1: Gathering Ideas

When you are assigned a prompt like the one in this workshop, you might want to jump right in and start writing. There are some things, however, that you should do before you write. This step is all about the process of selecting a poem, reading it carefully, and beginning to find a focus for your essay.

Reading and Making Observations

We cannot write an essay analyzing a poem or an excerpt from a play without first taking the time to read and interpret it. Since we do not initially know which observations will contribute to our analysis, we must fully annotate the text. Our notes should reflect our growing understanding of figurative language and the questions or ideas that emerge as we read. In this excerpt, from near the end of the play, Macbeth's wife has just committed suicide and all of Macbeth's enemies are moving against him. An annotated version of the excerpt might look like this:

She should have died hereafter;
There would have been a time for such a word.
Tomorrow, and tomorrow, and tomorrow,
Creeps in this petty pace from day to day,
To the last syllable of recorded time;
And all our yesterdays have lighted fools
The way to dusty death. Out, out, brief candle!
Life's but a walking shadow, a poor player,
That struts and frets his hour upon the stage,
And then is heard no more. It is a tale
Told by an idiot, full of sound and fury,
Signifying nothing.

A shift away from Macbeth's reaction to his wife's death, and toward a broader discussion of the meaning of life.

Repetition

Personification: Tomorrow is "creeping."

Metaphor: Life is being compared to a candle, which goes out quickly.

More personification

Another metaphor: Life is a minor actor.

Another comparison: Life is just a meaningless story.

Reading and Making Observations

Select a poem from this chapter or from another source, or select a different excerpt from *Macbeth* with which you connect. Your selection should include multiple examples of figurative language. When you have decided on a poem or an excerpt, read it twice — first to make sure you understand it and then to begin thinking about how the use of figurative language might relate to a theme of the work. Using the precediing sample as a model, make notes about the text and complete the following steps:

1. What is literally happening in the poem? Perhaps write stanza-by-stanza summaries.
2. Annotate the poem by asking questions and noting examples of figurative language and other poetic elements. See the Skill Workshop in this chapter (pp. 921 to 927) or Chapter 2 (pp. 67 to 68) if you need a refresher on figurative language.
3. Identify key moments, words, and phrases that shed light on the poem's speaker or the excerpt's character. See Chapter 2 (p. 54) for additional information on the speaker in poetry.
4. Comment on any shifts you may have seen. (See p. 925 to review shifts in poetry.)

Finding a Focus

While making detailed annotations is helpful for analyzing a poem, a vast collection of notes can be daunting. Before beginning to write the essay, you need to find patterns or observations in your notes that reveal insights about the poem and its theme. Selecting a few annotations to focus on is a good first step. Expanding on those can help you draw connections among them. For example, here are some initial thoughts on our sample excerpt from *Macbeth*:

- "Life is but a poor player": This metaphor, which compares life to a minor actor, is more than just imagery. The audience learns at this moment about the value Macbeth places on the actions he has taken in life: *Perhaps it just doesn't matter, because it's all just a show*. Because our excerpt comes from a larger work, we need to keep the rest of the play in mind as we consider what actions he might be referring to. At this point, near the end of the play, he has murdered people himself and engineered the murders of others, all for the purpose of gaining power. And, though he has successfully carried out his plans, he seems to feel unfulfilled. He may be lamenting his manipulation by the Weird Sisters and the feeling that his life is no longer under his control. He is just an actor playing a role in a play he didn't write.
- "It is a tale / Told by an idiot, full of sound and fury": Another metaphor that compares life to a story written by someone who knows little and cares for nothing. Is this fate that had been controlling him, which now he realizes has no meaning? "[F]ull of sound and fury," probably refers to an accumulation of action, words, and deeds that are ultimately meaningless.

Although we may not fully understand the meaning of the excerpt yet, we have made strong observations that can help us develop our analysis. We can probably say that the excerpt addresses the topic of whether or not life is meaningful. We don't necessarily need to make an interpretation about the text yet; we are simply narrowing down our ideas into a manageable focus for our essay.

Finding a Focus

Return to the text you have selected for your analysis and look carefully at the annotations you have made. Just as we did with the excerpt from *Macbeth*, try to identify the main topic of the piece. Consider the following:

- What are some repeated language choices?
- Are there any significant shifts in setting, time frame, or tone?
- How does figurative language help to communicate key ideas?
- What patterns or trends have you identified at this point?
- What possible themes do you see emerging?

Use your responses to the preceding questions to help you determine a manageable focus for your work with the piece. If you have trouble identifying a focus, perhaps you should select a different poem, or a different excerpt from *Macbeth*. And keep in mind that if you are using an excerpt from a longer work, as we are doing with *Macbeth*, that you will want to consider how the excerpt you selected relates to the work as a whole.

Step 2: Planning the Essay

Now that you've identified, read, and annotated your chosen poem or excerpt, and you've thought about a possible focus for your essay, you have a deep enough understanding of the text to begin planning your essay. This step will walk you through writing a thesis and organizing your ideas in preparation for drafting your essay in Step 3.

Developing a Working Thesis

Whether it's a thesis statement for an essay or a topic sentence for an analytical paragraph, the process remains the same: Introduce the idea you will explore and take an interpretive stance on it. Don't just tell readers the focus of your essay; tell them what your position on that topic is. We know that the focus of our essay will be Shakespeare's use of figurative language to communicate an idea about power and meaning in life, but our thesis statement should make a claim that we need to prove. Having a strong thesis clarifies your thinking and sets up a strong argument for your analysis. Poetry is complex and multifaceted. Multiple people could read the same poem and arrive at different interpretations; therefore, your thesis should reflect your specific ideas about the poem.

For the topic we have been modeling in this workshop, we might write a thesis like the following:

WEAK THESIS

In this essay, I will discuss the famous "tomorrow and tomorrow speech," which is the last soliloquy from *Macbeth*.

This thesis relates to the given prompt, but it does not take a stance. The purpose of a thesis is not simply to skim the surface of the task, but rather to make a claim that needs to be explained and supported. Here is another take on the thesis:

WEAK THESIS

Macbeth, the main character in this excerpt from the play *Macbeth*, describes what happens after his wife dies and how it affects his outlook on life.

While this thesis centers on the main character, it summarizes more than it analyzes. Based on this thesis, we still do not comprehend what point Shakespeare might be making.

To meet the requirements of the prompt (p. 1050), our thesis should address a theme of the work. In the case of our model, that means we need to keep the context of the play as a whole in mind. Macbeth has schemed and murdered his way to power. However, according to this soliloquy, his actions and their results have left him feeling like his life is meaningless. Identifying the actions Macbeth reflects on here and his feelings about them helps us zero in on a central point — a theme — that Shakespeare is trying to communicate to his audience. Our thesis should express that theme.

WORKING THESIS

In the famous "tomorrow and tomorrow" speech from Act 5 of *Macbeth*, Shakespeare uses extended metaphors and imagery to show just how depressed and desperate Macbeth has become by the end of the play, suggesting that the empty, selfish pursuit of power renders life meaningless.

This thesis provides a notion of how Shakespeare uses figurative language to communicate a specific idea about power and meaning in life.

While this working thesis is a single sentence, you shouldn't be surprised to see a thesis that is more than one sentence. The length of the thesis is dictated by the complexity of the prompt. Also, your thesis does not have to list the poetic devices that you will discuss, although that would be another acceptable approach. After all, there are many versions of this working thesis that could lead to a successful essay.

Developing Your Working Thesis

Using the poem or the excerpt from the play that you selected, write a working thesis that analyzes the complexities of the speaker or character and takes an interpretive stance on the meaning of the poem or that portion of the play. Remember that your thesis should introduce the idea you want to explore and take a position on that idea. A strong thesis is debatable, meaning that reasonable people could disagree with your position. Share your thesis with a partner to make sure that it meets the criteria for a strong thesis described on page 1053.

Identifying Points from the Thesis

Now that you have turned your focus into an interpretative stance by writing your thesis, the next step is to prove that your interpretation is valid. At times, it may seem that poetry is so subjective that readers can draw any conclusions they want. However, while poetry by its very nature allows for multiple interpretations, your analysis has to be a valid reading of the text. You must prove your case by citing evidence directly from the text and adding your own commentary.

Let's return to our model from *Macbeth* to think through this step. Based on our working thesis, what exactly do we need to prove?

WORKING THESIS

In the famous "tomorrow and tomorrow" speech from Act 5 of *Macbeth*, Shakespeare uses extended metaphors and imagery to show just how depressed and desperate Macbeth has become by the end of the play, suggesting that the empty, selfish pursuit of power renders life meaningless.

- **Point 1:** Macbeth is depressed by various events, including the death of his wife.
- **Point 2:** Macbeth is desperate and willing to go to extremes in the final part of the play.
- **Point 3:** Shakespeare suggests that the empty, selfish pursuit of power renders life meaningless.

Are these points true? They sound reasonable, but we need to back them up with specific evidence. That's the goal of writing an analytical essay — to prove our points, just as we would in defending an argument about a real-world issue.

Identifying the Points from Your Thesis

Using the working thesis you created earlier, identify the points that you will have to prove throughout your essay. This step will help you determine what evidence you will need to gather and what the topics of your body paragraphs will be. Be sure that you draw a conclusion about the theme of the text.

Gathering Evidence

Now that you have a thesis and you know the points you want to prove, you need to return to the text and your annotations to gather evidence. Allow for the possibility of shifting your interpretation of the poem or excerpt based on this step. If you find that you don't have enough textual evidence to support your points, adjust your thesis to reflect your more informed understanding of the work.

To make sure you are connecting your evidence to your thesis, you might want to use a chart like the following one. It can help you think through the purpose of each quotation and how it connects to your larger point. Here's how we might begin to fill out a chart for our model analysis.

WORKING THESIS

In the famous "tomorrow and tomorrow" speech from Act 5 of *Macbeth*, Shakespeare uses extended metaphors and imagery to show just how depressed and desperate Macbeth has become by the end of the play, suggesting that the empty, selfish pursuit of power renders life meaningless.

Quotation	How the quotation supports my point
"Life's but a walking shadow, a poor player, That struts and frets his hour upon the stage, And then is heard no more."	Shakespeare uses two different metaphors here, comparing life to "a walking shadow" (quite depressing) and "a poor player," which shows that Macbeth thinks we are just all minor actors who do our little lines and then disappear (also quite depressing).

For our model essay, we would complete an entry like the preceding one for each quotation we are thinking of using. Our finished chart will include more than we need, and we'll be in a good position to choose the quotations that provide the best support for our thesis.

Gathering Evidence

Return to the poem or excerpt you have chosen and gather evidence to support your working thesis. Remember that whether you use note cards, take notes in a document, or fill in a graphic organizer like the one shown earlier in this chapter is up to you. This activity is a good opportunity to try out a system and see how it works. If you are unable to identify at least four or five quotations from the text that support your thesis, you might want to consider either revising your thesis or selecting a different poem or excerpt. The quotations you select should be examples of figurative language because that is the focus of the prompt.

Organizing the Essay

Effective essay writing requires careful planning and a systematic approach. Now that you have developed a thesis statement, defined the points that need to be proven in the essay, and gathered appropriate textual evidence, you need to consider how to present this information.

For a poetry analysis essay, these are some of the organizational structures to consider:

- *Organize by sequential analysis*: With this approach, you delve into the interpretation of the poem following the order of the poetic lines. You might not analyze each line, but you would interpret sets of lines that go together, from the beginning to the end of the poem. Sometimes this means that you'll analyze the first stanza, followed by the second, and so forth. But other times you might identify beginning, middle, and ending segments around which to organize your analysis.
- *Organize by poetic devices*: With this approach, you structure your essay based on the various poetic techniques that you'll discuss in support of your thesis. For instance, one paragraph might discuss the role of figurative language while another paragraph might focus on the role of imagery in the poem.
- *Organize by points of analysis*: A more complex approach is the development of an essay based on the ideas that are derived from your thesis. You can use each of the points you've identified based on your thesis (p. 1054) to develop a topic sentence for each of your body paragraphs.

Organizing Your Essay

Review the three organizational structures discussed and consider which one might work best for your essay. Sketch an outline for the body of your essay based on the structure you selected. As you complete this activity, you might decide that a different structure is better for your essay. At that point, sketch a new outline. With a partner, talk through the essay structure each of you has chosen, share feedback, and discuss other methods of organization, if needed.

Step 3: Drafting the Essay

At this point in this workshop, you have drafted a thesis, identified suitable evidence, and considered the organizational structure that your essay might take. Now it is time to begin drafting your essay. The following discussion will guide you through writing body paragraphs, an introduction, and a conclusion.

Writing Body Paragraphs

When you present your ideas, you must make your point, frame your examples of figurative language, and explain how the two are connected with commentary. If we begin to incorporate our point, evidence, and commentary in a paragraph, it might look something like this.

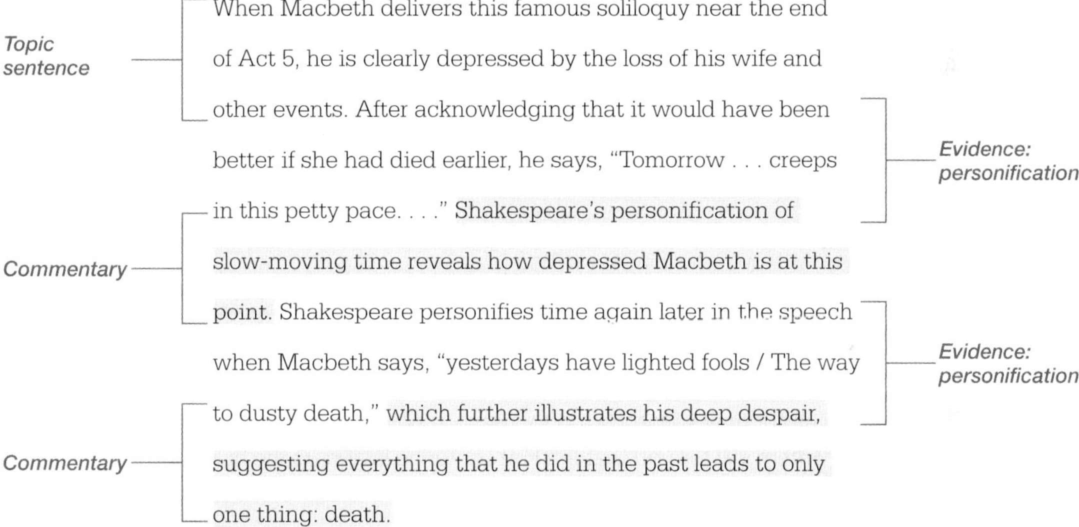

What we have created here is a short, focused analytical paragraph, including evidence and commentary that connects that evidence to our point.

Another point from our working thesis that we need to explain is that this depression leads Macbeth to become desperate, especially toward the end of the play. If we were to follow the same steps we took when writing the body paragraph above, we would have a second body paragraph discussing Shakespeare's use of figurative language related to this point. Then, we might have another body paragraph that explains how all of these choices help Shakespeare communicate the idea that a selfish pursuit of power renders life meaningless.

The number of paragraphs in the body of your essay will depend on the complexity of your thesis. Be sure to explain how examples of figurative language assist the author in presenting a theme. Depending on your organizational structure, you might do this within each paragraph, or you might have a separate paragraph about the theme.

Writing Body Paragraphs

Using the preceding steps as a guide, write a body paragraph for your own working thesis. Be sure that it includes a topic sentence that states your point, incorporates at least two pieces of textual evidence regarding figurative language, and explains with commentary how your evidence supports your point. Share your body paragraph with a partner, who can help you make sure that your interpretation guides your writing. Then, return to your working thesis (p. 1054) and the organizational structure you identified (p. 1056), and draft the remaining body paragraphs for your essay. Again, the number of paragraphs you need will depend on your purpose and the complexity of your topic.

Introductory Paragraph

The point of the introductory paragraph is to engage your reader and create interest in the topic. A standard introduction has three parts:

1. The hook
2. The context and connection to the piece
3. The thesis

The Hook

The hook is about drawing readers in and getting them thinking about the kinds of ideas at play in your analysis. This is a great place to raise questions or identify issues. No one is expecting you to have the answers to these questions or solutions to these problems. For an essay on this excerpt from *Macbeth*, for example, we might want to raise ideas about how someone too focused on power might struggle to find meaning in life. Many writers will tell you that the first sentence is always the hardest to write. Here are examples of how we might begin our introductory paragraph about *Macbeth*:

- *Question.* What makes life meaningful? Humans have discussed and debated this question for thousands of years. Some people have concluded that it should be about helping others, while others have decided it's about gaining and maintaining power.
- *Definition or a fact.* Shakespeare's *Macbeth* is based on a real-life Scottish warrior who became king after killing King Duncan in 1040. However, that is about the only thing that the real and the fictional Macbeth have in common. Historical evidence suggests that the real Macbeth was a just, kind, and legal ruler of the country.
- *Statement.* Shakespeare is considered to be one of the greatest writers in history, producing more than thirty plays and over one hundred sonnets, through which he continues to torture students 400 years after his death.
- *Story or anecdote.* When I was twelve years old, I stole a video game for my PlayStation. Yes, I felt a little uncomfortable, but mostly I felt powerful, having gotten away with doing something wrong. At least, that's how I felt *at first*. It wasn't long before the real guilt set in.

Context and Connection to the Piece

Once we have a hook, it's time to show our readers how the ideas we've brought up apply to the poem we are about to analyze. We might also need to give them some necessary background information. Connecting the hook to the text doesn't have to be elaborate. It's usually a simple connecting statement that might include a brief summary of the poem and the author and title.

The Thesis

The connection to the piece should lead your reader smoothly into your thesis statement, which you drafted earlier in this workshop. A thesis often appears at the end of the introduction.

Putting all of the pieces together, here's what an introduction could look like for our sample essay about *Macbeth*:

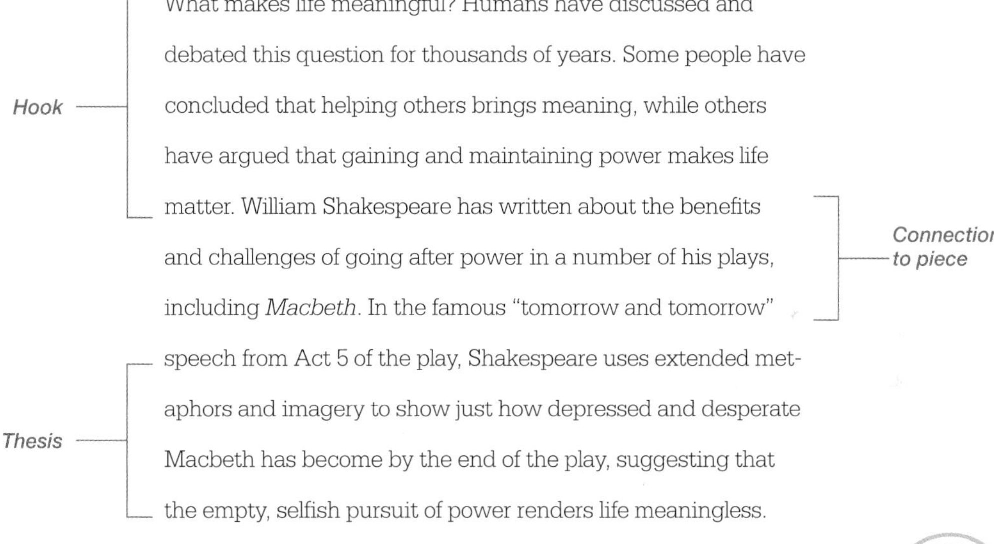

What makes life meaningful? Humans have discussed and debated this question for thousands of years. Some people have concluded that helping others brings meaning, while others have argued that gaining and maintaining power makes life matter. William Shakespeare has written about the benefits and challenges of going after power in a number of his plays, including *Macbeth*. In the famous "tomorrow and tomorrow" speech from Act 5 of the play, Shakespeare uses extended metaphors and imagery to show just how depressed and desperate Macbeth has become by the end of the play, suggesting that the empty, selfish pursuit of power renders life meaningless.

Drafting Your Introduction

Using our sample introduction as a guide, write a draft of your introductory paragraph. Think about the way you want to hook the reader and how you want to lead into your thesis statement with a connecting statement that includes the author and title. Work with a partner to make sure each of you has an introduction that grabs the reader's attention and connects smoothly to the text and your analysis.

Concluding Paragraph

Effective conclusions provide closure by reasserting the thesis and main points of the essay. Instead of simply repeating yourself as you rephrase your thesis and findings, make sure to convey a deeper understanding of the topic. Ideally, you will present your observations within a broader context. What does your essay suggest about society, people, or the environment? The conclusion should bring completeness and closure to the reader with the satisfaction that your assertion is a sound one. Notice how this draft of a concluding paragraph for our sample analysis of *Macbeth* relates to the thesis and situates Macbeth's condition within the broader context of how people perceive power.

> Macbeth clearly has suffered over the course of this play, mostly because of his own blinding ambition and ruthless quest for power. It's not hard, though, to have some sympathy for him, especially in his soliloquy before his own death. Throughout this "Tomorrow" speech, imagery and figurative language communicate Macbeth's desperation. But Macbeth is only one character in the play. Because he dies, his world view doesn't prevail. Macduff and Malcolm present other views of leadership that reveal what a just and ethical use of power can look like.

Drafting Your Conclusion

Write a concluding paragraph for your essay. Remember to relate it to your thesis and to the points in your body paragraphs. To add greater sophistication to your essay and possibly to avoid repeating what you have already stated, try connecting the situation facing the character or speaker to humanity in general.

Step 4: Finalizing the Essay

Now that you have a complete draft of your analytical essay, you can move on to the final steps in the writing process: revising and editing. These two acts are sometimes thought of as being the same, but they're not. Revision is when you look back at large-scale structural elements of your essay, such as how well you support your thesis, what kinds of examples you use, how effective your word choices are, and to what extent you have led your reader easily through your essay. Editing, on the other hand, focuses on specifics such as grammar, spelling, and other conventions. Editing is usually the very last thing you do before you finalize your essay, looking carefully for any errors that you may have made. The following are suggestions for you to consider as you finalize your essay.

Revising

Revising gives you a good opportunity to think again about your essay's purpose and audience. In most cases, your audience will be your teacher, or an external evaluator in the case of a standardized test. In both situations, that means using a somewhat formal tone, but your writing can still be engaging for you and your audience.

Reread your essay for the following:

- Look back at your **thesis**. You drafted this early on in the workshop; does it still relate to the analysis you wrote? Does it take an interpretative stance on the poem or excerpt from *Macbeth* that you chose to work with? If you have additional questions about this topic, you may want to work through Revision Workshop 1: Effective Thesis and Essay Structure (p. 1064).
- Look back at your **supporting examples**. Does the evidence effectively support your thesis? Look at Revision Workshop 4: Appropriate Evidence and Support on page 1076 if you need more assistance.
- Look back at your **body paragraphs**. Have you balanced the evidence with your own **commentary** about how that evidence supports your thesis? If not, consider looking through Revision Workshop 3: Balanced Evidence and Commentary (p. 1073).
- Did you avoid overly **summarizing** the poem or excerpt? Although some summary may be necessary for establishing context, summary is not analysis. Look back at Chapter 1 for more help with reading literature for understanding, interpretation, and style (p. 14).
- Did your **organizational structure** hold up over the course of your essay? Did you make it easy for your reader to follow your points? Look at Revision Workshop 5: Effective Transitions (p. 1082) or Revision Workshop 2: Effective Topic Sentences and Unified Paragraphs (p. 1068) if you need more support.
- Does your **introduction** hook the reader and provide context for understanding the text you analyze? Does your **conclusion** wrap up your essay without sounding too repetitive? Work through the exercises in Revision Workshop 8: Effective Introductions and Conclusions (p. 1097) if you need more practice.
- Did you use **present tense verbs** in your analysis? Literature *lives*, so your analysis should discuss how the author *uses* literary devices and *presents* the speaker.
- In general, did you use **third-person point of view** and avoid using pronouns such as *I* and *you*? Exceptions to this rule can sometimes be made for your introduction and conclusion.
- Are your **language choices** appropriate and effective for your audience and your purpose? Consider looking at Revision Workshop 6: Effective Syntax (p. 1087) and Revision Workshop 7: Effective Diction (p. 1093) for more practice.

Editing

Remember, editing is the very last thing you'll do before finalizing your essay. You and your teacher know better than anyone the types of spelling, grammar, and convention errors you need to focus on in your writing development, so be sure to refer to one or more of the Grammar Workshops that start on page 1101.

Continuing the Conversation

Throughout this chapter, you have been reading texts and thinking about power. At the beginning of the chapter and after each of the readings, you had opportunities to consider ideas related to the following essential questions:

- What different types of power do people have?
- Is the desire to gain power just part of human nature?
- When is the pursuit of power constructive? When is it destructive?
- How do individuals react to gaining or losing power?
- In what ways do gender identity, age, race, ethnicity, and other factors affect how people gain and use power?

The sections that follow will give you an opportunity to revisit and respond to some of those questions as you think further about power by connecting these ideas to yourself, to texts you read, and to the world outside of the classroom.

Connections to Self

Think back on the texts you have read, responses you have written, discussions you have participated in, and ideas you have considered during your work with this chapter. Use the following questions to help explore how the issues raised in this chapter connect to your life and experience.

1. When in your life have you felt most powerful or powerless? What conditions led to these feelings of power or powerlessness?
2. What elements of your identity — including your age, gender identity, past experiences, family, and culture — make you feel more or less powerful?
3. What people, things, or places, or events in your life have most influenced how you think about power?
4. Which of the texts that you read in this chapter has most influenced how you think about power? Why?
5. Which of the protagonists from this chapter would you like to spend time with? Why? What would you ask them about the power they have wielded, lost, or gained? Or, which protagonist would you definitely not want to spend time with? Why?

Connections to Texts

Use the following questions to make connections among the texts in this chapter and to consider what insights the texts provide into the essential questions. As you respond, make specific references to **two or more texts** you read in this chapter.

1. Create a dialogue between two characters from two different texts in this chapter. What would they say to each other about the power they have wielded, gained, or

lost? How would they respond to each other? Consider differences in time period and setting in your dialogue.

2. Social norms around gender can affect how much power a person has. Compare the ways that protagonists in two or more texts have more or less power because of socially prescribed gender roles. Examine the ways those characters gain or lose power. You may want to consider the following texts in your discussion: "Sweat," *Macbeth*, "The Tale of the Kiss," and "A Power of Our Own."
3. Some texts in this chapter focus on the relationship between violence and power. Compare two or more characters in the texts that you read, examining their use or rejection of violence as a method of gaining or maintaining power. How successful is each character in using or avoiding violence to gain or stay in power? You may want to consider the following texts in your discussion: *Macbeth*, "Lather and Nothing Else," and "Sweat."
4. Power and leadership are often connected. Compare the leadership styles of characters in texts from this chapter. Explain the relationships between leadership and power that those characters embody. You may want to consider the following texts in your discussion: "Ghost," *Macbeth*, "Ozymandias," and "Lather and Nothing Else."

Connections to World

Think back on the texts you have read, responses you have written, discussions you have participated in, and ideas you have considered during your work with this chapter. Use the following questions to help explore how the issues raised in this chapter play out in the world at large.

1. Identify one or two political, cultural, or social leaders who are using their power in beneficial or destructive ways. What methods do these leaders use to gain and hold onto power? Why might you support or oppose them?
2. What social institution — school, religion, media, or government, for example — has the most power in society today? Why? How does it acquire and use its power? What limits its power?
3. Describe a law, policy, or rule that you feel demonstrates a responsible or irresponsible use of power. What makes it fit your definition?
4. How do factors such as gender identity, race, and socioeconomic status determine how much power a person has?
5. "Institutional racism" has been defined by Solid Ground, a nonprofit organization working on issues of poverty and racism, as "the systematic distribution of resources, power, and opportunity in our society to the benefit of people who are white and the exclusion of people of color." In what specific ways does institutional racism demonstrate and sustain its power in the United States? How are individuals and groups working to dismantle that power?
6. What inequities do power imbalances create? These could be imbalances in economic, political, or other types of power. Describe a shift in power that might help alleviate the inequities you've identified.

Revision Workshops

Young adult novelist Robert Cormier said, "The beautiful part of writing is that you don't have to get it right the first time, unlike, say a brain surgeon. You can always do it better, find the exact word, the apt phrase, the leaping simile." Revision is an essential, but often overlooked, step in the writing process, and is the time when you look back at large-scale structural elements of your essay, such as how well you support your claim, what kinds of evidence you use, how effective your word choices are, and to what extent you have led your reader easily through your essay. The idea behind the Revision Workshops that follow is that every piece you write has something else that you can work on. The key to becoming a stronger writer is to begin to identify for yourself those areas of improvement. The activities in these workshops ask you to return to a piece that you are currently writing or have recently finished so that the work you do in these workshops is immediately relevant to your needs.

workshop 1 Effective Thesis and Essay Structure

When we write an essay, we are generally trying to convey a point, or even multiple points. We might be creating an argument, telling a story, or providing insight into literature we have read. Regardless of our reason for the essay, we must provide a structure that helps the reader follow our point(s) easily. Clarity is important in writing, just as it is in speaking. Think about it: if you give directions to your house in a random order, you may never get that pizza delivered. So, in order to create clarity for your reader, your essay — in general — should contain three components: an introduction (containing your thesis), body paragraph(s), and a conclusion.

In this workshop, we will ask you to take a close look at how effective your thesis statement is and how well it aligns with the topic sentences of your body paragraphs.

While we will be modeling this process through a literary analysis essay, we will also point out how it might be applied to an argumentative essay.

Crafting a Thesis

Your thesis statement is a sentence that provides your claim and/or the main point of your essay. The thesis is the foundation of your essay. Consider the foundation of a building: if it is weak, the building may crumble. Your thesis needs to provide a strong foundation so that your ideas are clear and focused. A weak thesis will lead to an essay that crumbles under scrutiny.

To get started, let's consider the following prompt given after reading the short story "Harrison Bergeron" by Kurt Vonnegut.

> *American writer Kurt Vonnegut often wrote about the tendency of humans to create dystopias, sometimes by accident or with the best of intentions. Carefully read Vonnegut's story, "Harrison Bergeron," in which the quest for complete equality creates a dystopian world. Then, in a well-written essay, analyze how Vonnegut uses literary elements and techniques to portray his complex attitude toward the idea of equality.*

So, the prompt always asks a question, or gives you something to consider. Your job is to answer that question. But in order to do that, look closely at the prompt to understand what the question is. Does it have more than one part? In this case, we need to answer two questions.

> . . . ***how Vonnegut uses literary elements and techniques*** *to portray his complex attitude toward the idea of equality.*

This prompt asks both what the author's attitude is and how he conveys it in the text. It's important to answer BOTH questions. What's not important is to list every element or technique he uses. Just choose one or two useful ones to focus on.

Before we begin writing, we need to determine our answer to the prompt. What will your thesis statement be? Let's look at the following statements in response to "how Vonnegut uses literary elements and techniques to portray his complex attitude toward the idea of equality."

WEAK THESIS

In the short story "Harrison Bergeron," Vonnegut uses irony and symbolism to display his attitude towards the enforcement of equality.

This thesis makes a common mistake. The student mentioned some techniques used by the author, but without mentioning the author's *point*. Remember, literary devices and elements are tools used by authors to create meaning, but they are not the meaning itself. This thesis does not discuss what the author's attitude towards equality is.

WEAK THESIS

In the short story "Harrison Bergeron," Vonnegut displays a complex attitude toward equality.

This thesis is too vague. The student says the author has a "complex attitude towards equality." That's just repeating the prompt. What does that mean? What is his attitude? How is it complex? Be precise in your answer.

WEAK THESIS

In the short story "Harrison Bergeron," Vonnegut warns us about the dangers of the use of technology: it can be used to replace humans.

This thesis makes a clear statement of theme that Vonnegut illustrates in the story, but it doesn't address the prompt, which also asks students to identify the literary techniques that the author employs.

WORKING THESIS

In the short story "Harrison Bergeron," Vonnegut uses dialogue and physical descriptions of his characters to expose the dangers of government-enforced equality, which could only be possible through suppression and control.

Now we have an answer! The student has stated that Vonnegut considers the pursuit of absolute equality dangerous and explains both *why* (suppression and total control), and *how* (through dialogue and physical descriptions of his characters). This thesis also provides a structure for the body paragraphs, which will support the two components of the answer: characters who are suppressed, and characters who are controlled. Now the student has a roadmap to use while writing.

If you are currently working on an argumentative rather than a literary analysis essay, the elements of a thesis are roughly the same. Your thesis should clearly state the claim that you are hoping to prove, as well as the main reasons you are planning to explore. Imagine that you were writing an argument about the policing policies in the United States.

WEAK THESIS

I think that we need more police reform to address recent shootings of unarmed citizens.

This thesis only states the writer's position on the issue, but does not provide a roadmap for the argument. It is also lacking in the specifics of "reform."

WORKING THESIS

Because the police are often asked to engage in activities that are outside of their expertise, cities and towns across the country need to revise their use of force policies, require all officers to wear body cameras, and reinvest in social service programs.

In this thesis, we not only get the writer's claim but also the main areas of focus that the essay will address.

ACTIVITY **Check Your Thesis**

Take a look at the thesis statement in the essay you are currently revising. Did your prompt have more than one question? Does your thesis answer all components of the question? Does it take a position on the issue? Does it suggest how your essay might be structured? Show your thesis to a classmate to receive feedback.

Revising Topic Sentences

Now that you have settled on a thesis, you are ready to build support for your idea. The purpose of body paragraphs is to provide evidence and details in support of your thesis. In order to stay on track and fully support your thesis, it is always a good idea to do some brainstorming as part of your pre-writing process. What evidence/ideas in the text support your claim? You may not end up using everything you brainstormed. However, you will have a range of evidence to choose from.

After you have done a close reading of the literature you are analyzing and have gathered your notes, or have researched the topic of your argumentative essay, you are ready to support your thesis statement. But how are you going to organize all of that evidence? How are you going to structure your essay? That's where topic sentences come in. The topic sentences of your body paragraphs are claims that define the points you'd like to make in your essay. Your reasons and/or evidence then support those claims.

Let's see what this looks like in practice. Again, here is our working thesis:

WORKING THESIS

In the short story "Harrison Bergeron," Vonnegut uses dialogue and physical descriptions of his characters that expose the dangers of government-enforced equality, which could only be possible through suppression and control.

The topic sentences of your paragraphs should be supporting statements to the thesis. While no specific number of body paragraphs is required, you should certainly be able to come up with at least two or three topic sentences that dig into your thesis in more detail and talk more about what it's claiming. For instance, here are some of the claims (though certainly not all of them) that can be made about our working thesis:

- Vonnegut develops characters through dialogue and description who experience suppression.
- Vonnegut develops characters through dialogue and description who experience control.
- These characters help Vonnegut to expose the dangers of government-enforced equality.

These are very clear areas of focus suggested by the thesis, and they can lead to a very clear essay structure when made into topic sentences.

Here are a few possible topic sentences for this essay:

- The government in "Harrison Bergeron" has created equality through suppression of excellence — as exemplified by its treatment of the title character.
- In order to maintain equality, the government must use fear and pain to exercise complete control of its citizens, as it has done with George and Hazel.

Notice that both of these topic sentences relate directly back to the thesis statement. Make sure your topic sentences are not just summary statements from the story. A topic sentence *must* be an arguable claim.

Again, if you are currently working on an argumentative essay, the process remains the same for aligning your topic sentences with your thesis. Here is the working thesis for the argument in favor of police reforms:

WORKING THESIS

Because the police are often asked to engage in activities that are outside their expertise, cities and towns across the country need to revise their use of force policies, require all officers to wear body cameras, and reinvest in social service programs.

The topic sentences that could be derived from this thesis might look like this:

- Too often, when arresting or restraining a suspect, police rely on tactics that can lead to injury or death.
- Video footage from police body cameras will be an essential part of reform because it gives the public evidence of the encounter with a suspect.
- Because of cuts in social programs, police are too often asked to intervene in domestic and mental health situations for which they are not trained.

Notice how each of these topic sentences takes a portion of the thesis to examine, but each one is also a claim in itself.

ACTIVITY Check Your Topic Sentences

Choose a topic sentence from a body paragraph in an essay that you are currently working on. Meet with a partner and explain how that topic sentence is derived from your thesis. Ask your partner whether or not the topic sentence makes an arguable claim and relates directly to your thesis.

culminating activity

Return to the essay that you have been working on and highlight the thesis statement. Then, highlight each of your topic sentences in a different color. Check that each topic sentence makes an arguable claim and that each is related directly to the thesis statement. If not, be sure to revise accordingly.

workshop 2 Effective Topic Sentences and Unified Paragraphs

As we build support for an argument or analysis, we think about various points that support our position. We want our topic sentences to lead our readers along our line of reasoning. This means we want our paragraphs to be unified, meaning that they focus just on proving the claim in the topic sentence, which makes our reasoning clear and convincing.

In this workshop, you will evaluate and revise your topic sentences and check that your paragraphs are unified. We will be working with Amy Tan's short story, "The Rules of the Game," as we look at samples of effective and ineffective topic sentences and examine unity in the body paragraphs. If you are working on a revision of an argumentative essay, we will include some relevant samples to assist you as well.

At the end of this workshop, you will be able to apply a critical eye to your own writing and revise your paper to make it stronger and more effective.

Examining Topic Sentences

An effective topic sentence accomplishes two goals. First, it introduces a claim that makes a point that is useful for proving your overall thesis. Second, it leads your reader to an understanding of what a body paragraph will be about. As you plan your writing, think about which claims to make, in order to ultimately prove your thesis and convince your reader that your argument or interpretation is correct.

Choosing these argumentative claims is your first step in building your essay. These reasons why you believe your position is correct will become your topic sentences. Ideally, your reader should be able to read from topic sentence to topic sentence to follow your line of reasoning and see the argument at a glance. For now, let's keep it straightforward and put your topic sentence as the first sentence in each paragraph. However, please know that your topic sentences can appear anywhere within your paragraph, especially as you become more comfortable with writing analytical or argumentative essays.

One error that many students make with topic sentences is writing a sentence that summarizes or provides simple facts, rather than writing a topic sentence as a claim. Let's look at some examples. These are sample topic sentences for an essay on the development of Waverly Jong's character in "Rules of the Game." Waverly Jong is a young chess expert who clashes with her traditional and domineering mother.

WEAK TOPIC SENTENCE

Waverly Jong learns how to play chess by studying books and by playing with adult chess players in the park.

This sentence is not a claim, as it is not arguable. It simply states a fact. This would not make a very effective topic sentence.

WEAK TOPIC SENTENCE

Waverly's most influential experiences while learning chess happened in the park by playing with an adult chess player named Lau Po.

This topic sentence is a little better than the first one, because it asserts that Waverly's experiences in the park are influential. However, it is not specific enough to lead to a strong interpretive paragraph that will make a convincing point in the paper.

EFFECTIVE TOPIC SENTENCE

Waverly approaching and interacting with Lau Po, the chess player in the park, reveals her developing assertiveness and determination.

This is the best of the three sentences. It presents a strong claim about the *effect* of Waverly's experiences in the park with Lau Po by identifying the personal qualities that Tan would like her reader to note are growing in her main character.

If you are writing an argument rather than a literary analysis, the elements of an effective topic sentence remain the same. As an example, imagine that you were writing an argument about the need for expanded electives in your school. The following are examples of topic sentences about one part of that argument: the connection to future careers.

WEAK TOPIC SENTENCE

School is boring to me because it doesn't have anything to do with what I want to do later in life.

This is just a personal opinion, rather than a claim. While many students might agree with this opinion, it doesn't take a position that can be argued.

EFFECTIVE TOPIC SENTENCE

For students to be engaged in their schoolwork, they need to be able to make connections to the real world and to future career opportunities.

This is a stronger topic sentence because it is a claim: there are people who might think differently about the causes of student engagement. Also, it is focused on the idea of careers.

ACTIVITY **Examining Your Topic Sentences**

1. Write your thesis statement from the piece you are currently revising.
2. Then, select one topic sentence.
3. Evaluate the topic sentence as either weak or effective, and explain why. These questions may help you to examine your topic sentence:
   - Is the topic sentence a claim? Does it make an arguable statement that must be supported and "proved" by evidence?
   - Does the topic sentence simply summarize?
   - Look at your thesis. Does the topic sentence help to build a convincing case for your thesis?
4. Revise the sentence as needed.

Building Paragraph Unity

What is paragraph unity? Paragraphs are unified when they are focused on proving one claim. Unity begins with a strong topic sentence. From there, all of the evidence and commentary must focus on supporting that claim. You must be choosy about what goes into your paragraph, and when you are revising, you must critically evaluate every sentence in your paragraph. Ask yourself these questions:

- Does each sentence belong here?
- Does each sentence relate to and support the claim in my topic sentence?
- Is my evidence the best evidence to prove this particular claim?
- Am I using commentary to explain how this evidence proves my point?
- At the end of my paragraph, do I circle back to my overall thesis, trying to tie my paragraph to my thesis?

Commentary is the key to unity. As you might recall, any time you use a piece of evidence, you must add commentary after it to explain how it proves your point. While the purpose of a piece of evidence might be obvious to you, it's likely not obvious to your readers. You have to tell them why that evidence is important. This is the connective tissue for building your body paragraphs, and for building your argument as a whole.

Let's examine some revisions to improve the following sample paragraph. This is a paragraph analyzing development of Waverly Jong's character in the story "Rules of the Game" (p. 316). Because different assignments, classes, and teachers have different requirements for citing a source, we have opted not to cite any sources here. For formal guidelines for documenting sources in an English class, see the MLA guidelines in the back of this book.

ORIGINAL

Waverly's approaching and interacting with Lau Po, the chess player in the park, reveals her developing assertiveness and determination. Waverly sees some old men playing chess. "Want to play?" she asks one of the men (Tan, par. 30). The fact that Waverly walks right up to the man and asks him to play without asking her mother's permission shows that Waverly is growing up and becoming more assertive. The man teaches her rules and secrets about how to play chess. "By the end of the summer, Lau Po had taught me all he knew, and I had become a better chess player." Through Waverly's interest in chess, her mother is also trying to understand the best way to be an American, telling Waverly, "Every time people come out from foreign country, must know rules." These rules become an important part of the story since Waverly's mother becomes more and more involved in her chess playing, even though Waverly does not always like it, telling her "It's just so embarrassing." Waverly and her mother found an uneasy connection to each other once she began interacting with Lau Po in the park that day.

Even though this paragraph begins with a strong topic sentence that makes a claim, it is not particularly unified. Notice that it is supposed to be focused on Waverly's assertiveness and determination. But, in the middle of the paragraph (with the highlighted sentence), it switches its focus to the relationship between Waverly and her mother. The writer got a little off track and strayed too far from the topic sentence. This is very easy to do in a literary analysis, because there are often many pieces of evidence that you want to use. Let's look at a revision:

REVISION

Waverly approaching and interacting with Lau Po, the chess player in the park, reveals her developing assertiveness and determination. Waverly goes to the park and sees old men playing chess. She runs home and gets her chess set and then comes back and asks them to play. "Little sister, been a long time since I play with dolls," one man says to her. He thinks because she is a girl, she is there with some toys other than a chess set. Waverly shows him it is a chess set. They start playing and he shows her many moves that will help her beat other people. These moves have interesting names such as "The Double Attack from the East and West Shores." Waverly doesn't ask her mother for permission to play chess with these people. This shows Waverly is becoming assertive around her mother. She shows her determination when she keeps coming back to play chess all summer and learns many new tricks that she later uses to beat everyone she plays with. Waverly shows she is taking charge of her life.

Looking at the topic sentence, there are two strong ideas presented here — that Waverly approached the elder Lau Po, and how she then interacted with him. Assertiveness and determination are the qualities that develop in Waverly. These developments need to support the main idea underpinning the entire essay as presented in the thesis — that Waverly becomes a young woman who gains power over her own life. The evidence and the commentary in this revision all focus on Waverly herself. While there are references to her mother in this revision (in the highlighted section), this time the examples and explanation are in support of Waverly's assertiveness. The paragraph furthers the student's argument that Waverly's character development is leading to more power and control of her own life.

If you are writing an argument rather than a literary analysis, the idea of paragraph unity is the same. Make sure that you are examining and developing a single idea in each paragraph. Let's look at some examples of possible paragraphs about the need for more electives in high school.

ORIGINAL

For students to be engaged in their schoolwork, they need to be able to make connections to the real world and to future career opportunities. Sometimes our work in high school does not seem relevant. For example, just about every day in my math class, someone asks my teacher, "When are we ever going to use this?" The answer the answer that teacher gives is usually something like, "doing your taxes" or "calculating a loan payment," but we're usually not convinced. Math just doesn't seem too relevant. Neither does history class. We usually just talk about a lot of stuff that happened in the past and the class is really big so it's hard to hear everyone sometimes. Gym is sometimes good because I know it's important to get lots of exercise and stay healthy, but it's not like I'm going to be in the NBA or anything.

This paragraph starts off with a clear topic sentence about the importance of schoolwork being relevant and connected to careers. However, while the student writer examined the different ways that schoolwork is or is not connected to the real world, other than the last reference to the NBA, there is no mention of careers. At times, the paragraph feels like a summary of what the writer likes and doesn't like about school (see the highlighted lines), so this paragraph lacks unity and focus on the topic sentence.

REVISION

For students to be engaged in their schoolwork, they need to be able to make connections to the real world and to future career opportunities. Sometimes our work in high school does not seem relevant. For example, just about every day in my math class, someone asks my teacher, "When are we ever going to use this?" If the math class were focused on something like math and construction, or engineering, or cooking, students would see both the relevance and the connections to their futures. In history class, we usually just talk about a lot of stuff that happened in the past, but it would be better if we connected it to real-life events that are happening today in our own city. Even though I know that I'm never going to play in the NBA, a class like gym is important to help us stay healthy today and in the future.

This revision keeps much of the same evidence, but it is far more unified, because each of the examples is explained in terms of the real-world connections and the impact on the future.

ACTIVITY Building Paragraph Unity

Look back at the essay you are revising, and revise one paragraph to improve its unity. Then show your revision to a partner and see if they are getting a clear idea of your point in the paragraph.

culminating activity

Look back at the essay you are revising. Use these questions to help guide your revision of your body paragraphs for unity:

- Is your evidence related to your topic sentence, or is it only somewhat relevant?
- Do you get off topic or stray too far from your topic sentence? If so, would that be more effective in a separate paragraph?
- Where can you identify commentary that refers to your thesis? Is there a smooth and clear connection between your evidence in this paragraph and your overall argument?

workshop 3 Balanced Evidence and Commentary

As you develop an essay on any topic, the most important thing you can do is put your ideas forward. You need to support your ideas with evidence, but it is just as important to explain your ideas with commentary. Commentary is your voice, your own explanation of how the evidence supports your point.

Chapter 4 (p. 128) offers details on how to critically examine your sources to use as evidence and includes instruction and examples on how to integrate evidence and commentary. Here we will take a deeper look into developing a balanced approach to presenting evidence and providing commentary on your topic, focusing on two key questions:

- Do you have enough commentary so that your voice remains central?
- Is your commentary insightful and related to your overall purpose?

To address these questions, we will be working with Sherry Turkle's opinion piece called "Why These Friendly Robots Can't Be Good Friends to Our Kids" (p. 604), which appeared in the *Washington Post* in 2017. We will examine sample paragraphs using evidence and commentary in a close reading analysis of Turkle's argument. If you are writing your own argument, rather than analyzing someone else's, this instruction and these examples will also apply to your writing task. When you complete this workshop, you will be able to apply your observations and skills to your own writing and examine how you are developing your own ideas with a balance of evidence and commentary.

Examining Quantity of Evidence Versus Commentary

Balancing compelling evidence with insightful commentary is the goal. You don't want your paragraph to be mostly evidence, or a just a summary of the evidence. Nor do you want your commentary to be the entire paragraph. With the former problem, your own position won't be as prominent as you would like. With the latter, your paragraph won't be as convincing as you would like since it won't be based on a solid foundation of evidence to support your views. Because different assignments, classes, and teachers have different requirements for citing sources, we have opted not to cite any sources here. For formal guidelines for documenting sources in an English class, see the MLA guidelines in the back of this book.

Let's take a look at some examples. We've highlighted the text evidence.

POOR INTEGRATION OF EVIDENCE

Sherry Turkle's article on sociable robots for kids argues that the robots are detrimental to a child's development of real empathy. She says: "But whereas adults may be able to catch themselves in such thoughts and remind themselves that sociable robots are, in fact, appliances, children tend to struggle with that distinction. They are especially susceptible to these robots' pre-programmed bids for attachment. So, before adding a sociable robot to the holiday gift list, parents may want to pause to consider what they would be inviting into their homes." Turkle's inclusion of the difference between adults and children helps the reader to understand her argument against sociable robots for children.

Notice how the large block of textual evidence leaves little room for the student's commentary to control the main idea in this paragraph. So, how do we fix it? One way is to use shorter quotations as evidence. Does this student writer really need all three sentences from Turkle, or would one be enough? In general, you will want to avoid large blocks of evidence like this sample. Instead, you can include one sentence, or even just phrases or words from the text in quotations as your evidence.

Let's look at another example, again with the evidence highlighted:

MORE EVIDENCE THAN COMMENTARY

Sherry Turkle's article on sociable robots for kids argues that the robots are detrimental to a child's development of real empathy. She states that robots are "machines whose art is to put children in a position of pretend empathy." Turkle says, "Empathy is a capacity that allows us to put ourselves in the place of others, to know what they are feeling." Because robots "have no emotions to share," it is clear that they are not appropriate companions for children and parents and caregivers should be careful about the time children spend with robots.

This paragraph does not make the same mistake as the first sample: there are smaller blocks of text and just a few words from Turkle in some places. Where this paragraph is off the mark, however, is that the highlighted evidence makes up about half of the overall paragraph. In other words, this student writer's own voice and argument is dominated by Turkle's words and ideas. A good rule of thumb is to have about twice as much commentary as evidence, which lets your own ideas remain central.

Finally, here is a model paragraph with a nice balance of evidence and commentary:

BALANCED EVIDENCE AND COMMENTARY

Many people believe that children should grow up learning to empathize with others. Sherry Turkle argues that robots are detrimental to a child's development of real empathy because playing with robots relies not on the "psychology of projection but the psychology of engagement." In short, they no longer see the toy as a projection of themselves. The robot is a thing that needs to be entertained and maintained. But isn't that a kind of empathy? Perhaps, but Turkle states that children will attach to the robot and not learn to have real relationships. Rather than true empathy, the robots are "machines whose art is to put children in a position of pretend empathy." Turkle compares the innocence of playing with a doll to the eeriness of a toy that "has power over you, too." Clearly this is a dramatic, and possibly worrisome, shift in how children play.

This revision begins with two sentences that establish the purpose of the paragraph. Each piece of evidence is followed by a sentence or two of commentary describing why the evidence is important. This paragraph balances commentary with evidence in order to maintain control of the intended point for the paragraph and paper as a whole. Look back at the previous paragraphs to notice how much more in balance the commentary is with the evidence in this one.

ACTIVITY **Examining the Quantity of Evidence Versus Commentary**

Look back at a paragraph in the essay you are currently revising, and highlight all of the evidence. Assess how much evidence you have included. Is it taking up a large proportion of your paragraph? Is there perhaps not enough evidence? Is there evidence that is excessively long, and perhaps could be shortened? Finally, revise your paragraph so that it has a good mix of your voice and evidence.

Improving the Quality of Your Commentary

Just as important as making sure your voice isn't overwhelmed by the amount of evidence you provide is making sure you are writing commentary that expresses your ideas and your position rather than summarizing the evidence. This is one of the most common errors students make. Look at this sample paragraph with the commentary highlighted:

SUMMARY INSTEAD OF COMMENTARY

Traditional dolls, according to Turkle, allow children to "project thoughts and emotions onto them" and work out troublesome feelings, such as guilt or sadness, that they may be having. However, the sociable robot toys have a very different approach. The robots tell children "they have emotions, friendships, even dreams to share." The robots have dreams and emotions, and this can be confusing for children. Instead of the child driving the relationship with the toy, the toy drives the relationship and "has power" over the child as the child tries to react and respond to the demands of the toy. Turkle tells the reader that the toys have power over children, and this helps her make her argument convincing. She convinces her readers that these toys are not helping children but hurting them because of the demanding nature of these toys.

In this example, not only is there not enough commentary, but the student is merely echoing the evidence instead of making a statement that uses the evidence to further the point he or she is making. Notice how the student writer mostly restates Turkle's ideas into his or her own words. The goal of the commentary is to explain how the evidence you include supports the points you are trying to make. A good technique to help with this might be to create a graphic organizer like the following one, in which you place the evidence you think you want to include on the left and your explanation for it on the right. An example from the evidence in the paragraph above is included:

Evidence	Explanation of the Evidence
The robots tell children "they have emotions, friendships, even dreams to share."	This shows that robots are different than old-fashioned dolls because robots manipulate the children into thinking that they have actual real emotions, just like humans.

If you are struggling with identifying the differences between summary and commentary, consider using some of the following words or phrases that can often lead you into explanation, rather than summary:

- This proves ___________
- This illustrates ___________
- This means that ___________
- Therefore, we can conclude that ___________

REVISED PARAGRAPH

Even though some robot manufacturers suggest that robots are no different than the dolls children have always played with, there are significant differences. Traditional dolls, according to Turkle, allow children to "project thoughts and emotions onto them" and work out troublesome feelings, such as guilt or sadness, that they may be having. However, the sociable robot toys have a very different approach. The robots tell children "they have emotions, friendships, even dreams to share." This shows that robots are different than old-fashioned dolls because robots manipulate the children into thinking that they have real emotions, just like humans. Instead of the child driving the relationship with the toy, the toy drives the relationship and "has power" over the child as the child tries to react and respond to the demands of the toy. Clearly, this is far different from a doll that has no real power over a child. A child can imagine the emotions a doll might express, but the robot actually expresses them out loud as well as through facial expressions and tone of voice. Parents and caregivers should be extremely cautious with these types of robots.

Not only is there more commentary than evidence in this paragraph, but the quality of the commentary is higher because it explains how that evidence supports the main point about the dangers social robots might pose to children. With the amount and the quality of the commentary, this paragraph demonstrates that the writer's own voice is central.

ACTIVITY **Improving the Quality of Commentary**

Look back at a paragraph in the essay you are currently revising, and highlight all of the commentary. Then, ask a partner to assess the quality of the commentary. Does it offer analysis of the evidence, or merely summarize the evidence? Revise your paragraph to improve the commentary.

culminating activity

Return to the essay you have been revising and highlight your own commentary in one color and the evidence in another. *Your* words should appear to be a significantly larger proportion of the paragraph than the evidence you are using. *Your voice* is making this argument, and it must remain in control rather than allowing the evidence to drive your argument. Then, review your paragraphs one by one. Examine each one critically. Use this final checklist to tie together all of the skills relating to evidence and commentary that you have worked on in this workshop.

- Is your evidence mostly short, integrated words and phrases from the text you are writing about? Have you removed any quotations longer than two lines of text?
- Is your commentary clear? Does it further your point?
- Does your commentary make your voice prominent and your ideas understandable?
- Have you removed repetitive commentary that merely echoes or summarizes the evidence you have presented?

workshop 4 Appropriate Evidence and Support

Like a lawyer in the courtroom, when writing an evidence-based analysis or argument, your job is to provide evidence that supports your case. You must examine the information available, establish a position, and present evidence to support that position.

First, we must consider: What is evidence? You might recall from your work in Chapter 3 that evidence is any information used to support a claim. There are many kinds of evidence, from personal experience to statistics, and each kind can serve a different purpose in your argument. In Chapter 4, we talked about how to assess the credibility of a piece of evidence by looking at its relevance to the topic, currency, biases, and other factors. So, as you look at the evidence in your writing and work through this workshop on appropriate evidence and support, keep those things in mind.

In this workshop, you have the opportunity to practice providing evidence to support a claim you have made, addressing the following three questions:

- Is there enough evidence?
- Is the evidence varied?
- Is the evidence relevant?

This workshop is most applicable to when you are writing your own argument, rather than when you are analyzing a piece of literature or a nonfiction. However, we identify places below where the activities might be relevant to analytical writing.

Examining Your Amount of Evidence

The first question you should ask about your writing is, "Do I have enough evidence to prove my point?" Let's start by reading this sample paragraph that uses evidence (highlighted) from John Taylor Gatto's essay "Against School" (p. 428) to support a claim about education in our country today. Because different assignments, classes, and teachers have different requirements for citing sources, we have opted not to cite any sources here. For formal guidelines for documenting sources in an English class, see the MLA guidelines in the back of this book.

ORIGINAL PARAGRAPH

Education today is designed to create students who conform rather than think. John Taylor Gatto, a three-time Teacher of the Year who taught for thirty years, compared schools to "cell-block-style forced confinement" for "forced schooling." Students and teachers report to schools with identical little rooms, sit in identical little desks, and study curriculum that doesn't vary much from school to school. Therefore, it's clear that schools are purposefully created to get their students to conform.

This paragraph makes a claim:

Education today is designed to create students who conform rather than think.

The student also provides some evidence for the claim:

- John Taylor Gatto, a three-time Teacher of the Year who taught for thirty years, compared schools to "cell-block-style forced confinement" for "forced schooling."
- Descriptions of the conditions of school: set times, identical desks, and similar curriculum.

As you saw in Chapter 3, an argument can be supported by personal experience, facts and statistics, and expert opinion. Are you persuaded from this paragraph alone that school is designed to create conformity? Probably not because, when considering the evidence, the student has provided information from only one source, John Taylor Gatto. The student has also included a general comment about the conditions of school, though we are unsure who is making those observations. In order to be persuasive, we have to have enough evidence to prove the point we want to make. How much evidence you need depends on the complexity of your topic and the length of your assignment. But, surely at the sophomore level in high school, you should expect to include more than two pieces of evidence as in the sample above. Look at this revision with evidence also highlighted:

REVISED PARAGRAPH

Education today is designed to create students who conform rather than think. John Taylor Gatto, a three-time Teacher of the Year who taught for thirty years, compared schools to "cell-block-style forced confinement" (par. 4) for "forced schooling." If a teacher who has been awarded his state's highest award believes that schools are like prisons, who are we to doubt his experience? Additionally, researcher Bijan Kazerooni, who studied the curriculum of elite private schools, found that "the loss of individualism . . . causes students to crack under all the pressure due to the inability to express their own personal interests." If schools truly cared about individuality, they would allow for multiple opportunities for students to express themselves. Every day that I come to school, I see students and teachers report to identical little rooms, sit in identical little desks, and study curriculum that doesn't vary much from school to school. Therefore, it's clear that schools are purposefully created to get their students to conform.

Now we have a paragraph that is at least moving in the right direction of having enough evidence with the addition of the research conclusion and the clear attribution of the descriptions of school as personal experience. Is it enough to prove the claim in the topic sentence? Probably not, since it is a very large topic, but it is an improvement.

If you are writing an analysis rather than an argument, a good rule of thumb is that you should have at least two to three examples from various parts of the text that you are analyzing in each paragraph. This is important to show that it is a pattern that the writer employed rather than just a single occurrence.

ACTIVITY **Examining Your Evidence**

Choose a paragraph from the text-based analysis or argument that you are currently revising. Identify the claim in the paragraph and then highlight the evidence used to support that claim. Show your paragraph to a partner who should tell you whether or not you have included enough evidence to support the claim you made.

Using Varied Types of Evidence

One thing to keep in mind as you are developing the support for your argument is that you want to not only have enough evidence, but also varied types of evidence. We established that John Taylor Gatto could certainly qualify as an "expert" in the field of education. However, he does not present much in the way of facts and statistics to prove his point about education. As a result, we might need to look at other sources to get a variety of types of evidence. The following are a few other sources who have weighed in on the topic of education that you may have seen in Chapter 7.

Here are some of organizational psychologist Adam Grant's thoughts on education from his *New York Times* article, "What Straight-A Students Get Wrong" (p. 373):

- "The evidence is clear: Academic excellence is not a strong predictor of career excellence" (par. 4)
- ". . . research shows that the correlation between grades and job performance is modest in the first year after college and trivial within a handful of years" (par. 4)

- "Academic grades rarely assess qualities like creativity, leadership and teamwork skills, or social, emotional and political intelligence" (par. 5)

Here are Peter Gray's thoughts in his *Psychology Today* article, "Children Educate Themselves: Lessons from Sudbury Valley" (p. 383):

- "Four-year-olds at the school have the same vote as do older students and adult staff members in all of this" (par. 3)
- "No staff members at the school have tenure" (par. 3)

Alexandra Robbins followed various high school students for a year in her book, *The Geeks Shall Inherit the Earth* (p. 410), and reached the following conclusions about the high school experience:

- "Only 22 percent of U.S. youth socialize with people of another race" (par. 4)
- "The No Child Left Behind Law, a disproportionate emphasis on SATs, APs, and other standardized tests, and a suffocating homogenization of the U.S. education system have all contributed to a rabidly conformist atmosphere that stifles unique people, ideas, and expression" (par. 3)
- ". . . popular cliques are more conformist than other groups" (par. 35)

And finally, here are some thoughts from Albert Einstein, widely considered to be one of the greatest thinkers in history, as delivered in his speech, *On Education* (p. 453):

- "The aim must be the training of independently thinking and acting individuals" (par. 4)
- "It seems objectionable to treat the individual like a dead tool" (par. 11)
- "If a person . . . has learned to think and work independently, he will surely. . . . better be able to adapt to progress and changes" (par. 11)

So, let's sort some of this evidence into the different types that we discussed in Chapter 3 (p. 91).

Personal Experience and Anecdotes	Facts and Data/ Statistics	Scholarly Research and Expert Opinion
"Four-year-olds at the school have the same vote as do older students and adult staff members in all of this"	"Only 22 percent of U.S. youth socialize with people of another race"	"Research shows that the correlation between grades and job performance is modest in the first year after college and trivial within a handful of years"

Now look at how this evidence can be included in a revision of the earlier paragraph with the additions highlighted. Because different assignments, classes, and teachers, have different requirements for citing a source, we have opted not to cite any sources here. For formal guidelines for documenting sources in an English class, see the MLA guidelines in the back of this book.

REVISED PARAGRAPH

Education today is designed to create students who conform rather than think. John Taylor Gatto, a three-time Teacher of the Year who taught for thirty years, compared schools to "cell-block-style forced confinement" for "forced schooling." *Expert opinion* Teachers and students report to schools with identical little rooms, sit in identical little desks, and study curriculum that doesn't vary much from school to school.

According to researcher Alexandra Robbins, the students within this system respond to this factory-like setting and reportedly "view life as a conveyer belt" while in high school. Under the guise of equity, lawmakers have continued to ensure that schools conform. As Robbins notes, "only 22 percent of U.S. youth socialize with people of another race." The danger of conformity is that students will lose the ability to think for themselves, to problem solve, to create. Peter Gray, whose own children went to an alternative school intended to foster individuality noted that, "Four-year-olds at the school have the same vote as do older students and adult staff members in all of this." John Taylor Gatto laments that, "School trains children to obey reflexively" rather than to think "critically and independently." If our students are to meet the challenges of a constantly changing world, they will need minds capable of creativity and flexibility.

Facts and statistics

Personal experience

Expert opinion

Notice how including each of the different types of evidence creates a balanced argument that is likely to be more convincing to your reader.

This applies mostly to the writing of your own argument. In general, when you are writing a literary or rhetorical analysis, you will focus on a single text, so you probably will not have a variety of types of evidence.

ACTIVITY Using Varied Types of Evidence

Return to the paragraph that you revised in the previous activity. Label each piece of evidence as Personal Experience, Facts and Statistics, or Scholarly Research/Expert Opinion. Do you have a balance of varied types of evidence? What could you add that might provide more variety?

Assessing Relevance of Your Evidence

So far in this workshop, you have tried to add *more* evidence to a paragraph and you revised it to include a *variety* of evidence. Now it's time to consider how *relevant* your evidence is to your claim. When you are writing an argument, you must avoid just plopping in evidence for support. Every piece of evidence must help prove the claim, and each piece should represent a different point on the issue in order to move your argument forward.

So, let's return to the claim in our sample paragraph:

Education today is designed to create students who conform rather than think.

The additional sources we looked at on page 1077 all deal with education in some way. But which ones help to prove the point about school and conformity? Just because the evidence deals with the same topic doesn't guarantee that it is relevant to the point we want to make. Let's look back at the paragraph that we created earlier with a variety of evidence, and ask ourselves whether this evidence directly relates to the point we're making. Note that some of the evidence is labeled with a number that we will explain below.

Education today is designed to create students who conform rather than think. John Taylor Gatto, a three-time Teacher of the Year who taught for thirty years, compared schools to "cell-block-style forced confinement" for "forced schooling." Teachers and

1

students report to schools with identical little rooms, sit in identical little desks, and
study curriculum that doesn't vary much from school to school. According to
researcher Alexandra Robbins, the students within this system respond to this facto-
ry-like setting and reportedly "view life as a conveyer belt" (par. 3) while in high school.
Under the guise of equity, lawmakers have continued to ensure that schools conform.
2 As Robbins notes, "[o]nly 22 percent of U.S. youth socialize with people of another
race." The danger of conformity is that students will lose the ability to think for them-
selves, to problem solve, to create. Peter Gray, whose own children went to an alterna-
3 tive school intended to foster individuality noted that, "Four-year-olds at the school
have the same vote as do older students and adult staff members in all of this," John
4 Taylor Gatto laments that, "School trains children to obey reflexively" rather than to
think "critically and independently." If our students are to meet the challenges of a
constantly changing world, they will need minds capable of creativity and flexibility.

1. This piece of evidence is relevant because it compares school to a prison, which insists on conformity to rules.
2. While this is an interesting statistic, it is just about the percentage of students who meet with different kinds of kids. Because there's no mention of conformity or its pressures, this might not be relevant.
3. The first part of this evidence when we learn that Gray sends his children to a school that fosters individuality might be relevant, but the actual quote is about kids and adults working together. It's not clear how Gray's quote supports the ideas of conformity.
4. The last piece of evidence is directly relevant because Gatto states that schools try to make children "obey" rather than think.

Ok, so most of evidence here was relevant, but the student clearly has some work to do to make it more closely aligned to the claim. If you find yourself in this position, you could return to the original source to see if there is a more relevant quote to include. Alternatively, you could look for an entirely different source. Look at the following revision with the changes highlighted, which tries to relate more directly with the claim about conformity and school.

REVISED PARAGRAPH

Education today is designed to create students who conform rather than think. John Taylor Gatto, a three-time Teacher of the Year who taught for thirty years, compared schools to "cell-block-style forced confinement" for "forced schooling." Teachers and students report to schools with identical little rooms, sit in identical little desks, and study curriculum that doesn't vary much from school to school. According to researcher Alexandra Robbins, the students within this system respond to this factory-like setting and reportedly "view life as a conveyer belt" while in high school. Under the guise of equity, lawmakers have continued to ensure that schools conform. As Robbins notes, "The No Child Left Behind Law, with its disproportionate emphasis on

> SATs, APs, and other standardized tests, and a suffocating homogenization of the U.S. education system have all contributed to a rabidly conformist atmosphere that stifles unique people, ideas, and expression." The danger of conformity is that students will lose the ability to think for themselves, to problem solve, to create. Albert Einstein believed that "[w]e must train independently thinking and acting individuals," but John Taylor Gatto laments that, "School trains children to obey reflexively" rather than to think "critically and independently." If our students are to meet the challenges of a constantly changing world, they will need minds capable of creativity and flexibility.

Notice how the highlighted evidence is more directly related to the ideas of conformity and independent thinking than the previous evidence. While this example comes from an argumentative essay, you will ask yourself similar questions about relevance when you are writing a literary or rhetorical analysis essay. Just because you include quotes from the text you are analyzing, it doesn't necessarily mean that they are the most relevant ones to help prove your thesis.

ACTIVITY Assessing Relevance of Your Evidence

Return to the paragraph that you have been revising throughout this workshop and explain how each piece of your evidence is either relevant or not relevant to your claim, in the way that we did on page 1080. Revise any of the sentences that include evidence that you decided was not relevant.

culminating activity

Throughout this workshop, you have been working with just one of your body paragraphs. Now, go ahead and look closely at the remaining paragraphs. Highlight each piece of evidence, and ask yourself the following questions:

1. Do I have enough evidence in each paragraph?
2. Do I have a variety of types of evidence in each paragraph?
3. Is each piece of evidence relevant to my claim and the topic sentence?

Receive feedback from a partner about how well you have used evidence in your essay.

workshop 5 Effective Transitions

One of the goals of any piece of writing is clarity. Writers want readers to follow their ideas and understand exactly what is being communicated. When ideas are being presented, writers should provide links to connect these ideas together, creating a train of thought that is easily followed by the reader. In fact, think of a train. Each car is connected with a hook. If one of those hooks is missing or comes undone, the train disconnects and cannot reach its destination intact. Writing is much like that train. All of your ideas need to be hooked together so that your communication can remain clear to the reader. If you are missing a link, the reader may lose the train of thought and become confused about the message you are trying to communicate. We call these links "transitions." They can be a single word, a phrase, or a sentence intentionally included to create clear communication.

In this workshop, you will explore various ways to link your ideas together, creating transitions to provide clarity for your readers. Transitions are necessary in any type of writing, whether it be a paragraph or a research paper that is ten pages in length. Since much of the writing you will be asked to do will be expository, we will model the use of transitions in an analytical essay about *The Tragedy of Macbeth*, a play by William Shakespeare. Note, however, that the ideas included here can apply easily to an argumentative essay or any other mode of writing.

You will choose a piece you are working on to apply the techniques in the activities that follow. The goal is to include meaningful and effective transitions in your writing. Throughout this workshop, you might want to refer to a list of selected transitional words and phrases, which can be found in the Resources section of the book's digital platform.

Linking Ideas by Purpose

The goal of this workshop is not to have you start throwing in a lot of transitional words and phrases randomly into your writing. Rather, it is for you to understand when it might make sense to include them to assist your reader. In this section, we will walk you through some of the most common reasons that you might consider integrating transitional words and phrases into your essays.

Showing Support and Drawing Conclusions

Oftentimes in analytical and argumentative writing, you have to demonstrate a connection between your evidence and the way that it supports your position. Key words and phrases for this purpose are: *in other words, for one thing, as an illustration, for this reason, notably, including, surely, in general, for example, to emphasize, as can be seen, generally speaking, given these points, as has been noted, for the most part, after all, in fact.*

Look at these examples of how the writer connects the evidence and his or her position about an aspect of Macbeth's character:

- Generally speaking, Macbeth acts as a tyrant in the last half of the play, illustrating how he has lost the honor and loyalty he demonstrated at the beginning.
- Macbeth isolates himself from the rest of humanity, notably when he learns of his wife's death while alone in his room. For the most part, Macbeth has no one but himself to turn to.

Showing Cause and Effect

Similar to showing support and drawing conclusions, sometimes in your analytical or argumentative writing, you need to prove that one thing led to another. This might include an example that proves a point you are making about a piece of literature, or that a real-life event caused something else to happen as part of your argument. Key words and phrases for this purpose are: *as long as, for the purpose of, since, while, with this in mind, in order to, seeing that, so that, when, because of, due to, as a result, in that case, for this reason, consequently, therefore, accordingly.*

Here are some examples of how the writer demonstrates a cause between the evidence and the effect on his or her position about the play:

- Since Macbeth continues to commits unspeakable acts of violence even after seeing the results, for this reason, we should conclude that he is unredeemable.
- Because of the witches' prophesies, Macbeth behaves as if his choices have no meaning; therefore, he stops fighting his fate, giving in to it instead.

Showing Similarity or Opposition

Sometimes in your writing you want to show how one example or piece of evidence is similar to or different from another. While this is particularly effective in argumentative writing, the examples below show how transitions can be used for this purpose in a literary analysis essay. Key words and phrases for this purpose are: *in addition, not to mention, to say nothing of the fact, equally important, by the same token, also, moreover, of course, likewise, similarly, additionally, although this may be true, in contrast, on the other hand, on the contrary, at the same time, in spite of, even so, though, then again, but, unlike, even though, although, instead, however, nevertheless, regardless.*

- Macbeth kills the king and his own best friend, to say nothing of the fact that he brutally murders the wife and children of his rival. Moreover, he is mostly unaffected by his wife's suicide.
- Unlike Malcom, Macbeth chooses ambition over loyalty, even though he might be a victim of the witches' interference.

Showing Order or Sequence

A final purpose for which you might use transitional words and phrases in your writing is to assist your reader to understand the order or sequence of events either within the text you are analyzing or within your own piece. Key words and phrases for this purpose are: *at the present time, from time to time, at the same time, to begin with, as long as, first, second, third. . . , finally, after, until, then, when, once, next.*

- First Macbeth met the witches, next he told his wife, then finally he killed Duncan.

ACTIVITY Adding Transitions based on Purpose

Choose a paragraph from a piece that you are currently working on. Look back through that paragraph and identify one or more of the following purposes that you might be trying to achieve:

- Showing support and drawing a conclusion
- Showing cause and effect
- Showing similarity or opposition
- Showing order or sequence

With those purposes in mind, look closely at the sentences within that paragraph. Do you have any transitional words or phrases included to help you achieve those purposes? If not, add ones from the lists above that might assist your reader. If you do have some, evaluate how effective they are and revise them accordingly.

Linking Ideas for Paragraph Coherence

At the beginning of this workshop, we shared the metaphor that transitions are like the connectors of a train. In the previous section, the transitional words and phrases were mostly about connecting a single train car to another. But what about the whole train? This section of the workshop will focus on looking beyond the sentence level to consider your paragraphs. The next section will focus on the entirety of your essay.

As you likely know from other workshops in this book and other classroom instruction, a solid body paragraph of an analytical or argumentative essay usually consists of three elements: a topic sentence, some evidence, and your commentary about that evidence. Transitions between each of these parts are a great way to build what is called *coherence* within a paragraph, meaning that the paragraph flows logically from sentence to sentence. Most of the effective transitional words and phrases that build coherence are the same as those you examined in the previous section, so it is mostly a matter of perspective. Instead of looking at just one or two sentences for your revision, you should be looking at the whole paragraph to see its flow. Read through the first paragraph that follows. Then compare its coherence with the second one, which has several transitional words and phrases underlined. Because different assignments, classes, and teachers have different requirements for citing sources, we have opted not to cite any sources here. For formal guidelines for documenting sources in an English class, see the MLA guidelines in the back of this book.

ORIGINAL PARAGRAPH

Macbeth delivers this famous soliloquy near the end of Act 5. He is depressed by the loss of his wife and other events. Macbeth acknowledges that it would have been better if she had died earlier, saying, "Tomorrow . . . creeps in this petty pace." Shakespeare's personification of slow-moving time reveals how depressed Macbeth is. Shakespeare personifies time in the speech when Macbeth says, "yesterdays have lighted fools / The way to dusty death," which illustrates his deep despair. Everything that he did in the past leads to only one thing: death.

REVISED PARAGRAPH

When Macbeth delivers this famous soliloquy near the end of Act 5, he is clearly depressed by the loss of his wife and other events. After acknowledging that it would have been better if she had died earlier, he says, "Tomorrow . . . creeps in this petty pace." Consequently, Shakespeare's personification of slow-moving time reveals how depressed Macbeth is at this point. Additionally, Shakespeare personifies time again later in the speech when Macbeth says, "yesterdays have lighted fools / The way to dusty death," which further illustrates his deep despair. As a result, everything that he did in the past leads to only one thing: death.

To be clear, it is not that the revised paragraph is somehow "better" just because it has *more* transitional words and phrases. In fact, an argument could be made that it actually includes too many. The goal of looking at the paragraphs in this way, however, is to see how the revised paragraph is intentionally trying to move the reader through the ideas of the paragraph as smoothly and clearly as possible.

ACTIVITY **Revising for Paragraph Coherence**

Return to a piece that you are currently working on and choose a different paragraph than you did for the previous activity. Read through the paragraph two or three times, out loud if possible. Consider whether or not the paragraph flows easily and has coherence. Does your reader know when you are shifting to a new idea? Or building on a previous one? Are the examples you use clearly identified as evidence or as conclusions? Ask a partner to read it as well to check for coherence and to make any suggestions for transitional words or phrases that might make it easier to read.

Linking Ideas for Essay Coherence

Now it's time to look at the last aspect of transitions — how a piece of writing flows from paragraph to paragraph within the whole essay. Oftentimes, when we are writing an essay, we build it paragraph by paragraph. That means that our paragraphs might read as if they are not connected to each other. A topic sentence is intended to communicate the main idea of that paragraph, but can the first sentence in a paragraph also link to the previous paragraph? And can the last sentence in a paragraph somehow connect to the first one of the next? These are the questions that we're going to consider in this section of the workshop. Instinctively, you know how this works, but too often you may have seen it done badly. For example, you might have seen a student essay in which the first body paragraph begins, "First," and the second one says, "Second," or "Next," and the last body paragraph starts with "Finally." The idea behind this approach is certainly a good one. It's effective at leading the reader through the ideas of the essay. However, the execution makes the writing sound formulaic and bland.

The best way to approach gaining coherence in your overall essay is to focus in on the ending of one paragraph and the beginning of the next and employing some of the transitional words and phrases you've been working with throughout this workshop. At the same time, you need to consider how you can connect the paragraphs with similar ideas.

Look at the sections from the following sample essay. First is the end of a body paragraph on Shakespeare's use of personification in *Macbeth*. Next, you'll see the beginning of a paragraph on his use of imagery.

ORIGINAL

. . . Additionally, Shakespeare personifies time again later in the speech when Macbeth says, "yesterdays have lighted fools / The way to dusty death," which further illustrates his deep despair. As a result, everything that he did in the past leads to only one thing: death.

Shakespeare uses imagery to illustrate Macbeth's deteriorating mental state. For example, on the night that Macbeth kills Duncan, Banquo notes that "There's husbandry in heaven; / Their candles are all out," which illustrates just how dark Macbeth has become.

It's clear that the student here has a topic sentence about Shakespeare's use of imagery that was probably written as part of a separate paragraph without really considering how it might fit in with the previous paragraph about Shakespeare's use of personification. This is why it is important to consider how the paragraphs flow together. Without any transitions between these paragraphs, the essay reads like two separate, unrelated ideas. Read the revision that tries to connect these paragraphs both through the use of a transition and also by connecting with the idea raised at the end of the first body paragraph. The revisions are highlighted.

REVISION

. . . Additionally, Shakespeare personifies time again later in the speech when Macbeth says, "yesterdays have lighted fools / The way to dusty death," which further illustrates his deep despair. As a result, everything that he did in the past leads to only one thing: death.

And death is something that Macbeth clearly has a lot of experience with. In addition to his use of personification, Shakespeare employs imagery to illustrate

Macbeth's deteriorating mental state. For example, on the night that Macbeth kills Duncan, Banquo notes that "There's husbandry in heaven; / Their candles are all out," which illustrates just how dark Macbeth has become.

While the topic sentence of the second paragraph remains the same, the addition of the sentence and the transitional phrase makes for a smoother connection between the two ideas.

ACTIVITY Revising for Essay Coherence

Return to a piece that you are currently working on and look carefully at the ending of one paragraph and the beginning of another. What can you add to make the flow between them smoother? Can you add a transitional word or phrase? Can you connect the paragraphs through the ideas in each?

culminating activity

So far in this workshop, you have been working with making connections between ideas and developing coherence within and between two paragraphs. Now, it's time to look carefully through your entire essay asking the following questions:

1. Have I linked all of my ideas based on their purposes?
2. Do all of my paragraphs have coherence and flow smoothly?
3. Do all of my paragraphs connect to those that come before and after?

Receive feedback from a partner about how well you have used transitional words and phrases in your essay.

---

workshop 6 Effective Syntax

A lot of times when we are writing, we are just hoping to be able to communicate our ideas as quickly, efficiently, and clearly as possible. Your writing, however, should also strive to be memorable, interesting, and varied. For that reason, you should always go back after drafting and revise for syntax — the arrangement of the words in your sentences — that can lead to more effective communication.

In this workshop, you have an opportunity to practice revising your syntax by examining your sentence beginnings, sentence variety, and sentence types. Since much of the writing you will do this year will take the form of analytical essays, we'll model these revision techniques with a sample body paragraph of an essay about a poem called "An Irish Childhood in England: 1951" (p. 519) written by Eavan Boland.

Choose at least one paragraph from an essay that you are currently working on to apply these techniques in the activities that follow.

Examining Syntax

The first step in thinking about how to revise your writing for its syntax is to make sure that you have a clear understanding about what's happening in each of your sentences within a paragraph. To get started, read this sample analytical paragraph about the poem "An Irish Childhood in England: 1951." We've numbered each sentence. Because different assignments, classes, and teachers have different requirements for citing sources, we have opted not to cite any sources here. For formal guidelines for documenting sources in an English class, see the MLA guidelines in the back of this book.

> **(1)** The speaker in Eavan Boland's poem laments the effects of forgetting about her life in Ireland. **(2)** The speaker wishes that "sleep" could "restore" all that she has lost by leaving her home country. **(3)** The speaker worries that she has lost her sense of self and what's defined her has been taken away. **(4)** She especially feels this way because she does not feel welcomed in her new environment. **(5)** The speaker's interaction with the teacher augments this feeling when the teacher reminds her, "You're not in Ireland now." **(6)** The speaker's connections to her native country have faded, and the void is not filled by an English identity.

This is a perfectly fine paragraph that communicates its ideas about the speaker clearly. However, take a look at this chart that identifies aspects of the six sentences in the paragraph:

Sentence #	First Words (Part of Speech)	# of Words	Ending Punctuation	Internal Punctuation
1	The speaker (noun)	16	period	none
2	The speaker (noun)	15	period	none
3	The speaker (noun)	15	period	none
4	She (pronoun)	15	period	none
5	The speaker's (noun)	19	period	1 comma
6	The speaker's (noun)	19	period	1 comma

Of the six sentences in this paragraph, five of them begin with "The speaker." While there certainly are times when you might want to repeat a particular sentence structure for a specific effect (called "parallelism"), in this case, the repetition of the exact same sentence beginning is likely to get monotonous for your reader. One of the ways to achieve more lively writing is to avoid the repeated patterns of your sentences. By charting the paragraph this way, several weaknesses become immediately clear. Not only does the writer start each sentence with a noun — and often the same word — but each of the sentences is almost the same length and has the same ending punctuation. Only two of the sentences have any internal punctuation, which means that they are almost all the same type.

ACTIVITY Examining Your Syntax

Choose a paragraph from the piece that you are currently revising and chart it as we did in the preceding example.

Sentence #	First Words	# of Words	Ending Punctuation	Internal Punctuation

Then, draw some conclusions about what you notice:

- Do all or most of your sentences start in a similar way? Do your sentences usually begin with a noun?
- Do you have some variety in the lengths of your sentences?

- Do all or most of your sentences end with periods?
- Do your sentences include any semicolons, colons, dashes, or other internal punctuation?
- Overall, how varied is your sentence structure in this paragraph? What changes might make your writing more lively, varied, and engaging?

Varying Sentence Beginnings

We noticed that the first three sentences all begin with "[The] speaker," which does not sound interesting to the reader. An easy way to break up this pattern would be to use a pronoun instead in sentence #2.

EXAMPLE: **(1)** The speaker in Eavan Boland's poem laments the effects of forgetting about her life in Ireland. **(2)** The speaker wishes that "sleep" could "restore" all that she has lost by leaving her home country.

REVISED: The speaker in Eavan Boland's poem laments the effects of forgetting about her life in Ireland. **She** wishes that "sleep" could "restore" all that she has lost by leaving her home country.

In English, sentences often begin by stating the subject of the sentences as the writer of the paragraph above did. This construction, however, can be varied, so that sentence #3 could instead begin with a phrase that describes the speaker:

EXAMPLE: **(1)** The speaker in Eavan Boland's poem laments the effects of forgetting about her life in Ireland. **(2)** She wishes that "sleep" could "restore" all that she has lost by leaving her home country. **(3)** The speaker worries that she has lost her sense of self and what's defined her has been taken away.

REVISED: The speaker in Eavan Boland's poem laments the effects of forgetting about her life in Ireland. She wishes that "sleep" could "restore" all that she has lost by leaving her home country. **Worried that she has lost her sense of self, the speaker feels that what's defined her has been taken away.**

Sometimes sentences need to be combined, in order to both mix things up and to draw a tight connection between two ideas, as in this revision, which combines the ideas in sentences 4 and 5.

EXAMPLE: **(1)** The speaker in Eavan Boland's poem laments the effects of forgetting about her life in Ireland. **(2)** The speaker wishes that "sleep" could "restore" all that she has lost by leaving her home country. **(3)** The speaker worries that she has lost her sense of self and what's defined her has been taken away. **(4)** She especially feels this way because she does not feel welcomed in her new environment. **(5)** The speaker's interaction with the teacher augments this feeling when the teacher reminds her, "You're not in Ireland now."

REVISED: The speaker in Eavan Boland's poem laments the effects of forgetting about her life in Ireland. She wishes that "sleep" could "restore" all that she has lost by leaving her home country. Worried that she has lost her sense of self, the speaker feels that what's defined her has been taken away. **"You're in Ireland now," her teacher says, reinforcing the fact that**

the speaker's connections to her native country have faded and the void is not filled by an English identity.

As you look at the last revised paragraph above, you'll see that now only two sentences begin with "The speaker . . ." whereas the original had four. The point of this exercise is not to alter every sentence, but rather to become more aware of how your sentence structures can affect your readers.

ACTIVITY Sentence Beginnings

Look back at the paragraph that you analyzed with the chart earlier and revise two or more of the sentences by varying how some of them start. Show your revision to a partner to see if your changes are more effective than your original.

Varying Sentence Lengths

Almost all of the sentences in the original sample paragraph were between 15 and 19 words, which is monotonous for readers. Varying sentence lengths keeps your readers' attention and lets you create emphasis. Short sentences, for example, can create a sense of urgency or punch, whereas longer sentences may feel smooth and flowing and allow you to develop complex ideas. If you are familiar with music, you might think of short sentences as being staccato, while long sentences are legato. Often, writers will use changes in sentence length or sentence types to create rhythmic effects. The most common is to follow a series of long sentences with a short one to create impact. However, the pattern can work the other way as well.

Notice the impact of this technique in this excerpt from Jane Austen's *Pride and Prejudice*:

> Mr. Bennet was so odd a mixture of quick parts, sarcastic humor, reserve, and caprice, that the experience of three-and-twenty years had been insufficient to make his wife understand his character. **Her mind was less difficult to develop**. She was a woman of mean understanding, little information, and uncertain temper.

The suddenness of the short length of the second sentence, especially in contrast to the very long sentence that precedes it, emphasizes the differences between the two characters. Again, think about the effect of writing with this type of syntactic variety. You are actually able to communicate information to your readers not only with the words you select, but also with the length of the sentences in your writing.

Let's look back at the model paragraph we've been revising, and notice what happens when we add a short sentence in the middle of the paragraph.

EXAMPLE: The speaker in Eavan Boland's poem laments the effects of forgetting about her life in Ireland. She wishes that "sleep" could "restore" all that she has lost by leaving her home country. Worried that she has lost her sense of self, the speaker feels that what's defined her has been taken away. "You're not in Ireland now," her teacher says, reinforcing the fact that the speaker's connections to her native country have faded and the void is not filled by an English identity.

REVISED: The speaker in Eavan Boland's poem laments the effects of forgetting about her life in Ireland. She wishes that "sleep" could "restore" all that she has lost by leaving her home country. Worried that she has lost her sense of self, the speaker feels that what's defined her has been taken away. **She is truly alone.** "You're not in Ireland now," her teacher says, reinforcing the fact that the speaker's connections to her native country have faded and the void is not filled by an English identity.

Not only does this additional short sentence break up the pattern of roughly the same number of words in each sentence, but its shortness directs the reader to the impact being away from her home has had.

ACTIVITY Varying Your Sentence Length

Return to the piece that you are revising (and maybe to the paragraph that you charted earlier) to see if there are places where you can revise your sentence length to add variety and/or to add a short sentence to create an impact on your reader, as in the example above. Show your revision to a partner to see if your changes are more effective than your original.

Varying Sentence Types

As you saw in the chart of the example paragraph earlier, all of the sentences ended with a period, and only two included any kind of internal punctuation. Thus, all of the sentences are of the same type. The ending punctuation is one clue to this. Remember, you can ask questions in your writing, so you would end with a question mark. You can also show emphasis by using an exclamation point (though this is not regularly used in academic, expository writing). The biggest clue to the sentence type, though, is that there is little internal punctuation. All of the sentences in the sample paragraph are what we call "simple sentences," as defined below. A goal for your writing, as you become more advanced in your skills, is to try for as much variety in the types of sentences you construct.

- **Simple sentences** can grab the reader's attention or provide information in a direct and simplistic way. If you use too many, however, your writing can come across as amateurish, choppy, or bland. A simple sentence contains one independent clause. An independent clause is a group of words that contains a subject and verb. It's called "independent" because it can stand by itself and still make sense.

  The speaker in Eavan Boland's poem laments the effects of forgetting about her life in Ireland.

- **Compound sentences** can be used to emphasize balance, to compare or contrast ideas, convey cause-effect relationships, or group similar ideas together. Compound sentences contain two independent clauses joined by a comma and a conjunction or by a semicolon alone. The following examples are revisions of the sample paragraph:

  The speaker in Eavan Boland's poem laments the effects of forgetting about her life in Ireland, and she wishes that "sleep" could "restore" all that she has lost by leaving her home country.

or

The speaker in Eavan Boland's poem laments the effects of forgetting about her life in Ireland; she wishes that "sleep" could "restore" all that she has lost by leaving her home country.

- **Complex** sentences also can emphasize balance, but they contain an independent clause and one or more dependent clauses. A dependent clause is a clause that does not make sense when it stands alone. The following is a revised sentence from the sample paragraph with the dependent clause underlined:

  Because the speaker worries that she has lost her sense of self and what's defined her has been taken away, she wishes that "sleep" could "restore" all that she has lost by leaving Ireland.

So, when you are thinking about varying your sentence types, you should consider where you can ask questions, use exclamation points (if appropriate for your purpose and audience), and when you can use more compound or complex sentences. In the original below, which has already been revised for sentence beginnings and length, most of the sentences are simple sentences. Look at how much more lively and engaging the writing is when we have taken the time to vary the types of sentences we use.

ORIGINAL: **(1)** The speaker in Eavan Boland's poem laments the effects of forgetting about her life in Ireland. **(2)** The speaker wishes that "sleep" could "restore" all that she has lost by leaving her home country. **(3)** The speaker worries that she has lost her sense of self and what's defined her has been taken away. **(4)** She especially feels this way because she does not feel welcomed in her new environment. **(5)** The speaker's interaction with the teacher augments this feeling when the teacher reminds her, "You're not in Ireland now." **(6)** The speaker's connections to her native country have faded, and the void is not filled by an English identity.

REVISED: Because the speaker worries that she has lost her sense of self and what's defined her has been taken away, she wishes that "sleep" could "restore" all that she has lost by leaving Ireland. Telling the speaker that "You're not in Ireland now," her teacher adds to that feeling of loss and isolation. Torn from home, she is all alone. Even though the speaker's connections to her native country have faded, the void is not supplanted by an English identity. Is she English, Irish, both, or neither?

ACTIVITY Sentence Types

Return to the piece that you are revising, or the paragraph that you charted earlier and identify all of the simple sentences you used. Then, revise one or more of those simple sentences into a compound or a complex sentence. Show your revision to a partner to see if your changes are more effective than your original and if you have constructed them properly.

culminating activity

Return to the essay you have been revising and choose a different paragraph that you have been working with throughout this workshop. Then, follow these directions:

1. Chart your sentences like you did earlier on p. 1088.
2. Revise the paragraph by applying all three of the elements you've explored: beginnings, lengths, and type. Be sure that you are making the changes that reflect how you want to communicate your ideas; don't change just for the sake of change.
3. Show it to a partner to reflect on how the changes in sentence variety affect the reader and have made your writing more engaging and lively.

workshop 7 Effective Diction

As you probably already know, "diction" refers to word choice. Choosing words appropriate to your particular type of writing and your audience is key. For example, in writing a scientific lab report, you would choose words that are accurate rather than creative. In writing a personal narrative, on the other hand, you would have more freedom to choose words that build imagery and stimulate the imagination.

There are a few basic rules that generally apply to all good writing when it comes to diction. How important it is to follow these, or how frequently you might be able to ignore these rules, would be determined by who your audience is and what your purpose is. If it's a formal academic setting, like most of the work you write in English class, you would be wise to follow these rules whenever possible.

In this workshop, we'll practice different ways of considering your diction in an argument you may be writing as well as a literary or rhetorical analysis essay. And throughout, you will return to a piece that you are currently working on to look for places where you can revise your diction.

Considering Your Audience and Purpose

The first thing you should consider when you are thinking about diction is the audience and the purpose of what you are writing. Of course you would choose different words in a text message sent to a friend than you would in an essay for your English teacher. Part of this concerns the level of formality. When you are writing a piece for school, you are generally expected to take on a scholarly, academic voice. However, when you are writing a text to a friend, you might be much more informal, likely including slang, abbreviations, and emojis, most of which would seem out of place in a rhetorical analysis essay. If you were writing a piece of fiction or a narrative for English, your diction would probably include lots of vivid details and description that would seem quite inappropriate for a lab report for science. The latter writing would instead include scientific terms and measurements that are appropriate to that purpose.

In the case of an analytical or an argumentative essay, your level of formality might be high. However, your purpose is to persuade your audience that your interpretation of a text or your position on an issue is a sound one, so you absolutely should use strong verbs and detailed descriptions whenever possible to engage and persuade your audience. Look, for instance, at the following section from an essay called *A Small Place* by Jamaica Kincaid who is questioning the value of tourism and the effects it has on her country Antigua:

> An ugly thing, that is what you are when you become a tourist, an ugly, empty thing, a stupid thing, a piece of rubbish pausing here and there to gaze at this and taste that, and it will never occur to you that the people who inhabit the place in which you have just paused cannot stand you, that behind their closed doors they laugh at your strangeness (you do not look the way they look); the physical sight of you does not please them; you have bad manners (it is their custom to eat their food with their hands; you try eating their way, you look silly; you try eating the way you always eat, you look silly); they do not like the way you speak (you have an accent); they collapse helpless from laughter, mimicking the way they imagine you must look as you carry out some everyday bodily function.

There are a lot of highly charged and brutal words in here to describe the tourists that make her purpose extremely clear. It is also interesting to consider Kincaid's audience: she directly addresses the tourist as "you," adding a more direct critique of tourism.

While you might not have the opportunity to use quite such powerfully descriptive diction when you are writing a literary or rhetorical analysis, you can still include words that make it clear that your interpretation is an accurate one. For instance, here is an introductory paragraph of an analysis of Kincaid's argument. Note that there is a clear purpose to draw the reader into this essay through the diction:

> Haven't most of us been a "tourist" in some way? Even if we haven't gone to another country, we have visited a local landmark to enjoy a carefree day with friends or family. We probably didn't think of ourselves as being "ugly," nor did we imagine that others saw us that way. Yet in *A Small Place*, author Jamaica Kincaid takes the "ugly tourist" to task in ways that may shock or surprise her readers. With strong emotional language and parenthetical asides, she develops a sarcastic, critical tone toward the tourists who visit Antigua seeking temporary escape and pleasure.

ACTIVITY Considering Your Audience and Purpose

Look back at the piece you are currently revising. Who is your intended audience? How might this affect your diction? What is your purpose? How might this affect your diction? Look closely at one paragraph of this piece and look for words or phrases that seem appropriate for your audience and purpose. Do you notice any that seem inappropriate either because of their level of formality or other reasons?

Keeping Connotation in Mind

Now that you have thought about how your word choice needs to reflect your audience and purpose, the next element to consider is the emotional impact that your diction might have on your reader. You may have already learned that the "denotation" of a word is its dictionary definition, whereas its "connotation" extends that literal meaning to include the feelings associated with that particular word.

Look, for instance, at another description that Kincaid offers about a tourist who leaves home to visit somewhere different: "you make a leap from being that nice blob . . . to being a person visiting heaps of death and ruin and feeling alive and inspired at the sight of it." The definition of a blob is "a drop of a thick liquid or viscous substance." However, it's clear that Kincaid is interested in the connotation of the word here: someone who is fat, lazy, and useless. Any other word would not have communicated quite the same emotion to her readers, nor would have some of her other word choices here, such as "heaps of death" or "inspired."

While writing an argument, like Kincaid is doing, certainly allows for a broader range of connotative choices, you still have lots of options for effective diction choices in a literary or rhetorical analysis writing. Look, for instance, at these two paragraphs of a rhetorical analysis of Kincaid's essay; the second one includes words and phrases highlighted for their diction.

ORIGINAL The language Kincaid uses to describe the tourist both physically and psychologically includes a lot of criticism. Toward the end of the essay, she writes that the ugly tourist is a "nice blob just sitting like a boob in your amniotic sac of the modern experience." Ultimately, she says the tourist is "an ugly, empty thing, a stupid thing, a piece of rubbish pausing here and there . . ."

REVISION The language Kincaid uses to describe the tourist both physically and psychologically is loaded with sharp criticism. Toward the end of the essay, she brutally claims that the ugly tourist is a "nice blob just sitting like a boob in your amniotic sac of the modern experience." Ultimately, she dismisses the tourist as "an ugly, empty thing, a stupid thing, a piece of rubbish pausing here and there . . ."

Compare the emotional qualities of the original word "says" with "dismisses" in the revision. Both are accurate, but the new diction creates an urgency and a clear idea about how the writer is interpreting Kincaid's choices. There are many words at your disposal when writing a literary or rhetorical analysis rather than words like "says," "includes" or "describes" to characterize what an author might be doing in a text. Consider words like these: *argues, believes, reports, suggests, claims, advocates, supports, condemns, observes, concedes, recommends, asserts.*

ACTIVITY Keeping Connotation in Mind

Go back into one paragraph of the essay that you are currently revising. Look closely at your diction. Are there words that you could change so that they include more emotional associations? Or words that could make your analysis of a text clearer and livelier? Be sure to keep your audience and purpose that you examined in the previous section in mind as you make any changes.

Being Concise

Stating your ideas without a lot of extra words can make your writing stronger and clearer. It's called being concise. Here are some examples of wordiness, along with some ways that you can trim them for conciseness:

Wordy Diction	Concise Diction
because of the fact that	since
at that point	when or then
all of a sudden	suddenly
in order to	to
has the ability to	can

Some phrases are just filler and you might want to consider cutting them altogether. Oftentimes, no meaning is lost when they are cut from your writing. They can be the writing equivalent of saying "ummm." Here are some examples from an analysis of the Kincaid piece we've been looking at. In each case, the underlined wordy phrase could likely be deleted.

- "The point I'm trying to make is that Kincaid is way too harsh toward the tourists who are actually making Antigua better economically."
- "The fact of the matter is that tourists likely contribute to well over half of Antigua's economy."
- "The thing is Kincaid is so angry that her word choices often get in the way of her argument because the tourists won't listen to her."
- "For all intents and purposes, Kincaid makes an essential point about the ways that tourists feel superior to those who live there."
- "It is important to note that not all tourists are like how Kincaid describes them."

ACTIVITY Being Concise

Look carefully at one paragraph of the piece you are currently revising and try to identify places where your language might be a little wordy. Revise those sentences to make the language more concise, making sure that the meaning remains roughly the same. Show your paragraph to a partner to see if he or she can identify any additional wordiness.

culminating activity

Throughout this workshop, you have been looking very closely at a single paragraph from the essay you are currently revising. Now, spend some time with the rest of your piece and examine its diction. Working with a partner, consider the following:

1. Is your diction appropriate for your audience and purpose?
2. Do you include words with the most effective connotation?
3. Have you revised words or phrases for conciseness?

Introductions and conclusions can be the hardest parts of an essay to write. It's difficult to know where to begin, and conclusions can sometimes seem like just repeating yourself. What makes things a bit easier is knowing the purpose of both of these pieces and remembering that they don't have to be perfect the first time. Draft something and then revise to strengthen it.

In this workshop, we will be modeling the writing of a rhetorical analysis essay of "Bully and the Pulpit" by DeRay Mckesson (p.196). We will focus specifically on how to start this essay in an engaging way and wrap it up in a satisfying manner. And even though the samples here will be of an analytical essay, everything included is relevant to the writing of your own argumentative essay as well.

Revising Introductions

As you likely remember from the Writing Workshops in this book, most introductions have three pieces:

a. The hook

b. The context

c. The claim (thesis)

For this Revision Workshop, we will focus on the hook and the context, because Revision Workshop 1 covers the claim or thesis in detail.

Effective Hooks

The hook is how you grab your reader's attention. It could be an interesting anecdote, a relevant quotation, a startling statistic, or an observation or question. The hook isn't just there for shock value; it has to be relevant to your thesis and your argument as a whole. The hook should be intriguing; it should make readers want to read further in your essay. Let's take a look at some examples of different types of hooks. that come from various pieces in this book.

PROVOCATIVE STATEMENT

I taught for thirty years in some of the worst schools in Manhattan, and in some of the best, and during that time I became an expert in boredom. — John Taylor Gatto, *Against School*, p. 428

INTRIGUING QUOTATION

As the saying goes, "All the world is mad except for me and thee, and I'm not too sure of thee."

This is the reaction many of us have when people express opinions that differ markedly from our own. And then, of course, we try to change their minds. — Denise Cummins, *How to Get People to Change Their Minds*, p. 181

RHETORICAL QUESTION

I saw the Martin Luther King movie the other day, how many of you saw that? — Dolores Huerta, *UCLA Speech*, p. 190

INSIGHTFUL OBSERVATION

Something is happening in Memphis; something is happening in our world. — Martin Luther King Jr., *I Have Been to the Mountaintop*, p. 211

STARTLING STATISTIC

Imagine that 7 out of 10 working Americans got fired tomorrow. — Kevin Kelly, *Better than Human*, p. 590

Now that we have a wide variety of types of hooks to choose from, let's look at a few possible hooks we might use for our rhetorical analysis of Mckesson's argument, based on this thesis statement:

In "Bully and the Pulpit," Mckesson draws an analogy between white supremacy and a school-yard bully, and argues effectively that neither one can be dealt with through "a strategy centered on opposition" alone, but by creating a vision of a future with no bully in it.

WEAK HOOK

Like many in this nation, DeRay Mckesson has had to deal with bullies.

This is a bland general statement and a little too obvious. A general statement can still be intriguing, surprising, establish common ground, or otherwise draw the reader in. This particular general point, however, does not do any of those things, though it does a decent job of connecting to the thesis. Let's examine another.

WEAK HOOK

Bullying is wrong and no one should get bullied.

While the instinct to begin an essay with a broad statement like this is not necessarily bad, it still needs to be an interesting statement. Very few people would object to this statement, so it is not particularly engaging. It also is a little too literal, since we know that the bully that Mckesson is talking about is that of white supremacy.

STRONG HOOK

DeRay Mckesson is haunted. Our nation is haunted. In both cases, the ghost left a deep mark upon the psyche — a wound that has never fully healed.

When you read this hook, you immediately start asking questions: A ghost? Is this a real ghost or just a symbol? Is it the same ghost haunting both Mckesson and our nation? What kind of wound did it leave? Why didn't it heal? There are many ways to write a good hook, but if your hook gets your audience to start asking questions, that means they are curious and engaged. That's a good start.

ACTIVITY **Revising Your Hook**

Return to the piece you are revising. Try out two or three of the approaches listed above for a hook. Which ones do you like best? Are any of them overly broad? Are they clichés? Do they connect to the thesis? Do they get the reader to ask questions and wonder about the topic? Now, choose one that you think is most effective and add it to the piece you are working on.

Providing Context and Making a Connection

Once you have a hook, you need to build a bridge between it and your thesis or your claim, if you are writing an argumentative essay. Since your hook is likely to be a statement not specifically about the text that you're analyzing or the position you take on an issue, you need to provide context to show how your general statement relates to the text. In short, you need to build a connection to the text being analyzed. The hook is also your last statement before the thesis or claim. In addition to building a bridge, this context section generally includes the background information the reader needs to understand the thesis or claim that follows.

For instance, the example hook that we selected in the previous section talks about ghosts. So part of the work this context statement needs to do is to move us from the figurative ghosts to a discussion of the analogy of the bully in "Bully and the Pulpit." Let's try it:

Hook

DeRay Mckesson is haunted. Our nation is haunted. In both cases, the ghost left a deep mark upon the psyche—a wound that has never fully healed. All these years later, civil rights activist Mckesson confesses that he still thinks about the bully who tormented him as a child, and he contends that America is still being tormented as well. This time it's not by a single school-yard bully, but by white supremacy, which he argues uses similar tactics. In his essay "Bully and the Pulpit," Mckesson draws an analogy between white supremacy and a school-yard bully and argues effectively that neither one can be dealt with through "a strategy centered on opposition" alone, but by creating a vision of a future with no bully in it.

Context

Thesis

If you are writing an argument rather than an analysis, the format of this part of your introduction will be similar, but you will have to be sure that you define any key terms and provide any necessary historical information that might be included in your claim, so it flows smoothly.

ACTIVITY **Context and Connection**

Return to the piece you are revising and analyze your introductory paragraph. Highlight the hook in one color and the thesis in another. Label the remaining sentences as context and connection. Then, ask yourself the following questions:

- Are any of my sentences neither context nor connection?
- Does my context provide all the information my readers need before they begin reading my essay?
- Is my connection smooth?

Based on your responses to these questions, revise your introduction in order to strengthen it.

Writing a Conclusion

Conclusions are tricky. You need to wrap up your essay, but just doing a quick summary of your argument or analysis is, frankly, boring. You need to do more than just summarize, but what? Ideally, your conclusion should answer the question: "So what?"

If you're writing a persuasive argument, this question is oftentimes easy to answer. Your conclusion might include a call to action, or you might want to leave your readers with a lasting impression that could change how they think about the issue. Oftentimes, a return to pathos, the emotional core of an argument, is a great ending: a story or image that tugs again at your reader's heart.

In an academic analysis, this question might be asking why your argument is important to the world. On the other hand, it could just be asking why the analysis is important in order for us to understand the text. Your conclusion is your opportunity to present a deeper understanding of the topic, or to talk about its significance.

Let's look at a conclusion for our sample Mckesson essay:

> Mckesson doesn't just rail against white supremacy and tell us how bad it is. Instead, he gives us a way to end it. The value of Mckesson's analogy is that it takes something as overwhelming and abstract as white supremacy and gives it substance. Once he gives this ideology form — once we are able to think of white supremacy as a basic school-yard bully — it's much easier to come up with ways to defeat it. Treating a cultural mindset like a school-yard bully is a powerful strategy to help all of us think concretely about how to end this problem that has haunted us for years, and begin to heal the nation's wounds.

This conclusion makes a few different moves. The first sentence sets up the "So what?" by presenting an alternative. The conclusion stresses the practical importance of Mckesson's analogy. Why is it important? Because this way of thinking could change the world. The conclusion ends with a call-to-action of sorts: Let's heal the nation's wounds. Finally, this conclusion makes another clever move, which is that it refers back to the hook. That sort of "book-ending," as it's sometimes called, gives a satisfying sense that the analysis has come full circle. Even a conclusion of an analytical essay can be a place of some rhetorical flourish and make your reader glad he or she made it to the end of your piece.

ACTIVITY Revising Your Conclusion

Return to the essay you are revising and look at your conclusion. Ask yourself the following questions:

- Does my conclusion summarize my findings?
- Does my conclusion answer the question, "So what?"
- Does my conclusion have a call to action?
- Does my conclusion demonstrate a deeper understanding of the topic?

If you only answered "yes" to the first question, then go back into your conclusion and try to revise it using one or two of the strategies found in this list.

culminating activity

Now that you have revised both your introduction and your conclusion, it's time to read them together to see how they fit with each other. Ideally, these two parts should work in tandem, maybe with the introduction raising a question that the conclusion answers or expands on. Or, maybe they both include a quotation by the same person. Perhaps the statistics raised in both parts of the essay complement each other. Take this opportunity to bring your introduction and your conclusion together in a way that is satisfying for the reader.

Grammar Workshops

Guide to Useful Terms and Concepts for Understanding Grammar

active voice	active voice verbs show that the subject of the sentence does the action	We made a mistake.
adjective	a word that modifies a noun or pronoun; adjectives often answer questions such as *which? how many? what kind?*	Mr. Everett scolded the two rowdy children.
adverb	a word that modifies a verb, an adjective, another adverb, or a clause; adverbs often answer the questions *where? when? how? why? to what extent? under what conditions?*	His gratingly loud voice always bothered me, but it was especially bad in the park.
antecedent	the noun, pronoun, or phrase that a pronoun refers to	The contestant who answers the most questions correctly will win the jackpot. (pronoun "who" refers to antecedent "contestant")
clause	a group of words that includes a subject and a verb	My grandmother made a cake. (*independent clause*) You are wonderful. (*independent clause*) Because we liked the movie (*dependent clause*)
collective noun	a noun that indicates a group or collection of people or things: *team, group, committee, audience, bunch*	The team threw up its hands.
comparative	a form of an adjective or adverb used to compare two things; many adjectives form the comparative with *-er*, and many adverbs form the comparative with *more*	My brother is taller than I am. She works more quickly than Jack does.

(*continued*)

Guide to Useful Terms and Concepts for Understanding Grammar

compound noun	two or more nouns joined with *and*, *or*, or *nor*	Neither Juan nor his brothers took the class. The drummer and the bassist kept the beat.
coordinating conjunction	a word that connects words, phrases, or clauses of equal importance: *for, and, nor, but, or, yet, so*	The girl laughed, but her mother got angry.
correlative conjunction	a two-part conjunction	either . . . or, both . . . and, neither . . . nor, not only . . . but also, just as . . . so, whether . . . or
helping verb	a form of *be* or *have* or other verbs (*will, would, can, could, should, may, might, must*) that work along with a main verb	I am going home. You may need help. They have been friends for years. He had not started the project.
indefinite pronoun	a pronoun that does not refer to specific people or things: *everyone, someone, everything, anything, nothing, either, none, all, much*	Everyone loves tacos.
independent clause	a clause with both a subject and verb; a clause that does not include a subordinating conjunction	Both boys will arrive on time.
intransitive verb	a verb that does not take an object	Go over there and lie down.
irregular verb	a verb that does not follow a regular pattern; most irregular verbs are irregular in the past tense form and/or in the past participle form, but some common verbs (*be* and *have*) are also irregular in the present tense	We shook hands. (irregular past tense form; a regular verb would add *-d* or *-ed*) We have shaken hands. (irregular past participle form; a regular verb would add *-d* or *-ed*) I am hungry. (irregular first person present tense form; a regular verb would use the base form) He has your address. (irregular third person present tense form; a regular verb would add *-s*)
linking verb	a verb that indicates a state of being, rather than an action; linking verbs do not take objects, but are followed by subject complements that take an adjective form: *be, look, appear, seem, feel, sound, smell*	The soup smelled good. You seem angry. We feel terrible about the misunderstanding. She is correct.

Guide to Useful Terms and Concepts for Understanding Grammar

noun	a word that names a person, place, thing, or idea	The children sulked as their father fed them vegetables. Anger is bad for your health.
noun phrase	a phrase that functions as a noun in a sentence	Imagining possibilities is my job. (The phrase *imagining possibilities* acts as a noun and serves as the subject of the sentence.)
number	singular or plural verb	He eats pasta. (verb agrees with singular subject) They eat their vegetables. (verb agrees with plural subject)
object	the noun or pronoun (or noun phrase or clause) that receives the action of a transitive verb	She sent a package.
passive voice	passive voice verbs show that the subject of the sentence is being acted on; passive voice uses a form of the helping verb *be* plus a past participle	A mistake was made.
past participle form	the form of a verb, usually ending in *-ed*, used with a helping verb to form perfect tenses	They have been friends for years. (*have been* is a present perfect verb phrase) He had not started the project. (*had . . . started* is a past perfect verb phrase)
person	first person (*I, we*), second person (*you*), or third person (*he, she, it, they*) point of view	I am watching you. (verb agrees with first person subject) You have my attention. (verb agrees with second person subject) She plays remarkably well. (verb agrees with third person subject)
phrase	a group of words that lacks a subject, a verb, or both	without a care in the world
present participle	the form of a verb, usually ending in *-ing*, used with a helping verb to form continuous tenses	He is thinking of a song he used to know.
pronoun	a word that stands in for a noun, another pronoun, a noun clause, or a noun phrase: *I, me, you, he, she, it, him, her, we, us, they, them*	We were best friends until she moved and we lost touch.
relative pronoun	*who, which, that* used as the subject of a dependent clause, with the antecedent in another clause	The contestant who answers the most questions correctly will win the jackpot. (relative pronoun begins the dependent clause "who answers the most questions correctly")

(*continued*)

Guide to Useful Terms and Concepts for Understanding Grammar		
subject	part of a sentence or clause that tells who or what is doing an action, occurring, or existing; an essential part of a clause or sentence	My grandmother made a cake. You are wonderful. Both boys will arrive on time.
subject complement	an adjective that follows a linking verb and describes the subject of a sentence	The soup smelled good. (*good* describes *the soup*) You seem angry. (*angry* describes *you*) We feel terrible about the misunderstanding. (*terrible* describes *we*) She is correct. (*correct* describes *she*)
subordinate clause (also called dependent clause)	a clause that includes a subordinating conjunction; a clause that cannot stand alone	Because we liked the movie (*Because* is a subordinating conjunction)
subordinating conjunction	a connecting word that makes a clause dependent (unable to stand alone): *after, although, because, before, if, even if, since, unless, until, when, while*	After you ate lunch Because we liked the movie Until the light turned green
superlative	a form of an adjective or adverb used to compare more than two things; many adjectives form the superlative with *-est,* and many adverbs form the superlative with *most*	Dan is the tallest person on the team. Of all the employees, Rashida writes most effectively.
transitive verb	a verb that takes an object	We made a mistake. (the verb *make* is transitive; the object, *mistake*, shows what is made)
verb	an action, state, or occurrence; an essential part of a clause or sentence	My cousin made a cake. You are wonderful. Both boys will arrive on time.
verbal	words that are made of verb forms but do not function as verbs	Driving makes me nervous. To sleep late was a treat.
verb tense	verb tense shows whether the verb's action or state happened or will happen in the past, present, or future; tenses include past, past perfect, present, present perfect, future, and future perfect	*past:* You wanted a car. *past perfect:* You had wanted a car for years when you finally got one. *present:* You want a car. *perfect:* You have wanted a car for years. *future:* You will want a car someday. *future perfect:* You will have wanted a car for years when you finally get one.

Understanding Active and Passive Voice

The voice of a verb indicates whether the subject of a sentence is acting or being acted on.

For definitions and examples of grammar concepts—key to understanding active and passive voice—see the **Guide to Grammar Terms** table *on pages 1101–1104.*

Active Voice

Active voice means that the subject of the sentence is doing the action.

> The guidance counselor advised him to take challenging classes.

The subject is *guidance counselor,* the verb is *advised,* and the object is *him.* The guidance counselor is doing the advising, so the sentence is in the active voice.

Passive Voice

Passive voice means that the subject is being acted on by someone or something. A passive voice verb phrase includes a form of *be* plus a past participle.

> He was advised to take challenging classes.

The subject is *he,* and the verb is *was advised.* This sentence doesn't say who was doing the advising; if it did, it would say something like this: *The guidance counselor advised him to take challenging classes.*

Revising Inappropriate Passive Voice

Passive voice is not always wrong. However, when it is used inappropriately, it can make sentences vague. In general, you should use the active voice in academic writing, because it clearly indicates who is doing what, and because it makes the prose more immediate.

> INAPPROPRIATE PASSIVE VOICE
> The championship will be won by us.

The performer of the action should be the subject of this sentence unless the writer has a good reason to emphasize the championship and de-emphasize those who will win it.

To change passive voice to active voice, identify the doer of the action. If it is a pronoun, as in this case, change it from an object form (*me, her, us, them,* and so on) to a subject form (*I, she, we, they,* and so on). Make the doer the subject of the sentence and change the verb from the passive form (a form of *be* plus a past participle) to the active form in the same tense.

> ACTIVE VOICE
> We will win the championship.

Breaking the Rule: Uses of the Passive Voice

Note that the passive voice is useful in some circumstances, such as when you don't know who did the action or when you want to emphasize the recipient of the action rather than the doer.

> APPROPRIATE PASSIVE VOICE
> Several seniors were swindled out of their savings.

Those doing the swindling may be unknown, or the writer may want to focus attention on the seniors who were tricked — or both. The passive voice is appropriate in either case.

You may see the passive voice used fairly often in some kinds of professional writing. In journalism, for example, the passive voice emphasizes the recipient of the action, who may be more newsworthy than the doer of the action.

> APPROPRIATE PASSIVE VOICE
> John McCain was first elected to the Senate in 1986.

The writer wants to emphasize the senator rather than the voters who elected him. In addition, using the passive voice is expected or even required in much scientific and technical writing.

APPROPRIATE PASSIVE VOICE

Study participants were asked to describe what they had seen.

Although the active voice often produces more energetic writing, don't avoid the passive voice if using it is conventional for the type of writing you are doing or if you can use it purposefully to achieve appropriate emphasis or another desired effect.

ACTIVITY 1 Identifying Passive and Active Voice

In the following sentences, underline the complete subject and double-underline the verb or verb phrase. Then, identify whether the sentence is in the active voice or the passive voice.

EXAMPLE: The children were sitting listlessly under the only tree on the playground. *Active*

1. According to scientists, bird populations are declining in North America.
2. The players were discouraged by a string of defeats.
3. After the accident, recommendations were made for improving safety at the intersection.
4. Servers are expected to report their tips.
5. The guidance counselor will be conducting a workshop on college applications this afternoon.

ACTIVITY 2 Changing Passive Voice to Active Voice

In each of the following sentences, change any passive-voice constructions to active voice.

EXAMPLE: As I jogged around the lake at dawn, the attention of a stray dog was attracted by the sound of my footsteps.

REVISION: *As I jogged around the lake at dawn, the sound of my footsteps attracted the attention of a stray dog.*

1. When the pigeons were startled by a barking dog, the whole flock ascended from the parking lot with loudly flapping wings.
2. The bridge was weakened by the rushing flood waters that came with the spring thaw.
3. Mistakes were admitted by the police officers during the press conference, but the crowd did not think the apology went far enough.
4. The dessert appeared after a spectacular banquet had been served by our hosts.
5. Free tickets were being given by the promoters to anyone who had a valid student ID.

ACTIVITY 3 Revising a Paragraph for More Effective Use of Passive and Active Voice

The following paragraph, written for a general audience, includes some inappropriate use of the passive voice. Revise the paragraph to make more effective use of active voice. Note that not all sentences require revision. Be prepared to explain why you decided to make any change.

Cats have long been seen as aloof and uninterested in human companionship. Even cat lovers may believe that cats are motivated more by a desire for food than by an interest in social interaction when they seek out human beings. But it has been suggested by several recent studies that cats do, in fact, bond with human companions. Cats domesticated themselves in prehistoric times — unlike dogs, who were intentionally domesticated by humans. Could it be that cats actually like to spend time with people, or that at least some cats like to be around some people some of the time? The answer given by scientists who study cats is a clear "yes." In one study, cats were brought to an unfamiliar place by their owners, and then the cats were left alone for a while to look around. When the owners returned, a majority of the cats acknowledged the familiar humans right away and then continued investigating the new space. It is believed that this behavior shows "secure attachment" in the same way that babies feel attached to caregivers. Other studies show that cats know their own names, even if they do not always come when they are called by humans, and that familiar humans are preferred over strangers by cats. Dog lovers may not be persuaded by such research that cats care about humans as much as dogs do. However, people who love cats will probably be happy to hear that affection for its owner can actually be felt by a cat and that the bond between human and cat can at least sometimes be mutual.

ACTIVITY 4 Revising Passive and Active Voice in Your Own Writing

Look over the most recent writing you've done to see if you have used the passive voice in any inappropriate ways. As you review, revise any inappropriate uses of passive voice you find. If you find any examples of passive voice that you believe are appropriate and serve a specific purpose, write a note explaining why you believe they do not require revision.

workshop 2 Adjectives and Adverbs

Understanding Adjectives and Adverbs

Adjectives and adverbs are both modifiers that help make your writing more lively and specific. Adjectives modify nouns and pronouns; adverbs modify verbs, adjectives, and other adverbs.

Common problems with adjectives and adverbs happen when writers confuse adjectives and adverbs or have trouble using comparative and superlative forms appropriately.

For definitions and examples of grammar concepts key to understanding adjectives and adverbs, see the ***Guide to Grammar Terms*** *table on pages 1101–1104.*

Revising Adjectives and Adverbs

In informal speech, many people use adjectives in place of adverbs, most often saying *real* instead of *really, good* instead of *well,* and *bad* instead of *badly.* They also use adverbs in place of adjectives, especially after linking verbs such as *feel.* In formal writing, be sure you choose the right word for the job.

To check for adjective-adverb confusion, identify the word or phrase being modified. If it is a verb, an adjective, or another adverb, make sure the modifier is an adverb.

Adjective Used When Adverb Is Needed

The cow must have jumped real high to get over the moon.

An adjective, *high,* is being modified. The modifier should be an adverb, not the adjective *real.*

REVISION

The cow must have jumped really high to get over the moon.

If the modifier follows a linking verb such as *seem, feel,* or *be,* the modifier should be an adjective.

Adverb Used When Adjective Is Needed

She felt badly about her angry words.

The modifier follows the linking verb *felt,* so the modifier is a subject complement, and the word being modified is the subject, *she.* The modifier should be the adjective *bad,* not the adverb *badly.*

REVISION

She felt bad about her angry words.

Using *Well* Correctly

Finally, take extra care with the word *well,* which is usually an adverb but also serves as an adjective when it means "healthy": *I am not well today.*

WELL AS AN ADVERB

They work well together.

WELL AS AN ADJECTIVE

Two weeks after the fever began, he was finally well again.

Using Comparative and Superlative Forms

When you use adjectives and adverbs to compare two or more things, you'll need to use comparative (*happier, more effectively*) and superlative (*happiest, most effectively*) forms. Comparative forms of many short adjectives add *-er,* while superlative forms typically add *-est.* Comparative forms of most adverbs use *more,* while superlative forms typically use *most.* However, many adjectives and adverbs have irregular comparative or superlative forms.

Wrong Form of Comparative or Superlative

The most common problems with comparative and superlative adjectives and adverbs include using the wrong form, using a comparative when a superlative is needed (or vice versa), and using double comparatives or superlatives.

If you aren't sure of the standard comparative or superlative form for a particular adjective or adverb, check a dictionary.

The day at the water park was the ~~funnest time~~ *most fun* I ever had.

The speech was poorly written, and his delivery was even ~~worser~~ *worse*.

Comparative-Superlative Confusion

If you are comparing two items, use the comparative form. If you are comparing three or more items, use the superlative.

When my brother and I used to race, he was always ~~fastest~~ *faster*.

Two people — *my brother* and *I* — are being compared, so the comparative form is needed.

The doctor asked some of the ~~stranger~~ *strangest* questions she had ever heard.

She has heard more than two questions in her lifetime, so the superlative form is needed.

Double Comparatives or Superlatives

Using double comparatives or superlatives is seen as an error in academic and formal English.

> The visiting team was ~~more~~ better prepared than the local one.

> Her ~~most~~ hardest task was developing self-confidence.

Breaking the Rule: Using Adjectives and Adverbs Informally

Once you understand how to use adjectives and adverbs appropriately in formal and academic writing, you may notice adjectives used in place of adverbs, double comparatives and superlatives, and other nonstandard usage in writing that aims for an informal tone — for example, in advertisements (like Apple's *"Think different"* slogan) or dialogue. Using adjectives and adverbs informally, the way many speakers do, can give your writing a casual flavor that may be appropriate in some situations.

ACTIVITY 1 Identifying Problems with Adjectives and Adverbs

In each of the following sentences, underline every adjective and double-underline every adverb. If the sentence contains an error, identify the problem. If the sentence is correct, write *Correct*.

EXAMPLE: The dog smelled badly, so we gave him a bath.

PROBLEM: *An adjective should follow a linking verb like "smelled," but "badly" is an adverb.*

1. She felt terribly sick and performed poor on the test.

   PROBLEM: ______

2. My mother and father argue about which of them does the most work around the house.

   PROBLEM: ______

3. The exhausted boy behaved badly in the grocery store.

   PROBLEM: ______

4. People who get a small amount of exercise are usually more healthier than people who sit all day.

   PROBLEM: ______

5. The engine was running smooth until the car began to cross the desert at the hottest time of the day.

   PROBLEM: ______

ACTIVITY 2 Revising Adjective and Adverb Errors

Correct any adjective or adverb errors in the following sentences. If the sentence is correct as written, write *Correct.* Be prepared to explain why you made each revision.

EXAMPLE: I could not have asked for a more better friend.

REVISION: *I could not have asked for a better friend.*

1. July is one of the hotter months of the year in Chicago.

   REVISION: ______

2. We were glad we had camped out overnight to get tickets to the concert because the line was real long by morning.

   REVISION: ______

3. Both teams played poorly, and the result was one of the boringest games Karina had ever seen.

   REVISION: ______

4. Suddenly, the rain stopped, and a spectacularly beautiful double rainbow appeared.

   REVISION: ______

5. The cake looked delicious, but it tasted terribly.

   REVISION: ______

ACTIVITY 3 Revising a Paragraph for Adjective and Adverb Problems

The following paragraph was written for a general audience and may include adjective and adverb problems. Revise the paragraph to correct any issues you identify.

Copenhagen, the capital of Denmark, tops many lists as the world's bestest city for riding bicycles. More bicycles than cars cross the city each day, with near 40% of Copenhagen residents biking regularly to work. Infrastructure in the capital city encourages biking. Copenhagen is fairly flat, so bike riders do not face any real difficult hills or other obstacles. For short trips, Copenhagen residents seem to feel badly about driving when they can bike instead. For longer trips, however, cycling to work instead of driving has not always seemed like the best option. Commuting by bike must be easy, or people will not do it. Therefore, planners have tried to ensure that biking is the most fastest way to get to work, even for those who live outside Copenhagen. Biking distances of more than three or four miles used to be difficulter than it is now. But the towns surrounding Copenhagen have built bike superhighways separated from roads to encourage cyclists to ride to the capital. These bike superhighways, with well-maintained pavement and lights, allow even long-distance riders to bike safe in Denmark. When biking is the efficientest way to travel, who needs a car?

ACTIVITY 4 Revising Adjectives and Adverbs in Your Own Writing

Look over the most recent writing you've done to see if you have used any adjectives or adverbs in nonstandard ways. As you review, revise any adjectives and adverbs you find that are likely to seem like mistakes to your readers. If you find any adjectives or adverbs that you used to create dialogue, an informal tone, or a specific effect and that seem to serve their purpose, write a note explaining why you believe they do not require revision.

workshop 3 Capitalization

Understanding Capitalization

Capitalization marks proper nouns, proper adjectives, and many words in titles of books, films, and other works, as well as the first words of sentences and lines of poetry. Following conventions for capitalization can help prevent confusion.

For definitions and examples of grammar concepts key to understanding capitalization, see the ***Guide to Grammar Terms*** *table on pages 1101–1104.*

Proper Nouns and Proper Adjectives

A proper noun is the name of a specific person, place, or thing. Proper nouns are always capitalized, and so are the proper adjectives that are formed from proper nouns.

PROPER NOUN	PROPER ADJECTIVE
Charles Dickens	Dickensian

In some cases, a noun may be capitalized when it is part of a name, but not capitalized when it is a common noun that refers to a generic instance.

PROPER NOUN	COMMON NOUN
Cuyahoga River	a river
Psychology 101	reverse psychology
Washington Monument	a monument

Proper nouns and proper adjectives typically fall into the following categories:

NAMES, TITLES PRECEDING NAMES

Barry Jenkins
Mighty Mouse
Senator McCain

NATIONS, NATIONALITIES, LANGUAGES

Argentina
Puerto Rican
Spanish

PLACES

Rockaway Beach
Columbus, Georgia
Main Street

MONUMENTS, STRUCTURES, SHIPS, TRAINS, AIRCRAFT, SPACECRAFT

Vietnam Veterans' Memorial
Grand Central Terminal
USS *Indianapolis*
Acela
Spirit of St. Louis
Apollo 13

ORGANIZATIONS, BUSINESSES, ACADEMIC AND GOVERNMENT INSTITUTIONS, SPECIFIC COURSE NAMES

League of Women Voters
General Electric
Harvard University
Federal Bureau of Investigation
Introduction to Sociology

BRANDS

Sensodyne
Android

ERAS AND HISTORICAL EVENTS

the Jurassic period
the Civil War

DAYS OF THE WEEK, MONTHS, HOLIDAYS

Tuesday
September
Thanksgiving

RELIGIONS AND RELIGIOUS TERMS

Hinduism
Holy Week
the Qur'an

Titles

Most words in titles and subtitles of creative works such as films, books, articles, and songs should be capitalized. In general, capitalize the first and last word of a title or subtitle and all important words. Typically, you will not capitalize *a, an,* or *the,* most prepositions, the word *to,* or coordinating conjunctions such as *and* and *or* unless they are the first or last word of a title or subtitle.

It's a Wonderful Life

Pride and Prejudice

"I Want to Hold Your Hand"

Revising Unnecessary Capitalization

Capitalizing words that don't need to be capitalized may be an even more common problem than failing to capitalize proper nouns. The following categories often cause problems.

Unnecessary Capitalization of Titles

Professor Mary Jackson was my history ~~Professor~~ *professor* last semester.

Don't capitalize titles or occupations such as *doctor except* when they directly precede a person's name (*Dr. Brown*).

Unnecessary Capitalization of Relationship Word

My ~~Father's~~ *father's* Aunt Annie has always been my favorite relative.

Don't capitalize a family relationship word unless it is used as a substitute for a name or as part of a name.

We asked Dad to give his advice.

Unnecessary Capitalization of a Compass Direction

The path of the eclipse moves ~~West~~ *west* to ~~East~~ *east*, beginning in the Pacific Northwest.

Don't capitalize compass directions (*north, south, east, west, northwest,* and so on) unless you are using them to refer to a geographical region.

Unnecessary Capitalization of Seasons

What classes are you taking this ~~Fall~~ *fall*?

Don't capitalize seasons (*spring, summer, fall, winter*).

Breaking the Rule: Changing Conventions for Capitalization

Some people's names and brands use unconventional capitalization. If a brand or product uses capital letters in the middle of a word, as in *iPad or FedEx,* write the name as given in company advertising or on the product itself. Capitalize a person's name following the person's own preferences: *bell hooks, Valerie van der Graaf.*

ACTIVITY 1 Identifying Capitalization Errors

In the following sentences, write *Missing* if any required capitalization is missing, *Unnecessary* if there is unnecessary capitalization, or *Correct* if the sentence includes no errors in capitalization.

EXAMPLES: Felicia and her Husband spent their Winter break in Alabama. *Unnecessary*

We went to grandma's house after school. *Missing*

1. When Spring comes, I want to see the Rocky Mountains.
2. During the depression, senator Huey Long of Louisiana introduced a program to limit individual wealth.
3. The committee meeting will be cancelled for the next two Tuesdays.
4. She is a Film major, but her favorite class last semester was Human Biology.
5. Harold would like to buy a new iphone next year, so he took a part-time job at Johnson's Garden Depot.

ACTIVITY 2 Revising Capitalization Errors

Revise each of the following items to correct capitalization errors.

EXAMPLE: The Washington state department of transportation operates Ferries from Seattle to Bainbridge Island.

REVISION: *The Washington State Department of Transportation operates ferries from Seattle to Bainbridge Island.*

1. My father chose Hans Christian Andersen's Fairy Tale "the Little Mermaid" as a bedtime story because he was familiar with the Disney Movie.

   REVISION: ______________________________

2. The doctor told Mrs. Sandoval that she should get a flu shot before the New Year.

   REVISION: ______________________________

3. She studied spanish and art history before she decided to become a Librarian.

   REVISION: ______________________________

4. Congress unanimously chose George Washington to lead the continental army during the American revolution, but as Commander-in-Chief, he accepted no wages.

   REVISION: ______________________________

5. The Empire state building has appeared in many films, including *King Kong* and *Sleepless In Seattle*.

   REVISION: ______________________________

ACTIVITY 3 Revising a Paragraph for Capitalization

The following paragraph was written for a general audience and may include problems with capitalization. Revise the paragraph to correct any problems you find. Some sentences may not contain errors.

New York City has a number of statues of female figures, including Central Park's statue of Alice from *Through the looking glass.* However, of all the city's Public statues, only five feature women who actually lived. Visitors will find two of the five in Riverside Park along the Hudson river. One is a statue of Joan Of Arc, a french martyr who lived in the

Fifteenth Century. The other is Eleanor Roosevelt, who was first lady of the United States throughout world war II. Bryant Park is home to a statue of Gertrude Stein, the Author of *the Autobiography of Alice B. Toklas.* The intersection of Broadway and 39th Street is known as Golda Meir square and features a bust of Meir, a woman raised in the American midwest who became Israel's first female Prime Minister in 1969. The fifth is a statue of Harriet Tubman, who escaped from slavery and helped dozens of others flee to Freedom. Fortunately, several new statues of women from History are planned. A statue featuring suffragists will include Elizabeth Cady Stanton and Susan B. Anthony, who fought for a woman's Right to Vote, and Sojourner Truth, whose speech "Ain't I a woman" noted that african american women needed the Vote as well. In addition, the "She built NYC" campaign is creating several new Monuments to pioneering women. If all goes well, New York City may soon have more statues of women to look up to.

ACTIVITY 4 Revising Capitalization in Your Own Writing

Look over the most recent writing you've done to see if you made any errors with capitalization. As you review, add any missing capital letters and change any unnecessary capital letters that you find.

workshop 4 Comma Splices and Run-On Sentences

Understanding Comma Splices and Run-On (Fused) Sentences

A comma splice is a sentence with two independent clauses, each one able to stand on its own, that are connected with nothing more than a comma.

COMMA SPLICE

Bad weather threatened the harvest, the storm clouds suddenly separated and revealed blue skies.

A run-on sentence, also called a fused sentence, runs two independent clauses together without any kind of punctuation or conjunction.

RUN-ON

Bad weather threatened the harvest the storm clouds suddenly separated and revealed blue skies.

"Bad weather threatened the harvest" and "the storm clouds suddenly separated and revealed blue skies" are both independent clauses that could be separate sentences. Connecting them with a comma alone results in a comma splice, and connecting them with no punctuation between them results in a run-on sentence.

Both clauses include subjects (*Bad weather* and *the storm clouds*), and both include verbs (*threatened* and the compound verb *separated and revealed*). Neither begins with a subordinating conjunction, which can turn an independent clause into a subordinate clause.

To understand and fix comma splices and run-ons, you'll need to recognize independent clauses, which must include a subject and a verb and do *not* begin with a subordinating conjunction such as *because.*

*For definitions and examples of grammar concepts key to understanding comma splices and run-ons, see the **Guide to Grammar Terms** table on pages 1101–1104.*

Revising Comma Splices and Run-Ons

Comma splices and run-ons can cause problems for readers because the relationship between the two independent clauses isn't clear. When you fix an inappropriate comma splice or a run-on sentence, you have several options. Each option connects the ideas in different ways, so which method you choose is up to you and depends on what you want to communicate.

Separate the Clauses into Two Sentences

If the ideas in the two independent clauses are not closely related, you can use a period to separate the independent clauses into two complete sentences:

> Bad weather threatened the harvest. The storm clouds suddenly separated and revealed blue skies.

Join the Clauses with a Semicolon

A semicolon can separate two independent clauses in a single sentence. Revising this way suggests a closer connection between the clauses than making two separate sentences.

> Bad weather threatened the harvest; the storm clouds suddenly separated and revealed blue skies.

Adding a conjunctive adverb such as *however* after the semicolon adds more information about the relationship between the clauses.

> Bad weather threatened the harvest; however, the storm clouds suddenly separated and revealed blue skies.

Join the Clauses with a Comma and a Coordinating Conjunction

Connecting independent clauses with a comma and a coordinating conjunction (*for, and, nor, but, or, yet, so*) indicates that the two clauses are equally important and closely connected.

> Bad weather threatened the harvest, but the storm clouds suddenly separated and revealed blue skies.

Rewrite One of the Independent Clauses as a Subordinate Clause

If one of the clauses is less important, or leads to the other clause, you can make it a dependent clause by beginning with a subordinating conjunction.

> Although bad weather threatened the harvest, the storm clouds suddenly separated and revealed blue skies.

Adding the subordinating conjunction *although* to the beginning of the first clause creates a subordinate clause that can be joined to the independent clause that follows. (Notice that when you begin a sentence with a subordinate clause, you should follow it with a comma.)

> Bad weather threatened the harvest until the storm clouds suddenly separated and revealed blue skies.

Adding the subordinating conjunction *until* to the beginning of the second clause creates a subordinate clause that can be joined to the initial independent clause. This revision emphasizes the bad weather, not the blue skies that followed. (Notice that when the subordinate clause follows the independent clause, you don't usually separate the clauses with a comma — unless the subordinate clause begins with *although* or another conjunction that shows contrast.)

Breaking the Rule: Appropriate Uses of Comma Splices

Once you understand what comma splices are and how to avoid creating them by mistake, you may start to notice comma splices in writing that aims for an informal tone — for example, in advertisements and social media messages. Used intentionally, comma splices, especially those that include very short clauses, can help writing sound casually conversational.

> My sister saves, my brother splurges. I'm somewhere in between.

As with any literary technique, comma splices should be used with care. In academic and other formal writing, many readers will always see a comma splice as a mistake. For that reason, you should think about your audience before you decide to include a comma splice.

ACTIVITY 1 Identifying Comma Splices and Run-Ons

Underline every independent clause in the following examples. Identify any comma splices or run-ons. If a sentence is correct, write *Correct.*

EXAMPLES: The squirrels in the park are fearless, one tried to steal my lunch. *Comma splice*
Although they are fun to watch, people should not feed them. *Correct*

1. Vintage film posters can be expensive, but fans of old movies may be able to find moderately priced copies.
2. The chair was bright yellow, the color seemed appealing to me but revolting to my sister.
3. South of town is a reservoir where people swim in warm weather the water is cool and inviting.
4. She left her jacket in the cafeteria when she came back, it was gone.
5. Try to listen to him politely, ignore everything that he asks you to do.

ACTIVITY 2 Revising Comma Splices and Run-Ons

Rewrite each of the following items to eliminate the comma splices and run-ons. Revise each item in two different ways, using any of the methods discussed above for fixing comma splices and run-ons.

EXAMPLE: The palm trees whipped back and forth a hurricane was coming.

REVISION 1: *The palm trees whipped back and forth; a hurricane was coming.*

REVISION 2: *The palm trees whipped back and forth because a hurricane was coming.*

1. In centuries past, people wore makeup to hide blemishes sometimes the makeup contained deadly ingredients, such as mercury or lead.

   REVISION 1: ______________________________

   REVISION 2: ______________________________

2. Every town in the county contributed a float to the annual parade, local high schools sent marching bands led by drum majors and baton twirlers.

   REVISION 1: ______________________________

   REVISION 2: ______________________________

3. Knowing how to cook is an important part of sticking to a budget if you have to buy prepared food, you will spend more money.

REVISION 1: ____________________

REVISION 2: ____________________

4. The house sat on a corner lot, when snow fell, Roberto had to shovel two sidewalks instead of one.

REVISION 1: ____________________

REVISION 2: ____________________

5. The setting sun lined up precisely between the tall buildings, a red-orange glow lit up both the sky and the faces of pedestrians.

REVISION 1: ____________________

REVISION 2: ____________________

ACTIVITY 3 Revising a Paragraph for Comma Splices and Run-Ons

The following paragraph was written for a general audience and may include comma splices and run-ons. Revise the paragraph to correct any problems you find. Some sentences may not contain errors.

Knolling is a method of arranging objects, the arrangement places items in straight lines or at right angles to each other. The term "knolling" was invented by a janitor who worked for a furniture designer in the 1980s the janitor, Andrew Kromelow, liked to arrange and photograph his tools in clean lines and rows that reminded him of the company's Knoll furniture. Curators may use knolling to depict collections in intriguing ways. Museums display items such as pencils, flyswatters, and mobile phones using knolling visitors may find the patterns more interesting than any individual object. Knolling, sometimes called "flat lay," can also be a way to look at all the small parts that make up a whole for instance, some knollers have taken photos of all the items they are taking on a trip. Other knolling experiments include lining up many similar items by color, a photo of pieces of toast arranged each slice from untoasted to burned. Recently, some larger-scale knolling has made a splash on social media, with paramedics and firefighters lying on the ground at right angles next to their vehicles and gear the images are captured by drone. Viewers may think at first that these pictures show toys and dolls, they show life-sized equipment and real human beings. Many people find something very pleasing about the orderly arrangement of everyday objects, images of knolled items that are well organized and well photographed can attract a lot of attention online. Who knows those images may also inspire others to get knolling.

ACTIVITY 4 Revising Comma Splices and Run-Ons in Your Own Writing

Look over the most recent writing you've done to see if you have created any comma splices or run-ons. As you review, revise any comma splices or run-ons you find that are likely to seem like mistakes to your readers. If you find a comma splice that you used intentionally and that seems to serve its purpose, write a note explaining why you believe it does not require revision.

Understanding Coordination and Subordination

Workshop 4 (see p. 1114) explains how to use coordination and subordination to fix run-on and comma splice errors. Coordination and subordination are not simply correctness issues, however. They are ways of joining parts of sentences to emphasize important ideas, give readers information, and vary rhythm. Knowing how to use them well can make your writing clearer and more interesting to read.

Coordination joins two ideas with a **coordinating conjunction** to show that both ideas are equally important. Subordination joins two ideas with a **subordinating conjunction** to show that one idea is less important than the other.

For definitions and examples of grammar concepts key to understanding coordination and subordination, see the ***Guide to Grammar Terms*** *table on pages 1101–1104.*

Coordination

Coordinating conjunctions join ideas of equal importance. The coordinating conjunctions are *and, but, for, nor, or, so,* and *yet.* Coordinating conjunctions can join **words** (*Maxine and Jackson*), **phrases** (*a box of chocolates or a dozen roses*), or **independent clauses** that could stand on their own as sentences (*I sat at the desk, but I could not study*). When you use coordinating conjunctions to join clauses, place a comma before the conjunction.

The conjunction you choose tells readers something about the relationship between the clauses joined.

COORDINATION TO SHOW ADDITION

Maxine picked up the books from the library, and Jackson returned them.

COORDINATION TO SHOW CHOICE

Your mother might like a box of chocolates for her birthday, or you could give her flowers.

COORDINATION TO SHOW CONTRAST

We were tired, but we were too excited to sleep.

COORDINATION TO SHOW RESULTS

The bus was late, so we started walking to school.

Subordination

Like coordination, subordination links ideas and shows the relationships between them. However, subordination de-emphasizes one clause to indicate that the other clause is more important. The less emphatic clause, called a **dependent clause** or **subordinate clause**, is indicated by a subordinating conjunction. Dependent clauses such as *when I woke up* cannot stand on their own as sentences because their sense depends on information in another clause. When the dependent clause comes first in the sentence, you should put a comma after it; when the dependent clause follows an independent clause, no comma is used.

Some common subordinating conjunctions show how clauses are related in time (*before, after, until, while, when*), indicate cause and effect (*because*), or show that the relationship between the clauses is conditional (*if, although, unless*).

SUBORDINATION TO SHOW TIME

After Maxine brought the books home, Jackson started to read them.

SUBORDINATION TO SHOW CAUSE AND EFFECT

We started walking to school because the bus was late.

SUBORDINATION TO SHOW A CONDITIONAL RELATIONSHIP

If you give your mother flowers, you will delight her.

Relative pronouns such as *who*, *which,* and *that* can also introduce dependent clauses called **relative clauses**. Relative pronouns may refer to an antecedent in an independent clause. In such cases the relative clause usually acts as a modifier, describing the antecedent. In other cases, relative clauses can act as nouns and serve as the subject or object of an independent clause.

Relative Clause to Modify Antecedent

My sister, who prefers to keep her things tidy, hates sharing a room with me.

The relative pronoun *who* refers to the antecedent *sister*. The relative clause *who prefers to keep her things tidy* describes the sister. Subordinating the sister's preference for tidiness emphasizes the main idea, that she *hates sharing a room with me*.

Relative Clause Acting as a Noun

He said that he would wait.

The relative clause *that he would wait* acts as a noun in this sentence. It serves as the object of the verb *said*.

Simple, Compound, Complex, and Compound-Complex Sentences

A *simple sentence* consists of a single independent clause.

SIMPLE SENTENCE

A skunk walked out of the woods.

A sentence that joins two or more independent clauses with coordination is called a *compound sentence.*

COMPOUND SENTENCE

A skunk walked out of the woods, but it ignored me.

A sentence that joins two or more clauses with subordination is called a *complex sentence.*

COMPLEX SENTENCE

A skunk walked out of the woods *as I was walking my dog.*

Finally, a sentence that joins clauses with both coordination and subordination is a *compound-complex sentence.*

COMPOUND-COMPLEX SENTENCE

A skunk walked out of the woods *as I was walking my dog,* but it ignored me.

Joining Ideas with Coordination and Subordination

You can use coordination and subordination to transform short, choppy simple sentences into writing that is clearer and more interesting to read, as the following example shows.

NO COORDINATION OR SUBORDINATION

Marisol woke up. The sun was rising. She heard a strange sound outside. It was surprisingly loud. A pigeon was building a nest. Marisol thought. Baby pigeons might be fun to watch. They also might keep her awake.

REVISED

Marisol woke up as the sun was rising. She heard a strange sound outside, which was surprisingly loud. A pigeon was building a nest. Marisol thought that baby pigeons might be fun to watch, but they also might keep her awake.

The first two sentences in the revision are complex sentences that use subordination; the third remains a simple sentence; and the fourth uses both coordination and subordination to form a compound-complex sentence.

Sentences that are all roughly the same length and all follow roughly the same pattern can be boring for readers. Mixing things up with a combination of shorter and longer sentences, and using a combination of coordination and subordination to form compound, complex, and compound-complex sentences, helps to keep readers interested. Because only you can decide what you want to emphasize in your writing and what you want readers to know about the relationships among your ideas, you have many choices to make about coordination and subordination as a writer.

ACTIVITY 1 **Identifying Coordination and Subordination**

Underline every independent clause in the following sentences, double-underline every dependent (subordinate) clause, put parentheses around coordinating conjunctions, and put brackets around subordinating conjunctions. Then, identify the type of sentence.

EXAMPLE: Everyone told me [that] I would like camping, (but) I hated the bugs, (and) I could not sleep [because] I heard noises. *Compound-complex*

1. Because her headache had lasted for three days, she asked her doctor for migraine medication.
2. Seeing ladybugs in the garden makes me happy, and they are astonishingly good at killing pests such as aphids, so that fact makes me even happier.
3. People who drive too fast can cause accidents, but people who drive too slowly are equally dangerous.
4. We had planned to spend the day at the beach until we learned that only local residents were allowed to swim there.
5. Although the dog had never seen a Frisbee before, it turned out to be extremely good at catching one in midair, so we included it in our game.

ACTIVITY 2 **Revising Sentences with Coordination and Subordination**

Revise each of the following sets of simple sentences to create the type of sentence indicated.

EXAMPLE: The children played in the apple orchard in the spring. Bees covered the blossoms.

COMPLEX: The children played in the apple orchard in the spring when bees covered the blossoms.

1. The moving truck stopped outside the house. Movers began to carry boxes out and load them.

   COMPOUND: ______________________________

2. The hallway was dark and uninviting. The single lightbulb had burned out.

   COMPLEX: ______________________________

3. Maya's mother was angry with her. Maya had skipped school. Her mother refused to let her go to her friend's slumber party.

   COMPOUND-COMPLEX: ______________________________

4. It was the middle of summer. The sun set late. My little nephew did not want to go to bed before dark.

   COMPOUND: ______________________________

5. The neighborhood sponsored a mural by a local artist. The neighborhood had pulled together through tough times. The artist had studied abroad and returned.

   COMPLEX: ______________________________

ACTIVITY 3 Revising a Paragraph with Coordination and Subordination

The following paragraph consists mainly of simple sentences. Revise to make the paragraph more readable using coordination and subordination.

An event called NaNoWriMo happens every November. NaNoWriMo is short for National Novel Writing Month. You may want to write a novel. You should try it. Over the course of the month, you try to write 50,000 words. You can complete a short novel by the end of November. The daily total exceeds 1600 words. Completing 50,000 words makes you a winner. Nobody else has to see the writing. It does not have to be polished. Most participants simply try to pound out a complete first draft. They do not edit their work. They do not expect to end up with a perfect manuscript. November has just thirty days. That does not allow time for careful revision. Of course, you can continue work on your drafts after November ends. In fact, doing so is encouraged. Some books have been drafted during NaNoWriMo. They were later published. One writer even got a movie deal from a book. She wrote it during NaNoWriMo in 2006.

ACTIVITY 4 Using Coordination and Subordination in Your Own Writing

Look over the most recent writing you've done to see if you can use coordination or subordination more effectively to vary your sentences and keep readers interested.

workshop 6 Commonly Confused Words

Understanding Homophones

Many commonly confused words are homophones, words that sound the same but are spelled differently and have different meanings. If you use the wrong one, you may confuse or distract your readers.

For definitions and examples of grammar concepts key to understanding homophones, see the ***Guide to Grammar Terms*** *table on pages 1101–1104.*

While computer spellcheckers have made a huge difference for writers, spellcheckers cannot catch homophone errors because a wrong homophone is nevertheless a correctly spelled word. Finding and correcting homophone errors requires that you learn commonly confused words so you can avoid choosing the wrong one.

Revising Commonly Confused Words

These word groups are some of the most commonly confused. If you aren't sure where to begin to avoid homophone problems, start by learning to differentiate this manageable number of homophones.

accept/except

Accept is a verb that means *receive or agree.* *Except* is a preposition that means other than.

We accept the blame for eating all the plums except the unripe one.

advice/advise

Advice is a noun, and *advise* is a verb that means *give advice.*

Their advice was usually helpful, but I wanted someone else to advise me on this matter.

affect/effect

Generally, *affect* is used as a verb, and *effect* is used as a noun.

Our advice had no effect on his behavior, but it affected his view of us.

it's/its

It's is a contraction meaning *it is* or *it has. Its* is a possessive pronoun meaning *belonging to it*.

Everything in the dining room is in its proper place, so it's time to welcome the guests.

lead/led

Lead is a noun and refers to a metallic element. *Led* is the past tense of the verb *lead* (which rhymes with *seed*).

He led Professor Plum to the conservatory and accused him of murder with a lead pipe.

loose/lose

Loose is an adjective meaning *not tight* or *unrestrained. Lose* is a verb meaning *misplace.*

My sandal strap was loose, so I was afraid I might lose my shoe.

sight/site

A *sight* is something that is seen. A *site* is a place.

We went to the site hoping to meet others interested in the cause, but there was no one in sight.

than/then

Than is used in making comparisons; *then* is an adverb that answers the question *When?*

Carlos is taller than Marty now, but wait a few years and see what happens then.

their/there/they're

Their is a possessive pronoun meaning *belonging to them. There* is an adverb that answers the question *Where? They're* is a contraction that means *they are.*

Go over there and take their phones away. They're disrupting the class.

to/too/two

To is a preposition meaning *toward* or part of an infinitive verb form (*to be*). *Too* means *also. Two* is a number.

The two hikers were going to Brixton, too, so we gave them a ride.

weather/whether

Weather is a noun that refers to the atmospheric conditions. *Whether* is part of a correlative conjunction, *whether . . . or.*

Whether the weather cooperates or not, the wedding will happen tomorrow.

who's/whose

Who's is a contraction meaning *who is* or *who has. Whose* is a possessive pronoun that means *belonging to whom.*

Ahmed wants to know whose car we're taking and who's driving.

you're/your

You're is a contraction meaning *you are*. *Your* is a possessive pronoun that means *belonging to you.*

You're the one who answered your phone during the meeting.

ACTIVITY 1 Identifying Homophone Errors

In the following sentences, underline any word that is incorrectly used. If the sentence contains no homophone errors, write *Correct.*

EXAMPLE: If you eat at there restaurant, you're meal will be expensive but delicious.

1. The temperature this morning is much colder then yesterday, so remember too bundle up.

2. The coach told us to play as if we could not loose, but some of us could not accept his advise.

3. Patricia led the horse to it's stall.

4. The fishermen checked the weather forecast, wondering how their catch might be affected.

5. Anyone who's visiting the sight tomorrow must wear a hard hat.

ACTIVITY 2 Revising Homophone Errors

Revise each of the following items to correct homophone errors.

EXAMPLE: The man who's dog dug up our yard would not except responsibility for the damage.

REVISION: *The man whose dog dug up our yard would not accept responsibility for the damage.*

1. The neighbors held one of there loud parties and invited everyone accept Thomas.

REVISION: ______________________________

2. The site of my family waiting at the airport too meet me made me wonder weather moving away had been a good decision.

REVISION: ______________________________

3. A round-trip bus ticket is less expensive than two one-way tickets, but if my little brother looses it before the return journey, its not worth the cost.

REVISION: ______________________________

4. The pitcher through the ball wildly, and it past by the startled batter's ear.

REVISION: ______________________________

5. Your going to need you're wallet if you're planning to buy something to eat.

REVISION: ______________________________

ACTIVITY 3 Revising a Paragraph for Homophone Errors

A spellcheck found no problems with the following paragraph written for a student audience. Revise the paragraph to correct any homophone errors that you find. Some sentences may not contain errors.

You can find information online about almost any news story your interested in. However, its not always easy to tell weather what you've read is true. Their are different kinds of "fake news" and misinformation, and some are more harmful then others. Honest mistakes can be made buy anyone, including a professional journalist. Reputable news sources will publish corrections if material in they're publications turns out too be incorrect. At the other end of the spectrum is deliberate misinformation, which happens when an article is published by someone who's hole purpose is to trick you. Sometimes people create false stories for the money that advertising can bring; others want to influence people's beliefs or even make them loose faith in the idea of truth itself. If a story seems to outrageous to be true, it probably is, so the best advise is to investigate on your own. You should no that people are more likely to share information that confirms what they already believe. Never simply except that information is correct because you read it on a popular sight, because it has been shared widely, or because it tells a story you want to hear. A little research can help you find out the facts behind a story that might have lead you to believe a lie. To fight misinformation, do you're homework!

ACTIVITY 4 Revising Homophone Errors in Your Own Writing

Look over the most recent writing you've done to see if you have made any errors with homophones. As you review, correct any errors that you find.

workshop 7 Fragments

Understanding Fragments

A sentence fragment is a group of words that looks like a sentence but isn't a complete sentence. A sentence must include at least one independent clause, and it must have a subject and a verb. If any of those elements is missing, it's a fragment.

A fragment may happen when a writer treats a phrase or subordinate clause as if it were a complete sentence.

*For definitions and examples of grammar concepts key to understanding fragments, see the **Guide to Grammar Terms** on pages 1101–1104.*

PHRASE FRAGMENT

Barking and chasing the waves. The dog ran into the ocean.

"Barking and chasing the waves" is not a complete sentence. It has no subject and no complete verb, so it is a phrase, not an independent clause.

PHRASE FRAGMENT

The dog failed to catch the foam. But did not stop trying.

"But did not stop trying" has no subject, so it is neither a complete sentence nor an independent clause. The phrase is part of a compound verb (*failed . . . but did [not]stop*).

PHRASE FRAGMENT

The dog looked for help. With a funny expression on its face.

"With a funny expression on its face" is not a complete sentence. It includes no subject and no verb, so it is a phrase, not an independent clause.

SUBORDINATE CLAUSE FRAGMENT

Another dog stared for a while and then wandered away. Because the waves seemed impossible to catch.

"Because the waves seemed impossible to catch" is not a complete sentence. Although it has a subject (*the waves)* and a verb (*seemed),* the subordinating conjunction *because* means that it is a subordinate clause, not an independent clause.

Revising Fragments

To fix a fragment, you can either join it to another sentence or rewrite the fragment to turn it into a complete sentence.

JOIN A FRAGMENT TO ANOTHER SENTENCE

Barking and chasing the waves, the dog ran into the ocean. The dog failed to catch the foam but did not stop trying. The dog looked for help with a funny expression on its face. Another dog stared for a while, and then wandered away because the waves seemed impossible to catch.

TURN A FRAGMENT INTO A SENTENCE

The dog ran into the ocean. It was barking and chasing the waves. The dog failed to catch the foam. However, it did not stop trying. The dog looked for help. It had a funny expression on its face.

Another dog stared for a while and then wandered away. *The waves seemed impossible to catch.*

Notice that rewriting a fragment as a complete sentence may involve adding or removing words — or both.

Breaking the Rule: Appropriate Uses of Fragments

Once you understand what fragments are and how to avoid creating them by mistake, you may start to notice fragments in writing by professionals and experts. Used intentionally, fragments can be an effective way to add emphasis.

> We drove for hours, and finally we saw a motel. *Old and shabby, yes, but open.*
>
> The pillow exploded, and the feathers went everywhere. *On the bed. On the floor. Out the window.*

As with any literary technique, fragments should be used with care, but a good fragment can have a profound impact on your reader.

ACTIVITY 1 Identifying Fragments

Underline any fragments you find in the following examples. (Some items may not contain a fragment.)

EXAMPLE: My favorite comedy series is too unconventional. For my parents.

1. If more people lived downtown. The streets would not be deserted at night. The neighborhood is eerily quiet after dark.
2. Corn on the cob is my favorite summer treat. When local corn is ripe in August, I eat it every day. Not even ice cream tastes better.
3. Although zombie movies are usually horror films. Zombies can appear in any genre. Even comedy films.
4. Every afternoon, the plaza is filled with skateboarders. Practicing their jumps. While tourists record every move on their phones.
5. Because the train station needed repair, the city decided to demolish it. Inspiring a campaign to save the classic building. It was over 150 years old.
6. As Mary began the last mile of the marathon, the sun came out. A rainbow crossed the sky. Looking up, she felt she might finish after all.

ACTIVITY 2 Revising Fragments

Rewrite each of the following items to eliminate the sentence fragments. Revise each item in two different ways: (1) combine the fragment with a complete sentence, and (2) rewrite the fragment as a sentence of its own.

EXAMPLE: After the music stopped. The crowd waited patiently, hoping for another song.

REVISION 1: After the music stopped, the crowd waited patiently, hoping for another song.

REVISION 2: The music stopped. The crowd waited patiently, hoping for another song.

1. Because Roberto needed to stop for gas. He realized he would be late to work that morning.

   REVISION 1: ____________________

   REVISION 2: ____________________

2. Creepy gargoyles staring down from the top of the cathedral. The statues are also spouts that move rainwater away from the building.

   REVISION 1: ____________________

   REVISION 2: ____________________

3. The jewel thieves were athletic as well as bold. Hopping over an iron fence and scaling the museum's walls.

   REVISION 1: ____________________

   REVISION 2: ____________________

4. Annoyed by my constant questions. My sister marched into her room and slammed the door.

   REVISION 1: ____________________

   REVISION 2: ____________________

5. The players celebrated their historic victory. With the crowd's deafening cheers still ringing in their ears.

   REVISION 1: ____________________

   REVISION 2: ____________________

ACTIVITY 3 Revising a Paragraph for Fragments

The following paragraph was written for a general audience and may include fragments. Revise the paragraph to correct problems with fragments. (You may determine that some fragments are appropriate; if so, be prepared to explain why you made the choice not to revise them.)

In the late 19th century, the notorious Dalton Gang committed several train robberies in Oklahoma. Which made people compare the outlaws with other well-known thieves of the West. Such as Jesse and Frank James. According to contemporary sources. Bob Dalton was the mastermind of the gang, which included his brothers Grat and Emmett.

Because Bob Dalton wished to outdo the James Gang. He created a plan to rob two banks in the town of Coffeyville, Kansas. On the same day in 1892. Unfortunately for the Daltons, news of their plan had leaked. In addition, the Dalton family had once lived near Coffeyville. Where Emmett had gone to school. Therefore, their faces were familiar to the townspeople. The daring daylight robbery went badly wrong for the outlaws. By the time the shooting had stopped. Bob and Grat and two other members of the gang had been killed, and Emmett, the youngest Dalton, was badly wounded. Having survived the Coffeyville robbery. Emmett served fourteen years in a Kansas penitentiary. Where he was described as a model prisoner. After his release, he and his wife went to California. Emmett later wrote a book. And made silent films about the Dalton Gang, even acting in one. Unlike his brother Bob, however. Emmett was not particularly interested in being famous. He ended up with a successful career in construction. Building houses in Hollywood.

ACTIVITY 4 Revising Fragments in Your Own Writing

Look over the most recent writing you've done to see if you have created any fragments. As you review, revise any fragments you find that are likely to seem like mistakes to your readers. If you find a fragment that you used to create a special effect and that seems to serve its purpose, write a note explaining why you believe it does not require revision.

workshop 8 Misplaced and Dangling Modifiers

Understanding Misplaced and Dangling Modifiers

Modifiers are words, phrases, or clauses that act as adjectives and adverbs, clarifying or adding shades of meaning to your writing. Modifiers need to be positioned near the words they modify. Misplaced and dangling modifiers can cause confusion or unintentionally comic effects.

For definitions and examples of grammar concepts key to understanding misplaced and dangling modifiers, see the ***Guide to Grammar Terms*** *table on pages 1101–1104.*

Revising Misplaced and Dangling Modifiers

Misplaced Modifiers

The solution to a misplaced modifier is to revise the sentence so that readers don't have to guess at its meaning.

MISPLACED MODIFIER

Two FBI agents gave a presentation on the psychological makeup of the killer in the conference room.

In this sentence, the modifier is "in the conference room," which was intended to tell the reader where the presentation took place. Because the modifier is misplaced (placed too far from the word it modifies), it seems to be saying that the killer is *in the conference room*.

REVISION

Two FBI agents gave a presentation in the conference room on the psychological makeup of the killer.

Squinting Modifiers

If a misplaced modifier is positioned so that readers can't tell which of two words it is supposed to modify, it is called a squinting modifier. The solution for squinting modifiers, too, is to revise the sentence so readers will understand which word is being modified.

SQUINTING MODIFIER

Speaking a new language often helps students learn vocabulary words.

Should students *speak often*, or does speaking *help often?*

POSSIBLE REVISIONS

Speaking often in a new language helps students learn vocabulary words.

Speaking a new language can often help students learn vocabulary words.

Moving the word *often* — and making changes to the wording of the sentence — allows the writer's meaning to be completely clear.

Dangling Modifiers

Sometimes the word or words being modified may be left out of the sentence completely. The modifier in such cases is called a dangling modifier. Although readers may be able to guess what the dangling modifier refers to, they shouldn't have to guess — and dangling modifiers can still be confusing or unintentionally comical. To correct a dangling modifier, decide what the modifier is supposed to modify. Then, revise the sentence to include that missing element, either by making it the subject of the main clause or by revising the dangling modifier as a clause that includes the missing word or words.

DANGLING MODIFIER

Spot used to chase Monica, as a puppy.

The phrase *as a puppy* seems to modify the noun *Monica*, who is not a dog.

POSSIBLE REVISION

As a puppy, Spot used to chase Monica.

The modifier is probably supposed to modify *our dog,* so changing *As a puppy* to *When our dog was a puppy* eliminates the dangling modifier.

ACTIVITY 1 Identifying Misplaced and Dangling Modifiers

In each of the following sentences, underline the modifier. If it is misplaced, squinting, or dangling, identify the problem. If the sentence is correct, write *Correct*.

EXAMPLE: Cackling and flapping, the henhouse erupted in a loud commotion. *Dangling*

1. Efficient and well-managed, the diner served a remarkable number of hungry local residents every morning.
2. Writing a summary quickly taught the students to look for main ideas.
3. Denying that the graffiti was mine, four cans of spray paint in my locker seemed to provide proof of guilt.
4. Two witnesses pointed out the suspect who had stolen the prize poodle in the police lineup.
5. Making a terrible screeching noise, Aunt Lucille noticed that the car's brakes were faulty.

ACTIVITY 2 Revising Misplaced and Dangling Modifiers

Correct misplaced, squinting, and dangling modifiers in the following sentences by revising each sentence in two different ways.

EXAMPLE: After leaving an envelope hidden in the hollow tree, the secret of the neighborhood's most mysterious house was revealed.

REVISION 1: *After the old man left an envelope hidden in the hollow tree, the secret of the neighborhood's most mysterious house was revealed.*

REVISION 2: *After leaving an envelope hidden in the hollow tree, the old man revealed the secret of the neighborhood's most mysterious house.*

1. Covered in cat hair, guests avoided the sofa in the lobby of the quaint little inn.

   REVISION 1: ______________________________

   REVISION 2: ______________________________

2. The radio announcer proclaimed a great military victory over a crackling speaker.

   REVISION 1: ______________________________

   REVISION 2: ______________________________

3. Laughing often makes people feel more optimistic.

   REVISION 1: ______________________________

   REVISION 2: ______________________________

4. Carrying a bushel of rutabagas home from the farmer's market, an unexpected dinner was sure to follow.

   REVISION 1: ______________________________

   REVISION 2: ______________________________

ACTIVITY 3 Revising a Paragraph for Misplaced and Dangling Modifiers

The following paragraph may include dangling and misplaced modifiers. Revise the paragraph to correct any issues you identify.

Advertising often makes a difference in the success of a product. Clever and memorable, products with great ads attract customers. Consider the billboards for Burma-Shave, a brand of shaving cream that dotted U.S. highways from 1927–1963. Americans' fondness for driving slowly resulted in the spread of billboard advertising. With a series of six or seven red billboards, each featuring one line of a comic rhyming poem, motorists waited for the punch line on the next-to-last billboard. The final sign always revealed the product name, "Burma-Shave." Increasingly famous, people driving along the highway loved the clever campaign. Proudly announcing, "If you/Don't know/Whose signs/These are/You can't have/Driven very far," motorists enjoyed being in on the joke. However, the days were numbered of Burma-Shave's success. Although showing no signs of being tired of the billboards, highways improved and cars went much faster. At fifty or sixty miles per hour, the distance needed between the billboards became too great. The Burma-Shave brand disappeared. Now in the Smithsonian Museum's collection, however, people will probably remember the Burma-Shave ad campaign better than they remember most modern billboard advertising.

ACTIVITY 4 Revising Misplaced and Dangling Modifiers in Your Own Writing

Look over the most recent writing you've done to see if you have used any misplaced or dangling modifiers that might confuse readers. If you find any, revise them.

Understanding Parallelism

Parallelism, or parallel structure, uses repeated grammatical forms to show relationships between similar parts of sentences. Parallel structure is commonly found in lists and comparisons. However, you can use parallelism for many other purposes, including highlighting logical relationships, improving sentence clarity, creating rhythm, and adding emphasis.

For definitions and examples of grammar concepts key to understanding parallelism, see the ***Guide to Grammar Terms*** *table on pages 1101–1104.*

Revising for Parallelism

When you join two or more items in a list or series with a coordinating conjunction such as *and*, make sure that all the items in the list are parallel to one another.

Lack of Parallelism in a List

A great leader should know how to plan, how to inspire, and should take responsibility for mistakes.

The items in the list are *how to plan, how to inspire,* and *should take responsibility for mistakes.* The first two have parallel structures, but the third does not.

PARALLEL

A great leader should know how to plan, inspire, and take responsibility for mistakes.

Lack of Parallelism with a Coordinating Conjunction

Is there anyone here able to drive me downtown or who can lend me a bicycle?

The phrases joined with the coordinating conjunction *or* — *able to drive me downtown* and *who can lend me a bicycle*, — are not parallel.

PARALLEL

Is there anyone here who can drive me downtown or lend me a bicycle?

In this revision, both phrases work with *who can,* so the parts are parallel.

When you use a two-part correlative conjunction such as *either . . . or,* be sure to use parallel structures with each part of the conjunction.

Lack of Parallelism with a Correlative Conjunction

He wanted not only to learn French, but also an introduction to French culture.

The phrase after *not only* begins with an infinitive, *to learn*. The phrase after *but also* begins with a noun phrase, *an introduction,* so the structures after each part of the conjunction are not parallel.

PARALLEL

He wanted not only to learn French, but also to get an introduction to French culture.

If you make a comparison, be careful to use parallel structure for the items you are comparing.

Lack of Parallelism in a Comparison

Asking forgiveness is often easier than to get permission.

The items being compared are *asking forgiveness* and *to get permission.* The structures are not parallel.

PARALLEL

Asking forgiveness is often easier than getting permission.

ACTIVITY 1 Identifying Problems with Parallelism

In the following sentences, underline items that need to have parallel structures. If the structures are parallel, write *Correct*. If they are not parallel, write *Incorrect*.

EXAMPLES: The soccer players in the park are wearing team jerseys from Argentina, from Brazil, and one player appears to support France. *Incorrect*

Either you give me my money back or I report you to the Better Business Bureau. *Correct*

1. We could not assemble the bicycle kit because it had a missing seat, broken spokes, and someone wrote terrible instructions.
2. The actors were prepared not only to say their lines but also gave a thrilling performance.
3. You have a good chance of getting the job thanks to your polished resume, flexible schedule, and retail experience.
4. Cooking for friends is more relaxing and less expensive than to go out for dinner.
5. After a week of trying out for the soccer team, Harry wanted to snack, sleep, and he planned to catch up on movies over the weekend.

ACTIVITY 2 Revising Problems with Parallelism

Rewrite each of the following items to eliminate any problems with parallelism.

EXAMPLE: Civilians who fly an American flag must either take it down at dusk or they should illuminate it.

REVISION: *Civilians who fly an American flag must either take it down at dusk or illuminate it.*

1. Keeping succulent plants alive is easy if you follow simple guidelines: water them very rarely, provide indirect light, and the soil should be well drained.

   REVISION: ______________________________

2. Before last weekend's hiking trip, we stocked up on high-energy snacks, reviewed the trail maps carefully, and we forgot to fill the car's gas tank.

   REVISION: ______________________________

3. She could either keep working on the essay past midnight or she could get up before dawn to finish it.

   REVISION: ______________________________

4. Singing in the chorus, building sets with the stage crew, and costume design are good ways to participate in the drama club.

   REVISION: ______________________________

5. Construction meant that pedestrians had to walk across a busy intersection, up an unpaved path, and go along a muddy ditch to get back to the sidewalk.

   REVISION: ______________________________

ACTIVITY 3 Revising a Paragraph for Problems with Parallelism

The following paragraph includes problems with parallelism. Revise any errors that you find. Some sentences may be correct as written.

Anyone who has ever wished either to reduce clutter or who does not want to take care of a large home might be interested in tiny house living. To be officially "tiny," a house must have an area of less than 400 square feet. Most tiny homes are not only small but also offer a lot of efficiency. Residents of tiny homes typically sleep in a loft space, own furniture that serves more than one purpose, and for entertaining, they go elsewhere. People who are attracted to life in tiny houses may be interested in living simply or to go off the grid. Living simply can be possible in a tiny house because it is usually less expensive to maintain one than the upkeep of an ordinary house. Nevertheless, much depends on whether the house is on a foundation or on wheels, whether or not the homeowner also owns the land, and on local regulations that the homeowner may have to comply with. As some tiny house residents have noted, living in a very small space is easier in a community than when the resident is isolated. In that case, a good way to test living in a tiny space in a vibrant community may be to live in an urban apartment.

ACTIVITY 4 Revising Problems with Parallelism in Your Own Writing

Look over the most recent writing you've done to see if you have made any errors with parallel structures. As you review, revise any parallelism problems you find.

workshop 10 Pronoun-Antecedent Agreement

Understanding Pronoun-Antecedent Agreement

When you use a pronoun such as *it, them,* or *which, the* pronoun refers to another word — a noun, noun phrase, or another pronoun — called the antecedent. Pronouns have to agree with the antecedent in number and gender.

Pronoun-antecedent agreement problems usually come up in just a few situations, when the antecedent is one of the following:

- A compound joined with *and, or,* or *nor*
- A collective noun
- An indefinite pronoun
- A singular noun without an identified gender

Revising Pronoun-Antecedent Agreement

To fix pronoun-antecedent agreement problems, identify the pronoun and its antecedent, and then revise the pronoun, the antecedent, or the whole sentence to eliminate the agreement error.

For definitions and examples of grammar concepts key to understanding pronoun-antecedent agreement problems, see the ***Guide to Grammar Terms*** *table on pages 1101–1104.*

Compound Antecedents

One common type of pronoun-antecedent agreement error involves compound antecedents joined with *and, or,* or *nor.* If a compound antecedent uses *and,* you should use a plural pronoun.

Agreement Error with Compound Antecedent

Both Mr. Devere and his son used his knowledge of sports to find a career.

The compound antecedent *Mr. Devere and his son* refers to two people, not one, so it requires a plural pronoun.

REVISION

Both Mr. Devere and his son used their knowledge of sports to find a career.

If the compound antecedent uses *or* or *nor,* you should make sure that the pronoun agrees with the closer part of the compound antecedent.

Agreement Error with Compound Antecedent

Either Anita or the boys spend her afternoon at the museum daily.

The parts of the compound antecedent are joined with *or,* so the pronoun should agree with the closer antecedent, *boys,* not with *Anita.*

REVISION

Either Anita or the boys spend their afternoon at the museum daily.

Note: If the revised sentence sounds strange, try switching the parts of the compound antecedent to see if the sentence improves. If changing the order doesn't help, try revising the sentence.

Collective Noun Antecedents

Another trouble spot for pronoun-antecedent agreement involves antecedents that are collective nouns, which are usually singular unless the members of the group are acting as individuals.

Agreement Error with Collective Noun Antecedent

The crowd roars their approval.

The verb *roars* suggests that the collective noun *crowd* is acting as one unit, so a singular pronoun is needed.

REVISION

The crowd roars its approval.

Antecedents with Indefinite Pronouns

Traditionally, indefinite pronouns such as *everyone, anyone,* or *none* have been considered singular antecedents, even when they seem to include more than one person. If you use a plural pronoun with a singular indefinite pronoun antecedent, many readers will consider it an error.

Agreement Error with Indefinite Pronoun Antecedent

Does anyone have a credit card with them?

Using the plural pronoun *them* with the grammatically singular *anyone* is sometimes seen as a pronoun-antecedent agreement error.

POSSIBLE REVISION

Does anyone have a credit card with him or her?

This revision is very formal, and some readers may find it awkward.

POSSIBLE REVISION

Does anyone have a credit card?

In this case, omitting the pronoun is a good revision strategy.

Avoiding Sexism

Singular nouns that refer to a category of person *(student, gymnast, physicist)* can also cause problems. Decades ago, using a singular masculine pronoun with such antecedents was considered appropriate, but many readers today find it sexist and awkward to use *he* and *him to* refer to a person who does not identify as male. Because some readers also don't consider a plural pronoun such as *they* appropriate for singular antecedents, you will have to think carefully about revising such sentences.

Agreement Issue with Singular Pronoun Antecedent

A student driver must recognize that their car can be dangerous.

Many readers — but not all — will see a pronoun-antecedent agreement error between the antecedent *driver* and the pronoun *their.* (See the "Breaking the Rule" section that follows for more information.)

SEXIST REVISION

A student driver must recognize that his car can be dangerous.

Any student driver who does not identify as male is excluded in this revision.

POSSIBLE REVISION

Student drivers must recognize that their cars can be dangerous.

This revision makes the generic *driver* plural, so the pronoun *their* agrees.

POSSIBLE REVISION

A student driver must recognize that a car can be dangerous.

In this revision, the problematic pronoun is eliminated.

Breaking the Rule: Changing Standards for Pronoun-Antecedent Agreement

Once you understand what pronoun-antecedent agreement is and how to avoid agreement problems, you may start to notice the "singular *they*" appearing in journalistic writing and other edited texts. The use of *they* to refer to grammatically singular indefinite pronouns such as *everyone* has often been called an error in formal writing (for example, in sentences such as *Everyone must receive their immunizations*), even though it is commonly used in speech as a way to avoid the sexist use of *he* or the awkward and excessively formal *he or she.* In recent years, however, many publications and writers have begun to accept *they* as agreeing with a singular antecedent that could refer to a person who does not identify as male.

The winner of the speaking contest will have their choice of several prizes.

Be aware that some readers may not know that the restriction against the "singular *they*" is changing. You may still want to avoid the "singular *they*" if your audience won't realize that you have made an informed decision to use it.

The winner of the speaking contest can choose among several prizes.

The winner of the speaking contest will have a choice of several prizes.

ACTIVITY 1 Identifying Problems with Pronoun-Antecedent Agreement

In each sentence, underline the pronoun and double-underline the antecedent to which the pronoun refers. If there is a pronoun-antecedent agreement error or related issue in the sentence, briefly explain the problem. If there is no problem, write *None.*

EXAMPLE: Everyone waiting for an interview should leave his résumé at the desk.

PROBLEM: *The pronoun is sexist; it does not agree in gender with the antecedent "everyone."*

1. Either the Santana sisters or Marcus should give their speech at the beginning of the ceremony.

   PROBLEM: ______________________________

2. Can someone let me borrow his or her phone?

   PROBLEM: ______________________________

3. The waiting crowd waved its hands and shouted wildly when the singer entered the hotel lobby.

PROBLEM: ______________________________

4. A soldier should obey his commanding officer at all times.

PROBLEM: ______________________________

5. Give the documents to Ms. D'Souza and the attaché when they arrive.

PROBLEM: ______________________________

ACTIVITY 2 Revising Pronoun-Antecedent Agreement Errors

Underline the pronoun and double-underline the antecedent in each of the following items. Then, rewrite each sentence in at least two different ways to correct problems with pronoun-antecedent agreement. Be ready to explain your choices.

EXAMPLE: The cat and the rabbits ate its food in separate rooms.

REVISION 1: *The cat and the rabbits ate their food in separate rooms.*

REVISION 2: *The cat and the rabbits ate in separate rooms.*

1. A writer can create his own schedule, but flexibility is sometimes a mixed blessing.

REVISION 1: ______________________________

REVISION 2: ______________________________

2. Everyone should try to resolve their interpersonal problems through direct, open communication.

REVISION 1: ______________________________

REVISION 2: ______________________________

3. Either cooking an elaborate meal or grabbing fast food can have their pros and cons.

REVISION 1: ______________________________

REVISION 2: ______________________________

4. The parliament has met their obligation to consider the law fairly.

REVISION 1: ______________________________

REVISION 2: ______________________________

ACTIVITY 3 Revising a Paragraph for Pronoun-Antecedent Agreement Errors

The following paragraph, written for a general audience, includes pronoun-antecedent agreement errors and other related problems. Revise the paragraph to correct any problems you find. Some sentences may not contain any errors, and some sentences may contain pronouns that would disturb only some readers. If you decide not to change a sentence, be ready to explain why.

Curling is a sport in which a team use their brooms to scrub an ice rink in order to make a big round rock slide smoothly to a target spot. But in addition to rocks and brooms, an unusual thing about curling is the fact that everyone who curls is supposed to be on their best behavior. The Curling Code of Ethics says that neither insults nor intimidation has their place in the sport. There are no referees to blow the whistle on a player who tries to hide their mistakes. Instead, someone who commits a foul by touching (or "burning") the curling stone is expected to say so, even if he knows that nobody else saw the foul. Both winners and losers are expected to show good sportsmanship and treat their opponents to a drink after the game ends. Curling may look odd, but anyone who treats honorable behavior as their sport's highest goal must be on the right track.

ACTIVITY 4 Revising Pronoun-Antecedent Agreement Problems in Your Own Writing

Look over the most recent writing you've done to see if you have any problems with pronoun-antecedent agreement. As you review, revise any mismatched pronouns and antecedents that are likely to confuse your readers. If you find anything that some readers might consider a pronoun-antecedent error but that you prefer not to change, make a note of your decision.

workshop 11 Pronoun Reference

Understanding Pronoun Reference

When you use a pronoun such as *it, them,* or *which,* the pronoun refers to another word — a noun, noun phrase, or another pronoun — called the antecedent. Pronoun reference problems occur when readers can't tell which word or words serve as the antecedent of a particular pronoun or can't identify any antecedent.

For definitions and examples of grammar concepts key to understanding pronoun reference, see the ***Guide to Grammar Terms*** *table on pages 1101–1104.*

Revising Pronoun Reference

To identify and fix problems with pronoun reference, identify the pronoun and then find its antecedent. If the antecedent is ambiguous, vague, missing, or otherwise unclear, rewrite the sentence to clarify the meaning.

Sometimes, the pronoun could refer to more than one antecedent.

Ambiguous Antecedent

Office policy bans personal phone calls, which many employees dislike.

Do many employees dislike the policy or the personal calls? The antecedent of *which* is unclear.

REVISION

Office policy bans personal phone calls, a rule that many employees dislike.

The revision clarifies that the pronoun *that* refers to the office policy against personal calls.

CLEAR REVISION

Office policy bans personal phone calls because many employees dislike them.

The revision leaves no doubt that the pronoun *them* refers to the phone calls.

At other times, the pronoun — usually *that, which,* or *it* — is so vague that readers can't tell exactly what part of a clause or phrase serves as the pronoun's antecedent.

Vague Antecedent

The bookshelves were filled to overflowing with paperbacks, hardcovers, and reference books, which contributed to the mess in the room.

Does *which* refer to a particular kind of book, to all the books, to the bookshelves, or to something else? The antecedent of *which* is vague.

CLEAR REVISION

The bookshelves were filled to overflowing with paperbacks, hardcovers, and reference books, a chaotic jumble that contributed to the mess in the room.

In this revision, the pronoun *that* refers specifically to the phrase *a chaotic jumble,* which restates the appearance of the shelves described in the independent clause.

Another problem occurs when a writer uses a pronoun such as *it, you,* or *they* without any real antecedent. This kind of usage is common in conversation, but inappropriate in formal writing.

Missing Antecedent

On this website, they suggest that the end of the world is coming.

Who are *they*? Here, the pronoun seems to refer to unknown people.

CLEAR REVISION

This website suggests that the end of the world is coming.

Removing the mystery pronoun *they* eliminates the confusion.

Finally, be aware that some readers object to using a possessive as an antecedent in formal writing.

Possessive Antecedent

Joanna's review showed how much she had loved the book.

Although readers can infer that *she* refers to Joanna, the sentence does not contain a noun that can be the antecedent of *she.* The possessive form *Joanna's* acts as an adjective rather than as a noun. Some readers will find such sentences ungrammatical.

CLEAR REVISION

Her review showed how much Joanna had loved the book.

The antecedent of *her* is now a noun, *Joanna.*

ACTIVITY 1 Identifying Problems with Pronoun Reference

In each sentence, underline the pronoun. If the sentence contains a pronoun reference problem, describe the problem. If there is no problem, write *None.*

EXAMPLE: Sonia told Maria that she should take a vacation.

PROBLEM: *The pronoun "she" could refer to either Sonia or Maria.*

1. Ed's sister announced that he had bought the winning lottery ticket.

   PROBLEM: ________________________

2. They said on the radio that the storm will bypass this area.

   PROBLEM: ________________________

3. The twelve-story building had an elevator until it was condemned.

   PROBLEM: ________________________

4. The students played cards until midnight and watched a couple of horror movies afterward, which may not have been a good idea the night before the physics final.

   PROBLEM: ______________________________

5. Three-year-old Sara put pretzels on a plate for her imaginary friend Sheela.

   PROBLEM: ______________________________

ACTIVITY 2 Revising Pronoun Reference Problems

Rewrite the following items to correct any problems with pronoun reference. If a sentence contains no error, write *Correct*.

EXAMPLE: Donna called Olivia to say that her dog had escaped.

REVISION: *Donna found that her dog had escaped, so she called Olivia.*

1. My brother's car is towed to the garage almost weekly, but he insists the car has many good years left.

   REVISION: ______________________________

2. Neville whispered to Mr. Middlebury that he needed to leave the party immediately.

   REVISION: ______________________________

3. During the kite-flying competition, enthusiastic kite handlers and onlookers cheered swooping and diving kites of all shapes and hues, which led to amazing photographs.

   REVISION: ______________________________

4. Valerie enjoys traditional French cooking because she loves butter and cream, but her sister tells her that too much fat is unhealthy.

   REVISION: ______________________________

5. The anchorwoman told every actress who came to the set that she needed a new contract.

   REVISION: ______________________________

ACTIVITY 3 Revising a Paragraph for Pronoun Reference Problems

The following paragraph, written for a general audience, may include unclear or missing antecedents or other pronoun reference problems. Revise the paragraph to correct any problems you find. Some sentences may not contain any errors.

Tom Blake's name may not be famous everywhere, but he is widely known in the world of surfing. They claim on Wikipedia that Blake was "one of the most influential surfers in history" because of his revolutionary design changes to the traditional surfboard. Blake was born in Milwaukee, Wisconsin, in 1902. He grew up near Lake Superior and first heard of surfing from an educational film in high school, which may have influenced his later choices. In Detroit in 1920, Blake met Duke Kahanamoku, who had helped to popularize surfing around the world. Blake believed he had invited him to visit his native Hawaii. In the 1920s, Blake and Kahanamoku became friends, and he both learned to surf and also studied antique surfboards in a Honolulu museum. Blake's innovations included hollowing out and reinforcing the surfboards of the era, which were too heavy for many people to carry. But according to modern-day board designers, Blake's greatest contribution to surfing involved adding a fin to the traditional board's flat bottom so it could be maneuvered in the water. Previously, a surfer had to dip one foot in the water to turn, and that made performance surfing difficult. In inventing lightweight finned boards, Blake made surfing a more accessible sport.

ACTIVITY 4 Revising Pronoun Reference Problems in Your Own Writing

Look over the most recent writing you've done to see if you have any problems with pronoun reference. As you review, revise any unclear or missing antecedents you find that are likely to confuse your readers.

workshop 12 Shifts in Pronoun Person and Number

Understanding Inappropriate Shifts in Pronoun Person and Number

In writing, a shift in person is a change in pronoun, such as from the second person *you* to the third person *someone,* that happens in the middle of a sentence or paragraph. A shift in number moves between singular and plural subjects. If you make shifts between person and/or number without a good reason, you may confuse your readers.

*For definitions and examples of grammar concepts key to understanding inappropriate shifts in pronoun person and number, see the **Guide to Grammar Terms** table on pages 1101–1104.*

Revising Shifts in Pronoun Person and Number

Shifts in person and/or number can make sense to readers when different people are the subjects of clauses in a sentence.

Intentional Shifts in Person and Number

I had a problem with my car, so my friends loaned me theirs.

The first-person singular subject of the first clause, *I*, and the third-person plural subject of the second clause, my friends, are different people, so shifts in both person and number are appropriate.

When shifts in person and/or number happen without a change in the people being referred to, such shifts can cause confusion.

Unintentional Shift in Person and/or Number

Anyone can find a job if you are willing to work hard.

The third person subject, *Anyone,* of the main clause and the second person subject, *you,* of the subordinate clause seem to refer to the same people, so this shift in perspective is confusing. By shifting to *you,* the writer may be aiming to avoid the choice between the awkward singular *he or she* and the traditionally plural *they* with the grammatically singular antecedent *anyone,* but the shift is not a good solution.

You have several options for revising shifts in person.

REVISION

You can find a job if you are willing to work hard.

If the writer is talking directly to readers, *you* is appropriate.

REVISION

Anyone who is willing to work hard can find a job.

Another option is to rearrange the sentence. Here, the writer avoids having to choose between *he or she* and *they* with the antecedent *anyone.* (See Workshop 10 on Pronoun-Antecedent Agreement for more information.)

Breaking the Rule: Changing Standards for Shifts in Number

You may have noticed the "singular *they*" in journalistic writing and other edited texts. The use of *they* to refer to grammatically singular indefinite pronouns such as *everyone* has often been called an error in formal writing (for example, in sentences such as *Everyone must receive their immunizations*), even though it is commonly used in speech as a way to avoid the sexist use of *he* or the awkward and excessively formal *he* or *she.* In recent years, many publications and writers have begun to accept *they* as agreeing with a singular antecedent when the gender of the antecedent is not known.

The winner of the speaking contest will have their choice of several prizes.

Be aware that some readers may not know that the restriction against the "singular *they*" *is* changing. You may still want to avoid the "singular *they*" if your audience won't realize that you have made an informed decision to use it.

The winner of the speaking contest can choose among several prizes.

The winner of the speaking contest will have a choice of several prizes.

ACTIVITY 1 Identifying Inappropriate Shifts in Person and Number

Determine whether each of the following sentences contains an inappropriate shift in person or number. If the sentence contains an inappropriate shift, explain the problem. If the sentence is correct as written, write *None.*

EXAMPLE: We followed the recipe, but you could tell the results were going to be disastrous.

PROBLEM: *Inappropriate shift from first-person "We" to second-person "you"*

1. A person may be absolutely certain that there are no monsters under the bed, but I still have to check.

   PROBLEM: ______________________________

2. Everyone already knows too much about our family history in this town.

   PROBLEM: ______________________________

3. Finding the discipline to practice a difficult new skill is not easy, but anyone can learn new skills if you practice them hard enough.

   PROBLEM: ______________________________

4. When I start feeling restless during the long introduction, you get worried that the comedian will have trouble winning over the crowd.

   PROBLEM: ______________________________

5. Most of us on the student newspaper have their specialties, which include feature writing, opinion writing, and photography.

   PROBLEM: ______________________________

ACTIVITY 2 Revising Inappropriate Shifts in Person and Number

Revise each of the following sentences in two different ways to correct any inappropriate shifts in person and number.

EXAMPLE: A vegetarian may have to explain to family members why you stopped eating meat.

REVISION 1: *Vegetarians may have to explain to family members why they stopped eating meat.*

REVISION 2: *A vegetarian may have to explain the decision not to eat meat to family members.*

1. One does not need to understand how and why dough rises if they want to bake bread.

   REVISION 1: ______________________________

   REVISION 2: ______________________________

2. For someone to be accepted to West Point, you have to demonstrate leadership skills and excellent academic qualifications.

   REVISION 1: ______________________________

   REVISION 2: ______________________________

3. As the child of immigrant parents, you felt like a cultural interpreter.

   REVISION 1: ______________________________

   REVISION 2: ______________________________

4. We were willing to wait overnight in the ticket line, but you weren't allowed to put chairs or sleeping bags on the sidewalk.

   REVISION 1: ______________________________

   REVISION 2: ______________________________

ACTIVITY 3 Editing a Paragraph for Inappropriate Shifts in Person and Number

Edit the following paragraph, written for a student audience, to revise any inappropriate shifts in person and number. If you decide that some shifts are acceptable, be ready to explain your reasoning.

Anyone who has studied a foreign language knows that you can rarely translate idioms literally. Those who create word-for-word translations will find that his or her results may sound comical — and may be very difficult to understand. For instance, most of us would not think twice about using an English expression like "It's raining cats and dogs" if you needed to indicate heavy rain. But if someone translates the literal words into another language, a listener may think they are trying to be confusing. A Portuguese-English phrase book published in 1855 by a man who spoke no English used a Portuguese-French phrase book and a French-English dictionary to create famously terrible translations. Even for readers who spoke no Portuguese, one was likely to find the English phrases mystifying and hilarious. Humorist Mark Twain said that the book was "perfect." People might agree that many expressions from the book, like "to craunch the marmoset," have a certain flair, even if you have no idea what they mean.

ACTIVITY 4 Revising Inappropriate Shifts in Your Own Writing

Look over the most recent writing you've done to see if you have created any inappropriate shifts in person and number. Revise any shifts you find that are likely to seem like mistakes to your readers. If some shifts seem acceptable to you, be ready to explain why you decided not to revise them.

workshop 13 Shifts in Verb Tense

Understanding Shifts in Verb Tense

In writing, a shift in verb tense is a change from one verb tense to another that happens in the middle of a paragraph or even in the middle of a sentence. At times, you will have a good reason to change tenses — but if you make such shifts without a good reason, they may confuse your readers.

For definitions and examples of grammar concepts key to understanding inappropriate shifts in verb tense, see the ***Guide to Grammar Terms*** *table on pages 1101–1104.*

Revising Inappropriate Shifts in Verb Tense

Shifts make sense to readers when the events being described in a sentence or paragraph happen at different times and require different tenses.

Intentional Shift

The castle burned down and fell into the swamp, but we will rebuild it.

The past tense verbs *burned* and *fell* make sense because the castle's destruction happened in the past. The future tense *will rebuild* makes sense because the rebuilding has not happened yet.

When the events of the sentence or paragraph happen at the same time, a tense shift is unnecessary and distracting.

Unintentional Shift

The castle stood on the edge of the swamp for years, and then it suddenly catches fire.

The shift from the past tense verb *stood* to the present tense verb *catches* is unnecessary and does not make sense in the sentence.

REVISION

The castle stood on the edge of the swamp for years, and then it suddenly caught fire.

If you're writing about literature, use the present tense to describe the actions of characters or to analyze what the writer does. You can think of literature as always happening right now, since readers can experience the work at any time.

Using the Present Tense to Write about Literature

Some of Jane Austen's best-loved heroines ~~were~~ *are* poor but plucky girls who unexpectedly end up with rich husbands.

Notice, however, that when you discuss the work's publication or anything about the work or the author that is tied to a particular time, the past tense is appropriate.

Austen herself ~~does~~ *did* not earn much from her novels during her lifetime.

The phrase *during her lifetime* places the information in this sentence in the past, so the past tense *did* is correct.

ACTIVITY 1 Identifying Inappropriate Shifts in Verb Tense

In each of the following sentences, underline all the verbs and verb phrases. If the sentence contains an inappropriate shift in tense, write *Shift*; if it is correct as written, write *Correct*.

EXAMPLES: Every August, the Perseid meteor shower fills the sky with light, so astronomers hope the weather will be clear. *Correct*

Startled, we leaped from our sleeping bags, and then we race away from the terrifying sound as fast as we can move. *Shift*

1. If you worked nearby, you would be able to spend less time traveling to the job.
2. As the morning sun's rays broke over the horizon, the vampire races toward home.
3. My dog Pickles escapes the yard and roams the neighborhood, but the little boy next door found him and brought him home.
4. When movie versions of Shakespeare's *Hamlet* are made, the actor who plays Hamlet was often forty years old, even though the play's hero was a college student.
5. The witness answered the defense attorney's questions without hesitation, but suddenly, during the cross-examination, he freezes.

ACTIVITY 2 Revising Inappropriate Shifts in Verb Tense

Revise each of the following sentences to correct any inappropriate shifts in verb tense. If the sentence is correct as written, write *Correct*.

EXAMPLE: Kittens' eyes ~~opened~~ *open* a few days after birth, and they start exploring their surroundings in three to four weeks.

1. A rainy gust from the storm blew the screen door open, and the children and their babysitter spend the next half hour moving several very startled tiny tree frogs back outdoors.
2. Most of the chocolate in Vivian's bag of Halloween candy had disappeared, but when she accused her sister of eating it, their mother admitted responsibility.
3. Marjane Satrapi's graphic novel *Persepolis* explored the author's rebellious youth when she was growing up in Iran in the 1980s.
4. According to psychological research, unskilled people often greatly overestimate their own abilities, a cognitive bias that was called the Dunning-Kruger effect.
5. The teenagers in town followed a long tradition of driving up and down Main Street on Saturday nights because there are few other entertainment options.

ACTIVITY 3 Editing a Paragraph for Inappropriate Shifts in Verb Tense

Edit the following paragraph to revise any inappropriate shifts in verb tense.

Is advertising as a profession doomed? This may seem like a strange question in an era when ads appeared everywhere. However, research suggests that the field of advertising had changed. Advertisers today have to contend with a constantly growing and changing number of platforms, from print to television to digital, and each required different kinds of advertising. For example, social media ads often appeared in the corner of a screen for just a few seconds, while television ads last thirty seconds or longer and aim to attract a viewer's full attention. Perhaps an even bigger problem for advertisers today, however, was that more people than ever before dislike ads so much that they are sometimes willing to pay more to avoid them. If social media users could pay a small fee never again to see ads about weird tricks to lose abdominal fat, will they do it?

ACTIVITY 4 Revising Inappropriate Shifts in Verb Tense in Your Own Writing

Look over the most recent writing you've done to see if you have created any inappropriate shifts in verb tense. As you review, revise any shifts you find that are likely to seem like mistakes to your readers.

workshop 14 Subject-Verb Agreement

Understanding Subject-Verb Agreement

The subject and verb(s) in a sentence have to agree in person and number.

Subject-verb agreement errors happen most often when a writer loses track of the subject of the sentence. Misidentifying the subject happens most often in just a few tricky situations:

- When words come between the subject and verb
- When the subject follows the verb
- When the sentence has a compound subject
- When the subject is a collective noun
- When the subject is an indefinite pronoun
- When the subject is *who, which,* or *that*
- When the subject is singular but ends in *–s*

For definitions and examples of grammar concepts key to understanding subject-verb agreement, see the ***Guide to Grammar Terms*** *table on pages 1101–1104.*

Revising Subject-Verb Agreement

Taking the time to identify the simple subject that the verb needs to agree with will help you fix — and avoid — subject-verb agreement errors.

Words between Subject and Verb

make

The flowers along the side of the road ~~makes~~ the long drive more cheerful.

Although the verb *makes* is closer to the singular noun *road*, it does not agree with the plural subject *flowers*. Look for prepositional phrases and other words that may come between the subject and verb, and be careful not to mistake any of them for the sentence's subject.

Subject Follows Verb

are

There ~~is~~ too many people here today.

The verb *is* does not agree with the plural subject that follows it, *people*. The word *there* is not a noun and is not the subject of this (or any) sentence.

Compound Subject

> My two dogs and my cat ~~runs~~ *run* into the kitchen, hoping to be fed.

The verb *runs* does not agree with the compound subject, *My two dogs and my cat,* which is plural because the two subjects *My two dogs* and *my cat* are connected with *and*.

> Either my cat or my two dogs ~~has~~ *have* broken the screen door.

The verb *has* does not agree with the simple subject *dogs,* which is plural. When the two subjects are connected with *or,* the verb agrees with the closer subject. If making the verb agree with the closer subject results in a sentence that sounds strange, try switching the parts of the compound subject (and, again, making the verb agree with the closer subject) to see if the sentence sounds better that way: *Either my two dogs or my cat has broken the screen door.*

Collective Noun Subject

> The committee ~~vote~~ *votes* on how to spend the bake-sale money.

The verb *vote* does not agree with the collective noun *committee,* which is usually singular unless the members are acting as individuals.

Indefinite Pronoun Subject

> Of the two candidates, neither ~~have~~ *has* earned our support.

The verb *have* does not agree with the indefinite pronoun *neither,* which is singular. Most indefinite pronouns take singular verb forms; a few (*both, few, many, several*) take plural verb forms; and a few others (*all, any, enough, more, most, none, some*) can be either singular or plural, depending on the context.

***Who, Which,* or *That* as Subject**

> Air conditioning does not cause colds that ~~comes~~ *come* in the summer.

The verb *comes* does not agree with the plural noun *colds,* which is the antecedent of the relative pronoun *that. Who, which,* and *that* may refer either to singular or to plural antecedents, so you will need to identify the specific antecedent to choose a verb that agrees with any relative pronoun.

Singular Subject That Ends in *–s*

> The news ~~continue~~ *continues* to be depressing.

The verb *continue* does not agree with the subject *news,* which is singular.

ACTIVITY 1 Identifying Subject-Verb Agreement Errors

Underline the simple subject or subjects of every clause in the following examples, and double-underline the verbs. Put any dependent clause in parentheses. Finally, mark any sentence that contains a subject-verb agreement error with *SV;* if the sentence is correct, write *C*.

EXAMPLES: In the sparrow's nest was two cowbird eggs. *SV*

The baby birds (that hatch from those eggs) will be much bigger than sparrows. *C*

1. A bag of marbles were given to each child at the birthday party.
2. There was no fingerprints anywhere on the museum cases that the jewel thieves had opened.

3. Neither of the specials that the waiter described sound good to me.
4. He and everyone who works at the school is planning ways to raise funds for the choir tour.
5. The bundle of letters, which was kept in a box in the writer's attic, is a discovery that has thrilled scholars.

ACTIVITY 2 Revising Subject-Verb Agreement Errors

Rewrite the following items to correct any subject-verb agreement errors. If a sentence contains no error, write *Correct*.

EXAMPLE: Bat populations in many parts of the country has been affected by a deadly disease called white-nose syndrome.

REVISION: *Bat populations in many parts of the country have been affected by a deadly disease called white-nose syndrome.*

1. Everyone in these hills have a story to tell about the way life used to be.
2. Was the rooster and the cat squabbling in the yard this morning?
3. The first joke does not even make Miss Stanton smile, but the final series of anecdotes causes her to laugh so hard that tears come to her eyes.
4. At the county courthouse is clerks waiting impatiently for the judge to arrive.
5. There is a couple of methods that may help you get rid of hiccups, but nothing is certain to work.

ACTIVITY 3 Revising a Paragraph for Subject-Verb Agreement

The following paragraph, written for a general audience, may include subject-verb agreement errors. Revise the paragraph to correct any problems you find. Some sentences may not contain any errors.

In the early 1930s, making a living by farming in some parts of the Great Plains were first difficult and then impossible. Native prairie grasses with deep roots that had once held the soil in place was uprooted over time so that farmers could plant food crops such as wheat. Then the rain stopped falling. In the resulting "Dust Bowl" conditions, strong winds picked up the dry soil and blew it around in "black blizzards" that was unstoppable and made the land barren. As a result, there was soon few surviving farms in the hardest-hit counties in the Texas and Oklahoma panhandles. Many families lost everything and was forced to move away from their farms. However, in the Dust Bowl region nowadays is many farms and ranches. Is a repeat of the 1930s conditions possible? According to scientists, the biggest problem for farmers remain a severe drought. Dry topsoil is simply more likely to blow away. But irrigation systems are in place in the region now that was unknown in the Dust Bowl era. In addition, the crops planted on an Oklahoma farm today has the ability to thrive on less water. Finally, thanks to the volunteers of the Depression-era Civilian Conservation Corps, who planted millions of trees in the 1930s, the Great Plains are now more resistant to the forces of soil erosion and destructive, unstoppable winds.

ACTIVITY 4 Revising Subject-Verb Agreement Errors In Your Own Writing

Look over the most recent writing you've done to see if you have made any subject-verb agreement errors. If you find any, revise them.

workshop 15 Verb Form and Tense

Understanding Verb Form and Tense

No sentence is complete without a verb, so understanding how verbs work is essential.

For definitions and examples of grammar concepts key to understanding verb forms and verb tenses, see the ***Guide to Grammar Terms*** *table on pages 1101–1104.*

Verbs give readers a lot of information about what happened and when it happened. Forming verbs and verb phrases effectively is essential for making your writing credible and clear.

Revising Verb Forms

Most verbs have five different forms — the base form, the past tense form, the past participle form, the present participle form, and the third person singular or -*s* form.

base	describe	have	go
past tense	described	had	went
past participle	described	had	gone
present participle	describing	having	going

An important exception is the verb *be,* which uses two present tense forms (*am* and *are*) instead of the base form *be,* which uses *is* as a third person singular form instead of a regular -*s* form, and which uses two past tense forms (*was* and *were*).

Most verbs, such as *describe* in the preceding table, are regular, which means that the past tense and the past participle are the same and are formed by adding -*d* or -*ed* to the base form. However, several dozen verbs are irregular, including *have, go,* and other very common verbs such as *eat, drink, sleep, see,* and *think.* The only way to be sure of the forms of an irregular verb is to look them up and learn the ones you don't already know.

The most common problems with verb forms occur with the past tense and past participle forms of irregular verbs. Using spoken and other nonstandard verb forms in formal writing can be very distracting for readers.

Choose Appropriate Past Tense Forms

NONSTANDARD

He swum as fast as he could, but he did not win the race.

STANDARD

He swam as fast as he could, but he did not win the race.

The standard past tense form of *swim* is *swam,* not *swum.*

Choose Appropriate Past Participle Forms

NONSTANDARD

The pizza finally arrived after the guests had went home.

STANDARD

The pizza finally arrived after the guests had gone home.

The standard past participle form of *go* is *gone,* not *went.*

Revising Verb Tenses

A verb's tense indicates when an action or state of existence happens.

Simple Tenses

The three *simple tenses* describe actions and states in the present, past, and future.

simple past	I *spoke*, he *danced*
simple present	I *speak*, he *dances*
simple future	I *will speak*, he *will dance*

The simple past uses the past tense form of the verb; the simple present usually uses the base form or the *-s* form of the verb; and the simple future uses the helping verb *will* and the base form of the verb. The simple present tense can indicate an action that happens regularly ("Class ends at 11:10") as well as a one-time action in the present; the simple present is also used for writing about literature, movies, and art ("Scout and Jem find Boo Radley intriguing").

Perfect Tenses

The three *perfect tenses* describe actions or events that last for some time. To form a perfect tense, you need a verb phrase that includes a form of the helping verb *have* and the past participle of the main verb.

past perfect	she *had eaten*, we *had walked*
present perfect	she *has eaten*, we *have walked*
future perfect	she *will have eaten*, we *will have walked*

Progressive Forms

The three *progressive* forms indicate ongoing actions or conditions in the past, present, or future. To indicate a progressive action, you need a verb phrase that includes a form of the helping verb *be* and the present participle of the main verb.

past progressive	I *was watching*, they *were waiting*
present progressive	I *am watching*, they *are waiting*
future progressive	I *will be watching*, they *will be waiting*

Perfect Progressive Forms

Perfect progressive forms combine progressive forms with a perfect tense to show actions or conditions that are ongoing and that last for some time.

past perfect progressive	I *had been watching*, they *had been waiting*
present perfect progressive	I *have been watching*, they *have been waiting*
future perfect progressive	I *will have been watching*, they *will have been waiting*

Breaking the Rule: Appropriate Uses of Nonstandard Forms

You may sometimes want to use nonstandard forms in informal writing or in dialogue that reports the way someone speaks. Used intentionally, nonstandard forms can show off a writer's ability to use multiple dialects or languages effectively, a skill that is sometimes called *code-switching.* As with any literary technique, nonstandard forms should be used in appropriate contexts. Be sure the reader will know that you are using the nonstandard form intentionally!

ACTIVITY 1 Identifying Nonstandard Verb Forms

In the following examples, underline the complete verb in every clause. Double-underline any verb forms that are nonstandard. Some sentences may not include any nonstandard forms.

EXAMPLE: My mother was angry that we had drank all the milk.

1. After the cattle had went to the watering hole, they stood calmly under the elm trees.
2. Her father asked why she had not wrote her aunt to thank her for the gift.
3. He throwed dozens of wild pitches, but the manager let him stay in the game.
4. The cat lay in the sun until the day grew warm, and then it went under a chair.
5. Before the car alarm started to go off, a garbage truck had drove down the street, and the workers had tossed each empty metal can back to the curb with a loud clang.

ACTIVITY 2 Revising Verbs

Revise each of the following items to correct any verb forms that are not standard. Some sentences may not require any correction.

EXAMPLE: As I set the envelopes on the table, I seen a car coming up the driveway.

REVISION: *As I set the envelopes on the table, I saw a car coming up the driveway.*

1. We thought we had overcame our nervousness before leaving for the party, but the moment we walked in the door, our anxiety returned.
2. Marie has rode competitively in equestrian events since she was nine years old.
3. The film suggested that if aliens had taken over the planet, few humans would have been able to tell the difference.
4. Sergio lay the tablecloth on the table and then sat the china dishes carefully on it.
5. Before Mark announced that he needed more volunteers, Fauzia had rose to say that she wanted to participate.

ACTIVITY 3 Revising Verbs in a Paragraph

The following paragraph, written for a general audience, includes verb form errors. Revise the paragraph to correct those errors. Some sentences may not contain any incorrect verb forms.

Many people enjoy crafting because they can create heirlooms and gifts out of items they have maked. Craft projects take time and effort, and a lot of crafters who have began with good intentions end up never finishing a project. Sometimes these people carry the project with them through life. Shannon Downey, who enjoys embroidery, has boughten unfinished sewing projects at estate sales and finished them for crafters who have past away. When she came across an unfinished quilt with hexagonal pieces representing all fifty states, she knowed she had to complete it. The quilter, Rita Smith, had died at 99. The hexagons had state birds and flowers drew on them, but only two had been stitched. Downey asked crafters from her Instagram feed to volunteer to help. Her request had took off. More than a thousand people had soon wrote to Downey offering to embroider a hexagon for the #RitasQuilt project. Downey embroiders, but she does not quilt, so she founded thirty quilters prepared to stitch the embroidered pieces together. "Humans are amazing. Community can be built anywhere," she wrote in an Instagram post. Many people following #RitasQuilt have spoke up to say that the project proves that "social media can be used for good."

ACTIVITY 4 Revising Verb Form Problems in Your Own Writing

Look over the most recent writing you've done to see if you've used any inappropriate verb forms. As you review, revise any nonstandard forms you find that are likely to seem like mistakes to your readers. If you find a nonstandard form that you used to create a special effect and that seems to serve its purpose, be ready to explain why it does not require revision.

Vocabulary and Word Roots

If your parents asked you to consent to a nonsensical plan to wake up everybody in the house with a light-sensor alarm clock, would you resent it, or would you be too sentimental to object?

The above sentence may not make much sense, except as an illustration of how word roots connect many words with related meanings. How many words in the preceding two sentences have as their basis the Latin root *sent* or *sens*, meaning "to feel"?

A *root* is the origin of a word, often from a different language. Recognizing the roots of words can help you understand their meanings. The words *consent, nonsensical, sensor, resent, sentimental, sentence,* and *sense* may all be familiar to you. But the root, meaning "to feel," might help you understand the meaning of an unfamiliar word, like *sentient*.

Many roots form new words by adding *prefixes* and/or *suffixes* to the root. The addition of the prefix *in-* and the suffix *-itive* turn the root *sens* into the word *insensitive*.

Below are some common roots, their meanings, and words derived from these roots.

Root	Meaning	Words
-audi- (Latin)	to hear	audible, auditory, audiovisual
-bene- (Greek)	good, well	benevolent, beneficial, benefit
-bio- (Greek)	life	biology, autobiography, biotech
-duc(t)- (Latin)	to lead, to make	conduct, education, induce
-gen- (Greek)	race, kind	genetic, regenerate, genre
-geo- (Greek)	earth	geography, geode, geometry
-graph- (Greek)	to write	graphite, autograph, paragraph
-jur-, -jus- (Latin)	law	injustice, jury, jurisdiction
-log(o)- (Greek)	word, thought	logical, sociology, dialogue
-luc- (Latin)	light	translucent, elucidate, lucid
-manu- (Latin)	hand	manuscript, manual, manufacture
-mit-, -mis- (Latin)	to send	transmit, mission, permission
-path- (Greek)	feel, suffer	sympathy, telepathy, pathos
-phil- (Greek)	love	philosophy, Francophile, philanthropy
-photo- (Greek)	light	photosynthesis, photocopy, telephoto
-port- (Latin)	to carry	transportation, portable, important
-psych- (Greek)	soul	psyche, psychiatry, psychic
-scrib-, -script- (Latin)	to write	transcription, scripture, unscripted
-sent-, -sens- (Latin)	to feel	sensitive, consensual, sentient
-tele- (Greek)	far away	television, telekinesis, telepathy
-tend- (Latin)	to stretch	extend, contending, distended
-terr- (Latin)	earth	terrain, extraterrestrial, disinter
-vac- (Latin)	empty	vacuum, vacation, vacuous
-vid-, -vis- (Latin)	to see	invisible, video, visor

MLA Documentation Style

The Modern Language Association (MLA) documentation style is a set of rules for citing sources in formal research essays. It is the most common style for English classes, but be aware that other disciplines follow other models. By documenting sources properly, you make it easier for readers to find the exact texts that informed your opinions and supported your claims. For a teacher grading your paper, your use of systematic citation shows that you have been conscientious in investigating the topic and have avoided plagiarism. For readers who are interested in your paper, your list of works cited can help them learn more about the topic. Rhetorically speaking, a properly documented research paper boosts your ethos and appeals to logos.

Guidelines for In-Text Citations

MLA documentation requires in-text citations that refer to a list of works cited — an alphabetized list of all the sources you've drawn from. Sometimes all the necessary information for an in-text citation fits in the body of your sentence:

> On page 162 of *Aerotropolis: The Way We'll Live Next*, authors John D. Kasarda and Greg Lindsay suggest that downtown Detroit was doomed as soon as automobiles made the railroads less popular.

But more often, you'll include some key information in parentheses just before the period. In this second example, the writer included the book title and authors' names in her sentence and thus only needed to provide the page number in parentheses.

> In *Aerotropolis: The Way We'll Live Next*, authors John D. Kasarda and Greg Lindsay suggest that downtown Detroit was doomed as soon as automobiles made the railroads less popular (162).

In this third example, there is no source information embedded in the sentence itself. As a result, the in-text citation includes both the authors' names and the page number. Note that the title isn't included. With the authors' names, the reader has enough information to find the relevant entry in the list of works cited.

> Although the growth of car manufacturing brought jobs to Detroit, America's drivable network of industrial cities and residential suburbs "bled entire cities dry: starting with Detroit" (Kasarda and Lindsay 180).

Guidelines for a List of Works Cited

Print Resources

1. Book with One Author

A book with one author serves as a general model for most MLA citations. Include author, title, publisher, and date of publication.

> Beavan, Colin. *No Impact Man*. Farrar, Straus and Giroux, 2009.

2. Book with Multiple Authors

> Kasarda, John D., and Greg Lindsay. *Aerotropolis: The Way We'll Live Next*. Farrar, Straus and Giroux, 2011.

3. Two or More Works by the Same Author

Multiple entries should be arranged alphabetically by title. The author's name appears at the beginning of the first entry but is replaced by three hyphens and a period in all subsequent entries.

> Gladwell, Malcolm. *Outliers: The Story of Success*. Little, Brown, 2008.
>
> ---. *What the Dog Saw, and Other Adventures*. Little, Brown, 2009.

4. Author and Editor Both Named

Vidal, Gore. *The Selected Essays of Gore Vidal*. Edited by Jay Parini, Vintage Books, 2009.

Alternatively, to cite the editor's contribution, start with the editor's name.

Parini, Jay, editor. *The Selected Essays of Gore Vidal*. By Gore Vidal, Vintage Books, 2009.

5. Anthology

Oates, Joyce Carol, editor. *Telling Stories: An Anthology for Writers*. W. W. Norton, 1997.

Selection from an anthology:

Washington Irving, "Rip Van Winkle." *Conversations in American Literature: Language, Rhetoric, Culture*, edited by Robin Aufses et al., Bedford/St. Martin's, 2015, pp. 435–48.

6. Translation

Wiesel, Elie. *Night*. Translated by Marion Wiesel, Hill and Wang, 2006.

7. Entry in a Reference Work

Because most reference works are alphabetized, you should omit page numbers.

Lounsberry, Barbara. "Joan Didion." *Encyclopedia of the Essay*, edited by Tracy Chandler, Fitzroy, 1997.

For a well-known encyclopedia, use only the edition and year of publication. When an article is not attributed to an author, begin the entry with the article title.

"Gilgamesh." *The Columbia Encyclopedia*, 5th ed., 1993.

8. Sacred Text

Unless a specific published edition is being cited, sacred texts should be omitted from the Works Cited list.

The New Testament. Translated by Richmond Lattimore, North Point, 1997.

9. Article in a Journal

The title of the journal should be followed by the volume, issue, and year of the journal's publication, as well as the page range.

de Botton, Alain. "Treasure Hunt." *Lapham's Quarterly*, vol. 4, no. 2, 2011, pp. 205–10.

10. Article in a Magazine

In a weekly:

Menand, Louis. "The Unpolitical Animal: How Political Science Understands Voters." *The New Yorker*, 30 Aug. 2004, pp. 92–96.

In a monthly:

Baker, Kevin. "Barack Hoover Obama: The Best and the Brightest Blow It Again." *Harper's*, July 2009, pp. 29–37.

11. Article in a Newspaper

If you are citing a local paper that does not contain the city name in its title, add the city name in brackets after the title. When citing an article that does not appear on consecutive pages, list the first page followed by a plus sign. The edition only needs to be included if it is listed on the paper's masthead.

Edge, John T. "Fast Food Even before Fast Food." *The New York Times*, 30 Sept. 2009, late ed., pp. D1+.

12. Review

In a weekly:

Davis, Jordan. "Happy Thoughts!" Review of *The Golden Age of Paraphernalia*, by Kevin Davies, *The Nation*, 23 Feb. 2009, pp. 31–34.

In a monthly:

Simpson, Mona. "Imperfect Union." Review of *Mrs. Woolf and the Servants*, by Alison Light, *The Atlantic*, Jan.-Feb. 2009, pp. 93–101.

Electronic Resources

13. Article from a Database Accessed through a Subscription Service

Apply the normal rules for citing a journal article, but follow this with the name of the subscription service in italics, and the Digital Object Identifier, if available.

Morano, Michele. "Boy Eats World." *Fourth Genre: Explorations in Nonfiction*, vol. 13, no. 2, 2011, pp. 31–35. *Project MUSE*, doi:10.1353/fge.2011.0029.

14. Article in an Online Magazine

Follow the author name and article title with the name of the magazine in italics, the date published, and the URL of the article.

Yoffe, Emily. "Full Metal Racket: Metal Detecting Is the World's Worst Hobby." *Slate*, 18 Aug. 2003, www.slate.com/articles/life/human_guinea_pig/2003/08/full_metal_racket.html.

15. Article in an Online Newspaper

Sisario, Ben. "Record Stores: Out of Sight, Not Obsolete." *The New York Times*, 29 Sept. 2009, www.nytimes.com/2009/09/30/arts/music/30private.html.

16. Online Review

Stevens, Dana. "Catcher in the MRI." Review of *50/50*, directed by Adam Levine, *Slate*, 30 Sept. 2011, www.slate.com/articles/arts/movies/2011/09/_50_50_reviewed_joseph_gordon_levitt_and_seth_rogen_as_pals_vs_s.html.

17. Entry in an Online Reference Work

"Eschatology." *Merriam-Webster*, 7 Apr. 2016, www.merriam-webster.com/dictionary/eschatology.

18. Work from a Website

"Wallace Stevens." *Poetry Foundation*, 2015, www.poetryfoundation.org/bio/wallace-stevens.

19. Entire Website

Website with editor:

Dutton, Dennis, editor. *Arts and Letters Daily*. Chronicle of Higher Education, www.aldaily.com. Accessed 2 Oct. 2009.

Website without an editor:

Academy of American Poets. 2016, poets.org. Accessed 13 Mar. 2015.

Personal website:

Mendelson, Edward. Home page. Columbia U, 2013, english.columbia.edu/people/profile/394.

20. Entire Web Log (Blog)

Holbo, John, editor. *The Valve*, www.thevalve.org/go. Accessed 18 Mar. 2012.

21. Entry in a Wiki

"Pre-Raphaelite Brotherhood." *Wikipedia*, 25 Nov. 2013, wikipedia.org/wiki/Pre-Raphaelite_Brotherhood.

Other Sources

22. Film and Video

Follow the title with the director, notable performers, the distribution company, and the date of release. For films viewed on the web, follow this with the URL of the website used to view the film. If citing a particular individual's work on the film, you may begin the entry with his or her name before the title.

The Hurt Locker. Directed by Kathryn Bigelow, performances by Jeremy Renner, Anthony Mackie, Guy Pearce, and Ralph Fiennes, Summit Entertainment, 2009.

Viewed on the web (use the original distributor and release date):

Nayar, Vineet. "Employees First, Customers Second." *YouTube*, 9 June 2015, www.youtube.com/watch?v=cCdu67s_C5E.

23. Interview

Include the name of the interviewer if it is someone of note.

Personal interview:

Tripp, Lawrence. Personal interview, 14 Apr. 2014.

In print:

Dylan, Bob. "Who Is This Bob Dylan?" *Esquire*, 23 Jan. 2014, pp. 124+.

On the radio:

Gioia, Dana. Interview with Leonard Lopate. *The Leonard Lopate Show*, WNYC, 19 July 2004.

On the web:

Gioia, Dana. Interview with Leonard Lopate. *The Leonard Lopate Show*, WNYC, 19 July 2004, www.wnyc.org/story/49925-dana-gioia.

24. Lecture or Speech

Viewed in person:

Kass, Leon. "Looking for an Honest Man: Reflections of an Unlicensed Humanist." Jefferson Lecture in the Humanities, Warner Theatre, Washington, D.C., 22 May 2009.

Viewed on the web:

Batuman, Elif. Boston College Lowell Humanities Series, 13 Oct. 2010, frontrow.bc.edu/program/batuman.

25. Podcast

Carlin, Dan. "King of Kings." *Hardcore History Podcast*, 28 Oct. 2015, www.dancarlin.com/hardcore-history-56-kings-of-kings.

26. Work of Art or Photograph

In a museum:

Hopper, Edward. *Nighthawks*. 1942, Art Institute, Chicago. Oil on canvas.

On the web:

Thiebaud, Wayne. *Three Machines*. 1963, De Young Museum, San Francisco, shop.famsf.org/Product.do?code=T636P. Accessed 2 Oct. 2013.

In print:

Clark, Edward. *Navy CPO Graham Jackson Plays "Goin' Home."* 1945, *The Great LIFE Photographers*, Bulfinch, 2004, pp. 78–79.

27. Map or Chart

In print:

"U.S. Personal Savings Rate, 1929–1999." *Credit Card Nation: The Consequences of America's Addiction to Credit*, by Robert D. Manning, Basic Books, 2000, p. 100.

On the web:

"1914 New Balkan States and Central Europe Map." *National Geographic*, maps.nationalgeographic.com/maps/print-collection/balkan-states-map.html. Accessed 25 Oct. 2013.

28. Cartoon or Comic Strip

In print:

Vey, P. C. *The New Yorker*, 10 Nov. 2008, p. 54. Cartoon.

On the web:

Zyglis, Adam. "City of Light." Buffalo News, 8 Nov. 2015, adamzyglis.buffalonews.com/2015/11/08/city-of-light/. Cartoon.

29. Advertisement

In print:

Rosetta Stone. *Harper's*, Aug. 2008, p. 21. Advertisement.

On the web:

Seamless. *The Washington Post*, www.washingtonpost.com. Accessed 4 Apr. 2016. Advertisement.

Glossary / Glosario

English | **Español**

A

act The major subunit into which the action of a play is divided. The number of acts in a play typically ranges between one and five, and the acts are usually further divided into scenes.

acto Unidad principal en la que se segmenta la acción de una obra de teatro. El número de actos de una obra de teatro oscila entre uno y cinco, y los actos están por lo general divididos en escenas.

---

active listening Listening that is focused and engaged.

escuchar con atención Escuchar con cuidado y empeño.

---

ad hominem Latin for "directed to the person," this fallacy refers to the specific diversionary tactic of switching the argument from the issue at hand to the character of the other speaker. If you argue that a park in your community should not be renovated because the person supporting the plan was arrested during a domestic dispute, then you are guilty of using an *ad hominem* fallacy.

ad hominem En latín, "dirigido a la persona." Esta falacia se refiere a la táctica de distracción que consiste en centrar el argumento no en el asunto en cuestión sino en el carácter de la otra parte. Si argumentamos que un parque de nuestra comunidad no debería ser renovado porque quien presenta el plan fue arrestado durante una disputa doméstica, usamos una falacia *ad hominem*.

---

ad populum (*See* **bandwagon appeal**.) Latin for "directed to the people," this fallacy occurs when evidence used to defend an argument boils down to "everybody's doing it, so it must be a good thing to do."

> You should vote to elect Rachel Johnson — she has a strong lead in the polls.

Polling higher does not necessarily make Senator Johnson the "best" candidate; it only makes her the most popular.

ad populum (*Ver* **sofisma populista.**) En latín, "dirigido al pueblo." Esta falacia ocurre cuando la evidencia que se usa para respaldar un argumento se reduce a decir "todos lo están haciendo, así que debe ser algo bueno."

> Debes votar por Rachel Johnson. Ella está a la cabeza de las encuestas.

El hecho de que esté de primera en las encuestas no significa que la Senadora Johnson sea la "mejor" candidata; solo la hace la más popular.

---

alliteration Repetition of the same consonant sound at the beginning of several words or syllables in sequence.

> Come live with me and be my love,
>
> And we will all the pleasures prove
>
> — Christopher Marlowe,
> "The Passionate Shepherd to His Love," (p. 61)

aliteración Repetición del mismo sonido consonántico al principio de varias palabras o sílabas en secuencia.

---

allusion Brief reference to a person, an event, or a place (real or fictitious) or to a work of art.

> The title of Maya Angelou's memoir *I Know Why the Caged Bird Sings* (p. 400) is an allusion to Paul Laurence Dunbar's poem "Sympathy" (pp. 70–71).

alusión Breve referencia a una persona, un suceso o un lugar (real o ficticio) o a una obra de arte.

> El título de la autobiografía de Maya Angelou *Yo sé por qué canta el pájaro enjaulado* (pág. 400) es una alusión al poema "Simpatía" (págs. 70–71) de Paul Laurence Dunbar.

analogy A comparison between two seemingly dissimilar things. Often, an analogy uses something simple or familiar to explain something complex or unfamiliar.

> Shawne Merriman is almost as big as the best offensive tackle who ever played and almost as fast as the best wide receiver who ever played. He is a rhinoceros who moves like a deer.
>
> —Chuck Klosterman, "Why We Look the Other Way," p. 849

analogía Comparación entre dos cosas aparentemente diferentes. Por lo general, la analogía se vale de algo sencillo o común para explicar algo complejo y poco común.

analysis To understand something by investigating its parts.

análisis Entender algo al investigar sus partes.

anaphora Repetition of a word or phrase at the beginning of successive phrases, clauses, or lines.

> But somewhere I read of the freedom of assembly. Somewhere I read of the freedom of speech. Somewhere I read of the freedom of press. Somewhere I read that the greatness of America is the right to protest for right.
>
> —Martin Luther King Jr., "I Have Been to the Mountaintop," p. 211

anáfora Repetición de una palabra o frase al principio de varias frases, oraciones, o líneas sucesivas.

anecdote A brief story used to illustrate a point or claim.

anécdota Breve historia que sirve para ilustrar el sentido de un argumento o una afirmación.

annotation The taking of notes directly on a text. For an example of annotation, see p. 10.

anotación Tomar notas directamente en un texto. Para ver un ejemplo de anotación, consulte la pág. 10.

antagonist Character in a piece of literature who opposes the protagonist: While not necessarily an enemy, the antagonist creates or intensifies a conflict for the protagonist. An evil antagonist is a villain.

> In William Shakespeare's *Macbeth* (p. 942), the witches serve as antagonists, fueling Macbeth's ambition, and using misleading prophecies to prod him toward his downfall.

antagonista El personaje de una obra literaria que se opone al protagonista; aunque no necesariamente un enemigo, el antagonista crea o intensifica el conflicto del protagonista. Un antagonista malvado es un villano.

> En *Macbeth* de William Shakespeare (pág. 942), las brujas hacen de antagonistas, pues encienden la ambición de Macbeth y usan profecías falsas para llevarlo a su perdición.

antithesis A syntax strategy in which two ideas are placed side-by-side for effect.

> America is an improbable idea. A mongrel nation built of ever-changing disparate parts, it is held together by a notion, the notion that all men are created equal, though everyone knows that most men consider themselves better than someone.
>
> —Anna Quindlen, from "A Quilt of a Country," p. 23

antítesis Oposición, o contraste, de ideas o palabras en una construcción paralela.

appeal to false authority This fallacy occurs when someone who has no credibility to speak on an issue is cited as an authority. A TV star, for instance, is not a medical expert, though pharmaceutical advertisements often use such celebrities to endorse products.

According to former congressional leader Ari Miller, the Himalayas have an estimated Yeti population of between 300 and 500 individuals.

apelación a una falsa autoridad Esta falacia ocurre cuando se cita como autoridad a alguien que no tiene credibilidad para hablar sobre un asunto. Por ejemplo, una estrella de TV no es un experto en medicina. Sin embargo, en los anuncios publicitarios de las farmacéuticas suelen aparecer celebridades que promocionan dichos productos.

Según el exlíder del congreso Ari Miller, los Himalayas tienen una población estimada de Yetis de entre 300 y 500 individuos.

appeals (*See* **rhetorical appeals**.)

apelaciones (*Ver* **figuras retóricas de apelación.**)

archaic diction Old-fashioned or outdated choice of words.

If this be error and upon me prov'd,

I never writ, nor no man ever lov'd.

—William Shakespeare, Sonnet 116, p. 56

dicción arcaica Elección anticuada o poco actualizada de palabras.

argument A process of reasoned inquiry. A persuasive discourse resulting in a coherent and considered movement from a claim to a conclusion.

argumentar Proceso de indagación razonada. Un discurso persuasivo que da como resultado el pase coherente y sopesado desde una afirmación hasta una conclusión.

Aristotelian triangle (*See* **rhetorical triangle**.)

triángulo aristotélico (*Ver* **triángulo retórico**.)

assertion A statement that presents a claim or thesis.

aseveración Enunciado que incluye una afirmación o tesis.

assonance The repetition of vowel sounds in a sequence of words.

Come live with me and be my love,

—Christopher Marlowe, "The Passionate Shepherd to His Love," p. 61

asonancia La repetición de sonidos vocálicos en una secuencia de palabras.

audience The listener, viewer, or reader of a text. Most texts are likely to have multiple audiences.

público Quien escucha, ve, o lee un texto. La mayoría de los textos suelen tener varios públicos.

authority Whether a speaker or a source is an expert in a field, either by education or experience.

autoridad Si un hablante o una fuente son expertos en un tema, ya sea por formación o por experiencia.

B

ballad A narrative poem made up of a series of quatrains. Ballads usually have rhyme schemes in which every other line rhymes, for instance *abac* or *abcb*.

romance Poema narrativo compuesto de una serie de cuartetos. Los romances suelen seguir patrones de rima en los que rima un verso de por medio, por ejemplo, *abac* o *abcb*.

bandwagon appeal Also known as *ad populem*, Latin for "directed to the people," this fallacy occurs when evidence used to defend an argument boils down to "everybody's doing it, so it must be a good thing to do."

sofisma populista Esta falacia (también conocida como *ad populum*, "dirigido al pueblo" en latín) ocurre cuando la evidencia que se usa para respaldar un argumento se reduce a decir "todos lo están haciendo, así que debe ser algo bueno."

bias A prejudice or preconceived notion that prevents a person from approaching a topic in a neutral or an objective way. While you can be biased *toward* something, the most common usage has a negative connotation.

parcialidad Un prejuicio o una noción preconcebida que impide que una persona se aproxime a un tema de una manera neutral y objetiva. Si bien podemos estar parcializados a favor de algo, el uso más común tiene una connotación negativa.

blank verse Unrhymed iambic pentameter.

> *See* William Shakespeare, "The Seven Ages of Man," p. 313.

verso libre pentámetro yámbico sin rima.

> *Ver* William Shakespeare, "Las siete edades del hombre," pág. 313.

blocking The actions of the people in a story. In drama, this refers to the movements and gestures and expressions of actors on stage. In fiction and nonfiction narratives, it refers to the descriptions of those movements, gestures, and expressions.

> Inside, my mother was cooking dinner while James followed her around the kitchen, handing her bits of paper he'd folded into unusual shapes. Even then, he had a knack for geometry.
>
> —Amy Silverberg, from "Suburbia!," p. 303

didascalia Las acciones de las personas en una historia. En las obras dramáticas, esto se refiere a los movimientos, gestos, y expresiones de los actores en escena. En las obras de ficción y narrativas, se refiere a las descripciones de dichos movimientos, gestos, y expresiones.

C

caesura A pause created by punctuation within a line of poetry that often mirrors natural speech.

> Men marched asleep. Many had lost their
> boots,
>
> But limped on, blood-shod. All went lame; all
> blind;
>
> —Wilfred Owen, "Dulce et Decorum Est," p. 225

cesura Pausa causada por la puntuación dentro de un verso poético que con frecuencia refleja el habla natural.

cacophony Harsh, discordant sounds, especially in poetry.

> The bickering of vowels on the buses,
>
> the clicking thumbs and the big hips of
>
> the navy-skirted ticket collectors. . .
>
> —Eavan Boland, "An Irish Childhood in England: 1951," p. 519

cacofonía Sonidos disonantes y estridentes, particularmente encontrados en la poesía.

character A person depicted in a narrative. While this term generally refers to human beings, it can also include animals or inanimate objects that are given human characteristics. Several more specific terms are used to refer to types of characters frequently employed by authors:

personaje Persona representada en una historia. Aunque este término se refiere por lo general a seres humanos, también puede incluir animales u objetos inanimados a los que se les atribuyen características humanas. Los autores usan términos más específicos para referirse a diversos tipos de personajes:

flat character A character embodying only one or two traits and who lacks character development; for this reason, a flat character is also called a static character. Often such characters exist only to provide background or adequate motivation for a protagonist's actions.

In *Macbeth* (p. 942), the Porter is a flat character. He is a gatekeeper at Macbeth's home and leads Macbeth to the king's chambers.

personaje plano Personaje que solo posee uno o dos rasgos y cuyo carácter carece de desarrollo; por tal motivo, los personajes planos también se conocen como personajes estáticos. Por lo general, estos personajes solo existen para presentar los antecedentes o para motivar las acciones del protagonista.

En *Macbeth* (pág. 942), el portero es un personaje plano. Vigila la entrada de la casa de Macbeth y lo escolta a las habitaciones del rey.

round character A character who exhibits a range of emotions and evolves over the course of the story.

In *Macbeth* (p. 942), Macbeth himself is a round character. He has complex motivations and various facets to his personality, and our understanding of him evolves over the course of the story.

personaje redondo Personaje que incluye una variedad de emociones y que evoluciona a lo largo de la historia.

En *Macbeth* (pág. 942), el propio Macbeth es un personaje redondo. Posee motivaciones complejas y una personalidad multifacética; nuestra comprensión del personaje va evolucionando conforme avanza el relato.

---

characterization The method by which the author builds, or reveals, a character; it can be direct or indirect.

direct characterization occurs when a narrator tells the reader who a character is by describing that character's background, motivation, temperament, or appearance.

The young woman was tall, with a figure of perfect elegance, on a large scale. She had dark and abundant hair, so glossy that it threw off the sunshine with a gleam, and a face which, besides being beautiful from regularity of feature and richness of complexion, had the impressiveness belonging to a marked brow and deep black eyes.

— Nathaniel Hawthorne, *The Scarlet Letter*, p. 46

indirect characterization means that an author shows rather than tells us what a character is like through what the character says, does, or thinks or through what others say about the character.

If you really want to hear about it, the first thing you'll probably want to know is where I was born, and what my lousy childhood was like, and how my parents were occupied and all before they had me, and all that David Copperfield kind of crap, but I don't feel like going into it, if you want to know the truth.

— J. D. Salinger, *The Catcher in the Rye*, p. 69

caracterización El método mediante el cual el autor construye, o revela, un personaje; puede ser directa o indirecta.

caracterización directa es cuando el narrador le dice al lector cómo es el personaje al describir sus antecedentes, motivación, temperamento, o apariencia.

caracterización indirecta significa que el autor no dice, sino que muestra cómo es el personaje a través de lo que dice, hace, o piensa este mismo o a través de lo que los demás dicen del personaje.

claim Also called an assertion or a proposition, a claim states the argument's main idea or position. A claim differs from a topic or subject in that a claim has to be arguable.

afirmación También llamada aseveración o proposición, una afirmación establece la idea o posición principal de un argumento. La diferencia entre un tema y una afirmación es que esta debe ser justificable.

climax (*See* **plot**.) The place where the tension of the rising action has reached its most significant place.

clímax (*Ver* **trama.**) Lugar en el que la tensión de la acción ha llegado a su punto más importante.

commentary In writing, commentary is the writer's discussion or analysis of a piece of evidence.

comentario En narrativa, un comentario es el análisis que el autor hace sobre cierta evidencia.

complex sentence A sentence that includes one independent clause and at least one dependent clause.

> In the early morning, when the alley was still quiet, I could smell fragrant red beans as they were cooked down to a pasty sweetness.
>
> —Amy Tan, "The Rules of the Game," p. 316

oración compleja Oración que incluye una oración independiente y al menos una oración dependiente.

compound sentence A sentence that includes at least two independent clauses.

> A hundred people might show up, and you've got to feed them.
>
> —Trevor Noah, "Chameleon," p. 348

oración compuesta Oración que incluye al menos dos oraciones independientes.

compound-complex sentence A sentence that includes two or more independent clauses and one or more dependent clauses.

> Twenty-eight percent of public school students and 21 percent of private school students report being bullied, and though inner-city kids are routinely portrayed in the press as menaces, the highest levels of bullying are reported among white kids and in nonurban areas.
>
> —Rebecca Solnit, "Abolish High School," p. 438

oración compleja y compuesta Oración que incluye una o dos oraciones independientes y una o dos oraciones dependientes.

concede (*See* **concession**.)

conceder (*Ver* **concesión.**)

concession An acknowledgment that an opposing argument may be true or reasonable. In a strong argument, a concession is usually accompanied by a refutation challenging the validity of the opposing argument.

> The human race, after all, is a pretty sorry mess, with our stubborn diseases, physical limitations, and short lives. Throw in humanity's jealousies, violence, and constant anxieties, and the transhumanist project begins to look downright reasonable. If it were technologically possible, why wouldn't we want to transcend our current species?
>
> —Francis Fukuyama, "Transhumanism," p. 612

concesión El reconocimiento de que un argumento opuesto puede ser verdadero o razonable. Cuando se trata de un argumento sólido, la concesión viene por lo general acompañada de una refutación que pone en juego la validez del argumento opuesto.

conflict The tension, opposition, or struggle that drives a plot. External conflict is the opposition or tension between two characters or forces. Internal conflict occurs within a character. Conflict usually arises between the protagonist and the antagonist in a story.

> In *Macbeth* (p. 942), the internal conflict is between Macbeth's ambition and his conscience. The external conflict is between Macbeth and the other rulers he is trying to remove in order to gain power.

conflicto La tensión, oposición, o lucha que permite que la trama se desenvuelva. Un conflicto externo es la oposición o tensión entre dos personajes o fuerzas. Un conflicto interno ocurre dentro del personaje. Un conflicto surge por lo general entre el protagonista y el antagonista de una historia.

> En *Macbeth* (pág. 942), el conflicto interno se da entre la ambición de Macbeth y su conciencia. El conflicto externo se da entre Macbeth y los demás gobernantes que está tratando de eliminar con el fin de ganar poder.

conjunction Words that connect things. Examples include *and,* and *but.*

conjunción Palabras que conectan cosas. Algunos ejemplos son: *y*, y *pero.*

connotation Connotation refers to meanings or associations that readers have with a word beyond its dictionary definition, or denotation. Connotations can be positive or negative, and they often greatly affect the author's tone. Consider the connotations of the words below, all of which mean "overweight."

> That cat is *plump*. That cat is *fat*. That cat is *obese.*

connotación Se refiere a los significados y asociaciones que los lectores tienen con una palabra más allá de su definición en el diccionario, o denotación. Las connotaciones son positivas o negativas, y por lo general influyen en el tono del autor. Tomemos por caso las connotaciones de las siguientes palabras, que significan "sobrepeso."

> Ese gato está *regordete*. Ese gato está *gordo*. Ese gato está *obeso*.

consensus In a conversation or an argument, reaching an agreement or compromise position that all participants can agree on.

consenso En una conversación o una discusión, llegar a un acuerdo o a una postura con la que todos los participantes estén de acuerdo.

consonance Repeating consonant sounds, most often found in poetry.

> I snapped beans into the silver bowl
>
> that sat on the splintering slats
>
> of the porch swing between my grandma and me.
>
> —Lisa Parker, "Snapping Beans," p. 459

consonancia La repetición del mismo sonido creado por consonantes en una secuencia de palabras.

context The circumstances, atmosphere, attitudes, and events surrounding a **text**.

> In March of 1968, Martin Luther King traveled to Memphis, Tennessee to lend his support and inspiration to the black sanitation and public works employees who were on strike for better wages and fair treatment. Violence between police and protestors had broken out at the rally on March 28. . . . "I Have Been to the Mountaintop" was delivered to an audience of supporters on April 3, 1968, and responds to that violence of a few days before. Tragically, this speech was King's last, as he was assassinated the following day by James Earl Ray, who confessed to the murder and died in prison in 1998.

contexto Las circunstancias, la atmósfera, las actitudes, y los eventos que rodean a un **texto**.

> En marzo de 1968, Martin Luther King viajó a Memphis, Tennessee para brindar su apoyo y servir de inspiración a los trabajadores sanitarios y empleados públicos de raza negra, quienes estaban de huelga en reclamo de mejoras salariales y un trato justo. Se habían producido enfrentamientos con violencia entre la policía y los manifestantes durante la marcha del 28 de marzo . . . El 3 de abril de 1968, pronunció el discurso "He ido a la cima de la montaña" ante parte de sus seguidores, en respuesta a la violencia de los días previos. Trágicamente, este fue el último discurso de King, ya que fue asesinado al día siguiente por James Earl Ray, quien confesó el crimen y murió en prisión en 1998.

context clues Determining the definition of an unknown word by looking at nearby words in a sentence or paragraph that you do know.

pistas del contexto Determinar la definición de una palabra mediante al resto de las palabras cercanas de una oración o párrafo que sí entiendes.

coordination A way of combining two sentences that uses a coordinating conjunction (and, but, or), and communicates that the two ideas in the original sentences are of equal importance.

> It's tempting to dismiss the notion of highly intelligent machines as mere science fiction, but this would be a mistake, and potentially our worst mistake ever.
>
> —Stephen Hawking, "Will AI Outsmart Us?," p. 616

coordinación El uso de una palabra u oración dependiente para conectar dos ideas de igual importancia.

counterargument An opposing argument to the one a writer is putting forward. Rather than ignoring a counterargument, a strong writer will usually address it through the process of concession and refutation.

> Another argument that college presidents make is that multigenerational enrollment helps improve the institutional ethos, tightening the bonds of community for those lucky enough to be admitted. That may be so, but it comes at a high cost in unfairness.
>
> —The Editorial Board of the *New York Times*, "End Legacy College Admissions," p. 104

contraargumento Argumento opuesto al que está presentando el escritor. Los escritores experimentados no ignoran los contraargumentos, sino que los someten a procesos de concesión y refutación.

couplet A rhyming two-line stanza.

copla Par de versos sucesivos que riman y que normalmente tienen la misma longitud.

cumulative sentence A sentence that completes the main idea at the beginning of the sentence and then builds and adds on detail.

> For those who like it, the faint insistent sweetness of *drooz* may perfume the ways of the city, *drooz* which first brings a great lightness and brilliance to the mind and limbs, and then after some hours a dreamy languor, and wonderful visions at last of the very Arcana and inmost secrets of the Universe, as well as exciting the pleasure of sex beyond all belief; and it is not habit-forming.
>
> —Ursula K. Le Guin, "The Ones Who Walk Away from Omelas," p. 746

oración acumulativa Oración que completa la idea principal al principio y luego añade algo.

currency How recent a source is. This might impact whether the source is current enough to be useful in support of an argument.

actual Qué tan reciente es una fuente. Puede ejercer un impacto si la fuente es lo suficientemente actual como para respaldar un argumento.

D

debate A discussion about a certain topic, in which conflicting arguments are presented and all parties argue in favor of a single side, rather than working toward a **consensus.**

debate Discusión sobre cierto tema, en la que se presentan argumentos opuestos y cada parte asume que su opinión es la correcta.

deduction A logical process wherein you reach a conclusion by starting with a general principle or universal truth (a major premise) and applying it to a specific case (a minor premise). The process of deduction is usually demonstrated in the form of a syllogism:

MAJOR PREMISE	Exercise contributes to better health.
MINOR PREMISE	Yoga is a type of exercise.
CONCLUSION	Yoga contributes to better health.

deducción Un proceso lógico en el que se llega a una conclusión a partir de un principio o verdad universal (premisa mayor) al aplicarle un caso específico (premisa menor). El proceso de deducción se suele ejemplificar con silogismos:

PREMISA MAYOR	El ejercicio es bueno para la salud.
PREMISA MENOR	El yoga es un tipo de ejercicio.
CONCLUSIÓN	El yoga es bueno para la salud.

denotation (*See* **connotation**.) The dictionary definition of a word.

denotación (*Ver* **connotación**.) La definición de una palabra del diccionario.

dialogue A conversation between two or more people.

> "If I tried to get away with it," said George, "then other people'd get away with it — and pretty soon we'd be right back to the dark ages again, with everybody competing against everybody else. You wouldn't like that, would you?"
>
> "I'd hate it," said Hazel.
>
> "There you are," said George. "The minute people start cheating on laws, what do you think happens to society?"
>
> — Kurt Vonnegut, "Harrison Bergeron," p. 738

diálogo Conversación entre dos o más personas.

diction A speaker's choice of words. Analysis of diction looks at these choices and what they add to the speaker's message. Formal diction is the use of more serious language, perhaps using longer or more obscure words, or words that are unlikely to offend. Informal diction is the use of language in a relaxed style, perhaps using slang terms or a conversational tone.

dicción Las palabras que decide usar una persona que habla. Un análisis de dicción identifica dichas palabras y aquello que añaden al mensaje de la persona que habla. La dicción formal es el uso de un lenguaje más serio, quizás con palabras más largas u oscuras, o palabras que en general no sean ofensivas. La dicción informal es el uso del lenguaje con un estilo informal, quizás con modismos o en un tono conversacional.

drama A type of storytelling meant to be performed in a live setting.

drama Contar una historia que se representa en un escenario.

E

either-or fallacy Also known as a false dilemma, in this fallacy the speaker presents two extreme options as the only possible choices.

> Either we agree to raise taxes, or our grandchildren will be drowning in debt.

falacia o-o En esta falacia, el hablante presenta dos opciones extremas como las únicas opciones posibles.

> O nos ponemos de acuerdo para subir los impuestos o nuestros nietos estarán ahogados en deudas.

elegy A type of poem expressing grief or sadness, written in response to a death. Elegies no longer have strict formal rules regarding length, rhyme scheme, or meter.

elegía Tipo de poema que expresa lamento o tristeza, escrito en respuesta a una muerte. Una elegía no sigue las reglas formales en cuanto a longitud, métrica, y rima.

end rhyme (*See* **rhyme**.)

rima final (*Ver* **rima**.)

English sonnet (*See* **sonnet**.)

soneto inglés (*Ver* **soneto**.)

enjambment A poetic technique in which one line ends without a pause and continues to the next line to complete its meaning; also referred to as a "run-on line."

> To be a good
>
> ex/current friend for R. To be one last
>
> inspired way to get back at R. To be relationship
>
> advice for L. To be advice . . .
>
> —Chen Chen, "When I Grow Up I Want to Be a List of Further Possibilities," p. 287

encabalgamiento Técnica poética en la que un verso termina sin una pausa y continúa al siguiente verso para completar su significado.

ethos Greek for "character." Speakers appeal to ethos to demonstrate that they are credible and trustworthy to speak on a given topic. Ethos is established by both who you are and what you say.

> My own experience in high school confirms this view. Playing football made me more confident; it gave me powers of resolve that I'd draw on later in life, and I'm grateful for those things. But it also made me more brutal. I came to crave the physical stimulation of the game—I came to like hitting and even being hit.
>
> —Mark Edmundson, from "Do Sports Build Character? Or Damage It?," p. 137

ethos "Carácter" en griego. El hablante apela al ethos para demostrar credibilidad y confiabilidad al hablar de cierto tema. El ethos viene establecido por quiénes somos y por lo que decimos.

euphony A series of words that produce a pleasing sound.

> I want you to be
>
> a student of impossible binds,
>
> a magician of
>
> a bloom from a fist,
>
> a dove from a dove from a dove.
>
> —Deborah Kuan, "Magic Lesson," p. 72

eufonía Una serie de palabras que producen una sonoridad agradable.

exposition (*See* **plot**.) In literature, the part of the story where the author provides background information about the characters, settings, or major ideas.

> There are three things Zinhle decides, when she is old enough to understand. The first is that she will never, ever, give less than her best to anything she tries to do. The second is that she will not live in fear. The third, which is perhaps meaningless given the first two and yet comes to define her existence most powerfully, is this: She will be herself. No matter what.
>
> —N. K. Jemisin, "Valedictorian," p. 695

exposición (*Ver* **trama.**) En literatura, la parte de la historia donde el autor expone los antecedentes de los personajes, el ambiente, o las ideas principales.

eye rhyme (*See* **rhyme**.)

rima visual (*Ver* **rima**.)

F

fallacy (*See* **logical fallacies.**)	**falacia** (*Ver* **falacias lógicas.**)
falling action (*See* **plot.**) A section of plot that includes those events immediately after the climax, during which the characters normally deal only with the results of the choices made during the climax.	**disminución de la acción** (*Ver* **trama.**) Sección de la trama que incluye los sucesos que vienen después del clímax, durante los cuales los personajes tienen que lidiar con las consecuencias de lo que hicieron en el clímax.
false dilemma (*See* **either-or fallacy.**)	**falso dilema** (*Ver* **falacia o-o.**)
faulty analogy A fallacy that occurs when an analogy compares things that are not comparable. For instance, to argue that we should legalize human euthanasia, since we all agree that it is humane to put terminally ill animals to sleep, ignores significant emotional and ethical differences between the ways we view humans and animals.	**falsa analogía** Falacia que ocurre cuando en una analogía se comparan cosas que no son comparables. Por ejemplo, argumentar que deberíamos legalizar la eutanasia en los humanos, dado que todos estamos de acuerdo en que es humano poner a dormir animales desahuciados, ignora ciertas diferencias emocionales y éticas entre la manera en que vemos a humanos y animales.
figurative language (figure of speech) Nonliteral language, often evoking strong imagery. Figures of speech often compare one thing to another either explicitly (using simile) or implicitly (using metaphor). Other forms of figurative language include personification, paradox, hyperbole (overstatement), understatement, metonymy, synecdoche, and irony.	**lenguaje figurado (figura retórica)** Lenguaje no literal, que por lo general evoca una imagen vívida; a veces es llamado tropo. Por lo general, las figuras retóricas comparan una cosa con otra de manera explícita (usando un símil) o implícita (usando una metáfora). Otros tipos de lenguaje figurado son: la personificación, la paradoja, la exageración (hipérbole), la atenuación, la metonimia, la sinécdoque. y la ironía.
flashback A section of plot that shows earlier parts of the story.	**evocación** Sección de la trama que muestra partes anteriores de la historia.
foil One common type of supporting character, whose purpose is to contrast with a main character in order to highlight an aspect or a trait.	**adlátere** Un tipo común de personaje secundario, cuyo objetivo es crear un contraste con el personaje principal para resaltar un aspecto o rasgo.
foreshadowing The introduction early in a story of verbal and dramatic hints that suggest what is to come later.	**presagio** La presentación a principios de la historia de pistas verbales y dramáticas que sugieren lo que vendrá luego.
form Refers to the defining structural characteristics of a work, especially a poem (i.e., meter and rhyme scheme). Often poets work within set forms, such as the sonnet, which require adherence to fixed conventions.	**forma** Se refiere a las características estructurales que definen una obra, sobre todo un poema (es decir, métrica y rima). Por lo general, los poetas trabajan con formas ya establecidas, como el soneto, lo que implica el uso de ciertas convenciones.
formal diction (*See* **diction.**)	**dicción formal** (*Ver* **dicción.**)

fragment An incomplete sentence. Usually fragments omit a subject, a verb/predicate, or both. Ingrid spent most of her day on the computer. Tweeting and posting to Facebook.	**fragmento** Oración incompleta. Por lo general, a los fragmentos les falta el sujeto, un verbo/predicado. o ambos. Ingrid pasó la mayor parte del día en la computadora. Tuiteando y publicando en Facebook.
free verse A form of poetry with lines that closely follow the natural rhythms of speech, not adhering to any specific rhyming or meter pattern. Traveling through the dark I found a deer dead on the edge of the Wilson River road. It is usually best to roll them into the canyon: that road is narrow; to swerve might make more dead. — William Stafford, "Traveling Through the Dark," p. 896	**verso libre** Tipo de poesía con versos que siguen de alguna manera el ritmo natural del habla, sin usar ningún patrón rítmico o métrico en particular.

G

genre A category of literary texts. Some literary genres include fiction, poetry, and drama.	**género** Categoría de textos literarios. Algunos géneros literarios son: ficción, poesía, y drama.

H

hasty generalization A fallacy in which a faulty conclusion is reached because of inadequate evidence. Smoking isn't bad for you; my great aunt smoked a pack a day and lived to be ninety.	**generalización apresurada** Falacia en la que se saca una conclusión falsa debido a que la evidencia es inadecuada. Fumar no es dañino; mi tía fumaba una cajetilla al día y vivió noventa años.
hook An opening of an argument with the purpose of getting the audience's attention. Mobilizing to confront the pandemic and, eventually, to reconstruct the shattered economy, requires not only medical and economic expertise but also moral and political renewal. We need to ask a basic question that we have evaded over these last decades: What do we owe one another as citizens? — Michael Sandel, "Are We All in This Together?," p. 843	**anzuelo** Apertura de un argumento con el propósito de llamar la atención del público.
hubris The Greek term for pride. In drama, hubris is the most common tragic flaw of a character.	***hibris*** "Orgullo" en griego. En las obras dramáticas, la hibris es el defecto trágico más común de los personajes.
hyperbole Deliberate exaggeration used for emphasis or to produce a comic or an ironic effect; an overstatement to make a point. In the first place, that stuff bores me, and in the second place, my parents would have about two hemorrhages apiece if I told anything pretty personal about them. — J. D. Salinger, *The Catcher in the Rye*, p. 69	**hipérbole** Exageración deliberada que se usa para hacer énfasis o para producir un efecto cómico o irónico; una exageración para decir algo importante.

I

iambic pentameter An iamb, the most common metrical foot in English poetry, is made up of an unstressed syllable followed by a stressed one. Iambic pentameter, then, is a rhythmic meter containing five iambs. Unrhymed iambic pentameter is called blank verse.

> With **in** his **ben** ding **si** ckle's **com** pass **come**
> —William Shakespeare, Sonnet 116, p. 56

pentámetro yámbico Un yambo, el pie métrico más común en la poesía inglesa, está formado por una sílaba no acentuada seguida de una sílaba acentuada. Por tanto, el pentámetro yámbico es una métrica rítmica que contiene cinco yambos. Un pentámetro yámbico sin rima se llama verso blanco.

---

imagery A description of how something looks, feels, tastes, smells, or sounds. Imagery may use literal or figurative language to appeal to the senses.

> All at once she bloomed. Huge, enormous, beautiful to look at from the salmon-pink feather on the tip of her hat down to the little rosebuds of her toes. I couldn't take my eyes off her tiny shoes.
> —Sandra Cisneros, "No Speak English," p. 491

imágenes Descripción de cómo se ve, siente, sabe, huele, o suena algo. Las imágenes pueden incluir lenguaje figurado o literal que apele a los sentidos.

---

indirect characterization (*See* **characterization**.)

caracterización indirecta (*Ver* **caracterización.**)

---

induction From the Latin *inducere*, "to lead into," induction is a logical process wherein you reason from particulars to universals, using inference in order to draw a conclusion, which is also called a generalization.

> Regular exercise promotes weight loss.
> Exercise lowers stress levels.
> Exercise improves mood and outlook.
> GENERALIZATION:
> Exercise contributes to better health.

inducción Del latín *inducere*, "llevar hacia," una inducción es un proceso lógico en el que razonamos desde elementos particulares a elementos universales, usando la inferencia con el fin de sacar una conclusión, que también se llama generalización.

> Hacer ejercicio promueve la pérdida de peso.
> El ejercicio disminuye los niveles de estrés.
> El ejercicio mejora el ánimo y la actitud.
> GENERALIZACIÓN:
> El ejercicio es bueno para la salud.

---

inference A conclusion drawn by looking at many pieces of evidence.

inferencia Conclusión que se saca a partir de muchas evidencias.

---

informal diction (*See* **diction**.)

dicción informal (*Ver* **dicción.**)

---

informed opinion A belief or judgment supported by evidence.

opinión bien fundada Creencia o juicio sustentado por evidencia.

---

inquiry The process of investigating an issue or idea.

indagación Proceso de investigar un tema o una idea.

---

integrating sources The process of including a piece of quoted evidence in a sentence.

integrar fuentes Proceso de incluir en una oración la cita de una evidencia.

---

internal rhyme (*See* **rhyme**.)

rima interna (*Ver* **rima.**)

---

interpretation An explanation of the meaning and significance of a text.

interpretación Explicación del significado y la importancia de algo.

---

inversion (*See* **inverted syntax**.)

inversión (*Ver* **sintaxis inversa.**)

inverted syntax An inverted clause or sentence is one that does not follow the standard subject-verb-object order.

Look like the innocent flower,

v *s* *o*
But be the serpent under it.
—William Shakespeare, *Macbeth*, p. 942

sintaxis inversa Una oración con sintaxis inversa es aquella que no sigue el orden tradicional sujeto-verbo-objeto.

irony, dramatic Tension created by the contrast between what a character says or thinks and what the audience or readers know to be true; as a result of this technique, some words and actions in a story or play take on a different meaning for the reader than they do for the characters. Macbeth, who trusts the Weird Sisters' prophecy about him, says of them:

Infected be the air whereon they ride,
And damned all those that trust them!
—William Shakespeare, *Macbeth*, p. 942

ironía, dramática Tensión que se crea por el contraste entre lo que dice o piensa el personaje y lo que el público o los lectores saben que es verdad; esta técnica da como resultado que algunas palabras y acciones de la historia u obra de teatro adquieran un significado diferente para el lector y para los personajes. Macbeth, que cree en la profecía de las Hermanas Fatídicas sobre él, dice sobre ellas:

irony, situational A discrepancy between what is expected and what actually happens.

See the ending of Amy Silverberg's story, "Suburbia!," p. 303.

ironía situacional Discrepancia entre lo que se espera y lo que realmente sucede.

Ver el final del cuento de Amy Silverberg "Suburbia!", pág. 303.

irony, verbal A figure of speech that occurs when a speaker or character says one thing but means something else. or when what is said is the opposite of what is expected, creating a noticeable incongruity. *Sarcasm* involves verbal irony used derisively.

And then the lover,

Sighing like furnace, with a woeful ballad

Made to his mistress' eyebrow.
—William Shakespeare, "The Seven Ages of Man," p. 312

ironía verbal Figura retórica que ocurre cuando el hablante o el personaje dice una cosa pero quiere decir otra, o cuando lo que se dice es lo contrario de lo que se espera, lo que genera una incongruencia notable. Sarcasmo implica el uso de la ironía verbal de manera burlona.

Italian sonnet (*See* **sonnet**.)

soneto italiano (*Ver* **soneto.**)

J

juxtaposition Placement of two things closely together to emphasize similarities or differences.

Straws, plastic caps, crushed cans,

in a three-block walk you could fill a sack.

As if we could replenish spirits quickly,

pitching containers without remorse

—who did we imagine would pick them up?
—Naomi Shihab Nye, "World of the Future, We Thirsted," p. 708

yuxtaposición Ubicación de dos cosas una al lado de la otra para hacer énfasis en las similitudes y diferencias.

L

limited omniscient narrator A character or persona that tells a narrative that is usually privy to the thoughts and actions of only one character.

narrador omnisciente limitado Personaje o persona que narra un cuento, pero que está al tanto de los pensamientos y acciones de solo uno de los personajes.

line A word or group of words arranged in a single row of a poem.

verso Palabra o conjunto de palabras dispuestas en un renglón de un poema.

logical fallacies Potential vulnerabilities or weaknesses in an argument. They often arise from a failure to make a logical connection between the claim and the evidence used to support it.

falacias lógicas Posibles vulnerabilidades o debilidades de un argumento. Por lo general, surgen de nuestra incapacidad de hacer una conexión lógica entre la afirmación y la evidencia que se usa para respaldarla.

logos (*See* **rhetorical appeals**.) Greek for "embodied thought." Speakers appeal to logos, or reason, by offering clear, rational ideas and using specific details, examples, facts, statistics, or expert testimony to back them up.

> While the displacement of formerly human jobs gets all the headlines, the greatest benefits bestowed by robots and automation come from their occupation of jobs we are unable to do. We don't have the attention span to inspect every square millimeter of every CAT scan looking for cancer cells.
>
> —Kevin Kelly, from "Better Than Human: Why Robots Will—and Must—Take Our Jobs," p. 590.

logos (*Ver* **figuras retóricas de apelación.**) "Pensamiento personificado" en griego. El hablante apela al logos, o razón, al ofrecer ideas claras y racionales y al usar detalles, ejemplos, hechos, estadísticas, o testimonios de expertos para respaldarlas.

lyric A form of poetry that expresses personal feelings, and is usually in the first person point of view. They must have a consistent meter and rhyme scheme to create a degree of beauty and musicality, but there are few other guidelines to this form.

lírica Tipo de poesía que expresa sentimientos personales y que suele estar escrita en primera persona. Su métrica y su rima deben poseer una consistencia que le otorgue cierta belleza y musicalidad, aunque también debe respetar otras pautas.

M

main idea The central point of a piece of writing or speech.

idea principal El tema central de un escrito o discurso.

metaphor Figure of speech that compares two things without using *like* or *as*.

> i already knew the exhaustion of hearing
> my name butchered by hammerhead
> tongues. . . .
>
> —Franny Choi, "Choi Jeong Min," p. 513

metáfora Figura del lenguaje que compara dos cosas sin usar *como* o *cual*.

meter The formal organization of stressed and unstressed syllables in a poem, measured in *feet*. A foot is distinguished by the number of syllables it contains and how stress is placed on the syllables — stressed (´) or unstressed (˘). There are five typical feet in English verse: iamb (˘´), trochee (´˘), anapest (˘˘´), dactyl (´˘˘), and spondee (´´). Some meters dictate the number of feet per line, the most common being tetrameter, pentameter, and hexameter, having four, five, and six feet, respectively.

patrón métrico La manera formal y regular en que están organizadas las sílabas acentuadas y las sílabas no acentuadas; se mide en *pies*. Un pie se distingue por el número de sílabas que contiene y por la manera en que las sílabas están acentuadas (´) o no acentuadas (˘). En los versos en inglés hay cinco pies comunes: yambo (˘´), troqueo (´˘), anapesto (˘˘´), dáctilo (´˘˘), y espondeo (´´). Algunos patrones métricos dictan el número de pies por verso. Los más comunes son: tetrámetro, pentámetro, y hexámetro, que tienen cuatro, cinco, y seis pies, respectivamente.

monologue In drama, a speech that a character gives to either themselves, the audience, or another character.

See William Shakespeare, *Macbeth*, Act I, Scene 5, ll. 1–28 (p. 953).

monólogo En las obras dramáticas, discurso pronunciado por un personaje a sí mismo, al público, o a otro personaje.

Ver William Shakespeare, *Macbeth*, Acto I, Escena 5, ll. 1–28 (pág. 953).

mood The feeling or atmosphere created by a text, usually related to the setting.

estado de ánimo El sentimiento o atmósfera que crea un texto, relacionado con el ambiente.

N

narration A mode of nonfiction that tells a true story; that part of fiction that is not dialogue and is told by a narrator.

narración Género de no ficción que relata una historia real; la parte de una obra de ficción que no es un diálogo y la cuenta un narrador.

narrator The character, or persona, that the author uses to tell a narrative, or story. Narrators may tell stories from several different points of view, including first person, second person (very rare), and third person.

narrador El personaje, o persona, que usa el autor para contar un relato narrativo, o cuento. Los narradores pueden contar historias desde varios puntos de vista, entre ellos: primera persona, segunda persona (muy raro), y tercera persona.

near rhyme (*See* **rhyme**.)

media rima (*Ver* **rima.**)

O

objective narrator (*See* **point of view**.)

narrador objetivo (*Ver* **punto de vista.**)

occasion The time and place a speech is given or a piece is written.

Mandela's "An Ideal for Which I Am Prepared to Die" (p. 205) was given in a courtroom during what is called the Rivonia Trial, in which Mandela was accused of a number of different crimes, and ultimately was found guilty of some of them and imprisoned for many years.

ocasión El momento y el lugar en el que se pronuncia un discurso o se escribe algo.

En lo que se conoció como el Proceso de Rivonia, Mandela pronunció ante el juez el "Ideario por el cual estoy dispuesto a morir" (pág. 205) Mandela fue acusado de distintos delitos, fue hallado culpable de algunos de ellos, y fue encarcelado durante muchos años.

octet A stanza with eight lines.

octeto Estrofa de ocho versos.

ode A poem that praises. Often in praise of nature, a person, or an event.

oda Poema de elogio o alabanza. A menudo se elogia la naturaleza, una persona, o un suceso.

omniscient narrator (*See* **point of view**.)

narrador omnisciente (*Ver* **punto de vista.**)

onomatopoeia Use of a word that refers to a sound, and whose pronunciation mimics that sound.

> There was the shriek of a door being torn from its hinges.
>
> — Kurt Vonnegut, "Harrison Bergeron," p. 738

onomatopeya El uso de palabras que se refieren a sonidos y cuya pronunciación imita dichos sonidos.

oxymoron A type of paradox made up of two seemingly contradictory words.

> Although she feeds me bread of bitterness,
> And sinks into my throat her tiger's tooth,
> Stealing my breath of life, I will confess
> I love this cultured hell that tests my youth.
>
> — Claude McKay, "America," p. 65

oxímoron Paradoja formada por dos palabras aparentemente contradictorias.

P

paradox A statement or situation that is seemingly contradictory on the surface but delivers an ironic truth.

> Bull Connor didn't know history. He knew a kind of physics that somehow didn't relate to the transphysics that we knew about. And that was the fact that there was a certain kind of fire that no water could put out.
>
> — Martin Luther King Jr., "I Have Been to the Mountaintop," p. 211

paradoja Afirmación o situación que es aparentemente contradictoria en la superficie pero que transmite una verdad irónica.

parallelism Similarity of structure in a pair or series of related words, phrases, or clauses.

> There will be more shuttle flights and more shuttle crews and, yes, more volunteers, more civilians, more teachers in space.
>
> — Ronald Reagan, *Challenger* Speech, p. 89

paralelismo Parecido de la estructura de un par o series de palabras, frases, u oraciones relacionadas.

passive voice A sentence employs passive voice when the subject doesn't act but rather is acted on.

> Once these disparate parts were held together by a common enemy, by the fault lines of world wars and the electrified fence of communism. . . .
>
> — Anna Quindlen, "A Quilt of a Country," p. 23

voz pasiva Una oración emplea la voz pasiva cuando el sujeto no actúa, sino que recibe la acción.

pathos Greek for "suffering" or "experience." Speakers appeal to pathos to emotionally motivate their audience. More specific appeals to pathos might play on the audience's values, desires, and hopes, on the one hand, or fears and prejudices, on the other.

> . . . I would watch God's children in their magnificent trek from the dark dungeons of Egypt through, or rather across the Red Sea . . .
>
> — Martin Luther King Jr., "I Have Been to the Mountaintop," p. 211

pathos "Sufrir" o "experimentar" en griego. El hablante apela al pathos para conmover emocionalmente al público. Algunas apelaciones más específicas al pathos tienen que ver, por una parte, con los valores, los deseos, y las esperanzas del público, y, por la otra, con los temores y prejuicios del mismo.

periodic sentence A sentence that starts with details and builds to the main idea.	**oración periódica** Una oración que comienza con detalles y luego desarrolla la idea principal.
persona Greek for "mask." The face or character that a speaker shows to his or her audience. I have done whatever I did, both as an individual and as a leader of my people, because of my experience in South Africa and my own proudly felt African background . . . — Nelson Mandela, "An Ideal for Which I Am Prepared to Die," p. 205	**persona** "Máscara" en griego. La cara o el personaje que el hablante le muestra al público.
personification Attribution of a lifelike quality to an inanimate object or an idea. Around our group I could hear the wilderness listen. — William Stafford, "Traveling through the Dark," p. 896	**personificación** Atribuirle vida a un objeto inanimado o a una idea.
Petrarchan sonnet (*See* **sonnet**.)	**soneto petrarquista** (*Ver* **soneto.**)
plagiarism The act of representing someone else's words, ideas, or research as your own.	**plagio** El acto de presentar como propias las palabras, ideas, o investigaciones de otra persona.
plot The arrangement of events in a narrative. Almost always, a conflict is central to a plot, and traditionally a plot develops in accordance with the following model: exposition, rising action, climax, falling action, denouement. There can be more than one sequence of events in a work, although typically there is one major sequence along with other minor sequences. These minor sequences are called subplots.	**trama** El orden de los sucesos en un relato narrativo. Casi siempre, la trama se centra en un conflicto y, tradicionalmente, la trama se desarrolla según el siguiente modelo: exposición, aumento de la acción, clímax, disminución de la acción, resolución. Puede haber más de una secuencia de sucesos en una obra; sin embargo, por lo general hay una secuencia principal junto a otras secuencias secundarias. Estas secuencias secundarias se llaman subtramas.
polemic Greek for "hostile." An aggressive argument that tries to establish the superiority of one opinion over all others, a polemic generally does not concede that opposing opinions have any merit.	**polémica** "Hostil" en griego. Argumento agresivo que trata de establecer la superioridad de una opinión sobre la de los demás; por lo general, en una polémica no se le concede ningún mérito a la otra parte.
point of view The perspective from which a work is told. The most common narrative vantage points are • **first person** Told by a narrator who is a character in the story and who refers to himself or herself as "I." First person narrators are sometimes unreliable narrators because they don't always have all the information, or because they might be biased. • **second person** Though rare, some stories are told using second person pronouns (*you*). This makes the reader a character in the story.	**punto de vista** La perspectiva desde la que se cuenta una obra. Los puntos de vista más comunes de un relato narrativo son: • **primera persona** Contado por un narrador que es un personaje de la historia y que se refiere a sí mismo como "yo." Los narradores en primera persona son a veces poco confiables porque no siempre ven todo el panorama o porque pueden estar sesgados. • **segunda persona** Aunque raramente, algunas historias se cuentan usando pronombres de segunda persona (*tú*). Esto da la impresión de que el lector es un personaje de la historia.

- **third person limited omniscient** Told by a narrator who relates the action using third person pronouns (*he, she, it*). This narrator is usually aware of the thoughts and actions of only one character.
- **third person omniscient** Told by a narrator using third person pronouns. This narrator is aware of the thoughts and actions of all the characters in the story.
- **third person objective** Told by one who reports actions and dialogue of the characters, and describes the setting, but does not move into the thoughts of any of the characters.

- **tercera persona omnisciente limitada** Contado por un narrador que relata la acción usando pronombres de tercera persona (*él, ella, eso*). Por lo general, el narrador conoce los pensamientos y acciones de un solo personaje.
- **tercera persona omnisciente** Contado por un narrador con pronombres de tercera persona. Este narrador conoce los pensamientos y acciones de todos los personajes de la historia.
- **tercera persona objetiva** Contado por alguien que narra las acciones y los diálogos de los personajes, y que describe el ambiente, pero que no está al tanto de los pensamientos de ninguno de los personajes.

---

propaganda The spread of ideas and information to further a cause. In its negative sense, propaganda is the use of rumors, lies, disinformation, and scare tactics in order to damage or promote a cause.

propaganda La difusión de ideas e información para promover una causa. En un sentido negativo, hacer propaganda implica el uso de rumores, mentiras, desinformación, y tácticas de miedo para perjudicar o promover una causa.

---

protagonist The main character in a work; often a hero or heroine, but not always.

> In Shakespeare's *Macbeth* (p. 942), Macbeth is the protagonist, though certainly not a hero.

protagonista El personaje principal de una obra; por lo general, es un héroe o heroína, pero no siempre.

> En *Macbeth* de Shakespeare (pág. 942), Macbeth es el protagonista, si bien no es el héroe.

---

purpose The goal the speaker wants to achieve. For example, Malala Yousafzai (p. 161) wrote her blog primarily to call attention to what she believed was an unfair situation — limitations on the educational opportunities available to women in her culture — but she also intended to criticize the regime that created such oppression.

propósito El objetivo de quien habla. Por ejemplo, Malala Yousafzai (pág. 161) escribía su blog principalmente para llamar la atención sobre una situación que le parecía injusta — las pocas oportunidades educativas para las mujeres de su cultura — pero también tenía la intención de criticar al régimen que había creado dicha represión.

Q

qualifier Words like *usually, probably, maybe, in most cases,* and *most likely* that are used to temper claims a bit, making them less absolute.

UNQUALIFIED Dogs are more obedient than cats.

QUALIFIED Dogs are generally more obedient than cats.

calificador Palabras como *usualmente*, *probablemente*, *quizás*, *en la mayoría de los casos,* y *seguramente*, que se usan para moderar un poco las afirmaciones y hacerlas menos absolutas.

SIN CALIFICADOR Los perros son más obedientes que los gatos.

CON CALIFICADOR Los perros generalmente son más obedientes que los gatos.

qualitative evidence Evidence made up of examples, facts, reason, or precedent. Qualitative evidence is not numeric.

> The extremists are afraid of books and pens. The power of education frightens them. They are afraid of women. . . . And that is why they killed many female teachers and polio workers in Khyber Pukhtoon Khwa and FATA. That is why they are blasting schools every day. Because they were and they are afraid of change, afraid of the equality that we will bring into our society.
>
> — Malala Yousafzai, "Speech to the United Nations Youth Assembly" p. 161

evidencia cualitativa Evidencia respaldada por razones, tradiciones, o precedentes. La evidencia cualitativa no es numérica.

quantitative evidence Things that can be measured, cited, counted, or otherwise represented in numbers — for instance, statistics, surveys, polls, and census information.

> Middle schools in North America have been called "the Bermuda triangle of education." Only 22 percent of U.S. youth socialize with people of another race. U.S. students have some of the highest rates of emotional problems and the most negative views of peer culture among countries surveyed by the World Health Organization.
>
> — Alexandra Robbins, from *The Geeks Shall Inherit the Earth*, p. 410.

evidencia cuantitativa Cosas que se puede medir, citar, contar, o representar de alguna manera con números—por ejemplo, estadísticas, encuestas, sondeos, y censos.

quatrain In poetry, a four-line stanza.

cuarteto Estrofa de cuatro versos.

R

refute (*See* **refutation.**)

refutar (*Ver* **refutación.**)

refutation Pointing out how the opposition either doesn't account for important issues or is outweighed by other considerations.

> Cop-cams strike a blow for truth, but they strike a blow against relationships. Society will be more open and transparent, but less humane and trusting.
>
> — David Brooks, Op-Ed in the *New York Times*, p. 103

refutación El proceso de revelar las debilidades de un contraargumento con el fin de respaldar nuestra propia afirmación.

relevance How clearly related a source is to the topic you're writing about. A relevant source can be a strong piece of evidence, while a source that is not relevant would likely be a weak piece of evidence.

relevancia Qué tan claro es el vínculo entre una fuente y el tema sobre el que se escribe. Una fuente de gran relevancia puede brindar una evidencia sólida, mientras que una fuente de escasa relevancia posiblemente brinde una evidencia débil.

resolution (*See* **plot.**) The working out of a plot's conflicts, following the climax.

resolución (*Ver* **trama.**) El desenlace de los conflictos de la trama tras el clímax.

rhetoric Aristotle defined rhetoric as "the faculty of observing in any given case the available means of persuasion." In other words, it is the art of finding ways of persuading an audience.

retórica Aristóteles definió la retórica como "la facultad de observar en cualquier caso dado los medios disponibles de persuasión." En otras palabras, es el arte de buscar las maneras de persuadir al público.

rhetorical appeals Rhetorical techniques used to persuade an audience by emphasizing what they find most important or compelling. The three major appeals are to ethos (character), logos (reason), and pathos (emotion).

figuras retóricas de apelación Técnicas retóricas para persuadir a un público al hacer énfasis en lo que se considera más importante o imperioso. Se puede apelar principalmente al ethos (carácter), logos (razón), y pathos (emoción).

rhetorical question Figure of speech in the form of a question posed for rhetorical effect rather than for the purpose of getting an answer.

> It frightens me because I wonder: do I have the right to represent the multitudes who have perished?
>
> —Elie Wiesel, Nobel Prize Speech, p. 119

pregunta retórica Figura que consiste en hacer una pregunta no para obtener una respuesta sino para generar un efecto retórico.

rhetorical situation (*See* **rhetorical triangle.**) The context surrounding a text, including who the speaker is, what the subject is, who the audience is, and the relationship among these three elements. The rhetorical situation also includes the author's purpose and the occasion that has prompted the text.

situación retórica (*Ver* **triángulo retórico.**) El contexto que rodea a un texto, incluyendo quién es el hablante, cuál es el tema, quién es el público, y la relación entre estos tres elementos. La situación retórica también incluye el propósito del autor y la ocasión que ha dado pie para que se produzca el texto.

rhetorical triangle (Aristotelian triangle) A diagram that illustrates the interrelationship among the speaker, audience, and subject in determining a text.

triángulo retórico (triángulo aristotélico) Diagrama que ilustra la relación que hay entre el hablante, el público, y el tema de un texto determinado.

rhyme The poetic repetition of the same (or similar) vowel sounds or of vowel and consonant combinations. A rhyme at the end of two or more lines of poetry is called an end rhyme. A rhyme that occurs within a line is called an internal rhyme. A rhyme that pairs sounds that are similar but not exactly the same is called a near rhyme or a slant rhyme. A rhyme that only works because the words look the same is called an eye rhyme or a sight rhyme. Rhyme often follows a pattern, called a rhyme scheme.

end rhyme

> When I was one-and-twenty
> I heard a wise man say,
> "Give crowns and pounds and guineas
> But not your heart away;
>
> —A. E. Housman, "When I Was One-and-Twenty," (p. 55)

rima La repetición poética de los mismos (o similares) sonidos vocálicos o de las mismas combinaciones de vocal y consonante. Una rima al final de dos o más versos se llama rima final. Una rima que ocurre dentro de un mismo verso se llama rima interna. Una rima que empareja sonidos parecidos pero no exactamente iguales se llama media rima. Una rima que funciona solo porque las palabras se ven igual se llama rima visual. Las rimas suelen seguir un patrón llamado patrón de rima.

internal rhyme

continually confused the light. In flight,

—Li-Young Lee, "For a New Citizen of These United States," p. 535

near rhyme or slant rhyme

What immortal hand or eye,
Could frame thy fearful symmetry?

—William Blake, "The Tyger," p. 74

eye rhyme

And if these pleasures may thee move,
Come live with me, and be my love.

—Christopher Marlowe, "The Passionate Shepherd to His Love," p. 61

rhyme scheme (*See* **rhyme**.) The pattern of rhyme within a poem. *See* the rhyme scheme of Shakespeare's Sonnet 116 on p. 56.

patrón de rima (*Ver* **rima.**) El diseño de rima de un poema. *Ver* el patrón de rima del soneto 116 de Shakespeare en la pág. 56.

rising action (*See* **plot**.) The events, marked by increasing tension and conflict, that build up to a story's climax.

aumento de la acción (*Ver* **trama.**) Los sucesos, marcados por una tensión y un conflicto creciente, que se acumulan y producen el clímax de la historia.

S

satire The use of irony or sarcasm as a means of critique, usually of a society or an individual.

sátira El uso de la ironía o el sarcasmo con el fin de criticar, por lo general, la sociedad o un individuo.

scansion The process of analyzing poetic lines to determine meter.

escansión El proceso de analizar los versos de un poema para determinar su métrica.

scene A minor subunit into which the action of a play is divided. Scenes typically divide the acts of a play.

escena Subdivisión secundaria en la que está dividida la acción de una obra de teatro. Comúnmente, las escenas dividen los actos de una obra de teatro.

sentence variety The strategic use of long and short sentences in order to spice up writing and keep readers focused.

variedad de oraciones Uso estratégico de oraciones cortas y largas para darle más color al relato y mantener la atención del lector.

sestet In poetry, a six-line stanza.

sexteto En poesía, estrofa de seis versos.

setting Where and when a story takes place.

She sat at the window watching the evening invade the avenue. Her head was leaned against the window curtains and in her nostrils was the odor of dusty cretonne. She was tired.

ambiente Dónde y cuándo tiene lugar una historia.

Few people passed. The man out of the last house passed on his way home; she heard his footsteps clacking along the concrete pavement and afterwards crunching on the cinder path before the new red houses. One time there used to be a field there in which they used to play every evening with other people's children. Then a man from Belfast bought the field and built houses in it — not like their little brown houses but bright brick houses with shining roofs.

— James Joyce, "Eveline," p. 340

Shakespearean sonnet (*See* **sonnet**.)	**soneto de Shakespeare** (*Ver* **soneto**.)
Shift In poetry, a significant moment in which both style and meaning change.	**giro** En poesía, momento importante en el cual cambian tanto el significado como el estilo.
signal word A word that signals that a quote is about to begin. Common signal words include *says*, *argues*, and *recommends*.	**palabra de aviso** Palabra que avisa que una cita está por empezar. Algunas palabras de aviso son *dice*, *argumenta*, y *recomienda*.
simile A figure of speech used to explain or clarify an idea by comparing it explicitly to something else, using the words *like*, *as*, or *as though*. Then the whining schoolboy, with his satchel And shining morning face, creeping like snail Unwillingly to school. — William Shakespeare, "The Seven Ages of Man," p. 313	**símil** Figura retórica que se usa para explicar o aclarar una idea al compararla explícitamente con otra cosa, usando las palabras *como*, *cual*, o *como si*.
simple sentence A sentence composed of one main clause without any subordinate clauses.	**oración simple** Oración compuesta de una cláusula principal sin cláusulas subordinadas.
slant rhyme (*See* **rhyme**.)	**media rima** (*Ver* **rima.**)
slippery slope fallacy In this fallacy, also known as the "floodgates fallacy," the effect the speaker is claiming is out of proportion to the cause, or illogical based on the cause. First they ban smoking in restaurants, next they'll ban french fries because they're bad for you too.	**falacia de la pendiente resbaladiza** En esta falacia, también conocida como "falacia de las esclusas," el efecto que el hablante está describiendo está fuera de proporción con la causa o es ilógico tomando en cuenta la causa. Primero prohibieron fumar en los restaurantes; luego prohibirán las papas fritas porque también hacen mal.
SOAPSTone A mnemonic device that stands for Subject, Occasion, Audience, Purpose, Speaker, and Tone. It is a handy way to remember the various elements that make up the rhetorical situation.	**SOAPSTono** Recurso mnemotécnico que, según sus siglas en inglés, significa: Tema, Ocasión, Público, Propósito, Hablante, y Tono. Es una manera muy conveniente de recordar los diversos elementos que forman la situación retórica.
soliloquy A type of monologue in which the character is in conversation with himself or herself.	**soliloquio** Tipo de monólogo en el que el personaje conversa consigo mismo.

sonnet A poetic form with fourteen lines. There are two primary types of sonnets, English (Shakespearean) and Italian (Petrarchan).

English (Shakespearean) sonnet This form, pioneered by William Shakespeare, is made up of three quatrains (four line stanzas) and a couplet (two line stanza), with a rhyme scheme of *abab cdcd efef gg*. This form is also written in iambic pentameter. The final couplet often represents a shift.

See William Shakespeare, Sonnet 116, p. 56

Italian (Petrarchan) sonnet Made popular by the Italian author Petrarch (Francesco Petrarca), this type of sonnet includes an octet (eight line stanza) and a sestet (six line stanza). The rhyme scheme of the octet is *abbaabba*. The rhyme scheme of the sestet varies, but is commonly *cdecde* or *cdcdcd*. The shift occurs between the octet and sestet.

soneto Composición poética de catorce versos. Hay dos tipos principales de sonetos: el soneto inglés (de Shakespeare) y el italiano (petrarquista).

Soneto inglés (de Shakespeare) Esta forma, cuyo precursor fue William Shakespeare, está formada por tres cuartetos (estrofas de cuatro versos) y una copla (estrofa de dos versos), y su esquema rítmico es *abab cdcd efef gg*. Esta forma también se escribe en un pentámetro yámbico. La copla final suele representar un giro.

Ver William Shakespeare, Soneto 116, pág. 56

Soneto italiano (petrarquista) Popularizado por el autor italiano Francesco Petrarca, este tipo de soneto incluye un octeto (estrofa de ocho versos) y un sexteto (estrofa de seis versos). El patrón rítmico del octeto es *abbaabba*. El patrón rítmico del sexteto es variable, pero suele ser *cdecde* o *cdcdcd*. El giro se produce entre el octeto y el sexteto.

sound The musical quality of poetry, as created through techniques such as rhyme, enjambment, caesura, alliteration, assonance, consonance, euphony, cacophany, onomatopoeia, and meter.

sonido Cualidad musical de la poesía cuando se crea con técnicas como la rima, el encabalgamiento, la cesura, la aliteración, la asonancia, la consonancia, la eufonía, la cacofonía, la onomatopeya, y la métrica.

sources The viewpoints of others, whether written, spoken, or presented visually.

fuentes Puntos de vista de los demás, bien sea escritos, hablados, o presentados visualmente.

speaker In nonfiction, the person or group who creates a text. This might be a politician who delivers a speech, a commentator who writes an article, an artist who draws a political cartoon, or even a company that commissions an advertisement. In poetry, the character or persona that the poet uses within a poem.

hablante En la no ficción, persona o grupo que crea un texto. Puede ser un político que pronuncia un discurso, un comentarista que escribe un artículo, un artista que dibuja una viñeta política, o incluso una compañía que manda a hacer un anuncio publicitario. En poesía, el personaje o la persona que el poeta usa en un poema.

stage directions (*See* **blocking**.) In drama, instructions within the play intended for the director or actor in order to accurately portray the scene.

[Thunder and lightning. Enter three Witches]
—Shakespeare, *Macbeth*, p. 943

acotaciones de escena (*Ver* **didascalia**.) En las obras teatrales, las instrucciones dirigidas al director o al actor con el fin de representar certeramente la escena.

stanza A grouping of lines in a poem, usually separated by a space.

estrofa Un grupo de versos separados de los demás, parecido a los párrafos en la prosa.

style The way a literary work is written. Style is produced by an author's choices in diction, syntax, imagery, figurative language, and other literary elements.

estilo La manera en que está escrita una obra literaria. El estilo surge de la dicción, la sintaxis, las imágenes, el lenguaje figurado y otros elementos literarios que escoge el autor.

subject In rhetoric, the subject is the topic of the text. What the text is about.

tema Aquello de lo que trata un texto. El asunto de un texto.

subordination A means of combining sentences that shows the relationship between two ideas. The dependent phrase or clause is structurally less important than the independent clause. A sentence created with subordination is called a complex sentence.

subordinación Forma de combinar oraciones que muestra la relación entre dos ideas. La frase u oración dependiente es estructuralmente menos importante que la oración independiente. Una oración creada mediante la subordinación se denomina oración compleja.

summarize To present the main idea and the main supporting or relevant details that reinforce the main idea of a text.

resumir Presentar la idea principal y los detalles de apoyo o más relevantes de un texto.

support Information that reinforces the main idea of a text.

apoyo Información que refuerza la idea principal de un texto.

symbol A setting, an object, or an event in a story that carries more than literal meaning and therefore represents something significant to understanding the meaning of a work of literature.

> In "The Tell-Tale Heart" (p. 75), the maddening heart beat represents the character's guilty conscience.

símbolo Ambiente, objeto, o evento de la historia que transmite más que el significado literal y que, por tanto, representa algo importante para entender el significado de una obra de literatura.

> En "El corazón delator" (pág. 75), el infernal latido del corazón representa el cargo de conciencia del personaje.

symbolism (*See* **symbol**.) Use of symbol in literature.

simbolismo (*Ver* **símbolo**.) Uso de símbolos en literatura.

syntax The arrangement of words into phrases, clauses, and sentences. This includes word order (subject-verb-object, for instance, or an inverted structure); the length and structure of sentences (simple, compound, complex, or compound-complex); and such devices as parallelism, juxtaposition, and antithesis.

sintaxis La manera en que están ordenadas las palabras, frases, y oraciones. Esto incluye el orden de las palabras (sujeto-verbo-objeto, por ejemplo, o una estructura invertida); la longitud y la estructura de las oraciones (simple, compuesta, compleja, o compuesta-compleja); y algunos recursos como el paralelismo, la yuxtaposición, y la antítesis.

synthesis Combining two or more ideas in order to create something more complex in support of a new idea.

síntesis Combinar dos o más ideas para crear algo más complejo que apoye una nueva idea.

T

text While this term generally refers to the written word, in the humanities it has come to mean any cultural product that can be "read" — meaning not just consumed and comprehended but also investigated. This includes fiction, nonfiction, poetry, political cartoons, fine art, photography, performances, fashion, cultural trends, and much more.

texto Si bien este término se refiere en general a la palabra escrita, en las humanidades ha llegado a significar cualquier producto cultural que se pueda "leer"—es decir, no solo que sea consumido y entendido sino, además, que haya implicado una investigación. Esto incluye ficción, no ficción, poesía, caricaturas políticas, bellas artes, fotografía, actuaciones, moda, tendencias culturales, y mucho más.

theme The underlying issues or ideas of a work.

> *Romeo and Juliet* suggests that love is a destructive force that, once unleashed, cannot be controlled.

tema Los asuntos o ideas subyacentes en una obra.

> *Romeo y Julieta* sugiere que el amor es una fuerza destructiva que, una vez desencadenada, no puede controlarse.

thesis statement The chief claim that a writer makes in any argumentative or explanatory piece of writing, usually stated in one sentence.

tesis Afirmación principal que hace un escritor en cualquier obra escrita de corte argumentativo; por lo general, se expresa en una oración.

tone A speaker's attitude toward the subject as conveyed by the speaker's stylistic and/or rhetorical choices.

tono Actitud del hablante dependiendo de los recursos estilísticos y retóricos que haya elegido para hablar de un tema.

topic sentence A sentence that contains a claim, and which defines the topic that will be talked about in a paragraph.

oración principal Oración que define el tema del que se hablará en un párrafo.

tragedy A serious dramatic work in which the protagonist experiences a series of unfortunate reversals due to some character trait, referred to as a *tragic flaw*. The most common tragic flaw is *hubris*, Greek for *pride*. *See* William Shakespeare, *Macbeth*, p. 942.

tragedia Obra dramática seria en la que el protagonista sufre una serie de reveses desafortunados debido a un rasgo de su personalidad conocido como *error trágico*. El error trágico más común es la *hibris*, *orgullo* en griego. *Ver Macbeth* de William Shakespeare, pág. 942.

tragic flaw A weakness in a hero's character that leads to his downfall. The most common tragic flaw is *hubris*, Greek for *pride*.

error trágico Debilidad de carácter del héroe que lo lleva a su perdición. El error trágico más común es la *hibris*, *orgullo* en griego.

tragic hero The protagonist in a tragedy. This character has a tragic flaw, which leads to his downfall.

héroe trágico El protagonista de una tragedia. El personaje sufre un error trágico, que lo lleva a su perdición.

transition word A word that signifies a change in thought while keeping writing cohesive. Common transition words include *so, therefore, because,* and *for instance.*

> I also believe that evolution implies there can be no qualitative difference between the brain of an earthworm and that of a human. It therefore follows that computers can, in principle, emulate human intelligence, or even better it.
>
> —Stephen Hawking, "Will AI Outsmart Us?," p. 616

término de transición Término que marca un cambio de pensamiento sin afectar la cohesión del escrito. Algunos términos de transición comunes son *por lo tanto, por tal motivo, y por ejemplo.*

U

understatement A figure of speech in which something is presented as less important, dire, urgent, good, and so on than it actually is, often for satiric or comical effect. Also called *litotes*, it is the opposite of hyperbole. In the following example, Lindy West understates her knowledge of this subject, but in the paragraphs that follow proceeds to demonstrate her full understanding of how noise-canceling headphones work.

> I am not sure what we thought the response of the world would be, but to see a fictional villainous version of yourself emerge from internet trolls and ideologues and Alex Jones, well, that certainly is something I never imagined.
>
> —David Hogg, "The Road to Change," p. 171.

atenuación Figura retórica en la que algo se presenta como menos importante, funesto, urgente, bueno, etc., de lo que realmente es; por lo general, se usa para crear un efecto satírico o humorístico. También se conoce como *lítote*; es el opuesto de hipérbole. En el siguiente ejemplo, Lindy West resta importancia a su conocimiento del tema, pero en los párrafos siguientes procede a demostrar su comprensión total de cómo funcionan los auriculares con cancelación de ruido.

unity The quality of a paragraph that is about a single subject, with all sentences in the paragraph dealing with that subject.	**unidad** Calidad de un párrafo que trata sobre un único tema y todas las oraciones de dicho párrafo tratan sobre ese tema.
unreliable narrator A type of first person point of view in which the narrator is biased, or doesn't give a full or accurate picture of events. Narrators may be unreliable because of youth, inexperience, madness, intentional or unintentional bias, or even a lack of morals. Authors often use this technique to distinguish the character's point of view from their own. Sometimes an author will use an unreliable narrator to make an ironic point.	**narrador poco confiable** Narrador que está parcializado y que presenta los eventos de la historia de manera parcial o imprecisa. Los narradores pueden ser poco confiables debido a que son jóvenes, inexpertos, están locos, están parcializados intencionalmente o no, o incluso carecen de moral. En general, los autores usan esta técnica para diferenciar su propio punto de vista del punto de vista del autor. A veces, el autor se vale de un narrador poco confiable para crear un efecto irónico.

V

villanelle A form consisting of five three-line stanzas and a final quatrain, with the first and third lines of the first stanza repeating alternately in the following stanzas.	**villanelle** Género poético formado por cinco estrofas de tres versos y un cuarteto final; el primer y el tercer verso de la primera estrofa se repiten alternativamente en las siguientes estrofas.

Text Credits

Nana Kwame Adjei-Brenyah, "The Era" from *Friday Black: Stories*. Copyright © 2018 by Nana Kwame Adjei-Brenyah. Reprinted by permission of Houghton Mifflin Harcourt Publishing Company. All rights reserved.

Michelle Alexander, "What if we're all coming back?" *The New York Times,* October 29, 2018. Copyright © 2018 by The New York Times Company. All rights reserved. Used under license. https://www.nytimes.com/

Maya Angelou, excerpts from I KNOW WHY THE CAGED BIRD SINGS. Copyright © 1969 and renewed 1997 by Maya Angelou. Used by permission of Random House, an imprint and division of Penguin Random House LLC. All rights reserved.

Lesley Nneka Arimah, "Glory," *Harper's Magazine,* March 2016. Copyright © 2016 by Harper's Magazine. Used with permission.

Edward C. Baig, "Cellphones at school: Should your kid have one?" *USA Today,* August 14, 2018. Copyright © 2018 USA Today. All rights reserved. Used under license. https://www.usatoday.com/

W. Haden Blackman, Richard Pace, and Bernardo Price, "Ghost" from *Where We Live: A Benefit for the Survivors in Las Vegas*. Copyright © 2018 by W. Haden Blackman, Richard Pace, Bernardo Price. Published by Image Comics, Inc.

Richard Blanco, "How to Love a Country" from *How to Love a Country: Poems*. Copyright © 2019 by Richard Blanco. Reprinted by permission of Beacon Press, Boston.

Eavan Boland, "An Irish Childhood in England: 1951." Copyright © 1987 by Eavan Boland, from AN ORIGIN LIKE WATER: Collected Poems 1967-1987 by Eavan Boland. Used by permission of W. W. Norton & Company, Inc.

Kathleen Boland, "A Writer's Insight: Amy Silverberg," *The Southern Review*, May 1, 2017. Copyright © 2017 by Kathleen Boland. Used with permission.

Nick Bostrom, "Transhumanism: The World's Most Dangerous Idea?" Copyright © 2004 by Nick Bostrom. Used with permission.

Rutger Bregman, "Why We Should Give Free Money to Everyone" from *Utopia for Realists: How We Can Build the Ideal World* by Rutger Bregman. Copyright © 2014, 2017 by Rutger Bregman. Translation copyright © 2016 by Elizabeth Manton. Used by permission of Little, Brown and Company.

Rosa Brooks, "In Defense of Killer Robots" from *Foreign Policy,* May 18, 2015, is reprinted by permission of the publisher.

Bill Bystricky, "When 16-Year-Olds Vote, We All Benefit," *Yes! Magazine,* May 23, 2018. Copyright © 2018 by Yes! Magazine. Used with permission.

David Callahan, excerpts from THE CHEATING CULTURE: WHY MORE AMERICANS ARE DOING WRONG TO GET AHEAD. Copyright © 2004 by David Callahan. Reprinted by permission of Houghton Mifflin Harcourt Publishing Company. All rights reserved.

Chen Chen, "When I Grow Up I Want to Be a List of Further Possibilities" from *When I Grow Up I Want to Be a List of Further Possibilities.* Copyright © 2017 by Chen Chen. Reprinted by permission of BOA Editions, Ltd., www.boaeditions.org.

Franny Choi, "Choi Jeong Min. " Originally published in *Poetry Magazine*, February 2016 issue. Copyright © 2016 by Franny Choi. Used with permission.

Sandra Cisneros, "No Speak English" from THE HOUSE ON MANGO STREET. Copyright © 1984 by Sandra Cisneros. Published by Vintage Books, a division of Penguin Random House, and in hardcover by Alfred A. Knopf in 1984. By permission of Susan Bergholz Literary Services, New York, NY and Lamy, NM. All rights reserved.

Judith Ortiz Cofer, "Abuela Invents the Zero" from AN ISLAND LIKE YOU by Judith Ortiz Cofer. Copyright © 1995 by Judith Ortiz Cofer. Reprinted by permission of Orchard Books, an imprint of Scholastic Inc.

Billy Collins, "On Turning Ten" from *The Art of Drowning.* Copyright © 1995 by Billy Collins. Reprinted by permission of the University of Pittsburgh Press.

Marie Colvin, "Marie Colvin: 'Our mission is to report these horrors of war with accuracy and without prejudice,'" *The Guardian,* February 22, 2012. Copyright © Marie Colvin. Used with permission.

Denise Cummins, "How to Get People to Change Their Minds," originally appeared in *Psychology Today,* February 25, 2016. Copyright © 2016 by Denise Cummins. Used with permission.

Lynne Curry, "The 'eat less meat' movement is growing. Does it distort science?" from *The New Food Economy*, September 5, 2019. Copyright © 2019 by Lynne Curry. Used with permission.

Kate Darling, "Extending Legal Protection to Social Robots" from *IEEE Spectrum.* Copyright © 2012 by Kate Darling. Used with permission.

Oliver De La Paz, "In Defense of Small Towns" from *Requiem for the Orchard.* Copyright © 2010 by Oliver De La Paz. Used with permission from University of Akron Press.

John Dever, excerpt from "Exploitive Inequality." Copyright © 2020 by Carnegie Council. Used with permission.

Cory Doctorow, "Printcrime" from *Overclocked: Stories of the Future Present.* Copyright © 2007 by Cory Doctorow. Reprinted by permission of the author and the author's agents, Scovil Galen Ghosh Literary Agency, Inc.

Emma Donaghue, "The Tale of the Kiss" from *Kissing the Witch: Old Tales in New Skins.* Copyright © 1997 by Emma Donaghue.

Mark Edmundson, "Do Sports Build Character or Damage it?" *The Chronicle of Higher Education,* January 15, 2012. Copyright © 2012 by The Chronicle of Higher Education. Used with permission.

Albert Einstein, Graduation Speech, from COLLECTED PAPERS OF ALBERT EINSTEIN (unpublished). Albert Einstein Archives — archival call number 74-917. Copyright © Hebrew University of Jerusalem. Reprinted by permission of Princeton University Press.

Margarita Engle, "Unnatural" from *Silver People: Voices from the Panama Canal* by Margarita Engle. Copyright © 2014 by Margarita Engle. Reprinted by permission of Houghton Mifflin Harcourt Publishing Company. All rights reserved.

Elena Ferrante, "A Power of Our Own," translated by Ann Goldstein, *New York Times,* May 17, 2019. Copyright © 2019 by The New York Times Company. All rights reserved. Used under license. https://www.nytimes.com/

News report titled "Wisconsin School Breaks Up Lunchtime Cliques With Assigned Seating" by Emily Files as originally published on npr.org on October 23, 2019, ©2019 Emily Files for National Public

Radio, Inc. and is used with the permission of NPR. Any unauthorized duplication is strictly prohibited.

Liana Finck, "illustrations" from PASSING FOR HUMAN: A GRAPHIC MEMOIR by Liana Finck, copyright © 2018 by Liana Finck. Used by permission of Random House, an imprint and division of Penguin Random House LLC. All rights reserved.

Jonathan Safran Foer, "Why We Must Cut Out Meat and Dairy Before Dinner to Save the Planet" was first published in *The Guardian* as an adapted excerpt from *We Are the Weather: Saving the Planet Begins at Breakfast* by Jonathan Safran Foer. Published by Hamish Hamilton, a division of Penguin Random House, in 2019. Copyright © 2019 by Jonathan Safran Foer. Reprinted by permission of Jonathan Safran Foer and Aragi Inc. All rights reserved.

Francis Fukuyama, "Transhumanism" from *Foreign Policy online,* Oct. 23, 2009, is reprinted by permission of the publisher.

John Taylor Gatto, "Against School: How Pubic Education Cripples Our Kids and Why" from *Harper's,* Sept. 2003. Reprinted by permission of the author.

Nikki Giovanni, "Knoxville, Tennessee" from *The Collected Poetry of Nikki Giovanni.* Copyright compilation © 2003 by Nikki Giovanni. Used by permission of HarperCollins Publishers.

Adam Grant, "What Straight-A Students Get Wrong," *The New York Times,* December 8, 2018. Copyright © 2018 by The New York Times Company. All rights reserved. Used under license. https://www.nytimes.com/

Peter Gray, "Children Educate Themselves: Lessons from Sudbury Valley," Psychology Today, August 13, 2008. Copyright © 2008 by Peter Gray. Used with permission.

Federico Guerrini, "By Giving Robots 'Personhood' Status, Humanity Risks To Be Demoted To The Rank Of A Machine," *Forbes.com,* January 16, 2017. Copyright © 2017 by Forbes. All rights reserved. Used under license. https://www.forbes.com/

"The Red Hat" from *Halfway Down the Hall,* © 1998 by Rachel Hadas. Published by Wesleyan University Press. Reprinted with permission.

Tim Hamilton, excerpts from RAY BRADBURY'S FAHRENHEIT 451: THE AUTHORIZED ADAPTATION, artwork by Tim Hamilton. Text copyright © 1953, renewed 1981 by Ray Bradbury. Artwork copyright © 2009 by Tim Hamilton. Reprinted by permission of Hill and Wang, a division of Farrar, Straus and Giroux.

"Education: Change is the only constant" from 21 LESSONS FOR THE 21ST CENTURY by Yuval Noah Harari, copyright © 2018 by Yuval Noah Harari. Used by permission of Spiegel & Grau, an imprint of Random House, a division of Penguin Random House LLC. All rights reserved.

"Once the World Was Perfect," from CONFLICT RESOLUTION FOR HOLY BEINGS: POEMS by Joy Harjo. Copyright © 2015 by Joy Harjo. Used by permission of W. W. Norton & Company, Inc.

Sam Harris, From LYING published by Four Elephants Press. Copyright © 2013 by Sam Harris. Reprinted by permission of the author.

Stephen Hawking, "Will Artificial Intelligence Outsmart Us?" from BRIEF ANSWERS TO THE BIG QUESTIONS by Stephen Hawking, copyright © 2018 by Spacetime Publications Limited; foreword copyright © 2018 by Eddie Redmayne; introduction copyright © 2018 by Kip Thorne; afterword copyright © 2018 by Lucy Hawking. Used by permission of Bantam Books, an imprint of Random House, a division of Penguin Random House LLC. All rights reserved.

Laura Hercher, "Designer babies aren't futuristic. They're already here," *MIT Technology Review,* October 22, 2018. Copyright © 2018 by MIT Technology Review. Used with permission.

Justin Herrmann, "Everything, Then Silence," *New Flash Fiction Review.* Copyright © New Flash Fiction Review. Used with permission.

Frederick Hess and Amy Cummings, "The Misguided Sliming of High-School Sports," *National Review,* February 7, 2019. Copyright © 2019 by National Review. Used with permission.

Monica Hesse, "The case of the Photoshopped female CEOs," *The Washington Post,* June 13, 2019. Copyright © 2019 by The Washington Post. All rights reserved. Used under license. https://www.washingtonpost.com/

Faith Erin Hicks, excerpt from FRIENDS WITH BOYS © 2012 by Faith Erin Hicks. Reprinted by permission of First Second, an imprint of Roaring Brook Press, a division of Holtzbrinck Publishing Holdings Limited Partnership. All Rights Reserved.

David Hogg and Lauren Hogg, "The Road to Change" from #NEVERAGAIN: A NEW GENERATION DRAWS THE LINE by David Hogg and Lauren Hogg, copyright © 2018 by David Hogg and Lauren Hogg. Used by permission of Random House, an imprint and division of Penguin Random House LLC. All rights reserved.

Arthur House, "The Real Cyborgs" first published in *The Telegraph,* Oct. 20, 2015. Copyright © 2015 by Telegraph Media Group Limited. Reprinted by permission of the publisher.

Dolores Huerta, Speech at UCLA, February 22, 1978. Copyright © 1978 by the UCLA Chicano Studies Research Center Library and Archive, Chicano Studies Research Center, UCLA. Used with permission.

Kristen Iskandrian, "Good With Boys." First published in *Zyzzyva.* Copyright © 2017 by Kristen Iskandrian. Used by permission of Brandt & Hochman Literary Agents, Inc. Any copying or distribution of this text is expressly forbidden. All rights reserved.

Shirley Jackson, "Biography of a Story," copyright © 1968 by Stanley Edgar Hyman; from COME ALONG WITH ME by Shirley Jackson, edited by Stanley Edgar Hyman. Used by permission of Viking Books, an imprint of Penguin Publishing Group, a division of Penguin Random House LLC. All rights reserved.

"The Lottery" from THE LOTTERY by Shirley Jackson. Copyright © 1948, 1949 by Shirley Jackson. Copyright renewed 1976, 1977 by Laurence Hyman, Barry Hyman, Mrs. Sarah Webster and Mrs. Joanne Schnurer. Reprinted by permission of Farrar, Straus and Giroux.

N. K. Jemisin, "Valedictorian" from *After: Nineteen Stories of Apocalypse and Dystopia.* Copyright © 2012 by N.K. Jemisin. Used with permission.

Ha Jin, "Children as Enemies" from A GOOD FALL: STORIES by Ha Jin, copyright © 2009 by Ha Jin. Used by permission of Pantheon Books, an imprint of the Knopf Doubleday Publishing Group, a division of Penguin Random House LLC. All rights reserved.

Mindy Kaling, "Don't Peak in High School" from IS EVERYONE HANGING OUT WITHOUT ME? (AND OTHER CONCERNS) by Mindy Kaling, copyright © 2011 by Mindy Kaling. Used by permission of Crown Archetype, an imprint of Random House, a division of Penguin Random House LLC. All rights reserved.

Kevin Kelly, "Better than Human: Why Robots Will—And Must—Take Our Jobs" from *Wired,* Dec. 24, 2012. Copyright © 2012 by Conde Nast. Reprinted by permission of the publisher.

Jamaica Kincaid, excerpt from A SMALL PLACE by Jamaica Kincaid. Copyright © 1988 by Jamaica Kincaid. Reprinted by permission of Farrar, Straus and Giroux.

Alex King, "Photographer Jason Larkin unpicks South Africa's complex present," *Huck Magazine,* September 4, 2015. Copyright

© 2015 by TCO London. Published 2015 by Huck Magazine. Used with permission.

Martin Luther King, Jr., "I've Been to the Mountaintop" is reprinted by arrangement with The Heirs of the Estate of Martin Luther King Jr., c/o Writers House as agent for the proprietor, New York, NY. Copyright © 1968 by Dr. Martin Luther King, Jr., copyright © renewed 1996 by Coretta Scott King.

Chuck Klosterman, "Why We Look the Other Way," *ESPN: The Magazine*, March 26, 2007. Copyright © 2007 by Chuck Klosterman. Reprinted with permission.

Debora Kuan, "Magic Lesson," *The New Republic,* April 13, 2018. Copyright © 2018 by Debora Kuan. Used with permission.

Marisa Lascala, "What Is Tiger Mom Parenting? Experts Say This Parenting Style Can Be Harsh, But Warm" by Marisa Lascala. Originally appeared on goodhousekeeping.com, Hearst Magazine Media, Inc. Used with permission.

Ursula Le Guin, "The Ones Who Walk Away from Omelas." First appeared in "New Dimension 3" in 1973, and then in THE WIND'S TWELVE QUARTERS, published by HarperCollins in 1975. Copyright © 1973 by Ursula K. Le Guin. Reprinted by permission of Curtis Brown, Ltd.

Li-Young Lee, "For a New Citizen of These United States" from THE CITY IN WHICH I LOVE YOU. Copyright © 1990 by Li-Young Lee. Reprinted with the permission of The Permissions Company, Inc., on behalf of BOA Editions, Ltd., www.boaeditions.org.

Ken Liu, "The Perfect Match," *Lightspeed Magazine,* Issue 31, December 2012. Copyright © 2012 by Ken Liu. Reprinted in The Paper Menagerie and Other Stories, Simon & Schuster, 2016. Used with permission.

Lela London, "This Is What The Future Of Robots Might Do To Humanity," *Forbes.com,* November 28, 2018. Copyright © 2018 by Forbes. All rights reserved. Used under license. https://www.forbes.com/

Amit Majmudar, "Dothead" from DOTHEAD: POEMS by Amit Majmudar, compilation copyright © 2016 by Amit Majmudar. Used by permission of Alfred A. Knopf, an imprint of the Knopf Doubleday Publishing Group, a division of Penguin Random House LLC. All rights reserved.

Nelson Mandela, excerpts from "Second Court Statement 1964" from "The Rivonia Trial, 1963-1964" from NELSON MANDELA: THE STRUGGLE IS MY LIFE (1986) are reprinted by permission of the Nelson Mandela Foundation.

DeRay Mckesson, "Bully and the Pulpit" from ON THE OTHER SIDE OF FREEDOM: THE CASE FOR HOPE by DeRay Mckesson, copyright © 2018 by DeRay Mckesson. Used by permission of Viking Books, an imprint of Penguin Publishing Group, a division of Penguin Random House LLC. All rights reserved.

Sarah Mirk, "It's Complicated Being a Feminist Football Fan." Copyright © 2015 by Bitch Media. Used with permission.

Frank Mitloehner, "Yes, eating meat affects the environment, but cows are not killing the climate," *The Conversation,* October 25, 2018. Licensed under CC BY-ND 4.0.

Toni Morrison, "The Work You Do." Copyright © 2017 by The Estate of Chloe A. Morrison. First Printed in *The New Yorker.* Reprinted by permission of ICM Partners.

Tahira Naqvi, "Paths Upon Water" from *The Forbidden Stitch, an Asian American Women's Anthology*. Copyright © 1989 by Tahira Naqvi. Used with permission.

Aimee Nezhukumatathil, "On Listening to Your Teacher Take Attendance" from *Oceanic.* Copyright © 2018 by Aimee Nezhukumatathil. Reprinted by permission of Copper Canyon Press, www.coppercanyonpress.org.

The New York Times Editorial Board, "End Legacy College Admissions," *The New York Times,* September 7, 2019. Copyright © 2019 by The New York Times Company. All rights reserved. Used under license. https://www.nytimes.com/

Viet Thanh Nguyen, "America, Say My Name," *The New York Times,* March 9, 2019. Copyright © 2019 by The New York Times Company. All rights reserved. Used under license. https://www.nytimes.com/

Leslie Nguyen-Okwu, "High School Shouldn't Guarantee Admission," *OZY,* February 10, 2017. Copyright © 2017 by OZY. Used with permission.

Trevor Noah, "Chameleon" from BORN A CRIME: STORIES FROM A SOUTH AFRICAN CHILDHOOD by Trevor Noah, copyright © 2016 by Trevor Noah. Used by permission of Spiegel & Grau, an imprint of Random House, a division of Penguin Random House LLC. All rights reserved.

Naomi Shihab Nye, "Famous" from *Words Under the Words: Selected Poems.* Copyright © 1995 by Naomi Shihab Nye. Used by permission of Far Corner Books, Portland, Oregon.

Naomi Shihab Nye, "World of the Future, We Thirsted" from *Cast Away* by Naomi Shihab Nye. Text Copyright © 2020 by Naomi Shihab Nye. Used by permission of HarperCollins Publishers.

Nnedi Okorafor, "Spider the Artist." © 2008 by Nnedi Okorafor. Originally published in *Seeds of Change,* edited by John Joseph Adams. Reprinted by permission of the author.

George Orwell, "Shooting an Elephant" from A COLLECTION OF ESSAYS. Copyright 1950 by Sonia Brownell Orwell. Copyright © renewed 1978 by Sonia Pitt-Rivers. Reproduced by permission of Houghton Mifflin Harcourt Publishing Company and Bill Hamilton as the Literary Executor of the Estate of the Late Sonia Brownell Orwell. All rights reserved.

Lisa Parker, "Snapping Beans," *Parnassus,* 23, no. 2 (1998). Copyright © 1998 by Lisa Parker. Used with permission.

Stephen Prince, "I'm a multimillionaire – and I think the tax system doesn't serve most Americans," *The Guardian,* November 22, 2019. Copyright © 2019 by Guardian News & Media Limited. Used with permission.

Excerpt from "Emotional Intelligence," *Psychology Today.* Copyright © 2020. Used with permission. www.Psychologytoday.com.

Anna Quindlen, "A Quilt of a Country," *Newsweek,* September 26, 2001. Copyright © 2001 Newsweek. Used with permission.

Amanda Ripley, "School Should Be About Learning, Not Sports," *The New York Times*, March 2, 2015. Copyright © 2015 by Amanda Ripley. Used with permission.

Alexandra Robbins, excerpt from *The Geeks Shall Inherit the Earth: Popularity, Quirk Theory, and Why Outsiders Thrive After High School* by Alexandra Robbins. Copyright © 2011 by Alexandra Robbins. Reprinted with the permission of Hachette Books.

Michael Sandel, "Are We All in This Together?" *New York Times,* April 13, 2020. Copyright © 2020 by The New York Times. All rights reserved. Used under license. https://www.nytimes.com/

George Saunders, "Sticks" from TENTH OF DECEMBER: STORIES by George Saunders, copyright © 2013 by George Saunders. Used by permission of Random House, an imprint and division of Penguin Random House LLC. All rights reserved.

Evan Selinger and Woodrow Hartzog, "The dangers of trusting robots," *BBC,* August 12, 2015. Copyright © 2015 by BBC. Used with permission. www.bbc.com/future.

William Shakespeare, "Macbeth" glosses from *The Bedford Shakespeare,* Bedford/St. Martin's (2015). Copyright © 2015 by Cambridge University Press. Reproduced with permission of the Licensor through PLSclear.

Warsan Shire, "Backwards." Copyright © 2014 by Warsan Shire.

Erin Shortell, "Sports vs. Education: A False Choice," *Harvard Political Review,* October 23, 2013. Copyright © 2013 by Harvard Political Review. Used with permission.

Amy Silverberg, "Suburbia!" *The Southern Review,* May 1, 2017. Copyright © 2017 by Amy Silverberg. Used with permission.

Lenore Skenazy, "Why I Let My 9-Year-Old Ride the Subway Alone" from *The Sun,* April 1, 2008. Reprinted by permission of the author.

Danez Smith, "alternate names for black boys" originally published in *Poetry Magazine,* March 2014 issue. Copyright © 2014 by Danez Smith. Used with permission.

Timothy Snyder, Excerpt(s) from ON TYRANNY: TWENTY LESSONS FROM THE TWENTIETH CENTURY by Timothy Snyder, copyright © 2017 by Timothy Snyder. Used by permission of Tim Duggan Books, an imprint of Random House, a division of Penguin Random House LLC. All rights reserved.

Rebecca Solnit, "Abolish High School," *Harper's Magazine,* April 2015. Copyright © 2015 Harper's Magazine. All Rights reserved. Reproduced from the April issue by special permission.

William Stafford, "Traveling through the Dark" from *Ask Me: 100 Essential Poems.* Copyright © 1966, 1998, 2014 by William Stafford and the Estate of William Stafford. Reprinted with the permission of The Permissions Company, Inc. on behalf of Graywolf Press, Minneapolis, Minnesota, www.graywolfpress.org.

A.E. Stallings, "The School of Dreams" from SELECTED POEMS by A.E. Stallings. Forthcoming from Farrar, Straus and Giroux in August 2021. Reprinted by permission of Farrar, Straus and Giroux.

Student Press Law Center, "'Courage in Student Journalism Award' goes to Burlington, Vermont high school editors who successfully fought censorship," *Student Press Law Center,* November 23, 2019. Copyright © 2019 by Student Press Law Center. Used with permission.

Adrienne Su, "The Chow-Mein Years in Atlanta" from *Peach State* by Adrienne Su, © 2021. Reprinted by permission of the University of Pittsburgh Press.

Amber Tamblyn, "I'm not Ready for the Redemption of Men," *The New York Times,* November 30, 2017. Copyright © 2017 by The New York Times Company. All rights reserved. Used under license. https://www.nytimes.com/

Amy Tan, "Rules of the Game" from THE JOY LUCK CLUB, copyright © 1989 by Amy Tan. Used by permission of G.P. Putnam's Sons, an imprint of Penguin Publishing Group, a division of Penguin Random House LLC. All rights reserved.

Hernando Tellez, "Lather and Nothing Else" from THE FLIGHT OF THE CONDOR: STORIES OF VIOLENCE AND WAR FROM COLOMBIA, edited by Jennifer Gabrielle Edwards. Copyright © 2007 by the Board of Regents of the University of Wisconsin System. Reprinted by permission of the University of Wisconsin Press.

Natasha Trethewey, "Enlightenment" from *Thrall: Poems* by Natasha Trethewey. Copyright © 2012 by Natasha Trethewey. Reprinted by permission of Houghton Mifflin Harcourt Publishing Company. All rights reserved.

Sherry Turkle, "Why these friendly robots can't be good friends to our kids," *The Washington Post,* December 7, 2017. Copyright © 2017 by Sherry Turkle. Used with permission.

Luisa Valenzuela, "The Censors" from *Open Door.* Copyright © 2000 by Luisa Valenzuela. Translation by Frank Thomas Smith. Used with permission.

Jose Antonio Vargas, "What America Looks Like From a Jail in South Texas," *The New York Times,* September 15, 2018. Copyright © 2018 by The New York Times Company. All rights reserved. Used under license. https://www.nytimes.com/

Kurt Vonnegut, "Harrison Bergeron," copyright © 1961 by Kurt Vonnegut, copyright renewed © 1989 by Kurt Vonnegut; from WELCOME TO THE MONKEY HOUSE by Kurt Vonnegut. Used by permission of Dell Publishing, an imprint of Random House, a division of Penguin Random House LLC. All rights reserved.

Lulu Wang and Ira Glass, "In This American Life Ep 585 In Defense of Ignorance: Act One What You Don't Know: WBEZ Chicago's *This American Life*," April 22, 2016. Used with permission.

Dyan Watson, "A Message from a Black Mom to Her Son," from *Rethinking Schools,* Volume 26, No. 3, Spring 2012. Copyright © 2012 by Rethinking Schools. Used with permission.

Carole Boston Weatherford, "You Go to My Head" from *Becoming Billie Holiday.* Copyright © 2008 by Carole Boston Weatherford. Published by WordSong, an imprint of Boyds Mills Press.

Lindy West, "We Got Rid of Some Bad Men. Now Let's Get Rid of Bad Movies," *The New York Times,* March 3, 2018. Copyright © 2018 by The New York Times Company. All rights reserved. Used under license. https://www.nytimes.com/

Wharton School, "Is Every Lie 'a Sin'? Maybe Not." Interview of Emma E. Levine and Maurice Schweizer, September 17, 2014. All materials copyright of the Wharton School of the University of Pennsylvania.

Elie Wiesel, "Nobel Prize Acceptance Speech," Dec. 10, 1986, reprinted by permission of The Nobel Foundation. Copyright © 1986 by The Nobel Foundation.

Alex Williams, "Will Robots Take Our Children's Jobs?" *The New York Times,* December 11, 2017. Copyright © 2017 by The New York Times Company. All rights reserved. Used under license. https://www.nytimes.com/

Austin Wilson, Seth T. Hahne, David C. Hopkins, "Harry Sloan, Barber" from *Re*pro*duct: Self-Applied.* Copyright © 2016 Austin Wilson. Published by Magnetic Press. Used with permission from the author.

Virginia Woolf, "Thoughts on Peace in an Air Raid," from *The Death of the Moth and Other Essays.* Copyright © 1942 by Houghton Mifflin Harcourt Publishing Company, Copyright renewed © 1970 by Marjorie T. Parsons, Executrix. Reprinted by permission of Houghton Mifflin Harcourt Publishing Company and The Society of Authors as the Literary Representative of the Estate of Virginia Woolf.

Malala Yousafzai, Speech to the United Nations Youth Assembly. Reproduced with permission of Curtis Brown Group Ltd, on behalf of Malala Yousafzai. Copyright © Malala Yousafzai, 2013 Malala Yousafzai's Speech to the United Nations.

Mark Zuckerberg, "The Facts About Facebook." Copyright © 2019 Dow Jones & Company, Inc. Republished with permission of Dow Jones & Company, Inc; permission conveyed through Copyright Clearance Center, Inc.

Index

M

N

T

U

V

W

Y

Z